FIRST CENSUS
OF THE UNITED STATES
1790

CONNECTICUT

HEADS OF FAMILIES

AT THE FIRST CENSUS OF THE
UNITED STATES TAKEN
IN THE YEAR
1790

CONNECTICUT

Originally Published: Government Printing Office
Washington, D.C., 1908
Reprinted: Genealogical Publishing Co., Inc.
Baltimore, 1966, 1972, 1980, 1992
Library of Congress Catalogue Card Number 72-6706
International Standard Book Number 0-8063-0523-1
Made in the United States of America

HEADS OF FAMILIES AT THE FIRST CENSUS
1790

INTRODUCTION.

The First Census of the United States (1790) comprised an enumeration of the inhabitants of the present states of Connecticut, Delaware, Georgia, Kentucky, Maine, Maryland, Massachusetts, New Hampshire, New Jersey, New York, North Carolina, Pennsylvania, Rhode Island, South Carolina, Tennessee, Vermont, and Virginia.

A complete set of the schedules for each state, with a summary for the counties, and in many cases for towns, was filed in the State Department, but unfortunately they are not now complete, the returns for the states of Delaware, Georgia, Kentucky, New Jersey, Tennessee, and Virginia having been destroyed when the British burned the Capitol at Washington during the War of 1812. For several of the states for which schedules are lacking it is probable that the Director of the Census could obtain lists which would present the names of most of the heads of families at the date of the First Census. In Virginia, state enumerations were made in 1782, 1783, 1784, and 1785, but the lists on file in the State Library include the names for only 39 of the 78 counties into which the state was divided.

The schedules of 1790 form a unique inheritance for the Nation, since they represent for each of the states concerned a complete list of the heads of families in the United States at the time of the adoption of the Constitution. The framers were the statesmen and leaders of thought, but those whose names appear upon the schedules of the First Census were in general the plain citizens who by their conduct in war and peace made the Constitution possible and by their intelligence and self-restraint put it into successful operation.

The total population of the United States in 1790, exclusive of slaves, as derived from the schedules was 3,231,533. The only names appearing upon the schedules, however, were those of heads of families, and as at that period the families averaged 6 persons, the total number was approximately 540,000, or slightly more than half a million. The number of names which is now lacking because of the destruction of the schedules is approximately 140,000, thus leaving schedules containing about 400,000 names.

The information contained in the published report of the First Census of the United States, a small volume of 56 pages, was not uniform for the several states and territories. For New England and one or two of the other states the population was presented by counties and towns; that of New Jersey appeared partly by counties and towns and partly by counties only; in other cases the returns were given by counties only. Thus the complete transcript of the names of heads of families, with accompanying information, presents for the first time detailed information as to the number of inhabitants—males, females, etc.—for each minor civil division in all those states for which such information was not originally published.

In response to repeated requests from patriotic societies and persons interested in genealogy, or desirous of studying the early history of the United States, Congress added to the sundry civil appropriation bill for the fiscal year 1907 the following paragraph:

> The Director of the Census is hereby authorized and directed to publish, in a permanent form, by counties and minor civil divisions, the names of the heads of families returned at the First Census of the United States in seventeen hundred and ninety; and the Director of the Census is authorized, in his discretion, to sell said publications, the proceeds thereof to be covered into the Treasury of the United States, to be deposited to the credit of miscellaneous receipts on account of "Proceeds of sales of Government property:"
>
> *Provided*, That no expense shall be incurred hereunder additional to appropriations for the Census Office for printing therefor made for the fiscal year nineteen hundred and seven; and the Director of the Census is hereby directed to report to Congress at its next session the cost incurred hereunder and the price fixed for said publications and the total received therefor.

The amount of money appropriated by Congress for the Census printing for the fiscal year mentioned was unfortunately not sufficient to meet the current requirement of the Office and to publish the transcription of the First Census, and no provision was made in the sundry civil appropriation bill for 1908 for the continuance of authority to publish these important records. Resources, however, were available for printing a small section of the work, and the schedules of New Hampshire, Vermont, and Maryland accordingly were published.

The urgent deficiency bill, approved February 15, 1908, contained the following provision:

That the Director of the Census is hereby authorized and directed to expend so much of the appropriation for printing for the Department of Commerce and Labor allotted by law to the Census Office for the fiscal year ending June thirtieth, nineteen hundred and eight, as may be necessary to continue and complete the publication of the names of families returned at the First Census of the United States, as authorized by the sundry civil appropriation act approved June thirtieth, nineteen hundred and six.

In accordance with the authority given in the paragraph quoted above, the names returned at the First Census in the states of Connecticut, Maine, Massachusetts, New York, North Carolina, Pennsylvania, Rhode Island, and South Carolina have been published, thus completing the roster of the heads of families in 1790 so far as they can be shown from the records of the Census Office. As the Federal census schedules of the state of Virginia for 1790 are missing, the lists of the state enumerations made in 1782, 1783, 1784, and 1785 have been substituted and, while not complete, they will, undoubtedly, prove of great value.

THE FIRST CENSUS.

The First Census act was passed at the second session of the First Congress, and was signed by President Washington on March 1, 1790. The task of making the first enumeration of inhabitants was placed upon the President. Under this law the marshals of the several judicial districts were required to ascertain the number of inhabitants within their respective districts, omitting Indians not taxed, and distinguishing free persons (including those bound to service for a term of years) from all others; the sex and color of free persons; and the number of free males 16 years of age and over.

The object of the inquiry last mentioned was, undoubtedly, to obtain definite knowledge as to the military and industrial strength of the country. This fact possesses special interest, because the Constitution directs merely an enumeration of inhabitants. Thus the demand for increasingly extensive information, which has been so marked a characteristic of census legislation, began with the First Congress that dealt with the subject.

The method followed by the President in putting into operation the First Census law, although the object of extended investigation, is not definitely known. It is supposed that the President or the Secretary of State dispatched copies of the law, and perhaps of instructions also, to the marshals. There is, however, some ground for disputing this conclusion. At least one of the reports in the census volume of 1790 was furnished by a governor. This, together with the fact that there is no record of correspondence with the marshals on the subject of the census, but that there is a record of such correspondence with the governors, makes very strong the inference that the marshals received their instructions through the governors of the states. This inference is strengthened by the fact that in 1790 the state of Massachusetts furnished the printed blanks, and also by the fact that the law relating to the Second Census specifically charged the Secretary of State to superintend the enumeration and to communicate directly with the marshals.

By the terms of the First Census law nine months were allowed in which to complete the enumeration. The census taking was supervised by the marshals of the several judicial districts, who employed assistant marshals to act as enumerators. There were 17 marshals. The records showing the number of assistant marshals employed in 1790, 1800, and 1810 were destroyed by fire, but the number employed in 1790 has been estimated at 650.

The schedules which these officials prepared consist of lists of names of heads of families; each name appears in a stub, or first column, which is followed by five columns, giving details of the family. These columns are headed as follows:

Free white males of 16 years and upward, including heads of families.
Free white males under 16 years.
Free white females, including heads of families.
All other free persons.
Slaves.

The assistant marshals made two copies of the returns; in accordance with the law one copy was posted in the immediate neighborhood for the information of the public, and the other was transmitted to the marshal in charge, to be forwarded to the President. The schedules were turned over by the President to the Secretary of State. Little or no tabulation was required, and the report of the First Census, as also the reports of the Second, Third, and Fourth, was produced without the employment of any clerical force, the summaries being transmitted directly to the printer. The total population as returned in 1790 was 3,929,214, and the entire cost of the census was $44,377.

A summary of the results of the First Census, not including the returns for South Carolina, was transmitted to Congress by President Washington on October 27, 1791. The legal period for enumeration, nine months, had been extended, the longest time consumed being eighteen months in South Carolina. The report of October 27 was printed in full, and published in what is now a very rare little volume; afterwards the report for South Carolina was "tipped in." To contain the results of the Twelfth Census, ten large quarto volumes, comprising in all 10,400 pages, were required. No illustration of the expansion of census inquiry can be more striking.

The original schedules of the First Census are now contained in 26 bound volumes, preserved in the Census Office. For the most part the headings of the schedules were written in by hand. Indeed, up to and

including 1820, the assistant marshals generally used for the schedules such paper as they happened to have, ruling it, writing in the headings, and binding the sheets together themselves. In some cases merchants' account paper was used, and now and then the schedules were bound in wall paper.

As a consequence of requiring marshals to supply their own blanks, the volumes containing the schedules vary in size from about 7 inches long, 3 inches wide, and ½ inch thick to 21 inches long, 14 inches wide, and 6 inches thick. Some of the sheets in these volumes are only 4 inches long, but a few are 3 feet in length, necessitating several folds. In some cases leaves burned at the edges have been covered with transparent silk to preserve them.

THE UNITED STATES IN 1790.

In March, 1790, the Union consisted of twelve states—Rhode Island, the last of the original thirteen to enter the Union, being admitted May 29 of the same year. Vermont, the first addition, was admitted in the following year, before the results of the First Census were announced. Maine was a part of Massachusetts, Kentucky was a part of Virginia, and the present states of Alabama and Mississippi were parts of Georgia. The present states of Ohio, Indiana, Illinois, Michigan, and Wisconsin, with part of Minnesota, were known as the Northwest Territory, and the present state of Tennessee, then a part of North Carolina, was soon to be organized as the Southwest Territory.

The United States was bounded on the west by the Mississippi river, beyond which stretched that vast and unexplored wilderness belonging to the Spanish King, which was afterwards ceded to the United States by France as the Louisiana Purchase, and now comprises the great and populous states of South Dakota, Iowa, Nebraska, Missouri, Kansas, Arkansas, and Oklahoma, and portions of Minnesota, North Dakota, Montana, Wyoming, Colorado, New Mexico, Texas, and Louisiana. The Louisiana Purchase was not consummated for more than a decade after the First Census was taken. On the south was another Spanish colony known as the Floridas. The greater part of Texas, then a part of the colony of Mexico, belonged to Spain; and California, Nevada, Utah, Arizona, and a portion of New Mexico, also the property of Spain, although penetrated here and there by venturesome explorers and missionaries, were, for the most part, an undiscovered wilderness.

The gross area of the United States was 827,844 square miles, but the settled area was only 239,935 square miles, or about 29 per cent of the total. Though the area covered by the enumeration in 1790 seems very small when compared with the present area of the United States, the difficulties which confronted the census taker were vastly greater than in 1900. In many localities there were no roads, and where these did exist they were poor and frequently impassable; bridges were almost unknown. Transportation was entirely by horseback, stage, or private coach. A journey as long as that from New York to Washington was a serious undertaking, requiring eight days under the most favorable conditions. Western New York was a wilderness, Elmira and Binghamton being but detached hamlets. The territory west of the Allegheny mountains, with the exception of a portion of Kentucky, was unsettled and scarcely penetrated. Detroit and Vincennes were too small and isolated to merit consideration. Philadelphia was the capital of the United States. Washington was a mere Government project, not even named, but known as the Federal City. Indeed, by the spring of 1793, only one wall of the White House had been constructed, and the site for the Capitol had been merely surveyed. New York city in 1790 possessed a population of only 33,131, although it was the largest city in the United States; Philadelphia was second, with 28,522; and Boston third, with 18,320. Mails were transported in very irregular fashion, and correspondence was expensive and uncertain.

There were, moreover, other difficulties which were of serious moment in 1790, but which long ago ceased to be problems in census taking. The inhabitants, having no experience with census taking, imagined that some scheme for increasing taxation was involved, and were inclined to be cautious lest they should reveal too much of their own affairs. There was also opposition to enumeration on religious grounds, a count of inhabitants being regarded by many as a cause for divine displeasure. The boundaries of towns and other minor divisions, and even those of counties, were in many cases unknown or not defined at all. The hitherto semi-independent states had been under the control of the Federal Government for so short a time that the different sections had not yet been welded into an harmonious nationality in which the Federal authority should be unquestioned and instructions promptly and fully obeyed.

AN ACT PROVIDING FOR THE ENUMERATION OF THE INHABITANTS OF THE UNITED STATES

APPROVED MARCH 1, 1790

SECTION 1. Be it enacted by the Senate and House of Representatives of the United States of America in Congress assembled, That the marshals of the several districts of the United States shall be, and they are hereby authorized and required to cause the number of the inhabitants within their respective districts to be taken; omitting in such enumeration Indians not taxed, and distinguishing free persons, including those bound to service for a term of years, from all others; distinguishing also the sexes and colours of free persons, and the free males of sixteen years and upwards from those under that age; for effecting which purpose the marshals shall have power to appoint as many assistants within their respective districts as to them shall appear necessary; assigning to each assistant a certain division of his district, which division shall consist of one or more counties, cities, towns, townships, hundreds or parishes, or of a territory plainly and distinctly bounded by water courses, mountains, or public roads   The marshals and their assistants shall respectively take an oath or affirmation, before some judge or justice of the peace, resident within their respective districts, previous to their entering on the discharge of the duties by this act required. The oath or affirmation of the marshal shall be, "I, A. B., Marshal of the district of ———, do solemnly swear (or affirm) that I will well and truly cause to be made a just and perfect enumeration and description of all persons resident within my district, and return the same to the President of the United States, agreeably to the directions of an act of Congress, intituled 'An act providing for the enumeration of the inhabitants of the United States,' according to the best of my ability." The oath or affirmation of an assistant shall be "I, A. B., do solemnly swear (or affirm) that I will make a just and perfect enumeration and description of all persons resident within the division assigned to me by the marshal of the district of ———, and make due return thereof to the said marshal, agreeably to the directions of an act of Congress, intituled 'An act providing for the enumeration of the inhabitants of the United States,' according to the best of my ability." The enumeration shall commence on the first Monday in August next, and shall close within nine calendar months thereafter. The several assistants shall, within the said nine months, transmit to the marshals by whom they shall be respectively appointed, accurate returns of all persons, except Indians not taxed, within their respective divisions, which returns shall be made in a schedule, distinguishing the several families by the names of their master, mistress, steward, overseer, or other principal person therein, in manner following, that is to say:

The number of persons within my division, consisting of ———, appears in a schedule hereto annexed, subscribed by me this —— day of ———, 179-. A. B. *Assistant to the marshal of* ——.

Schedule of the whole number of persons within the division allotted to A. B.

Names of heads of families.	Free white males of 16 years and upwards, including heads of families.	Free white males under 16 years.	Free white females, including heads of families.	All other free persons.	Slaves.

SECTION 2. And be it further enacted, That every assistant failing to make return, or making a false return of the enumeration to the marshal, within the time by this act limited, shall forfeit the sum of two hundred dollars.

SECTION 3. And be it further enacted, That the marshals shall file the several returns aforesaid, with the clerks of their respective district courts, who are hereby directed to receive and carefully preserve the same: And the marshals respectively shall, on or before the first day of September, one thousand seven hundred and ninety-one, transmit to the President of the United States, the aggregate amount of each description of persons within their respective districts. And every marshal failing to file the returns of his assistants, or any of them, with the clerks of their respective district courts, or failing to return the aggregate amount of each description of persons in their respective districts, as the same shall appear from said returns, to the President of the United States within the time limited by this act, shall, for every such offense, forfeit the sum of eight hundred dollars; all which forfeitures shall be recoverable in the courts of the districts where the offenses shall be committed, or in the circuit courts to be held within the same, by action of debt, information or indictment; the one-half thereof to the use of the United States, and the other half to the informer; but where the prosecution shall be first instituted on the behalf of the United States, the whole shall accrue to their use. And for the more effectual discovery of offenses, the judges of the several district courts, at their next sessions, to be held after the expiration of the time allowed for making the returns of the enumeration hereby directed, to the President of the United States, shall give this act in charge to the grand juries, in their respective courts, and shall cause the returns of the several assistants to be laid before them for their inspection.

SECTION 4. And be it further enacted, That every assistant shall receive at the rate of one dollar for every one hundred and fifty persons by him returned, where such persons reside in the country; and where such persons reside in a city, or town, containing more than five thousand persons, such assistants shall receive at the rate of one dollar for every three hundred persons; but where, from the dispersed situation of the inhabitants in some divisions, one dollar for every one hundred and fifty persons shall be insufficient, the marshals, with the approbation of the judges of their respective districts, may make such further allowance to the assistants in such divisions as shall be deemed an adequate compensation, provided the same does not exceed one dollar for every fifty persons by them returned. The several marshals shall receive as follows: The marshal of the district of Maine, two hundred dollars; the marshal of the district of New Hampshire, two hundred dollars; the marshal of the district of Massachusetts, three hundred dollars; the marshal of the district of Connecticut, two hundred dollars; the marshal of the district of New York, three hundred dollars; the marshal of the district of New Jersey, two hundred dollars; the marshal of the district of Pennsylvania, three hundred dollars; the marshal of the district of Delaware, one hundred dollars; the marshal of the district of Maryland, three hundred dollars; the marshal of the district of Virginia, five hundred dollars; the marshal of the district of Kentucky, two hundred and fifty dollars; the marshal of the district of North Carolina, three hundred and fifty dollars; the marshal of the district of South Carolina, three hundred dollars; the marshal of the district of Georgia, two hundred and fifty dollars. And to

obviate all doubts which may arise respecting the persons to be returned, and the manner of making the returns.

SECTION 5. Be it enacted, That every person whose usual place of abode shall be in any family on the aforesaid first Monday in August next, shall be returned as of such family; the name of every person, who shall be an inhabitant of any district, but without a settled place of residence, shall be inserted in the column of the aforesaid schedule, which is allotted for the heads of families, in that division where he or she shall be on the said first Monday in August next, and every person occasionally absent at the time of the enumeration, as belonging to that place in which he usually resides in the United States.

SECTION 6. And be it further enacted, That each and every person more than 16 years of age, whether heads of families or not, belonging to any family within any division of a district made or established within the United States, shall be, and hereby is, obliged to render to such assistant of the division, a true account, if required, to the best of his or her knowledge, of all and every person belonging to such family, respectively, according to the several descriptions aforesaid, on pain of forfeiting twenty dollars, to be sued for and recovered by such assistant, the one-half for his own use, and the other half for the use of the United States.

SECTION 7. And be it further enacted, That each assistant shall, previous to making his return to the marshal, cause a correct copy, signed by himself, of the schedule containing the number of inhabitants within his division, to be set up at two of the most public places within the same, there to remain for the inspection of all concerned; for each of which copies the said assistant shall be entitled to receive two dollars, provided proof of a copy of the schedule having been so set up and suffered to remain, shall be transmitted to the marshal, with the return of the number of persons; and in case any assistant shall fail to make such proof to the marshal, he shall forfeit the compensation by this act allowed him.

Approved March 1, 1790.

Population of the United States as returned at the First Census, by states: 1790.

DISTRICT.	Free white males of 16 years and upward, including heads of families.	Free white males under 16 years.	Free white females, including heads of families.	All other free persons.	Slaves.	Total.
Vermont	22,435	22,328	40,505	255	[1] 16	[2] 85,539
New Hampshire	36,086	34,851	70,160	630	158	141,885
Maine	24,384	24,748	46,870	538	None.	96,540
Massachusetts	95,453	87,289	190,582	5,463	None.	378,787
Rhode Island	16,019	15,799	32,652	3,407	948	68,825
Connecticut	60,523	54,403	117,448	2,808	2,764	237,946
New York	83,700	78,122	152,320	4,654	21,324	340,120
New Jersey	45,251	41,416	83,287	2,762	11,423	184,139
Pennsylvania	110,788	106,948	206,363	6,537	3,737	434,373
Delaware	11,783	12,143	22,384	3,899	8,887	[3] 59,094
Maryland	55,915	51,339	101,395	8,043	103,036	319,728
Virginia	110,936	116,135	215,046	12,866	292,627	747,610
Kentucky	15,154	17,057	28,922	114	12,430	73,677
North Carolina	69,988	77,506	140,710	4,975	100,572	393,751
South Carolina	35,576	37,722	66,880	1,801	107,094	249,073
Georgia	13,103	14,044	25,739	398	29,264	82,548
Total number of inhabitants of the United States exclusive of S. Western and N. territory	807,094	791,850	1,541,263	59,150	694,280	3,893,635

	Free white males of 21 years and upward.	Free males under 21 years of age.	Free white females.	All other persons.	Slaves.	Total.
S. W. territory	6,271	10,277	15,365	361	3,417	35,691
N. "						

[1] The census of 1790, published in 1791, reports 16 slaves in Vermont. Subsequently, and up to 1860, the number is given as 17. An examination of the original manuscript returns shows that there never were any slaves in Vermont. The original error occurred in preparing the results for publication, when 16 persons, returned as "Free colored," were classified as "Slave."

[2] Corrected figures are 85,425, or 114 less than figures published in 1790, due to an error of addition in the returns for each of the towns of Fairfield, Milton, Shelburne, and Williston, in the county of Chittenden; Brookfield, Newbury, Randolph, and Strafford, in the county of Orange; Castleton, Clarendon, Hubbardton, Poultney, Rutland, Shrewsbury, and Wallingford, in the county of Rutland; Dummerston, Guilford, Halifax, and Westminster, in the county of Windham; and Woodstock, in the county of Windsor.

[3] Corrected figures are 59,096, or 2 more than figures published in 1790, due to error in addition.

ERRATA.

LITCHFIELD COUNTY, CONNECTICUT.

The twelve towns in Litchfield county given below were returned under the heading, "Litchfield;" the population could not be separated, and the total, 20,342, represents the population, and the names given on pages 59 to 70, under Litchfield town, are the names of the heads of families of these towns, and not of Litchfield town alone:

Barkhamstead,	Hartland,	Salisbury,
Canaan,	Litchfield,	Sharon,
Colebrook,	New Hartford,	Torrington,
Goshen,	Norfolk,	Winchester.

Summary of population, by counties and towns: 1790.

FAIRFIELD COUNTY.

TOWN.	Number of heads of families.	Free white males of 16 years and upward, including heads of families.	Free white males under 16 years.	Free white females, including heads of families.	All other free persons.	Slaves.	Total.
Brookfield.................	189	267	219	522	7	3	1,018
Danbury...................	563	780	704	1,503	20	23	3,030
Fairfield..................	707	1,027	896	1,869	14	203	4,009
Greenwich................	527	801	638	1,572	32	89	3,132
Huntington..............	476	671	625	1,278	48	120	2,742
New Fairfield............	277	401	404	755	4	9	1,573
Newtown.................	445	723	635	1,342	10	64	2,774
Norwalk.................\	1,629	2,196	2,160	4,253	88	113	8,810
Stamford................/							
Reading..................	264	392	327	735	17	32	1,503
Ridgefield...............	351	488	461	989	4	5	1,947
Stratford.................	548	822	726	1,536	59	98	3,241
Weston...................	437	619	603	1,187	24	36	2,469
Total...............	6,413	9,187	8,398	17,541	327	795	36,248

HARTFORD COUNTY.

TOWN.	Number of heads of families.	Free white males of 16 years and upward, including heads of families.	Free white males under 16 years.	Free white females, including heads of families.	All other free persons.	Slaves.	Total.
Berlin.....................	452	631	561	1,258	11	4	2,465
Bristol....................	440	595	612	1,236	16	3	2,462
East Hartford............	473	790	670	1,519	7	30	3,016
East Windsor.............	481	715	563	1,281	33	8	2,600
Enfield...................	317	478	382	927	.....	13	1,800
Farmington..............	439	679	673	1,302	34	8	2,696
Glastenbury.............	468	639	672	1,323	71	27	2,732
Granby...................	489	674	669	1,226	21	5	2,595
Hartford.................	664	1,057	858	2,033	94	48	4,090
Simsbury................	424	657	649	1,256	12	2	2,576
Southington.............	389	540	504	1,038	16	12	2,110
Suffield..................	407	639	592	1,181	27	28	2,467
Wethersfield.............	685	950	816	1,924	52	64	3,806
Windsor..................	456	738	619	1,310	36	11	2,714
Total...............	6,584	9,782	8,840	18,814	430	263	38,129

LITCHFIELD COUNTY.

TOWN.	Number of heads of families.	Free white males of 16 years and upward, including heads of families.	Free white males under 16 years.	Free white females, including heads of families.	All other free persons.	Slaves.	Total.
Bethlem..................	178	275	243	534	.....	4	1,056
Cornwall.................	256	396	318	710	27	19	1,470
Harwinton...............	230	354	334	673	.....	6	1,367
Kent.....................	215	348	317	635	11	7	1,318
Litchfield................	3,361	5,206	4,931	9,912	199	94	20,342
New Milford.............	555	849	728	1,523	41	26	3,167
Southbury...............	308	485	369	842	19	23	1,738
Warren...................	146	199	207	373	5	6	790
Washington.............	268	442	399	818	11	5	1,675
Watertown...............	573	801	779	1,562	3	25	3,170
Woodbury...............	476	686	624	1,327	7	18	2,662
Total...............	6,566	10,041	9,249	18,909	323	233	38,755

MIDDLESEX COUNTY.

TOWN.	Number of heads of families.	Free white males of 16 years and upward, including heads of families.	Free white males under 16 years.	Free white females, including heads of families.	All other free persons.	Slaves.	Total.
Chatham.................	563	812	730	1,648	21	19	3,230
East Haddam............	472	702	592	1,400	35	20	2,749
Haddam..................	356	576	474	1,142	2	1	2,195
Killingworth.............	390	586	454	1,094	11	11	2,156
Middletown..............	944	1,240	1,266	2,684	56	129	5,375
Saybrook................	559	819	696	1,663	19	36	3,233
Total...............	3,284	4,735	4,212	9,631	144	216	18,938

NEW HAVEN COUNTY.

TOWN.	Number of heads of families.	Free white males of 16 years and upward, including heads of families.	Free white males under 16 years.	Free white females, including heads of families.	All other free persons.	Slaves.	Total.
Branford	384	565	504	1,108	36	54	2,267
Cheshire.................	440	592	507	1,192	31	15	2,337
Derby....................	553	751	727	1,414	52	50	2,994
Durham..................	209	315	214	526	7	9	1,071
East Haven..............	169	234	225	524	7	35	1,025
Guilford.................	728	951	714	1,732	22	41	3,460
Hamden.................	291	374	322	718	4	4	1,422
Milford..................	446	536	442	988	69	63	2,098
New Haven city..........	918	1,125	928	2,234	121	76	4,484
North Haven.............	238	320	275	626	8	7	1,236
Wallingford.............	656	846	784	1,667	26	52	3,375
Waterbury...............	552	734	717	1,460	14	12	2,937
Woodbridge.............	414	513	499	1,069	28	15	2,124
Total...............	5,998	7,856	6,858	15,258	425	433	30,830

Summary of population, by counties and towns: 1790—Continued.

NEW LONDON COUNTY.

TOWN.	Number of heads of families.	Free white males of 16 years and upward, including heads of families.	Free white males under 16 years.	Free white females, including heads of families.	All other free persons.	Slaves.	Total.
Not returned by towns....	5,692	8,224	7,183	16,478	729	586	33,200

TOLLAND COUNTY.

TOWN.	Number of heads of families.	Free white males of 16 years and upward, including heads of families.	Free white males under 16 years.	Free white females, including heads of families.	All other free persons.	Slaves.	Total.
Bolton...................	228	317	322	648	4	2	1,293
Coventry.................	336	512	515	1,079	17	7	2,130
Ellington................	171	285	220	534	15	2	1,056
Hebron..................	345	611	516	1,064	23	20	2,234
Somers..................	200	224	301	595	2	5	1,127
Stafford.................	315	476	445	956	4	4	1,885
Tolland..................	236	386	422	713	12	5	1,538
Union....................	100	150	162	318	.....	1	631
Willington...............	208	302	289	603	17	1	1,212
Total...............	2,139	3,263	3,192	6,510	94	47	13,106

WINDHAM COUNTY.

TOWN.	Number of heads of families.	Free white males of 16 years and upward, including heads of families.	Free white males under 16 years.	Free white females, including heads of families.	All other free persons.	Slaves.	Total.
Ashford..................	393	661	644	1,250	21	7	2,583
Brooklyne...............	177	352	302	633	30	11	1,328
Canterbury..............	288	501	387	975	16	2	1,881
Hampton................	201	338	303	680	10	1	1,332
Killingley...............	326	543	544	1,050	20	9	2,166
Lebanon.................	574	1,042	932	2,089	53	50	4,166
Mansfield...............	394	689	611	1,319	9	7	2,635
Plainfield...............	238	466	356	821	60	10	1,713
Pomfret.................	244	463	376	890	20	19	1,768
Thompson...............	333	562	555	1,138	5	7	2,267
Voluntown..............	290	487	435	915	14	21	1,872
Windham................	414	670	580	1,424	63	28	2,765
Woodstock..............	330	666	526	1,222	19	12	2,445
Total...............	4,202	7,440	6,551	14,406	340	184	28,921

Assistant marshals for the state: 1790.

DISTRICT.	NAME.
Fairfield county (part of)................................. Brookfield, Danbury, Fairfield, Huntington, and New Fairfield towns.	Daniel Bradley.
Fairfield county (part of)................................. Greenwich, Norwalk, and Stamford towns.	David Maltbie.
Fairfield county (part of)................................. Newtown, Reading, Stratford, and Weston towns.	Sam^el B. Sherwood.
Fairfield county (part of)............................ Ridgefield town.	John Keeler.
Hartford county................................... Berlin, Bristol, East Hartford, East Windsor, Enfield, Farmington, Glastenbury, Granby, Hartford, Simsbury, Southington, Suffield, Wethersfield, and Windsor towns.	John Dodd.
Litchfield county (part of)............................ Bethlem, Cornwall, Harwinton, Kent, New Milford, Southbury, Warren, Washington, Watertown, and Woodbury towns.	David Judson.
Litchfield county (part of).......................... Litchfield town.	Saml Marsh.
Middlesex county.................................. Chatham, East Haddam, Haddam, Killingworth, Middletown, and Saybrook towns.	Saml Canfield.
New Haven county................................. Branford, Cheshire, Derby, Durham, East Haven, Guilford, Hamden, Milford, North Haven, Wallingford, Waterbury, and Woodbridge towns, and New Haven city.	John Rutherford Throop.
New London county............................... Entire county.	Joshua Huntirgton.
Tolland county.................................... Bolton, Coventry, Ellington, Hebron, Somers, Stafford, Tolland, Union, and Willington towns.	Wm Williams.
Windham county.................................. Ashford, Brooklyne, Canterbury, Hampton, Killingley, Lebanon, Mansfield, Plainfield, Pomfret, Thompson, Voluntown, Windham, and Woodstock towns.	Eben^r Gray.

FAIRFIELD COUNTY.[1]

BROOKFIELD TOWN.

NAME OF HEAD OF FAMILY.	Free white males of 16 years and upward, including heads of families.	Free white males under 16 years.	Free white females, including heads of families.	All other free persons.	Slaves.
Stephens, Hezekiah, Jur.	2	2	2		
Morehouse, John	1	1	2		
Frank, Robin				7	
Wakeley, Lemwell	4	1	5		
Rugles, Eden	1		1		
Buckingham, Curtis	1		1		
Osborn, Israel	1		1		
Stephens, Hezekiah	1		2		
Brush, Joseph	1	1	1		
Starr, Giddeon	1		2		
Chase, Isaac	1	1	4		
Hull, Abraham	1		3		
Wileman, Lebeus	1	1	2		
Starr, Joseph	2		3		
Wileman, Richard	1	2	3		
Gregory, John, Jur	1	1	3		
Stephens, John	1	1	3		
Gregory, John	2		5		
Dunnen, Nathan	2		2		
Dunnen, Jeremiah	1	1	4		
Starr, Zarr	1	1	1		
Sturdevant, John	1		1		
Sturdevant, Timothy	2	4	3		
Barnum, Ebenezer	1		1		
Dunnen, John	1		2		
Penny, Jane			1		
Starr, John	1		2		
Hamblen, William	1		1		
Patch, Thompson	1	6	2		
Anderson, Daniel	1		5		
Lobden, Daniel	1	2	1		
Lobden, John	1	1	4		
Clark, Oliver	2		2		
Starr, James	2		3		
Brister, Isarel	2		2		
Lobden, Lewis	1		6		
Gray, Hezekiah	1		1		
Barnum, Isaac	2		2		
Veal, John	1	2	3		
Barnum, Ezbon	1	2	5		
Osborn, David	2	1	2		
Barlow, Nehemiah	3	1	3		
Bennet, David	1	2	2		
Burrit, Franses	1	1	2		
Osborn, James	2	1	2		
Camp, Abraham	1		1		
Camp, Levi	1	1	2		
Hubbell, Coleman	1	3	2		
Noble, Elethan	2	4	3		
Noble, Jesse	2	2	5		
Smith, Jehiel	1		2		
Palmer, Amme	2	1	1		
Bostwick, Benjamin	4		7		
Tomlinson, Joseph	3	2	3		
Rugles, Samuel	2	3	6		
Rugles, Joseph	4		2		
Knowls, Elezer	1	1	4		
Rudles, Timothy	4	2	3		
Like, Andrew	3	1	3		
Beeman, Josiah	1	1	4		
Bawlden, Tibbals	3	2	3		
Rugles, Abijah	4	1	6		
Rugles, Benjamin	1	1	3		
Bawlden, Thaddeus	4	1	3		
Warner, Martin	3		5		
Warner, Solomon	2		4		
Warner, Rugles	1	1	3		
Summers, Mark	1	1	3		
Hamblen, Elisha	1	3	1		
Keeler, David	1	1	2		
Keeler, John	1				
Keeler, Elisha	1		2		
Keeler, Nathan	1	3	5		
Nearing, Henery	1	5	2		
Smith, Ralph	1	2	3		
Nichols, William	1		1		
Rood, John	1	1	3		
Keeler, Sarah		1	2		
Hamblen, David	1		1		
Murry, Benjamin	1	2	1		
Mallet, Edmon	1	3	4		
Murrin, Nathan	1	1	6		
Wheeler, Daniel	1	3	2		
Murrin, Isaac	3	3	5		
Starr, Elijah	1	1	6		
Rugles, Bostwick	1		1		
Rugles, Ashbell	1		1		
Murrin, Levi	2		3		
Hawley, Liverius	1		3		
Nearnin, John H.	1		1		
Nearnin, Joseph	1	3	3		
Murrin, Samuel, Jur.	2	1	1		
Smith, David	1		1		

BROOKFIELD TOWN—continued.

NAME OF HEAD OF FAMILY.	Free white males of 16 years and upward, including heads of families.	Free white males under 16 years.	Free white females, including heads of families.	All other free persons.	Slaves.
Smith, Joseph	1	4	3		
Sherman, Rufus	1	1	2		
Bulkley, Luther	1		2		1
Towner, Nathanel	2	1	3		
Wheeler, Amos	2	3	3		
Lockwood, Isaac	1	1	5		
Northrop, Isaac	1	1	3		
Murrin, Samuel	2		2		
Murrin, Andrew	1	1	1		
Peck, David	1	3	3		
Peck, Miel	3	1	5		
Camp, Nathan	2	1	3		
Bunnel, Job	1	3	4		
Hawley, Nehemiah	2	1	2		
Hawley, Jedidah		2	1		
Dunnen, Joseph	1	1	1		
Hawley, Sarah			2		2
Cole, Elezer	1		1		
Dunnen, Woolcott	1	1	2		
Bennet, John	2	1	4		
Cox, William	1	3	4		
Dunnen, Reubin	1	1	4		
Keeler, John, Jur	1	2	5		
Dunnen, Giddeon	1	3	4		
Dunnen, Eli	1		1		
Dunnen, Luther	1	2	2		
Dunnen, Jered	1	1	2		
Booth, Abel	2	1	4		
Booth, Philo	2		1		
Jackson, Gershom	2	2	6		
Jackson, Ephraim	1	2	4		
Tredway, John	1	2	5		
French, Samuel	1	1	2		
Gun, Joseph	1		1		
Davis, George	1		2		
Wakelin, James	1		2		
Botchford, James	1	2	2		
Hurd, Jabesh	1		3		
Hurd, Abel	2		8		
Northrop, Enos	2	1	2		
Sherman, Zadock	3	2	4		
Smith, Ebenezer	3	1	3		
Smith, Sherman	2	2	3		
Smith, Joseph, 3d	1	2	3		
Smith, Richard	1	1	5		
Blackman, Ebenezer	1		2		
Blackman, Niram	1	1	1		
Blackman, Philo	1	1	2		
Hawse, Jabes	1		1		
Bostwick, Levi	3	5	4		
Taylor, Andrew	1	1	2		
Dunnen, John, Jur	2	3	4		
Stephens, Daniel	1	2	2		
Northrop, Mary			1		
Peck, John	1	2	3		
Sherman, Samuel	1	1	4		
Jackson, David	1	4	6		
Jackson, Daniel	1	4	5		
Brooks, Thomas	2		3		
Northrop, Wait	1		1		
Northrop, Anne	1		1		
Hawley, Isaac	2	1	4		
Dunnen, Liverius	2	2	1		
Northrop, Joshua, Jur.	1		3		
Northrop, Joshua	1		2		
Northrop, Asa	1	1	2		
French, Wells	1		1		
Judson, Joel	1	1	4		
Carman, John	1	1	3		
Wood, Preserve	1	2	2		
Northrop, Drake	1	2	2		
Knapp, Fransis	1	1	1		
Gun, Abel	1	2	5		
Brown, Samuel	2	3	3		
Peck, Hennery	3		2		
Northrop, David	2	1	2		
Stephens, Joshua	1		2		
Hallebert, David	1	2	3		
Stephens, Josiah	1		3		
Stephens, Ager	1	1	4		
Stephens, Eden	2		4		
Dibble, Ezra	1	1	3		
Dibble, Levi	1		1		
Dibble, Ezra, Jur	1		1		
Smith, Joseph	2	1	2		
Smith, Eli	2	2	1		
Smith, Amos	2	1	3		
Smith, Amos, Jnr	2		2		
Smith, Abel	1	3	3		
Gray, Isaac	2	2	3		

BROOKFIELD TOWN—continued.

NAME OF HEAD OF FAMILY.	Free white males of 16 years and upward, including heads of families.	Free white males under 16 years.	Free white females, including heads of families.	All other free persons.	Slaves.
Northrop, Andrew	1	3	3		
Picket, Thomas	2		3		
Platt, Nathan	1	2	3		
Brooks, Thomas, Jur	1	1	3		

DANBURY TOWN.

NAME OF HEAD OF FAMILY.	Free white males of 16 years and upward, including heads of families.	Free white males under 16 years.	Free white females, including heads of families.	All other free persons.	Slaves.
Wood, James	1	3	4		
Olmsted, Daniel	1		2		
Barnum, Josiah	1		4		
Griffin, Catherine		2	2		
Sanford, Joel	1	1	1		
Knapp, John	1		1		
Dightman, Thaddeus	2	2	2		
Wood, Samuel	3	3	4		
Washburn, Joseph	1	2	3		
Clark, Mary		1	3		
Wood, Daniel	1		3		
Wood, Daniel, Jnr	1	3	3		
Chapman, Joshua	1	1	1		
Wood, Nathan	2	1	5		
Barnum, John	1		2		
Dightman, Thomas	1		1		
Barnum, Noah	1	2	2		
Peck, Abijah	1	1	2		
Benedict, Michael	1		2		
Barnum, Eliphilet	1	2	4		
Andrews, Hannah	1		1		
Andrews, Samuel	1	2	3		
Stringham, Peter	1		1		
Benedict, Peter	1	2	4		
Hawley, Closen	1	1	5		
Brown, James	1	1	4		
Taylor, Major	2	2	5		1
Benedict, Eliakam	2	2	2		
Bennedict, Mary		1	3		
Hoyt, Comfort	1	3	3		
McClane, John	3	1	7		1
Clark, James	7	3	6		
Seib, James	1		2		
Rider, John	2	2	2		
Foot, Abel	1	1	2		
Douglass, Nathan	3	1	1		
Jarvis, Stephen	2		2		
White, Joseph M	7	3	4		1
Whiting, Frederick S	2	2	1		1
Wood, John	2		1		
Starr, Thomas	1	2	1		
Wood, David	1	2	4		
Church, Daniel	1		1		
Benedict, Joshua	1	1	6		
Mygatt, Eli	3	2	6		1
Ames, Everit	1	1	3		
Foot, Patience		1	3		
Clark, Joseph	3	2	2		
Smith, Josiah	2		1		
Peck, Eliakam	4	1	2		
Hodges, Ezra	1	2	4		
Hambleton, Paul	3	3	5		
Knapp, John	1	1	1		
Hambleton, John	1	3	3		
Maxfield, Joseph	1		1		
Porter, Joshua	1	1	5		
Seger, Daniel	1	3	1		
Hoyt, Thaddeus	1		4		
Morehouse, Thaddeus	1		2		
Comstolk, Stephen	2	2	5		
Picket, David	1		2		
Bass, Newcomb	1	3	1		
Starr, Ethel	1	1	1		
Starr, Nathanel	4	1	4		
Wileman, Timothy	2	1	1		
Brush, Stephen	1	1	1		
Wileman, Ezekiel	2	1	2		
Cornwell, John	1		1		
Cornwell, Nathan	1	2	1		
Steward, James	2		6		
Steward, Alexander	2	1	2		
Hoyt, Eli	4	2	2		
Hoyt, David	2		1		
Hoyt, Ager	1	1	3		
Hubbell, Ezra	2	1	2		
Nichols, Ebenezer	1	2	1		
Wileman, Isaac	1	2	1		
Benedict, Abraham	1		3		
Benedict, Abraham, Jnr.	1	2	3		
Gregory, Thomas	1	2	3		
Wileman, Noah	1	1	1		
Wileman, Isaac, Jnr	1	2	3		
Wileman, David	1	1	2		
Patch, Quint	1	1	2		
Patch, Ezra	1	3	1		

[1] No attempt has been made in this publication to correct mistakes in spelling made by the deputy marshals, but the names have been reproduced as they appear upon the census schedules.

FAIRFIELD COUNTY—Continued.

DANBURY TOWN—con.

NAME OF HEAD OF FAMILY.	Free white males of 16 years and upward, including heads of families.	Free white males under 16 years.	Free white females, including heads of families.	All other free persons.	Slaves.
Starr, Thomas, Jnr	1		1		
Bowton, Daniel	1	2	3		
Judd, Abner	1	1	2		
Judd, Thomas, 1	1		1		
Coles, Levi	2	1	2		
Nichols, Samuel	2	1	2		
Dibble, Elisha	2		2		
Judd, Thomas, 2	2	1	3		
Hoyt, Jonathan	2		1		
Picket, Ebenezer	1	3	6		
Hoyt, Enos	1	1	1		
Bowton, Eli	1	2	3		
Mygatt, Philo	1		4		
Dibble, Tar	1	1	2		
Hoyt, Daniel	1		3		
Daley, Benjamin	1	1	1		
White, Thomas P	2	5	3	1	
Knapp, Joshua	2		2		
Knapp, Daniel	1	2	4		
Judd, Jacob	2	3	4		
Hambleton, Silas	1		2		
Hoyt, Drake, Jnr	1		1		
Patch, William	1	2	3		
Wileman, Joseph	2	1	2		
Shute, Richard	2	1	5		
Hoyt, Justus	1	2	6		
Hoyt, Noah	4	4	3		
Stephens, Forward	1		4		
Stephens, Ezra, Jnr	1	1	7		
Stephens, Ezra	1	1	2		
Stephens, Samuel	1	4	3		
Peck, Levi	2	4	3		
Peck, Ezra	1	2	1		
Hays, James	3	1	3		
Hambleton, Joseph	1	1	1		
Hambleton, Eliakam	1		1		
Nash, Nathanel	1	3	2		
Knapp, David	1	1	2		
Hoyt, Daniel D	1		3		
Lenslee, Lemuel	1	2	3		
Lenslee, James	1	2	3		
Lindslee, Mathew	2		2		
Barnum, Judah	1	1	3		
Barnum, Seth	1	6	2		
Barnum, Joseph	2		2		
Barnum, Joseph, Jnr	1	2	1		
Barnum, Gabriel	1	1	4		
Hoyt, Nathan	1	3	3		
Hoyt, Starr	1	1	4		
Wilks, Mathew	1	1	2		
Barnum, John, Jnr	1	3	3		
Barnum, Olive			2		
Hoyt, John	2	1	3		
Barnum, Jesby	1		2		
Hoyt, Daniel	1		1		
Bennedict, Elezer	1	1	1		
Hawkins, William	1	4	3		
Wilks, Mathew, Jnr	1		3		
Knapp, Elnathan	3		3		
Knapp, Elnathan, Jnr	1		2		
Benedict, Timothy	1		4		
Roberts, William	2	1	2		
Barnum, Abijah, Jnr	1	1	1		
Knapp, James	2		2		
Picket, Ebenezer, Jnr	1		1		
Bouton, Mathew	2		4		
Benedict, David	1		3		
Boughton, Thomas	1	1	1		
Pierce, Joshua	1	1	2		
Weed, Throm	1	1	3		
Stone, Oliver	1	2	2		
Barnum, Nathanel	3		2		
Finch, Nathanel	1	1	4		
Hoyt, Eleazer	1	1	3		
Sturges, Moris S	1		3		
Barnum, Abijah	2	2	3		
Benedict, Asa	1	4	3		
Benedict, Samuel, 1st	1	1	1		
Benedict, Elijah	1	3	1		
Benedict, Asor	1	2	7		
Weed, Samuel	1		1		
Benedict, Samuel, 2d	1	2	2		
Weed, Azer	1	3	2		
Barber, Benjamin	2		1		
Pierce, David	2	2	2		
Weed, David	1	1	3		
Knapp, Henery	1	2	5		
Gregory, Nathanel	2	2	4		
Gregory, John	2	1	3		
Gregory, Samuel	1	3	2		
Combs, John	1	1	6		
Boughton, Joseph	1	1	2		
Weed, Ebenezer	1		2		

DANBURY TOWN—con.

NAME OF HEAD OF FAMILY.	Free white males of 16 years and upward, including heads of families.	Free white males under 16 years.	Free white females, including heads of families.	All other free persons.	Slaves.
Cook, Thomas	1	1	1		
Presbrey, Joseph	1		1		
Vinen, Josiah	1		1		
Gorham, Benjamin	1	1	6		
Peck, John	1	1	4		
Husted, Andrew	1	3	5		
Bennedict, Ephraim	1	1	2		
Barnum, Ezra	1		4		
Ludeman, John	1		1		
Trobridge, Isaac	2	1	1		
Barnum, Samuel	1		1		
Boughton, David, Jnr	4	1	2		
Boughton, Abijah	1		2		
Bowton, David	4		2		
Foot, John	3	3	4		
Bishop, Nathan	1	1	2		
Moss, Amasa	1	1	4		
Cook, Samuel	1		4		
Van Doosen, John	1		1		
Hoyt, Elijah	1	3	5		
Cook, Joseph P	3	1	4		
Phillips, Samuel H	1	2	1	1	
White, Ebenezer R	3	4	7		1
Cook, Joseph P., Jr	3	1	2		1
Gregory, Ebenezer	3		2		
Benedict, Noble	3	1	2		
Peck, Abijah	3		1		
Heneries, Elizabeth			1		
Barnum, Eleazer	1	3	5		
Church, Elizabeth	1		2		
Barnum, Stephen	2	3	3		
Barnum, Olive			2		
Barnum, Justus	3	2	4		
Agens, Andrew	1	2	4		
Brown, James	1	1	4		
Joyce, John	2	3	3		
Barnum, Benjamin, 1st	1		2		
Ambler, Stephen	1	1	3		
Combs, William	1	2	5		
Hawley, John	1	3	2		
Barnum, Benjamin, 2d	2	1	2		
Hubbell, Noah	1		1		
Roberts, Zelotus	1	5	2		
Porter, John	1				
Porter, Manoah	1	1	1		
Green, Orastus	1	1	2		
Gregory, Nathan	1		3		
Bartram, John	1	1	1		
Curtis, Samuel	2		1		
Curtis, Stephen	1		1		
Cummins, Asa	2	1	5		
Cato (Negro)				2	
Weed, Asa	1	5	1		
Castle, Peter	1	1	2		
Weed, Jonas	1		2		
Weed, Ephraim	1		2		
Seger, Eli	1	2	4		
Stephens, Eliphilet	2	2	5		
Stephens, Jonathan	1	2	5		
Stephens, Thomas, 1st	2		2		
Stephens, Thomas, 2	1	1	3		
Stephens, James	2	2	6		
Burrit, Philip	1	6	3		
Benedict, Theofelus	1	2	3		
Foster, Jesse	2	1	5		
De Forest, Elihue	2	1	2		
Taylor, Theofelus	1	1	4		
Taylor, John	1	1	3		
Taylor, Jonathan	2	3	3		
Bawlden, Samuel	1	3	4		
Bawlden, Calep	1		1		
Taylor, Zalmon	2	2	1		
Benedict, Jonas	2	3	5		
Whitney, Nathan	1	2	1		
Benedict, Lemwell	2	1	2		
Benedict, Stephen B	1		3		
Benedict, Ebenezer	1	2	3		
Benedict, Abigail			2		
Benedict, Nathan	1	2	4		
Taylor, Elezer	1	1	4		
Benedict, Thomas	2	2	5		
Welimar, Thomas	2	1	2		
Knapp, Noah	1		1		
William, Daniel	4	1	2		
Stone, James		1	3		
Bishop, Jonathan A	1		2		
Scofield, James	1		3		
Celogg, Eliphilet	3		5		
Peck, Stephen	1	3	3		
Rayment, Isaac	1	1	1		
Crary, James	1	3	2		
Phelmer, John	1		3		
Brunson, Ezra	1		4		

DANBURY TOWN—con.

NAME OF HEAD OF FAMILY.	Free white males of 16 years and upward, including heads of families.	Free white males under 16 years.	Free white females, including heads of families.	All other free persons.	Slaves.
Bettes, James	1	1	1		
Bettey, Daniel	1		1		
Brunson, Thaddeus	2		2		
Brunson, Amos	1		1		
Curtis, Stephen	2	2	3		
Platt, Joseph	2		6		
Peck, Eliphilet	1		1		
Wood, John	1		4		
Dean, John	1	1	1		
Osborn, Joseph	1	2	1		
Silik, James	1	2	3		
Dightman, Daniel	1	1	1		
Silik, Benjamin	1	2	5		
Silik, Nathanel	1	2	1		
Osborn, David	1		3		
Whitlock, Samuel	3	2	4		
Sturges, Joseph	1	1	7		
Knapp, Bracy	2	2	5		
Heacock, Samuel	1	1	3		
Benedict, Daniel	1		5		
Ambler, Peter	4	2	5		
Brooks, William	1		1		
Stalker, Anne		1	3		
Crowfoot, Ezra	1	1	3		
Mills, John	1	1	3		
Scofield, Stephen	1	4	2		
Crowfoot, Joseph	2	1	4		
Crowfoot, Seth	1	3	4		
Shove, Seth	2		3		
Shove, Levi	1	1	5		
Stone, Elizabeth		1	3		
Monson, Levi	1	1	4		
Washburn, Ephraim	3	1	3		
Ambler, John	1	1	2		
Wileman, Samuel	2		2		
Jube (Negro)				6	
Convass, Demor	2	2	1		
Wileman, Samuel, Jur	1	1	1		
Moris, Shadrack	2	1	3		
Shove, Daniel, Jur	2	2	5		
Shove, Daniel	1		3		
Stone, Levi	2	2	4		
Fielding, James	2	2	5		
Gregory, Monson	1	2	2		
Cosher, Benjamin	5	3	4		
Tweedy, Samuel	2	2	2		
Ambler, Squire	4		2		
Wileman, Abraham	2		3		
Benedict, Ezra	1	2	3		
Cheehan, Nathanel	2		3		
Hambleton, Joseph	3		3		
Bennedict, Calep, Jur	1	2	2		
Benedict, Calep	2	1	2		
Morris, Ephraim	1		2		
Morris, Samuel	3	2	4		
Hoyt, Daniel	1	3	4		
Starr, Rachel	1		2		2
Forgerson, John	1	1	1		
Carington, Daniel N	2	1	5		
Washburn, Edman	2		2		
Curtis, Reubin	1	5	4		
Smith, Samuel	1	1	1		
Benedict, Zadock	3		3		
Tucker, Thomas	3	2	3		
Knapp, Benjamin	4	1	5		
Starr, Jabes	1	2	3		
Comstalk, Daniel	2	1	2		
Porter, John	2	3	1		
Osborn, Levi	2	2	2		
Trobridge, John	2	4	4	1	2
Burr, Oliver	4	3	7		
Langin, Timothy	1	2	2		
Bennedict, Ashel	1		2		
Church, Winter	3	2	3		
Gregory, Nathan	2	1	1		
Gregory, Ezra	2		2		
Gregory, Mathew	1	1	2		
Stephens, Elijah	1		1		
Weed, John	1	1	4		
Starr, Rebekah			1		
Starr, Calep	4	5	3		
Finch, Peluk	1	2	2		
Finch, Jacob	2	1	3		
Phillips, Abiel	2	2	2		
Manson, Ebenezer	2	2	4		
Loveless, Richard	1		3		
Gregory, Deborah		1	3		
Benedict, Joseph	1	2	5		
Benedict, Ebenezer, Jur	1	1	2		
Benedict, Ebenezer	1		1		
Taylor, Timothy, Jur	2	1	3		
Whitlesey, Elisha	1	1	2		

FAIRFIELD COUNTY—Continued.

DANBURY TOWN—con.

NAME OF HEAD OF FAMILY.	Free white males of 16 years and upward, including heads of families.	Free white males under 16 years.	Free white females, including heads of families.	All other free persons.	Slaves.
Mygatt, Comfort	3		5		
Starr, Ezra	1	2	5		3
Jackson, Robert	1	2	2		
White, Fairchild	1	1	1		
Barnum, Eunice		1	2		
Hoyt, Comfort	2		1		
Glover, Christopher	2	5	3		
Bennedict, Thaddeus	1		2		
Curtis, Asa	1	5	3		
Cato (Negro)				5	
Brewer, John	1	4	4		
Starr, Jonathan	2		5		
Zimri (Negro)				5	
Taylor, Joseph	1				1
Bennedict, Comfort	1	3	2		
Bennedict, Jonah	1	2	2		
Griffin, William	1	1	2		
Flin, Thomas	1	1	2		
Andress, Eliakam	1	2	1		
Sperry, Benjamin	1		2		
Hoyt, Amos	3	1	2		
Osborn, Daniel	2	1	2		
Dibble, Daniel	2		1		
Dibble, Ezra	1		3		1
Daw, Isaac	3		2		
Taylor, Gilead	2	1	3		
Osborn, Moses	1		2		
Nikerson, Hannah	1		2		
Taylor, Lemwell	1	1	3		
Dibble, Nehemiah	5	2	3		
Judd, Daniel	2	2	4		
Judd, Elihue	1	2	2		
Gray, Justus	1	1	4		
Taylor, Eliakam	1	1	2		
Griffin, Jonathan	1	1	3		
Hall, David	1	1	2		
Judd, David	1	3	6		
Starr, Nathan	1		3		
Starr, Josiah	1	1	2		2
Starr, Eliakam	1		5		1
Starr, Zadock	2	1	3		
Starr, Mathew	1	2	5		
Wheeler, Philip	2	1	3		
Hays, Peter	1	2	3		
Trobridge, Stephen	1		2		
Bennedict, Joseph	1	1	2		
Bennedict, Levi	1	3	3		
Bennedict, Seth	1		3		
Andress, Robert, Jur	1	5	1		
Henery, Obediah	2	1	3		
Scogel, James	1	1	2		
Standley, Joseph	1		2		
Rockwell, Mercy			1		
Andress, Robert	1		4		
Trobridge, James	2	2	3		
Bennedict, John	1		1		
Bennedict, John, Jur	1	2	1		
Taylor, Thomas	2	1	2		
Heacock, Daniel	2	2	3		
Mathews, John	1	4	2		
Heacock, Benjamin	2		5		
Comstalk, Mercy		1	4		
Hoyt, James	1	3	6		
Barnum Levi	1		6		
Bennedict, Isaac	1		1		
Stove, Samuel	1	3	3		
Bunnel Gershom	1	1	1		
Bartram, James	2	1	5		
Burchard, Elijah	1		2		
Canfield, Samuel	1	5	3		1
Peck, Joseph	1		1		1
Barnum, Daniel	1	2	2		
Bennedict, William	1		6		
Holcomb, Luther	2	5	2		
Taylor, Samuel	1		3		
Taylor, Eli	2	1	3		
Bennedict, Nathanel	2	2	2		
Taylor, Thomas	2	2	3		
Silliman, Ebenezer	1	1	3		
Barnum, Lazerus	1	3	4		
Andress, John, Jur	1	3	1		
Andress, Eden	1	1	2		
Andress, John	1		1		
Taylor, Jabes	2		1		
Hubbell, Silevant	1	1	2		
Ferry, Eliphlet	2	2	5		
Roberts, Luke	2	3	4		
Taylor, Noah	2		5		
Starr, Samuel	2	2	5		
Taylor, John, Jur	3	2	4		
Peck, Benjamin	1		2		
Hoyt, Samuel	1				
Hoyt, Asa	1	1	2		
Peck, Calvin	1	1	3		
Hoyt, Jesse	1	3	1		

DANBURY TOWN—con.

NAME OF HEAD OF FAMILY.	Free white males of 16 years and upward, including heads of families.	Free white males under 16 years.	Free white females, including heads of families.	All other free persons.	Slaves.
Taylor, Silas	1	2	3		
Peck, Eliphilet	1	3	2		
Peck, Jesse	1	2	1		
Judd, Samuel	1		1		
Judd, Ebenezer	1		1		
Thompson, James	1	3	2		
Whitlock, Hezekiah	2	2	4		
Williams, Benjamin	1		3		
Whitlock, Seth	1		2		
Whitlock, John	2		2		
Whitlock, Ebenezer	1		4		
Whitlock, Nehemiah	2	1	4		
Whitlock, Squire	1		2		
Hoyt, Joshua	2	1	4		
Ferrys, Joshua	1		2		
Ferrys, Sarah			2		
Wakely, John	1	2	4		
Wileman, John	1	2	2		
Weed, James, Jur	1	2	2		
Weed, Jonas	2		1		
Crawfoot, Samuel	1	1	1		
Crowfoot, Sealee	1		1		
Crawfoot, Samuel, Jur	1		1		
Platt, Ebenezer	1		4		
Sealee, James	1	1	4		
Bennedict, Oliver	1	1	2		
Bennedict, Ira	1		1		
Hoyt, Samuel	1	1	7		
Benedict, Eliakam	1		1		
Bennedict, Benjamin	1		1		
Taylor, Eliad	1	1	3		
Elmer, Hezekiah	1	4	3		
Judd, Abigail			5		
Heacock, Ebenezer	2	1	3		
Lacy, Abel	1	1	2		
Baley, Benjamin	1	2	2		
Baley, Ebenezer	1	1	4		
Taylor, Phineus	1		1		
Taylor, Nathan	1		1		
Baley, Samuel	2	1	1		
Baley, Benona	1		1		
Taylor, Timothy	1	3	4		
Taylor, Joshua	1	1	2		
Taylor, Jabes, Jur	1	2	4		
Taylor, Jonathan	1	1	3		
Taylor, Ebenezer	1	2	4		
Crawfoot, Daniel	1	1	5		
Beebe, Edmond	1	1	2		
Barnum, Elijah	1		3		
Barnum, Ephraim	1		1		
Bennedict, Benajah	3	2	4		
Hoyt, Benjamin	1	1	3		
Barnum, Abel	1	2	1		
Barnum, David	2	3	3		
Ferry, Benjamin	1	1	4		
Barnum, Mathew, Jur	1	1	3		
Dibble, Thomas	1	1	4		
Dibble, Jeddediah H	1		1		
Dibble, Samuel	2	1	7		
Starr, Thaddeus	1	1	3		
Benedict, Hezekiah	1		3		
Bennedict, James	2	1	3		
Bennedict, Asel	2	1	2		
Bennedict, David, Jur	1	1	2		
Millson, Daniel	1	1	3		
Lacy, Aaron	2		2		
Bennedict, Nathanel	1		1		
Veal, Moses	1	2	3		
Beebe, Joseph	1	1	1		
Beebe, Joseph, Jur	1	2	4		1
Bennedict, Jonathan	1	4	4		
Bennedict, Lemuel	2		2		
Bennedict, Samuel	1		1		
Picket, Hannah	2	2	4		
Dibble, Nathan	1		4		1
Bennedict, Eleazer	1	2	2		
Starr, Jonathan	1	1	1		
Dibble, Eli	1	2	5		
Barnum, John	1	2	4		
Bennedict, Thomas	1		1		
Bennedict, Thomas	1		1		
Wood, Elijah	1	3	3		
Crawfoot, Mathew	1	1	4		
Crowfoot, Levi	2		1		
Starr, Joseph	2	1	2		
Starr, Joseph, Jur	3	2	2		
Crawfoot, Josiah	1		5		
Beebee, Ethel	1		1		
Beebe, Lemuel	1		2		
Beebe, David	1		5		
Beebe, Lemuel, Jur	1	2	3		
Barnum, Ephraim	1	4	4		
Barnum, Mathew	2	2	7		
Barnum, Joseph	1	2	1		
Jennings, Burrit	1		1		

DANBURY TOWN—con.

NAME OF HEAD OF FAMILY.	Free white males of 16 years and upward, including heads of families.	Free white males under 16 years.	Free white females, including heads of families.	All other free persons.	Slaves.
Hoyt, Nathanel	2	4	5		
Maxfield, Eber	1	1	1		
Hoyt, Thomas	2	1	2		
Williams, Thaddeus	1	4	4		
Hoyt, Eleazer	1		1		
Judd, Benjamin	1	1	1		
Weed, Solomon	2	3	2		
Bennedict, Hezekiah, Jur	1	4	3		
Williams, Hezekiah	1	1	4		
Beardslee, Daniel	1	1	2		

FAIRFIELD TOWN.

NAME OF HEAD OF FAMILY.	Free white males of 16 years and upward, including heads of families.	Free white males under 16 years.	Free white females, including heads of families.	All other free persons.	Slaves.
Burr, David	1		2		
Burr, David, Jnr	1	3	3		
Sherwood, Daniel	1	1	3		
Redfield, James, Jnr	1	1	3		
Bulkley, Abigail		1	2		
Oysterbanks, David	2	2	1		
Mills, Joseph	1	3	2		
Chapman, James	2	2	4		1
Oysterbanks, Isaac	1	1	3		
Sherwood, Moses	2	1	3		6
Craft, David	2	2	1		4
Hide, Joseph	2		2		4
Hide, John, Jnr	1		4		
Adams, Nathaniel	1	2	5		2
Oysterbanks, Joshua	1		4		
Redfield, Ebenezer	1		1		
Batterson, John	1	1	2		
Allan, Moses	2	1	1		
Raymong, Elijah	1	3	3		
Nichols, Moses	2	1	2		
Davis, Thomas	1	1	2		
Darrow, Daniel	1		2		
Beers, David, Jnr	1	3	3		
Meeker, Seth, Jnr	1	1	3		
Raymong, David	2		4		
Sherwood, Daniel	2	1	2		
Sturgis, Andrew	1	1	1		2
Batterson, Jorge, Jnr	1	1	5		
Gray, Giddeon	1	1	4		
Ogden, John	1	1	1		
Burr, Eunice	1		4		
Wynkoop, Grisel	1	1	3		
Chapman, Sarah	1		1		
Chapman, John	1		1		1
Chapman, Albert	2	3	2		
Couch, Josiah	2	1	3		
Gorham, Ebenezer	1	2	3		
Lockwood, Stephen	1	2	5		
Hurlbutt, Giddeon	1	5	1		
Bennet, Thomas	1	1	2		
Persall, John	1	1	2		
Persall, Samuel	2	1	2		4
Persall, Samuel, Jnr	1	1	2		
Bennet, Deliverance	1	2	4		
Hanford, Joseph	2	2	3		
Bennet, Hayns	1	1	2		
Hanford, John	1		2		
Godfry, Mary		1	3		
Jesop, Ebenezer, Jnr	1		1		
Hanford, Betty			2		
Clift, William	2		1		
Wood, Samuel	2	1	4		
Baker, Ebenezer	3	3	3		
Couch, Nehemiah	2	1	4		
Adams, Stephen	1	2	1		
Cable, Thomas	3	1	3		
Judah, David	1	3	4		
Smith, Samuel	1	3	5		
Gray, Solomon	3	1	2		
Allen, Gabriel	3	1	5		
Johnson, Nathanel	1		1		
Elwood, Richard	2	2	2		
Batterson, John, Jnr	1	1	1		
Squire, Seth	1	1	1		
Elwood, Hezekiah	2		4		
Elwood, Nathan	1	2	1		
Green, Samuel	1		3		
Batterson, James, Jnr	1		1		
Allen, Gershom	1		2		
Brothington, Daniel	1	1	5		
Disbrow, Justis	1	3	5		
Sherwood, Asahel	1	3	1		
Batterson, James	1		2		
Frasier, Daniel	2	1	3		
Burr, Daniel	3	1	3		
Ogden, Ebenezer	1	1	4		
Hide, John	2	1	1		6
Gorham, Joseph, Jnr	1	3	3		
Mills, Daniel	1	2	6		
Cooley, Hezekiah	1	1	4		
Goodsell, John	1	2	5		
Hanford, Jorge	1	1	2		

FAIRFIELD COUNTY—Continued.

FAIRFIELD TOWN—con.

NAME OF HEAD OF FAMILY.	Free white males of 16 years and upward, including heads of families.	Free white males under 16 years.	Free white females, including heads of families.	All other free persons.	Slaves.
Meeker, Benjamin	2	3	5		
Meeker, Seth	1		3		
Meeker, Joseph	3	1	2		
Sherwood, David	3	1	3		
Hull, Daniel	3	1	7		
Philips, Thomas	1	1	3		
Alvord, John	4	4	3		
Osborn, Levi	1	2	1		
Bradley, Daniel	2	2	4		
Jennings, Aaron	1	4	2		
Row, Ebenezer, Jnr	1		4		
Row, Ebenezer	4		5		
Wakeman, Giddeon	4	1	4		1
Burr, Talcott	2	1	4		1
Taylor, Samuel	4	1	2		
Andrews, John	1	1	3		
Cooley, John	1	1	1		
Wicks, Nathaniel	1		2		
Disbrow, Isaac	1		2		
Guire, Stephen	3	3	1		
Raymong, William	1		2		
Philips, John	2	2	4		
Couch, Giddeon	1	3	2		
Nash, Thomas	1	3	2		5
Nash, Thomas, Jnr	1	1	1		
Allen, Eliphilet	1	1	1		
Morehouse, John	1		2		
Wakeman, Joseph	1	1	3		3
Jerod, John	1	3	3		
Hanford, Hayns	1		2		
Allen, John	1		1		
Bennet, William	1	2	2		
Mosher, George	1	1	5		
Disbrow, Jason	2	1	2		
Bennet, Joseph	1	3	4		1
Bennet, Nathan	2	1	3		
Allen, Benjamin	2	2	4		
Bennet, Daniel	2	2	4		
Allen, Ebenezer	2	3	2		
Allen, Stephen	1	1	1		
Thorp, William	1		3		
Bennet, Moses	2		2		
Disbrow, Levi	2	1	3		
Bennet, James	2	3	2		
Thorp, Stephen	2		4		
Disbrow, Joshua	1	4	2		
Disbrow, John	1	3	1		
Gray, William	2		2		
Bennet, Jabez	2	1	3		
Bennet, Jesse	1	1			
Hill, Thomas	1	1	4		
Ripley, Hezekiel	2	1	3		1
Cable, George	2		4		
Disbrow, Thaddeus	1	1	1		2
Disbrow, Asahel	1	5	6		1
Disbrow, Jabez	1	3	3		
Disbrow, Elias	1	2	4		
Stratton, Cornelius	1	2	3		
Godfry, Stephen	2		4		
Godfry, Ebenezer	2	1	1		
Elwood, Abraham	1	1	1		
Elwood, Abijah	1	1	1		
Couch, Joshua	1		5		
Allen, Elethan	1	1	3		
Allen, William	1		3		
Burrit, Wakeman	2	2	5		
Chapman, Daniel	1	1	2		
Chapman, Denne	2		1		
Chapman, Lovel	1	2	3		
Banks, Talcott	1	2	4		
Godfry, Nathan	1	1	2	2	1
Patterson, John	1	2	2		
Raymong, William, Jnr	1	2	2		
Andrews, Thomas	1	3	1		
Couch, Simon	1	3	2		2
Davis, John	2	3	2		
Jesop, Ebenezer	1	1	4		5
Poor, Jonathan	1		2		
Batterson, William	1	2	8		
Morehouse, Samuel	1	1	2		
Morehouse, Ebenezer	3	3	2		
Morehouse, Abraham	1	2	2		
Morehouse, Eunice	2		1		
Batterson, George	3		3		
Morehouse, Groman	1		5		
Whitehead, Jehiel	3		4		
Jennings, David	1	4	4		
Burr, John	1	3	5		
Bulkley, Peter	2		2		
Bulkley, Abraham	1	2	3		
Godfry, Jonathan	1	1	1		
King, Richard	1		1		
Jennings, Joshua	5	2	4		
Osborn, Abigail			2		1
Osborn, Ebenezer	2	1	4		
Stratton, Joseph	2	3	3		
Bradley, Nathan	2	3	6		

FAIRFIELD TOWN—con.

NAME OF HEAD OF FAMILY.	Free white males of 16 years and upward, including heads of families.	Free white males under 16 years.	Free white females, including heads of families.	All other free persons.	Slaves.
Ogden, Samuel	1	2	1		
Ogden, Hezekiah	1	1	3		
Banks, Jonathan	3	3	3		
Blackman, John	1	2	5		
Perry, Joseph	1	2	1		
Murrin, Meeker	1	1	1		
Murrin, Abijah	2	4	2		
Burr, George	1		4		
Perry, Nathan	2	3	4		
Couch, Abraham	1	1	3		
Smith, Peter	1	5	2		
Smith, Samuel	1	4	1		
Thorp, Gershom	1	3	4		
Lion, Joseph, Jnr	1	1	1		
Banks, Gershom, Jnr	1	3	4		
Banks, Benjamin, Jnr	1	1	8		
Banks, Samuel	1		3		
Banks, Gershom	2		2		
Whitney, Samuel	1		1		
Whitney, Josiah	1	1	2		
Hubbard, Sarah				4	
Bradley, Frances	1		4		
Banks, Daniel	2		2		
Thorp, Jehiel	1	3	2		
Thorp, Ruel	1	2	4		
Holt, Daniel	1	2	1		
Gray, Siliman	2	1	1		
Banks, Nathan	1	2	2		
Banks, Elizabeth			1	1	1
Parrit, David	1	1	1		
Sherwood, Noah	1		1		
Banks, Moses	1	3	4		
Goodsell, Lewis	1	2	3		
Banks, Sarah				4	
Goodsell, James	1	3	3		
Smith, Daniel	1		1		
Smith, Ebenezer	1	1	2		
Sherwood, Jehiel	2	3	5		
Sherwood, Squire	1	2	1		
Whitney, Samuel	2	2	5		
Banks, John	2		3		
Sherwood, Joseph	2	1	5		
Sherwood, Elihue	3	1	5		
Hubbell, John	1		1		
Bradley, Adad	1	2	1		
Nichols, Ephraim	2	3	2		
Bradley, Albin	1		1		
Bradley, Seth	2	3	2		4
Rogers, David	4	4	2		2
Wakeman, John	4	1	2		
Goodsell, David	1		3		
Bradley, John	2		2		2
Oysterbanks, David, Jnr	1		1		
Bradley, Abel	2	2	5		1
Banks, Isaac	1		2		
Sherwood, Gershom	1		2		
Goodsell, Thomas	2	1	2		
Ogden, Moses	2	2	2		
Lion, Joseph	1		2		
Putnam, Aaron	1	3	3		
Banks, Elijah	1	1	3		
Murrin, Ebenezer	1		1		
Bradley, Elisha	3	2	5		
Mitchel, John	1	1	2		
Smith, Benjamin	2		2		
Bradley, Samuel	2	1	5		4
Bradley, Hezekiah	4	1	2		7
Bradley, Walter	2	2	2		1
Bulkley, Joseph	2	2	3		
Bradley, Zalmon	2		1		2
Jennings, Joel	1		6		
Jennings, John	2		2		1
Bradley, David	1		3		
Downs, Abel	1	1	1		
Brown, Samuel	1	1	1		
Downs, Chauncy	1	4	3		
Price, Zalmon	2		1		
Gray, Nehemiah	2	3	4		
Lion, Seth	2	1	2		
Downs, Joseph	1	1	2		
Downs, John	1		1		
Price, David	1		3		1
Gray, Joseph	1		1		
Downs, Mary		2	3		
Price, Hezekiah	1	2	2		
Wakeman, Thaddeus	2	2	3		
Williams, Huldah	1	1	1		
Williams, William	1	3	2		
Wakeman, Abel	1		2		
Wakeman, Gershom	3		2		1
Hubble, David	4	3	1		1
Dwight, Timothy	3	9	1	1	1
Bawlden, Dudley	1	2	2		
Middlebrook, Sylvanus	1	6	2		
Betts, Moses	2	2	2		
Grant, Darius	1		1		
Sherwood, Samuel, 1st	1	1	3		

FAIRFIELD TOWN—con.

NAME OF HEAD OF FAMILY.	Free white males of 16 years and upward, including heads of families.	Free white males under 16 years.	Free white females, including heads of families.	All other free persons.	Slaves.
Sherwood, Albert	4		4		
Redfield, James	2		2		
White, Jacob	3		2		
Middlebrook, Oliver	1	2	5		
Bradley, Peter	1	5	3		
Bradley, Mable		3	3		
Bradley, Joseph	2	1	4		
Hubbell, Gershom	2	3	2		
Sherwood, Ralph	2		2		
Lion, Jesse	1	1	2		
Burr, Jesse	1	2	2		
Sherwood, Increase	1		2		
Bradley, Elethan	2	1	4		
Bulkley, Turney	1	1	6		
Bulkley, Daniel	1		3		
Meeker, Daniel	2	2	4		
Dimon, Samuel	1	1	2		
Polley, John	1	3	1		
Bradley, Nathan	2	2	1		
Perry, Thomas	1	1	4		
Wakeman, Ebenezer	3	2	2		
Williams, David	1		3		
Wheeler, Daniel	3	3	5		
Burr, Ebenezer, 3d	1	2	1		
Burr, Timothy	1		1		
Burr, Zalmon	1		1		
Wakeman, William	5	1	3		
Burr, Ebenezer	1	3	3		
Nichols, Jesse	1	2	2		
Hill, William	2		2		
Nichols, Ebenezer	2	2	2		
Nichols, David	2	6	4		
Wakeman, Epaphras	2	2	5		
Hill, Eliphilet	1		1		
Burr, Joseph	1		1		
Burr, Increase	2	1	2		
Hawley, Catherin		1	3		
Wakeman, Moses	1		2		
Whitehead, Jeremiah	1		1		1
Wakeman, Liman	1	2	2		1
Whitehead, David	1	1	2		
Scudder, Roberd	1	1	1		
Jennings, Edmond	2	5	4		
Jennings, Enoch	1		1		
Bulkley, Nathan	1	2	3		
Bulkley, Peter	1		3		
Henneries, Samuel	1	3	6		
Henneries, Abner	1	3	4		
Willson, Jesse	1	1	1		
Jennings, Gershom	2	2	3		
Wakeman, Eli	1	1	1		1
Wakeman, John, 3d	1		4		
Adams, Ephraim	2	2	6		
Jennings, William	1	1	3		
Lion, Jese	1	2	2		
Gould, Samuel	1		1		
Willson, Robert	1	3	5		
Meeker, Stephen	1		2		
Parret, John	1		5		
Davis, Jabez	2		1		
Wilson, Samuel	2	2	2		
Staples, John	2	1	2		
Waley, Aaron	1	1	3		
Waley, Hezekiah	1		2		
Gould, Stephen	1		3		
Gould, Dimon	1		3		
Hull, Stephen	1		1		
Jennings, Thaddeus	1		3		
Gould, Echobod	1	3	2		
Gould, Jesse	1	4	2		2
Gould, David	2		2		2
Gould, Nathan	5		1		
Lion, Wakeman	1	1	1		1
Lion, Eliphilet	2		1		
Gould, Aaron	3	1	2		
Burr, Samuel	1	2	6		
Webb, Isaac	3	1	7		
Hill, Ebenezer	6	2	4		
Hill, Joseph	2				3
Wheeler, Thomas, Jnr	2	1	2		
Wheeler, Nathan	2	3	3		
Burr, Edmon	2	2	1		
Hull, Ezekiel	3	1	2		3
Goodsell, Epaphras	2	3	2		
Burr, Bud	1		1		1
Sherwood, John	2		2		
Sherwood, Eliphilet	1	2	4		
Sherwood, John, Jnr	1		5		
Middlebrook, Jonathan	1		2		1
Banks, Nehemiah, Jnr	1	5	3		
Banks, Nehemiah	1		2		1
Hull, Eliphilet	1		2		1
Sherwood, Daniel	4	2	3		1
Banks, Joseph	1	3	2		
Hull, John	4	1	3		
Fry, Thomas	1	1	2		
Banks, David	1		2		1

FAIRFIELD COUNTY—Continued.

FAIRFIELD TOWN—con.

NAME OF HEAD OF FAMILY.	Free white males of 16 years and upward, including heads of families.	Free white males under 16 years.	Free white females, including heads of families.	All other free persons.	Slaves.
Rayment, Daniel	1		4		
Bulkley, Gershom	5	4	3		
Osborn, Abel	1		2		
Sherwood, Sarah			1		
Gould, Luther	3	1	2		
Bulkley, Gershom, 2d	3	5	5		
Wynkoop, James	1		2		
Osborn, Daniel	2	1	3		
Osborn, John	1	2	4		
Osborn, Howes	1		2		
Osborn, Stephen	1	2	3	1	
Bulkley, James, Jnr	1				
Sheffield, Paul	2	1	2		
Burr, Wakeman	1	1	4		
Bulkley, Elihue	1	2	2		
Jennings, Nathanel	1	4	1		
Hubbell, Lidea	1	1	2		
Sherwood, Abel	1	1	1		
Pike, William	1	4	3		2
Thorp, Eliphilet	4	1	3		1
Cannon, Samuel	2	1	2		1
Perry, Miah	2		2		
Sturges, Solomon	1	1	3		
Sturges, Ebenezer	1	2	3	1	
Whitney, Peter	1	1	2		
Haleburd, Hosea	1		4		
Swords, Frances D	3		1		
Roberson, William	1		2		
Roberson, John	1	6	2		
Wicks, Alexander	2	1	2		
Perry, Jonathan	1	1	2		
Perry, Jabez	1	2	2		
Squire, Daniel	2	3	4		
Bulkley, Joseph	1	5	4		
Smith, Elnathan	1		2		
Perry, Peter	3	2	6		
Godfry, John	1	1	1		
Godfry, Hannah	3		2		
Osborn, David	2	2	1		
Spragg, Joseph	1		2		
Squire, Benjamin	1				
Perry, John	2		2		
Osborn, Ebenezer, Jnr	2	1	3		
Perry, Ebenezer	2		2		
Perry, Nathanel, Jnr	2		1		
Beers, Nathan	1		1		
Beers, Nathan, Jnr	1	3	4		
Beers, Samuel, Jnr	2	2	1		
Barlow, David	1		3		2
Barlow, Daniel	1	1	2		
Thorp, Jabez	2		2		1
Sturges, Dimon	1	2	3		
Sturges, Eward	1	1	1		
Parsons, Nathan	1		3		
Beers, Reubin	2	1	2		
Beers, David	3	1	1		
Beers, David, Jnr	1	1	1		
Beers, Joseph, Jnr	1	1	3		
Beers, Joseph	2		1		
Beers, Samuel	1	1	1		
Sturges, Abigail	2	2	4	1	
Bulkley, Joseph, 2d	1	2	3		
Barlow, Edmon	1	3	3		
Sturges, Hezekiah	2		2		4
Redfield, Lucretia	1		2		
Bulkley, Josiah	2	2	4		
Sturges, William	1	2	2		
Sturges, Hezekiah, Jnr	2		1		
Trubey, Answell	1	3	5		
Bulkley, Andrew	1		2		
Sturges, Benjamin	2		3		
Sturges, Jonathan	4	1	6		3
Sturges, Seth	4	3	1		
Darrow, Benjamin	1		2		
Roberson, John, Jnr	1		1		
Rollins, Aaron	1		3		
Osborn, Mable			2		1
Jennings, David	1	1	5		
Lewis, Lothrop	1	1	3		3
Bruster, Calep	1	2	3		
Wakeman, Ebenezer	2	2	2		2
Burr, David, 3d	3		2		3
Rowland, Andrew	3	2	2		2
Nichols, Hezekiah	3	2	3	1	
Smedley, Samuel	1		1		1
Rowland, Abigail	1		3		
Spalden, Rowland	1		3		
Runnels, Anne		1	3		
Jennings, Nathan	1		4		
Dimon, William	1	2	4		
Woodhull, Abraham C.	1		3		
Sturges, Abigail	1		1		
Burr, Thaddeus	1		2	1	5
Burr, Gershom	1		2		2
Malbey, Jonathan	2	1	6		1

FAIRFIELD TOWN—con.

NAME OF HEAD OF FAMILY.	Free white males of 16 years and upward, including heads of families.	Free white males under 16 years.	Free white females, including heads of families.	All other free persons.	Slaves.
Allen, David	4	3	3		
Bennedict, Jesse	1	1	2		
Penfield, Samuel	2	1	3		1
Elwood, Thomas	1	1	4		
Bulkley, Hannah	4	1	6		3
Hubbard, Justin	2	1	5		
Bulkley, Nathan	2		3	1	8
Hull, David	1		2		1
Palmitter, Geaner			1		
Fowler, Stephen	1		4		
Silliman, William	1		2		
White, Right	1	2	3		
Jennings, Moses	2	2	3		1
Bibbins, Israel	2	2	5		
Bulkley, Deborah	1		1		
Burr, Samuel, 3d	2	2	5		
Burr, Samuel, 1st	2		4	1	
Fourge, Sarah	1		1		2
Burr, Isaac	1	2	2		1
Hubbell, Jabez	1	1	2		
Hubbell, Isaac	3	4	3		
Abel, Elijah	1		1		4
Bulkley, Ebenezer	2		1		
Turney, Isaac	3	4	5		
Squire, Samuel	1		5	1	
Squire, George	1	2	5		
Nichols, Paul	3	2	6		
Hill, Joseph	1	1	4		
Squire, William	1	1	2		
Burt, Richard	1		1		
Penfield, James, Jnr	1		3		
Penfield, James	3		5		
Burr, Nehemiah	3	1	3		
Squire, John	2	1	2		
Holeburton, Thomas	1	2	3		
Siliman, Christian			3		
Squire, David	2	5	3		
Wheeler, Rebeckah			3		
Chancy, Woolcott	1	1	4		
Stone, Leman	2	1	3		
Bartram, Mary	3		3		
Sturges, Barlow	1	1	3		
Parret, Abraham	2	2	4		
Wheeler, Ichaburd	3		1		
Wheeler, David	1		3		
Wheeler, Chancy	1	1	4		
Adams, Stephen	1	1	3		1
Turney, Asa	1	1	2		
Staples, Thomas	1	1	1		
Turney, Aaron	1	2	2		
Squire, Joseph	1	4	4		
Warson, John	1	3	1		1
Gould, Elizabeth	1	2	2		
Buttonton, Walter	1	5	3		
Buttonton, William	1		1		
Williams, John	2	1	2		
Turney, Abel	1	1	2		
Carson, Walter	1	1	2		
Turney, Abiah	1	1	1		
Hays, Nathan	1		1		
Turney, Peter	1	1	3		
Burr, Charles	3	3	5		
Lewis, Jonathan	1		2		3
Gould, Talcott	1		3		
Gould, Isaac	1	1	2		
Nichols, Squire	1		1		
Dimon, Daniel	3	1	5		
Ogden, David	1	1	3		
Sherwood, Zalmon	1		3		
Ogden, Sturges	1	1	2		
Ogden, Jean			2		
Sherwood, Benjamin	2		1		
Sherwood, Seth	3	5	7	1	
Stratton, Samuel	1	3	4		
Stratton, John	1	1	2		
Jennings, Noah	1	3	2		
Bennet, Stephen	1	2	5		
Sealee, Ezra	2	3	2		
Meeker, Ichobud	1	6	3		
Hall, Ichobud	1	1	2		
Odle, Nehemiah S	1	1	2		
Sisco, Hannah	1		2		
Bennet, Thaddeus	1	3	2		
Tredwell, Abel	2	1	3		
Hall, William	1	1	3		
Hodgden, David	2	2	3		
Hall, Ebenezer	1		2		
Cary, William	1	1	1		
Patchen, James	1		2		
Patchen, Woolcott	1	2	4		
Morehouse, David	1		1		
Hall, Liman	1		1		
Hall, James	1		1		2
Squire, Samuel, Jnr	2	1	6		
Hubbell, Abel	2	1	5		

FAIRFIELD TOWN—con.

NAME OF HEAD OF FAMILY.	Free white males of 16 years and upward, including heads of families.	Free white males under 16 years.	Free white females, including heads of families.	All other free persons.	Slaves.
Sherwood, Samuel, 2d	1	2	4		
Morehouse, Isaac	1	2	5		
Morehouse, Elijah	1		1		
Jennings, Zacherius	1		1		
Morehouse, Abraham	1	3	3		
Wilson, John, Jnr	1	1	1		
Morehouse, Seth	2	4	4		
Wilson, Nathaniel	2		1		3
Willson, Isaac			2		
Hays, Nehemiah	1		1		
Willson, John	2		3		
Lion, Calep	3		4		
Jennings, David	3	1	2		
Morehouse, Peter	1	3	4		
Meeker, Abigail			2		
Meeker, Thankfull	2		2		
Jennings, Liman	1	3	5		
Willson, Jonathan	2		1		
Ogden, Bethuel	2		1		
Burr, William	1		4		
Smedley, James	2	1	4		2
Jennings, Jeremiah	3	2	2		
Squire, Ebenezer	1	1	5		
Jennings, Peter	1	1	4		
Osborn, Daniel	1		1		
Allen, George	2		3		
Staples, Thomas	2	1	1		
Jennings, Isaac	1	2	5		2
Burr, Peter	1	1	6	1	
Mallery, Levi	1		4		
Anebal, Antoni	1		1		
Phipeny, Nehemiah	2	1	4		
Pierson, John	1		2		
Smith, Joseph	2	3	2		
Jennings, Peter	1		2		
Wakeman, Andrew	2		3		2
Burr, Nathan	1	1	4		
Burr, Hezekiah	1	2	1		
Burr, Ebenezer, 2d	1		3		1
Silliman, Job					6
Osborn, Gershom	1	2	2		
Silliman, Mary		2	2		7
Noyse, Joseph	1	3	1		
Eliot, Andrew	1	2	5		3
Knapp, John, Jnr	1	1	5		
Silliman, Gould	1		4		
Silliman, Ebenezer	2		4		
McRay, James	2	2	3		
Morehouse, Abijah	1	5	3		
Davis, Joshua	1		3		
Patchen, Josiah	1	1	4		
Morehouse, William	2	3	6		
Morehouse, Uriah	1	1	1		
Patchen, David	1	2	2		
Knapp, James	3	1	2		
Knapp, John	2	1	2		
Meeker, Liman	1	1	1		
Meeker, Justus	1		1		
Vaune, Olive	1		4		
Knapp, Benjamin	1	2	3		
Hawley, Silas	1		2		
Nichols, John	2	3	6		
Hubbell, Richard	2	3	4		3
Shelton, Philo	1	2	3	1	
Burr, Aaron	2		2		
Burr, Osias	3	4	5		
Hubbell, Joel	1	1	2		
Meeker, Peter	1		2		
Burr, John, Jnr	1	3	3		
Tredwell, David	1	2	4		
Wheeler, Hezekiah	1		2		
Wheeler, Willson		1	4		
Odle, Sarah			1		
Wakelin, Abel	1	2	2		
Warden, William, Jnr	1	3	2		
Wheeler, Timothy	1	2	2		
Mallet, Lewis	1	1	6		
Wheeler, Benjamin	1		2		
Porter, John	2	3	2		
Wheeler, Samuel	1		1		
Odle, Isaac	1	2	4		
Bennet, Joseph W	1		2		
Beerdslee, John	1		2		
Hall, Joseph	2		4		
Hall, John	1		4		
Cable, Samuel	3		3		
Duncomb, John	1	3	4		
Holeburton, William	1	2	5		
Ross, Robert	1	1	2		
Fairweather, Benjamin	1				
Strong, Joseph	2	1	6		
Brothwell, Thomas	2				
Hull, William	1	1	1		
Hubbell, Aaron	1		3		
Buttonton, Nehemiah	1		1		

NAME OF HEAD OF FAMILY.	Free white males of 16 years and upward, including heads of families.	Free white males under 16 years.	Free white females, including heads of families.	All other free persons.	Slaves.
FAIRFIELD TOWN—con.					
Burr, Jesse, 2d	1	3	4		
Burr, Elijah	1	3	2		
Patchen, Elijah	1	5	2		
Hubbell, Giddeon	1	1	3		
Hubbell, Daniel	3		4		
Sherwood, Zachariah	1		2		
Meeker, John	1		1		
Sealee, Deborah		4	5		
Meeker, David	1		1		
Brothwell, Joseph	1		2		
Sealee, Seth	2	1	5		
Meeker, Hezekiah	1	2	4		
Cable, Rebekah			1		
Taylor, Anne	1		5		
Jackson, Nathan	2		2		
Hall, Benjamin	2		2		
Lacy, Daniel	2	4	2		
Lacy, Margeret			2		
Lacy, John	1		1		
Brothwell, Benjamin	1	1	3		
Lacy, David	1	2	3		
Bangs, Lemwell	1	4	3		
Fowler, Nehemiah	1	2	4		
Willson, Nathanel, Jnr	1	1	3	1	
Silliman, Seth	2		3		
Silliman, Samuel	2		1		
Knapp, Ebenezer	2	1	5		
Knapp, Daniel	2				
Willson, Amos	2	3	4		
Willson, Silliman	1		2		
Adams, Stephen	2		2	1	
Adams, Nathan	1		3	1	
Jennings, Mathew	1	1	2	6	
Hays, William	1		1		
Hays, Joseph	2	1	3		
Jennings, Ezra	2	8	3		
Willson, Daniel	3	2	3	1	
Willson, Ann	1		3		
Hallins, Abigail			4		
Jennings, Abel	4		5		
Jennings, Robert	1	1	1		
Hull, Jeddediah	2	1	2		
Sherwood, Reubin	1	2	3		
Sherwood, Sarah	1		1		
Sherwood, Benjamin, Jnr	1	2	3		
Bulkley, William	2	1	4		
Bulkley, James	1	1	3		
Robins, Ephraim	1	2	1		1
Banks, Ebenezer	2	1	5		2
GREENWICH TOWN.					
Hendric, William	1	3	5		
Jezup, Jonathan	5	2	4		
Peck, Moses	2	1	1		
Lockwood, Noah	1	2	1		
Husted, Joseph	1	6	2		
Adams, Joseph	1	2	2		
Waring, Henry	1	4	3		
Morris, Revd Robert	1		1		
Lockwood, Philip	1	3	5		
Lockwood, Samuel	2	2	4		
Lockwood, Andrew	1		2		
Lockwood, Edward	1	2	3		
Lockwood, Gilbert	2	1	3		
Bay, Thomas	1	1	4		2
Ferris, Samuel	3	2	1		
Jezup, Ebenezer	1		2		
Knapp, Charles	1		5		
Knapp, Timothy	3	1	5		
Lockwood, Mary (Wd)		2	2		
Palmer, Stephen	2	4	3		
Lockwood, Enos	3		2		
Ferris, Jeremiah	2	1	5		
Joyce, Sarah (Wd)			5		1
Ferris, Nathel, Junr	1	3	6		
Lockwood, Caleb	2	4	4		
Lockwood, Joseph	2		2		
Parrot, John	1	1	1		
Lockwood, Jonathan, 3d	1		2		
Lockwood, John	2	1	2		
Lockwood, George	2	4	4		
Sackett, Nathel	2	1	3		
Hobby, Thomas	1	1	4		
Hobby, Jabez Mead	1		4		
Hobby, Hezekiah	1	2	1		
Hobby, Charles	1	2	2		
Rundle, Timothy	2	2	3		
Peck, Joseph	4	1	5		
Johnson, Henry	4	2	4		
Rundle, Amy (Wd)	1	2	2		
Peck, Isaac	1	2	3		
Whiting, Samuel	2	2	2		
Peck, Jeremiah	1				
GREENWICH TOWN—con.					
Lockwood, Jonathan	1		2		
Lockwood, Abraham	2	1	3		
Lockwood, Frederick	1	2	2		
Peck, Samuel	4		1		
Peck, Ebenezer	2	2	6		
Guernsey, Samuel	1		2		
Knapp, Enos	3	1	3		
Rundle, Jeremiah	1		1		
Jezup, Silvanus	1	1	2		
Selleck, Joseph	1		2		
Peck, George	3		3		
Ferris, Stephen	1	2	2		
Lockwood, Stephen	1	1	1		
Peck, Roberts	2	2	2		
Whelpley, Abigail			2		
Adams, John	1	3	2		
Ferris, Jeduthan	4	3	5		
Ferris, Samuel	4	1	2		
Knapp, Jeremiah	2	2	4		
Reynolds, Samuel	1	1	3		
Sherwood, Nathan	1	2	1		
Palmer, B. (Wd)	1		5		
Goff, Peter	1	2	2		
Reynolds, Briggs	2	3	4		
Lane, John	1	1	4		
Whelpey, Anne (Wd)		1	4		
Titus, Daniel	1	2	4		
Titus, Samuel	2		3		
Knapp, David	1	1	1		
Knapp, Samuel	1		2		
Ash, Samuel	1	4	4	1	
Dayton, Abraham	1	2	3		
Palmer, John	3		3		
Simmons, Timothy (negro)					6
Weed, David	1	1	3		
Davis, Stephen	1	1	5		
Palmer, Smith	2	2	1		
Edgerly, John	1	2	2		
Knapp, William	1	1	4	1	
Reynolds, Daniel	3		3		
Whelpley, Ebenezer	1	1	2		
Howe, Jonathan	2		1		
Johnson, Thomas	2	4	4		
Johnson, William	1	2	4		
Pomroy, Joel	2	1	3		
Wilmot, Frank	1	1	2		
Ritch, John	1		2		
Ritch, Lemuel	1		3		
Ferris, Park	2	1	1		
Ferris, Shubeal	1		2		
Ferris, Moses	2		2		
Ferris, David, Jr	1	2	2		
Miller, John	1	2	3		
Mead, Edward	1		1		
Selleck, Silvanus	1	2	4		
Mead, Stephen	2		2		
Morrel, Jacob	2	4	1		
Titus, William	1	1	1		
Peck, Nathaniel	1	1	7		
Ferris, David	2		5		
Bush, Joseph	1		3		
Mead, Nehemiah	3		3		
Hubble, Jehiel	1	2	2		
Hitchcock, Joseph	1	2	1		
Fletcher, M. (Wd)	1		1		
Tenpany, Michael C	1		3		
Wilmot, Samuel	1		1		
Holly, Lois (Wd)	1	3	4		
Sacket, Joseph	3		3		
Mead, Jeremiah, Junr	2	2	4		
Hitchcock, Thomas	1	1	4		
Deforest, Samuel	1	1	3		
Peck, Isaac, 3d	1		1		
Mead, Israel	1	1	1		
Marshall, Andrew	3	1	5		
Marshall, Ezra	1	3	4		
Knapp, Gilbert	1		2		
Marshall, Isaac	2		9		
Holmes, Benjamin	2	2	2		
Mead, Andrew	2		1		1
Hobby, Benjamin	2		1		2
Hobby, Ebenezer	2	3	2	1	2
Brown, Bazaleel	2		1		
Hubby, Benjamin, Jr	1		2		
Mead, Titus	5	1	3		1
Mead, Jabez	1	1	1		
Mead, Titus, Junr	1	1	3		
Hobby, Joseph	2	2	3		
Hobby, Mills	1	1	4		1
Mead, Elkanah	2	1	2		
Knapp, Eben	2	3	4		
Mead, Jonah	2	3	4		1
Rundle, Solomon	2	3	3		
Hobby, Abraham	1	1	4		
GREENWICH TOWN—con.					
Close, Gilbert	1	1	1		
Hobby, Joseph, Junr	1	3	6		2
Rundle, Reuben	2	1	1		
Rundle, Samuel	1		4		
Reynolds, Horton	2	2	4		
Mead, Nathel, 3d	3	2	5		
Mead, Joshua	3	2	4	1	1
Knapp, Joshua, Jr	3	1	4		
Lyon, Caleb	1	1	4		
Lyon, Job	3		2		
Rundle, Elizabeth (Wd)		1	2		
Brown, Sherman	3	1	3		
Rundle, Nathaniel	2	1	3		
Knapp, Phebe (Wd)	1	2	4		
Brown, Josiah	1		3		
Brown, Levi	1	1	1		
Ritch, Mary (Wd)			2		
Close, Jonathan	1	1	1		
Ritch, Thomas	1	2	4		
Ritch, James	1	1	2		
Ferris, Oliver	1	1	5		
Lyon, Daniel, 3d	2		6		
Marshall, Thomas	1	1	4		
Reynolds, Joseph	2	1	2		1
Lockwood, Anny (Wd)	1		1		
Davis, Isaac	1		2		
Reynolds, Elihu	1	2	1		
Jezup, Elizabeth (Wd)	1	1	1		
Mosier, James	1	2	5		
Palmer, Elliot	1	1	1		
Palmer, Denham	2	4	1		
Studwell, Deborah (Wd)	2	1	2		
Studwell, Anthony	2	3	3		
Reynolds, Nathaniel	3	1	2		
Mead, Abel	1	1	6		
Reynolds, Philo	1		2		
Reynolds, Ezekiel	2	1	4		
Reynolds, Nathel, Jr	2	3	3		
Lockwood, Thaddeus	2	2	5		
Lockwood, Nathan	2	1	2		
Ferris, Nathaniel	3	2	6		
Ingersol, Nathaniel	3	2	5		
Knapp, Amy (Wd)			2		
Knapp, Rachel (Wd)			1		
Bush, William	1	1	2		1
Denton, Humphry	5		3		
Mead, Amos	3		2	2	4
Sacket, Justice	2	3	3		1
Seymore, Samuel	1	1	3		1
Mead, Jared	3	1	6	1	4
Hobby, John	3	2	5		
Hobby, Thomas, Junr	2	5	4		1
Holmes, Stephen	2		4		
Holmes, Isaac	1				
Hayes, Abraham	1		2		
Weed, Isaac	1	1	2		
Wilson, Benjamin	1	1	3		
Mead, Nehemiah, Jr	2	3	3		
Mead, Joseph	1	1	3		
Mead, Nathaniel, Junr	2	2	3		
Mead, Smith	1	4	1		
Lewis, Revd Isaac	4	1	4		1
Mead, Henry	3	1	5		
Mead, Matthew	2	2	6		
Wilson, Nehemiah, Junr	1		3		
Addington, John	2	1	3		
Avery, John	1	1	2		
Simmons Isaac	1		2		
Mead, John	2	2	3	2	1
Town, Jonathan	1	1	5		
Townsend, Coles	1	1	5		
Banks, James	2	1	6		
Lyon, Gilbert	3	1	3		
Lyon, Daniel	1	1	4		
Banks, Joseph	1	2	4		
Brundage, Joseph	2		1		
Lyon, David	1	3	3		
Wilson, Solomon	3		3		
Lyon, James	2	1			
Lyon, Benjamin			3		
Lyon, James, 3d	1	4	2	1	1
Lyon, Stephen	1		2		
Lyon, Shubeal	1	2	4		
Lyon, James, Junr	1	2	4		
Merrit, Abraham	1	2	2		
Taylor, Zebediah	1	1	2		
Lyon, Joshua	1	2	5		
Merrit, Jesse	1	1	1		
Merrit, Abraham	1	2	3		
Merrit, Solomon	3		3		
Mosier, Daniel	1		3		
Bacon, Ephraim	5	1	4		
Lyon, Gilbert, Junr	1	1	3		
Sherwood, Daniel	1	4	5		
Bearmore, Nathanel	1	2	5		

FAIRFIELD COUNTY—Continued.

NAME OF HEAD OF FAMILY.	Free white males of 16 years and upward, including heads of families.	Free white males under 16 years.	Free white females, including heads of families.	All other free persons.	Slaves.
GREENWICH TOWN—con.					
Lyon, Daniel	1	1	4	1	
Darrow, Sarah (Wd)			2		
Jordon, Wm	1		3		
Merritt, Eben	1	2	2		
Wilson, Amos	1		1		
Merrit, Nathan	2		4		1
Rathburn, Susannah			1		
Sherwood, Jabez	1		3		
Wilson, Nehemiah	1	3	3		1
Vanziekland, Minna	2	2	3		
Anderson, Jeremiah	1	1	1		1
Merrit, Jonathan	1		1		
Anderson, Joseph	1	3	1		
Strang, Jared	2	1	2		
Anderson, Isaac	1	3	6		
Reynolds, Nathan	2		2		
Merrit, Adam	1	2	1		
Lewis, Isaac	1	1	2		
Brundage, Sarah			2		
Eden, David	2		1		
Sutton, William	1	2	2		
Carrihart, Hacaliah	1	1	2		
Wilson, Jotham	2	1	1	1	1
Purdy, Daniel	1	2	4		
Anderson, Stephen	1	1	2		
Anderson, William	2		4		
Maynerd, Elisha	1	1	2		
Horton, Timothy	1	1	3		
Pine, Samuel	1	1	2		1
Green, Caleb	1	2	4		
Field, Aaron	2	2	3		
Cunningham, Abigail		1	3		
Clapp, Thomas	3	1	4		
Pughby, Samuel	1	2	5		1
Field, Uriah	6	3	8	1	
Clapp, Phebe (Wd)	2	2	4		
Nutt, Robert	1	1	5		
Jeffery (Black)				2	
Conklin, Mary (Wd)			3		
Bush, David	2	2	6	1	8
Peck, Ephraim	1	1	4		
Mesnard, John	2	2	3		
Studwell, Sarah (Wd)		1	2		
Fairchild, Ezekiel	1	2	2		
Studwell, Gabriel	1	2	3		
Smith, Isaac	1	3	3		
Knapp, Israel	3	2	7	1	3
Close, Hannah (Wd)	1		4		
Fitch, Col. Jabez	1	1	5		1
Grigg, Henry	1	1	1		
Grigg, Alexander	1		4		
Mead, Abraham	3	2	4		
Davis, Elisha	1		5		
Davis, Stephen, Jr.	1		2		
Howard, Daniel	1		5		
Close, Ellihu	1	2	1		
Reynolds, Ezra	1	2	4		
Mead, Abigail (Wd)	2	3	3		
Holmes, Reuben	3		3		
Mead, Ebenezer	2	2	6		
Lyon, Noah	1	3	2		
Darrow, James	1		3		
Betts, Sarah (Wd)	1	1	4		
Marshall, Gilbert	1	3	5		
Studwell, Henry	1		4		
Wood, David	4	1	5		
Ferris, Jabez	3	1	3		
Husted, Jared	1		2		
Ferris, Solomon, Junr	2	1	4		
Norcott, Dennis	1	1	3		
Johnson, Samuel	1	1	4		
Burley. Sarah (Wd)			6		
Burley, Silas	1	1	4		
Palmer, John W	1	6	3		
Palmer, Messenger	1	1	1	1	2
Palmer, Seth	2		3		
Quintard, Isaac	1	1	2		
Sackett, Peter	1	1	3		
Bush, Samuel	1	1	3		4
Banks, Elizabeth (Wd)		1	4		1
Banks, Daniel	1		1		
Banks, Benjamin	1	2	4		
Banks, Joshua	1	1	3		
Mead, Benjamin	2	1	3		1
Mead, David	2	1	1		
Mead, Whitman	1		3	1	
Rowel, Valentine	1		2		
Dayton, Amos	1	1	3		
Rowel, Wm	1	2	6		
Mead, Jehiel	3		3		
Mead, Eliphalet, Junr	2		1		
Mead, Henry, Junr	1		2		
Mead, Silas	4		2		
Mead, Calvin	2	1	2		
Cornwall, John	2	1	4		
Nash, Francis	5		3		

NAME OF HEAD OF FAMILY.	Free white males of 16 years and upward, including heads of families.	Free white males under 16 years.	Free white females, including heads of families.	All other free persons.	Slaves.
GREENWICH TOWN—con.					
Dun, Michael	2		1		
Reynolds, Israel	2	2	5		
Ireland, Job	1	1	2		
Tomkins, Oliver	1	3	3		
Ireland, Abraham	1	2	3		
Stokam, Reuben	1	3	3		
Bard, Alexander	1	1	2		
Sherwood, Nehemiah, Jr.	1		2		
Cherry, Poll		1	2		
Jermain, Elizabeth		1	1		
Mead, John, Junr.	1	1	6		
Hayes, Abraham, Jr	1	2	7		
Mead, Zacheus	1	1	5		
Wix, John	1	3	5		
Mead, Abigail (Wd)			1		
Mead, Jonathan	1	1	2		
Mead, Peter	2	2	4	1	
Husted, Abraham	4	3	2		1
Avery, Peter	2	3	4		
Palmer, Samuel, Jr	4	2	3		
Rundle, Amy (Wd)			4		
Palmer, Samuel	5		4		
Rundle, Phinehas	1	2	3		
Rundle, Samuel	2	1	3		
Hibbard, Nathaniel	3		3		
Finch, Nathaniel	3	3	2		
Brown, David	2	2	8		
MCaul, Angus	4	2	3		
Marshall, Henry	3	3	3		
Peck, Theophilus	2		3		
Peck, Gilbert	2		3		
Husted, Moses, Jr	1		2		7
Howe, Isaac	1	1	9		
Peck, Abraham	1	1	5	1	
Peck, Israel	2	2	2		
Peck, Samuel, Jr	2	2	5		
Peck, Isaac	1		1		1
Knapp, John	2	2	3		
Mead, Nathaniel	3		3	1	2
Beard, Robert	2	1	2		
Hibbard, Jonathan	1	3	3		
Lyon, Caleb, Junr	3	6	4		
Mead, Jasper	1	3	2		
Purdy, Ruth (Wd)	1	1	2		
Belcher, Elisha	2		5		1
Knapp, Jonah	2	4	5		
Lockwood, Israel	1	3	1	3	
Ferris, Ashford	2	2	2	1	
Knapp, Jonathan	1	4	5		1
Hobby, Seymore	1	1	1		
Holmes, Jabez	1	1	3		
Knapp, Shubeal	1	2	3		
Knapp, Joshua, 3d	1	1	1		
Knapp, Joshua	1	2	5		
Green, Charles	1		2		1
Husted, Nathan	1	1	4		
Worden, Roger	1	1	3		
Mills, Amos	4	1	2		
Reynolds, Elizabeth (Wd)			2		
Southerland, Roger	1	1	3		
Lockwood, Nathaniel	1	3	1		
Rundle, Rachel (Wd)			3		
Close, Odel, Junr	2	2	1		
Finch, Jonathan	2	3	7		
Brush, Benjamin	1	2	3		1
Brown, Nehemiah	3		2	1	1
Brown, Major	1	1	4	1	
Brown, Roger	3	2	4	1	
Holmes, Ebenezer	1	2	7		
Mead, Jesse	1	1	5		
Mead, Zebediah	2		4		
Clapp, Benjamin	1	2	3		
Clapp, Joseph	2	1	2		
Clapp, James	2	2	1		
Vanevert, Abraham	1	1	2		
Wood, Mary			3		
Sherwood, Gilbert	2		3		
Brown, Laurence	2		3		
Brundage, Gabriel	3	2	2		
Fairchild, Oliver	1	2	3		
Sutton, Benjamin	1	3	2		
Purdy, Nathan	1		1		
Merrit, Nehemiah	1	1	2		
Harmony, Nicholas	1	3	1		
Purdy, Elizabeth (Wd)			1		
Sherwood, Oliver	2		1		
Peck, David	1	1	6		
Sherwood, Elnathan	1	1	5		
Simmons, Jemimah (Wd)			1		2
Peck, Gideon	1	1	4		
Merrit, Nathan, Junr	1	3	2		3
Green, John	2	1	2	1	1
Miller, Andrew	2	2	3	1	
Merrit, Nathaniel	1	1	3		

NAME OF HEAD OF FAMILY.	Free white males of 16 years and upward, including heads of families.	Free white males under 16 years.	Free white females, including heads of families.	All other free persons.	Slaves.
GREENWICH TOWN—con.					
Wilson, Daniel	1	2	2		
Gunn, William	1	2	2		
Coe, Jonathan	1		1		1
Coe, Reuben	1	3	2		
Green, James	3	1	4		
Wilson, David	1	3	4		
Lewis, Daniel	1	4	4		
Wilson, Uriah	1		2		
Wilson, Joseph	1	2	3		
Peck, Solomon	1		1		
Knapp, Uriah	5	2	4		
Armer, Abigail (Wd)		1	2		
Lockwood, Samuel, Jr.	1	1	4		
Brown, James	2	3	3		
Lockwood, Amos	1	1	2		
Lockwood, Stephen	1	1	3		
Reynolds, Joseph	1	1	2		
Reynolds, Benjamin	2	2	4		
Reynolds, Joannah (Wd)		1	3		
Palmer, Winas	2	1	3		
Palmer, Jonathan	1		1		
Mills, Samuel	3	1	7		1
Mead, Ruth (Wd)	2	1	2		
Mead, Daniel	1	2	1		
Mead, Jotham	1	1	3		
Mead, Enos	1	3	2		
Close, Abraham	1	3	1		
Close, Joseph	4	1	4		
Knapp, Hannah (Wd)			2		
Finch, William	1	3	2		
Knapp, Anne (Wd)			4		
Finch, Timothy	3	3	3		
Finch, William N.	1	1	3		
Londen, John	1	2	7		
Husted, Peter	4	3	4		
Husted, Moses	1		1		
Numan, Platt	2	1	3		
Dota, William	1		1		
Peck, Benjamin	2	3	2		
Close, Odel	3	2	4		
Mead, Sibela (Wd)	1		1	1	
Reynolds, Ambrose	1	2	2		
Brown, Peter	1		1		
Knapp, Joseph	1	2	3		
Minor, John	1	2	7		
Howe, Ebenezer	1	3	4		
Palmer, Gideon	1	4	2		
Croney, Elizabeth		1	2		
Finny, Solomon	1	1	1		
Palmer, Enos	1		1		
Palmer, Titus	1	1	1		
Palmer, Israel	1	1	2		
Clason, Isaac	1		3		
Mosier, Henry	1	1	2		
Reynolds, Jonathan	1	2	4		
Mead, Shadrach	1		2		
Peck, Samuel, 3d	1		2		
Johnson, James	1	2	5		
Sherwood, James	2	1	5		
Lyon, Amos	1	2	5		
Finch, Timothy, Jr	1		4		
Ferris, Joseph, Junr	1	3	2		
Ferris, Thomas	1		3		
Ferris, Timothy	1	3	2		
Palmer, Levi	2	1	2		
Ferris, Josiah	3	5	4		
Blakely, Obidiah	1	2	3		
Husted, Benjamin	2	3	6		
Fisk, William	3	5	4		
Close, Benjamin	1	2	2		
Whelpley, Isaac	1		5		
Gerrineau, Peter	1	1	3		
Stockwell, Robert		1	3		
Lockwood, Sarah		2	1		
Rundle, Charles	1	3	1		
Lockwood, Shubeal	3		2		
Finch, Ezekiel	1		1		
Finch, Isaac	1	1	1		
Brush, Shubeal	3	4	3		
Lockwood, Gershom	2	2	4		
Wood, Lemuel	1	1	1		
Suard, Revd William	3	1	4		1
Peck, Aaron	2		5		
Hobby, David	2	6	3		
Hobby, Jonathan	1		1		
Howe, Silvanus	1	2	3		
Brush, James	2	3	4		
McKay, John	3	1	5		
Ferris, Joseph	1				
Finch, Jonathan, Jr	4	1	1		
Ingersoll, Simon	2	2	1		
Ingersoll, Elizabeth (Wd)			3		
Ferris, Solomon	1	2	3		

FAIRFIELD COUNTY—Continued.

NAME OF HEAD OF FAMILY.	Free white males of 16 years and upward, including heads of families.	Free white males under 16 years.	Free white females, including heads of families.	All other free persons.	Slaves.
GREENWICH TOWN—con.					
Hubbard, William	3	1	3		
Hubbord, Daniel	1		1		
Hubbord, Henry	4	3	6		
Mead, Edmond	4	5	4		
Banks, David	1	2	5		
Lockwood, Jonathan, Jr	1	3	6		
Ferris, Mary (Wd)	1	1	3		
Buxton, Dorras (Wd)			4		
Mead, Prudence (Wd)	2		2		
Mead, Jeremiah	4		3		
Parsons, Sarah (Wd)		1	3		
Gibbs, Hannah			2		
Ferris, Joseph	1		1		
HUNTINGTON TOWN.					
Beardslee, Hennery	2	2	2		
Davis, Benjamin	1	1	1		
Hambleton, Alexander	2	3	2		
Wakelin, Isaac	1	4	5		
Bennet, Daniel	1	3	5		
Hubbell, Mathew	2	1	4		
Hubbell, Giddeon	1	1	3		
Sherman, Walker	1		2		
Watkins, William	1	4	2		
French, Jeriel	2		2		
Hays, Stephen	1	2	2		
Winton, David, Jur	1	1	4		
Burr, Hosea	2	1	4		
Beardslee, Eli	1		3		
Winton, David	2	1	2		
Winton, Samuel	1	2	3		
Bundy, Ebenezer	1	1	3		
Beers, Lewis	1	1	1		
Tyrel, John	1	2	4		
Beach, Hezekiah	1	2	6		
Burr, Jehue	1	4	2		
Nichols, Philip	1	1	1		
Middleton, Peter				3	
Dimon, Nimrod				4	
Tredwell, Cato				4	
Watkins, Hezekiah	1		1		
Watkins, Abijah	1		1		
Prindle, Isaac	2	1	4		
Hubbell, David	1	1	5		
Lenenworth, Daniel	3		1		
Hubbell, William	1	2	2		
Tyrel, Amos	1	1	3		
Silliman, Data	1	3	5		
Beers, Archebus	1		3		
Rowel, Jacob	1	1	5		
Beers, Nathanel	1		2		
Blackman, Timothy	2		2		
Beardslee, Aaron	1	1	2		
Blackman, Asahel	1	1	1		
Pane, Samuel	1	2	4		
Burrit, John	2	4	5		
Pane, David	1	2	3		
Beardslee, Elizabeth		2	3		
Burr, James	3	1	6		
Vanostran, Aaron	2	3	4		
Niles, William	1	2	4		
Sears, Elijah	1	1	3		
Sears, Gershom	1	1	2		
Curtis, Isaac	1	3	6		
Mand, Dependence	2	1	3		
Albin, John	1	2	1		
Mallet, Philo	1	3	3		
Hawley, Jonathan	2	1	2		2
Hawley, Abel	1	2	4		
Hawley, Anne		2	2		
Hawley, Elijah	2	1	2		
Jackson, William	1		6		
Larkin, Joshua	1	2	6		
Wakelin, Samuel	2		1		
Dascomb, John	1	2	3		
Nichols, Benjamin	1		2		
Bradford, Hennery	3	1	4		
Nichols, Joseph	1	1	1		
Edwards, Ager	2	1	2		
Sears, Bartholomew	1		1		
Sears, Richard	1		1		
French, Jehiel	3	2	1		
Corney, Allen	1	1	2		
Odle, John	2	1	2		
Odle, Aaron	1	1	2		1
Hawley, Thomas	2	2	3		2
Man, Richard	1		2		
Elmer, Elijah	1	3	2		
Curtis, Timothy	1	3	5		
Sanders, Aaron	1	1	1		
Sherman, Nathanel	3	1	3		
Sherman, Phineus	4		6		
Sherman, Nathanel, Jur	1	3	2		
Picksley, David	1	3	3		
HUNTINGTON TOWN—continued.					
Sherman, Philo	2	1	3		
Hubbell, Jeremiah	2	1	3		
Sherwood, Ephraim	1	1	2		
Curtis, Jonathan	1	4	3		
Curtis, Abel	2	3	4		
Porter, Nathanel	2		2	1	
Hawley, Israel	1	3	5		
Hawley, Ephraim	1	4	2		
Northrop, Isaiah	2	3	5		
Hawley, Elias	1	3	5	1	
Curtis, Andrew	1		6	1	
Beardslee, Daniel	1	1	2	1	
Payn, Urana	1		2		
Booth, Nathan	2		1		2
Downs, John	1		6		
Booth, Lewis	1	2	1		
Hurd, Nehemiah	2		1		
Hurd, Abraham	1		1		
Beardslee, James	2		2		
Beardslee, Luke	2	1	2		
Wakeley, Samuel, Jur	1	3	1		
Hurd, Ebenezer	3	1	4		
Curtis, James	2	1	1		
Hawley, Giddeon	1	4	5		
Curtis, Robert	1	1	2		
Beardslee, Josiah	1	3	2		
Booth, Samuel	2	2	5		
Booth, Nathan, Jur	2	2	4		
Henman, Samuel	1	1	1		
Curtis, Elijah	1		1		
Booth, Silas	1	1	4		
Hurd, Mead	1	1	1		
Judson, Ezekiel	1	5	4		
French, Ebenezer	2	2	6		2
French, Othenial	1	3	3		
Judson, John	1		2		
Judson, John, 3d	2	2	3		
Beach, John	1		1		
Slane, Charles	3		1		
Judson, Ephraim	3	1	3		
Beardslee, Israel	2		3		
Farnum, Peter	2	1	4		
Daton, Benjamin	1	4	3		
Dunnen, Isaac	1	2	3		
Twiner, George	1	1	2		
Lewis, Walker	1	1	5	1	1
Lewis, Ebenezer	2	1	3		1
Beardslee, Elisha	3	4	2		
Barlow, Samuel	2	4	6		
French, James	1	1	3		
Reels, John	1	1	1		2
French, Abner	1	1	2		
Lewis, Wells	3	2	3		
Beach, Ebenezer	1	3	3		2
Hawley, Charrity			2	1	
Beardslee, Joshua	1	2	4		
Lewis, Fredrick	1	2	3		
Hawley, Ruth			1		
Cole, Hezekiah	2	1	3		
Rexford, Elisha	1		4		2
Lewis, Samuel	4		3		
DeForest, Nehemiah	2	2	5		2
Moss, Isaac	2		2		
Moss, Joseph	1		1		1
Tuday, Huldah			3		
Curtis, Ezra	2	2	7		
Smith, Heber	1	2	3		
Barnum, Eunice		1	3		
Moss, Daniel	2		4		
Beardslee, Philo	1		2		
Healey, George	2	2	2		
Beers, Barnabus	1		1		
Nichols, Elethan	1	1	2		
Hurd, Philo	1	3	2		
Osborn, Samuel	1		2		
Clark, Hezekiah	1		2		
Johnson, Ephraim	4		4		
Coban, Daniel	1	1	3		
Johnson, Ebenezer	1	3	5		
Nichols, Mansfield	2		4		
Judson, Phineus	1		4		
Munrow, John	1	3	1		
Clark, Elisha	3	6	3		
DeForest, Samuel	1	2	2		
Henman, Nathan	2		2		
Lewis, Thomas	3	3	1		
Booth, Nathanel	1	1	4		
Fairchild, John	3		1		
Fairchild, Joseph, Jur	1		3		
Dunnen, Abraham	2	2	3		
Barlow, Samuel	1		3		
Malery, Calep	1		1		
Mallery, Giddeon	1	2	2		
Mannon, Samuel	1		2		
Summers, Zacheriah S.	1	1	1		
HUNTINGTON TOWN—continued.					
Lewis, Birdsley	1	1	5		
Lewis, Everit	1	2	2		
Beardslee, Thaddeus	3	1	6		
Edwards, Willam	3	1	2		
Beardslee, George	2	1	2		
Mitchel, Zacheriah	1	1	2		
Beardslee, William	2	1	1	2	
Beardslee, Isaac	2		2		
Shelton, Benjamin	1	2	1		
Shelton, Daniel	2	2	2		5
Nichols, David	2		3		1
Nichols, Tiles	1	1	2		
Nichols, Nathan	2	2	2		
Nichols, James	3	2	3		
Lewis, Abel	2	2	2		
Thompson, Samuel	1	1	3		
Judson, Lemwell	1		1		
Judson, Lewis	2		1		
Thompson, Elihue	1	1	2		
Thompson, Jonathan	2		2		
Chitester, Moses	2	3	5		
Bennet, Silas	1	1	1		
Clark, George	1	2	3		
Thompson, David	1	2	1		
Beardslee, Benjamin, Jur	1	3	4		
Beardslee, Benjamin	3	1	3		1
Beard, David, Jur	1		1		1
Clark, John	1		1		
Beardslee, Thomas	1	4	4		
Beard, David	2	2	1		
Buckingham, Enoch	3	3	4		
Frasier, William	1	1	5		
Beardslee, Jered	3	3	5		
Wooster, Ephraim	2	3	6		
Hawley, Walleson	2	1	3		1
Beard, Charles	2		3		
Pool, John	2	2	3		
Lewis, Nathanel	1	2	4		1
Davison, Zacherius	2	3	2		
Hawley, Joseph	1	4	4		
Thompson, Abraham	1	3	1		
Loreing, Joseph	1		2		
Judson, Jonathan	1	2	2		
Blackman, Ruth		1	2		
Judd, Balmerim	2	3	4		
Beardslee, Lemwell	1	2	4		
Judson, Nathanel	2	4	4		
Gilbert, John	1	3	4		
De Forest, Hezekiah	1	2	4		
Mills, Jedediah	1				
Lewis, Ebenezer	1	1	3		
Lewis, Sarah			2		
Clark, Abraham E	1				1
Clark, Blagg	2	2	3		
Clark, Nathan	2		3		
Clark, Samuel	2		3		1
Newton, David	2		2		1
De Forest, Othenial	3	2	3		
Mills, Isaac	1		1		
Benton, Sealey	1		1		
Marks, Mordica	1	2	2		1
Eli, David	1	3	4		
Mills, Elisha	1	1	3	1	
Yates, John	3	1	3		
Beardslee, Stephen	2	2	2		
Lapener, Antony	1	2	2		
Thompson, Nathan	1		1		
Hide, Eliakam	1		1		
Hawley, Job	1	1	2		
Rines, Daniel	1	3	2		
Lester, John	1	1	1		
Bawlden, Elias	1	3	1		
Hide, Elisha	4		3		2
Shelton, Andrew	2	4	5		
Blackman, Eli	1		4		
Perry, David	1	4	2		
Sealee, Giddeon	1		2		
Wheeler, David B	1	2	3		
Wheeler, Elene			2		
Shelton, Zacheriah	1		2		
Hide, Samuel	1	2	1		
Kelogg, Martin	1		1		
Gilbert, Elihue	1	1	2		
Shelton, Samuel	1	4	5		
Lewis, Zacheriah	2		3		2
Hawley, Elijah	2	1	6		
Shelton, Jeremiah	1		3		1
Clark, Sarah			3		
Booth, Ashbell	1	3	4		
Babbet, Stephen	2		2		
Gilbert, Obediah	1	1	5		
Curtis, James	1	2	4		
Judson, James	1	4	1		
Carpenter, William	2		1		

FAIRFIELD COUNTY—Continued.

HUNTINGTON TOWN—continued.

NAME OF HEAD OF FAMILY.	Free white males of 16 years and upward, including heads of families.	Free white males under 16 years.	Free white females, including heads of families.	All other free persons.	Slaves.
Bailey, Hezekiah	3		2		
Hurd, Samuel	2		2	1	
Moss, John	1		3		
Wheeler, Nathan	1		3		1
Moss, Elihue	1	1	6		1
Scott, William	1	2	3		
Moss, Elizabeth		3	2		
Booth, Isaac	1	5	1		
Cable, Abner	1	2	2		
Clark, Nathan, 3d	2	1	1		
Hurd, Elethan	1	2	5	1	
Wheeler, Anne	2		2		
Lattin, David	1	1	5		
Blackman, Ephraim	1	4	3		
Jurden, David	1		1		
Smith, Eli	2	2	3	1	
Beardslee, Eliot	1		1	1	
Mathews, Giddeon	1	1	3		
Dick, Betty		2	3		
Beardslee, Zeph				3	
George, Amos	1	1	4		
Hawley, Anne			4		
Moss, William	1	1	3		
Hawley, John	1		1		
Beardslee, John	1	3	2	1	
Beardslee, Daniel	1		1		
Raymong, David	1	1	1		
Bostwick, Elethan H.	1	2	3	1	
Pulford, Lewis	1		2		
Hurd, David	1		4		
Hawley, Milton	3	1	3		
Mitchel, John	2		5		
Lattin, Thomas	3	1	5	1	
Judson, Samuel	2		2		
Basset, Hennery				3	
Laberee, James	2		2		
Laberee, Bennedict	1		1		
Blackman, Samuel	3		4		
Wells, Joana	2	2	5		2
Clark, James	2		5		
Clark, Nathan, 2d	1	2	3	1	
Blackman, David	1	2	4		
Willcox, John	2	1	6	2	
Willcox, David	1	1	5		
Hays, Elizabeth	1	2	4		
Judson, Isaac	3		3		
Willcox, Timothy	2		2	3	
Basset, John	1	2	8		
Wells, Zalmon	1		1	1	
Curtis, Elijah	1	2	4		
Piercy, Nathanel	1		1		
Beardslee, Hall	1		2	3	
Curtis, Silas	3	1	5		
McKune James	2	1	3		
Anebal, Ebenezer	1	1	2		
Beardslee, Moses	1	1	3		
Beardslee, Samuel	3	1	6	1	
Goodluck, London				2	
Raymong, Jesse	1		2		
Jurden, Edmon	2	2	4		
Sherman, Vincen	2	1	4		
Curtis, Hennery	1	2	3	1	
Curtis, Elihue	2	3	4		
Wetmore, Josiah	1		1		
Hick, John	1		2		
Tomlinson, Ager	1	2	4	1	
Shelton, Daniel	3		2		8
French, Joseph	1	3	2		
Shelton, Thaddeus	1	1	3	1	
Fanton, Jonathan	1		2		
Nodine, Fredrick	1	3	2		
Hays, Jesse	1	1	1		
Wheeler, Elisha	2		1		
Hibbard, Peter	1		2		
Beardslee, Abijah	2	2	2		
Hubbell, Elisha	1	5	3		
Hull, Samuel	1		1		
Hubbell, Giddeon	3	3	4		
Wheeler, Calep	2	2	3		
Wneeler, Elene			1		
Hubbell, Timothy	2	1	2		
Hubbell, John	2	3	7		
Hubbell, Mathew	1		1	4	
Levensworth, Giddeon	2	1	5		
Sissen, William	1	2	4		
Curtis, Stiles	1	1	4		
Levensworth, Edmon	2		6	1	
Patterson, Samuel	1	3	2		
Beardslee, David	1	2	2		
Sander, John M.	2	2	4		
Mills, James	1	2	4		
Patterson, Mark	1		4		
Patterson, James	1	1	1		
Platt, Moses	1	4	7		1
Blackman, William	2	1	3		

HUNTINGTON TOWN—continued.

NAME OF HEAD OF FAMILY.	Free white males of 16 years and upward, including heads of families.	Free white males under 16 years.	Free white females, including heads of families.	All other free persons.	Slaves.
Hamblin, Cornelius	2	1	2		
Hubbell, David, 2d	1		1		
Ransley, William	1	1	1		
Blackman, Joel	3		1		1
Birdslee, Joseph	3	2	3		3
Hawley, David	1		1		5
Judson, Ager, Jur	3	3	4	1	1
Judson, Ager	2		1		6
Beardslee, Calep	2	1	3		
Shelton, Elisha	1	3	4	1	
Lake, Jabes	3	1	3		
Downs, Joseph	1	2	1		
Judson, Silas	1	3	4		
Tomlinson, Beach	1	2	3		2
Wheeler, John	1	3	1		
Wheeler, Moses	2	4	2		
Summers, Luke	2	4	5		
Hill, Isaac	1	1	2		
Hill, Mary			2		
Mallery, Benajah	1		2		
Beardslee, Joseph	2	2	3		
Sealee, Liman	1	1	1		
Gilbert, Joel	1	1	2		
Gilbert, Ager	1	1	3		
Gilbert, Lemwell	1	1	4		
Beardslee, Samuel	1	1	3		
Gilbert, Abraham	2	2	2		
Gilbert, Thomas	1	1	4		
Judson, John	2		3		
Curtis, Temperence				2	
Beers, Tine		1		1	
Fulford, Edmon	1	1	1		
Garlic, Hennery	2	2	3		
French, Jonas	1	5	2		
French, Jonathan	1		1		
Lewis, Beach	2		3		
Curtis, Ephraim	2	2	2		
Wheeler, Moses	1	3	5		
Curtis, Levi	1	1	2		
Ellis, Timothy	1	2	4		
Shelton, Ager	2	1	4		4
Perry, James	1		1		
Brown, Ruth			1		
Perry, Abner	2		3		
Perry, Abner, Jur	1		2		
Curtis, William	1	2	6		
Calkin, Israel	1		3		
Curtis, Elethan	2		3		2
Shelton, James	2		2	1	
Dart, Job	1	5	3		
Perry, Elijah	1		1		
Perry, Abijah	1	1	2		
Perry, Joseph	1	1	2		
Bennet, Daniel	4	1	4		
Shelton, William	2	3	3		2
Shelton, Sealee	1	1	2		
Hull, Joseph	3	4	1		
Clark, Hezekiah	1	1	2		
Jellet, Canfield	2	1	2		
Clark, George	2	1	4		
Davis, William	1	2	4		
Moor, Robert	2	3	5		2
Mills, Samuel	1	1	1		1
Beers, Joseph	1		2		
Chatfield, Lemuel	3	2	1		
Wakelee, Josiah S.	1	2	3		
Nanneistran, Charles	3		3		
Hall, George	1	2	3		
Shelton, Joane			1		
Wakelin, David	1	2	3		
Shelton, Abijah	1		2		2
Shelton, Abijah, 2d	1	2	1		
Wakelee, James	4	3	4		3
Shelton, Noah			2		3
Stephens, Eliphilet	1		4		
Brown, Elisha	1	2	2		
Beardslee, Joseph	1		1		
Beardslee, Zepheniah	1	3	3		
Blackman, Samuel	1	3	2		
Wooster, Joseph L.	2		2	1	
Tomlinson, Curtis	4	2	4		4
Beardslee, Ager	1	2	2		
Lewis, Elijah	1		2		
Umphrevile, Patty	2	1	2		
Smith, Joseph	1	2	1		
Smith, Nathan	2	1	3		
Bennet, Nathan	1	3	5		1
Beard, Samuel	1	1	5		
Shelton, Eunice	1	2	5		
Howse, Zacheriah	1	3	5		
Beard, Joel	1	2	1		
Wells, Robert	1	3	3		
Wells, Giddeon	2	1	3		1
Wells, Daniel	2		4		
Wells, Abner	1	2	2		

HUNTINGTON TOWN—continued.

NAME OF HEAD OF FAMILY.	Free white males of 16 years and upward, including heads of families.	Free white males under 16 years.	Free white females, including heads of families.	All other free persons.	Slaves.
Cosher, Enoch	1	3	2		
Blackman, David	1	2	1		
Wooster, John	3		1		
Clenton, Antine	1		2		
Willcox, James	2		3		
Blackman, Jonas	4		2		
Birdsey, John	1		1		
Smith, Zalmon	2	1	2		
Sweetlove, Elis	1	1	2		
Harrop, Joseph	1		1		
Blacklidge, George				7	
Carsey, Devonshier				5	
Lewis, Floria				5	3
Blacklidge, Pamey	1	1	1		
De Forest, Nehemiah	1	1	4		
Vanorstrain, Aaron	1	1	3		
French, John	1		1		
Fairchild, Joseph	2		4		

NEW FAIRFIELD TOWN.

NAME OF HEAD OF FAMILY.	Free white males of 16 years and upward, including heads of families.	Free white males under 16 years.	Free white females, including heads of families.	All other free persons.	Slaves.
Hallebert, John	3		2		
Smith, Joseph	1	1	6		
Smith, Cornal	1	3	3		
Trobridge, Seth	2		1		
Rogers, Medad	1	2	2		
Beardslee, John	2	2	3		
Lacy, Anne				4	
Lacy, Chancy	1	1	2		
Bass, Joseph	1	1	6		
Fairchild, Enoch	2	1	4		
Beers, Noah	1	2	1		
Fairchild, Alexander	2		1		
Stephens, Eli	1	4	2		
Hoyt, Walter	1	2	4		
Scofield, James	1	4	4		
Beardslee, Josiah	2	3	4		
Beardslee, Nathan S.	1		1		
Stephens, Benjamin	2		2		
Beardslee, Giddeon, Jur	2	2	2		
Trobridge, John	1	1	3		
Beardslee, Phineus	3	1	2		
Beardslee, Obediah	1		2		
Beardslee, Elijah	1	4	2		
Beardslee, Zalmon	2	2	3		
Beardslee, Giddeon	2	2	1		
Knapp, Oliver	1	2	3		
Knapp, Moses	1	2	5		
Bass, Thomas	3		2		
Spencer, Samuel	2	1	3		
Knapp, James	1	1	2		
Penfield, Peter	2	3	1		
Penfield, Lewis	1	1	1		
Bass, John	2	1	3		
Man, Jabez	1		5		
Barnum, Zadock	2	3	7		
Barnum, Abel	3	1	4		
Wanzer, Nicholas	3	4	3		
Barlow, David	2	2	2		1
Wanzer, Moses	1	4	3		
Allen, John	3		2		1
Hallester, Giddeon	1	3	2		
Sutlow, Richard	2	2	4		
Towner, Zacheus	2		2		
Carpenter, Benedict	3		2		
Vaune, William	2	1	2		
Wanzer, Ebenezer	2	2	3		
Vaune, Benjamin	1	2	3		
Page, Abel	1	4	2		
Leach, Echabod	2	1	2		
Hevelan, Thomas	2	1	1		
Eastman, Joseph	2		2		
Wanzer, Abraham	1	1	2		
Leach, Mary	1	1	2		
Platt, David	1	3	3		
Conger, Ephraim	1	2	2		
French, William	1	2	2		
Hubbell, Ephraim	1	2	2		1
Hubbell, Amos	1	2	5		
Bennedict, Elezer	1	4	1		
Osborn, John	2	1	4		
Hatch, John	2		4		
Cowdry, John	2		2		1
Phelps, Joseph	1	5	4		
Sherwood, Nathan	1	4	3		
Sherwood, Ebenezer	1	2	1		
Hubbell, John	2	2	2		
Hatch, Hennery	1	1	2		
Bennedict, John	1	1	4		
Bartrum, Noah	2	2	2		
Bartrum, Isaac	1	2	2		
Prindle, Amos	1		2		
Leach, Daniel	2	1	4		
Richerson, Samuel	1	4	1	3	
Gregory, James	1	3	3		

FAIRFIELD COUNTY—Continued.

NAME OF HEAD OF FAMILY.	Free white males of 16 years and upward, including heads of families.	Free white males under 16 years.	Free white females, including heads of families.	All other free persons.	Slaves.
NEW FAIRFIELD TOWN—continued.					
Hallester, Jonathan	1	1			
Northorp, Abraham	2	1	1		
Northrop, Isaac	1	1	2		
Craw, Reubin	1	2	3		
Gorham, Meeker	1	2	2		
Lewis, Abraham	1	2	3		
Towner, Dan	3		2		
Prindle, Aaron	2	1	2		
Buck, Josiah	1	1	5		
Higgins, George	1	2	4		
Merchant, John	1	1	1		
Northrop, David	2		4		
Hungerford, Ezra	1	3	3		
Potter, Milton	1	2	1		
Wright, Abel	1		2		
Steward, Sylvanus	1	1	2		
Barns, James	1	1	6		
Howse, Edmon	2	1	2		
Phelps, William	2		1		
Carpenter, Barnard	1		1		
Carpenter, Isaiah	1	1	1		
Potter, James	3	3	4		
Hill, Jonathan	1		4		
Carpenter, Barnee	2	1	2		
Picket, Benjamin	2	1	1		
Picket, Polly I.		1	1		
Bennet, Benjamin, Jur.	1	2	3		
Yates, Paul	1		1		
Waring, Samuel	1	3	1		
Bennet, Benjamin	1		1		
Bennet, Daniel N.	1	2	4		
Hungerford, Mary	1		2		
Dutton, Joel	1	4	1		
Hungerford, Uriah	1	1	5		
Giddeons, Jonathan	2	3	5		
Tibbets, Obediah	1	5	3		
Graves, Ezra	1	2	2		
Graves, Jedediah	2		1		
Page, Jonathan	2	2	3		
Barns, Stephen	3	4	5		
Morehouse, John	3	4	2		
Barns, William	2	1	6		
Giddeons, Joseph	3		2		
Seman, Abraham	1	1	4		
Giddeons, William	3	4	3		
Babcock, Isaiah	3	3	3		
Bostwick, William	1	1	1		
Burley, Ebenezer	1		2		
Butts, Isaac	1	3	4		
Woodrough, Asa	1	1	3		
Tupper, Charles	1	4	3		
Nichols, Robert	1	2	3		
Morehouse, Hezekiah	1		3		
Sealee, Abel	3	1	6		
Briggs, Zepheniah	1	3	6		
Foster, Asa	1	1	4		
Kerbey, Robert	1		1		
Bradley, Ephraim	3	1	1		1
Hungerford, Isaiah	1	4	3		
Hallebert, Job	1	1	1		
Waring, Major	1	2	2		
Sealee, Bradley	3	1	3		1
Stewart, Elihue	1	3	1		
Stewart, Alexander	3	1	2		
Hungerford, Josiah	4	2	5		
Northrop, Amos	1	2	2		
Stewart, Alexander, Jur.	2	5	3		
Sanders, William	2	2	3		
Page, Samuel	1		7		
Pane, Aaron	3		2		
Draper, Giddeon	1		1		
Giddeons, Zebulon	1	3	1		
Buck, Daniel	1	2	1		
Holmes, Thatford	1	1	2		
Wane, Russel	2		3		
Sherman, Jesse	1		1		
Acorns, Daniel	2	1	5		
Wing, Thomas	3	3	6		
Bowdish, William	1		2		
Hubbell, Eleazer	2	3	4	1	
Penfield, John	1	5	6		
Wakeman, Seth	1	2	2		
Wakeman, Giddeon	1	1	2		
Pepper, Seth	1	1	3		
Pepper, Dan	1	2	4		
Leach, Amos	1		3		
Goud, William	1		4		
Sturdefant, John	1	2	5		
Sturdefant, Jonathan	1		3		
Ackley, David	2		4		
Bronson, Alford	1	1	2		
Cosher, Abel	1	3	5		
Osborn, Aaron	1	2	3		
Uvit, John	1	3	1		
Woodard, Asa	1	2	4		
NEW FAIRFIELD TOWN—continued.					
Mosher, James	1		4		
Hubbell, Giddeon	1		3		
Osborn, Jonathan	2	3	4		
Osborn, Reubin	2	2	3		
Conger, Joel	1	3	4		
Wileman, Paul	1	3	2		
Pepper, Stephen	2	2	4		
Pepper, Stephen, Jur.	1	1	5		
Stephenson, Stephen	1	3	3		
Wanzer, Eliud	2		3		
Rinevault, William	2	1	4		
Wanzer, Husted	1	2	3		
Buck, Abner	1	2	1		
Hawley, Isaac	1		1		
Barnum, David	1	3	1		
Chase, Giddeon	1	1	2		
Hevelan, Nathanel	1	1	1		
Stedwell, Roger	1	1	3		
Stedwell, Gilbert	1		3		
Brush, Thomas	1	4	6		
Heveland, Roger	2	2	3		
Heveland, Isaac	1	4	1		
Wakeman, Jeremiah	1		5		
Bradley, Jonathan	1	1	2		
Hall, John	1	3	2		
Hendrick, John	2	1	3		
Hubbell, Giddeon	1	2	3		
Wakeman, David	1		2		
Hubbell, Barrack	2		2		
Driskill, Timothy	1	2	2		
Gray, Joseph	1	2	3		
Rion, Jeremiah	1	1	5		
Cole, Hyman	1		1		
Stephens, Joseph	1		1		
Setle, Thomas	1		1		
Barnum, David	3	1	3		
Carlee, John	1	2	2		
Day, Jonathan	1		2		
Gorham, Echabod	2		2		
Barnum, Stephen	1	1	2		
Ball, Wait	1	2	6		
Hodge, Abel	1	1	2		
Hodges, Thaddeus	1	1	1		
Pardy, Stephen	1	2	2		
Pardy, Asher	1	1	2		
Sherwood, Abel	1	4	3		
Perry, Elisha	2		3		
Hodge, Thomas	1	3	2		
Gray, Elias	2	2	5		
Gray, Moses	4	2	2		
Hendrick, Samuel	1		1		
Stephens, Israel	1	4	1		
Oakley, Jeremiah	1	1	2		
Oakley, Gilbert	1		2		
Brush, Thomas, 2d	2	1			
Brush, Jonas	1	3	4		
Wakeman, William	1	3	3		
Beardslee, David	1	2	3		
Brush, Amos	1	2	4		
Beardslee, Nehemiah	2		5		
Bates, Isaac	1		1		
Fairchild, Andrew	2		2		
Rundle, William	2		7		
Nash, Eliakam	3		3		
Rundle, Experience			1		
Cleaveland, John	1	4	2		
Barnum, Timothy	1		1		
Barnum, Samuel	1		2		
Barnum, Timothy, Jr.	1	2	2		
Wheeler, Jedediah	2		3		
Wheeler, Samuel	2	3	7		
Hendrick, Benjamin	2		1		
Hendrick, Samuel	1		1		
Hendrick, James	2		1		
Disbrow, Joseph	1	1	4		1
Disbrow, Hennery	1	1	3		
Fealds, William	4		1		
Allen, Giddeon	2		3		
Wheeler, James	1	3	2		
Wheeler, Nehemiah	1	2	1		
Wheeler, Enoch	1		5		
Scribner, Osias	1	3	3		
Brush, Zacheus	1		1		1
Ball, Eliphilet	1	2	2		
Hambleton, John	1		2		
Disbrow, Asahel	1	4	5		
Dixon, George	1	1	4		
Fuller, Joseph	1	1	5		
Brown, Charles	1		1		
Hibbard, Elisha	1	1	5		
Hibbard, Nathanel	1		2		
Hoyt, Moses	3	1	3		
Osborn, Elezer	3	2	7		
Hall, Seth	2	2	1		
Taylor, Benjamin	1		3		
NEW FAIRFIELD TOWN—continued.					
Taylor, Thofelus	1	1	2		
Bulkley, Jonathan	1	3	5		
Bass, Benjamin	2		2		
Bass, Joseph	1	2	3		
Stephens, Ebenezer	4		3		
Brush, Stephen	2	1	1		
Bass, Elijah	1		5		
Stephens, Reubin	1	2	2		
Stephens, Daniel	1	3	3		
Kelogg, Martin, Jnr.	1	2	2		
Keelogg, Martin	2	1	2		1
Stephens, Amos	2	1	3		
Gregory, Ralph	1	2	3		
NEWTOWN TOWN.					
Tomlinson, Henery	1	2	3		1
Tomlinson, Josiah	1	3	2		3
Sharp, Jesse	1	2	5		
Sharp, Eliakim	1	1	6		
Wetmore, James	1	1	3		
Clark, Zachariah	5	4			1
Curtis, Benjamin	1	3	5		
Curtis, Nehemiah	2		5		2
Beardsley, Josiah	3	1	1		
Beardsley, Samuel	1		3		
Wadeling, Esther			1		
Shermon, Filo	2	2	4		
Shermon, Lymon	1	2	2		
Beardsley, Elias	3	2	2		
Hurd, Nirum	3	1	4		
Beardsley, Jonathan	3	2	2		
Hurd, John	2	5	6		
Peck, Ephraim	2	2	1		
Chambers, Asa	1	1	4		
Williams, Amos	1		3		
Bennitt, Abel	2	1	5		1
Platt, Josiah	3	1	6		
Bennitt, Amos	1	1	4		
Bennitt Richard	1	2	4		
Bennett James	2	1	2		1
Bennett, Thomas	3	4	3		1
Masters, James	1	2	2		
Sanford, Thomas	2	3	5		
Beardsley, Abigail (Wid.)	1	1	7		
Curtis, Filo	1	3	4		
Curtis, Abijah	4	2	2		3
Blackman, Edward	1	1	2		
Hubbill, Lewis	1	4	1		
Hubbill, John	2		3		
Allen, William	1	4	4		
Murrey, Pattern	2		3		
Beach, John, Junr.	1	3	4		1
Hubbill, Comfort	1	2	4		
Hubbill, Enoch	1	1	3		
Sanford, William	1		1		
Botchford, Joseph	2	2	4		
Bochford, Abraham	4		4		
Sanford, Hezekiah	2	3	5		
Baldwin, Isaac	2		4		
Sanford, John, Junr.	2	2	3		
Booth, Asael	2	2	6		
Booth, Olive (Wid.)	3	2	4		
Crowfoot, Stephen	2	1	6		
Cogswell, Asael	1		1		2
Sanford, James	2		7		
Sanford, Samuel	4		8		
Shermon, Lewis	1	2	6		
Baldwin, John	1	2	2		
Booth, Jonathan	1	3			1
Brau, Hanah (Wid.)	2	1	2		
Booth, David	3		4		1
Bennett, Caleb	1	2	2		
Booth, Abiel	1	2	2		
Booth, Daniel	2	3	6		
Chandler, John	5		2		1
Edmonds, William	1		2		
Curtis, Josiah	2	4	7		2
Bochford, John	2	1	2		1
Jerrold, Jabez	2	4	3		
Sherman, Ephraim	2	5	5		
Curtis, Matthew	3	1	3		
Farmon, Jeabud	2	3	4	1	
Lyon, Betty			2		
Bochford, Elijah	1	3	5		
Fairchild, William A	1	1	3		
Bochford, Jabez	2	1	3		1
Bochford, Abel	3	1	5	2	
Finney, Elded	2	4	4		
Gregory, Aaron M	1	2	4		
Farmon, Henery	1	1	4		
Booth, Phebe (Wid.)			2		2
Booth, Ezra	3	3	4		1
Burrill, Stephen	1	1	2		

FAIRFIELD COUNTY—Continued.

NEWTOWN TOWN—con.

NAME OF HEAD OF FAMILY.	Free white males of 16 years and upward, including heads of families.	Free white males under 16 years.	Free white females, including heads of families.	All other free persons.	Slaves.
Perry, Revᵈ Filo	1	2	3		1
Baldwin, Abraham	1		3		1
Beers, David	1	4	4		
Hull, Eliphalit	1	1	4		
Burch, William	2		1		
Wallis, Jacob	1	2	3		
Shepherd, John	2	2	2		
Thomas, James	1		3		
Bochford, Joel	1	1	3		
Foot, Peter	2	1	3		
Griffin, Abner	2	1	5		
Griffin, Amos	2	2	3		
Foot, Edward	2	5	6		
Deforest, Alexander	1	1	2		
Shepherd, Stephen	1	2	2		
Shermon, Ebenezer	1	2	5		
Tuttle, Daniel	2	1	4		
Kimble, Fitch	1	1	3		
Burch, William	1		1		
Hull, John	3		5		
Shepherd, David	2	4	7		
Northrop, Ruth (Wid.)	1		1		
Prindle, Lazarus	2		2		
Prindle, Philimon	1	1	1		
Prindle, Joseph	2		1		1
Prindle, Jonas	1		2		
Parmely, Noah	1	3			
Prindle, Sirus	1	1	3		
Prindle, Abiel	1	1	5		
Stilson, Benjamin	2		2		
Northop, Lawrence	1				
Northrop, Nathanᵉˡ	1	3	2		1
Ferris, Abel	3		3		
Northrop, Peter	1	2	3		
Northrop, George	1	2	1		
Northrop, Gideon	1	2	1		
Jellet, Abraham	2	2	5		
Jellet, Moses	1	2	1		
Shepherd, George	2	4	2		
Shepherd, Amos	2	3	4		
Burchin, William	1		1		
Jellet, John	1	2	2		
Glover, Elias	1	3	5		
Shepherd, Abraham	2	5	3		
Northrop, Nehemiah	2	1	5		
Northrop, Abel	3	1	2		
Northrop, William	2		2		
Foot, Daniel	1		2		
Brister, Joseph	1	1	1		
Washburn, Zebee	2	2	1		
Stilson, Jonathan	1		1		
Ferris, Peter	2		2		
Ferris, Samuel	1	1	6		
Northrop, John	2		2		
Betts, Abner	1	2	2		
Beers, Truman	1	1	3		
Beers, Sarah (Wid.)	2	1	3		
Beers, Oliver	1	1	6		
Beers, John	2	2	2		
Beers, Andrew	1	2	4		
Basset, Joel	1	1	1		
Ferris, Joseph	3		2		
Nichols, Richard	2		2		2
Beers, Elias	1		1		
Tousey, John	1		1		
Baldwin, Clark	1	3	4		
Baldwin, Sweeten	1	2	2		
Norton, Filo	4	3	2		
Peck, Isaac	1	3	4		
Peck, Elizabeth (Wid.)		1	5		
Williams, John	1	2	2		
Sharp, Thomas	1	3	5		
Griffin, Reubin	1	1	2		
Griffin, Joseph	2	2	3		
French, Gamaliel	1		3		
Tredwell, Timothy	1		2		
Johnson, John	2	4	4		
Stilson, Jacob	3		2		
Towsie, Donald	1	2	3		
Johnson, Abel	1	2	3		
Gray, Seth	1	1	3		
Chapman, Collins	1	1	1		
Peck, Matthew	2	3	5		
Lekes, Ephraim	2		2		
Bescoro, Nathan	1	1	3		
Prindle, Daniel	3	1	5		
Gilbert, Stephen	2	1	3		
Dimon, Gold	1				
Rowland, Jabez	2	3	5		
Raymond, Justin	2		4		
Tumey, John	1		2		
Platt, Jarvis	2	1	4		
Lacy, Richard	3		3		
Platt, Justin	1	1	2		
Gilbert, Seth	3	5	2		

NEWTOWN TOWN—con.

NAME OF HEAD OF FAMILY.	Free white males of 16 years and upward, including heads of families.	Free white males under 16 years.	Free white females, including heads of families.	All other free persons.	Slaves.
Beach, Lazarus	1	1	4		
Morgin, Hezekiah	2	2	4		
Underhill, John	2	2	3		
Basset, John	3	2	6		
Crowfoot, John	1	1	2		
Taylor, Ebenezer	5		1		7
Platt, Jesse	3	2	1		
Platt, Timothy	4		3		
Farmer, Filo	1		4		
Towsie, Zalmon	1	1	2		
Towsie, Filo	1		2		1
Crowfoot, Daniel	1	2	3		
Crowfoot, Isaac	1	1	1		
Crowfoot, John	1		1		1
Crowfoot, Elihu	1	1	2		1
Crowfoot, Molly (Wid.)	1		1		
Roberts, Thomas	3	1	3		
Shepherd, James	3	1	4		
Stilson, Israel	2	1	6		
Fairchild, Apheus	2	3	3		
Fairchild, John	1	1	6		
Shepherd, Merrit	1	1	1		
King, David	3	1	8		
Shepherd, Moses	1	2	8		
Fairchild, Ager	2		1		
Mills, Andrew	1	1	2		
Rample, George	1	1	3		
Fairchild, Jonathan	1	1	1		
Fairchild, Peter	1	2	2		
Fairchild, Silus	2	1	4		
Wheeler, Joseph	1	2	2		
Hubbill, Jepthan	2	1	4		
Prindle, Abijah	1	1	4		
Wheeler, David	1	1	2		
Fairchild, Seth	3	1	3		
Weed, Solomon	2	3	2		
Wheeler, Ann (Wid.)	1		1		
Wheeler, Jerusha (Wid.)			2		
Fairchild, James	1		2		
Fairchild, Filo	1	1	2		
Fairchild, James	1	2	3		
Shermon, Seth	1	2	3		
Shermon, David	2	1	3		
Foot, Joseph	1	2	6		
Fairchild, Zadoc	1	4	3		
Fairchild, Clemon	1		1		
Fairchild, Ebenʳ	2		2		
Foot, George	2	1	2		
Fairchild, Josiah	1	5	2		1
Winton, Daniel	1				
Summers, John	2		5		
Winton, Lockwood	1	1	2		
Sanford, Nathanᵉˡ	1	2	6		
Foot, Jehiel	1	2	1		
Summers, Robert	3		1		
Mills, Stephen	1		2		
Daton, Hezekiah	1	2	6		
Blackman, Josiah	1	2	5		
Blackman, Joseph	2		3		
Blackman, John	2		1		
Camp, Hezekiah	1		2		
Camp, Julius	1	1	3		1
Bochford, Clemon	1	1	5		
Bochford, Gideon	1	5	4		
Bochford, Theopholus	1				
Blackman, Reuben	1	2	3		
Shermon, Lemuel	3	1	5		
Baldwin, Amos	1	2	1		
Bochford, Gideon	4	2	3		1
Bennett, Abraham	2	1	4		
Parcks, Michael	1	2	3		
Glover, Benjamin	2		3		
Lacy, Sarah (Wid.)			2		
Bancraft, Oliver	1	2	2		
Elwood, Rion	1	8	2		
Turrel, Jared	3	2	3		
Chambers, Thomas	2	1	2		
Curtis, Nirum	1		1		
Burritt, Amos	1	1	6		
Hall, William	4	1	4		
Peck, Samuel	3	2	4		
Bobbit, Samuel	1	2	2		
Norton, Nathan	2	3	2		
Mills, Daniel	1	1	1		
Wheeler, Joseph	2		1		
Wheeler, Bennett	1		3		
Wheeler, Eli	1	1	4		
Peck, Ezra	1		3		
Peck, Sarah (Wid.)		1	3		
Peck, Heth	1		3		
Peck, Heth, Junʳ	2	1	2		
Peck, Nathaniel	2		1		
Burritt, Rebeckah (Wid.)			1		
Wheeler, Thomas	2	1	5		1

NEWTOWN TOWN—con.

NAME OF HEAD OF FAMILY.	Free white males of 16 years and upward, including heads of families.	Free white males under 16 years.	Free white females, including heads of families.	All other free persons.	Slaves.
Fulford, Oliver	2	6	2		
Booth, James	1	1	2		
Booth, Hezekiah	2		3		1
Glover, Daniel	1	1	6		4
Glover, James	4		2		2
Sanford, Jonas	2	2	6		
Sanford, Jonathan	2		8		
Sanford, Soloman	2	1	3		
Prindle, Samuel	2		4		
Glover, John	3	1	3		3
Osborn, Edward	1	1	2		
Sherborn, Benjamin	1	1	1		
Lattain, Jacob	2	2	4		
Lattain, Benjamin	2		2		
Lattain, Luke	2		9		
Morris, Amos	2	1	2		
Morris, Daniel	1	4	3		
Peck, Joshua	1	1	4		
Judson, Elijah	2	2	3		
Peck, Eli	2	1	4		
Malery, Mary (Wid.)			3		
Malery, Thomas	1	1	2		
Lattain, Joseph	2	3	4		
Shermon, Lymon	1	1	3		
Shermon, Filo	1	2	4		
Curtis, Zalmon	1	2	2		
Shermon, Elijah	2	1	2		
Shermon, Ezra	1	5	1		
Shermon, John	2	2	2		
Squire, William	1	2	3		
Cato (Negro)				6	
Beardsley, Abigail	2	1	7		
Hurd, Finious	2	3	4		
Beers, Eben	5	4	5		1
Johnson, Enoch	2	2	4		
Beers, Finious	1	2	2		
Warner, Molly			3		
Ferris, Zacheriah	1		2		
Walker, John	2	3	1		
Warner, Noadoc	1	1	5		
Shermon, Nathan	3		3		
Beach, John	1		4		2
Glover, Zalmon	2	2	2		
Hull, Elijah	2	1	6		
Wells, Isaac	2	3	1		
Foot, Tillo	1		3		
Hurd, Amos	6	1	5		
Foot, Peter	2	3	5		
Glover, Henery	3		4		
Hurd, Curtis	1	1	5		
Bochford, Moses	2	3	4		
Bochford, Jerid	3	1	3		
Stilson, Nehemiah	1	1	6		
Taylor, Stephen	1	2	1		
Foot, George	2	3	3		
Taylor, Nicholas	1	2	2		
Judson, Sarah			1		
Malery, Ebenezer	2	2	3		
Curtis, Stiles	1	1	2		
Judson, Abel	3	5	5		
Judson, Nathanᵉˡ	1	8	3		
Curtis, Gold	2	2	4		1
Tousey, Oliver	2		4		
Peck, Levi	2	1	2		
Peck, Henery	3	1	2		
Meeker, David	2		2		1
Glover, Solimon	1	2	7		
Peck, Shadrack	1	2	2		
Boscon, Patience		1	3		
Prindle, Jonathan	3	1	4		
Towsie, Isaac	2	1	2		
Towsie, Zalmon	3	1	4		
Heard, Oliver C	3		2		
Peck, Moses	3		5		
Nichols, Sarah	1	3	3		1
Nichols, Elijah	3	1	1		2
Shermon, Jotham	2	1	2		
Hinman, Mary			3		
Booth, Reuben	2	1	2		2
Mogenot, John	1	2	2		1
Strong, Nehemiah	2		3		
Johnson, Joel	2	1	3		
Pringle, Ephraim	1		3		
Whiting, Samuel	2	3	4		
Burritt, William	3	1	2		
Hinman, David	3	1	4		
Stilson, Bailey	1	1	3		
Shepherd, Gideon	1	2	3		
Perry, Bennitt	1	3	4		
Gilbert, John	1		2		
Baldwin, Caleb	3	1	1		1
Baldwin, David	1	2	3		1
Beers, Sirus	3	1	1		
Bagger, John	1	3	2		
Biscow, Sarah (Wid.)	1	2	2		1

FAIRFIELD COUNTY—Continued.

NEWTOWN TOWN—con.

NAME OF HEAD OF FAMILY.	Free white males of 16 years and upward, including heads of families.	Free white males under 16 years.	Free white females, including heads of families.	All other free persons.	Slaves.
Beers, Daniel	1		1		
Perry, Ezra	2	1	2		
Lee, Stephen	1		1		
Beers, Samuel	2	2	4		
Beers, Simeon	1	2	4		
Stilson, Abel	1	1	3		
Stilson, Vincent	2	1	3		
Peck, Ebenezer	4		1		
Ferris, Nathan	1	2	2		
Stilson, Elnathan	1		2		
Baldwin, Abigail	1		4		
Skidmore, Daniel	1	1	4		
Turrel, George	1	1	5		
Hurd, Ammon	2	5	4		
Upum, Wate	2		3	1	
Peck, Nathan	1	4	2		
Peck, Enoch	4	3	4		
Peck, David	2	1	2		
Peck, John	2	1	4		
Biscow, John	1	4	4		
Peck, Jabez	2	1	4		
Peck, Isarel	1	2	2		
Peck, Joseph	2	5	3		
Stilson, Thomas	1		2		
Whiting, James	1	3	5		
Peck, Asher	1	4	6		
Peck, Livenus	1	2	2		
Peck, Enos	1	3	4		
Nichols, Peter	3	1	3	1	
Nichols, Lemuel	1	1	4		
Nichols, Philo	1	1	1		
Judson, John	3		9		
Starling, David	2	1	1		
Starlin, Jacob	1		2		
Sherwood, Justin	1	2	1		
Stilson, Aaron	1	2	4		
Sherwood, Eben	3		3		
Taylor, Phineus	3	1	3		
Taylor, Phineus, Jr	1		3		
Summers, Gershom	3	1	3		
Burr, Noah	2	2	1		
Sherwood, Daniel	1	1	3		
Foot, Daniel	1	1	3		
Shepherd, Simeon	2	3	3		
Hurd, Jonathan	1	1	4		
Tousey, Abel	1	2	3	1	
Tousey, Rebecka(Wid.)	1	1	3		
Gray, William	1	1	6		
Dimon, Gold	1	2	5		
Willisson, John	1	2	2		
Blackman, Treuman	1	2	3		
Blackman, John, Junr	2	4	5		
Hawley, Benjamin	1	1	1		
Hatcher, Joshua	1	1	4		
Shermon, Matthew	1		5		
Hatch, Joseph	1	1	6		
Camp, Joel	4	2	2		
Blackman, James	3	1	3		
Trowbridge, Samuel	1		2		
Fairchild, Ranson	1	2	1		
Turney, John	1	3	2		
Turney, Nathan	2		2		
Hawley, Joseph	1	1	2		
Hawley, William	2	1	3		
Colson, Joseph	1	1	2		
Hawley, Jotham	1	2	1		
Hawley, Abel	2		3		
Baldwin, Mathew	1	2	5		
Lake, John	1	2	2		
Wheeler, Stephen	1	2	2		
Hennerics, Ellis	1		3		
Skidmore, Ephraim	2	4	5		
Skidmore, Amos	1	2	1		
Skidmore, Abel	1	3	3		
Skidmore, John	2	1	2		
Lake, Peter	1	2	3		
Lake, David	1	1	5		
Smith, John	1		1		
Turril, Amos	3	1	5		
Foot, Elisha	2	2	2		
Turril, Roger	3	1	3		
Booth, Abraham	1	1	2		
Turrel, Ruben	2	1	2		

NORWALK AND STAMFORD TOWNS.

NAME OF HEAD OF FAMILY.	Free white males of 16 years and upward, including heads of families.	Free white males under 16 years.	Free white females, including heads of families.	All other free persons.	Slaves.
Mott, Reuben	3		3		
Keeler, Anne (Wd)			3		
Rose (Negro)				2	
Harry (Negro)				4	
Jackson, Daniel	1	3	1		
Keeler, Nathaniel	2	2	2		
Seymore, Jonathan	1	1	2		
Mott, William	1	2	5		

NORWALK AND STAMFORD TOWNS--con.

NAME OF HEAD OF FAMILY.	Free white males of 16 years and upward, including heads of families.	Free white males under 16 years.	Free white females, including heads of families.	All other free persons.	Slaves.
Hoyt, Timothy	1	7	3		
Coza (Negro)				2	
Anne (Negro)				2	
Warson, Robert	3	1	7		
Syphax (Negro)				6	
Comestock, David, Jur	1	2	4	1	
Church, Ebenezer	5	1	3		2
Fitch, Thomas, Esqr	6		3	2	2
Marvin, Samuel	3		2		
Rogers, Mary (Wd)			5		
Gregory, Samuel	1		2		
Hanford, Daniel	1	2	2		
Fitch, Timothy	2	2	5		
Saunders, Jabez	2	1	3		
Wilson, Nathan	1	1	4		
Smith, Hutton	2	4	4		
Hyatt, Isaac	1	2	3		
Lockwood, Thomas	1		2		
Betts, Mary (Wd)	1		2		
Hendrick, Nathan	1	3	2		
Hyatt, Daniel	1	1	1		
Raymond, Josiah	2	3	4		6
Smith, James	2	2	1		
Raymond, Abigail(wd)			1		
St John, Wm, Junr	1	2	4		1
Smith, Hannah (Wd)			1		
Mallory, Polly (Wd)	1	1	3		
Fitch, Haynes	3	6	3		
Fitch, Rebecca (Wd)		1	2		
Waters, Robert	2		1		
Pope, Charles	1		1		
Hanford, Hezekiah	1	1	3		
Hanford, Hezekiah, Junr	1	4	2		
Fitch, James	2	1	2		
Fitch, James, Junr	1	1	2		
Hyatt, Mary (Wd)			1		
Gregory, Abraham	3	2	3		
Gregory, Seely	1	1	3		
Gregory, Ebenezer	1		3		
Mallory, Capt Nathan	2		3		
Smith, Sarah (Wd)			4		
Bessy, Bridget (Wd)			1		
Eversley, John	3		2		
Burnet, Revd Matthias	1	2	3		2
Bennedict, Elizabeth (Wd)			1		
Hall, Hannah			2		
Bartram, Job	1	2	4		1
Scudder, Elizabeth (Wd)			1		
Pomp (Negro)				3	
Mentor				4	
Peter (Negro)				3	
Ann (Negro)				3	
Grumman, Thomas	2		4		
Lockwood, John	3		3		
St John, William	1	4	3	1	2
Belding, Thomas	2		1	1	1
Betts, John	1	2	4		
Lockwood, Ebenezer	3	5	3		
Jarvis, Stephen	1				
Oglesby, Revd Geo	1	1	4		1
James, Hezekiah	3	4	4		
Lockwood, Hezekiah	1	2	4		
Fairchild, Samuel	1		2		
Knight, Doctr Jonathn	1	2	2		
Betts, Thomas	1	1	2		
Bennedict, William	2	1	4		
Canon, James	1		4		
Betts, Hezekiah	3	1	3		
Marvin, Seth	1	1	1		
Lockwood, Eliphalet	3	2	3		
Rogers, Uriah	1		5		
Beers, Nathaniel	3	2	5		
Camp, Richard	1	3	5		
Hanford, Jedediah	2		3		
St John, John	1	1	5		
Smith, Jeremiah	1	1	2		
Whitehead, Sibbely			1		
St John, Josiah	2	1	5		
St John, Stephen	2	1	1		
Hendrick, Peter	1	1	3		
Demmon, Nathaniel	5	1	5		
Lockwood, Matthew	1		1		
Thallter, Thaddeus B	1		1		
Betts, Elijah	1		2		
Betts, Isaac	1		1		
Betts, Isaac, Jun	1		1		
Everet, Richard	1	1	3		
Patrick, Ellen (Wd)			4		
Camp, Jonathan	3	1	4		
Scribner, Stephen	2	2	3		
Betty, James	1	1	4		
Gregory, Silas	1	2	3		
Gregory, Denton	1		1		
Gregory, Stephen	3	1	5		

NORWALK AND STAMFORD TOWNS--con.

NAME OF HEAD OF FAMILY.	Free white males of 16 years and upward, including heads of families.	Free white males under 16 years.	Free white females, including heads of families.	All other free persons.	Slaves.
Gregory, Samuel	1		1		
Gregory, John	2	1	6		
Beers, Samuel	1	1	3		
Cowley, James	2	2	2		
Rogers, Lemuel	1		1		
Camp, Isaac	2	2	6		
Camp, Isaac, Junr	1	1	1		
Jackson, Rachel (Wd)			3		
Harris, William	1	1	3		
Finch, Ruth			1		
Phillo, John	1	1	1		
Phillo, Isaac	1	1	2		
Olmsted, Reuben	1	2	2		
Stuart, Albert	1	3	1		
Olmsted, Silvanus	1		2		
Grumman, John	2		2		
Grumman, Jeremiah	2	1	2		
Grumman, Ezra	2	2	2		
Richard, Stephen	1		1		
Grumman, Nehemiah	1		2		
Abbott, Jedediah	1	2	3		
Betts, Abijah	2	1	4		
Hyatt, Elvin	1	2	2		
Grumman, Isaac	1	2	3		
Birrchard, Daniel	2	1	3		
Whitlock, Abel	1		2		
Church, Daniel	2	3	4		
Lambart, David	1	3	5		
Betts, Thaddeus	2	1	6		
Abbott, Seth	2	2	6		
Jarvis, Jesse	1		3		
Stuard, Simon	1	3	3		
Abbott, Ebenezer	3	3	4	2	3
Gayler, Elizabeth (Wd)	1	1	2		
Betts, Benjamin	2		4		
Paching, Ebenezer	1	5	3		
Rockwell, Joseph	1				
Whitlock, Mary (Wd)	1	1	2		
Dunning, Richard	1	1	2		
Raymond, Asahel	2	2	3		
Betts, Abigail (Wd)	2		2		
Betts, Daniel	1	2	1		
Betts, Jesse	1	1	2		
Raymond, Clapp	1	1	2		
Raymond, Clapp, Jr	1	3	2		
Belding, Samuel	1	4	1		2
Betts, Moses	1	2	4		
Sevans, David	1		2		
Deforest, Lemuel	2	1	2		
Ogden, Jesse	2	3	2		
Cole, Asa	1	1	5		
Rockwell, Joseph, Jr	1	3	1		
Wix, Stephen	1	2	1		
Starling, Samuel, Jr	1	4	3		
Hecock, Bethl	1				
Hecock, Nathanel	3	2	5		
Raymond, Seth	2	1	7		
Hendrick, Deodate	1	1	1		
Betts, Elijah		1	4		
Chitester, Abraham	2	3	2		
Patrick, Abraham	1	3	2		
Fox, Jonathan	1	5	2		
Betts, Stephen	3	1	2		
Raymond, Seth	1	1	7		
Raymond, Benjamin	1				
Hubble, Thaddeus	1		2		
Hubbell, Zadoch	1	1	5		
Hubble, Thomas	2	1	3		
Marvin, Matthew	3	2	2	1	1
Wescots, John	1	1	1		
Osborn, Jacob	2	2	2		
Cannon, John, Junr	1	3	4		2
Gilbert, Nathan	3		4	1	
Hecock, Noah	2	1	2		
Starling, Daniel	1		2		
Starling, William	1				
Starling, William, Jr	1	5	4		
Hollibert, Joseph	1	3	5		
Dikeman, Levi	1	4	5		
Betts, Reuben	2	3	5		
Mead, John Betts	1		1		
Stuart, Samuel	1	2	6		
Williams, John	1		1		
Marvin, Samuel, 3d	1	1	3		
Cole, Thomas	1	4	2		
Cole, Jonathan	1	1	2		
Nichols, James	1	4	3		
Starling, Samuel	1		3		
Belding, Asa	2	4	2		
Belding, David	2		4		
St John, Amy (Wd)	1	3	3		
Morgan, John	2	1	2	1	
Keeler, Philip	1	2	2		
Nash, Ebenezer	1	3	3		
Davis, James	1	2	3		

FAIRFIELD COUNTY—Continued.

NORWALK AND STAMFORD TOWNS—con.

NAME OF HEAD OF FAMILY.	Free white males of 16 years and upward, including heads of families.	Free white males under 16 years.	Free white females, including heads of families.	All other free persons.	Slaves.
Scott, Wm, Junr	2	2	3		
Bennett, Nathan	1	6	2		
Abbott, James	1	1	3		
Sanford, Nathan	1	1	3		
Denton, Benjamin	1		5		
Smith, Eliakim	1		2		
Keeler, Isaac	1		2		
Keeler, Elijah	1	1	3		
Birchard, Jesse	1	1	4		
Rogers, John	1	3	1		
Beers, Moses, Junr	1	1	1		
Scott, William	3	1	1		
Scott, John	1		1		
Scott, Aaron	1	1	1		
Seymore, Abijah	1	2	2		
Mead, Jeremiah	2		3		
Keeler, Timothy	2	1	2		
Keeler, Nathan	1	3	5		
Ayres, Benjamin	2	2	1		
Mead, Thaddeus	2	2	2		
Beers, Moses	2		2		
Keeler, Samuel	3	3	4		
Mead, Azor	1	1	2		
Keeler, Elizabeth			1		
Wescott, Elijah	1	2	3		
Mead, Matthew	4	2	4		
Comestock, Samuel	2	1	3		
Bigsby, Gracy (Wd)			1		
Thomas, Gregory	1		2		
Baker, James	1	4	4		
Olmsted, James	1	1	6		
Whitlock, Daniel	1		1		
Whitlock, Daniel, Jr	2	1	6		
Olmsted, Samuel	1	3	3		
Whitlock, David	1	1	4		
St John, John	3	2	2		
Nichols, Nehemiah	1		1		
Scofield, Peter	1	2	6		
St John, Isaac	3	1	3		
St John, Silas	1	1	4		
Morgan, James	3	3	3		
Betts, Matthew	1		1		
Tuttle, Enoch	1	1	4		
Gates, Samuel, Jr	1	3	2		
Gates, Moses	1	1	2		
Gates, Samuel	2		3		
Nichols, Enos	1	2	2		
Lyon, Palatia	1	1	2		
Nichols, Jonathan	1	2	4		
Boutain, Seth	1	1	3		
St. John, Ezra	1		2		
St John, Jonathan	1	4	1		
Gregory, Isaac	1		2		
Gregory, Isaac, Jr	1	2	1		
Jackson, Nathan	2	1	1		
Mead, Joseph	2	1	1		
Bennit, David	1	1	5		
Gunn, Aaron	1		1		
Black, Step (negro)				1	
Batterson, James	1	1	1		
Olmsted, Joseph	2	1	4		
Webster, Thomas	1	1	1		
Olmsted, Lydia (Wd)		2	3		
Olmsted, David	1	2	1		
Olmsted, Nathan	2	2	4		
Olmsted, James	3	3	3		
Thomas, Joseph	1	1	1		
Scribner, Uriah	1	2	4		
Nichols, Enoch	1		3		
Jackson, Mary (Wd)			1		
Nichols, Jeremiah	1		4		
Russique, Nathan	1	1	1		
Batterson, Pawel	1		2		
Stuart, Thaddeus	1	1	1		
Nash, William	1	1	4		
Buttersworth, John	1	1	2		
Smith, Henry	1	2	2		
Sterling, Thaddeus	2	1	6		
Elles, John	1	3	2		
Hanford, Theophilus	2		1		
Selleck, Uriah	1		1		
Hanford, Timothy	1	1	2		
Kellagg, Jonathan	2		4		
Johnson, Moses	1	3	3		
Stone, Elizabeth (Wd)			1		
Hoyt, Justice	2	2	4		
Hanford, Levi	2	1	2		
Hanford, Mary (wd)	2	1	3		
Hanford, Eliphalet	1	1	2		
Hanford, Ebenezer, Junr	1	3	2		
Hanford, Ebenezer	1		2		
Hanford, Samuel	1				
Hanford, Moses	2	3	5		1
Hanford, Samuel, Junr	2	2	2		
Hanford, Mary (Wd)		1	1		

NORWALK AND STAMFORD TOWNS—con.

NAME OF HEAD OF FAMILY.	Free white males of 16 years and upward, including heads of families.	Free white males under 16 years.	Free white females, including heads of families.	All other free persons.	Slaves.
Husted Thaddeus	1	2	3		
Sturges, Aquilla	1		4		
Seymore, Ezra	2	2	7		
Seymore, Thomas	2		1		
Hanford, Abraham	1	4	3		
Jarvis, John	1	1	3		
Bolt, William	3	1	4		
Reed, William	1		1		
Reed, William, Junr	2	3	1		
Kellagg, Isaac	2	1	3		
Waring, Eunice (Wd)		3	2		
Hanford, Alexander	1	2	1		
Reed, Abigail			2		
Reed, Thaddeus	2	1	1		
Reed, John	2	2	3		
Hayes, John	2		2		
Smith, Noah	1		1		
Waring, Jesse	1	3	2		
Whitmore, Solomon	1				
Younges, Richard	1	3	4		
Reed, Capt Eli	1	1	2		
Brown, Jesse	1	1	2		
Reed, Jesse	1	4	3		
Nash, David	2	2	2		
Street, Nathaniel	2	2	4		
Selleck, Nathaniel	1	2	4		
Bishop, Jacob	1	3	4		
Hanford, Levi	1	3	3		
Bennedict, Caleb	1	4	3	2	2
St. John, David	2	2	4		
Weed, Abraham	1	1	2		
Boutain, Eleazer	1		1		
Boutain, Eleazer, Junr	1	2	1		
Gray, Hannah (Wd)	1		2		
St. John, Selleck	1		2		
Silliman, Samuel C	1	1	1	1	1
Boutain, David	1	3	2		
Ambler, Mercy			1		
Silliman, Doctr Joseph	1	2	3		
Mitchel, Revd Justice	1	3	5		
Comestock, Aaron	1	3	3		
St John, Justice	1	1	3		
Comestock, Enoch	3	1	2		
Comestock, Moses	1	3	6		
Kellagg, Nathan	1	4	5		
Seymore, John	2	1	2		
Smith, Doctr David	1	1	2		
June, Jabez	1		3		
Tuttle, Abigail (Wd)	2		3		
Tuttle, Ebenezer	1		2		
Tuttle, Levi	1	1	1		
Bennedict, Isaac	2	3	4		
Betts, Stephen	1	2	4	1	1
Raymond, Ebenezer	2		2		
Raymond, John	1	3	5		
Tuttle, Eli	1		6		
Lockwood, Samuel	1	4	4		
Lockwood, Ephraim	3	4	4		
Kellagg, Samuel	4	1	4		
Elles, Jeremiah	1	1	6		
Lockwood, Jacob	3	5	5		
Waring, Solomon	1	1	4		
Green, Caleb	1	2	2		
Slason, Stephen	1	2	5		
Reynolds, Isaac	3	4	4		
Bennedict, Thaddeus	1	4	1		
Hoyt, Jonathan	1	2	6		
Raymond, David	1	2	3		
Marvin, Benjamin	1	2	3		
Duran, Joseph	1		4		
Seymore, Samuel	2	1	4		
Reed, Benjamin	2	2	4		
Burral, Samuel	4	2	1		1
Belding, John	3	1	2		2
Keeler, Isaac	1	3	2		
Fairweather, Hanford	1	3	3		
Bennedict, Thomas	2				3
Grummon, Samuel, Jr	5	2	1		1
Lockwood, John	1	1	2		
Kellagg, John	1		3		
Seymore, Phebe (Wd)		2	2		
Saunders, John, Senr	1	1	1	1	
Finch, Dan	1		3		
Phillips, Ebenezer	1		3		1
White, Peter	2	1	3		
White, Samuel	2	2	4		
Seymore, Anne (Wd)			1		
Bennedict, Nathaniel	3		2	3	3
Seymore, David	1	1	2		
Seymore, John	1		1		
Seymore, James	2	2	6		
Seymore, Rebecca (Wd)	1		3		
Renton, James	1	2	2		
Bennedict, Nathaniel, Jr	2	4	4		
Smith, Daniel	1		6		

NORWALK AND STAMFORD TOWNS—con.

NAME OF HEAD OF FAMILY.	Free white males of 16 years and upward, including heads of families.	Free white males under 16 years.	Free white females, including heads of families.	All other free persons.	Slaves.
Seymore, Seth	1	2	1		
Brooks, Lemuel	2	3	5		
Brooks, Lemuel, Junr	1		1		1
Brown, Jedediah	2	1	6		
Quintard, Peter	1	1	2		
Russique, Mary			2		
Raymond, Uriah	2	3	3		
Evertson, Evert	1		2		
Garner, William	1	1	1		
Smith, Eliakim	2	4	2		
Hoyt, Job	1	2	2		
Weed, Scudder	1	3	3		
Bloomer, William	1	3	3		
Scott, Eleazer	1	2	4		
Pickett, Peter	2	1	2		
Hoyt, Nathan	1		1		
Hoyt, Henry	1	1	3		
Hoyt, Asa	2	3	4		
Raymond, Nathel, Jr	2	6	3		
Raymond, Eliakim	1		2		
Whitney, Lois (Wd)		2	3		
Gibbs, Samuel	1	4	3		
Raymond, Naphtha	1	1			
Raymond, George	1		2		
Quintard, James	4	3	2		
Hoyt, Isaac	1	1	5		
Raymond, Nathaniel	1	2	4		
Seymore, William	1	1	1		
Raymond, Simon	1		2		
Hoyt, Sarah (Wd)	1		2		
Raymond, Hezekiah	2	4	2		
Raymond, Aaron	1		4		
Raymond, Moses	1	1	7		
Woods, Stephen	1	2	3		
Woods, Sarah (Wd)			1		
Boutain, William	2	2	6		
Boutain, Joshua	1	1	4		
Boutain, Sarah (Wd)			1		
Hoyt, Thomas	1	3	3		
Hoyt, Sarah (Wd)			4		
Raymond, Samuel	1	5	6		
Jones, Elijah	1	3	5		
Hoyt, John	1	1	3		
Briggsby, John	1	1			
Briggsby, Moses	1		2		
Briggsby, Joseph	1	1	2		
Saunders, Holmes	1	1	1		
Hoyt, Mary (Wd)		1	2		
Hoyt, Moses	1		1		
Marvin, Hercules	1	1	2		
Briggsby, Hopkins	1	1	2		
Briggsby, John	1	3	2		
Waring, Joseph, Jr	2	1	3		
Bessy, Peleg	1	1	4		
Brown, Nathan	2		1		
Boutain, Zarius	2	1	2		
Boutain, Samuel	1		3		
Knapp, Caleb	1	1	3		
Raymond, Paul	1	1	5		
Raymond, Edward	1	2	3		
Raymond, Gershom	1		5		
Raymond, Gershom, Jr	1	2	2		
Smith, Noah	1				
Morehouse, Sarah (Wd)			1		
Abbott, Eunice			1		
Abbott, John	2	1	2		
Abbott, Aaron	1		2		
Acorn, Thomas	1	3	3		
Green, Daniel	1	2	3		
Betts, Burrell	2	1	4		
Odel, Nathaniel	1	2	5		
Mead, Abijah	1		3		
Mead, Mehitable (Wd)			1		
Mead, David	1		1		
Burkout, Peter	1	1	2		
Chapman, Robert	1		2		
Keeler, Stephen	1	1	5		
Stone, Onely	1	1	1		
Nash, Edward	1		1		
Tuttle, Nathan	1		1		
Tuttle, Nathan, Jr	2		1		
Greenslit, Titus	1				
Richard, Abigail (Wd)	1		5		
Richard, Gershom	1	2	3		
Waring, Eliakim	3	2	4		
Richards, Nathan	2	3	4		
Richards, Rebecca (Wd)		1	2		
Neptune				5	
Price, David	1				
Nash, Nathan	3	1	2		2
Tayler, Paul	1	2	6		
Waring, Deborah (Wd)			4		
Blackley, Admer	2	2	4		
Tuttle, Jesse	2		1		
Arnold, Jacob	1	3	1		

FAIRFIELD COUNTY—Continued.

NAME OF HEAD OF FAMILY.	Free white males of 16 years and upward, including heads of families.	Free white males under 16 years.	Free white females, including heads of families.	All other free persons.	Slaves.
NORWALK AND STAMFORD TOWNS—con.					
Parks, James	1	3	2		
Kellagg, Enos	2	1	6		
Kellagg, Stephen	2	3	4		
Kellagg, Epenetus	2	3	6		
Saunders, John	1	2	4		
Fairweather, Thomas	2	1	2		
Kellagg, James	3	3	4		
Bennedict, Thomas, 2nd	1	1	3		
Fitch, John	3	2	8		
Fitch, Theophilus	1	3	4		
Fitch, Bushnel	1		1		
Fitch, Stephen	1	3	2		1
Smith, Peter	1	1	2		
Elles, Moses C	2	3	5		
Carter, Samuel	1	1	1		
Carter, John	1	1	4		1
Warley, Mary (Wd)			3		
Fitch, Abijah	2		3		
Hoyt, John, Junr	1				
Elles, Jeremiah B	4	2	6		
Selleck, Jacob	2	1	5		
Carter, Ebenezer	1	1	1		
Bennedict, Nehemiah	1				
Selleck, Thaddeus	1		1		
Hoyt, David	1	1	3		
Finch, Seth	1		2		
St John, Anna	1	1	3		
Auction, Thomas	1		3		
Hoyt, John	1	4	6		
Hoyt, Timothy	2	2	8		
Bennedict, Hezekiah	2	2	5		
Bennedict, James	2	2	4		
Bennedict, Ezra	1	2	7		
Bennedict, James, Jr	1		1		
Bennedict, Nehemiah, Jr	1	1	2		
Bennedict, John	2	1	4		
Gildersleeve, Finch	1	1	3		
St John, Caleb	1	1	2		2
St John, Hezekiah	1	2	9		
Fitch, Joseph	1	2	2		
Hoyt, Matthew	1	3	4		
Lockwood, James	2	2	4		
Smith, Samuel	1		3		1
Bennedict, Samuel	1		4		
Bennedict, Stephen	2	1	3		
Tuttle, David	2	1	1		
Keeler, David	1		3		
Hayes, Eunice (Wd)	1	1	2		
Smith, Phinehas	2	2	3		
Smith, Samuel, Junr	1	4	4		
Ressique, James	2		1		
Keeler, Daniel	1	1	2		
Keeler, Isaac	2	1	3		
Comstock, Abijah	2	1	2		
Raymond, Comfort	1	1	3		
Croford, Samuel	1	1	4		
St John, Matthew, Junr	1	1	4		
Hoyt, Thaddeus	2	1	2		
Croford, Ebenezer	1	1	4		
Holly, John	1		1		
Betts, Ruth (Wd)			2		
Richards, James, Junr	1	1	4		
Abbott, Jonathan	1	1	3		
Richards, Edmond	1	2	5		
Richards, Jesse	1	1	3		
Richards, James	2	2	3		
Clinton, Allen	1		2		
Hoyt, William	1	4	3		
Deforest, Isaac	1	2	3		
Keeler, Phinehas	2	1	3		
Deforest, Sarah (Wd)	1	2	1		
Keeler, Stephen	1	2	7		
Dunnin, David	1	4	3		
Gregory, Ezra	2	3	2		
Hecock, Ebenezer	1		5		
Nichols, Jonathan	1	1	2		
Joseph	1	2	6		
Baxto, Reuben	1	3	2		
Evans, Joseph	1	2	4		
Abbott, Enoch	1	2	6		
Betts, Silas	1		5		
Fitch, Seymore	1	2	3		
Raymond, Wm	2	1	2		
Comstock, Thomas	2	2	6		
Arnolds, Isaac	1		3		
Arnold, Isaac, Junr	1	1	2		
Croford, Joseph	1	2	1		
Hait, Elijah, Junr	3	1	5		
Birchard, Jemima (Wd)	2		2		
Birchard, James	1		3		
St John, Benona	2	3	2		
St John, Peter	3	2	5		
St John, Nehemiah	3	1	2		
St John, Stephen, Junr	1	2	2		
St John, Daniel	4		3		
NORWALK AND STAMFORD TOWNS—con.					
Whitney, David	2	1	2		
Comstock, Caleb	2	2	1		
Beers, Ezekiel	2		2		
St John, Nehemiah, Jr	1		6		
Platt, John	3	2	6		
Comstock, Sarah	2	1	4		1
Comstock, David	1	2	3		1
Comstock, Abijah, Jr	2	1	3		
St John, Matthias	2	1	4		
Clinton, Joseph	2		1		
Hunte, William	1		1		
Hodge, Job	1	2	2		
Robertson, Mercy			2		
Hoyt, Stephen	1	2	2		
St John, Phinehas	1	1	3		
Brown, Jonathan	1	2	7		
Waring, Joseph	1	1	1		
James (Negro)				5	2
Raymond, Jesse	1		2		2
Hanford, Nehemiah	3	2	7		
Waring, Enoch	1	1	5		
Raymond, Esther (Wd)			1		
Raymond, Abraham	1		1		
Hoyt, Water	1	2	1		
Chitester, Henry	1	1	2		
Chitester, Sarah (Wd)			1		
Marvin, Majr Ozias	2	4	3		1
Wentworth, Edward	3	3	5		
Selleck, James	4	3	5		2
Betts, Samuel	1	3	1		
Raymond, Wm	1	1	8		
Hoyt, Daniel	1	2	5		
Gregory, Jabez	2	1	1		1
Betts, William M	1	2	1		
Jarvis, William	1		1		
Isaacs, Isaac	1	2	2		1
Reed, Matthew	3	2	4		
Keeler, Samuel	1	3	2		
Sherman, Taylor	1	2	2		
Hoyt, Gould	4	3	2		2
Rogers, Hezekiah	1	1	3		
Rogers, Joseph	1	2	2	1	
Coneklin, John	1		2		
Adams, Aaron	1	3	2		
Adams, Mary (Wd)	1		2		
Hanford, Eleazer, Junr	1	2	3		
Taylor, Abijah	2	5	1	1	
Hollibert, James	3	3	2		
Betts, Jeremiah	1	2	2		
Nash, Aaron	1	1	1		
Burrel, Samuel, Jr	1		4		
Ketchum, Isaac	1	2	4		1
Finny, Elisha	1	1	2		
Taylor, Marthy (Wd)	1	1	5		
Patrick, Samuel	1	1	3		
Olmsted, Jesse	1		2		
Keeler, James	1	1	2		
Rockwell, John	2	3	3		
Keeler, Jeremiah	1		1		
Keeler, Aaron	1	1	2		
Keeler, Thaddeus	1	2	2		
Middlebrook, Samuel	5	4	4		
Morehouse, Jared	1		2		
Middlebrook, Somers	1	4	2		
Richard, John	2		1		
Gregory, Silas	1	1	2		
Gregory, Daniel	3	3	2		
Gregory, Aaron	2	3	3		
Gregory, Ebenezer	2	1	2		
Gregory, Isaiah	1	1	6		
Middlebrook, Jonathan	1	1	1		
Comestock, Nathan	1		2		
Comstock, Strong	2	4	2		
Dunning, Aaron	1		1		
Dunning, Daniel	1		1		
Nichols, Thaddeus	2	1	3		
Deforest, Ebenezer	1		1		
Dunning, Moses	2	2	2		
Stuart, Isaac	1	2	4		
Turrell, Nathaniel	2	2	3		
Waistcott, Jeremiah	3		2		
Wescott, David	3		2		
Gregory, Dolly (Wd)	1	2	4		1
Gregory, Moses	1	1	2		
Gregory, Thomas	2		2		
Gregory, Jeheel	1	1	1		
Rockwell, Clapp	2	2	3		
Gregory, Nathan	1	3	2		
Gregory, Ebenezer, Junr	1		2		
James, Peter	4	2	2		
Breto, Isaac	1	2	2		
Stuard, Sarah		1	1		
Betts, Stephen 3d	1		1		
Whitlock, Hezekiah	3	2	3		
Keeler, Justice	2	1	4		
NORWALK AND STAMFORD TOWNS—con.					
Newel, Frances	1	1	2		
Stuart, Sarah (Wd)			1		
Gregory, Rebecca (Wd)			2		
Jackson, Hannah			1		
Buttersby, Wm	1	4	3		
St John, Jesse	1		1		
St John, Nathan	1	1	2		
Lockwood, Sarah (Wd)		3	1		
Betts, Peter, Junr	1	1	1		
Betts, Samuel	1	2	1		
Marvin, David	1	2	3		
Bennedict, Mary (Wd)		1			
Keeler, Seth	2		2		
Hoyt, Jesse	1		2		
Holmes, Isaac	2	3	4		
Selleck, Isaac	1		2		
Hyat, Samuel	1	2	2		
Hoyt, Nehemiah	1	2	5		
Keeler, Luke	1	1	2		
Keeler, Aaron	1	3	1		
Betts, Daniel	1	2	2		
Cannon, John	3	1	2		1
Thatcher, Josiah, Jur	1	2	2		
St John, Anna (Wd)	2		2		1
Ritch, John	1	3	1		
Downs, Woolcot	1		3		
Bellknapp, Abel	2	4	3		
Jarvis, Henry	1	3	3		
Hanford, Hannah (Wd)			1		
Bolt, David	3	2	2		
Jennings, Jacob	2	1	7		
Betts, Peter	3	3	2		
Bennedict, Jesse	2	1	4		
Hill, Esther (Wd)			2		
Hyatt, John	2		1		
Lockwood, Martha (Wd)		3	3		
Jarvis, Samuel (Comp)	1	1	3		
Whitney, Abraham	2		3		
Whitney, Timothy	1	3	5		
Lockwood, Stephen	3	3	3		
Finch, William	1	1	2		
Lockwood, Joseph	2	3	3		
Keeler, Thomas	2	4	3		
Jennings, Seth	1		2		
Kellagg, Jarvis	2		6		
Gregory, Abijah	3	1	3		
Gregory, Moses	1	1	2		
Hyatt, Abraham	1	3	2		
Hanford, John	1	3	6		
Hanford, Uriah	1	1	3		
Betts, Seth	2	1	4		
Leonard, Timothy	1	1	2		
Lorain, David	1	2	2		
Squeer, Seely	1	6	1		
Griffith, Wm	1	1	1		
Abbott, Stephen	1	1	3		
Wright, Obadiah	2	1	7		
Bennet, Moses	1	5	4		
Dickenson, Deborah (Wd)			3		
Wright, Dennis	2	1	3		
Nash, Daniel	2	2	3	1	
Marvin, Barna	2	2	3		1
Hanford, Ozias	2	2	1		
Craft, Stephen	1	3	5		
Lockwood, Gershom	1	3	4		
Gorham, Samuel	1	3	2		
Couch, David	1		4		
Morehouse, Solomon	3	2	3		
Finch, John	2		4		
Cable, Benjamin	1		4		
Cable, Gershom	1		4		
Taylor, Levi	3	3	3		
Taylor, Gamaliel	1	1	3		
Toby, Samuel	1	2	3		
Scribner, Levi	1	3	3		
Nash, Micajah	1		3		
Scribner, Abraham	2	1	1		
Marvin, Ozias, Junr	1	1	6		
Hyatt, Thomas	1		2		
Platt, Samuel	1	4	3		
Platt, Jabez	1	1	2		
Platt, Joseph	1	1	1		
Marvin, Stephen	1	1	6		
Scribner, Enoch	2	3	3		
Scribner, Matthew	1	1	3		
Scribner, Thomas	1		1		
Tillet, James	1	2	3		
McNab, Alexander	2	2	3		
Cable, Martha (Wd)			2		
Saunders, Thomas	1		1		
Ketchum, Peter	2		1		
Beers, Nathan	3		2		
Blacksly, Benjamin	1	1	1		
Stuart, Justice	1				

FAIRFIELD COUNTY—Continued.

NORWALK AND STAMFORD TOWNS—con.

NAME OF HEAD OF FAMILY.	Free white males of 16 years and upward, including heads of families.	Free white males under 16 years.	Free white females, including heads of families.	All other free persons.	Slaves.
Archer, John	1	2	4		
Smith, John	2		4		
Barnes, John	2		1		
Barnes, John, Junr	1		2		
Nash, John	3	2	4		
Patrick, John	2	1	3		
Patrick, Noah	1	1	2		
Olmsted, Darius	2	3	3		
Scribner, Ezra	1		2		
Nash, Samuel	1	3	4		
Olmsted, Nathaniel	2	1	2		
Taylor, John	1	1	1		
Couch, Rachel (Wd)			1		
Bennet, Andrew	1		3		
Dikeman, John, Jr	1	2	1		
Dikeman, Daniel	1		1		
Cable, Ebenezer	1	1	1		
Sturges, Eliphalet	1	1	2		
Whitlock, Thomas	1	3	2		
Downs, William	2	1	3		
Sturges, Elias	1	2	2		
Jezup, Blackledge	1	4	5	1	3
Morehouse, David	1	2	5		
Green, William	1	3	2		
Betts, Enoch	3	3	4		
Jezup, Joseph	1	2			
Batterson, Stephen	1	1	2		
Patching, Abigail (Wd)			2		
Hendrick, Nathaniel	3		1		
Bennet, Silas	1		5		
Patching, Daniel	2		2		
Bennet, Ebenezer	1	4	5		
Bedient, Mordecai	1	2	2		
Gilbert, Benjamin	2	1	3		
Hecock, Thomas	1	1	1		
Hollibert, John	3	1	2		
Williams, Jacob	1	2	1		
Williams, Nathan	2	2	4		
Hollibert, Daniel	2	2	6		
Guyer, Luke	1		1		
Stuart, John	2	3	2		
Hollibert, Stephen	2		1		
Bedient, Jesse	1	1	1		
Bedient, John	1	1	2		
Knapp, Epenetus	1	2	4		
Morehouse, Samuel	1	2	2		
Bedient, Gilead	1	4	7		
Jezup, Blacklege, Junr	1		1		
Wright, Henry	2	1	1		
Hyatt, Stephen	1	1	5		
Fitch, Joseph P	1	1	1		
St John, Capt John	1	5	3		
Olmsted, Samuel	2	2	4		
Fitch, Samuel, Junr	1	2	2		
Stuart, Simeon	2	2	3		
Fitch, Samuel	2		4		
Fitch, Elijah	2	1	3		
Hanford, Phineas, Junr	1	3	3		
Stuart, Benjamin	2	1	1		
Olmsted, Reuben	1		1		
Leemmis, George	1	1	2		
Murray, Daniel	1	2	1		
Olmsted, Catharine (Wd)			3		
Olmsted, Samuel	2	2	5		
Olmsted, James	1		4		
Fitch, William	2	3	1		
Patrick, Ellen (Wd)			1		
Stuart, Ephraim	1	1	3		
Finch, Ichabod	1	3	2		
Patrick, Asa	1		2		
Waterbury, Cloe (Wd)		2	3		
Waterbury, Thaddeus	1		3		
Olmsted, James, 2d	1		1		
Phillo, James	1	1	5		
Olmsted, Phebe (Wd)		1	4		
Phillo, Benjamin	2	2	2		
Tuttle, Edmond	1	1	2		
Lockwood, Daniel	1	1	2		
Hanford, Levi	1		2		
Carver, Melzer	1	4	3		
Gregory, Josiah	2		2		
Taylor, Jonathan	2		3		
Burrell, Sarah			1		
Mills, John	4		2		
Finch, John, Junr	1	1	2		
Beers, James	1	3	2		
Morehouse, Michael	1	1	1		
Morehouse, Stephen	1	1	1		
Smith, Eunice (Wd)	2	2	4		
Sturges, Daniel	1	2	3		
Gillet, William	2	4	3		
Beers, Elnathan	1	1	1		
Smith, Joseph	1		3		
Chapman, Doctr Joseph	3	2	7		1
Tuttle, Peter	1	2	5		
Hanford, Eleazer	1		2		
Hanford, Stephen	2	4	5		
Adams, Peter	1	1	2		
Bennedict, Eli	1		2		
Wilson, Charles	1		2		
Webb, Samuel	1	4	3		
DMill, Anthony	1				
DMill, Joseph	1		1		1
Maltbie, David	2	1	1		
Hoyt, Samuel, 4th	1	1	4		
Holly, David	1	1	1		
Smith, Ezekiel	2	2	4		
Smith, Martha (Wd)			2		
Judson, John	3	3	5		
Weed, Smith	2	2	5		
Dibble, Revd Ebenezer	1		5		2
Arnold, Mary (Wd)			5		
Fifer, Simon	1	1	1		
Webb, Samuel, Jr	2	3	3		
Webb, David	3	1	2		1
Weed, Eliphalet	2		2		
Munday, Sarah	1	1	2		
Hoyt, John, Junr	3	2	4		
Davenport, Silas	4	2	4		
Hutton, Samuel	5		4		
Davenport, James, Esqr	3		3	1	10
Weed, Thaddeus	2		2		
Wedd, Ebenezer, Junr	2	3	6		
Hoyt, William	2	1	1		
Ferris, Revd Ebenezer	1	2	3	1	
Numan, Stephen	4	3	4		
Seymore, Daniel	2	1	2		
Holly, Nathan	2		3		
Brown, Enos	1	1	1		
Brown, Joseph	4	2	3		
Wilson, Elizabeth (Wd)	1		3		
Baul, Doctr J	1	2	1		1
Holly, John W	5	2	1	1	1
Bishop, Alexander	3	4	4		
Holly, Numan	1	2	3		
Bishop, Silas	3	1	4		
Webb, Epenetus, 3d	1	1	1		
Skelding, John	2	1	1		
Skelding, James	2	2	2		
Lockwood, Jared	1	2	2		
Wooster, Mary (Wd)			1		
Smith, Abigail			5		
Hubbard, Mary (Wd)			1		2
Jarvis, Martha (Wd)	1		2		
Quintard, Isaac	1		1	1	
Quintard, Peter	4		3		2
Jarvis, Joseph	7	2	4	1	2
Webb, Charles, Esqr	2		2		
Fitch, William	2	2	4	1	2
Nichols, James, Jr	1	2	2		
Guensey, Ezra	1	1	2		
Hoyt, Hannah (Wd)			2		
Gilman, Evans	1	1	1		
Avery, Revd John	1	5	2		
Judson, Joseph	1		1		
Crauford, Thomas	1		3		
Jagger, Joannah			1		
Mills, Alexander	1	1	1		
Mills, George	1		2		
Lockwood, Eliphalet	1		1		
Webb, Elizabeth, Jr (Wd)			2		
Toun, William	1		3		
Hecock, Samuel	1	4	1		
Smith, Peter	1	1	1		
Dascomb, Wm	1	2	3		
Webb, Jared	1	1	1		
Guernsey, Zacheus	1		2		
Scofield, Nathaniel	1		1		
Smith, Ethan	1	2	3		
Jones, Benjamin	1		2		
Jones, Capt Ebenezer	1	2	4		
Webb, Epenetus	2	1	3		
Webb, Elizabeth (Wd)			4		
Smith, Ezra	3	1	1		
Smith, Martha (Wd)			2		
Whitney, Justice	1	1	2		
Jones, Lewis	1		1		
Webb, Seth	1		1		
Webb, Ebenezer, Jr	2	2	1		
Knapp, Silvanus	2	2	4		
Selleck, Peter	2	1	1		
Smith, Mary (Wd)	1	1	2		
Lockwood, Jacob	1		2		
Hobby, Henry	1	4	4		
Finch, Ezekiel	1	1	7		
Brush, Benjamin	2		2		
Banks, Samuel	2		2		
Peck, Darius	1	1	1		
Dibble, George	3	3	9		
Hart, Joel	1		1		
Nichols, James	2		2		
Nichols, Moses	1	1	2		
Knapp, Nathan	2	2	3		
Selleck, Stephen	1	2	1		
Smith, Jesse	1	1	2		
Smith, Abraham			2		
Finchly, George			2		
Lockwood, Isaac	3	2	5		
Lockwood, Edmond	3	1	3		
Silleck, Peter, Junr	2	3	3		
Knapp, James	3		2		
Mead, Reuben, Junr	1	1	2		
Mead, Ezra	1		2		
Whitney, Daniel	1		1		
Palmer, Jeremiah	1	2	5		
Betts, Peter	1	1	2		
Lockwood, Daniel	3		3		
Clason, Stephen	2	2	2		
Clason, Samuel	1	1	6		
Clason, Enoch	1		2		
Wardwell, Jacob	2	2	4		
Knapp, Charles	2		3		
White, Jacob, Junr	1	1	4		
Thomson, John	1	1	3		
Brown, Rebecca, 2d (Wd)			2		
Hoyt, Nathaniel	2		1		
Knapp, James, Jr	1	3	2		
Hait, Samuel, 3d	1	4	4		
Bell, Abraham	3	1	3		
Dillabrose, Martin	1		4		
Hait, Joseph, Junr	1	2	3		
Weed, Aaron	5		3		
Weed, James, 3d	1		2		
Webb, William	1	2	1		
Waterbury, Nathaniel	1		1		
Waterbury, Jonathan	1	1	4		
Hoit, Mary			1		
Mather, Noyes	1	3	3		
Hoyt, Samuel, 5th	2	2	3		
Waring, Thaddeus	2	3	4		
Weed, John	2	1	4		
Clock, Jonas	2	2	3		1
Weed, Hezekiah	1	5	1		
Brookes, Anna (Wd)			1	1	1
Waterbury, David, Jr	2	1	4		
Waterbury, Phinehas	3	4	4		
Waterbury, Jemimah (Wd)			2		
Bishop, Jonathan	2	1	3		
Bishop, Samuel	1		2		
Smith, Jesse, Junr	1	1	4		
Youngs, Abraham	1	1	1		
Weed, Nathan	1	1	4		
Weed, Nathan, Junr	1	4	4		
Starr, Capt Nathanel	3	3	4		
Wooster, Ebenezer	1	2	2		
Lockwood, Charles	1		2		
Clock, Martin	1		1		
Clock, Martin, Jr	1		1		
Beachgood, John	2	1	2		
Brown, James	2		2		
Hait, Josiah	2	1	2		
Mather, Joseph	1	2	5		
Mentor, Thomas	1	1	2		
Waring, Nathan	1	4	1		
Waring, Elizabeth (Wd)		1	3		
Dixson, John	1	1	4		
Webb, Epenetus, Junr	2	1	2		
Marshall, Polly	1		1		
Waterbury, Janus	1	3	3		
Holly, Martha (Wd)			3		
Bunnel, Hannah			3		
Waterbury, John 4th	2		1		1
Kenworthy, Thomas	1		1		
Waterbury, Elizabeth			1		
Webb, Sarah (Wd)			2		
Bishop, Abijah	1	2	4		
Knapp, Daniel	1	1	2		
Whitney, Daniel, Junr	1	3	3		
Whitney, Jonathan	4	3	4		
Scofield, Elisha	1	1	4		
Green, Abraham	1	2	1		
Green, Mercy (Wd)			3		
Scofield, James	1	2	2		
Green, Amos	1		2		
Smith, Samuel	2	3	4		
Smith, Martha (Wd)			2		
Smith, John	1	3	4		
Fountain, Moses	1		1		
Bates, Nehemiah	1		3		
Clason, Solomon	1	1	3		
Smith, Whitman	1				

FAIRFIELD COUNTY—Continued.

NAME OF HEAD OF FAMILY.	Free white males of 16 years and upward, including heads of families.	Free white males under 16 years.	Free white females, including heads of families.	All other free persons.	Slaves.
NORWALK AND STAMFORD TOWNS—con.					
Clason, Seth	1		1		
Smith, Jabez	1	3	4		
Weed, Mercy (Wd)			4		
Nichols, Daniel, Junr	1	2	2		
Lounsbury, Monmouth	2	1	9		
Smith, Solomon	1				
June, Nathanel	1	3	4		
Davis, Abraham	1	1	3		
Reynolds, Richardson	1		1		
Lockwood, Jonathan	1		1		
Lockwood, Jonathan, Jr	1	2	2		
Austin, Isaiah	1	2	1		
Smith, Joshua	1		1		
Smith, Mary (Wd)		1	4		
Longwell, Stephen	1	1	3		
Stevens, James	1	3	1		
Austin, Samuel	1		2		
Shelp, Joseph	2		1		
Smith, Charles	4		2		
Hoyt, Ruth (Wd)			2		
Knapp, Samuel	2	1	5		
Comestock, Elizabeth (Wd)		2	1		
Hait, Jesse	1	1	2		
Hait, Jonathan, 3d	1	1	1		
Hait, Jonathan, Jr	2		3		
Mitchel, David	1	1	2		
Numan, Benjamin	3		3		
Hait, Seth	1		2		
Wheaton, Samuel	1	3	3		
Numan, Israel	1	1	5		
Numan, Clark	1		1		
Gale, Wm	2	2	2		
Numan, Samuel	1		2		
Numan, Nathaniel	2	1	1		
Carrigal, Henry	1	2	3		
Dunn, Reuben	1	3	4		
June, Silas	1	1	5		
Smith, John, Junr	1	2	1		
Smith, Eben	1		2		
Smith, Molly (Wd)	3		2		
Smith, Stephen	2	1	7		
Briggs, Ezra	1	1	2		
Briggs, Hannah (Wd)			2		
Lockwood, Thaddeus	2	1	1		
Briggs Hannah, Jr (Wd)		1	2		
Smith, Nathanel	2		4		
Smith, Daniel	2	1	3		
Briggs, Caleb	1	4	4		
June, Ezra	2		4		
June, Thomas	2		2		
Briggs, Stephen	2	2	3		
Ferris, Jonah	2	1	4		
Smith, Isaac	1	3	4		
Smith, Hannah (Wd)			1		
Smith, David, 3d	3		3		
June, Abner	2		5		
Gale, Isaac	1	3	3		
Numan, David	1	1	1		
Numan, Nehemiah	1		2		
Smith, Nehemiah	2	1	8		
Smith, David, Junr	1	1	1		
Smith, Nathel, Junr	2	2	3		
Hoyt, Frederick	1	1	4		
Hoyt, David	1	1	3		
Todd, John	5		1		
Sibley, Richard	1	1	2		
Numan, Ezra	2		2		
Waring. Hezron	1	2	2		
Scofield, James, Junr	1	3	2		
Whelpley, Amos	1		2		
Tredwell, Samuel	1	1	2		
Smith, Amos	2	1	4		
Mills, Nathel	1		2		
Ingersol, Elizabeth (Wd)			2	4	
Stuard, Aaron	1	2	2		
Lockwood, Gershom	1	3	1		
Waring, Linas	1		1		
Rockwell, Stephen	1		2		
White, Jacob	1		1		
White, William	1	3	3		
Waring, Jonathan	2	1	2		
Waring, Jesse	1	4	5		
Waring, Joseph	2		7		
Waring, Noah	1		4		
Holly, Stephen, Jr	1	1	3		
Lounsbury, Jacob	1	4	3		
Webb, Benjamin	1		2		
Webb, Nathaniel, jr	1		5		
Scofield, Billy	1	3	2		
Holly, Abraham	2	1	5		
Holly, Stephen	2	3	3		
Webb, Ebenezer	1	2	6		
June, Abisha		1	2		
NORWALK AND STAMFORD TOWNS—con.					
Youngs, Clemence	1		3		
Youngs, Benjamin	1	4	3		
Lounsbury, David	2	1	3		
Sherwood, Mathew	2		3		
Waters, Jacob	1	2	1		
Austin, Charles	1	2	3		
Lounsbury, Nathel, Jr	1	3	3		
Lounsbury, Nathel	1		1		
Galer, Reuben	1	2	3		
June, William	2	3	3		
Ferris, Ransford A	2	2	5		
June, Israel, Jr	2	3	2		
Lounsbury, Michael	1	4	4		
Smith, David	3	1	3		
June, Joshua	1	2	3		
Nichols, Robert	3	1	3		
Smith, Joseph	3		4		
Smith, Josiah	2		2		
Smith, Gould	1	4	4		
Scofield, Nathel, Junr	1	1	3		
Mead, Reuben	2		6		
Weeks, Henry	1	3	3		
Knapp, Peter	1	3	5		
Knapp, Jacob	1	1	3		
Hoyt, Thaddeus	4	2	6		
Wix, Bartholomew	3		3		
Knapp, Nathaniel	2		3		
Blanchard, Jacob	1	4	2		
Smith, Austin	1		2		
Smith, Austin, Junr	2	3	3		
Scofield, Abraham, Jr	1	2	2		
Webb, Nathaniel 3d	1	2	3		
Webb, Nathel	1	1	2		
Webb, Elisha	1	2	3		
Donald, Lewis M	3		2		
Lockwood, Nathaniel	1		3		
Waterbury, David	2		3		
Hoyt, Silas	3	2	5		
Hoyt, Josep, 3d	1	1	2		
Wilson, Mary (Wd)			3		
Brown, Mercy			2		
Scofield, Gideon	2		1		
Scofield, Israel	1				
Knapp, Usial	1	1	1		
Blanchard, William	2		1		
Hait, Isaac	2	1	3		
Ambler, Jacob	1	3	4		
Scofield, Jonas	1		3		
Waterbury, Enos	1	1	4		
Lewis, Jonathan	1	1	2		
Scofield, James, 3d	1		2		
Ambler, Joshua	1		1		
Weed, Ebenezer P	1	3	3		
St John, Hannah (Wd)	2		3		
Weed, Peter	1		4		
Ingersol, Mary (Wd)			2		
Smith, Gabriel	1	2	4		
Lounsbury, Gideon	2		2		
Knapp, John	1	1	1		
Hait, Elijah	1	3	3		
Scofield, Jacob, Jr	1	2	2		
Scofield, Silvanus, Junr	2	2	5		
Scofield, Epenetus	1	2	4		
Pardy, John	3	2	4		
Scofield, Daniel	1	2	2		
Scofield, Nathan	2	2	5		
Weed, Enos	2		3		
Mead, Eber	1	1	2		
Scofield, Samuel, Jr	2		2		
Dogharty, Andrew	1		3		
Lockwood, Titus	1	4	2		
Knapp, William	2	2	5		
Scofield, Jonathan H	1	1	2		
Buxton, James	3	4	5		
Buxton, Samuel	1	2	3		
Lounsbury, Enos	1	3	1		
Lounsbury, Nathan	1		1		
Ambler, Joseph	2	1	2		
Scofield, John	1	5	3		
Lockwood, Elizabeth (Wd)			2		
Lockwood, Josiah	1	1	1		
Lockwood, Hannah (Wd)		1			
Hawley, Elijah	1		3		
Jones, Ebenezer, Junr	1		1		
Lockwood, Freelove (Wd)			2		
Weed, Miles	3		1		
Mead, Sarah (Wd)			2		
Lockwood, Reuben	1	3	5		
Dibble, Solomon	1	1	5		
Buxton, John	2		1		
Buxton, Peter	2	1	2		
Lounsbury, Elijah	1	1	2		
NORWALK AND STAMFORD TOWNS—con.					
Lounsbury, John	2	1	3		
Dean, Ebenezer	2		2		
Weed, Jonathan, Junr	1	1	1		
Buxton, Mercy (Wd)			3		
Ayres, Bradley	1	1	4		
Scofield, Abraham	3	1	6		
Dan, Squire	2	2	5		
Scofield, Silvanus	1		1		
Scofield, Sarah (Wd)	1	1	3		
Scofield, Josiah	2		1		
Scofield, Weed	1	1	2		
Weed, Asahel	1	1	4		
Lockwood, David, Junr	1		7		
Scofield, Seth	1	3	2		
Scofield, Seeley	1	2	1		
Weed, Samuel	1		4		
Curtis, Jeremiah	2	2	3		
Deal, George	1		1		
Lounsbury, James	1	2	2		
Scofield, Josiah W	1		2		
Seely, John	1		3		
Seely, Obadiah	1	2	3		
June, Israel	1	2	3		
Jones, Enos	1		1		
Defres, Reuben	1	1	6		
June, Joel	1	2	1		
Jones, Josiah	1	2	4		
Reynolds, Peroz	1	1	2		
Hait, Jonas	4	1	3		
Hoyt, Epenetus	1		1		
Hoyt, Joseph, 4th	1		1		
Hoit, Nezer	1	1	3		
Hoit, Deodate	1	2	1		
Weed, Amos, Junr	1	1	4		
Weed, Amos	1		1		
Weed, Benjamin, Jr	1		5		
Weed, Jesse	1		4		
Weed, Israel	2	1	5		
Weed, Israel, Junr	2	2	4		
Weed, Ananias	1	3	3		
Shepherd, Revd John	1	2	4		1
Bishop, Stephen	1		1		
Bishop, Stephen, Junr	1	2	2		
Weed, Jonathan	2	2	4		
Weed, Seth, Junr	2		5		
Husted, Thaddeus	2	2	4		
Husted, Zebulon	1		2		
Weed, Jabez	1	3	6		
Weed, Gideon	1		1		
Weed, Abisha	1	1	2		
Weed, Benjamin	1	1	4		
Hoyt, James	1	1	1		
Provost, Samuel	1		1		
Scofield, Samuel, 3d	1	1	3		
Laurence, Timothy	2	1	5		
Hoyt, Elizabeth (Wd)	1		2		
Jones, Ephraim	1	1	4		
Davenport, John	4	2	6		
Scofield, Nezer	1	6	4		
Hoyt, Jesse, Junr	1	1	2		
Scofield, Samuel	2	1	1		
Scofield, David	1	1	1		
Curtis, Rebecca (Wd)		1	2		
Scofield, Reuben	3	3	3		
Scofield, Peter	2	1	4		
Scofield, Jacob	1	1	4		
Scofield, Stephen	1	1	4		
Scofield, Benjamin	2	5	3		
Scofield, Joseph, Junr	2	1	5		
Scofield, Warren	1	1	2		
Scofield, Josiah	1		1		
Scofield, Thaddeus	1	1	2		
Ayres, John	1		2		
Scofield, Edward	1	1	1		
Slason, Thomas	1	3	4		
Ferris, James	1	3	2		
Scofield, Uriah	1	3	4		
Brown, Nathel	2		2		
Scofield, Elias	1		2		
Hoyt, Josiah	1		3		
Finch, Hannah (Wd)	1		3		
Lockwood, Abigail (Wd)			2		
Wilmoth, Zopher	1	1	2		
Holly, Francis	2		2		
Curtis, Timothy	1		1		
Curtis, Jonathan	1	1	2		
Bell, Noah	2	3	4		
Bell, Stephen	1	2	1		
Chapman, William E	2	2	6		
Finch, Nathaniel	2	1	5		
Bell, Joannah (Wd)			1		
Bush, Samuel					4
Jezup, Samuel	1	4	4		
Jeffery, Samuel	1	1	4		
Tryon, Samuel	1	4	4		

FAIRFIELD COUNTY—Continued.

NAME OF HEAD OF FAMILY.	Free white males of 16 years and upward, including heads of families.	Free white males under 16 years.	Free white females, including heads of families.	All other free persons.	Slaves.
NORWALK AND STAMFORD TOWNS—con.					
Hait, Nathan	1		4		
Hait, Peter	4		3		
Hait, David	1	2	4		
Hoyt, John	3	1	2		
Scofield, Hait	1	2	2		
Holly, Increas	2		4		
Holly, Enoch	1		2		
Hull, Esther (Wd)		1	1		
Scofield, Jacob, 3d	1	1	2		
Holly, John	1		5		
Holly, John, Junr	1		2		
Crissy, Jesse	1	1	1		
Hait, Uriah	1	1	5		
Hait, Samuel, Junr	1		2		
Hoyt, Joseph	1	2	3		
Hoyt, Warren	1		1		
Crissy, Abraham	1		2		
Crissy, Nathaniel	1		2		
Crissy, William	1	2	4		
Crissy, Samuel	1		3		
Crissy, Mary (Wd)	1	1	3		
Seely, Abijah	2	1	5		
Seely, Abijah, Junr	1		1		
Leeds, Gideon	1	1	3		
Seely, Samuel	1	1	3		
Stevens, David	1	1	2		
Seymore, Jared	2	1	2		
Finch, Titus	2	2	3		
Bishop, Peter	1	2	3		
Weed, Wm	3	2	2		
Davenport, Deodate	3		9		
Davenport, Deodate	1	1	1		
Ayres, Jonathan	1	5	5		
Nichols, Daniel	1		3		
Young, Robert	1	2	1	1	
Webb, David, Junr	1	3	1		
Young, Samuel	1	3	2		
Stevens, Henry	1	1	3		
Weed, Ezra	1	2	4		
Jones, Samuel	1	1	2		
Stevens, Jonathan	1	2	5		
Weed, Ebenezer	2		2		
Hunt, John	3		3		
Brown, Abigail (Wd)		1	2		
Knapp, Hezekiah	2	4	4		
Hoyt, Jacob	1	1	1		
Hoyt, John, 3d	1		1		
Brown, Isaac	1	1	5		2
Brown, Jonathan	1		2		
Tryon, Benjamin	2	3	3		
Grey, Joseph	1	1	5		
Smith, Reuben	2	1	3		
Waters, Elisha	1	1	1		
Leeds, Carey	1	1	3		
Scofield, Gilbert	1	1	3		
Crissy, Nathel, Jur	1	2	2		
Young, Mary (Wd)			2		
Chittester, Abraham	2		1		
Waring, Martha (Wd)		1	1		
Chittester, Nathan	1		2		
Stevens, Hannah (Wd)			3		
Meaker, David	1		1		
Stevens, Solomon	1	2	4		
Wilkes, Augustus	1		1		
Stevens, Abner	3		2		
Allen, John	1	1	2		
Slason, Israel	1		6		
Slason, David	1	2	4		
Slason, Jonathan, Junr	1	2	1		
Stevens, Reuben	2	2	4		
Stevens, Daniel	1		1		
Slason, Jonathan	2	2	4		
Jones, Thomas	1	2	2		
Jones, Samuel, Junr	1	1	1		
Stevens, Abraham	1	4	4		
Stevens, Amos	3	6	2		
Stevens, John	2		3		
Brister, Soloman	1	2	3		
Jones, Reuben	1	2	4		
Lockwood, David	1	3	2		
Waters, John	1	1	2		
Stevens, Jacob	1	2	4	3	
Stevens, Amos, Junr	1	1	1		
Raymond, Luke	3	1	4		
Stevens, Seth	1		1		
Stevens, Isaac	1	1	2		
Scofield, Selleck	1		1		
Howard, Sarah		1	3		
Dan, Nathaniel	1				
Hoyt, Waterbury	1		1		
Dan, Nathan	1	3	2		
Weed, Jonas, 3d	1	4	2		
Howes, Noah	1	3	1		
Raymond, Lemuel	1	2	1		
Bebee, Lydia (Wd)			4		

NAME OF HEAD OF FAMILY.	Free white males of 16 years and upward, including heads of families.	Free white males under 16 years.	Free white females, including heads of families.	All other free persons.	Slaves.
NORWALK AND STAMFORD TOWNS—con.					
Chittester, David	1	3	2		
Penoyre, Martha (Wd)	3	1	1		
Penayre, Amos	2	1	3		
Howes, Prince, Junr	2		3		
Reed, Timothy	3	3	5		
Penoyre, Gould S	2	3	7		
Coggswell, Dunlap	2	5	2		
Howes, Prince	1		1		
Lockwood, Elnathan	1	1	4		
Bishop, Parsons	1		3		
Weed, Charles	3	1	3		
Weed, Abraham	1		1		
Comestock, Enoch	2	2	4		
Weed, Peter	1	2	6		
Weed, Enos	1		1		
Weed, Daniel	1	1	2		
Weed, James	1	1	4		
Weed, Josiah	2	1	5		
Weed, Jonathan, 3d	1				
Weed, Hannah			2		
Weed, Seth	2		2		
Boutain, Daniel	2	4	2		
Tucker, Isaac	1	1	2		
Peter (Negro)				4	
Stevens, Joseph	3	3	5		
Stevens, Joseph, Jr	1	1	2		
Talmage, Seymore	1	5	2		
Talmage, James	1		1		
Talmage, Jonathan	1	2	2		
Talmage, Bethiah (Wd)			3		
Smith, Joseph, Junr	2	1	8		
Wright, Dennis	1	2	3		
Jarvis, Catharine			2		
Jones, Asa	1		4		
Weed, Stephen	1	2	2		
Stevens, Obadiah	3	3	4		
Stevens, Sarah (Wd)		1	5		
Stevens, Admer	1	1	1		
Weed, Joel	1	5	1		
Hoyt, Nathaniel, Junr	3	1	4		
Waterbury, Nathaniel	2	1	2		
Hoyt, Jonathan	3	1	2		
Hoyt, Samuel	1	1			
Hoyt, Hanford	2		4		
Husted, Jonathan	2	3	3		
Holmes, John	1	1	7		
Waterbury, Wm	1	3	3		
Leeds, Mary (Wd)	3		3		
Leeds, Abraham	1	2	2		
Leeds, Elizabeth (Wd)	1		2		
Waterbury, Rebecca (Wd)			2		
Wilmot, Joseph	1	5	2		
Sherwood, Stephen	2		2		
Waterbury, Jacob	1		2		
Waterbury, Martha (Wd)			3		
Waterbury, John, Junr	1	3	6		
Bates, Gershom	2	3	5		
Brown, Francis	1	1	2		
Waterbury, Thankful (Wd)			3		
Weed, Silvanus	1	1	3		
Packeton, Dennis	1	2	1		
Selleck, Gershom	1	2	1		
Waterbury, John	1		2		
Seely, Jonas	1	1	1		
Leeds, Elisha	2		2		
Seely, Silvanus	1		1		
Seely, Silvanus, Junr	1	4	2		
Bennedict, Caleb	2	4	2		
Seely, Nathan	1	3	2		
Suard, Samuel	1		2		
Seely, Eliphalet	2	2	1		
Seely, Joseph	3	5	3		
Seely, Ebenezer	1	4	3		
Bates, John, Junr	3		2		
Bates, Charles	2	2	4		
Bates, Mary (Wd)	1		1		
Weed, Gideon, Junr	1	1	1		
Hait, Frederick, Junr			2		
Hayt, Ezra	1		2		
Weed, James, Jar	2	1	2		
Weed, Henry	1	2	1		
Weed, Mary (Wd)			7	1	
Brown, Rebecca (Wd)	4		3		
Slason, Jacob	3	1	2		
Slason, Zepheniah	2	3	2		
Weed, Gideon	4	4	5		
Andres, Jeremiah	1	1	3		
Andres, John	2	2	4		1
Bishop, Caty (Wd)			1	2	
Johnson, Elizabeth			1		
Wyatt, Sarah (Wd)		1	1		
Little, Ebenezer	1	1			

NAME OF HEAD OF FAMILY.	Free white males of 16 years and upward, including heads of families.	Free white males under 16 years.	Free white females, including heads of families.	All other free persons.	Slaves.
NORWALK AND STAMFORD TOWNS—con.					
Waterbury, Ebenezer	2		4		
Weed, Deodate	1	2	1		
Weed, Jonas, 4th	2		4		
Slason, Abraham	1		1		
Weed, Jonas	1				
Bell, Thaddeus, Jr	1	1	4		
Slason, Gershom	1	2	1		
Slason, Deliverance	1	2	1		
Dibble, Anne (Wd)			3		
Bell, John	2	2	2		
Bell, Jonathan	2	4	3		
Holly, Abraham, Junr	1	3	3		
Waterbury, James	1		2		
Weed, Mary, Junr (Wd)	1	1	2		
Bell, John, Junr	1		3		
Bell, Thaddeus	2	1	1		
Weed, Jonas, Junr	1	3	3		
Howe, Jacob	2	2	4		
Scofield, John, 5th	1		1		
Howe, Ebenezer	1		5		
Howe, Nathan	1	2	1		
Slason, Charles	1	1	2		
Howe, David	1		1		
Howe, Bowers	1	2	3		
Platt, Joseph Y	1	3	2		
Dibble, John	2	1	3		
Shaw, James	2	2	3		
Weed, Sarah (Wd)			1		
Walmsbey, William			3		
Weed, Benjamin, 3d	1		4		
Morehouse, Joshua	1		2		
Weed, John, Junr	1	2	2		
Seely, Esther (Wd)			2		
Clock, John	2	1	3		
Clock, Sarah (Wd)			3		
Clock, Comfort (Wd)			1		
Clock, Abraham	1	1	3		
Younges, Samuel	1	1	4		
Clock, Nathaniel	3	1	6		
Gotham, Daniel	2	5	3	2	
Selleck, Mary (Wd)			1	1	2
Selleck, Samuel	2	1	6		
Penoyre, Isaac	1	6	2		
Penoyre, Samuel	1	1	4		
Fancher, David	1		2		
Little, John	2	1	3		
Wilson, John	1	1	2	1	2
Gorham, Hannah (Wd)			2		
Selleck, Simeon	1	1	4		
Roberts, Amos	1	2	4		
Selleck, Nathan	1	1	2		
Seely, Wix	1	2	2		
Selleck, Edward	1	1	4		
Selleck, Daniel	2	1	5		
Lockwood, Daniel, Jr	2	3	3		
Betts, Benjamin	2	3	3		
Selleck, Seymore	1	2	3		
Selleck, Stephen, Jr	1	2	3		
Sudmore, Joseph	1	3	3		
Raymond, Stephen	1	1	3		
Mills, Ezra	2	5	2		
Scofield, Silvanus	1	2	2		
Provost, Thomas	1	1	2		
Petten, Samuel	3	2	2		
Fancher, Silvanus, Jr	1	1	2		
Ambler, Isaac	2		2		
Waterbury, Hannah (Wd)			1		
Waring, Samuel	1	1	4		
Waring, Mary (Wd)	1		1		
Waring, Sally (Wd)		2	4		
Waterbury, Wm, Jr	1	1	2		
Waring, Silvanus	2		1		
Hait, Nathaniel, 3d	1	3	2		
Street, Joseph	1		2		
Nich (Negro)				2	
Jack (Negro)				3	
Bates, William	1	1	1		
Whitney, Henry	1	1	1		
Whitney, Charles	1	2	2		
Matthias, Bethial (Wd)			2		
Whitney, Eliasaph	2	1	4		
Bates, David	1	1	3		
Bates, Jerom	1	3	1		
Mather, Revd Moses	2		1		
Hait, Elizabeth (Wd)		1	1		
Scofield, Josiah, Junr	2		5		
Scofield, Gershom	1	3	5		
Whiting, Samuel	1		2		
Scofield, Joseph	2	1	3		
Scofield, Henry	1	1	2		
Howe, Sarah (Wd)			2		
Fancher, Silvanus	1		3		
Fancher, David, Junr	1		1		

FAIRFIELD COUNTY—Continued.

NAME OF HEAD OF FAMILY.	Free white males of 16 years and upward, including heads of families.	Free white males under 16 years.	Free white females, including heads of families.	All other free persons.	Slaves.
NORWALK AND STAMFORD TOWNS—con.					
Selleck, Jesse	2	1	2		2
Morehouse, Gershom	1		5		
Knapp, Nathan, Junr	1	1	2		
Bates, Jonathan	2	2	3		
Bates, John	2	1	4		
Street, David	2	1	3		
Reed, Jonathan	1		1		
Mather, Samuel	1	1	1		
Gray, Daniel	1	1	2		
Bates, James	1		1		1
Waterbury, Benjamin	3		3		
Mosier, Rachel (Wd)			2		
Little, James	4	2	3		
Wardwell, Abigail (Wd)	1		3		
Waterbury, Deodate	1	1	1		
Waterbury, Epenetus	1	2	2		
Reed, Nathan	1	2	3		
Selleck, Wray	1	4	4		
Boutain, Nathan	1	1	2		
Weed, Mary (Wd)			1		
Belding, Benjamin	1	2	1	1	2
Waterbury, David, 3d	2		3		
READING TOWN.					
Dimon, Thomas	2		1		
Sanford, Hezekiah	1	2	2		1
Gray, John	3		3		
Andrews, Ebenezer	1	1	1		
Stratton, Stephen	2	5	1		
Andrews, Sarah			3		
Andrews, Seth	1	1	2		
Hull, John	1	2	2		
Gorham, Isaac	1		1	1	7
Gorham, Isaac, Junr	1	1	4		
Thorp, Lyman	1	1	1		
Fairchild, Abraham	2		2		
Fairchild, Stephen	1	3	1		
Fairchild, Samuel	1		2		
Fairchild, John	1	2	1		
Sanford, Oliver	3	3	6		
Morgan, Nathanel	1	2	3		
Godfry, Samuel	1		1		
Morgan, Joseph	1	3	4		
Banks, Jesse	2		3		
Banks, Jesse, Junr	1		1		
Banks, Joseph	2		2		
Gorham, Jaber	1		4		
Platt, Zebulon	2	1	3		
Platt, Hezekiah	3		4		
Lyon, Daniel	2		2		
Lyon, Nathan	1	2	3		
Beers, Gershom	1	2	1		
Platt, Mary			1		
Malery, Jonathan	2	3	4		
Lyon, Arel	2	2	3		
Lyon, Andrew	1		2		
Whitlock, Nathan	1	1	4		
Merit, Ebenezer	1	1	3		
Burr, Joseph	2	1	2		
Hill, Andrew	2		3		
Hill, Daniel	2	1	3		
Crowfoot, James	1	1	4		
Lyon, Filo	2	2	1		
Bulkly, Peter, Junr	1		1		
Bulkley, Aaron	2	1	7		
Hill, Aliel	1	1	2		
Meeker, Ephraim	1		1		
Malery, John	1		3		
Meeker, Ogden	1	1	1		
Mungo, Simeon	1		3		
Heron, William	2	1	7		1
Meeker, Jonathan	3		3		
Hill, David	1	1	6		
Hill, Ezekiel	2	2	5		
Starr, Thomas	1		1		
Beech, Lazarus	2		3	1	
Wheeler, Ephraim	2		2		
Marwell, Edward	1		4		
Wheeler, Seth	1		1		
Morgin, Abijah	1	1	4		
Dickerson, Zadoc	1	1	2		
Wheeler, Enos	3		4		
Wheeler, John	2		5		1
Sanford, John	1				
Hill, Daniel	1	1	2		
Sanford, James	2	3	2		
Jacson, Aaron	1		2		
Finne, Jesse	2	1	2		
Crofoot, David	2	1	4		
Leach, John	1	2	3		
Morehouse, Daniel	2		2		
Freeman, Thomas				2	
Bulkley, Peter	1	4	6		
Morehouse, David	1	2	3		
READING TOWN—con.					
Roberts, Philip				4	
Betts, Stephen	2	1	4		3
Napp, David	1		3		
Hull, Seth	5		5		
Perry, Elihu	1	2	4		
Whitlock, Ephraim	1	2	2		
Gray, James	1		4		
Napp, Rebecka		1	2		
Bloidell, Thomas	1	3	3		
Squire, Seth	1		3		
Devern, John	1		1		
Crowfoot, Israel	2	3	2		
Beardsley, Jesse	2	1	1		
Couch, Simon	1	1	2	1	3
Glover, Lemuel	1		1		
Drew, John	2	1	2		
Whitlock, Justus	1	1	1		
Whitlock, Nathaniel	1		2		
Fiarchild, Andrew	3		2	2	
Drew, John	2	6	2		
Morehouse, John	1	1	2		
MnRow, David	3	1	3		
Drew, Isaac	1	3	5		
Drew, Peter	1	2	2		
Judd, Elijah	1	1	4		
Lyon, Lemuel	1	2	2		
Manchant, Enoch	1		1		
Star, Eward	2	1	4		
Couch, Stephen	2	2	4		
Lyon, Grace		1	4		
Sanford, Aaron	2	2	3		1
Bartrum, Paul	2		3		
Platt, Isaac	1	1	4		
Hawley, Joseph	2	2	2		1
Hawley, William	3		1	1	1
Marchant, Chaney	2	3	4		
Marchant, Elenar	1		3		
Platt, Jonas	1	1	3		
Morehouse, Gershom	1	1	2		
Abbet, Thadeus	2		2		
Jarvis, Samuel	1	5	3		1
Rogers, James	2	1	6		1
Platt, Jonas, Junr	1	1	1		
Morehouse, Aaron	1	1	3		1
Sanford, Hezekiah	5		3		2
Starr, Levi	1	1	1		
Bartlett, Daniel	1	4	3		
Bartrum, Daniel	1	4	3		
Read, Eli	1		3		1
Read, Zalmon	1	3	2		
Read, Hezekiah	3	1	7		
Lynes, John	1	2	3		
White, Charles	1	3	4		
Rowland, Israel	1	1	2		
Rowland, Thomas	1		2		
Evans, Daniel	1	1	4		
Hamlinton, Benjamin	3	2	7		
Read, John	1	4	2		1
Hall, Ebenezer	1		3		
Adams, Joseph	3	1	3		
Munson, Theophelus	2	2	3		
Stoe, Robert	1	3	4		
Morehouse, Elijah	1	2	2		
Bartrum, David	2		6		
Gold, Samuel	2	1	4		
Banks, Hyat	1	4	1		
Patchon, Arael	2		1		
Adams, Abraham	1	2	6		
Griffin, Joseph	2	1	3		
Winecoop, John	1	1	2		
Persons, Timothy	1	1	3		
Persons, Daniel	1	2	1		
Mead, Jeremiah	2	1	1		
Benedict, Thadeus	2	4	2		2
Bartlett, Nathaniel	2		5		
Gray, Stephen	2		2		
Sanford, Lemuel	3	1	5		
Fitch, Arael	2		5	1	
Hull, John	2	1	3		
Couch, John	1		3		
Byington, John	1	1	3		
Salmon, Asael	3	1	2		
Smith, Samuel	4	1	3	1	
Hull, Zalmon	2	3	4		
Meeker, Isaac	1	1	2		
Napp, David	1		2		
Napp, Jonathan	2	2	3		
Lyon, Ezra	1	1	3		
Parsons, Elijah	1		1		
Hull, Peter	1	1	4		
Frost, Joseph	3	1	4		
Sanford, Seth	2		2		
Sanford, Ebenezer	1	1	2		
Sanford, Elias	1	1	2		
Barlow, Aaron	4	6	6	1	1
READING TOWN—con.					
Starr, David	2	3	4		
Starr, David, Junr	1		2		
Sanford, Peter	2		4		
Crowfoot, Uriah	2		3		
Sanford, Eli	2		2		
Sanford, Sarah			3		
Sanford, Ezra	2	1	3		
Smith, Reubin	1	1	4		
Burr, Elijah	2	1	4		
Coley, Jesse	1	1	2		
Jackson, David	2	4	5		
Couch, Elijah	3	4	3		
Couch, John	2	2	3		
Burr, Charles	1				
Sanford, Elnathan	1		1		
Sebens, Josiah	1	1	2		
Burr, Nathan	1	2	5		
Olmstord, Grace	1	1	5		
Peet, John	1	6	2		
Burr, Abel	1		1	1	
Burr, Seth	1	1	1		
Hull, Sirenus	1	1	2		
Hull, Chapman	1		1	1	
Lator, Preserv'd	2		7		
Bennitt, Shubel	2		3		
Platt, Isaac	1		3		
Platt, Philip	1		2		
Banks, Seth	2		3		
Laton, Abraham	1	1	3		
Burr, Ezekiel	1	2	3		
Banks, Thadeus	2	2	4		
Sanford, Biah	1	2	3		
Burr, Joel	1		2		
Bouton, David	2	1	2		
Couch, Thomas	1	4	3		
Green, Joseph	1	3	2		
Gray, Gilead	1	4	1		
Bento, Silus	2	1	4		
Coley, Gershom	2	1	2		
Smith, Lewis	1	1	1		
Jackson, Ezekiel	1	2	2		
Parsons, Abijah	1		4		
Davis, John	2	1	3		
Hillard, Jacy	2	1	3		
Meeker, Igaci	1		2		
Hull, Nehemiah	1	1	2		
Perry, Daniel	3	2	3		
Burr, Stephen	1		2		
Rumsey, Ephraim	1	2	4		
Bennitt, Miles	1	1	3		
Meeker, Seth	2	1	7		
Meeker, Elonyer	1	1	2		
Dikeman, Frederick	1	2	6		
Byington, John	1		1		
Bennit, Daniel	2	1	2		
Perry, John	1	1	3		
Sherwood, Isaac	3	2	2		
Sturges, Ebenezer	1	3	1		
Sturges, Perry	1	3	1		
Perry, Thadeus	1	3	4		
Sturges, Benjamin	1		2		1
Backsster, Arline	1	2	1		
Guire, John	1		3		
Morehouse, Beebe	1	2	3		
Guire, Thadius	1	1	3		
Parsons, Jonathan	1	2	3		
Lee, Silus	1	2	3		
Lee, Enos	1	3	1		
Malery, Daniel	2	1	3		
Malery, Samuel	1	2	3		
Hilliard, Thurstain	1		1		
Smith, Joel	2	1	2		
Andrews, Francis	1	2	3		
Bradley, Elijah	2	1	2		
Jackson, Stephen	1	1	3		
Guire, Samuel	1	2	2		
Mead, Uriah	1	1	3		
Hull, David	1	1	1		
Barlow, Gershom	1		3		1
Smith, Elieaser	1	2	2		
Bates, Justus	2		1		
Lee, Enos	3	1	5		
Lord, Gold	1	2	1		
Malery, Daniel	2		2		
Malery, Nathan	1	3	2		
Mead, Elias	1	2	2		
Sanford, Ezekiel	3	2	7		
Coley, Samuel	2		4		
Coley, Onisimus	3		5		
Darling, Benjamin	1	2	3		1
Sherwood, John	1	2	4		
Starr, Mijah	2	3	4		
Morgen, Joseph	1	1	3		
Wakeman, Timothy	2	3	5		
Wakeman, Jabez	2	4	1		

FAIRFIELD COUNTY—Continued.

NAME OF HEAD OF FAMILY.	Free white males of 16 years and upward, including heads of families.	Free white males under 16 years.	Free white females, including heads of families.	All other free persons.	Slaves.
READING TOWN—con.					
Gray, Justus	1	1	5		
Couch, Simon	1	4	4		
Gray, Joel	1		2		
Guire, Mathew	2		2		
RIDGEFIELD TOWN.					
Bradley, Phillip B., Esqr	2	2	5		
Keeler, Mathew	2	1	2		
Seymour, Matthew	1		2	1	1
Keeler, Matthew, Junr	1	2	2		
Keeler, John	3		4		
Waterous, John	3	2	4		
Jones, Ebenezer	2		3		
Jones, Ebenezer, 2d	1	1	1		
Rockwell, Thaddeus	2	2	7		
Rockwell, James	1	3	5		
Resiguie, James	2		4		
Resiguie, Jacob	2		2		
Resiguie, Jacob, 2d	1	1	2		
Scribner, Rachel		1	2		
Olmsted, Samuel	1	3	5		
Olmsted, James	1	3	3		
Keeler, Jeremiah	1				
Seymour, Thomas, 2d	1	1	2		
Sturgis, James	2		2		
Nash, Abraham	2	1	2		
Nash, Abraham, 2d	1	2	3		
Omsted, Nathan	2	1	3		
Keeler, Timothy	3		2		
Northrup, Aaron	3		2		
Baldwin, John	1		2		
Goodrich, Revd Samuel	1	1	4		
Morris, John	3		3		
Olmsted, Jared	2	2	7		
Kellogg, Daniel	2	2	3		
Kellogg, Nathan F	1	3	4		
Remerton, Stephen	1	2	3		
Bennitt, Trowbridge	1		2		
Hine, Newton	1	2	3		
Benedict, John, 2d	1	1	4		
Smith, Daniel, 4th	1	2	1		
Chitterster, Daniel	2		2		
Remington, Josiah	1	1	1		
Nash, Daniel	1	1	2		
Smith, Daniel, 2d	1	1	5		
Northrup, Josiah	1	3	4		
Keeler, Thaddeus	1	3	2		
Fairbanks, Samuel	2		2		
Northrup, Benjamin	1	2	1		
Mead, Jeremiah	1	2	3		
Benedict, John	1		2		
Benedict, Abijah	1	1	2		
Keeler, Martha			2		
Hoyt, Benjamin	3	2	2		
Olmsted, David	2	3	3		
Keeler, Timothy, Junr	3	2	6		
Olmsted, David, 3d	1		3		
Sturgis, Ward	1	1	1		
Saintjohn, David	1	1	6		
Keeler, David	1		2		
Nash, Riah	1	1	2		
Benedict, Jesse	3	1	3		
Seymour, Thomas	3	1	3		
Olmsted, Ebenezer	1	3	3		
Olmsted, Samuel, 2d	2	3	5		
Chambers, Nathan	1		6		
Northrup, John	1		3		
Olmsted, Mathew	1	3	1		
Northrup, Elisabeth	2	4	5		
Johnson, John	1	2	2		
Saintjohn, John	1	1	2		
Benedict, Ezra	1	2	2		
Smith, Azor	1		1		
Berry, George	1		3		
Barlow, John	2	2	5		
Betts, Eunice			2		
Hawley, Elisha	2	1	2		
Betts, Gideon	1		2		
Smith, Nathan	2	1	8		
King, Joshua	4		4		
Ingersol, Joseph	1	1	3		
Ingersol, Moss	1		2		
Barns, Ambrose	1	2	3		
Olmsted, Daniel	1		2		
Hawley, Thomas	5	3	3		
Olmsted, Daniel, 2d	1	3	4		
Hawley, Ebenezer	2	1	2		
Marvin, Uriah	2		3		
Gilbart, David	1	1	3		
Hawley, Hezekiah	1	1	3		
Gilbart, Ebenezer	1		3		
Foster, Joseph	1		2		
Smith, Jacob	2	1	1		
Seymour, Uriah	1		2		
RIDGEFIELD TOWN—con.					
Wilson, Ezekiel	3		2		
Smith, Benjamin	2	3	5		
Wilson, Jeremiah	1		1		1
Lobdell, Caleb	1		1		
Lobdell, Phillip	1	2	1		
Lobdell, Josiah	1	2	1		
Smith, Sarah, 3d (Ww)		1	1		
Dauchey, Nathan	3	1	5		
Keeler, Paul	1	2	5	1	
Sturgis, Thaddeus	1	1	5		
Mills, Denton	1		1		
Mead, Ezra	2	4	2		
Smith, Thomas	2		1		
Smith, Hezekiah, 2d	1	4	3		
Perry, David	1	4	3		
Dauchey, Phillip	1		3		
Sherwood, Benjamin	1	5	5		
Smith, Clemence	2	1	2		
Smith, Ebenezer	1	1	2		
Smith, Stephen	2	1	1		1
Smith, Thaddeus	2	1	2		
Stebbins, Joseph	1	1	5		
Bennit, Josiah	1	1	2		
Smith, James, 2d	3	1	4		
Osborn, Aaron	2	1	1		
Stebbins, Samuel	2	2	3		
Baker, Amos	2	1	4		
Stebbins, Benjamin	1		2		
Smith, Jeremiah	1	3	5		
How, Epenetus	2		6		
Olmsted, Ambros, 2d	1	1	2		
Waddy, Peter	1	5	1		
Olmsted, Ambros	2	1	4		
Stebbins, Ebenezer	1	3	4		
Smith, John	3	2	2		
Hall, Josiah	2	1	5		
Dowse, Mary		1	3		
Dauchey, Daniel	1	2	3		
Dauchey, John	1	2	7		
Dauchey, James	1	1	2		
Jones, John	2	2	5		
Folliot, Joseph	1				
Folliot, Bartlit	2		1		
Smith, Job	2		4		
Smith, Daniel, 3d	3	4	7		
Smith, Sarah, 2d		2	6		
Scott, Thomas	1	1	1		
Scott, James, 2d	1	3	2		
Deforest, Hezekiah	2				
Munson, Isaac	1	1	2		
Andros, Jonathan	1	1	3		
Burt, Theophilus	1	2	4		
Partrick, James	1	2	2		
Burt, Joshua	1	3	1		
Read, Elias	2	3	2		
Keeler, Levi	1	3	3		
Folliot, John	1	4	1		
Portman, Mary Ann			1		
Bennitt, Gabriel	2	2	3		
Smith, Levi	1	1	1		
Smith, Phinehas	1	3	4		
Folliot, Thankfull	1	1	3		
Deforest, Joseph	1		1		
Folliot, Jeremiah	1		1		
Sherman, John	2	1	5		
Mead, John	2		4		
Scott, Gideon	1	2	4		
Barnum, Abel	1	2	7		
Chapman, John	1		2		
Barlow, John, 2d	1		2		
Hyatt, Thomas	1	2	1		
Scott, David	2	2	2		
Smith, Gideon	1	1	2		
Smith, David	2	1	3		
Hyatt, Uzzeil	1	1	5		
Depeere, John	1	1	4		
Dann, Ezra	1	1	6		
Mead, Jaspar	1		4		
Mills, Stephen	1		4		
Dickens, Arnold	1	1	2		
Keeler, Daniel	2	1	6		
Whittock, Thaddeus	1	2	3		
Yabecomb, Gilbart	1		1		
Morris, David	1	1	2		
Scott, James	1		2		
Bowton, Timothy	1	2	2		
McFarden, Thomas	1		2		
Hoyt, Samuel	1	3	2		
Jones, Jacob, 2d	1	2	2		
Whitney, Henry	1		1		
Olmsted, Josiah	1	1	1		
Jenkins, Calvin	1		3		
Bears, Anthony	1	2	4		
Hoyt, David	2	2	5		
Jackson, Joseph	1	4	2		
RIDGEFIELD TOWN—con.					
Gates, Noah	1	2	2		
Jackson, John	1	2	3		
Price, Hurd	1	1	2		
Jackson, Daniel	1	1	4		
Bowton, Roger	1	2	2		
Price, Ebenezer	1		1		
Edmond, Robert	3	1	2		
Riggs, Joseph	1		3		
Smith, James	1		4		
Munro, Joseph	1	3	1		
Lee, Seth	1	1	3		
Lee, John	2	2	3		
Lee, Elijah	1	1	1		
Lee, Daniel	2	3	5		
Lee, Elias	1	1	1		
Williams, Solomon	1	1	3		
Gregory, Zaccheus	1		1		
Cain, Hugh	1		1		
Banks, David	1		1		
Bears, Nathan	1		3		
Olmsted, David, 2d	1	2	6		
Hull, Silas	3	1	3		
Keeler, Jabez	1	5	3		
Bowton, Avery	1	1	2		
Smith, Hezekiah	3		1		
Gray, Gilead	1	4	2		
Smith, Uriah	1	1	4		
Dean, Daniel, 2d	1		1		
Dean, Daniel, 2d	2	1	4		
Burr, Samuel	1	2	2		
Lobdell, Uriel	2	1	4		
Wheeler, Ichabod	2	3	3		
Whittock, Robert	2	2	5		
Rundle, Shubael	1	3	4		
Warren, Michael	1	3	4		
Resiguie, Alexander	1		1		
Munro, William	1	2	3		
Rundle, Charles	1	1	3		
Stebbins, Ann	1	1	2		
Dauchey, Vivus	2	2	2		
Bennitt, Isaac	1		3		
Bennitt, Daniel	1		1		
Resigue, William	2	2	4		
Bradley, Stephen	1		2		
Lobdell, Ebenezer	1	2	3		
Bradley, Daniel	1	1	1		
Livesay, James	1	3	2		
Olmsted, Justus	1	2	1		
Pulling, William	1	2	2		
Sherwood, Jonathan	1	2	4		
Olmsted, Justus, 2d	2	2	4		
Bryant, Samuel	1	1	1		
Mead, William	2	1	2		
Gilbart, Abner	1	4	4		
Sherwood, Nehemiah	3		3		
Bradley, Samuel	4	2	3		
Mead, Joseph	2	4	3		
Mead, Hannah			2		
Stewart, John	1		1		
Wilson, Thomas	2	1	3		
Whittock, Justus	1	2	3		
Scribner, Uriah	1		2		
Bryant, John	1	1	2		
Wood, Jonathan	1	1	4		
Wood, Andrew	1		2		
Bennitt, Stephen	2	2	3		
Sturgis, Elnathan	1		2		
Sturgis, Nehemiah	1	2	2		
Benedict, Gamaliel	1	1	2		
Starr, Sarah		1	4		
Brush, Eliphelet	2	3	6		
Smith, Elijah	4	1	3		
Sherwood Nathan	1		3		
Whitney, Capt Henry	2		3		
Benedict, Comfort	1	3	2		
Gates, Jonathan	4	1	6		
Foster, Jonah	2	1	2		
Pulling, Augustus	1	3	7		
Dolittle, Phinehas	2	2	2		1
Northrup, Thomas	1		2		
Sherwood, Reuben	2	3	3		
Pulling, Abigail	2		3		
Northrup, Nathanel	2		6		
Keeler, John, 2d	2	3	5		
Finch, Peter	1		9		
Saintjohn, Thomas	2		5		
Weed, Jacob	1	2	2		
Saintjohn, Samuel	2		2		
Barber, Benjamin	2	1	2		
Titus, John	2	2	4		
Wallace, William	2	1	8	1	1
Smith, Jabez	1	2	2		
Smith, Matthew	2		3		
Northrup, James	1	5	4		
Sellick, Jesse	1		1		

FAIRFIELD COUNTY—Continued.

RIDGEFIELD TOWN—con.

NAME OF HEAD OF FAMILY.	Free white males of 16 years and upward, including heads of families.	Free white males under 16 years.	Free white females, including heads of families.	All other free persons.	Slaves.
Rockwell, William	1		3		
Northrup, Matthew	1	1	3		
Birchard, Uriah	1		3		
Birchard, Isaiah	2		2		
Birchard, Jeremiah	1	1	4		
Rockwell, Elisabeth			1		
Leason, Prudence			2		
Wilson, Abner	2	2	5	1	
Deforest, Uriah	2	1	2		
Lynds, Benjamin	2	1	1		
Sherwood, Ebenezer	2		1		
Coley, Daniel	2	1	3		
Varnold, John	1	1	3		
Rockwell, Abraham	3	1	4		
Rockwell, Abijah	1	2	3		
Rockwell, Daniel	2	1	2		
Keeler, Samuel	1	1	3		
Benedict, Timothy	2	1	2		
Keeler, Timothy, 2d	1	1	1		
Camp, Revd Samuel	2	1	4		
Forrester, William	3	2	5		
Keeler, Nehemiah	1	3	4		
Grey, Joseph	1	1	4		
Osborn, Gamaliel	1		4		
Abbott, James	1	1	3		
Dykeman, Jonathan	1		3		
Abbott, Lemuel	1	1	3		
Abbott, Lemuel, 2d	1		2		
Abbott, Stephen	1	1	1		
Abbott, Silas	1	2	1		
Arnold, Peleg	1	1	2		
Leach, Christopher	1	2	2		
Osborn, Jonah	1	1	1		
Gates, Samuel	1		1		
Nickerson, Eliphaz	1	2	1		
Rockwell, David	2	1	5		
Crain, Zebulun	4	4	3		
Rockwell, Joseph	1		1		
Thomas, Recompence, 2d	2		3		
Whitney, Ezekiel	1	1	3		
Brush, Zophar	1	2	3		
Fairchild, Ezekiel	2	1	2		
Nickerson, William	1	1	2		
Nickerson, James	1		1		
Nickerson, Barack	1		2		
Osborn, Abigail	1	1	3		
Thomas, Recompence	1	2	2		
Perry, John	1		1		
Norris, Stephen	3	5	3		
Weed, Bartholomew	2	3	5		
Starr, Peter	1	2	2		
Scribner, John	1	3	4		
Rockwell, Isaac	1	1	1		
Stevens, Zachariah	2	1	6		
Porter, James	1		1		
Platt, Samuel	1	3	5		
Barber, Zachariah	1	4	2		
Porter, Elisabeth		1	3		
Stevens, Nathan	2	3	5		
Gorham, Lockwood	1		3		
Salmon, Stephen	1	1	1		
Sears, Comfort	1	1	6		
Sears, Knowles	1	3	4		
Brush, Phillip	1	2	2		
Sears, Daniel	1	1	1		
Gage, Thomas	1	1	1		
Gravy, Francis	1		2		
Keeler, Elijah	2	2	7		
Rockwell, Henry	1		1		
Rockwell, Ebenezer	1	2	1		
Pulling, Abraham	1	3	2		
Foster, Jonah	2	4	3		
Lee, William	1	1	3		

STRATFORD TOWN.

NAME OF HEAD OF FAMILY.	Free white males of 16 years and upward, including heads of families.	Free white males under 16 years.	Free white females, including heads of families.	All other free persons.	Slaves.
Judson, Pixly	1	1	1		
Wells, Agar	1	5	4		
Lewis, Isaac	2	1	1		
Pixly, Peter	1	2	3		
Hurd, Andrew	1	1	3	1	2
Benjamin, Elnathan	1	5	4		
Benjamin, Samuel	1		1		
Judson, Abraham	2	1	3		
Judson, Aaron	2	1	1		1
Jones, Elnathan	1	6	2		
Beardsly, Henery	3		1		
Beardsly, Matthew (Wid.)			3		
Burritt, Silus	1	1	2		
Beardsly, Ephraim	2	2	3		
Benjamin, Philip	1		4		
Benjamin, John	2	2	5		
Hawley, Abigail (Wid.)	1		4		
Brown, Isaac	3	3	3		

STRATFORD TOWN—con.

NAME OF HEAD OF FAMILY.	Free white males of 16 years and upward, including heads of families.	Free white males under 16 years.	Free white females, including heads of families.	All other free persons.	Slaves.
Benjamin, George	3	3	7		1
Fairchild, John	2	3	4		
Johnson, Samel W	1		1		2
Tomlinson, Phebe (Wid.)		1	3	2	1
Walker, Robert	1	1	7		4
Beers, Samel	1				
Beers, Josiah	1	1	4		
Collins, William B	1	3	2		
Hawley, Ruth (Wid.)			3		
Seirs, James	1	3	4		2
Peck, John	1	2	3		
Benjamin, John	1	2	4		
Curtis, Jonas	1		1		
Wells, Benjamin	3		2		
Wells, William	1	1	1		
Lilliston, James	1		3		
Hawley, Josiah	1	1	4		
Whiting, Joseph	1	3	3		1
Shelbey, Ebenezer	2	3	5		
Wakman, Ephraim	2	2	5		
Ufford, Samuel	1	3	4		
Ufford, John	1	2	4		
Ufford, Benjamin	2	3	4		
Cow, James	3	1	3		
Edward, Samuel	3	4	6		
Curtis, Agar	1	1	1		
Hurd, Jabez	1		1	3	
Cannon, Lewis	2		1	3	2
Gorham, Isaac	2		2		
Gorham, Nathan	1	2	2		
Allen, Eben	3	2	3		
Plum, Justis	1	1	4		
Gorham, Nehemiah	1	2	2	2	
Southard, Samuel	2	1	4		
Silly, John	3	1	6		
Warduher, Sarah			2		
Osborn, Marah			3		
Ward, Samuel	1	1	5		
Curtis, Thomas	2	5	2		
Paterson, Samuel	1	1	6		
Clark, James	3	1	7	2	
Curtis, Henery	1	1	6		
Wells, Joseph	2	3	3		
Wells, Legrand	2		2		
Well, Benjamin	1		3		1
Woodhull, Stephen	3	2	3		
Wheeler, Elnathan	2	2	3		
Curtis, David	1	1	5		
Curtis, Josiah	3		2		
Wheeler, Nathanel	2	1	5		
Wheeler, Ephraim	2	3	4		
Wheeler, Deborah			3		
Wheeler, Elnathan, Jur	1		2		
Lewis, George	1		2	2	1
Thompson, Stephen	1	1	1		
Judson, Stiles	1	1	5	1	
Wilcox, Anna (Wid.)	2	1	2		
Judson, Daniel	2		4	1	3
Curtis, Stephen	2		2	1	2
Gorham, George	1	1	2		
Brothwell, Hezekiah	1	4	1		
McCoy, Few	1	2	1		
Curtis, Nehemiah	3	3	5		
Wilcox, William	2		4		
Booth, Agar	1	2	2		
Booth, Daniel	4	1	2		
Well, Isaac	1	2	3		1
Blackman, James	1	2	3	1	
Blackman, James	1		1		
Bindy, Nathan	2		2	1	2
Cartly, Ezra	1		1		1
Cartly, Ezra	1	3	3		
Cartley, Zebelon	1	3	4		
Sherwood, David	1	2	4		
Clifford, Elizabeth			2		
Warden, William	2		1		
Hubbill, Abijah	2		1		
Hubbill, Eunice (Wid.)	1	2	2		
Wing, Charles	1		2		
Hoit, Eli	1	2	3		
Hawly, Elijah	2	1	4		
Hawley, Aaron	5		2		2
Hoyt, Hanah (Wid.)	1		1	1	1
Lymon, Robert	2	2	4		
Phipeny, Ebenezer	1	3	4		
Sturges, Lewis	1	2	2		
Porter, Samuel	1		2		
Davis, Clark	2		4		
Willard, William	1	4	1		
Hull, Stephen	3	2	1		
Napp, Daniel	2	1	3		
Shermon, Seth	2		2		1
Jennings, Eliphalet	1	1	2		
Hawley, Woolcut	2	2	2		

STRATFORD TOWN—con.

NAME OF HEAD OF FAMILY.	Free white males of 16 years and upward, including heads of families.	Free white males under 16 years.	Free white females, including heads of families.	All other free persons.	Slaves.
Summers, Jabez	1		2		2
Starlin, Stephen	1	2	1		
Starlin, Stephen, Jur	1		1		
Starlin, Abijah	3	2	2		
Wakely, Jonathan	2	1	4		
French, James B	2	3	3		
Dudley, Asel	1	2	2		
Hawley, Gregary	1	3	2		
Summers, Stephen	2	1	5		
Beach, Jabez	1	1	1		
Summers, Abijah	1	2	4		
Summers, Elnathan	1	1	4		
Ciely, Denton	1		4		
Nichols, Reubin	1		4		
Gregory, James	1		2		
Summers, Aaron	1	2	3		
Summers, Samuel	4		4		
Smith, John	2				
Peterson, Isaac	1	1	3		
Patchen, Salmon	1		3		
Seely, Elnathan	2	2	4		
Gray, Reuel	2	2	5		
Beardsley, Amos	2	2	4		
Edward, Isaac	1	4	4		
Seely, Agar	1	1	3		
Seely, Benjamin	2	2	5		
Burton, Joseph	2	1	3		
Hach, Ebenezer	1	1	1		
Beach, Isaac	1	1	1		
Beardsley, David	3		2		
Beardsly, David, Junr	2	3	1		
Beardsley, Aaron	2	1	1		
Hayns, John	2	2	3		
Edwards, Theophlus	1		1		
French, David	3	1	4		
French, Samuel	2	1	3		
French, John	2		3		
French, John	1	1	2		
Curtis, Jones	1		1		
Curtis, Edmond	3	1	4		
Wheeler, John	4		1		
Osborn, Nathanel	1	1	5		
Beers, Elnathan	1	2	2		
Beech, Jabez	3	2	3		
Hogden (Widow)			2		
Starling, Elijah	3	2	2		
Beche, David	2		1		1
Wanright, Wiliam	1		3		
Curtis, Edmond	3	5	2		
Booth, Silaman	5	2	4		
Summers, David	3	2	5		
Lane, Hanah			1		
Curtis, John	3	2	5		
Turney, Samuel	1		1		
Turney, Ephraim	1		2		
Walker, Eliakim	3		3		
Midlebrook, Stephen	2	1	2		
Midlebrook, Stephen, Jur	1	2	1		
Beers, James	1	1	2		
Tredwell, Sarah		1	5		
Turney, Robert	1		1		
Turney, John	1	2	4		
Midlebrook, Elizabeth	1	1	2		
Midlebrook, John	1		1		
Fairchild, Daniel	1		2		
Turney, John	1				
Whiting, David	1	2	1		
Midlebrook, Bine	1		2		
Fairweather, Zalmon	1	1	2		
Turney, David	2	2	8		
Turney, Elnathan	1	1	2		
Turney, Gershom	2	2	3		
Moyer, Nathaniel	3	3	3		
Boor, Jonathan	2	1	5		
Beebe, James	1	1	4		
Curtis, Joshua	1	1	1		
Wakely, Thomas	1	1	1		
Hawley, Elijah	1	2	1		
Jones, John	1		5		
Nichols, Jonathan	2	3	4		1
Man, Richard	1		2		
Cable, William	2	2	2		
Curtis, Judson	1	1	1		
Curtis, Judson, Junr	2	1	4		
French, Samuel, Junr	1		2		
Shermon, David	2	1	3		
Lewis, Samuel	1	4	3		
Duncan, Charls	2	2	2		
French, John	1	1	1		
French, Samuel	1	2	3		
Beech, Agar	2	2	3		
Booth, Isaac	1	2	2		
Ufford, John	2		5		
Ufford, Daniel	1		1		

FAIRFIELD COUNTY—Continued.

STRATFORD TOWN—con.

NAME OF HEAD OF FAMILY.	Free white males of 16 years and upward, including heads of families.	Free white males under 16 years.	Free white females, including heads of families.	All other free persons.	Slaves.
Booth, David	1		2		1
Booth, David, Junr	1		4		1
Ufford, Ebenezer	2	2	3		
Wetmore, Hezekiah	1	2	3		1
Seely, David	2	2	6		
Hinman, Jonas	1	2	3		
Booth, Filo	1	3	3		
Brinsley, Daniel	1		1	1	1
Coe, Zacheus	2	2	4	1	1
Coe, Aaron	1	2	5		
Lamson, Nathanel	1	1	4		
French, Phebe			2		
Ufford, Samuel	1	2	1		
Wakely, Anna			2	2	
Beech, Eliakim	1	3	3		
Hawley, Nero (Negro)				4	
Beebe, Ruth			3		
Edwards, Hezekiah	1		1		
Salmon, Richard	1	1	5		
Beach, Elizabeth	1	3	1		
Beach, Agar, Junr	2	1	2		
Beardsley, Lemuel	1	2	3		
Hawley, Epharim	2	1	2		1
Hawley, Andrew	1		2		
Hawley, Mable			1		
Diskom, Thomas	1		4		
Siely, Betty (Wid.)			2		
Peet, Daniel	1	3	4		
Starlin, Ephraim	3	2	5		
Borough, Ciely	1	2	3		
Summers, Daniel	1	2	5		
Hayns, Lemuel	1	4	3		
Ives, Daniel	1	1	4		
Wakely, Nehemiah	1		3		
Edwards, Elnathan	1		5		
Hubbill, Wiliam	1	2	6		
Rose, William	1	2	1		
Edwards, Nehemiah	2		2		
Edwards, David	1	3	3		
Edwards, Abel	1	2	3		
Edwards, Couh	1	1	3		
Edwards, Reuben	1	2	3		
Edwards, Thomas	2		3		1
Edwards, John, 3d	1	4	3		
Edwards, David	1		2	2	2
Edwards, John	4	3	6		
Hubbill, Benjamin	3		1		
Leman (Widow)			3		
Wells, David	2	1	2		
Wells, Gideon	1	1	1		
Hawly, Thomas	4		3		
Bennitt, Samuel	1	1	3		
Hanes, William	2	2	5		
Bulkley, Seth	1	2	3		
Sherwood, Stephen	2	1	4		
Wakely, Molly (Wid.)			1		
Seely, Elijah	1	1	1		
Siely, Abel	1	1	1		
Peet, Elijah	1	1	2		
Wakely, David	3	4	3		
Mitchel, Polly (Wid.)	1	3	1		
Beardsly, Benjamin	2	3	4		
Porter, Ephraim	1	4	4		
Porter, Thomas	3	1	3		
Mallet, Philip	1	4	3		
Gregory, Gilman	2	2	4		
Gregory, Enoch	2	2	5		
Tredwell, Sarah	1	1	6		
Beers, James	1	1	2		
Coswell, Caleb	2	1	2		
Hubbard, Icabud	2	2	4		
Gregory, Samuel	3	1	6		
Mallet, Joseph	2	1	3		
Gregory, Daniel	1	1	5		
Mallet, Seth	1	2	2		
Jones, John	1		5		
Midlebrook, Abiah	1	2	4		
Mallet, Zacheriah	1	3	5		
Whiting, David	1	1	2		
Jerrald, Jame	2	3	4		
Chambers, George	1		2		
Mallet, Samuel	2	2	3		
Mallet, Zalmon	1		2		
Mallet, David	2	1	5		
Mallet, Benjamin	1		1		
Newreshic, Lewis	1	1	1		
Mallet, Martha (Wid.)	1	2	3		
Mallet, John	1	1	2		
Siely, Phebe			1		
Mallet, David, Junr	2	3	3		
Bennett, Nehemiah	1		1		
Hall, Samuel	1	3	3		
Patterson, Hezekiah	2	1	3		
Osborn, William	4	2	4		
Curtis, Nehemiah	1		2		

STRATFORD TOWN—con.

NAME OF HEAD OF FAMILY.	Free white males of 16 years and upward, including heads of families.	Free white males under 16 years.	Free white females, including heads of families.	All other free persons.	Slaves.
Curtis, Samuel	1	1	3		1
Bennitt, Gidion	1		1		
Bennitt, Benjamin	1		1		
Daton, Andrew	1	2	4	1	2
Brooks, William	1	2	4		1
Fairchild, Robert	2	3	3		
Walker, Joseph	1	2			
Brooks, Polly (Wid.)	1		4	1	
Tomlinson, Abraham	1		6		
Alent, Thomas	2	1	2		1
Witmon, Victory	2				
Lewis, Phinus	1		1	1	
Stebens, Stephen	1	1	3		1
Curtis, Zelmon	1	1	2		
Deforest, Edward	1	1	2		1
McEuin, Abijah	1		3		
Judson, Abner	1	1	4		
Poor, Joshua	1	2	5		
Hubill, Ebenezer	3	4	3		
Deforist, Joseph	1	2	6		1
McEuin, Daniel	1		1		
McEuin, John	1	2	3		
McEuin, Matthew	2	1	4		
Coe, Ebenezer	2	1	2		1
Birdsie, William	1	1	1		
Borough, Josiah	1	1	2	7	
Porter, Stephen	2	2	1		2
Matcher, John	2	1	3		
Robert, Wiliam	1	1	2		
Beers, Joel	1		3		
Beers, Stephen	2		5		
Plant, Solomon	1	1	2		
Clark, Jerusha	2	2	4		
Shermon, John	1	1	3		
Jones, Jasper	1	2	2		
Nailer, John	1	1	3		1
Hows, Ebenezer	1		3		
Cornwall, Thomas	1	3	3		
Lyons, David	1	2	3		
Vos, Ebenezer	1		1		
Fulsora, Mary			2		
Beardsly, John	1	1	4		
Southard, William	1		2		
Curtis, Abijah	1	3	7		
Curtis, Elihu	1	2	2		
Curtis, Daniel	1	3	2		
Frost, Stephen	2	1	4		
Wells, William	1		2		
Thompson, David	1	1	5		
Thomson, John	1	1	5		
Brooks, Abijah	1	2	2		
Walker, Joseph	1	3	4	1	3
Magraw, John	1	1	3		
Booth, John, Junr	1	1	3		
Burritt, Hezekiah	1	1			
Burritt, Samuel	2		1		
Burritt, Joseph	2	2	4		
Gorham, Phebe			1	1	
Gorham, William	1	2	3		
Deforrest, Elihu	3	1	5		
Curtis, Samuel	2	2	3		
Cannon, James	1		3		1
Curtis, Jeremiah	2		3		
Burritt, Ephraim	5		3		
Russel, William	1	5	3		
Clifford, Elijah	2		1		
Stretton, Anna	2	3	6		
Nichols, Matthias	2	3	6		1
Osborn, Ephraim	1	1	6		
Elgar, Ezra	2		1		
Curtis, Charles	2	1	4		
Beardsley, Nathan	2	3	3		
Curtis, Esther (Wid.)	1		1		
Siely, Mable	1		1		
Beebe, Thomas	1	1	2		
Burrow, George	1	4	1		
Blackman, Phineas	2	1	2		
Wells, Hanah (Wid.)	1	1	3		
Jones, Molly (Wid.)			2		
Booth, John	4	2	1		2
Curtis, Joseph	3	4	3		2
Judson, Benjamin	3		3		
Beardsly, Abraham	3		3		
Beardsly, Curtis	1	4	3		
Booth, Hezekiah	1	2	2		
Booth, James	1	2	4		
Brooks, Isaac	1	2	2		
Curtis, Stiles	3	2	3		
Curtis, Edmond	3	3	6		
Curtis, Samuel	1	1	1		
Peck, Josiah	1	3	3		
Curtis, Henery	1				1
Peck, Tabitha	1		3		
Peck, Job	2	4	2		
Judson, Curtis	1	1	2		

STRATFORD TOWN—con.

NAME OF HEAD OF FAMILY.	Free white males of 16 years and upward, including heads of families.	Free white males under 16 years.	Free white females, including heads of families.	All other free persons.	Slaves.
Beers, Abner	2	1	2		1
Wells, James	2		4		
Wells, Elias	2	1	4		
Thomson, David	1		2		
Beers, Jabez	1		3		
Curtis, Andrew	1	1	2		
Clark, Samuel	1	3	2		
Peck, Judson	1	1	5		
Beers, Matthew	2	1	1		
Foot, Joseph	2		1		
Judson, William	1	2	4		
Curtis, David	1	4	3		
Curtis, Judson	1	1	1		
Curtis, Daniel	1	1	6		
Curtis, Agar	1	3	1		
Peet, Stiles	1	2	1		
Curtis, Lewis	2	1	6		
Walker, James	1		1		
Walker, James, Junr	1	3	2		
Nichols, Sarah (Wid.)	2		3		
Hurd, Gilead	3		1		
Shermon, Nathan	4	1	2		1
Pixley, William	1	1	2		
Nichols, Nathaniel	2	5	4		
Taulsom, Elias	2	1	3		
Lewis, Stiles	2	2	7		2
Crowel, Thomas	3	1	6		
Toby (Negro)				3	
Hubbill, Samuel	1	2	5		
Burrit, Stephen	4		2		
Peet, Bersheba (Wid.)	1	1	5		
Patterson, Charity			2		
Hubbill, Josiah	2	2	2		
Lewis, Judson	1	2	4		
Hubbill, John	2	2	3		
Lewis, Benjamin	3	1	3		
Lewis, Joseph	2		2		1
Lamson (Widow)			4		
Shermon, James	2	1	4		
Curtis, Fineus	1	1	6		
Curtis, Robert	2	1	2		
Curtis, Joseph	1	1	1		
Bibbons, Timothy	1	2	3		
Lampson, Nathanel	2	3	3		
Philips, Thomas	1		1		
Gorham (Widow)			2		
Whiting, Samuel	2	1	1		
Lewis, Filo	1	4	2		
Whiting, John	1	1	3		
Walker, Phebe (Wid.)			3		
Jones, Isaac	1	2	1		
Haris, Henery	1		3		
Barlow, David	1	3	3		
Osborn, Nathan	3	1	2		
Daton, Brewster	2	2	2		
Butler, Charles	1	1	3		
Lacy, Josiah	2	1	5		2
Peet, William	1	3	4		
Allen, Nehemiah	2		2		
Allen, James	1		3		
Baker, Jonathan	1	2	3		
Hawley, David	1		3		
Young, Daniel	3		2		
Clark, Ransom	4	1	2		
Smith, Justin	1		3		
Rose, Peter	1	1	2		
Hubbill, Amos	3	3	2		3
Hinman, Isaac	2	1	2		
Hubbill, Zalmon	4	1	2		1
Wilcox, Elisha	1		2		2
Sherwood, Samuel	1		1		
Brooks, Abijail (Wid.)			3		
Brooks, Benjamin	1	3	4		
Benjamin, Aaron	1	1	2		
Brooks, John	1		3		
Benjamin, Asa	1	1	1		
Beech, James	1		3		
Darrow, Nicholas	1	1	6		
Lake, Reubin	2		3		
Wells, Jedediah F.	1	1	4		
French, Gamaliel	1	1	3		
French, Benjamin	1		2		
Hall, Stephen	2	2	8		
Beardsley (Widow)			2	3	
Burrit, Charles	2		1		
Parish, Joel	1		4		
Burriss, Stephen	4	1	3		2
Burrit, Elijah	2		7		
Smith, Samuel	1		2		
Smith, Jonathan	1		3		
Borough, Griswell	1	1	2		
Booth, Samuel	3	1	4		
Siely, Michael	2		5		
Siely, Seth	2	1	3		

FAIRFIELD COUNTY—Continued.

NAME OF HEAD OF FAMILY.	Free white males of 16 years and upward, including heads of families.	Free white males under 16 years.	Free white females, including heads of families.	All other free persons.	Slaves.
STRATFORD TOWN—con.					
Nichols, Philip	3	1	4	1	3
Barlow, Thomas	1	3	4		
Nichols, William	1	1	7		
Diseum, Robert	3		1		
Siely, Michael	1		4		
Iarmgan, Jonathan	1		2		
Bangs, Lemuel	1		2		
Meeker, Isaac	1	1	1		
Hart, William	1	1	4		
Taylor, William	1		2		
Diseum, James	2		2		
Beardsly, Silus	1	4	1		
Nichols, Thomas (Neg.)				5	
Frost, Joseph	1	3	4		
Silemon, Hezekiah	2	5	5		
Lewis, Eli	1	1	2		
Lewis, Nathaniel S	2	1	3		
Lewis, Nathan	1	1	3		
Lewis, John	1	1	7		
Lewis, Judson	1	5	2		
Thomson, Nehemiah	1	2	3		
Thomson, Abijah	1	1	1		1
Burton, Samuel	1	2	4		
Wilcox, Ephraim	2	1	3		
Wilcox, Elnathan	1	2	2		
Wilcox, Nathan	2		3		
Beardsly, Jeremiah	2		1		2
Judson, Elihu	1	1	3		
Judson, John	1	3	2		
Wilcox, Gideon	1	2	1		
Wheeler, Samuel	1	3	3		
Pendleton, William	1	3	3		
Lewis, Stephen	1	2	3		1
Smith, John	2	1	4		
Wells, Philip	2	4	3		1
Thompson, Jonas	2		1		
Booth, Abel	1	2	8		
Hawly, Parson	2	1	1		
Wells, Samuel	1	2	2		1
Wells, Stephen	2		2		1
Booth, Hilkiah	2	1	2		
Curtis, Isaac	1		2		
Clark, John	1	2	2		
Juckets, Elijah	1		2		
Benson, Eben	1	1	2		
Booth, Abijah	3	2	3		
Dayton, Brewster	1	3	2		
Hawly, Edmond	1	4	1		
Curtis, Silus	1	5	6		3
Nodine, Lewis	1	1	1		
Russel, William	1	5	2		
Cojah, Elizabeth		2	2		
Blackman, Zacheriah	1	2	3		
Curtis, Elihu	1	3	6		
Curtis, John	3	3	3		
Birdsie, Thadeus	1	1	2		
Tomlinson, Jabez N	2	1	4		1
Birdsie, Ezra	2	1	6		
WESTON TOWN.					
Sherwood, John	3	2	5		4
Lyon, Andrew	1		1		4
Treadwell, David	2	3	2		
Jacson, Francis	1		5		
Osbone, Jeremiah	1	1	2		
Stratton, Thomas	1	2	2		
Siely, Ebenezer	1	1	3		
Siely, Nathaniel	3		3		
Johnson, James	2	1	4		
Gilbert, Thadeus	2	7	7		
Parrot, John	3	1	3		
Jewel, Hanah			3		
Cable, Ebenezer	1		2		
Bradley, Joseph	1		3		
Winton, Joseph	1	2	5		
Cable, Joseph	2		3		
Nichols, Daniel	1	1	4		
Redfield, David	2		2		
Wheeler, Ezra	1	4	3		
Winton, Ezra	2	3	1		
Lyon, Joseph	2	1	2		
Baldwin, Gabriel	4	1	5		
Sherwood, Amos	2	5	5		
Sherwod, Fanton	1		3		
Brindsmaid, Cyrus	1		2		
Brindsmde, Josiah	1		2		
Mills, Ebenezer	1	2	2		
Bennitt, Daniel	2	1	4		
Sanford, Josiah	2		5		
Gregory, Isaac	2	1	2		
Wheeler, Elnathan	1		2		
Siliman, David, Junr	3	2	8		
Bennitt, William	1	1	1		
WESTON TOWN—con.					
Wakeman, Daniel	1	1	2		
Sealy, Joseph	2	1	4		
Oakly, Miles	1	2	2		
Gilbert, Zalmon	1	1	5		
Hubbill, Isaac	1		2		
Sealy, Nathaniel, Junr	3	3	4		
Dursy, Thomas, Junr	1	1	3		
Hubbill, Timothy	2		3		
Siliman, David, 3d	1	1	1		
Jennings, Hezekiah	2	1	2		
Crowfoot, James	1	1	5		
Sealy, Ephraim	1	1	2		
Jennings, Nehimiah	2	1	4		
Duncam, Edward	1	1	2		
Gilbert, John	2		2		
Jennings, Hezekiah, Jr	1	1	2		
Wheeler, John	2	1	3		
Treadwell, David, Junr	2	1	2		
Oakly, Peter	1	1	2		
Wheeler, Gideon	1		1		
Mills, Ebenezer	2		3		
Foot, Nathan	1		1		
Hill, Wakeman	1	1	2		
Dimon, Benjamin	3	1	3		
Burr, Moses	2		5		
Adams, Abel	1	2	3		
Lyon, Zacheriah	2		6		
Odle, Daniel	1	2	1		
Judd, Reubin	1	2	2		
Sealy, David	1	1	4		
Hall, Aaron	1	3	5		
Hall, Mary		1	2		
Hall, Abel	3	1	1		
Bennitt, James	1	3	4		
Bennitt, Aaron	1		1		
Fairchild, Joel	1		2		
Wakelin, Samuel	1		1		
Fairchild, Noami			2		
Beardsly, Jabez	2		2		
Stratton, David	2	2	3		
Nethersmith, Matthew	2		1		
Summers, Henery	2		3		
Bennitt, John	3	1	2		
Oakly, Jerad	2	2	2		
Partlow, Abigail		2	2		
Shermon, Josiah	4		4		
Wadkins, Abel	1	1	2		
Jennings, Hezekiah, 3d	2	6	3		
Beach, Abel	1	2	1	1	
Wheeler, Dimon	1	1	2		
Lyon, Stephen	1	4	2		
Higby, Seth	1	3	3		
Garit, David	1	2	3		
Staples, Samuel	1	4	1		
Bennitt, Samuel	1		4		1
Siliman, David	2	2	2		
Jennings, William	1	2	3		
Bennitt, Thomas	1	2	3		
Silloman, Justus	2	1	2		
Sherwood, Matthew	1	2	2		
Silliman, James	1		2		
Sanford, Sarah			2		
Bennitt, Content			2		
Sherwood, Thomas	1		2		
Levitt, Josiah	1	3	3		
Sherwood, Daniel	2	1	2		
Hoyt, William	1	2	1		
Jackson, Daniel	1	1	1		
Jackson, John	2		2		
Jackson, Nathan	1		2		
Jackson, Aden	1		2		
Osborn, Jerad	1	1	2		
Sherwood, Thomas	1		1		
Hall, Byer	1	1	1		
Odle, David	1	2	2		1
Beers, Ephraim	3	1	3		
Beers, David	1	2	2		
Taylor, David	1	2	6		
Taylor, Baroch	1	2	3		
Whitehead, Nathaniel	1	3	4		
Wilson, Joseph	2	4	1		
Gold, Nathan	1	1	2		
Baker, David	1		2		
Squire, Arel	1	2	2		
Barlow, Nehemiah	1		2		
Coble, Daniel	3	2	2		
Goodsell, Samuel	1		1		
Bradley, Isaac	1	1	3		1
Wakman, Nathan	1	2	2		
Turney, David	1	4	2		
Jennings, Philow	1		2		
Sealy, Jesse	2	3	2		
Beach, Nathaniel	1	2	1		
Levet, Josiah G	1	3	2		
WESTON TOWN—con.					
Raymond, Ruth	1		1		
Jennings, Enoch	1		1		
Wadkins, William	4	2	4		
Winton, John	1		1		
Shermon, Andrew	1	2	1		
Summers, Isaac	1	1	4		
Summers, Elijah	1	1	2		
Fairweather, Samuel	1	1	1		
Fairweather, Jonah	1	1	2		
Winton, James	1	3	2		
Higgins, Isaac	1		2		
Higgins, Abraham	3	2	3		
Lacy, James	1	1	2		
Gilbert, Thomas	6	2	4		
Curtis, Job	1	3	4		
Curtis, Benjamin	2		1		
Curtis, John	1	4	3		
Whealer, Eliphalet	1	2	3		
Lyon, Ebenezer	2		5		
Bennit, Thadeus	2	2	4		
Murwin, John	1	1	5		
Wheeler, Calvin	1	1	6		
Jones, John	1	2	4		
Homes, Daniel	1		7		
Wheeler, Samuel	1	1	2		
Darling, Samuel	1	2	2		
Davis, Nathaniel	1	1	2		
Olmstead, Elijah	3	4	5		
Treadwell, Daniel	2	2	3		
Gray, Daniel	1		3		
Lyon, Walter	1	1	1		
Beardsly, Eliphalet	1	3	2		
Treadwell, Benjamin	1	2	1		
Bennit, Samuel	1	2	1		
Jennings, Abraham	1	4	5		
French, Ephraim	2	2	4		
Lyon, Zacheriah, Junr	1	2	3		
Halis, John	2	1	1		
Lacy, Joseph	1		5		
Wells, Samuel, Junr	1	1	5		
Wells, Samuel	3		3		
Wells, Nathan	1	1	2		
Lyon, Ezekiel	1	4	2		
Lyon, Sarah			2		
Fairchild, Gershom	1	1	2		
Lyon, Gershom	3	1	3		
Lyon, Daniel	2	1	5		
Lyon, Thomas	2	3	2		
Lyon,	1	4	3		
Lyon, Isaac	1	3	4		
Edwards, Isaac	1	1	1		
Cardwell, John	1	2	4		
Wakman, Samuel	2	1	3	1	3
Wakman, Elijah	1	3	3		
Wakeman, Samuel, Junr	1		4		
Wheeler, Jabez	1		2		
Wheeler, Nathan	2	2	4		
Olmstead, Daniel	1		2		
Olmstead, John	1	1	3		
Thorp, Hezekiah	1		3		
Thorp, Samuel	2	4	3		
Wakman, Lloyd	1	3	4		
Robertson, Jonathan	2		4		
Gilbert, Joseph	1	1	2		
Robertson, Jonathan, Junr	1		3		
Rockwell, Noah	1	2	4		
Bennitt, Nathan	3	3	5		
Rockwell, John	1	1	2		
Cable, Nehemiah	3	1	4		
Hambleton, William	1		1		
Gilbert, Reubin	1	2	4		
Bradly, William	2	1	2		
Fanton, Jonathan	2	3	4		
Godfry, Moses	1	1	3		
Cable, Ruth			2		
Morehouse, Daniel	2	1	3	1	1
Morehouse, Joseph	1		1		
Morehouse, Banks	1		1		
Dikeman, Hezekiah	1	1	2		
Lockwood, John	1	6	4		
Abrahams, George H	1	2	2		
Cole, Jonathan	1	4	4		
Patchen, Jacob	1	2	2		
Phinny, Jesse	3	1	2		
Duncan, Daniel	4	2	4		
Rockwell, Jonah	1	2	4		
Sturges, Ezekiel	1	1	3		
Sturges, Jabel	4	1	2		
Beers, Nathan	1	2	1		
Beers, Pinkany	1	3	2		
Bigsbie, Ebenezer	2	1	2		
Squire, Seth	1	1	3		
Squire, Stephen	1	1	2		

FAIRFIELD COUNTY—Continued.

NAME OF HEAD OF FAMILY.	Free white males of 16 years and upward, including heads of families.	Free white males under 16 years.	Free white females, including heads of families.	All other free persons.	Slaves.	NAME OF HEAD OF FAMILY.	Free white males of 16 years and upward, including heads of families.	Free white males under 16 years.	Free white females, including heads of families.	All other free persons.	Slaves.	NAME OF HEAD OF FAMILY.	Free white males of 16 years and upward, including heads of families.	Free white males under 16 years.	Free white females, including heads of families.	All other free persons.	Slaves.
WESTON TOWN—con.						WESTON TOWN—con.						WESTON TOWN—con.					
Gray, Anna			2			Bradly, Francis	1		2			Hilton, Adkisson	1		3		
Andrews, Silliman	3	2	5			Bradly, Gershom	1	1	4		2	Gray, James	2	1	2		
Rowland, Samuel	2	2	4			Bradly, Eliphalit	1	2	2		1	Coly, David, Junr	1		4		
Burr, Moses	1		5		1	Bradly, Gershom, Junr	1		2			Gray, Gideon	1		4		
Higgens, Tommy	1	3	1		1	Perry, Job	1	2	1			Gray, Nathan	1		4		
Higgens, John	1		1			Wakeman, Aaron	2		4			Morehouse, Andrew	1		2		
Ogden, Joseph	1	1	5			Banks, Austin	1	2	2			Lyon, Hezekiah	3	1	4		
Duncan, Jerard	1	3	2			Bradley, Levi	1	1	2			Taylor, Jonathan	1	1	1		
Squire, Sealy	2	4	4			Gilbert, Lewis	1	1	3			Dikman, John	1	1	1		
Sturges, James	1	3	4			Demon, Noah	2	1	2			Lockwood, Albert	1	2	4		
Lockwood, Gideon	1	4	3			Bradly, David	1	1	3		1	Adams, Nathan	3	2	6		
Squire, Thomas	1	1	4			Bradley, Lyman	1	6	8			Bulkly, Talcot	1	1	1		
Godfry, Jonathan	1	2	3			Stocker, Mary			3			Sherwood, Jabez	2	2	3		
Godfry, David	1		1			Davis, David	1	1	2			Sherwood, Seymour	1		2		
Godfry, Daniel	1	2	1			Davis, John	1		5			Smith, David	2	3	2		
Godfry, Silliman	2	2	4			Williams, Peter	3	3	2		1	Gorham, Shubal	2		2		
Osborn, William	1		3			Fanton, Hezekiah	1	3	4			Gray, Elijah	2	5	2		
Osborn, Isaac	1	4	3			Murwin, Nathan	1		3			Coley, Morehouse	1	1	2		1
Osborn, Hezekiah	3	1	3			Collyer, Thomas	2	3	3			Betterson, Joseph	1	2	4		
Patchen, George	4	1	6			Fanton, John, Junr	1	1	2			Coley, Ebenezer	5	1	4	3	5
Gilbert, Ebenezer	1	2	4			Sturges, Stephen	1	2	9			Crossman, Trowbridge	1	2	1		
Morehouse, Michael	1	2	2			Fanton, John	2		1		1	Thorp, John	1	2	2		
Brown, Elisha	2	2	3			Thorp, Ebenezer	1		5			Bennit, Elias	1	3	4		
Row, Daniel M	1		1			Thorp, Thadeus	1	5	2			Adams, Squire	2	1	1		
Row, Beniah M	2	1	5			Coley, Eliphalet	2		5			Adams, David	1		2		
Thorp, Gershom	1		3			Banks, Daniel	1	2	1			Adams, Silaman	1	3	2		
Thorp, Jacob	1		3			Thorp, Ebenezer, Junr	1		4			Coly, David	2	1	2		
Gorham, Jacob (Negro)				3		Thorp, Peter	1		1			Morehouse, Nathan	2	1	2		
Fanton, Gershom	1		1			Osborn, Ephraim	1	3	3			Marvin, Brush	1	1	2		
Wilkson, James	1		1			Dyars, James	2		2			Osterbank, Moses	2	1	4		
Thorp, Nathan	1	1	3			Blackman, Nehemiah	1	3	2			Dears, Benjamin	2		1		1
Banks, Joseph	1		5			Blackman, Daniel	2	1	4			Noyes, John	1	2	3		1
Banks, Thomas	1	3	3			Benton, Cyrus	2	3	3			Rowland, Jeremiah	2	3	2		
Nichols, Gold	1		3			Beleh, Josiah	1		4			Persons, Peter	3		3		
Treadwell, Joseph	1	1	4			Sly, Thomas	1	1	2			Morehouse, Jesse	1	3	2		
Lyon, Ephraim	3	1	4			Sawly, Thomas	1	2	1			Godfry, Elias	1	3	1		
Davis, Joseph	3	2	1			Green, Solomon	1		2			Beers, Ezra	1	1	2		
Thorp, Jabez	1	1	2			Smith, Seth	1		1		1	Godfry, Eleazer	1		1		
Williams, Elnathan	3	1	3			Hoyt, Seth	1	2	4			Godfry, David	1	3	2		
Platt, Jesse	2	2	5			French, Samuel	1	2	4			Godfry, Cristopher	1	3	2		
Gilbert, Andrew	3	1	1			Hawley, David	1		1			Beers, Isaac	1	1	1		
Hull, Moses	1		3			Hawley, Daniel	1	1	3			Rowland, Daniel	1	3	2		
Bradley, Ebenezer	1	2	2			Harris, Robert	1	3	3			Winkley, Henery	1	1	3		
Burr, Increase	1	3	2			Sherwood, Joseph	1	5	1		1	Bulkley. David	1	2	3		
Bennitt, Ezekiel	1		4			Hubbill, Nathaniel	2	1	4			Godfry, Isaac	1	1	2	1	
Shermon, Sarah				2		Prince, William	3	5	1	1		Siely, Abel	2		2		
Sturges, Moses	1	2	3			Bennit, Benjamin	2	1	4			Beers, Nehemiah	2	1	4		
Nichols, John	1	3	7	1		Hall, Esbon	1	3	4			Beers, Fanton	1	2	3		
Burr, Eliphalet	2		2			Beardsley Benjamin	2	3	5			Beers, Ephraim	2	1	2		
Nichols, Peter	1	2	6			Steward, Charles	1	3	3			Beers, Jonathan	1	1	6		
Banks, Hezekiah	2	1	5			Porter, Joseph	1	1	4			Brothington, Samuel	1	3	3		
foot, Levi	1	2	2			Porter, David	1	4	2			Coley, Jonathan	2	1	3		
Ryla, John	1	2	3			Gregory, Samuel	1		4			Coley, Jonathan, Jur	1	3	1		
Baker, Samuel	3	2	2			Daton, Sylus	1		3			Guire, Eben	1	2	2		
Jennings, Benjamin	3		1			Booth, Thadeus	1		7			Fanton, Zebulen	1	1	3		
Davis, Ebenezer	2	1	2			Bennit, Isaac	2	1	1			Gray, John	2	2	3		
Canfield, Ezekiel	1	2	5			Gilbert, Burr	1		3			Morehouse, Jabez	1		2		
Davis, Ebenezer	1		2			Bennit, Isaac	1					Lord, Sarah	2	2	7		
Cable, Isaac	2	1	2			Baily, Henery	1		2			Morehouse, David	1	2	5		
Dimon, John	1		4			Hubbill, Stephen	1	2	2			Wood, Obadiah	1	1	1		
Robertson, Seth	1	2	3			Booth, John	1		1			Wood, Samuel	2	1	2		1
Fanton, Abel	1		3			Broach, Mary		1	2			Adams, Joshua	1	2	3		
Murwin, David	3		2			Burton, Solomon	2	4	3			Sturges, Peter	2	1	3		
Bradley, Enos	1		1			Simers, Hezekiah	1	1	5			Lockwood, John	1	2	2		
Murwin, Seth	1		1			Turril, Daniel	1	4	2			Hutenack, Francis	2	1	2		
Murwin, Samuel	2		2			Gregory, Stephen	2	1	3			Sherwood, Samuel B	1	1	3		2
Rowland, Jonathan	2		3			Hubbill, Seth	1		5			Dikeman, Eliphalet	1	1	1		
Burr, John	1	1	2			Turril, Stephen	2	3	3			Andrews, Daniel	1	1	1	1	3
Parrick, Molly		2	4			Hubbill, Ebenezer	2		2			Andrews, Daniel, Junr	1	3	5		1
Murwin, Eppepras	1		3			Summers, Nathan	2	3	2			Fitch, Cuff (Negro)				9	
Fanton, Nehemiah	3	2	1			Thorp, David	1	3	5			Elwood, Joseph	1	2	4		
Treadwell, Thomas	3	1	2			Sherwood, Levet	1	1	2								
Treadwell, Nathan	1	1	1			Fairchild, Ephraim	3	1	3								

HARTFORD COUNTY.

NAME OF HEAD OF FAMILY.	Free white males of 16 years and upward, including heads of families.	Free white males under 16 years.	Free white females, including heads of families.	All other free persons.	Slaves.	NAME OF HEAD OF FAMILY.	Free white males of 16 years and upward, including heads of families.	Free white males under 16 years.	Free white females, including heads of families.	All other free persons.	Slaves.	NAME OF HEAD OF FAMILY.	Free white males of 16 years and upward, including heads of families.	Free white males under 16 years.	Free white females, including heads of families.	All other free persons.	Slaves.
BERLIN TOWN.						BERLIN TOWN—con.						BERLIN TOWN—con.					
Andrus, Moses	3		4			Booth, Thomas	1	1	2			Brunson, Noadiah	1		2		
Andrus, Nathaniel	1		2			Belden, Leonard	1	1	4			Booth, Stephen	1		1		
Atkins, Benjamin	2		3			Belden, Jonathan	3	1	4			Curtis, Ebenezer	1	3	2		
Andrus, Levi	3	1	3			Booth, Elisha	1	1	5			Churchill, Nathaniel	1	1	6		
Andrus, Hezekiah	1	2	5			Booth, Elisha	1	1	5			Churchill, Nathaniel, Jr	1	2	2		
Andrus, Hezekiah, Jr	1	1	1			Bass, Samuel	1	3	4			Clark, Abel	1	3	2		
Andrus, Josiah	1	1	3			Bassett, Cornelius	1		6			Churchill, Stephen	1	2	3		
Andrus, Joseph	2		5			Booth, Joseph	1	4	4			Churchill, Sage	1	1	2		
Andrus, Elijah	1	2	3			Booth, James	1	2	3			Cornwall, Robert	3	1	3		
Atkins, Hezekiah	1	2	2			Brunson, Elijah	1		2			Cadwell, Roderic	1		3		
Andrus, Moses, Jr	1	2	6			Brunson, Elijah, Jr	1	4	2			Clark, Solomon	1	1	4		
Booth, Nathan	1	1	1			Brunson, Samuel	1	3	3			Cone, Joshua	1	3	5		
Booth, Robert	1	1	3			Brunson, Nathan, Jr	2	4	2								

HARTFORD COUNTY—Continued.

NAME OF HEAD OF FAMILY.	Free white males of 16 years and upward, including heads of families.	Free white males under 16 years.	Free white females, including heads of families.	All other free persons.	Slaves.
BERLIN TOWN—con.					
Couch, Ebenezer	1		2		
Dewey, David	3		2		
Dewey, Josiah	1	2	2		
Dickenson, Samuel	1		1		
Dickenson, Samuel, Jr.	2	1	2		
Dickenson, Elijah	1	1	3		
Doolittle, Ephraim	2	2	4		
Daniels, David	1	2	3		
Daley, Samuel	1	1	2		
Dunham, David	1		2		
Eddy, Charles	2	4	5		
Frances, Elijah	2		3		
Frances, James	1	2	4		
Frances, Elijah, Jr.	1	1	1		
Frances, Justin	1	1	3		
Gridley, Oliver	1	1	5		
Griswold, Gideon	1		3		
Griswold, Ashbel	1	3	4		
Gladden, Samuel	1		1		
Goodrich, David	1	2	2		
Goodrich, Jediahah	1		2		
Gridley, Thomas	2	1	2		
Griswold, Experience			1		
Goodrich, Isaac	2		1		
Goodrich, Zenas	1	2	2		
Halet, Mabel		1	3		
Hart, Elijah	3	1	1		
Hart, Thomas	1	1	2		
Hart, Jehuda	2	3	5		
Hart, Benjamin	2	1	4		
Hart, Elizur	4	2	4		
Hart, Elijah, Jr.	2	4	2		
Hart, Judah	1	3	5		
Hinsdale, John	1		3		
Hinsdale, Elijah	3		5		
Hollister, Rebecca		1	5		
Hart, Bethel	1		4		
Hart, Elisha	1	2	5		
Hart, Asahel	1	2	4		
Hotchkiss, Lemuel	3	2	6		
Hart, Stephen	2		3		
Hills, David	2	1	1		
Hollister, Stephen	1	1	2		
Hotchkiss, Ludwick	1	3	4		
Hart, Aaron	1	1	3		
Hollister, Thomas	1	1	4		
Judd, Isaac	1		3		
Judd, Anthony	2	2	3		
Judd, Job	2	2	2		
Judd, James	1	3	4		
Judd, Daniel	1	2	2		
Judd, Mary			1		
Judd, John	3	1	2		
North, Asher	1	1	4		
Kilbourn, Timothy	1	2	6		
Kilbourn, Seth	1	2	2		
Kilbourn, Martha			1		
Lee, Isaac	1		1	2	
Lee, Isaac, Jr.	2	2	4		
Langdon, John	2	2	4		
Lewis, Adonijah	2	1	2		
Lusk, John	2		3		
Lusk, Elata			3		
Lusk, David	1		1		
Lusk, Seth	1	2	3		
Lusk, David, Jr.	1	2	3		
Lincoln, Simeon	1	2	3		
Ludington, Daniel	1	1	1		
Ludington, Collins	1		2	1	
Lewis, James				1	
Mather, David	2		3		
Mather, Joseph, Jr.	2	1	7		
Merrit, William	1		1		
North, James	3	4	5		
Ossgood, Jeremiah H.	1	1	3		
Pratt, William	1	3	4		
Pratt, Andrew	1		3		
Penfield, Phinias	1	2	5		
Penfield, Nathaniel	2	2	3		
Roberts, Aaron	1		1		
Roberts, Aaron, Jr.	3		3		
Recor, Michael	1		2		
Rugg, Solomon	1		3		
Rice, Abigail			4		
Smally, John	3		5		
Smith, Joseph	2	1	2		
Stanley, Timothy	3	2	4		
Stanley, Gad	3	2	6		
Smith, Samuel	5		2		
Smith, Elnathan	1	2	6		
Smith, Elijah	1	3	2		
Stanley, Seth	1	6	7		
Stanley, Lott	2	2	8		
Stanley, Noah	1	1	2	1	
BERLIN TOWN—con.					
Smith, Joel	1	3	2		
Stanley, Ruth	1		2		
Steele, Ebenezer	1		3		
Steele, Ebenezer	1	2	3		
Stedman, Charles, Jr.	1	3	3		
Steele, Josiah	1	2	4		
Steele, William	1	2	2		
Steele, Selah	1	1	2		
Shipman, Samuel	2	3	4		
Stedman, John	1	3	3		
Stedman, Thomas	1	4	2		
Stiles, Robert	1	2	2		
Seymour, Lewis	1	1	1		
Sagden, Thomas	1	3	4		
Smith, John	1		3		
Woodruff, Seth	1				
Woodruff, Amos	1	2	5		
Woodford, Bissel	2	2	3		
Webster, Joshua	1	2	3		
Wright, Joseph	1	5	1		
Wright, Reuben	1	3	4		
White, Ezra	1	1	2		
Whaples, Elezur	1	1	2		
Woodruff, Gad	1	1	1		
Wetherill, David	2	2	1		
Wright, Ann			4		
Warner, Thomas	1		3		
Atwood, Josiah	1		3		
Allyn, John B.	4	2	6		
Andrus, Amos	2		1		
Brunson, Jesse	1	2	5		
Brunson, Elnathan	1	1	4		
Brunson, Asahel	2	1	2		
Brunson, Luke	2	2	6		
Barret, Robert	2		2		
Belden, John	1		2		
Belden, John, Jr.	1	1	2		
Brown, Thomas	1		1		
Brunson, Titus	3		3		
Brunson, Nathaniel	1		1		
Brunson, Ebenezer	1	4	5		
Bailey, Jonathan	1	1	1		
Brunson, John	1		1		
Brunson, Roger	2	1	1		
Barns, Jonathan	2	3	3	1	1
Ball, Oliver	1	2	2		
Brunson, Abigail			2		
Cowles, Asahel	1		4		
Cowels, Samuel	1	2	3		
Cowles, Jabez	1	3	2		
Cole, Mathew	2	1	3		
Cole, Selah	1	1	4		
Cowles, Noah	2	2	4		
Cole, Gideon	1	2	7		
Cole, Stephen	2	3	3		
Cole, Nathaniel	2	1	1		
Crofoot, Epraim, Jr.	1	2	1		
Cole, Rebecca	1	1	4		
Cowles, Selah	1	2	4		
Cole, John	3	2	3		
Cole, Seth	1		4		
Dickenson, Moses	3	2	6		
Dunham, Barnabus	3	2	5		
Gridley, Abel	1	3	4		
Gridley, Clement	1	1	3		
Bilbert, John	1		1		
Gridley, Amos	2	1	2		
Gridley, Selah	1	2	3		
Gridley, Roger	1	4	2		
Goodrich, Seth	2	1	3		
Gridley, Judath			1		
Howard, Edward	2		2		
Hart, Gideon	1	1	2		
Hart, Thomas, Jr.	1	1	3		
Hooker, Elijah	3	5	3		
Hooker, Samuel	1	1	3		
Hart, Selah	2		3	1	
Hart, Roger	1	1	4		
Hooker, William	1	2	3		
Hart, Hezekiah	3		4		
Hurlbut, Calven	2	3	5		
Hart, Oliver	1		1		
Hart, Mathew	2		1		
Hart, Mathew, Jr.	1		1		
Hurlbut, Isaac	1		1		
Hills, Abraham	1		3		
Hills, Gideon	1	1	6		
Hill, Josiah	1		2		
Hill, Jonathan	2		1		
Hosington, John	1		2		
Hosington, Salmon	1		2		
Hart, Salmon	2	1	1		
Hopkins, Caleb	4	2	4		
Hopkins, Benjamin	2	1	5		
BERLIN TOWN—con.					
Judd, Hezekiah	1	1	5		
Jones, George	1	2	1		
Judd, Gideon	2	3	4		
Judd, Amos	1	1	2		
Kelsey, William	1	3	4		
Langton, Jonathan	1	2	2		
Lee, Samuel	1	1	1		
Lee, Oren	3	1	2		
More, Roswell	1	2	1		
Mather, Joseph	1	1	2		
Mark, Miles	1		2		
Measureall, Christopher	1		1		
Norton, Stephen	2	2	2		
Norton, Roger	1		3		
Norton, Roger, Jr.	1	3	6		
Norton, Josiah	2	4	4		
Parkerson, William	2	1	3		
Peck, Isaac	1		5		
Percival, James	3	2	4		
Percival, James, Jr.	1		3		
Peck, Joseph	1	2	6		
Peck, Oliver	3	3	2		
Peck, Samuel	2	1	1		
Peck, Eldad	2	1	2		
Peck, Amos, Jr.	2	1	5		
Peck, Amos	2		1		
Persons, John	4		3		
Peck, Mathew	1		2		
Prior, Mary			3		
Root, Thomas	2		3		
Root, Noah	1	1	6		
Root, Job	2	2	3		
Root, Daniel	2	1	3		
Sexton, Simeon	1		3		
Seymour, Jonathan	2		4		
Stockin, John	1	2	2		
Squire, Solomon	1		2		
Stanley, Martha			1		
Stanley, Elijah	2	2	3		
Stanley, John	1	3	2		
Stanley, Oliver	1	1	3		
Scovill, Ezra	1	1	4		
Stockin, Luther	1	3	2		
Smith, Allyn	2	3	6		
Smith, Asaph	1	1	3		
Shepard, Isaiah	1		3		
Smith, Solomon	1		2		
Tryon, James	2	1	4		
Upson, Benoni	1	2	4		
Wells, Joseph	2		4		
Wells, Joseph, Jr.	1	2	3		
Wells, Sylvester	2	3	2		
Williams, Gideon	2	3	4		
Wyard, Lemuel	1	2	3		
Wilkinson, Amos	1	1	4		
Winchell, Hezekiah	1	1	2		
Winchell, Solomon	1	1	2		
Winchell, Stephen	1	1	3		
Warner, Daniel	1	1	4		
Williams, Samuel	2	2	4		
Winchell, William	1	1	1		
Winchell, Salmon	1	1	1		
Winchell, Roger	1	1	2		
Andrus, George	1		2		
Allis, Abel	1		2		
Brandier, Elishama	2	3	2		
Buckley, Selah	1	1	2		
Barns, Eli	4		2		
Buckley, Elias	2		2		
Buckley, Elias, Jr.	1	3	1		
Benton, Jonathan	1		1		
Benton, Jonathan, Jr.	1	4	3		
Buckley, Benjamin	2		1		
Buckley, Jonathan	1	1	4		
Buckley, Oliver	1	2	2		
Belden, Ashbel	1		1		
Buckley, David	2	2	2		
Crutenden, Jonathan	1		4		
Clark, Ezekiel	1		3		
Cook, William	2	1	3		
Cook, Lucius	1		1		
Crofoot, Ephraim	1		1		
Crofoot, Joseph	2		5		
Cornwall, Nathaniel	1	2	3		
Curtis, Giles	1	1	3		
Clark, David	2	4	3		
Danielson, Deborah			1		
D. Wolf, Stephen	1	1	5		
Deming, Moses	1	1	2	2	1
Deming, Moses, Jr.	1	1	2		
Deming, Seth	2	4	2		
Deming, Lardner	1	2	1		
Deming, John	1	1	2		
Deming, David	1	1	2		

HARTFORD COUNTY—Continued.

BERLIN TOWN—con.

NAME OF HEAD OF FAMILY.	Free white males of 16 years and upward, including heads of families.	Free white males under 16 years.	Free white females, including heads of families.	All other free persons.	Slaves.
Deming, Jacob	1		1		
Dunham, Solomon	2	1	3	1	
Dunham, Warner	2	1	2		
Dunham, Elishama	1	2	1		
Deming, Israel	1	1	5		
Dickenson, Nathaniel	1		1		
Dickenson, Nathaniel, Jr	1		2		
Dickinson, David	1	2	3		
Edwards, Josiah	2	2	2		
Fuller, Ephraim	1		1		
French, Daniel	1		5		
Flagg, Solomon	2	3	4		
Galpin, Peat	2		2		
Galpin, Benjamin	2	1	1		
Galpin, Thomas	2	1	5		
Galpin, Joseph	1	2	3		
Goodrich, John	1	1	2		
Gilbert, Seth	1	1	7		
Gilbert, Moses	2	1	2		
Gilbert Hooker	1	1	4		
Gilbert, Jonathan	2	1	2		
Gilbert, Jonathan, Jr	1	1	2		
Gilbert, Thomas	1		1		
Gilbert, Mary			2		
Goodrich, Elias	1		3		
Goodrich, Salmon	1	1	1		
Goodrich, Asahel	1		2		
Hart, Samuel	1	2	4		
Hart, John	2		2		
Hart, Levi	2	1	3		
Hollister, Ephraim	2	2	2		1
Hubbard, William, Jr	1	1	1		
Hart, Asahel	2		1		
Hollister, Solomon	1	2	4		
Hubbard, Samuel	2	1	3		
Hubbard, William	2	1	2		
Hubbard, Abijah	1	2	3		
Hubbard, Jonathan	3	2	2		
Hubbard, George	2	3	3		
Hart, Zacheriah	2	1	2		
Hosford, Amos	1		5		
Hurlbut, Raphael	2	3	4		
Hurlbut, James	1	1	1		
Hurbut, Sarah			2		
Johnson, Samuel	2	2	5		
Kelsey, John	2	2	2		
King, Lois	1	2	6		
Kelsey, Stephen	1	2	2		
Kelsey, Charles	2	2	4		
Kelsey, Ezekial	1		1		
Kelsey Ezekial, Jr	1	1	5		
Kelsey, Asahel	2	3	3		
Lee, John	1		2		
Lee, John, Jr	1	2	2		
Loveland, Elisha	3	2	3		
Mitchel, Joel	1		2		
Norton, Andrew	2	1	3		
Norton, Samuel	1	1	3		
Norton, Isaiah	1	1	1		
Norton, Elnathan	2	1	3		
Norton, Elnathan, Jr	1		2		
Norton, Solomon	2	2	1		
Norton, Samuel	1	2	4		
Norton, Jedidiah	1		1		
North, Isaac	2		2		
North, Seth	1	2	7		
North, Levi	2	1	2		
North, Abel	1		2		
North, Jedediah	1	1	4		
North, Simeon	2	2	1		
Nott, Charles	1		2		
Nott, Charles, Jr	1	3	3		
North, Stephen	1	1	1		
North, Joseph	1	3	3		
North, Samuel	1		2		
Porter, Isaac	1	3	4		
Porter, Samuel	2		4		
Porter, Samuel, 2d	2	2	4		
Porter, Samuel, 3d	2		2		
Porter, Abel	2		6		
Porter, Aaron	2	1	4		
Porter, Abijah	2	3	2		
Porter, Joseph, Jr	1	1	2		
Peck, Joseph	3	1	4		
Peck, Jesse	2		3		
Paterson, Edward	2	2	1		
Paterson, Sherbail	3		3		
Paterson, Elizabeth			1		
Presby, Charles	3		3		
Riley, Roger	1	4	4	1	
Root, John	1		3	1	
Root, Asahel	1		2		
Richards, Joseph	3	1	6		
Richarson, Zebulon	2		5		
Steele, David	2	1	2		

BERLIN TOWN—con.

NAME OF HEAD OF FAMILY.	Free white males of 16 years and upward, including heads of families.	Free white males under 16 years.	Free white females, including heads of families.	All other free persons.	Slaves.
Sage, Jedediah	1	2	4		
Sage, Solomon	1	1	3		
Sage, Zadock	2	1	4		
Sage, Solomon, Jr	1	2	5		
Squire, Elias	1	2	4		
Sage, Jonathan	1	1	2		
Sage, Abraham	1	1	5		
Savage, Selah	1	1	3		
Savage, Seth	1	2	4		
Savage, Elisha	1	1	4		
Savage, Elisha, Jr	1	1	1		
Smith, Wait	2	2	3		
Smith, Josiah	1		4		
Stanley, Seth	1		4		
Sanford, Silas	1	1	3		
Sage, Oliver	1	1	1		
Sage, David	1		1		
Wilcox, Israel	1	1	5		
Wilcox, Josiah	3	2	5		
Wilcox, Samuel	1	4	1		
Wilcox, Sarah			2		
Wilcox, Jacob	1	4	3		
Webster, David	2	1	2		
Webster, David, Jr	1	1	3		
Wright, Abraham	1	4	3	1	
Willcox, Stephen	2	2	4		
Woodruff, Roswell	1	2	1		
Woodruff, Selah	1				
Watson, John	1	3	2		
Wilton, Luther	1	1	1		
Tryall, William	2	1	4		
Porter, Eliphalet	1	1	3		
Buckley, Richard	2		3		
Bishop, Ebenezar	1		1		
Green, Perry	1	1	1		
Fenn, Nathan	2		4		

BRISTOL TOWN.

NAME OF HEAD OF FAMILY.	Free white males of 16 years and upward, including heads of families.	Free white males under 16 years.	Free white females, including heads of families.	All other free persons.	Slaves.
Lewis, Roger	2	3	4		
Lewis, Eli	3	1	8		
Lewis, Abel	1	1	7		
Buck, Deborah			1		
Lewis, Josiah	1		1		
Lewis, Roger	2	2	3		
Lewis, Josiah	1	2	4		
Lewis, Samuel	3	3	4		
Lewis, Mark	1	2	2		
Thompson, Isaiah	3	1	3		
Roberts, Daniel	1	2	1		
Hart, Thomas	1	1	3		
Gaylord, Elizur	2		2		
Gaylord, Joseph	1		1		
Gridley, Luke	3		6		
Newill, Samuel	3	2	4		
Upson, Asa	2		2		
Upson, Asa, Jr	2	1	2		
Newill, David	3		3		
Root, Theodore	2		6		
Adams, Elisha	1		1		
Johnson, Chandler	1	2	2		
Holt, Josiah	1	1	1		
Hungerford, Levi	1	2	5		
Linsley, Keturah	1	3	4		
Hart, Gilbert	1		2		
Rowe, Joseph	3	1	2		
Hendrick, Abel	1	2	2		
Hitcheox, Nathaniel	2		2		
Carrington, Lemuel	2	3	4		
Mathews, Nathaniel	2		3		
Mathews, Nathaniel, Jr	1		2		
Shelton, Isaac W	1	1	5		
Arnold, Tennur	1	4	2		
Ives, Amasa	1	6	3		
Adams, Samuel, Jr	1	3	3		
Mathews, John	2	1	7		
Andrus, Noah	1	1	3		
French, Elisha	1	2	1		
Hart, Ithurel	1	2	2		
Hungerford, Thomas	1	3	7		
Mathews, Caleb	4	2	3		
Hill, Miles	1		1		
Hill, Dan	1	3	4		
Ives, Lent	1	3	5		
Gaylord, Joseph, 2d	4	2	3		
Gaylord, William	1		4		
Hitchcock, Harvie	1		1		
Roberts, Joseph	1	2	6		
Driggs, Daniel	1		2		
Kate, Isaac	1		2		
Hill, Gaines	1		2		
Ledyard, Charles	1	2	5		
Fuller, Simeon	2		2		
Fuller, Edmund	1		1		
Scovil, Abijah	1	1	4		

BRISTOL TOWN—con.

NAME OF HEAD OF FAMILY.	Free white males of 16 years and upward, including heads of families.	Free white males under 16 years.	Free white females, including heads of families.	All other free persons.	Slaves.
Hall, Samuel	2		3		
Obverd, Thomas	1	1	6		
Jones, Nathaniel	1		1		
Conwell, Benjamin, Jr	1	2	3		
Johnson, Daniel, 2d	1	2	1		
Brooks, Samuel	2	1	1		
Brooks, Samuel, Jr	1		1		
Benham, Joel	2		3		
Benham, James	1	4	1		
Tompkins, Phillip	1		4		
Hotchkiss, Elijah	1	3	2		
Spring, Timothy	1	2	4		
Wheeler, William	1	1	4		
Broock, Abraham	3	2	2		
Brooks, Isaac	2	4	3		
Linsley, Jacob	3	3	2		
Leming, Judah	1	1	3		
Johnson, Daniel	2		2		
Rowe, Stephen	2	3	2		
Peck, Lament	2	2	3		
Hungerford, Jacob	1	4	2		
Hungerford, Benjm	1		1		
Gridley, Hezekiah	2		1		
Ives, Ammon	1	1	2		
Barns, Daniel	1	4	3		
Gridley, Asahel	1	2	2		
Cogswell, Robert	1		3		
Peck, Zebulon	2	3	7		
Johnson, Daniel, Jr	1	1	4		
Jearoms, Canuy	1	2	4		
Barns, Thomas	2	3	4		
Roberts, Seth	1	2	2		
Thompson, Reuben	2	1	4		
Roberts, Jabiz	1		3		
Stone, James	1	1	3		
Allyn, Samuel	2	3	2		
Allyn, Abel	1	2	4		
Johnson, Amos	3	2	2		
Bartholumew, Jacob	3	2	5		
Upson, Friman	2	2	5		
Peck, Lyssim	1		4		
Byington, Joseph	2	4	4		
Mix, Timothy	2	1	3		
Ives, Enos	1	2	5		
Rogers, Nehemiah	2		1		
Rogers, Lent	1	2	2		
Lownsbury, Samuel	1		3		
Upson, Saul	1		4		
Byington, Noah	1	1	3		
Lownsbury, David	1		3		
Jearoms, William, Jr	1	1	4		
Mix, Prime				8	
Jearoms, Benjamin	1	1	2		
Jearoms, Willm	2		2		2
Freman, Peter				3	
Freeman, Cuff				3	
Adams, Samuel	1		1		
Lee, John	1	1	1		
Lewis, David	2	2	2		
Botchford, Theophilus	1	3	4		
Haddfull, James	5	2	5		
Yate, Abel	2	1	8		
Yate, Thomas	1		1		
Barns, Josiah	1	2	1		
Peck, Susanna			1		
Hendrick, John	1	1	1		
Hendrick, Daniel	1		2		
Hart, Benjamin	1	1	5		
Jeroams, Zerubbabel	1	3	3		
Bartholomew, Abram	1		3		
Wilcox, Benjamin	1	3	2		
Wilcox, John	1		2		
Webster, Aaron	1	1	5		
Richard, William	1	3	3		
Andrus, Ezekiel	1	1	8		
Gladden, Jedidiah	1	1	3		
Palmer, Judah	1	2	2		
Heron, Samuel	1	7	5		
Churchill, Benjm	2	1	3		
Churchill, Ira	1		1		
Churchill, Samuel	1	1	2		
Bradley, Abel	1		5		
Marross, Elisha	2	1	4		
Marross, Elijah	1	1	1		
Fox, Elisha	2	1	3		
Rich, Thaddeus	1	4	3		
Hall, Phebe			3		
Root, Natha H	1	1	6		
Frisleer, Levi	1	1	2		
Barns, Amos	2	1	2		
Barns, Judah	2	4	7		
Jearoms, Thomas	3	1	1		
Johnson, Simeon	1	7	5		
Johnson, Abigail	1		2		
Ives, Reuben	2	2	2		

HARTFORD COUNTY—Continued.

BRISTOL TOWN—con.

NAME OF HEAD OF FAMILY.	Free white males of 16 years and upward, including heads of families.	Free white males under 16 years.	Free white females, including heads of families.	All other free persons.	Slaves.
Lee, James	2		2		
Andrus, Lament	1	3	3		
Woods, John	1		2		
Lee, Wm	2	2	4		
Dannaly, John	1		1		
Wilcox, Elijah	4		1		
Gaylord, David	2	5	3		
Gridley, Hezekiah, Jr	1	2	2		
Mitchel, Wm	1	4	4		
Linsley, Jonth	2	3	4		
Rich, Wm	1	3	5		
Norton, Aaron	1	5	2		
Rich, Jno	1	1	3		
Roberts, Wm	1	3	3		
Mitchel, Jotham	1	1	3		
Robert, Gideon	1	3	4		
Roberts, Amasa	1	2	4		
Hungerford, Timothy	1	3	4		
Gaylord, Jno	1	4	3		
Cowles, Mary	1	1	1		
Gaylord, Jesse	3		2		
Gaylord, Elijah	2		3		
Gaylord, Elam	1		1		
Gaylord, Samuel	1		2		
Adams, Luke	2	1	5		
Trusdale, Joel	1	1	2		
Bowen, Bezahil	1	1	4		
Gridley, Moses	1		2		
Murray, Thomas	1		1		
Norton, Isaac	1		1		
Norton, Isaac, Jr	1	2	4		
Norton, Joel	1	5	2		
Gaylord, Jesse, Jr	1	1	4		
Beckwith, Samuel	1	1	5		
Dutton, Oliver	1	2	3		
Peck, Josiah	1	1	4		
Woodruff, Ezekiel	1		3		
Hungerford, Jehiel	1	3	3		
Smith, Elihu	1	2	3		
Hodgekiss, James	1		3		
Newill, Abel	3	2	4		
Cowles, James	2		2		
Clark, Daniel	2	1	3		
Hungerford, Stephen	2		3		
Norton, Isaac, 3d	1	5	4		
Clark, Joel	1	3	2		
Hayford, Ira	1		4		
Jearom, Asahel	1		2		
Hayford, Joseph	2	3	3		
Carrington, Natha	1	1	2		
Mathews, Wm	1		1		
Smith, John	1	1	1		
Carrington, Jonathan	1	3	7		
Loury, Samuel	1	4	5		
Barnes, Reuben	1	6	1		
Barnes, David	1	1	1		
Smith, John	1	1	2		
Garret, Jno	1	3	3		
Warner, Natha	1	1	2		
Scott, Ebenezer	1	1	1		
Wolcott, Theodore	2	2	1		
Stone, Joseph	2	2	1		
Spencer, Jared	1		3		
Foot, Ichabod	2	3	1		
Bartholomew, Jacob, Jr	1		1		
Chapman, Sabethial	1	2	4		
Peck, Seth	2	1	2		
Cone, Jereh	1	2	5		
Griggs, Elliot	1		1		
Chapman, Josiah	1		1		
Chapman, Josiah, Jr	1		1		
Boardman, Moses	1		1		
Churchill, Asahel	1	5	1		
Linsley, Aaron	2	4	3		
Mix, Timothy	1		3		
Stone, Christopher	1	3	1		
Stone, Solomon	1		1		
Hamlin, Dan	1	1	3		
Clark, Jude	3	2	4		
Clark, Marshal	1		4		
Grifiths, Danel	2		1		
Gillet, Ellick	1		2		
Gillet, Reuben	1	1	3		
Andrus, Ichabod	1		1		
Beckwith, George	3	3	6		
Hosmer, John	1	1	2		
Calver, Samuel	2		4		
Taylor, Wait	1		6		
Woodruff, Wm	1	2	4		
Eaton, Daniel	2	1	1		
Belden, Benjamin	2		2		
Fuller, Jesse	1	2	5		
Roberts, Lamberton	1	2	3		
Belden, Isaac	2		3		
Dorman, Israel	1	2	2		
Moses, Reuben	1	1	3		
Moses, Othaniel	1	2	4		
Brown, Elisha	1	3	3		
Page, Titus	1	2	2		
Barnes, Elijah	1		1		
Andruss, Samu I	1	2	3		
Andruss, Samu	2	2	2		
Andruss, Han	1	1	1		
Moses, Othaniel	1		3		
Barnes, Lois	1		1		
Fuller, Ambros	1	1	5		
Woodruff, Seth	2		3		
Griswold, Jeremiah	2	3	5		
Humphrey, Jiles	2	1	5		
Smith, Phineas	1	3	5		
Hill, Freeman					2
Starks, Ichabod	1		1		
Starks, Ichabod, Jr		3	4		
Woodford, Josiah	1	2	2		
Cornwall, Benjamin	1	1	1		
Nearing, John	1	4	4		
Pettibone, Chancey	1	4	4		
Smith, Joseph	1	1	2		
Petibone, Thodore	1	4	4		
Fuller, John	2	1	3		
Hicox, Freeman	1	1	3		
Mills, Job	1	1	3		
Mills, Jno	2		1		
Mills, Noah	1		2		
Foot, Samuel	1		3		
Higley, Ebenezer	1		2		
Smith, Grove	2		4		
Steele, Ebizur	1		2		
Teil, Joseph	1	1	3		
Woodford, John	3		4		
Gridley, Thomas	1	2	3		
Way, Joseph	3		5		
Boardman, Ephraim	3	2	4		
Brunson, Stephen	1	2	5		
Farnsworth, Phillip H	1	2	1		
Hart, Ambrose	1	3	2		
Hart, Bliss	1	3	2		
Beckwith, Thomas	2	3	5		
Stone, Natha	1	5	3		
Warner, Samuel	1	3	4		
Warner, Nathaniel	1		1		
Warner, John	1		3		
Parsons, Moses	2		2		
Curtis, Ethan	1	3	5		
Curtis, Robert	1	1	2		
Perkins, Reuben	2	1	4		
Perkins, Reuben, Jr	1		4		
Peck, Caleb	1	2	3		
Marks, David	1	2	2		
Wilmut, Thomas	1	4	2		
Cornwall, Cornilius	1	2	6		
Hamlin, Ebenezer	1		3		
Hamlin, Mark	2	1	2		
Miller, Jonth	1	1	5		
Hart, Simeon, Jr	1	1	2		
Hart, Simeon	1		1		
Hart, Marcus	1		2		
Friston, Zebulon	2	1	4		
Hotchkiss, Stephen	1		1		
Taylor, Elezur	2		1		
Driggs, Bartholomew	3	4	2		
Elton, Wm	1	3	2		
Spring, Ebenezer	1	1			
Hotchkiss, Simeon	1	2	2		
Brockway, Simeon	1	1	1		
Frisbey, Daniel	1		2		
Brockway, Samuel	1		1		
Brockway, Samuel	3	2	2		
Gillett, Jeremiah	1		2		
Hart, Noadiah	2		2		
Bristo (Negro)				1	
Hills, John	1	1	2		
Humphreys, Solomon	2	3	3		
Newton, Mathew	3	5	4		
Burdock, Joshua	1	1	1		
Burdock, Robert	2	2	5		
Willcox, Elias	1	3	3		
Crumby, Samuel	1	4	3		
Clark, Asa	1	1	3		
Davis, Roger	1		2		
Covey, David	1	3	2		
Hitchcock, Joel	1	1	2		
Hitchcock, Ashbel	1	1	2		
Woodruff, Timothy	2	1	3		
Woodruff, Timothy, Jr	1		1		
Stilman, Amos	1	3	4		
Neff, Arnold	2		1		
Palmeter, Jonth	1	1	1		
Palmeter, Benjamin	1				
Covey, Jared	1	2	4		
Covey, Elisha	1	1	3		
Covey, Silus	1		1		
Covey, Elijah	1		1		
Tubbs, Elisha	1		1		
Hotchkiss, Samuel	1	3	4		
Crandal, John	1	1	5		
Lewis, John	1		2		
Wilcox, John	1	1	1		
Davis, Jonth	2	3	4		
Pettibone, Aexander	1		2		
Hemecage, Abraham	1	4	5		
Bacon, Joseph	2		1		
Bacon, Roswell	1	1	1		
Lewis, Benjamin	1	1	8		
Bacon, Moses	1	1	6		
Rust, Alone	1		1		
Doad, Ezra	2	1	3		
Cleveland, Ezra	1	2	4		
Rust, Amos	1	2	2		
Covil, Ebenezer	1	2	2		
Lewis, Stephen	2		4		
Doad, Amos	1	1	4		
Doad, Stephen	1	3	1		
Willcox, Stephen	1	1	3		
Doad, Jesse	1	3	4		
Stephens, Joshua	2	1	6		
Wiard, Seth	2	1	6		
Woodruff, Asa	1		3		
West, Hezekiah	1	5	2		
Yate, Ezra	3	3	2		
Lewis, Elisha	1	1	1		
Lewis, Samuel	1	1	2		
Main, Ezekiel	1	1	2		
Lewis, Eno	1	1	3		
Burdock, Lewis	2	3	2		
Hotchkiss, Stephen, Jr	2	1	5		
Tubbs, Elisha	1		1		
Bunnel, Natha	1	1	2		
Benham, Ebenezer	2	1	1		
Webster, Justus	2		6		
Webster, Justus, Jr	1		1		
Tharp, Linus	1	2	3		
Park, John	2	2	4		
Robert, Freelove	1	2	1		
Bird, John	1		4		
Leming, David	1	1	3		
Bird, Ephraim	2		2		
Bunel, Daniel, Jr	1	1	2		
Smith, Samuel, Jr	1		2		
Smith, Samuel	2		8		
Smith, Joseph	2		1		
Turner, Ephraim	1	2	3		
Smith, Joseph, Jr	1	1	1		
Bellam, Lyman	1	2	2		
Smith, Amos	1	1	2		
Orsborn, Joseph	2	1	1		
Clark, Abel	1		3		
Roberts, David	1	1	6		
Robert, Martin	1		1		
Roberts, Benjamin	1	1	3		
Roberts, Jacob	1		2		
Little, Walter	1		1		
Bacon, Andrew	3	2	2		
Roberts, Jacob, Jr	1	4	4		
Clark, Dimon	1		3		
Bunnel, Bela	2		2		
Curtis, Simeon	1	1	4		
Frisbee, Hooker	1	1	4		
Brooks, Chancey	1	1	3		
Lawry, John	3	1	5		
Stedman, Lemuel	3	1	5		
Spencer, Joseph	1	1	2		
Brooks, Thomas	2	1	5		
Bunnel, Titus	2	1	2		
Lankton, Joseph	2	5	3		
Johnson, Asahel	2	3	6		
Bailey, Nathan	1	3	2		
Marks, Edward	1	1	3		
Marks, Zachariah	1	1	3		
Bunnel, Daniel	1	2	4		
Sedgwick, Samuel	1	2	3		
Phelps, Joshua	2	2	2		
Phelps, Joshua, Jr	1		2		
Johnson, Enock	1	2	6		
Whitmore, Jabez	4	3	4		
Warner, Samuel	1		2		
Warner, Samuel, Jr	1	3	3		
Brock, Phillis	1		2		
Meacum, Jeremiah	1		3		
Gaylord, Jos, Jr	1	5	2		
Barnes, Wise	1		2		
Barnes, Jonath	1		1		
Ferry, Joshua	1	1	6		
Winston, John	1	1	1		

HARTFORD COUNTY—Continued.

NAME OF HEAD OF FAMILY.	Free white males of 16 years and upward, including heads of families.	Free white males under 16 years.	Free white females, including heads of families.	All other free persons.	Slaves.
BRISTOL TOWN—con.					
Hart, Ard	1	1	2		
Hart, Lemuel	1	1	3		
Hart, Jude	1		1		
Hart, Amos	1	2	2		
Humphrey, Ozias	1	3	6		
EAST HARTFORD TOWN.					
Williams, Eliphalet	1	1	5		1
Pitkin, Daniel	4	2	3		1
Burnham, Augustus	2	2	2		
Wollcott, Roger	3		3	2	
Burnham, George	2	2	2		
Burnham, Eleazer	1	3	1		
Burnham, Thomas	1	1	1		
William, Joshua	3		5		
Williams, Jacob	4	2	4		
Anderson, Asahel	1		2		
Gilman, George	1	3	2		
Goodwin, Levi	2	1	3		
Cowles, Timothy	2	1	2		
Cowles, William	2		4		
Pitkin, Joshua	5	1	2		1
Pitkin, Nathaniel	1	2	3		
Pitkin, David	1	1	2		
Pitkin, Joseph	1		2		
Olmsted, Nathaniel	2	2	3		
Cowles, Eleazer	4	1	2		
Cowles, Ashbel	1	2	4		
Fowler, John	1		1		
Pitkin, William	2		4		
Pitkin, Ashbel	1	1	4		
Pitkin, George, Senr	2		2		5
Pitkin, Epaphras	4	1	3		1
Olmsted, William	2	1	4		
Olmsted, Stephen	1		1		
Elmore, Aaron	1	1	2		
Griswold, Shubael	3	2	1		
Stanly, Theodore	1	2	3		
Olmsted, Ashbel	2	2	5		
Olmstead, Ashbel, Jr	1	2	1		
Olmsted, George	3		4		
Olmsted, Asahel	2	2	5		
Olmsted, Thaddeus	2		2		
Olmsted, Samuel	3		5		
Olmsted, Samuel, Jr	1		1		
Cowles, Martha (Wid.)	2	1	6		
Pitkin, Elisha, Jr	1	3	2		2
Benjamin, James	2	1	3		
Pitkin, John	2	1	2		
Wyles, John	1	1	2		
Woodbridge, Samuel	5		2		
Woodbridge, Russell	1		2		
Benjamin, Jonathan	1	2	2		
Norton, Selah	1	1	7		
Meackens, Joseph	2		4		2
Merrow, Nathan	1	2	2		
Pitkin, Timothy	1		1		2
Flagg, Samuel	4	1	2		1
Holmes, John	1		2		
Ford, Mathew	1	2	3		
Woodbridge, Ward	2	1	3		
Porter, John	1	1	2		
Reynolds, John	2	3	4		
Burnham, Stephen	1	1	3		
Willcox, Jiles	1	1	5		
Buckland, Mary			3		
White, Lemuel	1	1			
Burnham, Moses	2		2		
Pitkin, Roger	2		2		
Pitkin, Isaac	1		1		
Selby, David M	1		1		
Blancherd, Eunice		1	3		
Hill, Solomon	2	2	6		
Pitkin, Jonathan	3	2	5		
Goodwin, John	2	3	4		
Goodwin, Joseph	1	3	4		
Bement, Makens	2	5	3		
Burnham, Theodore	1	1	1		
Arnold, Mary			2		
Williams, Elisha	1	3	6		
Treat, Theodore	1	2	2		
Burnham, Freeman	1		3		
Taylor, Giles	1	1	1		
Cotton, David	1	1	3		
Cotton, Samuel	4		3		
Burnham, Rhoderic	3	2	2		
Cheney, Benjamin	1		1		
Case, Thomas	2	1	7		
Chapman, William	1	2	7		
Gilman, Jonah	4		4		
Gilman, Nathaniel	2	1	3		
Kilbourn, Ashbel	1	3	1		
Gilman, Elizabeth	1		1		
Gilman, David	1		3		
EAST HARTFORD TOWN—continued.					
Williams, Daniel	1		2		
Williams, Phineas	1		1		
Williams, John	3	2	3		
Evens, Benoni	1	4	4		
Burr, Jonathan	2		1		
Burnham, Timothy	4		3		
Burnham, Samuel	1	2	1		
Burnham, Daniel	5	1	2		
Anderson, Timothy	1	1	3		
Burnham, Zenas	1	3	4		
Belden, Nathan	3	1	3		
Sage, John	2	2	1		
Olmsted, Aaron	1	2	5		
Olmsted, Jonathan	2	3	3		
Rippenier, Christopher	1		5		
Brown, William	1		1		
Rippenier, Asahel	1		3		
Olmsted, Epaphras	1		3		
Olmsted, Benjamin	1	2	3		
Williams, Edward	2		3		
Stanley, Jonathan	2	2	2		
Firbbs, Ichabod	2	1	4		
Kendall, John	1	1	3		
Keeney, Benjamin	1	2	4		
Norton, Samuel	1	2	3		
Roberts, Nathaniel	1	3	4		
Roberts, William	1	2			
Butler, Moses	2	3	2		
Hills, Timothy	2		1		
Skinner, John	1		3		
Tinker, Jonathan	2	2	2		
Pitkin, Elisha	6	2	1		5
Roberts, George	1	1	5		
Hurlbut, Samuel	1	1	3		
Pitkin, Thodore	1	1	1		2
Hurlbut, John	2	2	5		
Burnham, Aaron	1	4	6		
Olmsted, Michael	1		1		
Burnham, Jerusha		1	5		
Hurlbut, Joseph	3	2	4		
Reynolds, Charles	2		3		
Huntington, Silas	2	1	5		
Crosby, David	1	2	2		
Fowler, Samuel	2		3		
Bement, Edmund	1		2		
Jincks, Thankfull			1		
Bidwell, Eodias	1	2	2		
Bidwell, Ashbel	1	1	2		
Bidwell, Joseph	3	2	4		
Benton, Elisha	1		1		
Bidwell, Asenath		1	3		
Bidwell, Mary		1	3		
Bellows, Isaac	1		1		
Bidwell, Elisha	2	3	5		
Williams, Abraham	4	1	5		
Hays, John	3	3	4		
Gilman, Oliver	2	1	4		
Case, Richard	1	1	4		
Spencer, Gideon, Jr	3	2	6		
Lyman, William	1	4	3		
Kennedy, John	1		3		
Spencer, Gideon	2		2		
Spencer, John	2	4	4		
Kennedy, Samuel	2		6		
Pratt, Moses	2		4		
Roberts, Eias	2	1	9		
Roberts, Stephen	1	3	1		
Dallaby, Samuel	1	2	2		
Forbs, Thomas	1	1	6		
Forbs, Aaron	2	5	9		
Forbs, Timothy	2	3	6		
Forbs, Elijah	1	3	4		
Abby, Stephen	5		4		
Easton, Silas	1	2	6		
Corning, William	3	1	4		
Eaton, Justus	3		1		
Miller, Amaziah	1	2	5		
Abbey, Stephen, Jr	2		2		
Chandler, Jonathan	1	4	1		
Church, Samuel	3	3	1		
Bidwell, John	3	2	5		
Gulliver, Thomas	1	1	1		
Taylor, John	3	2	4		
Bidwell, Jonathan	2	1	6		
Evens, Elisha	1	1	2		
Abbey, Jeduthan	1	1	4		
Wallis, James	2	1	4		
Little, David	2	1	5		
Deming, Lemuel, Jr	1	2	2		
Warren, John	3		2		
Warren, Daniel	2		5		
Warren, Edward	1	3	3		
Wadsworth, Jerusha			2		
Kilbourn, Russell	3	2	6		
Easton, James	2	2	6		
EAST HARTFORD TOWN—continued.					
Deming, David	1	3	5		
Deming, Israel	1	4	2		
Wyles, Thomas	1	1	5		
Jutson, Roswell	2		6		
Risley, Benjamin	4		5		
Deming, Lemuel	1		5		
Williams, Timothy	3	1	6		
Risley, John, Jr	1	2	4		
Risley, John	2	1	5		
Williams, Joseph	4	4	5		
Roberts, Joseph	5	1	3		
Firbbs, Edward	2	1	2		
Bidwell, Samuel	3		7		
Treat, Mathias	2	1	7		
Ensign, Moses	1	1	1		
Hills, Epaphras	1	2	4		
Williams, Solomon	2		2		
Wells, Jonathan	3		4		
Wells, John, Jr	1	4	2		
Fox, Joneal	1	1	2		
Wells, John	4		4		
Butler, John	1	4	3		
Humphreys, William	1	2	2		
Smith, Eldad	4	3	6		
Risley, Richard, Jr	1	1	3		
Fox, Veniah	1	1	3		
Warren, Elisha	1		2		
Risley, Richard	2	1	3		
Risley, Eli	1	1	4		
Wyles, David	1		6		
Treat, Jonathan	1		2		
Hills, Jonathan	2		2		2
Hills, David	4		3		
Hills, Elisha	1	3	3		
Hills, Jonathan, 2d	1		2		
Hills, Caleb	1	1	2		
Hills, Mabel	1		4		3
Hills, Joseph	2		2		
Allyn, Othnial	1		2		
Smith, Joseph	1		2		
Risley, Jeremiah	1	1	2		
Wadsworth, Samuel	1	1	5		
Little, Deodat	3	3	2		
Warren, Ashbel	1	1	1		
Buckley, Hannah	1		5		
Smith, Samuel	2		4		
Porter, Moses	1		3		
Buckland, Charles	1	3	3		
Roberts, Jonathan	2		3		
Pratt, Russell	2	1	4		
Abbey, Nehemiah	1	2	5		
Chandler, Samuel	3	2	4		
Buckland, Daniel	1	4	3		
Spencer, John	1		4		
Roberts, David	1		1		
Smith, Nehemiah	1	2	1		
Smith, Moses	4	1	2		
Pratt, Eliab	3		2		
Risley, Joshua	3	2	6		
Hills, William	1	2	8		
Risley, Nehemiah	1	3	1		
Risley, Levi	1		1		
Vibbert, Jesse	1	2	3		
Vibbert, John	1	1	1		
Vibbert, James	2		1		
Risley, Stephen	2	3	6		
Wadsworth, William	2	4	3		
Arnold, Joseph	1	1	3		
Risley, George	1	2	2		
Easton, Samuel	1	2	1		
Firbs, Moses	2	1	6		
Treat, Richard	1	1	5		
Kentfield, John	1	3	5		
Phillips, John	2		5		
Porter, Nathan	1	2	3		
Ocolow (Negro)				3	
Kilbourn, Stephen	1	2	5		
Porter, John	2		3		
Brewer, Daniel	1	3	3		
Smith, John	2	3	3		
Hall, Timothy	1	2	4		
Jones, David	2		5		
Brainard, Ezra	1	1	3		
Porter, Job	2	2	5		
Keeney, Joseph	2	2	2		
Stebbin, Jonathan	1	1	2		
Porter, Isaac	1		3		
Risley, George, 2d	1		2		
Porter, Roger	3		2		
Porter, Benjamin	2	1	3		
Porter, William	1	1	3		
Porter, Elijah	1	2	2		
Fox, Ephraim	3		5		
Treat, Stephen	1	1	2		
Roberts, John	1	3	3		

HARTFORD COUNTY—Continued.

NAME OF HEAD OF FAMILY.	Free white males of 16 years and upward, including heads of families.	Free white males under 16 years.	Free white females, including heads of families.	All other free persons.	Slaves.
EAST HARTFORD TOWN—continued.					
Roberts, Samuel	1	2	2		
Roberts, Daniel	1	2	2		
Roberts, Benjamin	2	2	6		
Roberts, Ashbel	1	2	2		
Porter, Stephen	1	3	4		
Fox, Ephraim, Jr	1	2	1		
Wadsworth, Thomas	7	1	3		
Hills, Ashbell	3	3	2		
Bills, John	1	1	4		
Risley, Moses	1	1	6		
Ritter, Daniel	1	3	4		
Cowles, Samuel	1	2	2		
Loomis, Israel	1	1	3		
Risley, Jonathan	2	3	2		
Risley, Nathaniel	1	2	3		
Arnold, Samuel	4	2	3		
Hills, Ebenezer	1	4	4		
Hills, Eliphalet	1	2	4		
Hills, Elijah	1	4	1		
Hills, Russell, 1st	1	2	1		
Hills, Russell, 2d	1	2	4		
Deming, Elijah	1	1	1		
Burnham, David	2		4		
Burnham, Oliver	1	5	2		
Tryon, Aaron	1	1	5		
Gilman, Solomon, Jr	1	3	2		
Roberts, Timothy	3	2	5		
Gilman, Solomon	3	3	5		
Buckland, Aaron	2		5		
Chandler, Daniel	3		3		
Cooley, Chancy	1	1	1		
Buckland, Elisha	2	2	2		
Simons, Samuel	1	1	7		
Loomis, Solomon	1	1	3		
Evens, Samuel	1		1		
Evens, Samuel, Jr	1	2	2		
Fletcher, William	1	1	1		
Evens, David	2	2	2		
Skinner, Elias	1	1	1		
Bissell, Ozias	1	4	4		
Hammon, Jason	2	1	2		
Keeney, George	3	2	3		
Merryfield, Jonathan	1	1	5		
Evans, Moses	1	2	2		
Anderson, William	1				
Stibbins, Enos	4	3	4		
Dewy, Nathaniel	1	1	2		
Clark, Seth	1		1		
Brewer, Daniel	2		2		
Stedman, Nathan	1	2	4		
Stedman, Timothy	2	4	3		
Stedman, Comfort		4	3		
McKee, Elijah	1	1	2		
Corning, Malaca	2	1	2		
Olcott, Samuel	2	1	3		
Keeney, Alexander	1	2	4		
McKee, Joseph	3	1	3		
McKee, Robert	1	1	2		
McKee, Andrew	1	1	4		
McKee, Appleton	1	2	1		
McKee, Robert, Jr	1	2	4		
Webster, Eleazer	1	1	3		
McKee, Eleazer	1		2		
Olcott, Nathaniel	2		4		1
Webster, Ephraim	2	6	1		
Simons, Samuel	2	2	6		
Teal, John	1	3	2		
Spencer, Thomas, Jr	3	1	1		
Brewer, Daniel	1	1	3		
Spencer, Thomas	4		3		
Marsh, Allyn	1	2	6		
Marsh, Daniel	2		5		2
Cadwell, Reuben	1		2		
Olds, John	1		3		
Olds, John, Jr	2	2	3		
Wright, Aaron	3	3	5		
Case, David	3	1	3		
Case, David, Jr	1		2		
Case, Joseph	1		9		
Case, Ashbel	1		2		
Simons, John	2	3	5		
Simons, Israel	1	2	3		
Benton, Joseph	2	1	4		
Simons, Joseph	1	1	9		
Cadwell, John	1	3	5		
Cadwell, David	1	1	2		
Cadwell, Mathew	1		3		
Fox, Roswell	1	2	6		
Hills, Silus	1	1	5		
Hills, Amos	4	4	4		
Vibbert, James	3	3	4		
Loomis, Jonah	1	2	6		
Vibbert, David	1	2	4		
Glason, Moses	1	2	4		
Rich, Peter	1	1	2		
Griswold, George	1	1	4		
EAST HARTFORD TOWN—continued.					
McKee, Nathaniel	3	2	6		
Buckland, Peter	1	1	2		
Cheney, Timothy, Jr	1	2	1		
Bishop, Eleazer	1	1	2		
Deming, Benjamin	1	1	2		
McKee, John	1		5		
Bryant, Timothy	1		6		
Dewy, Nathaniel	3		4		
Chase, Gidiliah	1		1		
Brown, Benjamin	2	2	5		
Bartlet, Elizabeth	1	1	2		
Willson, Zilpah	1	1	3		
Wetherby, Seth	2	1	8		
State, Thomas	2		2		
Hills, Joshua	1	2	2		
Hills, Levi	1	4	1		
Hills, Nathan	1	1	3		
Hills, Reuben	1	2	2		
Hubbard, Jeremiah	4	2	5		
Treat, Henry	2	3	2		
Strickland, Benjamin	1	2	4		
Keeney, Thomas	9	3	6		
Keeney, Eleazer	3	1	4		
Keeney, Benjamin	2	1	5		
Keeney, Joseph	3	1	4		
Keeney, Simon	1		2		
Keeney, Simon, Jr	2	2	4		
Keeney, John	3	5	2		
Keeney, Richard	3	1	2		
Keeney, David, 2d	1	2	4		
Hale, Isaac	1	2	4		
Webster, Jonathan	1	1	2		
Hollister, Josiah	1	4	2		
Bidwell, Stephen	1		2		
Andrus, Ardon	1		2		
Woodruff, Gurdin	1	2	4		
Couch, Stephen	1	1	6		
Peck, Elijah	2	2	3		
Peck, Elijah, Jr	1	5	2		
Lucus, John	1	3	4		
Couch, John	3	4	2		
Minor, Christopher	2		2		
Wyllys, John	3		1		
Risley, Oliver	1		5		
Wallis, John	2	2	5		
Keeney, Isaac	2	1	4		
Dart, William	2		2		
Fogarson, Elizabeth		4	5		
Keeney, Elijah	1	1	6		
Skinner, Augustus	1	1	1		
Webster, Samuel	1	2	5		
Hollister, James	4	4	4		
Bidwell, Stephen	1		2		
Bidwell, Zebulon	1	3	3		
Bidwell, David	1		4		
Wallis, John	2	1	4		
Brown, Benjamin, Jr	1	2	1		
Peck, Daniel	1		5		
Keeney, Alexander	2		2		
Pitkin, Richard, Jr	3	2	5		
Pitkin, Richard	3	1	3		
Cheeney, Timothy	2		5		
Cheeney, Silus	2	1	2		
Phelps, Benajah	1	2	5		
Pitkin, Eleazer	1	1	2		
Man, Abeather	2	1	3		
Keeney, David	1	1	5		
Porter, James	1	2	5		
Skinner, Elias	1	3	4		
Man, Benjamin	1		1		
Cone, Russell	1	1	2		
Bryant, Ebenezer	2	1	4		
Evens, Ezekiel	1	2	1		
Cheeney, Asahel	2	2	2		
Smith, Ithemar	1	2	3		
Cone, Stephen	3	1	4		
Woodbridge, Deodat	1	3	5	1	
Clark, Caty	2		4		
Buck, George	1	1	3		
Skinner, Jonathan	1	1	3		
Swetland, Joseph	2		1		
Swetland, Benjamin	2		1		
Jones, John	2	2	2		
Lyman, Joseph	4	4	2		
Flint, John	1	4	2		
Flint, Joshua	2	3	4		
Swetland, Daniel	2	1	6		
Dewy, Thomas	1	4	4		
Kilbourn, Benjamin	2	1	3		
Benjamin, Samuel	2	2	3		
Millard, Andrew	1	3	3		
Deming, David	3		7		
Bissell, Russell	1	3	2		
Bishop, Samuel	1	4	1		
Little, William	1	3	2		
Landpir, David	1		2		
EAST HARTFORD TOWN—continued.					
Landpire, Abner	1	2	5		
Dart, Joseph	1		5	1	
Dart, Sarah			2		
Birdwell, Ozeas	1	3	5		
EAST WINDSOR TOWN.					
Burnham, Hannah		2	2		
Wood, Robert	2		2		
Wood, John	1		1		
Moseley, Timothy	1	3	2	1	
Bancroft, Abner	2		2		
Wolcott, Josiah	1		2		
Anderson, George	1		2		
Gillet, Benjamin	1	2	7		
Anderson, John	1		1		
Moreton, Abner	1		2		
Morton, Isaac	1	2	1		
Morton, William	1		2		
Chase, Berrey	1	2	3		
Rockwell, Joab	1		1		
Elmore, Timothy	1	1	4		
Elmore, Eliphalet	2	2	4		
Elmore, Stephen	1		3		
Elmore, Roswell	1	4	4		
Mills, Roswell	1	2	1		
Mills, Augustus	1	1	3		
Sutton, William	1		2		
Wood, Obediah	1	3	2		
Burr, Isaac	1	1	2		
Wood, James	1	3	2		
Anderson, John, Jr	1	3	4		
Kirkum, Philomon	1		2		
Holman, Ebenezar	2	2	4		
Elmore, Elizabeth		1	2		
Bancroft, Samuel	3	2	6		
King, Theodore	1	1	2		
Filley, Silvanus	1		1		
Diggins, Joseph	2		1		1
Wolcott, Permenis	2	1	3		
Fitch, Augustus	2		2		
Fitch, John F	1	1	2		
Elmore, Joseph	1	3	2		
Bancroft, Thomas	2	1	3		
Loomiss, Ezekiel	2	1	2		
Wolcott, Roger	2	1	2	1	
Daniels, Stephen	3		2		
Treat, Samuel	1	2	5	1	
Wolcott, Samuel	5	2	6		
Gibbs, Stephen	1	1	6		
Tudor, Samuel	2		3	1	
Tudor, Elihu	1	2	6		1
Evans, Josiah	1	3	1		
Webb, Abigail	2		3		
Avery, Samuel	2	1	4		
Walcott, William	3		2		
Loomiss, Giles	3	2	4		
Loomiss, Oliver	2	1	5		
Porter, Nathaniel, Jr	2	1	7		
Porter, Hezekiah	1		4		
Porter, Wareham	2		4		
McClure, Revd David	3	1	4		
Rockwell, Jemima			2		
Burnham, Abner	2	4	2		
Heyden, Daniel	4		4		
Stoughton, Russell	1		1		
Stoughton, William	1	1	1		
Wells, Esther			2		
King, Alexander	3	4	2		
Loomiss, John	1		3		
Loomiss, Luke	4		2		
Chapin, Eliphalet	3	1	5		
Read, Ebenezer	2	3	4		
Read, Justus	1		4		
Bidwell, Ephraim	1	2	3		
Wolcott, Benjamin	2	3	5		
Newbury, Joseph	3		2		
Newbury, John	1	2	3		
Beamont, Jona	1	1	3		
Hills, Anna			3		
Loomiss, Sarah			3		
Porter, Naomi		1	3		
Rockwell, Samuel	1	3	4		
Rockwell, David	1	3	2		
Newbury, Benjamin	1		2		
Newbury, Amasa	1	3	2		
Newbury, Chancey	1	3	4		
Skinner, Abijah	1		2		
Hosmer, Joseph	5	2	4		
Skinner, Benjamin	2	3	2		
Skinner, Azariah	1		2		
Phelps, Jerejah	3		1		
Phelps, Daniel	1		1		
Baxter, Frances, Jr	1	1	1		
Olcott, Asahael	1	1	4		
Olcott, Benoni	1		3		

HARTFORD COUNTY—Continued.

EAST WINDSOR TOWN—continued.

NAME OF HEAD OF FAMILY.	Free white males of 16 years and upward, including heads of families.	Free white males under 16 years.	Free white females, including heads of families.	All other free persons.	Slaves.
Olcott, Eli	1	1	2		
Wolcott, Erastus, Jr	1	2	2		
Wolcott, Honererable Erastus	3		1		
Wolcott, Albertus	1	1	4		
Loomiss, Benajah	1	1	4		
Wolcott, Ephraim	3		3		
Moore, Eli	1		3		
Moore, Wareham	1	4	3		
Sherman, Nathaniel	1	1	2		
Rockwell, William	3	1	5		
Drake, Moses	1		1		
Stroughton, Alexander	1	2	2		
Stoughton, Oliver	2		5		
Bliss, Stoughton	1	2	4		
Rockwell, Charles	1	1	4		
Flint, Archelaus	2	3	1		
Rockwell, Nathaniel	2	3	4		
Terry, Samuel	3	2	4		
Gilman, Benjamin	2		3		
Higley, Nathan	4	1	3		
Drake, Abiel	1	1	3		
Stoughton, Augustus	1	2	2		
Strong, Timothy	2	2	2		
Strong, Nathaniel	1		2		
Strong, Nathaniel, Jr	2	2	1		
Strong, John	1		1		
Strong, John	1	2	2		
Drake, David	1		1		
Preston, Samuel	1		1	1	
Sadd, Mathew	1		4		
Drake, Amasa	1	1	3		
Cook, Benjamin	4		2	1	
Drake, Reuben	3		2		
Grant, Ebenezer	1		1		
Grant, Roswell	3	1	2		
Grant, Aaron	2	1	3		
Grant, Azariah	1	1	6		
Virstille, William		1	3	1	
Foster, Oliver	1		3		
Loomiss, Amasa, Jr	1	1	3		
Bowers, Azel	1		1		
Mather, Charles	3	1	4		1
Crosby, Simon	1	3	2		
Bissell, Ebenezer	2	1	3		
Smith, John	1	1	4		
Dickerson, Obediah	2	3	5		
Grant, Aaron, Jr	1	1	3		
Grant, Reuben	1	1	1		
Grant, Benjamin	1		1		
Wells, Noah	3	1	3		
Wells, Mosses	2		1		
Day, Justus	1		2		
Day, Oliver	1	1	2		
Bissell, Epaphras	2	1	2	1	
Bissell, Aaron	3	1	3		
Bissell, Noah	2	2	5		
Watson, John	3	1	5	1	1
Bissell, Elisha	1	2	2		
May, Charles	2		2		
Burnap, Daniel	4		2		
Edwards, Rhodolfus	1		2		
Strickland, Richard	3		1		
Webster, Samuel	3		3		
Bissell, David	5		3		
Fenton, Francis	1	2	4		
Wolcott, Elezur	1		1		
Bissell, Jonathan	1	2	3		
Bissell, Justus	1	1	3		
Loomis, Elihu	1		1		
Moore, Nathaniel	1	1	3		
Morton, Elinor	1	1	1		
Smith, Samuel	1		4		
Wood, Ruth					
Bliss, Ellis	2		3		
Bliss, Anna			1		
Gaylord, Charles	1	3	1		
Mitchell, Oliver				5	
Chalke, William	1		3		
Stoughton, Elijah	2	1	4		
Gaylord, Abiel	1	6	5		
Bissell, William	2		3		
Bissell, Roswold	1	2	3		
Bissell, Nathaniel	1		1		
Cram, John	1	4	3		
Cahoon, Matha			3		
Elsworth, Joel	1		4		
Pelton, Nathan	2	2	3		
Pelton, Nathan, Jr	1		1		
Baxter, Levi	1	2	1		
Elsworth, Frederic	2	1	3		
Carpenter, Daniel	1	2	2		
Watson, Ebenezer, Jr	2	4	2		
French, John	1		2		
French, John, Jr	1	2	3		
Pinney, Jonª	1	1	2		
Putnam, David	3		1		
Watson, Robert	2	1	7		
Thompson, Alexander	1	2	1		
Bullard, Josiah	1	1	2		
Watson, Ebenezar	1		4		
Stoughton, Lemuel	5		6		
Watson, Sarah			4		
Watson, Samuel	2	3	1		
Wells, Lampson	2	1	3		
Shaw, David	1		8		
Phelps, Daniel	1		3		
Phelps, Obadiah	1				
Skinner, Samuel	1	3	3		
Richardson, Edatha		1	3		
Munsell, Martin	1	2	1		
Trumbull, David	2	4	2		
Skinner, Mary	1		1		
Clark, Oliver	1		1		
Baxter, Francis	2	1	3		
Stiles, Noah	2		1		
Prior, Joel	2	4	4		
Orsborn, Thomas	1	3	4		
McNight, Abigail			2		
Orsborn, Ezra	1	2	2		
Orsborn, Zebedee	1	3	3		
Orsborn, Benjamin			3		
Prior, George	1		2		
Orsborn, Rebecka			2		
Orsborn, Abel	1	3	3		
Osborn, Martha			1		
Orsborn, Ezekiel	2	1	5		
Pasko, Jonathan	1	2	2		
Morrison, John	1		2		
Parker, John	1		4		
Blodget, Elijah	1	1	2		
Heath, Stephen	3	2	6		
Bancraft, Isaac, Jr	3	3	7		
Abbey, Obediah	1	2	4		
Bancroft, John	4		3		
Fish, Levi	2	3	4		
Eggleston, Joseph	1		1		
Fish, Benjamin	1	2	2		
Booth, Aaron	1		3		
Pasko, Sarah	3	1	1		
Pasko, James	3	1	3		
Barber, Jonª	2		1		
Barber, Ashbel	1		1		
Barber, Oliver	3	1	4		
Barber, Shadrack	3	1	1		
Booth, Ephraim	2	1	5		
Pease, James	1	4	3		
Persons, William	3		3		
Allyn, Zacheriah, Jr	1	1	2		
Porter, Daniel	1	1	3		
Pease, Joel	2	2	3		
Fish, Jonª	1		1		
Utley, Joseph	2	2	2		
Kibbey, Phillip	1		2		
Elsworth, Daniel	1		5		
Phelps, Bethuel	1	2	2		1
Benjamin, Allyn	1	1	1		
Vorse, Samuel	2	1	2		
Chamberlan, James	2	1	1	1	
Chamberlan, James, Jr	1	1	2		
Fox, Ashbel	1	2	4		
Griswold, Roger	1		5		
Collins, Ebenezer	2		3		
Fish, Asa	1	1	4		
Munsell, Jacob	1		2		
Lord, Joseph	1	3	3		
Munsell, Silah	1	3	2		
Lord, Jeremiah	2		3		
Lord, George	1		1		
Holt, Ebenezer	2	1	3		
Booth, Calib	1	4	5		
Blodget, Abner	2	4	4		
Elmore, Joel	1	1	3		
Markum, Abigail			1		
Allyn, Samuel	3	2	3		
Allyn, Hezekiah	1	2	4		
Allyn, Samuel, Jr	1	1	2		
Vining, Alexander	1	4	2		
Bancroft, Edward	2	1	4		
Booth, Henry	1	1	3		
Burnham, James	1	1	3		
Fanning, Elisha	1	3	3		
Potwine, Thomas, Jr	1	4	3		
Wells, Hezekiah	4	2	5		
Potwine, John	1		2		
Wells, Joshua	2	1	3		
Potwine, Revd Thomas	3	1	3		
Warrener, Aaron	1		2		
Orsborn, Samuel	2	1	5		
Whipple, Abraham	1		1		
Watson, David	1		4		
Crane, Elishama	1		1		
Eli, Ephraim	2	3	1		
Orsborn, Daniel	6	2	3		
Allyn, Ebenezer	1	5	4		
Munsell, Thomas	1	1	2		
Elmore, Jacob	2		1		
Elmore, Noadiah	1	1	1		
Bartlet, Jonathan	1		1		
Chapin, Daniel	1	1	4		
Allyn, Peter	2		1		
Wolcott, Henery	2	2	3		
Bissell, John	1		1		
Bartlet, Samuel	3	1	4		
Stiles, Israel	1		1		
Stiles, Benoni	1	2	1		
Wolcott, Gideon	1		1		
Stiles, Asahel	2		4		
Wade, Dredley	1	2	2		
Brownley, Robert	2		1		
Clark, Jonathan	1		1		
Munsell, Corking	1	1	2		
Clark, Ebenezer	1		1		
Munsell, Hannah			2		
Bartlet, John	1	2	6		
Bissell, Moses	2		6		
Allyn, Benjamin	1		2		
Wolcott, Epaphras	1		5		
Wolcott, James	1	2	1		
Allyn, Joseph	3	1	2		
Cadwell, Levi	2	2	4		
Allyn, Solomon	2	1	3		
Allyn, Noah	1	1	3		
Simons, Silas	2	3	5		
Allyn, Luke	1	1	4		1
Stiles, Samuel	1	1	2		
Harper, James	1	2	3		
Thompson, John	1	2	3		
Thompson, James	1		1		
Thompson, William	3	2	2		
Thompson, John, Jr	2		3		
Munsell, Elisha	1				
Bullon, Jonª	1	2	5		
Belknap, Job, Jr	1	3	3		
Belknap, Job	1	1	1		
Brayman, Daniel	1	1	5		
Pease, Stephen	3		1		
Belknap, Deceius	1		1		
Pease, Peter	1	4	1		
Elsworth, Charles	1		1		
Elsworth, Josiah	1	1			
Persons, William	1		2		
Bancroft, Isaac	3	2	5		
Ferry, Nathan	1		2		
Lord, Jeremb, Jr	1	4	3		
Barber, Simon	2		5		
Loomiss, Roger	1	2	6		
Loomiss, John, Jr	3		2		
Janes, Daniel	4	3	3		
Chapin, Joseph	1	1	4		
Bissell, Jerijah, Jr	1	4	3		
Crane, Hezekiah	1		1		
Crane, David	2	3	4		
Crane, Hezekiah, Jr	3	1	5		
Crane, Rufus	1		2		
Blodget, Phinias	2	1	4		
Paine, Solomon	1		2		
Squires, Ezekiel	2		1		
Green, Jabez	1	1	3		
Green, Roswold	1	1	2		
Loomiss, Solomon	1	1	2		
Loomis, Hezekiah	1	1	2		
Abbey, Jeremiah	3	1	3		
Gay, Levi	1	2	5		
Paine, Rufus	1	3	2		
Paine, Stephen, Jr	1		1		
Paine, Eliazer	1	2	1		
Barber, George	1		2		
Crane, Aaron	1	4	3		
Squire, Daniel	1	2	2		
Chapin, Solomon	1	3	3		
Wolcott, Peter	1	1	3		
Sadd, Elijah	1	2	2		
Sadd, Elisha	1		1		
Sadd, John	2	2	2		
Bissell, Daniel	2	4	5		
Grant, Isaac	1		2		
Bissell, Jerijah	3	1	4		
Davis, Abel	1		5		
Freeman, Obed				8	
Allyn, Israel	2	2	4		
Armstrong, Rufus	1		3		
Bissell, Hezekiah	2	2	5		1
Webster, Daniel	1		1		
Elsworth, Benjamin	2		1		

HARTFORD COUNTY—Continued.

EAST WINDSOR TOWN—continued.

NAME OF HEAD OF FAMILY.	Free white males of 16 years and upward, including heads of families.	Free white males under 16 years.	Free white females, including heads of families.	All other free persons.	Slaves.
Elsworth, Job	1	1	1		
Elsworth, Solomon	5	3	4		
Morton, Alexander	1	2	2		
Drake, Gideon	1	1	3		
Starks, Ebenezar	1		1		
Morton, John	3	4	3		
Froet, Aaron	1	3	3		
Sangor, Nathaniel	2	2	2		
Charles (Negro)			1	3	
Wolcott, Simon	2		4		
Prior, Roswell	1		2		
Dawner, Edmund	2	1	2		
Orsborn, Jonathan	1		2		
Starkweather, Benajah	1		1		
Starkweather, Thomas	1	3	5		
Drake, Nathaniel	1				
Drake, Simeon	2		1		
Drake, Nathaniel, Jr	1	4	2		
Stedman, Stephen	1		1		
Stedman, Stephen, Jr	1	1	3		
Drake, Shubel	1		1		
Drake, Ebenezer	3		4		
McCivers, Daniel	1		1		
House, Eliphalet	1		1		
Stoughton, Shem	1	4	1		
Rockwell, Silvanus	1	3	3		
Rockwell, Joel		1	3		
Wolcott, Benjamin, 2d	1				
Rockwell, Amasa	1		1		
Grant, Justus	1	4	1		
Grant, Mathew	1	2	1		
Grant, Oliver	1		3		
Grant, Samuel R	1	1	3		
Keeney, William	1		2		
Foster, Peletiah	4		5		
Grant, John	1		3		
Grant, Edward C	4	1	1		
Johnson, Samuel	1	1	1		
Johnson, Feen	1	2	3		
Elmore, Augustus	1	1	2		
Smith, Joseph	2	3	3		
Kingsley, Salmon	1	1	2		
Kingsley, Oren	1	1	3		
Kingsley, Stephen	1		1		
Rockwell, Ephraim	1	4	2		
Corning, Nathan, Jr	1		3		
Corney, Nathan	3		3		
White, Freind	3	1	4		
Goodale, Walter	1	1	5		
Goodale, Ebenezer	3		2		
White, Henery	2	2	3		
Tryon, Aaron	1	1	5		
Evens, Allyn	1	1	2		
Fitch, White Roswold	1	2	1		
Fitch, Richard	1		2		
Elmore, Daniel	1	2	2		
Benjamin, Elisha	2	2	6		
Loomiss, Gideon	3		2		
Benjamin, Elisha, Jr	1	1	2		
Burkland, George	1	3	4		
Brunson, Beriah	1	2	2		
Ludd, Ezekiel	1		1		
Simons, Paul G	2	2	1		
Barber, Noah	2	1	4		
Munsell, Hezekiah	1	5	2		
Rockwell, Isaac	2		4		
Rockwell, Frances	1	1	2		
Fenton, William	1	1	1		
Green, Barzilla	2		1		
Green, Azel	1	3	5		
Cassee, Patrick	1	2	2		
Watrous, Nathaniel	1		2		
Strong, Israel	2	1	2		
Foster, Thomas	2	2	5		
Dorman, Stephen	1	2	1		
Stoughton, John	1	2	4		
Webster, Cyrenus	1	3	6		
Drake, Silas	2	6	3		
Lathrop, Thacher	2		3		
Lathrop, David	1	1	1		
Morton, Deodat	1	3	4		
Gibbs, Ebenezer	3	2	2		
Dart, Jabez	2	2	6		
Stoughton, Jonathan	1		2		
Grant, Hezekiah	1		3		
Rockwell, Ezra	1		1		
Rockwell, Daniel, 2d	1		2		
Smith, Samuel	1	3	6		
Woodbridge, Ashbel	1		1		
Grant, Gideon	2		3		
Grant, Gideon, Jr	1		3		
Grant, William	1		1		
Rockebell, Daniel	2	4	7		
Sadd, Thomas	1		1		
Sadd, Thomas, Jr	2	2	4		

EAST WINDSOR TOWN—continued.

NAME OF HEAD OF FAMILY.	Free white males of 16 years and upward, including heads of families.	Free white males under 16 years.	Free white females, including heads of families.	All other free persons.	Slaves.
Strong, Elijah	2	2	4		
Grant, Oliver, 2nd	1		1		
Skinner, Daniel	2		3		
Skinner, Oliver	2	2	3		
Filley, Mark	1	2	9		
Bissell, Timothy	1	2	2		
Bowers, John	1	2	3		
Bissell, Dan	2	2	5		
Bissell, Hannah			3		
Tuttle, Martha			3		
Rockwell, Ebenezar	3		2		
Rockwell, Ebenezar, Jr	1	1	4		
Rockwell, James	1	1	1		

ENFIELD TOWN.

NAME OF HEAD OF FAMILY.	Free white males of 16 years and upward, including heads of families.	Free white males under 16 years.	Free white females, including heads of families.	All other free persons.	Slaves.
Fish, Eli	1	3	2		
Pease, William	1	2	5		
Bullen, David	2		2		
Bullen, Christopher	1	1	3		
Pratt, Thomas	1	1	1		
Pease, Moses	1	1	5		
Pease, Moses, Jr	1	2	1		
Pease, Lemuel	1		2		
Avery, John	2	1	2		
Pease, Abiel	1		2		
Webster, Joel	1		2		
Markum, Isaac	1	1	1		
Allyn, Moses	4	1	5		
Allyn, Moses, Jr	1	1	1		
Allyn, Ebenezer	2		2		
Allyn, Elijah	1	1	1		
Warner, Eliphalet	2	2	4		
Hall, Israel	1		2		
Holkins, Joseph	1		1		
Holkins, Elijah	2	1	3		
Allyn, John	4		3		
Phelps, Noah	1		1		
Markham, Nathan	1		3		
Parsons, Benjamin, 2d	1	1	1		
Butler, James	1	2	7		
Holkins, Joel, Jr	1		2		
Starns, Levi	1	2	2		
Warner, John	2		1		
Warner, Hannah (Wd)			3		
Abbey, Richard	1	1	3		
Abbey, Richard, Jr	1	3	2		
Wilson, David	1	1	2		
Booth, John	1	2	3		
Booth, Joel	1		2		
Bement, Joseph	1		1		
Simons, Asahel	5		5		
Pease, Aaron, Jr	1	4	7		
Parsons, Ebenezer	1		5		
Lord, William	1		2		
Ward, Thomas	1		1		
Fenton, Truston	1		1		
Parsons, Joseph	2	3	4		
Parsons, Thomas	2	1	3		
Bemont, Edmund	1		1		
Bement, Dennis	1	1	7		
Holton, Elisha	1		4		
Parsons, Prudence (Wd)			1		
Parsons, Elijah	3	3	5		
Terry, Elijah	4		2		
Booth, Levi	2		2		
Sabin, Thomas	1				
Booth, Zacheriah	1				
Avery, Jonathan	1	2	3		
Olmsted, Joseph	2		2		
Booth, Joseph	5		6		
Pease, Ebenezer	2	1	4		
Prior, Isaac	1	3	5		
Knight, Joseph	3	1	2		
Knight, Thomas	1		1		
Higley, Jeremiah	1				
Pease, Sharon	2	1	4		
Simons, Joel	1	2	3		
Pease, Peter	1	2	2		
Griswold, Joseph	2	1	3		
Terry, Eliphalet, Esqr	2	3	6		
Meacham, John	6	3	2		
Potter, Elam	2	1	5		
Pease, Ephm	2	1	2		2
Pridden, Revd Nehemiah	1	1	3	1	
Parsons, Benjn	1		2	1	
Parsons, Simeon	1	1			
Chapin, Azubah (Wid.)	3	1	5		
Chapin, Nathaniel	1		3		
Chapin, Nathaniel, Jr	1	1	2		
Chapin, Simeon	1	1	1		
Pease, Zebulon	2	5	2		
Parsons, Peter	2	3	4		
Peirce, Joseph	1	2	3		

ENFIELD TOWN—con.

NAME OF HEAD OF FAMILY.	Free white males of 16 years and upward, including heads of families.	Free white males under 16 years.	Free white females, including heads of families.	All other free persons.	Slaves.
Reynolds, Samuel	1	1	4		
Prior, Azariah	1		2		
Churchill, Elijah	1	2	2		
McClester, John	1				1
McClester, Elizath (Wid.)			1		
McClester, James	1	2	2		
Ware, Daniel	1	1	2		
Terry, Colo Nathaniel	4	1	4		1
Feild, Doct Simeon	3	1	4		
Reynold, John, Esqr	2	3	7		
Olmsted, Hannah (Wid.)			1		
Olmsted, Asa	1	1	3		1
King, Obadiah	1		3		
Kibbe, Margaret (Wid.)	1	1	4		
Danna, Daniel	2		5		
Geer, Elihu	1	1	5		
Chandler, Nehemiah	1		3		
Terry, Ephraim	1	1	5		
Diggins, Augustus	1	1	4		2
Johnson, Jonathan	2	1	3		
Prior, Ebenezer	3		5		
Kibbe, Isaac	2	1	4		1
Kibbe, Gains	2	2	3		
Bush, Eli	1	1	3		
Hale, Samuel	1	3	6		
Stockwell, Reuben	2	4	4		
Terry, Samuel	1	1	1		
Terry, Benjamin, 2nd	1	1	2		
Hale, Israel	2		2		
Hillam, Eliphalet	1	5	5		
Hale, Thomas	1		2		
Hale, Eli	1	1	2		
Meacham, Elizabeth (Widw)			2		
Meacham, Benjamin	1	2	3		
Griswold, Benajah	1	2	2		
Green, Obadiah	1	1	4		
Green, Mary (Wid.)			4		
Anderson, Ashbel	1	1	4		
Parsons, Christopher	1		2		
Parsons, Lemuel	1	1	3		
King, Naum	3	4	3		
Rush, Joshua, Jr	1		1		
Pease, Noadiah	1	4	5		
Kingsbury, Joseph	2		3		
Monsen, Alexander	1	2	5		
Bucknel, John	4		3		
Metcalf, Thomas	3		3		
Fenton, Barry	3		3		
Terry, Selah	3	1	4		
Chaffer, William	1		7		
Abbey, Thomas, 2d	2	1	1		
Brooks, Zerah	3	3	5		
Alden, Amos	2	1	3		
Terry, Shadrack	3	2	3		
Brooks, William	1		1		
Parsons, Jonathan	4		2		
Parsons, Hezekiah	1		2		
Parsons, Hezekiah, Jr	1	5	2		
Collins, John	1	2	3		
Hale, John	1	4	3		
Terry, Selah, Jr	1	2	3		
Meachum, Simeon	1		3		
Terry, Zeno	1	5	4		
Handcock, William	2	1	5		
Chandler, David	1	3	5		
Chandler, Joseph	1	3	4		
Chandler, Joseph, Jr	2	1	1		
Rumvil, John	1	1	3		
Holkins, Joel	2		1		
Meacham, Asa	1		1		
Bugbee, Jonathan	1	1	3		
Kingsbury, Lemuel	3	4	4		
Bush, Jonathan	2	5	7		
Bush, Joshua	1		1		
Terry, Daniel	1	1	2		
Terry, Joseph	2	3	5		
Terry, Ebenezer, 2d	1		8		
Terry, Jacob	3		5		
Terry, Jacob, Jr	1		2		
Terry, Julus	1		2		
Parsons, Jabez	1		2		
Hale, Jona	1		3		
Pease, James	1	2	5		
Hale, David	1		1		
Hale, David, Jr	1	3	5		
Hale, Ebenezer	1	4	2		
Pease, Joseph	1		1		
Pease, Gideon	2		1		
Stanley, Benjamin	2		3		
Parsons, Wareham	2	2	5		
Simons, Benjamin	1		3		
Simons, Benjamin, Jr	1	5	4		

ENFIELD TOWN—con.

Name of head of family.	Free white males of 16 years and upward, including heads of families.	Free white males under 16 years.	Free white females, including heads of families.	All other free persons.	Slaves.
Button, Elias	1	3	2		
Perkins, Daniel	5		2		
Perkins, George	1	1	1		
Adams, Elijah	1	3	3		
Fairman, Ithemer	1		3		
Pease, John, 3d	2	3	4		
Allyn, Jonathan	1	2	2		
Gains, John	2	1	3		
Chapin, Jeremiah	1	1	2		
Pease, Gideon, 2d	1	2	3		
Pease, Isaac, 2nd	1	6	1		
Sabin, David	1	1	2		
Pease, Ezekiel	1				
Prior, Ezekiel	1		1		
Prior, Zacheus	3	1	5		
Pease, Simon	1	1	3		
Pease, Israel	3		1		
Comes, John	2	1	6		
Collins, Edward, Esqr	1		1		
Collins, Nathaniel	1	1	3		
Parsons, Eli	1	3	3		
Kibbe, Elisha	1		3		2
Bugbee, Nathaniel	2		2		
Pease, Samuel	1	1	2		
Pease, Edward, 2d	1	3	2		
Parsons, Shubel	1	3	4		
Pease, Hezekiah	2		6		
Eyers, Thomas	1	1	5		
Pease, Aaron	2		4		
Terry, Solomon	1	1	1		
Chapin, Eliphalet	1	1	2		
Pease, Jessee	1	2	3		
Parsons, Nathaniel	5	1	4		
Pease, John, 2d	2	3	2		
Peirce, Abner	1	2	1		
Pease, Samuel, 2d	2	2	5		
Parsons, John	2	5	3		
Phelps, David	1		2		
Phelps, David, Jr	1	4	2		
Phelps, Eldad	2		2		
Phelps, Eldad, Jr	1		3		
Abbey, Thomas	1	3	2		
Hubbard, Obediah	3		7		
Pease, David	2	1	5		
Hale, Daniel	2		4		
Pease, Stone	1	2	4		
Chapin, Ebenezer	4		5		
Root, Benjamin	1		2		
Root, Daniel	1	4	6		
Abbey, John	1		1	1	
Pease, Ephraim, 2d	1	3	1		
Abbey, Daniel	2	3	4		
Wright, Elezur	2		1		
Abbey, John, 2d	1	1	4		
Abbey, John, 3d	1		1		
Pease, Nathan	2	1	3		
Allyn, David	1		3		
Ingram, Ebenezar	2	2	3		
Thompson, Mathew	3		3		
Markum, Darius	2	3	4		
Meachum, Aaron	1	2	4		
Parsons, Shubab	1		1		
Collins, Eliphalet	2	4	6		
Thatcher, Thomas	2	1	2		
Terry, John	2		1		
Henry, John	3	2	7		
Henery, Gager	1	1			
Craw, Jonathan	1		1		
Craw, David	2	2	2		
Griswold, Jonah	1	4	4		
Griswold, Shubel	2	2	4		
Griswold, Solomon	1	1	6		
Griswold, Jehiel	1	4	3		
Shepard, Noah	1		2		
Gowdy, Samuel	2		3		
Gowdy, Robert	1		3		
Gowdy, William	1	2	3		
Jones, Caleb	1		2		
Jones, Caleb, Jr	1		1		
Jones, Ezra	1		2		
Gleason, Joseph	1		1		
Gleason, Jonah	1	1	1		
Gleason, Isaac	1	3	4		
Gleason, Solomon	1	1	4		
Gleason, Joseph, Jr	1	2	4		
Morrison, John	2		8		
Parsons, Edward	1		5		
Sexton, Thomas	3		1		
Fairman, Jared	1	1	6		
Sexton, Asabel	1		1		
Pease, John	1		1		
Pease, Simeon, 2d	1	2	1		
Pease, Isaac, 3d	2	3	3		
Terry, Aseph	1	2	4		
Baxter, Frances	1	1	1		

ENFIELD TOWN—con.

Name of head of family.	Free white males of 16 years and upward, including heads of families.	Free white males under 16 years.	Free white females, including heads of families.	All other free persons.	Slaves.
Billings, Thaddeus	1	2	2		
Billings, Eli	1		1		
Eaton, Samuel	1				
Eaton, Samuel, Jr	1	1	6		
Terry, Ebenezer	2	1	4		
Terry, Hirum	1		2		
Pease, Commins	1		1		
Pease, Heman	1	2	3		
Pease, Commins, 2d	1	3	5		
Pease, David, 2d	1	1	4		
Billings, Nathaniel	1	2	1		
Pease, Asa	1	3	2		
Pease, Timothy	1		2		
Pease, Edward	1	2	2		
McGrigery, John	1		3		
Terry, Jonathan	1		2		
Terry, David	1	9	3		
King, Benjamin	5	2	3		
King, Joel	1	3	2		
Hemingway, Samuel	1		2		
Marckum, Barzilla	3		2		
Parsons, Eldad	4	1	5		
Parsons, Asabel	1	3	3		
Meachum, Abner	1	2	2		
Olmsted, Simeon	2	5	3		
Chapin, Jabez	2	2	3		
Cooley, Noah	1	1	1		
Shepard, Noah	1		2		
Goold, John	1	1	1		
Wood, Edward	2		6		
Bush, Aaron	1		1		
Bush, Rufus	1	2	4		
Parker, Joseph	1		1		
Baxter, William	1	1	1		
Talcott, Elizur	3		1		
Parsons, Daniel	1	1	3		
Parsons, Daniel, Jr	1	1	1		
Hills, Jacob	1	1	4		
Emerson, Joseph	2	1	4		
Pease, Ruth (Wid.)		1	2		
Booth, John, Jr	1		1		
Booth, Daniel	1	2	4		
Meachum, Joseph	1		1		
Pease, Benjamin	8	4	16		
Pease, Elias	1	2	2		
Munsell, Zacheus	1	1	6		
Markham, Jehiel	2	1	4		
Markham, Justus	1	2	4		
Parker, Samuel	2	1	5		
Pease, Isaac	1	1	2		
Pease, Rufus	1	3	2		
Pease, George	1	2			

FARMINGTON TOWN.

Name of head of family.	Free white males of 16 years and upward, including heads of families.	Free white males under 16 years.	Free white females, including heads of families.	All other free persons.	Slaves.
Warner, Demus	1	2	3		
Gridley, Isaac	2	4	4		
Gridley, Jonathan	1		1		
Jones, Samuel	3		1		
Stedman, Elizabeth		1	2		
Gridley, Daniel	1	2	2		
Porter, Prudence					5
Gridley, Rezin	2		4		
Hamlin, John	3	3	2		
Hamlin, Oliver	1	1	1		
Hamlin, Phinias	1	1	2		
Gridley, Noadiah	3	1	4		
Cook, John	2	2	3		
Hotchkiss, Ladwick	1		1		
Hotchkiss, Josiah	2	1	3		
Root, Samuel	2	2	3		
Root, Elijah	1	1	7		
Root, Salmon	1	2	6		
Hills, Joseph	2	2	4		
Hills, Chancey	1	4	2		
Smally, Jacob	1	2	1		
Morse, Moses	1	3	3		
Wood, Eli	2	1	2		
Deming, Samuel	2		1		1
Deming, Benjamin	2		2		
Wilcox, Asa	1	1	1		
Wilcox, Jesse	1		1		
Frisbee, Zebulon	1		1		
Parsons, Isaac	2	1	4		
Richards, Seth	1	1	2		
Richards, Samuel	2		2		
Bishop, James	2	2	1		
Hooper, Asahel	4	1	3		
Carrington, Elizabeth		1	5		
Feney, Oziah	1	1	2		
Porter, Richard	3		2		
Evans, Luther	2	2	5		
Lawry, Daniel	1	4	3		
Hayford, John	1	4	3		
Gridley, Seth	1	4	3		

FARMINGTON TOWN—continued.

Name of head of family.	Free white males of 16 years and upward, including heads of families.	Free white males under 16 years.	Free white females, including heads of families.	All other free persons.	Slaves.
Root, Hezekiah	3	4	6		
Curtis, Solomon	1	1	1		
Parsons, Thomas	2	1	3		
Monger, Levi	1		4		
Parsons, Thomas, Jr	1	1	1		
Kenada, Asa	1	2	1		
Phinney, Oliver	1		1		
Phinney, Joshua	1	2	2		
Gridley, Ebenezer	2	2	2		
Willcox, James	1	2	3		
Comes, Phineas	2	2	8		
Burrows, Barzilla	2	1	2		
Burrows, Joseph	1	1	4		
Andruss, Ichabod	1	1	3		
Hamlin, Levi	1	1	3		
Shepard, Jesse	1	1	2		
Shepard, Amos	2	2	3		
Smith, Lydia		2	4		
Rowdan, James	1	2	3		
Hawley, Amos	2	4	5		
Churchill, Wm	3		1		
Hawley, Abel	1	2	6		
Crampton, Miles	2	1	4		
Hart, Thomas	1	5	4		
Hart, Ira	2	3	4		
Hawley, Ebenezer	1	6	3		
Elsworth, William	1		4		
Curtis, Abner	1		1	3	
Tubbs, Ammon	1	1	2		
Lee, Amos	2	2	3		
Bartholomew, Charles	1		4		
Rowe, Seth	1	5	4		
Curtiss, Jesse	1	2	5		
Sweet, Palmer	2	5	5		
Orvis, Zadock	2	2	4		
Barnes, Israel	1	4	2		
Alvord, Thomas G	3	2	3		
Wadsworth, Eliphalet	2		4		
Mildren, Huldah	1	1	2		
Cowles, Elias	3		2		
Elsworth, Mary			2		
Hayden, David	1	1	2		
Langdon, Joseph	2	4	5		
Sweet, Stephen	1	2	1		
Grindley, Alexander	2		1		
Byington, Jacob	3		3		
Scott, Ezekiel	2	2	5		
Scott, Elisha	2	1	6		
Wadsworth, Eunice			4		
Cowles, Ezekiel	5	3	4		
Welton, Joel	1	2	2		
Tubbs, Amos	1		1		
Wadsworth, Luke	2	3	7		
Wadsworth, Wm	2	3	2		
Hunt, James	3		2		
Clark, Levi	3		2		
Root, Timothy	4	1	3		
Root, Mark	1	1	3		
Cowles, Solomon, Jr	5	3	8		
Cowles, Isaac	4	3	5		
Bidwell, Theodore	3	1	4		
Kirkham, John	1	1	3		
Case, John	2	1	1		
Case, Corvil	1	2	1		
Curtis, Amos	1	3	4		
Cowles, Gideon	1		4		
Cowles, Enos	3	2	3		
Andruss, Timothy	2	1	2		
Kirham, Samuel	1	1	1		
Porter, Elijah	1	1	2		
Porter, Shubael	1	1	2		
Bull, Jonathan	2		2		
Bull, Martin	2		2		
Hawley, Isaac	2		1		
Lee, Thomas, Jr	1	1	2		
Porter, George	2		1		
Buckley, Thomas	2		1		
Bidwell, Isaac	3	1	4		
Wadsworth, Asahel	4	1	4		
Porter, Elijah, Jr	1	1	1		
Pitkin, Timothy	3		4		
Cowles, Thomas	2		3		
Lewis, Thomas	2	2	3		1
Cowles, Amos	2	1	3		
Deming, John	2		5		
Deming, Chancey	1		4		
Mix, John	1	2	5		
Jutson, Peter	1		1		
Shepard, Luther	1		2		
Lee, Seth	2	5	6		
Whitman, Solomon, Jr	2	3	5		
Pond, Phineas	1		1		
North, Reuben	1	1	5		
Woodruff, Oliver	2	2	6		
Woodruff, Lois	3	1	4		

Column headers for each panel:
- NAME OF HEAD OF FAMILY.
- Free white males of 16 years and upward, including heads of families.
- Free white males under 16 years.
- Free white females, including heads of families.
- All other free persons.
- Slaves.

FARMINGTON TOWN—continued.

Name	M16+	M<16	F	Other	Slaves
Woodruff, Timothy	1		2		
Woodruff, Abel	1	1	3		
Woodruff, Joshua	2	2	2		
North, Samuel	4	4	6		
North, Daniel	3	1	5		
Woodruff, Elijah, Jr	2	1	3		
Combs, Ebenezer	1		4		
Clark, Marvin	1	2	5		
Woodruff, Martin	2	3	5		
Hart, Joel	1	1	4		
Woodruff, James	1	2	4		
Hart, Lemuel	1	1	1		
Hooker, Joseph	2	4	2		
Hooker, Noadiah	2	3	7		
Loomiss, Joseph	2		2		
Cowles, Elijah, Jr	4	1	5		1
Cowles, Elijah	3		4		
Barker, Seth	2	1	3		
Hart, Asa	1	3	5		
Root, Samuel, Jr	2	4	2		
Warren, Samuel	2	2	4		
Porter, Joseph	3	1	5		
Merrill, James	1	4	1		
Root, James	1	2	3		
Goodrich, Elijah	1	4	4		
Hart, William	2	3	4		
Alvord, Thomas G., Jr	1	2	2		
Judd, James	2	2	5		
Clark, Amos	2	2	1		
Hart, Gad	1	3	3		
Strong, Elisha	2	1	5		
Clark, Mathew	1	2	2		
Rice, Memusan	1	4	2		
Curtis, Gabriel	2	2	2		
Curtis, Hannah			3		
Curtis, Silvanus	2	1	3		
Curtis, Peter	4	1	4		
Hart, John	1	3	2	1	
Hull, Eliakim	2	2	2		
Andrus, Obadiah	1		5		
Lewis, Phineas	3		4		
Thompson, Luke	1	1	7		
Nott, Gershom	1				
Curtis, Eleazer	2		3		
Curtis, Daniel	1		2		
Richards, Samuel, Jr	2	1	2		
Lee, Thomas	2		2		
Hooker, Roger	3	1	3	1	
Gleason, Isaac	2		2	1	
Hosmer, Timothy	2	5	3		1
Hill, Amos	1	3	5		
Andrus, Theodore	1	2	3		
Hicks, James	1		2		
Porter, Noah	1	2	4		
Judd, Wm	3		2		
Judd, William S	1	1	1		
Street, Thankfull		2	3		
Whitman, Solomon	1	1	2		
Whitman, Elnathan	1	1	3		
Porter, Amos	1	1	2		
Welton, Benjamin	1	2	2		
Porter, Jesse	1	1	3		
Pratt, Mabel			2		
Clark, Salmon	1	1	1		
Norton, Reuben S	1	2	3		
Smith, Thomas	2		2		
Smith, Samuel	2		4		
Thompson, John	1	1	5		
Gillet, Abraham	1	2	3		
Reynolds, John	3		3		
Woodford, Roger	1	5	3		
Newill, Thomas	3	3	3		
Roads, Joseph	2	2	4		
Woodruff, John	1	3	4		
Woodford, Charles	1	3	3		
Humphry, Ralph	1		1		
Dyer, Joseph	1	2	2		
Woodruff, Aaron, Jr	1	1	3		
Lewis, Elijah	1	2	2		
Woodruff, Judah	3		5		
Treadwell, John	2	2	6		
Woodruff, Joseph	2	1	3		
Thompson, Nathaniel	1	2	3		
Welton, Solomon	1	2	2		
Hayden, David, Jr	1		1		
McKeinster, John	1		1		
Buck, Isaac	3	3	6		
Gridley, David	1	3	5		
Peck, Samuel	2	1	1		
North, John	1	3	4		
North, Seth	1	1	1		
Parks, Prudence		1	3		
Hull, Abraham	1	2	4		
Judd, Elizur	1	2	3		
Bird, Joseph	1	3	3		
Wadsworth, Hezekiah	3	5	4		
Barnes, Amos	1	2	4		
Porter, John	2	2	6	1	
Porter, Lemuel	1	1	1		
Hooker, Elnathan	2	1	2		
Rowe, Isaiah	2	1	5		
Youngs, Joshua	1	3	1		2
Rowe, Samuel	1		2		
Barns, Moses	1	2	4		
Barns, James	3	3	7		
Brunson, Stephen	5	4	4		
Woodruff, Reuben	1	3	5		
Woodruff, Noah	4		3		
Woodruff, Solomon	1		3		
Clark, Dan	3		2		
Whittlesey, Abner	1	1	3		
Hinman, Amos	1		5		
Hayford, Elisha	1	1	1		
Cook, Roswell	2	2	2		
Winstone, John	1	2	2		
Hayford, John	1		1		
Potter, Philemon	1	3	4		
Peck, Abel	1	1	3		
Tooley, Lemuel	1	2	2		
Beckwith, Mabel		2	2		
Woodruff, Elisha	2	4	4		
Beckwith, Jonah	1	2	1		
Perry, Thomas	1		2		
Woodruff, Aaron	2	1	4		
North, Eli	2	2	6		
North, Asa	1	2	4		
Parsons, Joshua	2	2	1		
Cowles, Daniel, Jr	1	1	1		
Porter, William	1	2	6		
Hart, Reuben	1	1	3		
Cowles, Daniel	2	2	4		
Woodford, Elijah	1		5		
Lusk, James	3	3	3		
Cowles, Ziba	2	2	4		
Hawley, Reuben	1	6	3		
Thomas, Zelpha			2		
Brister, David	1	3	5		
Fullar, John	1	2	1		
Fullar, Josiah	1	1	2		
Norton, Jedidiah	2		2		
Tillotson, Elias	2	1	4		
Hart, Samuel	1	1	2		
Hart, Lent	1	4	2		
Hart, Munson	1		4		
Peterson, Charles	1	3	3		
Tillotson, Ashbel	1		2		
Woodruff, Moses	1	4	2		
Woodruff, Appleton	1	2	2		
Gridley, Obed	1	1	3		
North, Lott	1	3	2		
Hosford, Ezekiel	4		3		
Pratt, Elisha	3		2		
Langton, Solomon	1	1	3		
Kelsey, Amos	1	2	3		
Gridley, Elijah	3		5		
Thomson, Jonathan	3	1	3		1
Thompson, Daniel	1	1	2	1	
Andrus, Elijah	3		5		
Thompson, Samuel	3		2		
Langdon, Ebenezer	3	1	4		
Norton, Ichabod	2	2	3		
Gillet, Noah	1	4	2		
Gillet, Isaac	1	1	1		
Gillett, Noadiah	1	1	1		
Gillett, Amos	2		1		
Willcox, Jesse	1		2		
Willcox, Eleazer	1	2	2		
Willcox, Ezra	1	1	3		
Willcox, Josiah	1	2	4		
Bishop, Benjamin	1		1		
Bishop, Samuel	1		1		
Bishop, Thomas F	1		2		
Hart, Gideon	2	2	4		
Hart, Anthony	1	1	2		
Thomson, Timothy	1		2		
Thompson, Thomas	1	4	4		
Woodford, Ezekiel	1	4	3		
Miller, Anna	1	1	3		
Miller, Job	1	2	2		
Miller, Reuben	1	2	2		
Miller, Ebenezer	1		2		
Ford, Wm	2	4	2		
Ford, Thos	2	4	6		
Hawley, Rufus	3	3	2		
Miller, Daniel	1		4		
Thompson, Levi	1	2	6		
Thompson, Asa	1	2	2		
Thompson, Ruth			4		
Thompson, Barnabas	1	4	3		
Miller, Elisha	2	4	5		
North, David	1		2		
Lewis, Oliver	1	1	4		
Woodford, Wm	1	2	5		
Woodford, Selah	1	1	2		
Woodford, Samuel	1	1	3		
Everist, Solomon	2		2		
North, Isaiah	2	1	5		
Woodford, Elijah	1	4	4		
Woodford, Joseph	4	2	6		
Woodford, Wm, Jr	2	3	3		
Woodford, Dudley	1	4	4		
Norton, Bethuel	3	2	3		
Marshall, Eliakim	3		2		
Miller, Elijah	1		3		
Miller, Jonathan	2		1	1	
Woodford, John	1		2		
Woodford, Amos	1	1	2		
Cummings, Samuel	1		1		
Ingham, Jonth	2	1	3		
Ingham, John	1		1		
Ingham, Isaac	1	1	4		
Andrus, Mary			2		
Hart, Elnathan	2		1		
Hart, Lineus	1	2	1		
Judd, Calvin	1		6		
Hinox, Salmon	1	1	1		
Hart, Ambrose	2	1	3		
Woodruff, Thomas	2		1		
Woodruff, Medad	1	3	1		
Woodruff, Gedar	1	1	1		
Woodford, Isaac	2	4	3		
Thompson, Lott	1	1	6		
Woodruff, Eldad	2	4	3		
Woodruff, Micah	2	2	4		
Woodruff, Joseph	2	5	4		
Woodruff, Zebulon	2		1		
Foot, Jacob	2	1	4		
Hart, James	1	1	2		
Durren, Stephen	1	1	3		
Potter, Nathaniel	4		1		
Chidsuy, Joseph	1	4	4		
Hart, Hosea	1		3		
Alderman, Timothy	1	2	2		
Bunnel, Joseph	1		3		
Tillotson, Daniel	2	1	3		
Brockway, Joseph, Jr	2	2	4		
Soper, Timothy	3	3	2		
Sturdivant, Azor	2	1	2		
Miller, Noah	2	2	3		
Edson, Teracy	2		3		
Brockway, Joseph	1		5		
Frisbee, David	3	1	5		
Northway, Joseph	2	3	3		
Talcott, Job	3	2	4		
Sturdivant, James	1	2	3		
Studivant, Ozar	1	2	2		
Gleason, David	1	5	1		
Gleason, Samuel	1	1	4		
Curtis, Gran	1		3		
Norton, Samuel	1	4	4		
Thompson, Abel	1	3	2		
Hawley, Elijah	1	2	2		
Woodruff, Lott	4	1	5		
Hawley, Joseph	2	2	2	1	
Hawley, Gad	1	2	3		
Gridley, Timothy	2	3	3		
Harrington, Elisha	1	2	7		
Selden, Joseph	2	3	4		
Standley, Samuel	1	1	2		
Standley, Samuel, Jr	1	4	5		
Sedgwith, Stephen	2	1	3		
Sedgwith, Stephen, Jr	1	2	1		
Curtis, Josiah	1	3	2		
Belden, John R	2	1	5		
Olds, Ebenezer	1		3		
More, Simeon	1	2	4		
Goodwin, Morgan	3	1	2		
Farnsworth, Samuel	1	1	1		
Wells, Bayza	2	4	2		
Wells, George	1	1	3		
Wells, Elisha	1	1	1		
Wells, Elisha, Jr	1	2	2		
Grimes, John	4	2	6		
Fisher, Timothy	1	2	3		
Merrill, Moses	2	2	3		
Shepard, Thomas	1	1	4		
Rawley, Daniel	1				
Cadwell, Peletiah	1	5	2		
Parsons, Hezekiak	1	3	4		
Lord, Elisha	1	1	4		
Cadwell, Mathew	2	1	2		

HARTFORD COUNTY—Continued.

FARMINGTON TOWN—continued.

NAME OF HEAD OF FAMILY.	Free white males of 16 years and upward, including heads of families.	Free white males under 16 years.	Free white females, including heads of families.	All other free persons.	Slaves.
Olcott, Jediah	1		3		
Cadwell, James	2	4	3		
Burr, Noadiah, Jr	1	3	2		
Burr, Salmon	1	1	1		
Burr, Theodore	1		1		
Burr, Samuel	2		3		
Smith, John	1	1	2		
Burr, Titus	2		3		
Burr, Noadiah	3	3	6		
Burr, Isaac	1	2	4		
Allyn, John	1	2	4		
Burr, Eunice		2	1		
Kilbourn, Josiah	1	1	2		
Barnes, Simeon	1	3	3		
Barnes, Hartwell	1	2	2		
North, Ashur	1	3	4		
Johnson, Prince				5	
Auguster, Ceasar				4	
Freman, Amos				3	
Buttler, Benjamin				7	
Kitt (Negro)				4	
Nelson, Isaac				4	

GLASTENBURY TOWN.

NAME OF HEAD OF FAMILY.	Free white males of 16 years and upward, including heads of families.	Free white males under 16 years.	Free white females, including heads of families.	All other free persons.	Slaves.
Alger, Ashbel	2	5	4		
Andrus, Daniel	1	2	3		
Avery, Abraham	1	1	4		
Andrews, Joseph	1	2	2		
Anderson, Sawney				4	
Alger, Roger	1	1	3		
Anthony (Negro)				3	
Bidwell, Isaac	1	5	3		
Bidwell, Hezekiah	1		1		
Brooks, Joel	1	5	4		
Brau, Jonathan, Esqr	1	2	4		
Benton, Ebenezer	1	1	5		
Bidwell, Joseph	2	3	3		
Bidwell, Ephraim	1	2	1		
Bill, Aaron	1	3	3		
Bidwell, David	1		2		
Bill, Elizur	2	3	2		
Bill, Isaac	1	1	7		
Benton, Edward	1	1	2		
Benton, Josiah	2	2	4		
Bidwell, Jonathan	2	2	7		
Bidwell, Rebecca	1		2		
Bidwell, Allyn	1	1	3		
Bidwell, Samuel	1	1	3		
Bumter, Shorum				2	
Coleman, Asaph	2	2	3		
Chapman, Jonah	2	2	3		
Caswell, John	2	1	5		
Camp, Talcott	1	4	3		
Covil, Ephraim	3	1	2	1	
Case, Rachel (Wid.)	2		4		
Chapman, Tenant	1	1	2		
Chapman, Jehiel	1		1		
Chapel, Solomon	1	1	3		
Chapman, Amasa	2	2	1		
Chapman, Asahel	1		3		
Conley, John	1	1	4		
Densmore, Obadiah	1	4	3		
Easton, Ephraim	1		1		
Elles, Revd John	2	1	6		
Easton, Timothy	1		1		
Emons, Susanna			1		
Fox, Obadiah	1	3	3		
Flanckin, Banabas	1	3	2		
Fox, Samuel	1	1	3		
Fox, Hosea	1				
Fox, Joseph	1		2		
Fox, Joseph, Jr	1	2	4		
Fox, Eleazer	1	1	2		
Fox, David	1		2		
Fuller, Barnabas	1		2		
Fox, Asa	1	1	3		
Farris, Rhoda			2		
Fruman, Samson				4	
Goodrich, Isaac	1		3		
Goodrich, Wait, Jr	1		1		
Goodrich, David	1		1		
Goodrich, David, Jr	1	1	1		
Goodrich, Noah	2	3	1		
Goodrich, Wait	2	1	3		
Goodrich, Jehiel	1	5	2		
Goodrich, Eliakim	1	3	2		
Goodrich, Roswell	1	1	2		
Goodrich, Elisha	2	1	4		
Goodrich, Abigail	1		3		
Glosender, John	1	1	1		
Goff, Elisha	1		3		
Gains, Nathaniel	2	1	2		
Gains, Dan	1	1	1		
Gains, John	1	2	4		

GLASTENBURY TOWN—continued.

NAME OF HEAD OF FAMILY.	Free white males of 16 years and upward, including heads of families.	Free white males under 16 years.	Free white females, including heads of families.	All other free persons.	Slaves.
Hale, Elijah	1	2	4		
Hale, Asahel	1		2		
Hodge, Roswell	1	1	1		
Hollister, Jonathan	1		3		
Hodge, Eli	1		3		
Hollister, Stephen	2	1	5		
Hale, Joseph, Jr	1	3	3		1
Hale, Gideon	4	3	5		
Hale, Elisha	2	2	5	1	
Hale, Theodore	3	1	5		
Hale, Timothy	2		2		9
Hale, David	4		5		
Hale, Ruth	1		4		3
Hollister, John	1	5	5		
Hale, John	1	1	2		
Hale, Mathew	1		2		
Hollister, Joseph	1		2		
Hubbard, Eleazer	2		3		
Hale, David, Jr	1	1	4		1
Hale, Joseph	2		2		
House, Samuel	1	4	4		
Hubbard, David	1	3	1		
Hollister, Abraham	1		2		
Hollister, John	1		5		
Hale, Abagail			2		
Hodge, Elijah	2	2	3		
Hubbard, Prudence		1	3		
House, Benjamin	2	1	3		
Hollister, Roswell	3	2	2		
Hale, George	1		3		1
Hale, Josiah	2	2	5	4	
House, Eleazer	1	2	2		
House, John	1	1	4		
Hollister, Amos	2	2	3		
Hills, Joseph	2	2	4		
Hollister, Joseph, Jr	1	4	3		
Hodge, John	2	1	2		
Hale, Charles	4		1		
Hollister, David, 3d	1	1	3		
Hodge, Jonathan	1	4	2		
Hale, Benjamin	2	2	4		
House, Elijah	1	2	2		
House, George	1	2	2		
House, Elizabeth			2		
Hunt, John	1		1		
Hunt, Samuel	1	2	2		
Jop, John	1	1	2		
Kilbourn, Mary	1	1	2	1	
Kilbourn, Abraham	1		1		
Kibbard, Jonathan	2		3		
Lyman, Samuel	2	1	3		
Lewis, Abel	1	1	2		
Loveland, Lazarus	1	3	2		
Loveland, Deborah	1	1	5		
Loveland, Eli	1	1	5		
Loveland, Solomon	1	2	4		
Loveland, Thomas	1		1		
Lannd, Hannah			2		
Moseley, William	2	1	5		
Moseley, Syphax				5	
Miles, Daniel	2		2		
Miller, Mathew	2	1	6		
Matson, Thomas, Jr	1	3	4		
Miller, William, Jr	1		3		
Matson, Joseph	2	3	3		
Miller Elizur	1	2	3		
Matson, Thomas	1		1		
Miller, William	3	1	3		
Miller, Abijah	2	1	5		1
Moseley, Susanna			1		
Moseley, Ebenezer	1	3	2		
Miller, John	3	2	6		
Moseley, Joseph	5	1	1	1	2
Moseley, Demish	1	2	5		
Moseley, Eunice		2	3		
Moseley, Richard				3	
Nicholson, Frances	1	2	4		
Nichols, Nicholas	1	2	2		
Nicholson, Joel	1	2	2		
Nicholson, Ambrose, Jr	2		2		
Nicholson, Ambrose	2		3		
Olive, Neptune				4	
Simbo, Prince				5	
Plummer, Ebenezer	1		2		2
Plummer, Isaac	2	2	2		
Pratt, David	1	1	3		
Pratt, Daniel	1		1		
Pratt, Mansah	1	4	4		
Pease, David	1	2	2		
Pulsifer, Joseph	3		2		
Pulsifer, Sylvester	1		3		
Price, Samuel	1	4	3		
Polly, John	1	3	1		
Peirce, Philip	2	1	6		
Potter, Edward, Jr	1	2	1		

GLASTENBURY TOWN—continued.

NAME OF HEAD OF FAMILY.	Free white males of 16 years and upward, including heads of families.	Free white males under 16 years.	Free white females, including heads of families.	All other free persons.	Slaves.
Pulsifer, Huldah		2	2		
Pierce, Mary		1	2		
Pease, Peter	1		4		
Rice, Eliphalet	1	4	3		
Rice, John	1	2	1		
Rice, Samuel, Jr	1	1	2		
Rice, Samuel	2	2	2		
Risley, Benjamin	2	1	2		
Risley, Job	2	1	2		
Robertson, David	2	2	1		
Risley, Joseph	1	2	3		
Risley, George	1	3	2		
Ranson, Harris	1		3		
Smith, Jonathan	1				
Strickland, Stephen, Jr	2	4	3		
Stevens, George	1	2	3		
Smith, Hannah					
Sellew, John	2	4	5		
Stratton, Samuel, Jr	1	2	6		
Shipman, Stephen, Jr	1		1		
Shipman, John	2	1	5		
Smith, Jedediah	1	2	1		
Shipman, Stephen	1	1	1		
Smith, Ebenezer	1		1		
Smith, Benjamin	1	1	4		
Stevens, Timothy	1	2	4		
Strong, John	2	1	3		
Stocking, Ansel	1		3		
Stevens, Thomas	3		3		
Stevens, James	2	2	3		
Stevens, Peter	2	3	2		
Stevens, Josiah	2		2		
Stratton, Samuel, 3d	1	2	4		
Stevens, Elijah	2	3	5	1	
Smith, William	1		2		
Smith, Richard	1	1	1		
Smith, Elihu	1	3	2		
Stratton, Samuel	1	1	5		
Smith, Abraham	2		4		
Smith, Bathoheba			2		
Stevens, William		5	4		
Smith, Manoah	1		3		
Smith, Samuel, 2d	1	2	3		
Sellers, Phillip	3	5	7		
Starr, John	1	1	3		
Scott, Thomas	1		5		
Scott, Joseph	1	2	2		
Stoddard, Ebenezar	2		2		
Stocking, Elisha	1		2		
Strickland, Simecn	1	2	4		
Talcott, John	2	1	2		
Talcott, George	2	3	5		
Tryon, Thomas	1	2	2		
Talcott, Nathaniel	2		4		2
Tryon, Noah	1	2	3		1
Talcott, Elizur, Jr	1	3	7		
Treat, Peter	2	1	1	1	
Tryon, Elizuh	3	5	5		
Treat, Samuel	2		6		
Taylor, Samuel	1	1	3		
Treat, Dorotheus	1	1	2		
Treat, Charles	2		3		
Talcott, Annar			2		
Taylor, David	1		2		
Taylor, Azariah	1	4	1		
Taylor, Joseph	1	2	3		
Talcott, Abraham	1	2	2		
Taylor, Jonathan	1		5		
Talcott, Elizur	1		1		1
Tryon, William	2	1	2		
Taylor, George	1	2	4		
Talcott, Nathaniel, Jr	3	1	2		
Tryon, William, Jr	1	3	4		
Treat, Elisha	2	1	3		
Talcott, Ruth			3		
Talcott, Oliver	2	1	3		
Treat, Gershom	1	2	1		
Tenant, Caleb	1	1	4		
Wheelar, Elnathan	1	1	1		
Woodbridge, Howel	2	5	5		
Whiting, Isaac	1		3		
Willis, Eunice	1	1	3	2	1
Wickham, David	1		2		
Ward, Daniel	4	1	3		
Wheelar, Lazarus	1	2	4		
Welles, Samuel	1		4		
Welles, Joseph	1	3	2		
Wright, Isaac	1	2	4		
Welles, John	2	3	3		
Welles, Samuel, Jr	2	2	3		
Welles, Ephraim	2	1	3		
Welles, Jonathan	4	1	5	1	
Wells, Isaac	1	2	3		
Woodbridge, Theodore	1	2	4		
Wright, Samuel	3		3		

HARTFORD COUNTY—Continued.

NAME OF HEAD OF FAMILY.	Free white males of 16 years and upward, including heads of families.	Free white males under 16 years.	Free white females, including heads of families.	All other free persons.	Slaves.
GLASTENBURY TOWN—continued.					
Webster, Joshua	1	2	2		
Wares, Joseph	1	2	4		
Warren, John	1	1	3		
Welles, Elijah	1		1		
Wells, Thaddeus	1		1		
Williams, Jerusha			3		
Wright, Joseph	1	3	1		
Wheelar, Silent			2		
Waterman, Asahel	1	1	3		
Andrews, Charles	5	3	5		
Andrews, Stephen	1	1	1		
Andrews, Elisha	1		3		
Andrews, Elisha, Jr	1	2	2		
Andrews, John	1	2	4		
Andrews, Benjamin, Jr	1	1	5		
Andrews, David	1	2	6		
Andrews, Benjamin	3		3		
Baker, Ephraim	1	5	6		
Buck, William	1	4	3		
Brooks, Josiah	1	1	3		
Brooks, Samuel	3		2		
Boles, Ezra	1	4	4		
Brewer, Dorothy			4		
Blish, Thomas	1	2	2		
Brooks, William	1		3		
Brooks, Samuel, Jr	3	1	4		
Covell, Eliphalet	1	3	3		
Covell, Jonathan	1		6		
Covell, Elijah	2	4	2		
Covell, Philip	1	4	3		
Covell, James	1	1	1		
Couch, Elisha	1	3	2		
Covell, Samuel	2	1	4		
Daniels, David	1	2	3		
Dutton, William	1	3	2		
Dealing, Samuel	2	1	1		
Dickinson, Nathan, Jr	1	1	1		
Dickinson, David, 3d	1	3	3		
Dickinson, David, Jr	2	2	4		
Ellis, Revd James	1	1	1		1
Smith, Mabel			3		
Fox, David, Jr	1	2	3		
Fox, Lemuel	1	1	4		
Fox, Levi	1	1	2		
Fox, Richard	1		1		
Fox, Isaac	2	2	3		
Fox, Jonah	2	1	5		
Fox, Thomas	1		4		
Fox, Amasa	1	1	1		
Fox, Amos	1	4	3		
Fox, Israel	1	2	2		
Fox, Stephen	1	2	4		
Fox, Ebenezer	1	2	6		
Fox, Martha	1		3		
Goff, Aaron	2	1	3		
Goodale, Ebenezer	2	2	3		
Goodrich, Elijah H	1	1	1		
Goodale, Thomas	1		2		
Goodale, Joseph, Jr	5	3	6		
Goodale, Joseph	2		4	1	
Gosler, Timothy	3	2	4		
Gosler, Asa	3	1	3		
Gibson, Samuel	3		9		
Goodale, Isaac	1		1		
Goodale, Avary	1		2		
Goodale, Henery	2		3		
Hills, Samuel	1		1		
Hills, Samuel, Jr	1	3	2		
Hills, Israel	1	1	2		
Hollister, Elisha	4	1	4		
Hollister, Aaron	1	2	4		
Hollister, George	1	2	5		
House, Lazarus	2	4	3		
Holmes, Charles	1	5	5		
Hale, William	2	1	4		
Huxford, William	2		2		
Hollister, Thomas	1	1	6	1	
Hubbard, Elizur	2	3	3		
Hollister, Gideon	2	1	3		
Hills, Daniel	1	3	2		
Hills, Josiah	1	2	4		
House, William	1	2	5		
Hale, Frary	2	1	4		
Hollister, Israel	1	3	6		
Holden, Jonathan	1	2	2		
House, Israel	1	4	2		
Hollister, Asahel	1	1	2		
Holden, John	3		1		
Huxford, John	1		4		
House, Mathew	1	2	4		
Hale, Edward	1	2	1		
How, Elisha	4	1	6		
House, Joel	1	1	2		
Hale, Elizur	2	3	2		
Hale, Isaac	2	1	1		1
GLASTENBURY TOWN—continued.					
Hills, Elisha	1	5	3		
Homes, Appleton	1	6	4		
House, Daniel	2	2	4		
House, Abner	1	3	3		
Hunt, Thomas	3	1	5		
How, John, Jr	1	2	3		
Hollister, Ichabod	1	3	4		
Hodge, Benjamin	1	2	3		
Hodge, Benjamin, Jr	2	3	1		
Hollister, Nehemiah	1	2	5		
Hollister, Theodore	2	1	3		
Hollister, Nathaniel	1	2	4		
Hollister, Elizur	2	2	1	1	
Hollister, David, Jr	1	2	3		
Hale, Thomathy, Jr	1		2		
Holden, Jonathan, Jr	1		3		
Hills, John	1	1	3		
Hubbard, Elizur, Jr	2	2	3	1	
Hills, Libbeus	1	1	2		
Holmes, William	1		1		
Hildrieth William	3	2	4		
Huxford, William	1		1		
Jones, Parker	1		1		
Jones, Moses	1		1		
Ingham, Joseph	1	2	4		
Jones, Lemuel	2	2	6		
Johnson, Levi	1		2		
Kuney, James	1	1	4		
Kimberly, Mary			3		
Loveland, John	1	1	2		
Loveland, Aaron	1		1		
Loveland, Elizur	2		8		
Loveland, Levi	2	3	4		
Loveland, Peletiah	3	3	5		
Loveland, Nathan	1	1	2		
Moseley, Timothy	3	1	3		
McLean, James	3	2	5		
Nye, Solomon	1	1	4		
Nye, Milatiah	1		1		
Nowland, Samuel	2	2	7		
Newil, Sarah			2		
Parsons, Samuel	1		4		
Risley, Thomas, Jr	1		3		
Risley, David	1		3		
Riley, Charles	2		1		
Risley, Reuben	2	3	5		
Risley, Thomas	1	1	2		
Smith, David	1		1		
Smith, Asa	1	3	2		
Smith, Samuel	3	2	3		
Simons, Joseph	2	4	4		
Sparks, Reuben	1	2	5		
Shirtliff, Jonathan	1		5		
Sparks, Thomas	1	4	1		
Strickland, Stephen	1		2		
Skinner, Benjamin	1	1	3		
Standish, Jeremiah	2	2	6		
Strickland, Howel	1	1	1		
Strickland, Nehemiah	3	1	2		
Strickland, Stephen, 3d	1	3	2		
Smith, Isaac	2		2		
Richardson, William	1	3	2		
Strickland, Nehemiah, Jr	1	3	2		
Talcott, Jonathan	1	3	1		
Tubbs, Lemuel	2	1	2		
Treat, Jonathan, Jr	1	2	1		
Treat, Jonathan	1		1	1	
Treat, Charles	1	4	2		
Talcott, Isaac	1	2	5		
Tucker, Benjamin	1	4	3		
Tryon, Joseph	4		4		
Tryon, George	1	2	2		
Talcott, Jabez	1	1	1		
Tubbs, Ezekiel	2	1	1		
Tryon, Isaac	1	5	4		
Williams, Isaac	1	1	2		
Wilden, Peleg	3	2	2		
Wire, John	2	3	4		
Wire, Nehemiah	1	2	4		
Wickham, Hezekiah	3	1	5		
Wickham, Hezekiah, Jr	1	3	2		
Waters, David	1	3	1		
Wright, Daniel	1		3		
Ackley, Stephen	2		3		
Bigelow, David	2	2	3		
Blish, David	3		4		
Chamberlain, William	2		3		
Chamberlain, Elizabeth			1		
Chamberlain, Benjamin	1	2	3		
Dunham, Levi	1	5	2		
Dickinson, Thomas	2	1	4		
Dickinson, Nathan	1	4	4		
Dickinson, David	1		3		
Dewey, John	1	3	4		
GLASTENBURY TOWN—continued.					
Finley, David	1	1	3		
Finley, John	1	1	2		
Finley, Solomon	1	1	1		
Foot, Israel	1	3	4		
Finley, Samuel	2	1	2		
Loveland, Thomas	3		3		
Phelps, Timothy, Jr	1		1		
Phelps, Timothy	3	3	1		
Phelps, John	2	1	3	1	
Burden, Jerry				3	
Skinner, Abraham, Jr	1		2	1	
Skinner, Deborah	1	1	4		
Strong, Amos	2	2	4		
Skinner, Abraham	2	1	3	1	
Waters, Gideon	1	1	2		
Warren, Henery	1		1		
Robberdore, August				4	
Allyn, Peter				5	
Janes, Frederic				8	
GRANBY TOWN.					
Holcomb, Hezekiah	1	1	2		
Holcomb, Daniel	3	1	2		
Holcomb, Hezekiah, Jr	2	5	5		
Holcomb, Jesse	2	3	3		
Holcomb, Noah	2	1	6		
Alford, Josiah	3	1	3		
Alderman, Thankfull (Wid.)	1	1	2		
Barnes, Abraham	1	2	2		
Griffin, Benoni	3		1		
Griffin, Abraham	1	1	1		
Holcomb, Joshua	1	3	4		
Holcomb, Caleb	1	2	4		
Winchel, Jehiel	1	1	4		
Moore, Job	3	1	1		
Crome, Samuel	1	6	4		
Adkins, Daniel	1	1	1		
Hayes, Daniel, Jr	1	2	2		
Toping, Josiah	2	1	3		
Toping, Josiah, Jr	1	1			
Griffin, Stephen, 2d	3	2	2		
Higley, David	3	1	2		
Edwards, Henery	2		3		
Hayes, Daniel	1		2		
Heyes, Enock	1	2	2		
Hayes, Honora (Wid.)	1		4		
Baker, Samuel	2	1	3		
Johnson, Asa	3		4		
Pettibone, Chancey	2	3	5	1	
Phelps, Isaac	1	2	9		
Pettibone, Ozias	3		4	5	
Jeut, Roger	1	1	2		
Rowe, Abijah	2	1	3		
Rice, Peter, Jr	1	1	2		
Rice, Joel	1		1		
Smith, Jediah	1	2	3		
Smith, James	1	1	6		
Hays, Joel	3	1	2		
Hayes, Rufus	1		2		
Hayes, Amos	1		1		
Dibol, Benjamin	1		1		
Dibol, Heman	1	1	1		
Hillyer, Pliny	1	2	5	2	
Gold, Gurdon	1		1		
Dibol, Levi	1	3	2		
Rice, Peter	1		2		
Rice, William	1		1		
Drownd, Nathaniel	1	3	1		
Ates, Abraham	1	3	2		
Dibol, Benjamin, Jr	2	2	3		
Smith, Roger	1	2	2		
Brown, Justin	1		1		
Smith, Widow			1		
Gillett, Elijah	3	1	2		
Hayes, David	1	3	3		
Hayes, Silus	4		3		
Hayes, Samuel	3		2		
Hayes, Pliny	1	1	2		
Hayes, Simeon	1		1		
Hayes, Samuel, Jr	1	1	4		
Wright, Benjamin	1	1	4		
Moore, Oliver	1		1		
Holcomb, Elihu	1		1		
Barnard, David	1	5	3		
Hill, Elijah	1	2	2		
Hurlbut, Jehiel	1	2	2		
Cook, Benjamin	1	4	2		
Salter, Rachel			1		
Higley, Jonathan	1	3	5		
Higley, Mary			1		
Alderman, Gad	1	2	2		
Alderman, Lott	1	1	1		
Swan, Joseph	1	6	1		

HARTFORD COUNTY—Continued.

GRANBY TOWN—con.

NAME OF HEAD OF FAMILY.	Free white males of 16 years and upward, including heads of families.	Free white males under 16 years.	Free white females, including heads of families.	All other free persons.	Slaves.
Eno, Elisha	1	4	3		
Griswold, Joseph	1		1		
Griswold, Joseph, Jr	1		1		
Alderman, Joseph	1		1		
Alderman, Joseph, Jr	1	2	2		
Alderman, Timothy	1	2	2		
Skinner, Hezekiah	1		1		
Griffin, Thomas	3		4		
Griffin, Thomas, Jr	1		3		
Alderman, Elnathan	2	3	2		
Cook, Darius	1	6	2		
Holcomb, Abel	1	2	4		
Alderman, Elijah	1	3	5		
Holcomb, Simeon	2	1	5		
Messenger, Israel	1	1	3		
Messenger, Amos	1		2		
Messenger, Nathaniel	2		4		
Messenger, David	1	2	3		
Messenger, Daniel	1	1	2		
Couch, David	2	1	7		
Hayes, Oliver	1	3	4		
Gozzard, Moses	2	3	3		
Perring, Elisha	2	1	4		
Hugens, James	4	1	2		
Higley, Ozias	2	3	4		
Higley, Asa	2	1	3		
Holidy, Amos	1	5	3		
Hayes, Benjamin	3	2	5		
Hayes, Jacob	1	2	2		
Griffin, Joab	1	4	3		
Straten, Hannah	3	3	1		
Hicock, Jiles	1		1		
Hayes, Andrew	3		7		
Hayes, Andrew, Jr	1	2	2		
Hays, Ezekiel	2	2	2		
Kilbourn, Lemuel	1		2		
Kilbourn, Filo	1	1	1		
Holidy, John	1		1		
Strong, Elnathan	2	3	4		
Holcomb, Phineas	2	1	3		
Holcomb, Criss	1		1		
Holcomb, Nahum	1		1		
Holcomb, Reuben	1		1		
Holcomb, Noadiah	1	3	3		
Gozzard, Martin	3	7	3		
Gozzard, Abel	2		1		
Copt, Alexander	3	1	3		
Gozzard, John, Jr	1	2	2		
French, Asher	1		5		
Willcocks, David	1	1	4		
Hays, Benajah	1	3	1		
Hodgkiss, Ambrose	1		2		
Cosset, Timothy	2		3		
Bemon, Aaron	2	3	4		
Pratt, Nathaniel	1	3	3		
Gillett, Joseph	1	2	3		
Gillett, Benoni	1	3	2		
Hays, Seth	2	1	5		
Gozzard, Isaac	1	2	4		
Brewer, Benjamin	2	1	2		
Gozzard, John	1		2		
Gozzard, Nathan	3	1	5		
Gozzard, Ebenezer	1	1	1		
Gozzard, Ebenezer, Jr	1	2	2		
Gozzard, Levi	1	2	2		
Gozzard, Rufus	1	2	1		
Gozzard, Nicholus	1	1	5		
Griffin, John	1	4	2		
Messenger, Elijah	2		1		
Holcomb, Peter	2		3		
Holcomb, Asahel, 3d	1	1	3		
Holcomb, Peter, Jr	1	3	1		
Holcomb, Ebenezer	1	1	1		
Holcomb, Abel, 2d	1		1		
Owen, Elijah	1	1	1		
Holcomb, John G	1	2	1		
Gillett, Othenial	1				
Gillett, Othenial, Jr	1		3		
Gillett, Buckler	1	5	1		
Gillett, Ephraim	1	2	1		
Holcomb, Adonijah	1	2	6		
Gozzard, Ezra	1	1	1		
Gozzard, Ezra	1	2	2		
Gozzard, Luther	1		1		
Case, Abel	1		4		
Swaine, Benjamin	1	2	5		
Andrus, Ashael	1	2	3		
Andrus, Abner	1		3		
Weed, Aaron	2	2	5		
Bacon, Nathaniel	2	1	4		
Matson, Dorcas (Wid.)	1	1	1		
Weed, Deborah			1		
Weed, Moses	1	3	3		
Weld, Benjamin	1	1	2		
Bacon, Celi	1		2		
Wright, Jeremiah	1	1	4		
Case, Micah	1	2	4		
Case, Rufus	1	2	3		
Humphrey, Timothy	1	2	4		
Gillett, Adne	1	1			
Case, William	1				
Wright, John	1	1	2		
Holcomb, Dan	2	3	5		
Griffen, Nathaniel	3		1		
Holcomb, Ozias	4	2	2		
Holcomb, Ozias, Jr	1	1	1		
Pratt, Timothy	1		3		
Reed, John, Jr	2		2		
Read, Rusell	2	1	2		
Rice, John	2	1	4		
Rice, Jessee	1	1	2		
Phelps, Hezekiah	1	1	1		
Phelps, Hezh, 2d	1		3		
Vining, Richard	2	3	3		
Grigny, Dan	1		1		
Wrathbun, Daniel	1	2	1		
Higley, Joel	2	1	5		
Phelps, Abel	3	2	4		
Banthore, Wm	2	2	2		
Frasure, Daniel	3	1	4		
Griffen, Absalom	1	2	2		
Fletcher, Ephraim	2	2	8		
Holcomb, Benajah	2	6	2		
Post, Aaron			2		
Holcomb, Roger, Jr	1		1		
Coset, Reuben	1		2		
Compstock (Widow)			1		
Bulloph, Jonathan	1	2	3		
Phelps, William	1	2	3		
Phelps, Timothy	1		3		
Gains, Solomon	2	1	2		
Cobler, Thos	1	4	4		
Humphry, Ozias	1		2		
Rice, Pedi			1		
Rice, Jonah	1	4	2		
Butolph, Levi	1	1	2		
Cap, Job	2	2	2		
Holcomb, Silus	1	1	1		
Clemens, Fardy	1		2		
Clemens, William	1	2	2		
Colton, Elizabeth (Wid.)			1		
Copt, Frances	2		2		
Gaines, Luther	1		1		
Williams, Wm	1	3	5		
Hayes, Dudley	1	1	4		
Hays, Dudley	1	1	4		
Holcomb, Consider	2	3	5		
Gillett, Azariah	1	5	2		
Gillett, Nathan	3	4	2		
Holcomb, Roger	2	1	8		
Read, Benjamin	2	3	3		
Gozzard, Fille	2	2	5		
Read, John	1				
Read, Abner	1	3	2		
Hayes, William, Jr	1	1	7		
Barber, Joseph	1	2	1		
Hoskins, John	1		1		
Dibol, Moses, Jr	1	2	2		
Burr, Asa	1	2	1		
Griffin, Mathew	1		3		
Dibol, Dan	1	2	3		
Burr, Zebina	1	2	3		
Hilyer, Seth	2	2	3		
Messenger, Nathaniel	1		1		
Spring, Silvester	1		2		
Holcomb, Elijah	4		2		
Holcomb, Elijah, Jr	1	2	2		
Read, Martin	2	2	2		
Gains, Daniel	2		4		
Slater, Benjamin	2	2	3		
Moore, Ozias	3	1	3		
Holcomb, Asa	2		2		
Hays, William	1		1		
Holcomb, Nathaniel	1		1		
Juett, Joseph	2	2	2		
Phelps, Reuben	1	1	7		
Clark, Samuel	1	1	3		
Bacon, Mary (Wid.)	1		2		
Holcomb, Eli	1		3		
Pease, Naomi (Wid.)			1		
Hawley, James	1	1	3		
Hawley, Thomas	3	1	2		
Forward, Abel	1				
Sage, Seth	1	1	5		
Spencer, Ebenezer	1	3	2		
Egeton, Ebenezer	2	1	3		
Egeton, Ebenezer, Jr	1		2		
Segar, John	1		3		
Segar, Augustus	1		2		
Case, Noah	1		1		
Case, Roger	1		4		
Read, George	1	1	1		
Read, David	1	1	2		
Case, Noah, Jr	1	2	4		
Case, Simeon	4	4	3		
Case, Obed	1	1	1		
More, Damanes	1		1		
More, Jehiel	1	1	2		
More, Benjamin	1		1		
Case, Richard	3	4	5		
Case, Phineas	1	1	5		
Case, Richard, Jr	1	3	4		
Taylor, Russell	1	4	1		
Miller, Moses	1	1	5		
Miller, Ichabod	1		1		
Case, George	1	2	3		
Forward, Jesse	1	4	3		
Holcomb, Ahas	1		1		
Veits, Benoni	1		1		
Veits, Luke	1	3	5		
Stephens, Thomas	1	2	3		
Hays, Zenas	1	1	3		
Holcomb, Ezekiel, Jr	1	2	1		
Gillett, Jabash	1	2	3		
Gillett, Jacob	1				
Alderman, Epephras	1	1	5		
Veits, Abner	2	4	3		
Rice, Joseph	2	3	4		
Ormsby, Levi	1	1	1		
More, Rideout	1	1	3		
Veits, Seth	2	4	5		
Roe, Titus	1	2	1		
Gillet, Zacheus	1	1	1		
Stephens, Edmond	2	1	2		
Griffin, Michael	2	2	2		
Griffin, Elizabeth			1		
Veits, James	1	2	3		
Veits, Jonathan	2				
Phelps, Elijah	2	1	2		
Phelps, Shubel	1	1	1		
Miller, John	1	1	4		
Stephens, Phinias	1	3	4		
Griffin, Elijah	1	4	6		
Griffin, Seth	1	4	6		
Orsborn, David	1	3	2		
Miller, Alexander	1				
Brown, Joseph	1	3	2		
Holcomb, Obed	1		2		
Holcomb, Masa (Wid.)	2	3	3		
Holcomb, David	3		1		
Holcomb, David, Jr	1				
Bull, Abner	2	1	3		
Griffin, Stephen	2	2	4		
Roe, Daniel	1	2	1		
Pike, William	1	1	1		
Holcomb, Ezekiel	2	3	4		
Granger, Israel	2	2	2		
Halawa, Daniel	1		1		
Griffin, Stephen	1		2		
Hilyer, James	1		1		
Hillyer, Asa	2	2	2		
Hillyer, Theodorus	1	1	3		
Dunn, Samuel	1	3	5		
Spring, Thomas	3	2	4		
Spring, Silvester	2				
Burr, Adonijah	1	2	1		
Dibol, Moses	1	1	3		
Dibol, Reuben	1	1	3		
More, Shadrack	1		2		
More, Shadrack, Jr	1	2	2		
More, Roger	1	1	2		1
Huse, Abraham	1	3	2		
Wadsworth, Timothy	1	1	5		
Moore, Eli	1				
More, Reuben	1				
Davis, William	1		5		
Bell, Elisha	1	2	3		
Willcox, John	1		4		
Williams, David	1	1	3		
Gillett, Isaac	2	1	6		
Holcomb, Nathan, Jr	1	3	3		
Clark, Eliphalet	1	3	3		
Phelps, Noah	1	3	4		
Gillett, Levi	1	2	3		
Jones, Hezekiah	1	2	3		
Cushman, Solomon	3	2	3		
Phelps, Abijah	2	3	4		
Phelps, Levi	1	3	4		
Cook, Jacob	2	1	4		
Winchell, Mary	2	1	1		
Winchell, Simeon	1		1		
Kellogg, Oliver	1		1		
Enos, David	1	1	3		
More, Jonah	2		1		

HARTFORD COUNTY—Continued.

NAME OF HEAD OF FAMILY.	Free white males of 16 years and upward, including heads of families.	Free white males under 16 years.	Free white females, including heads of families.	All other free persons.	Slaves.	NAME OF HEAD OF FAMILY.	Free white males of 16 years and upward, including heads of families.	Free white males under 16 years.	Free white females, including heads of families.	All other free persons.	Slaves.	NAME OF HEAD OF FAMILY.	Free white males of 16 years and upward, including heads of families.	Free white males under 16 years.	Free white females, including heads of families.	All other free persons.	Slaves.
GRANBY TOWN—con.						GRANBY TOWN—con.						HARTFORD TOWN—con.					
More, Joel	3	4	3			Barnes, Isaac	2	3	3			Bruster, Prince	2	3	7		
More, Nathan	2	2	5			Huckins, James	2		1			Bolles, Samuel	1	1	2		
Griswold, Alexander	2	3	3			Huckins, Jonathan	1	1	2			Beebe, Adam	1	2	1		
Clark, David, Jr	1	3	3			Day, Roswell	1	1	3			Caldwell, John	2	2	6		
More, Joel, Jr	1	1	1			Day, Lues	1	6	3			Colton, Aaron	3		3		
Clark, David	5	1	4			Day, Timothy	1	3	3			Colt, Peter	2	2	6		1
Clark, Cefus	1	1	1			Johnson, Daniel	1	4	3			Colt, Elisha	2		2		
Ross, William	1					Berwick, Elisha	1		1			Calder, John	3	1			
Skinner, Roswell	1	3	3			Hoskins, Elijah	1	2	3			Caldwell, George	1		2		
Winchell, Oliver	1		4			Gillett, Nathaniel, Jr	2	4	6			Caldwell, —*	1		2		
Thompson, Edward	1	1	3			Gillett, Nathaniel	1		1			Cadwell, Elizabeth			2		
Thompson, Edward, Jr	1		5			Gillett, Timothy	1	1	2			Chenevard, John	4		5		
Thompson, Edmund	1	1	2			Holcomb, Ezra	5	2	2			Corning, Ezra	2	3	3		
Lews, Simeon	2	2	3			Miller, Samuel	1	2	5			Cotton, Daniel	2	1	3		
Winchell, Elisha	3		2			Rowley, Roswell	1	1	4			Cadwell, Hezekiah	2	2	4		
Winchell, Elisha, Jr	1	4	2			Strickland, Joseph	1	1	1			Corning, Asa	6	1	7		
Winchell, Grove	1	2	2			Strickland, Joseph, Jr	2	1	2			Cadwell, Abram	2		2		
Thompson, Jemima			1			Forward, Joseph	4	1	3			Cables, John	1	3	4		
Winchell, Jehiel	1					Forward, Reuben	1	2	3			Church, George	1		2		
Hoskins, Alson	3	1	2			Phelps, Ebenezer	2	1	6			Chapin, Aaron	3	2	3		
Winchel, Nathaniel	2	3	3			Phelps, Nathaniel	3		2			Cook, Aaron	2	1	4		
Parker, Reuben	4	1	1			Phelps, Nathan	1	1	2			Church, Caleb	4	2	2		
Clark, Joel	2	2	3			Phelps, Eliphalet	1	1	4			Caldwell, Charles	1	1	6	1	
Clark (Wid.)			1			Phelps, Nathaniel, Jr	1		1			Cook, John	1	1	9		
Phelps, Ruth (Wid.)	1		3			Adams, Ephraim	1		1			Collins, Robert J	1	3	4		
Clark, Jesse	2		4			Wilkinson, Oliver	1	1	1			Cadwell, Nehemiah	1		4		
Rockwell, William	1		1			Lyon, Aaron	1		4			Cadwell, Nehemiah, Jr	1	3	3		
Holcomb, Asahel, Jr	3	1	2			Leus, Hezekiah	3	2	1			Church, Asher	1	2	3		
Gooid, David	1	3	2			Kilbourn, James	1		1			Cadwell, Jeduthan	2	3	4		
Hillyer, Andrew	1	2	4			Bacon, James	1		4			Cook, James	2	1	1	1	
Holcomb, Asahel, Jr	3	1	1			Strickland, Asahel	1	4	4			Church, James	1		1	1	
Holcomb, Asahel, 4th	1	1	2			Colton (Wid.)		1	3			Cook, William	1	2	2		
Holcomb, Oliver	1		2			Ross, Timothy	1		3			Chapman, Alpheus	1		1		
Phelps, Basheba	2	1	3			Averett, Samuel	3		2			Church, Joseph	1	1	4		
Gillett, Joab	1	2	3			Clark, Aaron	1	1	2			Chapman, Andrew	1	2	3		
Hill, John	1		2			More, Isaac	1		2			Chapman, Silas	1	2	3		
Wright, Uring	1		2			Jones, Daniel	1		1			Cadwell, Ruth			3		
Dewy, Isaac	1		1			Hays, Levi	1	3	2			Curtis, Daniel	1		2		
Dewey, David	1	4	3			Holcomb, Martha (Wid.)			1			Clark, Ebenezer	2		3		
Dewey, Isaac	1	1	5									Clapp, Oliver	2	2	5		
Dewey, Aaron	1	1	3			HARTFORD TOWN.						Coop, David	2		2		
Copt, Alexander	3	1	2									Center, John	1	1	3		
Perring, Elisha	2	1	4			Andrus, Silvanus	1	1	5			Church, Timothy	1	1	2		
Kendall, Noadiah	2	4	4			Ames, David	1	1	1			Collier, William	1	3	4		
Totten, Dorcas			2			Avery, John	1	4	5	2	1	Doolittle, Enos	1	4	3		
Lampson, Joseph	1		2			Anderson, James	3		4			Denniss, Ebenezer	1		1		
Lampson, Ebenezer	1	2	2			Adams, William	1		6	1		Day, Samuel	1	2	2		
Lampson, Benjamin	1	1	3			Alford, Alpheus			6			Dickenson, Moses	1		1		
Lampson (Wid.)			1			Alford, Lydia (widow)			2			Danforth, Edward	3	1	4		
Haley, Israel	2		4			Adams, Ebenezer	2		2			Day, Joseph	2	2	1		
Lampson, Elnathan	3		2			Bull, Thomas	2	2	4			Drake, Martha			2		
Lampson, Samuel	2	2	3			Bull, William	1		2			Davis, Philip	1		2		
Hubbard, Elijah	4	3	3			Bull, George	4		2			Egleston, Elihu	2	2	6		
More, Ruth			4			Bull, Caleb	3		4			Ellery, William	3		4		
Holcomb, Judah, Jr	2	2	3			Bull, James	3	1	2	1	1	Ensign, Thomas, Jr	2		1		
Holcomb, Judah, Esqr	2		2			Bull, Hezekiah	1		4	1		Ewing, William	2		2		
Gilbert, Ichabod	2	3	2			Bull, Frederic	4	2	4	2		Fish, Miller	5	1	3		
Hays, Obadiah	1	3	3			Bull, David	2	2	6	2	1	Flagg, Joseph	1		2		
Ford, Adonijah	1	3	4			Bull, Isaac	2	3	3			Fowler, Benjamin	1	1	4		
Ford, Mathew	1		1			Brunson, Isaac	2	1	1	2	2	Fish, Eliakim	1		2		
Holcomb, Joseph	2	1	4			Burr, Samuel	3	2	6	1		Flagg, Jonathan	2	3	3		
Holcomb, Joseph, Jr	1	2	2			Burr, Timothy	3		1			Fry, John	1	1	2		
Cosset, Asa	2		4			Burr, Moses	3		4			Goodwin, John	2	1	3		
Perring, Ruth			3			Byington, Joel	3	4	6			Goodrich, Chancey	3		2		
Coley, Noah	2	2	3			Bolles, John, 2d	3	1	3			Goodman, Richard	2	1	4		
Cosett, Rana	1		2			Bunce, Isaac	1					Gove, William	2		3		
Cosset, Silas	1	4	1			Beebe, Adonijah	2	2	2			Goodwin, George	3	4	5		
Hillyer, James, Jr	1	3	3			Burr, George	1	5	4			Goodwin, William	2	4	3		
Willcox, Sadoss	2	3	3			Beckwith, Samuel	3	1	6			Goodwin, Theodore	1	1			
Robbins, Appleton	1	1				Burr, William	3	2	4			Goodwin, Russell	1		1		
Trumble, Ephraim	1		1			Bigelow, Daniel	1		1			Goodwin, Anna (Wid.)	2	3	4		
Phelps, Roswell	1	2	1			—*, Nathan	2	1	3			Goodwin, James	3	2	4		
More, Micah	1	1	1			Barnard, Joseph	1		2			Gray, Edward	1	3	4		
Forward, Samuel	1	3	5			Belair, Thomas	2	1	3			Goodwin, Samuel	2	1	2		
Bates, Zopha	1		2			Burnham, George	1	5	3			Goodwin, David	2	2	2		
Booth, Samuel	1	1	2			Barnard, Samuel						Goodwin, Jonathan	1	1	3		
Phelps, Roger	1		1			Beckwith, Josiah	4		2	1		Goodwin, Allyn	1	1	2		
Attwet, Oliver	1	2	3			Bunce, John, Jr	1	3	1			Goodwin, Mary			3		
Owen, Alvin	2	1	4			Barnard, Ebenezer	2	1	4			Goodwin, Timothy	1		3		
Bates, Lemuel	3	1	1			Dwight, —*	4		1			Grist, Joseph	1		2		
Gay, Richard, Jr	1	4	3			Bradley, Aaron	2	3	3			Goodwin, Asher	1	1	1		
Gay, Richard	2	1	3			Buner, Timothy	2	2	5			Goodwin, Mary			3		
Cornish, Joseph	1	1	2			Burkitt, Uriah	3		6			Hinsdale, Daniel	4	2	6	4	
Cornish, Elizabeth			1			Bolles, John	4	2	5			Hart, Joseph	2	1	4	4	
Buck, Eliphalet	2		2			Burkitt, Thomas	1	3	3			Hosmer, James	5	2	4		
Morse, Chester	1	2	5			Burkitt, John	1	1	2			Hopkins, Asa	3		7		
Strong, Eli	2	1	4			Bryant, Benjamin	1	1	2			Hopkins, Thomas	2	2	4	1	
Bartlet, Sylvanus	1	3	5			Burt, Consider	3	1	7			Hall, John	1	3	3		
Gillet, Oliver	1	2	3			Burr, Joseph	1	1	3			Hall, Asaph	1	1	2		
Burr, Adonijah, Jr	1	3	2			Blanott, James	2	2	2			Hall, William	1		2		
Jones, Levi	1	3	2			Benton, Asa	1	2	4			Hequimburgh, Charles	2	1	2		
Crittenton, Samuel	1		2			Brainthwait, Robert	4		4			Henery, James	1		3		
More, Horace	1		2			Bunce, Jerusha			3			James, Webster	1	2	5		
More, Obed	1	1	3			Bolles, Stephen	2	3	1			Herrod, Jesse	1		2		

* Illegible.

HARTFORD COUNTY—Continued.

HARTFORD TOWN—con.

NAME OF HEAD OF FAMILY.	Free white males of 16 years and upward, including heads of families.	Free white males under 16 years.	Free white females, including heads of families.	All other free persons.	Slaves.
Jones, Nathaniel	1		1		
Johnson, Shadrach	1	1	2		
Imley, William	1	4	4	1	
Indicott, John	1	4	3		
Jeffery, John	2	3	6		
Jepson, James	1	1	4		
Janes, Jonathan	6	2	7	1	1
Jones, John	1	1	2		
Jones, Daniel	4		8		1
Jones, Julius	2	3	4		
Jones, Samuel P	1		4		
Judd, Reuben	2	4	4		
Judd, Simeon	1	1	4		
Jones, Pantry	1		2		1
Jones, Benjamin	1		1		
James, John	2	3	5		
Knox, James	1	1	2		
Kingsbury, Andrew	1	1	5		
Knox, William	2	2	3	2	
Knox, Jennet (Wid.)	1	1	8	1	
Kelsey, Levi	1	3	4		
Kilbourn, Freeman	2	2	5		
Kilbourn, Samuel	1	2	3		
Kellogg, Charles	1		1		
Lyman, Timothy	2	1	3		
Leffingwell, John	4	1	5		
Leidlie, Hugh	3		1		
Lawrence, John	2	1	5		
Lawrence, William	2	2	5		
Lowell, Willibe	4	4	4		
Lord, John Haynes	3	2	5		
Leffingwell, Joshua	2	1	2		
Lord, John H., Jr	1				
Larkum, John	1		1		
Loud, Asa	2	1	1		
Larkum, Rhoderic	1	1	5		
Lamb, James	1	1	2		
Lee, George	1		3		
Marsh, Mary	1		5		
Moseley, William	1	2	2		
Morse, William	1	2	2		
Morgan, John	2	1	3		
Merrill, George	1		3		1
Marsh, Samuel	4	1	4		
Merrill, Hezekiah	1	5	3		
Murray, Cotton	1		3		
Marsh, Jesse	2	1	2		
Moore, Ebenezer	3	1	4	1	
McAlpine, John	1	2	4		
Marsh, John	1	3	2		1
Morgan, Devill	1		3		
Marsh, Samuel, 2d	5		6		
Mire, William	1	1	3		
Mason, Isaac	1	1	2		
Nichols, William	1	1	3	1	
Nevins, John	1	1	3		
Newill, James	1				
Olcott, Joseph	1	2	5		
Ogden, Jacob	1	1	8		
Olcott, Roderic	1		1		
Olcott, Samuel	2		5		2
Olcott, Jonathan	1		2		
Oakes, David	1	1	2		
Olcott, Theodore	2		4		
Olcott, Hezekiah	1	2	3		
Olcott, Timothy	1				
Oakes, Isaac	2	3	4		
Olcott, Daniel	2		3	1	
Olcott, James	1	2	4		
Olcott, William, 2d	2	1	3		
Pratt, James	1	1	3		
Porter, Solomon	1	2	2		
Phillips, Joseph	2		2		
Pratt, William, Jr	1		2		
Pomeroy, Ralph	4	1	3	1	2
Pratt, Zacheriah	1	1	1		
Pratt, George	1		1		
Pratt, William	5	2	2		
Phelps, Daniel, 2d	1	1	2		
Pratt, Joseph	2	1	3		1
Patten, Nathaniel	3	1	4		
Perkins, Jabez	3	4	1		
Perkins, Enoch	1		3	1	
Patten, Ruth (Wid.)			6		
Root, Jesse	3	1	2	1	1
Root, Jesse, Jr	1		2	1	1
Roberts, John	1	2	6		
Rowland, William	1		2		
Ramsey, Jonathan	1	2	2		
Roberts, Jonathan	1	2	4		
Roberts, Aaron	1	1	2		
Roberts, John, 2d	1		1		
Ritter, John	1	1	1		
Spencer, Lina		1	3		
Shortman, William	1	2	2		

HARTFORD TOWN—con.

NAME OF HEAD OF FAMILY.	Free white males of 16 years and upward, including heads of families.	Free white males under 16 years.	Free white females, including heads of families.	All other free persons.	Slaves.
Sloan, Robert	1	2	2		
Suitar, John	2	2	5		
Stackhouse, Stacy	3	4	3		
Steele, Thomas	4	4	4		
Spencer, Thomas	1	2	1		
Skinner, Daniel	1		2		2
Spencer, Theadore	1	1	2		
Spencer, Epaphras	1		4		
Spencer, Timothy	2	3	5		
Spencer, Ashbel	2	3	5		
Spencer, Michael	1	2	2		
Sheldon, James	2	2	3		
Sheldon, John	1		2		
Sheldon, John, Jr	1	5	5		
Skinner, Daniel, Jr	1	2	2		
Spencer, Benjamin	2	1	3		
Sanford, Thomas	3	2	5		
Spencer, John, Jr	1	2	4		
Smith, George	2	2	2		
Seymour, Asa	1	1	1		
Sloan, Thomas	3		4		
Seymour, Hezekiah	1	3	2		
Shepard, Ashbel	1	1	3		
Skinner, Theodore	1	2	3		
Shepard, Richard	2	3	5		
Skinner, Elisha	1	5	1		
Sanford, Isaac	2	1	6		
Skinner, William	1	1	1		
Seymour, Thomas, Esqr	8		3	1	
Seymour, Robert	1	1	4		
Strong, Revd Nathan	2	2	3	1	
Skinner, Jared	1	1	3		
Shepard, Charles	1		2		
Shepard, Uriah	1		4		
Shepard, Elisha	1	4	2		
Skinner, John	1		4		1
Shepard, Timothy	2		1		
Sloan, Robert	1	2	4		
Sanford, Zach	1		2		
Savage, Luther	1		2		
Stanley, Roswell	1	1	3		
Stanley, Frederic	1	2	5		
Tiley, James	1	2	4		
Talcott, Samuel	2		1		1
Talcott, Samuel, Jr	2	2	4		
Talcott, Joseph	1	1	2		1
Thomas, John	3	4	4		
Toocker, Joseph	3	3	7		
Tisdale, Thomas	5		3		
Trumble, John	1	2	5		
Tiley, Samuel	1				
Turner, Samuel	1		3		
Turner, Caleb	2	2	2		
Taylor, Jonathan	1		1		
Vibbert, Elisha	1	3	5		
Hatten, William	1		1		
Wadsworth, George	1		3		
Weare, William	3		3		
Woodward, Caleb	1	1	1		
Wadsworth, Samuel	2		3		3
Wadsworth, Thomas	1		3		
Wadsworth, Rachel (Wid.)		2	4		
Wadsworth, David	1	2	1		
Wadsworth, Joseph	2	3	4		
Wadsworth, Roger	2	3	8		
Wadsworth, Elisha	1		1		
Wadsworth, Jeremiah	5	1	8		4
Wadsworth, Gurdon	1	1	5		
Wells, John	3		4		
Wells, Ashbel, Jr	5	2	6		
Wells, Thomas	1		2		
Winship, Samuel	2	1	4		
Washbourn, Noah	5	1	9		
Wells, James A	1		4		
Watson, John	5	1	2		
Waggoner, Henry	1	1	2		
Wadsworth, James	1	3	3		
Wadsworth, Henry	1	2	3		
Wadsworth, Abigail	1	1	2		
Webster, Noah, Jr	2		4		
White, John	1	1	8		
Waters, Thomas	1		1		
Wadsworth, George	1		3		
Wyllys, Samuel	2	3	3		
White, Consider	1		2		
Winchell, John	1		1		
Andruss, William	1	2	2		
Andruss, William, Jr	1		2		
Allyn, John	3	2	4		
Ashton, Joseph	2		4		
Brunson, Mathew	1	2	4		
Bigelow, Alvin	1		1		
Barnard, William	1	1	4		
Butler, Norman	2		4		

HARTFORD TOWN—con.

NAME OF HEAD OF FAMILY.	Free white males of 16 years and upward, including heads of families.	Free white males under 16 years.	Free white females, including heads of families.	All other free persons.	Slaves.
Brainard, Adonejah	2	1	1		
Bigelow, Elisha	2		1		
Bigelow, Elisha, Jr	1	2	3		
Brau, John	2		1		
Bunce, Elizabeth (Wid.)		3	2		
Butler, Daniel	1	2	6		
Bigelow, Jonathan	1	3	2		
Bunce, Roderic	1	1	3		
Barnard, Ashbel	2	2	2		
Benton, John	1		2	1	
Bunce, James	1	3	4		
Butler, Jonathan	2		3		3
Barret, Elijah	1	1	1		
Bigelow, Jame	2		7		
Bunce, Daniel	1	1	4		
Barrett, Jere	1		1		
Bunce, Asa	1	3	2		
Bigelow, John	1	2	3		
Barnard, Dorios	2	3	1		
Barnard, John	4	1	4		
Bigelow, Joseph	2				
Bull, Jonathan	2	2	6		
Bigelow, Josiah	1		2		
Bowen, Consider	3	1	2		
Benton, Nathaniel S	1		1		
Boardman, William	2	1	3		
Bliss, David	1		2		
Bliss, Isaac	3		3		
Bull, Aaron	1	2	7		
Boardman, Revd Benjamin	1		1		3
Benton, Samuel	1	2	6		
Babcock, Elisha	2	5	4		
Butler, Henry	1	2	1		
Barnard, Ebenezer, Jr	2		3		
Beach, Miles	3	2	4	1	
Butler, Richard	2	1	5		
Butler, Moses	1		4		
Bull, Amos	1	1	4	1	1
Benton, John, Jr	1		2		
Benton, Josiah	1	2	2		
Bunce, Joseph	1		1		
Buckland, Joshua	1	3	2		
Bunce, John	1		4		
Benton, Ruth (Wid.)			2		
Clapp, John	1		1		
Carter, John	1	4	4		
Carter, Gidion	2		1		
Clapp, Roger	1		3		
Church, Timothy	1	3	3		
Chapman, Jonathan	1	2	3		
Clerk, Josiah	2	1	3		
Clapp, Thomas	1	1	4		
Carter, Joel	1		1		
Clark, Samuel	1	2	6		
Clapp, Elijah	1	2	3		
Cole, Jacob	1	2	4		
Chester, Star	3	1	4		
Dodd, John	3	1	2		
Dodd, Elisha	2	4	2		
Dodd, Timothy	1	3	4		
Dodd, Susan (Wid.)		1	3		
Diggins, Luke	1	1	1		
Ensign, Moses	1	1	1		
Ensign, Thomas	1		2		
Ensign, James	2	1	3		
Ferry, Moses	1	2	6		
Frances, Asa	7	4	3		
Greenwood, Parson	1	2			
Grear, Mathew	1		1		
Camp, James	1	1	1		
Hender, Thomas	1	3	4		
Humphreys, Joseph	2	2	4		
Hide, Ezra	1	1	1		
Hinsdale, James	1	1	2		
Hopkins, Moses	1		2		
Hutchinson, Stephen	2	4	3		
Hempsted, Joshua	2		4		
Hempsted, Josiah	1		4		
Hosmer, William	1	2	3		
Hooker, William	2	1	3		
Hinsdale, Amos	1		4		
Hopkins, Lemuel	1		4	1	
Hildrup, Thomas	1	5	3		
Hudson, Barzilla	7	2	7		
Howell, Ryal	1	1	3		
Hunt, Alexander	2		3		5
Hadlock, Reuben	1	2	3		
Hinsdale, William	1	3	2		
Holland, Benjamin	1	5	1		
Jones, Isaac	1	1	2		
Kneeland, Samuel	2		2		
Kilbourn, James	1	2	4		
Kepple, John	1		2		
Kilbourn, John	1				

HARTFORD COUNTY—Continued.

NAME OF HEAD OF FAMILY.	Free white males of 16 years and upward, including heads of families.	Free white males under 16 years.	Free white females, including heads of families.	All other free persons.	Slaves.
HARTFORD TOWN—con.					
Loomis, George	1		2		
M'Lean, Niel	2	6	3		
Merrill, Charles	2	3	3		
Mygatt, Abigail			2		
Nichols, James	1	3	2		
Nichols, Eunice (Wid.)		1	1		
Olmsted, James	1	5	5		
Phillips, Richard	1	2	1		
Rumbule, Phillip	1	1	3		
Seymour, Charles	2	1	3		
Smith, Moses	1	4	5		
Steele, Jonathan	1	1	4		
Skinner, Jonathan	1	4	1		
Steele, Timothy	2	1	4		
Seymour, Aaron	1	3	3		
Seymour, Asa	2		3		
Seymour, Michael	2	1	2		
Seymour, Thomas Y	2	1	3		
Skinner, Stephen	1	2	3		
Seymour, Zebulon	4		4		
Steele, John	2	3	1		
Skinner, Nathaniel	1	5	3		1
Seymour, Daniel	3	1	5		
Shepard, John	1		7	2	
Skinner, Richard	3	2	4		
Steele, Rachel (Wid.)			4		
Steele, Lemuel	1	3	7		
Seymour, Joseph Whiting	1	1	2		
Seymour, Richard	2	1	4		
Seymour, Freeman	1	3	5		
Sheldon, Joseph	1		3		
Sheldon, Roderic	1	1	3		
Saunders, Abel	1		5		
Steele, James, Jr	1	3	2		
Seymour, George	2	1	6		
Sheldon, Joseph, Jr	1		1	2	
Steele, James	3		4		
Seymour, Calvin	1	1	1		
Shepard, Mary	1		3		
Tryon, Lydia (Wid.)			2		
Taylor, Roswell	1		2		
Taylor, Jesse	1	1	3		
Taylor, James	2	3	3		
Turner, Peletiah	1	2	3		
Tucker, Isaac	1		2		
Webster, Mathew	2		1		
White, John, Jr	1	1	5		
White, John	2		4		
Webster, Samuel, 1st	1		2		
Webster, Medad	2	2	3		
Warren, Elizur	1	1	6		
Warner, Eli	3		2		
Wells, Elisha	1		1		
Waters, Benjamin	1		3		
Webster, Samuel, 2d	1	3	5		
Wyllys, George	3	3	5	1	1
Winship, Joseph	4	1	5		
Wills, Jonathan	3		2		
Warren, Dorus	1	1	2		
Wood, Benjamin	2		1		
Waters, William	1		2		
Waters, Benjamin, Jr	1	1	2		
Woodbridge, Joseph	1	3	6		
Whitman, Abigail	1		3		
Wheelar, Joseph	2		2		
Wheeler, Samuel	1	1	3		
Willson, Stebbins	1	2	4		
Waterman, Robert	1	3	2		
Wales, Horatio	1		1		
Wadsworth, Reubin	1	2	3		
Williamson, Dorotha		1	2		
Wyman, Solomon	1		1		
Wattles, Roswell	1		4		
Hull, Prince				3	
Cutas, Aaron				2	
Boston (Negro)				4	
Boston, Junior				3	
Rese, Willobe				6	
Sheldon, Prince				6	
Dege (Negro)				3	
Popp (Negro)				2	
Bear, Joseph	2	1	1		
Butler, Zacheus	2	1	4		
Brainard, Nathaniel	1	1	3		
Balch, Jonathan B	3	3	5		
Brau, Henry	2	4	4		
Brau, Moses	1	1	3		
Brau, Lenas	4	1	1		
Butler, Gideon	2	5	3		
Brau, Thomas	1	1	3		
Belden, Simion	1		1		
Beardsly, Frances	1	3	2		
Combes, William	1	3	3		
Center, Agnes	1	1	4		
HARTFORD TOWN—con.					
Cadwell, Thomas	1	2	4		
Cadwell, Hezekiah	2	4	2		
Cadwell, Aaron	1	3	4		
Cadwell, Joseph	2	1	5		
Cadwell, Rhoda	1	2	2		
Con, Robert	1		2		
Dean, John	1		3		
Frances, Elias	1	2	6		
Flagg, Abijah	3	2	4		
Frances, Hezekiah	1	2	2		
Frances, Roswell	1		1		
Gaylord, Moses	1	3	4		
Goodwin, Titus	1	1	2		
Goodman, Asa	2	1	5		
Goodman, Richard	3	1	7		
Goodman, Thomas	1	1	2		
Hooker, Daniel	3	3	6		
Heath, Peleg	2	1	3		
Henery, Aaron	1	1	1		
Hosmer, Elizabeth			2		
Hurlbut, Amos	1	1	5		
Kelsey, Zacheus	1	2	4		
Loomis, Zedekiah	1	1	2		
Lyman, Ichabod	2	4	2		
Love, Charles	1	1	2		
Lawrence, Amos	1	1	3		
Merry, John	2	2	6		
Merrill, Gideon	1	3	3		
Merrill, Samuel	1	2	2		
Merrill, Thomas	4		3		
Merrill, Thomas, Jr	1	3	4		
Perkins, Revd Nathan	1	3	4		
Perkins, Caleb	2	2	6		1
Page, Levi	1	2	2		
Merrills, Anna			4		
Steele, Ebenezer	1	3	4		
Steele, Allyn	1	2	2		
Steele, Joel	1	1	3		
Steele, Frederic	1	1	2		
Steele, Moses	1	4	3		
Sedgwick, Abram	1		3		
Shepard, Stephen	2	1	5		
Shepard, Ashbel	1	2	5		
Sedgwick, William	4		3		
Seymour, Timothy	1	4	5		
Stillman, David	2		2		
Wells, Ashbel	1	1	5	2	
Whiting, Allyn	3	1	4		
Whiting, Nathan H	2	1	1		
Whitman, William	2		3		
Wadsworth, Elisha, Jr	1	1	2		
Whitman, John	1	1	2		
Whitman, Samuel	2	1	2		
Whitman, John, Jr	4		5		
Wells, Ebenezer	3	1	2		
Whiting, Joseph	2	2	4		
Whiting, Gurdin	1		1		
Whiting, William	1	1	3		
Bevins, Ebenezer	3	1	3		
Butler, Joseph, Jr	3	1	3		
Butler, David	3	3	5		
Butler, Abel	1	2	3		
Bidwell, Amos	3		4		
Belden, Rositer	1	1	2		
Butler, Joseph	1		1		
Croswell, Cabel	1	3	3		
Crosby, Ebenezer	1	2	5	1	
Colton, Joseph	2	1	6		
Colton, Abijah	1	5	4		
Collins, Seth	2	1	4	1	1
Caldvin, David	1		1		
Cadwell, Aaron	1	1	2		
Deming, Gideon	2	3	5		
Ensign, Elijah	2		6		
Ensign, Solomon	2		6		
Fox, Elisha	1	1	1		
Faxton, Ebenezer	3	3	7		
Gray, Abial	1		1		
Gilbert, Benjamin	2	1	2		
Gilbert, Charles	2	1	2		
Gilbert, Jonathan	2	1	2		
Goodman, Moses	2	5	4		
Gibbs, Clark	1		2		
Griswold, Josiah	3	1	4		
Hurlbut, Fitch	1	1	3		
Hurlbut, Joseph, Jr	1	3	3		
Hurlbut, Christopher	5	1	3		
Hurlbut, Eli	1	1	3		
Hopkins, Stephen	2		2		
Hopkins, William	1		2		
Hurlbut, Lemuel	3	4	6		
Keyes, Amasa	1	3	9	1	1
Kellogg, George	2	1	5		
Kellogg, Ezekiel	1	2	6		
Love, William	1		2		
HARTFORD TOWN—con.					
Latimore, Wickham	1		3		
Merrill, Jacob	1	1	2		
Merrill, William	1		4		
Morgan, Charles	2		4		
Mix, Elisha	1	1	6		
Merrill, Nathaniel	1	1	5		
Merrill, Abram	2		4		
Mills, Jedediah	3	3	6		
Pelton, Jesse	1		3		
Olmsted, Timothy	2	1	1		
Olmsted, Thomas	2	1	4		
Olmsted, Frances F	1	1	2		
Rowe, David	1	2	1		
Skinner, Joseph	2	1	2		
Seymour, Nathaniel	2	1	2		
Seymour, Allyn	1	3	4		
Seymour, Charles	2	2	5		
Steele, Aaron	2	1	3		
Seymour, Norman	1	4	2		
Seymour, Moses	1		3		
Seymour, Aaron	1	5	4		
Stanley, Hannah (Wid.)	2	1	2		
Seymour, John	2		4		
Seymour, Eli	1	1	2		
Stanley, Allyn	1		3		
Stanley, Anna (Wid.)	1	3	4		
Smith, Alvin	2	1	2		
Smith, Frances	1	3	1		
Shepard, Sarah			2		
Stanley, Amaziah	1	2	3		
Stanley, Noadiah	1	2	3		
Stanley, James	2	1	1		
Tryon, Mary			2		
Tryon, William	1		5		
Wadsworth, Daniel	1		3	1	
Webster, Daniel	1	1	4		
Wells, Elisha	1	1	2		
Waters, Joseph	1	1	2		
Winter, Jonathan W	1	1	1		
Webster, Noah	2	3	3		
Webster, Isaac, Jr	1	3	2		
Webster, Stephen	3	3	4		
King, Erastus	1		1		
Miller, Charles	2	1	4		
Sage, Calvin	1	2	3		
Webster, Isaac	2	1	2		
SIMSBURY TOWN.					
Mosses, Michael	2	4	3		
Humphrey, Lott	1		4		
Petibone, John	2		3		
Humphrey, Sylvanus	2	2	1		
Harrington, Elisha	1	2	3		
Phelps, David	3	2	3		
Smith, Peter T	1	1	2		
Phelps, Noah A	1	2	3		
Humphrey, Jonathan	2	1	2		
Cornish, James	3	1	4		
Cornish, Joel	3	1	3		
Cornish, Elisha, Jr	1	3	4		
Humphrey, Amasa	1	1	4		
Humphrey, Amaziah	1		7		
Cornish, George	1	2	3		
Humphrey, Elisha	3	2	3		
Case, Giles	1	2	2		
Humphrey, Martin	2	1	3		
Andruss, William	1	1	2		
Penny Abner	1	5	4		
Humphry, Asa	1	2	1		
Humphrey, Nathaniel	2		2		
Andrus, Richard	1	1	4		
Goodrich, Stephen	1	2	3		
Humphrey, Campbell	2		4		
Starter, James	1	1	1		
Ferry, John	2	1	4		
Case, Arial	1	1	1		
Case, Job	2	3	2		
Case, Charles, Jr	2	1	3		
Case, Charles	2	1	3		
Terry, Samuel	1	2	3		
Humphry, Daniel	3	2	2		
Case, Amasa	4	1	4		
Terry, John G	2	3	5		
Eno, Jonathan	2	2	6		
Humphreys, Joseph	1	3	6	4	1
Risley, Samuel	1	1	2		
Higley, Anna			3		
Case, Levi	1		2		
Brown, Joseph	1	1	2		
Viney, Elias	3	5	2		
Brunson, Oliver	1	5	3		
Owen, John C	1		3		
Falmon, Benjamin	1	2	6		
Birdwell, John	1	1	2		

SIMSBURY TOWN—con.

NAME OF HEAD OF FAMILY.	Free white males of 16 years and upward, including heads of families.	Free white males under 16 years.	Free white females, including heads of families.	All other free persons.	Slaves.
Mountain, Jonathain...	1		5		
Phelps, Noah...	4	1	2		
Ensign, Isaac...	3	4	4		
Weston, Noah...	1		1		
Pennyfur, Darius...	1	1	4		
Pettibone, Jacob...	2	1	3		
Payson, John...	1	1	8		
Robe, Andrew...	1		2		
Smith, Ebenezer...	1	3	4		
Bidwell, James...	1	3	2		
Woodbridge, Theodore.	1	2	3		
Case, Reuben...	1	3	4		
Robbs, Phineas...	1	1	3		
Case, Jonathan...	2	1	1		
Stebins, Revd Samuel..	3	1	3		
Case, Israel...	1	3	3		
Case, Isaac...	1	1	3		
Phelps, Jonathan...	3	2	1		
Bird, Amy...	1	2	3		
Andrus, William...	1		3		
Witch, Benjamin...	1		2		
Pettibone, Dudley...	2	1	3		
Eddington, Isaac...	2		4		
Humphrey, Jonathan..	2	1	5	1	
Pettibone, Jonathan...	2	6	4		1
Tuller, Joseph...	2	1	2		
Smith, James...	3	3	2		
Case, Bartholomew...	3	5	2		
Tuller, Abel...	1		4		
Case, Roger...	3		7		
Petibone, Joseph...	3	2	6		
Petibone, Abel...	2		4		
Tuller, Elisha...	4	1	3		
Latemore. Wait...	4	1	2		
Case, Benajah...	3	2	5		
Case, Jediah, Jr...	1	1	4		
Case, Jediah...	2	1	3		
Pettibone, Abijah...	1		3		
Filer, Asa...	1	1	2		
Willcocks, Isaac...	1		1		
Hiccock, Daniel...	1		1		
Wilcocks, Elijah...	3	2	7		
Woodford, Levi...	1	1	2		
Phelps, Samuel...	3	3	2		
Phelps, Daniel...	1	2	3		
Grant, Joshua...	1	3	4		
Hill, Jediah...	1	1	2		
Onsted, Daniel, Jr...	1	3	3		
Hiccock, Helener (Wd)..		3	2		
Barber, Jared...	1		1		
Barber, Martha (Wid.).			4		
Alford, Nathaniel, Jr...	1	1	1		
Humphrey, Margeret (Wid.)..	2	4	4		
Dealy, Jeremiah...	1	1	1		
More, Jacob...	1		2		
Humphrey, Michael....	2	1	2		
Alderman, Eli...	1	2	3		
Hill, Eliazer...	2	1	2		
Alderman, Jonathan...	1	1	1		
Alderman, James...	1	2	3		
Alderman, Jonathan, Jr	1		2		
Adans, Timothy...	1	1	5		
Alderman, Thomas...	3		4		
Thomas, Samuel...	1	3	4		
Andrews, Asahel...	1				
Humphrey, Levi...	1		3		
Reed, Silas...	2	5	2		
Adams, Roderic...	2	5	2		
Case, George, 2d...	1	2	3		
Case, Roswell...	1	3	2		
Hoskins, Ashbel...	1	2	4		
Hoskins, Asa...	2	2	3		
Tiffery, Humphrey...	1	2	4		
Hoskins, Daniel...	1	1	3		
Hoskins, Asa...	1		2		
Hase, Zedikiah...	1	1	4		
Hase, Benjamin...	1	1	1		
Andrus, William...	2		1		
Slater, Shered...	1	2	1		
Well, Abijah...	1	2	2		
Bulloph, Daniel...	1		3		
Bulloph, Benoni...	1	1	2		
Tuller, Joseph, Jr...	2	2	4		
Phelps, Ozias...	1	2	2		
Bacom, Maskel...	3	2	2		
Hoskins, John...	1		4		
Hoskins, David...	1	3	2		
Andrus, Hezekiah...	1	2	7		
Hoskins, Ezra...	3	1	4		
Tuller, Samuel...	2	4	4		
Bacon, Masket, Jr...	3	1	3		
Moses, Zebne...	1	2	1		
Holcomb, Benajah...	1		6		
Holcomb, Benajah, Jr.	1	3	2		

SIMSBURY TOWN—con.

NAME OF HEAD OF FAMILY.	Free white males of 16 years and upward, including heads of families.	Free white males under 16 years.	Free white females, including heads of families.	All other free persons.	Slaves.
Hendrick, Philemon...	2		4		
Edgerton, Jonathan...	1	1	2		
Edgerton, Jedediah...	1	1	2		
Case, Seth...	2	2	5		
Case, Amasa, Jr...	2	4	3		
Tuller, Reuben...	1	1	6		
Willcocks, Roswold...	1		2		
Case, Moses...	1	1	7		
Buell, Solomon, Jr...	1	4	3		
Buell, Solomon...	2	2	3		
Buell, William...	1	1	2		
Thomas, David...	1	2	5		
Buell, William...	1	1	2		
Case, Thomas...	1		1		
Wells, Israel...	1	2	1		
More, Arcena...	1	2	2		
Robe, Andrew, Jr...	1	1	4		
Andrus, Jacob...	4	4	4		
Grimes, Joseph...	2		3		
Fletcher, John...	2	3	5		
Case, Abel...	1	2	2		
Case, Asa...	1	2	5		
Jutson, Elisha...	1	2	1		
Phelps, Daniel, Jr...	1	3	4		
Bacon, Daniel...	1	2	2		
Barber, Joel...	3	1	4		
Barber, Joel, Jr...	1		3		
Tuller, Jacob...	3		3		
Bud, Abijah...	2	1	3		
Seward, Charles...	1	2	5		
Priest, Asa...	1	1	3		
Lilley, Moses...	2	2	4		
Higley, Isaac...	1	1	4		
Onsted, Daniel...	1	1	2		
Hill, Elijah...	1	1	4		
Grant, Joshua...	1	2	5		
Case, Isaac, Jr...	3	1	2		
Case, Solomon...	2	1	5		
Tuller, Elijah...	3	1	5		
Tullar, Joel...	1	1	1		
Tillotson, Zenas...	1		1		
Tullar, Elijah, Jr...	1	1	3		
Wilcocks, Elijah. Jr...	1	1	2		
Willcocks, Simeon...	1	1	2		
Willcocks, Elisha...	4	1	2		
Higley, Simeon...	1	1	6		
Higley, Bruster...	1		1		
Higley, Enoch...	1		3		
Terry, Solomon...	4	2	4		
Higley, Seth...	3	2	6		
Wilcock, Roger...	2	3	5		
Case, Martin...	1	1	2		
Vates, John...	1				
Cotton, Eliakim...	1	2	1		
Adan, Oliver...	3	1	2		
Haskings, Shubael...	5		3		
St. John, Elijah...	2	1	2		
Russell, Jesse...	1	2	4		
Olmsted, Francis...	1	2	1		
Case, Aaron, 2d...	1		2		
Wilcox, Aaron...	4	1	5		
Case, Joseph...	3	1	2		
Laurence, Samuel...	1	1	2		
Andrus, Jonathan...	1	2	3		
Tullar, Samuel...	3	4	3		
Cornish, Daniel K...	1		2		
Higley, Sylvester...	1		1		
Pinney, Aaron...	3	3	3		
Pinney, Jonathan...	4	2	3		
Pinney, Levi...	1	2	4		
Cook, Eleazer...	1	4	2		
Todd, Ambrose...	1		3		
Loomis, Frances...	1	3	7		
Foster, Zacheus...	1	2	7		
Mitchelson, Eliphalet...	4	4	3		
Eno, Isaac...	1		3		
Eno, Ive...	1	2	4		
Trall, Ezekiel...	2	3	6		
Adams, Abel...	1	3	5		
Adams, Mathew...	1	1	3		
Griswold, Elisha...	4	1	7		
Griswold, Elisha, Jr...	2		4		
Pratt, Ezra...	1	1	3		
Comes, Ebenezer...	1	2	3		
Kilbourn, Lemuel...	1	2	3		
Griswold, Alexander...	1		3		
Clark, Daniel...	1		4		
Seger, Michael...	3	3	5		
Seger, Joseph...	3	2	3		
Wilson, John...	1	1	3		
Griswold, Joel...	3	1	3		
Eno, Reuben...	1	3	2		
Griswold, Elijah...	1	1	2		
Hoskins, Robert...	2		3		
Case, Aaron...	1	2	4		

SIMSBURY TOWN—con.

NAME OF HEAD OF FAMILY.	Free white males of 16 years and upward, including heads of families.	Free white males under 16 years.	Free white females, including heads of families.	All other free persons.	Slaves.
Barnard, Ebenezer...	1	2	3		
Barnard, Samuel...	2	3	4		
Barnard, Frances...	2	4	3		
Adams, William...	1	2	6		
Eno, Samuel...	1		2		
Gillitt, Joab...	1	1	5		
Piney, Abraham...	3	7	9		
Tuller, James...	1		2	1	
Tuller, Eli...	2		4		
Eno, Joel...	3		4		
Woodford, Solomon...	1	4	3		
Kilbourn, Timothy...	2		1		
Case, Caleb...	4	1	3		
Case, George...	1	3	3		
Case, Alexander...	1	4	3		
Barber, Thomas, 3d...	2	2	3		
Case, Zenas...	4	2	3		
Case, Benjamin...	2		4		
Brown, Eleazer...	1	2	3		
Foot, Elisha...	2	2	7		
Case, Ashbel...	1	4	2		
Goodwin, Joseph...	2	3	5		
Foot, Grove...	1	3	1		
Roberts, Lemuel...	2	2	6		
Roberts, Nathaniel...	2	2	5		
Fitch, Selah...	1		1		
Case, Josiah...	1	4	3		
Willcocks, Daniel...	3	3	4		
Marshall, Alexander...	1	1	3		
Moses, Timothy...	2	1	3		
Adams, Hosea...	1	2	2		
Nall, Mock...	1	1	4		
Fox, John...	1		1		
Bliss, Ebenezer...	1	2	2		
Case, Darius...	1	1	4		
Adams, David, Jr...	1		2		
Adams, David...	2		2		
Adams, Ezra...	2	2	4		
Adams, George...	1	1	2		
Willcocks, Jedediah...	1	2	2		
Priest, Darius...	1	2	3		
Grimes, Elisha...	4		4		
Grimes, Elisha, Jr...	2		3		
Adams, Sarah (Wid.)...	2		6		
Foot, John...	1	1	2		
Foot, John, Jr...	1	2	2		
Brown, Hannah (Wid.).	3	1	4		
Case, Ephraim B...	1	1	2		
Moses, Daniel...	1	3	2		
Moses, Aaron...	2		3		
Spencer, Caleb...	2	1	2		
Clarkland, James...	2		2		
Buttles, Joseph...	1	1	3		
Latimore, Jiles...	3	3	3		
Malson, Asa...	3	1	2		
Willcox, Amos...	1	3	3		
Latimore, Jonathan...	3	1	7		
Humphry, Ruggles...	1	1	2		
Spencer, Roswell...	1	3	3		
Willcocks, Robert...	1		3	1	
Mills, Ezekiel...	4	1	2		
Grimes, Daniel, Jr...	1	3	1		
Grimes, Daniel...	4	1	2		
Adans, William...	1		3		
Willcox, Ira...	1		1		
Willcox, Charles...	1	2	5		
Willcox, William...	1	5	2		
Beach, Elihu...	1	2	4		
Moses, Elihu...	4	1	4		
Curtis, Eliphalet...	2	2	3		
Curtis, Eliphalet, Jr...	2	3	4		
Humphry, James...	1	1	1		
Cavelu, Thomas...	1	1	4		
Grimes, Isaac...	2	1	9		
Case, Abraham...	3	3	5		
Case, Fithin...	2	3	4	1	
Humphry, Charles...	3	2	4		
Case, Daniel...	2		2		
Case, Zacheus...	2	3	2		
Leit, Samuel...	3		2		
Leit, Daniel A...	2		2		
Tuller, Isaac...	2		3		
Case, Hosea...	2		6		
Case, Joseph A...	2		2		
Bidwell, Thomas...	1	1	1		
Willcocks, Ezra...	3	3	5		
Willcox, Isaac...	1	3	6		
Case, Isaac...	1	3	1		
Anderson, Daniel...	2		8		
Noble, William...	1	3	5		
Till, Joseph...	1		4		
Case, Elias...	1	2	3	1	
Dill, Solomon...	2	1	2		
Dycer, Thomas...	2	1	3		
Dycer, Thomas, Jr...	1	1	1		

HARTFORD COUNTY—Continued.

SIMSBURY TOWN—con.

NAME OF HEAD OF FAMILY.	Free white males of 16 years and upward, including heads of families.	Free white males under 16 years.	Free white females, including heads of families.	All other free persons.	Slaves.
Dycer, Solomon	1	1	3		
Humphrey, Frederic	1	6	4		
Adams, Benjamin	2	1	5		
Bacon, Frances	2	3	2		
Case, Ozias	1	3	3		
Case, Jerre	2	2	2		
Case, Daniel	2	4	4		
Humphrey, Ezkiel, Jr	1		1		
Dyer, Daniel	2	2	4		
Dycer, Benjamin	1	2	1		
Dyer, Daniel	2	2	4		
Humphrey, Ezekiel	2	3	6		1
Garrett, Frances	2	3	2		
Garrett, Rufus	2	4	3		
Humphrey, Samuel	3	1	5		
Humphrey, Oliver	3	5	2		
Humphrey, Samuel	1	1	4		
Gleason, Chancey	2	1	2	2	
Firbbs, Alisha	2	2	2		
Alford, Nathaniel	2	2	4		
Mills, Jared	2	4	5		
Case, Daniel	2	4	1		
Case, Dudley	2		2		
Tuller, Amasa	1	1	2		
Higley, Obed	1	1	3		
Taylor, Noadiah	2	1	3		
Case, Elisha	3	3	5		
Case, Truman	1		2		
Harrington, Hezekiah	1	1	6		
Merring, Moam	1	2	5		
Seager, Joseph, Jr	4		4		
Seager, Elijah	1	4	1		
Crocker, John	3	2	4		
Barber, Michael	1	1	1		
Humphrey, Ichabod	1	1	1		
Petibone, David	1		3		
Hoskins, Abel	1	1	1		
Hubbard, Thaddeus	1	2	1		
Barber, Thomas	2	2	4		
Barber, Elijah	1	2	4		
Barber, Jesse	1	2	2		
Barber, Samuel	3	1	3		
Barber, John	1		2		
Barber, Jonathan	1	1	2		
Humphrey, Theophilus	1	3	4		
Taylor, William	2	1	4		
Taylor, Ozias	1	1	5		
Bacon, Joseph	1	2	3		
Barber, John, Jr	1	3	6		
Case, Hosea, Jr	1	1	2		
Messinger, Isaac	3		6		
Barber, Michael	1	2	3		
Humphrey, Abram	1	1	1		
Taylor, Ruth (Wid.)			1		
Barber, Reuben	1	4	4		
Mills, Amasa	2		4		
Hillick, Jeremiah	1	2	2		
Mills, Ephraim	1	3	4		
Barber, Bildad	3	3	4		
Taylor, John E	1		2		
Adkins, Josiah	1	2	5		
Roberts, Anna (Wid.)			2		
Eno, Abel	1		1		
Piney, Darius	1	1	1		
Kingson, Joseph	3	2	4		
Simons, Reuben	3		2		
Fosbury, John	1	4	2		
Enos, David	2		3		
Willcox, George	1	1	1		
Burdee, George	1	4	2		
Bacon, James	1	5	4		
Johnson, William	1			3	
Richards, Sarah (Wid.)	1	1	2		
Richards, Samuel	1		1		
Humphrey, Solomon	2	1	2		
Thomas, Solomon	1		2		
Case, Edward	1	2	5		
Case, Solomon	1	2	3		
Case, Timothy	1	1	4		
Case, Jacob	4	1	3		
Case, Jessee	2	2	5		
Case, Elias	4	3	4		
Case, Abel	1	3	3		
Case, Silas	1	4	3		
Case, Simeon	1		1		
Crocker, John	2	2	3		
Mills, Gideon	2	2	7		
Hill, John	1		4		
Hill, Jedediah	1	3	1		
Moses, Abram	2	2	3		
Hill, Darius	1	3	4		
Humphrey, Jonathan	2	1	6		
Case, Uriah	2	3	8		
Cornish, Daniel King	1		2		

SOUTHINGTON TOWN.

NAME OF HEAD OF FAMILY.	Free white males of 16 years and upward, including heads of families.	Free white males under 16 years.	Free white females, including heads of families.	All other free persons.	Slaves.
Smith, David	1	1	4		
Smith, Harvey	1		1		
Smith, Simeon	1	1	2		
Potter, Paullinus	1	1	3		
Toot, Robert	1	3	3		
Smith, David, Jr	3	5	5		
Tyler, Jacob	4	3	2		
Root, Joel	1		3		
Bunnel, Joseph	2		1		
Woodruff, Lydia	1		3		
Woodruff, Samuel	3		4		
Potter, Rhoda			2		
Woodruff, Jonathan	2	1	1		
Woodruff, Elisha	2	4	5		
Hash, David	1		2		
Rice, Mathew	1		5		
Leavingston, John	1		1		
Tish, Solomon	1	1	3		
Tish, Isaac	1	1	1		
Curtiss, Samuel	3	3	4		1
Root, James	1		5		
Root, Stephen	1	1	1		
Day, Horatior	1	3	2		
Lewis, Hart	2	3	4		
Tryon, John	1	4	6		
Norton, Charles	3	3	3		
Day, Stanley	1	4	2		
Norton, Elnathan	1	2	4		
Ives, Samuel	1	2	3		
Lyman, Noah	1		2		
Wheador, Thomas	1	1	7		
Newill, John	1	3	4		
Tisdale, William	1	3	2		
Newill, Josiah	1	1	1		
Newill, Amos	1	1	2		
Johnson, Barnabas	1		1		
Bradley, Dan	2	4	2		1
Durham, Silvanus	4	2	3		
Peck, Eleazer	2		2		
Hungerford, John	1	4	2		
Bradley, Hemingway	1		2		
More, Roswell	1		1		
Bradley, Ichabod	1		2		
More, Roswell, Jr	1	2	1		
Judd, Eunice	2		2	1	
Lewis, Isaac	1		3		
Winchell, Dan	1	1	2		
Dunham, Solomon	1	1	3		
Munson, Solomon	1		2		
Munson, Jeros	1		1		
Smith, Isaac	2	1	4		
Bradley, Nathaniel	1	3	3		
Bradley, James	1		3		
Judd, Immer	1		1		
Judd, Immer	1	4	3		
Hazard, Stuart	2	4	2		
Finch, Elam	1	3	1		
Mass, Elihu	1	2	1		
Dayton, Israel	1	1	2		
James (Negro)				2	
Clark, Enos	2	2	4		
Pratt, Stephen	1	2	3		
Pratt, Christopher	1	2	1		
Webster, Philologus	1	2	2		
Wilcox, Justus	1	1	2		
Beckwith, Harey	1		2		
Andrews, Josiah, Jr	1	3	2		
Woodruff, Asa	1	1	4		
Graniss, Aaron	1	2	2		
Frisbee, Ichabod	2	2	1		
Cogswell, David	3		3		
Cogswell, David, Jr	1		3		
Langton, Daniel, Jr	2		4		
Langton, Daniel	3	1	4		
Langton, Job	1	1	1		
Langton, Asahel	1	1	1		
Langton, Ruth			2		2
Gridley, Joseph	2		2		
Gridley, Ard	1		1		
Gridley, Ashbel	1		3		
Gridley, Noah	3		1		
Mertin, Jethro				2	
Newill, Simeon	1	2	3		
Gridley, Elisha	1	2	3		
Munson, Stephen	1	2	1		
Deming, Mertain	1		1		
Newill, Mark	1		6		
Deming, Lucy	2		2		
Whitcomb, Hiram	2	2	3		
Newill, Pomeroy	1	1	6		
Newill, Isaac	1		1		
Newill, Isaac, Jr	1	3	5		
Langton, Seth	2	1	3		
Curtiss, Solomon	3	2	6		

SOUTHINGTON TOWN—continued.

NAME OF HEAD OF FAMILY.	Free white males of 16 years and upward, including heads of families.	Free white males under 16 years.	Free white females, including heads of families.	All other free persons.	Slaves.
Lewis, Jabish	1	1	4		
Dunham, Cornelius	2	3	7		
Gridley, Asahel	1	2	2		
Smith, Ezariah	1		3		
Case, Jonathan	1	1	5		
Carrington, Samuel	1		1		
Carrington, Samuel, Jr	1	2	2		
Clark, Silas	2	2	3		
Clark, Ezra	1		2		
M cKein, James	1	1	3		
Hunt, Joel	1	1	3		
Peck, Eliakim	1		1		
Peck, Thomas	1		1		
Peck, Eliakim, Jr	1	3	2		
Peck, Isaac	1	2	3		
Peck, Selah	1	1	1		
Beckwith, Mervin	1	4	5		
Brunson, Benjamin	1		2		
Hart, Roswell	2		3		
Hart, John	1		1		
Hart, John, Jr	1	3	4		
Andrews, Jonathan	1		1		
Andrews, Jonathan, Jr	2	1	3		
Barnes, John	1		3		
Hart, Amos	2	1	2		
Hart, Chancey	1	1	1		
Bradley, Nehemiah	1	1	2		
Palmer, Judah	1	2	2		
Clark, Ephraim	2	1	5		
Sloper, Hannah	2		2		
Sloper, Ursula (Wid.)	1	1	3		
Pardee, David	1	1	3		
Newill, Charles	1	2	2		
Larking, Scovill	1	2	2		
Coles, Thos	2	1	5		
Barnes, Allyn	1		1		
Johnson, Stephen	2	4	3		
Hitchcock, Samuel	1	1	4		
Hitchcock, Samuel, Jr	1	3	2		
Hitchcock, Caleb	1	2	4		
Lewis, William	1		1		
Atwater, Herman	1	1	3		
Mathews, Moses, Jr	1	5	4		
Hitchcok, Amos	1		2		
Andrews, Thomas	1		1		
Andrews, Josiah	2		6		1
Parsons, Amos	1		1		
Barrett, William	3		6		
Potter, Martin	1		1		
Munson, Esther	1	1	2		
Barnes, Jona, Senr	1		2		
Royal, Jonathan	1	1	2		
Deming, Selah	1	1	1		
Lewis, Job	3	2	3		
Lewis, Seth	1		4		
Curtiss, Jeremiah	1		2		
Curtiss, Jonathan	3	2	2		
Robertson, William	3	2	3	1	1
Chapman, Levi	1		3	1	1
Lewis, Timothy	2	4	4		
Atkins, Charles	1	2	2		
Atkins, Abigail			3		
Allyn, Daniel	1	1	5		
Root, Jonathan	1		2		
Root, Jonathan, Jr	2	1	6	1	1
Andrus, Samuel	1	1	6		
Hart, Levi	2	3	1		
Lee, Timothy	1	5	6		
Church, Samuel	1	4	2		
Andrus, Obadiah	1		2		
Andrus, Eleazer	3	1	2		
Peck, David	2	3	5		
Wadsworth, Theodore	3	1	2		
Howd, Whitehead	4		4		
Clark, Elisha	1	1	3		
White, Isaac	2	5	2		
Crittenton, Nathaniel	1	2	4		
Hitchcock, Josiah	1	2	3		
Hitchcock, Ambrose	1		2		
Woodruff, Jason	1	2	3		
Dawson, Timothy	1	2	3		
Curtiss, Ezekiel	1	2	3		
Clark, Ithurill	1	1	4		
Clark, Lewis	1		1		
Carter, Jacob	1		1		
Carter, Levi	1		2		
Carter, Elihu	2		2		
Crittenton, Amos	1	1	3		
Woodruff, Levi	1	3	3		
Smith, James	1	2	2		
Jones, Nathaniel	3	3	4		1
Brunson, Silas	1	1	1		
Barnes, Nathan, 3d	1	3	3		
Page, Ranor	1	3	2		

HARTFORD COUNTY—Continued.

SOUTHINGTON TOWN—continued.

NAME OF HEAD OF FAMILY.	Free white males of 16 years and upward, including heads of families.	Free white males under 16 years.	Free white females, including heads of families.	All other free persons.	Slaves.
Beacher, Nathan	1	1	2		
Graniss, Joel	2	2	4		
Clark, John	1		1		
Hart, Samuel	1	1	2		
Carter, Daniel	1	3	3	2	
Woodruff, John, Jr	1	4	2		
Woodruff, John	1	2	2		
Squires, Samuel	3	1	2		
Blakely, Laban	1	2	2		
Graniss, Stephen	2	2	3		
Mathews, Moses	1		1		
Cook, Martin	1	1	2		
Carter, Abel	1	1	3		
Carter, John	2	4	3		
Dutton, Benjamin	1		1		
Dutton, Timothy	1	2	2		
Dutton, Benjamin, Jr	1		2		
Brunson, Phineas	1		2		
Thompson (Wid.)		1	1		
Peck, Joel	2	1	3		
Norton, Ebenezer	1	4	5		
Durvin, Jonathan	1	1	2		
Clark, Abraham	1	2	3		
Bunnell, Amos	1	1	3		
Clerk, Timothy	2		2		
Criessee, Gold	2	1	3		
Carter, Abel	2	2	5		
Dutton, Moses	1	1	2		
Dutton, Joseph	1	2	2		
Cook, Robert	1		2		
Hall, Jacob	1	2	5		
Bracket, Joel	1		2		
Dutton, Samuel	1		2		
Webster, Lucy	1		3		
Brunson, Isaac	1	2	2		
Baldwin, Samuel	1	2	3		
Hooker, Bryon	2		1		
Hart, Varlines	1		3		
Coles, Ashbel	2	2	3	1	
Clark, Azenath	1	2	2		
Dayton, Samuel	1	3	4		
Woodruff, Phinas	2	1	2		
Fields, John	1	2	2		
Pardee, Daniel	1	2	2		
Ward, Rufus	1	1	2		
Bray, Asa	2	1	3		
Bray, John	1		2		
Woodruff, Robert	1	1	5		
Dickenson, George	3	1	4		
Woodruff, Isaac	2	1	5		
Woodruff, Obed	1		1		
Shepard, Samuel	1		2		
Shepard, Samuel, Jr	1		3		
Shepard, Nathaniel	1	1	3		
Hutson, Daniel	2	2	3		
Sloper, Ambrose	2		2		
Lewis, Chancey	1		2		
Brunson, Joel	1	2	1		
Woodruff, Amos	4		5		
Newill, Samuel	1	1	1		
Dickson, William	2	1	5		
Hitchcock, Stephen	2		2		
Hart, Hawkins	1		2		
Woodruff, Mary			2		
Barnes, Asa	2	4	3	1	
Barnes, William	3		4		
Barnes, Benjamin	1	1	4		
Barnes, Nathan, 2d	1	1	1		
Cowles, George	1	2	2		
Louse, Abram	1	2	1		
Root Josiah	1	2	3		
Cowles, Josiah	5	2	4		
Upson, John	3	4	5		
Smith, Samuel	2	1	3		
Hawley (Wid.)			2		
Persons, Abraham	1		1		
Upson, Amos	5		2		
Upson, Josiah	2		2		
Upson, Timothy	3	2	2		
Moss, Theophilus	1	2	2		
Barnes, Nathaniel	1	1	2		
Lewis, Nathan, Jr	4	1	3		
Lewis, Asahel	3	1	3		
Merriman, Ebenezer	3	5	3	1	
Lewis, Lemuel	4	1	2		
Merriman, Pevis	1	1	2		
Barnes, Nathaniel D	1		1		
Hitchcock, David	1		8		
Elwell, Isaac	1	3	3		
Noal, David	2	2	2		
Finch, Joseph	3	2	1		
Thrash, John	1		5		
Thrash, Samuel	2	3	3		
Neal, Aaron	1		2		
Thrash, Reuben	1	3	3		

SOUTHINGTON TOWN—continued.

NAME OF HEAD OF FAMILY.	Free white males of 16 years and upward, including heads of families.	Free white males under 16 years.	Free white females, including heads of families.	All other free persons.	Slaves.
Thrash, Oliver	2	2	1		
Adkins, Samuel	1	3	5		
Neal, John	1	2	2		
Merriman, Chancey	1	3	4		
Whitman, Jonathan	2		3		
Jude, Ellin	2		4		
Neal Timothy	1		1		
Neal, Elijah	1	2	2		
Merriman (Wid.)			5		
Durin, Jonathan	1		1		
Durin, Noah	1	2	1		
Plant, James	1	3	4		
Reryy, Solomon	1		3		
Upson, Josiah	2		3		
Boardman, Catharine		1	2		
Bradley, Benjamin	1	3	3		
Goodsell, Samuel	1	3	3		
Porter, Joshua	1	2	5	3	
Pardee, Samuel	1		4		
Alcock, Jesse	2	1	5		
Gerens, Russell	1	3	2		
Blakeley, Abner	1	1	1		
Churchill, David	1	1	5		
Baley, William	1	4	2		
Johnson, Ebenezer	1		3		
Baley, James	1		2		
Bruckot, Samuel	2		1		
Carter, Jacob, Jr	3	2	4		
Adkins, Chancey	1	3	5		
Sorith, Elkany	1	2	5		
Wire, Daniel	1	2	1		
Duplax, Prince					5
Carter, Isaac	1	3	2		
Powers, Barnabas	1	1	3		
Neal, Noah	2	1	2		
Clark, Israel	1		1		
Wire, Aaron	3	2	3		
Rice, Elijah	1	2	3		
Baley, James	1	2	3		
Smith, William	1		1		
Beacher, Joseph	2		2		
Collins, Abel	2		2		
Pond, Moses	2	3	3		
Johnson, Ebenezer	1		4		
Johnson, Levi	1		5		
Thornton, Samuel	1	1	3		
Horton, Elisha	1	2	4		
Beacher, Joseph, Jr	1	2	2		
Beacher, John	2				
Beacher, Hezekiah	1		1		
Beacher, Erastus	1				
Scariott, Nathan	1	2	3		
Scariott, James	1	3	1		
Scariott, Johnson	1		3		
Bradley, Timothy	3	2	5		
Bradley, Mise	1	1	2		
Beacher, Amos	2	2	3		
Robberts, Eli	1		2		
Plumb, Simeon	3	1	3		
Plum, Solomon	1		1		
Beacher, Abel	3		5		
Peck, Justus	1	1	4		
Peck, Elisha	1	2	1		
Beacher, Walter	1	2	1		
Finch, Gideon	2	3	3		
Minor, Joseph	1	2	2		
Talmadge, Ichabod	2		4		
Linsley, Braniard	1		2		
Upson, Thomas	1	1			
Bracket, Zeuer	1	2	5		
Bracket, Amos	1	3	2		
Cleveland, Lemuel	1	2	1		
Smith, Joseph	2	1	2		
Cleveland, Johnson	1	1	4		
Lane, Elijah	1	2	4		
Lane, Joel	1	2	3		
Gillet, Ebenezer	1	2	3		
Harrison, Jabez	1	1	3		
Stephens, William	1	2	3		
Hanson, Aaron	2		1		
Potter, John	2		1		
Allcox, Daniel	3		6		
Stedman, Selah	1	3	2		
Tuttle, Abraham	1	2	2		
Carter, Stephen	1	1	2		
Johnson, Daniel	2	1	3		
Adkins, Luther	1	1	5		
Brunson, John	2	1	2		
Carter, Jonathan	1	4	3		
Barnes, Philimon	1	1	5		
Barnes, Mark	1	1	2		
Parker, Joseph	2	1	2		
Upson, Isaac	1	2	2		
Lewis, Nathaniel	3	2	4		
Barnes, Farrington	1	2	1		

SOUTHINGTON TOWN—continued.

NAME OF HEAD OF FAMILY.	Free white males of 16 years and upward, including heads of families.	Free white males under 16 years.	Free white females, including heads of families.	All other free persons.	Slaves.
Coles, Calvin	2		6		
Gillett, Nathan	1	2	4		
Gillett, Zachariah	1	1	6		
Hall, Heman	1	2	7		
Harrison, David	1	3	4		
Harrison, Mark	1	3	5		
Mathews, Epaphras	3		1		
Hall, Curtiss	2	1	6		
Barnes, Nathan	1		2		
Tuttle, Zenas	1		2		
Johnson, Daniel, Jr	1	1	1		

SUFFIELD TOWN.

NAME OF HEAD OF FAMILY.	Free white males of 16 years and upward, including heads of families.	Free white males under 16 years.	Free white females, including heads of families.	All other free persons.	Slaves.
Phelps, Oliver	3	2	3		2
King, Alexander	4	1	5		
Leavitt, John	1		1		
Granger, Gideon	1	1	2	1	
Sheldon, Phineas	3	1	3		
Leavitt, Thaddeus	2	1	3		
Granger, Amos	1	3	2		
Gay, Revd Ebenezer	2		2		5
Graham, Revd John	1	2	1		
Hasting, Elder John	4	1	4		
Granger, Zadoc	2		2		
Kent, Elihu	2		3		
Granger, John	1		2		
Hitchcock, Aaron	1		2		
Remington, Jona	1				
Granger, Abraham	2	1	3		
Hanchett, Oliver	5	1	5		
King, Josiah	3	1	3		
Sheldon, Simeon	3	1	5		
Pomeroy, Isaac	2	3	3		
Lovijoy, Phineas	2	1	5	1	
Granger, Oliver	2	4	5		
King, Ashbel	4	3	2		
Owen, Isaac	3	1	6		
Kent, John	1	2	3		
Granger, Abner	3		7		
Sheldon, Ebenezer	2	2	4		
Loomis, Luther	3	2	6		2
Phelps, Daniel	1	2	3		
Clark, Reuben	1	3	3		
Trumbul, Eli	1	3	6		
King, Thaddeus	2	3	2		
Williston, Consider	3	2	2		
Hale, Samuel	3	4	2		
Notton, Jona	2		1		
Swan, Timothy	1	1	3		
Austin, Seth	1	1	4		5
Granger, Gideon, 2d	1	1	1		
Pease, Joseph	5	1	5		2
Pease, Zeno	1	1	4		
Pease, Seth	2	2	2		
Burbank, Seth	1	2	1		
Granger, Charles	4		3		
Hanchett, Ezra	1	1	2		
Leavitt, John, 2d	1	2	3		
Wilcocks, Ruth			3		
Wilcocks, Aaron	1	3	3		
Robbins, Ephraim	1	2	6		
Granger, Beldad, 2d	1	1	1		
Kent, Anna	1		2		
Taylor, Gad	4	2	6		
Alden, Howard	1		3		
Field Pardont	1	1	2		
Huntington, Hezekiah	1	1	1		
Kent, Elisha, 2d	1	3	3		
Kent, Johnth Kellogg	2	3	2		
Kent, Hannah			3		
Kent, Augustus	1	3	5		
Austin, Calvin	2	3	4		
Thompson, Ardon	2	3	4		
Sheldon, Martin	2	3	3		
Sheldon, Jonathan	2	1	4		
Sheldon, Jonathan, Jr	1	1	2		
Rice, Elezer	2	1	6		
Phelps, Oliver	1	1	3		
Sheldon, Rachel	2	2	5		
Griswold, Collins	2	1	3		
Sheldon, Benjamin	1	1	3		
Sheldon, Jacob	2	3	4		
Sheldon, Daniel	1		2		
Sheldon, Gersham	2		1		
King, Oliver	1	1	2		
Harmon, Cephas	2		1		
Kent, Benajah	2		1		
Kent, Amos	2		3		
Southwell, John	2	1	5		
Austin, Caleb	4	2	5		
Spencer, Eliphalet	1		5		
Truesdall, Asa	1	4	2		
Kent, Joseph	2		6		
Hatheway, John	1	1	2		

HARTFORD COUNTY—Continued.

SUFFIELD TOWN—con.

NAME OF HEAD OF FAMILY.	Free white males of 16 years and upward, including heads of families.	Free white males under 16 years.	Free white females, including heads of families.	All other free persons.	Slaves.
Lacey, Sizzardus	1		4		
Hathaway, Seth	1	2	5		
Spencer, Rebeca		1	2		
Rising, Nathaniel, 2d	1		2		
Spencer, Hezekiah	3	1	8		
Spencer, Daniel	1		4		
Palmer, Saul				4	
Spencer, Augustus	1	4	2		
Austin, Uriah	1		2		
Austin, Uriah, 2d	2	1	2		
Remington, Benjamin	2	2	4		
Remington, Isaac	1	2	3		
Remington, Simeon	1	2	3		
Pomeroy, Nathaniel	1	2	2		
Remington, Asa	3	1	4		1
Middleton, William	1		3		
Harmon, Phineas	3		3		
Sheldon, Oliver	1	1	6		
Gillett, Daniel	2	1	1		
Lacey, Jasper	1	2	2		
Parsons, Oliver	1	1	1		
Trumbull, Shadrack	1	1	6		
Hale, Timothy	1		2		
Austins, Samuel	3	1	2		
Rising, Jonathan	4		3		
Rising, Eli	1	1	1		
Rising, Paul	4	3	6		
Hathway, Ebenezer	4		2		
Todd, David	2	3	5		4
Rowe, Moses	1	4	4		
Rowe, John	3	5	5		
Kirtland, John	4		3		
Bester, Daniel	3	5	4		
Pierce, Luther	1		1		
Cleveland, Frederic	1		8		
Hyde, Roger Eb^a	1	3	2		
Hathaway, Asabel	1	1	5		
Kellogg, Jonathan	3		2		
Pemberton, Thomas	1	3	3		
Olds, Joseph	1	1	1		
Lyman, Thaddeas	1		2		1
Olds, Josiah	2		2		
Olds, Josiah, 2nd	2	4	2		
Phelps, Timothy	5	2	2		
Phelps, Aaron	3		6		
Gunn, Elisha	1	1	1		
King, David	3	1	6		
Sheldon, John	1		1		
Sheldon, Josiah	1	3	3		
Remington, Abijah	1	2	4		
Peter (Negro)				3	
Hastings, Benjamin	2	3	5		
Remington, Elijah	2	1	3		1
Allyn, Reuben, 2d	1	1	2		
Allyn, Ebenezar	1	1	5		
Allyn, Reuben	1	3	5		
Leavitt, Enoch	1	1	3		
Hastings, Abijah	2	2	2		
Granger, Julius	1	2	2		
Granger, Elijah	2	2	7		
Remington, Amos	1	3	4		
Hastings, Joseph	2		4		
Remington, Stephen	1	2	9		
Remington, Hosea	1	1	2		
Remington, Thomas	1	2	5		
Barnard, Jacob	1	1	3		
Granger, Jacob	1	1	3		
Granger, Samuel	2	1	4		
Hathway, Martin	1	1	1		
Pomeroy, Amos	1	1	2		
Smith, Abisha	1	2	2		
Pomeroy, John	3	1	3		
Hathway, Samuel	1		2		
Hathway, Ebenezer	1	2	2		
Hathway, John King	1	6	3		
Hathway, Joel	2	5	3		
Austin, Thomas	3	3	3		
Smith, James	1	3	4		
Smith, Ichabod	1	2	5		
Smith, Seth	3		1		
Pomeroy, Asa	1	3	4		
Pomeroy, Abigail	1	1	3		
Palmer, Timothy	2	1	8		
Mather, Increase	4		3		
Hoskins, Simeon	1	1	2		
Spencer, Samuel	3	2	3		
Street, James	1		1		
Ives, John	1	1	2		
Rowes, Stephen	1		1		
Smith, Medad	1	1	1		
Smith, Joseph	2	1	9		
King, Joseph, 2d	2	2	5		
Parsons, Ebenezer	2	2	1		
Leavitt, Joshua	2	2	3		
Monrow, Benjamin	1		3		

SUFFIELD TOWN—con.

NAME OF HEAD OF FAMILY.	Free white males of 16 years and upward, including heads of families.	Free white males under 16 years.	Free white females, including heads of families.	All other free persons.	Slaves.
Hopkins, Jonathan	3	1	2		
Barnard, Edmund	3	2	6		
Addams, Zeb	2		1		
Addams, Zeb, 2d	1	1	1		
Thompson, Mathew	1	2	1		1
Sikes, Gideon	1	1	3		
Woodcoalk, Wm	3	1	1		
Grovener, Moses	2	3	3		
Grovner, Wm	1	1	1		
King, Jonathan	1	1	3		
Perpoint, Joseph	1	1	2		
French, John	1	4	4		
Hall, Libeas	1	1	1		
Adams, Zadock	3	1	4		
Fowler, Bildad	1	3	3		
Adams, Zadock, 2d	1		2		
Adams, Asabel	1		1		
Sykes, Victory	1		2		
Sykes, Samuel	2	4	5		
Lane, Dan	1		1		
Allyn, Gidion	1		4		
Allyn, Gershom	2	3	5		
Sykes, Paul	1	2	3		
Sykes, David	1	2	1		
Sykes, Victory, 2d	1	4	1		
White, Nathan	2	3	5		
Feany, William	1				
Sykes, Lott	2	2	4		
Sykes, Jonathan	1	1	1		
Stiles, Chauncey	1		2		
Kent, Joel	1	1	2		
Kent, Diana	2	2	4		
Kent, Thomas	1	4	2		
Adams, Samuel	3	2	5		
Larnard, Amariah	1	1	3		
Adams, Moses	2	1	2		
Kindall, Simion	1	3	2		1
Loomis, Nathaniel	1	2	3		
Blunder, Samuel	1	2	1		
Tobin, James	2		2		
Fuller, Joseph	4		3		
Granger, Benjamin	2	1	2		
Lewis, John	1	1	2		
Beebee, Ephraim	1	3	1		
Lane, Gad	1	5	3		
Kent, Seth, 2d	1	3	1		
Gardner, Sherman	1	2	3		
Kent, Zeno	1	3	2	1	
Kent, Seth	1		2		
Granger, Joseph	1	1	2		
King, William	2	1	4		
King, Seth	1	2	3		
Beckwith, William	1	4	4		
Norton, Seth	1	6	3		
Dewy, John	3		3		
Tucker, Asa	3		3		
Norton, Daniel	1		2		
Rising, Nathaniel	4		5		
Rising, John	1	4	3		
Smith, Eldad	1		1		
Parsely, Robert	1		1	1	
Pero (Negro)					5
Howard, Joseph	1		3		
Parmeley, Elihu	2	3	3		
Lewis, John, 2d	1	1	2		
Lewis, John	1	4	2		
Hathway, Charles	3		5		
Hathway, Thrall	1	3	4		
Wootworth, Timothy	1		1		
Hathway, Charles, 2d	1		2		
McMorin, John	2	2	2		
McMoran, John, 2d	1	1	5		
Hall, Nathaniel	1	1	2		
Hall, John	1		2		
Spary, Elijah	1	1	3		
Hough, Justin	3	1	3		
Harmin, Benjamin, 2d	2	3	4		
Spears, Moses	2		3		
Spears, Asabel	1	1			
Pomeroy, Darkis					2
Harmin, Benjamin	1		1		
Harmon, Iaguish	1	2	3		
King, Nathaniel	1		1		
King, Dan, 2d	2	2	5		
Hitchcock, Chancey	2	1	2		
Hanchett, Luke	3	2	7		
Hanchett, John	1		2		
Robbins, Elijah	1	1	2		
Hanchett, David	1	3	7		
Hanchett, John, 2d	1	1	1		
Hubbard, Philip	1		1		
Austin, Joseph	2		4		
Austin, Joseph, 2d	2	3	4		
Norton, John, 2d	1	3	2		
Mark (Negro)					9

SUFFIELD TOWN—con.

NAME OF HEAD OF FAMILY.	Free white males of 16 years and upward, including heads of families.	Free white males under 16 years.	Free white females, including heads of families.	All other free persons.	Slaves.
King, Joseph	1		2		
Wiggins, Josiah	2	2	3		
Parsons, Reuben	2		4		
King, Isaac	2	1	5		
Copty, Anna	1		2		
Graham, Daniel	2		1		
King, Gideon	4		3		
Harmon, Samuel	2	3	6		
Sheldon, Elijah	3		3		
Wyman, Ebenezer	2	1	5		
Gains, Samuel	1	2	3		
Ingraham, Jeremiah, 2d	1		3		
Caton, Elizabeth			2		
Harmon, Elias	3	4	4		
Hale, Joseph	1		2		
Rowes, Gad	1	4	3		
Spencer, Simeon	1	2	3		
Spencer, John	1	1	3		
Spencer, Reuben	3	2	4		
Harmon, Ebenezer	2	1	2		
Harmon, Israel	1	3	3		
King, Theodore	1	3	5		
Sheldon, Thomas	1	2	2		
Gillett, Elihu	1	1	2		
Pomeroy, Epephras	1	1	1		
Pomeroy, Sarah	1	1	6		
Pomeroy, Abagail			2		
Warner, Thaddeus	2	2	1		
Scott, William	3	4	6		
Feland, Thomas	2	3	3		
Nelson, Jereh	2	1	7		
Nelson, Hosea	1	2	2		
Nelson, Sarah			4		
Denslow, Benjamin	1	3	5		
Ingraham, Jeremiah	3		4		
Warner, Eli	2	1	5		
Taylor, Thad	3	2	5		
King, Ashur	3	1	5		
Warner, Samuel	2	3	5		
Gillet, Isaac	1	1	3		
Dunam, Jabez	2		2		
Dunam, Jabez, 2d	1	2	1		
Phelps, Ebenezer	1	1	2		
Rising, James	1		3		
Lillie, Jonathan	1	1	2		
Bush, Moses	1	3	3		
Rising, Elijah	1	2	2		
Rising, Abel	2	2	3		
Rising, James, 2d	1	1	1		
Rising, Jonah	1	2	1		
Rising, Joel	1		2		
Spencer, Elisha	3		4		
Stiveson, Abner	1	1	3		
Brown, John	1	1	2		
Warner, Isaac	1		2		
Warner, John	1		2		
Warner, John, 2d	1	1	2		
Edwards, David	1	4	1		
Trumbull, Levi	2	2	3		
Olds, Stephen	1	1	2		
Rocket, Josiah	3		2		
Parmatree, Joshua	1	2	2		
Trumbull, Luther	1	1	3		
Spencer, Elihu	1	1	1		
Rising, Ebenezer	1		1		
Pease, Justin	2	2	5		
Warner, Nathaniel	1		4		
Gillett, Calvin	1		3		
Warner, Silas	1	1	4		
Warner, Richard	1	2	3		
Trumbull, Oliver	1	2	6		
Remington, Elijah, 2d	1	2	3		
Abbey, Justin	1	1	2		
French, Amasa	1	2	2		
Stratton, John	2	1	3		
Stratton, John, 2d	1		2		
Norton, Freegrace	2	3	4		
Cannon, Joseph	4	5	3		
Blakely, Baley	1	4	4		
Miller, Mike	2	1	1		
More, Samuel	1	1	1		
Moore, Daniel	2	1	1		
Phelps, Silas	1	2	2		
Phelps, Elijah	2	2	3		
Linsey, Robert	1	6	3		
Edwards, Jonathan	2		3		1
Calver, Nathaniel	1	2	2		
Phelps, Judah	1	4	3		
Warner, Moses	2	2	6		
Granger, Elisha	2	3	4		
Bellamy, Abner	1	1	4		
Granger, Elisha, 2d	1	1	1		
Granger, Elihu	1	1	1		
King, Eliphalet	6	5	3		
King, William	3		3		

HARTFORD COUNTY—Continued.

NAME OF HEAD OF FAMILY.	Free white males of 16 years and upward, including heads of families.	Free white males under 16 years.	Free white females, including heads of families.	All other free persons.	Slaves.
SUFFIELD TOWN—con.					
King, Seth	1	3	2		
Norton, Simeon	2	4	3		
Leicester, Daniel	1	2	3		
Bissell, Isaac	1	4	3		
Granger, Bildad	2	2	3		
Granger, Epaphras	1		2		
Remington, Nathaniel	1	1	1		
King, Ebenezer, 2d	1	1	2		
Hitchcock, Apollos	1	5	1		
Towsley, Mike	1		3		
Dunlap, Brias	1	1	3		
Remington, Nathaniel	2	1	3		
Shaddock, Moses	1	1	2		
Burbank, Ebenezer	4	3	5		
Abbey, Peter	1		2		
Granger, Enock	2	1	3		
Tuffie, Robert	1	1	3		
King, Ebenezer	3	2	6		
King, John	1	1	1		
Leavitt, Stephen				2	
Harmon, Joseph	1	3	2		
Kindall, Amos	1	1	2		
Kindall, Joshua	1	1	4		
Kindall, Sarah	1	2	4		1
Pease, Levi	1	2	1		1
Lewis, Ezra	1	2	1		
Hill, Stephen	2	3	5		
King, Fidello	1	1	3		
Granger, Rufus	1		1		
Cobbin, Josiah	1		2		
Granger, Eli	1	2	3		
Williams, William	2	2	1		
King, Dan	4	2	9		
Archer, Thomas	2	1	2		
Archer, Thomas, 2d	1	3	2		
Holiday, William	2	4	5		1
Holiday, Naoma		2	4		
Allyn, Chester	2	2	3		
Tiley, Asa	1	3	2		
Scott, Benjamin	1		1		
Nelson, Jeremiah, 2d	1		2		
WETHERSFIELD TOWN.					
Deming, Henry	4	1	9		
Fosdick, William	1	3	3		
Fosdick, Aanna			3		
Bacon, Richard	5	3	2		
Stevens, Isaac	2		1		4
Webb, Joseph	4	4	8	1	4
Boardman, Elihu	1	1	4		
Farnsworth, Joseph	1	1	2		
Chester, Stephen	2	1	4	3	1
Dorr, Samuel	2	4	4		
Stanley, George	1		3		
Hitchcock, Brenton	1	1	2		
Woodward, ——	1		2		
May, Samuel, Jr	1	6	3		
Gains, James	1		1		
Latimer, Bezu	2	3	1		
Willard, Josiah	2		1		
Draper, Aaron	1	2	6	1	
Balik, Ebenezar	1	1	2		
Wright, Elijah	2	3	2		1
Morrison, Hannah		2	1		
Barnard, Samuel	2	1	2		
Beardsley, Hezekiah	2	1	1		
Wright, Ashbel	1				
Wright, David	1	1	2		
Wright, Josiah	4	1	2		
Fosdick, Ezekiel	1	1	1		
Riley, Levi	1	1	3		
Seymour, Elisha	3		1		
Deming, Richard	1	2	5		
Loveland, John	3	2	3		
Deming (Wid.)	1	1	2		
Baxter, Elisha	1		5		
Griswold, Elisha	1		1		
Griswold, Margeret	1	1	5		
Griswold, Frederic	1	1	3		
Buckley, Sarah	1		2		
Dupu, Lims	1		4		
Combs, Andrew	1		3		
Wright, Josiah, Jr	1		2		
Hulbut, William	3	1	3		
Hurlbut, Elijah	1		1		
Hurlbut, Stephen	1	2	2		
Moses, Clerk	1		2		
Hurlbut, Thomas	4	1	2		
Tente, Ammon	1	1	2		
Goodrich, John	1	4	3		
Bumbo, Harry	1	2	1		
Stilman, Elisha	2	1	3		
Russell, Timothy	1	2	2		
Wells, Samuel, 2d	1	1	2		
WETHERSFIELD TOWN—continued.					
Dix, Leonard	1	4	1		
Dix, Jacob	2	1	1		
Wright, Ebenezer	1		2		
Dix, Charles	1	1	3		
Dix, Elisha	1	3	2		
Boardman, Elisha	1	1	1		
Johnson, James		2	2		
Dillins (Wid.)			1		
Churchill, Samuel	2	1	2		
Montgue, Richard	2	2	2		
Montague, George	1		2		
Churchill, Jesse	3		2		
Bunce, Richard	1		1		
Churchill, Levi	1	2	3		
Combs, Joseph	3	1	4		
Willard, Simon	2	4	3		
Hatch, Moses	1	1	3		
Blin, Hosea	1	5	3		
Wells, Thomas, 2d	2	2	3		
Kibby, John	1	3	2		
Kibby, Dorothy		1	3		
Smith, Joseph	1		1		
Smith, Levi	1	1	2		
Griswold, Ozias	3	3	7		
Griswold, Jerusha	1	2	2		
Rockwell, Samuel	1	1	5		
North, Salmon	2		1		
Kibby, William	1		1		
Hatch, Zephaniah	4		2		
Hatch, James	1	1	4		
Durham, David	2		1		
Waterbury, Joseph	1	2	2		
Adams, Joseph	1	2	2		
Warner, Robert	1	3	2		
Montague, Moses	1	2	1		
Montague, Anna	1		3		
Montaigue, Seth	1	2	3		
Adams, John	1	1	4		
Adams, Amasa	1	3	3		
Blin, Solomon	1	1	3		
Blin, William	1	2	5		
Robbins, Joshua	2	1	3		
Robbins, Joshua, 2d	1		2		
Robbins, Asa	1	1	1		
Latimer, John	1		3		
Blin, Gershom	2		5		
Blin, Samuel	2	2	4		
Warner, John	2	1	2		
Ray, Flint	1	2	6		
Adams, Benjamin	4	1	7		
Havins, Thomas	1	3	2		
Pembleton, ——	1	2	3		
Adams, Camp	2	1	7		
Warner, William	1	2	3	1	
Williams, Elisha	1		3		2
Crane, Abraham	4		4		
Crane, Joseph	1	3	3		
Crane, Hezekiah	1	4	5		
Loveland, William	1	2	3		
Marks, William	1		3		
Harris, Hosea	3	1	3		
Hart, Josiah	1	1	6		
Dix, Moses	3		4		
Putman, John	1	1	1		
Loveland, William	1	2	3		
Barrett, Selah	2	1	3		
Griffin, Simon	2	1	2		
Kibby, Richard	1	1	2		
Crane, Ruth			3		
Kibby, Thomas	2	1	1		
Crane, Curtis	1	3	3		
Dix, Sarah			4		
Crane, Ruth	2		2		
Dickenson, Hannah			2		
Dickenson, Lucy	3	1	3		
Coleman, Thomas	1	1	4		
Denniss, Allyn	2		1		
Brooks, Jonathan	1		3		
Hurlbut, Simion	1	3	4		
Gooner, Quash					6
Robbins, Elisha	1	2	3		
Robbins, Oliver	4	2	4		
Robbins, Appleton	2	2	6		
Wells, Jonathan	1	1	1		
Hurlbut, Nathaniel	1		1		
Hurlbut, Nathaniel, 2d	2	2	2		
Horner, Thomas	2		1		
Benton, John	2	1	6		
Warner, Prudence			2		
Warner, Aaron	1	1	2		
Warner, John, 3d	1	1	3		
Belden, Rebecca	1	7	1		
Belden, John	2		1		
Warner, John, 2d	1	2	6		
Robbins, David	1		3		
WETHERSFIELD TOWN—continued.					
Welles, Elisha	1	3	2		
How, Elisha	1	2	1		
Buckley, Charles	1	2	3		
Buckley, John	1		3		
Treat, John	1	3	2		
Treat, Charles	2	1	2		
Treat, Damarus			2		
Smith, Josiah	3		3		
Smith, James	1	1	2		
Buckley, Benjamin	1	3	3		
Clark, Roger	1	1	3		
Palmer, Elizabeth			1		
Hudson, John	1	3	2		
Neff, John	1		3		
Dana, Thomas	3	3	3		1
Smith, Israel	3	1	4		
Smith, Jonathan	4		2		
Loomis, Silas	1		2		2
William, Ezekiel	2	2	3	1	2
Webb, Ebenezer	1		1		
Webb, Ezra	1	1	2		
Fontaine, Luke	1	1	2		1
Burnham, James	1	5	3		
Kilbourn, Abigail	1		1		
Clark, Mary			2		
Giles, Samuel	1		2		
Neuson, Thos	3		6		1
Deming, Elezur	1		7		
Williams, Samuel W	1		6		2
Warner, Thomas	1		1		
Treat, Elisha	1		2		
Riley, Samuel	2	2	2		
Boardman, Charles	3		4		
Riley, Christian			3		
Frances, James	1	5	3		
Gladden, Josiah	1	4	1		
Chester, John	2	3	9	5	4
Strong, William	1		3		
Willard, Stephen	2	2	4		
Beadle, Jonathan	3	2	6		
Storrs, Prince	1	1	1		
Hurlbut, Elijah, Jr	1	1	1		
Hurbut, Thomas, 2d	1	1	4		
Boardman, Levi	1	2	1		
Abbey, George	1	1	3		
Fosdick, James	1	1	1		
Mathews, Hugh	1		1		
Kibby, Christopher	1	2	4		
Sampson, Will				7	
Moreton, John	2		3		
Deming, Justus	1	1	1		
Porter, Aaron	1	1	4		
Buckley, Solomon	1	3	5		
Palmer, Isaac	1	3	2		
Welles, David	1	2	3		
Riley, Levi	2		2		
Row, John	1	3	2		
Burnham (Wid.)		1	1		
Burnham, Jeremiah	1	2	4	1	
Marsh, John	1	3	6		
Riley, Ashbel	2		4		2
Aysault, Daniel	1	1	3		1
Tryon, Moses	1	4	4		
Williams, John	1		2		
Belden, Simeon	4		5		
Beldin, Ezekiel P	1	1	5		2
Peirce, Samuel	1	2	4		
Mitchel, James	2	4	2		3
Mitchel, Stephen Mix	3	5	5		3
Brigden, Michael	2	2	3		
Riley, Justus	4	2	5		
Deming, William	2		2		
Deming, James	2	2	4		
Deming, Josiah	4	3	5		
Stilman, Samuel	1	1	3		
Chadwick, William	3	1	2		
Stilman, Joseph	4	2	6		
Stillman, Allyn	1	1	2		
Robbins, Levi	4		1		
May, William	2	1	4		
May, Hezekiah	1		1		
May, John	1	4	3		
Buckley, Frances	1	3	4		1
Goodrich, Abigail			5		
Goodrich, John	2	1	3		
Buner, Sarah	2		2		
Buner, Jona, Jr	1	1	2		
Talcott, Moses	1		1		
Talcott, Mary	1		2		1
Talcott, Ebenezer	4	1	3		
Talcott, Samuel	1		2		
Deming, William, Jr	1	2	3		
Porter, Abigail	1		2		
Butler, Frederic	1		5	1	
Wells, Bille	4	1	3	1	

WETHERSFIELD TOWN—continued.

NAME OF HEAD OF FAMILY.	Free white males of 16 years and upward, including heads of families.	Free white males under 16 years.	Free white females, including heads of families.	All other free persons.	Slaves.
Noah, Will				4	
Woodhouse, Samuel	1	1	4		
Stilman, Nathaniel	4		2		
Stillman, Allyn, Jr	1		2		
Griswold, William	1	2	1		
Griswold, Timothy	3	2	2		
Curtis, Samuel	1	3	6		
Woodhouse, Anna	2		3		
Wolcott, Josiah	1	1	1		
Stilman, Natha, Jr	1	2	4		
Hanmer, Sama	1	2	6		
Hanmer, Frances	3		4		
Hanmer, John	1				
Goodrich, Nathaniel, Jr	3	3	2		
Combs, Josiah	1		6		
Weston, Benjamin	1	1	7		
Woodhouse, Samuel	3		4		
Woodhouse, William	1		3		
Boardman, Samuel	1	2	5		
Buck, Samuel	1		3		
Buck, John	2		5		
Woodhouse, John	2	4	7		
Woodhouse, Abijah	1	2	3		
Dabloughhai, Jona	1		3		
Buck (Wid.)		1	3		
Latimor, Solomon	2		5		
Wells, Eli	1	2	5		
Wells, Chester	5	1	5		
Wells, Theodore	1		4		
Wells, Solomon	4	1	3		
Goodrich, Josiah	2	4	5		
Deming, Abel	1	3	7		
Deming, Daniel, Jr	1	3	5		
Butler, Joseph	2	2	3		
Wells, Prudence		1	3		1
Wells, John	3	1	1		
Tryon, Abijah	1	2	2		
Tryon, Josiah	1		1		
Standish, John	1		2		
Stoddard, Epephras	1	1	6		
Deming, Simeon	1	1	3		
Will, Jephet				7	
Brendly, John	1	2	3		
Beck, Josiah	1		1		
Buck, Josiah, Jr	1	2	4		
Buck, Daniel	2	5	3		
Deming, Peter	1	2	4		
Deming, Anora			2		
Standish, James	1		1		
Wright, Nathaniel	3		1		
Wright, Moses	1	2	3		
Wright, Elizur	2	1	3		
Butler, Roger	1	2	2		
Goodrich, Nathaniel	2	1	3		
Goodrich, Israel	1	1	2		
Butler, John	1	1	6		
Butler, Josiah	2	3	5		
Butler, Hezekiah	1	1	1		
Butler, James	2	2	3		
Butler, William	1	2	3		
Butler, Theodore	1	2	2		
Willis, Ichabod	3		5		
Oconoland, Patrick	1				
Curtis, Josiah	1		1		
Curtis, Levi	1	2	5		
Frances, Josiah	3	1	5		
Curtis, James	1		1		
Denniss, Dusen	1		1		
Deming, Abigail			1		
Deming, Hannah	1	1	5		
Deming, Moses	2		2		1
Wells, Samuel, 2d	2		3		1
Wells, Hezekiah	1		4		
Wells, Josiah	1	1	2		
Frances, John	4	1	4		
Deming, Josiah, Jr	1	2	3		
Goodrich, David	4	3	4		
Deming, Jessee	1		1		
Deming, John	1	1	4	1	
Wells, Ruth		1	1		
Franciss, Timothy	2	1	3		
Hanmer, James	1	1	9		
Flowers, Joseph	3	1	3		
Flowers, Simeon	1		3		
Lewis, Joseph	1	5	2		
Clark, Ambrose	1	1	3		
Payne, Ambrose	1	3	3		
Coleman, Peleg	2	1	2		
Porter, Israel	2	2	2		
Clark, Theodore	2		2		
Harrison, Theodore	1	3	3		
Clapp, Norman	1	2	1		
Write, Lucy		1	2		
Bunce, Josia	2	4	4		
Newbury, —	1		2		
Deming, Ebenezer	1	2	4		
Hale, James	1	2	4		
Hale, Elizabeth	1		1		
Hale, Benezer	1	1	1		
Curtis, Thomas	2		3		
Goodrich, Joseph	2	1	3		
Brown, Edward	2	1	2		
Wolcott, Samuel	1	1	2		
Wolcott, William	1	2	1		
Wolcott, Solomon	2	3	3		
Wolcott, Elisha	1		1		1
Wolcott, Elisha, Jr	1	2	4		
Robbins, Josiah	1	2	3	1	
Robbins, Josiah, 2d	1	1	1		
Robbins, Robert	1		1		
Andrus, Elijah	2		4		
Willis, Seth	1	1	4		
Wells, Joseph	1	1	2		
Wells, Elijah	1	3	8		
Wells, Christopher	1		2		
Wells, Joshua	2		3		
Wells, Joshua, Jr	1	1	1		
Wells, Gideon	1	1	1		
Wells, Levi	1	1	1		
Morgan, Levi	1	1	2		
Roods, William	2	2	4		
Roods, William, Jr	1	1	2		
Roods, Alexander	3	3	5		
Roods, Mary			1		
Combs, Joseph, Jr	1		2		
Blin, Unni	1		2		
Woolcut, Huldah	1		2		
Bunce, Jona	1	4	3		
Warner, Daniel	4		5		
Warner, Levi	1	1	3		
Warner, Rhoda	1		2		
Warner, Hannah			2		
Boardman, Elnathan	1		1		
Boardman, Elijah	2	2	2		
Robbins, Zebulon	1	2	2		
Robbins, Abigail			2		
Robbins, John	2	2	3		
Boardman, Jona	1				
Boardman, Jonathan, Jr	1	2	1		
Boardman, Hannah	1		3		
Boardman, Jason	1	1	3		
Price, Richard	2	1	5		
Adams, James	1	2	3		
Robbins, Elijah	1	2	1		
Griswold, William	2	1	5	4	
Deming, Jonth	2		6		
Riley, Jabez	2	1	5		
Morton, Benjamin	1	3	3		
Morton, Abigail			2		
Buckley, Charles, 2d	1	1	3		
Robbins, Jason	1		1		
Smith, David	1	1	1		
Warner, Wait	1	2	2		
Edwards, John, 2d	1	3	3		
Edwards, John	3		3		
Demmack, Joseph, Jr	1	1	1		
Simons, William	2	2	2		
Church, Joseph	2		3		
Stebbins, Joseph	1		3		
Buckley, Prescott	2	1	7		
Bull, Aaron	1	1	2		
Hosford, Aaron	2	2	4		
McCombs, Andrew	1	1	2		
Riley, Stephen	4	1	1		
Stillman, William	1	2	2		
Stanley, James	1		2		1
Riley, John	5	1	2		
Ames, Philemon	1		2		
Ames, William	1		1		
Ames, Abagail			3		
Robbins, John, Jr	2		3	1	
Goodrich, Elizur	1	2	2		
Goodrich, Isaac	1	1	2		
Grimes, Alexander	2	6	4		
Deming, Asa	1	1	4		
Pomeroy, Rachel			2		
Buckley, Prudence		1	3		
Goodrich, William	2	1	3		
Belden, Bildad	1	3	4		
Stoddard, Ebenezer	1	1	2		
Chauncey, Eunice			2		
Belden, Ezra	2		1		
Whitmore, Hezekiah	1	2	2		
Grimes, Josiah	2		4		
Grimes, Abigail	1		2		
Webb, William	1		1		
Ames, William	1	2	2		
Williams, Jacob	1		6		
Williams, Israel	1		2		
Higgins, Joseph	1	2	2		
Bradley, David	1		3		
Williams, Moses	1		3		
Bradley, William	1	2	3		
Hart, Seth	3		3		
Williams, Daniel	2		5		
Huntington, Josiah	1	3	4		
Buckley, Justus	1	2	2		
Foster, Samuel	2		6		1
Benton, Esther		1	3		
Nott, William	1	2	2		
Nott, John	2		1		1
Goodrich, Ichabod	1		3		
Ames, Benjamin	1		4		
Butler, Samuel	2		1		
Buckley, Paty			3		
Williams, Elias	1	1	1		1
Williams, John	2	3	3		
Collins, David	3		3		
Price, George	1		1		
Williams, William	2	2	4		
Robbins, Wait	2	3	3		1
Robbins, Abijah, 2d	2		5		
Robbins, Frederic	2	4	4		
Robbins, Simeon	1	3	5		
Goff, Josiah	4	1	4		
Riley, Ackley	1	1	1		
Dickenson, Elias	4		2		
Buckley, Wetherby	1	1	5		
Riley, Jacob	2	1	3		3
Calender, Elisha	1	3	7		1
Buckley, Jehiel	1	1	2		
Price, Jonathan	1	2	4		
Danforth, Thomas	3		5		1
Robbins, Jacob	2	3	3		
Riley, Roger	1	3	2		
Gibbs, John	2	1	6		
Colver, Edward	1	1	2		
Holmes, Jonas	1		3		
Lewis, John	1	2	3		1
Williams, Jehiel	2	4	5		
Goodrich, Israel	1		4		
Demmonck, Joseph	2		3		
Belden, Mary			2		
Samburn, Jedidiah	1		1		
Goodrich, Ebenezer	4	1	3		
Goff, Gideon	1		3		
Goodrich, Thilcon	2	2	4		
Selm, Patience			1		
Deming, Frances	1		1		
Boardman, Return	2		1		
Goodrich, Roger	2	3	2		
Cowing, Lois			1		
Churchill, Josiah	1		1		
Goodrich, Elijah	2		3		
Goodrich, Alpheus	3	1	4		
Goodrich, Jerusha	1		1		
Wilson, Silus	1		3		
Smith, Susanna			1		
Holmes, Levi	1		2		
Hands, Jonathan	3		3		
Buckley, Joseph	1	4	4		
Buckley, Edward	1	1	4		
Demmick, Samuel	1	2	1		
Boardman, Frederic	1		1		
Griswold, Mercy			2		
Holmes, Thomas	1		2		
Cleveland, Joseph	1		3		
Williams, Ephraim	4	3	2		
Smith, Ezekiel	1	2	4		
Buckley, Christian	1		1		
Goodrich, Elihu	1		1		
Williams, Levi	1		2		
Wilkinson, John	1		1		
Wright, Benjamin	1	1	2		
Hammond, James	1	3	1		
Wright, Daniel	1	1	2		
Griswold, Jehiel	1	3	3		
Goodrich, Gurdin, Jr	1		5		
Mildram, Leydia			3		
Miller, David	1		3		
Miller, Joseph			1		
Riley, Sarah			2		
Goodrich, Oliver	2	3	3		
Jager, Abraham	1	2	2		
Goodrich, Temperance			1		
Mitchel, Calvin	1	1	2		
Butler, Gideon	1	2	2		
Holmes, Daniel	1		2		
Buckley, Hosea	1	3	4		
Buckley, Gersham	1		3		
Butler, Benjamin	1	4	3		
Curtis, Wait	3		1		
Curtis, Josiah	1		1		
Butler, Joel	1	1	1		
Griswold, Constant	1	3	2		
Miller, Nathaniel	3	2	4		
Rash, Jeremiah	1	3	2		
Butler, Simeon	1	1	3		

HARTFORD COUNTY—Continued.

WETHERSFIELD TOWN—continued.

NAME OF HEAD OF FAMILY.	Free white males of 16 years and upward, including heads of families.	Free white males under 16 years.	Free white females, including heads of families.	All other free persons.	Slaves.
Butler, Richard	1	1	1		
Butler, Zeebah	1		6		
Butler, David	1		2		
Collins, James	2	2	4		
Collins, Robert	2		1		
Collins, Abial			3		
Smith, Manus	2		1		
Butler, Stephen	1		2		
Russell, Jonathan	1	2	3		
Russell, Thomas	2	3	4		
Boardman, Levi	1	1	1		
Collins, Levi	1	1	4		
Buckley, Jonathan	1		2		
Buckley, Stephen	1	3	3		
Miller, Jerusha			3		
Goodrich, Gurden	2	1	3		
Marsh, John	1		2		
Marsh, John, Jr	1		3		
Marsh, Eli	1	1	2		
Bunce, Thomas	1	3	4		
Goodrich, Seth	1	2	1		
Dickenson, Josiah	1	2	3		
Dickenson, Wait	1	2	5		
Dickenson, Ozias	1	5	5		
Dickenson, Obadiah	1	1	2		
Riley, Jasper	1	2	2		
Belden, David	1	5	2		
Belden, Asa	1		3		
Belden, Elisha	1	1	2		
Belden, John	1		3		
Belden, Jeremiah	1		3		
Deming, Jiles	1		4		
Deming, Leeman	1	1	2		
Deming, Asahel	1				
Wright, Jiles	1	2	2		
Ceaser (Negro)				3	
Collins, Simeon	2	2	2		
Belden, Abraham	1	2	2		
Wright, Justus	2		3		
Stow, Ebenezer	1	1	4		
Holmes, John	2	2	2		
Belden, Otho	1	2	3		
Belden, Richard	2		1		
Belden, Richard, Jr	1	2	2		
Blin, Hezekiah	2	1	3		
Blin, David	1		1		
Blin, Peter, Jr	1	3	3		
Blin, Peter	1		2		
Blin, Martha	1		1		
Blin, Justus	1	1	2		
Belden, Aaron	4		2		
Belden, Moses	1	1	4		
Belden, Silas	1	1	3		
Wright, Charles	1	1	6		
Buckley, Theodore	1	1	3		
Sanford, Justus	1	1	3		
Dix, Benjamin	1	2	3		
Wolcott, Josiah	1	2	4		
Goodrich, John	1	4	5		
Goodrich, David	2	3	2		
Webster, Amos	1	3	1		
Steele, Joseph	1	3	3		
Deming, Ephraim	1		2		
Deming, Hannah	1	1	4		
Deming, Elias	1	3	3		
Wolcott, Caleb	1		2		
Rockwell, Oziah	1	2	3		
Lark, Levi	1	1	3		
Butorick, Edward	1		1		
Churchill, Charles	1	1	2		
Churchill, Solomon	1		1		
Churchill, Samuel	1	4	3		
Churchill, Levi	1	3	5		
Deming, Jara	3		4		
Deming, Elizur	2	2	3		
Deming, Eliakim	1		3		
Deming, Frances	1	1	2		
Squire, John	2	2	2		
Richardson, Isael	1	1	2		
Blin, James	2		3		
Wright, Abijah	1		4		
Wright, Esther	2	1	4		
Hurlbut, John	1	2	4		
Hurlbut, Mathew	1		2		
Robbins, Unni	3	1	5		1
Wolcott, George	2	1	4		
Hurlbut, Elias	1	1	5		
Gibbs, Lemuel	1	2	1		
Deming, Robert	1	2	2		
Blin, Jonathan	2		5		
Belden, Joshua	3	1	6		
Whaples, Eli	1	1	3		
Whaples, Reuben	1	1	1		
Holmes, Lemuel	1		4		
Phelps, Ephraim	1	1	4		

WETHERSFIELD TOWN—continued.

NAME OF HEAD OF FAMILY.	Free white males of 16 years and upward, including heads of families.	Free white males under 16 years.	Free white females, including heads of families.	All other free persons.	Slaves.
Lowry, David	2		3		
Andrus, Eli	1				
Andrus, Abel	3		4		
Kilbourn, Eunice			2		
Kilbourn, Simon	1		3		
Wentworth, Sion	1		1		
Lusk, James	1	1	3		1
Stoddard, Solomon	1		1		
Andrus, Elizur	2	2	5		
Wells, Simon	1	3	2		
Andrus, Fitch	1	1	3		
Buck, Amos	2	2	4		
Wells, Jamus	4	3	6		
Wells, Elijah	2		5		
Atwood, Asher	2		3		
Wells, Roger	1	2	3	1	
Kellogg, Martin	2	1	3		2
Smith, Obadiah	1	2	4		
Boardman, Israel	1		1		
Williams, Elijah	1	1	3		
Russell, David	2		4		
Andrus, Elias	1	1	3		
Latimore, Luther	2	1	3		
Landers, Samuel	3		3		
Frances, Roger	1	1	1		
Wells, Absalom	1	1	4		
Wells, Robert	1	1	2		
Wells, Robert, Jr	1	2	2		
Whittlesey, Lemuel	2	2	4		1
Hurlbut, Levi	3	4	3		
Churchill, Joseph	1	2	2		
Coslet, Frances	1		1		
Andrus, Sarah			1		
Dickenson, Ebenezer	2		1		
Dickenson, Wait S	1	2	2		
Frances, Josiah	2	1	2		
Frances, Justus	2	3	2		
Taylor, Benajah	1	1	2		
Merrill, Ebenezer	2	1	2		
Wells, Levi	1		1		
Kellogg, Martin, Jr	1	2	6		
Willard, Daniel	2		2		
Willard, Daniel, Jr	2	2	1		
Deming, Frederic	1	1	1		
Stoddard, Jonathan	3		3		
Guinea (Negro)					1
Camp, Joseph	1	3	5		
Stoddard, Dorothy		2	2		
Stodard, Joseph	1	2	2		
Stoddard, David	1	1	4		
Walcott, Abigail			3		
Kellogg, Stephen	1	2	3		
Kellogg, Joseph	1	1	1		
Hunn, Enos	1	2	4		
Hinsdale, Zadock	2	2	6		
Seymour, Elias	2	1	6		
Seymour, Ashbel	1	4	2		
Seymour, Thankfull	1		2		
Fox, Thomas	1		1		
Pomp (Negro)					5
Kellsey, Enoch	3	1	4		

WINDSOR TOWN.

NAME OF HEAD OF FAMILY.	Free white males of 16 years and upward, including heads of families.	Free white males under 16 years.	Free white females, including heads of families.	All other free persons.	Slaves.
Alford, Jonathan	2	4	1		
Baldwin, Thomas	1	3	5		
Brown, Ephm	3	1	3		
Denslow, Elijah	3		6		
Mather, Joseph	3		2		
Brown, Elias	1	3	1		
Strong, Elisha	1	3	7		
Benton, Elihu S	2	1	5		
Benton, Thomas	2		3		
Sill, Richd L	1	3	2		
Sill, John	1	3	4		
Allen, John, Ju	1	2	2		
Wells, James	2	1	2		
Howard, Nathl	1	4	1		
Ellsworth, Migail			2		
Chaffee, Hezh, Jur	3	1	2	2	1
Chaffee, Hezekiah	3		3	1	
Hooker, James	1	1	7	1	
Allen, Hannah			1		
Gibbs, Charity	3		1		
Elsworth, Ebenr	1	3	4		
Porter, Daniel	1	3	3		
Mack, Andrew	1	4	1		
Strong, Sarah			1		
Filer, Samuel	1		2		
Mather, Cotton	1		7		
Daboll, Jonathan	2	3	4		
Thrall, Eliza	2	1	4		
Wilson, Moses	2	3	4		
Allen, John	1	1	3		
Allen, Charles	1	1	1		

WINDSOR TOWN—con.

NAME OF HEAD OF FAMILY.	Free white males of 16 years and upward, including heads of families.	Free white males under 16 years.	Free white females, including heads of families.	All other free persons.	Slaves.
Hooker, Horrace	2	2	6		
Russell, Cornelius	1	2	4		
Mather, Elijah	3	1	1		
Elsworth, Eliza			2		1
Gillet, Alme	1	2	1		
Allen, Joseph	1		3		
Drake, Dorson	3	1	1		
Elsworth, Giles	2		2	1	
Elsworth, Jonah	3	3	3		
Elsworth, Grove	1	1	2		
Barker, Ethan	3		1		
Russel, Wm	2	2	4		
Mather, Elijah, Jur	1		1		
Chapman, Taylor	3	1	1		
Mather, Eliakim	3	1	2		
Marshal, Amos	1	1	3	1	
Stiles, Samuel	2	1	5		
Stoughton, Israel	1		5		
Stoughton, Elisha	1	2	3		
Miller, Roswell	1		2		
Allen, Saml Ju	1	1	3		1
Woolcott, Alexr	1	3	2	2	
Rice, Aaron	1	1	1		
Hoskins, Ezekiel	2	2	4		
Gaylord, John	1	1	3		
Allen, Saml W	1	1	4		
Mather, Azariah, Ju	1		3		
Holcomb, Elijah	1	1	2		
Pinney, Eliza	2		1		
Stiles, Ashbel	2		4		
Stiles, Job	2		2		
Elsworth, Honbl Oliver, Esqr	2	2	5	1	
Elsworth, David	2	3	4		
Hindsdale, Theodore	3	5	4		
Haydon, Thomas	3	1	4		
Bissel, Ebenr F	2	1	1		
Thrall, David	1	2	3		
Thrall, Jesse	1	2	2		
Haydon, Isaac	1	2	5		
Munsel, Alpheus	2	2	2		
Haydon, Nathl	1		2		
Lamberton, Obed	1				
Lamberton, Moses	1	1	3		
Osburn, Jacob	1		2		
Bissel, Josiah	2	1	2		
Bissel, Hezih (Wid.)		1	2		
Welch, Lemuel	1	1	5		
Haydon, Ezra	2	2	6		
Phelps, Bildad	3		5		2
Bissel, Ebinr F., Ju	1		1		1
Haydon, Nathl Ju	4	2	4		
Haydon, Levi	4	4	4		2
Haydon, Ebenr	1	1	4		
Picket, Phinehas	3	2	5		
Ensign, Amos	2	1	1		
Haydon, John, Ju	1	1	6		
Haydon, Oliver	1		1		
Haydon, John	3	2	3		
Tucker, Gideon	1		3		
Sheldon, Remember	1		2		
Denslow, Joseph G	1		3		
Russel, Jacob	2	4	4		
Mather, Azariah	1		4		
Gaylord, Eliakim	2		1		
Gaylord, Eliakim, Ju	1		2		
Denslow, Martin	2	2	2		
Herskill, Jabez	2	5	5		
Denslow, Samuel	1		3		
Fish, David	1	3	1		
Eli, Daniel	1	1	2		
Gaylord, Eliazer	1	1	6		
Pinney, Martin	3	1	4		
Burge, Peletiah	4	3	3		
Dexter, Seth	2	3	6		
Clark, Oliver	1	3	6		
Sperry, Elijah	1		4		
Wing, Lydia	1	1	2		
Wing, Moses	2		2		
Allen, John	2	4	6		
Drake, Lora	1		2		
Abby, Saml, Ju	1	2	1	1	
Barber, Elijah	4		4		
Talcott, Danl	3	4	3		
Barber, Josiah	1		2		
Barber, Josiah, Jur	3	5	2		
Allen, Saml	2		2		
Barber, Thoms	3		1		
Barber, Eli	1		2		
Barber, Reuben	1	1	3		
Mills, Elijah	1	1	3		
Drake, David	3		2		
Drake, Phinehas	2	1	3	1	
Allen, Fitts	2	1	3		
Allen, Benja	2				

HARTFORD COUNTY—Continued.

WINDSOR TOWN—con.

NAME OF HEAD OF FAMILY.	Free white males of 16 years and upward, including heads of families.	Free white males under 16 years.	Free white females, including heads of families.	All other free persons.	Slaves.
Drake, Samuel	2				
Sheldon, Selah	1	2	2		
Wisland, Amos, Ju	1	1	3		
Drake, Phinehas, Jur	1	2	4		
Wesland, Joseph	1		4		
Moore, Thos	1		3		
Barber, Moses	3	1	3		
Barber, Aaron	1	1	4		
Loomis, Joseph, Ju	2	1	3		
Barber, Benoni	1		1		
Loomis, Jerajah	5		3		
Loomis, Nijah	1		2		
Warner, Loomis	4		3		
Loomis, Benajah	5	5	3		
Strong, Abel	1	3	4		
Elggleston, Thoms	3	4	1		
Loomis, Watson	1	1	1		
Loomis, Jedidiah	1		1		
Loomis, Jed, Jur	1	4	1		
Loomis, Dan	1		2		
Warner, John	2		2		
Cook, Wm	1		1		
Alford, Jeremiah	1		1		
Moore, Asa	1		3		
Bestor, John				5	
Roberts, James	2	1	5		
Halsey, Phillip	2	2	1		
Moore, Edwd	2	2	3		
Chandler, Isaac	3	1	2		
Moore, Roger	1				
Moore, Elisha	3	2	3		
Phelps, Augustus	2	1	4		
Eggleston, Ephm	1	1	5		
Mather, Oliver	3	4	2		
Phelps, Ebenr	1	1	3		
Moore, Hannah	1		2		
Filley, John	5	1	3		
Allen, Jonah	1		1	1	
Newbury, Roger	2	2	6	1	1
Allen, Henry	2	1	3		1
Drake, Elihu	2	1	3		
Francis, Wm	1	1	2		
Woolcott, Christopher	3	2	5		
Woolcott, George	3	2	5		
Utley, Joseph	2	2	3		
Mather, Increase	1		2		
Phelps, George	1	2	2		
Fitch, James	2		2		
Loomis, Abiah	2	2	4		
Loomis, George	1	3	6		
oomis, Odiah	1		2		
Holcomb, Elijah	1		3		
Roberts, Oliver	2	1	1		
Fuller, Obadiah	1	2	4		
Palmer, Benja	1		5		
Cook, Elisha	1	1	4		
Brown, Stephen	1	3	5		
Barber, Jerijah	6		4		
Gillet, Danl	2	1	5		
Phelps, Roger	2	1	3		
Phelps, Danl	1	1	1		
Palmer, Jonathan	3		2		
Eno, Ashbel	2		4		
Wilson, Phinehas	3	3	2		
Phelps, Lanclot	1	2	3		
Brown, Peter	2	1	3		
Colt, Jabez	2		2		
Barber, Jonah	2	2	3		
Bolls, Ruth			2		
Barber, Gideon	1	3	3		
Marshall, Eliakim	1		3		
Marshal, Eliakim, Jur	3	1	2		
Palmer, Joel	3	2	3		
Barber, David, Ju	1	3	3		
Dalton, Joseph	1	1	1		
Filley, Elisha	2	3	3		
Moore, Theophilus	1		1		
Allen, Moses	1		1		
Cook, Jonathan	2		1		
Rowley, Thomas	1	2	3		
Cook, Noah	1	1	4		
Cook, Shubael	1	3	2		
Wesland, Robert	1	1	2		
Cook, Josiah	3		2		
Cook, Theophilus	5		3		
Filly, Amos	2		1		
White, Moses	1	4	4		
Drake, Dudley	1	2	2		
Phelps, Cornelius	1		2		
Rowland, David S	4	1	4		
Phelps, Oliver	2	2	4		
Phelps, James	2	2	3	1	
Phelps, Timothy	2	1	3		
Palmer, John	1	5	2		
Phelps, Job, Jur	1	3	5		
Griswold, Jonah	2	1	1		
Rigly, Richard	2		3		
Moore, Benjn	3	1	1		
Denslow, Reuben	1		1		
Pinney, Judah	2	2	3		
Pinney, Isaac	1	1	2		
Griswold, George	2		5		
Griswold, George, Ju	1		1		
Griswold, Francis	1		1		
Barns, Abel	2	4	2		
Griswold, Joab	1	1	4		
Griswold, Joab, Ju	1	1	2		
Griswold, Elihu	1	1	7		
Griswold, Elijah	2	1	2		
Griswold, Ziba	3	3	7		
Marshall, Elisha	2		1		
Marshall, Timothy	1		1		
Holcomb, Saml	2		2		
Owen, Aaron	1		1		
Phelps, Wm	1		3		
Phelps, Eli	1		2	1	
Griswold Abel	2	5	3		
Holcomb, Roderick	1	1	2		
Griswold, Nathl	2	1	4		
Griswold, Timothy	1		2		
Holcomb, Martin	4		3		
Phelps, Enoch	1		1		
Holcomb, Martin, Jur	3	3	3		
Holcomb, Joseph	3	1	6		
Griswold, Edwd	2	2	5		
Blanchard, Jere	5		1		
Mills, Naomi			2	3	
Beebee, ——	1	1	2		
Griswold, Thomas	1	1	1		
Porter, George	1		2	1	
Wilson, Calvin	1	1	4		
Barnerd, Joseph	3	2	6		
Ross, John	2	2	5		
Alford, Joseph	2	3	4		
Griswold, Sylvanus	5	2	2		2
Phelps, Josias	2		2		
Phelps, Josiah, 2d	1	1	3		
Owen, Nathl	2	2	3		
Phelps, John	3	1	4		
Phelps, Isaac	3	1	2		
Phelps, Job	1	2	3		
Barna, Joseph	2	1	4		
Griswold, Isaac	1	3	5		
Case, Benoni	2	2	5		
Phelps, Shadrack	2		1		
Balcom, John	2	2	2		
How, Edwd	1	2	2		
Day, Isaac	1	2	2		
May, John	1		4		
Griswold, Hezh	1		1		
Miller, Abner	1	1	2		
Minor, John	1	2	2		
Thrall, John	1	1	1		
Latimer, Alexr	2		2		
Phelps, Jacob	1	1	5		
Lawrence, Amos	1	1	2		
Glazier, John	1	1	1		
McLean, John	1	3	4		
Waters, Bevil	1	2	2		
Filley, Moses	2	5	3		
McLean, Abia	1	2	2		
Parsons, Doctor	2	1	2		
Loomis, Andrew	1	4	3		
Clark, Roger	1	2	3		
Gillet, Jonah	1	3	5		
Gillet, Jonah, 2d	2	1	2		
Clark, Asahel	1		2		
Thrall, Isaac	1	2	5		
Loomis, Lydia			2		
Clark, John	2	2	4		
Latimer, George	1	1	3		
Loomis, Stephen	1		1		
Clark, Solomon	1	2	4		
Eggleston, Saml	2	3	6		
Eggleston, Nathl	1		1		
Wilson, Joseph	2	2	4		
Gillit, Levi	1	3	2		
Hoskins, Asa	1	2	2		
Gillit, Aaron	1	1	2		
Hoskins, Zebn	1		3		
Loomis, Elijah	1	1	5		
Loomis, Reuben	1		1		
Loomis, Abijah	1	1	3		
Loomis, Jacob	1	3	4		
Gillit, Amos	2	1	3		
Allen, Jonth	2	3	1		
Allen, Solomon, Ju	1	1	4		
Gillit, Abel	2	1	2		
Grimes, Simeon	1		2		
Lewis, Samuel	2	1	2		
Steel, James	1		1		
Drake, Joseph	2	3	2		
Stoughton, Saml	2	2	4		
Hubbard, Asa	1	1	3		
Hubbard, Nathl	1	3	2		
Bidwell, Jonathan	1	3	6		
Hubbard, John	1	3	1		
Allen, Elisha	1		2		
Allen, Alexr	1	3	1		
Allen, Thomas	1	2	5		
Tiler, Roger	1	3	4		
Burr, Amos	1	1	2		
Wilson, Hezh	1	1	3		
Allen, George	1	1	3		
Wilson, Abiel	1	1	3		
Webster, James	3	1	4		
Webster, Joseph	3	2	2		
Webster, Hezh	2		1		
Grant, David	2		2		
Allen, Solomon	2	3	3		
Hubbard, Timothy	2	2	5		
Risley, Zach	1	2	5		
Hubbard, Abner	1		2		
Clark, George	1	2	5		
Palmer, Jehiel	3		1		
Marshal, Saml	1		1		
Barber, Hepzibah			3		
Marshal, Sam, Jur	1	2	1		
Sanford, Robt	1	3	3		
Woodward, Oliver	1	2	3		
Cadwell, Theodore	1	2	3		
Palmer, Jonathan, Ju	1	1	2		
Filly, Jonathan	3		3		
Ackley, Abner B	3		3		
Hitchcock, Caleb	2	1	4		
Bissell, Col. Hezh	1	2	6	1	
Gillit, Deborah			3	4	
Elmer, Eliakim	1	1	1		
Butler, Nathl	2		3		
Wait, Wm	1	1	3		
Andrus, Saml	1	3	5		
Barton, Wm	1		1		
Elmer, Phinehas	2	1	3		
Fitch, Luther	1		1		
Barber, James	2	7	2		
Drake, Noah	1		1		
Mills, Elijah	1		1		
Clark, Hosea	1	2	3		
Drake, Moses	1	1	4		
Skinner, Isaac	2		2		
Skinner, Isaac, Ju	1	1	4		
Delanna, Wm	2		1		
Hoskins, Increase	4	1	4		
Higby, Job	3				
Wills, Roger	3	4	6		
Gillit, Abel, Ju	2	4	4		
Mills, Elijah	1		3		
Mills, Fredk	1	2	2		
Latimer, Hezh, Ju	1	2	4		
Newberry, Thomas	2		4		
Hoskins, Eli	2	1	5		
Rowley, Saml	1		1		
Filly, Luke	2		1		
Filly, Jesse	2		1		
Filly, Timothy	1		1		
Filly, David	1	2	2		
Rowley, John	1		3		
Rowley, Reuben	1		3		
Rowley, Philander	1	2	2		
Rowley, Roger	1	2	3		
Hempsted, Joshua	1	1	2		
Hall, Benajah	1	1	2		
Woolcott, Solomon	1	3	3		
Cook, Eli	1	1	1		
Latimer, Hezh	2	1	3		
Parsons, Hezh	1		2		
Parsons, Pelitiah	1		4		
Fitch, Joseph	3	1	2		
Cook, Job	1		2		
Mills, Diadema			2		
Griswold, Simon	2		2		
Barns, Stephen	2	2	3		
Cook, James	1	2	6		
Riley, Nathl	1		7		
Fusbury, Anna			3		
Gray, Wm	1	2	2		
Cook, Abner	2	2	2		
Eggleston, Jonathan	2	1	3		
Clark, Ira	1	3	2		
Wilson, Joel	1	3	4		
Brown, Ezra	2	1	8		
Wilson, Joel	1		2		
Gray, George	1		2		
Phelps, Charles	1		1		
Phelps, Charles, Ju	1		2		

HARTFORD COUNTY—Continued.

WINDSOR TOWN—con.

NAME OF HEAD OF FAMILY.	Free white males of 16 years and upward, including heads of families.	Free white males under 16 years.	Free white females, including heads of families.	All other free persons.	Slaves.
Phelps, Oliver	1	1	1		
Brown, Samˡ	2	1	3		
Griswold, Solomon	3	1	8		
Phelps, Aaron, Ju	1	1	2		
Phelps, Aron	4	1	4	1	
Enos, Samˡ	1	4	2		
Manley, Allen	3		1		
Filly, Aaron	1	1	4		
Brown, Zadock	1	2	3		
Brown, Benjⁿ, Ju	1	2	2		
Cotton, Samˡ	2	2	3		
Brown, Benjⁿ	1		2		
Brown, Joseph	1	2	2		
Filley, Jonathan	3	1	2		
Parsons, James	1	4	4		
Brown, Alpheus	1	2	4		
Cook, Joel	1	2	2		
Cook, Pinny	1	1	3		
Kirk, Thomas	1	2	2		
Thrall, John	1		1		
Hickoks, Ebenʳ	1	5	1		
Griswold, Matthew	2	2	3	1	
Olden, Isaac	3	3	3	1	
Thrall, John, 3ᵈ	2	5	2		
Thrall, ——*	1	3	3		
Owen, ——*	1	1	2		
Elsworth, ——*	1	1	4		
Hubbard, A——*	1	1	2		
Phelps, Azariah, Ju	1	1	3		
Mather, Nathˡ	2		3		
Marshal, Samˡ	1				
Owen, Stine	1				
Owen, Elijah	4	4	2		
Hollida, Daniel	1		3		
Phelps, Azariah	3	2	4		
Winchel, Elihu	1	1	1		
Pinney, John	4		3		
Hutchins, John	1	1	1		
Nungers, Israel	3		4		
Brown, John	1				
Eno, James	1	2	3		
Perkins, Joel	1	1	3		
Thrall, Benjⁿ	1	2	3		
Adams, Silas	2	1	4		
David, Samˡ	1		2		
Hendrick, John	1				9

LITCHFIELD COUNTY.

BETHLEM TOWN.

NAME OF HEAD OF FAMILY.	Free white males of 16 years and upward, including heads of families.	Free white males under 16 years.	Free white females, including heads of families.	All other free persons.	Slaves.
Allen, Amos	5		2		
Allen, Samuel	2	5	4		
Ambler, David	4		5		
Atwood, John	2	3	4		
Atwood, Gideon	1				
Brace, Elisha	3	1	5		
Barnum, Tila	1	2	6		
Brownson, Abraham	4	1	2		
Baldwin, Jacob	3	1	9		
Baldwin, Eli	1	2	2		
Bellamy, David	3	1	4		1
Bellamy, Samuel	1	3	3		
Butler, Darius	1	2	1		
Bishop, Amos	2	2	5		
Bishop, Dan	2	2	6		
Bishop, Daniel	1	2	2		
Bishop, Billy	1	1	1		
Beach, Dan	1		4		
Beacher, Hezekiah	2	2	2		
Bird, Lucy	1	4	2		
Bird, Atwood	1	5	4		
Burritt, William	1	1	5		
Blois, Francis	1	3	5		
Bacon, Josiah	1		3		
Bradley, Daniel			1		
Burton, Nathan	2	2	3		
Botsford, Daniel	2		2		
Brown, David	1	2	7		
Bishop, Deborah			3		
Baldwin, Joseph	1	2	7		
Clark, Amos	2		5		
Clark, Friend	1	2	4		
Clark, Joshua	2	2	3		
Churchel, Jonathan	1		1		
Churchel, Oliver	1		2		
Crane, Robart	3	1	4		
Cowles, Levi	1	3	2		
Cowles, Asa	1		2		
Curtis, Asa	2	1	4		
Curtis, James	1	1	2		
Camp, David	3	1	3		
Camp, David, 2ᵈ	1	1	2		
Chapman, Nathaniel	1		5		
Chapman, Michael	1	1	2		
Chapman, Nathan	1		2		
Dunning, Elias	3	1	2		
Davies, William	2	1	7		
Doolittle, Thomas	4		2		
Doolittle, Abner	1	1	1		
Doolittle, John	1	2	3		
D. Wolf, Levi	1	1	1		
Everit, Daniel	2	1	4		
Everit, Eunice	1		3		
Eagleston, James	1	5	4		
Ford, Thomas	2	2	6		
French, Gideon	1	1	3		
Frisbie, James	2	1	3		
Frisbie, Amos	2	2	3		
Frisbie, Jacob, 2ᵈ	1	1	3		
Frisbie, Jacob	2	1	1		
Frost, Joseph	1	1	2		
Foot, Robart	1		2		
Gordon, John	2		1		
Gordon, George	1		2		
Gaylord, Aaron	2	1	5		
Galpen, Moses	1		2		
Galpen, John	2	3	4		
Guitteau, Joshua	1		2		
Guitteau, Simeon	1				
Green, Eleazer	1	3	4		
Green, Eleazer, 2ᵈ	1	1	4		
Guernsey, Richard	1	2	3		
Gillet, Wheelor	3	2	4		
Goodrich, Waitstill	2		2		
Green, Eleazer	1	2	5		
Hill, Jonathan	2	1	3		
Hill, David	1	1	5		
Hand, Stephen	1		2		
Hand, Elias	1	3	4		
Hawley, Benjamin	3		3		
Hawley, Moses	2	3	4		
Hawley, Enos	3		7		
Hawley, Silas	2	4	2		
Hawley, Azor	1				
Hannah, Robart	1	3	5		1
Hannah, James	1	3	1		
Hannah, Alexander	3		5		
Hannah, Margaret			1		
Hannah, Daniel	1	1	3		
Hine, Dan	3	1	5		
Hine, Dan, Jur	1	3	3		
Hinman, Enos	2				
Hinman, James	1				
Hall, Ebenezer	1	1	3		
Hall, Bristor	2				
Hitchcock, Abel	1	3	3		
Hitchcock, Benjamin	2	1	4		
Hitchcock, Jared	2	3	2		
Hitchcock, Lydia			3		
Hull, Titus	3	3	7		1
Jackson, Theophilus	1	3	4		
Jackson, Samuel	1		4		
Jackson, Daniel	1	3	3		
Judson, Abner	3		2		
Kason, Alexander	2	1	4		
Kason, Archibald	1	1	1		
Kason, James	5	2	4		
Kason, James, Jur	3	4	5		
Knap, Moses	2	3	3		
Linsley, Timothy	1		3		
Lewis, Oliver	1		5		
Lewis, Ezekiel	1	4	5		
Lambert, Nehemiah	1		1		
Leavitt, David	1		2		
Leavitt, David, Jur	3	1	6		1
Meiggs, Phineas	1	2	3		
Meiggs, Jesse	1	1	2		
Martin, William	4		1		
Martin, Lucy			1		
Martin, William, 2ᵈ	1	1	2		
Martin, Simeon	1		2		
Martin, Andrew	2		1		
Martin, Seth	2	1	4		
Minor, Jonas	1		2		
Munger, Merriman	1		1		
Munger, Lewis	2	1	2		
Munson, Ephraim	1		2		
Parmely, Oliver	3	1	4		
Parmely, Oliver, Jur	1		2		
Parmely, Samuel	1		2		
Parmely, Ebenezer	1	2	1		
Peet, Samuel	3	1	5		
Peet, Richard	1	3	3		
Prentice, John	1	2	5		
Prentice, Christopher	3	4	5		
Parks, Anna			3		
Parks, Elizur	1		4		
Purkins, Ebenezer	1	2	3		
Prichard, James	1	1	2		
Robarts, Noah	1	1	5		
Rose, Mabel			1		
Runney, Julius	2		3		
Robartson, Solomon	1	1	3		
Smith, Jonathan	1		2		
Smith, Jonathan, Jur	1	4	2		
Stoddard, Curtis	1	2	2		
Stoddard, Elisha	1				
Stoddard, John	1	1	2		
Sherwood, Amy			1		
Skilton, Avery	1	2	4		
Stilson, Joseph	1	1	2		
Stilson, Josiah	1	4	3		
Stilson, Abel	1	3	3		
Steel, John	3	1	5		
Steel, Daniel	1	1	2		
Steel, Elisha	2	3	6		
Steel, John, 2ᵈ	2	2	3		
Strong, Daniel	2	4	2		
Strong, Timothy	4		4		
Strong, Samuel	1		1		
Stevens, Dan	1	1	1		
Stiles, David	1	3	1		
Smith, Daniel	1	4	1		
Stoddard, Giddeon	1		1		
Thomson, Henry	1	3	4		
Twiss, John	2	1	2		
Thomas, Enoch	1	3	2		
Thomson, Levi	2	4	3		
Thomson, Aaron	2	2	3		
Thomson, Thomas	1	1	3		
Thomson, Samuel	1	1	3		
Thomson, Zacheriah	2	2	4		
Wheelor, John	3	2	4		
Wheelor, Elizur	1		4		
Way, Philemon	1	1	4		
Way, Roswell	1	1	2		
Tucker, Daniel	1	2	1		
Church, Joshua	2		4		
Johnson, Truman	1		3		

CORNWALL TOWN.

NAME OF HEAD OF FAMILY.	Free white males of 16 years and upward, including heads of families.	Free white males under 16 years.	Free white females, including heads of families.	All other free persons.	Slaves.
Abbott, Daniel	2	3	1		
Andrews, Andrew	1	4	3		
Allen, Ebenezer	1	3	1		
Angel, Henry	1		2		
Allen, Elijah	2	4	3		
Andrews, Caleb	2	1	2		
Andrews, Lyman	1	1	2		
Abbot, Samuel	1		3		
Abbot, Gold	1		2		
Beardsley, Jeames	1				
Bennham, Oliver	1		3		
Bristol, Sarah		1	1		
Brownson, Jacob F	1	1	2		
Buel, Jesse	1		7		
Bacon, Ebenezer	1	4	4		
Bierce, Austin	4	1	3		
Bierce, Isaih	1	3	5		
Baldwin, Aaron	1	2	2		
Bierce, Jeames	1		2		
Beardsley, Nehemiah	1	3	6		1
Burges, Samuel	2	4	4		
Bonney, Titus	2	1	2		
Bierce, Joseph	4	6	3		
Bradford, John	1		3		
Bradford, Jeames F	1		3		
Bartholomew, Jesse	1	2	4		
Bell, Benjamin	1	1	1		1
Brownson, Timothy	1		1		

* Illegible.

LITCHFIELD COUNTY—Continued.

NAME OF HEAD OF FAMILY.	Free white males of 16 years and upward, including heads of families.	Free white males under 16 years.	Free white females, including heads of families.	All other free persons.	Slaves.	NAME OF HEAD OF FAMILY.	Free white males of 16 years and upward, including heads of families.	Free white males under 16 years.	Free white females, including heads of families.	All other free persons.	Slaves.	NAME OF HEAD OF FAMILY.	Free white males of 16 years and upward, including heads of families.	Free white males under 16 years.	Free white females, including heads of families.	All other free persons.	Slaves.
CORNWALL TOWN—con.						**CORNWALL TOWN—con.**						**CORNWALL TOWN—con.**					
Bordwin, Azeriah	1	2	4			Hollister, Gershom	1	1	6			Stewart, Daniel	2	1	4		4
Birdsey, Ebenezer	1	2	2		1	Heart, Silas	1	2	3			Swif, Rufus	1				4
Bonney, Jarius	1		4			Hyatt, Jesse	1	1	6			Scovil, Joseph	1	1	3		
Bryan, Saviah			2			Harrisson, Daniel, 1st	3		2			Sedgwik, John A	1				
Bonney, Perez	3	3	5			Hall, Hezekiah	1	1	3			Stewart, Joseph	1	1	4		
Bearce, Jeames, Junr	3		4			How, Deliverance	1	2	1			Sedgwick, John	6	3	6		
Bristol, John	1		1			Hurlburt, Osias	2	1	3			Sleet, Eliphet	1				
Bristol, Nathan	1		2			Heart, Titus	3	1	4			Stertin, Jeames	3	3	6		
Bristol, Amos	2	3	6			Harris, David	1	3	1			Stead, John	3	2	3		
Baldwin, Henry	1	2	4			Hochkins, Joseph	1	1	4			Seward, Nathan	1	3	2		
Benedict, Moses	1	1	4			Heart, Elias	1	2	2			Shephard, Ebemener	1	1	3		
Brown, Daniel	8	1	2			Hartshorn, Joshua	1	2	3			Scott, Obediah	1		2		
Bates, Isaac	2	1	6			Hineman, John	1		1			Smaiey, Enoch	1		1		
Bailey, William	2	1	7			Jackson, Charles	1		1			Squire, Abijah			2		
Brownson, Jacob, 2d	2	1	2			Jackson, Ebenezer	2	2	5		1	Stewart, Oliver		1	2		
Bierce, Hezekiah	3	1	5			Ives, Abel	3	1	2			Tanner, Consider	1	4	4		
Bell, Ruth	1		4			Johnson, Amos	3	4	4			Tanner, Trial	1	3	4	8	1
Bassot, Samuel	1		1			Jackson, Isaih	1	2	1			Tanner, William	2	1	4		
Bartholomew, Joseph	1	4	2			Jeffery, Ebenezer	2		1			Thorn, Abel	1	3	5		
Baldwin, Joseph	1	1	2			Johnson, Philemon	2		3			Tuttle, Joel	1	3	2		
Bishop, Ebenezer	1		4			Jones, Zachariah H	2	1	1			Tyler, Adonijah	1		1		
Baldwin, Joannah	1		1			Johnson, William	1	2	4			Thomson, Martha	1		2		
Bliss, Simeon	1	2	5			Judson, Abel	2	1	3			Wilcox, Samuel	3		2		
Beach, Linus	1	1	2			Jackson, Ephm	1	1	3			Wilcox, Zadock	1	1	4		
Clark, Silas, 2d	1		2			Jennings, Lemuel	3	1	4			West, Josiah	1	1	5		
Clark, David	1	2	7			Johnson, Amos	1		2			Wickwin, Samuel	4	1	2		
Cotter, Andrew	1					Luddington, Nathaniel	1	2	1			Wright, John	2	1	3		
Clark, Hezzekiah	1	1	7			Lorain, Calvin	1	1				Wadsworth, Samuel	7		3		
Clark, Benjamin	1	1	1			London, Charles	1		1			Wadsworth, Joseph	2	3	4		
Carter, Hezekiah	2		6			Linsley, Ephraim	1	1	2			Willougheby, Salmon	1	2	3		
Cornwell, Eden B	1	1	1			Kellog, Judah	2	2	3		1	Wadsworth, Jeams	1	2	3		
Chiddester, William	2	3	1			Kutland, Jeames	2	2	2			Wickwin, Richard	1		2		
Clark, Nehemiah	2	1	2			Miner, Joseph	3		1			Wickwin, Nathan	1	1	2		
Catlin, Roger	2	2	3			Miles, Joseph	1	1	1			Wood, Samuel	1		2		
Cother, John	1	1	2			Miles, John	1	3	2			Wilson, Thomas	1	1	1		
Carter, Philo	1		2			Mallery, Eliakim	3	3	4			Wells, John	1	3	4		
Carter, Salmon	1					Mead, Philip	1	5	3			Wood, Jonathan	1	1	2		
Clather, Ambrose	2	3	3			Millard, John, 1st	1	1	4			Young, William	1	3	3		
Carter, John	3	2	2			Millard, John, 2d	5	2	5								
Camp, Amos	2	2	2			Morey, Asa	2	3	1			**HARWINTON TOWN.**					
Clark, Silas	2	2	2			Marvin, Nehemiah	2		6								
Crocker, Jonathan	2	1	4			Miles, Stephen	1		1			Andrews, Silas	3	1	5		
Crammer, William	1	1	1			Miles, Levi	1					Alford, Eli	2	3	1		
Cole, Seth	1	2	4			Millard, Joel	1	1	1			Austin, Dan	1	1	4		
Croner, Hannah	2	1	4			Millard, Nathan	1	1	4			Ames, Benjamin	1	1	1		
Cadley, George	1		3			May, Edward	1		1			Abenatha, William	2	2	5		
Dean, Benjamin	3	2	3			Marion, David	1		3			Alford, Joab	3		3		
Dean, Samuel, 2d	1		1			North, Stephen	1	1	3			Austin, Reuben	1		1		
Dibble, Silas	1	1	3			Olcott, John Easton	1	2	2			Alford, Alexander	2	3	5		
Dibble, Jonathan	1		1			Payne, Rufus	1	5	3			Andrews, David	1		1		
Dibbe, John	1		1			Pratt, Abner	1	1	6			Alford, John	1	3	4		
Dean, Samuel, 1st	2		1			Pierce, Isaac	1	1	4			Bawaj, Thomas	1	2	2		
Dean, John	1	2	5			Pierce, Joshua, 3d	1					Bartholomew, Jacob	1	3	3		
Dibble, Isaac	1		2			Proston, Stephen	1	2	5			Butt, Sabria	1		1		
Dibbe, Benjamin	1		2			Pratt, David, 2d	1	1	6			Barber, John, 1st	2		1		
Dibble, Israel	3	2	2			Pratt, David, 1st	2		2			Barnes, Benjamin	2	1	7		
Dibble, George	2		4			Peck, Bennoni	2	1	3			Bill, Elijah, 1st	1	1	4		
Dean, Reuben	1	2	2			Pratt, Jasper	1	2	3			Bill, Elijah, 2d	1	2	1		
Dean, Reuben, 2d	1		1			Paterson, Elkana	2	1	4			Bristol, Reuben, 2d	1		1		
Dickerson, Asahel	1	2	3			Pierce, Levi	3		4			Barber, John, 2d	2	2	2		
Dean, Thomas	2	1	2			Pierce, Joshua, 1st	1		1		1	Barnes, Zopar	2	5	1		
Dextar, Sarah			2			Pierce, Joshua, 2d	3		2			Butler, Josiah	2		2		3
Dickerson, Elijah						Proston, David	1		2			Barber, Reuben, 1st	4		2		
Dibbe, Clemens	1	1	3			Patterson, Mathew	2	2	3			Bull, John	4	1	4		
Emons, Soloman	1	3	5			Pierce, John	2	1	2			Barber, Simeon	1	3	2		
Everest, Daniel	1	5	4			Pierce, Seth	3	2	8			Bartholemew, Jeames	1		1		
Emons, Asaph	2	3	2			Rogers, Grace			2			Bartholemew, Reuben	3	2	6		
Emons, Simeon	1	2	2			Rogers, Edward	4	2	9			Barber, Abner	1	2	3		
Emons, Asa	1	1	3			Rogers, Timothy	1	3	3			Bull, Jesse	2		2		
Emons, Woodruff	1		1			Rogers, Noah, 2d	1		2			Brownson, Selah	1	4	1		
Everston, Hannah		2	4			Reed, John	1	1				Bartholemew, John	1		2		
Freedom, Jack				4		Rexford, Samuel	1		1			Barber, Judah	1		1		
Foot, Jesse	2	1	6			Rogers, Noah	6	3	5		1	Bartholemew, Andrew	2	4			
Fox, Reuben	1	2	5			Reed, Holly	1					Bartholemew, Submit	1		3		
Ford, Oliver	1	3	4			Rouse, Elijah	3		1			Baron, Aaron	1	2	5		
Ford, Thaddeus	1	2	4			Rexford, David	3	2	4			Butler, Stephen	1		4		
Gold, Hezekiah	1	1	2			Russel, Ichabod	1	2	4			Brown, David	1	2	3		
Gold, Benjamin	2	2	3			Saunders, Joshua	1		3			Barber, Asahel	1	1	3		
Gipson, Samuel	2		3			Swift, Heman	3	2	3		3	Bearce, Jeames	1		4		2
Gerrard, Jesse	1	1	1			Swift, Elisha	1					Bristol, Reuben, 1st	2	2	3		
Gold, Joseph Wakefield	1	1			1	Saunders, Ithamer	3	3	5			Barber, Reuben, 2d	2	1	4		
Graves, Asahel	2	1	2			Scovil, Jacob	1		2			Bartholemew, Benja	1	3	2		
Green, Samuel, 1st				4		Saunders, Zelotes	2	3	4			Barber, Timothy	1	1	4		
Green, Samuel, 2d				5		Stewart, John	1	1	4			Bradley, Joel	1	2	3		
Green, Jacob				6		Shewood, Hannah	2	1	4			Blakeley, Enos	1	3	1		
Hallhet, John	1	3	4			Steel, Elijah, 1st	1	1	2			Barnes, Moses	2	3	3		
Holcomb, John	1	1	5			Steel, Elijah, 2d	1		4			Blakeley, Jonathan	1		2		
Hawkins, Abram	4		4			Scovil, Timothy	2		2			Basto, William	3	1	3		
Harrisson, Daniel, 2d	2	2	1			Steel, Mathew M	1	1	4			Blakeley, Silas	1	2	3		
Harrisson, Noah	3		4			Stewart, Stephen	1	2	4			Baldwin, W. Samuel	1	4	3		1
Hineman, Partrick	1		1		3	Scovil, Samuel, 1st	4		3			Bartholemew, Margett			1		
Hurlburt, Joab	1	1	7			Sawyer, Samuel	2	1	6			Bull, Michael	1	2	2		
Heart, Soloman	4	1	4			Scovil, Stephen	1	1	3			Butler, Jesse	1	2	1		
Heart, Phineas	2	1	2			Stephen, Nathaniel	4	1	5			Curtis, David	2	4	5		
Hopkins, Josiah	1	5	2			Scovil, Samuel, 2d	1	1	2			Castle, Joel	2	4	2		

LITCHFIELD COUNTY—Continued.

NAME OF HEAD OF FAMILY.	Free white males of 16 years and upward, including heads of families.	Free white males under 16 years.	Free white females, including heads of families.	All other free persons.	Slaves.
HARWINTON TOWN—con.					
Crow, Damaras			1		
Catlin, Joel	2	4	2		
Cook, Oliver	2		5		
Catlin, Jacob	5		6		
Cooler, Isaac	1	1	2		
Catlin, Dan	2	1	4		
Cook, Samuel	2		3		
Catlen, Daniel	2	3	4		
Catlen, Lewis	1	1	3		
Cleveland, Isaac	2		4		
Conley, Wm Gaylord	1	1			
Catlin, Abijah	2	2	6		
Catlin, Grover	2		1		
Catlin, Hezekiah	1	1	3		
Cook, Joseph	5	1	4		
Castle, Isaac	1	4	2		
Cook, Scad	1		4		
Cott, John	1	1	2		
Catlin, Jacob, 2d	1	1	3		
Cook, Sylvanus	1	1	3		
Cook, Titus	1	2	2		
Cott, Jonth Hanson	3		7		
Catlin, Elisha	2	2	2		
Catlin, Isaac, 1st	1	1	2		
Cook, Daniel	1	2	4		
Catlin, Isaac, 2d	1	4	1		
Catlin, George, 2d	1		4		
Catlin, Jonathan	2		3		
Cook, Joab	1		1		
Catlin, Grover	1	2	3		
Cook, Jonathan	2	1	1		
Cook, Thomas	2		1		
Catlin, Abram	1		3		
Cook, William	2		4		
Curtis, Molly		1	2		
Carter, Stephen	1		2		
Deer, Eli	2	3	4		
Davies, John	2		2		
Davies, Nathan	3		2		
Davies, Jeames	1	1	4		
Elden, John	1	1	1		
Ely, Jacob	1	7	2		
Evins, Asahel	1	1	1		
Frisbie, Jabez	2	2	4		
Foot, Darius	1	1	2		
Fitch, John	1	3	4		
Frisbie, John, 1st	2		6		
Frisbie, John, 2d			4		
Filley, Jonah	1	1	3		
Frisbier, Isaac	2	1	2		
Frisbier, Enos	1		2		
Griswold, Janna	1		1		
Gillott, Joel	2	1	3		
Gilbert, Jabez	2	3	4		
Griswold, Asa	1	1	4		
Griswold, Benjamin	1	1	4		
Grannis, Enos	2	3	2		
Gridley, Abel	3	2	3		
Gridley, Silas	2	3	2		
Graves, Stephen	2	2	2		
Gaylord, Chauny	2	4	3		
Gaylord, Elijah	2		2		
Harvy, Thos	1	4	1		
Hall, Elisha	2		3		
Hale, Curtis	2	3	5		
Hinsdale, Samuel	1	2	2		
Haydon, Elijah	2	3	3		
Hopkins, Hezekiah	2	2	8		
Haydon, Joseph	2	3	4		
Hopkins, Uriah	2	2	3		
Hopkins, Benjamin	1				
Hungerford, Mathew	1	3	6		
Hungerford, Joseph	1	1	3		
Hough, Benoni	1	1	2		
Homestone, Timothy	2	2	4		
Homestone, Joseph	1	2	5		
Homestone, Abram	1	1	4		
Hill, Asa	2	2	1		
Hungerford, Tertius	1				
Homestone, Abram, 2d	1				
Haydon, Samuel	1	2	2		
Haydon, William	2		4		
Hinsdal, Ezra	3	3	6		
Harvy, William	1	2	2		
Johnson, Ebenezer	2	2	4		
Johnson, Benoni	1	1	1		
Johnson, Hamlen	1	2	2		
Johnson, Christopher	4	5	3		
Johnson, Ira	1		3		
Johnson, Samuel	1	2	6		
Johnson, Elisha	1	4	2		
Johnson, Rufus	1	2	1		
Jones, George	1	1	3		
King, Joseph	1		6		
Kellogg, Allen	1	1	1		
HARWINTON TOWN—con.					
Kellogg, Azeriah, 1st	1	1	3		
Kellogg, Azeriah, 2d	1	1	5		
King, David	2	2	2		
King, Lydia			1		
Lee, Sarah			1		
Leach, Hezekiah	1	3	4		
Lanston, Jeames	1	3	4		
Loomis, Isaih	1		4		
Lee, Theodore	2	1	3		
Loomis, Ebenezer	1	1	5		
Loomis, Noah	1	1	5		
Loomis, Giles	1		3		
Moody, Thomas	3	3	4		
Meachum, Jeremiah	1		3		
Meriam, George	1	1	4		
Morse, Amasa	3	4	5		
Merrill, Mead	1	1	3		
Merwin, Stephen	2	2	3		
Mechum, Nehemiah	1		3		
Mechum, Seth	2	1	2		
Main, Ezekial	1	2	3		
Mansfield, David	2	1	6		
Meriam, William	2	3	4		
Morse, Chauncy	1	3	4		
Munson, Levi	3	2	1		
Olcott, Jeames	2		2		
Pierpont, Robert	3		5		
Pond, Josiah	1				
Phelps, Oliver	1		2		
Prindle, Mack	5	2	5		
Phelps, Josiah	2	1	3		
Phelps, Samuel, 1st	2		2		
Perkins, Abner	2	3	3		
Peck, Gideon	1	3	1		
Peck, Solomon	1	1	3		
Phelps, Samuel, 2d	1	1	2		
Potter, Jesse	1		1		
Preston, John	3	1	5		
Phelps, Uri	1	1	3		
Royce, Nehemiah	2	1	3		
Roseter, Jonathan	1	1	6		
Roseter, Amos	1	2	6		
Rogers, Hezekiah	2	1	5		
Smith, Amasa	1	2	4		
Smith, Jesse	1	2	1		
Smith, Asa, 1st	1	1	3		
Smith, Asa, 2d	1	2	3		
Smith, Jeremiah	1	2	2		
Stone, Edmond	1	2	1		
Stone, William	2	2	4		
Scovil, Ezekial	5	4	3		
Scovil, Joseph	3	2	4		
Scovil, Daniel	1	1	1		
Spencer, Silas	1	3	5		
Skinner, Ashbel	4		4		
Skinner, Thomas	1	2	6		
Skinner, Ira	1		2		
Stephens, Joshua	2	3	5		
Sperry, Ebeneza	1	1	2		
Stoddard, Wells	2	1	1		
Toles, Jacob	1	3	2		
Tiler, Jonathan	1	3	1		
Tinsdale, Samuel	2	1	2		
Williams, Thomas	1	1	2		
Wisson, Samuel	1		1		
White, Nathaniel	1	2	5		
Webster, Charles	2	2	6		
Wooden, Calvin	2	1	3		
Webster, Cyprian	2		3		
Webster, Amos	3	1	2		
Woodruf, Jesse	1		2		
Wilson, John, 1st	1				
Wilson, Eli	4	4	5		
Wilson, Abner	1	4	5		
Wilson, John, 2d	1	3	2		
Wilson, Daniel	2	2	4		
Wilcox, Moses, 1st	2		2		
Wilcox, Moses, 2d	1	1	1		
Watkins, John	1	2	1		
Watkins, Henekiah	1	1	2		
Williams, Joshua	1	1	4		
KENT TOWN.					
Berry, Joseph	2	1	3		
Berry, Nathaniel	5		6	1	
Bates, Joseph	1	2	6		
Beacher, Samuel	2	1	3		
Beacher, Abram	3	5	3		
Brown, Benjamin	4		6		
Benson, Noah	1	1	1		
Beebee, Daniel	3	2	4		
Barnum, Amos	1	1	4		
Beardsley, Ephraim	3	2	4		
Beardsley, David	1	3	3		
KENT TOWN—continued.					
Beardsley, Jabez	3	3	5		
Barnum, David	3		1		
Bates, Ichabod	2	3	3		
Betts, Jesse	1		3		
Botsford, David	1		4		
Barnes, Philip	2	3	6		
Beebee, Daniel, 2d	1	1	2		
Beardsley, Philo	3	2	2		
Benedict, Jesse	3	2	1		
Benedict, John	1	2	3		
Benedict, Elijah	2	2	3		
Bull, Jacob	3	1	6		
Beach, Mary			4		
Brownson, Levi, 1st	1		5		
Brownson, Silas	1	3	2		
Brownson, Wm	1		2		
Brownson, Levi, 2d	1	3	2		
Beamont, Tracy	1	3	2		
Barnum, John	2	2	3		
Boardwell, Joel	2	2	6		
Bailey, John	1	2	2		
Berry, Ebenezer	2	3	6		
Barley, Michael	1	3	1		
Barlow, John	3	2	6		
Bently, Mary			1		
Bostwick, Ebenezer	1	1	2		
Chamberlain, Leander	1	1	1		
Curtis, Hannah		1	1		
Chamberlain, Samuel	2	2	4		
Caswell, Julius	2		2	2	
Converse, Elijah	3		2		
Chamberlain, Elizur	2	1	1		
Comstock, Abijah	2	1	2		
Comstock, Gershom	1		3		
Coleman, Aaron	2	1	1	1	
Comstock, David	1		2		
Campbell, Thomas	1	1	2		
Carter, Israel	1	2	4		
Comstock, Eliphlet	1		1		
Carter, Ithiel	1		1		
Chamberlain, Nathan	1	4	2		
Chamberlain, Peleg	1	1	5		
Comstock, Peter	1	2	3		1
Carter, Heman	2		2		
Chamberlain, Jirah	1	1	3		
Case, Aaron	1	4	2		
Chamberlain, Bartlet	1	3	3		
Curtis, Martin	1	1	5		
Clark, Cyrenus	1	1	2		
Calhoun, John	1	4	4		
Canfield, Andrew	1	2	3		
Chase, Mary	1		1		
Carter, Buel	1		1		
Chapman, Ben Thomas	1		3		
Dailey, Jeames	1	2	1		
Dalton, John	1	1	1		
Dayton, Isaac	3	1	6		
Delano, Sylvanus	2	3	3		
Dayton, Jonah	1	2	6		
Delano, Aaron	2	2	3		
Dye, Daniel	1		2		
Dodge, Stephen	3	4	5		
Dunham, Isaac	1	1	6		
Dye, Elizabeth			3		
Eliot, Nathan	6	1	3		3
Eliot, Abraham	2	3	3		
Edward, Mary	2	3	4		
Eaton, Moses	1	2	3		
Elton, Joseph	1	3	3		
Freeman, Call				4	
Fairchild, Ezra	1		1		
Fairchild, Abel	1	2	2		
Fairchild, Stephen	2		2		
Fuller, Jeremiah	2	1	1		
Fuller, Ephraim	2	1	5	1	
Fuller, Jacob	4	1	7		
Fuller, Benajah	1	2	4		
Fuller, Oliver	2		5		
Fuller, Abram	3	2	5		1
Felch, Ebenezer	1	3	1		
Fairchild, Samuel	1		3		
Freeland, Robert	1	2	5		
Ghoram, Wakeman	1		2		
Gibson, Isaih	1	2	4		
Gregory, Fairweather	1		1		
Ghoram, John	3	1	2		
Geer, Ezra, 1st	2		2		
Geer, Ezra, 2d	1	4	2		
Gillet, Jonathan	1	3	1		
Geer, Elijah	1	1	1		
Gregory, Stephen	1	1	5		
Geer, Nathaniel	1	1	2		
Greegory, Samuel	1	2	3		
Greenill, Daniel	1	1	3		
Gibbs, Robert	1		3		

LITCHFIELD COUNTY—Continued.

Name of head of family.	Free white males of 16 years and upward, including heads of families.	Free white males under 16 years.	Free white females, including heads of families.	All other free persons.	Slaves.
KENT TOWN—continued.					
Hatch, Nathaniel	4	2	5		1
Hubbel, Abijah	1	4	5		
Hall, Asa	3	3	6		
Hath, Jethro	3		6		
Hopkins, Noah	1	2	2		
Hubbel, Jedediah	1		1		
Hubbel, Samuel	1	1	2		
Hall, Mary	1		1		
Hopson, John	1	1	1		
Hill, Daniel	2	1	2		
Hill, Jonathan	1	3	2		
Hubbel, David	1	3	2		
How, Leavitt	2		2		
Hoit, Ebenezer	2		3		
Rust, Abel	2	1	5	1	
Ross, Daniel	2	2	3		
Ross, Asher	2	2	2		
Sileman, John	3		5		
Sturtevant, Samuel	2	1	5		
Stewart, Silas	1	1	4		
Swift, Barzilla	3	4	4		
Swetland, Joseph	1	1	2		
Sturtevant, Zebedee	3	2	2		
Skiff, Nathan	4	3	5		
Smith, Noah, 1st	2	2	4		
Skiff, Joseph	5		2		
Smith, Noah, 2d	1	1	3		
Segar, Joseph	1	1	5		
Smith, Elias	1		1		
Smith, Moses	1	1	1		
Seeley, Elizabeth			2		
Sloson, Nathan	3	2	4		
Skieff, Stephen	4		2		
Spooner, Ebenezer	3	3	4		
St. John, Timothy	2	1	2		
Stuart, Jeames	2	2	5		
Swift, Asaph	2	2	5		
Stevenson, Jeames	1	1	3		
Smith, Noah Day	2	1	3		
Stanton, Sarah	1		1		
Stewart, Robert	1		2		
Townsend, Caleb	1	2	3		
Thair, Ezekiel	1	2	2		
Thomson, Elizur	3		3		
Thomson, Daniel	1	2	3		
Terrill, Daniel	2		2		
Tuttle, Gideon	2	1	3	1	
Tayler, Hugh	1	2	3		
Terrill, Abel	1	5	4		
Waller, Samuel	1		1		
Waller, Elijah	2	2	4		
Waller, Peter	1	2	6		
Worden, Joseph	1	4	3		
Whitney, Stephen	2		4		
Winegar, Handriks	1	3	2		
Winegar, Mary	2	1	2		
Winegar, Samuel	1	1	1		
Wilson, William	1	5	2		
Whitten, Thomas	1	2	3		
Hall, Timothy	1	3	1		
Judd, Comfort	1	3	3		
Judd, Philip	2		2		
Judd, Marthew	2	3	3		
Judd, Joseph	3		3		
Johnson, Daniel	1		1		
Keeney, Sylvester	1	1	1		
Lee, Daniel	1		2		
Leonard, Silas	2	2	3		
Lane, Richard	1	3	4		
Lane, Ephraim	1	1	1		
Lane, John	1		1		
Lake, Samuel	1	1	5		
Lynde, Reuben	1	3	4		
Morgan, Caleb	1	1	2		
Martin, Manassat	2		4		
Main, John	1	1	2		
Main, Hannah	1		2		
Morey, Thomas	2	2	4		
Morris, Thomas, 1st	1	1	2		
Morris, Thomas, 2nd	1	2	2		
Morgan, David	2	3	5		
Morgan, Jonathan	2	2	1		
Mills, Hannah	1	1	3		
Morgan, Samuel	1		4		
Mills, Peter	1	3	3		
Miller, Samuel	1	2	3		
Murray, Chloe			3		
Main, Caleb	2	2	3		
Main, Jonathan	1	4	5		
Mills, Bradley	1		2		
Morgan, Jeames	1	2	2		
Norecey, George	1		1		
Norton, Silas	2	1	4		
Nichols, Lewis	2	2	2		

Name of head of family.	Free white males of 16 years and upward, including heads of families.	Free white males under 16 years.	Free white females, including heads of families.	All other free persons.	Slaves.
KENT TOWN—continued.					
Noble, Israel	4	2	5		
Phelps, Ebenezer	1	3	1		
Piet, John	2	2	6		
Pratt, Peter	2		3		
Payne, John	3	3	6		
Pratt, Joseph	2	2	4		
Pratt, Noah	2	1	4		
Peck, Ebenezer	1	3	1		
Percy, Ebenezer	2	3	4		
Parish, Oliver	1	1	2		
Read, Hezekiah	4	2	3		
Roots, Daniel	1	4	2		
Ranson, John	2		2		
Roots, Gideon	1		3		
Rust, Levi	3	2	3		
LITCHFIELD TOWN.					
Smith, Jacob	3	2	4		
Russell, William	2	4			
Granger, William	2	3	1		
B——*, Solomon	1	1	2		
Blake, Richard	2	4	5		
Crosbey, Simeon	1	1	1		
Kilborn, Jeremiah	1	2	2		
Griswold, Median	1		5		
Smith, Charles	1		2		
Moodey, Mary			2		
Stone, Heman	1		1		
Griswold, Jonathan	1	1	6		
Bartholomew, Noah	2	2	4		
Smith, Charles	2		1		
Smith, David	1	2	4		
Cluff, Isaac	1				
Waugh, John	1	1	1		
Tthroop, Dan	1	2	4		
Throop, Joseph	1		2		
Throop, Benjamin	1	4	4		
Bishop, Miles	4	1	3		
Hand, Timothy	2	3	5		
Linley, Adam	1		2		1
Parmerly, Reuben	1	2	3		
Potter, Joel	1	3	1		
Johns, Benjamin	3		2		
Stone, Stephen	4		6		
Luddington, Eliphalet	1	1	3		
Throop, William	3	3	5		
Kannak, Hugh	3	1	4		
Westover, Joseph	2	2	2		
Moss, Asahel	3		3		
Waugh, Robert	2	2	6		
Waugh, Thomas	1		1		
Waugh, Samuel	1	1	2		
Zitaw, Jehon	2	3	4		
Smedley, Nathan	1	3	5		
Comstock, Calvin	1		2	1	
Foot, Timothy	2	1	2		
Stoddard, Moses	3	2	4		
Orton, Hezekiah	1		1		
Waugh, Alexander	2	2	3		
Wickwire, James	1	2	3		
Keling, Asahel	1	1	4		
Churchel, Moses	1		3		
Page, William	1	1	2		
Page, Daniel	1	2	4		
Stone, William	1	1	2		
Landon, James	1	1	2		
Bissel, Benjamin	1	3	4		
Dickenson, Molly	1	1	2		
Dickenson, Reuben	2	1	3		
Benton, Ebenezer	4		5		
Sanford, Joseph	1	4	3		
Sanford, Joseph	1	1	3		
Peck, Asa	1	1	1		
Woodruff, Nathaniel	1	1	4		
Woodruff, Philoe	2	3	3		
Woodruff, Andrew	1	3	6		
Camp, Abel	5	2	6		
Mansfield, Joseph	3	2	4		
Harrisson, Thomas	2	1	3		
Ensign, Samuel	4		4		
Harrison, Thomas	1	1	1		
Harrison, Levi	2	1	4		
Harrison, Elihu	3		2		
Fraust, Samuel	1				
Rigs, Jeremiah	1	3	4		
Woodruff, Anna			2		
Woodruff, John	1	1	2		
Woodruff, Solomon	1	1	1		
Woodruff, Charles	1	1	1		
Woodruff, Oliver	1	1	2		
Harrisson, Ephraim	1		3	1	
Steel, Mary	2		2		
Mattoon Gorham	1	4	3		

Name of head of family.	Free white males of 16 years and upward, including heads of families.	Free white males under 16 years.	Free white females, including heads of families.	All other free persons.	Slaves.
LITCHFIELD TOWN—con.					
Martin, Sam'l	1	2	2		
Collins, Charles	2		2		
Witton, Stephen	3		1		
Hubbard, Josiah	1	1	7		
Noth, Seth	1	1	2		
Romain, Daniel	2	3	2		
Smith, David	1	3	2		
Bishshop, Samuel	1	3	3		
Carter, Nathan	1	3	4		
Butler, Abel	3	2	2		
Mott, Samuel	1	2	2		
Ovatt, Samuel	1	1	1		
Ovatt, Samuel	3	5	3		
Murrin, Fowler	2	3	4		
Ovatt, Benjamin	2	5	5		
Norton, Aaron	3	5	4		
Catlin, Elisha	1	1	1		
Norval, Nathaniel	1		1		
Atwood, Harvey	1		1		
Buel, Timothy	3	2	5		
Norton, Nathaniel	1	1	4		
Miles, Isaac	1	3	4		
Sheppard, Josiah	1		1		
Driggs, Martin	1	2	1		
Merrill, Samuel	1		2		
Kilbron, John	1	2	1		
Lee, Rejoice			1		
Lee, Samuel	2	2	2		
Ganes, Moses	1	2	5		
Paine, Abraham	1	1	5		
Paine, William	1		4		
Paine, William	2		3		
Paine, Ebenezer	1		2		
Richard, Aaron	3	2	4		
Messenger, Reuben	1	1	3		
Willey, Jonathan	1		3		
Pike, Samuel	3		2		
Humpheys, Benonah	3	1	3		
Seymore, Elijah	1	3	5	3	
Sheppard, Phinehas	2	2	5		
Dikerson, John	1	2	4		
Ollcott, Thomas	1	2	3		
Olcott, James	2	4	3		
Roberts, Martin	1	1	4		
Towner, Elijah	2	1	2		
Towner, Ephraim	1	4	3		
Baldwin, Isaac	2		2		
Burrel, William	2	1	1		1
Higby, Patience		1	2		
Lawrence, Jonas	2	2	2		
Lawrence, Isaac	1		2		
Cobb, William	1	1	1		
Tubbs, Simeon	3	1	4		
Peet, William	1		1		
Kingsbury, Joshua	1		2		
Hide, Saml	2	2	5		
Wadsworth, Ebene	3		2		
Woodard, David	1	1	4		
White, Jedediah	1	3	2	1	
Whitney, Joshua	3	3	4		
Dutcher, Rulef	3	1	3		7
Hamlin, Reely			2		
Buckenham, Isaac	1				
Hantchet, Silvanus	3	3	4		
William, William	1	2	5		
Jule				5	
Hamlin, Thomas	2	3	4		
Gibbs, Silvanis	1	1	4		
Omsted, Hezekiah	1	2	6		
Collins, Justice	2	1	4		
Elmore, Saml	3	1	5		
Jewitt, Anney			1		
Rockwell, Saml	3	1	3		
Canfield, Darius	1	1	4		
Pardee, James	2	1	2		
Pardee, Jonathan	1	1	2		
Vandoore, Charles	1		2		
Grinnun, John	1		1		
Betts, Ezekiel	1	2	3		
King, George	5	3	6		
Evetts, James	1		2		
Smith, Asher	2	2	3		
Beach, Jacob	3	1	3		
Beach, Francis	1	1	1		
Rogers, Abeather	1	1	3		
Butler, Abel	1	4	3		
Dicingson, Thomas	4	1	3		
Dikingson, Thomas	1	2	1		
Sherman, Tesua	1		5		
Wilson, Job	2		2		
Roberts, Seth	1	2	3		
Squire, Justice	1	1	3		
Beach, William	1	3	1		
Baldwin, Bruin	2	4	4		

* Illegible.

LITCHFIELD COUNTY—Continued.

LITCHFIELD TOWN—con.

NAME OF HEAD OF FAMILY.	Free white males of 16 years and upward, including heads of families.	Free white males under 16 years.	Free white females, including heads of families.	All other free persons.	Slaves.
Hills, Seth	1	2	2		
Brown, William	1	1	1		
Humphrey, Simion	1	1	2		
Merrills, William	2	1	3		
Merrills, Jonathan	1	1	2		
Merrills, Jonathan	1	1	3		
Case, Dudley	4		4		1
Sievell, James	1	2	2		
Humphrey, Roswell	2	1	1		
Bidwell, Thomas	4		4		
Bidwell, Riverious	1	2	5	3	
Garrot, John	1	2	6		
Lenin, Justice	3		4		
Taylor, Obadiah	1	1	3		
Nobles, William	1	2	5		
Wallen, William	1	1	2		
Ives, Nathan	1	2	2		
Coles, Joseph	2	3	3		
Ensign, Eliphalet	2	1	2		
Pitkin, Stephen	3	3	3		
Flowers, Gabrial	1	3	2		
Henderson, John	2	7	3		
Henderson, James	3	6	3		
Tyler, Amos	1	2	2		
Teplay, Ashbel	2	3	4		
Ward, John	2	3	4		
Duglis, Moses	3	5	5		
Hurd, William	1	2	3		
Tracy, Uriah	1	1	5	1	
Buell, Salmon	2	3	4		
Barnes, Reuben	2	1	6		
Collins, John	3	2	5	1	1
Addam, Joseph	1				
Allen, John	1				
Marvin, Raynold	1		1		
Kirbey, Ephraim	1	1	4		3
Stanley, Rufus	1				
Ruggles, Philoe	1				
Dyre, Eliphalet	1				
Martial, Deota			1		
Morril, Robert	1				
Bishshop, Seth			2		
Bishop, Seth, 2d	1	2	3		
Spencer, Zacheus	2	3	5		
Persons, Eliphas	3	1	3		
Griswold, John	1	3	3		
Landon, Thadeus	1	3	1		
Parmeley, Mary			3		
Fry, Rena	1	1	1		
Dear, George	1	3	3		
Motthop, Stephen	1		2		
Chase, Lot	1	1	2		
Bristor, John	1				
Burghes, Joseph			2		
Burges, Benjamin	1		1		
Griswold, Asahel	2	3	7		
Smith, Eli	2	3	3		
Whitmore, Clark	1		2		
Emmons, Williams	1	2	4		
Dickemon, Ruth			2		
Spencer, Samuel	1				
Spencer, William	1				
Wright, Jonathan	2	4	7		
Perry, Israel	1	4	3		
Catlin, Bradley	1	3	3		
Whitmore, Timothy	2	1	2		
Baker, Constant	2	2	5		
Burges, James	1	4	1		
Gibbs, Truman	1	3	2		
Peck, George	1		3		
Coles, Stephen	1		4		
Pitkin, Timothy	1		1		
Baley, Joseph	3		4		
Standley, Timothy	3		1		
North, Ezekiel	1	4	6		
Norton, Oliver	1		4		
Landon, Ozias	1	1	3		
North, Joseph	4	3	6		
Norton, Alexander	3	2	4		
Waddoms, Solomon	3	2	4		
Griswold, Jiles	5	1	5		
Norton, Andrews	4	2	1		
Kettell, Jonathan	5	1	5		
Nash, Samuel	1		1		
Goold, Thomas R	1	1	3		
Sill, Elisha	2	1	4		
Hale, Ebenezer	1		2		
Mayo, Elisha	1	1	1		
Hale, Adino	3		3		
Lockwood, Seth	1	2	6		
Nash, Josiah	2	3	3		
Nash, William	1	2	9		
Brick, Moses	2		4		
Kellogg, Martin	1	2	3		
Merrills, Joseph	2	1	6		

LITCHFIELD TOWN—con.

NAME OF HEAD OF FAMILY.	Free white males of 16 years and upward, including heads of families.	Free white males under 16 years.	Free white females, including heads of families.	All other free persons.	Slaves.
Mix, Isaac	1		1		
Stephens, Aaron	1	1	1		
Sandiforth, Daniel	1	3	9		
Seymore, Noah	1	3	2		
Burnington, Ebenezer	1	3	2		
Watson, Zachariah	1	3	3		
Merrills, Marten	1		4		
Tryon, Ely	1	2	3		
Merrills, Aaron	1	4	5		
More, Josiah	1	1	1		
Cotton, William	1	2	2		
Bissel, Benjamin	2	3	2		
Goodman, Thomas	1	1	4		
Mather, Charles	2	2	3		
Northawey, James	1	4	5		
Watson, Levi	4		3		
Wells, Asahel	1		3	1	
Grow, Ambroser	1	1	5		
Averiss, Isaac	2		4		
Demmich, Solomon	1	3	3		
Averiss, Ethan	2	1	4		
Gibson, Roger	1		3		
Williams, John	3	3	1		
Dickenson, Elisha	2	1	2		
Dickenson, Ebin	1				
Sawyer, Nathaniel	3	1	6		
Gauslin, John	1	3	4		
Ichabud, Seth	1	1	2		
Camelon, John	1	3	4		
Nilger, Sam	1	2	5		
Minord, Frederick	3	1	4		
Beebe, Amasa	1	3	2		
Youngs, Soloman	1	2	3		
Chapman, Nehemiah	1		3		
Chapman, Caleb	1		2		
Bester, Seth	3	4	5		
Coblium, Stephen	3	1	3		
Bester, Job	1	3	2		
Leanard, Benjaman	1	3	3		
Benjamin, Phinehas	1	1	2		
Smith, Theophelus	1	1	2		
Smith, Theophelus, 2d	1	3	3		
Smith, Levi	1	2	4		
Jackson, Amos	1	3	3		
Hollister, Elisha	3	1	4		
Chappel, Silas	1	2	1		
Wilson, John	1	2	3		
Miller, Joshua	3	7	3		
Lovel, Joseph	2		6		
Denham, Jonathan	2	1	3		
Studley, Joshua	2	2	5		
Allen, Thomas	1		1		
Bailey, Joseph	3	1	4		
Sturdephant, George	1				
Swift, Philoe	2				
Pangman, Adonijah	1		3		
Lenley, Joseph	2		4		
Monroe, Younglove	1		2		
Griswold, Adonijah	1	3	3		
Monroe, Noah	1	2	3		
Hamlin, Benjamin	1	2	4		
Warren, Nathan[1]	1	1	1		
Goold, Job	3		1		
Dicks, Charles	2	1	2		
Noth, Juna	1	2	6		
Noth, Noah	2		3		
Rhiney, Daniel	1	3	2		
Hurlburt, Levi	1	1	3		
Leason, Noah	1	2	4		
Aglestone, Joseph	2	3	4		
Smith, Gidian	1	2	5		
Philer, Stephen	2	2	5		
Coe, Abner	1	1	4		
Martial, Thomas	5	1	3		
Philer, John	1	1	3		
Hill, Benona	2	1	4		
Philer, Silas	2	3	3		
Drake, Noah	1	2	1		
Sheppard, Stephen	1		3		
Agard, Solomon	1	2	3		
Leach, Caleb	1	5	1		
Loomise, Abraham	1		3		
Martial, Abner	3		2		
Drake, Joel	2	4	3		
Thrall, Noah	2	1	3		
Whitmore, Samuel	1		3		
Burr, John	2	3	4		
Stanley, Comfort	1		1		
Marther, Richard	1	2	2		
Burr, Reuben	2	2	4		
Burr, Russel	2	3	3		
Hudson, Daniel	2	1	5		
Stephens, Samuel	3		5		
Deming, Daniel	3	4	4		
Haydon, Agustin	3	5	6		

LITCHFIELD TOWN—con.

NAME OF HEAD OF FAMILY.	Free white males of 16 years and upward, including heads of families.	Free white males under 16 years.	Free white females, including heads of families.	All other free persons.	Slaves.
Elmore, Abiath	2	1	2		
Bierr, Hial	1	3	3		
Austin, Thaniel	1	3	3		
Frasier, George	1		4		
Loomise, Michael	1	3	1		
Brown, Stepen	1		3		
Miller, Ebenezer	1	1	2		
Doolittle, David	2		4		
Phernil, Benjamin	1	2	4		
Loomise, Roswell	1		3		
Roberts, Henry	1	3	2		
Philer, Ulissies	1	2	5		
Tuttle, Clem	1	2	2		
Tuttle, Isaac	2	2	5		
Cook, Shubel	1	1	3		
Shatdock, William	1	2	3		
Babcok, Elias	3	1	2		
Babcock, Rufiel	1	2	1		
Martial, Joseph	1	1	1		
Gibson, Ephraim	2		4		
Rowlenson, Asa	2	4	1		
Rowlenson, John	2		2		
Rowlenson, William	1	1	2		
Rowe, Samuel	3	2	4		
Howe, Stephen	1	4	3		
Barden, Seth	2	2	3		
Southland, Beldwin	2	1	1		
Deming, Daniel	2	2	3		
White, John	1	2	3		
Woodruff, Elias	2	2	1		
Pates, Elisha	1	2	1		
Landers, Joseph	1		1		
Hollister, David	2	2	3		
Onton, Joseph	1	1	5		
Croker, Oliver	2		4		
Goodrich, Ashbel	1		1		
Marsh, Isaiah	2		6		
Hamlin, Polley			1	1	
Gillet, Jonathan	3	1	1		
Rennalds, Joel	1	2	2		
Griffin, Thomas	4	2	3		
Roland, David	3	2	9		
Youngs, William	1	1	2		
Chapman, William	2	2	3		
Chapman, Pelatiah	1	2	5		
Foster, John	3	1	5		
Clark, William	1	2	2		
McDonald, Jerrents	1	1	3		
Hollester, Nathan	1		3		
Landen, Martha			6		
Hollister, Joshua	1		2		
Lovell, Joshua	2		4		
Homer, David	1	1	3		
Stanley, Comfort	1	3	3		
Austin, David	2	1	2		
Ward, David	1	1	2		
Watter, Daniel	3	3	1		
D Wolf, Benjamin	1	1	2		
Swett, John	2	1	5		
Watter, John	1	5	3		
Cook, Arijah	1	1	5		
Watter, Henry	2	1	1		
Basten, John	1		2		
Munson, Caleb	1		1		
West, Judy	1	1	2		
Crissey, David	1	1	3		
Woodruff, Hezekiah	2		5		
Woodruff, Isaac	1		1		
Hart, Luke	3		3		
Allen, John	1	1	3		
Russel, David	3	2	2		
Crissey, Israel	1		3		
Aglestone, Daniel	1	1	2		
Wolf, Daniel	1		2		
Right, John	2	4	3		
Right, Charles	2	4	4		
Right, Freedom	2		6		
Smith, Zebina	2	1	1		
Grenell, Michael	1	2	5		
Smith, Jonaiah	2	3	4		
Balcome, John	1	2	6		
Palmer, Reuben	1	2	2		
Palmer, Zazaries	1	3	1		
Palmer, Solomon	1	1	1		
Palmer, Benjamin	1	4	3		
Morey, Abijah	1	2	3		
Mills, Chancy	2	1	3		
Mills, David	2	2	3		
Mallery, Elisha	1	2	6		
Dunnam, Jonathan	2	4	4		
Mallery, Amos	2		1		
More, William	2		4		
White, Isaac	2		4		
Sawyer, Jesse	2	1	3		
White, Samuel	2	3	2		

LITCHFIELD COUNTY—Continued.

NAME OF HEAD OF FAMILY.	Free white males of 16 years and upward, including heads of families.	Free white males under 16 years.	Free white females, including heads of families.	All other free persons.	Slaves.	NAME OF HEAD OF FAMILY.	Free white males of 16 years and upward, including heads of families.	Free white males under 16 years.	Free white females, including heads of families.	All other free persons.	Slaves.	NAME OF HEAD OF FAMILY.	Free white males of 16 years and upward, including heads of families.	Free white males under 16 years.	Free white females, including heads of families.	All other free persons.	Slaves.
LITCHFIELD TOWN—con.						**LITCHFIELD TOWN—con.**						**LITCHFIELD TOWN—con.**					
Smith, Jacob	2	2	5			Belknap, Jonathan	1	1	4			Dudley, Miles	1	1	2		
Sheldon, George	1		2			Johnson, Chancy	1		2			Tibbots, Thomas	3		2		
Peck, Frederick	1	1	5			Palmer, Simeon	1	3	6			Burr, Eben^r	1		6		
Landon, George	1		2			Rickerson, Martha		1	3			Rice, John	1		4		
Knap, Jabez	3	2	6			Green, John	1	2	6			Wilcox, Hesana	2		3		
Scordam, Henry	1	2	1			Gleason, Ruful	1		2			Cotton, Michael	1	3	2		
Curtiss, Aaron	2		3			Tom					6	Galor, Timothy	2	1	2		
White, William	1	3	1			Watson, John	3	2	4			Turner, Barts	3		1		
Mills, Aaron	1	1	1	4		Thompson, Amos	1				4	Goodwin, William	1	1	2		
Churk, Nathan	1	2	2			Sedgwick, Mary			5			Thomson, Levi	3	2	3		
Leanard, Fellows	3		1			Fanning, Sarah			3			Hall, Abraham	1		3		
Blakesley, Samuel	1	2	4			Pardy, Saml	2	3	3			Hall, Sam	1	1	1		
Pierce, William	2	2	3			Manning, David	2		3			Hall, Abraham, 2^d	1	1	3		
Cameron, Lauchland	1					Dormond, Garsham	1	2	3			Goold, David	4	3	6		
Richeron, Thomas	1	1	3			Bennet, Edmond	3	3	4			Bell, Jude	1		1		
Comering, Jacob	1	2	5			Persons, Enoch	3	2	1			Jinks, Eben	1	1	3		
Horton, Elisha	2		2			Sanford, David	1	1	2			Humphey, Hoseah	4		2	1	
White, William	2		7			Summers, Asahel	2	1	2			Sheppard, Zebulon	1	1	4		
Landon, Rufus	1	3	2			Comp, Joel	2	2	3			Cadey, Lemuel	2	3	6		
Landon, John	1		1			Pettit, Solomon	1		1			Johnson, Jacob	2	4	5		
Landon, David	1		4			Hamlen, Nathen	3	5	3			Tyler, Banijah	1		1		
Landon, James	2		3			Cheseton, Samuel	1		2			Lowrey, Nathan	2		3		
Avery, Elisha	2	1	5			Swift, Wilard	1	2	3			Hammon, Dudley	2	1	6		
Commins, Jacom	1					Furgason, Daniel	1	1	3			Howe, Elisha	1		3		
Vaun, William	1					Dota, Timothy	2		1			Hale, Elihu	1		1		
Towsby, Vistory S	3	4	7			Fuller, Benjamin	1		4			Mott, Jonathan	1		2		
Tousbey, Samuel	2	1	1			Commel, Daniel	1		3			Bailey, Salmon	1	2	1		
Loveland, Ziie	1	1	1			Ruxford, William	1	3	3			Yale, Elisha	1	1	4		
Ensign, John	2	5	6			Minor, Joel	2	3	3			Merrills, Jeptha	1	1	3		
Smith, Seth	4		2			Gedion, John	2	2	4			Yale, Elisha, 2^d	1	1	3		
Knickabocker, Isaac	2	2	3			Andrews, Nehemiah	2	4	2			Howe, Jeremiah	4	1	3		
Knickabocker, John	1	2	2			Hutchins, Anna			2			Johnson, Timothy	1		2		
Rowlin, Luke	1	3	2			Hankok, Rachel			3			Johnson, Isaac	1		2		
Knickerbocker, Solomon	2	4	4			Lane, Enos	3	3	3			Johnson, Levi	2	1	2		
Heath, David	1	1	1			Hutchins, Benjamin	1	1	2			Howe, Joel	1	3	1		
Knickerbocker, Saml	2	2	3			Wilcox, Jeremiah	1		3			Harriss, Daniel	1		1		
Allen, Mathew	1		1			Church, Aaron	1	2	3			Brown, Jerry	3		4		
Knickerbocker, Abraham	3	3	6			Smith, Martin	2	2	3			Brown, John	1	3	2		
Parmerley, Theodore	2	1	5			Spensor, Jessee	1	1	2			Daming, Joel	2	2	3		
Hill, Medad	3	2	2			Smith, Havilah	2	1	1			Root, Caleb	1		1		
Parmeley, Abraham	1		3	1		Andrews, Nehemiah	2	2	7			Barns, Gideon	2		3		
Lewis, Ebenezer	1	1	4			Giddings, Benjamin	1	3	2			Clark, Reuben	2		1		
Barber, Sarah		2	2			Akins, Acker	1		2			Smith, Asahel	2	2	2		
Holbrooks, Nathaniel	1	1	3			Turner, Daniel	1		2			Harger, Jabesh	1	4	3		
Hoopkins, Stephen	1		2			Lawrence, John	2	1	3			Inenka, Charels	1	1	4		
Hopkins, Samuel	2	1	3			Humphrey, Dudley	1	1	3			Cleavland, Aaron	1		3		
Thompson, John	1		1			Mottbey, Johial	1	1	1			Perkins, Jason	1	4	3		
Thompson, John	1		2			Watter, Joel	2		3			Phelps, Samuel	3	1	2		
Baldwin, Stephen	1	1	1			Watter, Heman	1		1			Phelps, Samuel	2	1	4		
Porter, Seth	1	2	1			Watter, Elijah	1	2	3			Crosbey, Obed	1	1	4		
Beach, Fisk	2	1	5			Mack, Daniel	2	3	3			Crosbey, Samuel	1	3	3		
Rice, Josiah	3	1	3			Mills, Edan	1	3	1			Miller, Allen	1	2	2		
Carrington, Mabel	2	1	4			Nettleton, Joshua	2	2	2			Bates, Oliver	2	3	4		
Beach, Edmond	2	2	4			Pomeroy, Simean	1	2	4			Hungerford, James	1	1	5		
Beach, Edmond	2	1	7			Mills, Laurance	1	1	2			Bushnel, Daniel	2		5		
Beach, Adney	1	2	5			Derby, John	1		1			Hale, Reuben	1	1	5		
Chapen, Samuel	4		2			Lettleton, Roger	1	1	1			Allen, Titus	2		1		
Merrills, Miah	3	1	4			Austen, Saml	1		3			Treet, John	1	2	5		
Merrills, Jared	1		3			Lewis, Edward	2	1	3			Fox, Jabes	1	1	1		
Merrills, Elijah	3		4			Mills, Michael	4	1	4			Kilborn, Epephras	1	1	3		
Adams, William	1	3	6			Phelps, Frind	1	1	6			Woodbridge, Samuel	1		5		
Merrills, Asher	2	1	5			Pardy, Ebenezer	1	2	1			Brau, Charles	1		5		
Goodwin, Michael	1	5	4			Laurance, Grove	1		1			Dewey, Lenar	1	3	3		
Merrills, Benjamin	2		5			Giddings, Joshua	1	4	3			Smith, Reuben	2	4	2		
Bardock, Amos	2	3	5			Brockway, Edward	4	2	9			Deming, Roswell	1	2	1		
Goodwin, Moses	1	2	3			Spensor, Samuel	1	1	2			Clark, Rufus	1	3	3		
Goodwin, Elzer	4		6			Gildersleaves, Obadiah	1	1	2			Jakeway, Daniel	1	1	3		
Goodwin, Tiras	1	2	2			Brockway, Moses	1	1	1			Root, Enoch	3	1	7		
Mills, Moses	2	1	2			Merrit, Sam	1	1	3			Lappedal, Peter	1				
Hale, Reuben	1	1	3			Beach, Sam	1	2	2			Goodrich, Isaac	1	3	4		
Barnes, Timothy	1	1	3			Jones, Benjaman	1	2	2			Pettit, Saml	4		2		
Barns, Israel	1		3			Tuttle, Isaah	1	3	3			Goold, Jonathan	1	2	4		
Goodwin, Jonothan	3		4			Jones, Asahel	1	2	4			Reed, Ethiel	2	1	3		
Cadwell, Phinehas	1	1	4			Hart, Hawkins	3	2	3			Pettit, John	2				
Bennams, Samuel	1	1	1			Munson, Ephraim	1	3	2			Lilley, David	1	4	3		
Merrills, Eliakim	1		4			Munson, Wait	1	1	3			Marchant, Elijah	1				
Bennom, Johial	1	1	4			Gates, Theophelus L	1	2	5			Botsford, Ephream	1				
Smith, Josiah	1		1			Comore, Stephen	1	2	3			Williams, Eastes		2	1		
Bennom, Samuel	1	2	2			Betts, Bena Jah	2		5			Botsford, Epriam, 2^d	1	3	6		
Norton, Miles	2	5	4			Bills, Benajah	2		5			Marines, Ephriam	2	1	4		
Roberts, John	1		1			Rewick, Owen	1	1	2			Pratt, Abreham	1	1	3		
Coleman, Josiah	4		5			Reed, Benia	1		1			Sprague, Jonathan	2		3		
Newel, Nathan	1		1			Fox, Ephraim	1	1	2			Chamberlain, Isaa	2	3	7		
Newel, William	1	1	4			Clark, John	1	1	2			Guy, Danl	3	2	4		
Spalden, Barbara			3			Bills, Joshua	1		2			Pardee, Isaac	2	1	3		1
Sperry, Charles	1					Danniels, Pelletiah	1		2			Wanright, Thomas	1	1	2		
Whitney, Stephen	1					Shovel, Michael	2	3	5			Heath, Obadiah	1	1	2		
Howe, Philop	1	3	3			Phillip, William	1		1			Heath, Hezekiah	1	3	3		
Presson, David	1	1	2			Church, Abisha	1	1	2			Heath, Mehitabel			1		
Stephens, Daniel	1	1	2	1		Cowdrey, Moses	2		5			Guy, Margaret	3	1	6		
Brownwell, Aaron	1	3	2			Mechum, Isaac	1	4	5			Guy, John	1				
Burt, Abraham	3		3			Church, Uriah	1	1	2			Marchant, Unice	1		2		
Brownwell, Edward	1	6	2			Perkins, Phinehas	3	1	1			Marchant, Ashbel	1	4	2		
						Perkins, Eliphas	1	5	4			Sprague, Simeon	2	1	8		
						Mechur, Levi	1		2			Waldo, Syprean	3	2	3		

LITCHFIELD COUNTY—Continued.

LITCHFIELD TOWN—con.

NAME OF HEAD OF FAMILY.	Free white males of 16 years and upward, including heads of families.	Free white males under 16 years.	Free white females, including heads of families.	All other free persons.	Slaves.
Kelsey, Noah	1	1	2		
Bull, Jonathan	2	1	2		
Parmer, William	1	3	4		
Reed, Jonathan	2	1	2		
Treet, Isaac	1	1	2		
Barsley, John	2		1		
Foster, Polley			1		
Jennins, Charles	2	2	3		
Jewit, Caleb	2		3		
Cole, David	4	2	5		
Chapman, Noah	1		1		
Averitt, John	1	1	2		
Gregory, Joseph	4	2	1		
St John, Joel	1		1		
Harris, David	3	2	5		
Seers, Stephen	1	1	5		
Wolcott, Claudeus	1	1	3		
Pardee, George	2		1		
Pardee, Moses	1	2	3		
Sanford, Ezra	1		3		
Curtiss, Nathanl	2	1	4		
Colkins, Elije	2	1	4		
Colkins, Elija	1	1	1		
Blake, Marana	1	2	5		
Taylor, Joseph	1	3	5		
Carr, William	1	2	4		
Carr, Robert	1		3		
Cook, John	1	3	2		
Miller, William	1	2	2		
Phelps, Abraham	1	1	3		
Ives, Abner	3	3	7		
Ives, Jotheam	2	3	3		
Phelps, Elijah	1	4	3		
Carter, Ether	1	4	3		
Dibbie, Daniel	1	2	4		
Eno, Eliphealet	2		1		
Furgeson, James	2	3	7		
Brooker, John	1	1	3		
Cruner, Peter	1	5	2		
Luice, Ezekiel	1	1	2		
Northaway, Ozias	2	2	4		
Luice, Elisha	1	1	1		
Woodruff, Marten	2	4	4		
Wright, Jeremiah, No 1	1	3	4		
Shelden, Ephephsas	3	4	3		1
Knap, Timothy	1	1	1		
Kenton, Stephen	2	3	4		
Fowlar, Noah	1	5	7		
Avret, Israhel	2	5	5		
Barber, Ely	1	3	3		
Yale, James	1	1	2		
Lyman, Ebenezer	1	2	4		
Beach, Wait	3	1	6		
Whitmore, Joel	2		3		
Leach, Nathanl	1	1	4		
Lyman, Caleb	3		6		
Mastial, Raphel	3		3		
Bancroft, Noadiah	2	2	3		
Phelps, Jonathan	1	1	2		
Phelps, Benjamin	4		2		
Curtiss, Zebulon	2	1	5		
Northerum, Ebenr	3	1	4		
Grant, Matthew	3		2		
Thrall, Pardon	1	1	4		
Wilkinson, Jonathan	1	1	6		
Fauster, Daniel	1	1	3		
Sage, Daniel	1	1	5		
Truscoat, Solon	1	3	2		
Colking, John	2	2	2		
Reed, Moses	1	1	2		
Worden, Ebenezer	1		1		
Right, Jonathan	1	1	2		
Wright, Elisha	1	2	2		
Worthey, Benjamin	1	2	4		
Corkings, Silas	1		1		
Fuller, Joseph	1	1	2		
Fuller, Joshua	1	3	5		
Lyman, Simeon	1	2	5		
Dibble, Ebenezer	1	5	5		
Hynes, George	1		1		
Boness, Amos	1	4	5		
Hill, Michael, 2d	1	2	4		
Hill, Michael	1		1		
Fuller, Johiel	1	1	1		
Strong, Joel	1	1	2		
Tickner, John	2	5	5		
Deming, Hezekiah	2		3		
Rossiter, Benjamin	2	1	5		
Cowls, Joseph	3	4	4		
Barney, Thomas	1	4	5		
Osmon, Thomas	2	1	3		
Burrell, Charles	2	3	3		
Bukley, Joseph	2	3	4		
Hinsdale, Jacob	2	1	4		
Holcomb, Elijah	2	1	5		

LITCHFIELD TOWN—con.

NAME OF HEAD OF FAMILY.	Free white males of 16 years and upward, including heads of families.	Free white males under 16 years.	Free white females, including heads of families.	All other free persons.	Slaves.
Holcomb, Abraham	2	2	4		
Buckley, Samuel	3	3	3		
Holcomb, Noah	3	3	5		
Rice, Chaney	1		1		
Buckley, Joseph	2		2		
Cowle, Jasen	1		3		
Hinman, Joseph	2	3	2		
Right, John	1		3		
Fellows, Abia	4	3	2		
Marsh, Thankful			2		
Lester, Andrew	1		4		
White, George	1	1	2		
Bill, Jonathan	1	1	2		
Bill, Jonathan, 2d	1	1	6		
Wright, Ephraim	2	2	1		
Spensor, Thomas	2		2		
Bushnal, Thomas	1	1	4		
Rimington, Elihu	1	2	2		
Banning, David	2	1	1		
Banning, Saml	1		1		
Adams, Daniel	1		2		
Bishnel, Alexander	3		6		
Selvey, Ephraim	1	2	5		
Bush, Aaron	1		2		
Cole, Thankful			3		
Brayne, Asahel	2	2	4		
Selvey, William	2		2		
Hayner, Asahel	1		3		
Emmons, Lydia	2	4	6		
Right, Ephraim	1	1	5		
Mills, Timothy	1		2		
Case, Joseph	1	3	4		
Mills, Samuel	1	4	3		
Roberts, Nathaniel	2	2	2		
Mason, Elijah	2	3	5		
Mills, Constant	1	1	2		
Wilson, Joseph	2	1	6		
Gaylor, Adward	1	2	3		
Gaylor, Ammon	1	1	2		
Wilcox, Hosea	1	2	3		
Lee, Miles	1	4	3		
Humphrey, Michael	1		1		
Humphrey, Pelatiah	1	2	1		
Foot, Asa	2	4	4		
Corols, Ebenezer	5	2	4		
Gaylor, Benjamin	1	1	2		
Bradley, John	1	1	2		
Mills, Joseph	4	1	3		
Case, Asahel	4		4		
Pettibone, Isaac	1	3	3		
Norton, Stephen, 2d	1	1	1		
Norton, Stephen	4		3		
Lawrence, Nehemiah	2	1	2		
Lawrence, David	1	3	5	6	
Baccus, Silvenus	2		4		
Marsh, Rufus	1	1	3		
Pease, Calvin	1	2	1		
Spaldwin, Edward	4	1	4		
Plumb, Frederrick	1	2	1		
Peet, Anna		3	1		
Brooks, John	1	1	4		
Turner, Saml	2	1	1		
Howe, Nathan	1		2		
Baldwin, John	3	1	4		
Waid, Josiah	1		5		
Gillet, Jonathan	1	2	4		
Lane, Ashbel	2	1	3		
Rathborn, Job	3	1	4		
Ward, Abijah	2		1		
Kingsbury, William	1	3	3		
Williams, James	1		1		
Smith, Nodeah	2		3		
Stephens, Abel	2		8		
Hewit, Benjamin	1	2	5		
Evans, John	1	2	6		
Pardee, Thomas	2	1	3		
Moxom, Adonijah	2	3	3		
Randol, John	2	1	3		
Randol, Solomon	1		2		
Ranal, Job	1	1	2		
Jewit, Alpheus	1	1	4		
Jones, Andrew	2	2	5		
Pease, Allen	1		2		
Blakmore, Simeon	1		1		
Farling, Mechum	1	3	4		
Lockwood, Unice	1	3	3		
Slade, William	1		2		
Bard, Nathan	1		3		
Bard, Nathan	4	2	6		
Chapman, Elijah	2		1		
Downs, David	2	3	4		
Osmon, Thomas	2	1	4		
Karnes, Aaron	1	1	5		
Wilcox, Thomas	1		3		
Hunt Russel	4	1	4		

LITCHFIELD TOWN—con.

NAME OF HEAD OF FAMILY.	Free white males of 16 years and upward, including heads of families.	Free white males under 16 years.	Free white females, including heads of families.	All other free persons.	Slaves.
Hunt, Salmon	1	3	1		
Hare, Silas	1	1	3		
Gilbert, Rachel	1	4	1		
Suttey, Saml	4		3		
Seward, Daniel	1		1		
Crosbey, Sim	2	1	3		
Wildar, Ephraim	1	2	5		
Newton, Abraham	2		6		
Robinson, John	1		4		
Coe, Timothy	1	1	4		
Carnfield, Danl	1	3	4		
Cowdrey, Jacob	3	3	3		
Sheppard, Olver	1	2	2		
Galard, Nathan	1		4		
Williams, Israel	1	3	1		
Newton, Abner	1		2		
Bushnel, Saml	1		1		
Goodwin, Seth	1	2	1		
Allyn, Jonathan	1	1	2		
Senior, Danl	2	3	7	1	
Hunt, James	3		1		
Goodrich, Benjamin	2	1	2		
Curtiss, Josiah	1	1	3		
Peck, Isaac	1		1		
Hubard, Edmond	1	3	2		
Deen, Urah	1		1		
Carrier, Benjamin	3	1	4		
Deen, John, 2d	4	2	7		
Dean, Oliver	3		5		
Squire, Jessee	2	3	1		
Deen, John	2		5		
Hug, Isaac	1	3	2		
Barton, Andrew	1	1	4		
Hosford, Anne	1		3		
Hosford, Timothy	1	1	6		
Huntington, James	2	2	5		
Chamberlain, Joel	1	4	2		
Hug, William	1	1	2		
Curtiss, Samuel	3		6		
Rowley, David	1	1	1		
Deen, Salmon	1		2		2
Holeburd, Timothy	1		3		2
Holeburd, William	2	1	1		
Holiburd, John	1	1	1		
Hunt, Russel	2	1	2		
Right, Elizer	2	1	4		
Churchel, Benjamin	1	3	3		
Smith, Elijah	2	5	5		
Barns, Torhand	1	1	4		
Grenold, Samuel	1	1	1		
Spencer, Job	3	1	5		
Spencer, Job, 2d	2		3		
Spencer, Eliphas	2	2	2		
Owen Abner	2		2		
Miner, Asahel	3	5	4		
Sharman, James	1		1		
Ballard, Jessee	1	1	2		
Smith, Grove	2	3	4		
Seymore, David	2		3		
Shelden, Moses	2	2	4		
Rolepau, Lettie			1		
Sheldon, Ezra	1	1	7		
Norton, Lot	3	3	1		2
Kelsey, William	2		5		
Ely, Richard	1	5	2		
Jennins, Timothy	1	1	1		
Fitch, Elisha	1	1	2		
Burress, Joseph	3	2	3		
Conklin, Thomas	2	3	7		
Tausly, Matthews	3		2		
Chapman, Tutus	3	1	2		
Williams, Bennajah	2	1	3		
Williams, Ephraim	1		3		
Chamberlain, Abner	1	2	2		
Hubbard, Joseph	3	1	4		
Owen, James	2	1	7		
Goodsell, John	1		1		
Eveth, Daniel	1	3	2		
McLin, John	1	2	1		
Strong, Adonijah	2	4	4		1
Marvin, Martin	1	1	1		
Benton, James	1	1	1		
Chapman, Nathan	1		2		
Beebe, William	1	1	2		
Jack				1	
Bissel, John	1	1	5		
Walton, William	4		4		
Reed, Joel	2	1	2		
Reed, Stephen	3		2		
Roberts, Elisha	2	2	4		
Merills, Heck	2	2	3		
Marsh, Anos	1		3		
Marsh, Job			3		
Merills, Soloman	1	3	3		
Barnes, Charles	3	2	4		

LITCHFIELD TOWN—con.

NAME OF HEAD OF FAMILY.	Free white males of 16 years and upward, including heads of families.	Free white males under 16 years.	Free white females, including heads of families.	All other free persons.	Slaves.
Croe, Roger	1	2	2		
Marsh, John	1	1	3		
Marsh, Job	3	2	3		
Sheppard, Daniel	2	2	3		
Andruss, Eli	2	4	6		
Neal, William	1	2	2		
Neal, Aaron	1	1	1		
Neal, Enoch	1	2	3		
West, Aaron	1	1	3		
Thorp, Earle	2	1	2		
Dorson, Sibe		2	4		
Lone, Isaac	1	3	4		
Merrills, Siprean	1	2	4		
Andrews, Nehemiah	4	4	3		
Tucker, Ephraim	2	1	3		
Seymore, Uriah	5	1	4		
Stephen, John	1		1		
Wright, Ezekiel	2	1	3		
Graves, Hubbard	1	2	2		
Andrews, Ezra	1	1	4		
M'Canasy, Betty		3	5		
Rust, Stephen	1	2	1		
Seymore, Elias	1	1	5		
Hursted, Roger	1		1		
Gilbert, Jessee	1		2		
Atkins, James	1		1		
Russel, Elisha	1		2		
Cadwell, Isaac	1	2	4		
Goodwin, Ebenr	2	4	5		
Goodwin, Ebenr	1		3		
Petton, John	1		1		
Seymore, Hezekiah	2	4	3		
Omsted, Roger	2	1	3		
Merrills, Bena	3	7	7		
Shelden, Roger	2	4	5		
Marsh, Jonathan	4		5		
Marsh, Daniel	1	5	4		
Etton, Recompence	1	4	2		
Hinsdale, Elisha	1	2	1		
Goodwin, Jessee	1	2	2		
Johns, Joel	1	3	3		
Kelsey, Enoch	7	1	3		
Rowley, Levi	2	3	6		
Smith, John C	1	2	1		2
Smith, Cotten M	3	3	5	4	
Hunt, Isaac	4	2	2		
St. John, Silas	2	2	4		
Everitt, Isaah	3	4	4		
Hubbord, William A	1	2	4		
Warner, Austin	2	1	2		
Smith, Paul	1	1	1		2
Canfield, Saml	3	1	5		
Smith, Paul, 2d	1	1	3		
Tuller, John	3		7		
Dota, Timothy, 2	2		1		
Furgeson, Daniel	1	1	3		
Strong, Josiah	2	1	2		
Backen, Daniel	1	2	2		
Goodrich, Elisha	1	1	3		
Goodrich, Elizabeth			2		
Goodrich, Joel	2	3	2		
Pettit, Joel	2		2		
Burr, Walter	1	3	6		
Ashley, Abreham	1	3	3		
Holibert, Saml	1	2	2		
Basset, Joshua	3		3		
Williams, Wait	2	3	1		
Holibert, Elisha	2		4		
Bartlet, Russel	1	4	3		
Taylor, Augustin	1	1	2	3	2
Smith, Phinehas	2	4	3	1	
Gallow, Joseph	2		2	1	
Backen, Ebenses	2	1	4		
Goodwin, John	1		5		
Clark, Daniel	1	2	1		
Squre, Hulda			2		
Goodwin, John P	3	4	4		
Elmore, Elja	3		1		
Goodrich, William	2	3	5		
Freeman, John	1	1	1		
Wadsworth, Josiah	1	5	4		
Hawley, Saml	1	2	5		
Bennedick, Benjamin	1	1	4		
Bennedick, Timothy	3	1	5		
More, Simon	1		4		
Andrews, Danl	2	1	4		
Cook, Timothy	1	3	2		
Richard, Roswell	1	2	3		
Pardy, Charles	2	2	2		
Richard, Elishu	1	1	2		
Richard, Jedediah, 2d	1	5	2		
Richard, Jedediah	1	1	2		
Butler, Stephen	1		4		
Butler, Hezekiah	1		2		
Bishop, Mimsa	1		2	1	

LITCHFIELD TOWN—con.

NAME OF HEAD OF FAMILY.	Free white males of 16 years and upward, including heads of families.	Free white males under 16 years.	Free white females, including heads of families.	All other free persons.	Slaves.
Walter, Moses	1	1	1		
Walter, William	2		2		
Walter, Clark	1				8
Orvis, Reuber	1		1		
Stephens, Saml	1	2	2		
Jakins, George	1		2		
Halley, Samul	2		3		
Dimmick, David	2	2	1		
Crevath, Samul	2		2		
Gillet, John	1	2	4		
Benedick, James	1	2	3		
Benedick, Francis	3		4		
Hawlley, Elisha	1	3	3		
Stephans, Simeon	3	2	2		
Orvis, David	1	3	4		
Grant, Roswell	1		3		
Hungerford, Reuben	3	2	4		
Chamberlain, William	1	2	3		
Chamberlain, William	2		2		
Alverd, David	1		3		
Bacon, John	1	1	3		
Holiburt, Martin	1		1		
Nash, John	2		3		
Noth, Martin	1		2		
Elmore, Joseph	1	1	2		
Knap, Joshua	1	2	6		
Everit, Josiah	1	1	2		
Holiburt, Saml	4	2	4		
Evaritt, Ebenezer	2		2		
Avery, Daniel	1	5	1		
Everitt, Ebenezer	1	3	2		
Wood, Barney	1	2	1		
Smith, Samuel	1	1	3		
Chapman, Robert	3	2	2		
Wilson, Peter	5	1	3		
Tobins, John W	1		2		
Chapman, Robert	1		3		
Tobins, James	1	4	1		
Goodrich, Abner	1	3	3		
Warner, Amasy	1	1	4		
Wix, Rebacah			1		
Pomp					7
Fortier, Benjamin	1	3	4		
Jones, James	1	2	3		
Gibson, Eliezer	1	2	3		
Benjamin, Phinehas	1	3	4		
Morey, Nathaniel	1		1		
Frisbie, Hezekiah	3	4	4		
Shaddock, Joseph	1				
Spensor, Alexander	4		2		
Spensor, Hezekiah	1	1	2		
Hunt, Phinehas	1	2	4		
Lawrence, John	1	1	1		
Hooker, Jessee	1	2	5		
Pratt, Joel	1	2	5		
Stephens, Roswell	1	2	3		
Knap, Luke	3	1	5		
Patrige, Stephen	1	4	3		
Daniels, Jonathan	1	2	4		
Stephens, Abel	2		8		
Tucker, Jedediah	1	3	6		
Darling, Abel	1	4	5		
Stephens, James	2	1	3		
Babcok, Elias	3	1	2		
Babcok, Rufus	1	2	1		
Martial, Joseph	1	1	1		
Butler, Jererd	3	3	4		
Sturdaphant, James	1	1	1		
Hills, Jessee	1		1		
Whitmore, Abel	2	3	2		
Whitmore, Saml	1	1	2		
Holibart, Martin	1		1		
Case, William	1	3	4		
Spensor, Thomas	1	1	6		
Braughton, Nathan	1	2	2		
Murrin, David	1	2	1		
Blackman, Truman	1		1		
Spalden, Isaac	1	4	3		
Cammel, John	1		6		
Brister, John	1	3	5		
Barden, Seth	3	2	6		
Barden, Ebenezer	1	1	2		
Barden, Timothy	1		1		
Merrills, Ephrm	1	1	4		
Welch, Danil	1	3	2		
Knap, Samul	2	1	3		
Gaylor, Joseph	5		5		
Gaylor, Ayer	1	1	4		
Gaylor, Marmory			3		
Toby, Abraham	2	2	2		
Gaylor, Saml	1		2		
Toby, Miles	1		1		
Surdephant, Abijah	1		1		
Toby, George	2	1	3		
Murrey, Jasper	1	2	5		

LITCHFIELD TOWN—con.

NAME OF HEAD OF FAMILY.	Free white males of 16 years and upward, including heads of families.	Free white males under 16 years.	Free white females, including heads of families.	All other free persons.	Slaves.
Stephens, Roswell	1	2	3		
Holt, Isaac	5	1	3		
Cravath, Saml	2	2	4		
Canfield, Danl	2	4	1		
Morse, Andrew	2		1		
McCune, Garsham	1		1		
McCune, Gersham	1	2	2		
McCune, Saml	1	3	4		
Smith, Eleazer	1	3	4		
Alverd, Elihu	2	1	5		
Wilcox, Elisha	1	2	6		
Blackman, Peter	3	1	4		
Smith, Samuel	4	3	5		
Church, Silas	2	2	4		
Bennet, John	2	2	1		
Keep, Jabez	1	1	3		
Jevel, Joseph	2	4	6		
Camp, Jacob	2	3	3		
Weeb, Isaac	1	1	4		
Wholer, John	2	2	2		
Vosburgh, Jacob	2	2	4		
Dacker, Jacob	1		1		
Hall, David	1		2		
Camp, Luke	2	2	3		
Weldon, Abraham	1	2	2		
Weldon, John	3	1	4		
Beemont, William	2		3		
Farnume, Philop	1	1	2		
Tuttle, Moses	2		3		
Latten, John	1		1		
Roach, William	1	1	5		
Stanton, Joshua	4	1	4		
Merchant, Joseph	1				
Mason, Peter	2	5	4		
Fletcher, Ebenezer	2	3	6		
James, Ethiel	2	2	4		
Parx, James	2	2	5		
Fitch, Thomas	1	3	4		
Sirdam, Tunis	4	1	6		
Dean, Joel	1	2	2		
Lalintice, Jacob	2		4		
Corney, Andrew	1	2	4		
Northorp, Joseph	3	3	6		
Trowbridge, James	2		3		
Camp, Abial	2	1	3		
Chapin, Phinehas	3	3	3		
Chapin, Charles	2	2	4		
Ball, Erastus	2		2		
Lotts, John H	1	1	1		
Camp, Joel	3	2	5		
Mix, Thomas	3	1	1		
Turner, Easter			2		
Pollett, James	1	1	3		
Eddy, Asa	2	2	3		
Coudry, Jonathan	1	1	2		
Whiting, Asa	3	3	2		
Bingham, Banajah	1	1	2		
Eddy, John	1	1	1		
Scott, Etheel	1	2	2		
Curtis, Madad	1		1		
Curtis, Sirus	1		1		
Hollister, Isaac	2	3	2		
Phelps, Elijah	4	1	4		
Monger, Reuben	4	3	6	1	
Lewis, Richard	1		2		
Akins, Henry	4	1	3		
Curtis, Soloman	1	2	2		
Camp, Moses	3	1	4		
Phelps, Darius	2	1	3		
Coy, Ephraim	1		1	1	3
Rice, Nathanl	5		2		
Rice, Asa	1	1	2		
Cole, Danl	2		2		
Beach, Abner	1	2	2		
Johnson, Zebediah	1	3	1		
Burr, Ebenezer	2	3	5		
Jones, Joseph	3	3	6		
Robons, Amenizsehana	3	4	3		
Pettibone, Jiles	2	1	7		
More, William	1	2	2		
Jailen, Isaac	1	2	2		
Phier, Horace	1	1	2		
Moodey, Philop	1	2	4		
Ranford, Joel	1	3	1		
Case, Amos	3	1	5		
Allyn, Josiah	1	1	6		
Sperry, Darius	1		2		
Ranford, Daniel	4	4	4		
Wilson, John	1	2	3		
Crane, John	3	2	3		
Johnson, Sherman	1		5		
Johnson, Jonothan	1	1	2		
Allyn, Aaron	2	1	2		
Wyldur, Jonathan	2	2	3		
Austen, James	2	1	5		

LITCHFIELD COUNTY—Continued.

LITCHFIELD TOWN—con.

NAME OF HEAD OF FAMILY.	Free white males of 16 years and upward, including heads of families.	Free white males under 16 years.	Free white females, including heads of families.	All other free persons.	Slaves.
Newill, Solomon	2	5	4		
King, Jonathan	1	1	4		
Johnson, Reuben	1		3		
Sheppard, Moses	2		5		
Sheppard, Joseph	2	1	3		
Ward, James	2	2	3		
Mason, Elisha	2	1	4		
Mason, Harmon	1		1		
Mason, Joshua	1		2		
Moss, John	1	3	5		
Gerret, Lydia		1	2		
Wallace, Richard	3	1	6		
Goodwin, Joseph	1	3	4		
Seely, Justice	2	1	2		
Seeley, Ebenezer	2	2	7		
Seely, Benjamin	1	1	3		
Seeley, Nathaniel	1		1		
Manning, Thomas	1		1		
McNiel, Isaac	3	2	3		
Loomis, Benjamin	2	2	5		
Clark, Urial	1	2	3		
Stacey, Samuel	1	2	4		
Agard, Noah	1	2	3		
Horford, John, 2d	2	1	2		
Horford, William, 2d	2		3		
Agard, Joseph	1	4	2		
Andrews, William	1		1		
Grant, Charles, 2d	2	5	5		
Agard, Mary			2		
Gerret, Joshua	2		3		
Gibbs, William	2		3		
Gibbs, William	1	1	3		
Baldwin, Isaac, 2d	2	4	3		1
Catlin, Thomas	2	1	2		
Skinner, Timothy	5	3	4		
Tallmadge, Benjamin	1	3	4	1	
Sheldon, Daniel	3	2	4		
Catlin, William	2	1	5		
Parmerley, Amos	2		3		
Parmerly, Amos	1	1	1		
Kilborn, Solomon, 2d	2	1	2		
Kilborn, Solomon	3		2		
Smith, Ruama		1	3		
Gates, Jehiel	1	4	2		
Bissel, Joseph	1	2	1		
Griswold, Zacheus	3	1	3		
Servant, James	1		3		
Merrills, Ephraim	1	1	2		
Wadhams, Moses	1	2	3		
Ripner, Samuel	1	2	2		
Wadhams, Seth	3	2	3	1	
Wadham, Jonathan	2	2	3		
Leach, Phebe	1	4	5		
Hoy, John	1		3		
Pratt, Isaac	2		3		
Pettibone, Judy			2		
Price, Paul		2	3		
Parmly, Standley	1	1	1		
Filley, Abraham	3	1	2		
Pettus				4	
Jud, Benjamin	1		2		
Kimberly, Jacob	2	3	5		
Preston, Samuel	2	2	4		
Stannard, Seth	1	3	1		
Hill, Huste	2	2	6		
Cook, Aaron	1	3	2		
Philley, Remambrance	2		4		
Smith, Heman	1	3	2		
Beach, Joel	2	2	2		
Basset, Samuel	2	2	5		
Ward, Danl	1		1		
Deer, Jonathan	1	2	1		
Deer, John	1		7		
Mott, Adam	1	1	3		
Goit, Richard	1	1	2		
Grovier, Danl	1	1	1		
Martial, John	1	2	2		
Leason, Noah	1		2		
Corbin, Danl	3		5		
Corbin, Peter	1		1		
Vitelo, John	1	2	3		
Loomis, Mindwal	2	1	4		
Avarice, Hannah	1	2	3		
Wilkinson, Jessee	2	1	4		
Andrews, Abraham	1	3	2		
Smith, Chancy	1	1	3		
Merrills, Aaron	1		3		
Stodard, Mary	1	1	4		
Kilborne, Lewis	1		3		
Kilborne, Benjamin	1	1	3		
Parmeley, Submit			1		
Bissel, Colvis	1	2	3		
Bissel, Archulus	1	2	3		
Joy, Submit			1		
Bissel, Abagail			2		
Stone, Deodama	1		3		

LITCHFIELD TOWN—con.

NAME OF HEAD OF FAMILY.	Free white males of 16 years and upward, including heads of families.	Free white males under 16 years.	Free white females, including heads of families.	All other free persons.	Slaves.
Bissel, Zebulon	1	2	4		
Bissel, Benjamin	1	3	3		
Thomas, Joseph	1	1	1		
Tryon, Joseph	1	1	3		
Tryon, John	3		3		
Stone, John	1	2	4		
Taylor, Simeon	1	1	2		
Kilborn, Jessee	1	3	5		
Kilborn, Jiles	2		3		
Howard, Ezekiel	2		2		
Monger, Elisha S	1	1	3		
Johnson, Lambard	1	2	2		
Smith, Phinehas	2	3	2		
Carter, Thadeus	1	1	2		
Clemmons, Abijah	1	1	2		
Orven, Phinehas	1	2	1		
Smith, Nathaniel	1		1		
Kilborn, Isaac	1	1	4		
Glass, James	1	3	3		
Smith, Reuben	2	1	2		
Kilborn, John	1		1		
Smith, Wait	1		1		
Baldwin, Stephen	2		5		
Stodard, David	2	1	2	1	
Catlin, Rhoda		1	2		
Kilborn, David	4	3	4		
Stodard, Daniel	1	1	2		
Johnson, Benjamin	1		2		
Odel, Daniel	1	2	4		
Hoskins, Daniel	1	3	4		
Roe, Daniel	1	3	5		
Hunt, Miloe	1		1		
Glover, Edward	3	2	3		
Kilborn, Jessee	1		2		
Bradley, Leming	2		2		
Bradley, Aaron	1	2	1		
Bradley, Comfort	1	1	1		
Smith, Nathaniel	3	2	3		
Palmer, William	1	1	4		
Pierpoint, Eveland	2	1	5		
Pierpoint, James	3	3	3		
Johnson, Luther	1		5		
Gibbs, Samuel	3		6		
Goodwin, Thomas	3	1	3		
Farnham, Seth	3	1	2		
Goodwin, Nathaniel	1	1	3		
Goodwin, Elizabeth	1		2		
Johnson, Jonathan	1	4	4		
Harrison, David	1	1	1		
Johnson, Elizabeth			1		
Pero					3
Deforrest, Isaac	1	2	2		
Gibbs, Benjamin	1		1		
Gibbs, Ethamon	1	1	3		
Linley, Joseph	2		4		
Peck, Elijah	2	2	6		
Huntington, Israel	1		2		
Peck, Levi	1	3	8		
Woodruff, Benjamin	1	1	6		
Woodruff, Jacob	1		2		
Woodruff, W. Right	1	1	2		
Woodruff, Jacob	2	2	3		
Barnard, Sam'l	1	1	1		
Barnard, Sam'l	1	4	2		
Gibbs, Justice	2	2	6		
Gibbs, Remembrance	3		6		
Gibbs, Eldad	1	1	1		
Morriss, James	2	5	3		
Woodruff, James	1	2	3		
Moss, Joseph	1	1	3		
Hall, Mary	1	1	1		
Smith, Frien	1		1		
Hall, Ephraim S	1	1	2		
Knap, Jerard	2	1	1		
Lyman, Ruth			2		
Hyde, Enoch	2				
Barns, Orange	1	1	1		
Perkins, John	1		1		
Smith, Elnathan	1				
Woodward, John	2		2		
Boardman, Oliver	1	3	3		
Colyer, Thomas	3	4	3		
Beach, Ebenezer	1	1	2		
Galpin, Amos	2	1	3		
Trowbridge, Thomas	3	2	1		
Bradley, Abraham	1	1	3		
Wessells, Lawrence	2	1	3		
Holley, Elnathan	2	2	3		
Marsh, Ebenezer	4		4		
Stone, Mary	3		2		
Marsh, John	3	1	2		
Beckwith, George	1	1	4		
Bull, Asa	1		4		
Catlin, Saml	2		6		
Crosbey, Jeremiah	1		1		
Wiling, John	1	4	3		

LITCHFIELD TOWN—con.

NAME OF HEAD OF FAMILY.	Free white males of 16 years and upward, including heads of families.	Free white males under 16 years.	Free white females, including heads of families.	All other free persons.	Slaves.
Church, Ebenezer	1	3	4		
Cesar				3	
Griswold, Josiah	1	3	2		
Fairchild, David	1	1	4		
Roberts, Jude	1	1	1		
Phelps, John	2		3		
Pettiborn, Elijah	1	6	2		
Merrills, Noah	1	4	2		
Porter, James	4	4	5		
Phelps, Daniel	1	2	3		
Wakefield, Partrof	1	4	1		
Forson, Benjamin	1				
Martin, Asahel	1	2	3		
Cowls, Ira	1	1	2		
Allen, Justice	1				
Walcott, John	1				
Andrews, Elijah	2		3		
Pitkin, John	1		2		
Brown, John	1				
Pepper, John	1				
Morgan, Nathan	1		1		
Simmons, Solomon	2		3		
Forbs, Elisha	2	2	2		
Simmons, John	1	1	3		
Simmons, Rufus	2				
Grannis, William	3		4		
Motthrop, Isaac	2	3	3		
Will					6
Potler, Israel	1	3	3		
Smith, Hezekiah	1	1	1		
Page, Aaron	1	1	1		
Page, William	1		1		
Bessel, Isaac	2	2	5		
Barnes, Samuel	2		4		
White, Ezra	5	2	6		
Coldgrove, Joseph	1		2		
Bogue, Daniel	1	2	2		
Handy, Clemens	4	1	8		
Norriss, Champfire	2	2	4		
Philley, Isaac	2		4		
Beaman, Elisha	14	2	4		
Wright, Jonathan	1		2		
Hewit, Joshua	1	1	1		
Prince					6
Blakesley, Saml	2	3	3		
Rockwell, Elijah	1	2	4		
Blye, Paphroe	1	1	3		
Rockwell, Elihue	1		3		
Rockwell, Joseph	1				
Rockwell, John	1	2	2		
Bidwell, Epiphras	1	1	3		
Enos, Daniel	2	1	2		
Bass, Anna		1	6		
Bass, Nathan	1	1	2		
Wright, Moses	3	1	8		
Barber, Benjamin	1	1	2		
Hall, Daniel	1	2	3		
Rockwell, Saml	17	4	3		1
Seymore, Stephen	1	4	2		
Hopkins, Thomas	2	2	1		
Taintor, Joseph	1	3	2		
Buckingham, Andrew	1		4		
Pinney, David	2		3		
Pinney, Grove	1		3		
Pinney, Abraham	1		3		
Watter, Samuel	1	2	3		
Aglestone, Daniel	3		3		
Martial, Josiah	1	3	4		
Howell, Edmond	2	2	2		
Chamberlain, Saml	1		2		
Chamberlain, Saml	2		3		
Sage, Enos	1	5	4		
Stilman, Roger	1	4	4		
Stilman, Appleton	2		3		
Stilman, Robert	1	2	2		
Hart, Josiah H	2		1		
Preston, Charles	1	3	3		
Munson, Medad	1	3	2		
Gordon, Lewis	1	2	1		
Scovel, Benjamin	1	2	2		
Reed, Josiah	2	3	2		
Little, Robert	1	2	3		
Crane, Martin	1		2		
Adam, Thomas	2	1	1		
Kimbald, Richard	1	1	4		
Stephens, Ebenezer	3		2		
Stephens, Joel	1		1		
Saunders, Thomas	1		2		
Smith, Nathen	1		1		
Evets, Stephen	1	1	4		
Beets, John	1		4		
Moore, Amos	1				
Pinkerton, William	1	1	1		
Thompson, Joel	1		1		
Thompson, James	1		2		
Raynolds, John	1	1	2		

LITCHFIELD COUNTY—Continued.

LITCHFIELD TOWN—con.

NAME OF HEAD OF FAMILY.	Free white males of 16 years and upward, including heads of families.	Free white males under 16 years.	Free white females, including heads of families.	All other free persons.	Slaves.
Whitmore, Sam¹	3	1	4	1	
Woodward, Serenus	3	4	2		
Johnson, Daniel	2	3	2		
Johnson, Sarah	2	1	2		
Johnson, Polly		2	1		
Landon, Abagail			2	1	
Lott, Peter	1		3		
Bushnel, Gideon	2	1	3		
Fitch, Hezekiah	3	5	4		
King, John	1		1		
Cole, Sam¹	1		1		
Piffer, Nathan C	1		1		
Murphey, James	1	1	1		
Palmer, Daniel	1		1		
Montgomeroy, Hue	1	1	2		
Whiting, William	1		4		
Bessel, John	1	4	2		
Wadhams, Abraham	2	5	3		
Landon, David	1		1		
Landon, David	1	1	4		
Wire, Thomas	2	2	5		
Mitcalf, John	1	2	4		
Brooks, Joseph	1	3	2		
Collins, Ambrose	2	5	3		
Loomice, Fitch	1	2	2		
Drigs, Daniel	2	1	4		
Fleskey, Mary			1		
Loomis, Asahel	1	1	5		
Loomis, Joel	1	4	5		
Loomis, Isaac	1				1
Taylor, Stephen	1	2	6		
Phelps, Juda			4		
Barber, Ellhue	1		1		
Austin, Andrew D	3	5	3		
Austin, Aaron	3	2	5		
Austin, Eliphalet	3	3	6		
Atwater, Aseph	2	2	5		
Wilson, Noah	3	1	4		
Wilson, Abijah	3	1	4		
Wilson, Noah	1	1	5		
Cook, Daniel	1	1	1		
Munson, John	3	1	4		
Munson, Nathaniel	2		3		
Beach, Daniel	2	1	4		
Hinman, Samuel	1	5	4		
Hart, David	1		2		
Bartholemew, Isaac	1	1	3		
Stephens, Abijah	1	2	5		
Cook, Daniel	1	2	2		
Webb, Jonathan	1	2	5		
Webb, Jonathan	1	1	1		
Webb, David	1	3	5		
Baldwin, David	1	3	2		
Cornwell, Samuel	3		4		
Thomson, Jonathan	2	1	3		
Norton, Daniel	6	2	6		
Howe, Joseph	2	1	4		
Wright, Jabez	3		2		
Gaylord, Joel	2		6		
Allyn, Joel	4	2	3		
Wilson, Amos	2	1	3		
Cook, Elihu	1		3		
Wolcott, Gye	2	2	2		
Loomiss, Richard	2	3	3		
Higly, Sarah			2		
Loomis, Doritha	2	1	2		
Leach, Joshua	1	2	5		
Stoddard, Ebenezer	1	1	3		
Leach, Ebenezer	1	2	3		
Baldwin, George	2		3		
Ray, Timothy	1		4		
Leach, Richard	2	3	4		
Holebrook, Abijah	2		1		
Deming, Roswell	1		1		
Perrey, Isaac	1	1	1		
Denison, Christopher	1	4	4		
Apley, Ezekiel	3	3	3		
Grannis, Robart	1	2	2		
McNire, James	1	2	5		
Judd, Ebenezer	2		5		
Bound, Joseph	1		3		
Bradley, Azariah	1	1	3		
Bacon, James	1	1	1		
Martial, Sarah	2	1	2		
Whitmore, John	2	2	4		
Miller, Asahel	3	1	4		
Barber, Choxhebe			1		
Schovel, Ebenezer	1		4		
Keyes, William	1	2	2		
Horskins, Theodore	1		2		
Hoanmen, Wait	1	1	4		
Ives, Lazarus	2	4	5		
Luther, Martin	1	3	4		
Orton, Darius	1	1	4		
Maltbey, Jseph	2	3	6		

LITCHFIELD TOWN—con.

NAME OF HEAD OF FAMILY.	Free white males of 16 years and upward, including heads of families.	Free white males under 16 years.	Free white females, including heads of families.	All other free persons.	Slaves.
Bartholmew, Sam¹	2	4	5		
Bonney, Junis	1	3	2		
Bonney, Asahel	1		6		
Tuttle, Noah	3	2	5		
Leach, Jonas	1	3	5		
Beach, Michael	1	1	3		
Squire, Clement	2	3	4		
Kellog, Samuel	3		4		
Merrils, Biezela	1		2		
Denison, William	2	2	5		
Kellog, Helmont	1	3	1		
Thompson, Stephen	3	1	2	3	
Thomson, Edward	1		1		
Roberts, John	1		5		
Lee, John	1	3	3		
Barns, Abel	1	3	1		
Reed, Moses	2		2		
Trumbull, Jonathan	1		5		
Bates, Martin	1	3	7		
Chapman, Reuben, 2d	1		1		
Chapman, Reuben	1	1	4		
Chapman, John C	1	2	1		
Landon, Ezekiel	2	2	3		
Bessel, George	2		2		
Grennold, Japer	2		1		
Landon, Ashbel	1	1	3		
Grennold, Seth	1	1	2		
Landon, Nathan	2	2	3		
Kyes, William	2	1	3		
Doud, Peleg	2	1	3		
Harrison, Jared	2	2	5		
Lewis, Hendrick	1	4	1		
Doud, Samuel	3	1	4		
Bossworth, Nathan	2	3	3		
Kelsey, Jonathan	1		2		
Colkins, Elisha	2	1	2		
Perrey, Benjamin	1		4		
Perrey, Amos	1	2	1		
Rowley, Simeon	2	1	3		
Hamlin, David	4	2	4		
Fuller, Ebenezer	1	5	3		
Evarts, Sam¹	1	4	3		
Evarts, Ebenezer	1	1	5		
Anderson, John	1	2	1		
Phelps, Ichabod	3	3	4		
Monger, William	1		1		
Tubs, Luman	2	1	1		
Deen, Seth	1		1		
Reed, Elias	1	4	7		
Holms, James	2	2	2		
Eldredge, John	2	2	4		
Reed, John	1		2		
Rowley, Johiel	1	2	3		
Cook, Joel	1		2		
Hitchcock, Daniel	1	2	2		
Parker, Benjamin	3		4		
Holscombe, James	1	1	2		
Goodhue, David	1		4		
Barber, Ephraim	1	2	3		
Case, Andrus	1	2	6		
Barber, David	1	2	2		
Rice, Sam¹	1	3	4		
Hart, Seth	3	3	3		
Messenger, Abner	2	2	2		
Wilcox, Johiel	1	3	2		
Barber, Abraham	4	2	3		
Barber, Jimsi	1	2	2		
Barber, Jacob	3	2	6		
Basset, David	2	2	4		
Olcott, James	3	4	3		
Thompson, Samuel	2		2		
Graves, Alexander	1	1	2		
Andrews, John	1	4	5		
Wilcox, Asahel	2	6	2		
Sacket, Aaron	2		3		
Buell, John	1	2	2		
Collens, Oliver	1	2	2		
Kilborn, Appelton	1	1	5		
Graves, William	1	1	1		
Jones, Eaton	1		2		
Allen, Joseph	1	1	4		
McNeal, Roswell	2	3	2		
Buel, Norman	1	2	3		
Buel, Archelus	1	3	2		
Cole, Joseph	1		2		
McNiel, Archebald	2		6		
Bull, Enunice			5		
Bull, George	2	1	2		
Peck, Rhoda	2	1	2	2	
Gillet, Amos	2		3		
Anderson, Joshua	2	1	4	6	
Catlin, Theodore	3	2	5		
Landon, David	2	1	2		
Parker, Ebenezer	1	1	3		
McNiel, Alexander	2		1		2

LITCHFIELD TOWN—con.

NAME OF HEAD OF FAMILY.	Free white males of 16 years and upward, including heads of families.	Free white males under 16 years.	Free white females, including heads of families.	All other free persons.	Slaves.
Phelps, Edward	3		2		
Catlin, Abel	1	2	5		
Peck, Mary	2	1			
Horford, David	1		3		
Gardenor, George	1	2	1		
Butler, David	1		2	1	1
Phelps, John	1	2	5		
Long, John	1				
Clark, Lyman	2	3	4		
Orsborn, John	1		1		
Atwood, James	1	1	4		
Addes, James	2	1	1		
Blin, Hosea	2	2	6		
Baldwin, Phinehas	1	2	2		
Taylor, Elisha	1	2	3		
Taylor, Joel	1	1	2		
Hebard, Nathan	1	2	6		
Whitmore, Caleb	1		1		
Wallace, Anna		3	1		
Phill				2	
Marsh, Ashbel	1	1	1		
Chapman, Caleb	1	1	2		
Taylor, Benjamin	1	1	4		
Smith, Henry	1	1	4		
Dickenson, Friend	1	4	2		
Taylor, Anna			1		
Pierce, Mary		2	7		
Baldwin, Ashbel	1	1	2		
Jones, Eliakim	1		4		
Matlocks, James	3		2		
Starr, Daniel	1	1	4		
Stanton, William	2		2		
Seymore, Samuel	2	1	3		
Earl, Rafal	1	1	2		
Seymore, Moses	4	3	5		
Barber, Ebenezer	2		1	1	
Sanford, Oliver	2		2		
Sanford, Jonah	2	1	3		
Cleavland, Benjamin	1				
Silkrigs, Jonathan G	1				
Emmons, Russel	1	4	5		
Emmons, Oliver	1		1		
Emmons, Abner	1		5		
Lampson, Daniel	2	1	1		
Woodruff, Levi	3	1	3		
Agard, Hezekiah	1	2	3		
Knap, Abraham	1	2	2		
Hinsdale, Elias	2	1	4		
Farnham, Nathan	1	1	2		
Trumbal, Ezekiel	1		3		
Gibbs, David	2	1	3		
Gibbs, Reuben	1	1	2		
Stodard, James	2	1	2		
Sanford, Moses	2		4		
Chase, Amos	3		3		
Farnham, Gad	2	2	5		
Emmons, Arther, 2d	2	3	2		
Bartholomew, Luther	1	1	3		
Emmons, Arther	1		1		
Emmons, John	3		2		
Emmons, Orrange	1	2	2		
Gallop, Benjamin	1		2		
Emmons, Phinehas	1	1	2		
Brown, Joseph	1	2	6		
Orton, Azariah	2	2	5		
Barns, Timothy	2	2	2		
Hall, John	1	2	2		
Farnham, John	1	1	2		
Orton, Sedgwick	1	2	3		
Dresser, Simeon	1	1	4		
Kelley, Elizabeth		1	2		
Barns, Enos	2		3		
Smedley, Ephraim	2	3	5		
Barns, Gift	2				
Ray, William	1	2	5		
Clark, Champion	1	3	1		
Moore, David	1	2	2		
Shether, Sam¹	1	1	1		
Culver, Zebulon	1	3	3		
Presson, Jermiah	1		2		
Culver, Zebulon	1	2	4		
Culver, Stephen	1	3	6		
Stone, Heber	1	3	6		
Woodruff, Samuel	2	6	5		
Woodruff, Nathaniel	1	1	1		
Poerpont, David	1	1	1		
Buell, David	1	2	4		3
Lewis, Daniel W	1				
Raymond, William	2	2	3		
Sheldorn, Sam¹	3	2	3		
Baldwin, Isaac	2	2	3		
Sprats, William	2	2	4		
Demming, Julius	3	3	4		1
Woolcott, Oliver	3	1			6
Reeve, Tapping	1	2	3		

LITCHFIELD COUNTY—Continued.

NAME OF HEAD OF FAMILY.	Free white males of 16 years and upward, including heads of families.	Free white males under 16 years.	Free white females, including heads of families.	All other free persons.	Slaves.	NAME OF HEAD OF FAMILY.	Free white males of 16 years and upward, including heads of families.	Free white males under 16 years.	Free white females, including heads of families.	All other free persons.	Slaves.	NAME OF HEAD OF FAMILY.	Free white males of 16 years and upward, including heads of families.	Free white males under 16 years.	Free white females, including heads of families.	All other free persons.	Slaves.
LITCHFIELD TOWN—con.						LITCHFIELD TOWN—con.						LITCHFIELD TOWN—con.					
Lewis, Osius	5	1	3			Moss, Ives	1		3			Owen, Aaron	1		1	1	
Barber, Stephen	1	2	1			Sanford, Zacheus	1	1	2			Chapin, Reuben	2	2	4		
Russel, Stephen	1	1	5			Webster, John	1	2	1			Sillick, Ezra	3	1	6		
Marsh, Elisha	2		3			Tharp, Asher	1		1			Sillick, Bethiel	3	1	5		
Clemmons, John	1	2	4			Smith, Joshua	1	1	6			Green, Nathaniel	2	1	4		
Agard, Judah	1	3	1			Smith, Elizabeth	1		2			Grinnol, Daniel	1	2	3		
McKinly, William	1	3	4			Crosby, Thomas	2	1	5			Lord, Elijah	1		3		
Marsh, Solomon	2	3	5		1	Webster, James	1	4	2			More, Samuel	2	1	2		
Sanders, John	1	2	5			Grant, Jesse	2	1	3			More, Samuel, 2d	3		3		
Smith, Benjamin	3		3			Garnsey, Noah	3	2	6			Averis, Jared	4	2	5		
Bishop, Silvanus	2	1	2			Moss, Levi	2	2	6			Lyman, Simeon	2	1	3		
Stone, Reuben	2	3	3			Moss, Amos	4	2	6			Wright, James	3	3	2		
Hughes, William	1	2	3			Bidwell, Elijah	1	1	3			Dickinson, Shirman	1		1		
Hayson, Saml	1					Webster, Charles, Jr	1	2	1			Tryon, David	1	1	4		
Bates, Sarah		1	3			Catlin, Uriel	3		4			Reed, Thomas	3	1	2		
Landon, John	1	3	4			Orsborn, Reuben	1	3	2			Truman, Thaniel	1	3	3		
Stone, Thomas	2	2	2			Murry, Philemon	2	1	4			Chapin, Charles	1	2	6		
Bishop, Calvin	1	2	2			Williams, Israel	1	3	1			Jewell, Eliphalet	3		3	1	
Woodcok, Saml	2	1	6			Perkins, John	1	4	2			Beller, Saml	1	2	3		
Woodcok, Jonathan	1					Johnson, Elias	1	2	4			Camps, Hezekiah	3	2	6		
Griswold, Jacob	2	1	1			Chamberlain, Moses	2	5	2			Lee, Miles	3	3	3		
Stocker, Thadeus	1	3	4			Bradley, Tina	3	1	4			Howse, Bene	2	2	3		
Denison, Chaney	2	1	2			Hotchkiss, Elihu	2	1	5			David, Daniel	2	4	2		
Stone, Silvanus	1	2	1			Mason, Luther	1	2	2			Peck, James	1	1	2		
Stuard, Loas			1			Webster, Stephen	4	3	4			La Clear, Francis	1		1		
Philips, Gideon	2	1	3			Rowes, Winthrop	1	2	6			Hall, Silas	1	3	8		
Benton, Nathaniel	2	1	5			Roberts, John	1	3	4			White, Jacob	2	3	4		
Howard, Joseph	1		7			Webster, Elijah	1	3	2			Scovel, Jonathan	4	1	6		
Benton, Daniel	1	1	1			Webster, Benjamin	2		1			Tyler, Solomon	1		3		
Swan, Nathan	2		4			Mason, Jonathan	1		2			Pierce, Silas	1	1	2		
Benton, Abraham	1		1			Mason, Rebacca	2		1			Thornton, Ezra	1	4	2		
Hermom, Nicholas	1		2			Peck, Benjamin	1	3	3			Watter, Pierce	1		1		
Gosling, Solomon	1	1	2			Seeley, David	1	3	1			Hawley, Samuel	1	3	4		
Stone, Jonah	2	3	5			Ives, John	2	2	5			Whiting, Christophar	1	3	3		
Baldwin, William	3	2	2			Shepperd, Joseph	1	3	2			Clark, Saml C	1	1	3		
Baldwin, James	2		4			Tuttle, Jery	1	1	3			Miner, Reuben	2		3		
Worter, Benjamin	1		2			Ford, Josephus	1		4			Miner, John	1	3	3		
Worter, Samuel	2	2	3			Allyn, Jonathan	1	1	2			Roberts, Saml	1	1	2		
Wilmot, John	1	3	2			Ludington, Aaron	1	1	2			Whealor, Isaac	1	1	1		
Taylor, John	1		3			Thorn, William	2		4			Norton, Levi	2	2	1		
Merrills, Truman	1		3			Barber, Reuben	1	1	1			Spensor, Stephen	2	1	6		
Humestone, Reuben	3	1	3			Wilson, William	1	2	2			Stanard, Abel	1	2	6		
Catlin, Alexander	3	1	6		1	Hays, Asahel	1	1	4			Church, John	1	3	3		
Yale, Elsa			2			Clinton, Samuel	1		4			Burton, Saml	1	2	2		
McNeil, Saml	1	3	4			Menter, Daniel	1	1	6			Spensor, Elisha	2	1	1		
Stone, Levi	3	3	4			Clinton, Henry	1	1	3			Austen, David	2	1	3		
Peck, Philoe	1	1	4			Keemann, Pelatiah	1	4	2			Martial, Danl	2	1	2		
Phelps, Ariah	1					Hokim, Eli	4	3	3	9		Phelps, John	3	3	3		
Kinney, Martha	2	1	5			Weed, Ezra	1	1	3			Phelps, Jedediah	1	2	2		
Phillips, Samuel	1	2	3			Tiffany, Samuel	1		4			Pease, Nathan	2	3	2		
Crissey, Presarved	1	1	2			Tayler, Abner	1	2	2			Gillet, William	1	1	3		
Phillips, Samuel	1	3	2			Tayler, Abner	1		2			Walter, William	4	6	8		
Lymans, Aaron	3		5			Zicke					5	Smith, Joseph	1	1	4		
Lymans, Aaron	1		4			Humphey, Ambrosi	1	2	5			Smith, Theodore	1		4		
Lymans, Hezikah	1	4	5			Daniels, Pelatiah	2		2			Turner, John	1		2		
Lymans, William	1	1	2			Daniels, Reuben	1	4	2			Turner, Hezekiah	1		1		
Rockwell, David	1	2	4			Gates, Jessie	2		4			Ives, Titus	5	2	2		
Crissey, Solomon	1		5			Cowder, Ambrose	1	3	1			Pease, Nathaniel	2	1	4		1
Russel, Stephen	2	3	3			Cowder, Asa	1	1	2			Pease, Obadiah	2		2		
Gowdy, Samuel	1	1	3			Shipman, Jonathan	3		3			Stephen, Zebulon	1	1	2		
Minor, Thomas	2	7	3			Yates, Aaron	1	3	3			Butler, Saml S	1		1		
Wilcox, Mosas	1	1	1			Phelps, Charles	2	1	3			Stephen, Nathaniel	5	1	3		
Barbarer, James	1	1	2			Belden, Ebenezer	1		1			Day, Thomas	2	2	3		
Andrews, Samuel	1	2	4			Clark, Thomas	3		3			Hatch, David	1	3	2		
Perkens, Gidian	1	1	2			Clark, Thaniel	2	2	5			Baley, Hendrick	1	3	1		
Terry, Joseph	1		1			Jones, Thomas	3		3			Pettiborn, Jiles	4	5	3		
Jones, William C	1	1	1			Kirbey, Joseph	1		2			Gitteau, Ephraim	3	1	1		
Jones, Isaac	1	1	5			Harkins, Nathan	2		2	1		Welch, Elijah	1		1		
Jones, Israel	1					Goodyer, Chancy	1		2			Stephen, Benjamin	1	3	3		
Jones, Saml	1	3	6			Parker, Stephen	1		2			Carter, Zebulon	1	3	3		
Jones, Thomas	1	4	5			Cole, Eleezer	2	1	2			Pinto, John	1	2	3		
Perkins, Phinehas	1	4	1			Gideons, David	4	5	7			Stephens, Andrew	1	3	2		
Chapman, William	2	3	5			Borden, Asahel	1	3	2			Whitmore, William	2		2		
Smith, Ephraim	1	2	4			Cone, Thomas	2	2	4			Daniels, John	2	3	5		
Swat, Pelix	1	4	5			Borden, John	4	1	4			Clark, Joel	1	5	4		
Barnes, Solomon	1	1	1			Ackley, Joel	2		3			Church, Uriah	1		5		
Palmer, Ambrose	1	4	3			Remand, William, 2d	6	1	3			Avery, William	2	4	4		
Tucker, Reuben	2	4	3			Bird, James	6	3	7			Luce, Joshua	1	2	3		
Mott, Lemul	1	2	1	2		Bird, Thomas	3	6	6			Millerd, Joel	1	1	2		
Loomis, Daniel	1	1	4			Crane, Ezra	2	3	1			Tobins, Meriah			1		
Preston, Benjamin	1	3	1			Bradley, Arial	2		3			Spensor, Abel	1				
Thompson, Elijah	1	1	4			Averist, Jahiel	1	2	4			Chafey, Joel	2	2	7	1	
Andrews, Abraham	2	1	3			Spencer, Asahel	1	2	6			Frink, Seth	1	2	2		
Andrews, Theophilus	1	4	4			Slater, Francis	4	3	5			Church, Johiel	3	1	3		
Kellogg, Seth	1	4	3			Bushnal, Saml	2		3			Church, Johiel, 2nd	1		3		
Thompson, Samuel	1	1	2			Brinsmade, John	3		2			Racksford, Joseph	1	3	3		
Benedick, Noah	1	2	4			West, Amos	1	1	1			Sciff, Samuel	3	2	6		
Wilkeson, Levi	1	3	2			Landon, Elisha	1	2	2			Stjohn, Thomas	3	1	4		
Benedick, Abijah	1	1	1			Hinsdale, Moses	1	2	4			St. John, Uriah	1		3		
Turner, Titus	2	3	3			Brinsmade, Saml	2	1	4			Youngslove, Saml	1	2	3		
Sanford, Moses	1	3	2			Pempille, John	1	2	3			Youngher, John	1	3	5		
Moss, Solomon	2	3	2			Averis, Elisha, 2d	1	1	5			Cartwright, Betty	1	3	1		
Washburn, William	3		3			Averis, Elisha	1		2			Sanford, Caleb	1	2	2		
Graves, Benjamin	1	1	3			Carter, Moses	3	1	5			Pardy, Johiel	1	3	2		
Little, Thomas	1	1	2			Dunbarr, David	1	2	3			Miller, Jairs	3		4		

LITCHFIELD COUNTY—Continued.

LITCHFIELD TOWN—con.

Name of head of family.	Free white males of 16 years and upward, including heads of families.	Free white males under 16 years.	Free white females, including heads of families.	All other free persons.	Slaves.
Ackley, Thomas	1		2		
Ackley, David	2		2		
Muxum, Sam¹	1		2		
Howel, Edward	1		1		
Abels, John	1	1	2		
St. John, Timothy	2	1	1		
Cube					3
St. John, Ezekiel	1		2		
Harriss, George	1		1		
Youngs, Benjamin	3	1	3	1	
Ranford, Arther	3		1		
Lord, John	1	3	3		
Youngs, Samuel	2	4	5		
Frink, Sam¹	1	2	5		
Everitt, Isaiah	2	4	4		
Skift, Benjamin	3	3	5		
Notts, Martin	3	2	2		
McClure, Robert	2	1	3		
Frisbey, Joseph	2	2	2		
Stannard, Samuel	2	2	5		
Griswold, Seth	1	2	3		
Barber, William	2		4		
Lucus, John	2	1	3		
Breneson, Ozias	4	1	3		
Ward, Amasa	3	3	3		
Stannard, Ezra	1	3	1		
Orvis, Roger	2	1	7		
Stephen, Simeon	1	1	2		
Buttler Josiah	1		4		
Walter, John	1	3	2		
Hotchkins, Saml	1	3	3		
Orvis Eleazer	3	1	7		
Stuart, Sam¹	2	2	2		
Bull, James	2	3	4		
Holt, Nicholas	1	3	4		
Holt, Eliza	1	1	2		
Kingsbury, Stephens	1	1	2		
Holt, Isaac	4		3		
Norton, Silvenus	3	3	2		
Northaway, Sam¹	2	5	3		
Knap, Hezekiah	1	4	3		
Spalding, Jacob	3	1	3		
Knap, Samuel	3	4	3		
Picket, Benjamin	1	2	3		
Hoddy, Daniel	1	1	4		
Green, Martin	1	1	6		
Whipple, Joseph	1		3		
Right, Justin	1	1	4		
Nash, Polley			2		
Wills, Seth	2	2	3		
Hoskins, Joseph	2	1	3		
Mills, Macy	2		2		
Coe, Matthews	4	5	4		
Brunson, Levi	2	1	6		
Brunson, Binonah	1	2	4		
Thompson, Elijah	1		1		
Coe, Zedediah	1	1	3		
Cane, Daniel	1	4	3		
Grisworth, Phineas	3	4	3		
Hamlin, Darling	1		3		
Hamlin, Amasa	2	2	3	1	
Hitchcocks, Sam¹	3		3		
Winages, Philip	1	3	2		
Lamb, Johiel	1	5	1		
Data, David	2	3	2		
Data, Ezra	1	3	1		
Kellogg, Olliver	2	1	5		
Griswold, Ezeriah	1				
Griswold, Ezeriah	1	2			
Griswold, David	1		2		
Strong, Joel	1	2	1		
Hunter, Nathaniel	1	2	5		
Whitford, John	2	1	3		
Griswold, Daniel	3	1	4		
Canfield, Judson	1	2	2	3	1
Lane, Jared	1	1	2		
Conklin, Benjᵃ	2	2	1		
Nott, Asa	1	4	5		
Gay, David	1	2	2		
Deming, Tom	1	1	2		
Shuster, John	1	2	4		
Riley, Sam¹	3	2	2		
Goodrich, Solomon	3	2	2		
Elliot, Tom	1	3	3		
Pellet, Enos	2		3	3	
Marshnite, Zebalon	1				
Pardee, Elijah	1	3	3		
Jay, Elizabeth	1	1	5		
Moses, Timothy	2	1	2		
Fellows, Joseph	3	2	4		
Demming, Bernard	1	1	3		
Brown, James	1	1	2		
Blakesley, Thomas	2	1	3		
Benedict, Benjaman	2	4	4		
Henshaw, James	2		4		
Elton, Ebenees	2	1	5		
Curtess, Seth	1		4		
Rockwell, William	3	1	4		
Lawrence, Anson	1	1	3		
Lawrence, Solomon	1	3	3		
Stowe, Sam¹	2	1	4		
Rood, Marines	4	3	3		
Clarke, Israel	1		1		
Fellows, Ephraim	2	2	3		
Fellows, Philemon	3	1			
Mix, Chancey	1			1	
Hopkins, Consider	3	1	1		
Marsh, Jonathan	2	2	4		
Merrills, John	2	1	3		
Gilbert, Thodah	2	1	5		
Smith, Martin	1		1		
Moody, Eben	2	3	6		
Bull, Asher	1	6	3		
Smith, Elizer	1	3	2		
Smith, Seth	3	1	4		
Flowers, Elijah	1	1	1		
Gilbert, Joseph	1	3	6		
Gillet, Matthew	2	2	6		
Hopkins, Roodrick	1	1	4		
Pease, Violet		1	1		
Gilbert, Theodosia			3	2	
Gillet, Michael	1	1	3		
Crittenton, James	1	2	4		
Jones, Benjamin	1	1	3		
Terrol, Lettie	3		5		
Wells, Benjamin	1	3	4		
Steel, William	1	3	4		
Shephard, Eldad	1		6		
Romnam, Meajah	1		1		
Thompson, Elisha	1	1	1		
Brace, William	1		2		
Richards, Silas	2	1	2		
Hutson, David	2	3	2		
Childs, Timothy	1	1	2		
Willoughby, Samuel	1		3		
Richards, Charles	3	1	3		
Hill, Samuel	2	2	4		
Francis, Samuel	1		1		
Hillhouse, Samuel	1	1	4		
Collins, Philo	2		3		
Willoughby, Josiah	1	3	1		
Fargoe, James	1		3		
Deming, Jonathan	2	1	4		
Brooks, Asahel	2		3		
Willoughby, Westil	2	2	5		
Riley, John	5	1	2		
Gilbert, Roda	2	2	6		
Knickabocker, John	1	2	2		
Hantchet, Joseph	3		2		2
Hantchet, Simeon	1	4	3		
Tupper, Sam¹	2	1	2		
Hantchet, Luny			1		
Hatchet, Jonah	1	3	4		
Vandusen, Content	2		2		
Barton, Roger	4	1	5		
Barton, Joseph	2	1	3		
Jackson, Jane			2		
Jackaway, Simeon	1	2	3		
Nickerson, Samuel	1	4	2		
Nickelson, Ezra	1	1	4		
Jackaway, Aaron	3	1	3		
Wollner, Zebulon	2	3	2		
Trupper, Thomas	2	2	5		
Hantichet, John	1		3		
Hantihet, Amos	2	3	2		
Jacobs, Tuel	1	4	3		
Hantchet, Ebenezer	2	2	6		
Thomas, Benjamin	1	1	3		
Knickabacker, John	1	1	3		
Sweetland, Aaron	1	1	1		
Nickerson, Uriah	2	1	2		
Nicherson, Archelus	1	1	2		
Tupper, William	2	2	4		
Allen, Stephen	2	1	3		
Baker, Martha	2	2	3		
Benton, Isaac	1		1		
Waters, John	2	2	4		
Graves, Haynes	2	2	3		
Graves, Ichabod	1	1	3		
Mecantire, Stephen	2	1	4		
Sellick, Noah	2	2	3		
Graves, Anna	1	1	1		
Johnson, James	2	2	3		
Covel, Zenus	1	2	1		
Griswold, George	1		1		
Chipman, Thomas		1	2		
Gane, Jude	2	3	6		
Bradley, Daniel	1	1	5		
Buell, Nathaniel	4	1	5		
Canfield, Joseph, 2d	1	1	5		
Canfield, Joseph	2	2	6		
Hoskins, Abel	1	1	4		
Markem, James	2	4	5		
Banning, Samuel	3	2	5		
Philley, Jasper	2		4		
Ormstid, Timothy	4	2	5		
Trafford, William	3	2	3		
Beebe, Elisha	1	6	5		1
Herford, Jeremiah	1	1	3		
Crofford, William	2	1	3		
Brown, Jacob	3		2		
Deming, Daniel	1		2		
Phelps, Simeon	1		4		
Bebee, Daniel	1	1	3		1
Bebee, Solomon	2	3	5		2
Deen, Nathaniel	2		3		
Deen, Roswell	1	2	3		
Deen, Asa	1	1	6		
Smith, Allen	1	1	3		
Butler, Samuel	2	3	3		
Wickwire, Ichabord	2	4	1		
Bebee, Isaac	2	3	4		
Towsley, Arial	1	1	1		
Wolford, Jeremiah	4	1	6		
Post, George	1	2	6		
Villey, Cornelius	7	2	2	2	
Burrill, Jonathan	1	2			
Gleason, Arial	2	2	4		
Hanmer, Benjamin	1	2	4		
Barns, Job	1	2	3		
Denmore, Patty			3		
Hoogaboom, Jeremiah	1		1		1
Burd, Jonathan	1		1		2
Ensign, John	2		1		
Loveman, Aaron	1	1	1		
Hunt, Robert	1	1	2		
Bowlis, George	1	3	4		
Peek, John	2	3	4		
Bushnal, Abraham	2	4	6		
Bowman, Lydia	1	3	1		
White, Elizer	2	1	2		
Beach, Chancy	1	6	4		
Robens, Easter		1	1		
Sayer, Jesse	1		·1		
Elmon, John	1		2		
Hale, Nathan	1	2	6	1	1
Johnson, Isaac	2		1		
Barney, Samuel	1	2	1		
Fuller, John	2		4		
Peck, Calvin	1	3	2		
Gray, Darias	1	2	2		
Swift, Elisha	1				
Corbey, Meriah			2		
Bunson, William	1	4	2		
Caldwell, James	1		2		
Wells, Samuel	1	2	3		
Wells, Noah	1		1		
Monroe, Nathan	1	2	4		
Fullerton, John	1				
Johnson, James	2	3	4		
Smith, Willard	1	2	3		
Doolittle, Jonathan	2	4	2		
Wallen, James	1	2	3		
Hood, George	1	1	3		
Fellows, Thomas	2		3		
Harrison, Stephen	2	3	5		
Mix, Martha		1	1		
Ormsby, Amos	1	1	1		
Franklin, John	3	2	3		
Watson, Hezikah	1	3	3		
Fellows, Lois			3		
Stephens, Stafford	3	1	4		
Watson, William	2	3	5		
Wadsworth, John	1	1	1		
Stanley, Nathan	3	1	4		
Bromwell, Ichabod	2		5		
Williams, Jacob	2		5		
Paxton, Allen	6		1		
Lawrance, Gidian	2	2	6		
Austin, Thadeus	2	4	2		
Lawrance, Nehemiah	2	2	4		
Burns, Simon	1	2	2		
Jerrum, Lyman	1	1	4		
Miller, Seth	1	4	3		
Lawrance, Nathan	4		3		
Stephens, Nathan	2	1	5		
Stephens, Oliver	1	2	2		
Lawrence, David	2		1		
Lawrence, Jerry	2				
Stephens, Zebulon	2	1	4		
Stephens, Henry	2	2	4		
Jackeway, Ebenezer	2	2	4		
Foster, David	1		2		
Atwood, William	1	2	6		
Miller, Samuel	2	3	2		

LITCHFIELD COUNTY—Continued.

LITCHFIELD TOWN—con.

NAME OF HEAD OF FAMILY	Free white males of 16 years and upward, including heads of families	Free white males under 16 years	Free white females, including heads of families	All other free persons	Slaves
Mack, Benjamin	1	1	1		
Coe, Elijah	1	1	4		
Han, Titus	2	3	5		
Benjamin, Samuel	1	2	2		
Mack, Zebulon	1	1	1		
Albertson, John P	2	1	4		
Stiles, Sam¹	1	3	3		
Evans, Benjamin	1		1		
Spelman, David	1	1	6		
Mack, Gurdan	1	2	2		
Money, Reuben	1	3	4		
Coe, Phinehas	1	3	2		
Ensignor, Daniel	1	3	2		
Burnham, Reuben	2	2	3		
Butler, Nathan	3	2	4		
Gonyard, Spensor	4	2	2		
Blakesley, Sam¹	1	1	5		
Porter, Thomas	1	1	3		
Miller, George T	2	1	1		
Plumby, Ebenʳ	1	2	2		
Olcott, Samuel	1	1	4		
Brown, John	2		1		
Sweet, Joseph	1	1	2		
Brown, Nathaniel	1		2		
Barber, William	1		1		
Norton, Levi	1	1	2		
Norton, Thomas	3	2	5		
Cady, Chester	1	1	2		
Burr, Daniel	1	1	7		
Beach, Lewis	1	3	3		
Beach, John	1	2	2		
Tibbots, Thomas	1	2	3	1	
Smith, Roda	1	1	4		
Balcomb, Elias	4	2	4		
Stanlif, Sam¹	1	2	2		
Lee, Nathaniel	1	2	5		
Brown, Edmond	3		2		
Cole, Noah	1	3	2		
Tibbles, Samuel	3	3	5		
Frank, Andrew	1	3	3		
Nott, Abraham	1	1	2		
Austin, Caleb	1		5		
Hinsdale, William	1	2	1		
Fannig, Daniel	4	1	5	2	
Tooley, Nabby			3		
Holmbeck, Abraham	2	4	4		3
Belden, Charles	2	1	4		
Belden, Charles	3		2		
Belden, Charles	3	5	2		
Jupiter					1
Hide, Uriah	2	1	8		
Beach, Zopher	1	2	4		
Gannan, Edward	1	2	5		
Bushnal, Abner	1	2	3		
Porter, Elisha	1		2		
Spensor, Frederick	1	1	7		
Stanley, Aaron	1	3	6		
Wildeer, Gamaliall	1	2	4		
Gilbert, David	1		2		
Ormsted, Isaac	2	2	3		
Spensor, Jonah	1	4	3		
Gun, Noble	1	2	3		
Cady, Josiah	1	3	3		
Wilard, Eunice			1	2	
Hall, Nathan	1	1	2		
Beldon, Bartholomew	1	2	4		
Haliburt, Elisha	3	2	2		
Cuff					5
Andrews, Benajah	2		3		
Deming, Pelog					1
Towrley, Levi	1	1	1		
Hinsdale, Joseph	3	1	2		
Kellogg, Elijah	3		2		
Kellogg, Joseph	2	2	6		
Root, William	2	1	6		
Philips, Benjamin	1		1		
Holcomb, Amasa	3	1	4		
Fellows, John	1	1	3		
Parmely, Aaron	1	5	3		
Whitney, John	3	2	1		
Whitney, John, 2d	2	1	3		
Austin, Levi	1	3	4		
Perry, Elisha	1	3	3		
Belcher, William	2	1	2		
Throil, Aaron	1	2	2		
Little, Otis	1	2	2		
Witing, Benjamin	2	2	2		
Bancroft, Emiam	1	3	3		
Holmes, Seth	4	1	3		
Sweet, Jonathan	4	2	6		
Parmely, Standly	1	1	1		
North, Ashbel	2	1	2		
Whiting, John	3		3		
Coe, Ebenezer	3		3		
Comins, Samuel	2	2	5		
Loomis, Isanor	2	2	5		
Thrall, Levi	2	2	3		
Brau, Ariel	2	5	2		
Spenscer, Aseph	1	1	3		
Aglestone, James	1		1		
Benedick, Buchnel	1	1	2		
Pratt, Adonijah	1		1		
Thrall, Daniel	1		4		
Beach, John	2	3	4		
Hodges, Ellane	3	3	4		
West, David	2	1	3		
Smith, Elisha	2	1	4		
Loomis, Joel	1		2		
Williams, David	1		1		
Loomice, Moses	2	1	4		
Loomice, Abner	1	2	3		
Jagger, Phinihas	1		2		
Loomice, Shiphra	4		6		
Loomice, Mary			2		
Beach, Samuel	2	1	4		
Loomice, Benona	1	1	1		
Beach, Abel	1	1	3		
Beach, Noah	1	2	3		
Loomice, Ephraim	4	1	3		
Grant, William	3	1	3		
Loomice, Ephraim	1	3	1		
Loomice, Aaron	1	1	1		
Martial, Aaron	1		3		
Bowley, Samuel	3	2	5		
Brunson, Ashbel	1	3	4		
Aglestone, Benjamin	3	3	4		
Wilson, Roger	2	3	3		
North, Remembrance	1	1	2		
Prichard, Eli	1	1	3		
Prichard, Simain	2	2	5		
Buell, Ashbel	1	2	2		
Colver, Reuben	1		3		
Buell, Peter	1	3	3		
Lord, Daniel	4	3	6		
Ames, Chancey	1	4	2		
Jones, Samu¹	1	2	2		
Lee, Love			2		1
Lee, William	1	4	4		
Colver, Azriah	1	5	3		
Humerston, Joel	1		4		
Hart, Titus	1	2	2		
Curtiss, Joseph	2	1	1		
Moss, David	2	3	3		
Hopson, Simeon	1	2	5		
Moss, Simeon	1	1	3		
Barnes, Oliver	1	4	3		
Bachelor, Reuben	3		3		
Preston, Noah	2	3	1		
Spercy, Allen	1	4	1		
Hall, Simes	1		1		
Hart, Ebenezer	1	4	2		
Hopkins, Harriss	2	1	4		
Hopkins, Harriss, 2d	1		1		
Bates, Henry	2	1	1		
Humerston, Titus	1	4	5		
Todd, Eli	1	1	2		
Atwater, Richard	1		3		
Curtiss, Daniel	1	1	4		
Way, Elijah	1	1	2		
Todd, Ebenezer	1	2	3		
Basset, Zopher	1				
Todd, Ebenezer	2		3		
Homerston, John	2	1	5		
Meriman, Amasa	1		1		
Sanford, Stephen	1	1	3		
Lee, Sam¹	1	2	1		
Hall, Nathaniel	1		3		
Hall, Eleizer	1		2		
Ramond, William	1	3	2		
Curtiss, Gideon	1	1	3		
Evans, Isaac	2	3	1		
Rice, Thadeus	1		2		
Cate,			6		
Jacobs, Heziran	1	1	1		
Barns, Josiah	1		4		
Hammon, Dudley	1	1	5		
Hammon, John	2	3	1		
Barns, Samuel	1		3		
Root, Phinehas	2	1	6		
Root, Asahel	3		3		
Thrall, Charles	2	2	5		
Thrall, Friend	1	5	1		
Harriss, Ebenezer	2	2	3		
Norton, Sarah	1	2	1		
Olcott, Harriet	1	4	3		
Ensign, Elizer	2	2	3		
Taylor, Prince	2	3	4		
Ensign, Timothy	1		2		
Robertson, Noah	1		2		
Hatch, Nathan	2	4	4		
Sutley, David	1	1	3		
Brau, Orange	1	4	3		
Beach, Ezekiel	2	2	2		
Goodrich, Giles	1	3	2		
Birkshop, Abraham	1		4		
Cowdry, Jacob	2	1	1		
Bushnel, Jedediah	3		3		
Crosbey, Timothy C	1		2		
Vreet, George	1	2	2		
Bates, Aaron	1	1	3		
Brau, Abel	2	4	7		
Bushnel, Stephen	2	5	4		
Barber, Samuel	3	1	1		
Bushnel, Martin	2	1	6		
Taylor, Chiles	1	2	4		
Hokim, David	2	2	1		
Root, Phinehas	1	1	3		
Phelps, John	2	3	3		
Judd, Alexʳ	1	1	1		
Messenger, Nathaniel	1		1		
Root, Joel	1		2		
Whitaker, Samuel	1	1	2		
Rowens, Richerson	1	1	1		
Smith, Azariah	1		2		
Bishop, Jesse	1	2	5		
Robens, Ephraim	1	2	2		
Osmon, Ashbel	1	1	4		
Cowls, Timothy	1	2	4		
Deen, Nathan	1	2	3		
Dibble, Margret			1		
Rudd, John	2		4		
Griswold, Sam¹	2	1	5		
Deming, Andrew	1	2	2	2	1
Bidwel, Eliezer	1	6	1		
Hoskins, David	1		1		
Simons, Wiliam	1		1		
Veets, David	4	2	4		
Kneeland, Isaac	3	3	5		
Mills, Sam¹	1	1	3		
Gowdey, James	1	1	2		
Bidwel, Joseph	2	1	1		
Seymour, Joseph, 2d	1	3	2		
Seymour, Joseph	2		4		
Rockwell, John	2	4	5		
Chub, Alexander	1	2	3		
Whitmore, Increase	1		1		
Coe, Robert	1	1	2		
Miller, Marcy			2	5	
Norton, Phinehas	2	3	2		
Colver, Titus	1		1		
Ells, Ozias	1		1		
Collens, Nathaniel	1	2	4		
Weldeer, Joseph	2	5	2		
Merrills, John	2	1	4		
Lewis, Nathaniel	1		2		
Hudson, John	1	1	3		
Beach, David	2	1	5		
Smith, Seth	1	1	4		
Shepherd, Stephen	1	2	3		
Francis, John	2	3	5		
Bumps, Simeon	3	1	2		
Gregory, Joseph	1	3	3		
Jones, Benona	1	3	3		
Cornwell, Isaac	1	2	3		
Richerson, Stephen	2	4	2		
Bampus, Nathan¹	2	1	2		
Nichelson, Sarah					
Allen, Pelletiah	3	2	4		
Pike, James	1		3		
Addams, Richard	3	3	5		
Andrews, Benjⁿ	1	2	1		
Case, Ozias	2	1	3		
Case, Ezra	1	2	5		
Jones, Isrehel	3	4	6		
Huff, Caleb	1	3	5		
Spencer, Thomas	1	3	3		
Reed, Jacob	1	2	3		
Taylor, Ebenezer	1		3		
Fuller, Thomas	3	2	4		
Fuller, Eliphelet	1	3	2		
Fuller, Samuel	1	5	3		
Beeman, Thomas	2	2	4		
Beeman, Thomas, 2d	1	2	2		
Moses, Martin	2	4	2		
Tiffeny, Timothy	1	2	3		
Burnham, Isaac	1		2		
Moses, Abner	1	1	4		
Moses, Ashbel	1	2	1		
Holmes, Urial	3	1	2		
Mechum, Joel	3	1	5		
Sawyer, Jacob	1	2	7		
Bushnell, William	1	2	1		
Lawrance, Arial	3	1	5		1
Lawrence, Arial	1		2		
Pettibone, Samuel	4	2	4		

LITCHFIELD COUNTY—Continued.

LITCHFIELD TOWN—con.

NAME OF HEAD OF FAMILY	Free white males of 16 years and upward, including heads of families	Free white males under 16 years	Free white females, including heads of families	All other free persons	Slaves
Comstock, Secajah	1		1		
Thrall, Eli	1		2		
Pettibone, Roswell	1		1		
Cole, Amasa	2	1	2		
Gaylor, Roegs	4	3	2		
Phelps, Joel	3	1	1		
Humphrey, Asahel	2	2	5		
Malbey, Zacheus	1	1	5		
Brown, Sam'l	1	1	2		
Malbey, Benjamin	2	4	5		
Cowls, Samuel	4	1	2		
Blackesley, Mathew	1		3		
Grant, Joel	2	2	4		
Boardman, Joseph	1	1	3		
Grant, Elijah	3		3		
Clark, Daniel	1	3	2		
Frisbey, Simeon	1		1		
Case, Asahel	1	3	3		
Foot, Luther	1	2	3		
Barber, Timothy	1	1	2		
Mills, Samuel	3	1	4		
Bushnell, Daniel	1	1	2		
Banning, Abner	1	5	3		
Bill, Daniel	1	2	3		
Mechum, Johiel	3		2		
Wildeer, John	3		3		
Gilman, Elihu	2		3		
Goodyer, Stephen	1		3		
Allen, Chancy	1	2	1		
Wildeer, John	1	1	3		
Beach, Sam'l	2		3		
Beach, Benonah	2	1	5		
Atkins, Hezekiah	2		7		
Atkens, Joseph	1	2	4		
Ketchum, Stephen	1	2	4	1	
Obriont, Partrick	1	3	3		
Marsh, Nehenemiah	1	2	3	1	
Dugliss, Benajah	3		6		
Baker, Elisha	2		2		
Cobb, Elijah W	2	1	3		
Tausket, Mary			1		
Kingsbury, Sam'l	5	1	3		
Spalding, John	1	3	2		
Adams, John	1	4	4		
Fordes, Samuel	4	1	2		
Spalding, Asial	1	2	1		
Forbes, John	1	2	2		
Mix, Daniel	1	1	1		
Cook, Ephraim	3	1	3		
Curtiss, David	1	1	2		
Jackson, John	1	3	4		
Wright, Seth	2	2	4		
Linley, Sam'l	3	1	2		
Gleason, Ephraim	2	1	5		
Cammel, John	1	2	1		
Hunt, Daniel	2		2		
Hunt, Daniel, 2d	1	4	3		
Marsh, Jessie	2	3	7		
Hucheson, Ezri	1	1	2		
Hucheson, Ezri, 2d	2	2	3		
Marvin, Joseph	1	1	2		
Huchenson, Daniel	1	3	5		
Jackson, Elijah	2	2	4		
Manfield, Ichabod	1		1		
Curtiss, Josiah	1	1	2		
Curtiss, Seth	2		2		
Cartright, Sam'l	5	2	6		
Abels, Slumon	1	3	5		
Abels, Elijah	1		1		
Howe, Jeremiah	1	2	1		
Norton, Medad	1	1	3		
Collins, Cyprian	3	2	2		
Smith, Chilleab	2	1	3		
Standley, William	2		4		
Lewis, Thomas	3	4	4		
Newel, Nathaniel	1	1	2		
Standley, Jessee	2	2	4		
Rice, Daniel	2		4		
Norton, Bird Eye	3	1	3		
Norton, Samuel	2	1	6		
Dorod, John	2	1	3		
Norton, Ebenezer	2	2	4		
Davis, Abraham	1		1		
Goodwin, Abigal	3	1	4		
Lewis, Elihu	3	3	3	1	
Lewis, Nehemeah	3	1	2		
Orsborn, Samuel	2	1	3		
Markham, Ezekiel	1	4	3		
Cole, John	2	1	7		
Gillet, Stephen	1	1	1		
Marsh, Jonothan	1		3		
Loomis, Joseph	1	2	3		
Steel, Isaac	1	1	5		
Starling, John	1	3	6		
Merrills, Sarah		2	2		

LITCHFIELD TOWN—con.

NAME OF HEAD OF FAMILY	Free white males of 16 years and upward, including heads of families	Free white males under 16 years	Free white females, including heads of families	All other free persons	Slaves
Cook, William	2		3		
Henshaw, Benjamin	5	1	2		
Chub, Rachel			3		
Kellogg, Abraham	1		2		
Chub, Mindwell			3		
Kellogg, Moses	2	1	3		
Kellogg, Abraham	1		2		
Merrills, Joel	1	1	2		
Kellogg, Noah	2	3	4		
Marsh, Moses	1		2		
Sheldon, Ely	1	3	3		
Ryder, Syvester	2	2	1		
Merrills, Phinehas	1	1	3		
Chapen, Phinehas	1	1	1		
Russel, Josiah	2	1	2		
Addams, Phinehas	2	1	2		
Homer, James	4		3		
Creny, John	1	2	4		
Jewel, Oliver	3	5	6		
Jewell, Oliver, 2d	1	2	2		
Dorsey, Jeremiah	2	2	2		
Uri, John	2		1		
Parmerter, William	1		2		
Herrick, Mary		2	2		
Moore, Daniel	2		1		
Moore, John	4	3	3		
Lee, Samuel	3	1	2		
Hutcheson, Asa	1	2	4		
Stanton, Elijah	3	2	5		
Mechum, Barnibus	1		2		
Meigs, Janne	2	1	3		
Weed, Belden	1	1	2		
Bruster, John	2	2	2		
Edgarton, Nathan	1	1	3		
Esmon, Nathan	1	1	3		
Avery, Sanford	1		2		
Tush, Joseph	1	1	4		
Johnson, Benjamin	1	2	2		
Reed, Ebenezer	1		2		
Reed, Peter	3		3		
Bingham, Daniel	2	1	5		
Bingham, Daniel, 2d	2	3	4		
Russel, John	2	3	3		
Smith, Gideon	3	1	3		
Sardam, Tunus	1	2	4		
Sardam, Andrus	4	1	3		
Harris, James	2	4	5		
Dutcher, Gabriel	1	3	4		
Beeman, Samuel	2	2	4		
Wood, John	1	2	4		
Nichols, Philoe	2		4		
Nichols, Caleb	4	1	3		
Dutcher, Ruluf, 3d	1	3	2		
Hinsman, Benjamin	1		1		
Sheldon, Elisha, 2d	1	2	3		
Abanatha, Jiles	1		2		
Sheldon, Elisha	1	1	1		4
Breant, Alexander	1	2	2		
Jacobs, Salley		1	1		
Vandooser, Abraham	3		3		
Peck, Isaac	2		5		
White, Herman	1	4	3		
Mallery, Samuel	1		3		
Doolittle, Jessee	1		2		
Griffin, Ezri	1		3		
Rogers, Jonathan	2	2	2		
Potter, Phinehas	2	2	3		
Doolittle, Jessee	2	1	2		
Potter, David	1		1		
Potter, Ebenezer	1	2	6		
Whealer, Nathan	1	1	2		
Potter, Daniel	1	3	2		
Potter, Elizer	1	2	7		
Whealer, Benjamin	1	2	2		
Miles, Lewis	1	1	1		
Rowley, Ebenezer	1	3	4		
Bragnord, Othniah	1	2	4		
Hatten, Stephen	1	2	4		
Jop, John	1	2	1		
Shaw, John	1	1	4		
Thompson, Zebulon	1	1	5		
Rogers, Simeon	1	1	4		
Wait, John	1		1		
Case, William	1	4	6		
Kellogg, Elizer	3	4	5		
Balcome, John	1	1	5		
Goodrich, Seth	1	3	5		
More, Abijah	2	3	6		
Whilford, Robert	1	1	2		
Cook, Richard	1	2	2		
Raydon, Ezri	1	3	5		
Catlin, Abraham	1	3	4		
Cleavland, Rufus	1	5	3		
Woodruff, Josiah	2	2	6		
Wead, Daniel	1	2	2		

LITCHFIELD TOWN—con.

NAME OF HEAD OF FAMILY	Free white males of 16 years and upward, including heads of families	Free white males under 16 years	Free white females, including heads of families	All other free persons	Slaves
Allyn, Cloe		2	4		
Weed, Jonas	1	1	6		
Phelps, Elkane	3	2	6		
Sweet, James	2	3	5		
Roberts, Poll	1	3	3		
Kellogg, Daniel	1	1	4		
Croe, Nathaniel	1	1	2		
Croe, John	1		1		
Mills, David	1		1		
More, King	1		3		
Barmer, James	1		3		
Messenger, Isaac	3	1	5		
Messenger, Elisha	1	1	4		
Messenger, Simeon	3	3	4		
Messenger, Moses	1	2	2		
Humphrey, Benona	4	1	3		
Merrit, John	2	2	5		
Merrit, James	2	2	5		
Case, Abner	1	5	4		
More, David	1	4	3		
Bliss, Jad	2		5		
Rice, Wait	1	3	2		
Jones, Evan	1	1	1		
Case, Simeon	1	1	2		
Parrey, John	1	1	3		
Copet, Marten	2	3	4		
Copet, Timothy	1	3	4		
Miner				10	
Harris, William	2		4		
Miller, Sam	1	1	4		
Case, Simeon	1	1	3		
Emmons, Jonathan	3		1		
Muxum, Benjamin	1	1	4		
Willer, William	1		1		
Geer, Charles	1	1	1		
Dotee, Sarah	1		3		
Knibloe, William	2		2		
Knibloe, Joseph	2		3		
Hatch, Ebezer	2	1	4		
Stafford, John	1	2	2		
Tobey, Jonathan	1	1	1		
Nash, William	1		2		
Tobey, Elisha	5	4	5		
Dillenor, Stephen	2	1	7		
Dillenor, Thomas	1	1	2		
Dextor, Silas	1	1	3		
Cate				8	
Brockwey, Watston	2	3	2		
Hunter, Ebenezer	1		2		
Norton, Gideon	1		1		
Willer, Daniel	1	2	3		
Tober, Daniel	1	2	6		
Muller, Samuel	1	4	4		
Tewisdel, John	1	4	3		
Winchel, Daniel	2	2	4		
Burgh, John	1	4	2		
Taylor, John	2		2		
Burgher, David	1	1	3		
Miller, Ebenezer	3	3	5		
Burgher, Sim	2	3	4		
Strong, John	2	3	5		
Griswell, Shubal	3		2		
Bissel, Elijah	1		1		
Blake, Elijah	2	4	3		
Bissel, Benjamin	3	1	3		
Gaylor, Nehemiah	2	1	4		
Gaylor, Joseph	1	2	2		
Gillet, Jabes	4	1	7		
Soper, David	3	2	3		
Woodward, Samuel	1	2	4		
Gillet, John	1	4	3		
Badelle, William	3	4	6		
White, Amy			3		
Mills, Sam'l J	2	3	4	1	
Cook, Jessee	3		3		
Gaylor, Elijah	3	1	2		
Marther, Zachariah	2	2	6		
Bissel, Hezekiah	1	3	3		2
Bissel, Ezekiel	1	3	2		
Bissel, Eliphet	1	2	1		
Bissel, Ebenezer	1	4	2		
Loomis, Timothy	1	4	5		
Kelsey, Rachel			2		
Kelsey, Nathan	1		2		
Elsworth, Thomas	2	2	4	1	
Rood, Moses	1	2	2		
Rood, Ebenezer	2	3	5		
Buel, Jonathan	4	1	2		
Tharp, David	3	3	2		
Logan, Samuel	2		6		
Seeley, John	1	1	6		
Wadhams, John	3	2	3		
Norton, Ashbel	1	1	2		
Buel, Jonathan	1	1	1		
Cook, Amasa	4		2		

LITCHFIELD COUNTY—Continued.

LITCHFIELD TOWN—con.

NAME OF HEAD OF FAMILY.	Free white males of 16 years and upward, including heads of families.	Free white males under 16 years.	Free white females, including heads of families.	All other free persons.	Slaves.
Norvel, William	1	1	2		
Lyman, Moses	4	2	5		
Cook, Moses	1	1	2		
Hagan, James	1		1		
Simmons, Perer	1	3	4		
Farnham, Peter	2		1		
Wheeler, Josiah	2		1		
Waterman, David	23	3	4		
Hawley, Luther	1	5	3	1	
Mingo, William				1	
Porter, Joshua	3		5		4
Wheeler, Lemuel	3		2	1	2
Coskins, Amos	1	2	2		
Davis, Jacobus	3	1	6	1	
Lord, Joel	2	1	3		
Lee, Robert W	1	2	4		
Ball, Daniel	4	2	4		
Griswold, John	1				
Williams, Polley			1		
Chittendon, Timothy	2	1	4		
Chittendon, Timothy, 2d	1	1	2		
Everts, Submit			1		
Everts, Maryan	2	1	3		
Eldridge, John	3	3	3		
Everts, Nathan	5	1	8		
Catoe				1	
Marsh, George	2	2	3		
Porter, Nicholas	2	2	3	1	
Atwood, Jedediah	1	2	4	1	
Miles, Stephen	1	1	3		
Beyhal, Richard	2	1	2		
Cook, Daniel	1		1		
Cook, Ezekiel	1	1	2		
Cook, Simeon	1		1		
Touslery, Joseph	2	1	4		
White, Israhel	3		4		
White, John	1	3	3		
Wood, Elijah	2	2	5		
Tousley, John	1	2	3		
Colkins, Justice	1	2	6		
Colkins, Silvanus	1	1	1		
Ware, John	1	1	3		
Willamson, John	1	3	1		
Hill, John	1		1		
Barriss, David	2		1		
Martin, Eliphalet	2	1	3		
Howe, John	2	1	2		
Gilbert, John	2	2	1		
Lyman, David	1	6	3		
Curtis, Job	3	1	4		
Lyman, Josiah	1	1	2		
Morris, Daniel		1	2		
Miller, David			2		
Cole Samuel	2		1		
Omsted, Roswell	2	2	2		
More, Josiah	2	2	4		
Dutton, John	2	2	5		
Watson, Levi	1	1	3		
Goodwin, Isaac	2	3	5		
Coe, Seth	1	1	4		
Foot, Roger	2	1	1		
Loomis, Brigadeer	1	1	4		
Austen, Isaac	1		4		
Soper, Joel	2	1	1		
Elmon, Alexander	1	5	3		
Dickenson, Susannah			4		
Austen, Joel	1	3	3		
Austen, Robert	1	3	4		
Austen, Reuben	1		1		
Lyman, Francis	1	2	4		
Tuttle, Elisha	2	4	4		
Hills, Justice	1	3	3		
Francis, Asahel	3		4		
Bunnel, Fradrick	2	1	2		
Porter, Benjamin	2	2	4		
Cuff					2
Tompson Solomon	1		1		
Thompson, Elisha	4	1	4		
Miles, Samuel	2	2	3		
Munson, Thomas E	2	1	6		
Thompson, James	2	1	5		
Starr, Ephraim	3	3	7		
Ives, Joseph	4	2	3		
Thompson, David	7		4		
Pratt, Silas	3	2	4		
Gordon, Samuel	1	2	2		
Lewis, Judy	1		1		
Merrills, Nathaniel	1	1	2		
Merriman, Ichabud	1	3	3		
Peck, Zebulon	1	2	1		
Hurlburt, Gidian	2	2	3		
Parmerley, David	1	1	3		
Veal, Joseph	2		3		
Landon, John	1	3	5		
Crompton, Ebenezer	3	4	4		
Clark, Lyman	2	2	4		
Marsh, James	2	2	2		
Webster, Charles	1	3	2		
Orton, Sam1	3	1	5		
Stoddard, Briant	1	3	5		
Marsh, Elijah	3	2	3		
Marsh, Ambrose	4		2		
Marsh, Titus	1	4	1		
Marsh, Thomas	1		2		
Peck, Cornelius	1		1		
Atwater, Abel	1	2	4		
Birdwell, Stephen	2	1	6		
Hart, Benjamin	1	2	6		
Marsh, Roger	5	3	3		
Humerston, Noah	3	2	3		
Peck, Reeve	2		1		
Peck, Asahel	1	2	1		
Hotchkiss, Eliphalet	1	3	1		
Landon, Seth	2	1	5		
Marsh, Rhoda	1	1	6		
Stone, James	2	1	4		
Lord, Leynde	4	1	4		
Addams, Andrew	2	1	5		
Punderson, Ahimea	1				
Beach, Jessee	1				
Cleaver, Tobias	1				
Gatta, John I	1				
Sterling, Elisha	1				
Barnard, Hersey	1				
Taylor, William	1				
Addams, Andrew	3	3	5	1	2
Griffith, Edward	1		1		
Champion, Judas	1		4		1
Barnes, Amos	1	2	3		
Smith, Reuben	3		6		
Peck, Reeve	1	3	2		
Baldwin, Daniel	1	3	6		
Baldwin, Nathaniel	3	3	3		
Baldwin, Patience			3		
Smith, Matthew	2		4		
Baldwin, Samuel	3		3		
Smith, Israel	1		3		
Baldwin, Samuel	1	2	3		
Bailey, Andrew	1	4	2		
Hurd, David	3	4	3		
Hall, Aseph	2	1	2		
Henman, Phenehas	3	2	5		
Humphry, Ashbel	4	1	2		
Kimbal, Jacob	2	3	5		
Standley, Timothy	1	2	3		
Standley, Elisha	1	2	4		
Filley, Jessee	1		3		
Fox, Stephen	1	1	2		
Covel, David	1	2	4		
Tyler, Abel	1	2	3		
Branton, Michael	2	2	1		
William, Isaac	2	1	2		
Parsons, Benjamin	1	5	2		
Pettibone, Abraham	3		4		1
Douglas, Samuel	3	1	8		
Ensign, Eliphalet	1	3	4		
Spensor, Nathaniel	2	4	5		
Spensor, James	1	2	4		
Basset, William	1	1	4		
Spensor, Michael	1	1	2		
Spenser, Ashbel	1	2	5		
Spensor, John	1	2	2		
Thompson, Eliphras	1	2	3		
Coles, Asa	2		3		
Coles, Theodore	2	3	2		
Tyler, Abial	2	1	1		
Lomise, Isaac	2	2	2		
Loomise, Israel	2	2	5		
Jones, Benjamin	1	1	3		
Wells, Timothy	2	2	2		
Woodruff, Solomon	3	4	6		
Merrells, Verijah	3	1	2		
Austin, Aaron	4	2	7		
Ives, Joseph	1	2	4		
Goodrich, Isaac	1	3	4		
Lord, Frederick	1	2	2		
Tyler, Jedior	2	5	3		
Gaylor, Wait	1		3		
Tyler, Amos	1	1	2		
Warren, Mea	1				
Wood, Elijah	2	2	5		
Barnes, Reuben	1	4	2		
Barnes, Timty	3		3		
Batterson, Hezekia	2	2	3		
Harvey, Joel	4	1	4		
Elvendolf, Tobias	1	2	2	1	3
Newel, Theodore	1		3		
Hensdale, Jacob	1	2			
Rowe, Solomon	1		2		
Rood, David	2	3	4		
Rood, Roger	1	4	2		
Granger, Phinehas	1	1	1		
Lawrence, Nathan	2	1	3		
Detne, Benja	1	1	3		
Benton, John	1	1	1		
Hewit, Gershom	1	2	7		
Pierce, Thomas	3		3		
Pierce, Amos	2	4	5		
Pierce, Sam1	2	3	1	1	1
Pierce, Pelahat	3	1	3	1	
Dunham, James	2	1	2		
Dunham, Isaac	1	2	1		
Pierce, Edward	1	1	1		
Fenn, Theophelus	2		4		
Fellows, Stephen	1	3	2		
Higbey, Isaac	1	1	3		
Bacon, Andrew	3	2	6		
Whitney, Cornelus	1		4		
Feeman, John	3	2	4		
Capen, Timothy	1	1	4		
Lawrence, Josiah	1		1		
Lawrence, Abel	1	1	1		
Green. Willard	2	1	3		
Burrel, Charles	2	1	2		2
Burroll, Obed	2	2	5		1
Green, Sam1	1	2	3		
Towner, Sarah	1	1	3		
Bailey, Ithamon	1	1	2		
Towner, Abi		2	1		
Beach, Linus	3	1	4		
Beach, Mines	1		1		
Ives, Levi	2	2	3		
Benten, Josiah	1		2		
Balwin, Elisha	1	1	3		
Newton, Isaac	2	2	3		
Beach, Israel	1	3	2		
Wetton, Elijah	2	1	3		
Humphrey, David	3	1	4		
Humphrey, Samuel	3		7		
Humphrey, Charles	1	1	4		
Wallen, John	1		2		
Wallen, Thomas	1	1	2		
Wallen, James	1	3	4		
Hill, James	1		8		
Paine, Jessee	1	1	4	3	
Wllen, David	1	1	4		
Coller, Olliver	2	2	2		
Wallen, Daniel	1	2	2		
Fox, Levi	1	1	2		
Coller, John	1		3		
Coller, Isaac	1		3		
Henman, Asher	3	3	3		
Chaugorn, Mary			2		
Merrills, Benajah	2		4		
Roberts, William	2	1	3		
Willcox, Asa	1	3	5		
Tayler, David	1	2	2		
Willcox, Philander	2		6		
Clark, William	1	1	2		
Hill, AGift	4	1	5		
Richard, Pelatiah	1	2	4		
Mills, Benjamin	3	1	4		
Mills, Dudley	1		1		
Merrills, Daniel	1		4		
Merrills, Daniel	1	1	4		
Barns, Roswell	3		1		
Humphrey, Noah	1	5	3		
Humphrey, Abraham	2	1	7		
Pain, Ezri	1		2		
Gibbs, Gersham	2	3	3		
Gibbs, Philoe	1	1	1		
Plumb, Sarah		1	2		
Griswold, Timothy	2		3		
Frisbey, Noah	2		1		
Frisbey, Noah	2		4		
Welch, David	5		1	2	2
Page, Asa, 2d	1	1	3		
Ackley, Sam1	1	1	2		
Landon, Daniel	1	1	2		
Smith, Rebecca	2		3		
Landon, Daniel	1	1	4		
Bradley, Ellihue	1	2	3		
Dickinson, Olliver	1	5	2		
Stewart, Nathan	2		9		
Buel, Eunice	2		5		
Welch, John	1	1	2		1
Carter, Sam1	1	1	2		
Clemmons, Abel	1	1	3		
Robinson, Jerard	1	1	3		
Dudley, William	1	1	2		
Landon, Abner	3		3		
Ludington, Stephen	1	2	1		
Gibs, Nathan	1				
Gibs, Lydia			3		
Brown, Stephen	1	1	4		
Gibs, Zadock	1	2	5		
Veal, Daniel	1	1	2		
Catlin, Charles	4	1	5		

LITCHFIELD COUNTY—Continued.

LITCHFIELD TOWN—con.

NAME OF HEAD OF FAMILY.	Free white males of 16 years and upward, including heads of families.	Free white males under 16 years.	Free white females, including heads of families.	All other free persons.	Slaves.
Graves, William	1	3	2		
Day, John	1		2		
Morgan, Daniel	1		1		
Orsborn, Joseph	1		3		
Lyman, Moses	1				
Bissel, John	2	1	4		
Page, Asa	1	3	3		
Page, David	1	3	3		
Smith, Benajah	2	2	4		
Page, Abel	1		2		
Catlin, David	1	4	3		
Can, Sarah		1	1		
Glass, John	1	2	2		
Smedley, Gideon	2	1	4		
Spencer, Ephraim	1	2	3		
Cane, Edward	2		6		
Doolittle, Benjamin	3	3	7		
Doolittle, Fraderick	1	2	3		
Churchel, Jonathan	1	2	5		
Beach, Abner	2	3	4		
Beach, Noah	1	2	2		
Ward, William	2	2	5		
Plumb, Ebenezer	3	4	6		
Colver, Joshua	1	1	3		
Strong, Anna	2		4		
Strong, Anna	1		1		
Palms, Andrew	1	1	3		
Buell, Solomon	1	3	4		
Russel, John	1	5	2		
Stone, Thomas W	1		2		
Griswold, James	1	1			
Ribborn, Jehiel	1	2	6		
Plumb, Stephen	1	3	5		
Webster, James	1		3		
Hislop, Alford	1	1	4		
Stoddard, John	3		5		
Collins, William	1	1	3		
Beach, Losior	1	2	3		
Griswold, Syphrona	1	2	2		
Tylford, Philathia	1	2	2		
Palmer, Job	1		1		
Gilbert, Calvin	1		1		
Beach, Sabin	1	3	5		
Beach, David	3		3		
Gilbert, Abner	1	2	2		
Coe, Levi	1	1	1		
Coe, Thomas	2	1	2		
Pardey, Eli	1	3	2		
Landon, Nathaniel	1	1	1		
Landon, Martha		3	2		
Orsborn, Jacob	2		1		
Orsborn, John	2	1	5		
Orsborn, Jeremiah	1	1	2		
Buel, Clive	1	2	3		

NEW MILFORD TOWN.

NAME OF HEAD OF FAMILY.	Free white males of 16 years and upward, including heads of families.	Free white males under 16 years.	Free white females, including heads of families.	All other free persons.	Slaves.
Bostwick, Elisha	1	2	2		6
Bostwick, Oliver	1	1	1		
Bostwick, Elizur	1	2	1		
Bostwick, Joseph, 1st	3	1	3		
Bostwick, Samuel	1		4		
Bostwick, Reuben, 1st	2	1	3		
Bostwick, Ben Ruggles	1	2	3		
Bostwick, Benjamin	3		2		
Bostwick, Jonathan	8		4		
Bostwick, Isaac	4	1	2		
Bostwick, Reuben, 2d	2	1	4		
Bostwick, Salmon	1		2		
Bostwick, David, 2d	1		1		
Bostwick, Amos	1	1	3		
Bostwick, Joseph, 2d	3		4		
Bostwick, Abel	1		2		
Bostwick, Zackeriah	1	2	2		
Bostwick, Ichabod	2	1	5		
Bostwick, Martin	1	2	3		
Bostwick, David, 1st	2	2	3		
Bostwick, Nathan	1	3	4		
Bostwick, John	1		1		
Bostwick, Medad	1	2	1		
Boardman, Sherman	3		4	3	
Bordman, Daniel	4		2	1	
Baldwin, Ebenezer	3	4	5		
Baldwin, Theophilus	2	2	5		
Bennett, Edward	3	4	4		
Brownson, Thomas	1		1		
Brownson, Reuben	1	1	3		
Botsford, Ena	2	3	5		
Beach, Ebenezer	1	2	3		
Bishop, Eler	1	2	4		
Britterfield, Simeon	1	1	1		
Beach, Isaac	2		2		
Baldwin, Jonah	1				
Baker, Jesse	1	1	3		
Baldwin, Isaac	1	2	6		

NEW MILFORD TOWN—continued.

NAME OF HEAD OF FAMILY.	Free white males of 16 years and upward, including heads of families.	Free white males under 16 years.	Free white females, including heads of families.	All other free persons.	Slaves.
Baldwin, Abiel	1	2	3		
Baldwin, Israel	1		3		
Baldwin, John	1	1	4		
Beacher, Elizur, 2d	3		3		
Beacher, Nathaniel	2		3		
Bell, Jeams	1	2	2		
Buck, Enoch	3	3	4		
Bennett, Caleb	1		2		
Bennett, Gershom	1	2	1		
Buckingham, Benjamin	3	1	5		1
Botsford, Nathan	2		2		
Brownson, Noah	3	3	2		
Brownson, Mathew	2	1	2		
Brownson, Benjamin	1	3	3		
Bennett, Abijah	2	1	2		
Beard, David	1		1		
Buck, Sam Beebee	1	1	6		
Buck, Jeames	2	1	3		
Benson, Benjamin, 1st	2		2		
Benson, Benjamin, 2d	1	3	5		1
Buck, Asaph	1		2		
Bradshaw, William	2	3	5		
Bears, Ezra	1	1	2		
Bears, Jeames, 1st	2		3		
Bears, Jeames, 2d	1		1		
Buck, Ezekiel	1		1		
Buck, Benton	1		3		
Buck, Israel	2	3	2		
Buck, Ephraim	1		1		
Bristol, Daniel	1	1	4		
Beach, Caleb	1	1	2		
Bradley, Moses	2		7		
Benedict, Aaron	3	2	4		
Beardsley, Silas	1		1		
Brownson, Asa	1	1	2		
Brownson, Ziba	2	2	3		
Botts, Reuben	5	3	5		1
Bristol, Richard	6	1	4		
Baldwin, Asahel	2	3	5		
Bradley, Timothy	2	4	5		
Brownson, Isaac	1		4		
Burwell, Stephen	1	1	2		
Barnes, Sarah		1	3		
Beach, Abijah Heny	2		2		
Baldwin, Simeon	1		3		
Bull, David	1		4		
Bryan, Nathan	1	2	5		
Bulkley, John	1		1		
Bristol, Arial	1	2	2		
Bass, Josiah	1	1	4		
Buckingham, Abel	2	5	2		
Beardsley, David	3		1		
Bushly, Ebenezer	1	2	3		
Bass, Daniel	1	1	1		
Burnham, Woolcott	1		5		
Booth, Elisha	1	1	4		
Betts, William	2		3		
Bobbett, Lemuel	1	2	2		
Bobbett, William	1	2	1		
Butler, Ezekiel	1		1		
Bush, Joel	2	5	2		
Benson, Bryan	1	1	1		
Benson, Ambrose	1		2		
Beacher, David	2	1	3		
Boardman, Homer	1	2	2		
Baldwin, Nathaniel G	1				
Beacher, John	2	3	8		
Bosworth, Joseph	1	5	3		
Camp, Job	2	4	2		
Couch, Samuel	3	2	3		
Collins, Amos	1		2		
Canfield, Ithamar	2	1	1	1	
Camp, Heath	2	1	3		
Clark, William	2	3	3		
Chatfield, Levi	1	5	2		
Clark, Daniel	3		5		
Clark, Isaac	1	1	4		
Comstack, Achilles	1		3		
Chittenden, Stephen	1	3	3		
Comstack, John	3		2		
Canfield, Heath	1	1	3		
Comstack, Samuel	2	1	2		
Camp, David	2	1	2		
Cole, Ichabod	1		2		
Chittenden, Giles	2	1	1		
Canfield, Philor	2	2	3		
Clark, Thomas, 2d	3		4		
Clark, Edmond	2	2	4		
Camp, Daniel	1	2	3		
Canfield, Jeremiah	2		1		
Canfield, John	1	2	4		
Canfield, Lemuel	1	4	3		
Cole, Nathaniel	2	2	4		
Couch, John, 1st	3	3	4		
Cole, Solomon	1		1		

NEW MILFORD TOWN—continued.

NAME OF HEAD OF FAMILY.	Free white males of 16 years and upward, including heads of families.	Free white males under 16 years.	Free white females, including heads of families.	All other free persons.	Slaves.
Camp, Riverius	1	3	1		
Camp, Israel	1		2		
Canfield, Ira	1		2		
Cole, Jesse	1	2	2		
Cole, Timothy	1		2		
Canfield, Oliver	5	1	3		
Carpenter, John	2	5	2		
Camp, Enos, 1st	1		1		
Camp, Enos, 2d	2	2	2		
Canfield, Samuel	4	2	3		2
Clark, Thomas, 1st	2	1	3		
Cable, David	1	1	3		
Clark, Richard	1	1	3		
Camp, John	1				
Clark, Jeames	1				
Canfield, Eunice			3		
Couch, John, 2d	1	1	3		
Cole, John	3	1	2		
Canfield, Elijah	1	2	4		
Clark, Joseph	1	1	2		
Crane, Isaac C	3				
Crane, Ezra	1		1		
Canfield, Azeriah	1	1	3		
Canfield, Levi	1	1	3		
Clark, John	1	2	4		
Camp, Nathan	1	4	3		
Collar, Isaac	1	2	6		
Corbin, Philip	1		2		
Canfield, Abel	1	2	3		
Canfield, David, 2d	1	1	7		
Canfield, David, 1st	3		1		
Deforest, Isaac	2	1	4		
Dean, William	1	2	1		
Dunning, Samuel	2	2	5		
Downes, Jonathan	3	1	2		
Downes, Lemuel	1	1	6		
Downes, Thomas	1		5		
Downes, Elijah	1	3	1		
Dayton, Eli	2	2	2		
Dunning, Ezra	1	2	2		
Deavenport, Benjamin	1	2	3		
Davies, Sarah			3		
Deavenport, David	1	2	3		
Deavenport, John	2		4		
Downes, Jonathan, 2d	1		4		
Everts, Stephen	1	2	4		
Earle, Benjamin	1	2	2		
Everit, Daniel	1	4	3		
Edward, Ebenezer	1	1	3		
Edward, Edward	1	1	5		
Ferris, David	2	1	2		
Ferris, Amasa	1	2	3		
Fenn, Joab	2		1		
Feris, Zachariah	3	3	4		
Fairchild, Abraham	1	4	5		
Fairchild, Eleazer, 1st	2	1	2		
Fairchild, Eleazer, 2d	1	2	1		
Fairchild, Abel	1	2	3		
Farrand, Samuel	2	4	4		
Ferris, Joseph	2	1	1		
Fenton, Solomon	1	2	5		
Fits Jerald, Partrick					
Ferris, Stephen	2	1	3		
Firman, Richard	2	3	4		
Fisher, N. Beacher	1		2		
Ford, Jonathan	1	1	3		
Gillet, Abel	1	1	3		
Ghoram, Phineas	1		3		
Gunn, Gidion	1	1	4		
Gunn, Abner	5		3	1	
Gunn, Epenetus	1	1	3		
Garlick, Read	2		3		
Garlick, Edmund	1		2		
Garlick, Samuel	1	1	5		
Gaylord, Benjamin	3	3	3		
Gaylord, Aaron	1	3	3		
Gaylord, Nathan	1	3	3		
Gaylord, Ebenezer	1	2	2		
Gunn, Abel	2	2	4		
Griswold, Stanley	1		2		
Ghorrum, David	2		1		
Garlick, Heath	1		3		
Gunn, Nathan	1		3		
Gaylord, William	3	3	2		
George, Jarus			3	2	
Gratis, Nancy				1	
Green, Jarus	1	1	2	4	
Gilbert, Hezekiah	1		4		
Granger, George	1	1	2		
Hill, David	1	1	4		
Hartwell, Samuel	2	3	3		
Holmes, Jeremiah	1		3		
Holmes, Nathan	1	2	3		
Hayes, Thomas	3	3	5		

LITCHFIELD COUNTY—Continued.

NEW MILFORD TOWN—continued.

NAME OF HEAD OF FAMILY.	Free white males of 16 years and upward, including heads of families.	Free white males under 16 years.	Free white females, including heads of families.	All other free persons.	Slaves.
Hendricks, Andrew	1	3	2		
Hunt, Lewis	1	2	4		
Hayt, Nathan	1	1	5		
Hitchcock, William	1	2	1		
Hustfield, Charles	1		2		
Hotchkiss, Ebenezer	1	1	2		
Hine, Noble	3	2	9		
Hitchcock, David	2	2	3		
Hull, John	2		5		
Hill, Silas	4	2	3		
Hine, Daniel	1	2	4		
Hill, Solomon, 1st	1		3		
Hallock, William	1	4	2		
Hartwell, Joseph	2	1	2		
Hurd, William	2	1	3		
Hurd, Abijah	1				
Hurd, Hinman	1		1		
Hine, Abel	5	1	4		
Hine, Stephen	1	3	1		
Hollister, Abel	5	1	4		
Hatch, Isaac	2	3	4		
Hotech, John	1	2	2		
Hill, Samuel, 2d	2	1	3		
Hill, Samuel	1		2		
Hitchcock, Ira	1	1	2		
Hawley, Joseph	1	2	4		
Higgins, Joseph	1		3		
Hornet, John	1	1	1		
Hendick, Eleazer	1	1	3		
Hurlbutt, David	1		3		
Hurlbutt, Hezekiah	1	1	1		
Hotchkiss, Solomon	1	1	2		
Hurlbutt, Gamaliel	1				
Hymes, Jeames	1		1		
Hitchcock, Nathan	1	3	3		
Hunt, Theophilus	1	2	3		
Hitchcock, Aaron	2		4		
Hubbel, Watrous	2		2		
Hitchcock, Daniel		2	2		
Hallock, Benjamin	3	2	3		
Hill, Solomon, 2d	1	4	2		
Jeasup, Jeames	1	1	4		
Jackson, Heny	2	3	3		
Jackson, David	1	2	5		
Jackson, Isaac	1		1		
Johnson, Isaac	1				
Jacklin, Thaddeus			5		2
Johnson, Peter	1		5		
Ingersol, Buggs	1	2	3		
Knowles, William, 1st	1		1		
Keeler, Ralph	1	2	3		
Knap, Joshua	2	2	2		
Knap, Francis	1	3	4		
Knowles. Arthur, 1st	2	2	3		
Knowles, William, 2d	1		5		
Keeney, Elias	1	1	5		
Keeler, Ebener	1	1	2		
Ketchum, Aaron	1	2	4		
Knowles, Arthur, 2d	1		2		
Lake, Jeames	1		3		
Lyon, Lois			3		
Lory, Chauncy	1	1	1		
Lynde, Daniel	2				
Lamson, William, 1st	1		1		
Lamson, William, 2d	3	2	4		
Lamson, Silas	1	3	1		
Lockwood, Josiah	2	1	1		
Lockwood, Nathaniel	2	2	5		
Lockwood, David	1	2	2		
Lynde, Joseph	1		1		
Leach, Jeames	1		1		
Lockwood, Jeames	1	1	3		
Lockwood, Israel	1	2	2		
Lockwood, Nathan	1		1		
Lowly, Volentine	2				
Lamson, Sarah			2		
Morehouse, Stephen	1	2	3		
Miles, Justus	4		1		
Morehouse, John, 1st	3	1	3		
Miles, Stephen, 2d	3	3	4		
Mygatt, Ben Star	1	1	3		
McMehan, Cornelius	1	3	4		
Marsh, John	1	4	4		
Merwin, Abel	2	2	2		
Mead, Samuel	1	3	4		
Morehouse, Lemuel	1				
Morehouse, Stephen, 1st	1	1	2		
Mygatt, Noah	2	3	1		
Merwin, David, 2d	2	1	3		
Marsh, Samuel	1	5	3		
Marsh, Joseph	1	2	5		
Millan, Jeames	1		2		
Merwin, John	2	2	5		
Merwin, David, 1st	3	2	5		
Merwin, Stephen	1	2	4		
Mygatt, Jonathan	3		6		
Masters, N. Shelton	3	2	2		
Marchant, Ezra	3		2		
Morehouse, Benjamin	1	1	1		
Morehouse, John, 2d	1		5		
McEwen, William	1		2		
McEwen, John, 1st	1		2		
McEwen, John, 2d	1	1	1		
Mead, Daniel	1	1	3		
Murray, Nathan	2	1	2		
Milligan, George	1	1	1		
Murray, Elisha	2		1		
Morehouse, Squire	1		1		
Mead, Benjamin	2		4		
Meker, Chauncy	1	1	2		
McKentin, Duncan	1	1	3		
Northrop, Joel	3		4		
Northrop, David	3	4	5		2
Noble, David	1	1	3		
Noble, Daniel	1	2	2		
Nichelson, Angus	4	3	6		3
Noble, Sylvanus	2		2		
Noble, Wakefield	1				
Noble, Ezra	3	2	4		
Nichols, Isaac	4	3	6		
Nichols, Daniel	1	1	6		
Norton, Robert	3	1	3		
Noble, Elisha	1	3	2		
Noble, Asahel	1		1		
Noble, Sherman	1	2	3		
Norton, Rowland	1	1	2		
Northrop, Caleb	1	2	2		
Northrop, Solomon	2	1	4		
Nichols, Samuel	1		1		
Nichols, Robert	1	1	3		
Owen, Daniel	1	1	6		
Osborn, Stephen	1	4	7		
Ovaitt, Thomas	1	2	2		
Olmstead, Richard	1	1	5		
Olmstead, David	1	1	4		
Ovaitt, Samuel	1	1	3		
Ovaitt, John	1	1	3		
Otis, Christopher	2		1		
Pickett, Daniel	2	1	2		
Platt, Ephraim	1	5	2		
Payne, William	5	3	6		
Picket, Abijah	1	3	5		
Platt, Jeremiah	3	1	2		
Prince, Samuel	1	3	3		
Prince, Edmond Howel	2	2	5		
Prince, Asa	2	2	5		
Phippany, Jeames	2	1	4		
Phippany, Archibald	2	1	1		
Platt, Epinetus	2	1	4		
Platt, Gideon	1	2	2		
Peck, Joseph	2		2		
Platt, Nehemiah	2	1	1		
Prout, Jesse	2	1	4		
Platt, Epinetus, 2d	1	2	3		
Peet, Elnathan	1		2		
Peet, Daniel	2	1	2		
Peet, Joseph	1		1		
Peet, Ithiel	1	2	2		
Peet, Samuel	3	1	2		
Peet, George	1	3	2		
Phippeney, Nehemiah	1		1		
Platt, Truman	1	1	2		
Platt, John	1	2	3		
Phillips, Philip					2
Phillips, Reuben					7
Philips, Samuel					6
Philips, Jeruel					4
Phenk, Daniel	1	1	1		
Peet, Lemuel	2	2	5		
Porter, Nathaniel	1		4		
Porter, Philo	1	1	2		
Palmer, Polly			1		
Peet, Nathan	1	3	4		
Peet, Thaddeus	3	2	5		
Payne, Ezekiel	2	1	1		
Rundle, Jeremiah	1		2		
Richmond, Ephraim	2	2	5		
Richmond, Jonathan	1	1	5		
Richmond, Edmond	1	3	1		
Read, Jacob	1	2	5		
Ruggles, Joseph	1	2	1		
Read, Jonathan Hanson	1	1	4		
Read, Asa	1	1	3		
Robberts, Abraham	1	2	2		
Robberts, John	3		3		
Ruggles, Artemas	1		1		
Rowe, Thomas	1	2	2		
Ruggles, Isaac Mathew	1	3	1		
Ruggles, Lad	5	1	3		
Smith, John, 1st	2	1	2		
Syllivan, Mott		1	2		
Sperry, John	2	2	2		
Sherman, Ezra	2		1		
Stilson, Revinus	1	1	6		
Stilson, Nathan	2	3	3		
Stewart, Nathaniel	2	1	5		
Sherman, Eli	1	1	1		
Sherman, Daniel	1	1	1		
Stilson, Truman	1	3	4		
Sanford, Benoni S	1	2	2		
Stone, Reuben	1	4	4		
Sherwood, Daniel	1		4		
Sherwood, Reuben	1				
Smith, John, 2d	2	1	2		
Sanford, Samuel	3	1	5		
Smith, Joel	1	4	2		
Sturtevant, John	2	2	3		
Starr, Josiah	3	2	4		
Sanford, Liffe	1	1	2		
Smith, Josiah	1		4		
Stone, David	1	1	2		
Stone, Asahel	3	3	2		
Stone, Benjamin	2	3	4		
Summers, Samuel	2		1		
Smith, George	1		1		
Summers, Andrew	1	4	3		
Sanford, Nehemiah	2	2	4		
Squire, Joseph	1	1	3		
Smith, Eli	2	2	4		1
Sanford, Nehemiah, 2d	1	2	2		
Smith, Nathaniel	1	1	3		
Summers, Oliver	1	3	1		
Smith, George Clark	1	3	4		
Sturtevant, John, 2d	4	1	1		
Stone, Benjamin	1	1	5		
Sperry, Jared	2	1	4		
Stone, Julius	2	2	5		
Stone, Canfield	1	2	4		
Stone, Daniel	2	1	3		
Stone, Benajah	1	3	3		
Strict, Henry	1		5		
Stone, Ithiel	1	2	3		
Sealy, Benjamin	1		1		2
Smith, Thomas	1		3		
Stilson, John	2		3		
Sturges, Augustus	1	2	2		
Squire, Ebenezer	1	1	2		
Shelley, Abram	1	2	2		
Sanford, Zacheriah, 1st	3	2	3		
Seeley, Joseph	1		1		
Seeley, Abner	3	1	2		
Scamehorn, Cornelius	1	1	2		
Smith, Abraham	1	1	2		
Sperry, Alexander	2	4	3		
Sanford, Zacheriah, 2d	1	2	3		
Stone, Trueman	1	1	1		
Sears, John	1		2		
Stewart, Stephen	1		4		
Tomlinson Jabez	1		2		
Thomas, Lemuel	1	1	3		
Territt, John	1	2	2		
Todd, Eli	2	1	4		
Territt, Caleb	3		3		
Territt, Isaac	1	3	3		
Treat, Gideon	2	5	2		
Towner, Benjamin	1		1		
Treat, John	2	1	3		
Trobridge, Ebenezer	1	3	2		
Treat, Abijah	1	2	2		
Taylor, Nathaniel, 1st	1		2		1
Taylor, Nathaniel, 2d	1	1	2		
Taylor, Nathaniel, 3d	2	2	2	1	2
Territt, Oliver	2	2	3		
Tucker, Uriah	3	1	4		
Taylor, William	1	2	2		
Treadwell, Agur	1		2		
Territt, Joel	1		3		
Taylor, Daniel	3	1	5		
Taylor, Abram	1	1	2		
Territt, Jeames, 2d	1	3	4		
Taylor, Eli	2	1	6		
Territt, Jared	1		2		
Taylor, Jeames	1	1	1		
Territt, Joab	2	1	4		
Thacher, Jacob					9
Territt, Enoch	1	1	2		
Treadwell, Hezekiah	1	4	3		
Territt, Nathan	1	3	6		
Territt, Caleb, 2d	1	2	5		
Trobridge, Daniel	1		2		
Titus, Noah	1	2	5		
Thair, Lemuel	1	2	4		
Territt, Stephen	1	2	4		
Tillotson, Thomas	1	1	2		
Videto, Jeames	4	1	2		

LITCHFIELD COUNTY—Continued.

NEW MILFORD TOWN—continued.

NAME OF HEAD OF FAMILY.	Free white males of 16 years and upward, including heads of families.	Free white males under 16 years.	Free white females, including heads of families.	All other free persons.	Slaves.
Vaughn, Philander	1	1	2		
Whiteley, William	1	4	2		
Wilkeson, Peter	7		3		
Wheeler, Dobson	1		1		
Wildman, Mathew, 2d	1	1	6		
Wilkeson, Augustine	1	1	1		
Woster, Peter	1	1	1		
Wooster, Isaac	1		2		
Wilton, George	2		1		
Wooster, Jabez	1		1		
Warner, Reuben	3	1	5		
Weller, Abel	2	2	7		
Wilkerson, John	2		1		
Weeks, Samuel	1	2	3		
Warner, Reuben, 2d	1	4	4		
Warner, Lemuel	1	1	1		
Warner, Asa	2	1	7		
Wildman, Josiah	2	1	4		
Warner, Elizuer	3		3		
Warner, John	1	1	6		
Warner, John, 2d	1	1	2		
Warner, Oliver	2	1			
Wildman, Matthew	1		3		
Winton, Abiel	1	2	1		
Wells, Thomas	3	2	5		
Wheaton, Esack	1	4	3		
Wildman, Joseph	2		1		
Wadhams, Ingersol	1	1	2		
Wadhams, Noah	2		1		
Wiggins, Arthur	1	1	4		
West, Samuel	1		5		
Williams, Jabez	1	3	3		
Welch, Paul, 1st	4	1	2		
Welch, Paul, 2d	1	3	4		
Williams, Ezra	1		3		
Wheeler, Jedediah	1		1		
Wooster, Sylvester	1	1	2		
Wilkeson, Abel	1		2		
Wilkeson, David	2	1	6		
Warner, Elijah	1	6	2		
Waller, Joseph	3	1	1		
Warner, Orange	5		3		

SOUTHBURY TOWN.

NAME OF HEAD OF FAMILY.	M16+	M<16	Females	Other free	Slaves
Allen, Edward	1		2		3
Allen, Gideon, 1st	1	1	2		
Allen, Gideon, 2d	1		2		
Allen, David	1		3		
Allen, Jonah	1	2	1		
Bateman, Stephen	2		6		
Brownson, Ebenezer	1		2		
Brownson, Ebenezer, 2d	1	2	4		
Benham, Japhet	2		2		
Bulford, John	1	2	3		
Brownson, Noah	2	1	3		
Buritt, Anthony	1	1	6		
Brownson, Elijah	5	3	5		
Bates, Elias	1		2		
Bristol, Gad	3	2	5		
Bristol, Gad, 2d	1	1	1		
Bown, Park	1	1	3		
Brownson, Abram	4		3		
Burr, William	2	1	2		
Bristol, Thomas	1				
Brises, Isaac	2	2	3		
Bristol, P. Brigs	1				
Bristol, Eliphlet	1		1		
Bristol, Justus	3	2	5		
Bristol, Truman	1		1		
Burritt, Oliver	2	2	3		
Barnes, Phineas	2	1	4		
Booth, Smith	1	2	5		
Baldwin, Joseph	2	4	2		
Botsford, Samuel	1		4		
Blackman, Lemuel	1	2	3		
Baldwin, Elijah	1	2	3		
Bates, Eliakim	1	2	1		
Birchard, Elijah	1		3		
Barlow, Dosin		2	2		
Brown, Thomas	1		2		
Bates, Josiah	4	3	2		
Beebe, Asahel	1		1		
Bassett, Daniel	2	3	6		
Bagley, Agnes		1	4		
Baldwin, Jerusha	1		3		
Brown, John	2	2	2		
Booth, Elijah	5	3	5		
Curtis, Israel, 1st	1		1		
Curtis, Israel, 2d	2	1	6		
Curtis, Joseph	2	1	3		
Curtis, Reuben	2		3		
Curtis, Benjamin	1	3	2		
Curtis, Nathan	3	1	4		
Curtis, Sarah			1		

SOUTHBURY TOWN—continued.

NAME OF HEAD OF FAMILY.	M16+	M<16	Females	Other free	Slaves
Curtis, Abijah	1	3	4		
Curtis, Daniel	1	1	1		
Curtis, Wait	1	1	1		
Coe, Amos	1	1	1		
Coe, Andrew, 2d	1	2	3		
Cande, Samuel	2	5	3		
Cande, Esther	1		2		
Cande, Timothy	2	1	2		
Cande, David	1	2	6		
Clark, Nathel C	2	2	5		
Coggwell, Asa	1	1	1		5
Curtis, Samuel	2		2	1	
Coe, David	1	3	5		
Chison, John	1		5		
Chatfield, Oliver	3	1	4		
Coe, Andrew	3	1	1		
Cumming, Simeon					
Drakeley, Samuel	2	3	7		
Demmon, Isaac	1				
Dudley, George	2				
Daniels, Samuel	2	1	4		
Downes, Aaron	2		2		
Downes, Nathan	2	1	1		
Downes, Benjamin	3		4		
Downes, Ebenezer	1	1	4		
Downes, Moses	2	1	2		
Downes, Truman	1	2	4		
Downes, Wildman	1	1	1		
Dawton, John	1	2	5		
Edmond, John	2	2	3		
Edmond, Jeames	2	2	2		
Fairchild, Curtis	2	3	2		
French, William	4	1	2		
Fabrique, Bartemus	4		2		
Fabrique, David	3	1	2		
Fairchild, Abijah	1	1	3		
Glasier, Jacob	1		1		
Graham, Curtis	2		2		
Garrett, John	1	2	4		
Garrett, Wait	2	2	2		
Garrett, Frances	1		2		
Guthrie, Ebenezer	4		2		
Gibbs, Moor	2	1	3		
Griswold, John	1	1	3		
Galloway, Peter					2
Goss, Richard	1	3	1		
Hinman, Truman	4	1	4		1
Hinman, Eleazer	1	3	2		
Hinman, Sherman	4	1	6		
Hinman, John	1	1	2		1
Hinman, Justus	2		2		
Hinman, Timothy	1	2	2		1
Hinman, David	2	2	1		
Hinman, Edward	3		3		6
Hinman, Lewis	1		1		
Hinman, Jonas	1	1	4		
Hinman, Jonas, 2d	1		2		
Hinman, Silas	1		3		
Hinman, Abner	1				
Hinman, Agus	1	2	2		
Hinman, Joel	1	3	5		
Hinman, Aaron	1	3	4		
Hinman, Benjamin	2		1		
Hinman, Samuel	1		1		
Hinman, Francis	1		3		
Hinman, Titus	1	1	2		
Hinman, Jonathan	1	2	2		
Hinman, Wait	2	1	2		
Hinman, Lemuel	1	1	6		
Hinman, Daniel	2	2	3		
Hinman, Adam	2		3		
Haun, Michael	1		3		
Hurd, Andrew	1		5		
Hurd, William	3	2	3		
Hine, Elisha	1	4	2		
Hicock, Amos	3	1	2		1
Hicock, Benjamin	3	4	5		
Hicock, Asa	1	2	4		
Hicock, Justus	1		1		
Hawley, Richard	3	1	3		
Hicock, Ithiel	3	1	2		
Hicock, Joseph	1		2		
Hicock, Joseph, 2d	1	4	2		
Hymes, John	1	1	2		
Hendrick, Zadock	3	1	5		
Hendrick, Daniel	1	1	2		
Hughs, Nathan	1	1	2		
Heaton, Elizabeth			1		
Hazen, Isaac	1	4	2		
Holbrock, Joseph	1	1	3		
Hicock, Silas	2	4	3		
Jhonson, Asa	2		3		
Johnson, David	3	1	2		
Johnson, Hyram	1	1	3		
Johnson, Solomon, 1st	1	4	1		

SOUTHBURY TOWN—continued.

NAME OF HEAD OF FAMILY.	M16+	M<16	Females	Other free	Slaves
Johnson, Solomon, 2d	1	2	2		
Johnson, Timothy	1	1	1		
Johnson, Gideon	2		3		
Johnson, Jeremiah	1	2	5		
Johnson, Amos	2	2	4		
Johnson, John, 1st	1		2		
Johnson, John, 2d	1		4		
Johnson, Justus	1	3	4		
Johnson, Jehu	1	3	5		
Jennings, Reuben	2				
King, Elizabeth			2		
Knap, Ebenr Kason	2	1	1		
Kimberly, Adam	1	2	6		
Kimberly, Thomas	1		1		
Lewis, Swignion	1	1	3		
Lewis, Nehemiah	2	2	3		
Lewis, Beach	1	3	1		
Lum, Henry	2		3		
Lumm, Adam	3	4	5		
Leavenworth, Gideon	5	1	2		
Leavenworth, John	1	1	3		
Little, William	2		1		
Mitchel, Mathew	2	3	1		
Mitchel, Simeon, 1st	1		3		1
Mitchel, David	1	5	2		
Mitchel, Jonathan	1	1	3		
Mitchel, Eleazer	3	1	3		
Mitchel, Warren	2	1	2		
Mitchel, Simeon, 2d	2	1	5		
Moseley, Ineross	2	1	3		
Munn, Jedediah, 2d	1	1	3		
Munn, Jedediah 1st	3		5		
Mumn, Samuel	1	2	5		
Mumm, David	1	3	3		
Mallery, David	1	2	4		
Mallett, Miles	1	1	2		
Mallery, John	3	1	6		
Mogg, Christian	1	1	2		
Miner, Jehu	1	1	5		
Munn, Asa	1	1	3		
Osborn, Timothy	2	1	2		
Osborn, Shadick	1	2	5		
Osborn, Barnum	1	1	2		
Osborn, Josiah	1	2	5		
Penich, Samuel	1	1	1		
Pierce, Joseph, 1st	2	2	2		
Pierce, Joseph, 2d	2	2	3		
Pierce, Abram	2	2	4		
Pierce, Titus	3	2	6		
Pierce, Nathan	5	3	2		
Pierce, Justus	3	3	4		
Pierce, Eunice			2		
Pierce, Elijah	2		3		
Pierce, Joel	3	3	3		
Peck, Elisha	2		1		
Peck, Zalmon	1	2	2		
Perkins, Elijah	1	3	2		
Peck, Abijah	1				
Page, Josiah	1	3	2		
Post, Joseph	1		3		
Penich, David	1	1	2		
Porter, Gideon	1		1		
Platt, William	1		2		
Platt, John	1	2	2		
Platt, Stephen	2	2	4		
Philips, Dolphin				4	
Perry, Josiah	1	5	6		
Perry, Lucana			3		
Parks, John	2		2		
Peet, Stephen	2	1	4		
Pardee, Eliphlet	1	1	5		
Peet, Johiel			2		
Russel, Benjamin	1	1	2		
Raynold, Solomon	1	1	3		
Richard, Truman	2	3	2		
Rigbey, William	1	2	4		
Starr, Robbin				2	
Smith, Samuel	1	1	2		
Smith, Elizabeth			1		
Spring, Samuel	1	1	1		
Stiles, Benjamin, 2d	2				
Stiles, Samuel	2				
Stiles, Truman	1		2		
Stiles, Benjamin	3	1	3		
Stiles, David	2	1	3		
Stiles, Nathan	1	2	2		
Stiles, Ephraim	3	1	5		
Stiles, Isaac	1		2		
Sanford, Joseph	2	1	2		
Sanford, Nathaniel	1	2	3		
Strong, Ebenezer	3		2		
Strong, Benjamin	1	2	8		
Strong, Silah	3	1	4		
Strong, Return	1		2		

74 FIRST CENSUS OF THE UNITED STATES.

LITCHFIELD COUNTY—Continued.

NAME OF HEAD OF FAMILY.	Free white males of 16 years and upward, including heads of families.	Free white males under 16 years.	Free white females, including heads of families.	All other free persons.	Slaves.
SOUTHBURY TOWN—continued.					
Strong, Adino	1	2	4		
Strong, Charles	1		4		
Strong, Elnathan	4		3		
Smith, Daniel	1		2		
Smith, Ebenezer	4	1	3		
Smith, Elijah	2	1	4		
Stone, Mansfield	2		2		
Stone, John	2	2	2		
Summers, Jonah	4		6		
Stoddard, Truman	1	1	2		
Squire, Joseph	1		2		
Squire, John, 2d	1	2	1		
Squire, David	4	2	7		
Squire, Stephen	2	1	6		
Sherman, Daniel	1	2	4		
Stanlif, Jeames	1	2	3		
Seward, Samuel	2		3		
Seward, Solomon	2	1	1		
Skeels, John	1	1			
Stoddard, Cyreamus	3		2		
Skeels, Ephraim	1		3		
Skeels, Ephraim, 2d	1	5	3		
Squire, Daniel	1	1	2		
Smith, Zepheniah	1	1	5		
Sperry, Ambrose	1	4	3		
Stilson, George	2		2		
Sperry, Alexander	2	4	4		
Sharp, Joab				5	
Tuttle, Nathaniel	1	2	3		
Thomson, Esther	3	1	6		2
Towner, Joseph	1		2		
Towner, Joseph, 2d	1	1	6		
Towner, John	2		3		
Tuttle, Noah	1	1	1		
Tuttle, Newton	1	1	2		
Treat, Bethuel	4	1	8		
Ward, Macork	3	4	2		
Ward, Bethuel	2		7		
Wheeler, Obediah, 1st	1	1	2		
Wood, Joseph	1		3		
Wheeler, John	2	1	4		
Wheeler, Zophas	1				
Wooster, Sylvester	2	1	4		
Wheeler, Amos	1				
Waggoner, Adam	1		2		
Waggoner, David	1	1	1		
White, Samuel	1	1	4		
Wheeler, Jesse	2		3		
Wheeler, Aden	2	3	6		
Wheeler, Asa, 1st	1	1	5		
Wheeler, Obediah, 2d	2		4		
Wheeler, Joab	1		2		
Wheeler, Ebenezer	1		2		
Wheeler, Agur	1	4	4		
Wheeler, Asa, 2d	1	1	1		
Wheeler, Johnson	2	1	2		
Wildman, David	2	1	2		
Wildman, Benjamin	1	2	3		
Ward, Zenas, 1st	2	1	3		
Ward, Zenas, 2d	1		2		
Wilmot, Jonah	2		2		
Warner, Noadiah	2	2	3		
Wilmot, Alexander	1	1	3		
Wooden, Philo	1	1	4		
Wooden, Millow	1				
Warner, Seth	1	2	2		
Williams	1	2	1		
Wolf, Christian	1	2	3		
WARREN TOWN.					
Andrews, Joseph	2	3	2		
Alger, Mathew	1	1	2		
Alger, Nathan	1	1	2		
Beamont, Timothy	1	3	2		
Beamont, Truman	1	3	2		
Beamont, Park	1	1	2		
Barnes, John, 1st	1		1		
Barnes, John, 2d	1	3	1		
Bliss, Sylvanus	1		2		
Bliss, Nezias	1	1	2		
Brownson, Asahel	2	1	3		
Brownson, John	1	1	3		2
Beach, Reuben	2	2	3		
Bery, Cyrus	1	2			
Bamont, Thomas	3		3		
Beamont, Matthias	1	1			
Beamont, Daniel	1		5		
Beamont, Abel	2	3	4		
Beamont, Nathan	1	1	2		
Barnes, Jasper	1		1		
Beardsley, Jeames	2				
Beamont, Ceasor				4	
Comstock, Abel	2	2	2		
WARREN TOWN—con.					
Comstock, Martin Luther	1	4	2		
Carter, Joseph	2	1	2		
Carter, Joseph, 2d	1	3	3		
Carter, Solomon	1	2	2		
Carter, Samuel	3	2	3		
Carter, Samuel, 2d	1	2	2		
Carter, Benjamin	1	2	1		
Carter, Adonijah	1	3	3		
Carter, Bennoni	1	5	2		1
Carter, Bradock	1	3	1		
Carter, Jirah	1	2	2		
Carter, Berzilla	1	1	1		
Cartis, Eleazer	1	3	2		
Cartis, Augustine	1	2	2		
Curtis, Lysander	1				
Curtis, Silas	1		7		
Curtis, Milton	1	1	1		
Dunning, Benjamin	3	1	8		1
Eldred, Ward	1		1		1
Eldred, Judah	1	2	2		
Eldred, Elisha	1	2	2		
Eldred, Samuel	1		2		1
Eldred, Jehoshaphet	4		2		
Finny, John	1	1	1		
Finny, John, 2d	1	2	1		
Finney, Jonah	1	2	4		
Finney, Sylvester	1		6		
Foster, Joseph	2	1	3		
Fuller, Amos	1		1		
Fuller, Abel, 1st	1	2	2		
Fuller, Abel, 2d	1	2	1		
Fuller, Adijah	1		2		
Fuller, Asahel	1	1	3		
Fuller, Daniel	2	3	3		
Fuller, Howard	3		3		
Gilbert, Ezra	2	1	2		
Gilbert, Truman	1	4	2		
Gilbert, Jabez	1				
Hitchcock, Jonathan	1		2		
Hubbel, Ephiaim	2	1	1		
Heart, Amasa	1	5	4		
Hawes, Samuel	1	2	3		
Hopkins, Prince	4	1	6		
Hopkins, Nathan	1		1		
Holmes, Peleg	1		3		
Holmes, Israel	1		1		
Holmes, Gershom	1	1	3		
Hopkins, Thomas	1				
Hopkins, Elijah	2	1	8		
Hopkins, Benjamin	1	1	1		
Hoyt, Stephen	2		2		
Hawes, Isaac	2	6	2		
Hurlburt, Solmon	1		4		
Hopkins, Joseph	1	1	6		
Isles, Joshua	1	1	5		
Judd, Obediah	1	2	2		
Judd, Nathaniel	1	1	2		
Johnson, Nathaniel	1	4	1		
Kent, Darius	2		4		
London, William	2		2		
Lord, John	1	3	1		
Lyon, Nathaniel	1		1		
Morris, Samuel	1	2	3		
Morris, Marget			2		
Niel, Titus	1	3	1		
Newcomb, William	1		1		
Palmer, Nathaniel	2	3	3		
Palmer, Ezekial	3	3	2		
Phelps, Truman	1	1	2		
Phelps, David	1	1	4		
Palmer, Elijah	2		2		
Patterson, John	1		2		
Peck, Phineas	1	2	4		
Peters, Joseph	2	1	5		
Palmer, Ebenezer	2		1		
Peet, Thaddeus	1		1		
Paush, Daniel	1	2	3		
Pendal, Mary		2	3		
Roots, Isaac	1	3	5		
Sturtevant, Pelg	1	3	5		
Strong, Eber	1		2		
Strong, Philip	1	2	1		
Strong, Amasa	3	3	1		
Strong, Caverly	1				
Swetland, Lewis	1	3	2		
Sacket, Alexander	1	2	2		
Sacket, Salmon	1	2	2		
Sacket, Reuben	1	1	3		
Sacket, Benjamin	1	3	3		
Sackett, Justus	3		3		
Spooner, Ebenezer	1	1	2		
Smith, Peabody	1	3	5		
Stone, William, 2d	1	1	1		
WARREN TOWN—con.					
Starr, Platt	1	2	3		
Swift, Nathaniel, 2	2	1	8		
Spooner, John	2	2	2		
Spooner, William, 2d	1	2	4		
Swan, Isaac	3	2	5		
Swan, Amos	3	2	3		
Saunders, Benjamin	2	1	4		
Spooner, Nathaniel	1	1	1		
Swift, Jabez	1		3		
Stone, Willim	1		2		
Spooner, William	1		2		
Starr, Peter	2	4	2		
Taylor, David	1	5	4		
Talmage, John	2		4		1
Tanner, Ephraim	2	2	5		
Taylor, Elias	1	2	4		
Taylor, Joseph, 2d	2	2	4		
Tanner, Ebenezer	2	1	2		
Thomson, George	1	1	3		
Thomas, John	1	1	5		
Webb, Josiah	1	1	1		
Whitlock, Samuel	1	1	5		
Whitlock, Joel	1				
Wedge, Isaac	1	3	4		
Wedge, Stephen	1	1	2		
Wedge, Asahel	2	1	3		
Woston, John	1	1	1		
Wicks, Zadock				1	
Whitney, Joseph	1	1	2		
Weston, Samuel	1	1	3		
WASHINGTON TOWN.					
Ackley, Hezekiah	2	2	3		
Addams, Benjamin	2	2	5		
Armstrong, Thomas	3	3	4		
Armstrong, Jeames	2	1	3		
Averill, Samuel	2	2	1		
Averill, Percy	2	4	5		
Allen, Cornelius	2	4	1		
Brown, John	1	2	7		
Baker, Ephraim	2	5	7		
Baker, Jesse	2	1	4		
Baker, Samuel	1	4	1		
Baldwin, Enos	2		4		
Baldwin, Enos, 2d	2	2	3		
Baldwin, Judah	3	1	3		
Baldwin, Asahel	1	2	5		
Baldwin, George	2		4		
Baldwin, John	1	1	4		
Barnes, Elijah	1	4	2		
Barnes, Asa	2	2	3		
Barnes, Eber	1	1	2		
Barnes, Samuel	1	2	1		
Barnes, Daniel	1	3	3		
Beadsley, Wells	1	3	3		
Brinsmade, Daniel	3	1	6		
Brinsmade, Daniel N	2	1	2		
Bosworth, Nathaniel	1		2		1
Bosworth, Nathaniel, 2d	2	5	4		
Burges, Jeames	3	1	5		
Burges, Ebenezer	1	3	2		
Bears, Ebenezer	1	1	1		
Bears, Philo	1	2	2		
Bears, Abel	1	3	3		
Bears, Mathew	1		2		
Bryan, Richard	3	3	4		
Byan, Jeames	1	4	3		
Byan, Zacheriah	1	2	3		
Bunce, Isaih	1		5		
Brown, Nathaniel	1	4	5		
Bosworth, Jeames Wood	2	2	4		
Beach, Benjamin	3	2	2		
Betts, Nehemiah	1		4		
Blackman, N. Cady	2		7		
Brainard, Hen'y	1	4	4		
Bulkley, Calvin	1		4		
Camp, Jonah	2	1	2		
Camp, Isaac	2	3	3		
Camp, Gideon	4	3	6		
Camp, Chauncy	1		1		
Camp, Daniel	1	1	1		
Calhoun, Joseph	2	1	2		
Calhoun, Jeames	3	4	5		
Calhoun, David	3	4	3		
Calhoun, Ebenezer	1	3	4		
Calhoun, George	1	3	5		
Calhoun, Tabitha	1	3	2		
Clark, Ebenezer	5	2	5		
Clark, Joseph	2	2	4		
Clark, Samuel, 2d	1	1	3		
Clark, William	1		3		

LITCHFIELD COUNTY—Continued.

NAME OF HEAD OF FAMILY	Free white males of 16 years and upward, including heads of families	Free white males under 16 years	Free white females, including heads of families	All other free persons	Slaves
WASHINGTON TOWN—continued.					
Clark, Daniel	1	1	2		
Clark, Marcy	1		1		
Canfield, Thomas	2	1	3		
Canfield, Nathaniel	2	2	3		
Coggwell, Roger	5	1	5		
Coggwell, Anna		2	3		
Cary, Joseph	1	2	2		
Curtis, Elizur	1	2	3		
Curtis, Joshua	2	2	3		
Curtis, Abel	1		3		
Cole, Thaddeus	1	2	1		
Cooper, Timothy	1		3		
Coggswell, Edward	3	1	5		
Coggswell, Edward, 2d	1	1	2		
Cheritree, Reuben	3	1	2		
Copley, Daniel	1	2	1		
Dean, Elijah	1	1	3		
Day, Jeremiah	3	3	3		
Davidson, John	1	1	3		
Davies, John	3	1	2		
Davies, John, 2d	3	1	3		
Davies, Walter	1	1	4		
Davies, Jeams John	1				
Davies, David	2	1	3		
Davies, Thomas	1		2		
Durand, Samuel	2	1	3		
Davidson, Elizabeth			1		1
Dan, Abijah	2	1	4		
Durker, Benjamin	4	3	6		
Durker, Jedediah	1	1	2		
Durkerson, Robert	1	4	3		
Easton, Joseph	3	3	4		
Foot, David	1	4	5		
Foot, Isaac	1	5	2		
Foot, Aaron	1	1	5		
Farrand, Jonathan	4	4	4		1
Farrand, John	2	2	3		
Frisbrie, Edward	3		6		
Farmer, Thomas	2	1	4		
Ford, Samuel	3	3	4		
Ferry, Joseph	1	2	7		
Ferry, Ebenezer	1	4	3		
Ferry, Ezra	1	1	2		
Fowler, Benjamin	2		2		
Fisher, Darius	1		1		
Finn, Daniel	1	2	3		
Galpin, Benjamin	2	1	3		
Gibson, Brinsmade	2	2	6		
Gibson, William	1	3	3		
Guthrie, Joseph	5	1	6		
Gunn, Phebe	2		1		
Goodsel, Isaac	1	2	3		
Goodsel, Thomas	3	2	3		
Goodsel, Timothy	3	1	2		
Guthrie, Jeames	1		4		
Guthrie, Abraham	1		3		
Hurd, Levi	1		3		
Handerson, William	1	1	1		
Holloway, John	1	2	3		
Hicock, Johnson	3	2	3		
Haslings, Seth	3	3	4		
Hicock, Nathaniel	2	1	3		
Hicock, Nathan	4	2	2		
Hicock, Nathaniel, 2d	1	1	3		
Hicock, Nathan, 2d	2	1	2		
Hicock, Elijah	1	2	1		
Hicock, Joel	1	1	3		
Hicock, Thaddeus	1		2		
Hartwell, Joseph	1	1	2		
Harrison, Gideon	1		3		
Herrick, Ephraim	1	2	3		
Hurd, Solomon	3	1	3		
Hurd, Sarah			1		
Hollister, Gideon	2	2	3		
Hollister, Gideon, 2d	2	1	3		
Hopson, William	2	1	3		
Howes, David	4	1	1		
Hinman, Michael	1	1	4		
Hine, Jonathan	3		4		
Hine, Andrew	1	2	2		
Hurlburt, Joseph	2	1	2		
Hurlburt, Samuel	3	1	2		
Holdridge, Hezekiah	1				
Hurd, Amos Asahel	1	2	2		
Hazen, Elijah	2	1	3		
Hanford, William	3	1	4		
Judson, David	5	4	5		
Judson, Abijail			2		
Jordan, John	1		2		
Johnes, Benjamin	1		1		
King, Oliver	1		2		
Keeney, Mark	2	1	1		
Krappen, Thomas	1	2	5		
Kimberly, David	2	3	3		
Keeney, John	1	1	1		
WASHINGTON TOWN—continued.					
Keeney, John, 2d	1		1		
Keeney, Jacob	1		2		
Keeney, Pearle	2	5	3		
Keeney, Lyman	1	1	1		
Knowles, Gid Benedict	1	1	1		
Keith, George	2	3	3		
Keith			3		
Kent, Eri	1	1	3		
Leavitt, Samuel	2	2	4		
Lacy, Ebenezer	1	1	2		
Lemmon, Robert	2	1	1		
Lemmon, Robert, 2d	1	2	4		
Loggan, Mathew	3	1	5		
Loggan, Jeames	2	2	4		1
Loggan, Johnson	1	2	1		
Lovejoy, Abner	1		4		
Libberty, Jeff				4	
Morse, Joseph	1		4		
Metcalf, Dan	1	2	3		
Marchant, Sarah			2		
Merwin, Noah	2	1	6		
Miers, Martin	1	2	1		
Mallerey, Elijah	2		3		
Mallery, Ithamar	1	2	3		
Mitchel, Elnathan	5		3		
Mitchel, Simeon	2	3	3		
Mitchel, David	4	5			1
Mitchel, Timothy	2		1		
Mitchel, William	1		6		
Mecher, David	1	1	2		
Moger, Jeames	1	1	1		
Munson, John	1	5	3		
Mayo, Elisha	1	1	3		
Mossley, Abner	2	2	4		
Munger, Joel	3		3		
Munger, Joel, 2d	1	1	2		
Mead, Jeames	2	3	2		
Newton, Ezekiel	3		2		
Norton, Isachar	2	2	3		
Norton, Joel	1	2	1		
Northrop, Amos	1	2	2		
Northrop, Elijah	1	2	2		
Nettleton, Daniel	1	1	1	1	
Oliver, Timothy				5	
Older, Hannah		1	3		
Patterson, Joseph	1		4		
Palmer, Zebulon	1		1		
Parish, Isaac	1	5	3		
Parish, Asa	1				
Parmely, Thomas	4	2	4		
Parker, Amasa	2	1	3		
Parker, Joseph	2		4		
Parker, Abner	2	1	3		
Parker, Abijail	1	1	1		
Parker, Thomas	2	3	5		
Parks, William	1	1	1		
Powel, John	2	2	6		
Pratt, Abijah	1	2	6	1	
Platt, John	1	2	4		
Platt, Zophar	1	2	3		
Peters, Eber	2	1	2		
Palmer, John	1	1	1		
Parmeley, Truman	1	2	3		
Pitcher, Truman	1				
Pitcher, Susannah		1	4		
Ranney, Nathan	1	1	3		
Royce, John	1	1	3		
Royce, David	3	1	4		
Royce, Mark	2	2	4		
Rude, Lester	1	3	4		
Rude, Caleb	2		2		
Rude, Caleb, 2d	1	3	5		
Reynolds, John	1		3		
Reynolds, David	1	2	1		
Sharp, William	1	2	6		
Smith, John	3	3	3		
Smith, John, 2d	2	2	4		
Smith, Moses	1	2	3		
Smith, Aaron	1	1	4		
Sherman, Peter	5	2	5		
Stoddard, Jeames	1	2	2		
Sherwood, Warren	2		3		
Swan, John	1	2	3		
Swan, Elizabeth			2		
Smith, Samuel	1		5		
Stilson, Eli	1	1	1		
Sharp, Eliakim	1	1	2		
Titus, Joseph	1	2	3		
Thorp, Peter	1	1	3		
Treat, Sam Peat	1		3		
Tracy, John	3		3		
Tracy, Silas	2	2	6		
Twiss, Samuel	1		2		
Tibbals, Nathan	1	2	1		
WASHINGTON TOWN—continued.					
Tuttle, Eli	4	3	5		
Tuttle, Jonathan	2		6		
Titus, Joel	3	5	6		
Titus, Onosimus	3	1	3		
Titus, Moses	1	2	1		
Treat, Bulah			3		
Woodruff, John	3	2	4		
Whittlesey, Martin	2	1	5		
Whittlesey, John	3	3	5		
Whittlesey, David	2	1	2		
Whittlesey, Joseph	1	3	2		
Wooden, Eri	1	1	3		
Wooden, Elias	1	1	3		
Wheaton, Sylvester	2		3		
Wheaton, Orange	1	3	3		
Warner, J. Ichabod	1	2	6		
Whitney, Hezekiah	1	1	3		
Walker, David	1		4		
WATERTOWN TOWN.					
Allen, Ebenezer	2	1	5		
Alling, Solomon	1	1	1		
Allen, Jeames	2	3	4		
Avery, Ambrose	1		3		
Atwater, Timothy	1	1	2		
Atkins, David	1	2	3		
Allen, Jeames, 2d	1	3	2		
Allen, David	2	4	4		
Atkins, Daniel	1	1	5		
Andrews, Justus	1		3		
Avint, Amos	1	2	3		
Allen, John	1	1	1		
Andrews, Reuben	1	4	3		
Andrews, William	1	2	2		
Avery, Benjamin	1	2	2		
Atwood, Joseph	1	2	2		
Andrews, Abram	1		2		
Atwood, Noble	2	3	1		
Atwood, Nathan	1	1	2		
Andrews, Ebenezer	1		1		
Blakeley, Bela	1		2		
Beckwith, Jeames	2		2		
Beckwith, Zacheriah	3		6		
Brown, John	1				
Basset, Levi	2	2	3		
Beach, Adna	1		3		
Bearnes, Ebenezer	1	1	2		
Brown, Hezekiah	1	1	1		
Barnes, Eliphlet	1	3	3		
Blakeley, Moses	2		4		
Barnes, Joseph	1		1		
Baldwin, Thaddeus	2	2	5		
Bunnet, Ambrose	2				
Blakeley, Joel	1	3	3		
Blakeley, Judah	3		3		
Bartholemew, Daniel	2	3	4		
Blakeley, Adna	2		2		
Blakeley, Eli	1	4	5		
Blakely, Sola	1	1	1		
Brownson, Amos	3		6		
Blakeley, Annis			2		
Barker, Eliphlet	2	4	2		
Bradley, Ebenezer, 2d	2	2	2		
Blakeley, Solomon	1	1	2		
Barnes, Eli	1				
Bradley, Jared	1				
Blakeley, Samuel	1	2	3		
Barker, Miles	1	1	1		
Brownson, Noah Matt.	1	1			
Blakeley, Micajah	1				
Blakeley, Ashur	3		3		2
Barnes, Nathaniel	3	1	5		
Blakeley, Amos	1		1		
Barnes, Daniel	1	4	2		
Barnes, Jonah	1	1	3		
Bradley, Philo	1	2	1		
Bradley, Ebenezer	1		1		
Brainard, Stephen	1		2		
Barnes, Caleb	1	1	2		
Baldwin, Israel	1	5	1		
Baldwin, Abel	1	3	1		
Bartholemew, Seth	2	1	2		
Bradley, Anor	1	3	4		
Beard, Azeriah	2	1	7		
Brown, William	2	1	3		
Brownson, Thomas	2		5		
Brown, Zera	1	3	1		
Bidwell, Jeremiah	2	1	4		
Belding, Amos	2	1	2		
Buckingham, Epenetus	2	1	4		
Buckingham, David	1	1	2		
Bidwell, Jacob	2	2	5		
Bradley, Nathaniel	2	1	3		
Baldwin, Alsop	2	2	3		

LITCHFIELD COUNTY—Continued.

WATERTOWN TOWN—continued.

NAME OF HEAD OF FAMILY.	Free white males of 16 years and upward, including heads of families.	Free white males under 16 years.	Free white females, including heads of families.	All other free persons.	Slaves.
Brownson, Levi	1	1	3		
Blakeley, Jared	1				
Brown, Samuel	1	1	3		
Brigh, Elijah	2	1	3		
Byan, David	2	2	6		
Baldwin, Theophilus	1	6	2		
Bryan, Benajah	2	1	3		
Baldwin, David	1	3	4		
Bassett, William	1	2	6		
Beard, Clark	1	1	1		
Barber, Samuel	2	2	3		
Beard, George	1		1		
Bunnel, Hezekiah	1		2		
Beckwith, Anna		2	2		
Beardsley, Ebenezer	2		3		
Baldwin, Samuel	1		2		
Blakeley, Thomas	2	2	4		
Brown, Daniel	1	4	2		
Castle, Amasa	1	2	6		
Castle, Abisha	1	1	2		
Castle, Richard	1	1	3		
Camp, Isaac	2	3	3		
Culver, Reuben	1	2	3		
Curtis, Jesse	2	1	1		
Cook, Justus	1				
Curtis, Joseph	2		2		
Camp, Samuel	2	2	4		
Camp, Ephraim	2	1	2		
Carrington, David	1	5	2		
Curtis, Samuel	2		3		
Cook, Phebe			2		
Cook, Arba	1	1	3		
Cook, Joel	1	1	6		
Curtis, Isaac	2		2		
Curtis, Jeames	1	3	1		
Camp, Benajah	1	1	3		
Curtis, Elihu	1	1	2		
Cooper, Jesse	1	1	2		
Cusley, Jesse	1				
Curtis, Miles	1		1		
Cole, Timothy	2	1	1		
Cowles, Ebenezer	2	1	3		
Curtis, Benjamin	1	3	2		
Curtis, Thomas	1		1		
Clark, Ichiel	1	4	2		
Curtis, Zadock	1	1	2		
Curtis, Oliver	1	1	7		
Cowles, Moses	1	2	3		
Cole, John	1				
Cook, Jonah	1	1	4		
Curtis, Phineas	1		3		
Culver, Daniel	3	1	3		
Cowles, Thomas	3	1	3		
Carrington, Eliphat	1	2	4		
Coe, Denman	1	2	5		
Clark, Oliver	1		2		
Clark, Gamaliel	3	3	5		
Castle, John	1	2	3		
Curtis, Eli	1	1	1		
Cutler, Young Lorer	4	1	3		
Castle, Simeon	1	2	5		
Dutton, Sarah	1	1	3		
Dunbar, David	1				
Dunbar, Amos	1	1	2		
Dunbar, Joel	1	2	3		
Dunbar, Aaron	2	2	4		
Dunbar, Miles	1	3	2		
Darrow, Titus	3	3	2		
Dodge, Ezra	1	1	2		
Dunbar, Joseph	1	2	2		
Doolittle, Eliasaph	1	5	4		
Darrow, Ebenezer, 2d	1	2	1		
Darrow, Asa	2	2	6		
Dutton, P. Samuel	2	1	2		
Dunbar, Jonathan	1				
Darrow, Ebenezer	1				
Dodg, Ira	1	1	4		
Dayton, Michael	1		2		
Dutton, Thomas, 3d	4	2	3		
Dayton, Justus	2	3	4		
Davies, Thomas	1	1	1		
Dayton, Lyman	1	1	2		
Dayton, Abel	1	1	1		
Doolittle, Uri	3	2	2		
Dutton, Thomas, 2d	2	1	3		
Dayton, Charles	2	3	3		
Dayton, Alexander	2		2		
Dayton, Isaac	1	2	1		
Dayton, David	1	2	5		
Dart, William	1	2	3		
Davies, Jonathan	1	1	2		
Dayton, Samuel	1	1	2		
Edward, Joseph	1	1	2		
Elton, Ebenezer	3	2	3		
Edwards, Josiah	1	1	1		
Elton, John	1	1	2		

WATERTOWN TOWN—continued.

NAME OF HEAD OF FAMILY.	Free white males of 16 years and upward, including heads of families.	Free white males under 16 years.	Free white females, including heads of families.	All other free persons.	Slaves.
Edward, Isaac	1	1	2		
Edward, Nathaniel	2		6		
Egleston, John	2	4	5		
Edward, Asahel	1	4	2		
Frost, Samuel, 1st	1		2		
Frost, Samuel, 2nd	1	1	1		
Finn, Joseph	2	3	5		
Ferris, Nathan	1	1	6		
Frost, Solomon	1	3	2		
Finn, Titus	1	3	5		
Foot, Amos	1	1	4		
Fulson, David	1	1	2		
Foot, David	1	4	4		
Finn, Thomas, 1st	3	1	3		
Foot, Samuel	1	1	3		
Foot, Thomas	1		2		
Foot, John	2	1	4		
Foot, Jacob	3	1	7		
Finn, Samuel, 3d	1				
Finn, Amos	1	4	2		
Finn, Thomas, 2d	1	1	4		
Fulford, John	2	1	8		
Foot, Thankful	2	1	6		
Finn, Faar	2	1	6		
Finn, Jason	1	1	5		
Finn, Jacob	2		7		
Finn, Jesse	1	3	2		
Finn, Ebenezer	1				
Finn, Samuel, 1st	1	1	2		
Finn, Aaron	3	3	3		
Finn, Samuel, 2d	3		5		
Ford, Amos	1	3	3		
Ford, Ebenezer	1		1		
Ford, Daniel	1	2	4		
Ford, Enos	1				
Fost, Elisha	1	1	2		
Farnham, John	2	1	1		
Fancher, Ithiel	1	1	3		
Fenton, Benjamin	2	2	1		
Foot, Simon	1	1	3		
Fancher, Sarah		1	3		
Fancher, Jeames	1		3		
Ford, Barnebas	1	3	3		
Gilbert, Elisha	1	2	4		
Grannis, Hannah		1	2		
Gridley, Hosea	1	2	5		
Goodyer, David	1	2	6		
Griggs, Solomon	1	2	4		
Griggs, Paul	1	2	1		
Goss, Ebeneser	3	1	2		
Gaylord, Jotham	1	3	2		
Gaylord, Enos	1	1	5		
Guernsey, Joseph, 1st	3	1	2		
Guernsey, Joel	1	2	2		
Guernsey, Ebenezer	3	1	3		
Guernsey, Daniel	1	3	2		
Guernsey, David	2		10		
Griggs, Noah, 1st	2		3		
Griggs, Noah, 2	1				
Givins, Shelden	1				
Guernsey, Eldad	1	1	2		
Guernsey, Southmayd	1	1	3		
Guernsey, Jonathan	2		2		
Glasier, John	1	1	1		
Guernsey, Joab	2		1		
Guernsey, Philo	1		3		
Guernsey, Chauncy	1	2	3		
Guernsey, Amos	1		7		
Guernsey, Joseph, 2d	1	1	3		
Guernsey, Abijah	2	1	5		
Guernsey, Samuel	2	1	4		
Guernsey, Thankfull			3		
Griggs, Jacob	1	1			
Gridley, Uriel	1	1	2		
Heaton, Abram	2	3	3		
Hornestone, Timothy	1		2		
Hall, Benjamin	1	2	1		
Holt, Daniel	1	2	2		
Homestone, David	1	1	3		
Hemmingway, Abram	2		4		
Hitchcock, Zachariah	1	8	5		
Homestone, Abel	1	2	3		
Heading, George	1	1	2		
Hull, Ira	1				
Hawley, Samuel	3		2		
How, Zachariah	2		2		
Homestone, Jose	1	4	3		
Homestone, Eliphet	2	3	5		
Homestone, Thomas	1	3	1		
Hough, Benoni	1	1	1		
Hill, James	2	3	5		
Hicocks, Joel	1		4		
Hotchkiss, Truman	1		2		
How, Samuel	1		4		
Hicocks, Samuel	1		1		
Hicocks, Amos	2	1	4		

WATERTOWN TOWN—continued.

NAME OF HEAD OF FAMILY.	Free white males of 16 years and upward, including heads of families.	Free white males under 16 years.	Free white females, including heads of families.	All other free persons.	Slaves.
Hard, Anson	1	3	1		
Hadeley, Gideon	1	1	3		
Hammon, Thomas	2	1	5		
Hubbat, Hezekiah	3		3		
Hicock, Ambrose, 2d	2	1	5		
Hungeford, Jonas	1	3	6		
Hicocks, Caleb	1				
Hicocks, Dick				3	
Hicocks, Jonas	2		2		
Hotchkiss, Titus	1	1	3		1
Hicocks, Samuel	1		1		
Hicocks, Daniel	2	3	6		
Hansson, Jared	3	1	3		
Hungerford, Joel	1	1	5		
Hubbard, Joel, 1	1	2	4		
Hicocks, William	4	2	5		
Hicocks, Joseph	1	2	2		
Hungerford, Jeames	1	2	3		
Hicocks, Phebe		1	2		
Hicocks, Jeames	1	2	3		
Hull, David, 1st	2	1	2		
Hicocks, Mary		2	4		
Hicocks, Jared	1	3	4		
How, Ephraim	2	3	4		
Hull, David, 2d	1		2		
Hubbard, Josiah	1		1		
Hitchcock, Samuel	1		4		
Hubbart, David	1	2	2		
Hicocks, Consider	1	4	4		
Hicocks, Ambrose	1	1	1		
Hicocks, Hinman	1	1	1		
Judd, Noah	4	3	3		
Judd, Allen	2	2	7		
Judd, Michael	1	1	2		
Judd, Levi	1	2	3		
Judd, Dennis	1	2	4		
Judd, John, 1	2		1		
Judd, William	1		1		
Judd, Asa	2	3	4		
Judd, Merriam	1		4		
Judd, Samuel	1	1	2		
Jones, Sarah		1	1		
Johnson, Isaac	2		1		
Johnson, Enos	1	3	2		
Jones, Timothy	1	1	2		
Ives, Elnathan	1	3	3		
Jerom, Robert	1	1	4		
Judd, Harvey	1	1	2		
Leavenworth, Asa	2	1	3		
Luddington, David	2		4		
Lewis, Samuel	1	1	2		
Loomis, Faith	1	1	2		
Loomis, Oliver	1	3	1		
Lewis, Thankful			2		
Lockwood, Ezra	5	3	4		
Matthews, William	1	1	3		
Munson, Almond	1	2	2		
Matthews, Lydia			1		
Mozier, Zebulon	1	4	3		
Matthews, Samuel	1	2	1		
Miller, Isaac	1	3	2		
Marchant, Thomas, 1st	2		3		
Morris, Isaac	1				
Morris, Amos	1	1	2		
Mead, Daniel	1	1	3		
Mopley, John	1				
Mallery, Jacob	1	2	2		
Munson, Obidiah	3		1		
Matthews, Aaron	1		1		
Marp, Benoni	1	1	2		
Merrills, Daniel	2	1	2		
Matthews, Daniel	1	1	2		
Martin, Samuel	1	2	3		
Merrills, John	2		2		
Merriam, Isaac	3	1	4		
Merriam, James	2	1	2		
Matthews, Thomas	2	1	4		
Merriam, Thomas, 2d	1		1		
Mattoon, Amasa	1	3	2		
Merriam, Joel	2	2	3		
Miles, Richard	1	3	4		
Merriam, Joseph	1	2	2		
Merriam, Christopher	3	2	3		
Merriam, Thomas, 1st	2	2	3		
Merriam, John	3	2	3		
Mattoon, John	1		3		
Merriam, Charles	3	1	2		
Matthews, Stephen	2		3		
Manoil, David	2	2	3		
Matthews, Phineas	1		2		
Munson, William	1	1	4		
Merriam, Marshal	1	2	4		
Merrills, Mabel	1		2		
McDaniel, David	3		3		
McDaniel, James	2	2	1		

LITCHFIELD COUNTY—Continued.

NAME OF HEAD OF FAMILY.	Free white males of 16 years and upward, including heads of families.	Free white males under 16 years.	Free white females, including heads of families.	All other free persons.	Slaves.
WATERTOWN TOWN—continued.					
Marchant, Thomas, 2d	1	1	3		
Munson, Heman	1	4	1		
Northrop, Joseph	1				
Northrop, Gideon	1	3	5		
Northrop, Joseph	1				
Northrop, Gideon, 2d	1	3	5		
Northrop, Joel	2	1	1		
Noble, Francis	1	1	4		
Northrop, Jonathan	2	1	4		
Nettleton, Joseph	1	1	6		
Nettleton, Joseph, 2d	1	1	2		
Nettleton, Susannah			2		
Osborn, Zadock	1	1	1		
Osborn, Amos	1	1	2		
Osborn, Abijah	1		3		
Osborn, John	1		5		
Osborn, White	1	1	3		
Peck, Samuel	1		1		
Preston, Caleb	3	3	4		
Potter, Eliahson	2	3	4		
Potter, Daniel	1	2	3		
Potter, Lake	2	1	3		
Potter, Jacob	1	2	3		
Potter, Samuel	3	2	4		
Potter, Demas	1				
Potter, Zenas	1		1		
Potter, Thomas	1				
Packer, Leut	2	3	2		
Painter, Thomas W	1	1	2		
Pond, Jonathan	3	2	5		
Pond, Bartholemew, 1st	2	3	3		
Pond, Ira	1	1	1		
Painter, John	2		4		
Penfield, Jesse	1	2	2		
Pond, Bartholemew, 2d	1	1	3		
Parde, Stephen	2	1	3		
Prindle, Chauncy	1	1	4		
Parker, John, 2d	1		1		
Painter, John, 2d	1		3		
Pulford, Dorcas			3		
Prichard, Elijah	1	2	2		
Prichard, Benjamin	1	3	4		
Peck, Simeon	2	2	2		
Prindle, David	1	3	8		
Parker, John	2	2	4		
Parker, Eli	1	1	3		
Peck, Jeremiah	1	1	4		
Prindle, Eleasor	1	1	3		
Porter, Ebenezer	2	2	4		
Pitcher, Jerusha	1	1	4		
Peck, Elezier	1		2		
Preston, Amasa	1	4	5		
Pond, Zera	1	1	1		
Richard, Gideon	1	1	3		
Ransom, Theophilus	2	3	4	1	
Richard, Ebenezer	1		3		
Raynold, Richard T	2	1	2		
Raynold, Samuel, Junr	1	2	6		
Richard, William	1				
Richard, Benjamin, 1st	1		1		
Richard, Benjamin, 2d	2	2	3		
Richard, Elizabeth	1	1	3		
Robarts, Jonathan	1	1	5		
Richard, Peter	2		2		
Roberts, Jesse	1	1	2		
Rockwell, Jabez	1	1	2		
Rockwell, Benjamin	1	3	2		
Royer, Samuel	2	1	6		
Royer, Jacob	1	4	4		
Rozer, David	1		6		
Sanford, David	2		1		
Scovill, William	1	3	1		
Sutliff, Abel, 1st	1		2		
Sutliff, Abel, 2d	3	1	6		
Sutliff, Lucas	1				
Sutliff, Samuel	1	2	1		
Sutliff, John	2	3	5		
Sutliff, David	1	3	2		
Sanford, Samuel	3	2	1		
Sanford, Daniel, 2d	2		2		
Sanford, Joel	1		4		
Sanford, Jesse	1		4		
Sanford, Ezekiel, 2d	1	1	1		
Sanford, Stephen	1		2		
Scamon, Stephen, 1st	1		2		
Simons, Amos	1	1	2		
Simon, Gideon	2	3	3		
Simon, Abel	3	2	4		
Skilton, David	3	3	3		1
Stanley, Selah	1	1	1		
Scovill, Samuel	1		2		
Scovill, Uri	1	1	2		
Scovill, Eli	1	2	1		
Scovill, Jesse	1	1	2		
Sperry, Lemuel	1				

NAME OF HEAD OF FAMILY.	Free white males of 16 years and upward, including heads of families.	Free white males under 16 years.	Free white females, including heads of families.	All other free persons.	Slaves.
WATERTOWN TOWN—continued.					
Smith, David	2	3	3		
Smith, Jeames	1		3		
Soughton, Oliver	1	3	4		1
Sanford, Ezekiel, 1st	1	2	5		
Sanford, Amos	1	3	1		
Smith, Isaac	1		1		
Smith, Stephen	2	1	3		
Simons, Joseph	2	4	3		
Southmayd, Samuel	2		4		
Scott, Hezekiah	2		3		
Scovill, Martha			3		
Stoddard, John	1	2	1		
Scott, Elicks	1	2	5		
Stow, Ebenezer	1	1	4		
Simons, Richard, 1st	1	1	3		
Stoddard, Sampson	1	4	4		
Scott, Jonathan	3	4	1		1
Smith, Wart	3	3	5		
Sitkuggs, Osi	1		2		
Scovill, Darius	2	4	2		
Stoddard, Wills	1		1		
Scovill, William, 2d	2	2	3		
Stilson, Amos	1	2	3		
Steel, Elijah	2	1	3		
Scott, Isaac	2	1	1		
Steel, Ashbel	2		4		
Strickland, Samuel	1	2	4		
Scott, Barnebes	1				
Scott, Ebner	1	2	3		
Sutton, Henr'y	1	1	1		
Smith, Eliphlet	1	2	4		
Smith, John	3	2	4		
Simons, Samuel	1	2	3		
Smith, Reuben	1		1		
Simons, Josiah	1	3	3		
Scott, Uri	1	1	1		
Singlehuff, John	1		3		
Scott, Eleazer, 2d	1	1	5		
Simons, Richard, 2d	1	1	1		
Scovill, Israel	1	2	6		
Scott, Woolfy	1	2	2		
Steel, Samuel	1		2		
Smith, Thomas	1		1		
Tuttle, John	1		2		
Truitt, Mattha	2	1	4		
Tomkins, Feanes	1	1	2		
Tomkins, Edmond	1	2	2		
Titus, Amos	1		4		
Turner, David	1	1	2		
Turner, Stephen	2	1	3		
Treat, Richard	2		3		1
Tuttle, Obediah	1	4	4		
Thomas, Samuel	1		1		
Tyler, Osias	3	2	4		
Tomlinson, Victory	2	2	2		
Tuttle, William	1	3	3		
Todd, Samuel	2		2		
Todd, Edmond	3		3		
Todd, Elam	1				
Tuttle, Noah	2	4	3		
Turner, Bethuel	1	2	1		
Todd, Lydia		2	3		
Tuttle, Stephen	1		2		
Upson, Rusel	1	1	2		
Upson, Joseph	1	2	6		
Upson, Noah	2	3	1		
Upson, Benjamin	1				
Warner, Jeames	2	2	5		
Warner, Noah	1	1	2		
Warner, Elijah	4	2	4		
Wright, Joseph Allen	1	1	2		2
Warner, John, 2d	1	5	3		
Warner, John, 3d	1	1	5		
Welton, Eli, 1st	1	1	5		
Welton, Eli, 2d	1	1	1		
Woodruf, Gideon	1				
Way, Thomas, 1st	2	2	3		
Way, Thomas, 2d	1		2		
Warner, David	1	1	2		
Warner, Aaron	1	2	2		
Warner, Osias	1	5	4		
Wooden, Amos	1	2	3		
Williams, John	1				
Weed, Jesse	3	2	6		
Way, Samuel	1	3	3		
Wright, Amos	1	1	2		
Worden, Thomas	1	2	5		
Wheaton, Sarah			2		
Williams, Thomas	1	1	6		
Wetmore, Elizabeth	3		1		
Watson, William	1	2	4		
Wade, Increse	1	3	2		
Welton, Jeames	1		2		
Woodruff, Samuel	1	1	2		
Warner, Elisha	2		1		

NAME OF HEAD OF FAMILY.	Free white males of 16 years and upward, including heads of families.	Free white males under 16 years.	Free white females, including heads of families.	All other free persons.	Slaves.
WATERTOWN TOWN—continued.					
Wooden, Asa	2	1	3		
Whitney, Ransford	1	1	2		
Welton, Jesse	1	2	4		
Woodruf, John	2	5	2		
Woodruff, Sarah	1	3	2		
Woodard, Elijah	2	1	4		1
Williams, Daniel	1				
Woodard, Antipas	2	2	2		
Woodard, Edward	1	3	2		
Wooard, John	1	1	3		
Woodruff, Lambert	1	4	1		
Welton, Stephen	1		1		
Welton, Dan	2		1		
Welton, Reuben	2	2	5		
Weiton, Josiah	1	2	3		
Woodard, Israel	3	2	4		
Williams, Timothy	2				
Woodard, Nathan	1	1	3		
Way, Abel	1		1		
Woodard, Abel	4	2	4		
Williams, Jeames	1	1	3		
Clark, Chauncy	1	1	2		
WOODBURY TOWN.					
Atwood, Elijah	2		3		
Atwood, Nathan	2	1	1		
Atwood, Jesse	1	2	4		
Atwood, Elijah, 2d	1	1	2		
Atwood, Oliver	1	1	3		
Atwood, Elisha	3	3	4		
Atwood, David	1	2	2		1
Abenatha, John	1	1	1		
Andrews, Benjamin	2	1	2		
Aspenwall, Abel	1	3	2		
Atwell, John	3	1	5		
Armstrong, Isaac	1	2	3		
Austin, Jesse	1		1		
Andrews, Thomas	1	1	3		
Atwood, Skillars	1		2		
Baron, Jabez	6	1	5		
Baron, Asahel	1	1	2		
Baron, Jabez, 2d	1	2	3		
Berham, Samuel	4		7		
Bradley, Searl	2	1	1		
Bradley, Jehiel	2	2	1		
Bears, Zacheriah	2	1	6		
Bull, Thomas	2		2		2
Bassett, Noah	2	2	3		
Bears, Lewis	1	1	1		
Bradley, Richard	2	1	5		
Benham, Phineas	3		3		
Baldwin, Andrew	3	1	4		
Brewster, David	1	1	5		
Brothwell, F. Joseph	2	1	4		
Benton, Jeremiah	2	2	1		
Brougtron, Amos	1	4	6		
Baldwin, Warner	1	1	1		
Baldwin, Parmale	1	3	4		
Benedict, Noah	3	2	2		
Beach, Enos	2				
Beach, John	1	2	2		
Beach, Joel	1		1		
Baker, Jacob	1	2	5		
Bates, Elias	1	3	1		
Brownson, Abram	2		1		
Brownson, Abram, 2d	1	1	1		
Brownson, Thomas	1	2	3		
Brownson, Abel	1	1	4		
Bassett, Samuel	1	1	8		
Bassett, Isaac	2	1	1		
Bailey, Charles	1	1	5		
Bailey, Thomas	1	1	2		
Blakeley, Dan	3	3	3		
Blakeley, Abram	1	1	2		
Blakeley, Tilley	2	1	2		
Bristol, Samuel	1	2	1		
Bulford, John	2	1	1		
Bostwick, Andrew	3	2	4		
Booth, David	1	4	1		
Booth, John	1	1	4		
Baldwin, Lucy	1		1		
Bears, Josiah	1		2		
Black, Esther					
Blancher, Nathaniel	1	2	4		
Blakeley, Jeames	1		1		
Barnes, John	1		2		
Brownson, Josiah	1		2		
Betts, Azor	1		1		
Beebe, Stephen	1	1	2		
Benham, Smith	1		2		
Boyd, Francis	2	2	2		
Bishop, William	1	1	3		
Curtis, John	3	1	2		
Curtis, David	3	2	6		

LITCHFIELD COUNTY—Continued.

WOODBURY TOWN—continued.

NAME OF HEAD OF FAMILY.	Free white males of 16 years and upward, including heads of families.	Free white males under 16 years.	Free white females, including heads of families.	All other free persons.	Slaves.
Cunnigham, Garwood H.	2	3	2		
Crawfoot, Jeames	3	2	2		
Cherway, Philmi	1	6	3		
Carr, Samuel	1	2	5		
Clark, John	1	3	5		
Cussrey, Daniel	2		2		
Coggshall, Daniel	1		3		
Camp, Charity	1		1		
Crammer, Amos	1	1	4		
Castle, Israel	2		2		
Castle, Simeon	1	2	5		
Castle, Abram	1	4	4		
Castle, Samuel	2	1	2		
Castle, Luke	1		1		
Castle, Peter	2	3	5		
Castle, Reuben	3	1	2		
Cap, C. John	1	2	1		
Clark, Benjamin	1	3	3		
Canfield, Thomas	2	2	3		1
Canfield, Thomas, 2d	2	2	4		
Chatfield, Yarmouth				3	
Crammr, Adam	1		1		
Castle, Booth	1	2	1		
Demming, Phineas	1	1	2		
Davidson, Jeames	2	3	4		
Deforrest, John	2	3	4		
Dean, Samuel	1		3		
Downes, Simeon	1		1		
Downes, Susannah		1	2		
Dailey, Justus	3	2	3		
Easton, Eliphlet	2		1		
Edward, John	2		1		
Eastmon, Benjamin	1	3	4		
Eastman, Vespatian	1		3		
Titus (Eatheopian)				3	
Edgiton, Samuel	1		1		
Eastmon, Azeriah	2	1	4		
Eastman, Abner	1		3		
Easton, Norman	1	2	5		
Elderkin, Jedediah	2	3	6		
Eastman, Federich	1	3	1		
Fairchild, Seth	1		5		
Flowers, Nathaniel	1	1	3		
French, Josiah	1	1	3		
Fusbrie, Ezekiel	2		3		
Fusbrie, Noah	1	2	3		
Galpin, Stephen	1		1		
Galpin, Stephen Curtis	1	2	4		
Galpin, Samuel	3	1	2		
Galpin Abram	1		3		
Galpin, Curtis	1		3		
Glover, Budsery	1	1	4		
Gorden, Alexander	2		3		
Gibbs, Simeon	1	2	3		
Gilchrist, Damaras		1	4		
Gillet, David	2	3	4		
Galpin, Susannah			3		
Griswold, Jonathan		1	1	4	
Hyde, Gideon	2	1	3		
Hurd, Nathan	1	2	4		1
Hurd, Graham	1	3	2		
Hurd, Andrew	3		2		
Hander, Shuball	2		2		
Huntington, Daniel	2	2	6		
Hine, Joel	1	2	1		
Hine, Jonah	1		2		
Hull, Daniel	2		1		
Hotchkiss, Reuben	1	3	1		
Hurlbert, Turman	2	5	1		
Hurd, Wait	1	2	5		
Hall, John	1		2		
Hunt, Isaac	2		2		
Hunt, Isaac, 2d	1	2	2		
Hunt, Seth	1	1	4		
Hunt, Gideon	3		1		
Hunt, William	1		2		
Hunt, Lydia	2		3		
Hand, Bendict	1	2	4		
Hinman, Ephraim	3	1	3		
Hurlbut, Amos	1	2	4		
Hurlburt, Thomas	1	3	2		
Hurlburt, Ebenezer	1		2		
Hurlburt, Gideon	1		2		
Hawley, Ann		2	4		
Hurd, Simeon	3	1	4		
Hurd, Curtis	2	2	6		
Hurd, Moses	1	2	3		
Hurd, Thaddeus	3	3	5		
Hurd, David	1	1	3		
Hurd, David, 2d	1	2	4		
Hough, Buel	1	3	5		
Hodge, Philo	2	1	4		
Hurd, Adam	1	3	3		

WOODBURY TOWN—continued.

NAME OF HEAD OF FAMILY.	Free white males of 16 years and upward, including heads of families.	Free white males under 16 years.	Free white females, including heads of families.	All other free persons.	Slaves.
Hall, William	1	2	3		
Hurd, Noah	1	2	2		
Hammon, David	2		1		
Hall, Mathew	1	2	4		
Hurlburt, Amos	2	1	2		
Hurlburt, Damaras	1		2		
Hurd, Zadock	2		3		
Heart, Jeames	1		1		
Hyde, Ebenezer	1	2	3		
Hurlburt, Gideon, 2d	1	4	5		
Hill, Aaron	1		4		
Hull, Stephen	1		1		
Hull, Ebenezer	3		5		
Hurlburt, Benjamin	3		4		
Hurlburt, Comfort			3		
Hunt, Ransom	1		1		
Hurlburt, Nathaniel	1		1		
Hurlburt, Joel	1	1	3		
Hurd, Nathan	1		1		
Hurd, Nathan, 2d	1		3		
Ives, Asa	1	2	2		
Ives, Anor, 1st	1	2	4		
Ives, Anor, 2d	1	1	1		
Irwin, Andrew	1		3		
Judson, Thomas	1	2	4		
Judson, Chapman	1	2	3		
Judson, Joseph	2	1	2		
Judson, Elisha	2	3	4		
Judson, Jonathan	2	4	5		
Judson, Gideon	2	1	4		
Judson, Isaih	1				
Judson, Benjamin	3	1	4		
Judson, John	1	2	1		
Judson, Noah	4	2	4		
Judson, Joshua	1				
Judson, Jeames	2	2	4		
Judson, Nehemiah	2	4	4		
Judson, Hollister	1		1		
Judson, Emm	1	2	2		
Judson, David	2	3	7		
Judson, Deborah	2	2	3		
Judson, Seth	1	1	1		
Judson, Daniel	2	1	9		
Judson, Nathan	1	1	4		
Jackson, David	2	2	6		
Jordan, Timothy	2	1	2		
Jackson, Comfort	1	2	2		
Judd, Daniel	2	1	3		
Jarvis, Thomas	1		1		
Keeler, Joseph	1	1	4		
Kimberly, Jedediah	1		2		
Kimberly, Benjamin	2	1	3		
Lyon, Bethuel	1		3		
Lamson, Abner	1	2	3		
Leavenworth, Amos	1	2	6		
Leavenworth, John	2	1	3		
Linsley, Abiel	2		1		
Leavenworth, David	2	1	3		
Leavenworth, Elihu	1	3	2		2
Leavenworth, Gideon	1	2	4		
Leavenworth, Moss	1	3	2		
Lucas, Israel	1	1	3		
Leavenworth, Esther			2		
Lacy, Ezra	1	1	3		
Martin, Solomon	1		2		
Martin, Amos	2	1	4		
Martin, John	2		4		
Martin, Elijah	3	1	4		
Martin, Nathan, 2d	1	2	2		
Martin, Abijah	1		2		
Martin, Jonas	1	3	5		
Martin, Samuel	1	1	3		
Martin, Nathan	2	3	2		
Martin, Gold	1		1		
Martin, Thankful			1		
Martin, Isaac	2	2	2		
Mallery, Gideon	1		6		
Mallery, Walker	2	3	3		
Mallery, Thomas	3		3		
Mallery, David	1	1	4		
Miner, Solomon	1	4	3		
Mallery, Aaron	2	2	4		
Miner, Simeon	1	2	4		
Miner, Gilbert	1	1	1		
Miner, Daniel	4	2	3		
Miner, Seth	2	1	4		
Miner, David	1	2	1		
Miner, Preston	1		3		
Miner, Mathew	1	1	4		
Miner, Jonas	1		2		
Miner, Andrew	4	1	2		
Miner, Benjamin	1	1	1		
Miner, Adam	1	1	3		
Miner, Nathan	1	1	3		

WOODBURY TOWN—continued.

NAME OF HEAD OF FAMILY.	Free white males of 16 years and upward, including heads of families.	Free white males under 16 years.	Free white females, including heads of families.	All other free persons.	Slaves.
Miner, John	2		5		
Miner, Samuel	1	2	2		
Miner, Thaddeus	3	1	3		
Miner, Jeames	1	3	3		
Miner, Joseph	1		2		
Miner, Adoniram	1	2	1		
Miner, Thomas	1		4		
Miner, Israel	4	1	5		
Miner, Seth, 2d	1		1		
Miner, Peace	2	2	4		
Miner, Peter	2		2		
Miner, Josiah	1	1	4		
Moramble, John	1		4		
Morris, Mathew	1	3	2		
Mitchel, Reuben	1	1	5		
Mitchel, Nathaniel	3	3	4		
Mitchel, John, 2	1	1	6		
Mitchel, Abijah	1	1	3		
Mitchel, John	3	1	2		1
Mitchel, Asahel	1		1		
Mitchel, Daniel	2		1		
Mitchel, William	2	1	2		
Marshal, Sarah	1	4	3		
Maverill, John	3	2	3		
Munn, Daniel	1	1	1		
Munn, John	1	2	1		
Munn, Abel	1	2	3		
Munn, Gideon	1	2	2		
Masters, John	1		1		
Masters, John, 2d	2	3	3		
Mauray, David	1		3		
Moody, Zimie	2		4		
Moody, Ebenezer	1	1	1		
Munger, John	1	2	5		
Mallery, John, 2d	2	3	2		
Mallery, David	1	2	7		
Mallery, Adna	1		1		
Mitchel, Beriah	1		1		
Mix, Abel	2		6		
Maltbie, Huldah	1	3	4	1	1
Manvil, Simeon	1	1	3		
Marshal, Seth	2		2		
Mitchel, Seth	1	2	3		
Mallery, John	1		1		
Nihols, Gideon	2	3	4		
Nettleton, William	1	2	4		
Nettleton, Josiah	1	1	3		
Norton, George	1		2		
Norton, Austin	1	3	3		
Northrop, Enoch	1		4		
Nichols, John	1				
Orton, Samuel	1	5	4		
Osborn, Nathan, 2d	1	2	3		
Orton, John	2	3	5		
Osborn, Nathan	2		1		
Odle, Walker	1	1	1		
Peet, Elnathan	2		2		
Pond, Dan	1	1	5		
Pond, Edward	2		5		
Pollard, Isaac	1		6		
Prentice, Ameziah	1	3	2		
Percy, Nathaniel	1		3		
Peck, Joseph	2	2	4		
Percy, Joseph	2		4		
Prentice, Thomas	1	1	3		
Prentice, Zackeriah	1		4		
Price, Benjamin	1	2	1		
Painter, Lamberton	3	1	7		
Paterson, Andrew	2	4	2		
Peck, Hezekiah	2	1	2		
Penery, Nathan	1	1	1		
Prentice, Ozias	1	2	2		
Prindle, John	1		(*)		
Pompey, London				1	
Pompy (negro)				4	
Roots, Amos	1	1	3		
Roots, John	3	1	4		
Roots, Thomas	1	1	4		
Roots, Jesse	1	1	1		
Roots, Jesse, 2d	1	1	5		
Roots, Amos, 2d	1		3		
Russel, Benjamin	1	6	2		
Roots, David	1	1	5		
Ransom, Russel	4	2	5		
Rumsey, Nathan	3		1		
Rumsey, David	2	3	2		
Rogers, Jason	1	6	4		
Roots, Joseph	1		3		
Roots, Colonel	1				
Rogers, Phineas	1	3	3		
Rummery, Sarah		1	1		
Rowel, Caleb	1	2	3		
Shelton, William	1	1	1		
Strong, Solomon	3	1	2		

*Illegible.

WOODBURY TOWN—continued.

NAME OF HEAD OF FAMILY.	Free white males of 16 years and upward, including heads of families.	Free white males under 16 years.	Free white females, including heads of families.	All other free persons.	Slaves.
Strong, John	2	2	2		
Spalding, Jonas	1	1	3		
Stoddard, Seth	1	3	2		
Stoddard, Israel	2	3	3		
Stoddard, Gideon	3		4		
Spalding, Oliver	1	1	2		
Stoddard, Eunice	2		3		
Stoddard, Philo	1	2	3		
Stoddard, David	2		2		
Stoddard, David, 2d	1	1	2		
Stoddard, Elisha	3	1	4		
Schuls, Samuel	1	3	3		
Shelton, Gershom	1				
Sanford, Nathan	1	2	4		
Scott, Adoniram	1		2		
Smith, Amos	1	2	1		
Smith, Frederick	1	1	2		
Smith, Nathaniel	2	1	1		
Smith, Samuel	1		2		
Smith, Thomas	1		1		
Shelton, Daniel	2	3	4		
Sherwood, Jonathan	1	3	4		
Sherman, Elijah	6	4	4		
Sherman, Daniel	1		2		
Sherman, Reuben	2		2		
Sherman, Daniel, 2d	1	1	4		
Sherman, Solomon	1		2		
Stoters, Jonathan	1		3		
Smith, Jonathan	1	1	6		
Squire, Nathan	1	1	1		
Squire, Thomas	1				
Squire, Amos	1	1	2		
Squire, Benjamin	1	1	3		
Squire, Thomas, 2d	1	2	5		
Smith, Phineas	2	1	2		
Smith, Richard	3		2		
Sherman, John	2		5		
Sherman, John, 2d	1	1	3		
Semour, John	1		1		
Semour, John, 2d	1	1	1		
Semour, Joseph	1	1	1		
Stoddard, Simeon	1	1	1		
Stoddard, Ichabod	1	2	3		
Smith, Kinner	1	2	1		
Smith, Asa	1		1		
Smith, Bethel	1	2	4		
Smith, Sabra		1	2		
Smith, Robert	1	2	2		
Sherman, Mathew	1	3	1		
Sherman, David	5	1	2		
Stoddard, Thaddeus	1		4		
Stoddard, Daniel	1	1	4		
Tuttle, Ezekiel	2		1		
Tuttle, Ayers	1	2	2		
Tuttle, Aaron	1		1		
Tuttle, Ephraim	1		2		
Tuttle, Andrew	3	3	4		
Tuttle, Daniel	1	2	6		
Tuttle, Abram	1	1	2		
Tuttle, David	2	3	2		
Tyler, Jeames	2	2	2		
Tyler, Jeames, 2d	1				
Tyler, Roswell	1		2		
Tomlinson, Isaac	3	1	3		1
Tomlinson, Timothy	1				
Thomson, Hezekiah	3	2	4		
Terrill, Lee	1	2	3		
Terrill, Timothy	1	1	3		
Towles, Nehemiah	2	3	2		
Towles, Ira	1	3	2		
Trobridge, John	2	3	1		
Taylor, Simeon	1	3	4		
Townsend, Ezra	1				
Thomas, Charles	2	1	4		
Thomas, John	1				
Thomas, Jeremiah	1	4	6		
Thomas, David	1	3	4		
Thomas, Ebenezer	2	3	4		
Thomas, Abram	2	1	3		
Thomas, Friend	1	1	3		
Talman, Ebenezer	1	1	2		
Talman, Josiah	1	1	1		
Tomlinson, Samuel	1	1	1		
Tomkins, Joseph	1	1	2		
Thayer, Cornelius	1	2	3		
Taylor, Charles	3		2		
Tuttle, Bostwick	1		2		
Tuttle, Samuel	1	3	4		
Terrill, Nathaniel	1	4	1		
Terrill, Jonathan	1	2	1		
Tyler, Ebenezer	1	1	6		
Thomas, Ira	1		2		
Torrence, Samuel	1	3	4		
Woodman, Samuel	1	3	4		
Walker, Peter	1	1	8		
Walker, Samuel	2	2	5		1
Way, Daniel	1		1		
Warner, Nathan	2	2	3		
Warner, Emm		1	5		
Warner, Benjamin	3	2	2		
Warner, Ebenezer	1		2		
Warner, Ebenezer, 2d	2	3	6		
Warner, Thomas	1	2	4		
Warner, Samuel	1	3	3		
Warner, Joseph	2	1	3		
Warner, Gideon	1	1	4		
Warner, Saul	1	3	2		
Warner, Esther	1		2		
Warner, David	1	1	3		
Warner, Rhoda		1	1		
Warner, Abijail			2		
Walker, Joseph, 2d	1	2	4		
Weller, Zacheriah	3		3		
Weller, Samuel	2	1	3		
Weller, Daniel	1	3	3		
Wells, Thomas	1	2	5		
Wilcox, Stephen	1	2	1		
Way, Isaac	1	2	4		
Wakeley, Henry	1		3		
Wakeley, Platt	1	1	2		
Williams, David	1	1	4		
Whitney, Samuel	1	1	1		
Welles, Elijah	1	1	4		
Walker, Joseph	1	1	1		
Warner, Enos	1	2	3		

MIDDLESEX COUNTY.

CHATHAM TOWN.

NAME OF HEAD OF FAMILY.	Free white males of 16 years and upward, including heads of families.	Free white males under 16 years.	Free white females, including heads of families.	All other free persons.	Slaves.
Akin, Reuben	1		3		
Abby, Samuel	3	1	3		
Abby, Benjamin	1	6	1		
Andrews, Daniel	1	3	1		
Akin, Samuel	1	3	2		
Ames, Nicholas	2	1	5		
Brown, Nathaniel	4		3		
Brown, Richard	1	2	4		
Brown, Ebenezer	1		1		
Baley, Abraham	2		4		
Baley, Recompence	3		2		
Bates, Job	1		2		
Bates, David	1	4	4		
Bates, Abner	1	1	2		
Bidwell, John	1	6	3		
Bartlett, John, Junr	2	1	5		
Bartlett, Moses	1	1	2		
Buck, Samuel	1	1	3		
Buck, Isaac	1		1		
Bowers, Benajah	1		1		
Blague, Joseph	2	1	2		
Brewer, Hezekiah	3		1		
Belcher, Jonathan	4	2	4		
Bacon, Beriah	2		3		
Bush, Moses	1		2		3
Bush, Jonathan	1	2	4		
Bush, George	1	1	2		1
Bliss, Thomas	1	1	3		
Bevins, Ezra	1	1	1		
Bush, Elisha	1				
Brown, Samuel	1	2	2		
Butler, John	1	1	2		
Boardman, Asa	1	1	3		
Goodale, Henry	2		4		
Crosby, William	1		1		
Freeman, Cato				4	
Dixon, William	4	3	7		
Dean, Phinehas	2	1	3		
Davis, Charles	1	2	3		
Diggins, Welles	1	1	4		
Edy, Seth	1	3	5		
Edy, Thomas	1	2	6		
Fox, John	2		2		
Bagley, David	1	4	2		
Goodrich, Charles	3		4		
Goodrich, Richard	1		2		
Goodrich, Jeremiah, Junr	2	5	5		
Goodrich, Joshua	2	1	5		
Goodrich, Solomon	3	1	2		
Goodrich, Reuben	1	3	3		
Goodrich, Charles, Junr	3		4		
Goodrich, Hezekiah	6		7		
Gildersleeves, Obediah	1		2		
Gildersleeves, Phillip	1	3	2		
Gleason, Joseph	1	3	1		
Gains, John	2	1	3		
Goodrich, Jeremiah	1		1		
Grimes, Joseph	2		1		
Hall, Samuel	1		1		
Hall, David	1	2	3		
Hall, Gideon	1		2		
Hall, Abijah	2	4	3		
Hall, Joel	4	4	4		
Hale, Benjamin	1		6		
Hale, Elisha	1	1	2		
Hale, Daniel	1		2		
Hale, Jonathan	2	3	5		
Hall, Isaac	1		2		
Hale, Jabez	1	2	3		
Hale, Elisha, Junr	1	1	2		
Hulbert, Gideon	3	1	2		
Johnson, Jessey	5	1	8		
Kellogg, Joseph	1	6	2		
Knowles, Giles	1	2	3		
Knowles, Isaac	1		1		
Knowles, Seth	1	2	2		
Lewis, Moses	1	1	4		
Lewis, George, Junr	2	2	4		
Lewis, George	1		3		1
Lee, Daniel	1	2	11		
Mc Corney, William	2		1		
Maharr, James	1	3	2		
Butler, Samuel	1	1	1		
Buck, Jeremiah	2	2	1		
Bartlett, Thomas	1	1	2		
Bartlett, John	1	1	2		
Babbett, Jacob	2	1	5		
Bebee, Richard	1		3		
Brewer, David	1		1		
Brown, Jonathan	2	1	2		
Bidwell, Daniel	2	3	6		
Crittendon, Daniel	1	2	4		
Cornwell, Thomas	1	1	5		
Cornwell, Nathaniel	2	4	4		
Cornwell, Samuel	1	3	2		
Cornwell, Andrew	1	3	2		
Chapman, David	2	2	4		
Casheny, William	1		1		
Chapman, John	1	4	3		
Chapman, Solomon	1	2	3		
Churchell, Joseph	3	1	2		1
Cooper, George	1		2		
Cooper, John	1		2		
Chapman, Caleb	1		1		
Ellsworth, John	1		5		
Churchell, Daniel	1	3	4		1
Cheany, Daniel	1	1	1		
Crosby, John	1		2		
Chipman, Ebenezer	1		3		
Chipman, Joseph	1				
Chipman, Barnabas	1				
Cooper, Thomas	1	3	4		
Cooper, Deliverance	1	1	3		
Cooper, Timothy	2	3	4		
Cooper, Harris S	2	1	1		
Chappell, Jonathan	1		2		
Mc Cleave, John	1	1	2		
Mc Corney, William, Junr	1		1		
Mc Comb, John	1		1		
Norton, Jedediah	1		2		
Norcott, Abner	1				
Overton, Seth	1	3	4		
Pelton, John	2		3		
Pelton, Ithamar	2	4	3		
Parmer, Aaron	1	2	3		
Potter, Ezra	2	3	5		
Phelps, Elisha	1	1	2		
Pelton, John, Junr	1		3		
Pain, Reuben	1	4	1		
Pane, Amasa	1	1	1		
Penfield, Simeon	1		2		
Penfield, Jonathan	2	1	3		
Penfield, John	4	1	4		

MIDDLESEX COUNTY—Continued.

CHATHAM TOWN—continued.

NAME OF HEAD OF FAMILY.	Free white males of 16 years and upward, including heads of families.	Free white males under 16 years.	Free white females, including heads of families.	All other free persons.	Slaves.
Penfield, Jessey	1	1	2		
Penfield, Samuel	1	1	3		
Penfield, Amos	1	2	4		
Penfield, Abel	1	1	3		
Penfield, Simeon, Junr	1	2	3		
Penfield, Abisha	1	3	1		
Penfield, Stephen	1	2	2		
Pelton, Johnson	1		1		
Pelton, Johnson, Junr	2	1	6		
Pelton, Josiah	3		4		
Pelton, Joseph	3		3		
Pelton, Joseph, Junr	1	3	2		
Pelton, Jonathan	1	2	3		
Pelton, Abner	1	3	4		
Pelton, Moses	1				
Harrington, Jeremiah	1	1	2		
Rensom, Peleg	1		1		
Pelton, Phinehas	1		1		
Robinson, David	3		2		
Reves, Samuel	1		1		
Ranny, Stephen	1		4		
Russell, Noadiah	2		2		
Russell, Timothy	1	1	3		
Ranny, George	2	2	4		
Ranney, Thomas	1	2	3		
Ranney, Stephen, Junr	1		2		
Reaves, John	2	1	3		
Rass, Noah	1		3		
Randal, John	1	3	5		
Rise, Benjamin	2		2		
Ranney, Jabez	1		1		
Strong, Revd Cuprian	1	4	5		
Sage, David, Esqr	1		4		
Sage, Joseph	1	3	2		
Sage, Noah	1	1	2		
Stocking, John	1		3		
Shields, James	1		1		
Schallenx, Abraham	2	3	3		
Schallennex, Gideon	1	4	3		
Savage, John	1	2	4		
Savage, David	1	2	1		
Savage, Luther	1	1	4		
Stantliff, James, Junr	1	1	3		
Smith, Noah	1		5		
Smith, Charles	1	1	1		
Stow, Daniel, Junr	1		2		
Stewart, Robert	1	1	2		
Sage, Enoch	2	3	6		
Sage, Abner	1	1	4	1	
Strickland, Abel	1	3	3		
Smith, Peter	2		3		
Stocking, David	3	1	1		
Goodrich, John	2	2	3		
Shepherd, John	2		2		
Strickland, Seth	2		4		
Shepherd, John, Junr	1		1		
Shepherd, Amos	1		4		
Shepherd, Elisha	4	3	2		
Shepherd, Daniel, Junr	2	2	6		
Stewart, Daniel	4	1	6	6	1
Stewart, Michael	2	1	5		
Stocking, Marshall	3		1		
Stocking, Moses	1	1	2		
Shepherd, George	1		1		
Shepherd, Noah	1				
Shepherd, Billy	1		1		
Shepherd, Elisha, Junr	1		2		
Gildersleeves, Phillip	1	3	2		
Shepherd, Daniel	3	2	6		
Stocking, Benjamin	2		2		
Tom, Stephen				6	
Ufford, John	1	1	4		
Ufford, Elakim	2	1	2		
Ufford, John, Junr	1				
Ufford, Jonathan	2	4	5		
Vansant, Christopher	1		2		
White, Ebenezer, Esqr	2	1	2		
White, David	1	1	3		
White, Noadiah, Junr	1	3	4		
White, Noadiah	3		4		
White, Joseph	1	4	3		
White, Josiah, Junr	1	4	3		
White, George	1		1		
Willcox, Joseph	1	1	4		
Willcox, Samuel	1	1	4		
Wright, John	1	3	3		
Woolcott, Joshua	1		1		
Waterman, Sylvenus	1	1	1		
Waterman, Samuel	1	1	3		
Willcox, Reuben	1	1	1		
Welles, Thomas	2	3	6		
Willcox, Aaron	3	2	3		
Witherel, Jonathan	1	3	3		
Warner, Deliverance	2	3	6		
Washbourn, John	1		2		

CHATHAM TOWN—continued.

NAME OF HEAD OF FAMILY.	Free white males of 16 years and upward, including heads of families.	Free white males under 16 years.	Free white females, including heads of families.	All other free persons.	Slaves.
Wright, Jonas	1	2	5		
Williams, William	1	1	3		
Ackley, Oliver	1	2	5		
Able, Ebel	2	3	4		
Akins, Thomas	1		1		
Akins, Thomas, Junr	1	2	6		
Akins, George	1		1		
Wood, Jason	1	1	5		
Brainard, Daniel	1	2	5		
Brainard, Seth	2	1	4		
Bevins, Benjamin, Junr	1				
Brown, Nathaniel	1	2	2		
Buckley, Chauncey	2		2		
Bradford, Jeremiah	2		2		
Brainard, Jepthia	1	3	2		
Bradford, Jeremiah, Junr			3		
Brainard, James	2	4	6		
Bowers, Jonathan	2	3	2		
Brainard, Simeon	2	1	3		
Brainard, Simeon, Junr	1	3	3		
Brainard, Ozias	2	3	7		
Hollester, David B	1		4		
Brainard, Nathan	2	4	6		
Hubbard, Royel	1	1	1		
Brooks, Samuel	1	3	5		
Crowell, Heman	2	2	5		
Cary, Josiah	1		3		
Cary, Wait S	1	2	2		
Cady, Ephraim	1		3		
Cook, Jonah	1		5		
Crittendon, Josiah	1	3	2		
Clark, Jonathan	1	2	2	2	
Clark, Elijah	1		3		
Cook, Mary	1		3		
Doan, Seth	3	1	2		
Doan, Asaph	1		3		
Doan, Nathaniel, 2d	2	1	1		
Doan, Nathaniel	2	1	3		
Dart, Josiah	2		4		
Doan, Timothy	1	2	3		
Daniels, Lemuel	1		1		
Daniels, Amasa	2	5	3		
Exton, William	1		3		
Edy, John, Junr	3		2		
Edy, John, 3d	1				
Freeman, Barnabas	1	1	5		
Fuller, Amasa	1	1	1		
Fuller, Abijah	1		2		
Fuller, Samuel	2		6		
Fuller, Thomas	1		2		
Freeman, Nathaniel	2	1	2		
Griffen, Joshua	1	1	4		
Goff, John	2	2	4		
Goff, Ezekiel	1	2	3		
Goff, Phillip	2		1		
Goff, Phillip, Junr	1		2		
Hubbard, Jedediah	2	2	3		
Higgins, Israel	2		4		
Higgins, Israel, Junr	1	1	2		
Hurd, Benjamin	2	2	3		
Higgins, Thesiah			2		
Wheat, Jonas	2	4	4		
Hosmer, Zacheriah	2	1	4		
Higgins, Lemuel	1		2		
Hosmer, Stephen, Junr	1		1		
Hosmer, Asa	1		3		
Holibard, Jehiel	1	2	4		
Holibard, Elisha	6	2	6		
Hurd, Joseph	1	2	5		
Higgins, Lemuel, Junr	1		2		
Hubbard, Jedediah	1		1		
Hubbard, Calvin	1		1		
Hubbard, Timothy	1		2		
Hurd, Jacob	2		2		
Hubbard, Abner	1	2	1		
Hurd, Jessey	1		2		
Hubbard, Jessey	1	2	1		
Hubbard, George	1	2	3		
Higgins, Timothy	1		2		
Holibard, David	2	2	6		
Hosmer, Stephen	1	2	2		
Hill, Daniel	1		2		
Hurd, Jacob, Junr	1	2	4		
Holibard, William, Junr	1	2	3		
Holibard, Reuben	2	2	1		
Johnson, Joseph	2	1	2		
Pelton, George	1		1		
Higgins, James	1	2	3		
Hubbard, John, Junr	4		5		
Higgins, Moses	4	3	3		
Mayo, Richard	2	2	4		
Polly, John	1		2		
Purple, Josiah	1	3	5		
Park, Joseph	1	1	7		

CHATHAM TOWN—continued.

NAME OF HEAD OF FAMILY.	Free white males of 16 years and upward, including heads of families.	Free white males under 16 years.	Free white females, including heads of families.	All other free persons.	Slaves.
Park, John	1	1	1		1
Rowley, Ebenezer	1	2	3		
Ranney, Amos	1	2	4		
Rowley, Gershom	1		2		
Rowley, Ithamar	1	2	4		
Rider, John	1	4	2		
Stocking, Reuben	3	2	6		
Strong, Caleb	1	4	6		
Shepherd, Elisha, Junr	1		2		
Strong, Benjamin	1	3	2		
Shepherd, Abel	1	3	6		
Smith, Enoch, Junr	1	3	3		
Smith, Daniel	2		2		
Smith, Enoch	1	1	3		1
Smith, Ralp	3	2	3		
Smith, Heman	1		3		
Skeel, Asa	2		3		
Smith, Lemuel	4		3		
Swaddle, Sarah			2		
Smith, David	4	2	5		
Smith, Timothy	1	3	2		
Seldon, Thomas	1	6	3		
Strong, John	1	3	2		
Stocking, Abner	1		1		
Smith, Michael, Junr	1	2	2		
Stocking, Amasa	1	2	3		
Taylor, Noadiah	3	2	5		
Smith, Benjamin	4	4	5		
Strong, Josiah	2	3	8		
Shepherd, Edward	2	1			2
Shepherd, Edward, Junr	1	1	2		
Sears Hezekiah	3	2	7		
Seldon, Aaron	1	2	4		
Smith, David	1	1	2		
Taylor, Noadiah	1		1		
Taylor, Elisha	1		1		
Selden, David	1	4	2		
Taylor, Samuel	4	3	8		
Shepherd, Thomas	1		2		
Snow, Ebenezer	1	1	2		
Wright, John	1		1		
Wright, William	2	1	7		
Young, Samuel	3	2	4		
Young, Elijah	1	1	2		
Ackley, Thomas	4		1		
Ackley, Stephen	3		5		
Ackley, Levi	1				
Alvord, Seth, junr	1	3	4		
Whitmore, Luther	1	3	3		
Alvord, Orin	1	1	5		
Alvord, Seth	1	1	2		
Ackley, James, Junr	1	1	2		
Ackley, Ezra	1	1	8		
Alvord, Rend	1	2	4		
Ackley, Elizabeth			2		
Ackley, Edward	1	1	5		
Bailey, Ebenezer	1	4	6		
Bailey, Robert	1	4	4		
Brown, Samuel	2	1	3		
Brown, Samuel, Junr	1	1	3		
Brainard, Othniel	1	1	1		
Bailey, James	2	1	4		
Bill, Erastus	1		2		
Bailey, Joshua, Junr	1		2		
Bailey, Joshua	3		1		
Bars, James	2		4		
Beebe, Comfort	1		1		
Babbett, Elijah	1	1	5		
Bevin, William	1		1		
Bevin, Isaac	1	3	5		
Bailey, Ichabod	1	1	3		
Bailey, Solomon	1		3		
Arnold, Gideon	1		3		
Arnold, Apollas	1	1	3		
Bewell, Joseph	3	2	3		
Colly, Stephen	1		1		
Carrier, Titus	3	1	2		
Comstock Jabez	1	1	3		
Cook, Richard	1	1	3		
Chapham, Elezier		1	7		
Carrier, Andrew	2		2		
Cole, Ebenezer	1	1	4		
Cole, Ebenezer, Junr	1		1		
Cole, Marcus	1	2	1		
Cole, Abner	1	1	1		
Cone, Nathaniel	1	2	5		
Clark, Nathaniel	1		2		
Bill, James	2	2			
Clark, John, Esqr	2		1		
Caswell, John	1		3		
Caswell, Joseph	1	1	5		
Cunning, George	1	1	4		
Clark, William	1		1		
Clark, David	2	3	2		
Cowdry, Thomas	1		4		

MIDDLESEX COUNTY—Continued.

NAME OF HEAD OF FAMILY.	Free white males of 16 years and upward, including heads of families.	Free white males under 16 years.	Free white females, including heads of families.	All other free persons.	Slaves.	NAME OF HEAD OF FAMILY.	Free white males of 16 years and upward, including heads of families.	Free white males under 16 years.	Free white females, including heads of families.	All other free persons.	Slaves.	NAME OF HEAD OF FAMILY.	Free white males of 16 years and upward, including heads of families.	Free white males under 16 years.	Free white females, including heads of families.	All other free persons.	Slaves.
CHATHAM TOWN—continued.						CHATHAM TOWN—continued.						EAST HADDAM TOWN—continued.					
Clark, Stephen	1	1	2			Smith, Isaac	1		1			Brainerd, Bezaleel	3		4		
Cowdry, Nathaniel	1		1			Smith, Isaac, Junr	3	2	4			Gates, Joseph	2	4	4		
Cole, Moses	2	2	8			Smith, Ralph	2	2	6			Gates, Joshua	2	1	4		
Cole, Hannah	1	2	3			Smith, Sparrow	1	1	1			Gates, Caleb	1	3	2		
Caswell, Jonathan	1	1	3			Strong, Adonijah	2	5	6			Gates, Iona	2	1	5		
Cook, Moses	2	2	5			Shepherd, Thomas	2	1	3			Olmstead, James	2		4	1	
Clark, Amos	1	1	3			Shattuck, Randal	2	2	3			Moseley, Thos, Esqr	1		1		2
Clark, Jabez	1	2	1			Smith, Haziel	1	2	3			Moseley, Jona O	1	1	2		6
Cowdry, Jonathan	1		1			Sears, Elkanah	2		2			Emmons, Joseph	3	1	2		
Clark, Aaron	1	1	1			Sears, Isaac	1	1	4			Parsons, Revd Elijah	2	1	3		
Dothick, Ananias	1	2	5			Sears, Willard	1		2			Wadkins, Ephm	1	1	5		
Davis, Comfort	2	2	4			Tennant, Moses	1		3			Peck, Elisha	2	1	2		
Daniels, Amos	1	2	1			Taylor, Stephen	1	1	2			Chapman, Polly		5	2		
Dailey, Joseph	1	3	3			Thomas, William	1		3			Worthington, Elias	1	1	2		1
Fuller, Timothy	1					Tubbs, Lemuel	1	1	2			Gates, Bezaleel	1	1	6		
Freeman, Sylvenus	1	2	2			Trowbridge, John, Junr.	1		3			Smith, Thos	1	1	2		
Freeman, Sylvenus, Junr.	1	1	2			Trowbridge, Jonathan	1	1	3			Champion, Israel	2		2		
Fuller, Judge	1		1			Welch, William	1	2	4			Champion, Reuben	1		1		1
Fuller, Ezra	2		2			Welch, John	1	4	3			Brainerd, John	2	3	6		
Goff, Samuel	1	1	3			Welch, Constant	1	2	5			Ackley, Elijah	3	2	5		
Goff, James	1	2	1			White, Phillip	1	1	4			Brainerd, Amasa	3	2	5		
Goff, Jonathan	1	1	1			White, Ephraim	1		3			Brainerd, Joshua, 2d	2		3		
Goff, Josiah	1	1	1			Smith, Ezra	2		2			Willey, David	1	1	4		
Goff, Jacob	1	1	2			Willey, John	3	1	2			Cone, Timo	2	2	5		
Griffith, Stephen	1	1	3			White, William	1	2	5			Cone, Ebenezer	2		4		
Goff, Benjamin	1		3			White, Moses	1		2			Cone, Phinehas	1	2	4		
Gates, Nehemiah	1	1	1			Waterhouse, Mary			3			Warner, Danl	1	1	6		
Chappel, Caleb	1	1	4			West, Lemuel	3	5	4			Warner, Oliver	3		1		
Gates, George	1	2	4			Wood, Joel	1	1	3			Warner, Joseph	3		1		
Harding, Olive	1		1			Witherel, Henry	2		1			Ackley, Stephen	2		3		
Harding, Ebenezer	1	2	6			Webb, James	2	2	5			Arnold, John	1		2		
Hall, Calvin	1		1			Ackley, James	2	2	7			Spencer, Jared W	1	3	2		
Hinckley, John	4	3	6			Ackley, Samuel	2	3	5		1	Ackley, Elijah	1	1	3		
Hall, Dewy	1	4	5			Brainard, John	4	4	7			Ackley, Amasa	2	3	3		
Harris, Ely	1	7	2			Brainard, Stephen	4	2	6			Warner, John	2		3		
Hall, Jabez	2		2			Comstock, Christopher	1		1			Beckwith, Francis	1	1	1		
Hall, Abijah, Junr	1		2			Mitchell, Zephcniah	1	1	2		1	Church, Joseph	3	1	3		
Hall, Ebenezer	2		2			Mitchell, Zephaniah, Junr	1	3	1			Spencer, David	1	2	4		
Hall, Seth	1	1	2			Mitchell, Asa	1	1	2			Willey, Jonathan	1	1	5		
Hodge, Samuel	1		1			Scovill, Lemuel	1	3	3			Gates, Brainerd	1		5		
Harding, Ephraim	1	5	2			Scovil, Abagail		1	5			Fuller, Nathan	1	1	5		
Harding, Nathaniel	3	5	4			Totten, Samuel	1		1	1		Brainerd, Joshua	1		1		
Hubbard, Seth	1	3	6			Trowbridge, Ebenezer	2		4			Spencer, Gideon	2		2		
Jackson, Salah	1	2	1			Usher, Robert	3	3	5		1	Andrews, John	1	3	2		
Johnson, John	1	2	5			Williams, Thomas	2	3	6			Andrews, Joseph	1	3	6		
Hallen, John, Junr	1	1	3			Miller, Daniel	2		2			Andrews, Zephaniah	2	3	1		
Hill, Samuel	1	1	1			Brooks, Mary		2	2			Lyon, Josiah	1	1	3		
Doolittle, Margaret			3			Cotton, James	1		1			Fuller, Thankfull			2		
Kilbourn, Samuel	1	1	5			Goff, Gideon	1		2			Warner, Jabez	2		3		
Knolton, Stephen	1		2			Hop, John	2	4	4			Warner, Seldon	1	1	1		
Keys, Nathaniel	1		3			Hosmer, Timothy	1	2	2			Gates, Timothy, Esqr.	2	2	5		1
Lucas, Samuel	2		3			Hallen, John	2	3	3			Tracy, Nehh	1	1	2		
Loveland, Daniel	1	1	2									Tracy, Gamaliel R	1		2		
Lewis, Nathan	2	1	4			EAST HADDAM TOWN.						Selbe, Wm	1		1		
Lord, Eliphalet	1											Selbe, Jereh	1	4	4		
Lucas, John	1		2			Chapman, Jabez, Esqr.	11		4	2		Mark, Hezh	3	4	2		
Mott, Samuel	2	1	3			Gailston, Willm	1	2	5			Wright, Saml	1	1	4		
Morgan, Amos	2	3	7			Percivall, Gordon	1	4	3			Gates, Thos	1		1		
Mott, Nathaniel	2	1	3			Palmes, Samel	1	4	1			Gates, Thos, Junr	1	1	1		
Markham, Nathaniel	1	2	4			Johnson, Elijah	1		5			Gates, Gideon	1		2		
Marklam, John	1		3			Wenslow, Jesse	1	3	4			Tracy, Susanna		1	4		
Welch, William	2	1	2			Bunnel, Frank					4	Smith, Matthew	1		2		
Markham, James	1	2	1			Warner, Hannah			2			Smith, Jereh	1	3	2		
Mathews, Asahel	1	1	2			Harvey, Willm	1	3	2			Spencer, Juda	2		4		
Newton, Asahel	3	3	2			Mitchell, Samel	1	1	6			Smith, Matthew, 2d	1	3	4		
Nobles, Jonathan	1		1			Sears, Matthew	3		1		2	Spencer, Mary			2		
Norcott, Reuben	1	2	3			Anable, Abrm	4	3	2			Spencer, Jonathan	1	2	2		
Norcott, William	2		5			Spencer, Abigail		1	2			Spencer, Simeon	1		1		
Niles, David	1	5	4			Huntington, Jno	2	2	5			Fuller, Stephen	1		1		
Niles, Elisha	1	1	3			Belding, Stephen	1	2	1			Parmer, Levi	3	2	5		
Norton, John	1	2	7			Atwood, Elijah	3	2	8			Ackley, Ephm	3	4	1		1
Parmela, Bryan, Esqr.	2	1	2			Atwood, Elijah, Junr.	1	1	2			Andrews, Thos	1	2	2		
Griffeth, Joshua, Junr.	1	1	2			Brainard, Eleazer	3		1			Fox, Saml	1	1	2		
Johnson, Isaac	1	2	4			Belding, David	1	2	4			Spencer, Solomon	1	2	3		
Parsons, Revr Lemuel	1	2	4			Thomas, David	1	3	3			Spencer, Silas	2	1	4		
Parmelee, John	1	3	3			Lord, Saml P.	5	3	6		3	Hall, Margaret			1		
Rich, Samuel	2	2	4			Tinker, Silvanus	3	1	5	1		Hall, Saml, Junr	1	1	1		
Tupper, Mayo	1	2	3			Champion, Epaphras	5	1	4	1		Hall, Saml	2	2	6		
Purple, Edward	2	2	6			Metcalf, Elijah	2	3	4			Hall, Thos	1	1	6		
Park, Daniel	2	4	5			Tinker, Temperance	1		3			Gates, Ephraim	1	3	6		
Parmela, Jonathan	1		1			Marshal, Thos	5	2	5			Spencer, Sarah			5		
Parmela, Jared	1	2	5			Green, James	4	3	4			Ely, Gabriel	2	4	4		
Rogers, Augustus	2		3			Lyon, Humphrey	3		6			Stocking, David	1	1	3		
Rowley, Asher	1	1				White, Amos	3	3	7		2	Hall, Abner	3	3	3		
Remsen, Joseph	1		4			Wacket (Freeman)				2		Olcott, Thos	2		2		
Remsen, Joseph, Junr.	1		4			Daniels, Thos	1		4			Cook, Gideon	2	5	2		
Rich, Cornelius, Junr	2	3	3			Cone, Robt	2	2	3			Hurd, Robt	1		2		
Rogers, Timothy	4		3			Harvey, Elisha	2	1	3			Hurd, Crippin	1	1	2		
Rich, Lemuel	1		2			Bonfoy, Permit	1		4			Bingham, Abel	1	1	3		
Ranney, David	1	1	2			Goodspeed, Nathan	1	2	5			Spencer, Zachariah	1	1	1		
Sears, Ebenezer	1		4			Crowell, Saml	1	3	2			Rowley, Isaac	1		2		
Sears, David	1		1			Spencer, David B	4	1	4			Parmer, John	1		3		
Sexton, Samuel	2	3	5			Ackley, Isaac C	2	2	4			Fuller, Wm W	1	2	3		
Sexton, Jessey	2	2	3			Cone, George	2	3	4			Dick (negro)				4	
												Huntington, Saml, Junr	2	1	3		

MIDDLESEX COUNTY—Continued.

EAST HADDAM TOWN—continued.

NAME OF HEAD OF FAMILY.	Free white males of 16 years and upward, including heads of families.	Free white males under 16 years.	Free white females, including heads of families.	All other free persons.	Slaves.
Huntington, Sam¹	1		3		
Cillerman, Wm	2	2	4		
Kilbourn, Jonathan	3		5		
Chapman, Isaac	2	3	6		
Chapman, Danˡˡ	1	2	4		
Clark, Uriah	1		2		
Cone, Elisha	2		3		
Comstock, Jacob	1	4	1		
Chappel, Joshua	1	1	2		
Williams, Elijah	1	1	2		
Chapman, Timo	2	2	3		
Williams, Charles	1	2	2		
Chapman, Francis	2		3		
Chapman, Ozias	4	4	6		
Hurd, Crippin	3	2	5		
Gates, Nathⁿ, 2ᵈ	2	2	3		
Rowley, Eleazer	3	2	6		
Ackley, Wm	3		7		
Gates, Danˡ	1	1	2		
Percival, John, Junʳ	1	1	2		
Percival, John, Esqʳ	2	1	5		
Fuller, David	3		2		
Fuller, Thoˢ	1	1	3		
Fuller, Jehiel, 2ᵈ	2	2	3		
Fuller, Jehiel	2	1	5		
Fuller, Jrad	1	1	2		
Taylor, Isaac	2	1	3		
Gates, Noadiah	2	4	3		
Gates, Phinehas	1	4	4		
Chapman, Caleb	1	4	5		
Chapman, Sam¹	1	2	3		
Pike, Mary			2		
Higgins, Elkina	2	1	2		
Higgins, Dolle			3		
Mobs, Sam¹	1	1	1		
Gates, Oliver	1	2	2		
Gates, Helen (Widᵒ)		1	2		
Cone, Joshua	1		1		
Cone, Hannah	2	1	3		
Cone, Noadiah	1	1	1		
Isham, John	1	1	1		
Higgins, Jedʰ	3	1	1	1	
Higgins, Stephen	1	2	4		
Hannibal, Joseph	1	1	3		
Chapman, Zachʰ	2	1	6		
Throop, Phebe		1	3		
Hurd, Thoˢ	1	4	2		
Fowler, Joseph	1	2	3		
Ransom, Amos	4	2	3		
Brainerd, Jared	1	1	3		
Starlin, Simon	3	5	2		
Mason, Cooley			1	7	
Spencer, Amasah	1	1	3		
Chapman, John	1				
Rowley, Lydia			2		
Clark, Sam¹	1	1	6		
Randal, Amos	1	1	3		
Usher, Hezʰ	4	4	5		
Comstock, Phebe			3		
Griffin, Geo	4	2	5	1	
Jewett, Nathan	4	1	4		
Brown, Danˡ	1	2	4		
Beckwith, Job	1		1	1	
Chaddock, Silas	1	2	2		
Baker, Mercy	2	1	1		
Beckwith, Barzilla	3	3	6		
Griffin, John	1	3	2		
Griffin, Lemel	5	3	3		
Griffin, Nathan	3		2		
Jewitt, Nathan H	1	2	3		
Jewitt, Sarah	1	1	7		
Williams, Thoˢ	1	2	2		
Bebee, Clark	2	1	2		
Maynard, John	2	2	5		
Dean, Sam¹	1	3	3		
Pran, John	1	1	2		
Rogers, Gordon	1	3	3		
Rogers, John	3	1	2		
Ackley, Simeon	2		2		
Hughs, John	1	1	2		
Spencer, Israel, Esqʳ	2		2		
Spencer, Ebenezer	1		1		
Spencer, Seldon	1	2	3		
Cone, Sam¹	1		1		
Cone, Roswell	2	1	3		
Parmelee, Phinehas	2		3		
Post, Sam¹	1	1	2		
Seldon, Joseph	1	2	5		
Comstock, Israel	1	1	2		
Willey, Sam¹	2		2		
Warner, Sam¹	1	1	1		
Willey, Ezra	1		2		
Warner, John, 2ᵈ	2	1	6		
Hungerford, Joseph	1	1	3		
Comstock, Jabez, 2ᵈ	1	1	4		

EAST HADDAM TOWN—continued.

NAME OF HEAD OF FAMILY.	Free white males of 16 years and upward, including heads of families.	Free white males under 16 years.	Free white females, including heads of families.	All other free persons.	Slaves.
Comstock, Jabez	3	1	4		
Holmes, Christopher	3	1	2		
Rawson, Erindol	3	2	4		
Hungerford, Robt	2		1		
Hungerford, Elijah	1	2	4		
Marsh, Lem¹	1	2	6		
Marsh, Edmond	2	2	3		
Usher, Oliver	1		2		
Warner, Joseph, 2ᵈ	2	2	2		
Hungerford, Robt, Jur	1	3	2		
Beckwith Nath¹	2	2	4		
Holmes, Elephalet, Esqʳ	2	2	4		
Wilbee, Abm	1		1		
Warner, Abm	1		1		
Miner, Caziah			1		
Cone, Juda	1		3		
Marsh, Sam¹	1		3		
Willey, Joseph	1		3		
Phelps, David	1	1	3		
Willey, Ephm, Junʳ	1	2	3		
Beckwith, Joseph	1		1		
Beckwith, Chauncey	1		3		
Beckwith, Joseph, 2ᵈ	1		2		
Beckwith, Stephen	1	1	3		
Harvey, Ithamar	1	2	1		
Lyon, Elizabeth		1	2		
Hungerford, Zachʰ	2	1	4		
Minor, Elihu	1	2	1		
Hunn, Saml	2	2	3		
Cone, Sam¹, 2ᵈ	1	1	3		
Dutton, Joseph	1		2		
Crosby, Levi, 2ᵈ	1	1	4		
Spencer, Reuben	1	2	4		
Parker, John	2	2	3		
Lord, Sam¹	1	3	1		
Andrews, Asael	1	4	3		
Vail, Revʳ Joseph	1	3	3		
Willey, Noah	1	4	4		
Freeman, Peter			1	3	
Willey, Seth	1	2	4		
Willey, Cyrus	1	1			
Willey, Titus	1				
Hoel, Edwd	1	3	3		
Hunn, Mary	1		2		
Little, John	1	3	4		
Phelps, Sam¹	1	1	3		
Hatch, Elnathan	1	2	5		
Banning, Joseph	1	5	3		
Crosby, Increase	1		3		
Crosby, Benjᵃ	1	1	2		
Dixon, Edwd	1	1	1		
Crosby, Levi	1		4		
Crosby, Elijah	1	1	2		
Bebee, John	1	1	4		
Dewey, Israel	1	1	2		
Jewet, Gibbins	2	1	4		
Willey, Aaron	1	1	1		
Stewart, John	1		2		
Spencer, Joel	2	1	3		
Hungerford, Nath¹	1	1	3		
Hungerford, Nath¹, 2ᵈ	1		2		
Mather, Augustus	1	2	4		
Spencer, Isaac, Jur, Esqʳ	2	4	2	1	
Cone, Mary	1		3		
Cone, Benjᵃ	1		3		
Gates, Zeprᵃ	1		3		
Cone, Jonᵃ	2	1	3		
Stewart, Benjᵃ	1	1	2		
Lyman, Revᵈ Wm	1		2		
Southmayd, Danˡ	1	2	4		
Spencer, Hannah	2		5		
Phillis (Freeman)			1		1
Buckley, Danˡ	1	1	2		
Otis, Charles	2	1	4		
Gates, Martha	1	1	4		
Estherbrooks, Hobert	2	1	9		
Rose, Hannah	1		2		
Dutton, Russel	1		2		
Dutton, Sam¹	2		1		
Minor, Turner	1	2	1		
Bebee, Brockway	3		3		
Burnham, Nath¹, 2ᵈ	2	1	3		
Cone, Wm	3	1	4		
Gates, Joseph, 2ᵈ	2	3	6		
Gates, Nathan	3	1	2		
Warner, Jabez, 2ᵈ	1	1	3	1	
Clark, Sterlin	1		3		
Bebee, Abner	4		5		
Ingraham, Elkinah	1	2	3		
Cone, George	1	3	4		
Fuller, Benjᵃ	1		2		
Fox, Ebenezer	2		3		
Fox, Moses	1		2		
Willey, Susannah			4		
Willey, Alford	1		2		

EAST HADDAM TOWN—continued.

NAME OF HEAD OF FAMILY.	Free white males of 16 years and upward, including heads of families.	Free white males under 16 years.	Free white females, including heads of families.	All other free persons.	Slaves.
Chapman, Simeon	2	1	4		
Ackley, Sam¹	1	1	1		
Bebee, Caleb	1	2	3		
Spencer, Timo	2	3	4		
Bebee, Avary	1		2		
Bebee, Phebee	1		1		
Fuller, Mary	3		2		
Wickwire, James	2		3		
Gilbert, Sam¹	2	3	7		
Ransom, Joshua	1	3	5		
Cone, Martin	1				
Marshe, Woodward	2	2	2		
Arnold, Enoch	2		3		
Miller, Sarah			3		
Lord, Elijah		1	3		
Dutton, Amasa	4	5	3		
Bebee, Nathan	1		3		
Fuller, Uriel	1	2	5		
Willey, John	1	1	2		
Willey, Jabez	1	1	3		
Gates, Nath¹	1		3		
Nolton, Thoˢ	1		2		
Clark, Asa	1	2	4		
Burnham, David	1		1		
Burnham, Sylvester	1		3		
Arnold, Ephm	1	2	6		
Willey, Josiah	1	2	1		
Wickham, David	3	1	5		
Gates, Sam¹	1		1		
Willey, Benaiah	1		3		
Arnold, Joseph	2		4		
Willey, G. Warren	1		3		
Ackley, Thoˢ	1		1		
Niles, Daniel	1		1		
Cone, Joseph	1		2		
Spencer, Jared, Esqʳ	1		2		
Swan, Jabez	2	2	6		1
Brainerd, Enoch	2		6		
Bebee, Ebenezer	1	2	2		
Ackley, Nath¹, 3ᵈ	2		5		
Olmstead, Daniel	1	3	3		
Rich, Isaac	1	4	5		
Brookes, Timothy	1	2	2		
Bebee, Hannah	1		1		
Niles, John	1	1	1		
Martin, Jonathan	2	5	1		
Ackley, Gideon	2		1		
Dickinson, Simeon	4	2	3		
Cone, Nehᵇ	1	2	6		
Andrews, Sam¹	1	2	2		
Emmons, Noadʰ	1	4	2		
Cone, Danˡ	1	1	7		
Lee, Wm	1	2	2		
Davis, Joseph	2		6		
Cone, James	3	4	3		
Cone, Silvanus	2	1	3		
Cone, Solomon	1	2	4		
Corkins, Aquilla	1		3		
Clark, Dan	2		4		
Cone, Israel	1	2	3		
Marsh, John	1		1		
Stewart, Wm	1		1		
Stewart, Wm, 2ᵈ	1	1	5		
Harvey, Robt	1		6		
Harvey, Amasa	2	5	2		
Fox, Joshua	1	1	6		
Harvey, Russel	2		1		
Anderson, Robt	1	2	3		
Spencer, Isaac	3	1	5		
Hungerford, Green	1	2	6	1	
Brockway, Enoch	1		4		
Harvey, Robt, 2ᵈ	2	4	2		
Hannibal, John	2	2	2		
Harvey, Jonᵃ	1		1		
Willey, Ephm	1	2	4		
Graves, Benjᵃ	1	1	1		
Harvey, Asa	2	2	5		
Mack, Richᵈ	1	1	1		
Graves, Elijah	2	2	4		
Harvey, Ithamar, Jr	1	1	3		
Harvey, Elisha	1	1	3		
Harvey, Zachra	2	5	7		
Beckwith, Ezekiel B	1	1	3		
Beckwith, Sam¹	1	6	2		
Robins (Black)				3	
Sparrow, Deborah	2	1	6		
Stewart, Sam¹	1	2	5		
Sparrow, Nath¹	2		5		
Burnham, Nathan	1		4		
Hinckley, Ebenʳ	1		2		
Bebee, Lydia			2		
Stewart, Joseph	1	1	3		
Fox, Ezekiel	2	1	2		
Spencer, Matthias	1	1	2		
Spencer, Reuben	1	2	5		

MIDDLESEX COUNTY—Continued.

NAME OF HEAD OF FAMILY.	Free white males of 16 years and upward, including heads of families.	Free white males under 16 years.	Free white females, including heads of families.	All other free persons.	Slaves.
EAST HADDAM TOWN—continued.					
Smith, Thos, 2d	3		2		
Jones, Diad	1	1	2		
Spencer, Wm	1	1	3		
Burnham, Joshua	3	2	2		
Bigelow, Joel	1	1	2		
Bigelow, Elisha	2		8		
Fox, Gershom	1	2	2		
Fox, Wm	1		3		
Ackley, Simeon, Jr	1	3	6		
Lord, Nathl	2	1	5		
Fuller, Levise			2		
Rogers, Thos	1	2	1		
Fuller, Noadiah	1		1		
Fuller, Noadiah, Jr	1		3		
Fuller, Danl	2	1	3		
Fuller, Elisha	2		2		
Arnold, John, Jr	3	2	4		
Morgan, Abijah	2	3	5		
Williams, Abm	1	1	4		
Church, Wm	1				
Church, Richd	2	1	1		
Church, Oliver	1		2		
Cone, Elihu	1	2	5		
Bebee, Willm	1		3		
Plum Green	1		4		
Williams, Phillip	2	1	2		
Stocking, Ellis			2		
Watson, John	1	1	2		
Watson, John, Junr	1	2	3		
Butler, Amos	1	3	2		
Lenneaux, Benja	1		2		
Church, Ira	1	1	5		
Olmstead, Jehd	3		5		
Olmstead, Roger	1				
Jones, Daniel	1		1		
Smith, Ignatious	3		4		
Smith, Jno H	2	1	2		
Sheppardson, Jno	1		1		
Sheppardson, Willm	1	2	5		
Pecker, Nathl	1		2		
Gates, Matthew	1	2	2		
Olmstead, Bates	2		3		
Beebee, Silas		2	2		
Beebee, Jehiel	2	1	3		
Gates, Timo, 2d	1	2	2		
Lord, Willm	1		1		
Emmons, Ithamar	2	1	5		
Emmons, Saml	3	1	3		
Olmstead, Oliver	2	2	2		
Emmons, Daniel	2		2		
Williams, Robinson	1	1	2		
Williams, Robinson, Jur	1	2	2		
Emmons, Ebenezer	2		1		
HADDAM TOWN.					
May, Revd Elerzer	3	1	4		1
Brainard, Hezh, Esqr	2		3		1
Church, John	1	2	3		
Church, Thomas	1	3	6		
Cone, Elisha	1		2		
Smith, Sylvenus	1	1	3		
Brainard, William	1	2	6		
Brainard, Eber	1	1	2		
Hazelton, Nathaniel	2		3		
Hazelton, Arnold	1	2	3		
Haden, John	1	1	2		
Cone, Samuel	1	3	2		
Hazelton, Simeon	1	1	3		
Hazelton, Hannah			1		
Fuller, Daniel	2	2	3		
Welles, Joseph	1		1		
Dart, Siras	1	1	2		
Arnold, Joseph	2	1	1		
Clark, James S	1		2		
Smith, Martha		1	1		
Smith, Hezekiah	3	1	6		
Merwin, Heman	1	1	2		
Kelsey, George	1	4	1		
Smith, William	4	2	3		
Smith, Daniel, Junr	5	4	3		
Chapman, Timothy	1	1	1		
Arnold, Samuel	4	2	5		
Clark, Samuel	2	1	5		
Smith, Reuben	2	2	3		
Smith, Elias	1	1	5		
Brainard, Nehemiah, Esqr	3	1	5		
Smith, Abisha	1	1	3		
Shaler, Bezeleel	2	2	7		
Brooks, Jonathan	1	2	4		
Brooks, Joseph, Esqr	3		5		
Brooks, Wakeman	2	1	2		
Brooks, James	1		1		
Thomas, Ebenezer	2		6		

NAME OF HEAD OF FAMILY.	Free white males of 16 years and upward, including heads of families.	Free white males under 16 years.	Free white females, including heads of families.	All other free persons.	Slaves.
HADDAM TOWN—continued.					
Thomas, Ebenezer, Junr	1	1	1		
Knowls, Elisha	2		3		
Knowls, William	3		3		
Wakeley, Asa	2	2	3		
Knowls, Richard	4		3		
Knowls, Richard, Junr	1				
Tibbels, Elizabeth			1		
Knowls, Walker	1	2	3		
Thomas, James	2	1	5		
Doane, Phinehas	3	1	7		
Hubbard, Joel	5		4		
Spencer, Elizur	1	2	2		
Spencer, Sarah			1		
Hubbard, Benjamin	1	1	3		
Hubbard, Moses	1	1	2		
Hubbard, Samuel	3		2		
Hubbard, Samuel, Junr	1	3	2		
Thomas, Henry	1	4	3		
Knowles, James	3	4	3		
Knowls, Joshua	1		1		
Woodruff, D	2	3	5		
Sutliff, James	1	2	2		
Hubbard, David	1	1	7		
Hubbard, Jeremiah	2		3		
Hubbard, Shalor	1	3	7		
Hubbard, Jeremiah, Junr	3	2	6		
Hubbard, Thomas, Junr	1		1		
Hubbard, Thomas	2	2	8		
Spencer, David	2		1		
Hubbard, Job	3	1	4		
Spencer, Abner	3		4		
Hubbard, Timothy	2		2		
Hubbard, Timothy, Junr	1		2		
Hubbard, Calvin	1	2	2		
Hubbard, Michael	1		1		
Hubbard, Aaron	2	2	7		
Hubbard, James	3		3		
Hubbard Jonathan	1	1	1		
Tibbells, Stephen	1	1	3		
Clark, William	2		3		
Clark, Adna	1	1	2		
Seward, John	1		1		
Burr, Joseph	1	1	4		
Towner, Daniel	1	1	1		
Brainard, Oliver	1	2	3		
Arnold, Christian	1	2	4		
Thomas, Evan	1		2		
Thomas, Roger	1	4	4		
Smith, Jonathan	4	4	4		
Wells, Oliver	1	1	6		
Brainard, Eliakim	4	1	4		
Brainard, Gideon	5		5		
Smith, James	1	1	3		
Smith, Hubbard	1	1	1		
Brainard, Jessey	1	4	3		
Smith, Frederick	1	2	3		
Smith, Stephen, Junr	1	4	4		
Porter, Ezra	1		2		
Brainard, Phinehas, Junr	2	2	4		
Towner, Timothy	3		2		
Willcox, James	1	1	1		
Willcox, John	3		3		
Burr, Benjamin	1	4	2		
Burr, Jonathan	1	4	3		
Burr, Nathaniel	2		1		
Porter, Edmund	3		3		
Smith, Aaron	3	1	2		
Smith, Jonathan	1		3		
Smith, John	3	2	6		
Smith, Stephen	1		1		
Tibbells, Eben	1	3	4		
Snow, Gideon	1	4	2		
Gloding, Daniel	1	1	5		
Willcox, William	1	1	1		
Spencer, Abigail			2		
Spencer, James	1		2		
Clark, Stephen	2	4	4		
Johnson, Didemus	1		2		
Pelton, James	2	3	5		
Taylor, Joseph	2	3	1		
Burr, Nathaniel	1		3		
Clark, Aaron	1		3		
Clark, Asher	1		2		
Auger, Isaac	2		2		
Tyler Timothy	1	1	1		
Higgins, Hawse	1	2	2		
Higgins, Cornelius	2	1	3		
Auger, Joseph	1		1		
Lewis, Thomas	1	1	4		
Lewis, Augustus	1	4	2		
Tyler, Abraham	2	3	2		
Tyler, Samuel	1	1	2		

NAME OF HEAD OF FAMILY.	Free white males of 16 years and upward, including heads of families.	Free white males under 16 years.	Free white females, including heads of families.	All other free persons.	Slaves.
HADDAM TOWN—continued.					
Tyler, Joseph	3	1	5		
Tyler, Thomas	1		2		
Tyler, Joseph, Junr	1		1		
Dickinson, Mehitible	1		3		
Dickinson, Obediah	1	4	5		
Dickinson, David	1	2	5		
Dickerson, Esther			1		
Dickinson, John	1	1	4		
Arnold, Martha			2		
Arnold, David	1	3	3		
Scovil, Josiah	2		5		
Scovil, John, Junr	1	3	3		
Tyler, Nathaniel, Junr	1	1	2		
Shaler, Samuel	1	2	2		
Shaler, James	1	3	2		
Smith, Charles	1		6		
Arnold, James	1	2	5		
Necho (Negro)				1	
Smith, Martha, 3d		3	2		
Dickinson, Stephen	2		2		
Brainard, Eliakim, Junr	1		2		
Brainard, Gideon, Junr	1		1		
Lewis, Samuel	2	2	7		
Venterhouse, John	3		3		
Dudley, Barzilla	3	1	5		
Shaler, Reuben	1	1	7		
Venterhouse, John, Junr	1		1		
Shaler, Hezekiah, Junr	1	1	1		
Sherman, Benjamin	1	1	3		
Shaler, Thomas	1	3	4		
Shaler, Asa	3	2	4		
Smith, Joshua	1	3	3		
Shaler Aaron	1	2	1		
Ely, William	1	1	4		
Ray, Peter	3	2	4		
Ely, Moses	1	1	2		
Ray, Levi	1		2		
Ray, Joseph	1		1		
Russell, Stephen	3	4	5		
Tyler, Nehemiah	1	1	3		
Ray, Isaac	2		2		
Rutty, Jonah	2	1	5		
Tyler, Simon	3	3	3		
Rutty, Asa	1		2		
Tyler, Nathan	4	1	3		
Smith, Wells	1	2	2		
Shaler, Simon	2	2	4		
Shaler, Jeremiah	1	1	3		
Ray, Nathaniel	1	1	3		
Shaler, Ezra	3		3		
Shaler, Hezekiah	1	2	3		
Miller, Daniel	3	3	4		
Finker, Samuel	4		5		
Ely, Jacob	2		6		
Ray, Jecaniah	1		3		
Ray, Daniel	1	1	4		
Ray, Constant	1		2		
Bates, Daniel	2	2	5		
Bates, Jonathan	1		3		
Southward, Andrew	1	1	3		
Brooks, Nathan	2	2	3		
Clark, Joseph	1	3	6		
Bates, Elihu	3		4		
Clark, Sarah	1		1		
Bates, Joseph	2		1		
Bates, Eleazer	3	1	6		
Bates, Amos	1	1	6		
Seldon, Seephas	1		5		
Selden, Edward	1		5		
Selden, Joseph	1		1		
Brainard, Josiah, Junr	5		5		
Clark, Robert	2	4	4		
Arnold, Samuel B	1	1	4		
Arnold, Jabez	6		5		
Arnold, Jacob	1	3	4		
Arnold, Benjamin	1	1	5		
Brooks, Jabez	2	3	5		
Brooks, Amos	1	2	3		
Brainard, Ezra, Esqr	3	3	4		
Brainard, Zadock	2	2	1		
Brainard, Josiah	1		2		
Young, Asaph	1	4	2		
Brainard, Dudley	1	1	2		
Brainard, Amos	1	1	1		
Tucker, Anner			3		
Brainard, Isaac	1	3	2		
Brainard, Jona	3	2	4		
Goff, Gideon	2	1	4		
Brainard, Robert	1	1	2		
Brainard, James	1	1	2		
Tallbard, William	2	2	4		
Brainard, Jessey	3	1	5		
Brainard, Cornelius	2	1	5		
Higgins, James	1		7		
Brainard, Jedediah	2	2	3		

MIDDLESEX COUNTY—Continued.

NAME OF HEAD OF FAMILY.	Free white males of 16 years and upward, including heads of families.	Free white males under 16 years.	Free white females, including heads of families.	All other free persons.	Slaves.
HADDAM TOWN—continued.					
Brainard, Jedediah, Junr	2	3	5		
Williams, Abraham	4	3	9		
Chapman, Reuben	3	2	3		
Brooks, Samuel, Junr	2	2	4		
Day, Elisha	3	1	4		
Selden, Elias	2	4	3		
Northum, Samuel	1	3	6		
Arnold, John	4	1	5		
Arnold, Joshua	1	4	5		
Cook, Amos	2	1	6		
Willson, John	1	1	8		
Bailey, Nehemiah	2	1	3		
Childs, James R	1	1	4		
Childs, Hannah	1	2	2		
Childs, Thomas	1	2	1		
Smith, Robert	2		2		
Childs, Sylvester	1	1	2		
Kelly, Rebecca			1		
Huntington, Jonathan	2	1	5		
May, John	1		3		
Boardman, Luther	3	1	2		
Sawyer, Ephraim	2	1	3		
Eddy, Seveus	3	3	3		
Brainard, David	2		6	1	
Smith, Elihu	2	1	3		
Scovel, William	2	1	3		
Boardman, Chloe		1	2		
Brooks, Samuel	3		5		
Bailey, William	3	3	5		
Wheeler, Job	2	2	6		
Clark, Samuel, Junr	2	4	3		
Bailey, John	1		1		
Bailey, Amos	1	4	3		
Bailey, Elizabeth			2		
Sutliff, Nathaniel	1		1		
Brainard, Martha	1		3		
Arnold, Joel	1		3	1	
Brainard, Zachariah	3	3	1		
Brainard, Elijah	2	3	5		
Brainard, Samuel	1	2	1		
Spencer, John	1	1	2		
Skinner, Richard	1	2	1		
Smith, David	1	2	1		
Skinner, Ebenezer	4		2		
Chapman, Jonathan	2	3	5		
Boardman, Jonathan	1	3	3		
Bonfey, Bananuel	1	3	4		
Higgins, Cornelius, Esqr	2	1	2		
Spencer, Joseph	2	1	4		
Spencer, Elihu	1	1	3		
Brainard, Prosper	3	2	3		
Spencer, Abigail		1	3		
Spencer, Stephen	1	6	1		
Spencer, William	1		1		
Whitmore, Samuel B	3		4		
Bailey, Desire	1	1	3		
Smith, Lewis	1		4		
Smith, John	2		4		
Smith, Israel	1		4		
Smith, John, Junr	1	1	4		
Smith, Phinehas	1	1	2		
Smith, Samuel	1		2		
Smith, Henry	1		4		
Clarke, Sylvenus	1	1	4		
Clarke, James	2	1	2		
Cone, Elisha, Junr	2		3		
Arnold, Ambross	1	1	6		
Spencer, Daniel	2	1	2		
Spencer, Elia	1	3	2		
Brainard, William	1	1	1		
Bailey, Oliver	2	5	6		
Scovil, Samuel	3	4	7		
Scovil, John	1	2	5		
Scovil, Joseph	1	3	2		
Harvey, Elisha	2		1		
Crook, Joseph	2	5	2		
Crook, Whitmore	1	2	3		
Bailey, Christopher	1		4		
Clark, William, Junr	1	3	4		
Bailey, Eliakim	1	1	1		
Brainard, Josiah, 3d	2	1	2		
Bradford, Robert	3		2		
Spencer, Elisha	2		5		
Crook, Thomas	1	1	1		
Brainard, Jeremiah	5		2		
Sutliff, John	2		2		
Brainard, Nathaniel	2	2	4		
McKnary, Martin	1	3	2		
Brooks, Abigail			2		
Crook, Shubell	4		4		
Johnson, John	1		4		
Bailey, Abijah	2	2	1		
Bailey, Timothy	1	2	1		
Hubbard, Giles	1	2	1		
Bailey, Jabez	3	2	6		

NAME OF HEAD OF FAMILY.	Free white males of 16 years and upward, including heads of families.	Free white males under 16 years.	Free white females, including heads of families.	All other free persons.	Slaves.
HADDAM TOWN—continued.					
Bailey, Ephraim	1		2		
Bailey, Gideon, Junr	4	5	5		
Bailey, Stephen	3	1	8		
Walkley, Richard	1	3	3		
Bailey, Caleb	2	1	5		
Treadwell, Humphrey	1		2		
Brainard, Daniel	2	1	4		
Sears, Charles	3	5	3		
Brainard, John	1	1	9		
Brainard, Heman	1	2	4		
Brainard, Phinehas	2		2		
Bailey, Amy		1	1		
Smith, James, 3d	1	1	3		
Smith, William	2	1	5		
Brainard, Bushnell	2		3		
Brainard, Aaron	1	2	7		
Cone, Reuben	1		3		
Cone, Noadiah	1	1	1		
Cone, James	2		6		
Thomas, Aaron	2	1	5		
Clark, Joseph, Junr	1	1	1		
Clark, Lydia		1	2		
Clark, Patience		2	2		
Clark, Hezekiah	2		2		
Clark, John	2	3	2		
Brooks, Joshua	2	3	3		
Wakeley, Solomon	3	4	3		
Corn, Noah	1	2	5		
Brooks, Abraham	1		7		
Dickinson, Joseph	3	2	4		
Arnold, Joseph, Junr	1	2	2		
Smith, Joseph	1		5		
Kelsey, Benjamin	1	2	3		
Johnson, Isaac	1	1	4		
Stannard, Samuel	1	3	4		
Brooks, Porter	1	2	6		
KILLINGWORTH TOWN.					
Towner, Daniel	2		3		
Towner, Reuben	1	4	2		
Towner, Samuel	1	1	1		
Rutty, Levi	3		2		
Stevens, Hubbell	2	1	2		
Griswuld, Nathaniel	1	2	3		
Parmela, Eliab	1	1	2		
Griswould, Moses	1	1	3		
Griswould, Ebenezer	1	2	4		
Rutty, John	1	1	3		
Clark, Abel	1		2		
Bowers, Zephaniah	2	6	2		
Haden, Jacob	1	4	3		
Parmalee, Nehemiah	1	2	6		
Parmalee, Daniel	1	2	3		
Parmalee, Rhoda	2		3		
Coan, Gaylor	1		1		
Willcox, Abel	5		2		
Willcox, Abel, Junr	1	2	5		
Nettleton, Samuel, 2d	2	3	5		
Pratt, Samuel	2		1		
Parmalee, Roswell	4	2	3		
Parmalee, Amos	1	3	4		
Stillman, George	1	2	3		
Griffen, Samuel	2	3	2		
Stone, Nehemiah	1	2	1		
Turner, Elizabeth			1		
Lord, Martin, Esqr	3	2	6		
Lane, Hezekiah, Esqr	3		3		
Graves, Abner	2	1	1		
Lane, Jabez	1	5	3		
Parmalee, Ozias	2	2	5		
Parmela, Constant	1	1	2		
Lane, Elisha	2	1	2		
Parmela, Cornelius	3		3		
Parmelee, Aaron	1		3		
Parmela, Josiah	2	2	7		
Isbel, Israel	1	3	2		
Parmela, Braini	1	3	1		
Parmela, David	1		1		
Parmela, Nathan	1		1		
Kelsey, Joseph	2		2		
Kelsey, Eber	1	2	4		
Kelsey, Uriah	2	1	4		
Parsons, Samuel, Junr	2	5	3		
Willcox, Abraham	1		1		
Willcox, David	2		4		
Graves, Sylvanus	3		5		
Lane, Joseph	3		3		
Lane, Joseph, Junr	1		2		
Hull, Nathan	3	1	4		
Lane, John	2		3		
Lane, Arunah	1		2		
Stephens, Peter	1	4	5		
Kelsey, David	1		1		
Kelsey, Jonathan	2	1	2		

NAME OF HEAD OF FAMILY.	Free white males of 16 years and upward, including heads of families.	Free white males under 16 years.	Free white females, including heads of families.	All other free persons.	Slaves.
KILLINGWORTH TOWN—continued.					
Kelsey, David, Junr	1		2		
Lane, John, Junr	1	1	4		
Turner, Jacob	1	1	2		
Blackslee, Daniel	1	2	3		
Davis, Henry	1	1	4		
Nettleton, James	3	2	3		
Bishop, Thalmeno	1	3	3		
Evarts, Joseph	1		2		
Norton, Moses	2	4	2		
Norton, Eli	1	2	1		
Norton, John	2	1	3		
Norton, Joel	1	2	3		
Nettleton, Daniel	1	2	3		
Davis, Lemuel	1	2	1		
Francis, James	1	1	1		
Francis, Susannah	1		4		
Francis, Daniel	1	2	6		
Linn, James	3		1		
Hull, Gurdon	1	2	3		
Stephens, Lois	1	4	4		
Griswould, Zenas	1	2	1		
Davis, Solomon	1	2	3		
Davis, Josiah	1	2	4		
Kelsey, Stephen	1	2	3		
Davis, James	2	4	2		
Davis, Martha	1	1	1		
Blakelee, David	2		2		
Brister, Bozaleel	1	4	4		
Hill, James	4	1	3		
Kelsey, Nathaniel	2		5		
Davis, Samuel	2		1		
Buell, Jeremiah, Junr	2	1	7		
Higgins, Sarah			1		
Kelsey, Bani	1		5		
Wheeler, Joseph	2	1	2		
Parmela, Elias	1	3	3		
Parmela, Ezra	1		2		
Parmelee, Jehiel	1	4	4		
Parmelee, Samuel	1	1	6		
Kelsey, Joel	1	4	2		
Isbel, Elias	2	1	3		
Chappell, Jonathan	1		1		
Davis, Samuel, Junr	2		3		
Kelsey, Aaron	1	1	3		
Stephens, Eliakim	1		1		
Nettleton, Josiah	1	1	3		
Nettleton, Isaiah	1		6		
Bewell, Jeremiah	1		1		
Buell, Bela	1	3	3		
Hull, Ezekiel	2		5		
Kelsey, Joseph, 2d	1		2		
Kelsey, Lemuel	1		2		
Franklin, Essi	2	6	4		
Franlin, Jonathan	1		2		
Franlin, Samuel	1	2	5		
Hull, Levi	1	3	3		
Clark, Thomas	1		1		
Clark, Aaron	1	1	2		
Nettleton, Samuel	2		4		
Jones, Daniel	3	1	1		
Parmelee, Abner	4		2		
Phelps, Alexander	1		1		
Harris, Jedediah	1	1	3		
Willcox, Nathan	2		1		
Willcox, Nathan, 3d	1	5	2		
Stone, Benjamin	1		1		
Willcox, Joseph	1	2	6		
Stone, Jedediah	2		5		
Stone, Jedediah, Junr	1	1	1		
Williams, Jonathan	1	1	4		
Jones, Phinehas	1	2	1		
Willcox, Joel	1	1	2		
Coan, Mulford	1	1	2		
Smith, Samuel	1	2	4	1	
Stephens, Samuel, Junr	1		1		
Willcox, Adam	3	1	3		
Brooker, Abraham	1		2		
Snow, John	4				
Snow, William	1		2		
Lebarron, David	1	2	5		
Isbel, Robert	1		2		
Nichols, Rebeca		3	1		
Hill, Noah	1	4	2		
Turner, Abraham	2	1	5		
Stevens, Samuel	3		5		
Stephens, Aaron	1	1	4		
Brooker, Abraham	1		3		
Hull, Lucy			3		
Willcox, Adam	3	1	2		
Crane, Elisha	2	1	3		
Crane, Elisha, Junr	1	1	3		
Peirson, John, Esqr	2		4		
Willcox, Benjamin	2		2		
Buell, William	1	2	3		
Butler, Houton	2	1	2		

MIDDLESEX COUNTY—Continued.

NAME OF HEAD OF FAMILY.	Free white males of 16 years and upward, including heads of families.	Free white males under 16 years.	Free white females, including heads of families.	All other free persons.	Slaves.
KILLINGWORTH TOWN— continued.					
Buell, Asa	2	3	5		
Hull, Joel	1		6		
Hull, Roswell	1	3	3		
Griswould, Nathaniel, 2d	1	1	3		
Kelsey, Daniel	1	3	3		
Parmelee, Daniel	2	1	2		
Kelsey, Elisha	1	1	3		
Kelsey, Martin	2	5	4		
Kelsey, Oliver	1		3		
Ely, Rev' Henry	3	1	5		
Pierson, Abraham, Esq.	2	1	3		
Pierson, Dodo	1	1	2		
Ward, Ichabod	1	1	2		
Watrous, Josiah	1		1		
Redfield, Sylvenus	1	2	6		
Porter, Ezra	1	3	3		
Hull, James	1	3	6		
Stevens, Thomas	2		1		
Stevens, Thomas, Junr	4	3	4		
Hull, Lemuel	1	1	2		
Pierson, Samuel	3		3		
Hull, Lemuel, Junr	1	1	1		
Evits, Jehiel	4		3		
Evits, Jehiel, Junr	2	1	3		
Houd, Edward	3	1	4		
Chittendon, Daniel	2	1	3		
Hull, Abner	2	1	5		
Kelsoy, Moses	1		3		
Hinkley, John	1	1	7		
Davis, Ebenezer	1	3	2		
Davis, Haydon	1		1		
Davis, Sibbell			3		
Kelsey, Martha	1		1		
Stevens, Reuben	5		2		
Nettleton, John	1	3	4		
Griswould, Samuel	1	2	4		
Willson, Elijah, Junr	1	3	3		
Walden, Nathaniel	1		3		
Willcox, Elijah	1		3		
Hull, Peter	1		1		
White, Dudley	3	1	4		
Hull, Josiah	2		1		
Hull, Josiah, Junr	1	1	3		
Kelsey, Augustus	1				
Nettleton, Hannah			1		
Nettleton, Damaras	1	1	4		
Nettleton, Joseph	1	1	1		
Nettleton, Abel	2	1	3		
Butler, Stephen	1		3		
Redfield, Peleg	1	1	1		
Pelton, Josiah	3	4	3		
Redfield, Ambros	1	3	3		
Dudley, Phinehas	2	4	3		
Willcox, Simeon	2	4	9		
Redfield, Constant	1	2	5		
Willcox, Ebenezer	2	1	3		
Dudley, Nathaniel	3		2		
Redfield, Seth	1	5	1		
Redfield, George	1				
Baldwin, Eliezer	1	2	1		
Redfield, Josiah	2	1	2		
Redfield, Tereny	1	1	3		
Chittenden, Doseth			1		
Farnham, Joseph, Junr	2		1		
Aldridge, Peter W	3	1	2		
Farnham, Joseph	2		1		
Griswould, Joseph	1	1	4		
Stevens, Rebecca			1		
Field, Daniel	1	1	4		
Griswould, Abner	1		2		
Griswould, Giles	2	1	2		
Griswould, Nathan	3	1	2		
Williams, Mary			2		
Crane, Rufas	1	1	1		
Wilman, Jonathan	1		1		
Hull, Eliakim	1				
Andrews, Silas	1		1		
Tooly, William	1	1	4		
Tooly, Hannah	2		1		
Hull, George, 2d	1	1	2		
Willcox, Nathan, 2d	1		7		
Hull, George	1		3		
Hull, Samuel	1	5	1		
Farnham, Abner	3	1	2		
Hull, Josiah	1	1	3		
Hull, Joseph	1	1	2		
Stephens, Elias	1	1	2		
Stevens, Jane	2	3	3		
Trall, Oliver	1		2		
Hurd, Abraham	3	2	1		
Hull, Abel	1		1		
Buell, David	2	2	7		
Buell, Jedediah	1	3	4		
Kellsey, Levi	1	1	3		
Buell, David, 2d	1		2		

NAME OF HEAD OF FAMILY.	Free white males of 16 years and upward, including heads of families.	Free white males under 16 years.	Free white females, including heads of families.	All other free persons.	Slaves.
KILLINGWORTH TOWN— continued.					
Kelsey, Ezra	1	1	2		
Buell, Nathaniel	1		2		
Spencer, John	1	1	3	1	
Willcox, Daniel	1	1	2		
Willcox, John	1		1		
Griffen, Jared	1		2		
Hurd, Caleb L	1	5	4		
Hurd, Seth	1	1	4		
Hurd, Esther	1		2		
Ward, James	4		3		
Allen, Gideon	3	1	3		
Kelsey, Ezra	1	1	3		
Buell, John	1	2	3		
Willcox, Stephen	2		5		
Hurd, Elnathan	2		1		
Hurd, Elnathan, 2d	1	1	3		
Hurd, John	1	1	4		
Griffen, Edward	1	2	2		
Griswould, Daniel	3	3	5		
Buell, Job, 2d	1	1	4		
Carter, Jonas	1		1		
Buell, Job	3		4		
Buell, Josiah, 2d	1	1	2		
Kelsey, Samuel	1	3	6		
Bewell, Josiah	3	1	3		
Buell, Benjamin	1		1		
Grace, Nicholass	1	1	2		
Stevens, Nathaniel	1		2		
Stevens, Phillip	2	1	5		
Hilliard, Joseph	3		4		
Crane, Elias	3		1		
Redfield, Daniel	1		4		
Marble, Betsey			2		
Young, Joseph	2	6	2		
Redfield, Margarett	1		3		
Buell, Jonathan	1	2	5		
Griffeth, Thomas	1	2	3		
Morgan, Theophilus	1	3	3		
Buell, Reuben	2		2		
Buell, James	1	1	2		
Turner, Isaac	1		3		
Merrill, Benjamin	2	1	4	1	
Buell, Azariah	2	1	3		
Kelsey, Amos	3	2	2		
Kelsey, Dan	4		3		
Kelsey, Reuben	1	2	2		
Carter, Jarah, Junr	1	1	2		
Pierson, Phinehas	2	2	3		
Willard, Peleg	2		2		
Willard, Elisha	1	1	2		
Carter, Hubbell	3	1	3		
Carter, Josiah	2		4		
Carter, Benjamin	2	1	3		
Carter, Sarah			3		
Grinnol, Barber	2		3		
Grinnol, William B	1	1	4		
Kelsey, Peter	2		5		
Redfield, Augustus	1	1	4		
Concklin, Esther			1		
Dewolf, Elijah	1		3		
Dewolf, Elijah, 2d	1	1	4		
Smith, Enoch	1	2	4		
Peck, Daniel	1	2	5		
Holmes, Cornelius	2		2		
Lane, Stephen	2	1	7		
Pierson, Patience			2	2	
Pierson, Jedediah	1	1	3		
Stevens, Jeremiah	1	2	3		
Lane, Thatcher	2	1	4		
Kelsey, Solomon	1		1		
Wright, James	1	3	2		
Rositer, John, 2d	1	1	2		
Kelsey, John	1		2		
Rositer, John	2		2		
Kelsey, Asa	1	2	4		
Stevens, Jonas	2	1	4		
Elderkin, James	2		2		
Elderkin, Elisha	1		3		
Wright, Job, Esqr	1	3	5		
Hilliard, Barzilla	2		3		
Eliott, Jerod, Junr	1		3		
Eliott, Jarod	2	1	4		3
Dibble, David	2	1	4		
Crane, Theophilus	3	3	4		
Kelsey, Nathan	1	2	1		
Griswould, Martin	1		1		
Willman, Zadock	3	1	3		
Wright, Nathan	1	2	4		
Chalker, Jessy	1	2	2		
Kelsey, Samuel, 2d	2	1	3		
Griswould, Josiah	2		2		
Chapman, Constant	1	1	2		
Lane, Noah	1	1	4	1	
Wright, Grace			1		
Merrill, Samuel	2	2	4		

NAME OF HEAD OF FAMILY.	Free white males of 16 years and upward, including heads of families.	Free white males under 16 years.	Free white females, including heads of families.	All other free persons.	Slaves.
KILLINGWORTH TOWN— continued.					
Griffing, James N	1	1	3		
Griffing, James	1				
Crane, Samuel	3	1	7		
Stevens, Elnathan	2	1	2		
Burrows, John	1	1	2		
Buel, Hiel	1	1	2		
Williams, Jonathan	1	1	5		
Peck, Augustus	2	1	1		
Buel, Hiel, 2d	1		1		
Redfield, Samuel	1		1		1
Redfield, Samuel, 3d	1		3		
Redfield, Eliphilalet	3	1	3		
Kelsey, Josiah	2	1	5		
Wright, Benjamin	1	1	3		
Stevens, Jared	1	3	5		
Merriam, George	2	1	2		
Redfield, Samuel, 2d	1	2	4		
Meryan, William, 2d	1		1	2	
Redfield, Sylvester	2	2	4		
Willcox, Joseph, 2d	4	1	5	1	2
Willcox, John	1	1	2		
Stanton, Adam	4	1	7		
Triseth, William	1	1	5		
Grifling, William	2	1	4		
Eliott, George, Esqr	5	1	4		1
Redfield, Simeon	1		2		
Belden, Samuel	2	1	4		
Mansfield, Revd Achileus	2	2	5		
Eliott, William	1	1	4		
Gale, Hannah			4		
Hull, Oliver	2	2	2		
Graves, John	2	1	1		
L'Homedieu, William	2		2		
Eliott, Aaron	1	3	4	1	
Baldwin, Aaron	1				
Grifling, David	1	1	1		
Hilliard, Walter	1				
Grifling, Benjamin	1		2		
Morgan, William, Esqr	1	3	4		4
Farnum, Ozias	1	3	4		
Kelsey, Silas	2	1	3		
Willcox, John, 2d	1	5	2		
Chatfield, Joseph	2	3	2		
Grifling, Daniel	2		2		
Farnum, Hill	1	2	3		
Wright, Reuben	1		1		
Elie (negro)				1	
Evarts, David	1	1	2		
Chatfield, Josiah	3	2	3		
MIDDLETOWN TOWN.					
Hamlin, Hon. Jabez, Esqr	2		4		5
Miller, Asher, Esqr	2	1	3		1
Hubbard, Elijah, Esqr	3	1	4		1
Phillips, George, Esqr	1	1	3		1
Starr, Elihu, Esqr	1	2	6		1
Otis, Jonathan	1		1		1
Wetmore, Ichabod	1	2	9		
Bull, Samuel	1	2	7		2
Fisk, Boze	3	2	2		1
Whittlesey, Chauncey, Esqr	2	1	5	1	
Starr, George	2	3	3		2
Woodruff, Ezekiel, Esqr	1	2	4		
Storrs, Lemuel	4	2	3	1	
Cooper, Lamberton	1	2	5		
Hobby, Winsley	2		2		2
Meigs, Giles	3	3	9		
Warner, Robert	4		3		1
Canfield, Samuel	4	1	5		
Sage, Ebenezer	2	1	5		1
Harrington, Abijah	1	1	2		
Sebor, Jacob	1	2	4		1
Richards, William	1	1	2		1
Cornwell, James	2	1	2		
Alsop, Richard	2	1	4		
Hall, Anna	1		2		2
Parsons, William W., Esqr	1		3		
Brown, Nathaniel, Junr	1	2	3		
Brewster, Jane	1	1	3		
Goodrich, Samuel	1	3	3		
Rawson, Elizabeth			1		
Hall, John E	1		1		
Talcott, Mathew, Esqr	3		2		1
Starr, Timothy	2		3		
Cleaver, William	1				
Bigelow, Elizabeth	2	1	3		3
Bigelow, Timothy H	1		2		
Eglestom, Bennet	1		3		
Sage, Joseph	1		2		
Southmayd, William	2	1	1		

MIDDLESEX COUNTY—Continued.

MIDDLETOWN TOWN—continued.

NAME OF HEAD OF FAMILY.	Free white males of 16 years and upward, including heads of families.	Free white males under 16 years.	Free white females, including heads of families.	All other free persons.	Slaves.
Hubbard, Nehemiah, Junr	4	1	3		
Tuch, Samuel	1	2	4		
King, Joseph	1		1		
Pierce, Samuel	1		1		
Cleaver, William, Junr	1		2		
Campbell, Andrew	2	3	6		
Nott, William	1	2	1		
Dickinson, John	1		4		1
Alsop, Mary		1	8		5
Williams, Isaac	1	1	2		
Nott, John	1	3	1		
Banks, Hannah			3		
Bailey, Hez	1	2	4		
Cotton, Samuel	1	2	3		
Brigden, Thomas	3	1	1		
Whitmore, Jacob, Junr	1		1		
Banks, John	1	1	4		
Hall, Samuel	1	1	3		
Redding, Edward	1		1		
Willis, Jamima			2		
Babb, Sarah			2		
Treadway, Amos, Junr	1	1	3		
Banks, William	1		3		
Saxton, Knight	1		2		
Hall, Thomas	3	2	4		
Pierce, Stephen	1	2	3		
Starr, William	2	1	4		
Rand, Robert	2	4	2		
Ranney, Jonathan	1	3	2		
Goodwin, Sukey		1	3		
Beamont, Mary		3	1		
Ingraham, Nathaniel G.	4	3	3	1	2
Hall, Jonathan A.	1		1		
Hinshaw, Joshua, Esqr	1	2	4		1
Tracy, Ebenezer	1		2	1	
Washbourn, Ebenezer	1	2	2		
Clark, Seth	1		1		
Pomeroy, Adino	2	2	5		
Powers, Timothy	1	3	3		
Whitmore, Jacob	2	2	1		
Pickett, Thankfull	1		1		
Hulbert, Hezekiah	4	3	8	2	
Wallworth, Daniel	1	4	2		
Douglass, William	1		3		
Starr, Thomas	1				
Redfield, Frederick	3	5	2		2
Goodwin, Thomas	1		2		3
Ginnason, Lucy			1		
Southmayd, William, Junr	1	1	1		
Fenno, Ephraim	2	2	1		1
Boardman, Timothy	3		3		
Paddack, Zackeriah	1		1		
Winship, Samuel	1	1	1		
Leverett, Mary	2		3		
Treat, Joseph	1	1	2		
Meigs, John	4	3	5		
Paddock, Seth	2	2	3		
Parsons, Mehitable	1	1	5	2	1
Whitebread, Elizabeth			2		
Treadway, Elijah, Esqr	1		1		
Knap, Isaac	1		1		
Knap, Greenfield H.	2		3		
Cunningham, Samuel	1	2	6		
Paddack, George	2	1	2		
Starr, James	2		3		
Treadway, Amos	2	1	2		
Treadway, Josiah	1	1	3		
Sumner, Susannah			2		1
Magill, Charles	1	2	6		
Warner, William	1	2	3		
Russell, John	1	1	2		
Fairchild, Samuel	1	1	3		
Clay, Stephen	2	1	3	1	1
Daney, Jonathan	3		2	1	
Gleason, Margarett			2		
Sumner, William	1	2	4		
Coy, Mary			2		
Goodwin, Thomas, Junr	1	1	4		
Henshaw, Mary			1		
Willis, Joseph	1	1	2		
Starr, Samuel, Junr	1		2		
Strong, Nathan	2	3	5		
Winborne, Prince	1		3		
Phillips, Thompson	3		3		
Sage, Comfort, Esqr	4		2		4
Davis, John, Junr	1	1	3		
Spooner, George	1		1		
Foster, John	1	1	1		
Banks, Mary			2		
Jarvis, Revr Abraham	1	1	1		2
Whitmore, Ebenezer	1	3	5		
Starr, Timothy, Junr	1	5	1		
Strong, Elizabeth	1		1		

MIDDLETOWN TOWN—continued.

NAME OF HEAD OF FAMILY.	Free white males of 16 years and upward, including heads of families.	Free white males under 16 years.	Free white females, including heads of families.	All other free persons.	Slaves.
Cornwell, Elijah	2	2	2		
Rockwell, Grove	1		1		
Cadwell, John	1	2	3		
Reardon, Simon	1	1			
Johnson, Oliver	1	1	2		
Tarbox, Benjamin	1		3		
Harris, John	1	1	2		
Paddack, John	1	3	6		
Frothingham, Samuel	1	2	9		
Fletcher, Mary			1		
Frothingham, Ebenezer	1		3		
Robbert, Elizabeth			1		
Joyce, William	1		2		
Paddack, Samuel	1	1	2		
Shaler, Nathaniel	3	2	5		1
Johnson, Ashel	2	2	3		
Starr, Josiah	1	2	3		
Paddack, Robert	1		3		
Loveland, Darcus			2	2	1
Redfield, Peleg	1	1	1		
Parsons, Stephen	2	5	5		
Sizer, Anthony	1	1	2		
Willcox, Abell	2	5	2		
Stow, John	1	2	2		
Robert, Aaron	1		2		
Johnson, Jonathan	2		8		
Powers, Edward	2	3	3		
Sizer, Daniel	1	3	3		
Hull, Trustum	1	1	2		
Buffham, Joshua	1	1	1		
Bill, Martha			1		
Nott, Mary			5		
Bill, Solomon	2		2		
Fuller, Asa	2	1	3		
Paddack, William	1	2	6		
Gilbert, Joseph	1	2	3		
Bill, Samuel	1		2		
Chamberlain, Samuel	2	6	6		
Henry, James	1	2	3		
Clark, Phebe			1		
Goodwin, Samuel	1		2		
Starr, Thomas, Junr	1		1		
Ward, William	1	3	2		
Darby, Partrick	1	3	1		
Starr, Joseph	1				
Kelly, Hannah			4		
Gaylord, Samuel	1	3	3		
Sheers, Rebecca			3		
Starr, Samuel	1		2		
Starr, Cloe			1		
Starr, William, Junr	1	3	2		
Redfield, William	3		3		
Stone, Ephraim	2		1		
Dickerson, John	1	2	2		
Huntington, Revr Enoch	3	1	7		
Hall, Joseph	1	1	1		
Meigs, Return Jona	1	1	2		
Hubbard, Jacob	1	2	2		
Ingham, Joseph	1		1		
Vandeuerson, William	1	2	3		
Starr, Anna			3		
Nichols, Lois	2	2	5		
Russell, Samuel	2	6	2		
Plum, Charles	1	2	4		
Starr, Nathan	5	2	6		
Cone, Joseph	2	1	6		
Whittlesey, Bula			3		
Nichols, Thadeus	1		3	2	1
Sage, Esther			1	3	
Starr, Vim	1		2		
Tuch, Comfort	2		2		
Bow, Isaac	1	4	3		
Tuch, Micajah	1		2		
Grace, John	1	2	2		
Pousley, Samuel	1		2		
Stow, Solomon, Junr	2		2		
Tuch, Benjamin	1	2	2		
Allen, Peter	1	1	5		
Williams, Benjamin	1	3	3		2
Magill, Arther	3	2	6		1
Ranney, Stephen	2		2		3
Cotton, Elihu	1	2	2		
Cotton, Elihu, Junr	1	1	2		
Taylor, Jonathan	1	2	1		
Cornwell, Timothy	1	2	2		
Jepson, William	1	1	2		
Giles, William	1		2		
Bridgham, George	1	2	2		
Warner, Hope			2	1	1
Tuch, Enoch	1		3		
Aird, David	1	2	1		
Cotton, John	1		2		2
Cotton, Timothy	1	1	2		
Gill, Abigail		1	3		
Johnston, Samuel	1	1	5		

MIDDLETOWN TOWN—continued.

NAME OF HEAD OF FAMILY.	Free white males of 16 years and upward, including heads of families.	Free white males under 16 years.	Free white females, including heads of families.	All other free persons.	Slaves.
Hosmer, Stephen T.	2	1	3		1
Hosmer, Lydia	1		5		1
Foster, Edward	1		3		
Plum, Jacob	1	2	3		
Doolittle, Abraham	1	1	1		
Doolittle, Joshua	1		2		
Hamlin, Peter				2	
Hollett, John	1		1		
Burnham, Ashbell	2	2	8		
Smith, Joseph	1	1	3		2
Lee, Josiah	1		1		
Keith, William	1	5	4		
Scott, Lucreatia			5		2
Powers, Gregory	1	2	3		1
Osborn, Daniel	1	1	3		
Mortimer, Phillip, Esqr	1				11
Munn, Olvir	3		3		
Fisher, Lydia			2	1	
Johonnot, Daniel	1	3	1		
Starr, Jehosaphat, Junr	2	4	2		
Wetmore, Hannah	2	1	4		
Plum, Reuben	3	3	5		
Rockwell, Edward, Junr	1	4	3		
Wetmore, Jno, Junr	1	2	2		
Sage, Francis	2	4	3		
Ranney, Stephen, Junr	1	3	2		3
Woodward, Moses H.	1	2	4		
Allen, Joel	1	2	2		
Cotton, George	1	1	3		
Osborn, John	2	3	6		
Hawkins, Sarah			2		
Sanford, Peleg	2		4		
Johnson, Samuel	1		1		
Johnson, Samuel, Junr	1	1	2		
Ranney, Samuel W.	1	2	3		
Plum, Wait	2		4		
Bacon, Joseph	1	1	3		
Hulbert, Thomas	2	2	8		
Peck, Timothy	1	1	3		
Arnold, Asa Amasa	1	1	4		
Richardson, Rowland	1	3	4		
Spencer, Elizabeth			1	4	
Rockwell, Desiah			2	1	
Southern, Thomas	1		3		
Higbe, Noah	1	2	4		
Mitchell, Mary			3		
Rand, Thomas	2	1	2		
Cuff (Negro)				4	
Florah (Negro)				2	
O'Daniel, Partrick	2	3	3		
Griffin, Mary	2	1	2		
Masterns, James	1	1	1		
Thainer (Negro)			3		
Sage, William, Junr	2	1	4		
Canfield, Seba	1	2	3		
Mackintire, Duncan	3	1	3		
Bacon, William	1	1	3		
Bacon, Rhoda (alias Hall)			2		
Mahanna, John	1		2		
Wetmore, Esther	1		1		
Wetmore,	3		2	1	
Stow, David	2	1	5		
Stow, Peter	1	1	5		
Griffin, Ebenezer	1	4	4		
Frasier, Mary			2		
Winthrop, Mark				4	
Starr, Joseph, 3d	1		2		
Danforth, Martha	2	1	2		
Plum, William, Esqr	1		2		
Russell, Daniel	2	3	2		
Cale, William	1	1	1		
Doane, Nehemiah	1		2		
Williams, Peter				2	
Ackraw (Negro)				2	
Greenfield, Thomas	1	1	3		
Redfield, Susannah			2		
Cornwell, William	1	1	1		
Brown, Nathaniel	1		4		
Lucas, Pricilla			2		
Gilbert, Asa	1	1	2		
Goodwin, Jacob	2	3	5		
Wright, Hannah			1		
Creamore, George	1				
Henshaw, Sarah			2		
Hill, Gershom				1	
Henshaw, Daniel	1		3		
Bacon, Isaac	1	1	3		
Southmayd, Jonathan	2	1	3		
Adkins, George	3		5		
Saxton, Jonathan	1		3		
Treadway, Phebe		1	3		
Driggs, Israel	2		5		
Barns, John	2	1	1		
Hubbard, Hey	2	3	2		

MIDDLESEX COUNTY—Continued.

MIDDLETOWN TOWN—continued.

NAME OF HEAD OF FAMILY.	Free white males of 16 years and upward, including heads of families.	Free white males under 16 years.	Free white females, including heads of families.	All other free persons.	Slaves.
Peck, Jessy S	1		1		
Rogers, John	2	1	5		
Doyle, John	1		6		
Whitmore, Francis	1		2		
Miller, Caleb	1	2	1		
Ames, Anthony	1	1	2		
Arnold, Ebenezer	3	1	5		
Tryon, Elee	1	6	2		
Trevana, Richard	1		2		
Markland, Jeremiah	2	2	5		
Driggs, John	1		2		
Brown, William	1		4		
Frothingham, John	1	2	2		
Robbard, Edward	1	3	5		
Ward, Samuel	1	2	5		
Butler, John	1		3		
Butler, Hannah			2		
Miller, Jonathan	1	3	4		
Miller, Edward	1	2	2		
Markham, Samuel	2	4	6		
Ward, John, 4th	2	1	3		
Bow, Samuel	1	1	3		
Sears, Nathan	1	2	3		
Cotton, John, 2d	1	1	2		
Miller, Jared	1		1		
Daniels, John	1		1		
Hubbard, Joseph	1		1		
Hubbard, Manoah	2	2	5		
Sumner, Elizabeth	2	1	5		
Hubbard, Eliphalet	3		2		
Hubbard, Manoah, Junr	1	1	3		
Weston, Darius	1		5		
Bow, Peleg	1	1	1		
Prior, Josiah	1	2	5		
Tryon, David	1	1	2		
Tryon, David, Junr	1		2		
Tryon, Elisha	1	1	3		
Tryon, Stephen	1	2	3		
Nancarow, Edward	1	1	2		
Bow, Amos	2	3	4		
Daniels, William	3		4		
Griswold, Josiah	1	1	3		
Robbard, Timothy	1	3	5		
Johnson, Elijah, Junr	1	1	3		
Johnson, Mary			1		
Brooks, David	1		3		
Hubbard, Abner	1		3		
Coe, Jessy, Junr	1		1		
Hubbard, Elias	1	1	1		
Bates, Joseph	1	1	2		
Clark, Giles	1	2	6		
Griswold, Moses	1	2	5		
Butler, Samuel	1	2	4		
Bow, Amos, Junr	1	2	1		
Bigelow, Frederick	1	4	2		
Johnson, Henry	1	2	3		
Lucas, Abner	2	1	6		
Brooks, Martha			2		
Brooks, Joseph B	1	1	2		
Young, Sylvanus	3	2	3		
Carrier, Samuel	1		1		
Bow, Abraham	2	2	1		
Whitmore, Stephen	2	1	4		
Cone, John	3	2	3		
Carrier, Israel	2	1	2		
Morgan, Simeon	2	2	3		
Morgan, Richard	1		1		
Morgan, Richard, Junr	1	1	3		
Morgan, Peter	1	1	4		
Whitmore, Ebenezer	2		1		
Whitmore, Jehiel	1		3		
Johnson, Seth	1	3	4		
Brooks, Noah	1	3	3		
Clark, Francis	2	1	3		
Sears, Stephen	3	2	3		
Swaddle, John	2	1	5		
Sears, John	2	1	3		
Simmons, Samuel	2		2		
Butler, Davney	2	1	4		
Thayer, Jonathan	3		3		
Cook, William	1		4		
Miller, Stephen	3	2	4		
Cunningham, Esther			1		
Turpin, Henry	1		3		
Driggs, Joseph	1	1	2		
Driggs, Joseph, Junr	2	6	3		
Pike, Charles	1		3		
Markham, Sarah			1		
Robbards, Collins	1	3	4		
Ward, Abigail	1		3		
Hubbard, Jonathan	2	2	3		
Prior, Jesse	1	4	1		
Robbards, Hinkeman	4		3		
Robbards, Noyes	1	1	4		
Butler, Samuel	2	1	2		

MIDDLETOWN TOWN—continued.

NAME OF HEAD OF FAMILY.	Free white males of 16 years and upward, including heads of families.	Free white males under 16 years.	Free white females, including heads of families.	All other free persons.	Slaves.
Augar, George	1		1		
Croe, Asa	1		1		
Robbards, Samuel C	3	1	4		
Tryon, Amos	1	2	3		
Hubbard, Abijah	1		5		
Hubbard, Oliver	2	1	3		
Hubbard, Caleb	1	4	4		
Bailey, Lowdon	1	2	4		
Hubbard, John	1	3	1		
Hubbard, Ephraim	1	2	4		
Hubbard, Ama			3		
Butler, David	1	1	2		
Clark, Daniel	2	2	4		
Prior, Daniel	1		1		
Prior, Samuel	1	1	1		
Prior, Elijah	1	1	1		
Hubbard, Solomon	3	2	2		
Johnson, James	1	3	2		
Johnson, Mehitable			2		
Johnson, Caleb	1	2	2		
Tryon, Caleb	1	1	5		
Bailey, Ephraim	1	2	1		
Sears, Elisha	2		2		
Hubbard, Jamansy			2		
Coe, Jessy	2	2	4		
Rich, Eliakim	1	3	1		
Johnson, Partrick	3		5		
Robbards, Nathaniel	1	1	6		
Gilbert, John	1	1	2		
Hubbard, George	4		3		
Clark, James	1	3	3		
Whitmore, Daniel	1	1	2		
Whitmore, Gordon	2	1	5		
Lawrence, Roman	1	3	3		
Clark, Lamberton	2	3	1		
Clark, Ambros	1	1	2		
Bidwell, Ashbell	1	2	4		
Davis, John	2		2		
Miller, Joshua	2	1	2		
Powers, Henry	1		1		
Goff, David	1	1	3		
Starr, Daniel	1	4	5		
Braddock, Michael	1		5		
Rogers, John, Junr	1	1	3		
Robbards, Nathaniel, Junr	1	1	2		
Lee, William	1	5	5		
Robbarts, Seth	1	2	6		
Johnson, Stephen	1	1	2		
Johnson, William	1	3	3		
Johnson, Freelove	1	1	5		
Johnson, Jedediah	2		2		
Harris, William	1	3	3		
Mitchell, Abner	2	1	6		
Johnson, Martha			2		
Clark, Oliver	3	2	5		
Markham, Ebenezer	1	4	3		
Whitmore, Timothy	1		4		
Tryon, Thomas	1		1		
Tryon, Abel	1	1	1		
Tryon, Josiah	1	1	2		
Tryon, Jessy	1		2		
Johnson, Timothy	1	1	5		
Robbards, Rachel			2		
Crowell, Edward	1	2	4		
Hubbard, Jeremiah	1	2	3		
Lord, James	1	3	2		
Roberts, Ebenezer	1	1	3		
Robbert, Adonijah	1	2	1		
Prout, John	1	2	4		
Tryon, Charles	4	4	5		
Prout, Darcy	1		3		
Johnson, Ebenezer	3		2		
Prout, Harris	2	1	3		
Brooks, Daniel	1	2	2		
Robbards, Jonathan	1	2	3		
Lee, Samuel	1		1		
Shattuck, Robert	1		1		
Harris, David	1	1	2		
Sizer, Lemuel	2	1	2		
Lee, Samuel, Junr	1		4		
Francis, Mary			2		
Brewster, Elisha	1	1	3		
Brooks, Jabez	1		2		
Brooks, Timothy	1		5		
Sizer, Eli	1	1	3		
Barrett, John	1		2		
Woodward, Sibbel			2		
Brooks, Jabez, Junr	2		2		
Brooks, Jabez	1	2	2		
Johnson, Jedediah, Junr	2	3	5		
Hedges, Isaac	4		6		
Robbards, Phinehas	1	2	3		
Robbards, Simeon	1		2		

MIDDLETOWN TOWN—continued.

NAME OF HEAD OF FAMILY.	Free white males of 16 years and upward, including heads of families.	Free white males under 16 years.	Free white females, including heads of families.	All other free persons.	Slaves.
Lucas, Samuel	2	1	3		
Blake, Samuel	1	2	2		
Whitmore, Beriah	1		3		
Robbert, Fenno	1		2		
Rockwell, Noadiah	1	3	2		
Hedges, Henry, Junr	2		2		
Prout, Oliver	1	2	2		
Crowell, John	2	1	2		
Crowell, John, Junr	2	2	3		
Starr, David	1	2	3		
Miles, Sarah			2		
Hall, Calvin	1		3		
Hall, Jacob	1	3	3		
Ward, Josiah	2	3	6		
Ward, Josiah, Junr	1	1	2		
Ward, John	2	1	3		
Ward, John, 5th	1	2	2		
Crowell, Samuel	1	2	3		
Blake, John	2		5		
Blake, Freelove	1	3	2		
Crowell, Solomon	1	2	3		
Crowell, Sarah			1		
Fairchild, Abigail	1		2		
Fairchild, Joel	1	3	3		
Crowell, Daniel	1	4	4		
Prior, Oliver	1	1	1		
Hubbard, Micah	1	3	5		
Lucas, Moses	1		1		
Lucas, Moses. Junr	1	2	7		
Hubbard, Noadiah	2	2	2		
Hubbard, Noadiah, Junr	3		1		
Barns, Daniel	1		3		
Barns, Martha		2	2		
Adkins, Thomas	2	2	4		
Starr, Jehosaphat	1		1		
Hubbard, Jabez	2		1		
Barns, Amos	1		3		
Barns, Mary	1		3		
Cornwell, Francis	2		3		
Storms, James				3	
Barns, Solomon	1	1	2		
Phillips, Peter				5	
Barns, Thomas	1	3	4		
Johnson, Jonathan, Junr	1		2		
Barnes, Ezekiel	2		1		
Barns, Giles	1	1	5		
Gilbert, Jonathan	1	1	3		
Hubbard, Nehemiah	3	1	2		
Gilbert, Jonathan, Junr	2	1	4		
Doolittle, Mrs. Hannah			4		
Adkins, Jessie	1	1	2		
Adkins, Samuel	1		3		
Cornwell, Timothy	3		1		
Adkins, Jabez	1	2	1		
Adkins, Samuel, Junr	2	2	3		
Lucas, Thomas	1	1	1		
Ward, Samuel, Junr	2	2	4		
Hall, John	3		4		
Potter, John	1		9		
Hubbard, Isaac	1	4	3		
Adkins, Ephraim	1		2		
Savage, Abijah	1	4	7		
Savage, Josiah	2	1	2		
Haskell, William	1	3	5		
Savage, Josiah, Junr	1	1	3		
Bishop, Leveritt	1	2	3		
Sage, Timothy	3	1	5		
Sage, Samuel	1	1	3		
Plum, Joshua	1		2		
Edwards, Daniel	2	2	5		
Doxey, Henry	1		1		
Arnold, Daniel	1		1		
Ranney, William	2	1	1		
Eliott, John, Esqr	1	1	3		1
Williams, John	2	2	2		
Frairey, Samuel	1	3	2		
Clark, James	1	5	2		
Chauncey, Nathaniel, Esqr	1		1		
Chauncey, Nathaniel, Junr	1	1	4		
Smith, Edward	1	2	5		
Smith, James	3	2	4		
Robinson, Robert	1		3		
Sage, Nathan	2	1	2		2
Ranney, Ebenezer	2	2	4		
Stocking, Daniel	1		2		1
Stocking, William	2	1	4		
Goodrich, Barsheba			3		
Stocking, Jozeb	1	3	3		1
White, Abagail			2		1
Gaylord, Jonathan	1	2	4		
Gaylord, Wm C	1	1	5		
White, Elias	1	1	2		

MIDDLESEX COUNTY—Continued.

MIDDLETOWN TOWN—continued.

NAME OF HEAD OF FAMILY.	Free white males of 16 years and upward, including heads of families.	Free white males under 16 years.	Free white females, including heads of families.	All other free persons.	Slaves.
White, John	3	4	8		
White, Timothy	2	4	3		
Stocking, Samuel	1		1		
Savage, Giles	1		1		
Savage, Solomon	1		4		
Ranney, Mary		2	1		
Savage, Nathaniel	1	2	3		
Kirby, Hezekiah	1	1	2		
Stow, Jonathan	1		2		
Savage, Stephen	1		2		
Ellis, Nathaniel	1	4	4		
Ellis, Daniel	1	3	3		
Robinson, James	2	3	1		
Willcox, Eliphalett	1	1	2		
Butler, Benjamin	1		3		
Butler, Comfort	3		2		
Hamlin, Daniel	1	2	3		
Riley, Joseph	1	1	5		
Willcox, Elisha	2	4	5		
Willcox, Ozias	3		2		
Savage, Sarah			3		
Savage, Amos	1		3		
Clark, Sarah	1		2		
McPherson, Joseph	1		2		
Ranney, Hezekiah	1	2	3		
Coy, Edy	1	3	1		
Savage, Naomy			2		
Willcox, James	1		2		
Gridley, Isaac, Esqr	2	2	3		
Spencer, Samuel	2	1	8		
Gipson, John	3	1	5		
Willcox, Lois			3		
Johnson, Seth	1	2	3		
Hart, Seth	2	2	1		
Ranney, Nathaniel	2		5		
Nichols, James	1	1	2		
Ranny, Joseph	1	3	3		
Sage, Amos	2	3	3		
Buckley, Revr Gershom	1	1	3		
Stow, Joseph	1	3	5		
Stow, Zebulon	1	5	2		1
Savage, Timothy	1		2		
Savage, Jonathan	3				
Bunnell, Joel	1	2	4		
Savage, William	2	1	2		
Miller, James	2	1	3		
Edwards, David, Junr	2		2		
Edwards, Churchel, Junr	1	1	2		
Sage, Solomon	1		3		
Sage, Elisha	3	3	5		
Sage, William	4	4	4		
Gibson, Timothy	2	1	3		
Kirby, Nehemiah	2		4		
Edwards, Churchell	1		1		
Sage, Solomon, Junr	1	2	2		
White, Aaron	2	1	4		
Robert, Recompence	1	3	3		
Ray, Benjamin	1	1	3		
Butler, Eli	2	1	8		
Kelsey, Israil	4	2	4		
Shepherd, Joseph	2	2	1		
Mildram, John	1	3	3		
Treat, John	1	2	1		
Savage, Stephen	1	1	3		
Savage, Martha			1		
Treat, Stephen, Junr	1	3	3		
Kirby, Daniel	2		1		
Kirby, Sarah	2		2		
Shepherd, Jered	1	2	3		
Stow, Zachariah	1		3		
Hamlin, William, Junr	3	3	6		
Hamlin, Abigail	2		4		
Cornwell, Hart	1		2		
Cotton, Thomas	1	1	1		
Cornwell, John	2	1	3		
McKey, Phinehas	2	1	2		
Ward, Joseph, Junr	1	2	2	1	
Savage, Samuel	1	3	5		
Clark, David	1	2	2		
Alvord, Daniel	3	2	5		
Gilbert, Benjamin	1		4		
Gilbert, Ebenezer	1		2		1
Gilbert, Allen	2	2	3		
Hamlin, William	2		2		
Hamlin, Harris	1		3		
Cane, James	1	1	2		
Ward, William	1	2	4		
Cotton, Elisha	1	3	4		
Brown, Hugh	1		4		
Cotton, Samuel	1	2	3		
Cande, John	1	4	3	1	
Cornwell, Caleb	1		4		
Johnson, Amos	2		1		
Ward, Joseph	1		4		2
Ward, Bela	1		3		
Gad, Marear				3	
Ward, Thomas	3		3		
Ward, Joshua	1	1	2		
Bacon, Jeremiah	4	3	6		
Campbell, Andrew	1		1		
Lathrop, John	1		3		
Doud, Cornwell	1	4	3		
Hough, Abigail			2		
Adkins, Joel	1	1	1		
Riley, Asher	1	3	4		
Butler, Gershom	4	1	3		
Thrasher, Bezaleel	2				
Redding, Samuel	1		1		
Miller, Hoze	1	1	6		
Hubbard, Roswell	1	2	1		
Thomas, Evan	1	2	3		
Plum, Abraham	3		3		
Sears, Peter				5	
Ranney, Abijah	1	2	5		
Riley, Julius	1	4	4		
Williams, Jehiel	3	1	7		
Stocking, Seth	1		3		
Kirby, Thomas	4	1	4		
Smith, Abner	3	2	3		
Hamlin, John	1	2	1		
Beldon, John	1		2		
Beldon, Benjamin	1		1		
Chamberlain, Theodore	1				
Sage, John	1		1		
Sage, Simeon	2	1	4		
Sage, Epaphras	1	1	5		
Sage, Hezekiah	3	3	5		
Smith, Nathaniel	1	2	2		
Sage, Lewis Samuel	1		2		
Sage, Lemuel	1	1	1		
Sage, Joseph	1	1	2		
Perry, Christiany			2		
Robinson, Lydia	1		1		
Savage, Daniel	1	1	1		
Sage, Giles	1	3	3		
Barnes, William	1	2	2		
Pryor, John	1	2	2		
Lane, Letitia			1		2
Robberts, Ruth			1		2
Clark, Jonathan	1		4		
Bivins, Ebenr	1	1	2		
Bacon, Ebenezer, Esqr	3	2	4		
Johnson, Asa	1	3	1		
Bacon, Sibbel			1		5
Plum, Samuel, Junr	2	1	3		
Plum, Samuel	1		3		
Plum, James	1	1	4		
Plum, Aaron	1	2	3		
Plum, Jessey	1	2	1		
Robberts, Jessey	1	1	6		
Gaylord, Elieazer	1		3		
Bacon, John	1		2		
Bacon, John, Junr	1	5	4		
Bonfy, Henry	2	5	2		
Hall, William	2		1		
Stow, Amos	1	1	2		
Clark, Benjamin	1	1	3		
Clark, Daniel	2	2	2		
Clark, Timothy	2	1	7		
Gouge, Nathaniel	1	2	2		
Johnson, Edward	2	1	3		
Willcox, Giles	2	3	5		
Doud, Benjamin	2	1	3		
Cotton, James	1		3		
Cornwell, Ashbell	1	4	4		
Doud, Richard	1	2	4		
Doud, Phebe			1		
Hatch, Josiah	1	2	3		
Elton, Bradley	1	3	3		
Hamlin, Patience			3		
Treat, Stephen	1	1	3		
Ranney, Comfort	1	1	1		
Bacon, William	1		1		
Clark, Joseph	1	1	2		
Roberts, Reuben	1		1		
Lewis, Naboth	1	1	1		
Minor, Revr Thomas	1	3	2		
Doolittle, Hannah			3		
Doolittle, David	1	1	1		
Doolittle, Joseph	2	1	1		
Doolittle, Alisha	1	1	1		
Clark, Michal	1		5		
Treat, Rebecca			2		
Cornwell, Isaac	2	5	4		
Cornwell, Nathaniel	2	5	3		
Melona, Michael	1	1	3		
Robberts, Ebenezer	1	2	3		
Geir, George	1	2	3		
Robberts, Abel	1		1		
Churchell, Amos, Esqr	1	3	4		
Willcox, John	3		4		
Graves, Joseph	1	2	7		
Boardman, Nathaniel	2	2	4		
Willcox, Jeremiah	1	3	5		
Dudley, Asahel	3	1	4		
Galpin, Samuel	1	2	3		
Willcox, Eli	1	2	3		
Robberts, Elijah	1		2		
Goodrich, Hosea	1		2		
Bailey, William	1		3		
Woods, Ruth		1	1		
Boardman, Nathan	1	2	4		
Willcox, John, Junr	2		3		
Willcox, Samuel	1		1		
Willcox, Elijah	2	3	4		
Willcox, Joseph	1	1	4		
Bacon, Stephen	1	2	3		
Warner, John	1	2	4		
Warner, Lois	1		2		
Bacon, Joel	2	2	6		
Bacon, Noah	3	1	3		
Norton, Aaron	2	2	7		
Norton, Isaiah	1		3		
Higbe, Ephraim	1	3	4		
Rexford, Benjamin	1	3	3		
Hall, David	1	2	3		
Higbe, Daniel	4	6	2		
Joppen, William	1		2		
Higbe, Zacheus	1	2	3		
Morgan, John	1	4	7		
Dudley, Isaac	1		3		
Higbe, Jeduthan	1	1	2		
Higbe, Amos	1		2		
Higbe, David	2	2	3		
Crofoot, Elisha	1	3	4		
Webster, Benjamin	1		2		
Higbe Lemuel	1		1		
Doolittle, Joel	1	1	2		
Bacon, Phinehas	2	1	5		
Adkins, Benjamin	1	2	3		
Allen, Ebenezer	2	3	4		
Bears, James	1	2	3		
Washbourn, Joseph	5	2	5		
Kentner, John P	1	2	3		
Kentner, Jeremiah	1		2		
Roberts, David	1	1	3		
Wetmore, Seth	4	4	6		2
Whitmore, Jessey	1	3	4		
Peter (Negro)				4	
Hart, Ebenezer	1	1			
Jones, James	1	1	1		
Merrow, John	1		4		
Merrow, Elisha	1		4		
Rockwell, Edward	3	2	2		
Kelly, Daniel	1	2	2		
Pratt, Jonathan	1	1	1		
Sizer, Abel	1	1	2		
Southmayd, Partridge	1	3	3		
Gears, Hezekiah	2	1	1		
Roper, Nathaniel	1	1	2		
Gilbert, Rhoda			2		
Southmayd, Giles	2	1	2		1
Hall, Daniel	2	4	4		1
Wetmore, Oliver	1	4	7	1	1
Cotton, Ebenezer	1		3		
Hall, Jabez	1		3		5
Hamlin, Charles	1	2	3		
Marks, William	1	1	1		
Miller, Giles	1		2		
Miller, Giles, Junr	1	1	2		
Coe, Nathan	2		6		
Coe, Nathan, Junr	1		2		
Griffin, Samuel	1	3	4		
Auger, Prosper	1	1	4		
Roberts, John	1		1		
Nichols, Silvenus	1	1	1		
Richards, Sarah			2		
Coe, John	1	3	4		
Beebe, Zachariah	1		2		
Ward, Edward	3	4	4		
Jopping, Daniel	2		4		
Guild, Jeremiah	1	4	3		
Ward, Abiel			2		
Guild, Samuel	2	2	6		
Hale, Hezekiah	1	2	7		
Robberts, Asahel	1	1	1		
Turner, John	1		3		
Clark, Daniel	2	1	3		
Clover, John	1	4	2		
Ward, James T	2	4	4		
Robberts, James	1	1	1		
Robberts, E. Merril	1		2		
Coe, Joseph	1	3	4		
Turner, Stephen	2	2	4		
Hoadley, Jehiel	2		3		

MIDDLESEX COUNTY—Continued.

NAME OF HEAD OF FAMILY.	Free white males of 16 years and upward, including heads of families.	Free white males under 16 years.	Free white females, including heads of families.	All other free persons.	Slaves.
MIDDLETOWN TOWN—continued.					
Hand, Benjamin	1		4		
Freeman, David	2		2		
Ward, John	2	3	5		1
Stow, Joshua	1	1	4		
Wetmore, Asa	2	2	7		
Johnson, Hezekiah	1		4		
Spencer, Ichabod	1	4	4	1	
Walker, James	1	1	3		
Roberts, David	3	2	2		
Hubbard, Robert	1	4	3		
Coe, David	2	2	7		
Birdsay, Hannah		2	5	2	
Miller, Elisha	3	1	5		
Kimball, Tyler	1	1	2		
Camp, Edward	1	1	5		
Camp, Lemuel	1	3	3		
Butler, Timothy	1	2	4		
Ward, William	2		4		
Babbett, William	1	1	5		
Ward, William, Junr	1	1	1		
Willey, Barzilla	3	3	5		
Miller, Icabod	2	2	3		
Wetmore, Joseph	2	5	4		
Miller, Seth	2	5	3		
Miller, William	1	2	6		
Stow, Elihu	3		4		
Auger, Justice	1	2	1		
Camp, Asahel	1		3		
Coe, David	1		4		1
Coe, Eli	1	3	3		
Coe, Seth	1	4	2		
Birdsey, David	2	1	2		1
Birdsey, John, Junr	1		5	1	
Lyman, David	3	4	6		
Birdsey, John	1		1		3
Birdsey, Abel	1	2	1		
Miller, Isaac, Esqr	2	2	7		1
Hubbard, William	1		2		
Coe, Elisha	1	2	5		
Miller, Brainard	2	3	3		
Miller, Hezekiah	1	2	3		
Hambleton, Mary		1	2		
Hawley, Stow	4	3	5		
Talcott, Hezekiah	4	2	4		
Parsons, Aaron	1		2		
Cone, Berial	1	2	4		
Daniels, William	1		1		
Miller, Jacob	1	2	3		
Birdsey, Abigail		3	3		
Miller, William	3	2	2		
Miller, Ambros	1	1	3		
Rockwell, Joshua	2	4	5		
Wetmore, John, 2d	2	1	4		
Wetmore, Daniel	1	1	2		
Turner, Jonathan	3		2		
SAYBROOK TOWN.					
Hotchkis, Revd Fredk W	1	1	1		
Hart, Willm, Esqr	1	1	2	3	3
Pratt, Humphrey, Junr	1	2	6		
Pratt, Humphrey	1		2		
Pratt, Elias	1	2	2		
Buckingham, Daniel	1	1	3		
Field, Saml	1	2	4		
Pratt, Benjamin	2	3	3		
Kirtland, Ambrose	5		2		
Williams, Charles	3	1	2		
Blague, Giles	1	2	3		
Tulley, Wm	1	2	4		
Dickinson, Richard	6	1	3		
Ingraham, Jno	1	3	5		
Ingraham, James	1		1		
Ingraham, Wm	1	1	4		
Ingraham, Daniel	3		3		
Pierce, Thomas	1	1	2		
Cochran, Jno	1	2	3		
Cochran, Jno, 2d	1		2		
Buckingham, Adonijah	2		5		
Beaumont, Samuel	1	2	4		1
Kirtland, Martin	1	1	4		
Kirkland, Charles	1		4		
Kirtland, Elizur	1	1	2		
Stilman, Saml	1	1	4		
Ingraham, Benjamin	1	1	1		
Tryon, Edward	1	1	2		
Newell, David	1	2	5	2	
Clark, Ezra	1	3	3		
Tully, Saml, Esqr	1	1	5		
Tully, Elias	1		6		
Shirtland, Saml	2		3		
Shirtland, Saml, 2d	1	2	4		
Lynde, Wm	2	2	1		2

NAME OF HEAD OF FAMILY.	Free white males of 16 years and upward, including heads of families.	Free white males under 16 years.	Free white females, including heads of families.	All other free persons.	Slaves.
SAYBROOK TOWN—continued.					
Morgan, Abraham	3	2	5	1	
Clark, Saml	2	1	4		
Clark, Rufus	1		2		
Hart, Saml	2	1	5		2
Hart, Jno	2	3	4		
Shipman, Elias	1	3	1		
Ingham, Thomas	2		2		
Pratt, Timothy	3	1	5		
Shipman, Samuel	3		2		
Shipman, Nathl	2	3	2		
Pratt, James	1	1	3		
Shipman, Jno	1	1	2		
Lord, Russel	2	3	2		1
Lord, Andrew	3	1	2		
Lord, Martha			2		
Hart, Elisha	2	1	4		1
Hart, Mary			2		1
Ely, Elisha	1	3	4		
Willard, Joseph	2	3	4		
Newell, Benjamin	1	1	2		
Chalker, Abigail			2		
Willard, Nathl	1	4	5		
Jones, Ezekiel	1		6	1	
Sandford, Rebekah	1		1		
Jones, Isaac	2	3	5		
Chalker, Ezra	1		1		
Lord, Mary			2	1	1
Jones, Parker	1	1	3		
Jones, John	1	1	1		
White, Oliver	1		1		
Lilly (Negro)				2	
Pratt, Seth	3	1	6		
Lord, Wm	1	1	3		
Lord, Joel	1		1		
Lord, Abiel	1		3		
Reave, Pnyryer	1	2	5		
Munn, Robert I	1	1	3		
Newell, Robert	3		3		
Newell, Robt, 2d	1				
Tryon, Asa	1	1	1		
Waterhouse, Wm	3		3		
Buckingham, Elizabeth	1		1		
Waterhouse, Jno	3		5		
Waterhouse, Ambrose	1		5		
Parker, Wm	1	3	4		
Griffin, Jno	1	1	5		
Ayer, Travis	1	1	3		
Ayer, Jno	1		3		
Sill, Richard	2	2	3		
Hill, Hiland	1	1	3		
Hill, Peleg	1	2	2		
Chapman, Elisha	1	4	4		
Chapman, Pinehas	3		3		
Chapman, James	1		2		
Chapman, Levi	2	5	5		
Bushnell, Pinehas	1		1		
Bushnell, Saml	1	1	2		
Bushnell, Handly	1	1	2		
Bushnell, Joshua	1		1		
Ely, Robert	2	1	3		
Bushnell, Nathl	1		2		
Bushnell, Elisha	1		1		
Bushnell, Nathl, 2d	1		1		
Bushnell, Daniel	1		2		
Lee, George	1		2		
Lee, Saml	1	2	3		
Bushnell, Elias	2	3	5		
Chalker, Alexander	1	1	3		
Chalker, Gideon	1		1		
Chalker, Moses	1	1	2		
Chalker, Oliver	1		1		
Bushnell, Jonathan	1		2		
Bushnell, Constant	1	4	3		
Bushnell, Nathan	1	2	5		
Dibble, John	3	2	3		
Dibble, Josiah	2	1	4		
Doty, Edward	2		2		
Doty, Benjamin	2	2	5		
Bushnell, Handly, 2d	1	1	2		
Jones, Ezra	1		2		
Doan, John	1	3	2		
Chapman, Wm	1	5	1		
Chapman, Benja	1		2		
Tryon, Edward, 2d	1		4		
Whittelsey, Hannah			1		
Ingham, Ebenezer	2	2	3		
Ingham, Wm	1	3	4		
Bushnell, Joseph	2		3		
Bushnell, Joseph, 2d	2	1	2		
Bushnell, Lemuel	1		2		
Bushnell, Lemuel, 2d	1	2	3		
Chalker, Jacob	3	3	4		
Ingham, Daniel	3		1		
Bushnell, Ira	4	1	2		
Bushnell, John	3	1	5		

NAME OF HEAD OF FAMILY.	Free white males of 16 years and upward, including heads of families.	Free white males under 16 years.	Free white females, including heads of families.	All other free persons.	Slaves.
SAYBROOK TOWN—continued.					
Jones, Gideon	3	1	2		
Chalker, Stephen	2	2	3		
Chalker, Abraham	1	1	5		
Jones, Thomas	2	1	3		
Jones, Israel	1		2		
Bushnell, Ira, 2d	2	3	5		
Babcock, Saml	1	2	6		
Shipman, James	1	1	4		
Sherman, Sarah			2		
Mather, Hannah			2		
Whittlesey, Azariah	2	1	5		
Sanford, Samel	1		2		
Sanford, Samel, 2d	3		2		
Whittelsey, Ambrose	2	1	3		
Whittelsey, Hezekiah	3	1	2		
Whittelsey, Ambrose, 2d	1	2	3		
Dudley, Saml	2		4		
Lord, Jeremiah	2		1		
Chapman, Esther			3		
Harriss, Deliverance			3		
Buckingham, Samel	2	1	4		
Dudley, Jedediah	1	1	7		
Whittelsey, David	1	1	1		
Magney, Lucretia			2	3	
Whittelsey, Saml W	1		2		
Boles, Edgecombe	1		3		
Dudley, Anne			4		
Dudley, Elisha	1	1	1		
Kirtland, Asa	1	5	3		
Shirtland, Wm E	2	1	5		
Bates, Isaac	2		1		
Shipman, Jno	1	1	2		
Glading, Wye	1	1	1		
Glading, Rebekah			2		
Glading, Ebenezer	2		1		
Glading, Silas	5		4		
Pratt, Jno Clark	1	2	3		
Pratt, Reuben	2		6		
Strakey, Stephen	2	1	2		
Starkey, Charles	1		4		
Pratt, Abraham	3		5		
Pratt, Jeremiah	1		1		
Pratt, Mary			2		
Pratt, Charity			3	1	
Pratt, Jones	1		3		
Pratt, Saml	3	1	4		
Tucker, Tabor	1	1	1		
Tucker, Richard	1	1	3		
Starkey, Noah	3	1	3		
Starkey, Willm	1		3		
Trip, Willm	1	3	5		
Hill, James	1	1	3		
Biggs, Willm	1	2	1		
Tiley, David	1		2		
Tucker, James	1	2	2		
Hill, Peleg	1		3		
Haydon, Elias	1	5	5		
Starkey, John	1	1	4		
Plumb, Joseph	1		2		
Darrow, Jno	3		1		
Haydon, Jacob	2	2	3		
Pratt, Asa, 2d	1	1	2		
Pratt, Jno	3	2	3		
Pratt, Asa	1		5		
Pratt, Jno, 2d	1	1	2		
Williams, David	2	1	6		
Williams, Ebenezer	1		1		
Pratt, Jane	1		5		
Scovell, Annah			2		
Williams, Jno	2		2		
Scovell, Noah	2	4	2		1
Lay, Saml	2	2	5		
Wilson, Nathl	2		3		
Parker, Saml	1	1	4		
Hayden, Eliakim	3	2	2		
Haydon, Nehemiah	1	3	2		
Haydon, Uriah	3		5		
Lay, Robt	2		3		
Haydon, Ebenezer	5		3		
Pratt, Zephaniah	4		4		
Tucker, Joseph	1	1	4		
Pratt, Phinehas	2	2	6		
Pratt, Susannah			4		
Phelps, Jno	1		2		
Pratt, Jabez	2		1		
Pratt, Ezra	2	4	2		
Pratt, Robert	2		3	3	
Denison, Mary			2		
Denison, Ebenezer	3		3		
Mather, Elisha	1	3	3		
Holmes, Anne	1		2	1	1
Ely, Revd Richard	2		4		
Clark, Danforth	3	1	6		
Williams, Richard	1	2	5		
Knot, Josiah	3	1	5		

MIDDLESEX COUNTY—Continued.

SAYBROOK TOWN—con.

NAME OF HEAD OF FAMILY.	Free white males of 16 years and upward, including heads of families.	Free white males under 16 years.	Free white females, including heads of families.	All other free persons.	Slaves.
Williams, Benjamin, 2d.	2	3	4		
Starkey, Timothy, Esqr.	2	4	4		1
Griswold, Selah	1	3	2		
Pratt, Phebe	1	1	4		
Williams, Samuel	1	7	3		
Post, David	5	3	4		
Post, David, Junr.	1	1	2		
Lucass, Saml	2	6	2		
Brockway, Elijah	1	2	3		
Denison, James	1	4	1		
Brockway, Ebenezer	2	1	3		
Jane, John	1	4	4		
Pelton, Wm	3	1	6		
Ward, Smith	3	2	4		
Stilman, Charles	1		3		
Pratt, Tabor	1	4	3		
Pratt, Ozias	1	3	3		
Pratt, Gideon	2	1	3		
Doan, Israel	2	2	6		
Buckingham, Reuben	1	3	3		
Buckingham, Lucy		3	4		
Pelton, Phinehas	1		5		
Denison, Robert	2	1	6		
Butler, Saml	1		6		
Champion, Stephen	1	1	4		
Grimes, Cyrus	1		4		
Buckingham, Saml	3	4	3		
Andrews, Ichabod	1	2	3		
Tucker, Timothy	4		6		
Bebee, Mary	1	1	3		
Williams, Benja	1		3	2	
Scovell, Elijah	2		5		
Hill, Willm	4	2	3		
Dibble, George	1		4		
Dibble, Martin	1	1	1		
Post, Phinehas	1	1	2		
Post, Nathan, 2d	2	1	3		
Post, Josiah	1	1	3		
Dennison, Jno	3	2	2		
Utter, Stephen	4		2		
Buckley, Abraham	1	4	2		
Platts, Jno	1	2	5		
Buckley, Jemima		1	2		
Leister, Eliphalet	1	1	1		
Platts, Dan	1	1	4		
Platts, Dan, 2d	1	1	2		
Jones, Saml, 2d	1	4	2		
Stephens, Amos	1	1	1		
Chalker, Daniel	2	5	4		
Stephens. Saml	4	3	5		
Tribble. James	1	2	1		
Bailey, Daniel	1	1	1		
Pratt, Ether	1		1		
Bushnell, Phinehas	1	2	7		
Bushnell, Jn. W	4	3	4		
Buckley, Conkling	3	2	5		
Buckley, Wm	2	2	9		
Doan, Joel	1	2	1		
Post, James	1	1	3		
Kelsey, Jeremiah	1		1	1	
Post, Isaac	1	2	5		
Doan, Elkanah	2	1	1		
Platt, Noah	1	1	3		
Cone, David	1		3		
Sandford, Lois		1	4		
Post, Jonathan	3		2		
Griffing, Abner	1	2	5		
Glading, Joseph	1	2	2		
Clark, George, 2d	1	1	2		
Clark, George	3		5		
Clark, Christopher	3	2	3		
Clark, Paul	1	3	5		
Buckingham, Hezekiah	1		2	1	
Pratt, Thomas	2	1	3		
Comstock, Saml	1		1		
Wardstark, Wm	1	2	2		
Drone, Prince	4		4		
Pratt, Damaras			3		
Bushnell, Ethen	2		1		
Parker, Huldah			1		
Pratt, Simeon	2	1	2		
Pratt, Jesse	1	3	2		
Pratt, Benajah	1		1		
Clark, Wm	1	1	3		
Clark, Beamont, 2d	1	1	1		
Clark, Beamont	3	2	5		
Waterhouse, Stephen	1	1	2		
Birkingham, Hosmer	1		1		
Comstock, Saml, 2d	4		4		
Bushnell, Reuben	1		3		
Parker, Sarah			2		
Parker, Jonathan	1	3	2		
Clark, Peter	4		5		
Pratt, Deliverance			3		
Southward, Nathan	3	3	6		

SAYBROOK TOWN—con.

NAME OF HEAD OF FAMILY.	Free white males of 16 years and upward, including heads of families.	Free white males under 16 years.	Free white females, including heads of families.	All other free persons.	Slaves.
Southward, Nathan, 2d.	1		4		
Reed, Cornelius	1	1	8		
Callon, Ducan M	2		3		
Shirland, Stephen	2		4		
Lord, Doty	2		1		
Kirtland, Abner	1	4	5		
Lord, Elijah	3		1		
Pratt, Benja	1		1		
Pratt, Jedb	4	3	2		
Pratt, Wm	2	4	6		
Denison, Jno, 2d	3	1	3		
Dunnen, Jno	1	2	3		
Scovell, Mathew	2	5	4		
Beebe, Molly	2	1	1		
Pratt, Mehitable			3		
Widger, Jno	1	2	1		
Havern Edward	1	2	2		
Williams, Lydia			1		
Snow. Edmond	3	1	4		
Bull, Edward	1	2	2		
Bushnell, Daniel, 2d	1		1		
Bushnell, Francis	1	2	5		
Bull, Jno	2	2	4		
Corbet, Joseph	1	1	4		
Bushnell, Daniel	2	2	4		
Graham, Jane		1	1		
Devotion, Revr Jno	1	1	3		
Chapman, Martha		1	5		
Chapman, Caleb	2	4	2		
Keley, Rueben	1	4	2		
Kebly, Jedediah	2		2		
Kelly, James	1		3		
Bushnell, Jonathan	2	2	2		
Chapman, Wm	1	2	4		
Worthington. Wm	1	2	2		
Denison, Jedediah	1	3	1		
Norriss, Oliver	1	2	2		
Chapman, Labbeus	1	1	3		
Stannard, Abner	2		3		
Stannard, Joseph	1	1	4		
Redfield, James P	1	1	4		
Stannard, Jno, 2d	1		4		
Denison, Saml	1		3		
Denison, Asa	1		3		
Post, Hezekh	1	1	2		
Bartholomew, Wm	1	2	3		
Kelly, Job	1	2	4		
Stannard, Job	1	1	1		
Kelly. Ephm	2	1	6		
Lay, Robert	1	2	6		
Jones, Benjamin	1		1		
Jones, Benja, 2d	1	1	2		
Stannard, Peter	1	3	2		
Stannard, Wm	1	1	3		
Ely, Jno	1	2	2		
Lay, Jona, Esqr	2		4	1	1
Lay, Ezra	2	1	2		
Reed, Abigail			2		
Lay, Nathl	1	1	1		
Bushnell, Benajah	1	1	4		
Dee, Elijah		2	4		
Lay, Jeremh	2	3	3		
Dee, Danl	1	3	4		
Mordock, Wm	2	1	6		2
Dee, Wm	1		3		
Dee. Mark	1	1	4		
Mordock, Willm, 2d	1	1	3		
Wood, Mary		2	5		1
Lay, Simeon	2	1			
Denison, Gideon	2	1	3		
Belden, Mary			2		
Hedges, Eleazer	1	1	3		
Bushnell, Hezekiah	1		1		
Bushnell, Asa	1	2	7		
Bushnell, Reuben	2	2	4		
Bushnell, Ebenezer	1	2	3		
Champion, Thomas	1		1		
Champion, Nathan	1	6	4		
Denison, George	1		1		
Denison, Stephen	1	1	3		
Plant, Ethel	1		3		
Whittelsey, Joseph	1	2	2		
Hill, Henry	1		2		
Ingraham, Wm	3	2	5		
Spencer. Willm	1	1	3		
Jones, Zebulon	1	2	2		
Spencer, Deborah	2	1	4		
Spencer, Caleb	1		1		
Post, Jno	2		3		
Hinkley, Ira	2	1	4		
Spencer, Toby				2	2
Jones, Augustus	2	1	4		
Jones, Phinehas	1		3		
Jones, Ephraim	1		2		
Jones, Saml	1	2	2		

SAYBROOK TOWN—con.

NAME OF HEAD OF FAMILY.	Free white males of 16 years and upward, including heads of families.	Free white males under 16 years.	Free white females, including heads of families.	All other free persons.	Slaves.
Stannard, Jno	2	1	4		
Clark, Jno	2	1	3		
Bushnell, Daniel	1	2	3		
Jones, Huldah		1	2		
Stokes, Richd	1	2	1		
Post, Jedediah	1		3		
Jones, Lewis	1	6	3		
Lay, James	3	2	2		
Post, Isaac	1		5		
Post, Joel	1	1	3		
Belding, Seymour	2	1	1		
Post, Benjamin	2	1	2		
Dibble, Jonas	2	1	3		
Dibble, Jno P	1	2	3		
Post, Nathan	1	1	2		
Post, Christopher	3	2	5		
Post, Enoch	2		1		
Post, Anne			3		
Spencer, Daniel	1	2	2		
Stannard, Jasper	1	1	2		
Jones, Norris	2	3	4		
Spencer, Joseph, 2d	1	5	4		
Spencer, Joseph	2	1	2		
Spencer, Peter	3	2	2		
Wright, Saml	2	1	2		
Hilliard, Bezaleel	2		7		
Stannard, Nathan	1	3	2		
Stannard, Ephraim	1	3	4		
Wright, Benja	1	2	3		
Chapman, Jedediah	1	1	2		2
Chapman, Jedediah, 2d.	1	4	2		
Lay, John	1	2	4		2
Wright, Josiah	3		4		
Wright, Martin	1		1		
Kelly, Gemaliel	1		1		
Wright, Jeremh	2		1		
L'Hommedieu, Henry	2	1	3		1
Denison, Joseph	2	3	4		
Towner, Abraham	3		6		
Carter, Joseph	2		2		
Lay, Asa	2	2	6		
Hunter, Robert	1		1		
Wright, Ezekiel	1	4	3		
Thompson, David	1	3	4		
Chittenden, John	1	2	2		
Post, Joshua	2	2	5		
Stevens, Aaron	2	2	4		
Stannard, Josiah	1	1	3		
Hull, Oliver	1	3	2		
Platts, Elisha	2	2	7		
Stannard, Temperance	1	1	1		
Benjamin, Richard	3	2	2		
Baldwin, Josiah	1		2		
Jones, Daniel	1		6		
Turner, Wm	1	4	2		
Mills, Revd Saml	1	1	6		
Buckingham, John	2	2	2		
Silliman, Thomas, Esq	1	3	3		
Canfield, Isaiah	1	2	5		
Southworth, Gideon	2		3		
Clark, Zelotes	1	4	4		
Waterhouse, Abraham	2		4		
Southworth, Martin	3	1	8		
Canfield, Joel	3	1	2		
Webb, Reynold	1	1	2		
Waterhouse, Jno	2	2	2		
Waterhouse, Austin	1	3	6		
Waterhouse, Elijah	1	1	3		
Southworth, Isaac	1	1	3		
Warner, Jona	2	3	4		
Leet, Edwd A	3	1	2		
Leet, Gideon	1		2		
Leet, Gideon, Junr	2	1	3		
Waterhouse, Abrm, Jr	1		2		
Southworth, Nancy			2		
Church, Saml	1	1	2		
Church, Simeon	1		2		
Webb, Stephn	2	1	2		
Webb, Mary			2		
Matery, John	1	4	3		
Webb, Patience			3		
Webb, Constant	1	2	3		
Webb, Calvin	1		1		
Willard, Danl	1	4	3		
Webb, James	2	1	4		
Parker, John	1	2	2		
Brooks, James	1	1	3		
Hough, Willm	2	1	2		
Waterhouse, Josiah	1	2	3		
Brooks, Simeon	2	2	3		
Bushnel, Doctr	1				
Douglass, Danl	4	2	5		
Douglass, Israel	3		6		
Clark, Reuben	2	2	4		
Barker, John	1	1	2		

MIDDLESEX COUNTY—Continued.

SAYBROOK TOWN—con.

NAME OF HEAD OF FAMILY.	Free white males of 16 years and upward, including heads of families.	Free white males under 16 years.	Free white females, including heads of families.	All other free persons.	Slaves.
Barker, Elisabeth	1		2		
Barker, Mary	1		3		
Stebens, Benony	1	2	5		
Clark, Zachr	1		2		
Clark, Jared	3	2	4		
Lewis, John	3		2		
Lewis, Andrew	1	1	2		
Lewis, Joseph	2	2	6		
Lyndes, Saml	3	1	5		
Stevens, Elijah	2	3	6		
Hambleton, James	1	3	2		
Andrews (Wido)			6		
Webb, Gidn	1		2		
Spencer, Michael	1	2	1		
Spencer, Dan	1	1	2		
Church, Philemon	1	2	5		
Cone, Aaron	2	1	2		
Foster, Alpheus	1	2	1		
Waterhouse, Benja	3	5	3		
Grant, James	1		2		
Franklin, Caleb	1	1	8		
Warner, Phinehas	2	3	2		
Shipman, Michael	1				
Ames, Samel	1		2		
Harriss, Nathl	1		3		
Shipman, Israel	3	1	3		
Southworth, Willm	1		5		
Waterhouse, Gideon	2	3	5		
Mason, Elijah	1	2	5		
Shipman, Joseph	2	2	4		
Lyel, Robert	1	1	2		
Clark, Grnt	1	1	2		
Shipman, Edwd	3	2	5		
Deangelous, Pascal	1	1	2		1
Warner, Willm	1	3	2		
Parmelee, John	1		1		
Mitchell, Wm	3	1	2		2
Newbury, Nathl	1		1		
Warner, David	1	1	2		1
Dudley, Cyprian	3		1		
Webb, Willm	2		4		
Baldwin, James	2		5		
McCollum, Danl	1	1	1		
Parmelee, Mable			2		
Deangelous, Lewis	1	2	2		
Spencer, Wo			2		
Whittelsey (Wido)			2		
Clark, Joseph	1				
Luke (Negro)				2	

NEW HAVEN COUNTY.

BRANFORD TOWN.

NAME OF HEAD OF FAMILY.	Free white males of 16 years and upward, including heads of families.	Free white males under 16 years.	Free white females, including heads of families.	All other free persons.	Slaves.
Page, Joel	1		3		
Lent, Othimel	1	1	3		
Linley, Isaac	3		3		
Linley, John	2	3	3		
Linley, Rufus	1	3	4		
Rose, Thomas	2	2	4		
Page, Samuel	2	1	3		
Page. Amos	1		2		
Barker, Edward	3	4	4		
Stint, Elizus	1	4	4		1
Russell, John	1	3	4		
Russell, Edward	1		2		
Plant, James	1		3		
Rose, Elizabeth			4		
Smith, Allen	1	2	4		
Goodrich, Phineas	3		3		
Goodrich, Gidion	1	2	4		
Goodrich, Bethrolma	2	5	4		
Towner, Jonathan	2	1	4		
Towner, Jacob	1	1	5		
Bradley, Jerad	1	5	4		1
Isaacs, Ralph	1		4	4	
Plant, Benjamin	2	1	3		
D'Berrade, Charles	2	1	1		1
Spinks, Richard	2	1	2		
Wheeton, Samuel	1		1		
Wheeton, Mary			1		
Grant, Margaret			3		
Tyler, Philomen	1	2	3		
Tyler, Joseph	2		2		
Tyler, Samuel	1	2	4		
Cason, Thomas	1	1	3		1
Waters, Temperance		1	5		
Linly, Sarah	1		4		2
Linly, Ebenezer	1		4		
Linly, Ebenezer, 2	1		2		1
Linly, Malik	1			4	
Chitsey, Roswell	2	4	2		
Lamphin, Oliver	1	1	3		
Cora, Rebecca		1	2		
Trip, John	2	2	3		
Linley, Obed	1	3	3		
Wheeton, Nathal	1		1		
Cooke, Elihu	1	2	1		
Gordon, Alexander	1	2	3		
Whitney, John	2		1		
Linly, Samuel	2	2	3		
Plant, Abraham	1	1	5		
Ford, John	1	2			2
Morris, Edmond	1		4		
West, Agnes			2		
Parmalee, Joseph	1	2	2		
Foot, Stephen	2	2	4		
Bradly, Timothy	3	2	6		
Monro, Sarah	2	1	1		
Butler, Charles	1	4	2		
Parrish, Ephraim	2		2		
McQueen, Trefina		3	3		
Porter, Stephen	1		2		
Parmalie, Timothy	1	1	1		
Baldwin, Nicodemus	1	1	5		
Barker, Russell	1	2	2		
Barker, James	1		1		
Barker, Abigail			1		1
Gordon, Lidia	1	1	3		
Tyler, Benjamin	1		4		
Morris, Timothy	5	1	4		
Rose, John	1		2		
Attwater, Jason	1		4		1
Parish, Jonathan	1	1	2		
Maltby, Jonathan	1	3	3		
Baldwin, William	1	2	4		
Butler, Benjamin	1	1	4		
Whiting, John	1	1	3		
Hubbard, John	4		1		
Tyler, Josiah	1	1	2		
Millins, Charles	2		1		
Harrison, William	2				
Sheldon, Asher	2		1		
Huggins, Hester	1		2		
Gold, William	3	1	5		2
Tyler, Samuel	1		3		
Barker, Archelus	1	2	4		
Blaxton, Sarah			1		1
Hull, Ambrose	1	2	1		1
Russel, John	2	2	5		
Welford, John	1	2	4		
Palmer, Jonathan	2	3	3		
Houd, Amie	1		2		
Ods, Martha	1		1		
Russell, Samuel	1	2	1		1
Stock, Moses	1				
Russell, Samuel	1	2	2		
Foot, Abraham	1		2		
Blackston, John	4	3	3		
Blakston, Stephen	2		2		1
Willford, Elizabeth		1	2		
Hubbard, Moses	1	2	5		
Foot, Ephraim	2	2	2		
Tyler, Peter	1	2	1		
Williams, Waram	1	1	2		
Russell, Penfield	4		5		
Blakston, Timothy	1	1	6		
Hoadly, Samuel	2	3	8		
Tyler, Obed	1		2		
Barker, Joseph	2		5		
Hays, Ezekeil	2	3	5		
Harrison, Farr	1	4	4		
Baldwin, Samuel	2		2		
Johnson, Timothy	1	2	3		
Beach, Elnathan	4	2	4		
Goodrich, James	1		5		
Frisbie, Samuel	2	1	4		
Tyler, Patty		1	2		
Tyler, Obed	3		2		
Beach, Ephrim	3	1	2		1
Beach, Ebenezer	1	3	5		
Norton, Thomas	1	2	3		
Bartholemew, Joseph	1				
Tyler, Soloman	1	2	3		
Barker, Benjamin	2	4	2		
Baldwin, James	2		3		
Baldwin, Gamliel	2		1		
Baldwin, John	3	2	5		
Harrison, Amie	1	2	3		
Marchall, William	1		1		
Barker, Samuel	1	1	2		
Harrison, Hester	1	1	2	1	
Harrison, Peter	1	3	6		
Beech, Harrison	1	1	2		
Bartholomew, Benjamin	1	1	6	1	
Garret, John	1	2	6		1
Rogers, Ephraim	3	2	6		
Frisbie, Thomas	2		6		
Ives, Joel	2	1	4		
Baldwin, Zacheus	1	3	3		
Rogers, Samuel	2	2	4		
Rogers, John	3	2	3		
Frisbie, William	1	2	3		
Hoadly, Jonathan	2	4	6		
Rogers, Stephen	2	1	2		
Hoadly, John	1		3		
Hoadly, Abigail			3		3
Jones, Jared	1	1	2	1	
Rogers, Isaac	1	3	4		
Frisbie, Edward	1	2	3		
Jailor, Steward	1	1	1		
Palmer, Jerad	1		1		
Palmer, Barnabas	1	2	1		
Jones, Daniel	1		3		
Cooke, Demebs	1	1	5		
Rogers, John	2	1	2		
Houd, Hendrick	2	2	5		
Cooke, Isaiel	3		1		
Rogers, Abraham	1	1	5		
Barker, Timothy	2	2	4		
Pond, Elias	1	4	3		
Frisbie, Ebenezur	2	2	4		
Monro, George	1		1		
Hotchkiss, Ira	1	1	3		
Frisbie, Rufus	1		2		
Frisbie, Philomon	1		1		
Hoadly, Samuel	2	4	5		
Fuller, Jemima			1		
Frisbie, Nathaniel	3	2	3		
Palmer, Isaac	1	5	2		
Frisbie, Mary	1		3		
Gold, Thomas	2	1	2		
Palmer, Nathaniel	1	2	4		
Palmer, Benjamin	3	3	4		
Fowler, Ely	1		4		
Hooper, James	2	2	2		
Hoadly, James	2	1	3		
Hoadly, Benjamin	1	1	2		
Frisbie, Joseph	1	2	6		
Frisbie, Mary	1	1	3		
Griffin, Aron	1	2	2		
Palmer, Phebe	1	1	3		
Norton, Joel	1		6		
Chittenton, Levi	1	1	3		
Monro, William	2	1	4		
Monro, Fredrick	1		1		
Hoady, Silas	1	2	3		
Gay, Amie	1		2		1
Baldwin, Noah	1	1	1		
Baldwin, Edward	1	1	2		
Hoadly, Ralph	1	3	2		
Hoadly, Abigal	1		4		
Butler, John	2		1		
Butler, Mathew	3	2	3		
Baldwin, Moses	1	2	1		
Page, Joseph	1		1		
Baldwin, Ephraim	1	4	5		
Harrison, Timothy, 2nd	1	3	3		
Harrison, Timothy	2	1	2		
Houd, Joel	1	3	3		
Baldwin, Samuel	3	2	6		
Baldwin, Aron	1	3	6		
Palmer, John	4		4		
Potter, Joel	1		4		
Palmer, Stephan	4	1	4		
Barker, Daniel	1		3		
Barker, Job	2		2		
Harrison, Abraham	2		2		
Harrison, Nathan	1	3	3		
Byinton, Benjamin	1		4		1
Woodward, Gaskin			2		1
Baldwin, Joel	2	2	3		
Baldwin, Daniel	3		3		

NEW HAVEN COUNTY—Continued.

NAME OF HEAD OF FAMILY.	Free white males of 16 years and upward, including heads of families.	Free white males under 16 years.	Free white females, including heads of families.	All other free persons.	Slaves.
BRANFORD TOWN—con.					
Byington, Jonathan	1	2	3		
Harrison, Daniel F	1	2	3		
Pomp (Negroe)				7	
Smith, Joseph	2	1	3		
Harrison, Jerad	1	1	5		
Rose, Justice	1	1	5		4
Harrison, John	1		2		
Harrison, Samuel	2		3		
Ecels, Samuel	2		2	1	
Russell, Timothy	1	1	3		
Rose, Daniel	1	5	3		
Hoadly, Daniel	3	3	4		
Russell, Ethal	1	2	3		
Tyler, William	2	2	5		
Russell, Ebenezer	2	1	1		
Russell, Jonathan	3	1	5		
Rose, Soloman	3		2		
Rose, Levi	1	3	1		
Asher, Gad (Negroe)				8	
Rose, Ruben	2	1	5		
Page, Ruben	1	1	2		
Ford, Lemuel	2	2	4		1
Mulford, Nathan	1	2	3		
Mulford, Barnabas	2	1	2		
Wheeton, William	3	3	2		
Page, Nathaniel	4		2		
Wheeton, Samuel	1	2	5		
Barker, Justice	1	1	3		
Wheeton, James	3		3		
Wheeton, Ruben	2	1	4		
Smith, Jordan	1		2		
Wheeton, Roswell	1	1	2		
Stone, Elihu	2		4		
Harrison, Jacob	1		4	1	
Harrison, Asael	2	1	3		
Page, Icabod	1	3	3		
Renholds, Hezekiah	2	4	3		
Bunnel, Josep	2	1	6		
Harrison, James	2	1	1		
Baldwin, Joseph	1	1	4		
Page, Jacob	1	2	1		
Hoffman, Samuel	2		2		
Cooke, Demetrus	1		1		
Harrison, Jeras	2	1	2		
Johnson, Henry	1		4		
Merrick, Jonathan	1	1	4		
Phillis (Negroe)				5	
Otis, Joseph (Negroe)				6	
Linly, Stephen	1	2	4		
Rose, Samuel	2	2	2		
Hale, Francis	1	2	3		
Hale, Hannah		1	2		
Linsley, Daniel	2	2	3		
Foot, Jonathan	3	1	3		
Rose, Nathan	1	1	4		
Rose, Samuel	3	1	3		
Boils, James	2	1	5		
Palmer, Asael	1	3	5		
Beers, John	1				
Trusdale, Ebenezur	1		1		
Molthrop, Joseph	1	1	4		
Linsley, Israel	4	1	3		1
Harrison, Justice	1	5	1		
Beers, Pitman	1		3		
Smith, Isaac	2	2	3		
Palmer, Elijah	1	1	2		
Bunnel, Jerus	3	1	6		
Page, Benjamin	1	1	3		1
Rogers, Josiah	1		5		
Rogers, David	3		4		
Rogers, Thomas	4		2		4
Pardie, Ebenezur	1	3	2		
Rogers, Thomas, 2	2	2	5		
Butler, James	1	1	1		
Robertson, John	1	2	3		
Smith, Dow	1	3	6		
Harlow, Sarah	1		2		2
Baldwin, Israel	1	4	3		
Monro, Andrew	4	1	5		2
Linsley, Elizabeth	1		3		
Bunnel, Jacob	4		2		
Auger, Peter	1	3	2		
Potter, John	1		1		
Potter, John, 2nd	1	4	1		
Plymouth, John	2	2	3		
Bunnel, Jacob	1	1	2		
Street, Louis		3	4		
Foot, Daniel	2	1	3		
Auger, John	1	3	4		
Foot, Daniel	1	1	2		
Hotchkiss, Hannah	1		1		
Frisbie, Jonathan	1	4	1		
Rogers, Ebenezur	2	1	6		
Rogers, Elihu	2	1	3		
Douglas, Hannah	1	1	3		

NAME OF HEAD OF FAMILY.	Free white males of 16 years and upward, including heads of families.	Free white males under 16 years.	Free white females, including heads of families.	All other free persons.	Slaves.
BRANFORD TOWN—con.					
Frisbie, Jacob	4	2	3		
Baldwin, Benjamin	1	4	2		
Goodsall, Lidia			2		
Johnson, Nathaniel	1		3		
Johnson, Rebecca			1		
Baldwin, Phineas	2		2	1	
Smith, James	3		1		
Finch, Jonathan	1	1	2		
Williams, Stephen	1	3	3		
Foot, Isaac	3	2	6		
Harrison, Wooster	1	1	1		1
Smith, Stephen	1	1	2		
Bennet, Abigal			1		
Barnell, John	1	3	3		
Hawkins, Stephen	1	2	2		
Tainter, Isaac	1	1	1		
Auger, John	1		1		
Auger, Joseph	1	3	3		
Foot, Elisha	2	1	1		
Foot, Samuel	3	2	3		
Tainter, Michael	1				
Tainter, Michael, 2nd	1	3	3		
Tainter, Medad	1	1	4		
Rose, Samuel	1	1	1	1	
Tyler, Jonathan	2	4	4		
Tyler, Isael	2	4	3		
Seymore, Roger	2	2	4		
Munson, Jonathan	1	3	3		
Ingraham, Isaac	1	1	7		
Bartholomew, Jonathan	2	3	5		
Noyce, Mathew	1		1		1
Williams, Deavenport	1	1	2		
Bartholomew, Samuel	1		1		
Bartholomew, Timothy	2	2	2		
Rogers, Josep	1	3	3		
Rogers, Joel	1		1		
Talmage, Soloman	2	2	3		
Rose, Amajia	1	2	2		
Tyler, Peter	2	1	4		
Tyler, Paul	1		1	1	
Norton, Abraham	1	1	2		
Farnum, Mary			1		
Wheeton, William	1	2	2		
Houde, Jude	1		1		
Bartholomew, Benjamin, 2nd	1	1	3		
Clarke, Jonah	1	1	3		
Pierson, Samuel	1	1	2		
Pierson, Benjamin	1		4		
Meigs, Felix	1		1		
Houd, Thankfull			1		
Baldwin, Elihu	3		6		
Baldwin, Sally	1	1	5		
Kimberly, Isaac	1	1	4		
Kimberly, Sherman	1	1	1		
Maltby, Benjamin	1		2		
Maltby, Benjamin, 2	2	5	3		
Maltby, Stephen	1	1	1		
Lindley, James	1	1	2		
Lindley, Josiah	4	2	4		
Ward, Ambrose	1	2	4		
Hoadly, Rufus	3	3	6		
Maltby, John	1	1	1		
Fowler, Josiah	1	3	2		
Maltby, James	1	1	3		
Lindley, Solman	2	2	1		
Foot, John	2	1	2		
Foot, Jerad	2		4		
Hoadley, Ebenezur	1		2		
Hoadley, Timothy	1	2	1		
Harrison, Edward	1	1	3		
Harrison, Amos	3	2	2		
Fowler, Josiah	3		2		3
Lindley, John	1	2	3		
Page, John	2	2	4		
Elwell, Samuel	1	1	3		
Thomas, William	1		2		
Frisbie, Mary			1		
Evens, William	1				
Roser, Malachi	1				
Todd, Lidia	1	1	1		
Bench, Phineas	1		1		
Finch, Ebenezer	2	3	2		
CHESHIRE TOWN.					
Newton, Joseph	1		3		
Newton, Abner	1		1		
Newton, Jerad	2	2	2		
Hull, Thelus	1	2	2		
Newton, Cloe	1	2	3		
Hull, Hannah	1	1	3		
Hull, Lidia	1	1	1		
Root, Moses	1	2	3		
Carrington, Daniel	1	2	2		

NAME OF HEAD OF FAMILY.	Free white males of 16 years and upward, including heads of families.	Free white males under 16 years.	Free white females, including heads of families.	All other free persons.	Slaves.
CHESHIRE TOWN—con.					
Morse, Mary			1		
Hull, Abeather	1	1	1		
Attwater, Jesse	1				
Winchell, Ezeriah	1				
Bishop, Jarad	1	2	3		
Hill, Jonas	2	3	5		
Hull, Abigal	1		1		
Parker, Job	1	4	3		
Rice, Rebecca			2		
Hull, Andrew, 2nd	1		4	1	
Brooks, Soloman	1	1	3		
Reynolds, Squire	1		1		
Root, Judah	2		1		
Mathews, Amos	1		1		
Badger, Fredrick	1		4		
Hull, Luther	1		1		
Parker, Thankfull	1	1	2		
Parker, Thomas	1		2		
Rice, Robert	5		3		
Parker, Levi	1		1		
Tuttle, Ebenezer	1				
Merriman, Amos	1		3		
Parker, Edward	1		1		
Parker, Edward, 2nd	2	2	2		
Parker, William	2	2	6		
Swift, Joseph	2	2	3		
Hall, Timothy	2	1	3		
Hall, Isaiah	2	2	1		
Hall, Amassa	1	2	5		
Hall, Timothy, 2nd	1	3	5		
Coles, Elisha	1	2	5		
Yale, Job	1	1	2		
Yale, Osiers	1	1	1		
Thomas, Enoch	1		1		
Thomas, Enoch, 2nd	1	2	6		
Rice, John	1		4		
Curtis, Edward	2	2	7		
Parker, Amos	2	1	6		
Sanderson, William	1	1	4		
Hough, Ambrose	1	1	5		
Bradley, Peleg	1		1		
Miles, John	2	2	6		
Bristol, Benjamin	1	1	1		
Liberty, Sharp (Negroe)				4	
Clarke, Amassa	1	4	2	1	
Cooke, Samuel	2		4		
Andrews, Eneas	1		1		
Clarke, Stephen	3		3		
Andrews, Thomas	1	3	2		
Ives, Abraham	4	1	6		
Hull, Samuel	1	1	2		
Hull, Epharus	1	1	2		
Hough, Ebenezer	2	2	5		
Goodyear, Edward	1	1	3		
Morse, Isaac	1	5	3		1
Munson Amassa	1	1	3		
Benham, John	2		3		
Benham, Warren	1	1	2		
Lewis, Amassa	3	1	3		
Bradley, Stephen	2	5	5		
Attwater, Samuel	1	1	5		
Lewis, Barnabas	2	1	5		
Benham, Uriah	2	3	4		
Ives, Zachariah	3	1	3		
Attwater, Timothy	1	3	4		
Hull, Andrew	2		4		
Webb, Jonah	1	2	2		
Hotchkiss, Daniel, 3rd	2	1	2		
Hudson, David	1	1	3		
Stevens, Willard	1	2	1		
Tuttle, Edmond	1		2		
Tuttle, Lazerus	2	6	6		
Tuttle, Jecobed	1	5	5		
Tuttle, Moses	1	1	2		
Tuttle, Samuel	1	1	3		
Tuttle, Ephraim	1	2	6		
Attwater, Thomas	1	1	3		
Persons, John	3		5		
Attwater, Ambrose	5	3	6		
Attwater, Moses	1	1	1		
Attwater, Lyman	1		1		
Conner, Elnathan	1	3	3		
Attwater, Elihu	2	1	3		
Bristol, Jonathan	1	1	2		
Andrews, Patience		1	2		
Hall, Jonathan, 2	1	3	6		
Hotchkiss, Ruben	1		2		
Bristol, Zelus	1	1	3		
Grannis, Eldad	2	1	3		
Lewis, Thankfull			3		
Andrews, Amos	1	1	2		
Bristol, Austin	2	2	2		
Winchel, Daniel	1		3		
Stedman, Sarah			2		
Attwater, Hannah	1	2	3		

NEW HAVEN COUNTY—Continued.

NAME OF HEAD OF FAMILY.	Free white males of 16 years and upward, including heads of families.	Free white males under 16 years.	Free white females, including heads of families.	All other free persons.	Slaves.
CHESHIRE TOWN—con.					
Bristol, Thankfull			3		
Stedman, Sarah			2		
Bristol, Gideon	1	2	5		
Hill, Jonah	1	2	5		
Hotchkiss, Mineman	2	2	1		
Page, Jared	2	5	3		
Bristol, Thomas	4		4		
Bristol, Ezra	1	2	2		
Gales, Nathaniel, 2	2		6		
Gales, Nathaniel	1	1	3		
Gales, Elias	1		1		
Parker, Ebenezer	2		2		
Parker, Jabez	1	1	2		
Lines, Erastus	1	2	4		
Jones James	1	4	1		
Bellamy, Arom	1		1	1	
Bellamy, Justus	2	5	4		
Cook, Cornelius	2		2		
Rice, Clarke	2		3		
Hull, Dick (Negroe)				2	
Bunnel, John	1		5		
Bunnel, Abner, 2nd	2	2	4		
Attwater, Ruben	1	1	3		
Barnes, David	1		1		
Doolittle, Isaac	1	2	2		
Hotchkiss, Bela, 2nd	1		4		
Hall, Benjamin	1		2		
Arnold, Lidia		2	2		
Bunnel, Abner	1		1		
Bunnel, Eneas	1	2	4		
Tyler, Ruth	1		3		
Hall, Charles C.	1				
Wainwright, Jonathan	1	5	3		
Potter, Eldad	1	3	2		
Hitchcock, Amassa, 2nd	1		1		
Hitchcock, Valantine	1	2	5		
Hotchkiss, Elijah	1				
Hotchkiss, Henry	1		2		
Hotchkiss, Jonah	2	3	2		
Bench, John	2	2	3		
Ives, Nathaniel	1		1		
Ives, Jotham	1	1	4		
Ives, Mathew	2	1	2		
Bradley, Moses	1		1		
Bradley, Oliver	2	3	3		
Bradley, Ruben	1	1	7		
Gales, Thomas	1	4	4		
Bristol, Dick (Negroe)				3	
Hitchcock, John L.	1		4		
Wilson, Benjamin	1		2		
Parker, Stephen	1	1	1		
Smith, Anna			1		
Twist, Benjamin	1		2		
Miles, Burrage	1		1		
Hull, Miles	2		2		
Hotchkiss, Jason	1	2	2		
Jolly, Martha			2		
Hotchkiss, Ambrose	1				
Lawrence, Elihu	1	3	2		
Hitchcock, Bela	2		3		
Beecher, Benjamin	1	2	6		
Wolcott, Abel	2	1	2		
Attwater, Stephen	1		3		
Attwater, Stephen, 2	2	1	4		
Attwater, Titus	1		1		
Mallery, Daniel	2	2	1		
Hitchcock, Asa	1	1	1		
Attwater, John	2	1	1		
Dalton, Daniel	3	1	4		
Attwater, Amos	1		4		
Sperry, Benjamin	2		5		
Clarke, Stephen, 2d	1	1	2		
Bunnil, Samuel	1	1	1		
Hitchcock, Mary			1		
Doolittle, Samuel	1		1		
Doolittle, Abner	1	2	3		
Doolittle, Ambrose	2		5		
Lewis, Ebenezer	1	1	4		
Doolittle, Barney	1				
Smith, William	1	1	2		
Hall, Ruben	1				
Andrews, Israel	1	3	4		
Turrel, Ephrahim, 2d	1	3	2		
Hall, Lidia	1	1	4		
Law, William	4	3	5	1	
Cornwell, Abijah	2	1	3		
Atkins, Eber	2	1	2		
Clarke, William	2		4		
Beecher, John	2	2	6		
Thompson, Samuel	2		1		
Thompson, Asa	1	1	3		
Parker, Caleb	1	2	4		
Clarke, Andrew	2	3	6		
McCurgen, Alexander	1		1		
Miriam, Icabod	1	1	4		
CHESHIRE TOWN—con.					
Bunnel, Israel	2	5	3		
Smith, John	1		1		
Ives, Ruben	1		1		1
Hull, Hannah, 3rd		1	3		
Hotchwick, Israel	1	1	3		
Stanley, Whiting	1	2	2		
Smith, Elam	2	1	3		
Thompson, Rockmary			2		
Johnson, Seth	1	3	5		
Doolittle, Ebenezer	3		7		
Doolittle, Benjamin H.	1	1	2		
Canfield, Timothy	1	2	3		
Bunnel, Louis			1		
Hitchcock, Rufus	2				
Hitchcock, Easter	1		3		
Doolittle, Silas	1		1		
Dorchester, Ruben	1	2	7		
Parker, Samuel	1	1	5		
Beach, Elnathan	3	1	5		
Hall, Jonathan	3	2	3		
Conner, Trisham	1		3		
Bench, Samuel	3	1	3		
Foot, John	2	3	3		
Andrews, Zinnus	1	1	1		
Talmage, Samuel	2		3	1	
Hotchkiss, Benjamin	1		1		
Hotchkiss, Bennan	1	1	4		3
Hotchkiss, Josiah	1		4		
Hotchkiss, Josiah, 2nd	4		4		
Meriam, Munson	3		4		
Meriam, Munson, 2	1		2		
Meriam, Samuel	1	1	3		
Cooke, Aron	1				
Jones, William	1		5		
Hotchkiss, Robert	1		4		2
Norton, Gold G	1	2	4		
Durrany, Samuel	1	1	3		
Durany, Andrew, 2nd	1		1		
Hitchcock, Amassa	1	2	6		
Hotchkiss, Willstell	3	1	2		
Hitchcock, David	2	2	3		
Hitchcock, Daniel	3	1	2		
Hitchcock, Icobed	1	1	3		
Brooks, David, 2	1		3		
Hitchcock, Amos	1	2	5		
Hitchcock, Anna		1	3		
Hitchcock, Harvey	1		1		
Deering, Andrew	3		5		
Brooks, Cloe	1	2	1		
Brooks, Gideon	1				
Mathews, Elizabeth			2		
Mathews, Ephrim	1	1	2		
Andrews, Samuel	1	2	2		
Andrews, Abel	3	1	2		
Andrews, Bela	2	3	4		
Peck, Elijah	1	3	2		
Upson, James	1	1	2		
Doolittle, Ezra	2	2	5		
Merriman, Lent	2	1	4		
Hall, John, 2nd	1	3	3		
Hall, John	1		1		1
Hall, William	1	4	4		
Rice, Nathaniel	1		4		1
Rice, Ruben	2	3	3		1
Page, Ruben	2	1	2		
Morse, Benjamin	1		2	1	
Rice, Levi	2		3		
Morse, Abigal			3		
Morse, Isaac Bower	1		1		
Morse, Jesse	4	1	3		
Morse, Samuel	1		4		
Morse, Thomas	2	1	3		
Flay, Diamond	1	5	1		
Brooks, Ebenezer, B	1	3	2		
Hotchkiss, Benjamin, 3.	1		3		
Brunson, Martin	2		2		
Martin, John	1	2	3		
Doolittle, Mosses	1				
Hotchkiss Benjamin	1	1	1		
Hotchkiss, Ruth			1		
Hoppen, Benjamin	1	1	1		
Martin, Elizabeth			2		
Hitchcock, Aron	2	1	2		
Attwater, Joseph	2	2	2		
Attwater, Benjamin	4		4		2
Benham, John, 2nd	2		5		
Wright Enos	1		3		
Munson, Peter	2	3	2		
Ives, Phineas 2	2		2		
Naham, Peter (Negroe)					3
Burr, Samuel	1	1	2		
Bunnel, Unice			1		
Andrews, Elizabeth			2		
Peck, John	2	2	3		
Peck, John. 2nd	1	1	3		
CHESHIRE TOWN—con.					
Peck Asa	1		1		
Mathews, Hester			1		
Walton, Francis	1	2	2		
Brunson, Ruben	2	2	2		
Stone, Sarah			2		
Smith, Titus	1	1	2		
Cay, William	1	3	2		
Doolittle, Ephrahim	1	1	1		
Brooks, David	2	2	7		
Bradley, Roswell	2	2	2		
Brooks, Jerry	2	1	5		
Doolittle, Amos	3	1	2		
Lines, Rufus	2	2	3		
Cooke, Mireman	1	3	1		
Cooke, Elizabeth			3		
Andrus, Phebe			5		
Peter (Negroe)				3	
Brooks, Thomas	2		3		
Smith, Cooper	1		2		
Curtis, Gilbert	1	1	3		
Daly, Giles	1	2	4		
Hitchwick, Jason	2		2		
Smith, Josiah, 2	1	1	3		
Hall. Hannah			3		
Spencer, Seldon	1	2	5		
Plump, Benoni	3	3	2		
Smith Ephrahim, 2nd	2	6	2		
Rice, Bennet	1	4	4		
Hotchkiss, Adonijah	1		2		
Doolittle, Benjamin	4		3		
Cooke, Samuel, 2nd	1	1	2		
Hotchkiss, Ephrim	1	1	2		
Freston, Ruben	3	1	2		
Brooks, Amassa	1	2	2		
Ren (Negroe)				3	
Ishmael (Negroe)				4	
Ives, Joel	1	1	2		
Ward, Timothy	1		4		
Hummiston, Jesse	1	1	3		
Bunnel, David	2		6		
Davis, Desire			1		
Bunnil, Ebenezer	1	1	2		
Thompson, Jesse	1	1	1		
Badger, Edward	1	2	6		
Jones, Elisha	1	3	3		
Morse, Titus	2	2	3		
Bunnel, Joel	1	1	2		
Morse, Nathaniel	4	1	3		
Sutton, William	1		1		
Webb, Gideon	1	1	3		
Barnes, Elija			2		
Brooks, Henry	1	1	2		
Brooks, Henry 2nd	1	4	4		
Talmage, Josiah	1	1	4		
Clarke, Samuel	3	1	8		
Gilkie, Peter	1	5	2		
Doolittle, Obed	1	4	3		
Ives, Phineas	1	5	2		
Blakely, Moses	2		2		
Morse, Moses	3	3	4		
Doolittle, Abraham	5		2		
Morse, Josiah	2		1		
Benham, James	1	1	4		
Collin, Joseph	1	1	5		
Prindle, Sarah			2		
Todd, Caleb	1	3	1		
Barnes, Ambrose	2	1	4		
Hall, Jerad	3	2	6		
Andrews, Nathaniel	1	1	2		
Todd, Hezekiah	1	1	3		
Hall, Jonah	1	2	1		
Peirpoint, Ely	1				
Tyler, Joseph	3	2	5		
Blackely, Moses	1	5	3		
Doolittle, Obed	1	2	1		
Brooks, Obed	1	2	2		
Tuttle, Moses, 2nd	1	2	4		
Bryant, John	1	4	4		
Beecher, Hezekiah	2	4	6		
Perkins, John	1	1	1		
Hotchkiss, John, 3.	1	1	3		
Hall, Ebenezer	1	1	2		
Hotchkiss, John, 2nd	4	1	3		
Williams, Aron	3		3		
Hotchkiss, Henry, 2nd	1	1	2		
Hotchkiss, Chauncy	1		2		
Hotchkiss, Lyman	1		1		
Turrel, Ephrim	3	5	5		
Williams, John	1	3	3		
Hines, Jared	1	2	2		
Smith, Jarad	1	3	2		
Hitchcock, Levi	1	1	3		
Smith, Ephrim	1		3		
Smith, Ephrim, 2.	1	3	2		
Smith, Israel	1	1	4		

NEW HAVEN COUNTY—Continued.

CHESHIRE TOWN—con.

NAME OF HEAD OF FAMILY.	Free white males of 16 years and upward, including heads of families.	Free white males under 16 years.	Free white females, including heads of families.	All other free persons.	Slaves.
Peck, Phineas	1	3	3		
Wilmot, Elijah	2		6		
Tyler, Isaac	2	1	1		
Tyler, Amos	1	1	1		
Turrel, Enoch	1		1		
Chatterton, Assael	1		3		
Tyler, Enos	1	1	3		
Hotchkiss, Jiles	1	1	3		
Minick (Negroe)				3	
Benham, Thomas	1	3	2		
Andrew, Simeon	1	1	3		
Russell, Riverus	1	2	4		
Burr, Jerad	1		3		
Tyler, Isaac, 2nd	2		1	1	
Sandford, John	1	3	6		
Hines, Ambrose	1		1		
Hine, Silas	1	2	2		
Hotchkiss, Robert	2		2		
Russell, Nicholas	1	1	1		
Ford, John	1		1		
Ford, Nathaniel, 2	1	1	2		
Ford, Nathaniel	3		1		
Hine, Ambrose, 2	1	2	4		
Wilmot, Amos	1		3		
Sperry, Joseph	3		2		
Doolittle, Joseph	2	3	3		
Sperry, Job	1	1	2		
Sperry, Rhoda		1	2		
McDonnal, Elves	1		2		
Brown, Nathan	2		2		
Brown, Isaac	1		1		
Barns, Edmond	1	1	4		
Sandford, Gideon	3		4		
Williams, Ruben	1	2	2		
Nettleton, Ely	1		3		
Wilmott, Joel	1	1	4		
Wilmott, Elijah	1	1	4		
Sandford, Henry	1	2	2		
Sanford, Archibald	1	2	2		
Wilmot, Asa	1	1	4		
Hotchkiss, Noah	2		4		
Hotchkiss, John	2		4		
Hotchkiss, Ebenezer	1	1	1		
Hotchkiss, Daniel	2				
Hitchcock, Lemuel	1	3	4		
Mathews, Joshua	2		2		
Ives, William	1		4		
Merriman, Jehel	1	1	3		
Merriman, Theophilus	1		2		
Cooke, Clum	2	2	3		
Doolittle, Ruben	1	2	1		
Bristol, Ruben	1		4		
How, Joseph	1	1	2		
Lewis, Caleb	1	1	4		
Morse, Joel	1	1	1		

DERBY TOWN.

NAME OF HEAD OF FAMILY.	Free white males of 16 years and upward, including heads of families.	Free white males under 16 years.	Free white females, including heads of families.	All other free persons.	Slaves.
Curtis, Oliver	1		2		
Curtis, Sheldon	1	2	3		
Craft, Edward	2	4	4		
Humphrey, Anna		2	4		3
Whitlesey, Joseph	1				
Carter, Margerit		1	2		
Hond, John	2		2	1	1
Kimberly, Liberty	1	1	1		
Humphreys, John	3	3	5		1
Burret, William, 2nd	1	1	2		
Smith, Abraham	3	1	2		
Smith, James	1		2		
Bartholemy, Claudius	2	1	5		
Burret, William	2	3	5		
Hull, Samuel	2	4	5	1	2
Baldwin, Elizabeth	1	1	5		
Whitney, Stephen	1		3		
Tucker, Zephaniah	2	2	3		
Mansfield, William	1		1		
Parson, Nathaniel	1		4		
Person, Abel	2	3	1		1
Siverana, Nicholas	2		6		
Hotchkiss, Leveret	1	1	2		
Hawkins, Hannah			2		
Horsey, Eunice		2	4		
Starks, Daniel	1	2	2		
Todd, Daniel	2	1	1		
Hotchkiss, Elizabeth	2	1	6		
Mansfield, Richard, 2nd	2	1	4		
Gibb, Edward	1	5	5		
Baldwin, Ruben	1	5			
Picket, Joseph	1		2		
Whitney, Henry	1	2	2		
Davis, Joseph	2	4	1		
Beers, John	1	1	2		
Clarke, Sheldon	2	1	4		1

DERBY TOWN—con.

NAME OF HEAD OF FAMILY.	Free white males of 16 years and upward, including heads of families.	Free white males under 16 years.	Free white females, including heads of families.	All other free persons.	Slaves.
Clarke, William, 2nd	1		2		
Grany, Ebenezer	2	4	4		1
Wheeler, Joseph	1	3	3	1	
Davis, Nathan	1	4	1		
Judson, Isaac	1		2		
Hitchcock, David	2	3	3		
Smith, Abijah	2	1	4		
Smith, Abraham	1	3	1		
Thompson, Abel	1	3	1		
Wilcox, Abijah	2		2		
Putt, John (negroe)				3	
White, Joseph	1	3	2		
Gorham, George	1	1	4		
Johnson, Peter	1		3		
Short, Joseph	3	5	1		
Holbrook, Daniel	4	2	8		
Parsons, Rena	2	1	5		
Lains, Henry	2		4		
Hale, Samuel	1	1	4		
Bradley, Eneas	3		2		
Bard, James	2	1	2	1	
Tuller, Martin	1		5		
Coe, John	1	2	4		
Hale, Abraham	1		2		
Phillip (Negroe)				6	
Johnson, Nathaniel	3	1	2		
Johnson, Philo	1	1	4		
Chatfield, Joseph	2	1	4		
Hawkins, Abraham	1		1		
Johson, Amos	1		4		
Baldwin, Timothy	2	1	1		3
Baldwin, Thadeus	1	3	6		
Baldwin, Timothy, 2nd	1	1	2		1
Riggs, Joseph	1	1	1		1
Riggs, Joseph, 2nd	3	2	4		
Waterhouse, Isaac	1	1	3		
Pope, Joseph	2	4	3		
French, Samuel	1		3		
Pritchard, Philo	1	1	2		
Hitchcock, Jonathan	1	1	2		
Hitchcock, Jonathan, 2nd	1	2	3		
Loveman, Joseph	1	2	2		
French, Francis	1	3	3		
Sherwood, Joseph	1	2	2	1	
Lovemond, Lewis	1		1		
Blake, David	1	2	3		
Prindle, Eneas	1	1	5		
Pease, Elizabeth			2		
Keeney, Ethiel	1				
Davis, Nathan	1	1			
Wooden, Stephen	1				
Whitney, William	1	2	3		
Whitney, Josiah	1	3	3		
Clarke, William	2	4	4		2
Hawkins, David	1	2	1		
Jackson, Jonathan	3	1	3		
Prindle, John	1	1	2		
Granis, David	1	2	4		
Hull, Abijah	3	2	6		4
Hawkins, Moses	1	2	2		
Hawkins, Isaac	1	2	2		
Hawkins, Eli	2		4		
Hawkins, Eli, 2nd	2	2	4		
Canfield, David	1	1	4		
Bassett, David	1	3	3		
Smith, Eneas	1	4	2		
Smith, Nathan	4		5		
Smith, Andrew	2		3		
Carpenter, Benjamin	2		1		
Smith, Isaac	1	3	3		
Davis, Benjamin	1	1	2		
Parson, Samuel	1	1	2		
Tomlinson, John	2	2	4		
Alling, Samuel	1	2	4		
Smith, Josiah	2	6	3		
Nevis, Calver	1		2		
Tomlinson, John	2	1	3		
Mucker, Ephraim	1	1	2		
Deforrest, Hannah	4	1	5		
D'Forrest, Gideon	3				
Marshall, Bryan	1	1	3		
Marshall, Isaac E	2	3	3		
Davis, Elias	1		1		
Nicoll, Daniel	1		2		
Tomlinson, Sarah			2		
Lyman, Sarah	1	2	2		
Yale, Thomas	2	1	4		
Lister, Murry	1		2		
Morse, Joseph	1	4	2		
Spencer, Joel	2	3	3		
Durand, John	1	2	3		
Morse, William	4				
Smith, Lucy		3	1		
Smith, William	1	2	3		
Durand, Noah, 2nd	1	4	3		

DERBY TOWN—con.

NAME OF HEAD OF FAMILY.	Free white males of 16 years and upward, including heads of families.	Free white males under 16 years.	Free white females, including heads of families.	All other free persons.	Slaves.
Durand, Elizur	3		5		
Tomlinson, Auger	2	1	5		
White, Daniel	1	1	1		
Voce, Adam	3	2	2		
Lum, Ruben	1	4	3		
Lum, Joseph	1		1		
Hull, Elizabeth			2		
Bassett, Benjamin	2	2	5		
Bassett, Amos	3	1	1	1	1
Tomlinson, Daniel	2	4	3		
Tomlinson, Nathaniel	2	2	6		
Beardsley, Jonas	2	3	6		
Webster, Obed	2	1	2		
Pool, John	2	1	3		
Pool, Samuel	1		1		
Pool, Mary		1	3		
Bassett, Joseph	1	1	5		
Bassett, James	2	4	3		
Bassett, Samuel, 3d	1		1		
Tomlinson, Benjamin	1		2		
Smith, Abner	1		2		
Bassett, Samuel	1	1	2		
Tomlinson, David, 2nd	2				
Durand, Noah	1		1		
Durand, Noah, 3rd	1		2		
Botsford, Ebenezer	1	1	3		
Botsford, Samuel	3		3		
Botsford, Neamiah	2	3	7		
Botsford, Ezra	1	1	2		
Foot, Ezra	1	2	3		
Tomlinson, Benjamin, 2nd	1	1	2		
Hawkins, Samuel	1	1	3		
Fairchild, Zachariah	2		2		
Hard, Wilson	1	1	2		
Canfield, Daniel	1	1	4		
Bassett, Isaac	1	1	2		
Smith, Enoch	1		4		
Bard, George	1	2	2		
Tomlinson, Russell	2	4	3		2
Holbrook, Abel	2	1	2		
Lewis, Ebenezer	2	1	4		
Fanton, Moses	2	1			
Lewis, Philo	1	3	2		
Tucker, William	1	2	2		
Manville, James	2	3	2		
Tomlinson, Webb	1	4	5		
Mansfield, Nathan	2	1	4		
Beeby, Martin	2	1	4		
Tomlinson, Henry	3	5	3		
Smith, Andrew	1	1	1		
Graham, Andrew	1	2	1		
Waterhouse, Andrew	1	3	2		
Holly, John	1	5	3		
Russell, Joseph	1		2		1
Russell, Samuel	2	2	3		
Lumn, Jonathan, 2nd	3	2	4		
Tomlinson, Elizabeth		1	2		
Wooster, Eprahim	1	1	1		
Tomlinson, Isaac	1	4	2		
Lumn, Jonathan	1		2		
Lumn, Samuel	1	1	1		
Lake, Elnathan	1		1		
Bassett, John	4	1	1		
Smith, Christopher	1	1	3		6
Holbrook, John	2	2	2	1	1
Holbrook, John, 2nd	1	2	3		
English, Clement	4		3		
Nettleton, Jonah	3	1	4		4
Jellet, Jeremiah	2	2	3		
Holbrook, Nathan	2	3	2	1	
Johnson, Timothy	2		3		
Johnson, Jeremiah	2	1	3		
Durand, Ebenezer	1	4	2		
Perkins, Ephrahim	4		3		
Smith, John	1	2	1		
Bunnel, Luke	1				
Wooster, Daniel	1				
Durand, Nemiah	1		3		
Durand, Joseph	1	1	2		
Chatfield, Bennh	1	1	3		
Chatfield, Isaac	1	3	3		
Bassett, Eben	1				
Chatfield, Dan	1		4		
Nicoll, Isaac	3	2	4		
Chatfield, John	1	4	3		
Chatfield, Gideon	1	3	3		
Durand, Elizabeth	2		2		
Bates, Elihu	1	2	3		
Bales, Benjamin L	1		1		
Bunnel, Isaac	1		2		
Pirkens, Daniel	2	1	2		
Wooster, Nathaniel	1		2	1	
Wooster, Arther	1		1		

NEW HAVEN COUNTY—Continued.

NAME OF HEAD OF FAMILY.	Free white males of 16 years and upward, including heads of families.	Free white males under 16 years.	Free white females, including heads of families.	All other free persons.	Slaves.	NAME OF HEAD OF FAMILY.	Free white males of 16 years and upward, including heads of families.	Free white males under 16 years.	Free white females, including heads of families.	All other free persons.	Slaves.	NAME OF HEAD OF FAMILY.	Free white males of 16 years and upward, including heads of families.	Free white males under 16 years.	Free white females, including heads of families.	All other free persons.	Slaves.
DERBY TOWN—con.						DERBY TOWN—con.						DERBY TOWN—con.					
Hawkins, Silas	1	1	5			Johnson, Phineas	1	2	4			Johson, Gideon	1				
Hawkins, Zachariah	2	1	2		2	Johnson, Timothy	2		4			Gaston, Joseph	1		2		
Hawkins, Isaac	1	3	1			Candie, Neamiah	2	4	3			Johnson, Eber B	1		4		
Hide, Daniel	1		1			Wooster, Thomas	2	2	4			Johnson, Levi	1				
Parker, Soloman	1	1	3			Riggs, John	3	3	6			Bosteck, Isaac	1		2		
Wooden, William	2		1			Twichett, John	2	1	4			Bosteck, Richard	1				
Lewis, William, 2nd	1	1	1			Twichet, Joseph	2	2	1			White, John	2	4	4		
Lewis, Charles	1	1	1			Twichet, Elizabeth			3			Leek, James	1		4		
Lewis, William	2	1	4			Botsford, John	1	3	4			Page, Edmond	2		3		
Wooster, Joseph	1	5	4			Dean, Icabod	1		2			Crawford, John	1		1		
Oatman, Samuel	2	2	3			Lyman, Russell	1	1	6			Loveland, Trueman	2	1	3		
Bryant, Isaac	1		2			Osborn, Jerard	1	3	3			Witmore, Turrel	2	1	4		
Wooster, Elizabeth	1	1	2			Twichet, Benjamin	3	1	7			Dayton, Phebe	2	1	5	1	
Warton, Abel	1	1	1			Twichet, Enoch	1	1	4			Beech, Benjamin	1	1	2		
Hawkins, Dameras	1					Wooster, Abel	2	2	1			Loveland, Ashbel	1	1	2		
Hide, Abijah	2	2	5			Osborn, Thomas	1		1			Swift, John	1	6	5		
Hide, Nathaniel	1		1			Wooster, Ebenezer	1	2	3			Renny, Medad	1	1	1		
Hull, Abel	1	3	4			Tucker, Samuel	1		2			Tomlinson, Levi	1	1	8		
Hide, Asael	1		2			Andrews, Ephrahim	1	3	2			Wooster, Henry	1				
Hide, Joseph	1	1	1			Bunnel, Charles	1	2	1			Wooster, Henry, 2nd	1		2	1	
Jones, Joseph	1	1	2			Bunnel, Ruben	1		2			Hawkins, Joseph	1	1	5		
Wentworth, James	1	1	2			Fairchild, Nathaniel	2		4			Roe, Daton	1				
Gibbons, John	1		1			Basset, Samuel, 2nd	1	2	4			Baldwin, James	1	2	2		
Hubbel, Joseph	1	1	1			Clarke, George	1	4	1			Chatman, Ruben	1	1	3		
Perry, Ezekiel	1		2			Tucker, Samuel	1	1	1			Plant, Hester	1	1	4		
Perry, John	1					Tucker, Jonah	1					Pritchard, James	1	2	4		
Parsons, Eli	2		4			Twichet, Ebenezer	1	2	2			Steel, Bradford, 2nd	1	1	1		
Tomlinson, Noah	1		2			Wooster, Samuel	1	1	3			Steel, Elisha	2	1	1		
Tomlinson, Noah, 2nd	1	2	4			Clarke, Thomas	2		3		1	Sandford, Samuel	1				
Hubbell, Richard	1	3	3			Basset, Abraham	2	1	3			Pritchard, Leveret	1				
Smith, Elizabeth	1	2	3			Bassett, Miles	1	1	1			Davis, Daniel	2	3	2		
Lumn, Jonathan, 3rd	1	4	4			Davis, John	2	3	2			Steel, Bradford	2		2		1
Hawkins, John	1	4	1			Church, John	2		2			Baldwin, Isaac	2	3	3		
Sperry, Jonathan	1	1	2			Churchill, John	1	3	1			Hine, Amos	1	1	2		
Kimberly, Thomas	1	1	3			Beecher, Samuel	2	1	4			Smith, Jesse	1	1	2		
Bassett, Edward	1	1	2			Riggs, Ebenezer	2	1	5			Hitchcock, Ebenezer	1	2	4		
Bassett, John, 2nd	2	2	2			Riggs, Edward	2		2			Hargor, Edward	1	1	6		
Griffin, Elizabeth	3		3			Hitchcock, Samuel	1	4	3			Cornish, John	1		2		
Griffin, Jonathan	1	2	1			Fairchild, Abiel	1	1	1			Bartis, Samuel	1		2		
Beardsley, Eliakim	2	2	4			Kelly, Mathew	1	1	3			Washborn, Josiah	2		2		
Bailey, Enock	1	2	4			Riggs, James	1	2	4			Wooster, John	4		2		
Wooster, Ebenezer	1		1			Carpenter, Henry	1		4			Wooster, John, 2nd	1	1	2		
Perry, Caleb	1	3	2			French, Nathaniel	1	1	3			Stiles, Dan	1		1		
Wooden, William, 2nd	1		5			Clarke, Thomas, 2nd	2	2	3			Wooden, Hezekiah	2	2	1		
Clarke, Abel	1	3	4			Johnson, Ebenezer	1		1			Canfield, Abiel	2	2	3		
Perry, Peter	1					Johnson, Ebenezer	2	2	2			Wooster, Marchant		1	3		
Wooden, Charles	1		2			Judd, Sally	1		2			Bassett, Abraham	1	3	3		
Wright, Mosses	2	1	7			Riggs, Moses	1	3	3			Holbrook, Philo	2	1	4		
Hawkins, Elizabeth	1	1	6			Hine, Heil	6		3			Fowl, Lewis	1	2	1		
Tomlinson, David	2	2	3			Smith, David	1		3			Wooster, Abraham	2		1		
Perry, Joshua	2	2	2			Hine, Hezekiah	2		6			Miles, Jonathan	2		6		
Wooding, David	1	1	2			Wilcox, John	1	5	1			Miles, Theophilus	1	2	7		
Perry, Gelverton	1	3	3			Sandford, Zadock	2	3	5			Grinall, William	1	1	4		
Pondman, Nathaniel	1	1	2			Clark, Hezekiah	2	2	2			Keiny, William	1	4	4		
Perry, Gideon	1	1	3			David, Riggs	1	2	2			Renny, Ebenezer	1	1	1		
Smith, Richard	1					Riggs, Joseph	2	3	5			Saben (Negroe)				7	
Perry, Ezekel	1		2			Roger (Negroe)				3		Hine, Thomas	2		4		
Wholf, Henry	1		3			Shubel (negroe)				4		Barty, John	1		4		
Bunnel, William	1	2	3			Johnson, Alexander	2	1	3			Deal, Charles	1	2	1		
Twichel, David	2	2	6			Johnson, Timothy	1		3			Harger, Philo	3		2		
Osborn, Joseph	3	1	2			Johnson, Nathaniel	1	2	3			Cambridge (Negroe)				5	
Perry, James	2	1	1			Johnson, Charles	1	2	3			Barnes, Icabod	1	2	5		
Dutton, Ose	1	2	4			Wheeler, Moses	2	3	6			Todd, Daniel, 2nd	1	1	3		
Sowers, Hannah			3			Cobin, Parish	2	2	4			Morris, David	1		3		
Strong, Josiah		2	3			Clarke, Moses	1	1	3			Plumb, Joshua	1				
Candie, Enos	1	2	3			Washboun, Bowen	1		4			Plumb, Samuel	2	2	5		
Henman, Eben, 2nd	2	2	3			Riggs, Thomas	1		4			Hawkins, Daniel	1		3		
Henman, Eben	1		1			Fairchild, Joseph	1	2	5			Putt, Christopher	1		1		
Henman, Ephrahim	1	2	3			Wheeler, Abel	2	1	2			Prindle, Ebenezer	2	1	4		
Scott, Justis	3	2	3			Wheeler, Louis			5			Hotchkiss, Eliphalet	1		1		
Trumbel, Elizabeth			1			Hicock, Ruben	1	1	2			Mansfield, Richard	2	1	4		1
Brunson, David	1	2	2			Lines, Joseph	1	1	2			Hotchkiss, Moses	1		2		
Minott, Lewis	2					Andrews, Ebenezer	1	2	4			Merrel, Timothy	1	3	1		
Hatch, Sherman	1	4	1			Mills, Asa	1	1	1			Smith, Abel	1	1	4		
Tucker, Gideon	1	3	2			Andrews, Simeon	1	3	3			Baldwin, Silas	1		4		
Hawkins, Peter	1	2	4			Potter, Joseph	2	1	4			Tucker, Reuben	3	1	2		
Bunnet, Hannah		1	2			Chatfield, Samuel	2		4			Tucker, Daniel	1		2	6	
Burret, Benedict	1		3			Osborn, Joshua	1	3	3			Frank (Negroe)				6	
Candie, Gideon	3	1	4			Wheeler, Nathaniel	2	1	2			Thompson, Jabez	2	4	4		
Bunnels, Hannah			1			Wheeler, John	1	3	3			Burns, Titus	1		5		
Candie, Moses	1		2			Edee, John	1	1	3			Hotchkiss, Thomas	1		1		
Buckingham, Nathan	3	1	4			Johnson, Hezekiah	1	1	3			Burns, Titus, 2nd	2	2	1		
Osborn, Naboth	1					Johnson, Asael	1	2	3			Peter (Negroe)				2	
Osborn, Joseph	1	5	1			Johnson, Joseph	1		3			Hawkins, Edward	2	2	2		
Townes, John	1	5	2			Peck, Ebenezer	1		3			Arger, Abraham	1	1	1		
Bradley, Benjamin	1	3	1			Peck, Bezeliel	1	1	3			Arger, Mary			3		
Candie, Caleb	3	5	5			Bristol (Negroe)				2		Arger, Ephrahim	1		2		
Buckingham, Ebenezer	3		3			Holbrook, Daniel	2	2	3			Charles, William	1		2		
Smith, David	1	2	1			Johnson, Isaac	2	2	4			Wooster, Daniel	1	2	4		2
Candie, Justice	1	4	2			French, Israel	1	1	3			Davis, Ruben	1	1	2		
Wheeler, Samuel	2	2	4			French, Enoch	1	2	3			Delamore, Joseph	2		2		
Buckingham, Jerad	1	1	1			Chatfield, Joel	1	3	2			Molthrop, Benjamin	2		2		
Turrel, Isaac	1	3	3			French, Charles	1	2	3			Molthrop, Benjamin, 2nd	1		2		
Twichet, David	2	1	4			Smith, Samuel	1	2	4			Tuttle, Annie					

NEW HAVEN COUNTY—Continued.

NAME OF HEAD OF FAMILY.	Free white males of 16 years and upward, including heads of families.	Free white males under 16 years.	Free white females, including heads of families.	All other free persons.	Slaves.
DERBY TOWN—con.					
Washbourn, John	1		1		
Row, Dan	1	2	2		
Blake, Ruben	1		2		
Humphries, Isaac	1	2	2		
Mark (negroe)					3
Clarke, Michael	1	2	6		
Dorman, Samuel	1	2	3		
Mitchel, Whitney	1		1		
Harger, Ebenezer	1	4	3		
Bartis, John, 2nd	1	1	1		
Clinton, Ebenezer	1	2	1		
Allen, David	2	1	3		
Smith, Joseph	1	2	2		
Harrison, Levi	1	1	1		
Hegleton, Abigail		2	2		
Davis, Isaac	1		3		
Peirson, Joseph	1	5	4		
Waters, Richard	1	1	4		
OCane, Jeremiah	1		4		
OCane, Joseph	1				
Davis, Jabez	1		2		
Peirson, Amos	2	1	1		
Peirson, Isaac	1	1	1		
Dyer, William	1	2	2		
Homstead, Joseph	1	5	1		
Hale, Beman	2	3	1		
Tucker, Zapthali	1	3	5		
Murry, Abraham	1	1	1		
Dove, Jack	1				
Curtis, Samuel	1				
Blake, Isaac	1	1	1		
Mansfield, Stephen	1	1			
Hotchkiss, Levi	2	2	5		
Chatfield, Ebenezer	1				
Gilbert, David	1				
Miller, Elizabeth			2		
Johnson, Mary			1		
Hatch, Euson	1	1	1		
Loveland, Clarke	1		1		
Loveland, Trent	1				
Northrop, Abigal			2		
Patchen, James	1		1		
Clarke, Ann		1	1		
Hinman, Philo	1	1	5		
Smith, Martha			2		
Taylor, Henry	1				
Gillon, James	1				
Turner, Henry	1				
Jones, James	1				
Phillips, Elisha	1				
Palson, Henry	1				
DURHAM TOWN.					
Hart, Samuel	4		3		
Coe, Morris	1	5	2		
Coe, Simeon	1	5	3		
Coe, Timothy	1	2	4		
Parmalie, Eliphas	4	2	3		2
Stow, Timothy	1	2	3		
Camp, Nathaniel	2	3	1		
Spencer, John	1	1	2		
Norton, John	1	2	4		
Wright, Joseph	1		3		
Wright, Joseph, 2nd	2	3	4		
Bartlet, Abraham	1	1	4		
Seward, Moses	4	2	2		
Bartlet, Samuel	2		3		
Bartlet, Abraham	1	1	3		
Meigs, Phineas	1	1	1		
Parmalie, Levi	1	1	2		
Camp, Elias	1	1	2		
Canfield, Asher	1	1	2		
Parmalie, Joel	1	1	2		
Parmalie, Camp	1	1	2		
Fowler, Caleb	3	1	6		
Camp, Ely	1	1			
Camp, Phebe			3		
Camp, Joseph	1	1	3		
Camp, Elias	2		3		
Johnson, William	1		1		
Ceasar (Negroe)					6
Parmalie, Daniel	1	2	4		
Parmalie, Hezekiah	1		2		
Camp, Ezra	2		2		
Larkins, Peter	1	2	2		
Norton, Stephen	2		2		
Norton, Stephen, 2nd	1	1	2		
Hall, Luther	1	1	2		
Strong, John	1	1	4		
Lose, John	1	2	1		
Southward, Joseph	1		1		
Crane, Jesse	1		1		
Crane, Zelock	2	1	3		
Wright, Samuel	1	3	1		

NAME OF HEAD OF FAMILY.	16+	under 16	females	other free	Slaves
DURHAM TOWN—con.					
Wright, Asher	1	1	5		
Ades, Thomas	1	1	2		
Strong, Thomas	3		4		
Johnson, John	4	1	5		
Scranton, Abraham	6	3	4		
Gillam, Benjamin	1		4		
Stow, Abraham	2	1	1		
Seward, Samuel	1		2		
Meeker, Daniel	2		1		
Kelsey, Stephen	2		2		
Rositer, Mary			2		
Bishop, Jonas	1		2		
Dimick, Daniel	1	2	5		
Burret, Israel	1				
Coombs, John	1	2	2		
Crocker, Jabez	3		3		
Choker, Jabez, 2nd	1	2	3		
Crane, Lucretia			1		
Crane, Mahitabel		2	4		
Crane, Fredrick	1	3	3		
Loveland, Titus	3	2	3		
Crane, Henry	1	3	5		
Hull, Joseph	1	1	2		
Hull, James	1		3		
Hull, Cornelius	3		1		
Hull, Sylvanus	1	2	7		
Francis, Titus		1	2		
Strong, Eliakim	1	2	3		
Arnold, James	1	2	2		
Hinman, Elihu	1		4		
Wells, Mary			2		
Hinman, James	2		5		
Chrittenton, Hopestill	1	1	1		
Loveman, John	1	1	3		
Strong, Medad	1	3	3		
Squire, Ebenezer	1	2	2		
Chauncy, Elihu	1		1		
Burrett, Charles	1		2		
Wadsworth, John M	2	2	2		2
Wadsworth, Hester	2		1		1
Squire, Abiather	2	1	3		
Hicock, James	2	2	2		
Beamont, Jedutham	1	1	1		
Camp, Samuel	2	2	1		
Wilkinson, John	1		1		
Goodrich, Elizur	2	1	2	1	
Camp, Ebenezur	1	1	1		
Chauncy, Elnathan	3		1		
Spencer, Stephen	1	3	1		
Spencer, Roger	2		1		
Wheeton, Chapman	1		2		
Meeker, John	1				
Wells, Jonathan	1				
Murry, Warren	1				
King, John	1	1	3		
Chittenton, Gideon	1	2	2		
Parmalie, James	1	1	2		
Wadsworth, James	1		2		
Burret, Richard	1	2	3		
Camp, Israel	3	1	2		
Hall, Timothy	4	1	6		
Gillman, Asher	1	2	1		
Hall, Sarah			3		
Gurnsway, Lemuel	1		3		
Carr, Clement	1	1	2		
Hull, Eliakim	1	1	2		
Picket, Benjamin	2		4		
Camp, Job	8		4		
Spelman, Elizabeth		2	3		
Smithson, Robert	3		3		
White, Charles	1	2	5		
Robinson, Ebenezur	1	4	2		
Gurnsey, Ebenezur	2	1	2		
Dunn, Timothy	1		1		
Norton, Hosias	1		1		
Norton, Noah	1		1		
Dunn, Timothy, 2nd	1	2	2		
Clarke, Nathaniel	1	3	3		
Tibbalds, Ebenezur	4		5		
Tibbalds, Joseph	2	2	1		
Tibbalds, James	2		2		
Coles, Jesse	2	1	6		
Robinson, James	2	1	1		
Robinson, Nathaniel	1	1	1		
Canfield, Gideon	2		1		
Robinson, Asher	2	1	4		
Robinson, Stephen	1		2		
Rose, Jiles	2		2		
Talcott, Noah	1	2	5		
Davis, Amos	1	1	2		
Parsons, Ithamer	2	2	6		
Lyman, Noah	2	1	2		
Coe, Ann			1		
Coe, Joel	1	1	2		
Parsons, Joseph	1	2	4		

NAME OF HEAD OF FAMILY.	16+	under 16	females	other free	Slaves
DURHAM TOWN—con.					
Parsons, Samuel	2	1	2		
Lyman, Thomas	2	2	3		1
Lyman, Abel	1		1		
Parsons, Simeon	2		1		
Coe, Charles	2	1	2		
Parsons, Sarah			1		
Parsons, Aaron	1	3	2		
Butler, William	1	3	3		
Coe, Abel	1	1	2		1
Coe, Abel, 2nd	1		2		
Coe, Josiah	1	1	3		
Coe, Asher	2		1		
Spelman, Rohda		1	3		
Belknap, Ebenezur	1		2		
Feild, Ambrose	2	2	3		
Chadock, Timothy	2		7		
Robinson, James	1	1	2		
Brag, Benjamin	1	1	2		
Squire, Phineas	2	1	2		
Squire, Thadeus	3		2		
Camp, Elnathan	3	2	3		
Butler, Jeremiah	6	3	5		
Lee, John	1		2		
Strong, Seth	1	1	2		
Camp, John	1		1		
Camp, Phineas	3	3	5		
Hall, John	4	1	3		
Parsons, Sam F	1	2	2		
Chamberlane, Asa	1	3	6		
Bishop, James	1		2		
Whiting, Samuel	1	1	1		
Murrain, Job	1		2		
Attwell, Mary		1	3		
Squire, Ambrose	1		1		
Parsons, Timothy	3	1	3		
Baldwin, Ruben	2	1	4		
Baldwin, Noah	3	1	3		
Pasons, Samuel	1	2	2		
Parsons, David	1		2		
Johnson, Thomas	1		1		
Rice, Simeon	1		1		
Weild, Samuel	2	1	7		
Brown, Ruben	1	2	1		
Percy, Jane			1		
Smith, Daniel	1		1		
Austin, Jesse	4		3		1
Cooke, Thomas	1		4		
Murrain, Miles	2	2	7		
Baldwin, A Bial	4		2		
Curtis, Abijah	1	2	6		
Guernsey, Richmond	1	1	1		
Coe, Ann			1		
Coe, John	2	1	4		
Fairchild, Edmond	1	1	4		
Bates, Samuel	2	1	5		
Bates, Samuel, 2nd	1	1	2		
Bates, James	1		2		
Bates, Daniel	1		2		
Newton, Burrel	4		2		
Bates, Curtis	1	2	3		
Southmay'd, Daniel	3		4		
Picket, James	1	1	1		
Squire, Samuel	1	1	2		
Stevens, Thomas	1	1	2		
Willcox, Ruben	2	1	3		
Smith, Joseph	1	4	4		
Camp, Hezekiah	1		2		
Camp, Rejoice	1	2	5		
Curtis, John	2	1	3		
Curtis, Hannah			1		1
Curtis, Anner			4		
Squire, Asher	1	2	4		
Johnson, John, 2nd	2		9		
EAST HAVEN TOWN.					
Hine, Henry F	1		1		
Huse, John	1	1	5		
Huse, Daniel	1	1	2		
Forbes, Johial	5	1	7		5
Nails, Abraham	1		3		
Pardie, Jerad	1	2	2		1
Pardie, Molly			2		1
Smith, Job	1	1	3		
Wetmore, Charles	1	1	3		
Day, Abigal	1	2	4		
Atkins, Abigal	1		4		
Bradley, William	1	1	3		
Smith, Ambrose	1	2	4		
Woodward, John, Junr	4	1	3		3
Tuttle, Joseph	3	3	4		
Banns, Isaac	1		4		
Pardy, Jacob	2	1	4		
Pardy, Abijah	1	2	4		
Pardy, Lidia			4		

NEW HAVEN COUNTY—Continued.

EAST HAVEN TOWN—con.

NAME OF HEAD OF FAMILY.	Free white males of 16 years and upward, including heads of families.	Free white males under 16 years.	Free white females, including heads of families.	All other free persons.	Slaves.
Pardy, Joseph	1	2	2		
Pardy, Leveret	1	2	2		
Pardy, Chandler	1	1	2		
Morris, Amos, Junr	1	2	8	1	
Morris, Amos	1	1	2		1
Morris, John	1	3	3		
Way, Timothy	2	1	3		
Smith, Samuel	1	3	5		
Smith, Benjamin	1	4	4		
Thompson, Timothy	3	3	4		
Bishop, Icabod	1	2	3		
Bishop, Charles	1		3		2
Eveton, William	2		1		
Ford, Anna		1	1		
Smith, Louis		2	3		
Potter, Levi	2		4		
Mallery, Mabel			2		
Hemmingway, Enos	1	2	4		1
Street, Nicholas	3	2	5		1
Ferring, Zebelun	2	4	4		
Chitsey, Ephrahim	1		2		
Hemmingway, John	1	2	2		1
Walker, Abigal			5		
Smith, Laben	1		2		
Hemmingway, Moses	1	3	3		
Smith, Nehamiah	1	3	3		
Thompson, Moses	1	2	5		1
Goodsell, John	1	1	2		
Goodsell, John, Junr	1	2	5		
Thompson, Amos	2	1	6		
Bradley, Josiah	2		4		
Bradley, Daniel	1	1	5		
Chitsey, Deborah			1		1
Mallery, Levi	1		1		
Bradley, Jacob	3	1	2		
Granis, Russell	1	1	1		
Davidson, Andrew	1	3	3		
Row, Mathew	1	2	4		
Bradley, Stephen	2		1		1
Bradley, Stephen, Junr	1	1	3		
Chitsey, John	1	2	6		
Walker, William	1	1	1		
Mallery, Mary	1	1	2		
Thompson, Stephen	1	4	3		
Austin, Joshua	2	4	2	1	
Bradley, Simeon	5	2	6		
Bradley, Sarah			2		
Bradley, Gurdon	1	3	5		
Bradley, Elijah	1	1	4		
Tyler, John	3	1	1		
Thompson, Stephen	1	1	2		
Luttenden, Samuel	1	1	2		
Mallery, Amos	1		2		
Hemmingway, Joseph	2	6	3		1
Andrus, Jedediah	1	1	4		
Forbes, Samuel	1		3		1
Bradley, Ezeriah	2	2	4		
Bans, Abraham	2	1	3		
Forbes, Levi	1	3	9		
Augur, Daniel	2	1	2		
Augur, Philomen	1	1	1		
Goodshell, Daniel	1	1	2		
Eagleston, Elizabeth		1	2		
Barnes, Levi	1				
Barnes, Samuel	2	2	3		
Huse, Rebecca		2	3		
Tuttle, Samuel	2	2	4		
Goodsell, Daniel	2		2		
Forbes, Isaac	2	2	2		2
Mallery, Benjamin	2	2	4		
Sheppard, Samuel	2	2	3		
Sheppard, Joseph	1	1	2		
Barnes, Nathaniel	1	2	3		
Sheppard, John	1	2	4		
Shepard, Stephen	2	2	3		
Granis, Mary		2	5		
Bradley, Edmond	1	1	3		
Sheppard, Thomas	2	2	5		
Bradley, Ely	2		4		
Banns, Ebenezer	2	2	4		
Russell, Joseph	3	2	2		
Dennison, Jesse	1	1	2		
Townsend, Samuel	1		2		
Hotchkiss, Joseph	1	1	3		
Andruss, Elisha	3	1	4		
Lucas, Richard	1	1	2		
Holt, Joseph	2		2		
Luddenton, Mary	2		5		
Granis, Joseph	3		1		
Bradley, Isaac	1	2	4		
Holt, Samuel	2	1	2		
Hotchkiss, Asa	1		2		
Russell, Edward	1		2		
Holt, Daniel	2	2	6		
Dinnison, John	1	4	4		

EAST HAVEN TOWN—con.

NAME OF HEAD OF FAMILY.	Free white males of 16 years and upward, including heads of families.	Free white males under 16 years.	Free white females, including heads of families.	All other free persons.	Slaves.
Burton, Ebenezer	1	2	2		
Mallery, Asa	1		4		
Granis, Isaac	2	2	4		
Tuttle, Christopher	1	1	4		
Tuttle, Stephan	1	2	4		
Smith, Stephen	2		2		3
Ludington, Jesse, Junr	1		3		
Smith, Lydia			3		
Smith, Caleb	1	1	2		
Tuttle, Isaac	1	1	3		
Landeraft, George	1	3	1		
Chitsey, Isaac	3	1	3		
Goodsell, Samuel	1	3	4		
Hunt, John	2	4	6		
Chitsey, Ebenezur	3		5		
Granis, Elihu	1		5		
Chitsey, Levi	1		6		
Chitsey, James	2		1		2
Thompson, Samuel	2	2	3		
Cuff (Negroe)					5
Dawson, Robert	1		2		
Smith, Samuel	3	2	4		
Smith, Mabel	2		3		
Dayton, Nathaniel	1	2	3		
Curtis, Phineas	1		4		
Cooper, Levi	1	1	4		
Holt, Ebenezer	1	2	2		
Clarke, Daniel	2		1		1
Robinson, John	3	1	3		
Robinson, Chandler	1		3		
Thompson, Joel	2	1	4		
Thompson, Jared	1	1	2		
Molthrop, Joseph	1	3	3		
Molthrop, Josiah	2	1	3		
Fuller, John	1		4		
Molthrop, Asher	1	1	2		
Molthrop, Ely	1		2		
Molthrop, David	1	2	4		
Pardie, Mabel			2		
Luddington, Jesse	2	1	3		
Russell, Lidia		1	1		
Banns, Ebenezer	2	2	3		
Hemmingway, Samuel	4	3	3		4
Harrison, Philemon	1	3	1		
Smith, Ira	1	1	2		
Davenport, Samuel	3	1	3		
Brown, Hannah	1	3	6		
Rowe, Ezra	1	5	4		
Rowe, John	2		2		
Mallery, Jesse	1	2	2		
Ludington, Rachel		1	4		
Thompson, Elizabeth			2		
Woodward, John	3	2	5		2
Chitsey, Abraham	2	2	5		
Pardy, Levi	2	1	3		
GUILFORD TOWN.					
Fowler, Noah, 2nd	1	1	4		
Walstone, Thomas	1	2	1		
Fowler, Minor	1	1	2		
Fowler, Noah	1		2	1	
Norton, Felix	2	4	5		
Norton, Elizabeth			2		
Norton, Rufus	1	4	3		
Norton, Molly			3		
Norton, Beriah	2		4		
Norton, John	3	1	2		
Leet, John	2	1	5		
Goldsmith, John	3		5		
Goldsmith, John, 2nd	1	1	2		
Jones, Aron	2	1	2		
Stone, Jerad	1		2		
Stone, Mercy			3		
Burges, John	1		1		1
Norton, Ashbel	1		1		
Norton, Jerad	2		2		
Benton, Jerad	1	2	2		
Stone, James	1	1	2		
Stone, Nathaniel	4	1	5		
Stone, Abner	1	2	4		
Benton, Samuel	3		1		
Hall, Isaac	2		3		
Hall, Stephen	1	2	2		
Hall, Philomen	3		2		
Johnson, John	1	3	2		
Saxton, Simion	2	1	3		
Curren, James	1	1	4		
Fowler, Andrew	3	2	4		
Hotchkiss, John	2		3		
Hotchkiss, Miles	1		2		
Spencer, Uriah	1		2		
Stone, Miles	1	1	5		
Chittenden, Ambrose	2		1		
Prince (Negroe)					2

GUILFORD TOWN—con.

NAME OF HEAD OF FAMILY.	Free white males of 16 years and upward, including heads of families.	Free white males under 16 years.	Free white females, including heads of families.	All other free persons.	Slaves.
Silas (Negroe)				2	
Leet, Jerad	1	1	3		
Fortner, Charles	1		3		
Morse, John	1		1		
Morse, David	1	4	3		
Leet, Daniel	2	1	2		
Leet, Ambrose	1	3	3		
Leet, Palatine	2	1	2		
Leet, Amos	1	3	6		
Leet, Joel	1		1		
Leet, Soloman	1		2		
Leet, Elijah	1	2	2		
Leet, Pharos	1	1	2		
Leet, Soloman, 2nd	2	4	3		
Leet, Thomas	1	1	1		
Leet, Victor	1	2	1		
Colvel, Nathaniel	1		1	1	2
Leet, Absolam	2	1	2		
Elliott, John	2	2	5	1	1
Elliott, John, 2nd	1		1		1
Kirkham, William					
Norton, Ebor	1		2		
Norton, Timothy	1		1		
Hill, Benjamin	1		2		
Bradley, Samuel	1	4	2		
Bradley, Joseph	1		2		
Bradley, James	1	1	1		
Kirkham, Benjamin	1	1	2		
Fowler, Beldad	1		1		
Chrittenden, Timothy	1	2	2		
Chrittenden, Nathaniel, 2nd	1	1	4		
Chittenden, Charles	1		1		
Mercer, Absolam	2	1	4		
Vail, Jonathan	1	1	1		
Hoadly, Samuel	1	1	1		
Hotchkiss, Samuel	1		2		
Hand, Joseph	1				
Ferral, George	1	1	4		
Shally, Ebenezer	1		1		
Leet, James	1	2	2		
Stevens, Samuel	1	1	4		
Fosdick, Abijah	1		3		
Stone, Levi	1		2		
Stone, Sibel	1				
Hunt, John	1	1	2		
Hall, John	1		1		
Parmalie, David	3	3	3		
Miller, William	2		4		
Berry, Richard	1	1	1		
Parmalie, Joseph	1		1		
Raney, Ruben	1		3		
Pendleton, Increase	2		3		
Pendleton, Joshua	1	1	1		
Barker, Ruth	1	1	4		
Elliott, Abigal	3		5		
Elliott, William	1	2	1		
Bishop, Johson	1		4		
Cadwell, Elias	1	3	2		1
Wells, Joseph	2	1	4		
Parmalie, Samuel	1	1	1		
Elliott, Nathaniel	1		2		
Parmalie, Andrew	1				
Waters, Sarah			2		
Chrittenden, Joseph	1		3		
Chrittenden, Samuel	1	1	3		
Hunt, Thomas	2		4		
Hunt, Thomas, 2nd	1	2	2		
Parmalie, Linus	1	2	3		
Parmalie, William	3		1		
Bartlet, Hooker	3	1	1		1
Graves, Nathaniel	2		1		
Griffin, Timothy	1	6	2		
Shelly, Timothy	1		5		
Smith, John	1	1	6		
Shelly, Joel	1				
London (Negroe)				2	
Hill, Henry	1	3	5		1
Crittenton, Seth	1	1	1		
Colwell, Charles	1		1		
Colwell, Ruth			1		
Redfield, John	2		2	2	
Redfield, John, 2nd	1	1	3		
Fowler, Amos	2		2		
Spencer, Mark	1	5	3		
Spencer, Miney		6	3		
Elliot, Joseph	1		1		
Fairchild, Mahitabel		4	2		
Hallock, Israel	1	1	2		
Fairchild, Asher	1	2	4		
Foot, Eli	1	5	5		
Powers, Thomas	1	2	6		
Hill, Thomas	1		1		
Johnson, Nathaniel	2		3		
Benton, Caleb	2	1	6		

NEW HAVEN COUNTY—Continued.

GUILFORD TOWN—con.

NAME OF HEAD OF FAMILY.	Free white males of 16 years and upward, including heads of families.	Free white males under 16 years.	Free white females, including heads of families.	All other free persons.	Slaves.
Landon, Samuel	1		3		
Handy, Anna			1		
Landon, Jonathan	1	1	2		
Landon, David	1	3	1		
Tuttle, Joel	4		8		
Stone, Medad	1		4		1
Collins, Pitman	1	1	2		
Chalker, Isaac	2	2	4		
Ward, Buley			1		
Griffin, Joseph	1	3	1		
Pyncheon, Joseph	1		2		
Bosston, Nathaniel	1	1	2		
Handy, Hetty		1	2		
Murry, Thankfull		2	1		
Johnson, Joel	1		1		
Pyncheon, Thomas R	2	1	4		1
Woodward, Rosswell	2	3	6		
Ruggles, Nathaniel	1		1		1
Griffin, Nathaniel	1		2		1
Ward, Thelas	1		3		
Spencer, Christopher	2	3	5		
Fowler, Elizabeth	2		3		
Lines, Benjamin	1	1	4		
Person, Submit		1	3		
Griffin, Jasper	1	1	1		1
Hubbard, Deborah	2	1	1		
Kimberley, George	1	3	3		
Chittenton, Caleb	1	1	1		
Stone, Bela	1		3		
Stone, Ruben	2		1		
Stone, Timothy	1	1	1		
Collins, Joel	2	2	4		
Crittenten, Nathaniel	2		1		
Crittenton, Bela	1		1		
Chrittenden, Nathaniel, 2nd	1		1		
Roberson, Samuel	1		1		
Stone, Abraham	2	2	4		
Roberson, Samuel, 2	1	1	2		
Shelly, Shubal	2	1	2		
Bishop, Seth	1		2		
Stone, John	1	1	2		
Veale, Joshua	1	2	5		
Stone, Soloman	1	1	2		1
Griffin, Joel	1	2	2		
Griffin, Peter	1		1		
Green, Joseph	1	1	1		
Stone, Benjamin	2	1	4		
Woodward, Abraham	1	3	2		
Stone, William	1		2		
Chittenton, Joseph	1	1	4		
Johnson, Samuel	3		2		
Johnson, Nathaniel	1		1		
Johnson, Samuel, 2nd	1	2	2		
Ruggles, Nathaniel	2	1	5		
Fowler, Joel	1		2		
Hotchkiss, Hannah			1		
Hemman, Aron	3	1	1		
Veal, Jonathan	2		6		
Norton, Elizabeth			3		
Frisbie, Benjamin	2	1	1		
Davis, John	1		3		
Hill, Thomas	3	1	2		
Redfield, Nathaniel	1	1	1		
Evetts, Elyers	1		2		
Evetts, Elyers, 2nd	1	1	2		
Scot, James	1	3	2		
Chittenton, Anna			3		
Benton, Jabez	3	2	2		
Scranton, Thomas, 2nd	1	1	2		
Scranton, Samuel	2		2		
Starr, William	2	1	3		
Starr, John	1	1	6		
Fowler, Abraham	1	2	3		
Hall, Eliphalet	2	1	2		
Evett, Lucy			2		
Lee, Samuel	1		2		
Lee, Levi	1	3	3		
Lee, Timothy	1	1	2		
Bishop, Jonathan	1		3		
Bishop, David	1		3		
Bishop, Jerad	1	2	1		
Hall, Benjamin	1		3		
Hall, Benjamin, 2nd	1	1	3		
Chittenton, Joseph	1		2		
Amos, James	1		1		
Smith, Samuel	1	1	3		
Downs, Griffin	1		2		
Hotchkiss, Eber	1	3	2		
Collins, Charles	3		2		
Lee, William	3	3	2		
Lee, Eton	3	1	2		
Evetts, Abraham	1	1	3		
Evetts, Samuel	3	2	3		
Ward, Andrew	2	1	3		
Stone, Joseph	2				
Dibble, Jane	1		1		
Benton, James	1		2		
Naughty, David	2	2	3	1	
Naughty, David, 2nd	1	2	1		
Johnson, Nathaniel	1		1		
Parmalie, John	1		2		
Parmalie, Joel	1	2	1		
Parmalie, James	1	2	1		
Parmalie, Eber	1		3		
Parmalie, Ruben	2	1	4		
Griswold, Joel	1	1	2		
Griswold, Thomas	1	1	2		
Griswold, Thomas, 2nd	1	1	2		
Griswold, Miles	1	1	3		
Davis, James	1		2		
Hall, Miles	1	1	1		
Stone, Luther	1	1	1		
Benton, Silas	4	3	1		
Hall, Mary			3		
Johnson, Hill	1	1	2		
Johnson, Miles	1	2	3		
Bishop, David	1	3	4		
Hotchkiss, Ebenezer	2	1	2		
Hotchkiss, Ruben	1		4		
Scranton, Thomas	1		1		
Scranton, Nathaniel	1	3	1		
Lee, Eber	1		1		
Evetts, Samuel, 3rd	1	1	2		
Bristol, Samuel	1	1	3		
Parmalie, John, 2nd	1	1	4		
Stanton, Daniel	2	2	5		
Scovel, John	2		3	1	
Wells, Joseph, 2nd	1		1		
Fowler, Elizabeth			1		
Hopson, Ebenezer	1	2	4	1	
Parmalie, William	1	2	2		
Graves, Ambrose	1		2		
Burges, Thomas	1		1		
Burges, Thomas, 2nd	3	1	5		
Handy, Samuel	1	2	3		
Hill, Nathaniel	1	1	2		
Hill, Anna			2		
Chittenden, Abraham	1		1		
Chittenden, Abraham, 2	2	2	3		
Colwell, Thomas	2		6		
Bartlett, Samuel	1	1	4		
Bartlett, Timothy	1	1	1		
Griswold, Ezra	1	1	5		
Griswold, John	1		1		
Griswold, Molly			2		
Parmalie, Nathaniel	1	3	3		
Fowler, Nathaniel	1		3		
Mann, Phillip	2		1		
Chittenden, Noah	1		5		
Collins, Darius	2		5		
Griffin, Jasper	1	4	2		
Crumbey, John	1	2	5		
Ackley, Rebecca			1		
Plum, Thankfull			1		
Bishop, Elizabeth			1		
Meigs, Nathaniel	1	2	3		
Davis, James	1	2	2		
Leet, John	1	2	2		
Rossell, Mons	1		2	2	1
Shelly, Ruben	1		1		
Fowler, Nathaniel	1	2	3		
Shelly, Ruben, 2nd	1	2	1		
Shelly, Medad	1		1		
Murray, Daniel	1	1	2		
Scovel, John	1	1	2		
Happen, Gideon	1		3		
Parmalie, Sarah			1		
Leet, Ruben	2	1	4		
Deming, Josiah J	1	4	2		
Seward, David	2		1		
Seward, David, 2nd	1		4		
Seward, Timothy	1	3	1		
Chittenton, Samuel	1		2		
Evets, Aron	2		3		
Evetts, Benjamin	2	2	2		
Chitenton, Benjamin	2	2	2		
Chittenton Abraham	1	3	1		
Chittenton, David	1	1	1		
Chittenton, Nathaniel	1		3		
Evett, Timothy	2		1		
Evett, Timothy, 2nd	1		1		
Crittenton, Joseph	1		3		
Crittenton, Huldy			1		
Evett, Isaac	2	4	3		
Evett, Daniel	1		3		
Evett, Samuel	2	2	5		
Norton, Hooker	1	3	3		
Norton Ruben	3		1		
Norton, Eber	1	1	1		
Norton, Aron	2	1	5		
Evetts, Jonathan	2		3		
Evetts, Ezra	2		2		
Stanton, John	1		1		
Evett, Moses	1		1		
Crainton, John	1		2		
Dudley, Thomas	2		1		
Dudley, Eber	1				
Bartlet, Joseph	3		3		
Dudley, Samuel	2		1		
Dudley, Jane			1	1	
Ward, Elizabeth			1		
Dudley, Amos	2	3	2		
Hotchkiss, Isaac	1	2	2		
Spinish, Nathaniel	1				
Dudley, Caleb	1		1		
Dudley, Nathaniel	1	2	3		
Dudley Abraham	1	2	2		
Dudley, Caleb 2	2	1	4		
Johnson, Benjamin	1		2		
Johnson, Nathaniel	1		1		
Benton, Seth	1		1		
Shelly, Lucy			2		
Hill, Thomas, 2nd	3	1	2		
Powers, Thomas, 2nd	1				
Norton, Ruben, 2	1	4	4		
Evett, David	1				
Cleaveland, George	1				
Hotchkiss, Amos	2		2		
Wilson, Lucy			1		
Shelly, Edmond	1	3	2		
Hull, David	1		1		
Hull, William	1		2		
Collins, Freind	1	2	3		
Ceasar (Negroe)					3
King, Charles	1	1	3		
Lee, Deborah			3		
Morse, John	1	2	2		
Stone, Edmond	1		2		
Ranney, George	1		2		
Crampton, David	1	2	5		
Manger, Ebenezer	1		1		
Manger, Ebenezer, 2d	1	2	2		
Manger, Jesse	1	3	1		
Stone, Thomas	1		1		
Cranton, Nathaniel	1		2		
Cranton, Nathaniel, 2d	1	2	2		
Stone, Seth	1	1	1		
Stone, Mary			3		
Bishop, Joiner	1		3		
Bishop, James	1		2		
Bishop, Hannah	1	1	2		
Bishop, Lines	1	1	3		
Bishop, Tabitha			1		
Bassett, Elisha	1	2	5		
Lee, Jonathan	1	1	1		
Lee, Jonathan, 2nd	1		2		
Smith, Jeffry	1	3	1		
Bassett, William	1	1	4		
Stone, Noah	1	1	2		
Bishop, Russell	1		2		
Wright, Benjamin	3	1	3		
Crumton, Jonathan	1				
Crumton, Jonathan, 2	2		1		
Shelly, John	1	1	3		
Cramton, Asbel	1	2	3		
Lee, Nathaniel	3		4		
Dudley, Jonathan	1	2	5		
Brown, Samuel	2		1		
Wilcox, William	2	2	2		
Willcox, Jonathan	1	3	4		
Bradley, Simry	4	1	5		
Veal, Nathaniel	1	3	2		
Hand, Icabod	1	4	3		
Judd, Jonathan	1	2	3		
Blakely, Oliver	1	4	3		
Conglin, Jacob	1				
Stone, Rachel			2		
Stone, William			1		
Lee, Fredreck	1		1		
Bradley, Timothy	2	3	4		
Bradley, Anson	1				
Feild, Joseph	3	4	4		
Feild, Luke	1	3	4		
Crittenton, Noah	2	1	6		
Munger, Simeon	2		1		
Munger, Josiah	1	1	2		
Crumton, Hull	2	1	1		
Crittenton, Edmond	1		1		
Munger, Willis	1	3	1	2	
Crumton, Darius	1		2		
Evett, Stephen					
Ripsey, Prinson	1	1	3		
Graves, Temperance			2		
Graves, Ezra	1		2		

NEW HAVEN COUNTY—Continued.

NAME OF HEAD OF FAMILY.	Free white males of 16 years and upward, including heads of families.	Free white males under 16 years.	Free white females, including heads of families.	All other free persons.	Slaves.
GUILFORD TOWN—con.					
Munger, Bela	1	1	5		
Munger James	2	1	3		
Graves, Ebenezer	3		4		
Graves, Irael	1		3		
Bishop, Ebenezer	1	2	4		
Graves, Luman	1	2	1		
Thompson, David	1	1	2		
Judd, Martha			2		
Bartlet, Ruben	2		2		
Bartlet, Ruben, 2nd	1		1		
Bartlet, Stephen	2		3		
Bartlet James	1	2	4		
Willcox, Ezra, 2	1	3	1		
Scranton, John	1	2	2		
Blakely, Abigal			3		
Monger, Lidia			2		
Monger, Johiel	1				
Evets, Ambrose	3		2		
Dow'd, Zachariah	1		1		
Dow'd, Zachariah, 2nd	1	2	3		
Dowd, Soloman	1	1	3		
Field, Timothy	1	2	6		
Graves, George	1	1	1		
Todd, Jonathan	1		1		
Scranton, Abraham	1	3	3		
Jones, John	1	4	3		
Dudley, Gilbert	2	1	2		
Lee, Silas	1		2		
Hill, Daniel	1		3		
Hill, Timothy	1		5		
Hart, Benjamin	4		3		
Graves, Simeon	1	1	3		
Graves, Timothy	1	2	1		
Graves, Elias	1	1	3		
Meigs, Timothy	2	1	5	1	
Bradley, Ashbel	1	1	1		
Hill, Ruben, 2	1	1	4		
Todd, John	1		1		
Todd, Jonathan	2	2	2		
Willcox, Benjamin	1	2	3		
Scranton Thomas	1	5	4		
Mann, Elisha	2		2		
Scranton, Theobald	1		1		
Graves, Eli	2		4		
Dudley, Bela	1	3	3		
Buckley, Aron	2	3	5		
Buckley, Moses	1		1		
Murry, Amassa	1		2		
Blakley, Moses	1	1	1		
Dowd, Joseph	3	1	4		
Dowd, Timothy	2	1	3		
Dowd, Ebenezer	4	3	1		
Willard, Julius	1	1	3		
Meigs, Elias	2		6		
Graves, Gilbert	1		3		
Crane, Elisha	1	1	6		
Hand, Edmond	2	2	1		
Willard, Elias	1	2	4		
Willard, Stephen	2		1		
Willcox, Nathaniel	2	2	5		
Meigs, Daniel	2	2	2		
Ward, Levi	3		3		
Willard, Hiel	1				
Hill, John	2	1	6		
Bradley, Gillard	2	1	3		
Bradley, Noah	5	1	1		
Meigs, Elish	2	4	4		
Hotchkiss, Thomas	2		4		
Murry, Abigal			4		
Parmalie, Pheneas	1				
Meigs, Lucy			2		
Munger, Lyman	1	2	2		
Graves, Ambrose	1		3		
Scranton, Josiah	1	2	5		
Murry, Jesse	1	2	2		
Murry, John	2	1	4		
Bishop, John	2		2		
Murry, Selah	1		1		
Hill, Abraham	1	1	2		
Hill, Ruben	1		1		
Hill, James	1	1	5		
Hill, Aron	1	1	3		
Norton, Jesse	1	1	2		
Bishop, Elias	1	1	2		
Bishop, John, 2	1		2		
Stannard, Elias	1	5	4		
Coe, Thomas	1	3	2		
Willcox, Joseph	1		3		
Willcox, Joseph, 2nd	1	1	3		
Coe, Jedediah	1		3		
Fenton, Israel	1		3		
Griswold, Jedidiah	2		3		
Griswold, Jedidiah, 2nd	1		2		
Willcox, Ezra	3		2		
Wheaton, Rufus	1		3		
GUILFORD TOWN—con.					
Willcox, Edmond	2	4	4		
Henderson, John	3		1		
Hand, Daniel	1		1		1
Hand, Daniel, 2nd	1	2	1		
Dowd, Miles	1	2	3		
Teal, Benjamin	1	1	4		
Willard, Jerad	1	1	5		
Willard, James	1		1		
Dudley, Josiah	1		1		
Dudley, Joseph	2		1		
Dowd, Abraham	2		1		
Dowd, Ruben	1	3	3		
Dudley, Simeon	1	3	4		
Forster, Christopher	1	2	3		
Forster, Thomas	1	3	2		
Dowd, Dedimos	2		3		
Griffiths, Benjamin	3	2	3		
Dowd, Asa	1		1		
Dowd, Asa, 2nd	2	2	4		
Meigs, Phineas	2		4		
Conglin, Joseph	1				
Murry, Curtis	1	2	1		
Bassett, Nathaniel	1	1	3		
Hill, Icobad	1	4	2		
Maltby, Jane			2		2
Forster, Sarah		3	3		
Munger, Timothy	1		1		
Munger, Timothy, 2	1		3		
Munger, Lines	1	1	2		
Munger, Josiah	1	2	1		
Blakley, Joshua	2		4		
Dowd, John	1		7		
Feild, Zacheriah	1	1	6		
Leach, Oren	1		1		
Field, Jedediah	1	1	2		
Meigs, Abigal	1		4		
Field, Icobad	1	1	2		
Cranton, Nathaniel	1	1	4		
Leach, David	1	2	2		
Cranton, Josiah	1	3	5		
Hall, Zebulon	1	3	4		
Cranton, Benjamin, 2	1	1	3		
Fowler, Asher	1		4		1
Calhoun, Josiah	1	1	1		1
Pardie, James	1		4		
Field, Samuel	3	3	3		
Johnson, Phineas	3		2		
French, Didimus	2	1	3		
Johnson, Ruben	1		2		
Johnson, Isaac	2		1		
Griswold, George	1	1	2		
Bishop, Eneas	4		2		
Dowd, Thomas	1		2		
Doud, Moses	2	1	4		
Doud, Job	1	2	6		
Crittenton, Soloman	1	2	2		
Cranton, Benjamin	1		1		
Cranton, Edmond	1		3		
Cranton, Luther	1	2	3		
Stevens, Nathaniel	1				
Stevens, Nathaniel, 2nd	2		3		
Scranton, Timothy	2		1		
Scranton, Timothy, 2	1	3	1		
Dudley, David	2		1		
Dudley, Elizabeth			4		
Bishop, Sussannah			2		
Munger, Miles	3	1	2		
Munger, Cabe	2	1	1		
Wheeler, Thomas	1		5		
Walkley, Ebenezer	1	4	3		
Bristol, Richard	1		2		
Chittenton, Daniel	1		1		
Hotchkiss, Noah	3	2	2		
Hopson, Amelia			2		
Hopson, John	1	1	1		
Norton, Noadiah	1	2	4		
Stone, Isaac	1	2	5		
Stone, Aron, 2nd	1	2	1		
Dudley, David	1				
French, Philomen	3		3		
Field, David	1	2	2		
Field, Benjamin	1	3	1		
Hill, James	1	2	4		
Cain, Latin	1		1		
Richmond, Jacob	4	1	3		
Richmond, Warner	1		2		
Richmond, Hannah	2	2	3		
Benton, Noah	2		2		
Dudley, Roswell	1		1		
Johnson, Nathaniel	1		1		
Johnson, Benjamin	1		2		
Spicer, Asher	1	2	2		
Fowler, Nathaniel	2	2	4		
Russell, Samuel R	1		1		
Fowler, Phineas	2				
GUILFORD TOWN—con.					
Russell, Timothy	2		3		
Fowler, John	1		1		
Fowler, Lucy	1	1	4		
Fowler, Samuel	1	1	1		
Chitsey, Nathaniel	1	1	1	1	
Chitsey, Bathsheba			1		
Baldwin, Timothy	1	2	6		
Cook, James	1	1	1		
Cook, Joshua	1		1		
Tom (Negroe)			1		
Dowd, Jeremiah	1				
Roseter, Timothy	1	1	2	1	
Norton, Gideon	1	1	1		
Norton, Abel	1		3		
Rochester, Benjamin	1		3		1
Kimberly, Abraham, 2nd	3	2	4		
Benton, Elihu	2	4	4		
Benton, Timothy	3	1	3		
Pond, Gad	2	3	3		
Johnson, Isaac	1	1	5		
Hall, Eber	2	1	3		
Benton, Lot	1	1	3		
Bartlet, John	3		3		
Bartlet, Daniel	2	1	1		
Philor, John	1	2	2		
Bray, Thomas W	1	6	5		
Crittenton, Hull	1		2		
Fowler, David	2		2		
Bishop, Samuel	3		2		
Fitch, Thomas	1		2		
Fitch, Samuel	2	1	2		
Dibble, Simus	2		1		
Bishop, Jesse	1	1	3		
Bishop, Hannah			2		
Fowler, William	1	3	4		
Dudley, Selah	2	2		1	
Fowler, Silas	2	2	6		
Hall, Ebenezer	4		3		
Rochester, Samuel	1	1	1		
Brooks, David S	1				
Wick, Edward	3	1	2		
Leet, Jarad	1	1	3		
Scranton, Torry	1	1	3		
Kimberly, Abraham	1		2		
Chittenton, Daniel	1	1	4		
Stevens, Timothy	1	2	3		
Dudley, Luther	1	5	1		
Elwell, James	1		1		
Dudley, Medad	4		4		
Dudley, Ambrose	1	1	2		
Tallman, Peter	3		6		
Fowler, Stephen	3	5	6		
Fowler, Hannah			2		
Hubbard, Ebor	3	1	2		
Bishop, Elizabeth			2		
Hubbard, Abraham	2	2	4		
Parmalie, Ambrose	1		1		
Stone, John	1	2	2		
Hubbard, Abraham, 2	1	1	2		
Wick, John	1		1		
Hubbard, John	1	1	1		
Griswold, Nathaniel	1	2	3		
Griswold, Noah	2		1		
Stone, Eber	1	1	2		
Stone, Ezra	2		2		
Dudley, Stephen	3				
Bishop, Nero	1	2	2		
Bishop, James	1	4	2		
Coan, John	1	2	1		
Coan, John, 2nd	1	1	2		
Fowler, Daniel	1		1		
Dudley, Jerad	1		2		
Dudley, Jerad, 2nd	1	1	2		
Barnes, Lemuel	1		2		
Blakley, Joseph	2		1		
Roseter, William	2	4	5		
Fowler, Theophilus	1	3	1		
Bartlet, George	1		2		
Cain, Patrick	1	2	1		
Leet, Stephen	1		2		
Chittenton, Simeon	1	2	4		
Rawlinson, Joseph	2		2		
Hill, Anna			2		
Looper, Samuel F	1		2		
Looper, Samuel, 2nd	3		3		
Brickwell, Zebulon	1	1	5		
Chittenten, Jerad	2	3	3		
Chittenton, Amos					
Chittenton, Anson	1	1	1		
Chittenton, Submit			1		
Scranton, Jerad	4	1	2	1	1
Coan, Simeon	1				
Philor, Joseph	3		3		
Fowler Ebenezer	1		1		
Fowler, Caleb	1	2	3		

NEW HAVEN COUNTY—Continued.

NAME OF HEAD OF FAMILY.	Free white males of 16 years and upward, including heads of families.	Free white males under 16 years.	Free white females, including heads of families.	All other free persons.	Slaves.
GUILFORD TOWN—con.					
Fowler, Oliver	1		1		
Collins, Daniel	1	1	1		
Collins, Samuel	1				
Collins, Ruth			2	1	1
Collins, Augustus	3	4	4		
Stone, John	3		6		
Grave, Benjamin	3		5		
Grave, Abraham	3		4		
Griffin, Robert	1		2		
Grave, Daniel	1		3		
Fowler, Ebenezer	1	3	3		
Russell, Ebenezer	1		3		
Rose, Joel	1	2	4		
McCane, Barnabas	1	4	6		
Atkins, Samuel	1		1		
Dibble, Simus, 2nd	1		2		
Bassett, Henry	1		2		
Fowler, Jonathan	3		3		
Fowler, Joiner	2	2	4		
Fowler, Josiah 2	1	2	6		
Elliott, Timothy	3	3	2		
Bishop, Ezra	1				
Tyler, Molly			1		
Dudley, Abigal			1		
Bails, Deborah			1		
Stone, Osborne	1	4	3		
Bishop, Timothy	3		2		
Bishop, Ruben	2	1	3		
Fowler, Soloman	1	2	3		
Wright, Daniel	1		1		
HAMDEN TOWN.					
Attwater, Medad	1	2	4		
Attwater, Abigal		1	3		
Attwater, Louis			2		
Attwater, Joshua	1	4	4		
Howell, Nicholas	3		3		
Attwater, David	1	1	3		
Attwater, Jerad	1	2	1		
Turner, Jabez	2	4	2		
Potter, Timothy, 2nd	1	1	4		
Turner, Abraham	1	1	2		
Turner, Elisha	1	1	1		
Turner, Gurden	2	4	5		
Potter, Philomon	3	3	2		
Cooper, Abraham, 2nd	1	1	2		
Potter, Joseph	2	1	4		
Mansfield, Ebenezer	2		4		
Potter, Timothy	2	1	3		
Gilbert, Joseph	2		1		
Potter, Chauncy	1	1	1		
Marsen, Stephen	1	1	3		
Mencer, William	1	1	1		
Potter, Medad	1		2		
Ball, Oliver	1		5		
Gill, John	1	2	3		
Gill, John, 2nd	1				
Hummiston, Samuel	1	4	5		
Gill, Ebenezer M	1	1	2		
Mansfield, Titus	3		1		
Tuttle, Daniel	1		2		
Peckham, George	1		1		
Peckham, George, 2nd	2		2		
Talmash, Daniel	1		3		
Tolmap, Daniel, 2nd	1	3	3		
Ford, Stephen	1	3	5		
Potter, Jesse	1		5		
Potter, David	1	1	3		
Potter, David	1		1		
Potter, Abel	1	1	2		
Ford, Joel	2		1		
Gilbert, Moses	2	1	1		
Cooper, Abraham	1		1		
Basset, Theophilus	1	1	2		
Basset, John	1		1		
Basset, Amos	1	2	3		
Ford, Moses	2		3		
Potter, Job	1	3	7		
Humiston, Joseph	2	2	3		
Potter, Thomas	1	3	3		
Ford, Jonathan	2	4	2		
Talmap, Hannah	1	3	2		
Howell, Nicholas	1				
Carrington, Elizabeth		1	1		
Turner, Timothy	1	1	1		
Ford, Jonah	1		1		
Potter, Moses	3	2	4		
Blakesley, Deborah			2		
Tuttle, Jabez	2	5	3		
Tuttle, Aexander	1	1	3		
Bassett, Abel	2		3		
Todd, Job	2	4	5		
Todd, Joel	3	1	5		
Ives, Alling	1	2	2		

NAME OF HEAD OF FAMILY.	Free white males of 16 years and upward, including heads of families.	Free white males under 16 years.	Free white females, including heads of families.	All other free persons.	Slaves.
HAMDEN TOWN—con.					
Martin, Samuel	1	1	2		
Tuttle, Aron	1	2	3		
Cooke, Samuel	1		4		
Gilbert, Grigson	1		4		
Andrus, Samuel	1	2	2		
Mix, Caleb	2	1	3		
Carrington, Elener	1		1		
Brooks, Benjamin	1	2	2		
Munson, Joshua	1		1		
Benham, Joseph	2	2	3		
Johnson, Noah	1	1	1		
Basett, James	2	1	4		
Wooden, Lidia	1		3		
Hinton, Nathaniel	3		1		
Leek, Thomas	1		2		
Leek, Thomas, 2nd	1	1	3		
Alling, Joseph	1		2		
Chrittenton, Jerry	3	1	2		
Mansfield, J	2	4	4		
Cooper, Alling	1	1	2		
Attwater, Samuel, 2nd	1	2	6		
Goodyear, Jesse	2	1	4		
Goodyear, Theophilus	3		2		
Goodyear, Titus	1	2	3		
Cooper, Beedy	1		1		
Attwater, Samuel	1		3		
Pardy, Joseph	1		2		
Bradley, Eli	2		2		
Pardie, Thomas	1		1		
Attwater, Caleb	1	4	2		
Thompson, Henry	1	3	4		
Bassett, Hezekiah	3	3	6		
Seelly, Isaac	1	2	2		
Bassett, Mabel			1		
Alling, Elisha	1	1	5		
Ives, Jonathan	1		1		
Ives, Jonathan, 2nd	1	1	2		
Ives, Elam	1		1		
Ives, James	3		2		
Pardie, Stephen	2	2	3		
Hotchkiss, Phebe			2		
Dickerman, Hezekiah	1	3	3		
Bradley, Levi	1	2	2		
Gilbert, Joseph	1	1	5		
Goodyear, Timothy	2	4	3		
Gilbert, Abraham	1		2		
Gilbert, Abraham, 2nd	1	2	2		
Dickerman, Amos	1		2		
Dickerman, Jonathan	2		2		
Chapman, Elisha	2	1	3		
Bellamy, Samuel	2		2		1
Dickerman, James	2	1	3		
Kimberly, Ezra	3	2	3		
Hubbard, Joseph	1	3	1		
Todd, Abner	3	1	4		
Dickerman, Chauncy	3	3	5		
Willis, Sarah			2		
Miles, Simeon	1		4		
Todd, Bethuel	1		1		
Munson, Justice	1		4		
Munson, Bazael	2		3		1
Bishop, Nathaniel	1	1	2		
Gilbert, John	2		2		
Beach, Asa	1		2		
McDonald, Abigal		1	1		
Dudley, Mercy			1		
Dickerman, Loley	1	2	5		
Dickerman, John	1	1	3		
Doolittle, Titus	1	1	6		
Johnson, Joseph	2	3	8		
Johnson, Joseph, 2nd	1		1		
Tuttle, Joatham	1	2	3		
Tuttle, Jesse	1	2	1		
Tuttle, Abigal			1		
Dickerman, Isaac	2	3	3		
Frisbie, Luman	2	3	3		
Bennet, Ebenezer			1		
Munson, Job	1	3	4		
Mansfield, Hannah	1	1	2		
Bradley, Amassa	1	1	1		
Haush, Joseph	1	4	2		
Bristol, Simeon	2	2	3		1
Bristol, George A	1	2			
Rice, Elisha	1	2	1		
Attwater, Stephen	2	1	5		
Bradley, Aron	1	1	3		
Bradley, Daniel	1		2		
Bradley, Daniel, 2nd	1	5	3		
Bradley, Joel	2	2	2		1
Bradley, Jabez	1		3		
Perkins, Elish	2	1	6		
Ives, Andrew	1		4		
Bradley, Amos	2	2	4		
Brooks, Abijah	1	2	1		
Brooks, Louis	1		2		

NAME OF HEAD OF FAMILY.	Free white males of 16 years and upward, including heads of families.	Free white males under 16 years.	Free white females, including heads of families.	All other free persons.	Slaves.
HAMDEN TOWN—con.					
Tuttle, Enos	1		1		
Tuttle, Enos	1	2	1		
Galend, Benjamin	1		1		
Galend, Benjamin, 2nd	1	2	4		
Ives, Thomas	1	1	2		
Tuttle, Hezekiah	2		4		
Perkins, Aron	1		1		
Doolittle, Caleb	3	1	3		
Perkins, John	1	2	5		
Sperry, John	1	1	2		
Bradley, Jason	4	2	4		
Alling, Mabel			3		
Alling, Nathaniel	3	1	1		
Peck, Jesse	1	1	1		
Alling, Eli	1		3		
Peck, Mosses	1	1	4		
Alling, Nathaniel, 2nd	1	1	3		
Spencer, Jabez	2		4		
Chatterton, Abraham	1		3		
Chatterton, Daniel	1		1		
Chatterton, David	1	1	1		
Hitchcock, Stephen	2		4		
Peck, Amos	3		4		
Roberts, Ebenezer	1	1	1		
Munson, Ezra	1		4		
Peck, Joseph	1		3		
Hitchcock, Lidia	1		3		
Andrews, John	1	1	5		
Hitchcock, Samuel	1	2	3		
Hitchcock, Jabez	1	1	2		
Attwater, Eneas	1	2	4		
Thomas, Isaac	3	2	4		
Bradley, Elven	2	2	3		
Attwater, Jacob	3		1		
Ives, Ezra	2	3	5		
Warner, Abigal		1	2		
Goodyear, Stephen	2	1	4		
Leek, Timothy	2		1		
Leek, Timothy, 2nd	1	2	2		
Dickerman, Jonathan, 2nd	1	2	5		
Andrus, Caleb	1		1		
Leek, Daniel	1		2		
Warner, David	1	4	3		
Goodyear, Asa	1				
Goodyear, Asa, 2nd	1	1	5		
Sugden, Lidia	1		3		
Bassett, Timothy	2	2	1		
Wolcott, Noah	4	1	5		
Alling, David	1		1		
Alling, Medad	2		1		
Warner, Hezekiah	3	3	2		
Warner, Benjamin	1		3		
Warner, Ebenezer	2		6		
Warner, Amos	1				
Warner, Jesse	1			4	
Warner, Samuel	1			2	
Warner, Ebenezer, 2nd	1				
Bradley, Gamaleil	2	2	4		
Crosby, Gad	1				
Pardie, Joel	1		1		
Goodyear, Gerad	1		1		
Doolittie, Easter			2		
Bracket, Hezekiah	1	3	1		
Bristol (Negroe)				4	
Wolcott, H			2		
Andrus, Caleb	1		1		
Warner, Jonah	1		1		
Potter, Amos	1		2		
Hitchcock, Ebenezur	2	1	3		
Hinton, Joseph	1	1	1		
Johnson, Timothy	1	2	4		
Alling, Joel	1		1		
Alling, Abraham	1	1	5		
Dorman, Benjamin	2		3		
Dorman, Daniel	1	3	2		
Gorham, Susanah	1	1	4		
Smith, Abraham	1	1	4		
Hitchcock, Ebenezur, 2nd	1	2	4		
Hummiston, David	1	2	3		
Munson, Isaac	2	1	3		
Alling, Charles	1	3	8		
Alling, Caleb	1		2		
Hitchcock, Lidia	1	3	2		
Munson, Jabez	1		2		
Munson, Eunice	1		2		
Munson, Levi	1	1	1		
Denshy, William	2		3		
Denshy, Eli	1	2	1		
Dorman, Joseph	1	2	2		
Dorman, John	1	1	3		
Dorman, Roger	1		1		
Dorman, Stephen	1				
Dorman, John	1	2	2		
Munson, David	1	2	2		
Boath, Jonathan	1	1	1		

NEW HAVEN COUNTY—Continued.

NAME OF HEAD OF FAMILY.	Free white males of 16 years and upward, including heads of families.	Free white males under 16 years.	Free white females, including heads of families.	All other free persons.	Slaves.
HAMDEN TOWN—con.					
Boath, Alexander	1	1	1		
Boath, Elisha	1		1		
Maneer, John	1	1	2		
Wooden, Isaac	1	1	2		
Andrews, Timothy	1		2		
Gilbert, Asa	1	1	3		
Tuttle, Amos	1		2		
Gilbert, Daniel	1	4	3		
Gilbert, Mathew	1		1		
Wooden, Jaben	1		1		
Reed, Peter	1	1	2		
Alling, Icabod	1	2	1		
Alling, Desire	1	1	3		
Mix, Thomas	1	2	3		
Bassett, James	1	1	1		
Jones, Pratt	1	1	1		
Dickerman, Louis			2		
Dickerman, Hezekiah	1		2		
Dickerman, Joseph	1		1		
Wooden, Nathaniel	2	1	2		
Wooden, Hannah	1		3		
Leforgess, Henry	1	3	5		
Wooden, Benjamin	1	3	3		
Hummiston, Nathaniel	2		1		
Attwater, Icabod	1	2	2		
Cooper, Samuel	2	5	2		
Cooper, Timothy	3		2		
Gilbert, Amos	1	2	2		
Gilbert, James	1		5		
Alling, Roger	1	2	2		
Hubbard, John	2	4	3		
Dorman, Samuel	1	2	1		
Attwater, Zopher	1	1	4		
Hotchkiss, Daniel	1	2	2		
Thomas, Caleb	1	2	3		
Whitty, John	1		1		
Demmons, Charles	1		1		
Ford, Daniel	1				
Ford, Edward	1				
Cooper, F			1		
MILFORD TOWN.					
Jellet, John	3	1	1		
Clarke, William	1	3	3		
Marren, John	1	2	3		3
Sadley, John	1	1	1		
Bens, Juno	1				
Baldwin, Soloman	1	1			
Baldwin, Daniel	1		1		
Platt, Isaac	1	3	3		
Purtree, John	2	1	7		
Plumb, Isaac	1		7		
Bush, Lindie	2		2		
Beach, Thomas	1	2	3		
Burrel, Samuel	2				
Burrel, Samuel, 2nd	1	2	2		
Jellet, John, 2nd	1	2	3		
Bunnel, John	1	5	1		
Pritchard, Nathaniel	1		1		
Burrel, Jeremiah	1	2	3		
Burrel, Daniel	1	2	3		
Beech, Thadeus	1		5		
Beech, Samuel	1	1	1		
Parker, James	1		1		
Plump, Joseph	1				
Plump, Joseph, 2nd	1	2	2		1
Murrain, Miles	1	5	3		1
Ellis, Samuel	1		1		
Ellis, Samuel, 2nd	1		2		
Ellis, Hester			1		
Ellis, Sibel		1	2		
Murdock, William	1				
Pritchard, Nathaniel	1		3		
Whiting, John	2	1	1		
Murren, Mary	1		1		1
Clarke, Rebecca			2		
Clarke, Amos	1	1	3		
Platt, Hannah	2	2	3		
Clarke, Samuel	2	3	2		1
Smith, Isaac	3	1	3		2
Platt, Joseph	1	1	2		
Davinson, William	1	3	3		
Nott, William	1		2		
Jellet, Benjamin	1	3	2		
Strong, John	1		2		
Trant, Philo	2	2	3		
Bryan, Oliver	1		4		
Pond, Elizabeth			3		
Camp, Joab	1	2	1		
Woodruk, Barnabas	2		2		
Sandford, John	1		1		
Sandford, Elisha	1	1	6		
Wolcott, John	1	2	4		
Sandford, Mother	1	2	4		
MILFORD TOWN—con.					
Fowler, Nathaniel	2		2		
Fowler, Anna	1	1	1		
Hoods, Catherine			1		
Jones, Isaac	3	3	4	1	
Lawrence, Katey		1	3		
Miles, John	4		5		
Green, Sarah	1		1		
Clarke, Mary			2		
Jones, John	1		2		
Woods, Titus	1	1	4		
Fowler, John	1	1	2		
Platt, Jiremiah	4		2		
Buckingham, John	2	2	3		2
Buckingham, Gedion	2	2	2		2
Bradley, Israel	2	6	2		
Goldsmith, Joseph	1		2		
Donalds, Samuel	1		1		
James (Negroe)				3	
Higby, Samuel	2		4		
Plumb, Samuel	1				
Wise, Samuel	1	1	3		
Pry (Negroe)				6	
Mallery, Mosses	1	1	1		
Clarke, Andrew	2	1	4		
Britton, Newton	1	1	3		1
Lockwood, William	1	1	3	1	
Carrington, Edward	2	2	5	1	
Sheldon, Hannah			2		
Sears, Francis	1		3		
Ingersall, Clement	1		3		
Green, Anna			2	1	
Glenny, William	1		3		
Mallet, Lewis	3	1	3		
Miles, Tilla	1	1	1		
Hepborn, Peter	4	2	5		
Perit, Peter	1		1		
Davidson, James	3		2		
Fowler, Nathaniel, 2nd	1		2		
Bristow, John	1		1		
Bryant, Joseph	1				
Galbin, Benjamin	1				
Mallery, Moses	2		1		
Bino, Watham	1				
Sacket, Daniel	1		2		1
Stow, Samuel	2		1		
Dickenson, Sylvanus	1	2	3	2	
Harpin, John	1		1	1	
Baldwin, Phineas	1	1	3		
Stow, William	1	1	2		
Barn, Daniel	1	2	6		
Murren, David	1	3	7		
Jellet, Zebulon	2	1	3		
Davidson, Joseph	1	1	1		
De Witt, Garret	1	2	3		5
Coggeshall, William	1	4	3		2
Bull, Henry	1	2	3		
Lartherbie, William	2	1	1		
Pond, Charles	1	3	5		2
Tomlinson, Abraham	3		3		
Baldwin, Asbeil	3	1	4		
Smith, Mary	1		4		
Arnold, Abigal			2		
Coggshall, Freegift	1				
De Wint, Garret N	1				
De Wint, Abraham N	1			1	
Tebbalds, James	1				
Nettleton, Nathaniel	1				
Goldsmith, Gilbert	1	1	2		
Baldwin, Heil	3	2	4		
Perit, Peter	2	1	1		
Mallet, John	1	1	1		
Vanduser, Thomas	1	2	2		
Hicock, Aron	1		1		
Gilbert, Katey		1	2		
Stow, Freelove			1		
Stow, Stephen	1	1	4		
Stow, John	1	3	1		
Thompson, James	1				
Ball, Benedah	3	1	3		
Bull, Temperance			1		
Miles, Daniel	2	2	3		
Goldsmith, William	1		4		
Goldsmith, James	1				
Goldsmith, James, 2nd	1	3	1		
Beardsley, John	1				
Gray, William	1	2	1		
Stevens, Eliphalet	1	4	1		
Tebbalds, Arnold	1		3		
Marchant, Ezra	1		2		
Gibbs, John	1		3		
Smith, Joseph	1	1	1		
Camp, Samuel	1	3	1		
Camp, Hail	1		1		
Peck, John	1		2		
Covert, Elerick	3	1	2		
MILFORD TOWN—con.					
Jillet, Eliphalet	1		1		
Baldwin, Thadeus	1	1	4	1	
Baldwin, Abraham	2		3		
Ceaser (Negroe)				3	
Whitney, Isaac	1		3		
Prime (Negroe)				2	
Wetmore, Joseph	1				
Beebie, Joel	1		2		
Plumb, John	2	3	4		
Anderson, Atiny	1	1	1		
Prime (Negroe)				6	
Miles, Theophilus	1	1	3		1
Bull, Jeremiah	1		2		
Baldwin, Isaac	1	1	3		
Mallery, Daniel	2	3	3		1
Baldwin, Jeremiah	3		4		
Baldwin, David	1		1		
Attwater, William	1	4	7		
Baldwin, Isaac, 2nd	1		2		
Gowsley, William	1		1		
Gunn, Isaac	1		2		
Clarke, William	3	2	6		
Northrop, Lazerus	1				
Camp, David	1	2	3		
Ford, Amos	1	2	1		
Bisco, Ruth			1		1
Baldwin, Elnathan	1	2	2		
Tomlinson, William	1		3		
Nettleton, Caleb	2	2	3		
Stow, Jedediah	1	3	3		
Baldwin, Advice			2		
Baldwin, Elisha	1				
Baldwin, Nathan	3		4		
Baldwin, Eliph	1	1	3		1
Tibbalds, Arnold	1		2		
Clarke, Jonathan	1	1	2		
Tibbalds, Benedick	1	2	3		
Tibbalds, Samuel	1	4	1		
Baldwin, Nathan, 2nd	1	2	2		
Bard, Abigel			1	1	
Mills, David	1	2	3		
Smith, Joel	1	2	3		
Clarke, Joseph	1	1	3		
Camp, Ezra	1	1	4	1	1
Ovet, Isaac	1		2		
Clarke, Abraham	1	1	4		1
Collins, John	2		1		
Tibbalds, David	1	3	2		
Camp, Mary	1		1		
Bard, Andrew	1	2	2		
Turrel, Samuel	1		3		
Turrel, David	1		3		
Clarke, Abel	1		3		
Hine, Samuel	2	4	2		
Tibbalds, Lemuel	1	1	4		
Baldwin, Josiah	1	2	5		
Northrop, Moses	1		3	1	
Smith, Hezekiah	2	1	2		
Smith, Caleb	3	3	5		
Bim, David	2	4	3		1
Camp, Elias	2	3	3		
Hine, George	1		3		
Basset, Samuel	1	3	3		
OCain, Antony	1		2		
Bassett, Samuel, 2nd	2		2		
Bassett, David	1	3	1		
Ovett, Ebenezer	1		6		
Smith, Ebenezer	1	2	3		
Peck, Abraham	1	1	3		
Northrop, Heth	1	3	2		
Nettleton, Thaddeus	2	2	1		
Ovett, Nathan	1	2	2		
Mallery, Daniel	1	2	3		
Basett, Isaac	1	2	3		
Bawley, John	1	2	2		
Clarke, Joseph	1	2	3		1
Peck, Benjamin	2	1	2		
Hine, David	1	3	3		
Beers, Benjamin	1				
Beers, John	1		2		
Tuttle, Andrew	1	2	1		
Tuttle, Andrew, 2nd	1		1		
Ford, John	1		5		
Ford, John, 2nd	1	1	4		
Ford, Thomas	1		4		
Ford, Thomas	1		1		
Botchford, David	1		1		
Botchford, Eli	1	1	1		
Peck, Samuel	2		1		
Peck, Stephen	2	1	1		
Gunn, Stephen	2		1		
Baldwin, Amos		1	2		
Baldwin, Edward	1	1	3		
Peck, Michael	1	6	4		
Smith, Jeremiah	1	2	1		

NEW HAVEN COUNTY—Continued.

MILFORD TOWN—con.

NAME OF HEAD OF FAMILY.	Free white males of 16 years and upward, including heads of families.	Free white males under 16 years.	Free white females, including heads of families.	All other free persons.	Slaves.
Carrington, Elias	2	2	4		1
Higgins, Timothy	3	1	5		
Hine, Joel	3		4		
Martin, Susannah			1		
Marchant, Mary			2		
Nettleton, Samuel	1		1		
Fern, Mary		1	2		
Clarke, Elizabeth	2		2		
Buckingham, Daniel	1	2	3		2
Talmage, Ezra	1		1		
Strong, Ephrahim	1		1		
Strong, Ephrahim	1	1	3		
Marshal, Joseph	2		1		
Marshall, John	1	1	3		
Northrop, Clement	1	1	6		
Deering, Samuel	2		3		
Deering, Andrew	1				
Deering, John	1	6	1		
Deering, Ann	2		3		
Clarke, Patty	1		1		
Clarke, David	2	4	4		
Burk, John	1				
Bristor, Elizabeth			2		
Sommers, Abel, 2	1	1	1		
Ashborn, Abigal			1		
Bristol, Phico	3	2	3		
Hatch, Daniel	1	4	3		
Newton, John	1	1	8		
Treat, Isaac	2		3		
Clarke, Enoch	1		2		1
Prudden, Jonathan	1	1	2		
Clarke, Neahh	1	1	2		
Treat, Joseph	2		1		2
Treat, Isaac	1	1	2		
Treat, Robert	1	1	2		
Storer, Joseph	1	2	3		
Hine, John	1	2	5		
Hine, Joseph	1	1	3		
Frost, Samuel	2	1	1		
Alling, Gidion	1	2	4		
Woods, Samuell	1	1	5		
Clarke, Amos	1		2		
Evans, Evan	1		1		
Newton, Jonah	2	1	5		4
Summers, Henry	2		2		
Summers, Isaac	1		2		
Smith, John	4		3		1
Gillet, Eliphalet	1		1		
Gillet, Jonathan	1		1		
Smith, Joseph	1	1	3	1	
Smith, Samuel	1	4	6	1	
Jack (Negroe)				5	
Peter (Negroe)				7	
Munson, William	1		2		
Rogers, Joseph	1		5		1
Smith, David	1	2	3		
Summers, Abel	3	1	5		
Munson, Daniel	1	4	6		
Benjamin, Berzeler	3	3	1		
Botsford, Aron	1	1	1		
Bassett, Mary			2		
Turrel, Mary			1		
Foot, John	1		2		
Simeon (Negroe)				2	
Joseph (Negroe)				3	
Ovet, Ellick	1		2		
Gunn, Anna	1		2		
Roseter, Timothy W	1		1		
Whiting, Joseph	1	1	2		
Baldwin, Thankfull			1		
Morris, Richard	1	2	2		
Merchant, Samuel	2		1		
Burn, David	1	2	4		
Nando (Negroe)				1	
Camp, Nathaniel	2	3	4		
Peck, John, 2nd	1	1	2		
Tomlinson, David	2				
Bristow, Nathan	1	6	2		
Bristow, Richard	1				
Clarke, Oliver	1		1		
Northrop, Abel	3	3	3		
Smith, Benjamin	1	1	3		
Lewis, Sarah			2		
Baldwin, Sibel			2		
Prindle, Charles	2	1	2		
Ovet, Isaac	1	1	2		
Summers, Agnes			1		
Botchford, Elnathan	1		1		
Fowler, Timothy	2	1	5		
Fowler, William	1	1	4		
Treat, Joseph, 2nd	1	1	5		
Hine, Aron	1	1	2		
Pardie, Joseph	1	1	3		
Clement, Isaac	1	1	1		
Treat, Robert	2	1	2		

MILFORD TOWN—con.

NAME OF HEAD OF FAMILY.	Free white males of 16 years and upward, including heads of families.	Free white males under 16 years.	Free white females, including heads of families.	All other free persons.	Slaves.
Treat, Jonathan	1		2		
Fenn, Sarah	2	2	2		
Priden, Samuel	1	3	3		
Woodruff, Joseph	2	1	4		
Platt, Joseph	1	1	3		
Mallery, Samuel	2		5		
Treat, Daniel	3	1	3		
Bukingham, Ephrahim	1	2	2		
Strong, Elnathan	1		1		
Stone, Samuel	2	3	3		
Clarke, Isaac	1	1	5		1
Andrews, Charlotte		1	2		1
Nettleton, Benijah	1		2		
Fenn, Aron	1		2		
Platt, Richard	3	1	2		
Hine, Stephen	1	1	2		
Woodruff, Phebe			1	1	
Joe (Negroe)				4	
Platt, Samuel	2		3		1
Platt, Sibel	2		1		
Clarke, Nathan	2		2		
Hine, Isaac	1	1	3		
Hine, Abraham	1	1	5		
Fenn, James	3	1	1		
Bassett, Edward	1	1	5		
Steward, John	1	2	2		
Pridden, John	1	1	3		
Priden, Fletcher	2		5		
Baldwin, Jerad	2	3	3		
Pritchard, Isaac	1	1	2		
Pond, Peter	1		1		
Tuller, David	1		2		
Colbrith, John	2		1		
Downs, John, 2nd	2	2	3		
Downs, John	1		1		
Bristol, David	1		1		
Welsh, Martha			1		
Treat, Edmond	1	1	1		
Malery, Benjamin	1		1		
Bryant, Heil	1		1		3
Smith, William	1	3			
Clarke, Enoch, 2nd	1	3	2		1
Platt, Gideon	2		2		1
Clarke, Elias	1	3	2		2
Treat, Samuel	1	1	3		
Clarke, Benjamin	1	2	3		
Rogers, Jonathan	1	2	3		
Bryant, John	1	3	2		
Fenn, Samuel	2	2	6		
Andrew, William	2	1	2		2
Bryant, Thomas	1		2		
Woodruff, Mathew	2	4	3		
Nettleton, Isaac	2	2	3		
Marks, Abraham	1	2	1		
Buckingham, Joseph	1				
Marks, Zacheriah	2		4		
Treat, Francis	1	1	2		
Treat, Richard	1		2		1
Treat, John	1		1		
Treat, John, 2nd	1		2		
Parker, Jeremiah	1		2		
Fenn, John	1		2		
Fenn, Isaac	1		2		
Welsh, Thomas	2	1	5		
Murrain, John, 3rd	1	3	3		
Pritchard, Martha			3		
Bryant, Heil	1		2		
Molton, Joseph	1	1	1		
Peck, Ephraim	1		1	1	
Jeff (Negroe)				2	
Gabriel, Peter	1	1	2		
Gabriel, Henry	1		3		
Bull, Benjamin	2		1	1	
Smith, Ebenezer	1		1		
Smith, Andrew	1	1	2		
Bull, Anna	1		2		
Peck, Hezekiah	1		1		
Baldwin, Justice	1		1		
Isaacs, Isaac B	1				
Warren, Jonathan	1				
Clarke, Thomas	3		3		
Mallery, Moses	1	3	4		
Treat, Stephen	1	1	1		
Murrain, John	1		1		1
Platt, Benjamin	1	2	3		
Isbell, Israel	1	1	4		
Treat, Elisha	1	1	2		1
Hooker, John	1	1	3		
Morris, Newton	1	1	2		1
Bradley, Jerad	1		2		
Hine, Titus	1	2	2		
Congo (Negroe)				4	
Pomp (Negroe)				3	
Law, Benedick	2	5	3		1
Lambert, Jesse	2	1	2		

MILFORD TOWN—con.

NAME OF HEAD OF FAMILY.	Free white males of 16 years and upward, including heads of families.	Free white males under 16 years.	Free white females, including heads of families.	All other free persons.	Slaves.
Stevens, Thomas	2		3		
Lambert, David	3	2	4		
Trussell, Elizabeth	1		1		
Ben (Negroe)				6	
Buckingham, Isaac	1		1		
Pardy, Josiah	1	2	7		
Woodruff, Mather	2	1	5		
Prindle, Josep	1		2		
Lambeth, David, 2nd	1	1	2		
Sacket, Jonathan	1				
Donnalds, Samuel, 2nd	1			1	
Isbel, Sarah			2		
Law, Jonathan	1		1		
Ovet, Hannah			2		

NEW HAVEN CITY.

NAME OF HEAD OF FAMILY.	Free white males of 16 years and upward, including heads of families.	Free white males under 16 years.	Free white females, including heads of families.	All other free persons.	Slaves.
Plymate, William	1	2	3		
Prinale, Charles	2	1	5		
Cooke, David	1		2		
Hood, William	1		1		
Bonticon, Sussanah			2		
Sherman, Molly			1		
Jocelin, Simeon	1		2		
Bishop, Israel	1	2	5		
Ells, Joseph	1	1	1		
Davis, Solomon, Junr	1	1	1		
Hitchcock, Samuel	1	2	3		
Bonticon, Susanah	1	1	2		
Bonticon, James	1				
Story, Nathaniel	2	2	3		
Lyman, Mary			3		
Covert, Samuel	3	1	2		
Higby, Cheney	1		2		
Hopkins, Thomas	3	1	2		
Hunt, Fredrick	2	6	2		
Stilman, Benjamin	1	2	2		
Gorham, Elias	1		2		
Gorham, Elizur	1		2		
Spencer, Nathaniel	2		3		
Townsend, Soloman	1	2			
Brown, Elizur	4		4		
White, Timothy	1	4	5		
Alley, William	1		1		
Kindley, Joseph	1	1	2		
Wooster, Mary			1		
Wooster, Thomas		6	3		
Hood, Samuel	1	1	2		
Smith, Seymore	1	1	3		
Wells, Gad	1		1		
Palmer, Elizabeth		1	1		
Brown, Henry	1		3		
Turner, Jesse	1	3	3		
Davis, Thomas	1	1			
Parmalie, Jeremiah	2	2	3		
Dana, Revd James	2	1	4		
Irwin, Sarah		3	1		
McKenzie, John	1				
Humiston, Mary Ann		2	1		
Warner, Jacob	1	2	1		
Peck, Thomas	1		1		
Holmes, Joel	1	3	3		
Tinker, Amos	1				
Tucker, Noah	1		7		
Hotchkiss, Eneas	1		2		
Warner, Joseph	1		2		
Leavenworth, Catherine		1	1		
Denis, Samuel	1		2		
Platt, Jerimiah	2	1	4		1
Broome, Samuel	3	2	6	2	
Hulse, Joseph	1	3	5		
Green, David	1	1	1		
Wells, Mosses	2		4		
Thompson, Timothy	2		4		
Smith, Joshua	1	4	5		
Hood, Richard	3		3		
English, Benjamin	1	4	5		
Tomlinson, Isaac	4	2	4		
Cooke, George	1		2		
Ray, Caleb	1	1	2		
Catlin, Thomas	1	3	2		
Tuttle, Abraham	2		1		
Cuff (Negroe)				3	
Punderford, John	1	3	3		
Montcalm, Mosses	1	3	4		
Brown, Jabez	1	3	3		
Storer, John	2	3	3		
Stilman, Ashbel	2	4	3		
Bonticon, Thomas	1		1		
Storer, Sarah			1		
Bonticon, William	1	1	4		
Sloan, Mary			2		
Mansfield, Ester			2		2
Woodward, Richard	4	1	2	1	2
Russell, Samuel	1		3		

NEW HAVEN COUNTY—Continued.

NAME OF HEAD OF FAMILY.	Free white males of 16 years and upward, including heads of families.	Free white males under 16 years.	Free white females, including heads of families.	All other free persons.	Slaves.	NAME OF HEAD OF FAMILY.	Free white males of 16 years and upward, including heads of families.	Free white males under 16 years.	Free white females, including heads of families.	All other free persons.	Slaves.	NAME OF HEAD OF FAMILY.	Free white males of 16 years and upward, including heads of families.	Free white males under 16 years.	Free white females, including heads of families.	All other free persons.	Slaves.
NEW HAVEN CITY—con.						NEW HAVEN CITY—con.						NEW HAVEN CITY—con.					
Sabins, Hezekiah	1	1	2	4	1	Lothrop, Unice			5			Gorham, Joseph	1	3	1		
Graham, John	1	2	3			Mix, Joseph, 2nd	2		3			Townsend, Elias	1	1	5		
Tharp, Joel	2	1	2			Munson, Stephen	1		3			Brown, Isaac	1		1		
Sherry, Joseph	1		3			Noyse, Paul	1	1	3			Phipps, Daniel Goff	1	3	3		
Lieke, John	1	2	3			Gardiner, David					6	Keif, Arthur	1	1	4		
French, Edmond	2	3	3		1	Adams, John	1	1	2			Austin, Elijah	3	4	4		
Griffin, Rossiter	1	1	2			Bell, John	1	1	1			Trowbridge, Joseph E	1		4		
Sandford, Benjamin	1	1			5	Dwight, Timothy	1	4	3			Trowbridge, Stephen	1	1	1		
Perit, Job	1		2			Nicoll, John	2	1	4		2	Gobine, Nicholas	1		1		
Burke, Edmond	1	1	2			Bradley, Joseph	2		2		2	Trowbridge, Stephen, 3rd	3				
Benedick, John	1	2	1			Mirriman, Silas	3		2			Thomas, Samuel	1		1		
Downs, Nathaniel	1		2			Mirriman, Marcus	1	1	3			Allen, Eneas	1		2		
Reiley, William	1	1	1			Turner, Enoch	1		2			Robinson, Catherine			1		
Lewis, Sussanah			1			Drake, Joseph	3	1	3			Dinah (Negroe)				1	1
Molony, Downey	1	2	1			Mansfield, Henry	1	1	2			Hubbard, Leveret	2	1	3	1	1
Trickey, Jerard	1	1	2			Sabin, Hezekiah, 2nd	1	4	2			Brown, Robert	5	3	4		
Jellet, Margret			2			Bradley, Abraham	2	1	3			Peck, Henry	1	1	5		
Wilson, Sarah			2			Huggins, Heaton	1		1			Trowbridge, William	1	2	2		
Mulford, David	2	1	1			Mansfield, Jerad	1		1			Larkin, Edward	1	3	3		
Reed, David	1		1			Bradley, Stephen	1	1	3			Oakes, Nathan	6	1	7		
Mulford, Barnabas	2	2	3			Street, John	2	1	1			Ward, Ambros	1		3		
Thatcher, John	1		2			Mix, Eldad	1	2	4			Peck, John	1	1	1		
Buckly, William	1		2			Morse, Abel	4	3	2		2	Gold, Thomas	1		2		
Sails, James	1	1	1			Fitch, Jonathan	5	5	3		1	Howell, Thomas	1		3		
Fenton, Nathaniel	2		4			Stilwell, Elias	1		3			Hubbard, Julia			1	2	
Peck, Gad	1		1			Huggins, John	1	1	3			Bartholemew, Israel	1	2	3		
Barber, Noah	2	1	2			Hotchkiss, Sussanah			3			Horcheild, William	2		1		
Walter, William	3	3	4			Spalding, John	4		1			Howell, Thomas, Jr	2	1	3		1
Miles, William	1	2	5			Horton, Samuel	2		2			Sacket, Hannah			1		
Townsend, Ebenezer	3	3	4			Townsend, Robert	2	4	5			Malone, Danael	1	3	2		
Smith, Edmond	1	1	3			Darling, Samuel	1	3	3			Hitchcock, Eliakim	2	2	4		
Collis, Daniel	3	1	5			Trowbridge, Stephen	2	2	4			Holly, Josiah	1	1	2		
Collony, Patrick	1	1	3			Howett, Joseph	3	2	4			Bailey, Elizabeth			2		
Sabins, Jonathan	1	1	6			Tritten, Elizb			1	1	3	Osborn, Stephen	5	5	4		
Little, Alexander	1		1			Attwater, Timothy	1	3	6			Granis, Benjamin	3	2	2		
Throop, John R	1	2	4			Bishop, Sylvanus	3		1			Miller, Caleb	1		1		
Miles, John, 3rd	1	3	2			Miles, John	2	1	1			Johnson, Thomas	1		3		
Trowbridge, John	1	3	3			Miles, Stephen	1		1			Yorke, Henry	2	2	6		
Bedford, Ad ——	1		1			Howell, Samuel	1		3			McNeil, William	1	1	4		
Collins, Luther	1		2			Beecher, Mary			3			Hugins, Ebenezer	1	4	4		
Peck, Ebenezer	4	2	2			Munson, William	1	3	4			Prat, Samuel	1		3		
Peck, James	1		1			Cleavland, Samuel	1	2	3			Alicocke, David	3		3		
Powell, William	2		2			Sisson, James	1	1	4			Ward, Ambrose, Jr	2	3	2		
Marsh, Robert	1	2	1			Hall, Abiel			3			Austin, Mahatibel			1		
Heyliger, John	2	4	4		1	Whiting, Sarah			1		1	Herrick, Stephen	1		5		
Wells, William	1	1	3			Whiting, Samuel	1		1			Austin, Jonathan	1		5		
Meloy, Edward, 2nd	1	1	2			Whiting, Jonathan	1		2			Hubbard, Revd Bela	1	4	5		
Phipps, Solomon	1		4			Whittlesey, Patty	3		3			Brigden, William	1	2	3		
Ward, John	1		1			Hotchkiss, Lent	2		3			Alling, Bet (Negroe)				3	
Davis, Thomas	2	2	3			Attwater, Thomas	1	3	4	1		Denison, Martha			4	5	
Brintnal, William	2	2	6			Northrop, Joel	1	5	3	1		Chrittenton, Dolly			2	3	
Phipps, David	1	2	4			Chatterton, Rodah			3	2		Burnet, Jeremiah	1	1	1		
Brown, Benjamin	2	1	1			Townsend, Jeremiah	1	1	3			Johnson, Robert	1				
Jocelin, Nathaniel	1		1			Prout, Margeret			1			Stone, Cyrus	1		2		
Brown, Francis	1	1	5			Forbes, Elijah	1	2	4		2	Peck, John	1	2	2		
Helmes, William	2	4	2			Brown, George	1	2	2			Ade, Aner	1	1	2		
Prentice, Jonas	2	1	5			Tuttle, Abraham, 2d	3	1	2	1		Mix, Jonathan	2	4	3		
Fanning, David	1	2	1			Allen, Stephen	1	1	5			Webber, John	1	1	2		
Forbes, Samuel	1		1			Lymar, Elihu	2		1		1	Beecher, Isaac	1		1		
Sherman, Samuel	2	1	3			Andrus, Phineas	3	4	3			Hoye, Nelly			1		
Gilbert, Miriam			2			Smith, George	1	3	2		1	Howell, Cheney	1	2	1		
Ward, Titus	1		1			Gorham, Isaac	1	1	2			McNeil, Archabald	1	3	1		
Dorman, Amassa	1	1	2			Gurnsey, Isaac	1		2			Mathews, Elizabeth			2		
Smith, Benjamin	1	1	1	1		Thompson, William	1					Sherman, William	2	1	7		
Crittenden, Lidia			2			Miles, Josep	1		1			Bonticon, John	1		1		
Sherman, Lemuel	1	3	1			Townsend, Woodbridge	1	1	1			Bradley, Abraham	1		1		
Lane, James	1					Keeney, Michael	1	1	2			Lyon, William	2		7		
Dougal, James	3	1	3			Forbes, Elias	1	1	4			Mix, Joseph	2	3	5		
Thomas, John	1		1			Morgan, Jacob	1	1	2			Lyon, Nathaniel	2		4		
Dorman, John	1	1	2			Harrington, Benjamin	1	1	3			Munson, Theophilus	1		2		
Sharper (Negroe)				2		Davis, John	1		3			Hill, Hannah		1	1	1	
Hubbard, William G	1		3			Hitchcock, Jotham	1					Beardsley, Ebenezer	3	2	2	1	
Hotchkiss, Stephen	3	3	3			Hatch, Zephaniah	1		1			Reed, Zackeriah	2	2	5		
Jack (Negroe)				1		Roberts, Josiah	1	1	4			De Witt, Peter	1		1		
Gorham, Abigal			2			Snow, Samuel	1					Attwater, Jeremiah	2	3	5		
Smith, Joseph, 3rd	2	2	3			Bills, William	3		3			McCraken, William	1	4	5		2
Lines, Ezra	1	1	4			Wallace, William	3	1	4			Cutler, Richard	1	4	7		
Dummer, Nathaniel	1		3			Miller, John	1		2		1	Cooke, John	3	3	2		
Dummer, Stephen	2	4	3			Davis, Enoch	1	1	3			Kimberly, Nathaniel	1	3	3		
Munson, Samuel	1	1	1			Benham, Elisha	1	1	5			Beecher, Sussanah			2	5	
Wilmot, Samuel	1	2	3			Rice, James	2		1		1	Beecher, John	1	1	1		
Dennison, Rohda			3			Perit, Antony	1		1		1	Cocker, James	1	1	1		
Pardee, Sarah	1	2	3			Brumham, John	1		2			Davis, James			2		
Bishop, Daniel	4	5	3			Trowbridge, Caleb	2	4	4			Miles, John, 3rd	3		4		1
Burret, Abel	3	2	4			Rice, Thomas	1				2	Beecher, Thadius	4		3		1
Mansfield, William	1	2	4			Trowbridge, Rutherford	2	2	5			Wetmore, Hezekiah	1		2		1
Ray, Martha			2			Morris, John	2	1	3			Austin, Asa	1	3	3		
Dummer, Abraham	1	1	2			Clarke, John	2	1	4			Turner, Seth	1		2		
Pinto, Polly		1	1			Kirby, Abner	1		2			Townsend, Isaac	3	2	5		
Bishop, Samuel	4		4			Trowbridge, Daniel	1		3			Eld, Richard	1	2	2		
Pinto, Jacob	1	1	3			Trowbridge, Joseph	1		3			Townsend, Neeland	4		2		
Bishop, Isaac	1	1	4			Trowbridge, Mahbel			1			Adams, Polly			2		
Todd, Michael	2		4		5	Trowbridge, Newman	3	3	1			Bradley, Hannah			3		
Chandler, John	1	3	4			Gorham, Timothy	1		1			Smith, Joseph	2		3		
Jones, Timothy	1	1	2		1												

NEW HAVEN COUNTY—Continued.

NEW HAVEN CITY—con.

NAME OF HEAD OF FAMILY.	Free white males of 16 years and upward, including heads of families.	Free white males under 16 years.	Free white females, including heads of families.	All other free persons.	Slaves.
Barney, Samuel	1	2	5		
Sabins, Sussanah			2		
Hubbard, Levi	2	1	2	1	
Cooladge, Henry	3	1	2		
Bates, Mosses	2	2	1		
Brigden, Jonathan	1	2	2		
White, John	1		1		
Carrington, Merrit	2	1	2		
Cooke, William	2	2	2		
Langmore, Alexander	1				
Brown, Jacob	3		2	2	
Gorham, Miles	1	6	2		
Austin, David	2		2		
Wise, John	1		2		
Wise, John, Junr	1		1		
Wise, Samuel	1		3		
Austin, John	3	2	3		
Crocker, Daniel	1	2	1		
Gilbert, Caleb	1		2		
Goodsell, Levi	1		1		
Clarke, Tim	2	2	2	1	
Ord, John	1		2		
Austin, William	1	3	2		
Rice, Archabald	1	1	1		
Austin, Lidia			1		
Bradley, Jonah	2		3		
Mix, Sarah			1		
Mix, Thankfull		1	3		
Lines, James	2		1		
Jack (Negro)				3	
Meloy, Edward	3	2	1		
Thompson, Joseph	3		6		
Ford, Caleb	2	2	4		
Chappel, Patience		1	5		
Otty, William	1		3		
Thompson, Jacob	1	1	6	1	1
Thompson, Jerad	1	2	2		
Thompson, Isaac	1	1	3		
Clause, John	1		4		
Alley, Joseph	1		3		
Gilbert, Elizabeth		2	3		
Gilbert, Isaac	2	2	5		
Bills, Thomas	3		2		
Bills, Thomas, 2nd	1		1		
Thompson, Jeremiah	1		1		
Dougal, David	1	2	4		
Gilbert, David	1	1	2		
Gilbert, Amos	1	2	4		1
Gilbert, Timothy	1	2	2		
Hull, Samuel	1	3	2		
Dodd, Bishop	1		2		
Barnes, Elizabeth		1	1		
Mix, Ester		3	1		
Doolittle, Isaac	1	1	4		
Noyce, William	2	2	4		
Beecher, David	2	1	4		
Hull, Joseph	2		2		
Fitch, Luther	5	3	4		
Thompson, Phebe			1		
Fitch, Nathaniel	2	5	3		
Green, Thomas	3		4		
Attwater, Joel	2	1	3		
Attwater, Ward	1		3		
Potter, Statia	1		1		
Townsend, Jeremiah	1	2	4		
Potter, Livi	1	1	1		
Green, Samuel	2		5		
Attwater, Jeremiah	3		2	1	
Stiles, Revd Ezra	2	1	6	1	
Beers, Elias	1	2	4		
Beers, Isaac	1	3	2		
Goodrich, John	2	3	4	1	1
Shipman, Elias	2	4	6	1	
Hubbard, Mary			2		
Perit, Thadeus	1	1	1		
Ingersal, Jonathan	2	1	5		
Chittenden, Ebenezer	1		2		
Chittenden, Timothy	1		1		
Buel, Abel	1	3	2		
Dagget, David	3	1	3	1	
Scott, John	1	2	4		
Clarke, Samuel	2	1	2		
Griswold, Samuel	2	2	4		
Gilbert, Margaret		1	3		
Brown, Stephen	1		4		
Baldwin, Theodore	1	1	4		
Mansfield, Daniel	1		1		
Graham (Widow)			2		
Osborn, Mahitabel	1		2		
Beecher, Hiram	1		4		
Gilbert, Elisha	1	1	3		
Beecher, Sarah			1		
Thompson, Sarah		1	3		
Gilbert, James	2	1	5	1	

NEW HAVEN CITY—con.

NAME OF HEAD OF FAMILY.	Free white males of 16 years and upward, including heads of families.	Free white males under 16 years.	Free white females, including heads of families.	All other free persons.	Slaves.
Williams, Hecter (Negroe)				4	
Potter, Noah	1		2		
Potter, Asa	1	1	3		
Geff (Negroe)				2	
Broughton, William	1		1		
Dagget, Jacob	1	1	5		
Hitchcock, Hannah			1		
Jocelin, Pember	2		4		
Attwater, Mary			1		
Punderson, Daniel	1				
Prescot, Benjamin	4	3	2		
Munson, Eneas	3	3	2		2
Beers, Nathan	1	2	5		
Phelps, Timothy	1				
Hotchkiss, Amos	1		1		1
Johnson, Abraham	1	1	1		
Ruben (Negroe)				2	
Sperry, Eber	1	1	2		
Gold, Peter	1		3		
Henry, John	1				
Attwater, Stephen	1	2	5		
Gorham, Samuel	1	3	3		
Mix, Samuel	1	2	4		
Mix, Elisha	1	1	4		
Mix, Hannah			1		
Hotchkiss, Obadiah	1		1		
Cooke, Miller	1	2	1		
Blakley, Tilley	1	1	2		
Burr, Josiah	1	2	6		
Page, Icabod	1	1	2		
Dagget, Micajah	1				
Chapman, Daniel	2	2	1		
Hart, Rebeca		1	2		
Cooke, David	1		2		
Macumber, Jeremiah	2				
Stevans, Leveret	1	1	4		
Cambridge, Ruth				2	
Chatfield, Heil	1		2		
Luke (Negroe)				4	
Chittendon, Beriah	1	2	2		
Griswold, Hannah			2		
Mansfield, Deborah			1		
Hale, Hezekiah	1	1	2		
Munson, Israel	5		3		
Munson, Joseph	4	2	6		
Mix, John	5	1	3		
Townsend, Timothy	1	1	4		
Doolittle, Amos	1	4	2		
Ford, Ezra	1		7		
Clarke, Parsons	2		2		
Townsend, John	2	1	3		
Grenough, William	1		2		2
Molthrop, Enoch	1		3		
Barnes, Darcus			1		
Bradley, John	1		1		
Dagget, Ezra	1		3		
Barney, Hanover	1	4	4		
Bradley, James	2	2	5		
Hotchkiss, Gabrael	1	1	2		
Wise, Rhoda			1		
Molthrop, Charles	1		3		
Hotchkiss, Hezekiah	2	2	5		1
Fisher, Hannah		2	2		
Hanson, Christan	1		2		
Thompson, Abraham	1		1		
Marumble, Abiel	1	1	1		
Alling, Samuel	1		3		
Parmalie, Sarah			2		
Dagget, Henry, 2nd	1	1	3		
Hotchkiss, Asa	1		1		
Doolittle, Isaac	3		1		
Hotchkiss, Josiah	1	3	3		
Burr, Sturgis	2	1	3		1
Prescot, James	4	3	4		
Dagget, Henry	1	3	4		
Ball, Stephen	2	1	3		
Sherman, Roger	3	1	8		
Baldwin, Simion	1	1	3	1	
Sherman, John	2	2	4		
Parmalie, Ebenezer	1		4		1
Peck, Joseph	1	2	4		
Hays, Ezekiel	4	2	6		
Lucas, Amaziah	1				
Leavenworth, Mark	1	1	2		1
Bradley, Phineas	4		5		
Clarke, Russell	2	1	5		
Smith, John	1	1	3		1
Whiting, William J.	1	1	5		
Chauncy, Charles	1	3	3	1	2
Leavensworth, Ely	1		4		
Volumn, Lenard	1		3		
Lamont, Mary Ann			2		
Edwards, Cuff (Negroe)				4	

NEW HAVEN CITY—con.

NAME OF HEAD OF FAMILY.	Free white males of 16 years and upward, including heads of families.	Free white males under 16 years.	Free white females, including heads of families.	All other free persons.	Slaves.
Dudley, Thomas	1		3		
Hatch, Amy			1		
Morrison (Widow)		1	1		
Rackerbrandt, John	1		3		
Newall, Joshua	2		5		
Dodd, John	1	3	2		
Gordon, Sarah			2		
Pierpont, John	2	3	3		
Miles, Elihu			2		
Butler, Justas	2	1	3		
Thatcher, Samuel	1	1	5	1	2
Goodrich, Elijur	2	1	4		1
Hillhouse, James	1	2	7	2	1
Dodd, Guy	1	2	5		
Smith, Joseph, 2nd	1	1	2		
Hillhouse, Mary		1	4		3
Hillhouse, William	1				
Higgins, Nemamiah	1	3	3		
Trowbridge, Joseph, 2nd	2	1	3		
Parmalie, Hezekiah	2	1	3		
Gibson, Hannah			3		
Tuttle, Richard	1		6		
Belfast (Negroe)				5	
Primus (Negroe)				3	
Smith, Israel	1		1		
Dixon, James	1		3		
Luke (Negroe)				3	
Parmalie, Simion	1	2	3		
Reed, Sussanah			3		
Mansfield, Richstead	1	1	6		
Mansfield, Moses	1		1		
Edwards, Revd Jonathan	3		4		
Woodhull, Richard	1				
Brainard, Joshua	1	1	2	2	
Lines, Major	1	3	6		
Lines, Ebenezer	1		1		
Jones, Isaac	1	4	4	1	
Ball, Hezekiah	1		3		
Bird, Sarah	1		3		
Breed, Newell	2	2	1		
Stillwell, Mary			2		
Dummer, Edward	1		1		
Edwards, Perpont	1	4	5		2
Burrel, Thomas	4	3	4		
Dwight, Samuel	1		2		
Hubbard, Daniel	1	2	1		
Wales, Revd Samuel	2	3	2	1	1
Feilds, Thomas	1	1	2		
Punderson, Thomas	3	3	3		
Punderson, Samuel	1	2	5		
Alling, Christopher	1	1	5		
Hotchkiss, Ely	2		3		
Reed, Daniel	2	3	1		
Gorham, Stephan	1	4	4		
Auger, Abraham	1	1	2		
Fry, Christopher	1		2		
Towers, Joshua	1	3	2		
Attwater, Holbrook	1	1	4		
Hill, Amos	1		1		
Hendrick, Coe	1	2	1		
Tuttle, Hezekiah	3		3		
Tuttle, Abner	1	2	1		
Alling, Hezekiah	1		1		
Ives, Levi	2	2	5		
Scott, William	1	1	4		
Benham, Lemuel	1	2	5		
Lenard, Tim (Negroe)				3	
Camp, Jesse	2	1	3		
Johnson, Peter	2	3	6		
Auger, Hezekiah	2	1	6		
Auger, Isaac	1	3	2		
Thompson, Abraham	3				
Mix, Anna			1		
Eli (Negroe)				6	
Tappen, John	1	1	2		
Nicolls, Christopher	1	1	2		
Hotchkiss, Hannah	1		2		
Attwater, Jonah	1		1		
Smith, John	1	1	3		
Hotchkiss, Eneas	1	1	4		
Harry (Negroe)				2	
Hibbard, Samuel	1	2	1		
Mix, Timothy	1		4		
Dorchester, Abigel			2		
Murray, James	1	2	4		
Robinson, Samuel	1	1	3		
Oshall, John	1		4		
Warner, John	2		3	1	
Osborn, Hill	1		2		
Hotchkiss, Nemamiah	1	3	2		
Peck, Nicholas	1				
Dagget, Sue (Negroe)				4	
Parrett, Martin	1	2	4		

NEW HAVEN CITY—con.

NAME OF HEAD OF FAMILY.	Free white males of 16 years and upward, including heads of families.	Free white males under 16 years.	Free white females, including heads of families.	All other free persons.	Slaves.
Gain (Negroe)				1	
Amey (Negroe)				3	
Lambert, George	1	1	2		
Talmage, Timothy	1		2		
Osborn, Mary			3		
Attwater, Eldad	1	2	3		
Ball, Oliver	1		3		
Upsom, Jesse	1	1	4		
Barnes, Ezra	1	1	1		
Place, Joe (Negroe)				2	
Jane (Negroe)				10	
Granis, Nathaniel	1	3	3		
Row, Stephan	2	1	3		
Osborn, Jeremiah	1		1		
Barnes, Soloman	1	1	4		
Alling, Roger	1		1		
Bracket, Mosses	1		3		
Munson, David	1	1	3		
Devenport, John	1		1		
Tuttle, Hoy	1	2	3		
Osborn, Benjamin	1	1	3		
Attwater, David	1	1	2		
Ball, Joseph	1		1		
Ball, David	1	1	1		
Brown, Bersheba	1	1	3		
Ceaser (Negroe)				3	
Humiston, Ebenezer	1	3	3		
Roles, James			1		
Burke, Flizabeth			1		
Pendergrass, John	1		1		
Gowan, William	1				
Hotchkiss, Leman	1				
Carr, James	1				
Potter, Seate	1				
McCoy, James	1				
Isaacs, Brown	1				
Sperry, Joseph	1				
Smith, Jesse	1				
Pickets, William	1				
Law, Francis	1				
McHolland, Hugh	1				
Parral, David	1				
Mathews, Thomas	1				
Lickleter, James	1				
Green, Daniel	1				
Hicks, Samuel	1				
Vanorden, John	1				
Clarke, Ebenezer	1				
Bates, Elias	1				
Smith, Joseph	1				
Law, Francis	1				
Tuft, Joshua	1				
Peet, Sherman	1				
McCurn, Malecton	1				
Dummer, Jonathan	1				
Little, Samuel	1				
Raymond, John	1				
Jennings, William	1				
Miller, Stephen	1				
Stephenson, Thomas	1				
Fenton, Jonathan	1				
Malery (Widow)			1		
Jutt, Joseph	1				
Dukerman, Elisha	1				
Smith, Thomas	1				
Bullard, Ely	1				
Dickerman, Joseph	1				
Mason, Peter	1				
Wilmot, Thomas	1		1		
Punderson, Lizey			1		
Wilmot, Ebenezer	1				
Beecher, Stephen	1				
Gourd, Thomas	1				
Mix (Widow)			1		
Hendrick, Sarah		1	2		
Mallery, Elinor			1		
Warner, Elizebeth		1	1		
Dennis, John	1				
Mahan, Phillip	1				
Clime, Pillip	1	1	2		
Atkins, Benoni	2	1	5		
Martin, John	1	1	1		
Bradley, Lewis	1	1	4		
Bradley, Elizabeth	1		1		
Bradley, Alexander	1	1	3		
Drowney, Mary			1		
Bradley, Hezekiah	1	1	5		
Chatterton, Stephen	1	1	1		
Hotchkiss, Lemuel	3	1	4	1	
Hotchkiss, Lyman	1	1	3		
Hotchkiss, Joshua	2		1		
New, John	1	1	2		
Hotchkiss, Silus	3	3	2		
Hotchkiss, Elijur	2	1	3		
Thompson, James	2	4	2		

NEW HAVEN CITY—con.

NAME OF HEAD OF FAMILY.	Free white males of 16 years and upward, including heads of families.	Free white males under 16 years.	Free white females, including heads of families.	All other free persons.	Slaves.
Downey, James	1		3		
Thompson, Elisha	4	3	5		
Moore, Francis	1		2		
Baldwin, Silas	1		2		
Bunce, David	2	3	2		
Heppborn, Lewis	1	1	4		
Osborn, Medad	2	2	5		
Hotchkiss, Caleb	1		1		
Hotchkiss, Punderson	2		3		
Hotchkiss, Elisha	1		3		
Thompson, James	1		3		
Bradley, Soloman	1		4		
Sperry, William	4	3	3		
Hotchkiss, John	1	1	1		
Sperry, Levi	1	2	3		
Way, Job	1		2		
Sperry, Edon	2	1	2		
Lines, Cornelius	1	1	1		
Bradley, Griffin	1		2		
Warner, Abraham	1		3		
Lines, Asbael	1	3	5		
Bradley, Erastus	1	1	3		
Bradley, Martha			3		
Culver, John	2	2	4		
Dickerman, Isaac	1	1	5		
Strong, Moses	1				
Dickerson, Benjamin	2	1	1		
Rexford, Phillip	1		1		
Baldwin, John	2	1	4		
Ball, Glover	1	3	3		
Ball, John	2	2	5		
Ares, William	1	3	1		
Harding, Fredrick	1		2		
Hull, David	2	4	1		
Johnson, Stephen	1		1		
Johnson, Abraham	1		3		
Sabin, Charles	1	1	3		
Alling, Daniel	4		4		
Alling, Philo	1	3	3		
Alling, Caleb	1	1	4		
Alling, Silas	2	3	3		
Chaise, Isaac	1		3		
Alling, Edward	1	1	1	1	
Russell, Samuel	1	3	4		
Beecher, Samuel	1	2	3		
Wolcot, Elisha	1	3	1		
Beecher, Medad	1		4		
Beecher, Raphel	1	1	6		
Beecher, Samuel	1		3		
Beecher, Lowes	1	1	3	1	
Alling, Amos	1	1	3		
Humpherville, Ebenezer	1		2		
Humpherville, Joseph	1	1	1		
Humpherville, Moses	1		2		
Humpherville, Lemuel	2	1	6		
Pardie, Moses	2		5	1	
Humpherville, Samuel	1		5		
Pardie, Sibel	2		3		
Humpherville, Samuel	1	1	2		
Smith, Nathan	3		4		
Smith, Gould	1		2		
Meloy, John	1	1	2		
Lancashire, Abigal			1		
Johnson, Eneas	2		3		
Johnson, Ebenezer	3	3	3		
Johnson, Lidia	1		3		
Alling, John	1	1	4		
Loyd, Jabez	1	1	5		
Thomas, Susanah			1		
Tuttle, Daniel	2		6		
Pool, Samuel	1		3		
Alling, Susannah			2		
Johnson, John	1	2	4		
Beecher, Moses	2		4		
Beecher, Moses, 2nd	1	1	2		
Alling, Joseph	3		4		
Alling, Stephen	2	3	4		
Thomas, Joseph	1	5	3		
Prindle, Joseph	2	1	3		
Prindle, Elisha	2	3	4		
Prindle, John	1	3			
Prindle, Elizabeth			3		
Prindle, Dina	1	2	3		
Benham, David	1		3		
Stebbens, Uriah	1	1	5		
Graham, Elenor			1		
Smith, Oliver	2	1	5		
Bristol, David	2	3	3		
Bristol, David, 2nd	1	1	1		
Jones, John	2		4		
Brown, Jonathan	2		3		
Benham, John, 2nd	1	2	2		
Benham, John	3	1	3		
Smith, Edward	1	1	5		
Benham, Gamaliel	1	2	3		

NEW HAVEN CITY—con.

NAME OF HEAD OF FAMILY.	Free white males of 16 years and upward, including heads of families.	Free white males under 16 years.	Free white females, including heads of families.	All other free persons.	Slaves.
Murrain, Jonas	1	2	2		
Murrain, Margeret			3		
Clarke, Thadeus	2	1	5		
Clarke, Merrit	1	7	1	1	
Clarke, Abigal	2		2	1	
Murran, Joseph	2		2		1
Platt, Josiah	1				
Platt, Anna	1	1	6		
Hoase, Sarah		2	5		
Down, Job	1	2	2		
Down, Benjamin	3	3	3		
Down, Nathaniel	2		3		
Plat, Mary			1		
Merrick, Josiah	1				
Hoy, Daniel	1				
Thomas, Asael	2				
Smith, Samuel B	1	4	4		
Smith, Phlomon	1	2	1		
Candie, Isaac	1	1	5		
Bingley, Hannah			1		
Kimberly, Asael	1	3	3		
Willington, Noah	2		3		
Candie, Samuel	1		5		
Kimberly, Nathaniel	1	2	3		
Kimberly, Silas	2	5	6		
Kimberly, Israel	1	2	2		
Kimberly, Mary			2	1	
Kimberly, Gilead	1	1	3		1
Reynolds, James	1		1		1
Reynolds, James B	1	1	2	1	
Reynolds, Fredrick	1	1	2		
Catlin, John	1		2		
Trowbridge, William	1		1		
Trowbridge, Samuel	1	1	1		
Stevans, John	1	1	1		
Williams, Joatham	1		2		
Bunham, Thomas	1	1	3		
Painter, Thomas	1	1	2		
Smith, Joseph	1		4		
Smith, Samuel	1		5		
Smith, Darcus	1	1	2		
Smith, Wharam	1		4		
Beecher, Isaac	1	1	4		
Smith, Benjamin	1	1	2		
Smith, Thomas	1		5		
Smith, Nathan	1	3	5		
Smith, George	1		1		
Smith, Jeremiah	2		6		
Alling John	1		4		
Smith, Benjamin, 2nd	1		2	4	
Steephens, Jesse		3	2		
Bemmer, Mary		3	2		
Bemmer, Nathaniel	1	1	2		
Ward, Thomas	1	1	1		
Trowbridge, David	1	1	4		
Clarke, Mary			4		
Toles, Bethsheba		1	1		
Clarke, Thompson	1	1	7		
Beldin, Jerad	1		1		
Belding, Rachel			3		
Steephens, David	1	3	1		
Smith, Titus	1	3	3		
Smith, Huldy	2		1		
Thomas, Rhoda		1	1		
Thomas, Aron	1	3	5		
Ward, Sibel		2	3		
Thompson, Stephen	1	1	2		
Smith, Eli	1	1	2		
Smith, Andrew	2	1	5		
James, Dolly	1	1	2		
Thomas, Edward	3	1	5		
Thomas, Daniel	1		1		1
Willoby, Christopher	1	1	1		
Thomas, Hester		2	2		
Johnson, John	1	2	1		
Smith, Nehamiah	1	1	2		
Smith, Justice	1	1	4		
Thomas, Benjamin	2	2	5		
Beecher, Titus	1		5		
Latherby, David	1		4		
Richard, John	2	3	5		
Clarke, Daniel	1		2		
Ward, Henry	1		2		
Thompson, Margeret	1		1		
Allen, Ebenezer	1	2	5		
Allen, Elijah	2		3		
Ward, John	1		3		

NORTH HAVEN TOWN.

NAME OF HEAD OF FAMILY.	Free white males of 16 years and upward, including heads of families.	Free white males under 16 years.	Free white females, including heads of families.	All other free persons.	Slaves.
Tharp, Titus	1	1	4	1	
Tharp, Mosses	1	1	2	1	
Benham, Samuel	1				
Thomas, Sarah			1		
Peter (Negroe)				3	

NEW HAVEN COUNTY—Continued.

NORTH HAVEN TOWN—continued.

NAME OF HEAD OF FAMILY.	Free white males of 16 years and upward, including heads of families.	Free white males under 16 years.	Free white females, including heads of families.	All other free persons.	Slaves.
White Sarah			3		
Hull, Abner	1		2		
Blakesley, Enos	1	1	3		
Barnes, Enoch	1		2		
Sandford, Jeremiah	1		1		
Tharp, Asa	1	1	1		
Todd, Samuel	1		1		
Barnes, Jonathan	1	4	1		
Smith, Abiel	1		2		
Bracket, Eneas	1		4		
Bracket, Eneas, 2nd	1	3	3		
Spencer, John	1		1		
Holly, Miller	1		2		
Doolittle, Joseph	1	3	3		
Tuttle, David	1		1		
Bradley, Diamond	1	3	3		
Bradly, Joseph	1		2		
Bradley, Thomas	1	2	2		
Day, William	3	1	5	1	
Ives, Noah	3	2	3		
Ives, Daniel	1	3	4		
Ives, Alling	1		1		
Ives, Sarah	1		5		
Walter, Mahitabel			2		
Walter, Jacob	2	2	2		
Todd, Seth	2	1	5		
Bracket, Giles	1	1	4		
Seeley, John	2	2	1		
Tuttle, John	1	1	4		
Ives, Sussanah			1		
Mix, Samuel	3		5	1	
Clarke, Caleb	2	1	4		
Cooper, Joel	1				
Cooper, Joel, 2nd	2	1	1		
Cooper, Justice	1		4		
Cooper, Joseph	1	1	4		
Mix, Stephen	1		1		1
Eaton, Timothy	1		6		
Eaton, Titus	2	1	1		
Brokes, Limeuel	1	2	2		
Tharp, Samuel	1		6		
Fowler, Jeremiah	1	4	5		
Mansfield, Richard	2	2	1		
Dayton, John, 2nd	1		2		
Tomlinson, Robert	1	1	4		
Starry, Nathan	1	1	8		
Munson, Walter	2		3		
Munson, Mansfield	1	1	3		
Passett, Joel	2	2	3		
Simmons, Joshua	1	3	4		
Cooper, Joseph, 2nd	1	1	2		
Ives, James	2	3	3		
Jacobs, Steven	2	3	7		
Jacobs, Eli	1				
Craine, William	1	2	5		
Tuttle, Simeon	1		1		
Darling, Joseph	1	1	3		
Arnold, John	1	1	4		
Bishop, Joy	1		1		
Todd, Enos	1	1	2	1	
Dayton, Jonathan	2	1	4		
Dayton, Cornelius	1	1	2		
Todd, Isaac	1	1	1		
Tharp, David, 2nd	4		1		
Tuttle, Deborah	2		1		
Tuttle, Abigal			2		
Tuttle, Joel	1	2	4		
Tuttle, Jonathan	2	1	3		
Eastman, Peter	2	1	2	1	
Bradley, Ebenezer	1		1		
Bradley, Ebenezer, 2nd	1				
Tuttle, Soloman	1	2	6		
Todd, Caleb	1	1	2		
Todd, Lyman	1		2		
Tuttle, Hezekiah	2	4	2		
Tuttle, Ethmah	4	4	3		
Tuttle, Isaac	1	1	1		
Buckley, Job	2	1	4		
Todd, Ethmah	1				
Tyler, Josep	1	2	5		
Todd, Titus	2	1	3		
Bracket, Samuel	1		1		
Bassett, Joseph	2	1	3		
Tuttle, Samuel	1	1	2		
Bishop, Simion	1	2	3		
Bishop, Benjamin	4	1	3		
Bishop, Joy, 2nd	3	2	5		
Blakesley, Seth	1	1	6		
Blakeley, Zelus	1	2	4		
Hill, Stepen	1		1		
Hill, John	1		3		
Blakesley, Caleb	1	3	3		
Tuttle, Ezra	2	1	3		
Bishop, Abel	3	3	2		
Bassett, Jehu	1		1		

NORTH HAVEN TOWN—continued.

NAME OF HEAD OF FAMILY.	Free white males of 16 years and upward, including heads of families.	Free white males under 16 years.	Free white females, including heads of families.	All other free persons.	Slaves.
Cooper, James	1		1		
Mansfield, Thomas	2		2		2
Humiston, Ephrahim	3	1	4		
Bradley, Justus	1	1	3		
Andrews, Mary		2	4		
Todd, Etham	1		4		
Tuttle, Limuel	1		2		
Turner, Edward	1	1	2		
Ralph, Jonathan	2	1	4		
Trumbull, Benjamin	2	1	5		
Stiles, Clarke	1	2	4		
Parker, John	1	1	4		
Jacobs, Enoch	1	2	3		
Todd, Daniel	1	2	4		
Todd, Joel	1		1		
Todd, Soloman	1		2		
Todd, Hezekiah	2	1	3		
Sacket, Joel	1		2		
Peirpoint, Samuel	2	1	4		
Todd, Bethuel	1	1	3		
Thomas, Josiah	1		2		
Selby, Abraham	1		1		
Selby, Abraham, 2nd	1	1	1		
Barnes, Benjamin	1	1	3		
Parker, Edmond	1	2	3		
Hull, Daniel	2		3		
Beach, Elasa	2	4	6		
Sacket, Soloman	1	2	4		
Ray, Enoch	2		3		
Sacket, Eli	1	4	4		
Ray, Thomas	1				
Beach, Giles	2	1	1		
Beach, Nathaniel	4	3	3		
Frost Titus	2	3	3		
Frost, John	1	1	2		
Frost, John, 2nd	1	1	1		
Sandford, Thomas	2		1		
Heaton, John	1	1	3		2
Heaton, John	2	2	3		
Burke, Ebenzer	1		2		
Stephens, Ashael	1	1	1		
Bracket, Richard	2		1		
Barnes, Justice	1	2	3		
Bracket, Levi	2	2	3		
Bracket, Benjamin	2	1	6		
Bracket, Abel	1	2	3		
Bracket, Stephen	1	2	2		
Button, Jedediah	1	2	1		
Barnes, Seth	2	2	3		
Barnes, David	1	2	2		
Houghton, Giles	2	2	1		
Ray, Levi	3	1	5		
Cooper, Caleb	1		3		
Barnes, John	2		4		
Heaton, Calhoun	3	2	2		
Sandford, Eliadia	1		3		
Humiston, Thomas	1		2		
Jacobs, David	1		1		
Jacobs, Soloman	1	3	2		
Bracket, Ebenezer	3		3		
Sandford, John	1	1	5		
Sandford, William	2	2	4		
Cooper, Thomas	2	1	1		
Bracket, John	2		1		
Bracket, Isaiah	1	3	2		
Barnes, Noah	1	2	3		
Cooper, Isaac	1	2	2		
Pardy, Eliphalet	2	1	2		
Pardy, David	1	1	3		
Pardy, James	1	1	4		
Pardie, John	1	1	3		
Cooper, Thomas	2	4	3		
Cooper, John	1	1	3		
Peirpoint, John	1	1	1		
Peirpoint, James	2	1	4		
Peirpoint, Joseph	2		1		
Barnes, Joshua	1	2	3		
Wolcutt, Thomas	1		3		
Peirpoint, Hezekiah	1	1	3		
Barnes, Joel	2	1	6		
Barnes, Jerry	1	1	2		
Perth, Andrew	1		2		
Peirpoint, Thomas	2	1	3		
Sacket, Samuel	3		3		
Bracket, Joseph	2	3	3		
Jacobs, Joseph	1	2	3		
Jacobs, Ezekiel	1	1	2		
Robinson, Mosses	1	2	3		
Todd, Gideon	1		6		
Blakesley, Philomen	1	1	2		
Blakesley, Amos	1	2	2		
Tharp, Abner	1		4		
Blakesley, Isaac	1	2	3		
Hubbel, Lewis	1	3	3		
Smith, John	1	1	1		

NORTH HAVEN TOWN—continued.

NAME OF HEAD OF FAMILY.	Free white males of 16 years and upward, including heads of families.	Free white males under 16 years.	Free white females, including heads of families.	All other free persons.	Slaves.
Smith, Thankfull		5	2		
Smith, James	1		2		
Smith, Thomas	1		2		
Smith, Lidia	1	1	2		
Peirpoint, Joseph	1		2		
Hull, Joseph	1		3		
Hull, Joseph, 2nd	1	5	3		
Turner, Caleb	1		1		
Hull, John	2	4	3		
Hull, Benjamin	1	2	2		
Hull, Amie	1		3		
Peirpoint, Benjamin	2	1	1		
Peirpoint, Giles	1	2	1		
Peirpoint, Joel	1		1		
Todd, James	1		1		
Todd, Yale	1	2	2		
Blakesley, Zopher	3		2		
Blakesley, Abraham	1	2	1		
Blakesley, Joel	2	2	5	1	
Clarke, Phineas	1	3	2		
Bassett, Jehu	1		4		
Clinton, Lawrence	1	1	2		
Johnson, Stephen	1	1	2		
Bradley, Zewer	1	1	4		
Bradley, Obed	3	1	3		
Blakesley, Jonah	1	2	2		
Tuttle, Ruben	1		1		
Jones, Samuel	1	2	2		
Bradley, Joel	1		2		
Blakesley, John	1		2		
Bassett, Daniel	2	1	2		
Bassett, Isaac	1	1	1		
Bassett, Lidia	1	1	2		
Bassett, Samuel, 2nd	1	4	3		
Bassett, Obed	1		3		
Bassett, Samuel	1		1		
Doolittle, Daniel	3	3	5		
Alling, Joathem	1	2	6		
Humiston, James	1	3	4		
Hayes, John	1		2		
Tharp, Timothy	1	1	3		
Bradley, Titus	3	2	5		
Tharp, David	3	2	1		
WALLINGFORD TOWN.					
Meeker, Nathaniel	1		1		
Gulbin, Oepas	1	1	3		
Butler, Comfort	2	2	5		
Scovil, David	1	3	3		
Yale, John	2	2	4		
Hubbard, Watts	2	2	4		
London, Charles	1	1	2		
Lark, John	2	1	2		
Lark, Solomon	1				
Edwards, Jonathan	1				
Farrington, Jeremiah	2	1	4		
Crane, Daniel	2	5	1		
Austin, Noah	2		2		
Wholf, Seth D	1	2	2		
Collins, Jonathan	2	3	4		
Hall, Rufus	2	1	4		
Collins, Edward	1		1		
Collins, Edward, 2nd	1	1	2	1	
Forster, Thomas	6	1	3		
Stow, Thomas	1	1	1		
Merriman, Jesse	1	2	2		
Merriman, Josiah	1	3	1		
Person, Joel	1		4		
Benham, Jerad	1	3	3		
Robinson, John	1		1		
Forster, Giles	1	4	5		
Forster, Timothy	2		2		
Merriman, Caleb	2		2		
Merriman, Caleb, 2nd	2	3	2		
Merriman, William	2		2		
Austin, John	1		1		
Merriman, Asaph	1	4	2		
Meriman, Nathaniel	2	1	3		
Merriman, Edmond	1	2	3		
Merriman, Benjamin	2	1	2		
Merriman, Jesse	1		1		
Miriman, John	1	2	5	1	
Mix, Joel	1		1		
Forster, Phebe	1		1		
Hough, Louis	2	1	4		
Hough, Samuel, 2nd	1		2		
Hough, Mathew	1	2	1		
Hull, George	1		2		
Barnes, Abel	1	1	1		
Hough, Philip	1		2		
Hough, James	2	4	3		
Scovel, Elizabeth	2	1	4		
Scovel, Elisha	2	1	4		
Hollebut, Daniel	1				

NEW HAVEN COUNTY—Continued.

NAME OF HEAD OF FAMILY.	Free white males of 16 years and upward, including heads of families.	Free white males under 16 years.	Free white females, including heads of families.	All other free persons.	Slaves.
WALLINGFORD TOWN—continued.					
Forster, David	1	2	3		
Shayler, Joseph	2	1	5		
Piper, Jude	1	2	4		
Ways, Abner	1	1	1		
Hall, Elizabeth	1	1	3		
Ways, John	2	1	2		
Ives, Timothy	1	2	5	1	
Hall, Enos	1	1	1		
Hall, Moses	1	1	2		
Gale, Mathew	1		1		
Hall, Elisha	1		3		
Ives, Amos	1	2	4		
Hull, Josiah, 2nd	1	1	2		
Hall, Brenton	3	5	4	1	
Hall, Daniel	2	1	4		
Yeoman, John	1	2	5		
Bin, Isaac	3		5		
Ives, Elnathan	2		3		
Yale, Jonathan	2	1	4		
Breford, Benjamin	1	2	3		
Andrews, Thomas	1	1	2		
Burres, John	2	4	3		
Yale, Nathaniel	2	3	3		
Yale, Daniel	1	3	3		
Yale, Anna			1		
Hough, Samuel	1	2	3		
Darling, Samuel	1	3	3		
Hall, Samuel	2	3	4	2	1
Collins, Daniel	2	2	4	1	
Lyman, Aron	1		1		
Willard, John	1		2		
Curtis, Levi	1		1		
Couch, John	1		1		
Couch, John, 2nd	1	3	1		
Yale, Noah	1		1		
Yale, Amiton	1		2		
Perkins, Simeon	2	3	5		
Coben, John	1		3		
Coben, James, 2nd	1	2	2		
Merriman, Joseph	3	1	4		
Andrews, Nicholas	1				
Andrews, Lidia		1	4		
Andrews, Moses	1	2	4		
Merriman, Ephrim	1	2	4		
Merriman, Aron	1	1	3		
Butler, Ezra	1		4		
Andrews, Sarah		1	1		
Bucket, Runnel	1				
Merriman, Samuel	1	1	2		
Todd, Caleb	2		3		
Merriman, Elisha	1	2	3		
Yale, Nathaniel	1				
Johnson, Israel	1	2	3		
Livenston, Daniel	1		1		
Griswold, Giles	1	2	6		
Lawrence, Elihu	1	3	2		
Merriman, Titus	2		3		
Merriman, Joel	1				
Carter, John	1		4		
Baldwin, Smith	1				
Baldwin, Nathaniel	1	1	1		
Collins, Giles	2	1	6		
Duglass, Nathaniel	1	1	4		
Douglass, Levi	1		3		
Holly, Abel	1		1		
Rice, Samuel	2	2	5		
Rice, Ezekiel	3	1	2		
Merriman, Amassa	2	3	2		
Livenston, Eunice			1		
Attwater, Isaac	1	3	3		
Miles, John	1		1		
Hotchkiss, Samuel	1		1		
Attwater, Eunice		1	2		
Attwater, Stephen	1				
Attwater, David	1				
Holt, Nathaniel	1	1	1		
Hall, Israel	2	2	4		
Rice, Amassa	1	2	5		
Hall, Aron	2	1	5		
Johnson, Silder	1		2		
Rice, Ezra	1	1	3		
Rice, Joel	1	4	4		
Johnson, Samuel	1	1	1		
Johnson, William B	1	2	3		
Cole, Ebenezer	2	1	2		
McKeys, Daniel	2		2		
Robinson, Theophilus M	1	2	3		
Robinson, Levi	1	1	5		
Hough, Oliver	1				
Holt, Aron	2		2		
Cowls, Timothy	2	2	4		
Cowls, Joseph	1		1		
Johnson, William	1	2	3		
Hall, Enos, 2nd	1	1	3		
Yale, Ashal	1	2	2		
WALLINGFORD TOWN—continued.					
Holt, Daniel	1	1	2		
Holt, Daniel, 2nd	1		1		
Holt, Benjamin	1		1		
Mitchell, Asaph	1	1	2		
Austin, Abel	4	1	5		
Andrews, Dana	2	1	3		
Levit, Samuel	1		1		
Yale, Noah	1		2		1
Yale, Joel	1	1	3		
Lyman, Phineas	1	2	4		
Hubbard, Isaac	2	2	4	1	
Yale, Nathaniel	1				
Defforrest, David	1				
Clarke, Lamberton	1		4		
Hall, Joatham	1		3		
Aubony, Susannah		1	2		
Ives, John	3	2	3		
Cooke, Benjamin	1	3	4		
Merriman, Thomas	1	1	4		
Brainard, David	1				
Francis, Joseph			5		
Merriman, Nathaniel	1	1	4		
Hall, Street	1		2		
Morse, Joel	1	3	1		
Metune, Ebenezer	1		2		
Molthrop, Timothy	1				
Matune, John	1	1	1		
Matune, Caleb	1		5		
Tharp, Elnathan	1	2	2		
Hall, Street T	1		1		
Ackley. Dina			4		
Alling, Archibald		3	4		
Curtis, Philip	1		1		
Curtis, Phillip, 2nd	1	1	1		
Curtis, Joseph	1		3		
Curtis, Joel	1	2	2	1	
Winston, John	1		2		
Durow, Daniel	1	3	2		
Reed, John	1	4	1		
Bertow, Benjamin	1		2		
Chipman, Joseph	1	3	2		
Hart, Timothy	1	3	2		
Ives, Amos	1	5	3		
Wade, Ebenezer	1	1	2		
Swift, James	1	2	6		
Jones, Nathaniel	1	1	2		
Jones, Ruben	1	1	3		
Hall, Isaac	4	3	3	1	
Hall, Eliakim	1		1		3
Hall, Hezekiah	1	3	8		
Hall, Eliakim, 2nd	1	2	8		2
Doolittle, Isaac	1				
Matune, Samuel	1	1	3		
Booth, John	1	2	5		
Hall, Asa	1	2	2		
Hall, Ezekiel	1		1		
Blakely, Joseph	1	1	3		
Fenn, Edward, 2nd	2		1		
Blakley, Joseph, 2	1	2	1		
Fenn, Austin	2				
Fenn, Edward	1	1	3		
Hall, Thomas	1		1		1
Ives, Sarah	2	1	5		
Hall, Amassa	2	3	3		
Matune, Isaac	2		3		
Hall, David	3	2	3		
Hall, David, 2nd	1	1	1		
Francis, Amos	1	3	4		
Francis, Jacob	1		2		
Francis, Joseph	3		2		
Ives, Abel	1		2		
Ives, John, 3rd	1	3	2		
Ives, Icobod	1	1	4		
London, Ambrose	1	1	2		
Hall, Giles	2	1	5		
Hall, Ephraim	2	2	4		
Hall, Joshua	1		2		
Hall, Samuel, 2nd	1				
Hall, Luben	1	1	3		
Hall, Benjamin	3	2	2		
Douglass, John	1	2	1		
Matune, Hester			2		
Andrews, Marvel	1				
Swift, Daniel	1				
Jolly, Martha			2		
Hotchkiss, Ambrose	1				
Baldwin, Elizabeth			5		
Atkins, David	2	1	2		
Graham, John	1		1		
Prout, John	1		2		
Miller, Constant	1	4	4		
Baldwin, Samuel	1	2	2		
Baldwin, Daniel	1		2		
Baldwin, Daniel, 2nd	1		2		
Yeamons, Elizabeth	1	4	3		
WALLINGFORD TOWN—continued.					
Hall, Phineas	1		2		
Hall, Phineas, 2nd	1	2	2		
Hall, Levi	1				
Hall, Benjamin	1				
Hall, Israel	1				
Hall, Joash	1	1	2		
Tharp, Jerad	1		1		
Wade, John, 2nd	1	1	1		
Hall, John	4	1	3		
Berry, Asael	1	2	4		
Whiting, Samuel	2	1	5		
Ives, Samuel	2	2	4		
Ives, Bazelel	2		2		
Ives, John	3	2	3		
Ives, Levi	1	1	3		
Curtis, Abel	4	2	4		
Hall, Isaac	4	4	6		
Freeman (Negroe)				4	
Perkins, Stephen	1	1	2		
Hough, Ensign	1	2	4		
Hall, Theophilus	2	2	4		
Carter, Benjamin	6	4	4		
Webb, John	1		1		
Baldwin, Ebenezer	1				
Mitchel, Moses	1		2		
Mitchel, Zenus	2	1	4		
Rinbal, Rachael			1		
Smith, William	1	1	1		
Curtis, Elisha	1	1	4		
Avery, Edmond	1	2	3		
Austin, Amos	1	3	4		
Smith, Elizabeth	1		2		
Voce, Jesse	1		1		
Cooke, Jesse	1		5		
Peck, Stephen	2	1	4		
Ives, Abijah	1	1	3		
Rice, Amos	4		3		
Clarke, Daniel	2	1	2		
Curtis, Jacob	1	1	2		
Hull, Eunice		2	3		
Rice, James	2	4	4		
Yale, Stephen	2	2	3		
Peck, Nicholas	2		2		
Murren, Thomas	4		5		
Andrews, Anson	2	4	2		
Clarke, Archibald	2		1		
Woodruf, Samuel	1	2	2		
Mix, Josiah	2	3	5		
Colly, George	1		1		
Carter, John	1		4		
Pane, William	1		1		
Day, Stephen	1	3	6		
Day, Israel	1		1		
Tuttle, Charles	2	1	4		
Beamont, Deoadah	1	1	3		
Peck, Samuel	2	1	6		
Chittenton, Benjamin	1	4	2		
Andrews, Stephen	3		3		
Barnes, Samuel	1	1	3		
Mansfield, John	3	1	1		
Cooke, Amos	1		3		
Morse, Ebenezer	3	1	4		
Johnson, Miles	1	3	3		
Street, Caleb	1	1	6		
Lewis, Samuel	3	1	4		
Carrington, Jerem	4	2	3		
Wettlesey, Elisha, 2	1	3	4		
Noyce, James	1		4		1
Bissinton, Robert	1		1		
Bissinton, Heil	2	1	2		
Hall, Prudence	2	2	2		
Ackley, Aron	2	3	6		
Bissinton, Asael	2	1	6		
Rogers, Gideon	3	2	5		
McCleave, John	1	1	2		
Merriman, Caleb	1	3	2		1
Persons, Aron	1	2	4		
Smith, Daniel	1	3	1		
Gales, Moses	2	1	2		
Street, Samuel	1		2		
Catlin, William	1		2		
Street, Elnathan	1		1		2
Potter, Jerad	1		2		
Hall, Charles	1	3	3		
Carrington, Jerh, 2nd	1	1	2		
Marks, James	1	2	3		
Marks, Levi	1	2	1		
Doolittle, Daniel	1		1		
Vanette, James	1	3	2		
Lovewell, Fredrick	1				
Downs, Elizabeth			1		
Downs, Sarah		1	2		
Ives, Fitch	1				
Ives, Elnathan	1				
Ives, Noel	1				

NEW HAVEN COUNTY—Continued.

NAME OF HEAD OF FAMILY.	Free white males of 16 years and upward, including heads of families.	Free white males under 16 years.	Free white females, including heads of families.	All other free persons.	Slaves.
WALLINGFORD TOWN—continued.					
Camp, Amos	1	1	1		
Hough, Joseph	1	1	2		
Hough, Joseph, 2	2	1	5		
Hart, Benjamin	1	1	5		
Yale, Samuel	1	3	2		
Rice, Justice	1	1	1		
Parker, Daniel	2	1	4		
Rice, Abner	1	4	3		
Rice, Moses	1		1		5
Rice, Amos	1	1	2		
Hough, Ephrim	2	3	5		
Hough, Andrew	1	1	4		
Hough, Lidia			1		
Baldwin, James	1	1	2		
Sanderson, William	2		3		
Davidson, John	1	1	1		
Berry, Thomas	1	1	2		
Cobin, Joseph	1	1	1		
Alling, Amby			1		
Rice, Joseph	1	3	3		
Gale, Elihu	1	3	5		
Andrews, Bartholomew	2	1	3		
Hull, John	1	2	3		
Wollcot, Samuel	1	3	2		
Austin, Ezra	1	1	4		
Hall, Andrew	1	1			
Tyler, Samuel	3	1	7		
Hough, Lent	1	1	3		
Hull, Charles	1	1	3		
Hull, Ebenezer	1	2	4		
Stanley, Abraham	1	1	1	2	
Adwick, William	1				
Bunker, James	1				
Dudley, John	2		3		
Hall, Joel	1	1	3		1
Newton, Aron	1	1	1		
Cooke, Ephrahim	3	4	3		
Parker, Arnold	1	1	2		
Ives, Abigal			1		
Davison, Samuel	1				
Davison, Anna			3		
Tyler, John	1				
Owing, Patience		1	2		
Tyler, Jerad	3	1	3		
Persons, Samuel	1		3		
Clarke, James	1	1	2		
Parker, Benjamin	1	2	3		
Hill, Molly			1		
Parker, Elliady	2		2		
Parker, Levi	1	3	3		
Rice, Thadeus	2		6		
Hitchcock, Nathaniel	1	1	5		
Beach, Mary	1	1	3		
Gales, John	1	1	2		
Preston, Samuel	3	3	4		
Parker, Joshua	2	3	7		
Distin, Josep	1	2	4		
Parker, Waitfull	1		1		
Parker, Charles	2	1	2		
Hummiston, James	2	1	2		
Hummiston, James, 2nd	1		1		
Ives, John	2	2	7		
Beach, Moses	1	2	2		
Beach, Titus	1				
Rice, Samuel	1		2		
Cobert, James		2	3		
Way, David	1	1	3		
Yale, Joel	1		3		
Cobert, Hannah			2		
Worthinton, Elizabeth		1	1		
Hitchcock, Hannah		1	4		
Parker, Gamaleel	2	3	2		
Parker, Ephrim	1	2	5		
Parker, Amos	1		3		
Hitchcock, Joash	1	1	2		
Beach, William	2		3		
Johnson, Dan	2	5	3		
Johnson, Soloman	3	2	4		
Beach, Stephen	1	4	5		
Conner, Elizabeth			3		
Bard, James	1		2		
Parker, Isaac	1	1	2		
Tyler, Jason	1	1	3		
Johnson, Dayton	3		2		
Parker, Joseph	2		7		
Beech, John	3	4	3		1
Cooke, Thaddeus	2		6		5
Preston, Benjamin	1		5		
Cooke, Samuel	2	4	4		
Preston, Titus	1	1	2		
Parker, Eliakim	1	1	4		
Dudley, Zebulon	2		4		
Hitchcock, Dan	1	4	5		
Johnson, John	1	1	2		
How, Noah	1	1	4		

NAME OF HEAD OF FAMILY.	Free white males of 16 years and upward, including heads of families.	Free white males under 16 years.	Free white females, including heads of families.	All other free persons.	Slaves.
WALLINGFORD TOWN—continued.					
Johnson, David	1	4	2		
Frost, Amos	1	1	2		
Tuttle, Beni	1		6		
Tuttle, Jonathan	2	1	3		
Tuttle, Jetus	1				
Johnson, Ephraim	3		3		
Johnson, Hezekiah	2	1	5		
Fitch, Lidia			3		
Dudley, Dyer	1	5	5		
Jones, Theophilus	1	1	2		3
Doolittle, Joseph	2		2		
Doolittle, Oliver	1	1	3		
Merriman, George	2	1	6		
Hall, Elihu	1	4	3		8
Benham, Lettice			3		
Hotchkiss, Anna			1		
Stephensen, John	1	4	2		
Munson, Eliphalet	1	3	1		
Jones, Nicholas	1		4		
Doolittle, Ruben	1	1	1		
Doolittle, Joel	2	2	2		
Jack (Negroe)				1	
Cooke, Molly		1	4		
Potter (Negroe)				2	
Cooke, David	1				
Kimberly, Thomas	1				
Fenn, Benjamin	1				
Hall, Benijah	1	1	3		
Mix, John	3	3	3		
Mix, Thomas	1				
Andrews, Nathaniel	1	3	2		
Andrews, Andrew	1		2	1	
Williams, William	1		2		
Ives, Charles	1	1	3		
Winchester, Amajh	1	2	3		
Ives, Joel	1				1
Ives, Joel, 2nd	1	2	3		
Morse, Jonathan	2	3	6		
Morse, Jonathan	1				
Morse, Levi	2	1	2		
Morse, Bemijah	1		3		
Kemp, Charles	1	1	1		
Yale, Elihu	1	1	2		
Jones, William	1		2		
Baldwin, David	2	2	4		
Hull, Jeremiah	1		4		
Hart, Nathaniel	3		3		
Rice, Hannah		1	2		
Hough, James	1	2	3		
Feild, Edmond	7		4		
Hull, John	2		3		
Hough, Joseph	1	1	2		
Hough, Joseph, 2nd	2	1	5		
Hendrick, John	1	3	3		
Ives, Ruben	1	1	1		
Curtis, Nathaniel	1	1	3		
Whittlesey, Elisha, 2nd	1				
Attwater, Caleb					
Yale Amassa	1	2	2		
Hall, Titus	2	2	4		
Smith, Elisha	2	2	4		
Sheppard. Isaac	2	1	4		
Honferd, Rubin	2	1	3		
Merriman, Elisha	1	2	4		
Hall, Sarah			3		
Sheet, Hester			2		
Parsons, Hester			1		
Cole, Hannah			2	1	
Scarrot, James	3	2	4		
Carter, Margeret			1		
Samson (Negroe)				2	
Attwater, Benjamn	1		1		
Cooke, Peter	2	3	2		
Stanley, Oliver	3	2	3		
Cooke, Caleb	2	1	4		
James, Rachael			1	1	
Rice, James	1				
Baldwin, Benja	1		1		
Voce, Charles	1		2		
Peck, Samuel, 3rd	1		2		
Cooke, Ambrose	2	1	7		
Peck, Peter	2	1	4		
Frisbee, Levi	1	1	1		
Miles, Daniel	1	2	4		
Austin, Elias	1		2		
Hull, Eldad	1	1	2		
Cooke, Isaac	1	1	5		
Ives, John, 4th	2	3	5		
Carrington, Timothy	1				
Carrington, Lemuel	1		1		
Cooke, Attwater	2	1	6		
Hull, Benjamin	3		3		
Tebbalds, Abner	1		1		
Lewis, Hester			1		
Cooke Meriman	2	4	6		

NAME OF HEAD OF FAMILY.	Free white males of 16 years and upward, including heads of families.	Free white males under 16 years.	Free white females, including heads of families.	All other free persons.	Slaves.
WALLINGFORD TOWN—continued.					
Jepbell, Abel	2	2	4		
Cooke, Hannah			1		
Doolittle, Isaac	1	1	1		
Peck, Abner	1	4	4		
Culver, Charles	1	1	2		
Culver, Benjamin	1		1		
Culver, Benjamin, 2nd	1	3	3		
Bracket, Titus	1	3	3		
Munson, Joshua	1	3	4		
Williams, Willoby	1	1	2		
Williams, Harmon	1		1		
Hall, Peter	2		1		3
Hall, Abell	1	1	2		
Hall, Abell, 2nd	1	1	3		
Hall, Daniel J	1	2	2		
Hall, Arael	1	1	1		
Hopson, Alvanus	2	5	4		
Hopson, Rue	1		4		
Tharp, Abner	1		2		
Hopson, Ashbel	1	4	5		
Hopson, Clement	1	1	2		
Hall, Aron	2	2	4		
Hall, Arael, 2nd	1	2	2		
Ives, Joseph	1		1		
Hall, Andrew	1	2	4		
Hall, Joel	3	2	2		
Batholomew, Andw	1	5	4		
Austin, Joshua	2	2	3		
Bartholomew, Isaac	1	5	4		
Bartholomew, Jona	1	3	3		
Avery, Abner	1	1			
Avery, Abner, 2nd	1	1	4		
Hopson, Samuel	2	3	5		
Page, Isaac	1				
Webber, Stephen	1	2	3		
Page, Balthus			3		
Austin, Joel	2	3	5		
Austin, Moses	1	1	1		
Cooke, Titus	1	2	2		
Dina (Negroe)				1	
Cooke, Chancy	1		1		
Cooke, James	1	1	2		
Culver, Hannah			4		
Culver, Samuel	1	2	3		
Culver, James	1	1	4		
Luttinton, Oliver	1	1	1		
Peck, Dan	2		1		
Culver, Ebenezer	1	1	3		
Culver, John	1	4	2		
Culver, Enoch	1	1	3		
Culver, Enoch, 2nd	1		2		
Peck, Samuel	2	3	5		
Todd, Heil	1	5	1		
Hull, Heil	1	6	2		
Hull, Peter, 2nd	2	5	3		
Cooke, Aron	3	3	4		2
Cooke, Abel	2	7	1		
Cooke, Stephen	1	3	3		
Cooke, Samuel	1	1	4		
Collins, Uriah	1		3		
Todd, Asa	1	2	6		
Munson, Joseph	2	3	3		
Whitney, Enos	1	2	2		
Munson, Samuel, 2nd	1	1	2		
Munson, Isaac	1	1	4		
Smith, Eli	2		2		
Munson, Samuel	3		1		
Lewis, Gerad	2	3	3		
Todd, Stephen	2		6		
Katlin, Isaac	1	1	6		
Munson, Ethel	1	2	3		
Doolittle, Samuel	1	1	3		
Alling, David	1	1	3		
Street, Glover	3	1	3		
Street, Samuel	1				
Rice, Thomas	1	1	3		
Street, Samuel, 2nd	1	1	2		
Alling, Daniel	2	2	4		
Alling, Enos	1	1	3		
Doolittle, Benjamin	1	2	1		
Doolittle, Charles	1	1	1		
Doolittle, Samuel, 2	1		1		
Thompson, Elihu	1		2		
Bartholmew, Moses	1	1	1		
Austin, Joseph	1	1	2		
Wright, Samuel	1				
Houd, Daniel			3		
Ward, Amie					
Johnson, Ward	1		2	1	
Barker, John	1		1		
Barker, Edward	2		3		3
Barker, Abigal	1	4	2		
Clinton, Jesse	1	1	2		
Catlin, Constant	2		4		
Ives, Caleb	1		2		

NEW HAVEN COUNTY—Continued.

NAME OF HEAD OF FAMILY.	Free white males of 16 years and upward, including heads of families.	Free white males under 16 years.	Free white females, including heads of families.	All other free persons.	Slaves.
WALLINGFORD TOWN—continued.					
Bracket, Elisha	1	2	4		
Thompson, Abel, 2nd	1		2		
Thompson, Abel	1		1		
Doolittle, Ann			1		
Doolittle, John	1		3		
Cornwell, Cornelius	1		2		
Doolittle, Johnson	1				
Bracket, Phebe			3		
Bracket, Martha			1		
Rice, William	1	1	1		
Plump, Seth	1				
Bracket, Jerad	1	1	1		
Spencer, Henry	1	3	2		
Rice, Jesse	1	3	3		
Abbot, Joseph	2	2	6		
Doolittle, Elizabeth		1	3		
Bradly, Isaac	2		1		
Clarke, Job	1	1	1		
Hall, Thankfull	1	2	4		
Eran (Negroe)				2	
Sharper (Negroe)				2	
Dutton, Eunice	1	2	3		
Dutton, Amos	1				
Hall, Stephen	1	1	2		
Hall, Samuel, 2nd	1	4	5		
Cooley, Arael	3	1	5		
Hall, Elisha	3	1	5		
Attwater, Jeremh	1				
Catlin, Jerham	3	3	3		
Cooke, Augistin	1				
Beevel, Martin	1	3	1		
Doolittle, Soloman	2	2	5		
Peck, Heil			3		
Yale, Hannah			3		
Hull, Harvey	1	1	3		
Rice, Lucy			1		
Bunce, John	1				
WATERBURY TOWN.					
Hecock, John	1	1	3		
Brunson, Ebenezur	2	1	3		
Brunson, Amassa	1		2		
Baldwin, Benjamin	1		3		
Hicock, Prosper	1		2		
Frost, Moses	1		3		
Tuttle, Hannah			3		
Taylor, David	1		2		
Johnson, Abner	1		3		
Frost, Jason	2		4		
Hopkins, Joseph	2	1	3	1	
Judd, Samuel	2	1	4		
Brunson, Mark	1	1	2		
Brunson, Ezra	2	1	3		
Fox, Ebenezer	1	1	3		
Harrison, Lemuel	1	1	1		
Leavenworth, Mark	1	1	2		1
Leavenworth, William	1	1	3		
Brunson, Stephen	1	2	4		
Scovel, Samuel	2	1	2		
Upson, Benjamin	3	1	3		
Beardsley, Levi	1	1	1		
Porter, Phineas	1	2	5		
Pritchet, David	1	2	4		
Baldwin, Isaac	3		4		1
Warner, Ephrahim	2	2	3		
Baldwin, Jonathan	1		4		
Baldwin, Noah	1	4	4		
Young, Happy			3		
Porter, Preserve	1	2	2		5
Porter, Timothy	2	2	4		
Nicoll, John	3	1	8		3
Welton, David	1	3	3		
Welton, Martha			1		
Pomp (Negroe)				4	
Judd, Stephen	1	1	3		
Cossett, John	2		2		
Brown, Daniel	3		1		
Silkrogs, Nicholas	1		3		
Richards, Huldy			2		
Whitney, James	3		2		
Brunson, Daniel	2	1	5		
Cooke, Charles	1		2		
Cooke, James	1	1	1		
Adams, Arael	1		1		
Adams, William	2		2		
Adams, Sebinus	1	1	3		
Scott, Samuel	1		3		
Scott, Ashley	1		2		
Adams, William, 2nd	2	2	2		
Scovel, Timothy	1	1	1		
Nicoll, Elizabeth			1		
Harrison, James	1				
Durand, Samuel	1				
Beardsley, Jabez	1				

NAME OF HEAD OF FAMILY.	Free white males of 16 years and upward, including heads of families.	Free white males under 16 years.	Free white females, including heads of families.	All other free persons.	Slaves.
WATERBURY TOWN—continued.					
Cooke, Sarah			1		
Hopkins, Jesse	1	1			
Holmes, Israel	1				
Nicol, Lidia			1		
Bolt, Louis			1		
Nicol, Sussanah			2		
Nicoll, Polly			1		
Welsh, Patrick	1				
Brunson, Joseph	1		4		
Porter, Daniel	1		1		
Welton, Hy	1				
Cooke, Moses	3	1	4		
McClaud, John	1		1		
Knolton, John	1		1		
Nicol, Richard	1		1		
Root, Eneas	1	4	3		
Nettleton, Elizh	2		5		
Nicol, Simon	1	2	5		
Hoadly, Lemuel	3	3	3		
Pritchett, Isaih	1	1	2		
Brecket, Zenus	2	2	3		
Preshell, George, 2nd	1	5	2		
Hotchkiss, Stephen	1	1	5		
Hotchkiss, Abraham	3	2	3		
Tyler, Ruben	1		4		
Ives, Steven	2	1	3		
Paine, Joseph	1	2	3		
Brunson, Samuel	1	2	3		
Paine, Thomas	1	3	3		
Hill, Jarad	2	2	3		
Hill, Obadiah	1	1	1		
Peirpoint, Ezra	1	2	3		
Hotchkiss, Eldad	1	1	2		
Blakley, Ebenezer	2	3	5		
Benham, Thomas	2	3	2		
Dutton, Thomas	1	1	2		
Hummiston, Joy	1		2		
Munson, Elizabeth	1	1	3		
Root, Samuel	1		4		
Mix, Samuel	1	3	1		
Mix, Eldad	2		2		
Mix, Levi	1		1		
Olds, Gersham	1	3	1		
Hodley, Andrew	1	1	2		
Callow, Miles	1		2		
Benham, Isaac	1		1		
Boxton, John	1		2		
Johnson, Cornelius	1		1		
Johnson, Jesse	1	1	5		
Johnson, Lyman	1	1	3		
Beech, Joseph	1				
Beach, Joseph, 2nd	2	3	4		
Beach, Asa	1	1	2		
Spony, Elizabeth	1	2	4		
Hoadly, Nathl	1		2		
Hoadley, Asa	2		3		
Munson, William	1	1	3		
Hummiston, Bennet	1	2	1		
Betram, Benjamin	2	1	1		
Benham, Shadreck	1	2	3		
Hitchcock, Benjamin	1	6	3		
Merriman, Joel	1	2	3		
Austin, Edmond	2	3	4		
Cartie, Phineas	1	3	7		
Johnson, Cornilus, 2nd	1	1	3		
Upson, Samuel	3	1	3		
Munson, Soloman	1	2	1		
Frost, David	2		3		
Frost, Jesse	1	1	3		
Bartholomew, Abial	1	2	1		
Bartholomew, Seth	1		4		
Bartholomew, Osi	1	3	2		
Frisbie, Ruben	1	3	5		
Warner, Ebenezer	1		1		
Warner, Justice	1	2	4		
Warner, Mark	1	2	4		
Austin, James	1		2		
Turrel, Amos	2		2		
Grillery, Daniel	1		2		
Wooster, Miles	1	2	6		
Pritchet, Roger	1		2		
Warner, Josiah	2	2	4		
Pritchet, Abraham	1	2	2		
Pritchet, Amos	2	3	4		
Welton, Levi	1	1	7		
Warner, Andrew	1	4	5		
Worthington, John	2	1	3		
Munson, Samuel	2	2	4		
Warner, James H	1	1	2		
Welton, Andrew	1	2	3		
Harrit, Stephen	1		2		
Welton, Stephen	1	3	4		
Barnes, Samuel	1	1	2		
Smith, Ephraim	2	4	1		
Welton John	2	3	5		

NAME OF HEAD OF FAMILY.	Free white males of 16 years and upward, including heads of families.	Free white males under 16 years.	Free white females, including heads of families.	All other free persons.	Slaves.
WATERBURY TOWN—continued.					
Welton, Oliver	1		1		
Warner, Ruben	1		1		
Welton, Richard	2	3	4		
Scott, Edmond	1	1	2		
Warner, Joseph, 2nd	2	2	4		
Frost, Samuel	1		1		
Taylor, Theodore	1	3	1		
Frost, Timothy	2		7		
Leavenworth, Thomas	1	1	1		
Turrel, Binjamin	2	1	3		
Scott, Zebulon	1		1		
Scott, Simeon	1	5	4		
Brown, Daniel	2		2		
Brown, Daniel, 2nd	1	3	5		
Brown, Asoph	1	1	4		
Brown, Elias	1	1	3		
Brunson, Michael	1	2	4		
Brunson, Asher	1				
Brown, Asa	1	2	3		
Merrill, Caleb	2		2		
Richards, Elizabeth	1	3	3		
Merrils, Nathanel	1	3	2		
Brunson, Sibey	4	5	6		
Munson, Hammon	2	1	3		
Clarke, John	1	2	1		
Brunson, Mary			1		
Hicock, Jesse	1	2	2		
Merrils, Icobad	1	1	3		
Tomkins, Elizabeth	1	2	2		
Buckingham, David	2	1	2		
Davis, Edward	1	1	1		
Tuttle, Jesse	1	2	1		
Warner, Elinor			1		
Welton, Amassa	1	1	5		
Wetmore, John	1				
Osborn, Isaac	1	2	2		
Hicock, Timothy	1	2	6		
Brown, James	4	1	2		
Orton, Guy	1		1		
Miles, Simon	1		1		
Brown, Ebenezer	1	2	3		
Leavenworth, Samuel	2	1	4		
Tomkins, Philip	2	1	4		
Warner, Abijah	1	2	6		
Warner, Ephraim	2		2		
Barnes, Jonathan	1	2	3		
Conder, Daniel	2	1	3		
Frost, Samuel, 2nd	1	2	2		
Frost, Isaac	1	1	3		
Sortune, Mary			3		
Bristow, Stephen		2	3		
Sanders, Nathaniel	1	2	3		
Hine, David	3		1		
Kellock, Morton	2	3	4		
Kellock, Joseph	1		2		
Merril, Elizabeth	1	1	2		
Benedick, Aron	2	2	5		
Thompson, John	3	2	7		
Morris, William	1	6	2		
Brunson, Rosswell	1	1	4		
Atwell, Thomas	1	2	3		
Munson, Caleb	1	5	1		
Clarke, John	2	1	2		
Hine, Benjamin	2	1	2		
Abbot, Daniel	1		1		
Abbot, David	1	1	2		
Nicoll, Samuel	1	2	2		
Morris, Major	1	4	4		
Scovel, Asa	1		2		
Scovel, Desire	1		1		
Nicoll, Benjamin	1		2		
Scovell, Seldon	1		3		
Scovel, Selah	2	2	3		
Fenn, Samuel	1	2	3		
Richardson, Nathaniel	1	1	3		
Richardson, Eber	1		3		
Bartholomew, Joseph	1		3		
Brunson, Levi	1		3		
Barnes, Thomas	1	1	3		
Richardson, Thomas	1	1	3		
Pritchard, Archibald	1	1	2		
Merril, David	1	1	5		
Judson, Eber	1	4	2		
Berman, Josiah	2	1	5		
Wilmot, Abijah	2	2	2		
Wilmot, Silas	1		2		
Crilley, Henry	1		1		
Brunson, Isaac	1	1	3		
Brunson, Ethal	1		1		
Brunson, Isaac, 2nd	2	1	2		
Brunson, Eli	3	1	6		
Brunson, Arael	2	1	4		
Brunson, Abel	2	3	4		
Brunson, Josiah	1	1	2		
Brunson Abel	2	1	4		

NEW HAVEN COUNTY—Continued.

WATERBURY TOWN—continued.

NAME OF HEAD OF FAMILY.	Free white males of 16 years and upward, including heads of families.	Free white males under 16 years.	Free white females, including heads of families.	All other free persons.	Slaves.
Brunson, Theo	1	2	5		
Brunson, Seth	1	3	3		
Brunson, Titus	2	3	3		
Brunson, Jesse	1	2	2		
Scovel, John	1		3		
Tyler, Daniel	1		3		
Tyler, Daniel, 2nd	1	3	2		
Tomkins, David	1	1	4		
Munson, Abner	2	3	4		
Munson, Caleb	1		1		
Munson, Benjamin	4				
Sackett, Siam D	1		2		
Brunson, Josiah, 2nd	2	4	2		
Brunson, David	1	1	3		
Newton, Miles	1	3	2		
Porter, Mark	1	3	3		
Hinman, Amos	1		3		
Porter, David	2	3	3		
Peck, Ward	1		4		
Porter, James	2	1	4		
Fenn, Benjamin	1		4		
Peck, Augustus	1	1	2		
Osborn, Abner	1	1	2		
Scovel, Amos	1	1	1		
Beman, Benjamin	1	3	3		
Porter, Timothy, 2nd	1	1	3		
Buckingham, Samuel	1	2	2		
Ratford, James	1	1	3		
Fenn, Gamaliel	1	2	3		
Bates, Benjamin	1	5	4		
Smith, Levi	1	3	2		
Scott, Ruben	1	1	1		
Scott, Abel	1	2	6		
Scovel, Noah	1	2	1		
Welton, Lemuel	1		2		
Areston, Gad	1				
Lewis, Silas	1	3	2		
Saxton, Ebenezer	1	1	2		
Scott, Amos, 2nd	1	1	1		
Wooster, David	2	1	8		
Scott, Ebenezer	1	1	4		
Harrison, Samuel	1	1	5		
Gunn, Samuel	3	3	2		
Scovel, Timothy, 2.	1	1	2		
Hotchkiss, Thelus	1		2		
Brunson, Andrew	2		4		
Bates, Gamaliel	1	2	3		
Adams, John	1	2	5		
Pritchett, John	2		3		
Pritchett, James	1		1		
Hall, Ezra	2	2	4		
Nicoll, Samuel	1		1		
Clarke, David	2		2		
Pritchet, George	1	1	3		
Clarke, Samuel	2	1	2	1	
Pritchett, John	1	1	4		
Wooster, Wait	1		2		
Sperry, Jacob	1	2	4		
Blakely, Ruben	3	2	3		
Porter, Elizabeth	2		3		
Chatfield, Daniel	3	1	2		
Sperry, Jesse	2	1	5		
Roberts, Joel	1	1	5		
Clarke, William	1	2	4		
Platt, Gideon	2	3	3		
Pardie, Phyphe			5		
Scovell, Amaziah	2	4	2		
Bradley, Enos	1	3	3		
Wooster, Elizabeth	1	1	3		
Pope, Jacob	1		2		
Scott, Enoch	2	1	2		
Cowell, James	1	4	2		
Thayer, Hester			2		
Upson, Daniel	2		2		
Hotchkiss, Arael	2	2	3		
Warner, Eneas	3	3	4		
Cambie, Noah	2	1	2		
Fulford, Titus	1		2		
Beebe, Elizabeth	1	1	1		
Frisby, Elizabeth	1		2		
Frisbee, John	1	1	1		
Anderson, Asa	1	2	1		
Wakely, David	2	1	2		
Wakely, Ebenezer	1		1		
Frisby, Charles	1	3	2		
Grilly, Sirus	1	2	3		
Grilley, Teuly	1		3		
Norton, Hseas	2	2	3		
Norton, Zebel	1	3	1		
Talmage, John	1	3	2		
Thrasher, Elnathan	1	2	3		
Frisby, Judas	1	2	4		
Upson, Ashbel	1	1	1		
Seward, Amos	1	1	4		
Wilcox, Philomen	1	1	2		
Scott, Timothy	1		3		
Dana, Daniel	1	2	2		
Stalief, Joseph	1		1		
Stalief, Joseph, 2nd	2	3	4		
Hopkins, Simeon	2	2	5		
Hopkins, Isaac	1		4		
Silkrags, Trunans		1	2		
Hotchkiss, Wait	2	3	2		
Obed (Negroe)				5	
Hotchkiss, Joel	1		3		
Norton, Noah W	1	1	2		
Tuttle, Daniel	3	3	5		
Byington, Benjamin	3	3	5		
Atkins, Joseph	3	2	5		
Talmage, Jacob	1	2	3		
Upson, Charles	1	5	2		
Mallery, Joseph	1	2	3		
Weston, Abraham	2	2	10		
Upson, Ezekiel	2		7		
Byington, Daniel	3	2	5		
Curtis, Abel	2	4	4		
Beecher, Amos	1	1	3		
Williams, Obed	1	5	7		
Thomas, James	1	3	4		
Alcock, James	1	1	8		
Rinny, John	1		2		
Barnes, Josiah	1	3	4		
Welton, Eliakim	1		1		
Welton, Eliakim, 2nd	2	2	2		
Alcocke, David	2	3	5		
Alcock, John	3		1		
Alcock, John, 2nd	1	2	1		
Alcock, Samuel	2	1	2		
Alcock, Soloman	1		3		
Wilton, Benjamin	1	2	2		
Richards, Street	2	2	3		
Wilson, Thomas	2	3	7		
Shatlief, Nathaniel	3	1	5		
Mills, John	1				
Rowley, Eli	1	1	3		
Rowley, William	1		2		
Rowley, William, 2nd	1	1	1		
Scott, Nathan	1	1	2		
Hicock, Abraham	1		3		
Nicoll, Samuel	1	2	3		
Nicol, Samuel	1	2	3		
Scott, Samuel, 2nd	1	2	1		
Frisbie, Israel	1	2	2		
Scott, John	1		2		
How, Daniel	1				
Gunn, Abigal	2	1	3		
Scott, Amos, 2nd	1	3	1		
Palmer, Samuel	1	2	3		
Scott, Joseph	1		1		
Smith, Ephrim	1		1		
Gunn, Jabamah	4	3	4		
Osborn, Thomas	2	3	3		
Osborn, Daniel	2		1		
Gunn, Nathaniel	2		6		
Gunn, Abel	1	2	1		
Peck, Joseph	1	1	1		
Webb, Nancy		1	1		
Osborn, Abraham	1		3		
Osborn, Abraham, 2nd	1		3		
Osborn, Andrew	1	1	2		
Osborn, Peter	1		1		
Osborn, Ezra	1	2	3		
Osborn, John	1		1		
Osborn, Daniel, 2nd	2		1		
Pits, Richard	1	1	3		
Bruster, Stephen	1	2	3		
Lownsby, John	1	1	2		
Cupper, Cornelius	1		2		
Judd, Roswell	1	2	6		
Porter, Samuel, 2nd	1	4	4		
Condy, Timothy	2		3		
Scott, Isaac	1	1	3		
Scott, Thadeus	1	2	1		
Scott, Abner	1		3		
Todd, Walter	1	1	3		
Judd, Chauncy	1	1	2		
Morgan, Isaac	1	1	2		
Porter, Samuel	1				
Porter, Ebenezer	1	3	3		
Judd, Isaac	2	1	1		
Williams, Ruben	1	2	2		
Williams, Mary			1		
Smith, Elizabeth			1		
Osborn, Elijah	1	3	3		
Smith, John	1	1	7		
Woodruff, Jonah	1	4	1		
Adams, Abraham	1		2		
Judd, Isaac, 2	1	3	4		
Adams, Ely	2	2	2		
Scott, Enoch, 2nd	1	4	1		
Lewis, David	1	2	4		
Warner, Stephen	3		2		
Scott, Gideon	1		1		
Scott, Caleb	1	1	3		
Scott, Samuel, 2nd	1	1	1		
Lewis, Eunice	1		3		
Porter, Nathaniel	1	2	4		
Spencer, Culver	2	1	1		
Hoadley, Culpeper	1	1	2		
Culver, Amos	2	2	4		
Buckly, Daniel	1	1	1		
Lewis, John	1		1		
Lewis, Samuel S	1	2	2		
Hoadley, Ebenezer	1	2	2		
Hoadley, Philo	1	1	1		
Chatfield, Samuel	1		4		
Chatfield, Samuel, 2nd	1		3		
Beebe, Ruben	1	4	6		
Camp, Samuel	1		4		
Reecher, Daniel	2	2	6		
Warner, Joseph	2	2	2		
Porter, Francis	1	3	4		
Caukins, Roswell	2	2	3		
Rush, Phebe			1		
Clarke, Chauncy	1	1	2		
Scott, Josiah	1		3		
Alcock, Isaac	1		1		
Lane, Daniel	1	1	1		
Minor, Caleb	1	1	2		
Stevens, Nathan	2	3	5		
Twicket, Joseph	1		1		
Bicket, David	1	1	2		
Byington, Jerad	1				
Minor, Jud	1		4		
Hine, Ebenezer	1		4		
Potter, Lemuel	2	3	3		
Turrel, Icobald	1	3	2		
Porter, Freeman	1	1	4		
Porter, Thomas, 2nd	2	1	3		
Hoadley, William	1	2	3		
Porter, Ashbel	2	1	2		
Porter, Asbell, 2nd	1	1	1		
Hoadly, Jude	2	1	2		
Stevens, Elijah	6	2			
Fowler, Abraham	2	2	3		
Turrel, Jerad	1	1	2		
Turrel, Isaiah	4	2	5		
Hicox, Samuel	2	1	5		
Hicox, Gideon	2		4		
Scott, Uriah	1		2		
Turrel, Oliver	1		2		1
Osborn, Arael	1		2		
Osborn, Amos	2	2	2		
Norton, David	1		2		
Norton, Cyrus	1	4	3		
Smith, Anthony	1	4	4		
Beebe, James	2	1	1		
Porter, Ezekel	1		2		
Morris, David	1	2	2		
Hine, Hezekiah	1	1	3		
Turrel, Israel	2	1	4		
Byington, Jerad	2	2	2		
Webb, Daniel	1	2	2		
Smith, Austin	2	1	2		
Beebe, David	1	3	7		
Osborn, Thaddeus	1		1		
Hichson, Eneas	1	1	2		
Ells, Linthell	1	1	5		
Wooster, Walter	2	3	2		
Beebe, Borden	1		3		
Hall, Prindle	2	2	3		
Ames, Samuel	1	1	2		
Hopkins, John	3		3		
Hopkins, David	1				
Gibbord, Timothy	3	3	2		
Horton, John	3		3		
Horton, Calvin	1	3	1		
Hotchkiss, Amos	2	2	3		
Turrel, Isaac	1	1	3		
Hopkins, Joseph, 2nd	2	1	4		
Philis (Negroe)				2	
Payne, David	1	1	5		
Hotchkiss, Gideon	4		2		
Hotchkiss, Eber	1	1	2		
Todd, Samuel	1	3	3		
Riggs, John	2	1	3		
Riggs, Abner	1	4	2		
Tinker, Absolum	1	3	4		
Hotchkiss, Fredrick	1		1		
Tyler, Abraham	1	3	4		
Turrel, Josiah	3	1	1		
Hine, Isaac	2	1	3		

NEW HAVEN COUNTY—Continued.

WATERBURY TOWN—continued.

NAME OF HEAD OF FAMILY.	Free white males of 16 years and upward, including heads of families.	Free white males under 16 years.	Free white females, including heads of families.	All other free persons.	Slaves.
Root, Joseph	1	5	2		
Spencer, Ansel	1		2		
Hickson, Gideon, 2nd	2		2		
Hickson, James	2	1	2		
Turrel, Enoch	1	3	2		
Beebe, Zina	2	4	2		
Morgan, Arael	1	2	1		
Paine, Philemon	1	1	1		
Burret, Benjamin	1	1	2		
Peck, David	1		3		
Farrel, Joel	1	1	4		
Lane, Asael	1				
Lane, Nathaniel	1				
Welton, Eliakim, 2nd	1		3		
Welton, Ebenezer	1		3		
Turrel, Elihu	1	2	2		
Smith, Austin	1		1		
Lewis, John, 2nd	3	2	2		
Grant, John	1	3	2		
Thomas, Elisha	1	4	4		
Higgs, John	1		2		
Lewis, Abraham	2		5		
Judd, Ebenezer	1	3	4		
Beebe, Joseph	1	3	3		
Frisbie, Josiah	1	1	1		

WOODBRIDGE TOWN.

NAME OF HEAD OF FAMILY.	Free white males of 16 years and upward, including heads of families.	Free white males under 16 years.	Free white females, including heads of families.	All other free persons.	Slaves.
Brown, Jonathan	1		2		
Bristol, Eunice	1	3	3		
Smith, Heil	1	2	1		
Baldwin, Richard	2	5	4		
Northrop, Isaac	1	2	4		
Baldwin, Enoch	1	5	4		
Baldwin, Charles	4	2	5		1
Pardie, Samuel	1	3	4		
Sandford, Moses	2		1		
Baldwin, Henry	1	1	3		
Baldwin, Henry, 2nd	1		4		
Osborn, Elisha	1	1	3	1	
Smith, Jesse	1	4	1		
Ford, Illard	1	2	3		
Andrus, Timothy	1				
Baldwin, Andrew	2		3		
Trent, Abijah	2	2	4		
Baldwin, Josiah	3	1	2		
Sandford, Isaac	2		1		
Sandford, Abel	1		3		
Tinker, Oliver	2		2		
Northrop, Job	2	2	2		
Hine, Charles	3	1	3		
Hine, Stephen	1	2	6		
Hine, David	1		2		
Newton, Samuel, 2nd	1		1		
Dibble, Philo	1	2	1		
Hotchkiss, Soloman	1	2	3		
Clinton, Laurence	1		2		
Clinton, Samuel	1	4	2		
Smith, Daniel	1	2	5		
Northrop, Job, 2nd	1	3	5		
Hine, Moses	1	1	3		
Booth, Walter	1	2	4		
Sperry, Richard	2		6		
Northrup, Philo	1	1	3		
Baldwin, Thomas	3	3	5		
Baldwin, Barnabas	3		2		2
Andrus, Elijah	1	1	4		
Baldwin, Barnabas, 2nd	1	4	1		
Downs, Seth	2	1	3		
Beecher, Ebenezur	2	2	2		
Beecher, Nicholas	1		1		
Beecher, Sarah			3		
Beecher, Enoch	1	2	2		
Beecher, Joseph	1	4	2		
Whiting, Sarah	1		4		
Andrews, David	1		1		
Andrews, Barnes	1		3		
Bradley, Andrew	1		1		
Bradley, Silas	1		2		
Peck, Molly			3		
Peck, Benjamin	1		4		
Osborn, Elijah	1	1	3		
Thomas, Ephrahim	1	2	4		
Bradley, Timothy	2		2		
Bradley, Wilmot	1	2	3		
Beecher, Jonathan	1		1		
Bradley, Timothy, 2nd	1	1	1		
Bradly, Charles	2	3	7		
Bradley, Benjamin	1		4		
Geers, Caleb	1	1	1		
Sperry, Nathaniel	1	2	4		
Thomas, Ruben	1		2		
Johnson, Samuel	1	3	3		
Peas, Mary			2		
Smith, Hezekiah	2	1	3		

WOODBRIDGE TOWN—continued.

NAME OF HEAD OF FAMILY.	Free white males of 16 years and upward, including heads of families.	Free white males under 16 years.	Free white females, including heads of families.	All other free persons.	Slaves.
Baldwin, Jerad	1		4		
Booth, Hester	1		2		1
Lines, James	1	1	2		
Dibble, John	4	1	3	1	
Lines, Samuel	2	1	2		
Lumsdale, Hatham	1	3	4	1	
Lines, Daniel	1	1	1		
Lines, Darus			1	2	
Jim (Negroe)				2	
Lines, Alvin	1	1	3		
Lines, Linus	1		3		
Beecher, Linus	1		1		
Adams, Rebecca			1		
Alling, Marahel	2	3	5		
Thomas, Amos	2	2	1		
Beecher, Ephrahim	1	2	6		
Sherman, Amos	2		3		
Sherman, Jese	1	1	1		
Johnson, Job	1	5	2		
Johnson, Isaac	1		2		
Johnson, Mary		2	2		
Sperry, Asa	1		2		
Howell, Henry	1				
Downs, Joseph	1	1	5		
Alling, Daniel	1				
Buckingham, John	1				
Smith, Israel	1		1		
Hine, David	1	1	2		
Clinton, Anson	1				
Platt, Nathaniel	1	1	4		1
Smith, David	1	1	3		
Beach, Benjamin	1	5	3		
Smith, Nathan	1		4		
Smith, Nathan, 2nd	1				
Peck, Phineas	2		2		
Peck, Samuel F	1	2	3		
Clarke, Lar	2	3	4		1
Gun, George	2	1	2		
Smith, Abel	1	3	3		
Clarke, Samuel	1		1		
Peck, Hannah		2	3		
Clarke, George	2	1	2		
Bradly, Alling	1	2	3		
Newton, Samuel	3	2	4		
Gilbert, Soloman	1	1	4		
Gilbert, Ely	1	2	2		
Ford, David	2	1	3		
Hemmingway, Isaac	1		3		
Murring, Joseph	1	1	2		
Murring, Fletcher	1	1	3		
Murring, Joseph, 2nd	1		4		
Newton, Enoch	2	1	3		1
Andrus, Judah	1	1	7		
Newton, Roger	1	1	3		
Russell, William	1	1	5		
Russell, Richard, 2nd	1	2	3		
Russell, Richard	1				
Perkins, Jonathan	2	1	2		
Perkins, David	1	2	4		
Main, Russel	1		2		
Perkins, Rachel			1		
Beecher, Burr	3	1	4		
Huntington Asa	3	1	3		
Russel, Stephen	1	2	2		
Hull, Amassa	1	2	2		
Walker, Webber	1				
Ford, Isaac	2		2	1	
Ford, Vincen	1		2		
Carrington, Allen	2	2	2		
Perkins, Amos	2	1	2		
Perkins, Elizabeth	1	4	2		
Perkins, Amos, 2nd	1	4	2		
Peck, Dan	1	1	4		
Peck, Henry	1	1	2		
Peck, Amie			1		
Parmer, Bethseba			2		
Hotchkiss, David	1	2	6		
Cooke, David	1		1		
Osborn, Samuel	3	2	4		2
Perkins, Elias	1	3	2		
Thompson, Thadeus	1	2	3		
Alling, Roger	1	3	4		
Smith, David	1	2	5		
Smith, Titus	1	1	3		
Smith Adney	1	4	2		
Johnson, Niamiah	2		2		
Russell, Daniel	1	1	8		
Sperry, Thomas	1	1	3		
Sperry, James	1	1	3		
Sperry, Caleb	1		2		
Sperry, Samuel	1	3	3		
Peck, Stephen	2	2	5		
Sperry, Lent	2	2	4		
Sperry, Amie			2		
Sperry, Samuel	1	3	5		
Salton, George	2	1	1		

WOODBRIDGE TOWN—continued.

NAME OF HEAD OF FAMILY.	Free white males of 16 years and upward, including heads of families.	Free white males under 16 years.	Free white females, including heads of families.	All other free persons.	Slaves.
Sperry, Ebenezer	2	1	3		
Sperry, Eliakim	2	3	3		
Sperry, Amos	1	2	2		
Sperry, Lidia			3		
Bradley, Abner	4	2	4		
Ford, Jesse	3	1	6		
Perkins, Unice		3	4		
Clarke, Elioney	2	1	2		
Darling, Thomas	2	2	1		
Darling, Abigal			3		4
Clarke, David	1		1		
Sperry, Asa	1	3	4		
Jim (Negroe)				5	
Clarke, Martin	1		3		
Sperry, David	2		3		
Sperry, Joel	1	3	3		
Marten, Francis	1	2	4		
Hotchkiss, Jonas	1	2	4		
Hitchcock, Eneas	2		1		
Carrington, Samuel	1	2	4		
Carrington, Noadiah	1		2		
Peck, Silas	1	1	2		
Carrington, Peter	1		2		
Syrus (Negroe)				2	
Dorman, Samuel	1	2	4		
Hull, Joel	1				
Pond, Phineas	1				
Clarke, Nathan	2	1	3		
Curtis, Nathan	1		1		
Allen, Elenor			1		
Andrews, Anna		1	3		
Hitchcock, Daniel	1				
Hitchcock, Phineas	1				
Hitchcock, Eneas	1				
Alling, Noah	1	2	2		
Alling, Lemuel	1	3	4		
Andrews, Caleb	1	1	6		
Humpherville, John	1	4	2		
Downs, Samuel, 2nd	1		2		
Brooks, Asshael	1	3	2		
Gilbert, Linus	2	3	4		
Downs, Samuel	2		1		
Downs, Ebenezur	2	1	5		
Downs, Felix	1		2		
Gilbert, Samuel	1	2	6		
Johnson, Jesse	2	2	3		
Goodyear, Joel	2	1	4		
Hotchkiss, Benjamin	2	1	4		
Beecher, Weeler	1		2		
Sandford, David	3	3	6		
Sperry, Isaac	1		5		
Morris, Asa	1	3	1		
Toles, Abraham	1	1	2		
Humpherville, Ebenezer	1	3	2		
Sandford, Stephen	1	2	5		
Dickerman, Timothy	1		1		
Toles, Lazurus	1	4	4		
Ceasar (Negroe)				5	
Beecher, Isaac	2	1	2		
Beecher, Hezekiah	1	3	4		
Peck, Hiram	1	2	2		
Hotchkiss, Elias	1	2	1		
Hotchkiss, Joel	1	2	6		
Peck, Sarah			1		
Peck, Elizabeth	1		4		
Wooden, Elizabeth	1	2	2		
Perkins, Archibald	1	3	3		
Wooden, John	3	3	3		
Tuttle, Nathaniel	2	2	4		
Wooden, Edmond	1	2	3		
Todd, Josiah	3	1	5		
Hotchkiss, Daniel	2	3	2		
Hotchkiss, Soloman	1	1	2		
Tuttle, Uriah	3	5	2		
Hammiston, Joel	1	2	2		
Wheeler, Joel	1	1	3		
Bradley, Ruben	3	1	3		
Ives, Abel	2		2		
Perkins, Adonijah	2	1	2		
Beecher, Hannah	2	1	3		
Bishop, Ebenezer	1	4	3		
Bishop, John	1				
Hotchkiss, Joel, 2nd	1	1	7		
Talmage, Alsop	1	2	5		
Beecher, Jesse	2	1	5		
Russell John	3	1	3		
Sperry, Simeon	3	1	5		
Thompson, Daniel	1		3		
Osborn, John	1		3		
Downs, Jacob	1	2	4		
Sperry, John	1		4		
Carry, Margaret	1				
Sperry, Lois	1				
Merriman, Moses	1	1	2		
Toles, Hannah			2		
Wooden, Cyrus	1				

NEW HAVEN COUNTY—Continued.

WOODBRIDGE TOWN—continued.

NAME OF HEAD OF FAMILY.	Free white males of 16 years and upward, including heads of families.	Free white males under 16 years.	Free white females, including heads of families.	All other free persons.	Slaves.
Todd, Rachael	1		5		
Hummiston, Abel	1	3	4		
Hummiston, Daniel	1		1		
Warren, Nathen	1	3	2		
Perkins, Ruben	2	3	4		
Sperry, Amie	1		1		
Sandford, Jonathan	1	2	2		
Barnes, Jacob	1	2	6		
Johnson, Hezekiah	1	2	4		
Johnson, Eliphalet	1	4	4		
Foot, Isaac	1	1	2		
Beecher, Isaac, 2nd	1		1		
Baldwin, Mathew	2		1		
Benham, Elihu	1	3	4		
Smith, Lamberton	2	1	2		
Thomas, Moses	1		1		
Smith, Ezekiel	1	4	3		
Wheeler, Simion	1	1	3		
Collins, Joel	1	2	6		
Turrel, Jesse	1	2	1		
Perkins, Israel	2		2		
Perkins, Rossannah			3		
Kimbal, Thomas	1	2	1		
Sperry, Ezra, 2nd	1		1		
Bencher, Justus	1	1	3		
Peck, Samuel	1	5	3		
Thomas, John	3	1	3		
Smith, Jonathan	1	3	4		
Sperry, Ezra	2		5		
Beecher, Daniel	3		2		1
Hitchcock, William	1		3		
Ball, Timothy	1	1	6		
Ball, Mary			2		
Hitchcock, Medad	2		1		
Lines, Abel	1	1	4		
Hotchkiss, Joseph	3	1	2		
Hotchkiss, Abraham	1	4	2		
Attwater, Jonathan	3		2		
Hooker, Hezekiah	1	2	1		
Sandford, Elihu, 2nd	1	3	1		
Holly, Stephen	1	1	1		
Holley, Stephen, 2nd	1		1		
Pane, Abraham	1	1	2		
Thomas, James	1				
Warren, Abigal			1		
Johnson, Eden	1	2	3		
Sperry, Elam	1		2		
Sperry, Ruben	2	2	3		
Sperry, N.	3	2	5		
Sandford, Elihu	1		2		
Hotchkiss, Samuel	1	1	2		
Perkins, Peter	4	1	4		
Wilmot, Walter	1	4	1		
Tuttle, Jeremiah	1	1	3		
Tolles, Jerad	1	5	2		
John (Negroe)				1	
Sperry, Demas	1	2	1		
Downs, Joseph	2	1	2		
Rinsley, Sarah			4		
Sperry, Elizabeth	2	3	6		
Tolles, Lamberton	3		8		
Thomas, Garthom	3		1		
Thomas, Noah	1	2	3	1	
Sperry, Hezekiah	1	3	8		
Peck, Timothy	1		1		
Attwater, Amos	1	1	3		
Hitchcock, Amos	2		1		
Martin, Israel	1		2		
Nelson, Silus	1	2	3		
Wolcot, Joseph	1		2		
Goodyer, Theophilus	1				
Goodyer, Simeon	1				
Beers, Nathan	1	2	3		
Alling, John	1				
Smith, Niamiah (Negroe)				2	
Rowland, Jesse	1	3	4		
Hoadley, Amasia	1	3	2		
Attwater, David	1	1	3		
Driver, Lidia		2	2		
Hummiston, Asa	1		2		
Russell, Robert	2		1		
Lownbury, Stephen	1	1	3		
Lownbury, Elias	1	2	1		
Peck, Chester	1				
Lownbury, Timothy	2		2		
Lownbury, Timothy, 2nd	1		2		
Hotchkiss, James	1	1	2		
Collins, Joseph	1				
Collins, Joseph, 2nd	1	1	1		
Collins, Benjamin	1		1		
Morris, Benjamin	1		3		
Turrel, Phineas	2	6	5		
Wilmot, David	1	1	4		
Wilmot, Volantine	1		1		
Wilmot, Volantine, 2nd	1	1	2		
Brown, Timothy	2	1	3		
Hotchkiss, Stephen	1		1		
Hotchkiss, Jabez	1		2		
Beacher, Jerad	2	1	3	1	
French, David	3	2	6		
Thomas, Hezekiah	2	1	3		
Hotchkiss, Eziekel	1	2	2		
Thomas, Amos	1	1	2		
Hine, Joel	1	2	3		
Pardie, William	1		2		
Attwater, Moses	1	1	3		
Newton, Christopher	1	3	3		
Buckhingham, Oliver	1	1	1		
Buckhingham, Abijah	1		1		
Sandford, Raymond	1	3	5		
Tim (Negroe)				5	
Underwood, John	1		1		
Nettleton, John	1	1	2		
Tyrell, John	1	2	2		
Andrew, Sarah		2	1		
Downs, Sarah			1		
Hotchkiss, Elisha	1	1	2		
Prince, Nathaniel	1	2	3		
Tyrell, Eliakin	1	5	2		
Tyrell, Philomin	1		2		
Warren, Edward	2	2	3		
Bino, Samuel	1		2		
Bino, Ruth			2		
Hotchkiss, Isaac	1	2	2		
Wheeler, James	1	2	6		
Northrop, Gideon	1	1	1		
Clarke, Aron	3	1	2		
Ward, Abel	1				
Smith, Poly Carp	1		1		
Beach, Samuel	1	1	2		
Clarke, Elizabeth	2	2	2		
Chatfield, Hannah	1				
Thomas, John, 2	1	1	2		
Tolles, Daniel	1	2	6		
Hotchkiss, Jacob	2	1	4		
Sacket, Jonathan	1		1		
Hitchcock, Joseph	1	1	3		
Hitchcock, Ebenezer	1	1	2		
Russell, John	2	1	7		
Tuttle, Caleb	1	1	3		
Johnson, Joseph	1	4	3		
Carrington, Abraham	1	2	3		
Carrington, David	1		1		
Hitchcock, Joseph	1	3	5		
Thomas, David	2	1	5		
Lines, Eber	1	1	3		
Lines, John	1		1		
Lines, Ebenezer	1		2		
Lines, Luke	1	1	3		
Sandford, Hitabel			1		
Baldin, Mathew, 2	1	1	1		
Clarke, Joseph	1				
Lownsbury, Lyles	1	3	1		
Beers, David	1		1		
Hotchkiss, Hetty			1		

NEW LONDON COUNTY.

NAME OF HEAD OF FAMILY.	Free white males of 16 years and upward, including heads of families.	Free white males under 16 years.	Free white females, including heads of families.	All other free persons.	Slaves.
Coburn, Samuel	1		2		
Able, Alpheus	3	1	3		
Perrigo, Ezekiel	1	2	3		
Bushnal, John	1	1	2		
Hartshorn, Oliver	1	1	2		
Dodge, Joshua	1	1	4		
Perkins, John	9	4	4		
Perkins, Levi	2	2	4		
Overton, Aaron	1		2		
Fuller, John	1	4	3		
Fuller, Jacob	1	1	1		
Fuller, Ebenezer	1	2	3		
Guy (Negro)				2	
Perkins, Frederick	4	2	4		
Perkins, Joshua	5	2	5		
Coburn, Cornelius	1	1	2		
Bishop, Mary	1	2	4		
Cutler, Daniel	2		6		
Cutler, Eleazer	1	1	3		
James, Saml	1		3		
Perrigo, John	1		1		
Manning, Luther	2	1	2		
Perrigo, Joshua	2		6		
Perrigo, William	1	2	4		
Tubs, Daniel	1	2	5		
Perrigo, William, Junr	1	2	4		
Cutler, Samuel	3	3	3		
Farnum, Elijah	1	4	2		
Kingsley, Diah	1	2	4		
Able, Zacheus	1		1		
French, Pheba	1		2		
Lee, Andrew	1	4	5		
Farnum, Henry	3	2	4		
Bushnul, Nathan	2	2	7		
Bushnul, Joseph	2	1	3		
Bushnul, Ezekiel	1	2	2		
Bushnul, Aaron	2	4	4		
Lovett, Saml	4	2	6		
Williams, John	1		2		
Grunstel, John	1	1	2		
Grunstel, James	1		2		
James, John	1		1		
Knight, Asa	2	1	2		
Cumstock, Daniel	1	1	2		
Webb, Jonathan	1	2	5		
Knight, Issabel			2		
Perrigo, Ebenezer	1	2	2		
Knight, David, Junr	1	2	4		
Knight, Phineas	2	1	3		
Knight, David	2	1	2		
French, Joseph	1	2	1		
Clark, David	1	1	1		
Hide, Asa	4	5	4		
Bishop, Joshua	1	2	2		
Bishop, Nathl	1		2		
Roathburn, William	1	2	3		
Mingham, John	3		3		
Smith, Elkanah	1	1	4		
Kingsley, Hezekiah	1	1	3		
Clark, Perry	4		5		
Petingall, Lemuel	2		2		
Simons, Thomas	1	1	1		
Bingham, John, Junr	1		4		
Bottom, James	1	2	4		
James (Negro)				7	
Peter (Negro)				4	
Davis, John	1	1	1		
Smith, Nathl	1	3	3		
Huntington, Barnabas	3		3		
Stephens, John	3	1	3		
Roathburn, Thomas	3	4	3		
Morse, Rufus	1	1	3		
Roathburn, Asa	1	2	4		
Bishop, Samuel	1	3	5		
Isaac (Negro)				5	
Adams, William	7	2	7		
Lewis (Negro)				8	
Avory, Jonathan	2	4	3		
Palmer, Asa	1	1	3		
Palmer, John	2	1	2		
Lothrop, Jedediah	1	1	4		
Burnham, Benjamin	3	1	3		
Bishop, Caleb	4	2	3		2
Potter, William	1	1	6		
Smith, Thomas	1	2	2		
Capron, William	1		1		
Williams, Ezra	1	1	3		
Burnham, Jedediah	1	2	3		1
Lapum, David	1		3		
Kinsman, Jeremiah, Junr	3	1	6		
Stephens, Moses	3	1	3		
Stephens, Levi	1		2		
Kinsman, Jeremiah	3		3	8	
Wintworth, William	2	5	4		
Crosby, Ezra	1	2	1		
Cleaveland, John	1	4	1		
Craps (Negro)				6	
Safford, Solomon	1	1	3		
Safford, Jedediah	2	1	5		
Hide, Barnabas	1	1	3		
Calkins, Able, Junr	2	1	5		
Braman, Daniel	1	1	3		
Thillam, Samuel	1		2		
Whaley, Theophilus	1		4		
Perkins, Olive	2	1	4		
Perkins, Joseph	1		1		
Perkins, Solomon	2	3	5		
Perkins, Jacob	4	2	4		
Fitch, John	1	2	3		
Bundy, Joshua	1		3		
Bottom, Daniel	1	1	4		
Bottom, Daniel, Junr	1		2		
Morrow, Thomas	1	1	2		
Whipple, Rebecka			1		

NEW LONDON COUNTY—Continued.

NAME OF HEAD OF FAMILY.	Free white males of 16 years and upward, including heads of families.	Free white males under 16 years.	Free white females, including heads of families.	All other free persons.	Slaves.
Bottom, Amaziah	1		2		
Kimball, Jedediah	1	4	3		
Sheldon, William	1	3	3		
Smith, Joseph	1		1		
Smith, Daniel	1	2	2		
Caulkins, William	1	1	3		
Pharough (Negro)				6	
Jackson, John	1	3	3		
Denison, James	3	1	6		
Jackson, Jonathan	1		1		
Clark, Ezra	2	4	6		1
Bishop, Ezra	3	3	4		
Bishop, Ebenezer	3	1	5	1	
Lothrop, Septemius	3	2	6	2	
Willoughby, Elijah	4	1	4		
Baldwin, Joseph	2		3		
Baldwin, Rufus	1	2	4		
Burnham, James	3	1	3		
Herrington, Andw	1		3		
Herrington, Stephen	1		1		
Lothrop, Simeon	3	2	4		
Clark, Andw	4	1	3	1	
Craft, Rhoda			2		
Clark, Samuel	1	2	2		
King, Joseph	2	1	3		
Goodel, Ruben	1	2	1		
Sly, Thomas	2		1		
Jehu (Negro)				6	
Larrance, Jonathan	2		3		
Gorton, Joseph	1	4	2		
Larrance, Samuel	2		1		
Read, Samuel	1	1	3		
Kuzer, Nathl	1	3	4		
Kuzer, Samuel	1		1		
Kirtland, Hannah	1		1		
Yerrington, Ruben	2	3	2		
Bishop, John	2		2		
Autherton, Isaac	1		3		
Branch, Stephen	3	4	4		
Read, Asa	1	2	5		
Read, Joseph	1		1		
Read, Amos	1	4	4		
Herrington, Joseph	2	1	2		
Eames, John	2	1	4		
Tracy, Jesse	3	5	5		
Tracy, Andw	1	2	4		
Tracy, Ebenezer	4	1	6		
Tracy, Elijah	2	1	2		
Smith, James	1		1		
Read, Jabez	2	1	3		
Read, John	1	3	5	1	
Baker, Enoch	3	1	3		
Gordon, Elexander	1	2	2	1	
Preston, Daniel	1	3	2		
Caulkins, Jonathan	1	1	3		
Button, Joshua	1		3		
Morgan, Elisha	2	3	8		
John (Negro)				3	
Cato (Negro)				3	
Eames, Cumfort	1		1		
Fanning, Charles	1	3	5		1
Jewet, Joseph	2		3		
Kimball, Levi	2	2	9		
Draper, Fisher	2		2		
Jewet, Eleazer	1		2		
Taylor, Nathan	1	3	3		
Brown, John	1	2	2		
Whealer, Parley	1	1	1		
Wilson, John	3	2	4		
Clark, Daniel	1		5		
Morgan, Dudley	2	2	4		
Smith, Samuel	1	2	4		
Norman, John	2	1	3		
Woodard, Ruben	1	1	4		
Smith, Jonathan	1		3		
Rose, Thomas	1	2	4	1	
Rose, Asa	1		5		
Rose, Sarah			3		
Moore, James	2		2		
Adams, Asael	2	2	4		
Sipeo (Negro)				6	
Geers, Roger	1	3	4		
Geers, Christopher	1		1		
Quive, Elijah	1		1	1	
Coit, Oliver	2	3	4		
Phillups, Genworence		1	2	1	
Tracy, Samuel	1		3		
Keeney, Benjamin	1	1	3		
Belshaw, William	3		3		
Phillups, Levi	1		1		
Phillups, Squire	1	3	3		
Phillups, Jonathan	1	3	2		
Keigwin, James	1	1	3		
Mulkins, John	1		2		
Lothrop, Azariah	1	3	2		
Pope, Ansil	1	2	5		
Kuzer, Elisha	1		1		
Davis, Samuel	1	3	5	6	
Moody (Negro)				6	
Rich, Solomon	1	1	2	2	
John (Negro)					1
Harris, Daniel	1		2		
Peter (Negro)				3	
Avory, James	2	2	5		
Geer, Robert	1		3		
Absolum (Negro)				6	
Avory, Gideon	2	3	5		
Avory, William	2	2	3		
Hatch, Elisabeth				1	
Jackson, Thomas	2		1		
Coit, Benjamin	3	4	4	1	
Quive, Lemuel	2	2	5		
Greene, David	2	2	7		
Greene, Winter	7	2	5		
Greene, John	1		3		
Belshaw, Joseph	1	3	6		
Gates, John	1	2	2		
Tucker, William	2	1	5		
Coit, Samuel	1		1		1
Quive, Henry	1	1	2		
Coit, Samuel, Junr	3	1	4		
Partridge, Asa, Junr	1		3		
Fanning, Frederick	1		2		
Smith, David	4	5	4		
Blunt, Ambrus	2	1	3		
Blunt, Walter	1	1	1		
Johnson, Stephen	4	1	4		
Waters, Lydia			1	1	
Walton, Daniel	2	1	8		
Austin, Thomas	3		2		
Walton, Oliver	2	4	5		
Clarke, Lydia			3		
Olin, Philup	3	5	5		
Blunt, Elisha	1	1	3		
Bennett, Daniel	2	5	3		
Fry, Peleg	1	2	4		
Gorton, Stephen	1		2		
Tylar, John	2	3	2	2	
Tylar, John, Junr	1	3	3		
Geer, Nathan	1	1	5		
Phillips, Jeramiah	2	3	4		
Coit, John	3	2	6		
Geers, Daniel	1		3		
Avery, John, Junr	1	2	4		
Lord, Nathl	2	2	5		
Yerrington, Abraham	1		2		
Tucker, Ephraim	2	2	3		
Adams, Daniel	1	2	2		
Gates, Mary	1		4		
Bennett, Jacob	2		2		
Parks, Ruben	1	1	1		
Cleft, Amos	3	1	3		
Pero (Negro)				5	
Pike (Negro)				6	
Tylar, Elisha	3	1	5		
Tracy, Lucy			3		
Tylar, Joseph	1	1	3		
Tylar, James	2	2	3		
Covey, Kinyon	1		1		
Cogswell, Nathl	4	1	3		
Kenney, Asa	2	1	3		
Brown, Jacob	1	1	2		
Bliss, Jona	2	1	1		
Potter, Gideon	2	4	6		
Baxter, Jesse	1		6		
Freman, Abigail	1		3		
Kenney, Jacob	4	3	2		
Bassett, James	1	2	4		
Cook, Thadeus	2	3	6		
Wade, William	1	1	1		
Cheesborough, Thomas	1	2	4		
Hatch, Jeremi	1		2		
Hatch, Elisha	1	1	2		
Gates, Daniel	3	3	3		
Absolum (Negro)					2
Stanton, Jabez	1	1	4		
Stanton, William	1		3		
Geer, Able	2	2	2		
Prentice, Manassa	2	2	2		
Morgan, James	2	1	5		
Geer, Lebeus	1	4	3		
Lester, Moses	3	2	6		
Geer, Stephen	1	1	2		
Geer, Elisha	2	1	6		
Bliss, Saml	1	1	2		
Bliss, Silas	2	1	2		
Whealer, Edward	1		1		
Smith, Darius	1		2		
Clark, Perry	2	1	2		
Parks, David	1		2		
Stanton, Jabez	2		6		
Bruster, Simon	4	1	7		2
Freman, Caleb	1		2		
Freman, Saml	3		4		
Freman, Peleg	1	1	5		
Freman, Mary	2		1		
Rude, Lydia	1		2		
Morse, William	1	1	5		
Morse, Daniel	2		2		
Morgan, Benjamin	1		2		
Geer, Silsbey	1		2		
Johnson, William	1		1		
Benjamin, John	1	1	3		
Palmer, Darius	1	2	3		
Nickols, William	1	2	1		
Prentice, Eleazer	3	1	2		
Lester, Elisha	2	2	5		
Leonard, Saml	2	2	3		
Stanton, Nathan	1	1	2		
Stanton, Robart, Junr	2		1		
Stanton, Robart	1		1		
Leonard, Saml, Junr	1	1	2	1	
Denison, Elijah	2	1	2		
Stanton, David	2		4		
Stanton, Saml	1	1	2		
Maine, Peres	1		2		
Burton, Israel	1		6		
Palmer, Gershom	1		2		
Ray, Daniel	2		4		
Bramin, Prudence	2	2	3		
Herrick, Israel	2	1	5		
Randal, Nathan	1	4	5		
Ray, Amos	1	3	4	1	1
Dorrance, Gershom	3		1		
Herrick, Isaac	1		2		
Herrick, Ephraim	1	2	5		
Wilbur, Joseph	1	5	2		
Kimball, Nathan	3	1	4		
Frink, James	1	2	2		
Stanton, David, Junr	1	1	5		
Brown, Parley	2	4	6		
Tylar, Samuel	3	1	4		
Bordman, Hezekiah	3	2	5		
Branch, Thomas	3	1	5		
Guile, Abraham	2		3		
Cook, Barton	4		6		
Cook, John	4	3	5		
Samson, William	1	1	3		
Sherman, Elisabeth			1		
Holly, Manchester			3	1	
Stuart, Alexander	1	3	8		1
Keeney, Ezra	2	1	1		1
Boardman, David	2	1	7		
Yemmons, Saml	1	2	2		
Rouse, Simeon	4		2		
Starkweather, Joseph	2	3	2		
Reynolds, Ebenr	2	3	3		
Lewis, Mary			3		
Maine, Peckham	1		2		
Killam, William	1		2		
Barns, Elijah	2	3	6		
Bromley, Preserved	1		1		
Starkweather, Ephraim	1	1	3		
Chapman, William	2		4		
Holt, Nathl	2	1	1		
Capron, Giles	2	1	6		
Pollard, Joseph	1				
Johnson, Benjamin	1		2		
Keeney, Gideon	3		4		
Herrick, Elijah	1		4		
Rose, Daniel	3	3	2	1	
Huntington, Andw	2	1	2		
Avery, Solomon	1				
Partridge, Elijah	1	3	1		
Partridge, Asa	1	2	3		
Love, Robart	1		1		
Weeden, Elijah	2	2	6		
Davis, Joseph	1	1	3		
Herrick, Nathan	1	1	1		
Herrick, Amos	1		3		
Partridge, James	1	3	6		
Belshaw, Nathan	1	1	2		
Bottom, Joseph	1		2		
Whealer, John	1	5	1		
Guile, Joseph	1	3	2		
Partridge, John	1		1		
Gates, Joseph	1	3	4		
Gates, Elijah	1			1	3
Wanton (Negro)			2		3
Whitman, John	1		2		
Partridge, Ruben	2	1	4		
Bennett, Elias	1	1	3		
Daniels, Oliver	3		3		
Woodard, Moses	1	2	7		
Geer, James	2	1	2		
Rose, Elisha	1		8		
Coit, Daniel	1	1	8	4	
Prentice, Elisha	1	1	4		

NEW LONDON COUNTY—Continued.

NAME OF HEAD OF FAMILY.	Free white males of 16 years and upward, including heads of families.	Free white males under 16 years.	Free white females, including heads of families.	All other free persons.	Slaves.
Cogswell, John	1	1	2		
Hartshorn Jonathan	1	2	2		
Guile, Samuel	2	1	4		
Keeney, Henry	1	1	2		
Ray, Stephen	1	2	2		
Ray, John	2	1	5		
Ray, Gideon	1		3		
Burton, Nathan	1		1		
Burton, Israel	1		3		
Hutcherson, Amos	2	2	5		
Bromley, Israel	1	3	2		
Parrish, Roswell	1	2	2		
Benjamins, Jedediah	1		1		
Brown, John	4	2	3		
Rix, Hannah	2		4		
Billings, Joseph	1		1		
Maine, Rufus	1	4	4		
Rix, Thomas	2	2	4		
Small, William	1		1		
Rix, Theophilus	1	2	3		
Woodburn, Pruda	1		3		
Amos, Elisabeth			2		
Lambert, Thomas	1	2	3		
Herrick, Eleazer	2	1	3		
Kimball, John	1		1		
Benjamin, Abiel	1		1		
Benjamin, Abiel Junr	1	6	3		
Benjamins, Ezra	2	2	3		
Badcock, Benjamin	2	3	4		
Geer, Jonathan	1		1		
Blodgett, William	1				
Frink, Diah	1	1	2		
Brown, Amos, Junr	1	2	3		
Grant, Wm	1	2	2		
Brown, Walter	2	2	3		
Brown, Amos	2	5	3		
Robins, Moses	2		4		1
Crasy, Robert	1	1	2		
Keeney, David	1	2	4		
Davis, Thara	2	2	4		
Halsey, Wm	2		3		
Safford, Thomas	2	1	5		
Guile, Elisha	1	1	2		
Frink, Andw	4		2		
Brumley, Christopher	1	4	5		
Safford, John	3	2	2		
Safford, Johnson	1	1	2		
Starkweather, Jesse	1	2	6		
James, John	2	2	6		1
Tylar, Caleb	2		3	1	1
Tylar, Joseph	2	2	3		
Spicer, Oliver	1		1		
Crasy, John	3	2	4		1
Palmer, George	1	4	3		
Tylar, Lemuel	2		2		
Peters, Nathan	2	2	5		
Morgan, John	3	4	5		
Forthsides, Charles	1	4	3		
Jones, Simeon	1		4		
Billings, Randall	3	5	1		
Palmer, Jesse	1	1	4		
Downing, John	1	2	3		
Parks, Hannah			1		
Edwards, William	1		1		
Smith, Jona	1	2	3		
Crasy, Robart, Junr	1		4		
Tracy, Isael	2	1	7		
Forbs, Nathan	3	1	2		
Andrus, Solomon	1		1		
Rude, Zachariah	3	2	2		
York, Elisha	2	3	5		
Cook, Cyprian	1	1	3		
Leonard, Nicholas	1		2		
Morse, David	2	4	3		
Brown, Walter, Junr	1	1	2		
Meach, Lucy	1		2		
Rude, Ezekiel	2	1	3		
Meach, Moses	2	2	5		
Smith, Asa	2	4	9		
Meach, Jacob	4	2	4		
Clark, Timothy, Junr	1	3	3		
Mott, Samuel	4	2	5	1	
Bestow, Calvin	3	1	3		
Bruster, Eunice		1	1		
Mott, Edward	3		7		
Downer, Joshua	4	4	3		1
Treat, Samuel	1		2		
Brown, William	1	3	4		
Rix, Nathan	1	1	2		
Gavett, John	1		2		
Morgan, James, Junr	1	1	2	1	
Button, Roswell	5	5	6		
Downer, Avory	1	3	1		
Tracy, Edward	1	2	3		
Brown, Amos, Junr	1		2		
Grant, William	1	1	3		
Winter, Frederick	3	1	8		

NAME OF HEAD OF FAMILY.	Free white males of 16 years and upward, including heads of families.	Free white males under 16 years.	Free white females, including heads of families.	All other free persons.	Slaves.
Plummer, Mary			2		
Gates, Ebenezer	1	1	1		
Chapman,Cumfort,Junr	1	2	2		
Avory, Richerson	1	1	3		
Dunwell, Stephen	1	1	3		
Winter, Amos	1	1	3		
Crandall, Benjamin	1	3	1		
Button, Mathias	1	3	4		
Parks, Elisha	2	2	2		
Stanton, Nathan	1	1	2		
Parks, Silas	1	1	2		
Parks, Elijah	2	4	4		
Geer, John W	1	4	2		
Parks, Paul	2	1	4		
Baley, Jeremiah	2		2		
Baley, Samuel	1		3		
Freman, Ebenezer	1		2		
Thomas, Abigail			3		
Avory, Ebenezer	2	3	5		
Story, Solomon	2	1	3		
Kimball, Elisha	1	4	4		
Winter, Ebenezer	1		1		
Halsey, Jeremiah	4	4	8	1	2
Parks, Roswell	1	3	2		
Parks, Abijah	1		3		
Parks, Abijah, Junr	1		1		
Parks, Asa	2	1	3		
Cook, Isaiah	2	4	3		
Woodard, Thomas	2	2	4		
Avory, Samuel	2		3		
Avory, David	1	2	2		
Avory, John	3	2	2		
Avory, Isaac	3	2	6		
Avory, Amos	2	1	3	2	
Winter, Jonah	1	2	3	1	
Swan, Timothy	1	5	3		
Thomas, Daniel	1	2	6		
Killam, Samuel	1	2	6		
Whipple, Luther	1	3	7		
Bruster, Jacob	1	2	4		
Gates, Thomas	2	1	2		
Gates, Cyrus	1	4	4		
Beard, William	3		2		
Chapman, Cumfort	3		1		
Gates, Daniel	3	2	6		
Prentice, Elisha	1	1	4		
Harris, Andrew	1	1	2		
Crasy, Oliver	3	1	5	1	
Bruster, Dorothy	1		2		
Bruster, Daniel	3	3	4		
Standish, Israel	1	1	4		
Standish, Amasa	1	4	4		
Gion, Luke	1	2	3		
Newton, Jacob	1	3	2		
Comb, Thomos	2		3		
Smith, Jonathan	1		4		
Holt, Jesse	1		5		
Jones, Stephen	1	1	1		
Smith, Silas	1	5	1		
Ruel, Elijah	1		1		
Roath, Daniel	1		2		
Roath, Rufus	1	2	3		
Randall, Joseph	2		3		
Roath, Betsy		1	2		
Wintworth, Amos	1		2		
Roath, Benjamin	2	1	5		
Peter (Negro)					3
Roath, Saml	2	1	2		
Roath, John	2	2	3		
Roath, Silas	1	2	4		
Cook, William	1	2	3		
Williams, Moses	1	1	1		
Roath, Joseph	1	2	3		
Downs, Sarah			2		
Rose, Peleg		3	2		
Bromley, Dewey	1	1	4		
Spicer, Daniel	1	1	3		
Spicer, Asa	1		2		
Mortimer, Benjamin	1		2		
Corning, Elisha	2	4	3		
Corning, Loami	2	3	3		
Corning, Samuel	1	1	1		
Coy, Nathan	1	3	2		
Wilcox, Elisha	1		2		
Wilcox, Joseph	1		1		
Cato (Negro)					5
Brown, George	1		1		
Longwood, Mathew	1		1		
Tracy, Elisha	1		1		
Gideons, Joseph	1	1	7		
Tracy, John	1	1	2		
Smith, Ephraim	1	1	5		
Avory, James	3	4	3		
Badcock, Ichabod, Junr	2	4	3		
Morgan, Simeon	1	1	3		
Buttors, William			2		
Williams, Moses, Junr	1	1	3		

NAME OF HEAD OF FAMILY.	Free white males of 16 years and upward, including heads of families.	Free white males under 16 years.	Free white females, including heads of families.	All other free persons.	Slaves.
Stilman, Zeporah			3		
Bruster, Jona, Junr	2	1	2		
Pride, Absolum	2		2		
Story, Jonathan	1	2	7		
Story, Ebenr	1	3	1		
Williams, Jesse	3		2		
Penninian, William	1		2		
Story, Mehitable		1	1		
Holdrige, William	2	1	1		
Winslow, William	1	2	2		
Craige, Robart	1		1		
Aderton, Samuel	1	3	3		
Ford, John	1	1	2		
Bruster, Jabez	3	5	3		
Bruster, Nathan	2	1	4		
Bruster, Elijah	3	2	3		
Harkness, John	2	2	6		
Capron, Simeon	1	2	3		
Bruster, Jonathan	3	3	3		
Allen, Ebenezer	1		1		
Clark, Roger	1	1	2		
Pollard, Barsheba			2		
Pollard, Nabby			3		
Wight, John	1		4		
Worthington, Dan	1	5	4		
Rust, Prudence		1	4		
Punderson, Ebenezer, Junr	1	1	4		2
Page, Philemon	1	1	2		
Punderson Ebenezer	1		2		
Billings, Benjamin	1		1		
Billings, William	1		1		
Whipple, Jonathan	1	3	2		
Holerige, Elisha	1	1	2		
Capron, Samuel	3	3	5		
Rose, Joseph	2		4		
Thurber, Luther	1		1		
Whipple, Elijah	1	2	2		
Pollard, John	1	1	2		
Chapman, Obadiah	1	1	4		
Whipple, Joseph	2	1	3		
Brown, Elias	3	3	3		1
Badcock, Ichabod	3	1	5		
Brown, Eunice			2		
Kimball, Moses	3		2		
Kimball, Asa	1	2	3		
Stodard, Mortimer	2	2	4		
Standish, Levi	1		4		
Starkweather, Richard	1		3		
Badcock, Christopher	1	1	5		
Read, Christopher	1		3		
Badcock, Joseph S	1	1	5		
Prince (Negro)				1	4
Huntley, Thomas	1	2	2		
Brown, David	1	1	3		
Button, William	1		1		
Button, Shubael	1	1	1		
Teel, Joseph	5	4	3		
Bruster, Silas	1	1	2		
Williams, Samuel	2		5		
Williams, Simeon	2		1		
Crandall, Christopher	1	3	2		
Gideons, Solomon	1	5	5		
Pembleton, Joshua	2	3	6		
Standish, Nathan	2	4	4		
Baldwin, Joseph	1	3	3		
Davis, John	1		1		
Guile, Nathan	1		3		
Bramin, John	2	2	5		
Read, Samuel	1	2	5		
Corning, Nehemiah	2		2		
Corning, Uriah	1	1	3		
Truman, Jonathan	2	2	3	1	
Pride, Asa	2		4		
Adams, Abraham	1	1	2		
Wight, Joseph	1		2		
Champlin, Silas	1	1	2		
Story, Jabez	2	1	2		
Pride, William	4	1	7		
Smith, John	2		3		
Benjamins, Asa	2	1	2		
Harvey, Ruth			2		
Weever, Elijah	1		2		
Vale, William	1	1	2		
Patterson, James	1	4	1		
Ellis, Samuel	1		2		
Harvey, Phillup	2	4	3		
Andrus, Jude			2		
Andrus, Joseph	1				
Saunders, Wait	2		3		
Badcock, Elihu	1	1	2		
Ginnings, Jonathan	1	1	3		
Saunders, Elisha	3	2	7		
Andrus, John	1		3		
Hasskall, Roger	2	2	3		
Fitch, Cordelia			3		
Hilyard, Benjamin	1	4	3		

NEW LONDON COUNTY—Continued.

NAME OF HEAD OF FAMILY.	Free white males of 16 years and upward, including heads of families.	Free white males under 16 years.	Free white females, including heads of families.	All other free persons.	Slaves.
Wilcox, Isaiah	1	2	2		
Fitch, Benaijah	2		2	1	
Fitch, Elijah	3		3	1	
Fitch, Thomas	1	1	2		
Fitch, Nathaniel	1	3	2		
Downs, Joshua	1		1		
Bushnell, Joseph	1	2	3		
Mix, Rufus	1	2	2		
Tracy, Moses	1		3		
Standish, Saml	1		2		
Morse, Mary	1		2		
Bruster, Joseph	1	4	2		
Parks, Moses	3	4	5		
Demming, Jabez	1	2	5		
Pride, Elijah	2	3	3		
Chote, Abigail			2		
Chote, John	1	1	4		
Harvey, George	1		2		
Cook, Asael	3	3	5		
Cook, James	1	2	3		
Grinell, Mathew	1	1	2		
Tracy, Joseph	1	2	1		
Rockwell, Samuel	1	3	3		
Bruster, Judah	1	3	5		
Larreby, James	1		2		
Davis, Samuel	2	2	3		
Cook, Elisha	2	2	4		
Cook, Daniel	2	1	4	1	
Spicer, Able	1	1	2		
Palmer, Jedediah	2	2	7		
Tracy, Miner	2	2	5	1	
Clark, John	3	2	2		
Aldrige, Jane	1		2		
Clark, Ebenezer	3	1	5		
Bruster, Simeon, Junr	3	1	6		
Ayrs, Nathan	6	2	6		
Stersy, Abigail	1		2		
Stersy, Consider	1	1	5		
Meach, David	4	1	6		
Will (Negro)					3
Morgan, Simeon	3	1	7		
Morgan, Daniel	2	3	5		
Herrick, Rufus	1		2		
Lester, Timothy	1	1	5		
Lester, Elijah	1	4	7	1	
Back, Elisabeth			1		
Graves, Jonathan	1	2	2		
Coit, Whealer	4	1	8		
Hart, Levi	1	2	2		
Herrick, Ephraim	1	1	3		
Austin, Edward	1		4		
Button, Joseph	2	1	4		
Morgan, Daniel, Junr	1	3	7		1
Swan, Elisha	3		7		
Sharp (Negro)				2	
Meach, Aaron	2	2	2		
Andrus, Eli	1	2	3		
Waldo, Cornelius	1		1		
Meach, Daniel	3	2	5		
Smith, Seth	1		1		
Smith, Chester	1	1	2		
Bromley, John	1	1	4		
Culver, Jeremiah	2	2	3		
Yerrington, Joseph	3		5		
Chapman, Adinah	1		3		
Button, Zebulun	1	2	1		
Starkweather, Athur	2	4	2		
Starkweather, Robert	1	1	3		
Starkweather, Charles	1	3	2		
Starkweather, John	1	5	3		
Kimball, John	2	1	4		
Prentice, John	3		4		
Prentice, John, Junr	1	1	1		
Prentice, Thomas	2		2	1	
Bruster, Elisabeth			2		
Prentice, Samuel	2	1	4		
Utley, Peleg	1	2	2		
Prentice, Joshua	2	3	3		
Smith, Joseph	5	3	2		
Denison, Avory	2	1	3		
Denison, Daniel	2	3	7		
Denison, Elisha	2	2	5		
Prentice, Lucy	1		3		
Eames, Joseph	2	3	3		
Crasey, George	2	3	2		
Sears, Remington	3	1	3		
Whealer, Ephraim	2	1	5		
Billings, Samuel	1		4		
Billings, Otis	1		2		
Billings, Samuel, Junr	2		1		
Swan, Edward	2	3	2		1
Swan, Thomas	3	2	5		2
Fanning, Richard	2	1	2		
Wilkinson, George	2	2	2		
Woodard, Caleb	2	3	5		
Worden, Sitorster	1	4	2		
Jones, Charles	1	1	2		
Eglestone, David	1	2	3		
Bentley, Ezekiel	1	4	2		
Woodard, Content	1		2		
Morgan, Jonathan	2	1	5		
Searls, William	1	3	4		
Swan, Patience	1	1	4		
Swan, David	1		1		
Swan, Charles	1	4	2		
Swan, Robart	2	2	4		
Brown, Silvanus	1	5	2		
Brown, Humphrey	1	1	2		
Swan, Nathan	1	4	3		
Smith, Thomas	1	1	6		
Swan, Timothy	1		2		
Ayrs, Joseph	2	1	5		
Browning, Jeremi	1	3	2		
Palmer, Michael	1	2	1		
Meach, Moses	5	3	5		1
Barns, Nehemiah	1	3	1		
Moore, David	1	1	3		1
Harvey, Peter	1	1	3		
York, Collins	2	1	3		
Frink, Hannah	1		2		
Hewet, Jonas	3	1	7		
Billings, Sanford	4	2	4		
Greene, Caleb	3		3		
Hewet, Henry	3		3		
Hewet, Simeon	1		2		
Hewet, Saml	1		4		
Hakes, George	1		1		
Hilyard William	1	2	3		
Baldwin, Theophilus	1		2		
Billings, Daniel	1	1	8		
Billings, Elisha	1	3	2		
Billings, Benaijah, Junr	1	1	3		
Billings, Benaijah	1		2		
Baldwin, Zeba	1	6	1		
Baldwin, David	3	1	4		
Baldwin, John	3	4	5		
Brown, Asa	2	4	4		
Swan, Jesse	2	3	6		
Lamb, Lemuel	3	4	3		
Herrick, Ebenr	1	1	1		
Woodard, Park	1		3		
Frink, Stephen	1	1	3		
Woodard, Asa	1		3		
Brown, Jesse	2	2	6		
Church, Nathl	1	4	1		
Searls, John	1	3	5		
Jones, Saml	1	1	2		
Jones, William	1		4		
Wilcox, Oliver	2	2	5		
Geer, Thomas	1	4	2		
Hodge, Benjamin	1	2	2		
Eglestone, Ichabod, Junr	2		1	1	
Briston & Philup (Negro)					2
Edwards, Peleg	3	2	4		
Eglestone, Ichabod	1	2	2		
Palmer, Jemima	1		2		
Eglestone, Ichabod, 3d	1		2		
Eglestone, Dennis	1	1	2		
Maine, Nathl	1	3	3		
Eglestone, Winlock	1	4	3		
Edward, Christopher	1		2		
Billings, Nathan	1	3	4		
Eglestone, Joseph	4	2	7		
Beba, Stephen	1		2		
Baker, William	1	1	4		
Crandall, Baley	1	3	2		
Crandall, Isaiah	1		5		
Eglestone, Benedick	2		6		
Hadsall, Stephen	1	1	2		
Burdrick, Ira	1	1	1		
Tiff, Joseph	2	2	1		
Tiff, John	1	1	3		
Mott, Jonathan	1		2		
Stafford, Andrew	1	2	6		
Crandall, Amos, Junr	2	3	4		
Austin, Edward	1	1	6		
Austin, Jedediah	1		2		
Austin, William	1	2	1		
Palmer, Stutely	1	2	4		
Whealer, David	1		2		
Tiff, Oliver	1	3	4		
Roads, Anthony	3	1	3		
Palmer, Wait	1		2		
Palmer, Mody	1		2		
Brown, Jabez	1	1	2		
Badcock, Timothy	2	1	3		
Palmer, Vorce	1	3	5		
Badcock, Joshua	4	5	4		
Lewis, Jonathan	1		3		
Cleaveland, Pheba			3		
Burdet, Thomson	1	3	4		
Downs, Joseph	2	4	5		
Palmer, William	1	1	6		
Palmer, George	1	1	1		
Coats, Rufus	1	3	2		
Coats, William	2		2	1	
Brown, Stephen	2	2	5		
Plumb, Samuel	1	2	4		
Palmer, Joseph	2		4		
Palmer, Gershon	1	3	3		
Palmer, Ethel	3	1	3		
Palmer, Elias Sanford	2	4	6		
Palmer, Ichabod	2		3		
Palmer, Peleg	1	1	1		
Lamphear, John	1	3	1		
Palmer, Gilbert	1	1	2		
Palmer, Sanford	1		2		
Crandall, Amos	1		2		
Bromley, Jesse	1	1	2		
Frink, Amos	3	2	3		
Darrow, Lemuel	1	1	3		
Thompson, Robart	1	2	4		
Thompson, James	4		3		
Thompson, James, Junr	1	3	3		
Roggers, Jonathan	2		2		
Thompson, Elexander	1		1		
Thompson, Moses	1		2		
Wilcox, Collins	1	2	5		
Young, Nicholas	1	1	7		
Worden, Nathl	2		3		
Taylor, Sanford	3	1	6		
Nun, Samuel	2		2		
Wilcox, Francis	2	3	1		
Wilcox, Daniel	4	5	4		
Northrop, Saml	1	1	2		
Weever, Jonathan	1	1	2		
Eglestone, Joseph	2		5		
Palmeter, Joseph	1	5	1		
Palmeter, Silas	1		5		
Palmeter, Paul	1	4	2		
Homes, Thomas	6		4		
Worden, Daniel	1				
Roggers, Jonathan	1		2		
Brown, Nehemiah	2	2	6		1
Brown, Christopher	2		7		
Popple, George	1	1	3		
Galley, James	1		2		
Dye, Easter			1		
Weever, Lodowick	1	2	1		
Chapman, Nathan	3	2	3		
Chapman, Amos	2	2	4		
Chapman, Joseph	3	3	5		
Chapman, Andrew, Junr	3	3	4		
Chapman, Nahum	1	3	2		
Crandall, Charles	2	1	4		
Parks, Malvin	2	3	4		
Brown, William	3		2		
York, Bel	3	1	3		
York, James	1	1	6		
York, Bel, Junr	2	1	8		
Lamphear, Shubael	1	1	2		
Lamphear, Roswell	1				
Maine, Lyman	1		2		
Maine, Jonas	1	2	2		
Yemmons, Thomas	1	1	1	1	
Brud, Jabez	1	1	4		
Brud, Joseph, Junr	1	1	5		
Brud, Allen	1		1		1
Bromley, Jabez	1	4	4		
Geer, Joseph	2		1		
Geer, George	1	4	1		
Northrop, Samuel	1	1	2		
Brown, Danl	3	1	5		
Coats, Wm, Junr	2	6	3		
Parks, Peter	2		3		
Burdick, Samuel	3	1	1		
Burdick, Abraham	3	3	4		
Coon, Lebues	1	1	1		
Parmeter, Joshua	1		2		
Burdick, Daniel	2		3		
Tanner, Joseph	1	2	2		
Palmer, Stephen	1	2	3		
Maine, Asa	3	1	5		
Maine, Asa, Junr	1		2		
Maine, Peter	1		1		
Maine, Peter, Junr	2	4	4		
Maine, Peter, 3d	1		1		
Heby, Christopher	3	2	2		
Cole, Sands	1		2		
Collins, Stephen	1	1	2		
Collins, Mehitable			2		
Brown, Nathan	1	2	4		
Langothy, Thomas	2	3	1		
Langothy, John	1	3	3		
Davis, William	1	1	2		
Maine, David, Junr	1	1	2		
Langothy, Benjamin	2	4	6		
Burdick, Elijah	2		3		
Allen, Ichabod	1		4		
Crandall, Peter	1		1		

NEW LONDON COUNTY—Continued.

NAME OF HEAD OF FAMILY.	Free white males of 16 years and upward, including heads of families.	Free white males under 16 years.	Free white females, including heads of families.	All other free persons.	Slaves.
Allen, John	1		1		
Spalding, Asa	1	3	5		
Roberson, John	3	1	6		
Wills, Thomas	2	4	5		
Greene, John	1	3	3		
Vors, Edward	1	1	1		
Reynolds, Thomas	1	2	3		
Welles, David	1	2	5		
Bentley, George	2		3		
Stanton, Joshua	4	4	6		
Wilcox, Nathan	2		3		
Wilcox, David	1		2		
Collins, Daniel	2	1	3		
Hall, Stephen	2	4	6		
Burdick, Ezekiel	1		3		
Miner, Asa	2		4		
Crum, Arnold	1	3	1		
Badcock, Paul	3	1	5		
Stanton, William	1		4		
Worden, Walter	1	1	2		
Palmer, Wm, Junr	1	2	2		
Palmer, William	1		3		
Loomis, Timothy	1	1	2		
Nugen, John	1		3		
Lewis, Beriah	1	4	5		
Richerson, John	1	1	3		
Pemberton, Stephen	1		3		
Dewey, Christopher	2	1	4		
Hall, Simeon	1	2	2		
Brown, Zebulun	1	1	4		
Church, David	1	1	3		
Allen, Jonathan	1		1		
Allen, Jonathan, Junr	1	1	5		
Collins, Amos	3	2	6		
Brown, Simeon	1	4	6		
Hall, Ruben	2	1	5	1	
Bentley, George, Junr	1	3	4		
Button, John	3	5	8		
Partlow, Thomas	1		2		
Partlow, Azariah	2	2	5		
Miner, Daniel	2		2		1
Crum, Joseph	3	2	6		
Whealer, Hannah			3		
Brown, Nathan, 3d	1	2	2		
Brown, Mathew	1		2		
Brown, Simeon	1		1		
Brown, Joshua, Junr	1		3	1	
Brown, Jeptha	1	1	2		
Brown, Josiah	1		3		
Larkin, Moses	1	1	2		
Frink, Samuel	1		2		
Dye, William	2	3	6		
Randall, Robart	2	6	2		
Brown, Nathan, Junr	3	2	5		
Bromley, David	2		4		
Palmer, Jonathan, Junr	1	1	7		
Welch, Charles	3	3	4		
Stanton, Robart	1	5	4		
Grant, Noah	1	3	3		
Brown, Jeremi	2	4	4		
Brown, James	1	2	7		
Brown, Eleazer	2	1	4		
Maine, Daniel	1	3	5		
Crandall, Ebor	2	1	4		
Thurston, Edward	2	4	5		
Maine, Amos	2	1	8		
York, John	3	1	6		
Homes, Joshua	3	3	4	1	
Homes, Edward	1	1	2		
Maine, David	2	4	4		
Maine, Timothy	3	1	3		
Maine, Timothy, Junr	1	1	4		
Maine, Benaijah	3	3	6		
Williams, William	1		1		3
Williams, William, Junr	1	2	1		
Williams, John, 2d	3	3	3		
Laws, John	1	1	3		
Utley, Elijah	3		1		
Badcock, John	2		2		
Homes, James	1	3	4		
Brigs, Ithamer	2	1	2		
Maine, Luther	1	1	2		
Bill, Joseph	1		6		
Hakes, Richard	5	6	7		
York, Allen	1		3		
Swan, Mary			4		
York, Jesse	3	2	2		
Peabody, Saml	2		2		
Peabody, Thomas	3	3	5		
Brown, Jedediah, Junr	1	5	2		1
Hammon, Thomas	1	3	6		
Fellows, Ephraim	2		6		
Homes, Jared	1	1	2		
Homes, Jeremi	1	4	6	1	
Homes, John	1	2	7		3
Smith, Lemuel	1	2	3		
Hewet, Isaac	1	1	4		
Williams, Benadam	1	4	4		4
Coats, John	3		4		
Coats, David	1	1	1		
Coats, Amos	1	2	2		
Grey, Robart	2	2	6		
Brown, David	1	1	2		
Thomson, Joseph	1	1	2		
Tiff, Oliver	1	4	3		
Coats, Bartholemu	1	2	5		
Stuart, Nathan	2	3	6		
Coats, Edward	1	1	4		
Coats, Betsy	2	2	4		
Williams, Isaac, Junr	1	2	6		2
Hilyard, William, Junr	2	1	3		
Hilyard, John	1		4		
Browning, Jeremiah	3	2	4	1	
York, Oliver	1	2	5		
Brown, Jared	1	2	3		
Harvey, Paul	1	2	4		
Ayrs, Joseph, Junr	2	5	4		
Hilyard, Azariah	1	3	1		
Newton, Ebenezer	1	1	5		
Miner, Simeon	2		3		
Avory, Elias	1		1		
Plumb, Nathl	1		3		
Plumb, James	2	4	4		
Brown, Jonas	2	1	6		
Miner, James	1	1	3		
Miner, Nathan	2		1		
Miner, Nathan, Junr	1		1		
Avory, Luther	1	4	3		
Stow, Samuel	1	2	3		
Burdrick, John	1	3	2		
Sisson, William	3	1	7		
Avory, Stephen, Junr	5	2	6		
Peckham, Thomas	1	2	2		
Swan, John	5	1	4		
Elliot, John	1	1	1		
Hewet, Rufus	2		2		
Avory, John	1		3		
Leeds, Jedediah	1	1	3		
Hewet, Elias	1				
Hewet, Rufus, Junr	1		2		
Peckham, John	2	1	4		
Peckham, Benjamin	1	3	4		
Whealer, Hosea	2	3	5		
Whealer, John, Junr	1	1	3		
Grant, Josiah	1	2	5		
Palmer, Nehemiah	2	1	7		
Elexander, James	1	1	5		
Brown, Robart	2	1	3		
Whealer, Thomas, 2d	1	2	3		
Roberson, William	1		1		
Grant, Amos	1	2	2		
Brud, Stephen	1	1	2		
Grant, Oliver	1		1		
Grant, Oliver, Junr	1	5	3		
Hewet, Dudley	1	1	3		
Avory, Christopher	1	1	2		
Avory, Christopher, Junr	1	1	1		
Hewet, Charles	4		4		
Brud, Joseph	1	3	3		
Whealer, Amos	1	3	3		4
Whealer, Jeremi	1				
Greene, John	2	4	3		
Brumley, Joshua	1	1	5		
Badcock, Nathl	2		4		
Brumley, David	2		3		
Denison, George	5	3	6		
Davis, Joseph	1	1	3		
Denison, Nathaniel	1		4		
Meach, Jonathan	1	2	2		
Gardiner, Abiel	4	2	3		
Vincent, William	1	2	3		
Burington, Eliphelet	1		1		
Noyce, James	1	1	1		
Hinckley, Thomas	1	2	4		
Helme, Oliver	2	2	4		
Richerson, Salmon	3		2		
Brand, Thomas	1	3	3		
Whealer, Sheppard	1	2	2	1	
Clark, Arnold	1	1	3		
Badcock, Elias	1		2		
Button, George	1		2		
Greene, Mathew	3		2		
Grant, Joshua	1	4	3		
Grant, Gilbert	1	1	4		
Grant, Noah, Junr	1	1	2		
Munsill, Phineas	2		2		
Whealer, John	2	1	1		
Whealer, John, 3d	1		3		
Niles, Surviah			2		3
Whealer, Thomas	2	1	5		2
Williams, Washam	2		3	1	
Williams, Washam, Junr	1		3		
McDaniel, James	1	2	1		
Grant, John	1	6	2		
Whealer, Paul	1	1	6		
Noyce, Joseph	3	2	5		
Frink, Isaac	3	1	4		
Champlin, Joseph	3		3		1
Palmer, John	1				
Hull, Latham	2	4	5		2
Utley, John	1	2	2		
Hull, Stephen	1		1		
Whealer, Joseph	1	7	1		
Whealer, Joshua	1		4		
Brown, Asher	1	4	3		
Geary, Thomas	1	3	5		1
Williams, Ephraim	1	1	1		2
Gibeons, John	2		6		
Otis, Jonathan	1	2	4		
Tosbery, John				5	
Fish, Jason	3	1	3		
Fish, Titus	2		2		
Fish, David	1	2	5		
Schoolcraft, Samuel	1		1		
Baley, David	2	1	6		
Baley, Able	1	3	3		
Bennett, Aaron	3	2	6		
Bennett, David	1		3		
Bennett, Elisha	1	3	5		
Hemstead, Robart	3	2	4		
Hemstead, Robart, Junr	1		2		
Hemstead, Samuel	1	5	3		
Lewis, Volentine	1	5	3		
Mulkey, Timothy	1	4	7		
Gallup, John	1	3	3		
Brumley, Simion	1	3	3		
Miner, Samuel	2	1	4		
Miner, Peres	1		1		
Whittles, Isaac	2	1	3		
Satille, Elisha	2	4	4		
Cheesborough, Christopher	1	4	1		
Williams, Ebenezer, Junr	1	1	2		
Williams, Nathl	1	3	2		
Williams, Thomas	1		2		
Miner, Richerson	1	1	6		
Avory, Stephen	2		2		
Denison, James	2		3		
Eldridge, Christopher	3		3		
Denison, Andw	3	3	2		
Miner, Daniel, Junr	1	4	4		
Wilcox, Robart	1	3	4		
Wilcox, Jeremi	1	2	1		1
Smith (Negro)				7	
Wilcox, Arnold	3		3		
York (Negro)				4	
Williams, Ebenezer	1	2	2		
Fish, Sirus	1		2		
Daverson, Christopher	2	3	2		
Daverson, Daniel	1	3	1		
Williams, Nehemiah	3		3		
Williams, Park	1	4	3		
Williams, Eleazer	1		6	1	
Hudson, John	3		3		
Williams, Gilbert	1				
Denison, Daniel, Junr	2	1	6		1
Williams, Uriah	1	2	3		
Williams, Isaac	1		4		
Denison, Joseph	1		1		1
Copp, Saml	1	3	9		
Denison, John, 3d	1	3	5		
Denison, Amos	2	2	4	1	1
Denison, Peleg	1	3	4	1	
Whipple, Amos	1	1	6		
Whipple, William	1		3		
Shaw, Amos	1	1	2		
Whealer, Lester	1	6	3		
Williams, Elisha	2	3	6		4
Denison, Joseph, Junr	1	5	6		
Amon (Negro)				7	
Lewis, Ichabod	1		1		
White, Mary	1		2		
Prince (Negro)				3	
Holdridge, Nathl	1	1	1		
Whittles, Isaac, Junr	1	2	3		
Denison, Oliver	1	2	3		
Stanton, Danl	3		3		
Witter, William	1	1	2		
Stanton, Saml, 3d	1	1	3		
Whealer, Richard	4	1	3		
Whealer, Jonathan	1		1		
Whealer, Jonathan, Junr	3		3		
Page, Joseph	3	1	5	1	3
Ingraham, Nathl	2	2	3		
Champlin, Charles	2	2	5		
Collins, Daniel	2	1	4		
Hubbard, Peter	1	2	3		
Gallup, Amos	2	3	2		
Stanton, Wait	2	1	1		

NEW LONDON COUNTY—Continued.

NAME OF HEAD OF FAMILY.	Free white males of 16 years and upward, including heads of families.	Free white males under 16 years.	Free white females, including heads of families.	All other free persons.	Slaves.
Dewey, Joseph	1		1		
Hallans, Amos	3	2	4	1	
Vincent, Joseph	1	4	10		
Hubbard, Eliphelet	2	4	1		
Cheesborough, Robart	1	3	6	1	
Palmer, Thomas	2	1	2		
Whealer, Elisha	1	1	1		
Randall, Thomas	2	4	8	1	
Hancock, Elihu	1		1		
Grey, Jonathan	1		2	2	
Dewey, Deborah	3	2	3		
Haley, Edmund	1	1	2		
Belshaw, John	3	1	1		
Fellows, Nathl, 3d	1	1	1		
Fellows, Nathl, 2d	4	1	4		
Fellows, Nathl	1		2		
Cheesborough, Nathl, 2d	3	4	4		1
Haley, John	3	1	4		
Hinckley, Able	4	1	4		
Noyce, Peleg	4	2	5	1	1
Welden, Jonathan	1	2	5		
Burdick, Nathl	1	1	3		
Williams, Robart	1	1	4		
Harvey, James	1		1		
Cheesborough, Zebulun, Junr	1	2	3		
Graves, Saml	2	5	4		
Buttles, George	2	1	4		
Hubbard, Eliphelet	2	1	3		
Eliot, James	1	1	2		
Patterson, Amasa	1	1	3		
Spargo, Edward	1	1	2		
Whipples, Joseph	2		3		
Whipples, Robart	1	2	3		
Hancock, James	1		3		
Hancock, Nathan	1	2	3		
Burdick, Elisha	2	3	4		
Jaquis, Robart	1	1	2		
Cheesborough, Nathl	2	2	5		
Irish, John	4	2	6		
Lewis, William	2	3	6		
Lewis, William, Junr	1	1	1		
Hancock, Joseph	1		2		
Dean, James	5	2	3	1	
Denison, Robart	1	2	4		
Cheesborough, William, 3d	1	6	3		
Baldwin, Silvester, Junr	1	1	3		
Denison, Beba	1	3	5		
Denison, Darius	1	3	6		
Miner, David	1	1	6		
Miner, David, Junr	1	2	2		
Slight, Joseph	1		2		
Miner, Rufus	3		2		
Miner, William	2	3	5		
Miner, Thomas	1	3	5		
Miner, Manassa	1	2	4		
Wilcox, Edward	1		2		
Wilcox, John	1	1	1		
Mason, Samuel	2		2	1	
Mason, Elnathan	1	2	3		
Mason, Andw	1		1		3
Denison, Pheba			2		
Wilcox, Ebenr	2		2		
Mason, Nehemiah	1	2	5		
Denison, George	2		4	4	
Denison, Nathan	1	2	1		
Brown, Joshua	3	2	6	2	
Williams, Joshua	2	1	2		
Williams, Mercy		1	4	2	
Brown, Peter	1	2	3		
Thomson, Nathl	1	2	2		
Palmer, Nathl	3	2	5	3	
Bell, Joseph	1	4			
Woodbrige, Dudley	4		2	3	
Denison, George, Junr	1	4	4	3	
Denison, William	1	2	4		
Stanton, William	1		3	3	
Stanton, Nathan	2	2	3		
Denison, Isaac	1	4	5	2	
Denison, Beeba, 2d	1	1	3		
Denison, Frederick	1		2		
Denison, Henry	1	4	4		
Adams, Simeon	1	4	6		
Williams, John	2		2	4	
Williams, John, 3d	3	3	6	3	
Gardiner, Abigail			1	2	
Niles, Nathan	6	1	3		
Parks, John	1	2	3		
Pero (Negro)				5	
Hallam, Abigail			2	2	
Quash (Negro)				3	
Gallup, Levi	1	2	2		
Gallup, Ezra	1	2	3		
Gallup, Silas	1	2	5		
Cheesborough, James	1		3		

NAME OF HEAD OF FAMILY.	Free white males of 16 years and upward, including heads of families.	Free white males under 16 years.	Free white females, including heads of families.	All other free persons.	Slaves.
Billings, Amos	2	4	5	1	
Frink, Isaac	2		6		
Whealer, Rufus	1	1	1		2
Randall, Jedediah	1	1	1	1	2
Dickerson, Ichabod	1		1		
Leeds, Thomas	1	2	3		
Miner, Peleg	2	2	2		
Denison, Elisha	4	1	4	1	2
Smith, Roswell	1	1	2		
Brown, Roswell	2	2	1		
Brown, Jedediah	3	1	4		
Randall, Roswell	1		2		
Randall, William	1	1	2		1
Baldwin, Asa	1	1	4		
Badcock, Joseph	1	1	2		
Frink, Asa	2	2	6		
Burdick, Christopher	3	2	2		
Brown, Samuel	3		4		
Randall, John, Junr	1	7	2		
Weever, Joshua	1	1	3		
Miner, Christopher	2	5	3		
Miner, Thomas	3	2	4		
Miner, James, Junr	1		2		2
Miner, Daniel	1				1
Brud, Lucy	2	3	2		
Brud, Nathan	2		3		
Brud, Nathan, Junr	1	1	1		
Brud, Oliver	1	5	2		
Brud, Samuel	1	2	2		
Whealer, Peres	1	1	2		
Miner, Peres, Junr	1		2		
Randall, John	4	1	4		4
Weever, Jonathan, Junr	1	3	6	1	
Allen, Thomas	2	3	4		
Swan, George	1	3	3	1	
Roads, Simon	2		1	2	
Stales, Adam	3	2	3		
Hinkley, Elijah	1	3	6		
Frink, Prentice	4	4	3		
Miner, Charles	1	2	8	1	
Barber, Henry	2	3	3		
Ingraham, Hezekiah	1	2	3		
Miner, Ephraim	1	1	2		
Will (Negro)					3
Dewey, David	1	1	2		
Otis, James	1	2	2		
Laten, Joseph	3	2	4		
Babcock, Henry	4		4		
Bradford, Alexander	1	1	2	1	
Stanton, John	3	1	2		
Blivin, John	1		2		
Sheffield, George	1	2	5		
Davis, John	1	3	3		
Davis, Thomas	2	2	2		
Hinckley, John	2	1	3		
Harvey, James	1	1	4		
Burdick, Peter	1		3		
Stanton, Thomas	3		3	4	
Will (Negro)				1	
Stanton, Eli	1		5		
Stanton, Jesse	1				
Peters (Negro)				2	
Baldwin, Jonathan	2		3		
Stanton, Job	2	3	3	1	
Badcock, Elihu	1	1	2		
Cuff (Negro)					5
Stanton, Thomas, Junr	1	3	5		
Stanton, Thomas	1	3	4		
Slack, Amos	2	1	2		
Palmer, Moses	1	1	4		
Badcock, Simon	1	3	4		
Hinkley, Nathan	1	2	6		
Brown, Joshua, Junr	1	3	1		
Dorrel, Thomas	2	3	4		
Hinkley, Mary		1	2		
Noyce, James	1		4	2	
Noyce, John	3		2	2	
Noyce, James, Junr	2	6	2	1	
Cheesborough, William, 2d	1	4	5	1	1
Palmer, William	1	1	2		
Palmer, James, Junr	2	2	2		
Palmer, Roswell	1		2		
Palmer, Hannah		2	1		
Stanton, Peleg	1	1	5	1	
Palmer, Samuel	1	5	2	2	
Badcock, Robart	2	1	4		
Palmer, James	2		3		
Crandall, Nathl	1	1	2		
Crandall, Paul	1	2	5		
Brown, William	1		2		
Lamphear, Benjamin	1		3		
Lamphear, Nathan	1	1	1		
Lamphear, Elisha	1	1	1		
Palmer, Ruben	1	1	2		
Palmer, Daniel	1	3	3		
Palmer, Denison	3	2	6		

NAME OF HEAD OF FAMILY.	Free white males of 16 years and upward, including heads of families.	Free white males under 16 years.	Free white females, including heads of families.	All other free persons.	Slaves.
Shaw, Peleg	1		3		
Slack, Able	1	1	2		
Slack, William	1	1	7		
Cheesborough, Asa	1	1	4		
Noyce, Gershom	1		1		
Burdick, Lodowick	1	1	2		
Cheesborough, William	2	1	3		
Tenny, Jeremiah	1	2	1		
Cheesborough, Saml	5	2	8		
Burch, Henry	2	2	6		
Loper, Abraham	1	1	3		
Cheesborough, Jedediah	5		4		
Cheesborough, Rebecka 3d			3		
Yemmons, Daniel	2	3	3		
Yemmons, Moses	3		4		
Palmer, Abijah	1				
Palmer, Simeon	1	1	4		
Palmer, Jesse	2		2		
Cheesborough, Amos	1		2		
Cheesborough, Saml, 2d	2	1	6		
Cheesborough, John	1		1		
Dennis, Betsy			2		1
Lewis, Asa	1	1	5		
Solomon (Negro)				3	
Miner, Hemstead	2		3		
Baldwin, Silvester	2	1	4		
Palmer, Noyce	4	1	5	2	
Thomson, Jedediah	1				
Thomson, David	1	2	5		
Cheesborough, Peleg	1	4	6	1	1
Cheesborough, Zebulum	3	1	5		
Phelps, Charles	3	1	5		
Phelps, Charles, Junr	1		3		
Lewis, Elisha	2		2		
Lewis, Elisha, Junr	1	2	3		
Hancock, John	1		3		
Cheesborough, Pheba	2	1	4		
Burdick, Oliver	1	1	5		
Johnson, Nathan	1	4	5		
Miner, Humstead, Junr	1		2		
Stanton, William, 3d	1		1		
Palmer, Henry	1		1		
Brown, Elias	1	1	2		
Burdick, Thomson	2	1	3		
Cheesborough, William, 4th	1		2		
Worden, Mary			2		
Stephens, Sarah			1		
Pero (Negro)				1	
Palmer, Asa	1	1	2		1
Pendleton, Andrew	1	1	3		
Palmer, Elijah	2	3	6		
Cheesborough, Bridgett	1		5		
Norden, Benjamin	4		3		
Homes, Silas	1	2	4		
Roathburn, Joshua	1		4		
Rothburn, Achors	1	2	1		
Sheffield, Achors	2		8		
Palmer, Amos	1	2	5		
Brand, Lucy			2		
Eales, Joseph	4		4		
Cutler, Benjamin	1	1	3		
Spencer, John	1	3	1		
Cables, Michael	2	2	4		
Billinghast, John	2		3		
Elliot, Mary	2		3		
Palmer, Nathan	2		2		
Palmer, Eliakim	1	1	3		
Cobb, Ebenezer	3	3	3		
Pendleton, Eunice			2	6	
Tripp, James	3	2	6		
Tripp, Nathl	1	2	1		
Rhoads, James	2		3		2
Brown, Stephen	1	1	2		
Niles, Paul	1		2		
Niles, Paul, Junr	1	1	1		
Stanton, William	1	1	1		
Tribe, John	1	1	1		
Sattille, Samuel	1	5	3		
Waldren, Lowis	2	4	3		
Cobb, Elkanah	1	3	2	1	
Miner, Clemment	2		1		
Miner, William	1		1		
Sheffield, Robart, Junr	1	3	3		
Bottom, Saml H	1	1	2		
Sheffield, William, 2d	1	1	1		
Denison, Mary		2	4		
Denison, John, 2d	1		1		2
Denison, John, 4th	1		3		1
Smith, Oliver	3	1	4		
Sheffield, William	1	4	2		
Terrett, William	2	2	3		
Hilyard, Oliver	1		2		
Ash, Michael	3	1	5		
Fanning, Gilbert	2	2	2		
Woodruff, Hezekiah	2	1	5		

NEW LONDON COUNTY—Continued.

NAME OF HEAD OF FAMILY.	Free white males of 16 years and upward, including heads of families.	Free white males under 16 years.	Free white females, including heads of families.	All other free persons.	Slaves.
Sanford, Elisha	3	1	3		
Rothburn, Volentine	1		1		
Niles, Sands	1		2		1
Cheesborough, Naboth	1	3	3		
Stanton, Samuel	2		2		
Stanton, Zebulun	2	3	3		
Burch, Billings	1	1	4		
Crary, Jonathan	1	1	4		
Larrey, John	2		3		
Smith, Nathan	2		1		
Palmer, Nathan, Junr	2	2	2		1
Smith, Edward	1	3	3		
Roberson, Thomas	2	2	2		
Wilcox, Joshua	1	3	3		
Sloane, William	1	3	2		
Durfee, James	1	3	2		
Fellows, Elnathan	2	2	4		
Brud, Prentice	1		5		
Burch, Samuel	1	2	4		
Palmer, Robart	1	2	2		
Palmer, Peleg	1	1	3		
Worden, Henry	1	3	2		
Swan, Joshua	4		3		
Potter, Hannah			2		
How, Mary	2		1		
Avory, Patience		1	2		
Hall, Joshua	2		3		
Ellis, Edward	1	2	4		
Wood, Gophar	1	3	2		
Gardiner, Thomas	1	1	1		
Hickcox, Thomas	2		1		
Fowler, Gideon	1		2		
Palmer, Amos, 2d	1	4	1		
Lewis, Sarah			2		
Bliss, Mary			3		
Hart, Lewis	1	1	2		
Stanton Azariah	1		3		
Lewis, Robartson	1	1	1		
Ammy, Emanuel	1	1	2		
Robbins, Ezekiel	1		1		
Bebe, John	1	1	3		
Crary, Humphery	1		2		
Copp, Joseph	1	1	3		
Stanton, Ebenr	1	1	2		
Hancock, Edward	1		2		
Hancock, Nathan	1	1	3		
Spencer, Caleb	1		3		
Mitchel, Moses	1		1		
Hancock, Zebulun	1	2	3		
Brown, Peleg	1	3	5		4
Brown, Mary	3		1		1
Homes, Jabez	1				
Hancock, Edward, 2d	2	1	7		
Rothburn, John	2	3	6		
Miner, Nathl	1		1	1	
Sheffield, Isaac	2		1		
Sheffield, Amos	1	1	2		
Sheffield, Isaac, Junr	1	4	2		
Dewey, Lemuel	2	1	2		
Cotterall, Thomas P	1		1		
Hancock, James	1	1	1		
Hancock, Nathl	1	1	3		
Rosseter, Elnathan	1	1	1		
Kinyon, Augustus	1		3		
Nugen, John	2	1	2		
Crary, Peter	6	2	3		
Smith, Benjamin	2	2	1		
Elles, Benjamin	1		2		2
McCurdy, John	1	4	3		
Sheppard, James	1				
Woodbridge, James	2		4		
Noyce, Thomas	3	3	3		
Lord, Danl	2	1	1		
Packer, Frelove			4		
Crandall, Jonathan	3	2	3		
Crary, Nathan	1	1	2		3
Crary, Isaac	1	5	3		
Dinah (Negro)				2	
Eldridge, Charles	2		1		
Eldridge, Charles, Junr	1		2		1
Eldridge, Saml	3	1	7		
Frink, Jabez	6		2		
Frink, Jabez, Junr	1		3		
Gallup, Jesse	1	2	5		1
Gallup, Samuel	3	2	7		
Gallup, Joshua	1	1	1		
Gallup, Josiah	1		1		
Gallup, Jacob	2	1	3		
Gallup, Nathan	4		4	1	
Gallup, Ebenezer	1	4	2		
Gallup, Henry	4		2		1
Williams, Seth	1	1	3	1	
Williams, Henry	2	1	1		
Holdrige, Benajah	2	5	5		
Freman, Hannah			3		
Morgan, Christopher	2	1	6		2
Stanton, Prudence	1	1	4		
Williams, Peleg	2	2	3		
Brown, Cumfort	1	2	3		
Morgan, John	1	1	2		2
Morgan, Stephen	2		4		
Billings, Stephen	1	1	3		3
Brown, Ezekiel	1	4	3		
Morgan, Rebecka			2		
Hilyard, Jonathan	2	4	4		
Morgan, Shapley	1	1	4		
Morgan, Shapley, Junr	1	1	1		
Morgan, William A	1	5	4		
Gray, Benjamin	2	1	5		
Allins, Ephraim	2	5	5		
Stanton, Thankfull	1		3		
Smith, Nehemiah	2		2		
Parks, Jacob	1	1	1		
Brown, Elkanah	1	1	2		
Billings, John	1	1	2		
Spicer, Sarah		2	4		
Giles, Thomas	3	2	4		
Bellows, Nathl	1		1		
Bellows, John	2		5		
Allen, James	2	3	5	1	
Brown, Nathl	1	1	2		
Brown, Ann		2	2		
Mallerson, Thomas	1	2	3		
Williams, Richard	3		2		
Williams, Isaac	1	3	4		
Allen, David	2		1		
Hewet, Elkanah	1	2	3		
Brown, Hannah		1	2		
Halsey (Negro)					3
Geer, Amos	2		7		
Geer, Ebenezer	1	2	1		
Geer, James	1		1		
Green, Joseph	1	1	2		
Brown, Ebenezer	2		7		
Geer, Robart	1		3		5
Stodard, Margarett			3		
Geer, Mary			2		
Geer, Richard	4	1	5		
Geer, Benjamin	2	4	4		1
Forthsides, Robert	1	1	3		
Chapman, Joseph, 2d	2	3	4		
Williams, Aaron	2		1		
Maynard, John	3		1		
Pettis, Benja	1		3		
Ethridge, Sarah	2	1	2		
Miner, John O	1	1	3		
Holdrige, Rufus	1	1	2		
Bayler, Noah	2	1	4		
Allen, Hannah	2	1	3		
Palmeter, Phineas	1	1	1		
Morgan, Ebenr	3		3		
Newton, Mark	2	2	5		
Newton, Agrippa	2	1	5		
Chapman, Joseph	2	1	4		
Spicer, Edward	2		3		
Allen, Tryall	2	1	4		
Perkins, John	1	3	5		
Lamb, Silas	1	1	4		
Lamb, Asa	1		3		
Lamb, Silas, Junr	1	2	1		
Steadman, Sarah			4		
Lamb, William	1	1	1		
Morgan, Nathan	1	2	3		
Avory, Simeon	2	6	3		
Morgan, Solomon	2		2		
Morgan, William	3	1	5		
Keeney, Aaron	2	4	5		
Dabol, Benjamin	1		4		
Belton, Jonas	1		1		3
Brown, Wm	1	4	6		
Brown, Geshom	4		3		
Gray, Phillup	5	1	3		
Perkins, Jacob	3	1	2		
Perkins, Mary			4		
Stanton, Saml	1	3	2		
Hallet, Thomas	1	1	5		
Parks, Hezekiah	1	6	2		
Fanning, Elisabeth	1		1		
Derby, Jedediah	2		1		1
Latham, Carey	1	2	5		
Latham, Joseph	4	6	3		
Williams, John	1		3		1
Williams, Carey	1	1	3		
Williams, Peter	1	2	3		
Stanton, Isaac	1		1		
Spicer, Oliver	2		4		
Spicer, Amos	1		4		
Avory, Benaijah	1	1	6		
Williams, Amos	1	1	3		
Williams, John, Junr	1		1		
Avory, Daniel	2	4	4		
Avory, David	1	2	3		
Chapman, Joshua	1	2	4		
Chapman, Amos	1	1	2		
Smith, Joshua	1		2		
Newton, Christopher	1		1		1
Lamb, John	1	2	1		1
Morgan, Israel	1		9		1
Powers, John	1	2	5		
Hide, Phineas	1	1	5		
Parks, Mary	1		3		
Meach, Aaron	1	1	1		
Fanning, Elkanah	2	1	1		
Avory, Jacob	2		2		
Avory, Theophilus	1	1	3		
Spicer, John	2	1	5		
Avory, Constant	2		1		
Avory, Theophilus, Junr	1	3	2		
Avory, James, Junr	4	2	3		
Standish, Israel	1	3	4		
Morgan, Jacob	1	2	1		
Spicer, Edward, Junr	1	6	1		
Avory, Isaac	2	3	6		
Smith, Saml	2		3		
Adams, Joseph	1	3	7		
Gates, John	1	1	4		
Pelton, Ebenr	1		1		
Andrus, Saml	1		1		
Newton, Saml	1		1		
Williams, Robart	1		5		
Avory, Jacob, Junr	1		3		
Chapman, David	1		1		
Chapman, Asa	1		2		
Andrus, Elisha	1	2	1		
Shoals, John	3		5		
Chapman, Levi	2	2	10		
Stodard, Robart	1				
Stodard, Robart, Junr	1	3	3		
Stodard, Danl	1	2	3		
Geers, Gurden	1	2	2		
Holdrige, William	1	2	4		
Bill, Benaijah	1	1	2		
Stodard, James	1		2		
Stodard, James, Junr	2	4	2		
Spicer, Silas	2	2	7		
Stodard, Deborah		3	2		
Allen, Thomas	1	5	4		
Allen, Mary	1	1	4		
Mallerson, Elisha	1	1	2		
Avory, John	2		2		
Avory, John, Junr	1	2	4		
Avory, Amos	1	1	4		
Smith, Job. I	1		3	1	
Starry, Oliver	2	2	2		
Bill, Joshua	1	2	3		
Newton, Able	2	3	7		
Shoals, Mary	2	2	4		
Marks, Aholiab	1	1	2		
Waldren, Isaac	1		2		
Stodard, Jonathan	1	1	1		
Stodard, Ichabod	4	3	4		
Williams, Christopher	1	2	2		
Newbury, Nathan	1	1	3		
Stodard, Mark	1		3		
Smith, William	2	5	5		
Hewet, Henry	1	1	3		
Pelton, Thomas	1		1		
Allen, Park	2		3	1	
Allen, Park, Junr	1		1		
Newton, Elijah	1	1	3		
Mallerson, Joseph	3	1	6		
Allen, Robart	1	1	3		
Allen, Thomas, Junr	1	2	2		
Elderkin, Elisabeth			3		
Morgan, Thomas	2	2	3		
Morgan, Thomas, Junr	1		3		
Chester, Charles	1		2		
Allen, Edna	1		2		
Elderkin, Roxa		1	2		
Allen, Joseph	1		3	1	
Stodard, Ralph, Junr	3	3	2		
Havens, Jonathan	1	4	2		
Avory, Nathan	1	3	2		
Mallerson, Ezra	1	1	3		
Mallerson, Roswell	1	2	3		
Lester, Amos	1	1	4		
Bill, Phineas	2	2	6		
Lester, Peter, Junr	2		1		
Baker, Saml	1	1	4		
Daton, Richard	2		3		
Rought, Daniel	1	1	2		
Badcock, Sarah			1		
Davis, Jasper	1	6	1		
Williams, Mary	3	1	2		
Jones, John	1	1			
Hallabutt, Ralph	2	1	5		
Widger, Andw	1	1	2		
Culver, Peter	2		3		
Auther, Elisha	1		1		
James (Negro)				4	
Allen, John	2		3		

NEW LONDON COUNTY—Continued.

NAME OF HEAD OF FAMILY.	Free white males of 16 years and upward, including heads of families.	Free white males under 16 years.	Free white females, including heads of families.	All other free persons.	Slaves.
Geer, Israel	1		5		
Geer, Jacob	4		1		
Clark, Ruben	1		1		
Allen, Nathan	2	1	2		
Allen, Elisabeth	1	1	3		
Latham, Thomas	2	2	3		
Smith, Saml, Junr	2	1	6	1	
Dirskall, Asa	1	1	3		
Widger, Eli	1	1	2		
Widger, John	1		2		
Ruff, Sarah		2	1		
Plumb, George	1	2	2		
Geer, Easter	1		3		1
Widger, Saml	4	2	5		
Smith, James, Junr	3	2	5		
Smith, Richard	1		2		
Smith, Richard, Junr	1	3	2		
Boles, Roberson	1		2		
Perkins, Solomon	3		4		
Perkins, Ebenr	2	1	2		
Perkins, Jacob, 2d	1		1		
Perkins, Elisabeth		2	3		
Swift, William	1	2	4		
Bill, Benjamin	3	1	3		
Avory, Amos	3	1	4		
Roberson, Flias	1		2		
Morgan, Temperance			1		1
David, David	1	1	3		
Stodard, Tabitha	1		1		
Sheffield, Paul	1		1		
Stodard, Silas	1	3	4		
Stodard, Wait	2		1		
Kennedy, John	1		2		
Williams, Thomas	1	1	3		
Lester, Asa	1	1	3		
Lester, Nathan	2	1	3		
Lester, Peter	2	1	2		
Allen, Amos	2	2	3		
Read, James	1	1	1		
Latham, Lucy	1	1	2		
Stodard, Ralph	1		1		1
Stodard, Vine	1	5	3		
Shoals, John	3		2		
Tammage, Elisha	1	1	1		
Avory, Hannah			2		1
Giles, Thomas, Junr	1	3	5		
Baley, Simeon	1	2	1		
Bundy, Robart	1	2	1		
Smith, James	3	5	5		
Smith, Saml, 3d	1		2		
Lamb, Hannah		1	1		
Starr, Joseph	1		1		6
Perkins, Rufus	2	7	2		
Perkins, Jabez	1	3	2		
Lewis, Joseph	1	1	2		
Lewis, Deborah		1	4		
Muxley, Joseph	1		4		
Dexter, Elisha	1	3	2		
Perkins, Youngs	1	3	2		
Hemmingar, John	1	1	2		
Smith, Jeremiah	2	2	1		
Woodworth, Asael	1		3		
Baley, Elijah	1	1	2		
Baley, Dudley	1	1	2		
Tayler, John	2	1	3		
Perkins, Mary			2		
Adams, David	1	1	2		
Fish, Thomas	1	1	5		
Fish, Jonathan	1		3		
Fish, George	1	2	2		
Niles, Nathl	3		3		3
Niles, Elisha	1	2	2		1
Baley, Obadiah	1	4	5		
Baley, Azubah			5		
Starr, John	2	1	5		
Culver, Amos	2		3		
Woodworth, Oliver	1		3		
Andrus, Benja	1	4	4		
Saunders, Gideon	2		4		
Woodworth, Joseph	1	1	3		
Adams, Saml	2		2		
Perkins, Obadiah	4	4	4		
Woodmansee, Joseph	1	1	2		
Baley, John	2	1	2	1	
Baley, Joseph	2	3	5		
Pembleton, Jabez	1	1	2		
Baley, Jonathan	3	1	2		
Daball, John	1		4		
Avory, James	2	2	2		
Avory, John	2	2	3	1	
Avory, Pruda	1		2	4	
Budington, Walter	2	2	4	1	
Latham, Christopher	3		3		
Wood, John	1		3		
Wood, William	1		3		
Wood, Saml	1		1		
Wood, John, Junr	1	1	2		
Starr, Vine	3	1	1		
Latham, Robart	1	1	1		2
Street, James	1		2		
Baley, Jona, Junr	2	4	1		
Ingraham, Elexander	1	3	2		
Lester, Saml, Junr	1	2	3		
Lester, Saml	1		1		
Knowls, Danl & Son	4		2		
Forthsides, Nathan	1		4		
Forthsides, William	1	3	2		
Woodmansee, John	1	3	6		
Wood, William, Junr	1	2	3		
Woodbridge, Micha	1	1	2		
Fanning, Thomas	1	2	1		
Culver, Thomas	1	2	4		
Latham, Christopher, Junr	1	2	2		
Lester, Christopher					
Lewis, Peleg	1	1	4		
Woodard, Lucretia		1	3		
Culver, Daniel	1	1	1		
Lester, Elisabeth			2		
Newton, Ama	1	1	5		
Starr, Thomas	1	1	5		
Starr, William	1	5	3		
Mills, James	2		3		
Lester, Mary	3		2		
Lester, Thomas	1	1	4		
Lester, Danl	1	1	2		
Lester, Sarah	1	1	3		2
Taylor, Job	1	2	6		
Shoals, Whealer	1	1	3		
Budington, Walter, Junr	1	4	6		
Badcock, Isaac	1	3	4		
Muxley, Jona	1		2		
Latham, Jasper	2	1	5	1	
Latham, Mary		1	5		
Barber, John	1	4	5		
Smith, Charles	2	2	4		
Gallup, Gardiner	1	1	1		
Andrus, James	1		4		
Brown, Peter	1	1	3		
Hill, Easter	1	2	2		
Fanning, Jona, Junr	1		4		
Muxley, Elisabeth	1		2		
Waterhouse, Amos	1	2	2		
Devenport, William	1	1	1		
Deball, Mary			3		
Deball, Saml	1	1	2		
Davis, Daniel	1		5		
Morgan, John	4	1	3		
Deball, John	2	4	3		
Turner, Amos	2	3	3		
Turner, Amos, Junr	1	1	1		
Turner, Ezekiel	2	1	3		
Avory, Peter	1	1	1		3
Daniels, John	1	3	2		
Shoals, Susanna		1	1		
Daniels, John, Junr	1	1	1		
Elexander, William	2		4		
Start, Daniel	1	1	3		
Allen, Miner	1	1	3		
Chalsea, Wm	1	1	2		
William (Negro)					8
Pharough (Negro)					3
Edgcomb, David	1	2	3		
Edgcomb, Jabez	1		2		
Avory, Thomas	3	2	7		
Smith, Rufus	3	1	2		
Edgcomb, Saml	3		2		
Edgcomb, Saml, Junr	1	1	1		
Smith, Jabez	1		3		1
Smith, Gilbert & Son	2	1	2		1
Smith, Denison	1		2		
Walworth, Joshua	1	1	4		
Chipman, Saml	2		4		
Niles, Thomas	4	2	2		
Daball, Nathan	1	2	2		
Lewis, William	1	2	2		
Chaple, Edward	1	2	4		
Stark, Solomon	1	1	4		
Stark, Daniel, Junr	1	1	2		
Whitman, Isaac	2	3	3		
Baley, John, Junr	1		1		
Whitman, Timothy, Junr	1	2	2		
Whitman, Timothy	2	1	3		
Culver, Moses	1	2	6		
Culver, Joseph	1		4		
Culver, Eunice	1		1		
Hart, Jemima	2		4		
Baley, Joseph, Junr	1	3	3		
Baley, Pethust	1		1		
Lamb, Timothy	3	3	6		
Lamb, Samuel	1	5	6		
Clark, Obed	1	3	2		
Heath, William	1	4	4		
Roads, William	1	1	2		
Mitchel, Francis	2	4	3		
White, Christopher	2	3	3		
Avory, Peter, 2d	1	1	1	1	1
Ledgyard, Ebenr, 2d	1		3		
Burdick, Walter	3	2	5		
Read, Alexander	1				
Warren, Thomas	1	1	2		
Williams, Peter	1	2	4		
Chester, Giles	1	1	4		
Darrow, Nathan	1	3	2		
Chester, Simeon	1	1	1		
Mason, Henry	1	3	2		
Lester, Lucretia		1	4		
Prentice, Amos	3	1	5		
Latham, Edward	3	1	2		1
Whealer, Ephraim	1		1		
Jeffers, Edward	2		1		
Baley, Ezekiel	1	2	1		
Baley, Elisabeth	1		2		
Latham, Elisabeth		1	3		
Avory, Rufus	3	4	2		
Ledyard, Ann		1	3	1	1
Harvey, John	1	1	3		
Leeds, Wm	2	3	4		
Ledyard, Ebenr	4	3	2		1
Avory, Ebenr	2		2		1
Griffen, John	1		2		
Gore, Able	1	1	3		
Latham, Betsy		1	3		
Thomson, Elisabeth		1	4		
Yerrington, Ezekiel	1		5		
Chipman, Saml, Junr	1		2		
Lankford, Joseph	1	1	2		
Leeds, Ann	1		2		
Latham, Jona	1		2		
Latham, William, Junr	2	4	6		2
Avory, Ebenr, 2d	1	3	4		
Avory, Pheba		2	3		
Avory, Caleb, 2d	1		2		
Chester, Isaac	2		2		
Chester, Thomas	3		5		
Avory, Latham	2	2	3	1	
Starr, Jesse	1	3	3		
Hawlet, Josiah	2		3		
Widger, John	1	1	2		
Primes (Negro)					5
Chester, Ann		1	1		
Latham, Ann		2	3		
Latham, Sigleton	1	2	4		
Dodge, Mary		1	5		
Brown, John	1	1	3		
Daniels, Frank	1	1	3		
Moore, Frederick	1	2	2		
Chipman, Christopher	1	5	2		
Thays, Thomas	1	1	1		
Williams, Theoda		1	7		
Williams, John, 3d	1		1		
Hall, Mary			2		
Avory, Youngs	1	1	3		
Avory, Park, Junr	1	2	3		2
Burch, Isaac	1	2	2		
Avory, Park	2		3		2
Ayrs, Daniel	1	2	1		
Brown, Jesse	2	1	4		2
Gallup, Joseph	3	1	4		
Morgan, Youngs	2	2	4		
Avory, William	3		3		1
Morgan, James	2		7		
Morgan, James, Junr	1	1	3		
Ceaser (Negro)				3	
Clark, Josiah	3	6	3	1	
Latham, William, 3d	1	2	2		
Hoskins, Ebenr	1	3	2		
Avory, Benjamin	1	3	5		
Champlin, John	1	1	4		
Davis, Robart	1	3	2		
Roggers, Amos	1	4	2		
Guard, Daniel	2		1		
Roggers, Ebenr	1	5	3		
Avory, Caleb	1	1	3		
Havens, Silvester	1	1	1		
Latham, Joseph	1	1	1		
Chipman, William	1	7	2		
Avory, Deborah	3	3	3		
Brand, Benjamin	1	5	3		
Burrows, Silas	2	1	5	1	
Crum, Charles	2	1	4		
Burrows, James	1	1	3		
Burrows, James	1	1	3		
Gaurd, Nathan	1		3		
Burrows, Joseph	1	1	4		
Tylar, Solomon	1				
Latham, Jasper	1	5	1		
Latham, John	1		1		
Latham, Joseph	1	2	3		

NEW LONDON COUNTY—Continued.

NAME OF HEAD OF FAMILY.	Free white males of 16 years and upward, including heads of families.	Free white males under 16 years.	Free white females, including heads of families.	All other free persons.	Slaves.
Morgan, Timothy	3	1	4		
Morgan, Sam¹	1	1	1		
Palmer, George	2	2	2		
Ashley, James	1		2		
Palmer, Elihu	1	1	3		
Morgan, Joshua	1	1	4		
Sawer, James	1		2		
Fitch, Hannah	3		1		
Potter, Thomas	1	1	2		
Burrows, Lemuel	1	1	2		
Burrows, William	1	1	3		
Ashby, Edward	5		2		
Williams, Solomon	1	4	3		
Rothburn, Elijah	1	1	5		
Burrows, Nathan, Junr	1	4	1		
Fish, John	1		1		
Fish, John, Junr	1		2		
Fish, Sam¹	1	3	1		
Tiff, Solomon	1	3	4		
Brice, Robart	1	3	2		
Burrows, Elisha	1		6		
Fish, Ebenr	1	2	4		
Gaurd, Elisha	1		3		
Gaurd, Sam¹	1		3		
Middleton, George	3		4		
Lewis, David	1	2	3		
Baker, Joshua	1	5	2		
Gates, Zebadiah	1	1	3		
Gates, Sarah	1		2		
Wilcox, Mary			1		
Taylor, Joseph	3	3	4		
Williams, Sam¹	1		2		
Brightman, Henry	2		3		
Brightman, Henry, Junr	1		2		
Latham, William	1	2	5		
Billings, Mary			1		
Smith, Simeon	1	2	7	1	
Walworth, Sarah	3		3		
Burrows, Sam¹	1	4	2		
Sabins, Sam¹	1		1		
Packer, Joseph	2		4		
Packer, Benjamin	1		1		
Packer, John	2	1	3		
Packer, John, Junr	1	1	4		
Packer, Surviah			1		
Ashby, John	1	2	3		
Packer, Elisha	2	4	6		
Packer, Abigail			2		
Packer, Joseph	1	2	8	1	
Parks, Joseph	2	3	4		
Volph, Anthony	1	1	3		
Burrows, Lemuel, Junr	2	1	5		
Packer, Dan¹	3	1	1		1
Packer, Elam	1		4		
Packer, Eldrige	1	1	2		
Packer, Edward	1		2	1	
Packer, James	1	1	3		
Niles, Sam¹	1	1	2		
Burrows, Nathan	2	2	9		
Eldrige, Thomas, 2d	1	2	1		
Niles, Nathan	1	1	2		
Burrows, Dan¹	2	1	4		
Enos, John	1		1		
Fish, Nathan	4		5		
Fish, Sands	1	1	1		
Parks, Joseph	3		2		
Parks, Thomas	2		1		
Smith, William, 2d	1	1	4		
Clark, Aaron	1		3		
Haley, Jeremiah	3	2	2		
Holdrige, Sam¹	1	2	4		
Stodard, Elisha	1	2	3		
Holdrige, Sam¹, Junr	1	2	4		
Parks, Nathl	3		4		
Denison, Jona	2		2		
Burnett, Rachel	2		3		
Prince (Negro)				2	
Welles, Thomas	1	3	3		
Welles, Walt	2		4		
Sisson, James	1	1	4		
Hix, John	2	2	2		
Haley, Caleb	2	1	2		
Morgan, Jesse	1	1	4		
Eldrige, James	1	2	5		
Clark, Francis	1	1	2		
Williams, Caleb	2	4	2	1	
Hix, John, Junr	1	1	3		
Fish, Aaron	2	1	4		
Fish, Sprage	1	1	1		
Langothy, John	1		2		
Crary, Nathan, Junr	1	3	6	1	
Burrows, Hubbard	1		1		
Burrows, Jona	2	1	6		
Ingraham, William	1		3		
Eldrige, Daniel	1		5		
Spicer, William	1	2	1		
Burrows, John	1		2		

NAME OF HEAD OF FAMILY.	Free white males of 16 years and upward, including heads of families.	Free white males under 16 years.	Free white females, including heads of families.	All other free persons.	Slaves.
Lydia (Negro)				2	
Baley, Thadeus	3	2	6		
Baley, Jedediah	1		1		
Burrows, Paul	1	4	5		
Williams, Sam¹, 3d	1	4	8		
Start, Ebenr	1		2		
Waterhouse, Jabez	3		3		
Waterhouse, Timothy	3	2	4		
Waterhouse, Timothy, 2d	1	3	1		
Enos, Joshua	2		9		
Gallup, Benadam, 2d	3	2	3		
Gallup, Benadam	1		3		4
Gallup, Isaac	1	1	2		
Morgan, Jedediah	2	1	5		
Lee, Joseph	1	1	2		
Geer, Robart	1	3	8		
Geer, David	2	3	4		
Rose, Robart	2		2		
Rose, Robart, Junr	2	1	4		
Swan, Elias	1	2	3		
Shadrack (Negro)				7	
Gallup, Nehemiah	1	3	3		
Williams, Sam¹, Junr	3	4	3		
Barns, Ezra	2	3	5		
Fish, Ambrus	2	1	3		
Fanning, Jona	1	1	1		
Fanning, Phineas	1	3	3		
Brown, William, Junr	1	2	3		
Fanning, David	1	1	4		
Steadman, John	1		1		
Steadman, Benjamin	2	3	5		
Jones, Samuel	3	2	6		
Miner, Joshua	1		3		
Dixon, John	1		1		
Dixon, Robart	1	2	3	2	
Williams, Wm	1		2		
Williams, William, 2d	1	3	3	2	
Williams, Elisha	1		2	1	
Williams, Joseph, Junr	1	1	4		
Williams, Joseph	1		2		
Wood, Elisabeth		1	5		
Stanton, Joseph	3	2	5		
Stanton, John	1	1	1		
Lucas, Park	1		2		
Holley, Joseph	1	3	3		
Fish, Elias	1	1	2		
Stodard, Increase	1		2		
Williams, Roger	1	1	5		
Brown, Nathl, Junr	1	2	6		
Brown, James	2	2	4		
Barns, Simeon	1		4		
Barns, Easter			1		
Packer, John, 3d	1	3	2		
Holdrige, Phineas	3	2	5		
Barns, Jesse, 2d	1		1		
Barns, Jesse	1	1	3		
Hewet, Stanton	2	2	1		
Lester, Ebenr	2	3	6		
Lester, Guy	1		3		
Smith, Moses	1	2	4		
Lee, Squire	2	2	4		
Eyrs, Elisha	2	1	5		
Brown, Gershom, Junr	1		3		
Brown, Ruben	1	2	2		
Parks, Mathew, Junr	1	2	2	1	
Hewet, Israel	1		4		
Bellows, Darius	1		4		
Bellows, Asa		1	1		
Noyce, Charles	1	2	2		
Worden, James	1		2		
Worden, Joseph	2	3	2		
Cumstock, Simeon	1	4	1		
Baker, Daniel	2	1	3		
Williams, Margaret	1	1	3		
Park, Stephen	1	1	3		
Lucas, William	2	1	4		
Grant, Beriah	1	2	4		
Brown, Amos	1	2	2		
Brown, Cumfort, 2d	1	2	3		
Morgan, Joseph	1	3	3		1
Roach, Thomas	1	1	2		
Thomas, Abigail			3		
Hubbard, William	1	1	2	1	
Isham, Joseph, 2d	1		2		4
Worthington, Asa	1	3	4		
Cook, John	1		3		
Wright, Dudley	2		3	3	
Watrus, John R	1	1	2		
Buckley, Charles, Junr	1	1	3		
Townshend, William	1	1	1		
Tainter, John	3		4	1	1
Tainter, Joseph	1		3		
Wack, Lydea		1	1	1	
Hall, William	1		3		
Clark, Darius	1	2	3		
Buckley, William	2		1		1

NAME OF HEAD OF FAMILY.	Free white males of 16 years and upward, including heads of families.	Free white males under 16 years.	Free white females, including heads of families.	All other free persons.	Slaves.
Foot, Daniel	2	3	2		
Whitney, Daniel	1		1		
Foot, Charles	2		1		
Clark, John	1	2	5		
Clark, Ezra, Junr	2	1	3		
Welles, John	2	4	4		
Buckley, Joseph	4	2	4		
Chamberlain, John	3	2	2		
Huntley, Harris	4	3	4		
Hall, Ephraim	1		1		
Bill, Annis			1	1	
Johnson, Joseph	1	2	4		
Burnham, Catharine			3		
Hazard, Samuel	2	5	6		2
Clark, Lucy		2	1		
Watrus, Theodore	1	2	3		
Clark, Elihu	3		2		1
Clark, Ezra	3		1		
Freman, Timothy	1				
Freman, Calvin	1	1	2		
Foot, Joseph	2	2	6		
Bridges, Edmund	2	3	4		
Foot, Hosea	3		3	1	1
Peter (Negro)				10	
Kellog, Russell	1	1	2		
Foot, Ruhamah	4		4		
Judd, Daniel	4		4		
Judd, Timothy	1	2	3		
Beckwith, Francis	1	1	1		
Pratt, John	1	3	5		
Albert, Obed	3	4	7		
Pratt, Daniel, Junr	3		2		
Pratt, Daniel	1		2		
Gillet, Ela	3	1	4		
Taylor, Joseph	3		3	1	3
Northam, Asa	1				
Northam, Jonathan, Junr	1	2	1		
Alvord, Rachel			1		
Kellog, Elisha	1	1	4		
Hatch, Benjamin	2		2		
Jones, Isaac	1	1	2		
M°Crackin, James	1	3	1		
Kellog, Israel	1	2	4		
Chamberlain, Roswell	2		5		
Adams, Sam¹	3		4		
Carrier, Isaac	1	4	5		
Staples, John	1	2	1		
Skinner, John	1	2	4		
Bass, Jonathan	1	1	4		
Pratt, Daniel, 3d	1	3	3		
Mitchel, John	1	1	2		
Mitchel, Amasa	1	1	2		
Mitchel, Joseph	1	1	1		
Mitchel, Asa	1		1		
Ransom, Joseph	1	3	4		
Reede, Rufus	1	4	4		
Woodworth, John	1	1	2		
Skinner, Stephen	1	4	3		
Strong, Amos	3	1	1		
Carrier, Samuel	3	3	4		
Carrier, John	2	3	2		
Bigalow, Ira	1	1	2		
Niles, Ambrus	2	3	5		
Niles, Darkas	1	1	2		
Drinkwater, Ebenezer B	1	2	3		
Carrier, Thomas, Junr	1	1	7		
Carrier, Joseph	3	1	4		
Skinner, Noah, Junr	1	1	1		
Foot, Asa	3	2	2		
Skinner, David	4	4	4		1
Eales, John	1	2	8		1
Buel, Elisha	2		3		
Foot, Roger	1				
Lord, Ebenezer	2	3	5		1
Fox, Appleton	1	3	4		
Lord, Epafras	1		1		3
Lord, John	1	1	1	1	
Lord, Ichabod	1	3	5		
Lord, Elisha	2	4	3		
Bowers, Ephraim	1	3	1		
Kneeland, Morey					
M°Call, Daniel	1	3	6		
Carter, Eleazer	2		3		
Deane, Abner	2		2		1
Strong, David	1	3	3	1	
Huntington, David	1	3	3		
Isham, Samuel	2	2	6		
Buel, Elijah	3		3		
Buel, Elijah, Junr	2	1	3		
Root, Benjamin	2	2	2		
Boles, Joshua	1	1	3		
Curtis, Benjamin	3	1	1		
Dayton, Henry	5	1	5		
Finley, Samuel	1	3	2		
Judd, Daniel, Junr	4	3	5		
Blush, Asa	1	1	2		

NEW LONDON COUNTY—Continued.

NAME OF HEAD OF FAMILY.	Free white males of 16 years and upward, including heads of families.	Free white males under 16 years.	Free white females, including heads of families.	All other free persons.	Slaves.	NAME OF HEAD OF FAMILY.	Free white males of 16 years and upward, including heads of families.	Free white males under 16 years.	Free white females, including heads of families.	All other free persons.	Slaves.	NAME OF HEAD OF FAMILY.	Free white males of 16 years and upward, including heads of families.	Free white males under 16 years.	Free white females, including heads of families.	All other free persons.	Slaves.
Caton, James	1					Crocker, Timothy	1	4	1			Otis, James	3				
Carrier, Thomas	4	1	4			Saxton, James	1	2	4			Brown, Ephraim	1	3	3		
Lord, Theodore	3	1	7			Doras (Negro)				2		Welch, Daniel, Junr	1	1	1		
Carter, Ezra	1	4	3			Shattuck, Robart	1	3	2			Welles, Amos	5	3	2		
Kneeland, David	2	3	5			Shattuck, David	1		2			Morgan, Joshua	1	3	4		
Adams, John	1		2			Loomis, Solomon	2	2	3			Welles, Ephraim	2	1	4		
Miller, David	2	2	3			Loomis, Samuel	1	2	3			Scovil, Solomon	2		3		
Strong, Ebenezer	1	2	4			Dunham, William	1	1	1			McCarter, John, Junr	1	1	4		
Ingraham, Jacob	1	2	5			Lewis, Sarah	2		2			Welch, Daniel	1				
Berry, Joseph	1	2	4			Lord, Ezekiel	1	2	4			Mason, Peter	2	1	3		
Curtis, Isaac	1		1			Umstead, John	4		3			Ways, John	1	1	3		
Willis, Jeduthan	1	2	4			Champion, Henry	3	1	2		2	Brown, Ezra	1	1	7		
Taylor, Stephen	1	1	4			Champion, Henry, Junr	2	2	4			Prince (Negro)				3	
Blush, Ezra	1	1	2			Worthington, Erastus	1	1	2			Rosseter, Stephen	3	1	4		
Blush, Easter			2			Carrier, Lovina			2			Randall, Arunah	1	4	3		
Stodard, William	1	1	1			Isham, Joshua	1		1			Rothburn, Able	1	3	5		
Ingraham, Jonathan	2	3	4			Foot, Nathl, Junr	1	2	4			Holms, George	1	3	6		
Coleman, Ebenezer	2	3	8			Carrier, Uriah	3	2	3			Holms, Saml	2	4	4		
McCall, Jacob	2	2	5			Smith, Elijah	1	3	3			Ransom, William	1	1	3		
Goff, Joshua	1		1			Wetmore, Joseph	1	4	2			Chamberlain, Fredom	2	1	2		1
Watrus, Lazarus	1	4	3			Isham, Isaac	2	1	3			Cremor, I	1		3		
Bigalow, Azariah	4	2	4			Isham, Isaac, Junr	1	2	6			Otis, Nathl, 3d	1	1	3		
Bigalow, Daniel	3	1	4			Bigsby, Green	1		1			Treadway, Asa	2	1	5		
Goff, Saml	1		3			Brainard, William	2	4	4			Beebe, Joab	1		2		
Goff, Cumfort	2	1	2			Cone, Cephas	1	2	5			Jones, Mary			1		
Goff, Charles	1	1	5			Fuller, Joseph	1	3	1			Lothrop, Ebenezer	3	1	4		
Goff, Cumfort, Junr	1	2	3			Gates, John	1		2			Gates, Josiah	4		2		
Goff, Squire	1	2	3			Devenport, Eliphalet	1	1	1			Gates, Thomas	1	3	3		
Goff, Gansey	1		1			Williams, Nathan	1	2	5			Gates, Able	1	1	2		
Isham, John	2	1	1			Buckley, Joshua	2	1	3	4	5	Gates, Saml	2	1	5		
Isham, Noah	1	1	2			Bigalow, Jonathan	1	1	4			Rothburn, Jonathan	1		2		
Watrus, Joseph	2		2			Bigalow, James	1		3			Rothburn, Moses	1	4	2		
Watrus, Henry	1		3			Swan, Asa	1	2	6			Rothburn, Joshua	1		1		
Adams, David	1		1			Roggers, Saml	1	3	2			Rothburn, Joshua, Junr	1		5		
Staples, Elijah	1		2			Buckley, Abigail			1		4	Harris, Joseph	1	1	4		
Staples, Benjamin	1		5			Buckley, Daniel	2	3	3		1	Harris, Nathl	3	3	7		
Staples, Elijah, Junr	1	1	4			Welles, Chaunsey	1	4	3			Homes, John	1	3	4		
Adams, Benjamin	1		2			Brown, Stephen	1	3	2			Buckley, Peter	4	1	5		1
Adams, Benjamin, 2d	1		2			Buckley, David	2	1	5			Chapman, Abner, Junr	2	1	1	1	
Warner, Nathl	1		1			Dodge, Thomas	3		6			Newton, Asael	1	1	4		
Foot, Nathl	1		1			Johnson, John	1		1			Way, Barsheba	4		2		
Foot, Aaron	2	3	5			Quash (Negro)				2		Buckley, Peter, Junr	3		5		
Day, Abraham	1		2			Vira (Negro)				3		Randall, Asa	3	2	4		
Day, Elijah	1	2	2			Webster, Stephen	1		2			Randall, Silvester	2	2	4		
Babbit, Jacob	1		1			Webster, Elisabeth			3			Randall, Rufus	1	2	5		
Hill, Thomas	2		3			Webster, Levi	3		1			Brown (Negro)				3	
Williams, Weeks	1		1			Hopson, John	1		1			Randall, Abraham	1	3	2		
Williams, Daniel	1	4	2			Buckley, Roger	5	4	3	2	3	Tennant, John	1	2	2		
Williams, Elijah	1	5	4			Kellog, Abigail	1		2			Stark, Silas	2		4		
Watrus, Timothy	2	4	1			Kellog, Ebenr	1	2	4			Welles, Oliver	4	5	4		
Bigalow, Ezra	2	1	2			Kellog, Butler	1		1			Randall, Elias	2	1	2		
Brown, Saml	1	4	1			Tainter, Charles	2	1	9	2		Palmer, George	1		4		
Gifford, Caleb	1	1	3			Buckley, Elijah	1	2	1			Palmer, Humphrey	1	1	3		
Scovil, Judah	3		7			Gillet, Nehemiah	2	1	5			Palmer, Christopher, 2d	1		1		
Crocker, Joseph	1	2	2			Burnham, David	1	1	4			Allen, Ichabod	1		1		
Dunham, Eleazer	1	1	1			Gillet, Joseph	3	3	6			Randall, Joseph	2		3		
Dunham, Eleazer, 2d	1		3			Fuller, Elijah	1	2	3			Vibber, Thomas	3	2	5		
Miner, David	2	1	1			Fuller, Hannah	1		5			Wightman, Allen	2	3	3		
Worthington, Gad	1	1	5		1	Fox, Jacob	1	3	4			Palmer, Christopher	3	1	5		
Day, Joseph	2		3			Roberson, Samuel	1		2			Bouge, Jeremiah	1	1	5		
Skinner, Noah	1		1			Worthington, Abigail	1	3	2	2	2	Randall, Amos	1	2	3		
Skinner, Saml	1	2	2			Buckley, James	2	3	7			Palmer, Elias, Junr	1	2	3		
Taylor, Ezra	1	2	2			Boham (Negro)				5		Morgan, Jonathan, 2d	1	1	4		
Sexton, George	1	2	3	1		Clark, Nathl	2		2			Palmer, Elias	5	2	2		
Sexton, Betsy	1		3			Clark, Gurdon	1		2			Juba (Negro)				3	
Day, Amasa	2	1	5			Gillet, Joseph, Junr	1	1	3			Cavarly, John, Junr	1	1	1		
Day, Jesse	1	2	2			Mun, Isaiah	2		3			Beeba, Peter	1		3		
Day, Asa	1		1			Strong, Ambrus	3	2	2	1		Cavarly, John	1	1	2		
Prince (Negro)				2		Roggers, Josiah	1	1	6			Cavarly, Phillup	3	1	2		
Foot, Adonijah	1	1	3			Bettis, Thomas	1		1			Hall, Joshua	1	4	5		
Foot, Ruben	1		1			Chamberlain, Nathl, Junr	1	2	1			Otis, Nathl	2	6	6		
Northum, Jonathan	3		5			Gillet, Lydia	3	1	6			Wright, Azariah	5	1	7	1	
Lothrop, Oliver	1	1	5	1		Archer, Crispass	1		4			Clark, Daniel	3		5		
Watrus, Samuel	2	2	3			Puffer Sarah			3			Kellog, Samuel	2	1	4		1
Tracy, Daniel	2	2	1			Strong, Zebulun	4	1	4			Hill, Abner	2	1	4		
Young, Robart	1	1	2			Coleman, Daniel	1	2	3			Morgan, Jonn	1	3	2		
Ramsdale, Ezra	1	3	2			Watrus, William	1		1			Edward (Negro)				6	
Brown, Amasa	1	1	3			Welles, Israel W	2	1	2			Kellog, Daniel	2	3	3		
Peter (Negro)				2		Little, Ephraim	1	3	3			Kellog, Amos	2	3	2		
Pomp (Negro)				3		Wright, Mehitable			2			Chamberlain, Jarus	1	1	1		
Susanna (Negro)				2		Chamberlain, Nathl	2		2			Rowley, Jesse	1	2	4		
Jack (Negro)				5		Chamberlain, Erastus	1	2	3			Boston (Negro)				5	
Yemmons, David	1	5	5			Wright, John	2	3	5	1		Jefferson, Joseph	1	2	2		
Yemmons, Sarah			2			Jacob (Negro)				4		Skinner, Thomas	4		3	1	
Isham, John, Junr	2	2	2	7		Carter (Negro)				10		Watrus, John	4	2	7	1	
Blish, John	2	2	5		1	Bennett, Daniel	2		1			Buckley, Charles	2	6	4		
Woodbridge, Timothy	1	1	2	5		Coleman, Ambrus	1	2	1			Little, Justin	1	2	2		1
Williams, Charles	2	1	1			Dale, Saml	1		1			Mather, Gibeons	2	1	1		
Robins, Robart	3	3	5			Mariner, Mary			4			Brud, John	2		2	1	
Sabins, Phenias	2	3	3			Kellog, Abner	1	3	5			Buckley, Eliphelet	1	2	7		
Isham, Joseph	1	1	1			Chamberlain, Job	2		1			Pomroy, Noah	2	1	4	1	
Jones, John	1	2	1			Welles, Ann			1			Foot, Abigail			3		
Bigalow, John	3		5			Welles, Martin	2	4	3			Hall, William	1	1	3		
Bigalow, Sarah			4			Isham, Daniel	4		4			Cone, Simon	3	2	6		1
McCan, Francis	1		2			Otis, John	3	1	4			Kitterfield, Elisabeth		2	2		
Crocker, Simeon	1	3	3			Otis, John I	1	2	3			Kilburn, David	4	2	6		
Herrick, Isaac	1	1	1									Baker, Asa	2		2		

NEW LONDON COUNTY—Continued.

NAME OF HEAD OF FAMILY.	Free white males of 16 years and upward, including heads of families.	Free white males under 16 years.	Free white females, including heads of families.	All other free persons.	Slaves.
Graves, Asa	1	1	2		
Ceaser (Negro)				2	
Wyles, David	1	3	5		
Kilburn, Elijah	2	3	5		
Beadle, Benjamin	2	6	5		
Keeney, Jonathan	2	1	2		
Beckwith, Jasper	1	2	3		
Wolcott, Solomon	2	2	4		
Chapman, Gideon	2	3	3		
Chapman, Abner	1		1		
Bigalow, Asa	3	3	3	3	
Graves, Peter, Junr	2		4		
Ransom, Amy	1	1	2		
Newton, Israel, Junr	1	1	4		
Newton, Israel, 3d	1		3		
Beeba, Robart	2		3		
Newton, Israel	1		1		
Newton, Asa	1	2	3		2
Ransom, Asael	1	2	6		1
Newton, Able	1	1	1		
Newton, John	1		1		
Ransom, Amasa	1	3	4		1
Morgan, Saml	2	4	4		
Jones, Amos	3	1	4		
Jones, Amos, 3d	1		4		
Rothburn, Job	1	5	4		
Purple, David	1	1	2		
Newton, James	1	2	1		
Bigalow, Bond	1	3	3		
Chapman, Elisha	2	1	2		
Chapman, Ichabod, Junr	2	2	4		
Chapman, Gidion, Junr	1	2	3		
Loverige, Edward	3	1	5		
Ransom, Bliss	4	4	4		
Lester, Jonathan	1		1		
Kilborn, Elisabeth			2		
Eads, Eleazer	1		2		
Graves, Arvil	1		1		
Chapman, Noah	1	1	4		
Jones, Amos, Junr	2	4	4		
Tiffany, Philomon	1		4		
Loverige, David	1		2		2
Sipro (Negro)				6	
Craw, Jesse	2				
Church, Saml	1	3	5		
Warner, Elihu	1		3		
Loomis, Samuel	4	1	3		
Williams, Enos	1	2	3		
Gustin, Walter	1	2	3		
Treadway, John	1	1	7		
Tarball, William	2	2	5		
Denison, Gilbert	1	1	2	2	
Worthington, Elijah	5	1	2		
Way, John	1	1	1		
Worthington, William	1	2	5	1	
Dean, Christopher	1	3	3	1	
Worthington, Joel	2	3	3		1
Miller, Thomas	3	2	3		
Chapman, William	2	1	4		
Kilburn, Hezekiah	2		1		
Ferman, John	1	2	6		
Marshall, Jeremiah	3	3	5		
Bergen, Mercy				2	2
Treadway, Charles	1		2		
Treadway, Elijah	1	2	4		
Chapman, Jonathan	1	3	4		
Ferman, David	1		1		
Welles, Joshua	1				
Daniels, Asa	3	3	4		
Domine (Negro)				3	
Dodge, Beajamin	1	3	4		
Otis, Nathl, Junr	1	1	2		
Rothburn, Jona	1		2		
Waters, Saml	2	1	2		
Beckwith, Caleb	1	1	1		
Beba, Easter			4		
Warner, Nathan	1		1		
Warner, Oliver	1	3	2		
Bacon, Pierpoint	2		1	1	6
Gardiner, William	2	3	3		
Loomis, Israel	3	2	4	1	
Dodge, Jonathan, Junr	1	2	7		
Dodge, Jonathan	1		1		
Dodge, Daniel	1	1	3		
Morgan, Abigail	1	2	4		
Buel, Jacob	3		2		
Loomis, John	4	4	2		
Morgan, Benjamin	1		3		
Graves, Peter	1	1	1		
Morgan, William	1	1	2		
Gardiner, William	1		2		
Ransom, James	4		4		1
Peck, Elias	2	2	5		
Treadway, James	1		2		
Jones, Jabez	3	2	3		
Jones, Jabez, Junr	1	2	2		
Hambleton, Abial	1	1	1		

NAME OF HEAD OF FAMILY.	Free white males of 16 years and upward, including heads of families.	Free white males under 16 years.	Free white females, including heads of families.	All other free persons.	Slaves.
Lothrop, Daniel	1	1	3		
Loverige, Noah	1		2		
Loverige, John	1		1		
Carter, John	3		2		
Carter, Clark	2	3	1		
Treadway, Alpheus	1	1	2		
Harris, Elias	1		3		
Sheridan, Mary			2		
Hambleton, James	1		3		
Hambleton, James, 2d	1	2	2		
Loverige, Abner	1	3	4	1	
Loverige, William	1	4	2		
Waterman, Zebulun	2	3	3		
Treadway, David	1	1	6		
Hambleton, Gurdon	1				
Henry, Robart	1	4	4		
Treadway, Abigail	1	1	4		
Williams, John	4		4		
Henry, John	3	4	6	2	
Towser, Richard	2	2	3		
Towser, Julias	2	1	5		
Fassion (Negro)				3	
Beba, Timothy	2	2	2		
Duglass, John	1	1	2		
Duglass, Robart	1				
Seabury, John	2		3		1
Mumford, John	5	3	7	1	3
Beba, Clark	3	1	3		
Pomp (Negro)				7	
Miner, Jonathan	1	1			
Ransom, Israel	1	3	1		
Ransom, James	1	2	2		
Tiffany, Ebenr, Junr	1	2	3		
Tiffany, Ebenr	5	1	5		
Baker, Matthias W	1	1	1		
Chapman, Abraham	1	2	3		
Story, Saml	1	1	4		
Wood, David	1		2		
Wood, David, Junr	1		1		
Perkins, Jona	3		6		
Perkins, Joshua	2	3	2		
Eames, Lucy			2		
Beckwith, Ephraim	1	1	4		
Huntley, Hoel	1	2	2		
Mackintosh, Lothlin	1	2	2		
Huntley, Benaijah	3		1		
Bouge, James	3		3		
Huntley, Nehemiah	1		2		
Clark, Danl	2	4	6		
Tillotson, Simeon	1		2		
Wood, Margarett		2	5		
Bouge, James, Junr	1		1		
Beckwith, Daniel	1	3	1		
Daniel (Negro)				4	
Lee, Benjamin	1	2	4		
Eames, John	1	2	2		
Armstead, Joseph	1	5	2		
Park, Lee	2		2		
Lee, Seth	1	2	5		
Pratt, Edward	1	3	2		
Leach, Manassa	2	3	6		
Mather, Frederick	1	3	4		
Mather, Eleazer, Junr	1	5	2		
Tillotson, Mary	1		1		
Mather, Eleazer	1		1		
Emerson, Stephen	1		2		
Minor, Ebenr	1	2	2		
Rise, Ruel	3	1	3		
Beba, Azariah	1	3	2		
Cuff (Negro)				4	
Phillups, Michael	1	1	4		
Way, Peter	1	1	4		
Mitchel, George	2	2	1		
Colt, Samuel	2	5	2		
Spencer, Ichabod	2	4	3		
Wright (Negro)				5	
Pumham (Negro)				4	
Saml (Negro)				6	
Sipro (Negro)				5	
Beba, Lemuel	1	1	5		
Roggers, Gedion	1	1	1		
Griffin, Joshua	1	1	2		
Griffin, Nathan	1	1	3		
Griffin, Jasper	2	1	3		
Griffin, John	1	2	3		
Griffin, Sarah	3	2	4		
Lord, John	6	2	6		4
Tinker, Joshua	2	2	4		
Huntley, Lydia			3		
Colt, Harris	2		4	1	
Phelps, Thadeus	1	1	6		
Gould, James	2		4		
Gould, John	1	1	4		
Gould, Walter	1	1	4		
Colt, Desire	2	1	3		2
Bingham, Elijah	3	1	3		
Lee, Stephen	1	1	3		

NAME OF HEAD OF FAMILY.	Free white males of 16 years and upward, including heads of families.	Free white males under 16 years.	Free white females, including heads of families.	All other free persons.	Slaves.
Higgins, David	1	2	3		
Marvin, Timothy	4	4	4		
Gould, James, Junr	3	1	5		
Mervin, Elisha	2		2		
Mervin, Joseph	1	2	2		
Anderson, Thomas	3	1	4		
Harvey, Joseph	2		4		
Prince (Negro)				5	
Lee, Abner	1	1	3		
Lee, Dan	1	1	2		
Lord, Abner	1		2		
Lord, Abner, Junr	1	1	5	1	1
McCary, Saml, Junr	2		2		
McCary, Elisabeth	3	3	4		
Otis, Robart	2		1		
Otis, Robart, Junr	1		1		
McIntosh, Rachel			2		
Ely, Seth	3	1	5		
Mingo (Negro)				3	
Rothburn, Ebenezer	2		2		
Ransom, Stephen	1	2	3		
Cumstock, Joab	2		4		
Bouge, Richard	1		1		
Cumstock, Abner	2	1	4		
Cumstock, Abner, 2d	1	4	1		
Cumstock, Asa	3	1	5		
Cumstock, Easter	2	1	3		
Cumstock, Hezekiah	1	1	2		
Matson, William	2	2	3		2
Peck, Daniel	4		4		
Church, Josiah	1		5		
Church, John	1		2		
Hains, Charles	3		2		
Seldon, Elijah	1	3	2		
Warner, Chapman	1	1	4		
Brooks, Saml	1	2	3		
Fox, Joshua	1	1	1		
Alwood, Mariam			3		
Warner, Jonathan	2		2		1
Warner, Selden	1	2	1		
Selden, Elisabeth	1		1		
Selden, Dudley	1				
Selden, Ely	2		5	1	
Lorther, Levi	1	2	2		
Selden, Samuel	1	2	2		2
Church, Ezra	1	1	2		
Saunders, Saml	1	4	3		
Saunders, John	1		2		
Saunders, John, Junr	1	2	3		
Greene, John	1		1		
Miller, William	1		1		
Saunders, Simeon	1		3		
Pratt, David B	1	3	5		
Banning, John	1		3		
Brockway, Ezra	1		3		
Phelps, Mary		1	3	1	
Niles, Ambrus, 2d	1		3		
Niles, Ambrus	1	1	2		
Mentor, John	1		2		
Wood, John	1	1	4		
Beba, Abner	1	2	2		
Butler, William	1	3	4		
Cumstock, Jesse	2	1			
Phelps, Jonathan	1	1	1		
Smith, Phineas	1	1	3		
Cumstock, Noah	1	4	4		
Beba, David	2		2		
Emerson, Abraham	1	1	2		
Emerson, Abraham, 2d	1	2	3		
Harron, John	1	2	4		
Reynolds, John	1	2	3		
Phelps, Samuel	1	3	2		
Peter (Negro)				5	
Mitchel, John	2	1	5		
Brockway, Ebenezer	5	1	4		
Brockway, Zebulun	1	1	1		
Harrison, Elihu	2	3	2		
Curwin, Theophilus	1		3		
Brockway, Gamaliel	4	1	4		
Brockway, William	2		3		
Brockway, Richard	1		2		
Brockway, Richard, 2d	1		1		
Brockway, Clark	1		1		
Brockway, Eliphelet	2	2	5		
Brockway, Ezra	2		2		
Banning, Ebenezer	3	2	4		
Ely, Abner	1	2	4		
Ely, Elijah	4		3		
Wade, Hannah			1		
Miller, Elisha	1	1	1		
Brockway, Abner	1	5	1		
Laplass, Jonathan	1		1		
Brockway, John	2	1	1		
Brockway, Lowis	1		1		
Smith, Nathl	1	1	4		
Ransom, Ruben	3	2	1		
Rothburn, Saml	1		2		

NEW LONDON COUNTY—Continued.

NAME OF HEAD OF FAMILY.	Free white males of 16 years and upward, including heads of families.	Free white males under 16 years.	Free white females, including heads of families.	All other free persons.	Slaves.	NAME OF HEAD OF FAMILY.	Free white males of 16 years and upward, including heads of families.	Free white males under 16 years.	Free white females, including heads of families.	All other free persons.	Slaves.	NAME OF HEAD OF FAMILY.	Free white males of 16 years and upward, including heads of families.	Free white males under 16 years.	Free white females, including heads of families.	All other free persons.	Slaves.
Perkins, John	3	2	6			Miner, Daniel	3	1	5			Hudson, Stephen	2		4		
Sawyer, Ephraim	1	2	4			Peck, Samuel	1	1	6			Loveman, Susanna			1		
Harrison, Hipsebah		1	2			Peck, Darius	2	2	3			Auger, Roger G	1	2	4		
Ely, James	3	2	3			Burt, Joseph	2	3	4			Champion, Elisha	1		8		
Tiffany, Nathan	2	1	3			Beckett, Josiah	2	1	2			Champion, Lynds	1	2	1		
Lord, Saml	2	1	4			Roggers, Pheba			2	2		Champion, Roswell	1	2	1		
Marvin, Elisha, 2d	3	2	8			Roland, Benjamin	1	2	2			Havens, Edward	1	2	4		
Miller, Volentine	2	2	4			Hide, Elisabeth	2	1	4			Chadwick, Allen	1	3	3		
Wade, John	1	1	4			Lord, Joseph	1	1	5			Roland, Asael	1	1	2		
Wade, Abraham	1	1	3			Bennett, John	1		1			Roland, Levi	3	3	2		
Boon, Henry	2		5			Robins, Silas	1	2	3			Salem (Negro)				2	
Harvey, Joshua	1		1			Huntley, Zephaniah	1		1			Champlin, Nathan	3		3		
Brockway, Benjamin	1	4	2			Sill, Silas	1	2	3			Champion, Henry	2		1		
Butler, John	1		5			Sill, David F.	3	1	4			Peck, Joseph	1	2	1		
Sterling, William	3	5	3			Matson, Israel	2		3			Auger, Lucy			2		
Sill, William	1		3			Hall, Able	2	4	7			Suaney, John	2	2	4		
Hide, Elisabeth		1	1			Jerom, Elisabeth			1			Miner, Elias	2	3	2		
Mark, Ezra	2	1	8			Brockway, Elisha	1	3	4			Ray, Daniel	1		3		
Reaves, Israel	1		5			Woolf, Samuel	1	2	3			Robins, Nathan	2		3		
Howard, David	1	1	5			Sill, Samuel	1		4			Peck, Lebeus	1	1	3		
Ely, Amy	2	1	4			Wade, Elihu	4	1	5			Marvin, Mathew	2	2	6		
Ely, Gurden	1	1	2			Wade, Elisha	2		4			Champlin, William	1	1	3		
Tucker, Phillup	1	2	3			Read, Joseph	1		4			Minor, Seth	1	2	4		
Ely, Ann		2	4			Sill, John	2		3		1	Brown, Jeremiah	1		2		
Huntley, Mary			2			Beckwith, Watrus	3	1	2			Lay, Joseph	2		1		
Sterling, Jacob	1		5			Peck, John	2	3	5			Daniels, Daniel, 2d	1	3	1		
Sill, Giles	2	4	7			Noyce, Calvin	1	1	3			Welch, John	1		4		
Sterling, Samuel	4	1	4			Noyce, Joseph	1	2	1		2	Johnson, Stephen	1		6		1
Sterling, John	2	2	3			Noyce, William	2		1		5	Mather, Lucinda			2	2	
Brown, Henry	3	3	5			Noyce, William, Junr	1		3		1	Lay, John, 3d	1	1	1		
Sterling, Betsy			2			Clark, Silvanus	1	3	2			Watrus, Gershom	2	2	3		
Huntley, Elihu	1	2	5			Huntley, Asher	1		2			Watrus, Phineas	3		1		
Hays, Abigail	1		3			Wicks, Joseph	1		3			Daniels, Daniel	1		2		
Ely, Denison	1		1			Miller, Weltha			2			Champlin, Silas	1	2	1		
Stark, Samuel	1	1	3			Miller, Silas	1	2	6			Robins, Ezra	2	1	3		
Wade, George	2		2			Hill, Samuel	3		1			Robins, Elisha	2		4		
Tiffany, Mary			2			Marvin, Joseph	2	1	2			Lay, Elisha	3	2	3		1
Tiffany, Mary, Junr		2	3			Griswould, Mathew	4	2	3		1	Lay, William	4		5		1
Bump, John	2	4	2			Griswould, Mathew, 2d	3		1			Ingraham, Samuel	2		1		
Brooks, Silas	1	1	3			Griswould, John	3	2	6			Lee, Ezra	1		4		
Ely, Elihu	2	4	5			Noyce, John	1		1			Greenfield, James	1	2	3		
Selden, Ezra	3	1	5			Lay, Lee	1	4	4		1	Hobart, Saml	1	3	4		
Perkins, William	3	3	3			Denison, Easter		3	4			Smith, William	2	1	3		
Ely, Ezra	2		1			Champion, Ezra	1	2	3			Greenfield, Archibauld S.	1		2		
Miner, Wm	1	1	4			Watrus, Easter	1		1			Lay, John	2	2	4		
Ely, Adriel	2	2	5			Woolf, William D	2	1	4			Lay, John, 2d	2	1	3		
Ceaser (Negro)				7		York (Negro)					2	Johnson, Abigail	1	1	4		
Ely, Welles	3		2			Eldrige, Jonathan	2	5	6			Marvin, Benjamin	2	1	4		
Ely, Daniel	1		5			Huntley, Phineas	2	2	4			Porter, Edward	1		2		
Ely, Christopher	3	1	1			Smith, Richard, 2d	2	4	4			Hall, Daniel	1		1		
Ely, Marsh	1	1	6			Gardiner, Thomas	1		4			Parsons, Marshfield	1		4		4
Ely, Cullick	3	1	3			Beckwith, Phineas	1		4			McCurdy, Ann	2	1	3		
Ely, David	1	1	2		1	Miller, Ezra	1	1	5			Mather, Saml, Junr	3	3	9	1	4
Ely, Cullick, Junr	1		1			Smith, Amos	1	2	1			Kent, Mehitable			2		
Mack, Josiah	3	3	5			Wait, Loen	1	3	6			King, Paul	1		1		
Ely, Josiah	4	1	4			Griffen, Saml	3		3			Mather, Sarah			2		
Beckwith, George	1		2			Chadwick, Ruben	2	2	5			Tinker, Nathan	2	2	4		
Beckwith, George, Junr	1	2	4			Comb, Henry	1	2	1			Mather, Joseph	1		1		
Perkins, Samuel	1	1	2	1		Chadwick, Guy	2		3			Persons, John	1		5		
Perkins, Abraham	1	2	3			Chadwick, Hannah	1		4			Mather, Silvester	2		2		
Lord, Amos	1		2			Wait, Richard	2		1			Smith, Joseph	2	1	4		
Peck, Sarah	1		5			Wait, Remick	1	2	2			Tinker, Amos, Junr	1		3		
Munsill, John	2		3			Wait, John	2	2	4			Higgins, Benjamin	1	1	4		
Munsill, John	1		3			Miller, Joseph	1		1			Smith, Joseph, 4th	1	1	1	1	
Munsill, Thomas	1	2	1			Havens, John	1		3			Hollester, Lucretia	1	2	5		
Ely, Gabriel	1	1	5			Chadwick, Richard	1		3			Morgan, Elijah	3		3		
Mack, Samuel Junr	1	1	2			Chadwick, George	1		6			Smith, Ichabod	2	1	4		
Miller, Thomson	1	1	1			Chadwick, George, 2d	1		3			Mather, Jehaiada	3	1	5		
Ransom, David	1	3	3			Nevee, Peter	1	3	2			Beckwith, Roswell	1	2	5		
Mather, Samuel	2	1	4		1	DeWoolf, Stephen	1	2	3			Minor, Martin	2		4		
Lord, Daniel	4		4		1	Wait, Richard, Junr	3	2	5			Marvin, Zachariah	2	2	3		
Pierson, Peter	1	2	3			Lay, Robart	3		2			More, Able	1	1	3		
Lord, Marvin	1	2	4			Ingraham, Parnall			3			Tinker, Peter	1	1	2		
Lord, Benjamin	6	1	3			Wait, Joseph	2		3			Wilkerson, Malachi	1		6		
Lord, Ruben	2	2	6			Anderson, John	1		1			Mather, Timothy	1	2	4		
Lord, Sarah	1	2	3			Anderson, John, 2d	1	2	1			Mather, Timothy, 2d	3	2	4		
Lord, Josiah	1	2	1			Clark, John	1	2	1			Kellog, Martin	3	2	5		
Ransom, Edward	1	2	5			Beckwith, Saml	1	1	3			Marvin, Moses	1	1	4		
Giles, John	1	2	2			Walker, Joseph	1	2	2			Read, George	2		4		
Colt, Benjamin	1	1	2			Smith, Silvanus	2	1	5			Lamphear, Ruth	1		4		
Mather, Nathl	2	1	2			Tinker, Amos	1		1			Peck, Mathew	1	1	3		
Tinker, Stephen	1	2	1			Tinker, Joseph	2	3	3			Lay, Peter	1	1	2		
Lord, Enoch	4		3	1	5	Smith, Stephen	1		4			Peck, Jasper	3	3	5		
Lord, Richard	3		2			Watrus, Gideon	1	3	2			Marvin, Zachariah, 2d	2	1	3		
Glover, Jeremiah	1	1	1			Miner, Jesse	1		2			Tucker, Stephen	3	1	2		
Burnham, Joseph	1		4			Gilbert, John	1		2			Wood, David	3		8		
Burnham, James	1	1	2			Brockway, Elias	1	2	1			Clark, Gurdon	2	1	6		
Denison, Samuel	1	3	5			Champion, Elisabeth		1	2			Rogers, Able	1	1	3		
Clark, Roswell	3	1	6			Chadwick, Ezra	1		4			Marvin, Saml	2	3	4		
Smith, Latham	1	4	3			Champion, Stephen	1	1	5			Bartholick, Martin	1		1		
Dowsack, Gospur	3	3	2			Champion, Ruben	1	1	4			Bartholick, Thomas	2		2		
Higgins, Cristian	2		4			Baker, John	1		3			Fitch, Elijah	2		3		
Higgins, Silvanus	1		2			Chadwick, Stephen	1	2	3			Peck, Reynold	3	2	3		
Burnham, Josiah	1		3			Clark, Lemuel	1	1	1			Wilson, George	1	1	3		
Roggers, Ebenezer	1					Scovil, Martin	1	2	4			Peck, Martha	2	1	5		
Roggers, Able	1	1	3			Roland, Nathl	1		4			Peck, Hannah		2	4		
Roggers, Richard	1	3	1			Roland, Ezra	1		2			Peck, Latt	1		2		

NEW LONDON COUNTY—Continued.

Name of head of family	Free white males of 16 years and upward, including heads of families	Free white males under 16 years	Free white females, including heads of families	All other free persons	Slaves
Royce, Elisha	2	2	4		
Chadwick, James	1	1	2		
Bramble, John	1	1	4		
Wade, Martin	2	1	5		
Gillet, Joseph	1	3	4		
Tucker, Job	1	1	2		
Lester, Jeremiah	1	2	2		
Dorr, George	1	1	5		
Smith, Richard	2		3		
Lee, Thomas	2	2	4		
Griswould, Andrus	1	2	4		
Lee, Elisha	5	2	2		1
Lee, Elisha, Junr	1	1	4		
Griswould, George	2	2	5		
Beckwith, Martin	1		3		1
Keeney, Samuel	2	1	3		
Lester, Noah	1	3	6		
Lester, Joshua	1		2		
Lee, John M	2		1		
Gould, Francis	2				
Read, Enoch	1	2	5		
Mather, John	1		1		
Mather, John, 2d	2	2	3		
Hall, Ezra	3	3	5		
Gillet, Daniel	1	2	1		
Gillet, Ezra	1	1	2		
Gillet, Reynold	1	1	2		
Sill, Samuel	1		2		
Sill, Isaac	1	2	5		
Huntley, Martin	1	4	1		
Huntley, Jasper	1	1	2		
Roggers, Daniel	1	1	2		
Huntley, Amos	1	1	2		
Huntley, Rice	1		2		
Huntley, Marvin	1		2		
Munsill, Timothy	1	3	2		
Huntley, Ruben	1	3	2		
Huntley, James	3	3	3		
Pierson, Eli	1	3	2		
Roggers, Saml	3	1	2		
Roggers, Isaiah	2	2	2		
Minor, Jesse	3	3	4		
Peck, Dan	1	2	1		
Belot, John	1	2	1		
Beckwith, Lebeus	1		2		
Mack, William	1	1	3		
Mack, Ebenezer	1	1	2		
Smith, Ithamer	2		3		
Miner, Ebenr	1		1		
Miner, Whitfield	1	1	1		
Brockway, Edward	3		5		
Bouge, Elisha	1		2		
Bouge, John	1		3		
Gee, William	1		2		
Gee, Zophar	1	1	1		
Gee, William, Junr	1		2		
Peck, Silas	1		1		
Lewis, James	2	1	3		
Huntley, William	1		2		
Beckwith, Buel	1	4	3		
Smith, Samuel	4		2		
Tubs, John M	2		2		
Howard, David	1		2		
Read, Robart	1	1	2		
Huntley, Reynold	3	3	3		
Mack, Zophar	2	1	3		
Roggers, Jonathan	1	2	2		
Tubs, Ahimus	1	3	4		
Beckwith, Ezra	1	1	4		
Beckwith, Nathan	1	1	4		
Smith, Russell	2		2		
Peck, David	5		3		
Smith, Nehemiah	3		1		
Lewis, John	2	1	3		
Belshaw, Joseph	1		2		
Maxson, Tony	1	3	1		
Lewis, George	4	1	4		
Smith, Joseph	2		2		
Lee, Jason	2	2	5		
Beckwith, Jedediah	1		1		
Beba, Jedediah	1		1		
Ryon, James	3	1	2		
Smith, David	1	2	2		
Smith, Edward	1		1		
Kettles, Benjamin	1	1	1		
Smith, Seth	2	3	3		
Beckwith, Stephen	2		2		
Cumstock, Saml	2	3	4		
Tubs, Peter	1	2	2		
Smith, Elisha	1	1	2		
Johnson, John	3	1	2		
Johnson, Reynold	1	1	1		
Winslow, Job	3	2	5		
Roggers, Rowland	1	1	4		
Brown, David	3		2		
Lewis, Daniel	1	1	1		
Smith, Zadock	1	1	5		

Name of head of family	Free white males of 16 years and upward, including heads of families	Free white males under 16 years	Free white females, including heads of families	All other free persons	Slaves
Miller, George	3	6	3		
Bush, Amaziah	2	1	1		
George (Negro)				7	
Powers, Joshua	1	3	4		
Gorton, Benjamin	2	4	4		
Manwaring, Josiah	2		6		
Manwaring, Latham	1		1		
Manwaring, Adam	1	1	1		
Manwaring, Nathl	1	2	4		
Denison, William	2		2		
Denison, Ashbael	1	1	2		
Church, Fairbanks	1		7		
Lester, Andw	1	2	5		
Manwaring, Peter	1		3		
Beckwith, Perigreen	1	3	1		
Beckwith, Elijah	1	1	2		
Latham, Joseph	1	2	3		
Latham, David	1		1		
Latham, John	1	4	1		
Champlin, Edward	1	1	3		
Champlin, Caleb	1	2	1		
Champlin, Edward, 2d	1	1	1		
Dowsett, Amos	1	2	2		
Griswould, Saml	3		1		
Lewis, Sirus	3	1	2		
Smith, Joseph	1		4		
Roggers, Saml, 2d	2	3	3		
Way, Thomas	2	2	1		
Way, Elisha	1		6		
Way, Thomas, 2d	2		2		
Smith, Thomas	1		3		
Smith, Dudley	1	1	2		
Smith, Stephen	1		4		
Tillotson, Bela	1		4		
Tillotson, Isaac	1	1	2		
Tinker, Nathan	1	2	2		
Beckwith, Absolum	2	1	4		
Beckwith, Nathl	1		1		
Tillerson, John	3	2	4		
Huntley, Dan	1		1		
Watrus, Gordon, 2d	1	1	1		
Shipman, William	1		3		
Shipman, Abner	1	6	2		
Read, William	1	2	3		
Read, Pheba			4		
Tillotson, George	1	2	1		
Moore, John	2	4	4		
Tillotson, William	1		1		
Chapman, Ezekiel	1	1	2		
Avory, Silvanus	1	1	2		
Luther, Benjamin	1	1	1		
Tillotson, Daniel	1		1		
Avory, Pheba	1	2	5		
Avory, Martha	2		2		
Chapman, Amy	1		2		
Smith, Josiah	1		3		
Smith, Josiah, 2d	1	1	3		
Roland, Henry	1		2		
Tillotson, Simeon	1				
Chapman, Edward, 2d	1		2	1	
Chapman, Elisabeth		2	3		
Avory, Jona	1		1		
Avory, Abraham	1		3		
Way, George, Junr	2	1	5		
Tubs, John B	1		3		
Beckwith, Zenos	3	2	4		
Beckwith, Thomas	1	1	1		
Beckwith, Abner	1	2	1		
Brooks, Noah	1		4		
Moore, Eunice			1		
Tinker, Saml	1	3	3		
Lee, Lemuel	1	3	4		
Lee, Sabra			3		
Way, Daniel	2	2	4		
Spencer, Calvin	2		1		
Miner, Elisha, 2d	1		4		
Peckwith, Joseph	1		1		
Caulkins, Elisabeth		4	7		1
Wait, Thomas G	1		1		
Brockway, Woolston	1	3	4		
Miner, Elisha	1	1	1		
Miner, William	1	1	2		
Warren, Moses	1		1		
Warren, Moses, 2d	2	2			
Beckwith, Mary	1		2		
Way, Durin	1	1	1		
Moore, Joshua	1		5		
Moore, Deborah			4		
Ayres, Jona	2	1	1		
Ayres, Easter			2		
Huntley, Daniel, 2d	1	1	1		
Morgan, Jona	1	3	3		
Austin, Edward	1	4	5		
Hains, Elisabeth	1		4		
Sullard, Jacob	1		1		
Sullard, James	1		3		

Name of head of family	Free white males of 16 years and upward, including heads of families	Free white males under 16 years	Free white females, including heads of families	All other free persons	Slaves
Chapman, Peter	2		3		
Chapman, Edward	4	1	3		
Buckley, John	1		3		1
Miner, Easter	1		5		
Roggers, Peleg	1		1		
Way, Joseph	3		1		
Tinker, Durin	4	2	2		
Tinker, William	3	1	3		
Mack, Ebenr	2	1	4		
Dodge, Jeremiah	1	1	4		
Demay, Samuel	1		3		
Beckwith, Jesse, 2d	1	6	2		
Beckwith, Jesse	1	1	1		
Strickland, Peter	2	3	5		
Watrus, Gusdon	2	2	4		
Watrus, Pheba			2		
Moore, Joseph	1	1	2		
Tinker, William, 2d	1	2	1		
Moore, William	1		1		
Beckwith, Jonathan	1	1	4		
Miner, Champlin	1		1		
Roggers, Samuel, 3d	1	3	2		
Tinker, Silvanus	1		1		
Way, Reynold	1	2	4		
Miner, Stephen	1	2	2		
Bishop, Joseph	2	2	4		
Miner, Volentine					
Fox, Ezekiel	1		2		3
Fox, Brinton	1	4	3		
Austin, Joseph B	1		2		
Allen, Saml	1		2		
Fergo, Joshua, 2d	1	2	2		
Fergo, Joshua	1		1		
Scarot, Thomas	1	1	3		
Chaple, Danl	1	3	4		
Cobb, Benjamin	1		2		
Allen, Jason	3	2	3		2
Fox, Saml	2	4	4		1
Fox, Elisha	2	1	6		
Comstock, Zebulun	1	3	7		
Robarts, George	1		1		
Foresides, Timothy	1		2		
Foresides, Latham	1	1	2		
Lyons, John	2	1	3		
Condall, James	2	1	2		
Chaple, John	4	1	5		
Condall, Jonathan	1	2	3		
Roles, Daniel	2	1	3		
Cumstock, Jared	2	2	6		
Turner, Isaac	1	4	3		
Fergo, Robart	3		3		
Fergo, Stanton	2		1	4	
Scribner, Ann			1	4	
Chaple, Andrew	1	2	1		
Lester, Isaac	1		3		
Turner, Thomas	1		1		
Lester, Norman	1	1	2		
Stebbins, Edward	1	4	5		
Stebbins, Jabez	2	1	2		
Cumstock, Thomas	1		2		
Wickwise, Lucretia	1		2		
Cumstock, Ransford	2	3	4		
Cumstock, Peter	2	4	6		
Cumstock, Oliver	2	1	4		
Clayton, Peter	1	1	2		
Dolebear, John	2	3	4	1	3
Smith, Nathan	3		2	1	
Raymond, Joshua	2	1	5	1	2
Vallet, Jeremiah, 3d	4	2	6		
Baker, Joshua	1	2	2		
Cook, Roswell	2	2	3		1
Miner, George	1		1		
Atwell, Lucretia		1	2		
Atwell, Benjamin	3		3		
Atwell, George	1		2		
Lester, Elihu	1	1	2		
Capple, Nathl	1	2	2		
Dart, David	1	2	4		
Bishop, Thomas	1	3	5		
Dart, Solomon	3	3	4		
Chaple, Easter		1	7		
York (Negro)				2	
McFall, William	1	2	3		
Chaple, Richard	3		3		
Turner, Thomas, 2d	3	3	5		
Foresides, John	2	3	4		
Bishop, Sarah	1	3	2		
Thompson, John	1	2	2		
Bishop, John	1	1	3		
Bishop, Clemment	3	1	5		
Wix, James	1	2	3		
Miner, Ananias	1		2		
Prentice, Saml	1				
Bishop, Daniel	1	2	3		
Davis, Joseph	2		2		
Davis, Benajah	1	2	2		
Cobb, Simeon, 2d	1	1	2		

NEW LONDON COUNTY—Continued.

NAME OF HEAD OF FAMILY.	Free white males of 16 years and upward, including heads of families.	Free white males under 16 years.	Free white females, including heads of families.	All other free persons.	Slaves.
Davis, Micaijah	1	1	2		
Matimer, George	1	1	7		
Latimer, Jonathan	1	2	4		
Latimer, Henry	3		5		1
Baker, Josiah	2	1	5		
Colt, John	2	1	2		
Chapple, Lebeus	2	3	3		
Latimer, Amos	3	1	3		
Latimer, Nathan, 2d	1	3	2		
Latimer, Nathan	2		5		
Latimer, Hallam	1	1	3		
Martenus, Goodard	1	1	3		
Johnson, Larrance	1	4	1		
Boan (Negro)				7	
Miner, Samuel	2		1		
Beckwith, Saml	2	3	2		
Johnson, Lucy	1		1		
Mosier, Noman	2		3		
Manwaring, George	1	2	6		
Manwaring, George, 2d	1		1		
White, Ezekiel	1	1	4		
White, Ezekiel, 2d	1	1	2		
Cobb, Joseph	1		2		
Boles, Joseph	1	1	4		
Homes, Jabez	1	2	5		
Brown, Sarah	1	1	3		
Gurley, John	1	1	4		
Waley, James	4	1	4		
Johnson, Caleb	1		4		
Chaple, John	1	2	5		
Cobb, Simeon	3	1	6		
Chaple, Jedediah	1	2	3		
Swaddle, Saml	2	1	4		
Chaple, Ezekiel, 2d	3		5		
Chaple, William, 2d	3		2		
Austin, Jonathan	3	4	4		
Chaple, John, 2d	1	1	3		
Austin, Zebadiah	1		2		
Mosier, Stephen	1	2	2		
Miner, Volentine	1	2	1		
Brown, Cumstock	1	1	2		
Page, Joseph	1	1	1		
Chaple, William, 3d	1	2	3		
Chaple, Ezekiel	1	1	1		
Latimer, Samuel	1		1		
Fitch, Thomas	1	1	5		
Chaple, Saml	1	1	1		
Gilbert, Jona	3	1	3		2
Atwell, Benjamin	2		5		
Allen, Nathan	3	2	4		
Avory, George	1		2		
Turner, Mathew	4	2	4		
Turner, Perigreen	1	1	2		
Duglass, Joshua	2	2	4		
Loomis, Jacob	1	2	4		
Ransom, Elijah	2	1	8		3
Latimer, Stephen	1	1	4		
Condall, Daniel	1	1	4		
Dashon, Joseph	3	1	2		
Gallup, Thomas P	3		4		
Miner, Lebeus	1		2		
Miner, Zebadiah	1	1	3		
Eames, John	1		3		
Dolebear, Saml	2	1	2		2
Bliss, Pelatiah	1	2	2		
Bradford, Benjamin	1	1	1		
Roggers, Asa	1	2	5		
Homes, Elisha	1	1	4		
Roggers, Nathl	2		1		
Roggers, Nathl, 2d	1	2	3		
Roggers, Jabez	2		2		
Roggers, Ebenezer	2	2	3		
Harris, Ephraim	1	4	6		
Roggers, Gurdon	1	1	1		
Williams, John	3		4		
Beckwith, Jasper	2	1	3		
Burk, William	1	2	2		
Roggers, Alpheus	1	1	5		
Worthington, Sarah		1	2		
Worthington, Dan	1		1		
Derttrick, John	1	4	3		
Rothburn, Simeon	2	4	4		
Palmer, Able	2	4	2	1	
Whipple, Frederick	1	1	3		
Chester, Joseph	4	1	10		
Chester, Joseph, 2d	1	3	1		
Billings, Stephen	1	3	3		
Stanton, John	1	1	1		
Rothburn, Saml	1	2	2		
Roggers, James	1	1	2		
Waley, Samuel	1	4	3		
Whipple, Silas	3		2		
Turner, Joshua	1	2	2		
Allen, Stephen	1		1		
Moore, Miles	1		3		
Fergo, Nehemiah	1	2	1		
Darrow, Christopher	2	3	2		
Allen, Stephen, 2d	1	2	4		
Miner, Roswell	1	2	1		
Miner, Jonathan	3	2	2		
Thompson, William	3		1		
Thompson, Samuel	1		2		
Denison, George	1	2	4		
Miner, Joshua	1		1		
Miner, Lemuel	1	1	4		
Miner, Richard	1		2		
Chapman, Alpheus	2		4		
Miner, Abiather	2	1	3		
Fergo, William	1		1		
Chapel, Atwell	3	2	2		
Thompson, Nathl	1	2	4		
Chapman, Betsy			1		
Manwaring, Asa	1	1	1		
Atwell, Richard	1	1	5		
Dolbear, George	2	1	3		
Avory, Elihu	1	1	4		
Otis, Nathl	2	2	6		
Gardiner, David, 2d	1	6	4		
Beba, Amos	2	3	3		
Fish, Joseph	1	7	3		
Daniels, Asa	1	2	1		
Williams, Nathl	1	2	1		
Hopkins, Benjamin	1		4		
Avory, Isaac	1	2	3		
Roggers, Nathan	1		3		
Denison, Margarett	2		3		
Manwaring, Christopher	1		4		
Cumstock, Peres	1		2		
Avory, Amy			3		
Manwaring, John	1		1		
West, Joshua	1	2	2		
Cumstock, Nathl	2		7		1
Aplev, Roswell	1	1	3		
Willoughby, Bridget			1		
Willoughby, Bliss	1		1		
Cato (Negro)				6	
Ceaser (Negro)				5	
Hammon, Isaac	1	1	5		
Hammon, Joseph	1	1	4		
Cumstock, Joshua	1	1	1		
Crocker, John	1		2		
Hilhouse, John	2	1	4		2
Camp, Elither	1	1	2		
Raymond, Christopher	2	1	3		2
Hilhouse, Thomas	3	2	1		1
Bradford, Joseph	4	1	5		
Waley, David	1	2	3		
Leffingwell, Benjamin	2	3	5		
Payton, George	1		1		
Chapman, Jonathan	3		2		
Leffingwell, Caleb	1		1		
Nobles, James	1		1		
Nobles, James, 2d	1	2	4		
Nobles, William	1	3	3		
Hammon, Josiah	1	2	2		
Tracy, Moses	1	2	3		
Billings, Mathew	1	3	1		
Maples, Stephen	2	3	5		
Williams, Elisabeth			2		
Raymond, Josiah	2	2	1		
Partin, John	1	1	3		
Homes, Samuel	1	1	2		
Davis, John	2	4	2		
Hosmer, Graves	1		2		
Hilhouse, William	1		3	1	2
Raymond, Mulford	1	1	4	1	
Gardiner, John	1				
Raymond, Lemuel	1	2	1		1
Raymond, Lucy	1	1	1		1
Bill, Charles	1	2	6		
Hatch, Zephaniah	1	2	3		
Maples, William, 2d	1	2	4		
Bland, James	1	1	5		
Raymond, John	2	2	2		1
Waley, Elexander	1	2	2		
Waley, Jonathan	2	2	2		
Robbins, Mary			3		
Maples, Stephen, Junr	1	1	4		
Story, Samuel	1	1	3		
Munson, Henry	1	2	2		
Fitch, Joseph	3	1	3	1	
Fitch, Sherwood	1		2	1	
Avory, Thomas	1	1	2		
Vibber, Nathl	1	2	5		
Vibber, William	1	5	3		
Fitch, Andrus	2	3	4		
Maples, John	2		2		
Maples, William	2	3	5		
Munroe, Joshua	1	2	1		
Chapple, William	1	2	1		
Maples, Josiah	1	3	4		
Morris, James	1	3	4		
Bradford, Peres	3		2		
Homes, Seth W	2	2	3		
Roggers, Jaheil	1	1	6		
Roggers, Thomas, 2d	1	3	2		
Roggers, Andrew	1	2	2		
Chapple, James, 2d	1		2		
Dirskall, Daniel	1		2		
Mosier, Elijah	1		2		
Smith, Joseph	1	3	3		
Brown, Amy			3		
Lester, Silas		1	1		
Brown, Thomas	1		2		
Forthsides, Timothy, 2d	1	3	3		
Wickwire, Jonas	1	2	3		
Boles, Stephen	1	1	2		
Cumstock, James	2	3	3		
Church, Amos	1		2		
Church, Mary	1		2		
Falley, James	1		2		
Sheffield, Saml	1	1	6		
Cumstock, Mary	1		2		
Waterhouse, Thomas	1	3	2	2	
Cumstock, Nathan	1	2	5		
Cumstock, Jason	1	3	2		
Baker, Hepsibah		1	3		
Roggers, Martha		1	4		
Roggers, Joseph	1		3		
Shoals, Jabez	1	2	5		
Church, Mary, 2d	1	1	1		
Palmer, Ruben	1	2	5		
Condall, David	1	2	3		
Roggers, Jeremiah	1	1	5		
Condall, John	1		2		1
Cumstock, Elisha		2	3		
Cumstock, Daniel	1	1	4		
Amy (Negro)				1	
Whealer, William	1	3	6		
Church, Jonathan	1	3	4		
Vallet, Jeremiah, 2d	2		5		
Goff, William	2		1		
Roggers, James	1	2	1		
Roggers, Jonathan	1	1	1		
Cumstock, George	2		2		
Chapple, James	1		2		
Horton, James	4	1	2		1
Raymond, Nathl	2	2	2		1
Raymond, George	2		2		
Leach, John	2		4		
Wickwire, Jeremiah	4		2		
Bradford, Saml	2		4		
Roggers, Thomas	1		1		
Bradford, Nathl	1		1		
Hill, Jonathan	1	3	6		
Allen, Joseph	2		4		
Baker, James	1		1		
Baker, Jared	3		1		
Horton, Lebeus	1	2	2		
Chapman, Joseph	1	1	3		
Beckwith, Isaac	1	1	4		
Wood, Miss			2		
Boles, Thomas	2	1	6		
Perkins, Mary			3		
Baker, Gideon	2		3		
Tuttle, Pelatiah	1	3	1		
Church, Peleg	3	1	1		
Whealer, Ephraim	1		1		
Nickerson, Daniel	1	3	2		
Miner, Abiather	2		1		
Williams, Easter	1	1	1		
Horton, John	3	3	6		
Chapman, Nathl	2	2	1		
Adgate, John	1		4		
Adgate, Thomas	1	3	3		
Boles, Amos	3		4		
Rose, Rufus	1	2	2		
Smith, Ebenr	3		1		
Smith, Ebenr, 2d	1	2	5		
Whealer, Ephraim, 2d	1	6	6		
Williams, Oliver	1		2		
Cumstock, Joseph	1	4	6		
Atweil, Samuel	2		2		
Woodworth, Joshua	1	3	6		
Eames, Danl	1		6		
Adgate, Asa	1		1		
Church, Joseph	1	1	3		
Atwell, John	1		2		
Dersy (Negro)				4	
Eames, Ebenezer	1	1	1		
Brown, John	1	1	1		
Brown, Daniel, 2d	1		2		
Spink, Asa	1	1	4		
Roggers, Frederick	1		1		
Roggers, Asa	1		2		
Ceaser (Negro)				2	
Rebecka (Negro)				4	
Jewet, David H	2	2	5		1
Whealer, William	1	5	4		
Palmer, Saml	1		1		
Swaddle, Jemima		1	3		

NEW LONDON COUNTY—Continued.

NAME OF HEAD OF FAMILY.	Free white males of 16 years and upward, including heads of families.	Free white males under 16 years.	Free white females, including heads of families.	All other free persons.	Slaves.
Bishop, Betsy		1	1		
Waterman, Nehemiah	1		1		
Waterman, Nehemiah, 2d	4	1	2		
Gifford, Stephen	2		3		
Gifford, Susanna		2	1		
Birchird, Jesse	4	1	3		
Hilyard, Dennis	1	1	3		
Baldwin, Ebenr	1		1		1
Backuss, Oliver	1	1	3		
Waterman, John	3	1	4		
McCall, John	2	1	2		
Story, William	1	1	5		
Brown, Wm	1		4		
Johnson, Ebenr	4	1	3		
Edgcomb, John	1		3		
Lothrop, Simeon	2	1	2		
Lathrop, Andrew, Junr	1		2		
Avory, Nathl	1	1	1		
Tillotson, Saml	1	1	2		
Baulding, Eliphelet	2	2	7		
Bingham, Nathan	2	3	5		
Lothrop, Saml	2	1	3		
Persons, Joseph	2	1	4		
Deane, David	1	2	3		
Able, Jesse	2	2	3		
Able, Saml	1	1	2		
Squire, Josiah	1	1	1		
Backuss, Ozias	1	1	2		
Fitch, Asa	5	3	3	1	
Lothrop, Uriah	1	1	4	1	
Able, Theophilus	1	1	2		
Able, Simeon	3	1	5		
Birchird, Ezra	4		3		
Moredock, Jona	1	1	4		
Caulkins, Durkee	1	1	1		
Caulkins, Thomas	1		5		
Baker, Asa	2		3		
Throop, Wm	2	2	4		
Throop, Benja	3	1	4		
Edgerton, Lucy		1	4		
Roberson, Saml	1	3	3		
Downer, Richard	3	1	5		
Marshall, Abiel	1		1		
Allen, Jason	1	1	2		
West, Nathan	1		2		
West, Elias	2	1	5		
Lathrop, Asa	2	2	4		
Fox, Jemima			1		
Downer, Uriah	1	1	2		
West, Asael	3		1		
Whitman, Abraham	1		2		
Whitman, John	2	4	3		
Whitman, Volentine	2	2	3		
Smith, Elisha	1		1		
Woodworth, Asa	3	2	4		
Lamphear, George	1	2	1		
Houghf, David	2	1	4		
Houghf, Jabez	5		4		
Crocker, William	1	1	2		
Spicer, Elderkin	1		1		
Lothrop, Andw	2	1	6		
Woodworth, Benjamin	2		1		
Collins, Nathl	1		2		
Able, Hezekiah	2	1	6		
Woodworth, Benja, 2d	1	1	2		
Ford, Charles	1		3		
Fish, John	1	2	2		
Rudd, Daniel	1	2	5		
Balding, Oliver	1	2	3		
Whitman, Zorobable	3	1	5		
Harris, Benjamin	2	2	3		
Scott, John	2	1	4		
Houghf, Ebenr	2	1	3		
Waterman, Benjamin	2	1	5		
Johnson, John	1	2	3		
Hinson, William	1		4		
Hinson, William, Junr	1	1	1		
Sangor, Trijah	1		2		
Plumb, Peter	1		1		
Step (Negro)				1	
Samson (Negro)				4	
Tuley, Amos	1		6		
Fergo, Daniel	1	2	2		
Ammon (Negro)				6	
Ceaser (Negro)				3	
Fox, Roswell	3	1	4		
Read, Christopher	1	1	1		
Eames, Joseph	1	2	2		
Houghf, John	4	2	5		
Crocker, Thomas	1	1	3		
Crocker, Asa	1		1		
Durkee, Sabin	1		2		
Backuss, Ebenr	1	4	2		
Huntington, Isaac	2	1	3		
Huntington, Elijah	1	3	4		
Caulkins, Christopher	3		2		
Culver, Lemuel	1	1	5		
Eames, Josiah	1		2		
Woodworth, Jabez	2		3		
Huntington, Christopher	2		2		
Ford, Joseph	1	1	7		
Ford, Roswell	1		1		
Osgood, Josiah	1	1	2		
Lothrop, Zebadiah	3	1	2		
Woodworth, Ziba	1		1		
Gardiner, Gurdon	1	1	1		
Smith, Wm	2		3		
Fish, Nathl	2	2	6		
Fish, William	5	3	5		
Cardwell, William	1	4	4		
Bingham, David	2	1	2		
Walworth, Benjamin	2	4	3		
Lothrop, Jedediah	2		2		
Whiting, Caleb	3		2		
Avory, Ezekiel	1		2		
Gardiner, Stephen	1		4		
Gardiner, Daniel	2	3	3		
Gardiner, William	2	2	4		
Gardiner, John	1	2	3		
Gardiner, Jona	1		3		
Gardiner, Jonathan, 2d	1	1	3		
Gardiner, Lemuel	1		2		
Frink, Christopher	2	2	2		
Gardiner, Simeon	1	2	4		
Condon, Timothy	2		5		
Gardiner, David	1	1	3		
Avory, Samuel	2		5		
Gardiner, Isaac	1	2	2		
Gustin, Amos	1	3	4		
Fox, Jedediah	2	1	6		
Gardiner, David, Junr	1	2	5		
Minor, Daniel	1	1	4		
Vergoson, John	1	1	4		
Vergoson, Diah	1	1	3		
Loomer, Ebenr	1	1	3		
Leffingwell, Clark	1	1	4		
Roggers, Peter	1	2	2		
Nobles, Diah	1	2	5		
Lothrop, Sarah		1	2		
Leffingwell, Saml	1		1		
Leffingwell, Saml, 2d	1	1	5		
Leffingwell, Roswell	3		4		
Leffingwell, Presilla	1	1	5		
Leffingwell, Andrew	2	1	2		
Nobles, Mary	1		3		
Post, Stephen	1	2	1		
Beckwith, Lemuel	1		5		
Post, John	2	1	4		
Post, Nathl	1		2		
Gemina (Negro)				2	
Reynolds, Hezekiah			1		
Johnson, Eliphalet	1	1	3		
Loomer, Arnold	1		2		
Sangor, Asael	1		1		
Loomer, Lovina		1	2		
Ford, John	1	1	2		
Whitman, Daniel	1		1		
Senot, Thomas	1		4		
Gazer, Simon, & Dan	3	2	4		
Gardiner, Caleb	1	2	2		
Whitman, Amos	1	2	1		
Fagins (Negro)				5	
Harris, William	1	1	2		
Durkee, William	1	1	3		
Huntington, Thomas	1	1	3		
Lothrop, Jedediah, 2d	2	2	3		
Vergoson, Jeremiah	1		3		
Whitman, Israel	2		5		
Harris, Daniel	1	2	3		
Harris, Peter	1	2	3		
Metcalf, Jabez	1		1		
Wait, Marvin	1	2	4	1	2
Deshon, John	2		2		4
Wright, David	1	2	4		
Roberson, Archibauld	1		5		
Chapman, Elisabeth	5		2		
Caulkins, Pember	4		3	1	3
Melally, Michael	1	1	3		5
Latimer, Saml	3		3		
Latimer, Richard	1	1	3		
Pool, Thomas	2	1	3		
Deshon, Richard	4	2	4		1
Brainard, Jeremiah	1	2	5		1
Coit, Joshua	1	2	4		
Shaw, Thomas	2		5		1
Ceaser (Negro)				5	
Williams, George	2		10		3
Smith, Joshua	1	2	3		
Boles, Thomas	2	1	6		
Powers, Saml	3		4		3
Greene, Benja	2	1	5		
Strickland, Peter, Junr	2	2	3		
Greene, Christopher	2	1	5		
Boles, John & Son	3	1	5		
Hinman, Elisha	2	1	4		2
Hallam, George	1		1	2	2
Smith, David	3	1	5		4
Newbury, Davis	1	1	3		
Smith, Sarah			2		
Roggers, Elexander	3	2	6		
Roggers, Nathl	1		3		
Hambleton, John	2	1	2		
Hambleton, Gurdon	1	1	3		
Lester, Levi	1	3	3		
Boles, Deborah	1	1	1		
Roggers, John	1	3	4		
Walden, John	1	3	3		
Roggers, Mary			2		
Shaw, Thomas, 2d	1		1		
Whealer, Guy	1	2	3		
Avory, Frederick	1	2	3		
Whealer, Zachius	1		3	1	
Roggers, John, 3d	2	3	4		
Roggers, Saml	1		2		
Burns, Daniel	1	1	1		
Waterhouse, John	2	3	4		
Roggers, Saml, 2d	2	3	2		
Roggers, Lite	2		5		
Roggers, James, 2d	1	1	3		
Prentice, Easter	1	2	2		
Robart (Negro)				3	
Boles, Joshua	2	1	3		
Simons, Ann	1		3		
Frink, David	2	3	4		
Boles, Enoch	1	1	5		
Learned, Amasa	1	4	5	1	1
Richards, William	1	1	6		
Richards, Saml	2	1	5		
Bliss, Abraham	2	1	3		
Hallam, Robart	1	2	2		
Richards, Jabez	1	3	5		
Smith, Paul	1	1	3		
Smith, King	1	2	2		
Smith, Hezekiah	1	1	2		
Smith, Elijah	1		3		
Roggers, Jona	1				
Beba, Abijah	1	2	2		
Smith, John	1	3	2		
Smith, Hugh	1	4	3		
Smith, Simon	2	4	4		
Smith, Ezekiel	1	2	2		
Fergo, Thomas	1	3	3		1
Smith, Mercy			2		
Smith, Samuel	1				
Smith, Saml, 2d	1	3	5		
Smith, Daniel, 2d	1	1	3		
Smith, Daniel	4		4		
Luther, Levi	1	1	1		
Lee, Levi	2	1	5		
Dart, Roger	1				
Daniels, Peter	1	1	6		
Latimer, Lemuel	1	1	3		
Mago, Thomas	1	2	4		
Daniels, Nathan, 2d	2		6		
Chapple, Peter	1		1		
Dart, Saml	1		3		
Avory, Wait	1		3		
Walden, Elisabeth			1	1	
Thomson, Benjamin	1	3	2		
Chapman, Lemuel	1	1	7		
Lee, Edgcomb	1		5		
Strickland, Amos	1	1	3		
Strickland, William	1		3		
Strickland, Sarah	1		2		
Boles, James	1		4		
Boles, Joseph	3		1		
Dart, William	4		2		
Dart, William, Junr	1	1	3		
Sharp, Joseph	1	1	2		
Quinley, Jeremiah	1		1		
Quinley, Thomas	1	2	5		
Freman (Negro)				4	
Strickland, Peter	2		2		
Strickland, Peter, 3d	1		1		
Thomson, Charles	1		2		
Eames, Daniel	2		3		
Whipple, Titus	2	3	2		1
Duglass, Joseph	2	2	7		
Douglas, David	3		2		
Douglass, Stephen	1	3	1		
Eames, Saml	2	5	2		
Brooks, Daniel	1	1	2		
Dodge, James	1		2		
Gitchel, Joseph	1	1	2		
Dart, Ebenr	3	1	1		
Dart, Ebenr, Junr	1	1	1		
Waterhouse, Nathl	3	1	6		
Caulkins, Thomas	1		2		
Butler, John, Junr	1		2		
Prentice, Joseph	3	1	6		

NEW LONDON COUNTY—Continued.

NAME OF HEAD OF FAMILY.	Free white males of 16 years and upward, including heads of families.	Free white males under 16 years.	Free white females, including heads of families.	All other free persons.	Slaves.	NAME OF HEAD OF FAMILY.	Free white males of 16 years and upward, including heads of families.	Free white males under 16 years.	Free white females, including heads of families.	All other free persons.	Slaves.	NAME OF HEAD OF FAMILY.	Free white males of 16 years and upward, including heads of families.	Free white males under 16 years.	Free white females, including heads of families.	All other free persons.	Slaves.
Duglass, Thomas	3		8			Leach, Stephen	1	3	3			Caulkins, Jedediah	1	2	1		
Douglass, Daniel	2	5	2			Leach, Ephraim	1		2			Caulkins, Ezra	1	1	1		
Duglass, James	1		1			Culver, Joseph	1	2	1			Beckwith, John	1		3		
Duglass, Silvanus	1		2			Tinker, Joseph	1	1	4			Beckwith, Caleb	1		1		
Duglass, James, 2d	1		3			Whipples, John	3	1	4			Miner, Silvester	1	1	1		
Watrus, Elijah	3	2	4			Beba, Azariah	3		2			Beckwith, John, Junr	1	2	6		
Caulkins, Saml	2	1	3			Beba, Richard	1	1	2			Pember, Ezekiel	1		1		
Richards, Nehemiah	3	3	4			Leach, Daniel	1		2			Darrow, Ebenr	1	2	2		
Powers, Michael	1		3			Beckwith, Elisha	1	1	3			Gardiner, Benaijah	3	3	1		3
Powers, Joseph	1		3			Howard, John	1		1			Durfee, Sarah	1		3		6
Eames, Joseph	1	1	1			Chaple, Isaac	1	1	4			Taylor, Simon	1	3	4		
Powers, Michael, 2d	1	1	4			Thomson, James	2		3			Miner, Amos	1	1	3		
Holt, Wm	1		2			Latimer, Daniel	1	1	1		1	Prentice, Stephen	1	1	2		
Holt, Asa	1	3	1			Latimer, Pickett	1		2			Manchester, Thomas	1		2		
Chapple, Walter	2		2			Chaple, Isaac, Junr	1	1	3			Prentice, Stephen, Junr	1	2	3		
Chapple, William	1	1	3			Harding, Jeremiah	1	2	1			Beckwith, Frederick	3	1	5		
Way, Azariah	3		1			Atwell, Thomas	1		2			Brown, Charles	2	3	5		
Duglass, Saml	1	2	2			Hemstead, Jonathan	1	2	5		1	Beckwith, Noah	1	5	4		
Beba, Thadeus	2	1	3			Maynard, Stephen	4	1	7			Soper, John	1		2		
Caulkins, Lemuel	1	5	1			Ryan, Rebecka	1		2			Chapple, Wm	1	2	4		
Hall, Aaron	1	1	3			Staplin, Edward	1	1	1			Newbury, Richard	1	1	3		
Chapple, Barsheba	1		2			Richards, Edward	1	1	4			Newbury, Samuel	1	1	2		
Knight, John	1	1	3			Doyle, Peter	1	1	2			Maynard, Naomi		1	5		
Daniels, James	2		3			Chapman, Nathl	1		1			Darrow, William	1	2	3		
Daniels, Thomas	1	1	1			Harden, Thomas	3		4			Lester, Timothy	1		1		
Fox, Jesse	1		3			Williams, Daniel	1	1	1			Crocker, Jonathan	2	2	2		
Fergo, William	1	1	2			Chapman, Eliphelet	1	3	1			Mallery, David	1	2	4		
Champlin, Isaac	1	3	3			Clifford, Silvester	2		1	1		Beba, Rufus	2	1	1		
Watrus, Sarah			2			Clifford, Joseph	1	3	2			Tabor, Jeremiah	1		3		
Gibson, Roger	2		1			Read, Charles	1	2	5			Moore, William	2	1	4		
Phillups, John	2	2	3			Cannon, Robart	1	2	1			Daniels, Noah	1		1		
Daniels, Nehemiah	1		3			Chapman, Jason	1		4			Leach, David	1	2	2		
Daniels, Joseph	1	1	2			Marshall, Joseph	1	1	5			Tinker, John	1		3		
Butler, James	1		4			Boles, Saml	1	3	5			Tinker, John, Junr	1	1	1		
Butler, John	1	1	5			Avory, Charles	1	1	2			Durfee, Thomas	1		2		
Bishop, Jona	1	4	5			Richards, John	1		1		2	Shaw, Daniel	2	1	3		1
Daniels, Saml	3		1			Hatch, Deborah		1	2			Chapple, Elisabeth			1		
Fergo, Moses	3		2			Roggers, Ichabod	1	2	5			Chapple, Lydia		1	2		
Moore, Hannah			1			Richards, Nathl	2	1	4		2	Munro, Joshua	1	1	2		
Daniels, Jasper	1	1	1			Huntington, Jedediah	1	2	7			Tinker, Saml	1	4	1		
Crocker, Amos	1	1	4			Sistarre, Gabriel	2	3	4		3	Stebbins, John, 2d	1	1	1		
Daniels, Job	1	4	2			Green, Timothy	5	4	5		3	Fergo, Zacheus	1		2		
Daniels, Nehemiah, 2d	1		3			Burns, John	1	1	4			White, Hannah			2		
Morgan, William	1		1			Edgcomb, Jesse	2	1	4			Miner, Hugh	2		5		
Beckwith, Isaac	1	1	3			Chapman, Easter			2			Roggers, David	1	6	4		
Brown, Eleazer	1	2	4			Hemstead, Nathl, 3d	1	1	2			Davis, William	1	1	2		
Beba, James	3	1	6			Manwaring, Robart	3	2	5			Beba, Theophilus	2	1	3		
Hall, Joshua	3		2			Hemstead, Nathl, Junr	2	2	3			Beba, Othiniel	1	4	1		
Dart, Daniel	1	1	3			Richards, David	1		1			Darrow, Ebenr	1		3		
Strickland, John	3	8	2			Chapman, Hannah			2			Chapple, George	2	1	2		
Bartholemy, Saml	1	1	2			Hemstead, Benjamin	1	3	4			Badcock, Daniel	1	1	2		
Dart, James	1	2	2			Ashcraft, William	1	2	2			Beba, Jared	1		1		
Miner, Jabez	1		3			Froud, Robart	1				1	Miner, Samuel	1	3	3		
Gorton, Collins	1	2	4			Ashcraft, Edward	1	3	1			Tinker, Perry	1	1	1		
Avory, Elisha	2		1			Dart, Caleb	1	3	2			Beba, Ruben	1		2		
Manwaring, Isaac	1		4			Mosier, Saml	1		2			Finger, William	1	1	3		
Kenyon, Pain	1	3	2			Dart, Benja	1	1	3			Crocker, Amos	1	3	1		
Tabor, Saml	3	1	2			Dart, Ruth			3			Chapman, James	1	1	2		
Tabor, Saml, Junr	1	2	5			Beba, Saml, Junr	2	2	4			Holt, Daniel	2	3	4		
Page, Jeremiah	2	4	3			Chaple, Jesse	1	1	1			Truman, Daniel	2		3		1
Fosdike, Clemment	1	3	2			Chaple, Eunice		1	3			Fox, Edward	1		1		
Beckwith, Ezekiel, 3d	1		2			Manwaring, Jabez	1	1	1			Carter, John	1	1	1		
Crocker, Daniel	1	4	2			Leach, Mary			3			Henry, Daniel	1		3		
Wordon, Wait	1	3	2			Stebbins, Joseph	1		1			Harris, Joseph	2	2	2		1
Lane, William	1	2	4			Brown, Sarah			2			Miller, Jeremiah	3	1	4		2
Darrow, James	2	1	1			Chaple, Richard	1		2			Way, Jerusha	1		2		
Brown, Zachariah	1					Stebbins, John	1	2	2			Smith, John	1		3		
Crocker, Constant	2	1	2			Armstrong, Peter	1	1	3			Gardiner, Rufus	1		3		
Ayres, Elisha	1		4			Miner, Stephen	1		1			Hemstead, William	2	2	5		
Beba, Eliphelet	1	3	3			Miner, Lydia	1		2			Norris, Henry	1		2		
Keeney, William	1	4	2			Tinker, Benja	3		2			Keeney, Amos	1	2	3		
Horton, Benjamin	1		5			King, Charles	1		2			Watrus, Benjamin	1	1	2		
Daniels, Isaac	1		1			Tinker, Benjamin, 2d	1	1	2			Lewis, Joseph	1		1		
Manwaring, Thomas	1	1	6			Beba, Ephraim	1	2	5			Smith, Joseph	1		2		
Raymond, Caleb	2		3		1	Manwaring, Oliver	1	2	2			Teague, Jerusha		2	1		
Moore, Joshua	2		1			Crocker, Thomas	2	1	2			Cato (Negro)				3	
Crocker, Lydia		1	2			Crocker, Isaac	1	1	3			Fowler, John	1	4	2		
Chaple, Jonathan	1	1	2			Crocker, Stephen	2	1	5			Maynard, Ebenr	1	2	3		
Bishop, Susanna			2			Beckwith, Jason	1	2	1			Maynard, Christopher	1	2	4		
Beba, Joseph	1		1			Newbury, Stedman	1	3	4			Roggers, Ebenr	1		2		1
Clark, Nathl	1	2	5	2		Crocker, Joshua	1		2			Roggers, Thomas	1		1		
Bramin, Paul	1		4			Beba, Saml	1		1			Roggers, David	2		3		
Daniels, Nathan	1		6			Beckwith, Seth	1	2	2			Rogers, Zebulun	1	2	3		
Dart, Richard	1		1			Hicks, Saml	1	1	2			Rogers, Clark	1	1	4		
Stuart, Elisha	2		4			Crocker, Nehemiah	1	2	2			Rogers, Ephraim	1	1	4		
Morgan, Samuel	1		6			Smith, George	3	1	2			Rogers, Nathan	2		2		
Duglass, George	1		10		1	Mossett, Thomas	1	1	2			Rogers, Jona	1	3	1		
Duglass, William	3		3			Caulkins, Lydia		1	4			Rogers, Phineas	1	1	4		
Morgan, Grace			1			Morrison, Joseph	1		3			Westcott, William	2	4	4		
Morgan, John	1		1			Cumstock, Martha			1			Paeston, Shubael	1		3		
Whipple, Anthony	2		3			Howard, Sarah	1	2	2			Chub, Joseph	1	1	4		
Morgan, George	2	2	3			Lovett, Joseph	1	2	4			Darrow, Jedediah	2	1	1		
Bill, Timothy	1	1	1			Miner, Jonathan	1		6			Crandall, Phinias	2	1	4		
Baker, Sarah		1	2			Darrow, Zadock	2		2			Fox, Benja	1		3		
Baker, John		1	4			Darrow, Lemuel	1	3	4			Fox, Samuel	1		2		
Morgan, Edward	2		4			Howard, Daniel	1	1	5			Jerom, Richard	1	1	5		
Morgan, Phillup	2	1	2			Stuart, William	3	1	2			Rogers, James	1		1		4

NEW LONDON COUNTY—Continued.

NAME OF HEAD OF FAMILY.	Free white males of 16 years and upward, including heads of families.	Free white males under 16 years.	Free white females, including heads of families.	All other free persons.	Slaves.
Dayton, Joseph	1		1		
Daton, Ephraim	1	1	1		
Tabor, Pardon	2		1		1
Allen, Thomas, Junr	2	4	4		1
Beba, Jethro	1	2	3		
Brooks, Ezekiel	1		1		
Brooks, Ezekiel, 2d	1	3	1		
Rothburn, Wm	1	4	5		
Beba, Jona	1	1	2		
Beba, William	1	1	2		
Beba, Guy	1	3	6		
Beba, Jabez	1		2		
Beba, Paul	1		3		
Beba, Jabez, 2d	1	2	2		
Rogers, Daniel	1		2		
Chapple, Saml	1	3	5		
Tinker, Ezekiel	1	1	2		
Welles, Lucy			3		
Beba, Jeduthan	2	1	3		
Daton, Zophar	2		2		
Beckwith, Timothy, 2d	1	1	2		
Beckwith, Timothy	2	2	5		
Edwards, Roger	1		1		
Bur, Purcy	1	3	2		
Moore, William, 2d	3	2	5		
Rogers, Solomon	1	3	4		
Rogers, Stephen	1	2	2		
Rogers, Isaac	1	2	2		
Fowler, Morris	2	1	1		
Wix, Joseph	1	3	1		
Avory, Griswould	4		4		
Brown, Benja	3	3	3		
Maynard, James	1	2	3		
Brown, Jeremiah	2	4	5		
Jerom, Benjamin	1	5	4		
Brown, James	2	2	1		
Harris, Eliphelet, 2d	1		1		
Sprage, Lucy			2		
Wyllis, William	1		4		
Brown, John	1	1	4		
Harris, Eliphelet	2	2	4		
Harris, Daniel	1	1	4		1
Chapple, Alpheus	1		2		
Harris, Ezra	1		2		
West, Daniel	1		1	1	
Harris, Thomas	1	1	5		
Lester, John	2		4		
Harris, John	1		3		
Harris, Sarah	1		3		
Harris, Noah	1	1	1		
Harris, John, 3d	1	1	2		
Lester, Amos	1		2		
Harris, Walter	2	1	3		
Newbury, Mary			2		
Harris, Daniel, 2d	1	1	2		
Way, Nathl	1		2		
Kenney, John	2	4	3		
Keney, Danl	1	3	2		
Tinker, Edward	1		1		
Tinker, Josiah	1		1		
Tinker, Jeremiah	1		1		
Lewis, Mary		1	3		
Prentice, John	1	1	1		
Barber, Benjamin	1		1		
Harris, Nathl	1	4	2		
Rogers, Israel	1		3		
Harris, John, 2d	3	1	6		
Fox, Daniel	1		3		
Carrol, John	1	1	1		
West, Jabez	1		1		
Cumstock, John	1	2	4		
Harris, Roswell	1	1	3		
Darrow, Nicholas	1	3	5		
Harris, Henry	1	1	1		
Lewis, Edward	1		1		
Daniels, Jeremiah	1	1	2		
Paterson, James	1	1	4		
Fink, Adam	1		2		
Coit, Saml	1	1	2		
Coit, John	1		1		
Coit, Saml, 2d	1	4	1		
Mason, Saml	1	2	3		
Devenport, Welthy			4		
Mason, Japhet	1		1		
Thorp, Nathl	1	2	3		
Thorp, Nathl, 2d	1	1	1		
Stone, John	1	3	4		
Thorp, Ezekiel	1		3		
Thorp, Amos	1	1	4		
Davis, Ruben	1	1	2		
Holt, Thomas	2	2	2		
Miller, Frelove		1	1		
Wicks, Rebecka			1		
Ceaser (Negro)					2
Jones, Henry	1	1	3		
Dart, Prudence			4		
Harding, Thomas, 2d	1	1	6		
Perkin, Richard W	2	1	4	1	2
Winthrop, Frank	3	2	4		1
Howard, Wm	1	1	2		
Strowd, Richard	1		2		
Slater, Zerobabel	2	1	3		
Fellows, Joseph	1	2	2		
Melona, William	1	1	2		
Tinker, Daniel	1	3	3		
Fellows, Isaac	1		4		
Packwood, Joseph	1	1	6		
Rogers, John	1	1	5		
Hancock, Thomas	1	1	3		
Potter, Ann		2	3		
Sampson (Negro)				6	
Harry (Negro)				4	
Sarah (Negro)				3	
Gordon, John	1	2	3		
Bloyd, Margaret				1	
Whipple, John	1	1	1		
Phink, Adam	1		3		
Fernando, Frances	1	1	2		
Gesting, John	1		1		
Mason, Patience			2	4	
Smith, Henry	1	1	1		
Beebee, Burgess	1		1		
Culver, Christopher	1	2	2		
Beebee, Grace	3		6		
Ryon, William	1		5		
Holt, Jonathan	1	2	1		
Gristing, James	1	1	4		
Jones, Aaron	1	2	1		
Harris, James	1		1		
Harvey, ——	1	2	2		
Holt, William	1	1	2		
Squier, John	1		1		
Culver, James	1				
Crowly, William	1		1		
Dart, John	1	1	2		
Holt, Elizabeth	1	1	3		
Codner, Cata			2		
Coit, Patty	1	2	1		
Harris, Jasper	1		2		
Penveer, John	1		1		
Holt, Ebenezer	1		3		
Smith, James	2	1	2		
Watrous, Stephen	1	1	1		
Wheat, William	1		2		
Manning, Latham	1		1		
Hempstead, Nathl	1	1	2		
Hempstead, Samuel	1	1	1		
Proud, Robert	1		3		
Hempstead, Joshua	1	1	2		
Hamilton, Rebecca	1	2	1		
Miner, Turner	2	2	4		
Christophers, Peter	6	1	3	2	2
Coit, William	1		4		2
Wolcott, Simon	2	1	8		
Douglass, Richard	1		1		
Shields, Hannah			1		
Weaver, William			2		
Miner, Hugh	1	4	2		
Starr, Jonathan	1		2		
Freeman, Henry	1		3		1
Crawford, John	1	1	2		
Carroll, Nancy			2		
Silvia (Negro)				2	
Chapman, John	1	2	3		
Sherman, James	1	1	2		
Holt, Eben	3	2	4		
Rogers, Hannah		2	4		
Brown, Wheeler	3	5	3		
Turner, Sarah			2		
Coit, Joseph	2	3	4		3
Starr, Lucy			4		
Champlin, Elizabeth	2	2	4		
Bradley, Joshua	1	1	4		
Crocker, John	1	2	3		
Buddington, Walter	1		1		
Clark, John	1		1		
Watson, John	1	1	2		
Rockwell, Merit	1	2	2		
Harris, William	4	2	2		
Dodge, Ezra	1		1		
Ryon, Irena			1		
Short, Hannah		1	2		
Lampheer, James	1	1	7		
Gardiner, Mary	1		2		
Shepherd, John	1	3	4		1
Tilley, James	9	6	4		2
Miller, John	2	3	4		2
Winthrop, Ann			2		
Starr, Jonathan, Junr	1	3	7	1	
Starr, Jared	2	3	3	1	1
Way, John	1	1	6		
Avery, George D	2	3	1	1	
Fink, Jacob	1		3		
Saltonstall, Winthrop	1		2		3
Coit, Thomas, Junr	1	1	3		
Goddard, Ebenezer	1	3	2		
Hurlburt, Daniel	1		1		
Warner, ——	1		2		
Payne, Phoebe	2		1		
Norcute, John	1	1	3		
Buckley, Charles	1	3	4		
Fosdick, Nicoll	2	2	3		1
Mumford, Giles	1	1	4		1
Hempstead, Stephen	3	4	3		
Smith, Joseph	2		2		
Tabor, Job	2	4	6		1
Stimel, John	1	1	2		
Fergo, Hannah	1		1		
Tilley, John	1		3		
Dart, Job	1		3		
Proctor, Abel	1	2	4		
Douglass, Richard, 1st	1	3	4		
Rathbun, Job	1		1	1	
Wescott, Elizabeth	2		2		
Stockman, Jacob	1	3	1		
Spence, Deborah		1	5		
Jones, Thomas	1		3		
Manwaring, David	2		5		
Miner, Ephraim	2	1	5	2	
Douglass, Jonathan	2	4	2		
Starr, Joshua	4	4	4		1
Penniman, James	5	1	3		
Wheat, Samuel	2	4	3		3
Durivage, Nicholas	4	3	3		1
Stewart, William	2		4		2
Saltonstall, Gurdon	1	1	2		
Elliott, Clark	2		1		
Rogers, George	4	1	8		
Hill, James	1	5	2		
Luke, John	1	2	1		1
Law, Richard	2	2	3	2	1
Wild, John	2	1	3		
Matters, James	1	2	3		
Leech, James	1	1	2		
Young, Joseph	1		1		
Beckwith, David	1	1	3		
Clark, Isaac	1		3		
Dennis, John	1		2		
Craw, Sarah			2		
Richards, Daniel W	2	1	2		
Percival, Monsieur	1		3		1
Skinner, William	1	1	1		
Skinner, William, 2d	1	2	2		
Dickinson, Nathl	1	3	4		
Holt, Stephen	3	2	3		
Way, Ebenezer	1	2	1		
Harris, Peter B	1	1	6		
Burrows, Roswell	5		2		
Latimer, William	1	2	1		
Palmer, Hannah	1		1		
Edmunds, ——			2		
La Roche, John	1	1	2		
Chapman, Oliver	4		3		
Pero, Barsheba		1	3		
Emerson, Joseph	1	2	4		
Weeden, Isaac	1	1	3		
Angell, James	1	4	4		
Potter, Joshua	1	2	7		
Powers, Sylvester	1		2		
Rice, Thomas	1		2		
Wignall, William	1	2	2		
Miller, James	1		4		
Fish, Seabury	3		2		
Lathrop, John	1		2		
Douglass, Sperry	1	2	3		
Brooks, Jonathan	2	1	2		
Cottril, James	1		3		
Bloyd, John	1	1	4		
Smith, Asa	1		1		
Manning, Gamaliel	2				
Smith, Dayton			1		
Douglass, Ebenezer	1	3	6	3	
Brown, Joseph	1		1		
Richards, Mary	1		2		
Potter, John	3	4	2		
Potter, William	1	1	2		
Harvey, Thomas	1	1	1		
Harvey, William	1		3		
Hart, James	1	2	2		
Jack (Negro)				3	
Malay, Aliff			2		
Hempstead, Hallam	1	1	2		
Jeffery, Thomas	1		3		
Jeffery, James	1		2		
Nicholl, Owen	1	1	1		
Brooks, James	1		2		
Jeffery, Charles, 2d	2		6		
Hewitt, Nathaniel	3		2		
Bayley, Nathan, Junr	1	4	5		
Craw, Amasa	1		1		
Springer, John	1	2	3		

NEW LONDON COUNTY—Continued.

NAME OF HEAD OF FAMILY.	Free white males of 16 years and upward, including heads of families.	Free white males under 16 years.	Free white females, including heads of families.	All other free persons.	Slaves.
Woodard, John	2		1		
Jeffery, Moses	2	2	3		
Bayley, Nathan	2		2		
Manierre, Lewis	2	3	4		
Jeffery, Charles	1		1		
Whipple, Thomas	1	4	4		
Taylor, John	1		1		
Chapell, Edward	2	2	5		3
Colbert, Temperance		1	2		
Harris, Francis	1	1	3		
Holt, James	1	1	3		
Perry, Eliahim	1		2	1	
Dunton, Ebenezer	1	2	11		
Foster, Benjamin	1	1	2	1	
Waldo, John	1		1		
Simmonds, John	1	1	3		
Holmes, James	2	3	4		2
Treby, John	2	1	4		
Young, James	1	1	3		
Dyian, Philip	1	1	3		
Billings, Lament		1	7		
Rice, Mary			1		
Treby, Isaac	2		4		
Stacy, Rebecca			3		
Douglass, Mary			1		
Trott, Jonathan	3	1	4		
Mumford, David	3	1	4	1	1
Saltonstall, Nathaniel	1	2	1		
Robinsone, Patrick	2	3	3		
Bolles, Isaiah	1	5	4		
Gale, Luther	2		2		
Hewit, Gurdon	4	2	2		
Plumb, Samuel	1	2	2		
Lyman, Elisha	1	1	1		
Lee, Elizabeth			2		
Pool, David	1	2	4		
Cornhill, Job	3	2	5		
Powers, Sylvester	1	2	2		
Zants, Monsieur	1		4		
Manwaring, John	1		2		
Cheney, Samuel	1	1	1		
Newport, Sarah			1		
Clay, Patience	1		3		
Seabury, Samuel	2	2	4		3
Freeman, Mary			7		
Richards, Guy	1				
Allen, Thomas	1	1	2		1
Badet, Peter	1	1	2		
Coit, Boradel		1	5		
Belden, Samuel	3		5		1
Smith, Simeon	4	2	5		
Burrows, Daniel	6	2	3		
Stebbins, Lucy	1		1		
Walker, John	1	1	2		
Packwood, Nabby		1	2		2
Rogers, Fanny		3	1		
Owen, Joseph	1		2		
Champlin, John	3	3	2		
Lee, Thomas	1	3	1		
Prince, Kimball	1	2	2		
Adams, Bela	1		1	1	
Brooks, William	1	1	2		
Adams, David	1	1	3		
Newcomb, Sarah			2		
Sistarre, Gabriel, 2d	1	1	3	1	
Pitman, William	3	2	3		
Woodard, Abisha	5	3	7	1	
Plumb, John	1		3		
Goodard, Mary	1	2	3		
Merrils, Mary	1		4		
Saltonstall, Dudley	3		3		1
Hall, Sarah			3		
Dixon, Thomas	1	1	1		
Rudge, Sampson	1	2	3		
Wix, Deborah		1	2		
Thomas, John	1	1	2		
Smith, Ephraim	1	1	3		
Daniel (Negro)				2	
Bolton, James	1	1	2		
Crawson, Asa	1		3		
Thomson, Robart	1		3		
Markaniff, Charles	1		1		
Rogers, James	4	3	4		2
Burn, James	1		1		
Rogers, Jason	2	2	3		1
Deshon, Daniel	1	2	2		
Deshon, Henry	2	1	2		1
Susant, James	1		1		1
Fitsgerald, John	1	1	2		
Ward, Crittendon	1	1	2		
Channing, Henry	1	2	2	1	
Richards, Elisabeth			1	1	
Manwaring, Lydia			1		
Colefax, George	2	2	5		
Copp, Joseph	1	1	2		
Edgerton, James	1		2		
Blackley, John	1	1	3		
Deepu, John	1		3		
Blackley, Margaret			3		
Piner, Lydia			4		
Prentice, Ebenr	1	1	2		
Richards, Guy	3	4	7		
House, George	1	1	2		
Coats, Frederick	1		2		
Hallam, Edward	2		2	1	
Higgins, William	1	2	2		
Goodfaith, David	1	1	1		
Carrol, James	1	2	4		
Hurlbut, Elisabeth	3		5		3
Whittemore, Saml	1	3	3		
Gordon, John	2	3	2		
Winthrop, Elisabeth	1		3	1	
Sebor, Jacob	1	1	7		2
Saltonstall, Roswell	4	3	7		1
Hallam, John	1	3	3		1
Seabury, Saml, 2d	1	1	2		
Tabor, Wardon T	2		4		
Elliot, Daniel	1	4			
Young, James	1	1	4		
Jackson, John	1	2	3		
Wilson, Thomas	1		1		
Kimball, Chester	1	2	1		
Ward, John	2		1		
Stark, William	1		2		
Beba, James	1	2	2		
Miller, Henry	2		2		
Collins, Thomas	1	1	2		
Owen, John	2	5	7		
Stark, Benjamin	1	2	1		
Swain, Peter	1	2	2		
Colvin, Gabriel	1	1	2		
McDonald, Mathew	1		2		
Hall, Jenny			2		
Culver, Samuel	1	3	4		
Wally, John	1	1	1		
Simons, Chapman	1	1	4		
Williams, Visalamos	1	1	2		
Bush, Henry	2	1	2		
Simmons, Sarah			1		
Simmons, Sally			1	1	
Brooks, Thadeus	2	3	3		
Rogers, Benjamin	2	4	4		
Briggs, William	2	2	4		
Peters, James	1		2		
Gardiner, Henry	1		1		
Shapley, Mary	2		1		
Colefax, Abigail			3		
Hinman, Cate			4		
Hichcox, Ebenr	1		2		
Chapman, Danl	1		2		
Griswould, Elisha	1		3		
Griswould, Saml	3	2	6		
Lord, Nathan	2	7	5		
Mills, Mehitable			2		
Roberson, Nathan	3	1	3		
Gideons, Nathl	2	2	5		
Fillemore, Cumfort	2	3	6		
Fillemore, Amaziah	1	1	3		
Kingsley, Eliphelet	2		3		
Armstrong, Isaiah	1	4	1		
Griswould, Ebenr	4		5		
Armstrong, Bela	1	4	3		
Barker, John	4	2	6		
Barker, John, 2d	1		2		
Backeus, Ezekiel	1	1	2		
Armstrong, John	3		3		
Armstrong, Amos	3	3	3		
Armstrong, Asa	2		2		
Kingsley, Alpheus	1	2	5		
Fox, Martha			2		
Kingsley, William	2	2	2		
Ellis, John	2	1	5		
Ladd, Samuel	3		2		
Ladd, Ezekiel	2	1	6		
Samson, Joseph	2	1	4		
Bruster, Stephen	2	2	2		
Ladd, Jeremiah	3	1	2		
Hazen, Moses	2		3		
Hazen, Joseph	1	1	1		
Ladd, David, 2d	1	1	4		
Ladd, Jedediah	1		4		
Ladd, Andw	1		1		
Story, Ephraim	1		2		
Smith, Joshua	2		2		
Smith, Joshua, 2d	1		2		
Cook, John	1	2	2		
Ladd, Abner	3	2	6		
Armstrong, James	1	1	2		
Huntley, Calvin	1	1	3		
Smith, John	3		3		
Smith, Saml	1	1	3		
Armstrong, Hope	2		2		
Armstrong, Pelatiah	1		2		
Sabin, Benajah	2	1	2		
Taylor, John	1		2		
Ayres, Joseph	3		3		
Ayers, John	1		1		
Ayers, Squire	1	2	5		
Ayers, Timothy	1	5	3		
Abell, Martin	1	1	2		
Abell, Parnell	1		2		
Peck, Phinehas	3	3	3		
Samson, Jonathan	1	2	2		
Ladd, Joseph	2	2	3		
Hyde, Joseph	2	2	2		
Stoddard, Solomon	2		2		
Edgerton, Ariel	1	3	3		
Scott, Joseph	3	3	4		
Munsell, John	1	2	2		
Edgerton, Elizabeth			2		
Edgerton, Samuel	2		4		
Edgerton, Zebulon	1		3		
Gazer, John	4		4		
Abell, Cherub	1	2	1		
Barstow, Yetonce	2		4		
Currin, Phinehas	1	4	1		
Bourne, Amos	1		2		
Hyde, Mary			2		
Hyde, Isaac	2	1	2		
Hyde, Elihu	2	1	2		
Armstrong, Lee	1	2	3		
Perry, Seth	1	1	8		
Gazer, Levi	2	1	3		
Denison, Eleazar	4	3	5		
Rogers, John	1	1	1		
Manning, Josiah			2		
Edgerton, Nathan	1		2		
Edgerton, Hannah		1	3		
Belshaw, Thomas	3	2	4	1	
Gazer, Daniel	2	1	4		
Gazer, Aaron	2		1		
Hyde, Vaniah	1	2	3		
Barker, Mary	1		1		1
Ladd, Daniel	2	3	7		
Tracy, Josiah	1		2		
Tracy, Calvin	1	2	3		
Tracy, Eliphalet	1		2		
Smith, Asahel	1		4		
Tracy, Elisha	2		3		
Throop, Cary	3		3		
Ellis, Benjamin	1	1	3		
Hyde, Daniel, Junr } Rogers, Uriah	2	3	1		
Hartshorn, Zebadiah	1	1	2		
Kingsbury, Daniel	1		1		
Pepper, Michael	1	1	1		
Sholes, Miner	1	1	2		
French, Joshua	2	1	3		
Edgerton, Jos. Kingsbury	1	1	4		
Hartshorn, Nathan	1	2	3		
Hartshorn, Sarah			2		
Hartshorn, John	1		1		
Edgerton, Zebulon, Junr	1	3	2		
Woodworth, Amasa	1	1	3		
Nott, Abigail			1		
Smith, Abner	1	3	3		
Peck, Darius	2	1	1		
Munsell. Henry	4		5		
Bugby, Samuel	1	3	2		
Hyde, Asa	2	2	3		
Pember, Jacob	1	2	3		
Hyde, Mehitabel			2		
Hyde, Matthew	1	3	1		
Ingraham, Joseph	1		1		
Ingraham, Rachel			2		
Grunslit, Benjamin	1	1	2		
Hyde, Eli	3	1	7		
Hyde, Thomas	2	1	4		
Rudd, Jonathan	2	1	1		
Rudd, Samuel	1	1	2		
Huntington, Elisha	1	2	4		
Rudd, Prosper	1	3	3		
Woodworth, Amos	2	1	3		
Abell, Oliver	1	4	1		
Hyde, Solomon	1	2	3		
Camp, James M	2	3	4		
Rogers, Uriah, Junr	2	1	3		
Hyde, Abel	1	1	3		
Tracy, Peter	2		1		
Hyde, Joshua	1		6		
Fessenden, Samuel	1	1	2		
Fox, Edmund	1		2		
Lebbeus (Negro)				9	
Wood, Phinehas	1	1	1		
Crocker, Ezekiel	2	1	2		
Crocker, Diah	2		2		
Backus, Asa	2		2		
Calkins, Hugh	1		1		
Hartshorn, Andrew	1	1	4		
Griswold, Diah	1		2		

NEW LONDON COUNTY—Continued.

NAME OF HEAD OF FAMILY.	Free white males of 16 years and upward, including heads of families.	Free white males under 16 years.	Free white females, including heads of families.	All other free persons.	Slaves.
Penhally, Richard	1	4	2		
Hazen, Jacob	2	1	4		
Armstrong, Ezra	2		5		
Hartshorn, Ebenezer	1		1		
Hartshorn, Eben, Junr	2	2	5		
Ladd, David	2	2	3		
Deans, Levi	1	1	3		
Willes, Henry	2		2		
Willes, Joshua	1	1	1		
Nott, Samuel	2	2	4		
Waterman, Ezekiel	2	2	2		
Packer, John	2	1	3		
Sanford, Kingsbury	1	4	3		
Sanford, Bethiah	1		4		
Starr, Abigail			3		
Lathrop, John	2		1		
Hyde, Joseph, Junr	1	2	3		
Willes, Jabez	1		1		
Ellis, William	1	1	4		
Ellis, Daniel	2	1	2		
Peck, Joseph	1	1	3		
Peck, Syril	1	2	7		
Hyde, Ezekiel	2		2		
Chapman, Stephen	1	2	4		
Smith, Obadiah	1	1	3		
Backus, Eunice		3	2		
Hartshorn, Elijah	1	1	2		
Smith, Joshua, 3d	2		1		
Smith, Andrew	2	2	5		
Smith, Sarah	1		2		
Fox, David	3	1	2		
Hyde, Taber	2		1		
Hyde, Andrew	1	3	4		
Hyde, Benjamin	1	1	3		
Hastings, Roswell	1	3	3		
Hastings, Dan	1	1	1		
James (Negro)					2
Champion, John	1		2		
Champion, Henry V	3	2	5		
Forry, Micajah	1		4		
Metcalf, Eliphalet	2	1	1		
Ellis, Stephen	2		3		
Tracy, Joshua	1	1	2		
Huntington, Azariah	3	1	3		
Sabin, Elijah	1		1		
Sabin, Jedediah	1	1	1		
Tracy, Josiah, Junr	2		7	1	
Tracy, Hezekiah	1	1	3	1	
Tracy, Dudley	1	2	3		
Tracy, John	3	1	5		
Bentley, Eleazar	1		2		
Edgerton, Elisha	2	2	5		
Edgerton, Abel	1	1	4		
Tracy, Naomi		1	3		
Edgerton, Hezekiah	2	2	6		
Edgerton, Hezekiah, Junr	1		2		
Tracy, Daniel	4		4		
Hyde, Taber, Junr	1	2	2		
Tracy, John, Junr	1	2	3		
Lathrop, Ephraim	1	2	2		
Fitch, Benjamin B	2		1		
Hyde, Daniel	4	1	5		
Mason, David	2	1	5		
Johnson, Isaac	1	2	2		
Johnson, Oliver	1		2		
Lathrop, James	1		3		
Lathrop, Ezekiel	1	1	3		
Lathrop, Abigail			1		
Lathrop, Arunah	2	1	3		
Maynard, James	1	1	3		
Pettis, Ichiel	1	2	3	1	
Lathrop, Walter	1		3		
Lord, Sylvanus	1		3		
Tinney, Asa	1	5	4		
Tinney, Reuben	1	1	3		
Tinney, Mary			1		
Lathrop, Priscilla	2		2		
Bret, William	1		1		
Hewitt, Jedidiah	4	1	2		
Cary, Diah	1		1		
Hyde, Sarah	2	1	2		
Backus, Joshua	1	1	2		
Abell, Ira	1	2	1		
Lilly, Amariah	1	3	5		
Giffords, Samuel	2	1	4		
Rogers, James	3		5		
Rogers, Eleazar	1		2		
Edgerton, Simon	2	1	2		
Edgerton, Stephen	1	1	3		
Tracy, Jabez	1	1	5		
Ellis, Joseph	2	1	3		
Birchard, John	1	2	6		
Armstrong, Joseph	1		1		
Armstrong, Phinehas	1	1	6		
Armstrong, Elijah	2	1	2		
Armstrong, Jabez	1	3	2		

NAME OF HEAD OF FAMILY.	Free white males of 16 years and upward, including heads of families.	Free white males under 16 years.	Free white females, including heads of families.	All other free persons.	Slaves.
Lathrop, Darius	1		2		
Griswold, Abell	2	1	2		
Morse, John	1	5	5		
Lathrop, Jonathan	4	1	3		
Lathrop, Zachariah	2	4	6		
Chappell, Nathan	1		1		
Lathrop, Jeremiah	2	3	5		
Caulkins, Daniel	1		2		
Abell, Caleb	1	1	2		
Allen, Hezekiah	1	1	2		
Lord, Lucy	2		3		
Woodworth, Asa	1	1	2		
French, Samuel	1		2		
French, Daniel	1	2	2		
Smith, Roger	1		3		
Wentworth, Elizabeth			1		
Kirtland, Jabez	1	3	2		
Bushnell, Jason	1	2	2		
Kirtland, Joshua	1	4	2		
Downing, Christopher	1		1		
Perkins, Robert	1	4	5		
Woodworth, Asa, Junr	3		3		
Burnham, James	1		1		
Burnham, Roger	1	2	2		
Abell, Thomas	2	1	7		
Burnham, Samuel	1		1		
Tracy, Jabez, Junr	1	1	2		
Tracy, Daniel	1		3		
Tracy, Esanlus	1	2	1		
Quy (Negro)				2	1
Lathrop, Jabez	1	1	1		
Lathrop, Lucy	2	1	2		
Hughes, John	2	1	1		
Allen, John	2	3	4		
Jack (Negro)				1	
Leech, Elijah	1	4	3		
Jones, Rufus	1	2	3		
Johnson, Nathan	2	1	3		
Kingsley, Josiah	2		3		
Kingsley, Eleazar	1	1	8		
Bushnell, David	1	4	3		
Bushnell, John }	1	1	4		
Bushnell, Mary }					
Meeker, Josiah	1	1	1		
Jones, Amos	1	1	2		
Bushnell, Jonathan	1		1		
Bushnell, Jonathan, Junr	1	2	2		
Lord, Hezekiah	1		3		
Williams, Solomon	1	4	4		
Walbridge, Gustavus	1		1		
Walbridge, Ebenezer	1		1		
Wall, James	1	2	4		
Brown, Samuel	1		2		
Yeomans, Joshua	1	3	3		
Reeves, Ebenezer	2	1	3		
Barker, William	1	3	2		
Bushnell, Elisabeth	1	1	3		
Hazen, Jacob	1	1	1		
Wayres, Archibald	1		2		
Derly, Blanchard	1	2	4		
Derly, Blanchard, Junr	1		1		
Belshaw, Samuel	1	4	1		
Lunt, Sarah			2		
Leffingwell, Matthew	6	1	3		
Bushnell, Caleb	2		3		
Bushnell, Richard	1	2	2		
Parish, Nathaniel	2		2		
Leffingwell, Phinehas	1	6	3		
Fitch, Gideon	1		4		
Fitch, Gideon, Junr	1		2		
Huntington, Jared	1	4	4		
Goodell, Benjamin	2	1	4		
Ormsby, Samuel	2	1	4		
Senter, John	1		5		
Giffords, Jeremiah	2	1	7		
Morgan, Darius	1	2	2		
Giffords, John	2	1	2		
Starr, Jona	6	2	6	2	1
Carew, Eliphelet	2	4	6	2	
Leach, Thomas	1		2		
Hazen, Darius	1	4	2		
Williams, Ashur	1	4	1		
Lathrop, Jedidiah	2	1	4		
Pitcher, Elijah	3	6	2		
Burnham, Elias	2	3	4		
Burnham, Zaccheus	1		1		
Willet, Joshua	1		3		
Lathrop, Zephaniah	3	1	5		
Roath, Frederick	1	1	1		
Carpenter, Alfred	1	2	1		
Palmeter, Jesse	1		1		
Maples, Jona	1		5		
Woodworth, Jasper	3	1	2		
Adams, Solomon	1	2	4		
Woodworth, Simeon	3		1		
Mumford, Thomas	3		5		1
Coit, Thomas	3	2	4		3

NAME OF HEAD OF FAMILY.	Free white males of 16 years and upward, including heads of families.	Free white males under 16 years.	Free white females, including heads of families.	All other free persons.	Slaves.
Lehomidieu, Grover	3	4	7		
King, Walter	2		5		
Bruster, Seabury	2	2	2		
Carew, Simeon	2	1	3		
Lester, Jona	3	3	3		
Niles, Robart	2	1	2		
Geers, Squire	1	2	5		
Ewen, Edward	1	2	2		
Story, Henry	1	1	2		
Story, Henry, 2d	1	1	2		
Story, James	1	1	1		
Herrick, Elijah	2	3	4		
Deolph, Prissillah			3		
Story, Ephraim	2		2		
Lester, William	1	2	2		
Wattles, Elijah	1		4		
Wade, James	2	2	4		
Hall, Daniel	1	2	4		
Parker, Timothy	2	2	3		
Tracy, David	1		1		
Leffingwell, Mathew, 2d	1	1	2		
Bryan, Timothy	1	1	1		
Beckwith, William	1	1	1		
Gilbert, George	1	1	4		
Beckwith, Nathan	1		1		
Jeffers, Peter	1	1	2		
Waterman, John	2	1	4		
Waterman, Peter	1	1	3		
Elderkin, John	1	2	3		
Wade, Jona	1		1		
Webb, John	3		3		
Willet, John, Junr	1	1	2		
Murry, Semore	1	2	2		
Billings, Alpheus	2	3	6		
Vorce, Wm	1	2	3		
Sutliff, Jannah	1		3		
Geer, Uziel	2		3		
Williams, Elijah	1	1	4		
Chapman, Nancy		1	1		
Fitch, Hannah		1	4		
Baker, John	1	2	2		
Peirce, John	3		2		
Day, John	1	3	4		
Willet, John	1		2		
Willet, Jedediah	1	1	1		
Ewen, Edward, Junr	1	2	1		
Hewet, Solomon	3	2	3		
Larrance, Jona	1		2		
Calkins, Hugh	1		1		
Whiting, Ebenr	3	4	6		2
Destouch, Sirace	1		1		7
Whipple, Joshua	1		3		
Baker, Pemberton	1		3		
Ceaser (Negro)				4	
Craige, Mary		1	4		
Kelley, John	2		2		
Cheney, Abiel, 2d	1	1	5		
Brooks, Gurdon	1	1	2		
Barker, Stephen, 2d	1		1		
Day, James	3	2	2		
Williams, Joseph	5	3	6		2
Fitch, Ebenr	2	1	3		
Cowdre, Isaac	1	1	4		
Woodworth, Darius	1	1	2		
Brud, John	2		5		1
Huntington, Jona	3		3		
Huntington, Daniel	2		2		
Clemment, Jeremiah	1		2		
Braddock, John	1		2		
Smith, Jona	1	2	4		
Osburn, David	1	3	2		
Christee, James	2	3	4		
Leffingwell, Hart	2		2		
Lord, Jabez	1	3	4		1
Dennis, Benjamin	1	1	2		
Coit, Farewell	1	1	2		
Holden, Phineas	1		2		
Tracy, Isaac	2	2	3		
Backeus, Betsy	1	2	9	1	1
Denison, Benadam	1	3	6		1
Backeus, Ezra	1	2	3		
Kelley, Daniel	1		2		
Loring, Surviah		4	2		
Brud, Shubael	1	1	4		
Swaddle, John	1	1	2		
Burdett, Edward	1	1	2		
Fillemore, Timothy	1	1	2		
Read, Mary			3		
Stephens, William	1		2		
Barker, Stephen	2	4	2		
Culver, Stephen	1		2		
Lanman, Peter	4	1	5		
Daverson, Brazilla	4	1	4		
Perkins, Erastus	1	4	3		
Daverson, William	1		2		
Marvin, Elihu	1	1	4		
Coit, William	6	1	5		1

NEW LONDON COUNTY—Continued.

NAME OF HEAD OF FAMILY.	Free white males of 16 years and upward, including heads of families.	Free white males under 16 years.	Free white females, including heads of families.	All other free persons.	Slaves.
Whipple, Zephaniah	1	4	1		
Peabody, Asa	1	1	3		1
Peabody, Prentice	1	3	5		
Young, Nabby			2		
Huxley, Eunice			2		
Kelley, Hezekiah	4		2		
Tylar, John	2	1	6		
Buswell, Lemuel	2	2	3		
Bingham, Simeon	1		1		
Story, Solomon	1	2	3		
Choat, Eunice			2		
Vale, Christopher	2	1	3		
Welcop, John	1	1	2		
Brown, William	1		1		
Young, John	1	1	4		
Wilber, Jeremiah	1	2	1		
Thomas, James	1		1		
Freman, Hezekiah	2	1	5		
Warren, Lemuel	1	1	4		
Corning, John	2	1	1		
Whipple, Wm	1	1	4		
Dennis, Russel	2	1	3		
Howland, Joseph	4	2	9		
Moore, David	2	4	3		
Lamb, Jesse	1		1		
Harris, Jeremiah	2	5	5		
Perkins, Andw	2		5		
Perkins, Hezekiah	2	3	3		
Lothrop, Lydia	2	4	5		
Perkins, Jabez	3		2		
Hambleton, Jonas	4		4		
Hambleton, Solomon	2		3		
Kingsley, Eunice			2		
Leffingwell, Hart, 2d	1		1		
Smith, Zebadiah	1	2	5		
How, Abner	3	2	4		
Bruster, Phillup	1	1	1		
Backeus, Erastus	1	2	1		2
Ginnings, Zephaniah	2	2	2		
Perkins, Jabez, Junr	3	1	3		
De Witt, Jacob	1	2	3		
Lothrop, Elijah, Junr	3	3	4		
McCurdy, Lynds	2	2	4		
Huntington, Levi	2	3	6		
Norman, Joshua	2	1	4		
Wetmore, Izrahiah	1	1	1		1
Demming, Elizer	1		1		
Bill, Ephraim	3	1	2		2
King, Thomas	5	3	4	1	
Cheney, Abiel	1		1		
Lathrop, Samuel	1		3		
Silsby, Polly			1		
Smith, Daniel	1	1	4		
Smith, Jona	1	2	2		
Barrett, William	3		2		
Coit, Benjamin	1	2	3		
Demming, Wm	1		4		
Wattles, Henry	2		3		
Brooks, Benjamin	1	1	3		
Roath, Ebenezer	1	1	3		
Badcock, Thomas	1	3	1		
Champlin, Rowland	3	4	4		
Jones, Benjamin	2		4		
Easter (Negro)				3	
Frisby, Jonathan	1	1	3		
Corning, Deborah			2		
Waterman, Ignatius	1		3		
Winchester, Amaziah	2		2		
Disskoll, Adam	1	3	2		
Elderkin, Frederick	1		4		
Buswell, Lemuel, Junr	2	1	1		
Rockwell, Elisabeth	2		2		
Clemment, Peabody	2		1		
Kelley, Joseph	1		3		
Gordon, George	1	1	2		
Daverson, ——			1		
Trapp, Caleb	1		4		
Moore, Jona	1		1		
Edwards, David	1		3		
Farnum, John	2	2	1		
Trapp, Saml	1		1		
Joy, Richard	1		2		
Crandall, Samuel	2		3		
Brooks, Guy	1		3		
Rogers, Nehemiah	1		1		
Cullis, James	1		4		
Bates, Henry	1	1	2		
S (Negro)				7	
Leffingwell, Benaijah	3	1	2		
Joy, William	1	1	5		
Joy, William, Junr	1		3		
Trapp, Ephraim	1	1	3		
Hinckley, Vorce	1	1	5		
Elderkin, Martha		1	2		
Coy, David	1	2	1		
Arnold, Caleb	1	1	2		
Strange, Hannah			1		
Bliss, Elijah	1				
Bliss, Thomas	2		2		1
Silsby, Jona	1	1	2		
Smith, John, 2d	1	4	2		
Roath, David	2		4		
Roath, Joseph	1	1	6		
Roath, Jona	1				
Roath, Stephen	1		1		
Roath, Eleazer	1	2	3		
Roath, Saml	2	3	2		
Roggers, Presilla			3		
Lamb, John	1	1	1		
Culver, Benjamin	1	1	1		
Headen, Noah	2		4		
Winchester, Joel	1		3		
Dennis, Saml	1	2	3		
Sutliff, John	1	2	2		
Mchagan, Dennis	1				
Elderkin, James	1		1		
Sherman, John	1	2	2		
Smith, Patience		1	1		
Hill, John	1		2		
Hendricks, Benjamin	1	1	2		
Billings, Henry	1	1	1		
Keeney, Newcomb	2	2	1		
Carew, Daniel	1	1	3		
Fanning, Thomas	3	1	5		
Huntington, Frederick	2	1	4		
Corning, Bliss	2	2	2		
Shipman, Nathl	5	1	2		
Dennis, George	1		3		2
Moore, John	2	3	5		
Derby, Erastus	1		1		
Lothrop, Elijah	2	1	3		4
Lothrop, Simon	1	2	2		1
Weston, Amaziah	2	1	3		
Leffingwell, Elisha	1	2	5		
Goodel, Silas	1	1	5		
Cato (Negro)				5	
Bena (Negro)				6	1
Kingsley, Joseph	3		4		
Leffingwell, Hezekiah	2	1	5		
Savage, Cornelius	1	3	1		
Hendricks, Daniel	1		1		
Nicols, John	1	1	2		
Castle, Anthony	1	2	4		
Reynolds, Joseph	3	2	5		
Barral, Lewis	1	2	2		
Bliss, John	5		2		
Williams, Hezekiah	1	1	3		
Fanning, Ann			1		
London (Negro)				2	
Pettis, Abigail			1		
Leffingwell, Thomas	2		3		
Coit, Joseph	2		2		
Leffingwell, Saml	1		6		
Linkhorn, James	1		2		
Winter, Abner	1		3		
Winship, Philemon	1	1	1		
Richards, John	1	2	3		
Norman, Caleb	1		1		
Marsh, Jonathan	1	1	4		
Leffingwell, William	1	2	3		
Leffingwell, Christopher	5	2	10		
Firgo, Elisha	1		1		
Cox, William	1		4		
Harland, Thomas	6	7	7		
Williams, Thomas	4	1	2		
Primus (Negro)				2	
Huntington John, 2d	3	3	5		
Billings, Mary			3		
Hubbard, Thomas	2	6	2		
Bushneel, Ebenr	1	1	2		
Cleaveland, Irena			1		
Carew, Ebenr	7	3	5		
Lothrop, Zebadiah	1		3		
Avory, Richard	3		2		
Maynord, Asael	1		2		
Rockwell, Amy			2		
Manning, Rockwell	1	1	2		
Lothrop, Rufus	2	1	2	2	1
Lothrop, Joshua	2	1	3	1	2
Case, Simeon	2		2		
Lothrop, Jerusha	1	1	3		
Lothrop, Thomas	2	3	5		1
Coit, Daniel	2	1	6	1	1
Adgate, Eunice	3		2		
Case, Saml	2	1	3		
Cobb, Nathan	3	1	5		
Brown, Surviah			2		
Coney, Edward	1	1	3		
Mix, James	1	2	2		
Case, Ebenr	1	1	2		
Beba, David	1		1		
Case, Asael	1		1		
Pots, Christopher	2	2	2		
Burchird, Gideon	2	1	3		
Burchird, Elisha	3	3	2		
Avory, Samuel	2	3	4		
Huntington, John	2		1		
Huntington, Felix	5	2	7		
Huntington, Ezra	1	3	5		
Huntington, Benjamin	2	1	3		
Tracy, Daniel	3		6		
Darrow, Michael	1		1		
Post, John	1	1	1		
Lothrop, Darcas			2		
Danforth, John	3		5		
Danforth, Hannah			3		
Spicer, Joshua	1		2		
Larthly, Mary		1	2		
Hall, Nathan	2		1		
Grist, Ann			4		
Huntington, Elisha	1	3	3		
Lancaster, John	3		2		
Strong, Joseph	2	2	3		1
Huntington, Zachariah	2	2	4	1	1
Huntington, Joshua	2	1	4		
Tracy, Mundator	2	3	4		
Able, Hannah		1	1		
Huntington, Andw	2	3	5		
Tracy, Saml	3	1	3		
Jones, Parmenus	1		3		
Huntington, Saml	2		4	2	1
Gale, Joseph	1	2	2		
Abbot, Danl	1	3	5		
Leach, Jeremiah	2	1	2		
Townshend, Nathl	1	2	3		
Huntington, Simeon	2	2	6		
Nevins, David	5	7	5		
Charlton, Charles	2	2	5		
Lothrop, Asa	3		6		
Young, Thomas	1	2	3		
Carew, Joseph	2		3		
Turner, John	1		3		
Sam (Negro)				4	
Mix, John	1	2	5		
Roggers, David	2		1		
Gilden, Issabell			2		
McDonald, Elexander	1	1	2		
Miner, Seth	2	2	3	1	
Sloakum, Edward	1		2		
Dean, Saml	1	1	2		
Carpenter, Joseph	4	2	6		
Brown, Jesse	1	3	4		1
Griswould, Roger	2	3	2		
Carpenter, Gardiner	1		2		
Peck, Bela	2	2	2		1
Jones, Ebenr	3		3		
Spalding, Asa	1	1	3		
Stockwell, Elisabeth		1	1		
Manning, Diah	1	1	5		
Cole, Mary			2		
Lord, Eleazer	3	1	3	1	
Lord, Abigail			2		
Lord, Daniel	1	1	1		
Lothrop, Azariah	5	3	6	1	3
Leffingwell, Bela	1		1		
Wedge, David	1		1		
Otis, Joseph	1	1	2		
Backeus, Elisabeth		2	2		
Backeus, Rufus	7	3	4		
Backeus, John	2		3		
Jack (Negro)				1	
Backeus, Elijah	6	2	3	1	1
Noyce, Dolly			1		
Woodbridge, Samuel	2	2	6	1	
Prince (Negro)				3	
Roggers, Theophilus	1	1	3		
Pomp (Negro)				1	1
Sutton (Negro)				2	
Caulkins, Andw	1		2		
Waterman, Arunah	1	5	5		
Waterman, Lucy	1		3		
Yale, Joseph	1	2	4		
Waterman, Eunice	1		2		
Tracy, Andw	4	2	6	1	
Roggers, Zabdiel	2	4	10		
Ornsby, Ephraim	1		4		
Winter, Jacob	2	2	3		
Tracy, Fridirick	1	3	6		
Marshall, Thomas	1	1	2		
Hide, James, 2d	3	4	4		
Hide, Abiel	3	3	5		
Waterman, William	2		4		
Griswould, Isaac	1	1	5	1	
Clark, Elisha	1		1		
Silva (Negro)				2	
Lord, Simon	1	1	4		
Wintworth, Lemuel	1	3	4		
Culver, Jonathan	5	2	6		
Hide, Ebenr	3	2	5		
Hide, James	2	1	2		
Gibeons, Gerard	1	1	3		

NEW LONDON COUNTY—Continued.

NAME OF HEAD OF FAMILY.	Free white males of 16 years and upward, including heads of families.	Free white males under 16 years.	Free white females, including heads of families.	All other free persons.	Slaves.
Waller, Silas	1	2	2		
Collier, John	2		3		
Waller, Hannah			1		
Avory, Elisha	1	1	4		
Thatcher, John	1	4	1		
Clark, Watrus	2	4	3		
Thomas (Negro)					5
Poor house	2	2	3		
Huntington, Simon	4	1	2	1	
Huntington, Saml, Junr	1	1	4		
Huntington, Daniel	1		1		
Richerson, Asa	2	2	5		
Roath, Robart	1				
Griswould, Joseph	2	1	3		
Lamb, Richard	2	2	3		
Carew, Palmer	2	1	4		
Gilson, Jona	1		2		
Thatcher, Saml	1	2	2		
Huntington, Eliphelet	2	2	5		
Dennis, George, 2d	1	1	5		
Caulkins, Simon	1	1	1		
Thomas, Ebenr	2	5	6		
Tracy, Jared	2	2	6		
Cleaveland, Aaron	3	3	5		
Armstrong, Worth	1	2	3		
Barret, Ezekiel	1	3	2		
Sabins, Sarah	1	1	2		
Wintworth, Abigail			1		
Belshaw, Jona	1		2		
Lord, Ebenr	1		4		
Chapple, Nathan, 2d	3		3		
Morgan, William	3	1	3		
Frost, Ebenr	1	4	4		
Tracy, Nathan	1	1	3		
Duglass, Daniel	1		4		
Giffords, Saml, Junr	1	1	1		
Thomas, Thomas L	4	3	5		
Bryan, John	2	1	4		
Brigden, Timothy	1	2	1		
Thomas, Simeon	2	1	5		
Dulongpre, Ann	1	1	3		
Tracy, Peres	2		2		
Able, Joshua	1	1	2		
Waterman, Uriah	2		2		
Huntington, Benjamin	7	1	6		
Grover, Ebenr	1		3		
Hartshorn, Rufus	1		3		
Bride, Ann			1		
Bristo (Negro)				4	
Hide, Zebadiah	2	2	3		
Tracy, Philemon	1	1	2		
Tainter, Joseph	1		3		
Hide, Elisha	1	1	4		
Mansfield, William	1	1	7		
Chapman, Joseph	1	2	5		
Doyle, Richard	1		1		
Johnson, Eliphelet	1	2	3		
Wade, Sarah			1		
Reynolds, Gamaliel	2		3		
Nutter, John	2		4		
Post, Saml	2		3		
Latham, Peter	1	2	6		
Arnold, Prudence	1		4		
Will (Negro)				6	
Ark (Negro)				5	
Avory, Ann			2		
Waterman, Timothy	2		3		2
Turner, Phillup	2	1	6		
Trumbull, John	2	6	4		
Tracy, Uriah	1		3		
Collier, Benja	2		2		
Baker, Ephraim	3	1	2		
Tracy, Elisha	1		3		

TOLLAND COUNTY.

BOLTON TOWN.

NAME OF HEAD OF FAMILY.	Free white males of 16 years and upward, including heads of families.	Free white males under 16 years.	Free white females, including heads of families.	All other free persons.	Slaves.
Coleman, Jno, Jr	1	1	2		
Coleman, Jno	1	3	2		
Waterman, Ezra	3	1	4		
Talcot, Josu	2	3	5		
Phillips, Elijah	4	1	4		
Fowler, James	2	1	2		
Chapman, James	1	4	2		
Herkin, Aaron	1	1	5		
Hollister, Appleton	1	2	2		
Bartletts, Char			2		
Post, Jos	2		3		
Griswould, George	1	1	3		
Ringe, Isaac	1	2	1		
Cone, Jared	2		2		
White, Joel	1		1		
Alvert, Saul	3		3		
White, Jabez	1		5		
White, Elijah	5	2	4		1
Bliss, Mrn	1	1	2		
Clark, Em	1	1	1		
Strong, Aaron	2	4	3		
Spencer, Timo	1	5	3		
Taylor, Jno	1	1	2		
Webster, Jos	1		3		
Andrews, Elisha	1	1	3		
Skinner, Richard	1		2		
Skinner, Uriah	1	1	2		
Skinner, Saml	1	1	2		
Clark, Jno	4	1	2		
Fox, Jacob	1	3	5		
Skinner, Richard	2		1		
Skinner, Daniel	1	6	3		
Farmer, Aaron	1	1	2		
Gay, Icabod	1		2		
Phelps, Israel	1		5		
Littel, Wm	1		2		
Hubbard, Nathl	1	4	1		
Taylor, David	4		1		
Strong, David	2		1		
McColton, Rev	2	1	3		
Wanner, Davd	4		4		
Carver, Ebenr	2	3	3		
White, Thos	2	3	4		
Cone, Jared, Jr	1	1	3		
Alvert, Saul, Jr	4	3	3		
Griswould, Danel	2		2		
Woodworth, Saml	1		1		
Dart, Wm	1	2	1		
Strong, Ebr	1	2	1		
Brownson, Jabez	1	1	2		
Dart, Jno	1	1	2		
Goodrich, Moses	1	3	8		
Howard, Benja	2	1	2		
McKee, Nathl	1	3	3		
Gay, Pearce	1	1	1		
Howard, Jno	1	2	4		
Strickland, Jonas	2	3	4		
Howard, Benja, Jr	1	1	2		
Goodrich, Crafts	1		2		
Strong, Leroy	1	2	2		
Strong, Nathn	2		1		
Bingham, Asa	2	1	3		
Strong, Judas	1	1	1		1
Strong, Charles	1	1	1		
Lyman, Jacob	2	1	3		
Isam, Timo	6	2	4		
Tolcot, Jona	1	2	3		
Atherton, Simo	1	4	4		
Swetland, Luke	1	1	4		
Bishop, Thos	2		2		
Dart, Jona	2	1	3		
Lomis, Elijah	2	1	7		
Dart, Jona	1	1	2		
Lomis, Amasa	1	2	2		
Lomis, Abner	1	3	3		
Lomis, Jacob	2		3		
Lomis, Charles	1	2	6		
Webster, Thos	1		2		
Webster, David	3	1	4		
Bishop, Jno	2	4	4		
Bishop, Saml	1	2	2		
Raynolds, Ruben	1		2		
Lomis, Levy	1	4	5		
Lomis, Andrew	1	1	2		
Huckins, Joshua	1	1	1		
Huckins, Jno C	1	1	1		
Bowing, Jno	1	1	1		
Dart, Alvin	1	1	1		
Lomis, Thos	1	4	2		
Trumbull, Benjn	1		1		
Colton, Jona	2	2	5		
Lomis, Mathew	2		2		
Ringe, Thos	2	2	1		
Skinner, Israel	2	1	4		
Robinson, Benjn	1	2	4		
Skinner, Jona	3		3		
Carver, Saml, Jr	2	2	5		
Hamman, Elijah	2	1	2		
Hamman, Nathl	4	6	7		
Carver, James	2		2		
Bruce (Widow)		1	2		
Welles, Benja	2	1	4		
Smith, Victore	1	1	3		
Wilson, Wm	1	4	5		
Howard, Saml	1	1	2		
Hoskins, Wm	3	1	3		
Risley, Richard	2		1		
Tolcot, Elijah	1	3	3		
Tucker, Jos	2	1	3		
Tucker, Em	1		1		
Welles, Elezer	2	1	1		
Welles, Jarred	1		2		
Tolcot, Jno	1	1	5		
Marchall, Icabod	3	1	6		
Carver, Jno	2	4	3		
Carver, Jos	5	2	4		
Dewey, Sola	1	3	5		
Tucker, Elijah	3	1	7		
Tolcot, Benjn	5		4		
Olcutt, Ezekl	3	1	3		
Daniels, Jno	3		1		
Walker, Jno	3		5		
Johns, Abijah	2	2	3		
Daniels, Jno., Jr	1	2	3		
Walker, Jno, 2d	2	2	1		
Pain, Wm	1		2		
Pain, Benajah	1		3		
Lomis, Jos	1	1	3		
Evans, Thos	1		1		
Hyde, Jos	2	2	4		
Tolcot, Seth	3		3		
Tolcot, Justus	1		3		
Rude (Widow)			2		
Tolcot, Caleb	2	1	2		
Simons, James	2	5	2		
Ellis (Widow)			2		
Dart, Jno	2	1	4		
King, Elijah	3	1	4		
King, Saml	2	1	3		
Fields, Thos	1		3		
Chapman, Thos	1	4	5		
Webster, Asahel	2	1	2		
Root, Daniel	1		2		
Byers, Leonard	1		5		
Skinner, Ruben	2	2	6		
Chapman, Leml	2	2	5		
Ladd, Elijah	3	3	4		
McClen, Alexander	3	2	5		
McClen, Lethman	1		3		
Brownson, Allin	1	1	1		
Taylor, Nathl	1	3	3		
Ryder, Cornelius	1	2	4		
Hunt, Abner	2	1	4		
Dorchester, David	2	3	2		
Dorchester, Danl	1	1	5		
Lomis, Elijah, jr	1	1	2		
Fowler, Gordan	2	2	5		
Lomis, Roger	2		4		
Dorchester, David, Jr	1	2	6		
Lomis, Roswel	1		4		
Pain, Jno	1	2	5		
Lomis, Hezekiah	1	2	4		
Grant, Elnathan	1		4		
Hall, George	1		4		
West, Ira	1	4	5		
Grant, Cyras	4	2	6		
McVay, Jno	3		3		
Walden, Em	1	2	1		
McKinna, Alexander	2	4	2		
Brown, Eber	2	1	3		
McKinna, Alexander, Jr	1	1	1		
Cheesbrooks, Jabez	2	3	5		
Chapman, Nathn	1	4	1		
Hunt, Wm	1		1		
Driggs, Jno	3	2	6		
Hawkins, Eliakim	3	1	6		
Smith, David	4	1	4		
Simons (Widow)	2		2		
Lord, Danl	2	2	1		
Ladd, Ezekl	1		2		
Chapman, Jona	2		1		
Chapman, Eleze	1	1	3		
Ladd, David	1	1	4		
Chapman, James	1	1	1		
Pain, Roswel	4	2	6		
Sparks, Jno	4		1		
Tolcot, Saml	1		1		
Lomis, Elijah	3	1	4		
Brown, Wm	1	5	2		
Lord, Benjn	2		3		
Carpenter, Noah	3	3	3		
West, Abel	1	1	4		

TOLLAND COUNTY—Continued.

Panel 1

NAME OF HEAD OF FAMILY.	Free white males of 16 years and upward, including heads of families.	Free white males under 16 years.	Free white females, including heads of families.	All other free persons.	Slaves.
BOLTON TOWN—con.					
Brownson, Isaac	2	2	2		
Perry, Jos	1	4	4		
Tonkum, Peter	1	2	2		
Fich, Jm	3		3		
Webster, Elijah	1	5	2		
Smith, Jona	2	2	2		
Thrawl, Leml	1	1	1		
Shrinner, Elijah	1	3	3		
Millard, Levit	1	1	2		
Flint, Tolcot	2	1	2		
Tucker, Jona	1	2	2		
Bissel, Luthry	1	1	2		
Johnsin (Widow)		1	1		
Foot, Noah	1	3	5		
Wiles, Jonas	2		1		
Tolcot, Benja, 2d	1	2	3		
Kellogg, Rev. Em	2	1	2		
Strong, Jacob	1	1	1		
Chapman, Phineas	1	1	7		
Kellogg, Eber	2		3		
Emerson, Jabez	1	2	3		
King (Widow)			2		
King, Lelah	1		2		
King, Dawn	1	5	4		
King, Ruben	1	2	5		
King, Gidn	3		3		
King, Stephen	2	1	3		
King, Oliver	2	3	1		
King, Daniel	1	1	2		
Sage, Ruben	1	3	2		
Pearl, Joshua	2	3	4		
Skinner, Jno	2	1	3	1	
Richardson, Ezekiel	1	3	2		
Webster, Ransford	1		2		
Johns, Thos	1	1	5		
King, Leml	2		3	3	
COVENTRY TOWN.					
Porter, Noah	1	3	8		
Cook, Jesse	2	1	8		
Porter, Isaiah	1	1	1		
Porter, Jona	2	1	4		
Bruster, Benjn	1	3	1		
Buel, Benja	2	1	7		
Brewster, Israel	1	1	3		
Little, Saml	2	2	4		
Brown, Abm	1		1		
Chamberlain (Widow)			2		
Kingsbury, Wm	1	2	1		
Badcock, Jno	1	3	4		
Baxter, Wm	1	1	5		
Carpenter, Wm	3	1	4		
Chapple, Stephen	2	2	4		
Lamb, Benja	2		3		
Allin, Saml	2		1		
Grover, Isaac	1	1	4		
Barnard, Jos	2	1	2		
Carpenter, Elipt	3	1	8		
Bissel, Mathew	1	1	5		
Miner, Isaac	1	2	4		
Woodward, Moses	1	4	3		
Woodward, Nathl	4	2	5		
Hawkins, Jos	2	3	4		
Hatch, Dan	1	4	2		
Hunt, Gad	2	3	3		
Root, Ezra	1	2	4		
Jewet, Icaood	3	1	3		
Jewet, Icabod, 2d	1	1	3		
Edgerton, Jabez	1	1	2		
Edwards, Adonijah	1	1	4		
Ladd, Saml	2		2		
Molbourn, Godfry	1		1		
Tiffany, Ol	1		4		
Malbone, Charles	1	1	3		
Manning, Andrew	2	2	3		
Scripter, Sime	1		1		2
Dorman, Danl	1		4		
Cogswell, Benjn	2	1	4		
French, Abner	1	6	3		
Dean, Wm	1	4	3		
Cogswell, Amos	1	3	7		
Hunt, Sime	3		1		
Wintworth, Ezekiel	1		2		
Gurley, Phineas	1	2	5		
Chamberlain, Edman	1	3	1		
Wintworth, Ebenr	2	1	4		
Herrick Jos	2		1		
White, Saml	1	2	3		
White, Jona	1	1	1		
Lyman, David	1	1	1		
Brown, Ebenr	1	1	2		
Thompson, Jona	1		2		
Root, Nathl	1	3	4		
Brown, Jos	1	4	3		

Panel 2

NAME OF HEAD OF FAMILY.	Free white males of 16 years and upward, including heads of families.	Free white males under 16 years.	Free white females, including heads of families.	All other free persons.	Slaves.
COVENTRY TOWN—con.					
Edwards, Warham	1	2	1		
Richardson, Amos	2	1	5		
Swetland, Levi	2		4		
Robinson, Saml	3	1	2		
Brown, Thos	2	1	3		1
Pomeroy, Elenr	2	3	5		
Tolcot, Jos	2	3	4		
Parker, Jos	1	1	3		
Page, Gad	1		2		
Chapple, Noah	1	2	2		
Crocker (Widow)			3		
Devensport, Thos	2	1	8		
Parker, Josiah	1		1		
Parker, Nathan	1	3	2		
Case, Tuball	1	2	1		
Edwards, Jame	1		2		
Richardson, Justus	1	4	3		
Wright, Elijah	2	1	5		
Wright, Elijah, 2d	2	1	1		
Turner, Robt	1		2		
Richardson, Stephen	2	1	3	2	
Case, Benjm	2	3	2		
Avery, Amos	1	1	3		
Walbridge, Jno	1	1	2		
Walbridge, Leml	1	2	1		
Reddington, Jno	2		3		
Kingsbury, Saml	3	1	3		
Richardson, Jona	3		2		
Hendy (Widow)			2		
Fowler, Israel	3		7		
Ellis, Nathl	1	4	3		
Lomis, Daniel	4	2	6		
Lomis, Dan	1	4	5		
Lomis, Elisha	2	2	2		
Andrews, Em	4	1	3		
Waldo, Nathan	1		3		
Brewster, Jacob	2	1	5		
Wheldon, Jona	2		3		
Manley, Joseph	2	2	3		
Lomis, Jno	3	2	6		
Hibbard, David	2		2		
Parmer, Nathl	2	4	1		
Lomis, Danl, Jr	1	1	2		
Wheeler (Widow)		2	4		
Brewster, Peter	2	1	4		
Hunt, Elipht	3	1	4		
Page, Elias	1	2	3		
Hibbert, Silas	2		1		
Strong, Reve N	2	1	3		
Carpenter, Noah	3	3	4		
King, Silas	4		7		
Fuller, Jona	2	2	3		
Badger, Danl	1		2		
Badger, Danl	1		3		
Badger, Moses	1	4	4		
Pearce, Oliver	1		1		
Carpenter, Levi	3		3		
Carpenter, Elijah	2	2	2		
Wilson, Rust	2	1	2		
Johns, Elihu	1	4	4		
Coolly, Saml	2	2	3		
Bourns, Wm	1	3	3		
Waldo (Widow)	1	1	3		
Willson, Wm	1		2		
Field, Saml	1		2		
Wilson, Jno	1	3	2		
Long, Lemuel	2	1	1		1
Long, Lemuel, 2d	1	5	1		
Porter, Abel	2	1	5		
Kingsbury, Eber	3	2	6		
Avery, Jabez	1	1	3		
Hilyard, Jos	1	1	1		
Lyman, Elijah	1		4		
Avery, Amos	2	2	3		
Bockwell, Amorialo	2	2	2		
Kingsbury, Em	2	2	4		
Vislon, Elijah	1		1	6	
Ladd, Jno	2		2	2	1
Crosman, Eber	1	2	4		
Dow, Em	1	4	1		
Jud, Thos	3		4		
Parker (Widow)			1		
Hale, David	5	1	8		
Porter, Thos	2	1	1		
Wright, Nathel	2	1	4		
Grant (Widow)			2		
Parker, Soln	2	2	5		
Gears, Jedediah	1	3	5		
Huchinson, Em	1	3	4		
Doubleday, Jos	3		3		
Devenport, Umphry	1	3	2		
Ellis, Jno	2	3	5		
Hale, Richard	1	1	4		
Devenport, Benjn	2	2	1		

Panel 3

NAME OF HEAD OF FAMILY.	Free white males of 16 years and upward, including heads of families.	Free white males under 16 years.	Free white females, including heads of families.	All other free persons.	Slaves.
COVENTRY TOWN—con.					
Lyman, Asa	1	3	4		
Dorman, Dudley	2	1	4		
Parker, Canda	3		2		
Howard, Nthel	2	2	2		
Dow, Levy	1	4	2		
Dow, Calvin	1				
Porter, Uriah	1		2		
Taylor, Jno	2	1	3		
Rose, Timo	3	6	3		
Huntington, Rev. J	1	3	5		
Fich, Jno	1	3	4		
Devensport, Richard	1		1		
Parmerly, Jno	1		2		
Brigham, Tiphet	1		3		
Robinson, Danl	2	1	7		
Dow, Em, 2d	1	3	3		
Robinson, Saml	2	2	3		
Cushman, Minerva	1		6		
Manning, Calvin	1	3	6		
Curtis, Bilvad	1	2	1		
Meade, Jno	1	2	2		
Allin, Sam	2		1		
Coleman, Eber, 2d	1	2	4		
Warin, Martin	1	2	4		
Coleman, Em	2	4	3		
Boinington, Oliver	2	5	3		
Cook, Jesse	1	2	4		
Coleman, Nathl	1	1	4		
Coleman, Timo	1		4		
Robinson, Jno	2	2	6		
Robinson, Ralph	1		2		
Standley, Moses	2	1	2		
Fields, Benn	2	3	6		
Robinson, Danl	1	4	6		
Carpenter, Timo	2	1	5		
Stanly, Caleb	1	3	3		
Rose, Frederick	1	1	4		
Turner, Jos	1		1		
Turner, Saml	1		1		
Denty, Mathew	1	2	4		
Grover, Benjn	1	1	4		
Porter (Widow)	1		3		
Carpenter, Jos	2	3	5		
Brigham, Thos	1		2		
Strong, Benajah	3	1	6		
Root, Medad	1	1	5		
Root, Jno	3		5		
House, Jona	1		5		
Greenleaf, David	1	1	3		
Cristee, Jno	1	2	1		
Hawkins (Widow)			2		
Hawkins, Rodolphus	1	4	2		
Langdon, Chancey	1		2		
Root, En	3	1	6		
Root, Jesse	4	1	3	1	3
Ripley, Jm	1	1	4		
Fitch, Heny	1	1	1		
White, Adno	1	5	2		
Root, Wm	3		3		
Ripley, Jabez	1	3	4	1	
Parme, Gersham	2		10		
Brigham, Don	1	3	6		
Sherman, Jabez	2		5		
Richarson, Hezekiah	1	2	7		
Sanford, Elisha	1	2	4		
Ringe, Danl	1		4		
Carpenter, Silas	2	2	2		
Rose, Jehiel	3	2	2		
Ringe, Wm	2	2	4		
Edwards, Sola	1	2	2		
Dorman, Amos	3	1	4		
Edward, Warham	1		2		
Brown, Richard	1	4	3		
Brigham, Gersham	1	1	4		
Dunham, Stephen	1	1	2		
Brown, Elepht	2	1	4		
Devensport, Richard	1	4	5		
Dunham, Elezer	2	2	2		
Dimock, Timo, Jr	1		4		
Rose, Saml	2	3	4		
Dimock, Timo	3	1	3		
Dimock, Danl	1	3	4		
Carpenter, Jno	1		2		
Sprague, Perez	2	1	2		
Coleman, Levy	1		2		
Robinson (Widow)	1	3	5		
Fuller, Jos	1	3	3		
Fich, Pen	1	1	3		
Robinson, Hezekiah	1	1	2		
Robinson, Isaac	2	2	2		
Robinson, Jno	2		2		
Robinson, Wm	3	3	3		
Woodworth, Josi	1	2	3		
Fitch, Jos	1		1		
Fitch, Abner	1		1		

TOLLAND COUNTY—Continued.

NAME OF HEAD OF FAMILY.	Free white males of 16 years and upward, including heads of families.	Free white males under 16 years.	Free white females, including heads of families.	All other free persons.	Slaves.
COVENTRY TOWN—con.					
Turner (Widow)	2		2		
Fitch, Abner, Jr	3	4	4		
Cook, Nathl	1	2	3		
Hamman, Zephn	2		4		
Babcock, Zebulon	2	4	4		
Babcock, Robd	1		2		
Edwards, Benajah	2		5		
Cook, Shubal	2	1	1		
Babcock, Wm	1		2		
Babcock, Roger	1	2	3		
Cushman, Atherton	3		3		
Babcock, Robd	3	1	3		
Turner, Amos	1		2		
Turner, Jethro	2	5	5		
Brown, Nathl	1	2	2		
Cushman, Em	1	4	4		
Coleman, Saml	3	3	5		
Coleman, Asa	2	1	7		
Rust, Nath. W	1	2	4		
Larriby (Widow)			2		
Turner, Caleb	1	1	4		
Curtis, Heny	3		3		
Meads, Jno	1	1	3		
Manley, George	2	2	3		
Badcock, Timo	1	1	2		
Ladd, Elisha	1	2	2		
Badcock, Elihu	3	2	2		
Baker, Timo	2	5	3		
Baker, Blund	1	1	5		
Baker, Asa	1	2	4		
Timons, Elijah	1	1	2		
Dow, Umphus	2	2	5		
Johnes, Saml	1	3	3		
Jones, Elias	1	3	3		
Jones (Widow)	2		2		
Peters (Widow)		2	1		
Fieldon, Jno	1	2	6		
Hows, Asa	1	3	2		
Lomis, Israel	1	5	2		
Sprague, Saml	2	1	5		
Sprague, Saml, Jr	1		5		
Lomis, Zadock	3	1	7		
Sprague, Elisha	1	2	5		
Lockwood, Rev. S	2		2		1
Walbridge, Saml	1	1	3		
Mordoch, Jona	2	2	7		
Walbridge, Jona	2	3	3		
Thompson, Thos	1	1	1		
Skinner, Daniel	1	1	2		
Jones, Benjn	2		1		
Jones, Silas	2	2	1		
Jones, Noah	3	2	7		
Lyman, Silas	1		1		
Blackman, Aaron	1	3	2		
Blackman, Benjn	2	2	2		
Blackman, Benjn, Jr	2	1	2		
House, Benjn	1	6	2		
Lyman, Joab	3	2	6		
House, Sam	2	1	5		
Smith, Experience	1		1		
Badger, Enoch	2	4	8		
Blakeman, Elijah	1		1		
Wheldon, Jno	2	1	4		
Dow, Pelitiah	1		7		
Simon (Widow)	1	1	2		
Daggett, Isaiah	1	5	2		
Dagget, Saml	1		1		
Lawrence, Heny	1	2	3		
Hendy, Elipt	2	5	3		
Lomis, Nathl	2	4	2		
Aynsworth, Jno	1	1	3		
Babcock, Jno	1		3	1	
Aynsworth, Ebenr	3		2		
Robinson, Em	1	1	3		
Burnap, Christopher	1	2	5		
Patten, David	3		2		
Lomis, Heny	1		2		
Barnaby, James	1	1	1		
Dart, Levi	1		1		
White, Danl	2	2	6		
Burnap, Abm	3		4		
Badcock, Danl	1	3	2		
Crocker, James	1	1	2		
Richardson, Em	1	1	4		
Kingsbury, Nathl	1	2	3		
Kingsbury, Jos	1	2	7		
Atherton, Elijah	2	3	6	3	
McCoy, Jno	1	1	2		
Fitch, Jm	1	1	3		
Fitch, Jeptha	1	2	3		
ELLINGTON TOWN.					
Steel, James	4	1	6		
Mills, Stone	3	1	2		
Chapman, Jabez	1	1	2		
ELLINGTON TOWN—con.					
Kingsbury, Dur	1		3		
Pomler, Elija	3	1	3		
Bingham, Ithm	1	1	2		
Hyde, Mathew	4		3		
Maher, Dan	1	2	1		
McCray, Jno	1	1	3		
Bartlet, Elepht	1		1		
Warner, Daniel	3	2	2		
Denison, Jona	1	1	3		
Stephens, Heny	2	1	5		
Hombbord, Isaac	3		3		
Reed (Widow)	1	4	4		
Parker, Jno	1	1	4		
Barber, Jona	2		6		
Porter, Jno	1	1	2		
Wise, Ruben	1	1	3		
Kingsbury, Some	1		3		
Cushman, Alverton	1		3		
Smith, Jno	1		1		
Smith, Isaac	1		2		
Wadsworth, Icabod	2	2	4		
Goodale, Eler	1	2	2		
Clark, Danl	1	4	4		
Emerson, Jabez	1		2		
Wallis, Wm	1		6		
Wallis, Wm	1	1	2		1
Goodrich, Thos	3		2		
Kenada, Thos	1	2	4		
Smith, Moses	1	2	5		
Spears, Wm	4	1	5		
Bakon, Jno	1	4	2		
Fuller, Jacob	3	1	4		
Belnap, Sima	2		4		
Peas, Jona	3	3	4		
Daman, Natha	1	2	1		
Stiles, Jno	1	2	1		
Warner, Saml	1	1	1		
Bingham, Ithm	2	1	5		
McCray, Wm	3	1	3		
McCray, Calvin	1	1	2		
Pearse (Widow)	1		1		
Pearse, Em	2		3	1	
Stone, Stephen	1		1		
Stone, Dane	1	1	2		
Strong, Phineas	2	1	2		
Holton, Timo	4	4	7		1
McKnite, Jno	2	1	3		
Jennings, Em	2	2	3		
Thompson, Saml	2	2	3		
Thompson, Israel	1		2		
Thompson, Luther	1		1		
Thompson, Wm	2	5	3		
Elsworth, Charles	1	3	3		
Hamblengton, Paul	1		5		
Hamblengton (Widow)	3	1	2		
Scovel, Isaac	2	3	3		
Parsons, Saml	2		2		
Sanger, Danl	1	1	3		
Belnap, Frances	1	1	2		
Green, Danl	1	1	5		
McKinstry, Elezer	3	3	7		
Whitney, Jos	1	2	3		
Barkley, Jona	2		4		
Snow, Sylvanus	1	2	3		
Davis, Daniel	1		3		
Parker, Em	1	1	2		
Levit, Jame	1	2	4		
Abbot, Moses	1	1	1		
Buckley, Alexander	1	1	2		
Charter, George	1	5	4		
Penna, Elezear	2	1	7		
Blodget, Josiah	2	3	3		
Penna, Jos	5	1	4		
Cotton, Isaac	1	2	1		
Abbot, Joseph	4	3	6		
McKinna, James	2		2		
McKinna, James, 3d	1	4	4		
McKinna, Andrew	1	2	6		
McKinna, James	1		1		
McKinna, Wm	3	2	6		
Chapman, Saml	2	2	3		
Elsworth, Daniel	3		3		
Elsworth, Gordon	3		6		
Nash, Eben	3	4	5		
Kimball, Adm	1	1	3		
Baker, Let	1	3	5		
Craw, Jno	4	1	3		
Varnum, Wm	1	3	3		
Little, Rufus	1		2		
Fuller, Frederick	1	2	2		
Snow, Natha	3		2		
Buckley, Alexander	3	1	4		
Parker, Jno	1	2	2		
Mug, Icabod	2		1		
Tayler, Jno	1	3	3		
Cross, Jno	1	1	2		
ELLINGTON TOWN—con.					
Fitch, Medin	2		2		
Wells, Levi	3		4	1	
Isam, Benjn	2		1		
Carpenter, Ruggles	1		2		
Allen, Jos	1	1	2		
Hall, Jno	3	2	4		
Gifford, Siba	2	2	5		
Bartlett, Edm	3	1	1		
Nucrum, Saml	1	3	5		
Waldo, Bethuel	3		3		
Johnson, Convus	1		1		
Foster, Charles	1	1	2		
Chapman, Hoseah	1	2	4		
Chapman, Jabez	2	3	6		
Grant, Jona	1	2	4		
Pomber, Andrew	2	1	2		
Sessions, Saml	2	2	5		
Purple, Ezra	1	4	4		
Mills, Peter	1	2	2		
Graton, Nathl	1	1	2		
Clark, Warham	1	2	5		
Smith, Grace	1		4		
Hare, Stephen	1	1	3		
Jones, Danl	1		2		
Uttley, Timo	1		1		
Uttley, Stephen	1		1		
Hills, Elijah	3		1		
Charles, Jno	2		2		
Grover, Edm	1		3		
Pease, Thos	1	3	3		
Woodworth, Jesse	1		4		
Andrews, Saml	2	5	4		
Shurtliff, Jno	1		5		
King, Saml	3	2	7		
Torry, Elijah	1	2	4		
Newton, Jno	1	2	4		
Jinks, Jno	3		3		
Braman, Jos	1	2	2		
Newton, Moses	1	2	2		
Warner, Phillip	2	2	4		
Durfy, Eber	1		3		
Russel, Eben	3	1	5		
Lomis, Justus	1	1	5		
Dewey, Josu	1	1	2		
Porter, Ruben	1	2	4		
Russell, Hezekiah	3	2	9		
Brag, Edwd	1		1		
Sabine, Thos	2	1	2		
Newel, Nathl	5		6		
Porter, Jos	1	1	2		
Carver, Ralph	1	1	1		
Woodworth, Peleg	2		2		
Banister, Levi	1	1	7		
Durfey, Jos	1	2	3		
Buck, Eben	3		1		
Bradley, Ruben	3		4		
Chubbuck, Eben	2		3		
Chubbuck, Nathl	1	1	1		
Charter, Allen	1	1	2		
Charter, Jno, Jr	1	4	3		
Ray, Adonijah	5	1	3		
Aldridge, Nathan	4		3		
Keath, James	2	1	2		
Slawter, Anthony	1	3	5		
Frost, Josu	1	3	3		
Fentons, Old			3		
Slawter, Moses	1	3	4		
Briant, Danl D	1	1	4		
Edson, Benjn	1	1	3		
Bigsbee, Jno	1		2		
Demming, Aaron	1	2	2		
Negros (Free)				15	2
HEBRON TOWN.					
Button, Jos	1		3		
Button (Widow)	1		3		
Isam, Jos	1	2	1		
Hutchinson, Jona	2	1	3		
Culver, David	6		4		
Sumner, Ruben	3		3		
Webster, Elijah	2	2	2		
Skinner, Danl	5	1	2		
Wells, Bateman	1	2	7		
Wells, Rufus	1	3	5		
Ingram, Danl	2		3		
Wells, Shipman	2	1	1		
Sawyer, Jno	1	1	1		1
Phelps, Elezer	1	1	5		
Wells, Thos	3	1	4		
Horton, Eli, Jr	4		4		
Hutchinson, Jos	1	1	2		
Hutchinson, Jabez	1		3		
Post, Jedediah	2		4		
Post, David	3	4	3		
Merrils Jno	4		3		

HEBRON TOWN—con.

NAME OF HEAD OF FAMILY.	Free white males of 16 years and upward, including heads of families.	Free white males under 16 years.	Free white females, including heads of families.	All other free persons.	Slaves.
Post, Jos	2	5	4		
Fieldon, Saml	1	1	4		
Brown, James	1	2	1		
Ellis, Jabez	4		3		
Tolcot, Wm	1	1	4		1
Post, James	2		3		
Brown, James	1	5	1		
Curtis (Wid.)	1	1	2		
Calver, David	1	3	1		
Curtis, Jno	1		2		
Wright, Jude	1		1		
Horton, Saml	1	1	4		
Davis, Zephn	1	3	4		
Tolcot, Gad	3	2	3		1
Daniels, Ezekl	3	2	2		
Gears, Saml	2	2	3		
Dunham, Timo	5	1	5		
Dunham, Isacc	1		2		
Perrin, Sola	1	3	3		
Root, Josa	1	1	6		
Sumner, Wm	1		4		
Finley, Jno	2	1	3		
Roswell, Nehm	1	1	3		
Hall, Amos	2	2	5		
Ford, Luther	1	2	2		
Rollow, Zachary	3	1	2		
Mc——, Jos	3		3		
Bucks, David	2	2	4		
Allin, Wm	2	2	3		
Root (Widow)			1		
Rollow, Wm	4	2	4		
Post, Jacob	2	1	3		
Post, Thos	4	2	3		
Norton, Soln	2	1	4		
Gilbert, Saml	4	3	4		3
Cass, Jos W	2	1	3		
Brown, Thos	2	2	4		
Graves, Elijah	1	3	4		
Sutton, David	1		2		
Pratt, James	1		1		
Peters, Jno	2		3	1	
Peters, Jona	1	1	4		
Peters, Wm	1	2	2		
Willes, Thos, Jr	2	2	5		
West, Ruben	2	3	2		
Brown, Ezekiel	1	2	1		
Bliss, Abel	1	1	3		
Lothrop, Revd J	3		2		
Wells, Jno	2	4	2		
Post, Gordan	4	2	4		
Huchinson, Jno	1	1	1		
Huchinson, Jona	2		3		
Huchinson, Israel	1	2	1		
Gilbert, Jno	1		1		
Phelps, Icabod	1		2		
Phelps, Icabod, Jr	1	1	4		
Tillotson, Elezr	2	1	2		
Bushnoll, Danl	2		1		
Brown, Danl	1	4	2		
Trumbel, Asa	3	2	8	1	1
Hall, Seth	1		2		
Hall, Jona	1	2	3		
Mc——, Ralph	1	3	7		
Wilcocks, Jehiel	2	4	5		
Horton, Stephen	2	2	4		
Horton, Sampson	1	1	4		
Ingram, Jos	1	2	4		
Darbay, Wm	3	4	2		
Root, Danl	3	1	4		
Case, Roger	3	2	3		
Loveman, Alpheas	2	3	4		
Wartis (Wid.)	3		2		
Buck, Wm, Jr	2	3	2		
Fox, Abm	1		2		
Fox, Jael	1	3	1		
Root, Ebenr	1	2	4		
Acheley, Jno	1	2	4		
Root, Jona	3	3	3		
Phelps, Soln	1	1	1	4	
Phelps, Soln, Jr	1	2	3		
Phelps, Ashbel	2	1	2		1
Nothenn, Elijah	3	1	3		
Tillotson, Elezer	2	1	7		
Bewel, Wm	2		1		
Curtis, Ruben	2	4	5		
Owen, Aziel	1		3		
Owen (Wid.)	2		4		
Carrver, Amos	1	1	1		
Phelps, Ruben	1	4	4		
Smith, Nathn	3	1	1		
Hosford, Danl	3	5	6		
Collings, Luis	1	1	1		1
Hosford, Enos	2		5		
Nelomd, Jona	3	3	6		
Kellogg, Danl	3		1		
Kellogg, Elijah	3	1	1		

HEBRON TOWN—con.

NAME OF HEAD OF FAMILY.	Free white males of 16 years and upward, including heads of families.	Free white males under 16 years.	Free white females, including heads of families.	All other free persons.	Slaves.
Smith, Nathl	1	1	2		
Hosford, Dudley	2	1	9		
Bowls, Wm	2	6	3		
Darbey, Danl	1		1		
Gillet, Aaron	1	2	2		
Rayman (Wid.)		1	2		
Jones, Gid	2	1	2		
Jones, Benajah	3	1	5		
Smith, Benjn	2	1	3		
Kellegg, Moses	2	1	5		
Fuller, Nathel	2	3	6		
Darbey, Nthel	1		2		
Kellogg, Moses, Jr	1		2		
Kellog, Martin	1	1	1		
Fuller, Nathl	2	3	5		
Darbey, Nathl	1		2		
Phelps, Ruben	1	3	3		
Smith, Benjn	2	1	4		
Kellogg, Martin, Jr	1	1	1		
Root, Jonah	2	4	3		
Horton, Ezekiel	3	2	5		
Norton, David	1	1	3		
Brown, Jona	3	2	6		
Chapple, Jno	3	1	3		
Chapple, David	1	1	1		
Cone, Zachy	3	4	3		
Sutton, Jno	2		3		
White, James	3	2	8		
Swetland, Joel	2	2	1		
Sanger, Soln	1	1	3		
Jones, Jona	3	1	4		
Jones, Saml	1	4	1		
Bingham, Stephen	4	4	3		
Bewel, Jno	7	4	6		1
Parker, Jos	1	3	5		
Townsend, David	1	1	3		
Blackman, Wm	1	3	5		
Powel, Aaron	1	2	2		
Clark, Benia	3	1	2		
Kingsbury, Denson	2	1	4		
Swetland, Azariah	2		3		
Swetland, Peter	3	3	3		
Swetland, Aaron	2	3	3		
Wells, Timo	2	1	3		
White, Adonjah	1	4	4		
Townsend, David, Jr	2	1	4		
White, James	1	1	4		
Hows, Luke	1		1		
Lomis, Ahiel	2		2		
Lomis, Jos	2		2		
Buel, Benjn	3		3		3
Cone, Zachy	3	4	2		
Jones, Gid, Jr	1	1	2		
Jones, Abner	3	2	3		
Jones, Oliver	2		2		
Mervin, Elihu	2	1	4		
Barker, Aaron	1	2	4		
Kelleg, Jno	2	1	3		
Pepone, Silas	2	1	1		
Jones, Ezekiel	4	3	9		
Danish, Jona	1	1	3		
Tuch, Richard	1	1	1		
Danish, Ezkl	1		2		
Danish, Neham	3	1	6		
Jones, Samuel	2	4	5		
Jones, Joel	4	1	2	1	
Beach, Jno	1		1		
Archer, Amasa	1	1	2		
Jones, Jedediah	1	1	3		
Dean, Amos	2	2	5		
Risley, Saml	2	4	4		
Washbourn, Levi	1	2	6		
Archer, Benjn	1	2	3		
Peas, Nhel	1	1	3		
Chapman, Em	1	2	2		
Wright, Enos	1	2	3		
Northam, Jno	1	2	1		
Mc——, Orlander	1	1	2		
Hamblin, Eben	1	2	5		
Wright, Saml	1	3	5		
Darbey, Jos	1	1	4		
Niles, Nathl	1	3	3		
Cullom, George	1	1	1		
Felcher, Miael	1	1	3		
Dunnum, Jona	1	1	3		
Jillitt, Israel	1		3		
White, Death	4		3		
Ford, Isaa	3	3	5		
Brown, Amasa	1	2	4		
Gay, Joel	1	2	3		
Parker, Peletiah	3		6		
Porter, Danl	1	3	2		
Parker, Wimans	1	1	4		
Stiles, Aaron	2	1	4		

HEBRON TOWN—con.

NAME OF HEAD OF FAMILY.	Free white males of 16 years and upward, including heads of families.	Free white males under 16 years.	Free white females, including heads of families.	All other free persons.	Slaves.
White, Jos	4	1	6		
Beach, Elijha	3	1	5		
Mann, Abijah	3	2	5		
Skinner, Benjn	3		2		
Skinner, David	1	1	2		
Beach, Elijha	1		2		
Somers, Sylvester	5	5	7		
Dunnum, Jona	2	1	2		
Felcher, Michael	1	1	2		
Porter, Nehemiah	2	3	5		
Carver, David	4		2		
Carver, David, Jr	1	4	1		
Root, Dan	1	1	2		
Phelps, Horner	1	2	4		
Porter, Joel	3	3	4		
Porter, Increas	1	3	5		
Webster, Martin	1	1	5		
Anabal, Anson	1	3	3		
Badger, Neha	2		1		
Gillit, Ezekl	4		2		
Pomeroy, Elihu	1	4	2		
Gillit, Charles	1	1	1		
Gillit, Amasa	1		3		
Barber, Bela	3	2	3		
Corkins, Jedediah	1	1	2		
Bliss (Wid.)	1	1	10		
Fuller, Roger	3	5	9		
Phelps, Aaron	2	2	4		
Townsend, Jona	1	2	1		
Kellogg, Revd Mr	2	1	3		
Gilbert, Sylvester	2	4	5		2
Dutton, Timo	6		5		1
Jones, Joel	3		2		
Phelps, Eber	2		5		
Gilbert, Jno	1	4	9		1
Strong, Elezer	2		2		
Strong, David	1	3	5		
Stiles, Stephen	4	2	7		
Bessel, Levi	1	5	4		
Filer, Saml	3		3		
Coleman (Wid.)	1		3		
Phelps, Amos	7	2	3		
Man, Joel	3	3	2		
Huntington, Soln	3	3	6		
Barber, Stephen	1		2		
Barber, Stephen, Jr	3		3		
Phelps, Abner	1	1	3		
Tillotson, Abm, Jr	2	2	1		
Root (Wid.)	1		2		
Root, Abel	2	2	2		
Rude, Jno	2	3	5		
Wintr, Niolas	1	1	3		
Mann, Jos	3	1	2		
Barber, Obd	1	1	2		
Norton, Francis	2	3	7		
Stewart, Jno	2	3	3		
Tillotson, Abm	2	2	1		
Phelps, Syvanus	2	1	4		
Root, Caleb	4	1	3		
Bliss, Elis	1	3	6		
Marble, Thos	2		2		
Owen, David	2	1	5		
Root, Dan	2		2		
Beach, Azariah	2	1	4		
Backus, Ezra	3	1	3		
Phelps, Jos	2	1	1		
Phelps, Jos, Jr	1	1	6		
Buel, Icabod	2	1	2		
Strong, Phenias	1	1	4		
Phelps, Roswel	1	1	3		
Phelps, Saml	1	1	2		
Mann, Jno	1	1	3		
Mann, Andrew	3	3	3		
Man, Elijah	2	3	7		
Burge, Jona	1	1	4		
Porter, Gaylan	2	2	1		
Tarbox, Jona	1	4	5		
Townsend, Jona	2	2	4		
Phelps, Cornelus	2	1	2		
Phelps, Roger	1	2	8		
Basset, Abel	1	1	3	1	
Phelps, Sylvanus	2	1	4		
Bissel, Hezekiah	3	1	5		
Phelps, Frederick	1	2	3		
Gillet, Jno	1	1	3		
Barber, David	2	3	3		
Wass, Jno	2		6		
Baxter, Aaron	1	2	4		
Carver, Alderich	1		1		
Leanarvas, Jno	1	1	1		
Barber, Stephen	3	1	2		
White, Daniel	1		1		
Parmer, Stephen	2	2	3		
Got, Danl	2		3		
Burge, Jno	1	3	3		
Tayler, Benja	1	2	4		

TOLLAND COUNTY—Continued.

NAME OF HEAD OF FAMILY.	Free white males of 16 years and upward, including heads of families.	Free white males under 16 years.	Free white females, including heads of families.	All other free persons.	Slaves.
HEBRON TOWN—con.					
Parmer, Jos^u	1		3		
Tayler, Jn°	1	1	4		
Dewey, Aaron	1	2	7		
Jones, Saml, Jr	2	3	2		
Wartis, Jos.	3	2	4		
Wartis (Wid.)			1		1
Phelps, Elihu	1	1	1		
Wartis, Enos	1	1	1		
Cutting, Zadock	1	1	1		
Wartis, Phel^n	1				
Foot, Ambros	1	3	1		
Ingram, Nathl	2	1	2		
Foot, Stephen	1	2	2		
Crouch, Thos	3	7	3		
Crouch, Ruben	1		1		
Clark, Noah	1	1	2		
Got, Jn°	1	1	2		
Crouch, Christopher	2	2	4		
Tarbox, David	3	5	4		
Porter, Tim°	3		3		
Tarbox, Zenas	1	3	4		
Tarbox, Sol^n	2	1	4		
Tarbox, Godfry	1		4		
Parmer, Saml	2		1		
Rus, Jn°	3		3		
Bridge, Asa	1	2	3		
Cutting, Isaac	1		4		
Porter, Jonah	1	5	4		
Wright, Saml	2	1	3		
Barber, Oliver	3	3	5		
Barber, Obedi	1	3	4		
Tillotson, Jn°	1		2		
Wartis, Jn°	1		2		
Fuller, Eber	1		3	9	
Housie, Elijah	5		5	1	1
Yonguer, Ebn^r	1	2	3	7	
SOMERS TOWN.					
Chapin (Wid.)	2	1	7		
Thompson, George	1	1	4		
Chapin, Moses	3	1	5		
Wood, Harber	3	1	2		
Newcrum, Du^r	4	2	2		3
Pease, Joel	1	1	3		
Kibbe, Bildad	1	1	4		
Cooly, Luke	1	3	1	1	
Dickinson, Noah	3	4	6		
Cooly, Nathl	2	2	4		
Prentice, James	2		6		
Howard, Jos.	2		3		
Howard, Charles	1	1	1		
Dunbar, Jabe.	1		2		
Kibbe, Lemuel	1	5	2		
Kibbe, Israel, Jr.	2	1	2		
Fuller, Stephen	1	3	3		
Kibbe, Danl	2		1		
Kibbe, Frederick	1	1	1		
Elmer, W^m	1	2	3		
Phelps, Benjn	2	2	3		
Kibbe, Jed^h	1	3	4		
Kibbe, Israel	1		1		
Kibbe, Ed^d	1	3	5		
Burge, Jon^a	1	4	3		
Fuller, Ja^s	1	1	6		
Russel, Jn°	2	1	7		
Russel, W^m	1		3		
Cooly, James	3		2		
Sheldon, Charles	2	3	6		
Hall, Saml	4	2	3		
Davis, Isaac	1	1	3		
Spencer, Isr^l	2		3		
White, Sam.	1	2	4		
Purchase, Thos	1	1	1		
Wardwell, Nath^el	1		2		
Hall, Jos^a	1	2	3		
Hall, Alpheus	1		1		
Hall, Veasny	3	3	3		
Kimball, Saml	2	2	4		
McGregory, Eben^r	1	2	4		
Hall, Zadock	1	1	4		
Hall, Libny	1	1	4		
Swetland, Thos	1	1	3		
Pease, James	1	1	2		
Clark, Amo^s T	2	1	3		
Allen, Asa	2	4	2		
Hall, Luke.	2	1	4		
Jones, David	1	3	3		
Brace, David	1	2	4		
Wallice, Ab^m	1	2	5		
Slate, Ezek^l	3	3	2		
Billings, Saml	2	3	4		
Lomis, Phillip	1	1	5		
Pease, Col^n	2	2	3	1	

NAME OF HEAD OF FAMILY.	Free white males of 16 years and upward, including heads of families.	Free white males under 16 years.	Free white females, including heads of families.	All other free persons.	Slaves.
SOMERS TOWN—con.					
Pease, David	3	3	7		
Parsons, Seth	1		2		
Pease, Saml	1		3		
Ward, Jacob	1		3		
Wood, Danl	3	3	1		
Jones, Danl	1		2		
Jones, Silas	1	2	7		
Spencer, Obed^h	1	2	6		
Shephard, Isaac	2	1	2		
Spencer, Jon^a	2	1	3		
Spencer, Eber	2	1	2		
Spencer, Hezekiah	3	2	4		
Spencer, Hez., Jr	1	2	4		
Goudy, Alexander	1	1	3		
Shepherd, Jacob	1	1	5		
Billing, Jn°	2	2	4		
Billings, Sol^n	2		2		
Collings, Jn°	1	2	4		
Fords, Jn°	1	1	3		
Fords, Jn°, Jr	1	3	1		
Billings, Elijah	2	2	3		
Jones, Isahar	2	3	4		
Halbert, Jabes	1	4	3		
Jones, Stephen	2	2	3		
Jones, Benjn	2	2	4		
Ward, James	1	2	5		
Chaffee, Serrel	1	2	4		
Collins, Jabez	2	3	4		
Parsons, Nathl	2		1		
Parsons, Stephen	1		3		
Kibbe, Joel	1	2	1		
Parsons, Ezra	2	1	3		
Kibbe, Gordon	1		1		
Kibbe, Elijah	1	1	1		
Pease, Noah	3	2	2		
Raynolds, Saml	1	1	2		
Davis, Corn^s	1		1		
Backus, Revd. C	1	1	3		
Pitkin, Thos	1	1	3		
Pitkin, Calvin	1	1	2		
Dwight, Alpheus	1	2	1		
Fowler, David	2		3		
Meacham, Saml	2		5		
Allen, Nathl	2	3	5		
Davis, Aaron	1		2		
Morehouse, Thos	1		2		
Root, Tim°	1		6		
Root, Jos.	1	3	1		
Chapin, Seth	1		1		
Jones, Benjn	1		2		
Pitkin, Paul	1	3	2		
Chapin, Saml	1	4	4		
Chapin, Elias	2	1	1		
Chapin, Aaron	2	1	3		
Davis, Jobe	2	2	1		
Davis, James	1	2	4		
Root, Jacob	3		1		
Root, Eben^r	1	1	3		
Kibbe, Moses	1	2	3		
Ladd, Jn°	1	1	3		
Buck, Thos	2	1	2		
Elis, Oliver	1		6		
Hunt, Jos.	1		1		
Hunt, Peter	1	3	2		
Richardson, Stephen	1	3	4		
Wood, Danl	1		1		
Buel, Joseph	3	2	4		
Wardwel, David	3		2		
Kibbe, Peter, Jr	1	2	1		
Parsons, Stephen	1		1		
Richardson, David	1		1		
Pease, Stephen	2	1	3		
Richardson, David, Jr.	2	1	2		
Horton, Moses	1	3	1		
Cosly, George	2	1	5		
Wood, Jn°	6	1	3		
Burton, Christopher	1		2		
Pratt, Eliakim	1		2		
Pomeroy, Jos^a	3	1	2		
Pomeroy, Jn°	5	1	5		
Felt, Saml	2	5	5		
Buck, Isaac	1	1	1		
Wood, Josiah	1	1	1		
Jenning, Benjn	1		1		
Adams, Sol^n	1	1	4		
Parsons, W^m	1	2	3		
Buckley, Danl	1	2	2		
McGound (Wid.)		1	2		
Cooly, Ruben	1		2		
McGee (Wid.)		2	4		
Burbanks, Danl	1	4	5		
Kibbe, Peter	4		2		1
Sykes, Ruben	3	1	4		
Kibbe, Amoriah	1	5	3		1

NAME OF HEAD OF FAMILY.	Free white males of 16 years and upward, including heads of families.	Free white males under 16 years.	Free white females, including heads of families.	All other free persons.	Slaves.
SOMERS TOWN—con.					
Pease, Levi, Jr	1		3		
Kibbee, Tim°	1		4		
Felt, David	1	2	2		
Hamblenton, Asa	2	3	2		
Sexton, Stephen	2	2	3		
Prentice, Jn°	2	1	2		
Jones, Benj^a	1	3	2		
Orcutt, Jacob	2	2	3		
Morehouse, David	1	1	2		
McLlewer, David	1	1	5		
Luce, Luke	2	2	2		
Parsons, Seth	2		3		
Kibbe, Elisha	3	1	3		
Kibbe, Zerah	2		1		
Pease, Noah	1	1	1		
Pease, Giles	2	1	1		
Pease, Richard	2	2	3		
Pease, Robt	1	2	5		
Sexton, Joseph	4	2	2		
Sexton, Joseph, 2^d	2	4	4		
Saxton, Daniel	1	2	5		
Collins, Jos.	1	5	2		
Jones, Jiles	1	1	2		
Brace, Lt.	1	2	4		
Brown, Jn°	3	1	3		
Cooley, Thos	5	3	5		
Fuller, W^m	1	1	2		
Pease, Alphe.	1	1	2		
Tiffany, Nathl	2		4		
Painter, Jn°	1	1	6		
Purna, Peter	1				
Inman, Edward	3	1	5		
Prat, Ashbel	1	2	4		
Pollet, Robt	2	3	4		
Ford, Jos.	1	1	1		
Coy, David	3	2	5		
Phillips, Jon^a	2		6		
Horton, Aaron	1	3	3		
Winchester, Benjn	2	3	5		
Dwight, Jos	1	2	2		
Fords, Tim°	3	3	5		
Meacham, Jo^s	4	2	4		
Scott, W^m	1	3	1		
Utley, Asahel	1	1	2		
Kibbe, Tim°, 2^d	2	3	2		
Fuller, Lukus	3	2	3		
Kibbe, Elijah	1	2	2		
Kibbe, Edward	1		1		
Kibbe, Noah	1	1	1		
Cook, W^m	1	3	1		
Prentice, Stephen	1		1		
STAFFORD TOWN.					
Agar, Jos^u	1	2	3		
Alden, Jos^u	3	1	4		
Alden, Elisha	4	3	4		
Amadown, Jn°	1		4		
Addams, Sol^n	1	1	1		
Avery, Jabez	3		4		
Abbot, Stephen	1		1		
Blodget, Josa	4	1	3		
Bass, Codsida	1	1	1		
Babcock, Hozeah	1		2		
Bolton, Danl	1	2	5		
Butler, Zeb^di	2	1	4		
Blodget, Ab^m	2	2	4		
Bloget, Tim°	1	1	5		
Blodget, Sylvanus	2	1	3		
Blodget, Danl	2		2		
Blodget, Paul, 2^d	1		4		
Blodget, Paul	1		4		
Bass, Zeph^h	1	2	1		
Bascom, Danl	2		2		
Bartlett, E^m	2	2	4		
Bartlett, Saml	2	3	4		
Bigsbee, Sol^m	1		1		
Bradley, Mercy			3		
Bradley, Jonah	1	1	3		
Carpenter, Jn°	1	3	1		
Carpenter, W^m	1	2	2		
Chaffee, Darius	1		1		
Clark, Neh^m	1		1		
Carue*, Rev^d M^r	1				
Cross, Sam	1	5	3		
Convus, Jesse	2		4		
Convus, Jos.	1	2	6		
Convus, Darius	1		2		
Convus, James	1	6	2		
Convus, Asa	1	3	4		
Cross, Stephen	1	2	3		
Crandal, Urich	1	1	1		
Crandal, Abijah	1		2		
Cushman, W^m	3	3	6		

*Nonresident.

TOLLAND COUNTY—Continued.

STAFFORD TOWN—con.

NAME OF HEAD OF FAMILY.	Free white males of 16 years and upward, including heads of families.	Free white males under 16 years.	Free white females, including heads of families.	All other free persons.	Slaves.
Carpenter, Jno	3	1	3		
Carpenter, Nathan	1		3		
Convus (Wid.)		1	3		
Convus, Josi	2	1	6		
Cushman, Solm	3	1	2		
Convus, Sola	1	2	5		
Coy, Aaron	1	1	1		
Colebourn, Eben	4	2	4		
Colebourn, Saml	2	1	2		
Colebourn, Jos	1	4	5		
Colebourn (Wid.)	1	1	1		
Colebourn, Danl	1	3	4		
Colebourn, Ruben	1	3	5		
Convus, Joseph	1	2	3		
Convus, Stephen	2	1	4		
Canvil (Wid.)		1	2		
Cross, Noah	2	4	4		
Cushman, Nathl	1	2	2		
Chapman, Jno	2	3	4		
Cushman, Isaac	1	2	2		
Chaffee, Amos	2	2	3		
Cady, Ruben	1	4	2		
Cady, Asa	1	1	4		
Cady, Jesse	1	1	7		
Cady, Abner	1	2	2		
Cady, Jedediah	1		5		
Cady, Hez	1	3	3		
Chapin, Elias	1	1	3		
Chapin, Aaron	1	3	4		
Carpenter, Danl	1		3		
Carpenter, Moses	1	2	1		
Carpenter, David	1	1	2		
Cushman, Urich	1	1	2		
Kimbal, Daniel	1	4	2		
Dunoty, Francis	1		2		
Dunbar, Benja	1	3	3		
Drake, Levy	2	5	2		
Davis, Jo	1		1		
Davis, Danl	1	1	1		
Davis, Noah	3	3	5		
Davis, Moses	3		1		
Davis, Jesse	1		4		
Dimock, Sylvanus	2	1	2		
Davis, Benja	2		2		
Davis, Benjn, Jr	1	1	2		
Davis, Noah, Jr	1	3	3		
Davis, Jno	1	1	6		
Davis, Aaron	3	3	3		
Davis, Leml	1	4	3		
Edson, Eliab	2	2	3		
Eaton, Jno	2	4	3		
Edson, Calvin	2		4		
Edson, Jacob	3	1	6		
Edson, Peter	1	2	3		
Edson, Levi	2	1	4		
Estes, Stephen	1	5	3		
Eaton, Aaron	4	1	3		
Elethrop, Saml	1	2	1		
Elethrop, Jno	1		3		
Ellis, Timo	1	1	2		
Ellis, Cyrus	2	1	1		
Ellis, Benjn	4		4		
Ellis, Jos	1	2	3		
Eaton, Wm	1	1	2		
Eaton, Saml	1	1	4		
Foster, Revd Mr	1		3		
Fuller, David	2	1	4		
Fuller (Wid.)			1		
Forget, Jno	2	1	5		
Forget, Elijah	1	4	2		
Fish, Elijah	2	1	2		
Fuller, Wm	1	1	6		
Fuller, Hez	1	2	1		
Fuller, Saml	3	1	1		
Foot, Isaac	1	4	3		
Fays, David	2	2	3		
Guthery, Saml	3		3		
Gibs, Josi	1	1	4		
Gay, Eben	2	2	4		
Gilman, Wm	2		2		
Green, Jno	1	1	4		
Gordon (Widow)	1		3		
Gordon, Gardner	1		3		
Hall, Moses	1	3	2		
Hyde, Em	3		4		
Hyde, Em, Jr	1	2	3		
Hickson, Jos	1		1		
Hickson, Nathl, Jr	1	2	6		
Hall, Em	3	1	3		
Hodg, Jno	1	1	1		
Hornes, David	1	1	4		
Harris (Wid.)	1		3		
Harris, Robt	1	2	3		
Harris, Eben	1	3	2		

STAFFORD TOWN—con.

NAME OF HEAD OF FAMILY.	Free white males of 16 years and upward, including heads of families.	Free white males under 16 years.	Free white females, including heads of families.	All other free persons.	Slaves.
Harwood, Jno	2	2	5		
Hall, Wm	3		2		
Holmes, Josi	2	1	3		
Holmes, Jona	1		2		
Hows, Israel	2	2	4		
Hyde, Nathl	1	2	3		
Hitchcock, Jona	1	2	2		
Johnson, Seth	2		2		
Hunt, Jesse	4		5		
Holloway, Danl	1	1	4		
Johnson, Nathl	3	1	3		
Jones, Elijah	1	3	4		
Johnson, Sampson	1		1		
Jennings, Robt	1		4		
Johnson, Ebenr	1	1	3		
Johnson, Em	1	4	2		
Johnson, Abner	1	1	6		
Johnson, Jona	3	3	6		
Igard, Benja	1	3	6		
Johnson, Charles	1		1		
Johnson, Abel	1	1	2		
Johnson, Nathan	2	3	4		
Johnson, David	2	1	4		
Jinks, Wm	2	4	2		
Kendal, Eben	1	3	2		
Kent, Josi	2		3		
Kent, Jabez	3	1	4		
Kent, Benja	2	2	6		
Lyon, Lymon	1	3	5		
Lard, Wm	3	1	2		
Leach, Calvin	1	2	4		
Lull, James	2		2		
Lee, Saml	1	1	2		
Little, Robt	1		1		
Molton, Salmon	1	4	1		
Molton, Jona	3	1	2		
Molton, Barnard	1	2	3		
Molton, Eben	2	1	3		
Miller, Cornelius	1	1	1		
Maker, Danl	3		2		
Molton, Stephen	3	1	2		
Molton, Stephen, Jr	1	2	2		
Morse, James	4	2	6		
Mercy, Jno	1		1		
Moulton, Howard	3	2	6		
Moulton, Jos	1		1		
Miller, Cornelus	1	1	1		
Marchal, Ruben	1	2	6		
Newton, Jona	1	1	2		
Nedom, Dan	1		2		
Nedom, Nehm	2	1	3		
Nelson, Wm	1	2	1		
Nelson, George	1		5		
Knox, Adam	1	2	2		
Nash, Phneas	1	3	4		
Orcutt, Timo	1	1	2		1
Orcutt, Nathl	2		2		
Orcutt, Jabez	1	3	5		
Orcutt, Stephens	1	4	1		
Orcutt, David	1		2		
Orcutt, Icabod	2		4		
Orcutt, Solm	2		2		1
Orcutt, Natha	2		2		
Orcutt, Danl	2		2		
Pinna, Isaac	2	1	3		
Phelps, Jno	3	1	4		
Phelps, Jose	2		2		
Pooler, Jno	1		1		
Pool, James	2	3	4		
Pool, Jona	3	1	2		
Perry, Ruben	1	3	4		
Parsons, David	7		6		
Pattin, Nathl	3	4	4		
Pattin, Wm	3	1	4		
Pulnam, Cornelius	1	2	1		
Pattin, Jno	2	3	4		
Parker, Or	1	1	2		
Pease, Jno	1	2	2		
Richardson, Isaac	1	3	3		
Richardson, Natha	1		4		
Richardson, Gershom	1	1	4		
Richardson, Jno	1		2		
Ross, Wm	1	1	4		
Russel, Isaac	2		3		
Ryder, Benja	1	3	3		
Rockwell, Saml	4	1	7		
Smith, David	1	2	1		
Sessons, Benj	1	2	2		
String, David	3	2	6		
Smith, Abijah	1		1		
Strickland, Saml	1	3	2		
Stanton, Robt	1		1		
Sawyer, Cornelius	2	3	3		
Searls, Jno	1	2	3		
Scott, Stephen	1	1	5		

STAFFORD TOWN—con.

NAME OF HEAD OF FAMILY.	Free white males of 16 years and upward, including heads of families.	Free white males under 16 years.	Free white females, including heads of families.	All other free persons.	Slaves.
Stoel, Robt	1	2	4		
Scott, Philip	1	1	3		
Saxton, George	1	2	2		
Stone, James	1		4		
Sanger, Jno	2	1	3		
Townsend, Benjn	1		2		
Torry, James	2	5	3		
Townsend, Jno	1		1		
Townsend, Gibs	1		3		
Thrasher, Eben	2	2	3		
Thrasher, Christopher	3	1	3		
Thrasher, Sampson	1	1	3		
Thrasher, Noah	1	3	3		
Tupper, Solm	1		1		
Torry, Jame, Jr	2	2	2		
Torry, Amos	1	1	3		
Torry, Ezra	1	2	4		
Thompson, Asa	1		2		
Thompson, Heny	2	1	1		
Thrasher, Josu	1	1	1		
Willard, Rev. I	1	1	4		
Wardwell, Eber	1	5	3		
Whisler, Zadock	1	1	2		
West, Abbe	1	2	2		
Wakefield, Levy	1		4		
Wakefield, Elijah	1		3		
Wakefield, Jno	1		2		
Walbridge, Amos	4	2	5		
Walbridge, Wm	1	3	4		
Wallis, James	1	1	2		
Washbourn, Ezra	2	5	3		
Whore, Edw	1		2		
Washbourn, Ezra, Jr	2		1		
Web, Eliph	1	2	5		
Wakefield, Ziel	1	2	2		
Washbourn, Wm	1	1	3		
Washburn, Solm	1		1		
Washbourn, Nathn	1	1	3		
Washbourn, Soln	2		5		
Washbourn, Moses	1	2	6		
Whittikar, Abm	1	1	2		
Washburn, Wm	2	1	5		
Wood, Nathn	1	2	3		
Wood, Abner	3	2	7		
Warner, Moses	1	2	5		
Whittikar, Jona, 2d	1		5		
Wood, Natha	1	2	4		
Whittikar, Stephen	1	1	3		
Welch, Jude		1	1		
Whittikar, Jona	3	1	3		
Winter, Jos	1	5	4		
Woodworth, Charles	1	4	3		
Washburn, Nehm	1	2	2		
Wesley, Wm	1		1		
Webster, Jos	2	3	2		
Burrows, Amos	1	2	1		
Phillips, Jno	1		4		
Burge, Edwd	1	4	3		
Bester, Jno	2		4		
Foot, Jesse	1	5	3		
Barret, Benja	1	2	4		
Barret, James	1	3	1		
Barret, Jno	1	1	1		
Russel, Rider	1		1		
Allden, Zephn	1		2		
Pasco, Jno	1		3		
Pasco, Jona	2	3	3		
Fuller, Jose	2		5		
Skinner, Jo	2		3		
Avay, Danl	1	3	4		
Gager, Saml	1		3		
Bester, Abel	1	1	5		
Dimock, Amasa	2	1	4		
Dimock, Timo	1	1	1		
Dimock, Jno, Jr	1	2	2		
Clust, Jona	3	1	3		
Carton, Caleb	1	3	3		
Eaton, Saml	1	2	1		
Dimock, Jno	3		1		
Burows, Jona	1	2	5		
Bourns, Moses	1	3	2		
Clust, Timo	2	1	2		
Rice, David	1	1	5		
Allin, Saml	1	2	5		
Sawyer, Jno	2	1	3		
TOLLAND TOWN.					
Holmes, Nathel	2	2	3		
Nye, Jno	1		2		
Hinkley, Icabod	4	3	10		
Holmes, Jazaniah	1	3	3		
Tyler (Widow)			4		
Eaton, Jno	4	1	2		
Eldridge, Solomon	1		4		

TOLLAND COUNTY—Continued.

TOLLAND TOWN—con.

NAME OF HEAD OF FAMILY.	Free white males of 16 years and upward, including heads of families.	Free white males under 16 years.	Free white females, including heads of families.	All other free persons.	Slaves.
Fellows, Isaac	2	3	4		
Nye, Samuel	2		4		
Nye, Hezekiah	1	4	1		
Hows, Ebenr	2	4	2		
Scott (Widow)			2		
Lothrop, Jno	3		4		
Bradley, Jabez	2	3	5		
Lothrop (Widow)	1		2		
Davis, Jos	1		2		
Robinson, Joshua	3	1	4		
Harvey, Nathan	2		4		
Rawdin, Thos	2	1	3		
Crandal, Samuel	2	1	4		
Bester, Jno	2	1	3		
Barnard, Moses	1	1	3		
Barnard, Wm	1	1	1		
Robinson, Ruben	1	1	2		
Cook, Stephen	1	1	3		
Holbrook, Elias	3	3	4		
Avery, Asael	4		2		
Steel, Elezer	3		3		
Steel, Ashbel	1		1		
Stearns (Widow)		1	3		
Barns, Jona	2	1	1		
Chapman, Isham	1		4		
Grant, Em, Jr	1		3		
Shepherd, Benoni	2	1	5	1	
Williams, Wilks	1	1	3		
Grosvenor, Wm	2		2	1	
Spencer, Ebenr	1	3	3		
Bond, Thadeus	4	1	3		
Williams, Rev. N	4		2		
Howard, Asa	1	1	1		
Howard, Thos	3	6	3		
Steel, Stephen	2		2		
Steel, Perez	1	3	4		
Woodward, Elisha	2		2		
Parker, Phineas	1	1	4		
Parker, James	1		3		
Luce, Jos	1	1	4		
Cobb, David	2	3	2		
Steel, Elezr, Jr	1	4	1		
Norris, Jno	2	2	5		
Thomas, Jno	2	1	1		
Hammon, Elezr	1	3	6		
Lomis, Simon	1	2	1		
Tupper, Jos	2	5	2		
Hawkins, Jno	1		1		
Hawkins, George	1	4	4		
Tonkum, Gid	1		1		
Grover, Jabez	1	1	1		
Edwards, Jabez	2	3	2		
Caswell, Lemuel	1	4	4		
Carpenter, Timo	1	1	1		
Carpenter, Comfort	2	1	3		
Grover, Ebenr	4	4	6		
Rawding, Ezra	1	2	1		
Whipple, Saml	4	2	1		
Lomis, Soln	2	5	3		
Winslow, Jno	1	1	1		
Griggs, Jno	1	2	6		
Yongue, Moses	1	2	3		
Norris, Benjn	4	1	2		
Hammon, James	1	4	7		
Ryder, Jno	3		3		
Humphries, Saml	1	1	5		
Grover, Jno	5	2	4		
Clap, Increas	1	5	4		
Barrows, Wills	2	2	2		
Baker, Thephilus	2	2	5		
Webster, Timo	1	1	4		
Cobb, Jeduthron	4	3	6	1	1
Hilyard, Miner	3	2	3		
Jennes, Amos	3	1	2		
Stearns, Jos	1	4	4		
West, Soln	1	2	5		
Cobb, Daniel	2	1	2		
Baxter, Simn	1	2	3		
Studley, Jos	2	4	5		
Griggs, Saml	1	1	3		
Barrows, Jno	2	2	1		
Edgerton, Oliver	1	2	4	1	1
Hews, Danl	1	2	4		
Edgerton, Danl	3	4	6		
Haskel, Elijah	1	3	3		
Hart, Jno	1	1	3	1	1
Long (Widow)			2		
Griggs (Widow)	1		3		
Squire, Danl	3	1	3		
Goodspead, Nathl	1	1	1		
Steel, Jno	2	2	7		
Wheeler (Widow)		1	2		
Crow, Simon	1		3		
Warren, Jno	2	3	5		
Cheedle, Rufus	1		1		

TOLLAND TOWN—con.

NAME OF HEAD OF FAMILY.	Free white males of 16 years and upward, including heads of families.	Free white males under 16 years.	Free white females, including heads of families.	All other free persons.	Slaves.
Lothrop, Icabod	1	1	1		
Whiton, Elijah	1	1	3		
Lothrop, Hope	2	5	6		
Carpenter, Simo	1	1	3		
Luce, Jona	2		4		
Mumford, Irad	1	4	4		
Alford, Jno	1	2	3		
Richardson, Lemul	3	3	4		
Benton, Jacob	1	2	4		
Benton, Danel	1	1	4		
Scott, Zebediah	2		1		
Luce, Mark	2	1	3		
Kenndy, David	2	1	4		
Abbot, Jno	1	1	4		
Willes, Soln	3	2	3		
Burge (Widow)			2		
Stimpson, Stephen	3	2	6		
Davis, Benjn	1		3		
Paulk, Ammi	1	2	3		
Polk, David	1	1	1		
Griggs, Josu	2	1	4		
Robinson, Eber	3	2	3		
Whittlesey, Saml	1		2		
Stimpson, Thos	2		1		
Hatch, Elezer	3	1	6		
Lothrop, S. (Widow of)			1		
Baker, Titus	2		1		
Baker, Titus, Jr	1	1	2		
Weston (Widow)	1		3		
Baker, Danl	2	2	6		
Baker, Ebenr	2	1			
Welles, Thos	1	4	1		
Baker, Jos	3	2	2		
Cady, Amos	2	3	4		
Cady, Nahum	2	1	6		
Field, Danl	3	1	4		
Reed, Shubal	4		3		
Reed, Saml	1	2	3		
Kaggan, Saml	2	1	4		
Hull, Stephen	3	4	5		
Delano, Sylvanus	1		1		
Polk, Em	1	2	3		
Strong, Elnathan	3		3		
Tobey, Saml	1	4	3		
Eaton, Soln	1	3	2		
Shurtliff, Jno	1		1		
Chapman, Eliakim	1	2	3	7	
Chapman, Elijah	3	1	1		
Chapman, Elijah, Jr	2	2	4		
Chapman, Ashbel	1		3	2	1
Chapman, Simo	3	5	2		
Chapman, Samuel	1		1		
Stanley, Jno	2	2	4		
Baker, Jno	1		1		
Baker, Haman	2		3		
Kingsbury, Nathel	3	1	5	1	
Aychinson, Bazzallet	4	2	4		
Aychinson, Baza, Jr	1	2	2		
Johnson, Elihu	2	2	6		
Kingsbury, Nathl, Jr	2	1	4		
Kingsbury, Rust	1	2	5		
Cartson, Jno	1	3	3		
Cartson, Darius	2	2	3		
Blodget, Silas	2		1		
Benton, Timo	3		4		
Peck, Jos	1	1	2		
Aberns, Saml	3		2		
Aberns, Saml, Jr	2		1		
Smith, Danl	4	4	3		
King, Saml	1	1	5		
Ladd, Elial	2	2	2		
Post, Jazaniah	1	1	4		
Sessions, Amasa	1	1	5		
Ladd, Akijah	1	1	1		
Newel, Danl	1	1	1		
Betts, Timo	1	1	4		
Huntington, Jno	1	2	1		
Huntington, Elisha	1	2	2		
Huntington (Widow)			4		
Baxter, Alexander	1	2	3		
Benton, Jona	1	4	3		
White, Ebenr	1	2	2		
Benton, Cyrus	1	6	3		
Ladd, Jona	2		2		
Wheelersom, Jos	1		1		
Smith, Allan	1		1		
Isham, Asher	1		3		
Boothe, Peter	1		5		
Russel, Jona	2	1	6		
Ryder, Enos	1	1	3		
West, David	1	3	2		
Baker, Jno, Jr	2	1	5		
Preston, Enos	1		3		
Ward, Obediah	1	2	2		
Heath, Simo	1	5	2		

TOLLAND TOWN—con.

NAME OF HEAD OF FAMILY.	Free white males of 16 years and upward, including heads of families.	Free white males under 16 years.	Free white females, including heads of families.	All other free persons.	Slaves.
Heath, Isaac	1	1	2		
Able, Asa	1		1		
Burchard, Walter	1	1	3		
Carpenter, Ruben	2	2	5		
Ingersol, Richard	1	1	1		
West, Jabez	1	1	2		
West, Ruful	2		4		
West, Job	3	1	3		
Hows, James	1	1	2		
Delano, Barna	1	1	4		
Wilson, Jacob	1	2	3		
Jewet, David	2	3	5		
Baker, Seth	1	2	1		
Ryder, Saml	1		3		
Wood, Jno	2	1	7		
Ladd, Saml	3	2	3		
Bates, Jos	1				
Baxter, Jedediah	1	2	1		
Hare (Widow)			2		
Borac, Jared	1				
Rogers, Benjn	1		2		
Heney, Asa	1	2	4		
Barton, Elkane	1		3		
Lillibridge, Thos	2	2	3		
Lillibridge, Jon	1	3	3		
Hartch, Jos	2	4	7		
Cogswell, Wm	1	1	2		
West, Jm	2	2	5		
Baker, Elezer	2	1	2		
Morgan, Joshua	2	3	4		
Carlton, Richard	1	3	2		
Baldwin, Asa	1	1	4		
Woodward, Amos	1	1	6		
Harth, Alma	2	2	6		
Grant, Em	4	2	2		
Grant, Eber	1	2	4		
Dornah, Edward	2	2	4		
Marnard, Zachariah	1	1	3		
Howard, Stephen	1	3	2		

UNION TOWN.

NAME OF HEAD OF FAMILY.	Free white males of 16 years and upward, including heads of families.	Free white males under 16 years.	Free white females, including heads of families.	All other free persons.	Slaves.
Williams, Wm	3		3		
Foster, Edward	2	4	4		
McKnawt, James	1	1	1		
Gay, Amasa	1		3		
Walker, Benjn	1		1		
Walker, Timo	2	2	5		
Lewes, Jona	2	3	6		
Newel, Nathl	2	2	5		
Walker, Benjn, 2d	1	2	3		
Sprague, Thos	2	1	5		
Write, Saml	1	2	4		
Sessions, Ebenr	2	1	2		
Merriman, Edw	3		2		
Taylor, Thos	2	2	4		
Horton, Ezra	1	3	4		1
Bowls, Lemuel	1	2	1		
Trimklin, Ic	1	1	3		
Childs, Penuel	1	4	2		
Armer, Benjn	2		1		
Moses, Jno	1		3		
Moses (Wid.)	1		2		
Armer, James	1	5	2		
Badger, Jm	4	2	5		
Armstrong, Elias	1		1		
Munger, Jno	2	3	1		
Armer, James	2		2		
Stone, Jos	2		5		
Merrifield, Ithm	1		1		
Coy, Levy	1	2	2		
Clark, Jno	1	2	3		
Convus, Josi	1		1		
Sessions, Abijah	3	1	7		
Bates, David	1	2	3		
Pearce, Francis	1	2	2		
Olney, Ezekl	3	4	5		
Crawford, Saml	3		4		
Burley, Soln	1	2	6		
Convus, Benjn	1	1	3		
Howard, Manassa	1	1	2		
Lally, Jos	1	1	1		
Lawson, Thos	2		3		
Coy, Archabal	1	1	3		
Lawson, Robt	1	1	3		
Farebanks, Jos	2	3	4		
Paul (Wid.)			2		
Lawson, David	1		2		
Mattason, Wm	2	2	3		
Hows, David	2		3		
Lawson, Jno	3	1	2		
Paul, Robt, 2d	2		2		
Convus, Noah	1	2	3		
Eneas, Jos	1	3	2		
Hunt, Jno	1	3	3		

TOLLAND COUNTY—Continued.

UNION TOWN—con. / WILLINGTON TOWN

NAME OF HEAD OF FAMILY.	Free white males of 16 years and upward, including heads of families.	Free white males under 16 years.	Free white females, including heads of families.	All other free persons.	Slaves.
Utley, Jona	1	3	7		
Backus, Jos	1	2	1		
Rube, Jno	1	3	4		
Gasby, Caleb	2	2	5		
Shaw, Gid	1	3	3		
Abbot, Wm	2	3	5		
Sessions, Jno	2	3	4		
Sessions, Waller	1		3		
Leach, Robt	1	1	1		
Martin, Saml	1		2		
Newel, Jacob	2	2	4		
Burley, Jacob	1		4		
More, David	1	3	3		
Godman, Jno	3	1	3		
Paul, Robt	1		2		
Sessions, Nathl	1	2	5		
Kenna, Nathan	2	4	3		
Sprague, Jame	1	1	3		
Thompson, Jame	1		2		
Hiscock, Stephen	1	2	3		
Griggs, Jos	3	3	5		
Morris, Henry	1	1	1		
Wales, Soln	2	2	4		
May, Rufus	1	2	4		
String, Saml	2		8		
Dodge, Nathl	1	1	5		
Twist, David	2		5		
Fisk, Jno	1	3	3		
Bass, Jos	1	1	1		
Whiton, Caleb	1	2	3		
Munger, Edw	1	5	3		
Sessions, Nathl	1	2	5		
Wales, Elijah	1	4	4		
Rothbone, David	1	1	1		
Strong, Alexander	1	2	5		
More, Wm	2	3	2		
More, James	4	4	2		
More, James	1	1	1		
More (Wid.)	1	1	3		
More, Icabod	1	1	3		
Lomis, Abner	2	1	3		
Burley, Jos	2	3	5		
Booth, Isaac	1		3		
Thompson, David	2	3	1		
Holt, Seth	1	1	4		
Semans, Abel	2	1	3		
Paul, Mathew	2		4		
WILLINGTON TOWN.					
Nye, Benjn	3	4	4		
James, Amos	2	1	2		
Merrick, Stephen	2	1	5		
Farley, Jno	3		8		
Farley, Saml	1	2	1		
Parsons, Jos	2	1	2		
Merrick, Thos	1		1		
Merrick, Timo	3	1	2		
Merrick, Jno	2		1		
Merrick, Jno, Jr	1	3	2		
Johnson, Wm	1	1	3		
Hinkley, Jno	1	2	3		
Hinkley, David	1	1	2		
Abby, Saml	2		1		
Bates, Danel	1		1		
Hatch, David	3		6		
Fellows, Varny	2		4		
Nobles, Revd. G	2	2	3		
Nobles, Soln	1	1	1		
Holmes, Abel	1	3	4		
Kenada, Jona	1		4		
Rice, Jno, Jr	1		1		
Olcut, Caleb	1	1	4		
Sparkes, Jos	1		1		
Jennings, Nathl, 2d	1	2	2		
Jennings (Wid.)		1	2		
Hows, Haman	2	1	4		
Weston, Jona	1	2	2		
Curtis, Ramson	2	4	3		
Marcy, Zebediah, 2d	1		4		
Davis, George	1	1	2		
Clyder, Jos	2	5	4		
Fuller, Elisha	3	1	2		
Pearl, Richard	1	4	3		
Pearl, Frederick	1		2		
Flint, Asher	2	1	1		

WILLINGTON TOWN—con.

NAME OF HEAD OF FAMILY.	Free white males of 16 years and upward, including heads of families.	Free white males under 16 years.	Free white females, including heads of families.	All other free persons.	Slaves.
Church, Asa	2	3	4		
Sanger, Azariah	3		2		
Vintin, Seth	1	3	1		
Thare, Shadrick	1	1	5		
Peery (Wid.)		1	1		
Niles, James	2	2	4		
Perry, Saml	1	1	1		
Thompson, Jno	2	2	3		
Works, Heny	2	4	2		
Pool, Timo	1	2	1		
Whitmore, Jacob	1	4	3		
Jacobs, Jos	1		1		
Lillibridge, Benjn	2	1	2		1
Jinnings, Thos	1		1		
Tyler, Broadstreat	1	1	3		
Tyler, James	1		2		
Jennings, David	2		2		
Cummings, Sime	1		4		
Tyler, Broadt, 2d	1		2		
Sibley, Jno	2	1	2		
Sanger, Noadt	2	2	6		
Mackintosh, Andrew	2	2	3		
Dorman, Micajah	3		1		
Davis, Jno	1	1	2		
Davis, Avery	1	2	3		
Amedown, Jedediah	1	3	3		
Hewit, Danl	1	3	4		
Lillibridge, David	2	1	4		
Lillibridge, Clark	1		3		
Sawying, Jno	2	1	3		
Pomeroy, Noah	1	1	1		
Pearl (Wid.)			1		
Hastings, James	3		2		
Amadown, Moses	1	1	4		
Flint, Jona	1	3	1		
Amadown, Henry	4		2		
Andrews, George	3	1	3		
Smith, Jno	3	2	5		
Wever, Benjn	1	2	3		
Johnson, Jno	3	1	6		
Johnson, Danl	1	1	3		
Chapman, Jason	1	2	4		
Albray, Peter	1	1	2		
Jennings, Nathan	2	1	3		
Goodale, Jno	1	2	3		
Hewit, Asa	1	1	1		
Johnson, David	1	1	2		
Mane, Josa	1	1	3		
Mane, Ruben	1	2	1		
Mane, Elias	2		2		
Mane, Andrew	1		1		
Robinson (Wid.)	1		3		
Robinson, Bethul	1	2	6		
Robinson, Sabin	1	1	3		
Mane, Andrew, Jr	1	1	5		
Fuller, David	2	2	2		
Weber, Thos	1	3	6		
Wheeler, Jos	1		3		
Nelson, James	1		1		
Fisk, Rufus	1	2	5		
Weber, Jno	1		1		
Culver, James	1	2	4		
Wever (Wid.)	1	1	5		
Wever, David	2		5		
Sibley, Ezra	1	1	4		
Scripter, James	3	3	6		
Stanton, Saml	1	3	5		
Damock, Geduthon	1	3	2		
Peck, Thos	3	1	1		
Newcum, Jos	1	4	3		
Carie, Nathl	2	2	4		
Scripter, Jno	2	1	2		
Gleason, Elezer	1	3	4		
Fenton, Elijah	2		2		
Fenton, Jno	2	1	2		
Fenton, Nathl	1	3	2		
Thompson, Justus	1	1	2		
Thompson, Jona	1	1	6		
Dimack, Jos	1	1	2		
Root (Widow)	1	2	2		
Taylor, Elisha	1	3	4		
Pearl, Timo	2	1	3		
Johnson, Saml	1	4	3		
Fenton, Elezer	3	1	3		
Taylor, Thos	1	3	5		
Holt, Caleb	1	3	1		

WILLINGTON TOWN—con.

NAME OF HEAD OF FAMILY.	Free white males of 16 years and upward, including heads of families.	Free white males under 16 years.	Free white females, including heads of families.	All other free persons.	Slaves.
Crocker, Jos	3	1	5		
Sawing, George	1	4	4		
Brown, Jas	2		3		
Eldridge, Jesse	2		1		
Eldridge (Wid.)		1	2		
Eldridge, Jos	1	1	5		
Eldridge, Zooth	2	3	4		
Crocker, Zebn	2	1	2		
Crocker, Stephen	1		2		
Dumnum, Saml	1		1		
Vintin, Saml	1	2	4		
Crocker, Saml	1		5		
Root, Nathl	1		3		
Scott, Jos	1		1		
Rice, Jno	1		2		
Holt, Nathl	2		1		
Holt, Nathl, 2d	1	1	3		
Preston, Darius	2	1	4		
Weston, Abm	1	2	3		
Weston, James	3		4		
Grant, Minor	1	4	2		
Holt, Andrew	1		2		
Holt, James	3	2	3		
Holt, Timo	2		2		
Wheeler, Asa	1	3	4		
Buknall (Wid.)		1	3		
Johnson, Elisha	2	1	3		
Eldridge, Wm	1	3	1		
Scott, Jn	3	1	2		
Hull, Hazard	1	4	2		
Topliff, Clement	3		3		
Utley, Jno	2	1	5		
Richardson, Jno	1	3	4		
Fenton, Elezr	1	3	2		
Holt, Philn	1	1	1		
Fuller, Danl	2		3		
Root, Nathl	2		2		
Vintin, David	1		2		
Stoel, Samuel	1	2	2		
Stoel, Asa	1	1	2		
Hancks, Elijah	1	4	3		
Eldridge, Micajah H	1	1	2		
Fuller, Danel	2		3		
Jennings, Nathl	1	3	2		
Hatch, Justus	1	1	3		
Pearl, Timo	2	1	3		
Fenton, Saml	1		5		
Fenton, Asa	2	4	6		
Fenton, Adonijah	1	4	2		
Fenton, Soln	1	1	1		
Fenton, Luke	1		2		
Fenton, Jos	1		7		
Rice, Thos	2	1	2		
Pearle, Oliver	1	2	3		
Glayer, Silas	3	2	5		
Antissel, Silas	1	4	7		
Antissel, Pheneas	1	4	2		
Smith, Jos	3		4		
Preston, Darius	1	1	1		
Britt, Em	2	1	4		
Parks, Jona	2	2	3		
Cushman, Elezer	1		2		
Cushman, Elezer, 2d	1	3	6		
Cushman, Elipht	1	2	2		
Cushman, Thos	1	1	1		
Johnson, Abel	1	2	3		
Holt, Elijah	2		4		
Dunton, Saml	2	3	3		
Rice (Wid.)			2		
Heath, Ebenr	2	1	2		
Lee, Danl	1	4	5		
Marcy, Zebh	2	1	5		
Stiles, Galo	2	1	11		
Holt, Isaac	2	2	6		
Case, Jno	1		1		
Woodward, Abner	1		1		
Teel, Isaac	1	2	3		
Root, Timo	1	1	5		
Becknal, Elezer	1	1	1		
Demock, Jos	1	1	2		
Belnap, Jon	1	3	1		
Brown, Shubal	1		1		
Jenning (Wid.)		1	2		
Fenton, Jno	1		1		
Sibley, Moses	1	2	2		
Johnson, Isaac	2		2		17

WINDHAM COUNTY.

ASHFORD TOWN.

NAME OF HEAD OF FAMILY.	Free white males of 16 years and upward, including heads of families.	Free white males under 16 years.	Free white females, including heads of families.	All other free persons.	Slaves.
Wright, Nathan	4	1	4		
Knolton, Thomas	2	4	3		
Knolton, Ezra	1		3		
Reed, Mathew	2	3	2		
Phillips, Augustus	1	1	2		
Squire, Ephraim	1	3	5		
Johnson, Sam¹	3		2	1	
Johnson, Sam¹	2	1	2		
Preston, Abraham	1	3	5		
Bugbe, James	2	2	5		
Russ, Azariah	3	1	4		
Tappin, Richard	1		2		
Snow, Oliver	2	1	1		
Southward, John	1		5		
Snow, Stephen	4		3		3
Bugbe, Sam¹	1	2	4		
Woodward, John	2	1	3		
Clark, Benjⁿ	3		3		2
Snow, Jonᵃᵗʰ	1	1	3		
Stebbins, Thomas	2	3	5		
Webb, Jabez	1	2	3		
Smith, Sarah			2		
Bicknall, Zachᵃʰ	3		3		
Bicknall, John	3	1	4		
Welch, Solomon	1		4		
Fletcher, Benjⁿ	1	3	2		
Cross, Nathan	1		3		
Fletcher, Richard	3		4		
Snow, Simon	1	2	1		
Yeomans, John	1		1		
Aspenwell, Peter	4		3		
Wright, Benjⁿ	1	2	4		
Chaffee, Josiah, Jnʳ	1	1	1		
Eldridge, Stephⁿ	1	1	1		
Eaton, Elisabeth		2	2		
Parker, Reuben	1	1	1		
Abbe, Isaac	3		1		
Owen, Ebenʳ	1	1	6		
Owen, Eleazʳ	2	2	3		
Fay, Jedediah	4	1	5		
Donset, Jonathan	1		4		
Cummins, David	2	1	8		
Sibley, Ezekel	2	1	1		
Fay, Jedʰ, Jnʳ	1	2	3		
Hale, John	3	5	5		
Warner, Thomas	1	1	1		
Dunham, John	2	1	1		
Connel, Jereʰ	1	1	6		
Sharp, Solomon	1	2	6		
Maine, Thoˢ	2	3	4		
Smith, Ebenᵉ	1	1	4		
Knowiton, Abraham	5	3	3		
Farnam, Manassa	2	1	3		
Wickwire, Solomon	1		1	2	
Spearks, Isaiah	1	4	4		
Hanks, Benjⁿ	1	2	3		
Dyer, James	2		9		
Bragg, Thomas	1	2	4		
Farnam, Stephen	1		2		
Farnam, Benjⁿ	1	3	2		
Poor House	3		3		
Chaffee, Jonᵃᵗʰ	1		1		
Slater, Benjⁿ	1	5	3		
Smith, George				11	
Walker, Sam¹	1	2	4		
Walker, Ebenʳ	1	2	3		
Walker, James	1		3		
Waker, Mary	3		2		
Chaffe, Josiah, Senʳ	3	1	5		
Robinson, Timothy	2		3		
Bugbe, Amos	1	1	7		
Bugbe, Josiah	2	1	2		
Porter, Abigal			4		
Warren, John	4	1	7		
Knolton, Dani¹	2	1	3		
Butler, Stephen	1		2		
Hall, Robert	1	3	2		
Tiffany, Ezek¹	1	1	1		
Woodward, Joseph	4	1	3		
Walker, Benjⁿ	3		5		
Watkins, Pheneas	1	1	1		
Lamb, Nathan	1	3	5		
Hanks, John	2	3	2		
Hannam, Justus	1		3		
Whiton, James	1	2	8		
Huges, Jonᵃᵗʰ	1	2	2		
Chaffee, Dareus		2	2		
Birchard, Prince	3		6		
Dimmock, Elias	3	1	4		
Waker, Sam¹, Jnʳ	1	1	4		
Marcy, Sam¹	2	2	3		
Person, Benjⁿ	4		4		
Dimmock, Dan¹	1	3	5		
Farnam, Solomon	2	2	3		
Russell, John	2		3		

ASHFORD TOWN—con.

NAME OF HEAD OF FAMILY.	Free white males of 16 years and upward, including heads of families.	Free white males under 16 years.	Free white females, including heads of families.	All other free persons.	Slaves.
Gasper, Joseph	1		2		
Hall, Job	2	2	2		
Stanley, Jeremʰ	2		2		
Whiton, Whitfield	1	2	3		
Buffington, William	1	1	2		
Chapman, Benjⁿ	2	2	5		
Hill, Thomas	1	5	2		
Haws, Eli	2		5		
Pratt, Benjⁿ	1	1	1		
Knox, Sam¹	1	5	2		
Snow, Stephen, Jnʳ	1	1	3		
Potter, Silas	2	5	5		
Hillyard, Isaac	1		1		
Dimmock, Timothy	1	1	5		
Knox, William	1	2	4		
Freemans, John					2
Hall, Uriah	1	3	3		
Grosvenor, Ezra	1	3	3		
Wilcox, Thomas	5	3	3		
Robins, Clark	1	1	4		
Robins, Benjⁿ	1	3	3		
Curtiss, Henry	1	1	2		
Young, Thomas	1	3	3		
Kingsbury, Sam¹	3		2		
Bass, Sam¹	2	4	6		
Snell, William	1		2		
Snell, William, Jnʳ	1	2	1		
Preston, Hovey	1	2	5		
Eldridge, Hezekiah	1	3	3		
Eaton, Josiah	1	3	2		
Henfield, William	1		1		
Eastman, Peter	3	2	1		
Brook, Abijah	3	1	2		
Preston, John	2	1	4		
Preston, Medinah	3	1	4		
Amadown, Joseph	2	4	6		
Ward, Ichabod	2	2	5		
Whiton, Joseph	1	6	7		
Whiton, Hannah	2		5		
Smith, Simeon	4	2	7		
Smith, Ezra	1		1		
Huntington, Thomas	2	2	4		
Dudley, Nicholas	1	1	2		
Howard, Lucy			1	2	
Brooks, Nath¹	1	3	1		
Craine, Roger	1	1	5		
Sanders, Duty	1		3		
Bozworth, John	2	3	5		
Grant, Hamlinton	2	1	1		
Sanders, Isachar	1	2	5		
Sanders, Stephen A	1	1	1		
Keyes, Sampson	2	1	5	1	
Knolton, Fredrick	1	1	4		
Utley, Sam¹	2	3	2		
Moseley, Luther	1		3		
Barker, Joshua	3	4	3		
James, Benjⁿ	2	2	5		
Palmer, Benjⁿ	2	3	2		
Chaffee, Jonathan	2	2	4		
Smith, Asa	2	1	4		
Utley, Abigal	1	1	3		
Royce, William	1		4		
Bishop, Jereʰ	2	1	2		
Phillips, Elijah	3	2	6		
Palmer, Joseph	3	5	6		
Lewis, Dan¹	1	2	6		
Chapman, Jacob	2	2	4		
Chapman, Penelope			2		
Marcy, Thomas	2	1	2		
Byles, Ebenʳ	3	3	8		
Knolton, Mehitabel	1		3		
Johnson, Marver	1	1	5		
Preston, Jareb	2	3	7		
Ellis, John	3	2	5		
Brown, Mary		2	5		
Heath, Ebenʳ	1		3		
Torrey, David	1	2	2	1	
Dana, Jacob	2		3		
Messinger, Elisabeth	1	1	4		
Preston, Zephʰ	1	1	2		
Dana, Jedediah	1	3	5		
Burnam, Joseph	3	3	3		
Clark, Elephᵗ	1	2	2		
Badcock, Timothy	2	2	4		
Smith, John	1	2	3		
Snow, Joseph	2	2	3		
Snow, Benjⁿ	1	1	6		
Snow, Bela	1	1	2		
Hende, Joseph	1	4	1		
Hende, Caleb	2		2		
Ewings, Thomas	1		4		
Brown, David	2	3	5		
Snow, James	1	3	3		
Kendal, Eli	2	1	3		

ASHFORD TOWN—con.

NAME OF HEAD OF FAMILY.	Free white males of 16 years and upward, including heads of families.	Free white males under 16 years.	Free white females, including heads of families.	All other free persons.	Slaves.
Kendall, Isaac	1	1	3		
Clark, John	1	3	3		
Clark, Israel	2	1	2		
Leonard, Benjⁿ	2	1	1		
Triscot, Joseph	2	2	6		
Howe, James	1	3	4		
Boutle, Ezra	3		3		
Snow, Sam¹, Jnʳ	2	2	4		
Abbot, Stephen	2		1		
Snow, William	2	5	7		
Mercy, Reubin	5	1	6		
Macy, Mathew	1		4		
Chandler, Stephen	1	1	1		
Howe, Nehehʰ	2		5		
Perkins, Isaac	3	4	4		
Cook, Aaron	2	1	2		
Simmons, Abel	4	4	5		
Davis, Willard	2	1	3		
Preston, Zera	1	3	4		
Dow, Abel	2	1	2		
Woodward, Jason	3	2	4		
Gould, Jonathan	2	1	2		
Wilson, Jacob	1		2		
Pond, Enoch	2	3	6		
Mason, Ebenʳ	2		2		
Russell, Benjⁿ	1		2		
Leamphere, Sam¹	2	2	3		
Burnam, Isaac	3	2	5		
Richards, Thaddeus	2	2	4		
Bullard, Calvin	1	2	3		
Chubb, William	1		4		
Chapman, David	1	4	6		
Smith, John	1	1	3		
Loomis, Abner	3		5		
Snow, Sam¹, Senʳ	1	1	2		
Mason, John	1	2	2		
Eaton, Ebenʳ	2	2	5		
Dowe, Abel	1	1	2		
Dowe, Cyrus	4		2		
Watkins, Jedediah	1	3	3		
Sumner, Edward	4	2	3		
Payne, Noah	1	5	8		
Abbot, John	5	4	7		
Tucker, Rufus	1	4	2		
Brown, John	1	2	4		
Broughton, John	1	1	4		
Owen, Benjⁿ	2	2	4		
Burlington, Nathan	1	2	2		
Watkins, Amasa	3		4		
Scarborough, Stephen	1	2	3		
Brown, Obediah	1		2		
Humphrey, Lucy		2	1		
Russell, James	1	2	2		
Hynes, James	2	2	2		
Wales, Nathan	1	4	3		
Kyes, Solomon	3		5		
Brown, Ambrose	1	1	2		
Dean, Simeon	1	2	4		
Bartlet, Dan¹	3	6	6		
Rogers, Moses	1	1	4		
Works, Joseph	2	2	9		
Bozworth, Allen	3		6		1
Frinck, Mary	1	3	2		
Watkins, Sarah			4		
Cheedle, Increase	2		2		
Bozward, Ebenʳ	5		5		
Works, John	3		2		
Spalding, Josiah	5	1	5		
Watkins, Thaddeus	1	2	2		
Fitz, Daniel	1	2	1		
Wright, Ebenʳ	3	2	10		
Allen, David	2	4	2		
Howard, Ephraim	4		7		
Watkins, William	1	1	1		
Scarborough John	2		1		
Scarborough, Joseph	1	1	2		
Briggs, John	1	3	1		
Hiscock, David	1	4	3		
Allen, Timothy	4	1	1		
Bugbee, Isaiah	3	2	4		
Carpenter, Hezᵃ	3	3	5		
Bugbee, Jesse	1	5	2		
Parkhurst, ——	3	1	2		
Carpenter, Dan	1		1		
Fisher, Olcott	1	3	4		
Howard, Sam¹	3	1	3		
Carpenter, Joel	2		1		
Howard, Jonᵃᵗʰ	2	3	5		
Coats, Benjⁿ	1		1		
Judson, Andrew	1	5	3		
Pettis, John	4	2	8		
Bowen, Joseph	3	2	2		
Bowen, John	1	1	3		
Bowen. Barre	1	1	1		
Burnam, John	1	3	2		

WINDHAM COUNTY—Continued.

ASHFORD TOWN—con.

NAME OF HEAD OF FAMILY.	Free white males of 16 years and upward, including heads of families.	Free white males under 16 years.	Free white females, including heads of families.	All other free persons.	Slaves.
Snow, Robert	3		2		
Parrish, Eliphaz	1	3	4		
Badger, John	1	3	3		
Cheney, Benjn	2	2	4		
Sumner, Robert	1	1	3		
Horton, Moses	1		2		
Badger, Ezekel	2	1	2		
Russell, John	1	5	3		
Case, Elipht	1		3		
Strickland, Nathl	1		1		
Tufts, Peter	1	3	2		
Sumner, John	2	2	5		
Foster, Stephen	1		2		
Tufts, Aaron	3	3	6		
Beamus, Jonathan	1	3	6		
Mumford, Jeremiah	1	2	2		
Bowls, David, Jnr	1	1	3		
Nichalls, Jonathn	2	2	4		
Kendal, Joseph, Jnr	1	2	1		
Averil, John	1	2	1		
Kendall, Joseph	4	3	4		
Bowls, David	2	2	4	2	1
Chamberlin, Edmond	1	4	6		
Bozworth, Aaron	1	4	7		
Badger, Ezra	1	2	1		
Havens, Jeriah	1	1	2		
Sumner, Benjn	4		4		
Kendal, Smith	1	2	1		
Carperter, Comfort	1	2	2		
Work, Josiah, Senr	2	1	3		
Sumner, James F	2	2	5		
Sumner, Samuel	2	3	5		
Works, Ingolsby	2	1	3		
Sumner, Ebenr	3	1	6		
Clap, Seth	1	4	1		
Simmon, Abel, Senr	1	3	4		
Havens, Simons	2	2	3		
Burnam, Nathan	1	3	2		
Lyon, Nathan	1	2	1		
Beamous, Ephraim	3		1		
Wilson, Elias	1		2		
Lyon, Ephraim	3	1	5		
Eastman, Ebenr	4		3		
Chapman, Jonathan	1		3		
Chapman, Jonan, Jnr	1	6	3		
Chapman, Jonah	3	3	2		
Mason, Ebenr	1	6	3		
Peck, Joseph	1	3	2		
Peck, Lyda			3		
Peck, John	2	1	2		
Clark, Leml	2	4	2		
. . w, Arunnah	1	2	4		
Spring, Saml	3		1		
Spalding, Ephraim	2	2	4		
Wilson, Jacob, Jnr	1	4	2		
Snow, Billarky	1	3	3		
Dodge, Ephraim	1	1	3		
Bullard, Luther	1	1	3		
Bullard, William	3		2		
Harton, Moses, Jnr	1	2	3		
Sanders, Eseck	2	6	7	1	
Angell, Stephn	1	1	3		
Craine, Roger	1	2	4		
Smith, Hubard	1	3	3		
Dimmock, Isaac	2	2	4		
Lewis, Enock, Senr	1		1		
Lewis, Israel	1	5	1		
Kyes, Edward	2	4	2		
Brown, Roswell	1	1	1		
Walker, Stephen	1	4	1		
Chaffee, Joseph	2	4	5		
Holt, Ezekiel	1		1		
Lawson, Ebenr	1	3	3		
Fanam, Asa	3		4		
Sheppard, James	1		1		
Ward, Phebe			1		
Kasson, Saml	1		1		
Kasson, Saml, Jnr	1	2	1		
Walker, Ephm	2	1	2		
Chapman, Joseph	2		3		
Chapman, Elias	2	2	3		
Chapman, Thomas	1		1		
Chaffee, David	3	2	4		
Abbe, Jonathan	2	3	5		
Robins, David	1		1		
Loomis, Danl	2	2	3		
Miller, Solomon	1	1	3		
Henfield, Benjn	1	2	3		
Loomis, John	1	2	2		
Walker, Ebenr, Jnr	1		1		
Walker, William	3	1	3		
Walker, Ebenr, Senr	1		1		
Backus, Adonijah	2	1	3		
Smith, Abijah	1		3		
Suitleif, Sylvester	2	1	3		
Tyler, Saml	1	2	1		

ASHFORD TOWN—con.

NAME OF HEAD OF FAMILY.	Free white males of 16 years and upward, including heads of families.	Free white males under 16 years.	Free white females, including heads of families.	All other free persons.	Slaves.
Tyler, Job	2	1	3		
Chapman, Christopher	1	1	4		
Johnson, Reubin	1	3	2		
Rathbon, John	2	1	3		
Barney, Mary		1	3		
Coy, Luke	1	1	2		
Chapman, Thomas	3		2		
Chapman, Oliver	1	1	1		
Brown, Danl	1	4	1		
Brown, John, Senr	3		3		
Burnam, Freeman	1	1	3		
Kyes, Edward	1	5	1		

BROOKLYNE TOWN.

NAME OF HEAD OF FAMILY.	Free white males of 16 years and upward, including heads of families.	Free white males under 16 years.	Free white females, including heads of families.	All other free persons.	Slaves.
Harras, Reuben	1	4	7		
Rogers, Josiah	1		3		
Harris, Paul	1	1	6		
Brown, John	1		4		
Allen, Parker	1	1	3		
Harriss, Ebenr	1	1	1		
Scott, William	1	1	3		
Harris, Saml	1	6	3		
Perrit, Joseph	2	1	4		
Staples, Abel	1	4	3		
Cady, Ebenr	1	3	2		
Withy, Eunice			1		
Stanton, Thomas	2	1	5		
Benjamin, Barzl	1		2		
Dean, Saml	3	1	4		
Merrit, Thomas	3	1	5		
Davison, Peter	3	3	2		
Litchfield, Eleazr	1	2	3		
Hewit, Stephen	1	2	4		
Tyler, Asa	2	3	4		
Winter, Nathan	2	1	4	1	
Alworth, James	4	2	4		
Winter, Josiah	2	2	1		
Pooles, Amasa	1	3	2		
Copeland, James	3	2	3		
Cady, Gideon	2	1	5		
Cady, Asail	1	1	2		
Fasset, John	1		3		
Roe, Isaac	2	1	3		
Downing, Jededh	3	2	5		
Frazier, John	1	1	2		
Randal, Jobe	1		3		
Davison, Joseph	3	2	4		
Davison, Joseph, Jnr	1	1	4	1	
Bacon, Nehemiah	2		3		
Cady, Benjn	3	1	5		
Cady, Jonathn	1	1	3		
Bowman, Walter	1	4	6		
Cady, John	3	2	3		
Searls, Salter	3	4	3		
Clark, Caleb	2	1	3		
Bowman, Elisha	3	3	4		
Geers, John	3	3	3		
Morgan, Roswell	1	2	3		
Brown, Alpheus	2	3	5		
Carder, ——	2	1	2		
Shepard, Benjn	2		2		
Shepard, Whitmore	2	1	3		
Litchfield, Israel	3		3		
Litchfield, John	3	2	4		
Baker, John	4	1	5		
Quivy, Amasa	1	1	2		
Baker, Joseph, Jnr	2	1	2		
Fuller, Josiah	1		3		
Adam, William, Sen	7	1	7		
Cady, Naham	1	1	3		
Clark, Moses	1		2		
Clark, Danl	1	1	5		
Palmer, Thaddeus	1	3	2		
Cady, Uriah	1	1	4		
Cady, Danl	2	2	6		
Hastings, Dyeer	4	2	7		
Baker, Stephen	2		5		
Putnam, Reubin	1	5	1		
Goodale, Abijah	1	1	3		
Litchfield, Uriah	1		2		
Cook, Danl	1	1	1	1	
Sterns, Daniel	3	1	3		
Baker, Erastus	4	2	3		
Spalding, Ebenr	4	3	3		
Payne, Seth, Jnr	2	2	5		
Baker, Stephen	1	3	4		
Gilbert, Eleazr	2	3	6		
Whitney, Josiah	2		6		
Tyler, Danl, Jnr	4	6	4		
Jefford, John	2		2		
Herrick, Benjn	2	1	4		
Herrick, Rufus	2				
Finch, Stephen					6
Tyler, Danl	3		3		1
Miles, Joshua	5	2	4		

BROOKLYNE TOWN—con.

NAME OF HEAD OF FAMILY.	Free white males of 16 years and upward, including heads of families.	Free white males under 16 years.	Free white females, including heads of families.	All other free persons.	Slaves.
William, Benjn, Jr	1	2	6		
Pike, John, Jr	4		3		
Stephens, John	1	2	3		
Allen, Joseph	1	1	7		
Pike, Jona	2	2	2		
Kindal, David	1		2		
Kindal, John	1		5		
Eaton, Ezekl, Jr	3	1	7		
Pellet, Jonan	2	1	6		
Butts, Saml	4	1	6		
Copeland, Jonan	1	3	3		
Peirce, Timaus	2	3	5		
Peirce, Dillano	2	4	4		
Dorrance, James	2	2	4		
Smith, William	4	2	4		
Murdock, Andrus	6	1	3		
Woodward, Ward	2	5	5		1
Cogshall, Nathl	3	2	3		
Allen, Jabez	2	2	6		
Darke, William, Jr	2	6	5		1
Weaver, John	1		1		
Weaver, Rimington	1	3	4		
Whittiker, Saml	1	1	1		
Adams, Peter	4		5		
Adams, Philemon	3	3	3		
Miles, Thomas	1	3	4		
Wilson, Ignatus	1		2		
Hubard, William	3	1	2		
Prince, Abel	2	1	1		
Adams, Shubael	1	2	2		
Weaver, Anna			4		
Hubard, Ebs	1	2	3		
Denison, David	1	1	4		
Adams, Noah	3	1	3		
Hulet, Nehemh	1	1	4		
Kelly, William	3	5	5		
Ashcraft, Jedediah	2	3	6		
Ashcraft, John	3	1	4		
Howard, Charles	2		2		
Adams, Ephraim	1		3		
Adams, Abner	2		2		
Tyler, Joseph	2	2	4		
Frost, Jonas	3	1	4		
Darke, James	1	1	2		
Fogg, Danl	1		2	7	4
Badcock, Jereh	2	1	4		
Brown, Shubael	2	3	3		
Cady, Eliakim	1	3	4		
Eldridge, James	4	6	6	3	2
Withy, James	4	2	5		
Hide, Jakey & Co	2	3	5		
Scarborough, Ebenr	1	2	5		
Scarborough, Saml	2	4	6		
Barret, William	1	3	5		
Gilbert, Wilks	1	4	6		
Williams, Saml, Jnr	2	5	2		
Pike, James	4		6		
Deaolph, Charles	2	6	2		
Pike, Willard	1	1	3		
Smith, Thomas	3	1	3		
Spalding, Caleb	4		2		
Spalding, Abel	2		2		
Prince, Timothy, Jnr	2	1	4		
Cushman, Isaac	3	2	7		
Peirce, Benjn	3	2	3		
Payne, Seth	2	1	3		
Prince, Timoty	1		1		
Miles, Jesse	1	3	1	5	
Baker, Joseph	3	3	4		
Putnam, Danl	3	1	5		
Winchester, Jabez	1	1	5		
Cushman, William	1	4	3		
Phillemore, Willm	1		2		
Williams, Asa	1	1	4		
Fling, Lemuel	1	3	3		
Williams, Saml	1	3	3		
Frazier, Elijah	1	3	4		
Gilbert, Joseph	3	1	3		
Fasset, Adonijah	6	1	4		
Chapman, Amazh	3	1	5		
Collar, Jonathan	2	2	5		
Davis, Danl	1	3	4		
Malborne, Peter					3
Williams, Stephen	2	4	4		
Williams, Martha		2	2		
Williams, Roger	3	1	3		
Weeks, Ebenr	3	7	7		
Ingolls, Saml	3	1	5		
Williams, Saml	3		6		
Ward, Saml	2		1		
Putnam, Israel	3	2	5		1
Scarborough, Joseph	4	5	7		
Holmes, Nathl	1	1	1		
Cleavland, Pheneas	1		1		
Johnson, Stephen	1	2	2		
Cleavland, Joseph	2	2	3		
Dayley, Benjn					3

WINDHAM COUNTY—Continued.

CANTERBURY TOWN.

NAME OF HEAD OF FAMILY.	Free white males of 16 years and upward, including heads of families.	Free white males under 16 years.	Free white females, including heads of families.	All other free persons.	Slaves.
Wills, Gideon	2	1	3		
Cleavland, Eliphaz	2	2	2		
Amy, Christopher				2	
Amirell, Job				7	
Lyons, John	2	2	3		
Safford, Joseph	1	2	5		
Pellet, Hez^a, Jn	2	2	3		
Kendal, Phineas	2	3	4		
Backus, Elisha	3	1	3		
Backus, Stephen	3		3		
Payne, Luther	2		4		
Bingham, Gurdon	1	4	1		
Bingham, Luther	5		5		
Ward, Ichabod	2	2	4		
Fitch, Jabez	3	2	8	1	
Fitch, John	7	1	4		
Hough, Walter	3	3	3		
Lord, William	1	3	3		
Obrian, William	1	2	2		
Brewster, Walter	1	1	2		
Bacon, Abner	2	1	4		
Felch, Saml	2	1	4		
Andross, Fredrick	3	4	1		
Bacon, Jacob	2	2	2	1	
Spalding, Jacob	1	1	4		
Hough, Erastus	1		1		
Fisk, Darius	2	1	8		
Washburn, Eli	1	1	3		
Backus, Timothy	1	1	5		
Spalding, Ezekiel	2	1	3		
Aspinwall, William	1	3	5		
Tracy, Zurriah	1		3		
Cob, James	2		3		
Ainsworth, Anne			4		
Adams, Nathan, Jn	4	1	6		
Brown, Jede^h	1	1	3		
Johnson, Obediah	2	1	3		
Ainsworth, Nathan^l	1	2	5		
Hyde, Jonathan	4		3		
Finny, Joshua, Jr	2	2	4		
Fitch, Rebeca, Jr	1	1	4		
Dyer, James	4	1	8		
Adams, Roger, Jr	2		4		
Bawldin, Jacob	2	1	2		
Devenport, Paul	5	3	6		
Adams, Elihu, Jr	3	2	4		
Webb, Christopher	1	4	1		
Baldwin, David	2	2	3		
Justin, George	2	1	6		
Stearkweather, Bilchar.	1	1	4		
Carter, Saml	3	1	4		
Ainsworth, Joseph	4		5		
Adams, Phineas	2	1	1		
Cobb, Ephnah	2	1	3		
Payne, Solomon	4	1	5		
Edwards, Danl, Jr	3	2	4		
Dyer, Jareh, Sr	4	2	6		
Dyer, Elijah	5	1	4		
Finney, Asa	1		1		
Ainsworth, William	2	1	4		
Ainsworth, Willm, Jr	2	1	2		
Bennet, Eben^r	2	2	5		
Farnam, Joseph	2	4	3		
Justin, Nicholas	2		2		
Mott, Gershom	1		1		
Larrabe, Silas	1	1	3		
Dyer, Eben^r	1	3	3		
Whitford, David	1	1	4		
King, Elisha	1	2	2		
Gould, Edmond	1	2	2		
Morse, Charles	3	2	4		
Adams, Levi	1	1	2		
Stevens, Adams	2	3	6		
Adams, Parker	2	2	3		
Dulop, James	3	1	4		
Muth, Abiah	1	2	3		
Smith, Asa	1	6	4		
Leach, Mary			1		
Rude, Nathan	1	2	5		
Justin, William	1		2		
Green, Eunice		2	2		
Williams, Elijah	2	2	5		
Mott, Jere^h, Sr	3		4		
Lyon, Eben^r	2	3	2		
Kingsley, Jabez	1	1	1		
Rathbon, Joseph	1	3	2		
Rathbon, Sybil		2	2		
Justin, Walcott	1		1		
Lyon, Ephraim	1	2	4		
Smith, Benjn	1		3		
Apley, James	2	4	2		
Wentworth, John	2	5	4		
Dimmock (Wid.)	2		5		
Wentworth, William	1		4		
Allen, Pratt	1	1	1		

CANTERBURY TOWN—continued.

NAME OF HEAD OF FAMILY.	Free white males of 16 years and upward, including heads of families.	Free white males under 16 years.	Free white females, including heads of families.	All other free persons.	Slaves.
Cotton, Thos	1	1	3		
Morse, James	1	1	5		
Francis, John	1		1		
Winter, Asa	1	2	3		
Winchester, Andrew	1		2		
Brewster, Peleg	1		1		
Brewster, Jededi^h	1	3	4		
William, Isaiah	3	3	4		
Bennet, Elijah	1		2		
Payne, Esther			2		
Carver, David, Sr	3	2	7		
Park, Nathan	2	1	2		
Smith, Benjn	1		3		
Smith, John	2	1	7		
Butts, Josiah	1	3	3		
Adams, Bradford	1	2	4		
Herrick, John	4		3		
Fuller, Benjn	1	1	3		
Perkins, William	1		3		
Perkins, Leonard	1	2	1		
Adams, Thos, Sr	2	1	3		
Peck, Reubin	1	3	4		
Wood, Augustus	1	1	2		
Allen, Barnabas	1		5	1	
Allen, Jared	1	3	3		
Waldo, Edward	2	1	3		
Jewit, Thos	1	1	5		
Smith, Jacob	2		5		
Park, Reubin	2	1	3		
Parks, Simeon	2		5		
Butts, Sherekiah	4		2		
Butts, Gideon	1	2	2		
Butts, Eben^r	1		7		
Adams, Joseph	1	3	4		
Silsby, John	1		4		
Safford, Joseph	4	1	5		
Safford, Rufus	1	1	2		
Meach, Esther	1	2	2		
Parks, Eben^r	1	1	2		
Carter, Joseph	2		2		
Butts, Stephen	3	1	3		
Justin, Charles	1	2	1		
Parks, John	2	3	5		
Rose, David	2	3	7		
Rose, John	1	1	3		
Beston, John	2	2	7		
Bond, Jonas	1	1	3		
Beston, Saml	4	3	4		
Bond, William	1		6		
Wright, Saml	1	3	7		
Brown, Waldo	1		1		
Woodward, Peter	1	2	5		
Beston, John	1		2		
Winchester, Andrew	1		2		
Herrick, John	2		2		
Herrick, John	3	2	5		
Frost, Henry	2	2	5		
Adams, James	2	2	4		
Frost, Danl	1	2	2		
Leach, Joel	1	2	3		
Austin, Sarah	1		4		
Adams, Timothy	2	1	3		
Herrick, Asael	1	1	1		
Fish, Nathan	1	1	4		
Bingham, Gidion	1	1	2		
Adams, Saml	1	1	2		
Payne, Luther	2		4		
Kendal, Peter	2	2	2		
Smith, Jarus	1	4	2		
Johnson, Joel	1		2		
More, Joseph	4	2	5		
Pellet, Sarah	1	1	5		
Hough, John	1		3		
Buswell, Thos	2	2	3	1	
Cleavland, Timothy	4		4	1	
Payne, Saml	1	2	4		
Adams, Elishah	2	1	3		
Bacon, Joseph	1		1		
Cleavland, Perez	2	1	4		
Spalding, Pearl	1	1	2		
Pellet, Rufus	2	3	5		
Pellet, Joseph	2	3	2		
Adams, John	3	3	7		
Tyler, John	1		2		
Tyler, Zebulon	4		1		
Obrion, John	1	2	6		
Button, John	2	2	3		
Wheeler, John	3	1	4		
Bradford, John, Jur	1	2	4		
Bradford, Saml	2	1	5		
Bradford, Thos	3		4		
Adams, Saml	1	2	2		
Adams, Eben^r	1	3	4		1
Cady, Abijah	3		5		
Adams, Cornelius	1	5	6		

CANTERBURY TOWN—continued.

NAME OF HEAD OF FAMILY.	Free white males of 16 years and upward, including heads of families.	Free white males under 16 years.	Free white females, including heads of families.	All other free persons.	Slaves.
Stanton, Amon, sr	2	2	4		
Clark, Seth	1	1	2		
Simons, Francis	1		1		
Wheeler, Jonath^n	2	5	5		
Geer, Jacob	2		2		1
Warren, Moses	2	3	1		
Tyler, Oliver	1	3	4		
Smith, Mary			4		
Brown, Benjn	3	1	5		
Knowling, Asa	1	2	3		
Morse, Benjn	2	2	6		
Foster, Danl	2		4		
Litchfeld, David	2	2	4		
Constable, William	1		2		
Parrish, Lem^l	2	2	4		
Parrish, Roswell	1	2	3		
Falkner, Caleb	1	1	4		
Masi, Anthony	4		5		
Bradford, John	1	3	3		
Bradford, Josiah, sr	3	2	5		
Olney, Hez^a	2	3	9		
Hibard, Rufus	1	3	4		
Ransford, Joseph	1		1		
Ransford, David	1	1	6		
Ransford, Joseph	1	1	2		
Ransford, Richard	2	2	3		
Adams, William	1	1	3		
Carew, William	1		4		
Hyde, Josiah, Jur	1	1	1		
Hyde, Josiah	2		1		
Hyde, Neh^h	2		2		
thayer, Ezekiel	1	1	6		
Staples, John	3	4	2		
Johnson, Rufus	2		2	2	1
Glass, Silas	1	1	4		
Davis, Mary			4		
Burgess, Asa	1	3	5		
Downing, Henry	1	3	7		
Downing, Stephen	2	2	2		
Downing, Phineas	2	1	2		
Downing, Phineas, Ju	1	1	3		
Dowing, Danl	1	3	1		
Hebard, Eben^r	1	1	3		
Dowing, Jona^a	4		3		
Hebard, William	4	1	3		
Hebard, Willm, Jr	1	4	5		
Darbe, Eleaz^r	1		2		
Darbe, Rufus	1	2	4		
Douset, Joseph	1	1	4		
Williamson, Joseph	2	1	2		
Burge, Joseph	1	2	4		
Spiner, Elijah	1	3	2		
Henry, Saml	1	1	4		
Gordon, Alexander	3	5	5		
Parks, Peter, sr	2	2	2		
Parks, Jesse	1		2		
Backus, Isaac	2	1	3		
Backus, Nathan	1		4		
Shaw, William	1		2		
Waldo, Zach^h	2	1	2		
Sanders, Peter	1		3		
Williamson, Cornelious	1	1	2		
Williamson, Caleb	3		3		
Williamson, George	2	2	4		
Williamson, Caleb, Senr	1		1		
Raymond, Joshua	3	1	3		
Shaw, Benjn	1		1		
Avery, David	3	1	3		
Davis, Jonathan	1		3		
Hyde, Elasa	1	3	5		
Sheppard, Asa	2	1	2		
Bacon, Benjn, Jur	2	1	4		
Bacon, Benjn	4	1	3		
Johnson, William	4	1	6	1	
Hyde, Benjn	1	2	2		
Johnson, John	3	2	8		
Payne, David	1		3		
Cleavland, Moses, sr	4	2	5		
Stevens, Robert	1	1	2		
Hyde, Nathan	1	1	3		
Cleavland, Shubail	1	1	5		
Justin, Miner	1	2	1		
Hyde, Isaac	2	2	4		
Clark, Theoph^u	2	1	3		
Cleavland, Josiah	2	1	3		
Brown, Eben^r	3		4		
Hyde, Comfort	2	2	5		
Spalding, Thos	1	1	2		
Ransom, Saml	1	2	2		
Bacon, Asa	2	1	5		
Palmer, Elihu	3		4		
Chaffee, Eben^r	3	2	5		
Pike, Joseph	1		2		
Pike, James	1		2		
Pike Amos	3	1	3		

WINDHAM COUNTY—Continued.

NAME OF HEAD OF FAMILY.	Free white males of 16 years and upward, including heads of families.	Free white males under 16 years.	Free white females, including heads of families.	All other free persons.	Slaves.
CANTERBURY TOWN—continued.					
Harris, John	1	2	4		
Hyde, David	1	1	2		
Cleavland, Asa	2		2		
HAMPTON TOWN.					
Moseley, Flavel	2		2		
Utley, Saml	2	1	3		
Hammond, Josiah	3	1	7		
Goodale, Aaron	2	1	3		
Moseley, Joseph	2	3	5		
Moseley, Ebenezer, Junr	1	1	2		
Hovey, Ebenr	2	1	3		
Clark, Timothy	1	1	3		
Holt, Nehemiah	1	1	3		
Holt, Nehemh, Jnr	1		5		
Lamphear, Jedeh	2	2	4		
Lyon, Robert	1	1	7		
Moseley, Uriel	1	1	1		
Robins, Nathl	1		2		
Huntington, William	2	2	5		
Spearks, Lemuel	2	2	3		
Clark, Pheneas	2	4	5		
Ringe, John	1		1		
Ringe, Richd	1	1	4		
Martin, Richd	2	1	2		
Clark, Jonathn	1	1	2		
Robins, John	2		4		
Durke, Wm, Jnr	1	1	2		
Loomiss, Jonathan	2	2	6		
Robins, Mary		1	1		
Fuller, Daniel	3	1	4	1	
Hewit, Robert	1	2	2		
Utley, Amos	2	2	2		
Fuller, William	3	1	1		
Fuller, Joseph	2	5	4		
Stedman, Hannah	2	1	4		
Ford, Abraham	3	1	8		
Martin, Nathl	1	1	3		
Durke, Elipht	2	2	3		
Hodgkins, Thomas	2		3		
Holt, Paul, Senr	2		3		
Durke, Henry	3	2	4		
Holt, Abiel	2		2		
Burnam, Joseph	1	1	3		
Robinson, Clifford	1	4	1		
Clark, Ebenr	1	2	3		
Simons, Elijah	1	3	2		
Kennedy, David	2		3		
Bill, Roswell	2	1	4		
Flint, Danl	1	2	2		
Clark, Titus	1		1		
Clark, Danl	1	2	3		
Richardson, John	2	3	6		
Buck, Judah	2	2	7		
Walcott, Moses	2	3	3		
Martin, William, Jnr	2	2	4		
Butlar, William	1		2		
Butlar, Hannah			4		
Holt, Paul, Jnr	1	3	5		
Kingsbury, Jonath	3	5	7		
Utley, Amos, Jnr	1		1		
Flint, Benjn	1	2	4		
Clark, Jeremiah, Jnr	1	4	5		
Clark, Amos	1	1	1		
Clark, Jeremiah	1		1		
Martin, Joseph, Jnr	1	4	3		
Clark, Stephen	1	4	3		
Clark, Hannah			3		
Ford, Benjamin	1	2	4		
Ford, Amos	1	1	4		
Clark, Amos, Jnr	1	1	2		
Molton, Benjn	1	4	5		
Holt, William, Jnr	3	2	4		
Holt, Joshua	3	1	2		
Denison, Daniel	2	1	6		
Clark, John	1	4	2		
Allen, Saml	1		2		
Hovey, Jonath	3	4	6		
Joslin, David	3	1	5		
Avery, Abel	3	1	3		
Ford, Amos, Jnr	1	1	2		
Blanchard, Elias	2	1	3		
Jennings, Nathan	1	2	5		
Utley, Thos	2		7		
Kimball, Asa	1		1		
Abbot, Nathan	1		2		
Grow, Thomas	2	3	7		
Grow, Thomas, Jnr	3	3	9		
Pearl, Phillip	3	3	4		
Abbot, Henry	1	2	2		
Ford, Nathanel	2	2	1		
Martin, Benjn	2		9		
Cummins, Stephen	1	2	4		
Roger, Benjn				2	

NAME OF HEAD OF FAMILY.	Free white males of 16 years and upward, including heads of families.	Free white males under 16 years.	Free white females, including heads of families.	All other free persons.	Slaves.
HAMPTON TOWN—continued.					
Griffin, Ebenr	2	2	5		
Fuller, John, Jnr	1	1	2		
Fuller, John	4	2	4		
Fuller, Benjn	2	5	2		
Hammond, Hezekiah	3	3	2		
Moseley, Saml	2	1	4		1
Moseley, Ebenr	2	2	5		
Simons, Elijah	2		4		
Sessions, John	5	2	3		
Martin, George	2		3		
Ringe, Martha	1	1	4		
Orms, Hannah			1		
Hovey, John	4	1	4		
Brewster, John	3	1	4		
Stedman, Thos	4	3	4		
Greenslit, Joel	2	1	7		
Stedman, Thos, Jnr	2	1	4		
Fuller, Della			1		
Wheat, Benjn	1		3		
Collins, Josiah	1	1	4		
Jackson, Thos	2		1		
Crocker, Elizabeth			1		
Hovey, Chloe		1	2		
Brown, Henry	3	1	5		
Farnam, William	3		6		
Ormsby, Jereh	2	2	4		
Abbot, Asa	1	1	4		
Burnap, James	1	1	6		
Martin, Amasa	1	2	2		
Blanchard, John	1		1		
Cheedle, Benjamin	2		4		
Abbot, Benjan	1	2	4		
Abbot, Benjn, Jnr	1		3		
Parker, John	3		4		
Smith, Solomon, Jnr	2	1	2		
Fisk, Jonn, Jnr	1	3	2		
Burnam, Josiah	1	2	2		
Neff, William	1	3	2		
Randall, Elijah	1	2	5		
Porrage, Jabez					5
Burnam, Joseph	1	1	3		
Flint, Nathl, Jnr	1	1	4		
Upton, John	2	2	3		
Burnam, Danl	2	3	3		
Smith, Solomon	2	1	3		
Fuller, Abijah	2	4	5		
Elliot, William	3	2	4		
Fisk, David	2	3	6		
Spence, Silas	1	3	8		
Alsworth, William	2		6		
Dodge, David	2		2		
Rude, Jason	1	1	3		
Fenton, David	1		1		
Hebard, Warner	1		1		
Howard, Stephen	2		2		
Spencer, David	1	1	3		
Ashley, Abner	2	4	4		
Ashley, Joseph	1	3	4		
Jewit, Ebenr	2	1	5		
Smith, James	1	1	2		
Fuller, Jonathn	1	4	3		
Fuller, Aaron	3	2	3		
Kimball, Danl	2	1	2		
Durkee, Benjn	2	3	3		
Farnam, Zebudh	2	1	2		
Fullar, Thos	4	1	2		1
Durke, Andrew	2	3	5		
Dorrance, Alexr	1		1		
Dorrance, Saml	2	3	4		
Dorrance, Jereh	2	3	3		
Durke, Zebeh	3	2	6		
Holt, Zebeh	3	2	6		
Simons, Shubael	1	1	5		
Holt, Jonath	2	4	3		
Preston, Jacob	3	1	6		
Butts, John	1	1	2		
Martin, David	3	2	5		
Fuller, Saml	2	3	4		
Geer, Ebenr S.	1	2	1		
Downing, Jonath	1	1	5		
Cleavland, Silas, Jnr	2	1	3		
Waldo, John E	1	3	3		
Jewit, Benjn, Jnr	2	3	5		
Curtiss, John	4		4		
Curtis, John, Jnr	2	1	3		
Williams, Nathan	1		5		
Dorset, Joseph	2	1	4		
Snow, Abraham	2	2	5		
Bennet, Francis	1		2		
Keys, James	1		2		
Colborn, Edward	1		3		
Avery, Uriah	1	1	4		
Spalding, Amos	2	1	2		
Howard, William	5	4	6		
Howard, James	5	3	6		1
Bennet, Isaac	2	1	7		

NAME OF HEAD OF FAMILY.	Free white males of 16 years and upward, including heads of families.	Free white males under 16 years.	Free white females, including heads of families.	All other free persons.	Slaves.
HAMPTON TOWN—continued.					
Farnam, Hannah		1	1		
Farnam, Jereh	1	3	3		
Greenslit, Elijah	1	3	2		
Durkee, William	3	1	3		
Martin, Benjn	2		9		
Molton, Tabatha			3		
Martin, Joseph	1	2	3		
Flint, Nathl	2	1	2		
Flint, Phens	1	3	2		
Martin, William	3	4	6		
Jennings, Seth	1	3	1		
Meachum, Seth	1		1		
Rogers, Jeduthon	2		1		
Park, Jacob	1	5	3		
Burnam, Josiah	2	2	1		
Upton, Lucy	1		3		
Fisk, Jonathan	1		1		
KILLINGLEY TOWN.					
Hutchins, Silas	1	2	2		
Hutchins, John	1	4	2		
Hutchins, Amasa	1	1	1		
Hutchins, Shubal	1		6		
Hutchins, Ezra	2	5	3		
Sprague, John	2	1	4		
Key, John	1	6	2		
Barret, Amos	2	6	4		
Spalding, Benjn	2	1	6		
Kingsbury, Asa	2	2	3		
Cleavland, Jesse	2	3	5		
Wilson, Andrew	2	3	5		
Barret, Jonathan	2	3	4		
Farnam, James	2	3	4		
Farnam, Daniel	1	1	3		
Farnam, Eleazr	1		5		
Sprague, Danl	3	1	5		
Spalding, Davis	3	1	9		
Spalding, Nathl	2	1	3		
Wright, Saml	2		4		
Grover, Jonathan	3	1	5		
Reynolds, Alexander	2	2	2		
Leavens, Isaac	2	1	4		
Reynolds, Elisha	1	2	5		
Spalding, Simon	3	5	4		
Hutchins, Isaac	1	3	6		
Spalding, Zadock	1	4	4	2	
Danielson, James	2	2	2		
Fasset, Ruben	1	2	2		
Hutchins, Zadock	2	1	5		
Hutchins, Penuel	2	2	1	1	1
Stephens, Cypian	1		3		
Stearns, Elias	1	3	3		
Stearns, Boaz	1	4	5		
Stearns, Saml	2	1	4		
Davis, Barnabas	1	2	6		
Key, Wilson	1	1	2		
Key, Nathl	2	2	3		
Reynolds, John	1		1		
Reynolds, David	1	1	4		
Dixon, James	2	4	6		
Danielson, William	1		3		1
Dixon, Thomas	1	4	4		
Cundal, William	2	3	4		
Cheamberlin, Benjamin	2	2	1		
Hall, Thomas	1		2		
Bushee, Jonn	1	4	2		
Young, Caleb	1		4		
Danielson, Samuel	3	1	5	5	3
Robinson, Isaiah	1	4	5		
Day, Thomas	1	3	2	1	
Coller, Joseph	1		2		
William, Eleazr	2		1		
Fisher, John	2	4	3		
Green, Nathl	2		3		
Fuller, Peter				4	
Biggs, Adam			3		
Wheaton, Simon	1	1	5		
Fuller, John	3	3	2		1
Whiting, Cornelius	1	2	2		
Hulet, Allim	3	1	4		
Hulet, David	2	4	6		
Youngs, Othoniel	2	4	5		
Hulet, Mehitable			5		
Baker, Jonathan	1	2	2		
Davis, Gyas	1	3	1		
Petingall, Nathl	1		4		
Mitchell, Jothn	1		3		
Bassett, Isaac	2	2	3		
Warren, Ephraim	3	1	4		
Brewster, Nathl	1	2	5		
Clavland, Jacob	1	1	2		
Slater, Jeremiah			3		
Simmons, Benjn	3	3	3		
Young, Ezekel	1	2	3		

WINDHAM COUNTY—Continued.

KILLINGLEY TOWN—con.

NAME OF HEAD OF FAMILY.	Free white males of 16 years and upward, including heads of families.	Free white males under 16 years.	Free white females, including heads of families.	All other free persons.	Slaves.
Graves, Whitney	1		7		
Hicks, David	1	1	2		
Hopkins, Jenks	1	1	2		
Adams, Abel	3	3	9		
Slater, Abraham, Senr	2		3		
Slater, Abraham, Jnr	1	1	3		
Mattison, Royall	1	1	2		
Young, Joel	1	2	4		
Page, James	2		3		
Baker, Jonas	1	4	4		
Baker, Nathan	1	3	3		
Baker, Thomas	1		2		
Russell, John	3	3	2		
Baker, Joel	1	2	2		
Moffat, Mathew	1	6	2		
Spearks, Saml	2	2	3		
Moffat, Andrew	1	1	5		
Spearks, John	1	3	4		
Martin, John, Jnr	1	2	2		
Graves, Isachar	1	5	2		
Martin, John	1	1	2		
Tarbox, Caleb	1	1	1		
Woodcock Israel	1		5		
Hulet, Oliver	3	1	4		
Carey, Benjn	1	4	2		
Baker, Saml	1		2		
Kingsbury, Saml	1	3	2		
Jowls, John	1	2	2		
Short, Siloam	3	1	7		
Eaton, John & co	2	1	6		
Foster, Weaver	1	1	2		
Cady, David	1	3	3		
Day, Noah	1	3	5		
Eaton, Timothy	3		3		
Weaver, Constant	1	4	2		
Day, Jonathan	2	1	5		
Knight, David	1	1	2		
Cady, Joseph	2		1		
Dailey, Field	2		4		
Burlington, Benjn	1	1	2		
Day, Jonathan	1		1		
Whitney, Asa	1	1	2		
Day, Abner	1	3	3		
Bush, John	2	1	4		
Parks, Isaac	1	3	2		
Day, David	1	2	2		
Burlingham, Edmond	1	1	2		
Moffat, John	1	3	3		
Moffat, John, Jnr	1	3	2		
Day, Levi	1	3	2		
Smith, Elisha	2	6	4		
Day, Jonathan, Jnr	2	3	2		
Burlington, Hopkins	1	3	2		
Barrows, William	1	4	3		
Barrows, Thomas	1	2	4		
Bennet, Joseph	2		1		
Harridon, Benjamin	1	2	5		
Preston, Danl	1	2	4		
Twogood, Saml	1	1	2		
Pooler, Allen	2		2		
Adams, Abijah	3	1	3		
Whitney, Matthias	1	3	4		
Randall, James	1	2	3		
Sharp, Reubin & co	2		5		
Warker, Comfort	1	1	4		
Pidge, John	2	1	4		
Alswerth, John	1	2	3		
Owens, Josiah	4		7		
Cooper, Peter	2		2		
Durfee, John	1	1	4		
Anderson, Saml	1	3	3		
Eames, Saml	1	5	4		
Bates, Oliver	2		2		
Bowen, James	1	1	2		
Spalding, Silas	1	3	3		
Dexter, Andrew	2	1	4		
Day, Israel	1	4	3		
Day, Comfort	1	1	4		
Whitney, Jona	1	2	3		
Short, Seth	1		3		
Rude, Isaac	1	2	1		
Rude, Jacob	1	1	4		
Slack, Joseph	1	1	4		
Slack, William	2		2		
Winter, Nathan	2		3		
Day, Elias	1	4	2		
Dexter, Phillip	1	1	2		
Howard, Joseph	2	1	5		
Day, John	1	2	6		
Warren, Isaac	2	3	2		
Sanders, Prudence A			1		1
Boyden, Elham	3	2	2		
Selden, Caleb	2	4	2		
Allen, Caleb	3	3	5		
Allen, Thaddeus	1		2		

KILLINGLEY TOWN—con.

NAME OF HEAD OF FAMILY.	Free white males of 16 years and upward, including heads of families.	Free white males under 16 years.	Free white females, including heads of families.	All other free persons.	Slaves.
Whittemore, Joshua	2	2	5		
Weaver, Timothy	2	3	6		
Bordon, John	1		1		
Buck, Aaron	1	3	3		
Day, David	3	1	4		
Carder, John	2	3	5		
Mays, Ephraim	1	2	2		
Bassitt, John	4	1	3		
Whittemore, Danl	1	2	4		
Kinsbury, Jeduthan	3		5		
Russell, David	3		2		
Starkweather, Elijah	3		5		
Whitmore, Pearley	1	1	4		
Cady, Isaiah	3	1	5		
Mitchell, Zebudiah	1	1	1		
Warren, Eleazr, Jnr	2	5	3		
Coman, Stephen	1	1	3		
Hopkins, Charles	2	1	4		
Warren, Eleazr	4	1	3		
Warren, Ephraim	3	1	4		
Jurdon, Martin	1	1	1		
Cook, Stephen	1	2	1		
Fisher, Barzillia	3	1	4		
Dexter, Joseph	2	1	4		
Stevens, Oliver	2	1	2		
Aldridge, Abner	1	1	2		
Eames, Mack	2		3		
Lawrence, Elihu	2	1	4		
Lawrence, John	1		2		
Leach, Ebenr	2	1	4		
Bigford, Thomas	1	1	5		
Tucker, Richard	3	1	3		
Burges, William	1		2		
Burges, Thomas	2	2	5		
Bullock, Danl	1	1	3		
Chase, Edward	1	5	2		
Chase, David	2		2		
Chase, Oliver &c	3	3	8		
Campbell, Sylvanus	1	3	2		
Brown, Andrew	2	2	2		
Bartlet, Richard	4	1	4		
Mason, Pellatiah	3	3	7		
Whitney, Saml	1	2	2		
Mitchell, Ezekiel	1	1	2		
Campbell, William	1		1		
Cape, Demas					6
Tucker, Timothy	2	2	1		
Talbert, Benjamin	1	1	6		
Prague, Joseph	1	3	1		
Brown, Isaiah	1	4	2		
Horton, Jotham	2	4	2		
Brown, Stephen	2	4	4		
Wheelock, Saml	1		1		
Durfee, William	5		6		
Hopkins, Richard	1	1	3		
Turtels, Benjamin	2	1	4		
Bateman, Benjamin	2	3	5		
Aldridge, Levi	2	4	3		
Carpenter, Lou	3	3	3		
Smith, Joseph	1		1		
Laws, David	2	2	3		
Brown, Nathl	1		1		
Brown, Zachu	2	2	4		
Brown, Josiah &c	2	1	2		
Ferrows, Benjamin	1	3	5		
Covill, Ebenr	2	3	5		
Smith, John, Senr	1		3		
Herrington, Jonathan	3	1	3		
Herrington, Jona, Jnr	1		1		
Cutlar, Isaac	1	2	2		
Herrington, John	1	1	2		
Herrington, Othniel	1		1		
Smith, John	1	1	1		
Smith, Heza	1	1	5		
Cutlar, Roberd	1	2	5		
Corban, Elipht	1	2	3		
Babbet, Edward	3		2		
Beston, William	1	5	4		
Cady, Joseph	4	3	5		
Covil, Daniel &c	5		2		
Fisk, Ephraim	3	4	6		
Herrington, Jeremiah	2	1	2		
Bowen, Oliver	1	3	4		
Bartlet, Edward	1	1	5		
Collins, Richard	4		2		
Whitmore, Benjn	1	2	3		
Moffet, Eleazr	3		2		
Converse, Eleazr	1	2	5		
Leach, William	2	2	7		
Hull, Thomas	1	1	1		
Wilson, Ebenr	4		3		
Hartwell, Nathaniel	1		2		
Talbert, Jared	2	2	5		
Salsbury, Gilbert	2	5	4		
Covill, Saml	1	2	5		

KILLINGLEY TOWN—con.

NAME OF HEAD OF FAMILY.	Free white males of 16 years and upward, including heads of families.	Free white males under 16 years.	Free white females, including heads of families.	All other free persons.	Slaves.
Grow, Nathl	1	2	4		
Learned, James, Jnr	1	1	1		
Perry, Sylvanus	2	2	5		
Brooks, John	1		2		
Carpenter, Oliver	1	3	3		
Torrey, Anne	1	3	1		
Hawkins, Uriah	1	4	1		
Adams, Edward	1	2	2		
Learned, Theophilus	1	2	3		
Leavins, Rowland	2	3	5		
Key, Daniel	1	3	3		
Levins, Elisabeth	1	1	4		
Levins, Benjn	1		3		
Buck, Samuel, Jnr	1	2	3		
Howe, Isaac Cady	1	4	4		
Brown, David	1	2	2		
Wheaton, Resolved	2		5		
Whipple, Jesse	3	4	3		
Buck, Jonathan	1		1		
Buck, David	1		1		
Brown, Othniel	1	2	3		1
Waterman, Gideon	2				
Adams, Joseph	1	3	1		
Falshaw, John	6		6		
Deane, Ezra	3	2	4		
Peirce, William	2	3	2		
Cutlar, Ephraim	2		7		
Coop, David	2	2	3	1	
Howe, Sampson	2	5	5		
Atkins, Elisha	1	2	5		
Buck, David	3	1	3		
Learned, James	1	2	2		
Buck, Daniel	1		1		
Cady, Joseph	4	1	2		
Cady, Jonathan	3		4		
Kent, George	1	1	4		
Buck, Reuben	1	1	3		
Miles, Eleazer	1	1	1		
Buck, Samuel	3		2		
Spalding, Obedh	2	3	5		
Converse, Jesse	1		1		
Bishop, Parker	1	1	3		
Cutlar, Benjamin	2	3	7		
Johnson, Resolved	1	1	2		1
Torrey, Oliver	3	1	3		
Torrey, Hubard	3		2		
Torrey, Joseph	2		3		
Warner, Benjamin	4	1	6		
Converse, Jonathan	1	2	2		
Graves, John	2	4	4		
Wallin, Cornelious	3	1	5		
Cutlar, Peter	3	3	4		
Reynolds, David	1	1	3		
Brown, Nebudiah	4	3	8		
Babbet, Edward, Jnr	1		3		
Green, Edward	1	2	5		
Bowen, Eleazr	1	2	3		
Cutlar, Azariah	3	3	6		
Cutlar, David	1	2	2		
Leonard, Enoch	1		2		
Johnson, Aholiab	1	1	4		

LEBANON TOWN.

NAME OF HEAD OF FAMILY.	Free white males of 16 years and upward, including heads of families.	Free white males under 16 years.	Free white females, including heads of families.	All other free persons.	Slaves.
Kennie, Nathan	2	2	6		
Kasson, Joseph	1	4	3		
Brooks, Isaac	2		5		
Ford, Abraham	1		3		
Badcock, Nathan	2	3	1		
Seabury, Saml	2	1	2		
Manning, John	1	3	2		
House, John	3	5	7		
Avery, Joseph	3	4	5		
Payne, Joseph	2	2	6		
Payne, Joel	1	1	1		
Badger, Abner	1	4	2		
Clark, James				2	
Sprague, Benjn	1	2	4		1
Perkins, John	1	1	1		
Perkins, Thos	3	6	4		
Cook, John	2	1	2		
Wheeler, William	1	2	1		
Perkins, Saml	1	3	3		
Fitch, Jabez	3		3		
Dagget, John	2	1	2		
Hutchinson, Eleazr, Jnr	1	2	1		
Simms, William	4	1	6		
Hutchinson, Eleazr	3	1	4		
Hutchinson, Eleazr, 3d	2	1	2		
Reed, Danl	3	3	5		
Bill, Elisha	3	3	6		
Hutchinson, Saml	3	1	4		
White, Aaron	1		1		
Hebard, Lindon	1		1		
Deman, John	2		2		

WINDHAM COUNTY—Continued.

LEBANON TOWN—con.

NAME OF HEAD OF FAMILY.	Free white males of 16 years and upward, including heads of families.	Free white males under 16 years.	Free white females, including heads of families.	All other free persons.	Slaves.
Loomis, Asa	1	1	1		
Dunham, Daniel	2	3	8		
Little, Gamaliel	1	3	7		
Linkon, Abijah	4		1		
Barker, Priscilla	2	2	4		
Mason, Elijah, Senr	1	1	1		28
Throope, Dan	1	2	4		
Throope, Joseph	1	4	2		
Throope, Benjamin	1	3	4		
Payne, Seth	2	4	6		
Payne, Stephen	3	2	3		
Tisdale, Elijah	7	4	7		
Hutchinson, Daniel	1	1	1		
Hatch, Samuel	3	2	4		
Hunt, Walter	1	1	4		
Champion, Salmon	3	3	5		
Phelps, David	2	1	3		
Payne, Stephen, Jur	3	3	7		
Badcock, Elijah	2	3	4		
Lathrop, Zebulon	3	2	4		
Johnson, John, Jur	2	1	6		
Johnson, John	1		1		1
Snow, Abraham	1		1		
Payne, Benjn	2	2	4		
Badcock, Abijah	2	2	7		
Seabury, Abigal			4		
Stearkweather, Nathan	4		2		
Williams, George	5	5	5		
Payne, Benjamin, Jnr	1	1	2		
Bliss, Amos	3	1	8		
Tisdale, Eliphalet	1		2		
Turner, Mary	1	1	4		
Gross, Saml	1	2	3		
Tisdale, Ebenezr	1		3		
Hyde, Moses	3	1	4		
Williams, Honr William	2	2	4	2	
Trumbull, David	4	3	7		
Williams, Thomas	3	3	4		
Ely, Zebulon	1	2	4	1	
Huntington, William	2	1	3		1
Hyde, Elijah	3	2	6		
Abell, Caleb	2	1	6		
Medcalf, Eliphalet	1	3	5		
Medcalf, David	2	2	7		
Fitch, Andrew	1	3	2		
Huntington, William	5		2	1	
Brewster, Comfort	3	1	5		
Lovegrove, Edward	1	1	4		
Huntington, Oliver	3	3	5		
Beamon, Samuel	1	2	6		
Hyde, Elijah, Senior	1	1	3		
Russ, Jehiel	1	2	6		
Fitch, Ichabod	2	3	8		2
Hyde, Benjamin	3	3	5		
Mason, James F	2	1	3		
Waterman, Simeon	2	3	6		
Hyde, Samuel	4	2	7	1	
Little, William	4	1	7		
Pettiss, James	2	3	3	6	
Medcalf, Jabez	4	3	6	1	
Medcalf, Abigal			6	1	2
Medcalf, Zebulon	3		4		
Medcalf, Peter	1	1	2		
Alden, William	1	1	2		
Huntington, Andrew	1	4	4		
Lisk, Andrew	2	1	4		
Chappel, Oliver	1	3	5		
Flint, Martha		1	3		
McCawl, John	2	2	2		
Fitch, Abraham	3		4		
Loomis, Joseph	4	3	3		
Palmer, Nehemiah	2		2		
Bissell, Daniel	3	3	7		
Bewel, Abel	1		2		
Bewel, Josiah	1	2	5		
Bewel, William	1	1	6		
Palmer, Jabez	1	1	2		
Hyde, Daniel	1	2	5		
Brown, Sarah			2		1
Clark, James	4	2	7		
Williams, Isaac	2	4	4		
Williams, Vitch	2	1	4		
Bissell, Joseph W	4	2	4		1
Wattles, Oliver	2		9		
McCawl, Green	1	1	2		
Brown, John	2	2	4		2
Williams, Fredrick	1	2	2		
McCawl, Ozias	1	4	3		
Williams, Jonath	4		3		
Fowler, Adonijah	2	3	6	1	
Medcalf, Andrew	1		3	1	
Harris, Phillip	2	3	3		
Whitely, John	1	2	3		
Fowler, John	2		4		

LEBANON TOWN—con.

NAME OF HEAD OF FAMILY.	Free white males of 16 years and upward, including heads of families.	Free white males under 16 years.	Free white females, including heads of families.	All other free persons.	Slaves.
Lee, Solomon	1	3	3		
Waterman, Andrew	3	1	3		
Yeomans, Daniel	2	4	4		
Polly, Joshua	1		2		
Wattles, Joshua	1	4	1		
Badger, Abigal			3		
Jones, Daniel	1		4		
Ingraham, Daniel	3	1	5		
Bolls, Asa	3		7		
McCaul, Archs	3		2		1
Thomas, Elihu	1	1	7		
Hill, Phillip	2		1		
Wattles, Thos	1	2	4		
Fitch, Nathan	2		1		
Hunt, Jonath	1	3	5		
Wattles, Mason	2		1		
Wattles, Charles	1	2	5		
Thomas, Amos, Jnr	1	2	2		
Wattles, Belcher	1	2	3		
Wattles, Daniel	3	3	4		
Alden, Andrew	1		2		
Rogers, Nathanl, Senr	1	2	1		
Frink, William	5		8		
Medcalf, Ebenezr	3	2	4		
Capills, Thomas, & Josiah Rogers	2	1	4		
Lamphear, Elijah	2	2	2		
Coleman, John	2		2		
Harrison, Silas	1	3	4		
Coleman, John, Jnr	1	2	1		
Coleman, Jason	1	2	4		
Carter, James	2		2		
Dilla, Riva	1	3	8		
Waters, Aaron	3	3	3	1	
Miners, David	1	4	4		
Lee, Israel, Jnr	1	3	5		
Lee, Israel, Senr	2	3	3		
Mason, Jeremiah	4		4	1	2
Learned, Joseph	1		4		
Kingsley, Timoy	2		3		
Kingsley, Nathanl	1	2	6		
Payne, John	1	1	4		
Stark, Abiel	1	2	5		
Steark, Nathan	2	3	4		
Rogers, Jeremiah	1	2	3		
Lathrop, James	1	1	2		
McKensey, George	1	2	4		
Lathrop, Charles	2	3	4		
Lathrop, Abiel	1	1	6		
Thomas, Amos	2	4	8	1	1
Thomas, Abijah	4	2	4		
Hyde, William	2	5	4		
Bigelow, Otis	2	5	3		
Abel, Simon	2	2	5		
Bartlet, Chandler	1	3	5		
Bartlet, Judah	1	4	5		
Capells, John	2	3	5		
Thorp, Aaron	3	4	7		
Bartlet, Ichabod	2	3	3		1
Jordon, Asa	1	3	3		
Steark, Joshua	3	2	4		
Hobbs, Edmond	1		1		
Whitman, William	1	2	3		
Gay, Elisha	1	1	1		
Hill, Abner	1		1		
Mantle, Jacob	1	1	2		
Roger, Nathel, Jnr	2	1	5		
Stone, Timothy	4		3	1	
Hinkley, Dyer I	3		6	2	
Hinkley, Jared	4	1	3		
Dutton, Ambrose	1	2	2		
Shapley, John	1	3	2		
Bewel, Oliver	4		6		
Hinkley, Ebenr	3	1	3		
Thomas, Belcher	2	1	4	1	
Butler, Patk	2	1	3		
West, Ebenezr	4	1	5		
Sumner, Jonath	1	1	4		
Tillotson, Danil	2		4		
Clark, Dan	2	1	5		
Alden, Walter	1		2		
Martin, Anderson	1	2	4		
Smith, Frederick	1	1	1		
Hutchinson, Eleazer	2	1	2		
Hutchinson, Elisha	3	1	3		
Mason, Elijah, Jnr	2	2	4		
Terry, Ephraim	4	3	5		
Terry, Saml	1		2		
Coye, Joseph	1		2		
Webster, Josiah	3	1	4		
Smith, Jacob	1		3		
Smith, Elijah	1		2		
Bemount, Isaiah	1	1	4		
Smith, Abijah	3	1	2		
Bacon, Ebenezr	1	1	3		

LEBANON TOWN—con.

NAME OF HEAD OF FAMILY.	Free white males of 16 years and upward, including heads of families.	Free white males under 16 years.	Free white females, including heads of families.	All other free persons.	Slaves.
Howard, Caleb	2		2		
Loomis, Eleazr	1	2	4		
Waterman, Joseph	2	3	1		
Hyde, Zebediah	1	4	2	1	
Barber, Jeremiah	1	4	3		
Stearkweather, Nathl	1	1	6		
Dutton, Ebenr	2	1	3		
Abel, Joseph	1	2	7		
Southward, Beriah	3		5		
Leach, Joseph	4	1	4		
Lyman, Jonath	3	1	3		
Thomas, James	2	2	3		
Lyman, William	3	2	5		
Porter, Nathl	2		3	1	
Bushnell, Ebenezr	3	4	3		
Trumbull, Jonathan	1	1	5	2	
Robinson, Ichabod	2	1	3		3
Wood, Josiah	1	1	6		
Wattles, Denison	1	2	2	1	
Fitch, Isaac	1		3		
Taintor, John	1	1	4	1	
White, Enoch	2	3	3		1
Lisk, Ebenezr	1		5		
Gay, Asael	2	1	4		
Crowel, Ebenr	2	1	3		
Clark, John	2		3		1
Rockwill, Jonah	4	3	6		
Young, David	4	2	4		
Green, Robert	1		2		
Lyman, Jabez	1		3		
Strong, Oliver	2	1	2		
Payne, Dan	1	1	7		
Chappel, Caleb	1	1	6		
Strong, Daniel, Jnr	4	2	7		
Bozworth, Ichabod	1	2	4		
Strong, Daniel	3	1	3		
Loomiss, Thomas	2	2	6		
William, William, Jnr	2	2	3		
Clark, Jacob	1	1	1		
Clark, Jerom	3	1	3		
Loomiss, Thomas, Jnr	2	3	3		
Bartlet, John	3	3	4		
Brewster, Benjamin	3		2	2	1
Hall, Christopher	1	2	1		
Clark, Jonathan	1		4		
Williams, Jehiel	3	4	3		
Wilcox, Ephraim	1	1	4		
Clark, Andrew	1	1	2		
Clark, Nathan	1	1	3		
Clark, Silas	5		3		
Chappel, Amaziah	1	3	4		
Bliss, Ezra	4		1		
Hyde, Oliver	1		6		
Bill, Jonath	1	1	3		
Clark, Jared	3	1	4		
Clark, Daniel	3		5		
Abell, Solomon	2	2	6		
Abell, Elipht	1	2	2		
Abel, Danl	2	1	2		
Abel, Elijah	2	3	4		
Gurley, John	2	2	3		
Green, Robert	1		2		
Woodworth, Walter	2		2		
White, Sylvanus	2	1	4		
Dewey, Barzeliel	1	2	1		
Doubleday, Elisha	1	2	5		
Doubleday, Jesse	1	1	5		
Marsh, Anne	1		4		
Payne, Dan	1		2		
Williams, John	1		2		
McCaul, Roger	2	1	2		
Williams, William, 3d	2	3	4		
Williams, Charles	4	2	4		
Bascomb, William	2		4		
Cole, Jonathn	1	1	2		
Richardson, Humphrey	1		2		
Fuller, David	1		4		
Porter, Reuben	2	2	6		
Hunt, Saml	2	3	5		
Allen, Jared	1	3	2		
Spencer, Peter	3	5	3		
Williams, Isaiah	1	2	5		
Williams, Simon	4	1	7		
Stiles, Benjamin	2	2	4		
Palmer, Amos	1	2	4		
Cuningham, Peleg	1	1	2		
McCaul, Holbart	2	3	3	1	1
Bristol (Negro)				3	
Jeffords, Robin				5	
Bewel, Isaac	1	2	3		
Clark, Moses	1	2	3		
West, David	1	2	2		
Haynes, Daniel	1	3	4		
Haynes, Sylvester	1		4	1	
Bliss, Peltiah	1	1	3		

WINDHAM COUNTY—Continued.

LEBANON TOWN—con.

NAME OF HEAD OF FAMILY.	Free white males of 16 years and upward, including heads of families.	Free white males under 16 years.	Free white females, including heads of families.	All other free persons.	Slaves.
Tyler, Danl	4	1	4		
Clark, Roswell	1	2	4		
Wright, Mehitable	1	1	4		
Clark, Ambrose	1	2	1		
Coleman, Noah	2	4	3		
Williams, Ambrose	1	1	2		
Watrous, Jonath	1	1	3		
William, Israel	2	1	3		
Medcalf, Levi	1	4	3		
Bell, Oliver	6	2	9		
Medcalf, Reuben	2	1	3		
Brewster, Ichabod	3	3	6		
Wilcox, Abraham	1	3	3		
Bill, Abial	1	3	2		
Porter, Laton	1	1	4		
West, Levi	1	1	3		
Bascomb, Abial	1	1	5		
Spafford, Nathan	2	3	5		
West, Amos	1		1		
Webster, Zurvey	1	1	3		
Lamb, Rufus	2	1	5		
Harriss, Phillip	1	1	3		
Marsh, Dan	2	3	3		
Webster, Ruth	3	3	9		
Cuff (Wido.)				4	
Webster, James	2	4	9		
Bissell, Benjamin	1	3	2		
Bissell, Partridge	1	1	2		
Bissell, Joseph F	1		2		
Finney, Joseph	1	2	2		
Hill, Consider, Senr	3	1	4		
Hill, Darious	2	1	2		
Pryor, Azarior	3		6		1
Case, Levi	2	1	6		
Antrim, Francis	1	4	5		
Ward, William	1		4		
Calkins, Solomon	3		2		
Crocker, Simon	3		4		
Crocker, Adonijah	2	1	4		
Woodworth, Jeremiah	1	1	2		
Wills, Eleazr	1	3	1		
Clarck, Saml	1	2	5		
Smith, Elijah	1		4		
Tilden, Daniel	5	1	8		
Mason, James	1	3	8		
Snow, Francis	3	4	4		
Fitch, Ammi	3	2	3		
Seabury, Saml, Jnr		1	2		
Murdock, William	2	2	7		
Hovey, Nathan	1	2	2		
Swift, Rowland, Jnr	1	1	4		
Cheevers, Nathan	2	3	4		
Swift, Rowland	4	2	6		
Goodin, William	1	1	4		
Goodwin, Johnath	2	1	2		
Clark, Abigal	2	1	4		
Bailey, Elisha	2	1	2		
Ford, Jacob	1		2		
Davis, Lathrop	2	3	3		
Swift, William	2		1		
Thatcher, Abigal			2		
Bayley, Sexton	4	1	3		
Swift, Charles	3	4	6		
Kingsley, Oliver	3	1	2		
Kingsley, Asael	1	2	1		
Brooks, Thomas	1	1	2		
Newcomb, Jesse	1	5	3		
Newcomb, John	2	3	3		
Clark, Jonath	2	1	5		
Collins, Rufus	3	1	3		
Dewey, Abraham, Senr	2	1	4		
Dewey, Abraham, Jnr	1		2		
Collins, Eleazr	1	3	5		
Collins, Rufus, Jnr	1	4	4		
Kingsley, Timo	1		3		
Gillet, Isaac	2	4	3		
Beamont, William	1		2		
Beamont, Dan	1	2	2		
Scovil, Elizebith	2	1	4		
Hebard, Luther	1		1		
Hill, James	1		5		
Thatcher, Benjn	5		5		
Dingley, John	1		5		
Carpenter, Dan	1		3		
Carpenter, Paul	1	1	1		
Dewey, Solomon	1	2	3		
Fuller, Saml	1		2		
Fuller, Bezl	5	2	3		
Fuller, Abiaal	3	3	3		
Tickner, James	1		3		
Dewey, Israel	2	1	3		
Maxwill, John	2	2	3		
Dewey, Eliphalet	1		2		
Buckingham, Jedediah	5		2		
Buckingham, Thomas	1	1	5		

LEBANON TOWN—con.

NAME OF HEAD OF FAMILY.	Free white males of 16 years and upward, including heads of families.	Free white males under 16 years.	Free white females, including heads of families.	All other free persons.	Slaves.
Hill, Joseph	2	3	3		
Newcomb, Joseph	1	2	4		
Clark, David	3	3	7		
Allen, Joshua	3	2	6		
Hunt, Elijah	2	2	7		
Allen, Saml	2		4		
Hartshorne, Ezekel	2	2	5		
Woodworth, Ebenezr	1		3		
Woodworth, Elipht	4	4	8		
Fitch, Nathl	2	4	4		
Hunt, Eldad	2	5	2		
Brewster, Wadsworth	3	3	6		
Lyman, William	2		3		
Kingsbury, Asa	1	2	1		
Badcock, Amos	1	3	4		
Thomson, Saml	1	4	5		
Loomis, Nathan	1	2	5		
Manley, Sylvester	1	3	2		
Baxter, William	2	1	4		
Woodward, Israel	1		1		
Woodward, Eleazr	2	4	3		
Woodward, Israel, Jnr	3	2	4		
Gary, Thadeus	1		4		
Woodworth, Swift	1	3	4		
Lyman, Benjn	1	3	5		
Gary, Seth	1		1		
Garey, Elijah	1		2		
Tickner, Isaac	3	4	2		
Bliss, Henry	2	1	6		
Little, John	1	4	3		
Little, Gamaliel	2	2	7		
Wright, Jabez	1	1	2		
Wright, Jeriah	1	4	3		
Chapman, James	1		2		
Little, John	2	4	3		
Wood, Benjn	2		2		
Bliss, Saml	2	1	5		
Loomis, Simon	4	2	4		1
Clark, Simon	1	1	3		
Clark, Asael	2	4	5		
Clark, Flavel	1	1	2		
Brockway, Thomas	2	2	9		2
Leamphear, Jabez	1	1	4		
Barker, Saml	1		2		
Bill, Thomas	2		3		
Loomis, Joel	1	3	3		
Woodworth, James	3	1	5		
Guild, Saml	1	2	5		
Huntington, David	1	2	4		
Hunt, Eldad	2	5	4		
Dunham, Hannah			3		
Lyman, Jesse	4		4		
Bounce, Aaron	1	2	3		
Abbot, James	2	3	5		
Strong, David, Jnr	1		2		
Fish, Saml	2	1	4		
Helms, Christopher	1	1	4		
Newcomb, Paul	2	6	4		
Strong, David	2		4		
Sprague, Dan	2	1	3		
Crocker, James	1		2		
Gary, Eneas	1	2	2		
Nye, Silas	1		1		
Hyde, Nathl, Jnr	1	1	7		
Richardson, James	1	1	5		
Bennet, Hinchman	3		7		
Richardson, Eleazr	2	2	4		
Wright, Charles	1	2	5		
Hyde, Nathl, Senr	2		1		
Bennet, Simon	1		4		
Payne, James	1	3	2		
Marble, John	1	4	4		
Gary, Gilbert	2	3	4		
Garey, Ebenezr	2	2	6		
Woodworth, Jehiel	1	1	2		
Stearns, Roswill	2	3	4		
English, Abiel	1	2	4		
Woodworth, Lebens	3		3		
Treadaway, David	1	1	4		
Little, Gamaliel, Jnr	2	2	1		
Finney, David	3	1	4		
Prince, Abijah				3	
Yeomans, Giles	3		5		1
Sweatland, Jonah	1	4	5		
Treadaway, William	2	3	4		
Rude, Jeremiah	3	2	5		
Brown, Azariah	1		7		
White, Nathl	2	2	4		
West, Saml	2	1	8		
Phelps, Joseph	3	3	5		
Newcomb, Bethewel	2	4	10		
Post, Pheneas	1	5	5		
Thomas, Daniel	1	4	3		
Gates, Zebulon	1	1	3		
Chapman, Joshua	1	4	2		

LEBANON TOWN—con.

NAME OF HEAD OF FAMILY.	Free white males of 16 years and upward, including heads of families.	Free white males under 16 years.	Free white females, including heads of families.	All other free persons.	Slaves.
Beston, Joseph	1	1	2		
Cole, David	3	1	4		
Bliss, Elias	1		1		
Chappel, Elijah	1		5		
Sulard, Joseph	2	1	5		
Beston, Saml	1	1	4		
Pinney, James	4	2	6		
Loomis, Ezra	1		1		
Porter, Abraham	1	1	4		
Porter, Elikm	1	4	3		
Hoolbrook, John	1	4	3		
Brewster, Experience			4		
Bissell, Elisha	3	1	4		
Hunt, Joseph	3	2	7		
Thomas, Elipht	1	1	3		
Hoolbrook, Abel	2		3		
Brewster, Saml	1	2	1		
Porter, John	2	2	3		
Bennet, Robert	3		1		
Bliss, Zenas	1	1	1		
Loomiss, Joseph	2	1	2		
Wright, Joel	1	2	3		
Williams, John, Jnr	1	4	2		
Loomiss, Benoni	1	3	5		
Buckingham, William	1		2		
Williams, John	2	4	3		
Little, Consider	2	3	9		
Abel, Jonath	2	2	4		
Backus, Whiting	2	3	7		
Bailey, Isaac, Jnr	5	1	6		
Bailey, Isaac	2	2	3		
Medcalf, Saml	2	2	4		
Dewey, Elipht	1	2	3		
Gross, Simon	2	2	4		
Gillet, Isaac		5	3		
Gillet, Mary (Wido.)		1	4		
Gay, Saml	2	3	5		
Loomiss, Ezekiel	2	3	3		
Bliss, Samuel	3	1	6		
Loomiss, Abraham	2	2	4		
Bliss, Joseph	3		4		
Hyde, Nathl	2	1	4		
Lee, Nathan	1		3		
Loomiss, Jacob	1		4		
Goodwin, Saml	1	2	2		
Tilden, Ebenr	1	2	2		
Bailey, Saml, Jnr	2		3		
Brown, Thomas	1	1	2		
Bailey, Saml, Senr	2	2	3		
Clark, John	1		3		
Bettis, James	2		2		
Torrey, Asa	6	1	2		
Groscup, John	1		2		
Hoolbrook, Timoy	2	2	4		
Bailey, James	4	4	6		
Vaughn, Martha			2		
Dewey, John	1	1	4		
Loomis, Israel, Jnr	3	2	5		
Dewey, Danl	2	3	4		
Loomis, Simon	2	2	1		
Dewey, Woodward	2		2		
Hill, Ephraim		1	3		
Loomiss, Israel	1	3	7		
Loomiss, John	1	4	5		
Arnold, John	2	3	5		
Lyman, Fredrick	1		2		
Tiffeny, Recompense	1		2		
Syms, George	2	1	2		
Manning, Eleazr	1	1	3		

MANSFIELD TOWN.

NAME OF HEAD OF FAMILY.	Free white males of 16 years and upward, including heads of families.	Free white males under 16 years.	Free white females, including heads of families.	All other free persons.	Slaves.
Chaplin, Benjn	6	2	3		3
Storrs, John	2	1	2		
Lyon, Chester	1	2	2		
Mopley, Nathl	2	2	4		
Robins, Solomon	2	3	3		
Preston, Danl	2	2	3		
Edgerton, Abel	1		2		
Butler, Danl	2	2	2		
Williams, Lucretia		2	2		
Edgerton, David	1		2		
Edgerton, John	1	1	2		
Hartshorne, Andrew	2	1	1		
Phelps, Moses	2	3	4		
Storrs, Judah	3		5		1
Carey, Ebenr	3	2	5		
Clark, James	1	1	6		
Clark, Oliver	1	2	3		
Clark, Israel	4		4		
Clark, Lemuel	5		6		
Rust, Eunice	2	1	7		
Huntington, Whitman	3		2		
Clark, Nathan	2	2	1		
Gates, Susanna		1	4		

WINDHAM COUNTY—Continued.

MANSFIELD TOWN—con.

NAME OF HEAD OF FAMILY.	Free white males of 16 years and upward, including heads of families.	Free white males under 16 years.	Free white females, including heads of families.	All other free persons.	Slaves.
Owen, Timothy	3		1		
Tracy, Israel	1	4	4		
Stoel, Josiel	2	3	5		
Southward, Nathl	1	3	4		
Abbe, Solomon	2	1	2		
Curtiss, Mary			3		
Smith, Uriah	2	1	2		
Booth, Henry	1		3		
Balch, Vivian	1		2		
Balch, Israel	2	3	3		
Church, Abner	2	1	1		
Linkon, Lemuel	1	2	2		
Thompson, Jared	5		2		
Swift, Barzillia	3	4	4		
Bingham, Oliver	1	2	3		
Cushman, Joab	1		2		
Abbe, Nathan	1		2		
Hovey, Jonath	2	2	2		
Tilden, Ithamar	3	2	2		
Parker, Ephraim	3	1	4		
King, John	3		3		
Badger, Jonathn	1	4	3		
Porter, Saml	1	1	2		
Ainy, Ambrose	1		2		
Hartshorne, Joseph	1	2	6		
Stutson, Anne	1		3		
Bingham, Eleazr	3	2	5		
Stearkweather, Joel	2		3	1	
Keaton, ——	1		3		
Allen, Heza	3		4		
Ross, Ebenezr	2	3	3		
Trumbull, Walter	2	1	2		
Bawldin, Ebenezr	3	3	3		
Sessions, Leonard	1	1	2		
Hunt, John	2		2		
Hunt, Joseph	1	1	2		
Raies, Moses	1		1		
Hutchins, Benjn	2	1	2		
Adams, Lucy	2	1	3		1
Southward, Saml	4	2	9		
Martin, Ebenezr	1	5	2		
Stowel, Amasa	1	1	1		
Arnold, John	1		1		
Martin, John	1		2		
Whittemore, Joseph, Jr	1	2	1		
Sergeants, Saml	4	1	6		
Storrs, Mary		1	1		
Hearsay, James	1	2	2		
Southward, Josiah	1	1	6		
Storrs, Experience	3	1	4		
Conant, Eleazr	2	3	4		
Storrs, Dan	3	5	5		
Collins, Benjn	1		3		
Cushman, Isaac	1	1	2		
Aspenwell, Prince	2		4		
Hull, Elias	1	4	2		
Bibbens, Timothy	1	1	1		
Dodge, Edward	2	1	5		
Storrs, Amariah	4	1	4		
Whittemore, Saml	2				
Hartshore, Danl	2	2	4		
Barrows, David	1	4	3		
Abbe, Elijah	1	1	1		
Abbe, Solomon, Jnr	3	2	5		
Abbe, Bathsheba	1		1		
Hall, Josiah	3	1	3		
Campbell, Zuril	3	5	5		
McCaul, Eleazr	2	1	5		
Kidder, James	2	2	2		
Hopkins, Elisha	1	2	1		
Dodge, William	1	4	3		
McCaul, Mary			2		
Kitch, Benjn	1	3	1		
Storrs, Josiah	5	4	8		
Simons, Jonathan	2	1	1		
Calkins, James	1		4		
Conant, Sylvanus	1	3	7		
Freeman, Azariah	2	2	2		
Barrows, Phillip	1	1	3		
McCaul, Elijah	1	1	1		
Atwood, Heman	2	3	3		
Dunham, Elisha	1		3		
Fenton, Ebenr	1	3	1		
Atwood, Thomas	1	1	8		
Atwood, Hannah	1	1	4		
Atwood, Nathl	4	1	5		
Dunham, Bangs	2	3	2		
Philps, Nathl	2	1	4		
Phelps, Joseph	1		2		
Thomson, Joseph	1	1	6		
Fenton, Nathl	1	1	2		
Eaton, Nathl	1		2		
Russell, Benjamin	1	4	2		
Newcomb, Submit			5		
Brown, Jonathan	3	2	2		
Fenton, Rusba		3	2		
Fenton, Joseph	2		3		
Fenton, Ebenezr, Senr	1		1		
Fenton, Jonathan	1		2		
Dexter, Nathan	1	2	1		
Birchard, Joseph	2		4		
Conant, Seth	1	5	1		
Wheaton, Jacob	2	1	3		
Whitmore, Aaron	3	1	4		
Parker, James	1	3	4		
Harriss, Daniel	2	1	9		
Warner, Eleazr	2	2	5		
Bozworth, Nathl	1	2	3		
Barrows, Thomas	2	4	5		
Olcott, John	1	4	2	1	
Swift, John	4	2	4		
Upham, Noah	2	2	3		
Upham, Joseph	1		3		
Swift, Thomas	3	5	5		
Southward, Joseph	2	1	2		
Wood, Saml	2	2	7		
Bugbee, Hannah	1		2		
Jones, Jacob	2	1	3		
Russill, Thomas	1	1	1		
Balch, Henry	1	3	3		
Nichols, Jonathn	4		4		
Allen, Heza	3	1	4		
Huntington, Abner	4	3	7		
Plumb, Daniel	2	2	3		
Crain, Hezekiah	2	3	3		
Conant, Benajh	1		3		
Conant, Shubael	2	1	4		
Salter, Mary	1	1	4		2
Salter, John	3	1	3		
Southward, Constant	2		3		
Trumbull, William	1	1	6		
Campbell, Peter	1	1	2		
Hall, Theophilus	1	4	3		
Nicholls, Lemuel	2	1	3		
Triscatt, Dorathy			3		
Hovey, Jonathn	2	1	7		
Balch, William	1	2	2		
Hodges, Ephram	1	3	4		
Kennedy, Daniel	2	1	4		
Kennedy, Daniel, Jnr	1		1		
Fletcher, Seth	1	3	1		
Turner, Elijah	1	2	3		
Hanks, Benjan	2	3	3		
Fuller, Timothy	1	1	4		
Hanks, Uriah	3	2	3		
Newcomb, Thos	1		3		
Webster, Moses	1	2	5		
Royce, Asa	1	1	4		
Cross, Peter	4	2	4		
Nicholls, Thomas	1	1	2		
Thompson, Isaac	4	1	4		
Freeman, John	1	3	4		
Gurley, Zebulon	1	3	7		
Royce, Byram	1	1	3		
Parker, Zachariah, Jr	1		2		
Parker, Zachh	3		4		
Barrows, Ethan	1	2	3		
Baldwin, Danl	4		3		
Simons, Darious	2	3	3		
Shumway, Joseph	2	3	8		
Newcomb, Bradford	1	3	4		
Royce, Zurel	1	3	2		
Kidder, Nathl	1	1	5		
Eaton, Jacob	2		3		
Eldridge, Elisha	1	1	2		
Gilbert, John	1		3		
Cross, Ruebin	2		1		
Fuller, Timothy	1	1	4		
Parker, Joshua	2	2	4		
Anderson, Lemuel	1		3		
Barrows, Robert	2	3	5		
Sergeants, Isaac, Jnr	1		4		
Howe, Danl	4	1	2		
Storrs, Benjn	2	3	4		
Sergeants, Isaac	2	1	4		
Freeman, Skiff	2	4	5		
Davis, Joseph	2	1	4		
Davis, Elizabeth	1	1	2		
Freeman, Rebecca	1		3		
Baldwin, Joseph	1	3	3		
Dimmick, Lot	3	2	4		
Hovey, Jabez	1	3	4		
Dimmik, Hezah	1	3	1		
Marcy, Benjamin	1	1	3		
Royce, James	2	1	3		
Hovey, Enoch	2	1	2		
Hebard, Eliphaz	1	1	3		
Freeman, Edmond	1		2		
Hosmer, Eunice			3		
Thompson, Saml, Jr	1	1	1		1
Crain, Danl	1	3	4		
Johnson, William	1		2		
Pierce, Enoch	1	2	3		
Royce, David	2	3	2		
Royce, James, Jnr	1	4	3		
Royce, Solomon	1	4	3		
Royce, Phillip	2	2	4		
Bundy, John	2	2	3		
Dimmik, Joseph	1	2	3		
Kidder, Nathl, Senr	1	1	4		
Storrs, Royal	1		4		
Waldo, Jesse	1		3	1	
Waldo, Roger	2		1		
Molton, Asa	2		3		
Royce, David	1		1		
Molton, Mary		1	3		
Hovey, Aaron	3	1	3		
Bicknal, Moses	3	3	7		
Fairwell, Thomas	1	4	3	1	1
Finney, Joseph	1				
Thompson, Saml	3	2	4		
Freeman, Fredrick	2	3	5		
Johnson, William, Jnr	1		2		
Topliff, Calvan	4	2	5		
Peirce, Saml	1		4		
Peirce, Enoch	2		3		
Perin, Seth	3	5	2		
Beardly, Gershom	2	2	5		
Storrs, Cordial	1	2	2		
Calkins, James	2	1	3		
Dexter, Jonath	5	2	8		
Taylor, Joseph	3	1	1		
Russ, Stephen	1	2	3		
Turner, Prince	1	1	5		
Badcock, John	2	1	3		
Williams, Jesse	3	2	6		
Dunham, Jacob	1	2	2		
Peirce, Fred'k, & Jarum Topliff	2	1	2		
Parrish, Abigal	1	1	3		
Dunham, James	1	2	2		
Fuller, Jonathn	1	2	5		
Slater, Eleazr	1	5	5		
Johnson, Joseph	1		3		
Johnson, William, Jnr	1	2	2		
Reed, Nathan	1	1	1		
Evens, Arad	1	1	2		
Welch, Moses Cook	2	3	8		
Allen, Simeon	1	1	3		
Conant, Joseph	2		2		
Conant, Josiah, Jnr	1	3	3	1	
Wood, Timothy	1		1		
Ames, Amos	1	1	3		
Dexter, Silas	1	2	1		
Whitehouse, Thomas	1	1	3		
Cheamberlin, Oliver	2	4	2		
Turner, Saml	2	5	2		
Dimmick, Shubael	8	1	4		
Turner, Stephen	1		3		
Turner, Timothy	1	4	3		
Turner, Pheneas	1	3	4		
Dimmick, Edward	2	1	3		
Cheamberlain, Seth	1		1		
Reed, Amasa	3	2	5		
Barrows, Isaac, 2d	1	2	4		
Stewart, Thomas	1	1	2		
Waldo, Jesse, Senr	2	1	2	1	
Stewart, Saml	1	4	5		
Slater, Saml	1		2		
Badcock, Josiah	3	1	2		
Spafford, Jesse	3	1	3		
Dunham, Danl	3	1	2		
Dimmock, Elipht	1	3	3		
Dimmock, Oliver	2	4	4		
Nicholls, John	1		1		
Dunham, Danl	5		2		
Turner, Isaac	1	5	4		
Dunham, Phebe			3		
Dunham, Jonath	1	2	5		
Tilden, Joshua	2	2	7		
Dunham, Seth	2	2	5		
Medcalf, Ebenezr	5	1	7		
Wood, Timothy	1		1		
Brigham, Stephen	4	2	6		
Williams, Amariah	2	1	7		
Hovey, Joseph	3	3	5		
Utley, Oliver	1	1	4	1	
Wright, Chloe			4		
Willis, Willm			4		
Spafford, Abraham	1	1	2		
King, James	1	3	2		
King, Saml	2		6		
Simons, Elipht	1		2		
Barrows, Thomas	4	1	4		
Barrows, Eleazr	1	2	1		

WINDHAM COUNTY—Continued.

MANSFIELD TOWN—con.

NAME OF HEAD OF FAMILY.	Free white males of 16 years and upward, including heads of families.	Free white males under 16 years.	Free white females, including heads of families.	All other free persons.	Slaves.
Wright, Ebenezr	2	1	4		
Barrows, Jabez	3	2	4		
Abbot, David	1	2	3		
Hanks, Silas	2	1	6		
Beemus, Levi	1	2	1		
Huntington, Jonas	5	2	6		
Bennet, Jesse	1	1	2		
Bennet, Joshua	1		3		
Gurley, Jacob B	5	1	5		
Gurley, Daniel	2	6	2		
Gurley, Saml	3	1	5		
Gurley, Ephraim	2	1	1		
Gurley, Jonathan	2	1	6		
Willis, James	2	2	3		
Willis, Micajah	1	3	2		
Willis, James, Jnr	1	3	5		
Dimmock, Peter	3	1	7		
Turner, Eleazr	1		3		
Dexter, Isaac	2	1	3		
Dexter, Danl	1	1	2		
Craine, Heza	1	1	3		
Craine, Elisha	1	2	4		
Gurley, William	3	3	3		
Dexter, David	1	3	6		
Dunham, John	1	2	7		
Russ, John	1		3		
Wright, Amaziah	1	3	7		
Davis, Jonathn	2	1	3		
Davis, Thomas	3	1	5		
Wright, Eleazr	2	1	6		
Nichall, Saml	1	3	4		
Nichalls, Nathl	1	2	3		
Waters, Jacob	1		2		
Barrows, Solomon	1	3	3		
Bennet, Nathl	2		5		
Storrs, Thos	4	3	6		
Waters, Jacob, Jnr	2	4	4		
Bennet, Nathl, Jnr	1	3	5		
Turner, Phillip	1	3	1		
Cumins, William	1	3	2		
Snow, Ebene	1		3		
Barrows, Lemuel	3	1	4		
Conant, John	2	1	3		
Eldridge, Lemuel	2	4	3		
Barrows, Elisha, Jnr	1	2	3		
Hall, Nathl	1	2	5		
Hall, Gershom	2	1	3		
Barrows, Gershom	2	3	5		
Slate, Ezekel	2	1	6		
Barrows, Jabez	3	1	3		
Hall, James	2	3	5		
Hall, Susanna			2		
Whittemore, Joseph	1	3	2		
Bennet, Asa	1	3	3		
Barrows, Thos, 3d	1	4	3		
Barrows, Jesse	1	1	1		
Hall, Andrew	3	3	6		
Palmer, Nathan	4	1	5		
Nesbit, Nathan	1	1	3		
Barrows, Joshua	1	1	3		
Storrs, Saml	2	2	5		
Storrs, Jehiel	2	2	5		
Barrows, Isaac	2		1		
Bennet, James	1	2	6		
Barrows, Elisha	2	2	4		
Turner, Thomas	1	1	2		
Turner, Stephen	1	3	3		
Turner, Elijah	1		4		
Fitch, Josiah	2	4	6		
Hall, Nathl	4	2	5		
Davisson, Danl	1		2		
Harriss, John	1	2	4		
Stearn, Boaz	2	2	7		
Balcom, Joseph	2	2	5		
Hunt, Nathl	1	1	5		
Jacobs, Benjn	4	2	4		
Simons, Nathan	2	2	2		
Pryor, Joshua	3		2		
Perkins, Phillip	2	2	4		
Jacobs, Joseph	3	3	7		
Fuller, Ezra	1		2		
Smith, Solomon	1		1		
Arnold, Nathan	1	2	2		
Huntington, Eleazr	3	2	8		
Lane, James	4	1	4		
Huntington, Eleazr, Jnr	1		2		

PLAINFIELD TOWN.

NAME OF HEAD OF FAMILY.	Free white males of 16 years and upward.	Free white males under 16 years.	Free white females.	All other free persons.	Slaves.
Maxwell, James	2	3	4		
Aply, John	2		4		
Spalding, Saml	2	2	5		
Palmer, Walter	1	1	4	1	
Clark, Benga	1	1	2		
Phillips, Aaron	3		1		

PLAINFIELD TOWN—con.

NAME OF HEAD OF FAMILY.	Free white males of 16 years and upward.	Free white males under 16 years.	Free white females.	All other free persons.	Slaves.
Phillips, William	2	1	3		
Dowe, John	4	1	6		
Spalding, Stephen	2	2	3		
Sharkweather, Anne		1	2		
Dunworth, Charles	1	3	2		
Parks, Neheh	4	3	11		
Robinson, Josiah	2	3	6		
Collins, Peter	1		1		
Sharkweather, Richard	1	1	1		
Benjamin, Simeon	1	1	2		
Sweet, Benjn	1	4	2		
Cole, Spencer	1	1	2		
Dean, Josiah	1	1	5		
Spalding, Danl	1	1	2		
Whipple, Zebulon	4	1	5	1	
Dean, Christopher	1	1	4		
Phillips, Asa	2	2	4		
Glover, Nathan	2		4		
Badcock, Silas	1	2	1		1
Clark, Stephen	3	6	4	1	
Clark, Silas, Jr	2	6	2		
Crary, Benja	2	1	3	2	
Harris, Sears	3	1	3		
Gallop, John	2	1	4		
Kinsman, Newport				2	
Starkweather, Jekey	3	1	6		
Heard, Josiah	1	1	5		
Tanner, William	1	1	1		
Williams, Thoa	2	2	1		
Bailey, Caleb	1	1	1		
Gallop, Ebenr	2	1	2		2
Welch, John	2		2		
Woodward, Elias	7	1	8		
Satterlee, Nathl	5	2	5		
Dixon, William	2	3	3	1	
Harris, Nathan	5	3	5		
Rude, Joseph	1	3	2		
Pearks, Robert	1	1	3		
Sheldon, Eunice	1	1	2		
Spaldin, Jesse	1	1	3		
Hopkins, George	2	4	5		
Johnson, Sylvester	2		2		
Herrick, Andrew	3		3		
Colegrove, Jonathn	1	3	5		
Hall, Saml	3	1	6		
Bradford, James	2	2	4		
Palmer, Vose	1	1	2		
Andrus, Akel	2	2	4		
Pastelot, Aseal	2		1		
Pryor, Benjn	2	1	5		
Garey, John	1	2	5		
Hall, Stephen	2	1	4		
Gray, Jenney	2		4		
Sabin, Nathl	1	2	2		
Taylor, George	3	1	3		
Wilbar, William	1		2		
Nicholls, Joseph	1	1	2		
Phillips, John	4	2	4		
Webb, Joshua	2	2	2		
Potter, Nehemiah	1	1	2		
Clark, William	2	2	2		
Phillips, Joseph	2		2		
Shinger, Sarah	1		2		
Crandal, Christopher	1	2	5		
French, John	2	4	5		
Dexter, Saml	2	4	3		
Kenney, Manuel	4	2	4		
Sheppard, Reubin	3	1	5		
Douglass, James	2	2	4		
Simmons, Thoa	1	2	5		
Hall, Stephen	1	2	1		
Miller, Alexander, Jnr	2	1	2		
Murdock, George, Jn	2	4	7		
Dunham, Danl	2		1		
Burges, John	2	4	5		
Warren, Saml	3		2		
McCinster, Hugh	1	2	1	4	
Parks, Saml	1	3	2		
Corey, Josiah, Senr	1	1	3		
Marsh, Nathl	3	4	5		
Warren, Jotham	2	3	4		
Robinson, Ebenr & co	2	2	6	1	
Chase, Benjn	4	3	2		
Wood, Noah	4	1	3		
Boyd, Abraham	1	3	4		
Richardson, William	1	5	3		
Bordon, Joseph	1	1	4		
Bush, Stephen	1	1	4		
Levins, William	3		2		
Hall, Joshua	1		3	5	
Hall, Jona	1	2	6		
Dean, Abijah	2	1	6		
Hall, David	1		2		
Witbert, Abner, Sr	2		4		
Nicholls, Joseph	2		3		

PLAINFIELD TOWN—con.

NAME OF HEAD OF FAMILY.	Free white males of 16 years and upward.	Free white males under 16 years.	Free white females.	All other free persons.	Slaves.
Wheeler, Aaron	3		4		
Kingsbury, James	2	2	3		
Pierce, Samuel	2	1	3		
Fuller, Benjn	2	1	4		
French, Stuman	2	2	3		
Hall, John	2	1	1		2
Thurstone, Saml	1	3	3		
Wilson, Abraham	2	2	4		
Hall, John, Jnr	1	1	2		
Stranaham, James	3	2	4		
Hinsbury, Eben	2		2		
Walling, Ezekiel	2	2	5		
Wilch, David	1		2		
Kennedy, Mary	1		2		
Hill, Danl	3		5		
Wheeler, Moses	1	4	4		
Lane, Heza	1	2	5		
Ashbury, Thoa	1		1		
Parkhurst, David	2		5		
Hutit, Nathl	2		4		
Parkhurst, Job	1	3	4		
Parkhurst, Leml	3		2		
Millar, James	1	2	2		
Millar, Sanders	3	2	3		
Whipple, Jonathan				3	
Gallop, Jonathn	1	2	1		
Maine, Nathl	2	2	1		
Wall, William	2	1	2		
Spalding, Azariah	1	1	3		
Care, Ebenr	1	3	3		
Pope, Richd	5	2	5		
Parkhurst, Pierce	1	1	2		
Carey, Joseph	1	3	4		
Backus, Stephen	1	1	4		
Backus, Andrew	3	1	4		1
Spalding, Jonathn	1	2	4		
Wheeler, Ephraim	5	2	7		
Cutlar, William	7	2	4		
Hall, Joseph, Jn	2	3	2		
Champton, Paul	2	3	5		
Ansell, Nathl	3	1	2	1	1
Dunlop, Joshua	3	1	6		
Howe, Robert	1	4	5		
Burton, Uriah	2		2		
Spalding, Phillip	3	2	5		
Hall, Caleb, Jr	2	3	5		
Herd, Jacob	1	1	3		
Stern, Nathl	4	1	4		
Corey, Josiah	1	1	1		
Sheppard, Simon	3	1	2		
Pryor, Joseph	1	1	3		
Warren, Ezra	1	5	6		
Branch, Moses	5	1	4		
Dow, Saml	2	1	1		
Gallop, Benjn	1	2	4		
Douglass, John	3		5	7	
Stevens, Hepsibah, Sr			5		
Perkins, Elisha	6	9	7	1	
Hun, Jonathan	2	1	3		
Smith, Luther	1	1	7	1	
Herd, Thomas	1		1		
Perce, William	3		2		
Tuckerman, Jacob	2		1		
Bottom, Joshua	2	1	4		
Jones, Ephraim & co	3	4	6		
Badcock, Jack				8	
Eaton, Ebenr	5	3	6	1	
Robinson, William	1	2	1		
Bennedict, Joel	1	3	6		
Bottom, Abel	1		2		
Gordon, James	4	1	4		
Stevens, Jeduthan	1	1	6		
Lightfoot, Robert	2		2		
Farlin, Hitchcock	1	1	2		
Avery, John	2	1	2		
Fox, Saml	5	1	3	1	
Pierce, John	1	1	2		
Coops, Ebenr	1	1	2		
Pierce, Timothy	2		3		
Spalding, Andrew	3		4	1	
Spalding, Heza	1	1	4		
Spalding, Ezra	1	2	4	2	
Dorrance, George	2	1	2		
Ingraham, Reubin	2	1	4		
Dunlop, Ledly, Jn	2	4	3		
Peire, Thoa	3	2	3		1
Pierce, Josiah	1	4	4		
Spalding, Joseph	2	1	4		
Herrick, Andrew	1	2	3		
Sheppard, Joseph	2	1	4		
Spalding, Reubin	2	1	2		
Knight, Isaac	2	1	6	1	
Wheeler, Jonas	2	1	2		
Herrick, Elisabeth			4		
Parrish, Elijah	1	1	3		

WINDHAM COUNTY—Continued.

PLAINFIELD TOWN—con.

NAME OF HEAD OF FAMILY.	Free white males of 16 years and upward, including heads of families.	Free white males under 16 years.	Free white females, including heads of families.	All other free persons.	Slaves.
Wheeler, Sam¹	2	4	5		
Howe, Noah	1	1	2		
Cullar, William, Jr	6		3		
Cullar, Jonathan	1	2	1		
Lester, Timothy	5	2	6	4	
Sheppard, Abraham	4	2	5	1	
Sheppard, John	2	2	6	3	1
Thurston, David	2	1	2	4	
Compton, William	1	2	2		
Healey, Resolved	2	1	3		
Key, Uriah	2	1	3		
Key, Nath¹	2	1	5		
Davis, David	1	1	6		
Howe, Jonathⁿ	1	1	2		
Picket, John	1		2		
Knight, Sam¹	2	3	5		1
Parkhurst, Sam¹	2	1	4	1	
Sheppard, Stephen	2	2	4		
Parkhurst, Isaac	3	2	6		
Parkis, James	3		6		
Parkis, William	2	1	1		
Hammot, Jonathⁿ	3	2	6		
Cleavland, Truman	2		1		
Cleavland, Jesse	2	1	4		
Russell, Josiah	2	2	4		
Morse, Solomon	1	1	1		
Morgan, Isaac	4	1	6	1	
Smith, Sam¹	3	2	7		
Kenney, Cogshall	2	2	3		
Sheppard, Lyda		1	3		
Sheppard, John	2	1	9		
Kenny, David	3	3	6		
Austin, Caleb	1		2		
Johnson, Jacob	3	3	3	1	
Spalding, Miner	1	2	3		
Peise, Willard	1		2		
Cornet, Gideon	2		4		
Cornett, Gideon, 2d	1	1	4		
Bennet, Stephen	1		3		
Russell, Jonah	1	4	2		
Barber, John	1		2		
Morgan, Solomon	3	3	6		

POMFRET TOWN.

NAME OF HEAD OF FAMILY.	Free white males of 16 years and upward, including heads of families.	Free white males under 16 years.	Free white females, including heads of families.	All other free persons.	Slaves.
Grosvenor, Seth	4	4	9		1
Dyer, John	2	1	1		
Grosvenor, Ebenʳ	5	2	5		
Grosvenor, Lem¹	3	4	3	1	
Gorton, John	2	3	2		
Sabin, Josiah	2	1	2		1
Sabin, Willᵐ	1	2	5		
Ainsworth, Jededʰ	2	2	5		
Lee, Cyril	2	3	3		
Chandler, Henry	2	2	3		
Denison, Jabez	2	1	2		
Sabin, Joseph	1	3	4	1	
Whitwell, An	1	1	2		
Payson, John	3	2	7		
Chandler, Joseph	1	4	6	1	
Chandler, Peter	5	3	6		1
Underwood, Josiah	2	3	3		
Greggs, Sarah	1	2	5		
Shumway, Elijah	1	2	1		
Aplin, James	1	1	2		
Dresser, John	1	2	3		
Chub, Prentiece	3	1	7		1
Stephens, Nathan¹	1	2	3		
Goodale, David	4	3	3		
Fuller, Caleb	1	1	3		
Grosvenor, Oliver	2	3	3		
Laurence (Wido)	1		2		
Webster, Stephen	1	4	4		
Gary, William	5		3		
Gary, Josiah	1	2	2		
Cook, Eleazʳ	1		1		
Cook, Lot	2	1	3		
White, Dan¹	4	3	7		
Vose, Lem¹	2	2	4		
Bugbe, Thoˢ	1	1	3		
Smith, John R	1	4	4		
Sabin, Elihu	3	2	3		
Sawyer, James	3	1	1		
Perrin, Sam¹	3	1	3		
Lamb, John	1	3	5		
Clark, Sam¹	1	3	2		
Below, Peter	2	2	4		
Flying, Abijah	5	2	4		
Carpenter, Sam¹	1		2		
Dresser, Nathan	2	2	3		
Herrington, Elisha	1	1	3		
Leffingwell, Jerᵉʰ	3	1	6		
Gleason, Elisha	2	2	5	1	
Adams, Elihu	3		4		
Williams, James	1	1	4		

POMFRET TOWN—con.

NAME OF HEAD OF FAMILY.	Free white males of 16 years and upward, including heads of families.	Free white males under 16 years.	Free white females, including heads of families.	All other free persons.	Slaves.
Foster, Joseph	1	1	3		
Holmes, Ebenʳ	4	1	3		
Williams, Joshua	1	3	3		
Durkee, Benjⁿ	2	2	7		
Cotton, John	3		3		
Cotton, Simon	2	3	6		1
Smith, Benjⁿ	3	1	3		
Cheamberlin, Harvey	2		1		
Westcoat, Hukely	1	1	2	1	
William, Stephen	1	2	5		
Knight, Edward	3	2	5		
Inman, Thoˢ	5	3	4		
White, Adam	1	2	5	1	1
Dana, Elijah	2	2	3		
Ellis, Benjⁿ	3	2	5		
Hubard, Willard	1	2	4		
Mᶜintire, Benjⁿ	1	1	5		
Holmes, Benjⁿ	1	2	2		
Richmond, John	2		3		
Grosvenor, Asa	1	3	6		
May, Ithamar	2	3	5		
Sabin, Jonathan	3	1	3		
Bartholomew, Leonard	1		2		
Allen, Jonathan	2		3		
Allen, Nath¹	2	1	2		
Smith, Henry	1	1	2		
Underwood, Lott	2	1	2		
Sabin, Peter	2	3	6		
Carpenter, Simon	3		5		
James, Freeman	1	1	1		
Angel (Wid.)	1	2	3		
Cady, Penuel	2	1	4	1	
Kingsley, Pardon	4	1	4		
Sole, Jonathⁿ	1		1		
Phillips, Barnard	1	2	4		
Detray, Peter	1	1	3		
Child, Payson	2	1	2	2	
Cleavland, Aaron	2	3	7		
White, James	2		2		
Quithy, Phillip	1	1	3		
Waters, John, sr	3	2	5		
Liscomb, Thoˢ	1	1	6		
Collar, Isaac	1	2	2		
Brown, David	1	1	2		
Brown, Joseph	1		3		
Field, Jeremiah	3	2	4		
Putnam, Peter S	2	3	4		
Barry, John	2	3	9		
Williams, Nehemiah	1	2	5		1
White, Antipass	1	3	4		
Kinsbury, Ebenʳ	5	1	5		
Molhone, Evan	1	2	6		1
Newel, Dan¹	3		3		
Chandler, Josiah	3	2	4		
Waldo, Joanna			3		
Averill, Stephen	4	3	2		
Chandler, Philemon	1		3		
Fay, John	1		2		
Cornel, Ezekiel	4		3		1
Holmes, David	1		2		
Spalding, Reubin	4	1	2		
Stone, William	2	1	1		
Perry, John	1		1		
Jenkinbottom, Obediah	2		4		
Randal, Jonathan	2		2		3
Franklin, ——	3	2	4		
sharp, Caleb	2		2		
Goodale, Richard	1	4	7		
White, Jacob	2	1	4		
Griggs, Hezᵃ	1	2	4		
Chandler, Silas	2	3	6		
Grosvenor, Chester	1	1	3		
Wharton, James	1	2	5		
Dana, Sam¹	1	2	4		
Sharp, Gershom	1		4		
Cheedle, Elisabeth		1	2		
Sharp, Gershom, Secⁿᵈ	2	1	8		
Langworthy, Timothy	1	1	2		
Tucker, Ephraim	4	3	4		
Underwood, Timothy	1	1	1		
Capron, John	5		6		
Cargell, Benjⁿ	4	3	5	1	
Hosmer (Widow)	1	2	3		
Gregg, Joseph	1	2	3		
Sharp, Asa	3	4	5		
Sabin, Isaac	2	1	4		
Grosvenor, Thoˢ	4	2	4	1	2
Waldo, Sam¹	1	2	5		
Hall, Jonathⁿ	2	2	3	1	1
Hubard, Benjⁿ, Jnʳ	5	3	5		
Putnam, Aaron	2	1	5		2
Waldo, Abigene	1		5		
William, John	2	1	3		
Sabin, Joshua	2	1	4		
Howard, Caleb	1	1	8		

POMFRET TOWN—con.

NAME OF HEAD OF FAMILY.	Free white males of 16 years and upward, including heads of families.	Free white males under 16 years.	Free white females, including heads of families.	All other free persons.	Slaves.
Brayton, David	1	1	2		
Cleavland, Solomon	2	1	4		
Dresser, Ebenʳ	1		3		
Brayton, Thoˢ	2	2	4		
Sessions, Amasa	2	1	2		
Grosvenor, Amos	4	1	1		
Ingalls, Zebulon, sr	4	2	7		
Dresser, Sam¹	2		5		
Baxter, Robert	2	2	3		
Sessions, Squire	4		1		
Whipple, Sam¹	2	3	3		
Trowbridge, Dan¹	3	3	7		
Sawyer, Prescot	2		2		
Sawyer, William	2	2	2		
Cuningham, Peter	1	3	4		
Work, Alexander	1	1	2		
Trowbridge, John	2	1	4		
Grosvenor, Joshua, Jr	1	1	4		
Grosvenor, Joshua	3	1	4		
Wheeler, John	1	4	4		
Ruggles, Edward	3	1	4		
Stoddord, Ebenʳ	2	1	2		
Lyon, Zurviah	1	1	4		
Hoel, Ephraim	3	2	4		
Chace, Seth	4	3	4		
Slade, Jonathan	1	3	4		
Trowbridge, James	2	4	5		
Wheaton, James	1	4	3		
Mathson, Nathⁿ	1	1	3		
Osgood, Zachʰ	3	1	5		
Davison, Pheneas	1	1	5		
Osgood, Appleton	1	2	1		
Osgood, William, Jnʳ	2	5	2		
Hartshorne, Sam¹	2	1	3		
Stowel, Lemuel	4	2	7		
Coats, Elisabeth	1		2		
Utley (Widᵒ)		1	2		
Craft, Sam¹	3	2	6		1
Gould, Jonathⁿ	1		4		
Sumnar, Sam¹	4		6		
Ashley, Rachel	1	2	4		
Adams, Noah	2	2	2		
Greggs, Sam¹	2	1	6		
Utley, Stephen	2	2	5		
Ruggles, Benjⁿ	2	2			
Greggs, Nathan	1		3	2	
Greggs, David	2	2	3		
Dodge, Nehᵉʰ	2	2	5		
Lyon, Thoˢ	1	1	4		
Abbot, William	2		3		
Trobridge, Mary			2		
Lyon, Walter	1	2	2		
Goodale, Zachʰ	4	1	6		
Williams, Freelove		1	5		
Trusdell, Jeduthem	1	3	1		
Goodale, Caleb	1	2	2		
Goodale, Meachum	1	2	3		
Sharp, David	2	2	3		
Ingalls, Benjⁿ	2	1	2		
Kenny, Amos	3	1	5		
Sharp, John	3		2		
Stevens, Lemᵃ	1	3	2		
Raymond, Amazʰ	1	1	2		
Winter, Ephraim	1	1	4		
Plank, William	1	1	3	2	
Plank, Zebudiah	1		4	2	
Record, Silas	2		1		
Holmes, Jonathan	1	2	3		
Ingalls, Joseph	1	2	2		
Ingalls, Peter	1	3	5		
Sharp, Robert	2	2	5		
Bennet, John	2		1		
Dean, Nathan	2		1		
Sharp, Ruth		1	3		
Ingalls, David	1		5		
Webber, Benj	1		3		
Ingalls, John	2	1	4		
Sharp, Abigail	1		2		
Ingall, Thoˢ	1		2		
Goodale, Dan¹	2	1	3		
Allen, Benjⁿ	1	3	3		
Fish, Dan¹	1		3		
Pratt, Dan¹	2		1		
Copeland, William	1		3		
Warner, Jared	2	3	6	1	1
Stoel, Elisha	2	1	5		
Lord, Elisha	3	2	9		2
Ingalls, Lem¹	2	1	4		
Goodale, Amasa	1	3	6		
Ruggles, Edward	1	2	4		
Ingalls, Ephraim	2	1	4		
Boutwell, ——	1	1	3		
Field, William	1	2	2		
Stephens, Aaron	1		1		
Childs, Charles	1	1	6		

WINDHAM COUNTY—Continued.

POMFRET TOWN—con.

NAME OF HEAD OF FAMILY.	Free white males of 16 years and upward, including heads of families.	Free white males under 16 years.	Free white females, including heads of families.	All other free persons.	Slaves.
Force, Ebenr	1	1	2		
Sharp, William	3	2	4		
Cresey, Ebenr	2		2		
Payne, Nathan	1	3	6	1	

THOMPSON TOWN.

NAME OF HEAD OF FAMILY.	Free white males of 16 years and upward, including heads of families.	Free white males under 16 years.	Free white females, including heads of families.	All other free persons.	Slaves.
Johnson, Smith	3	2	5		
Halsey, Samuel	1	1	2		
Plank, Robert	1	2	6		
Brown, Jesse	1	4	5		
Underwood, William	1	1	4		
Gay, Elisha	4	1	4		
Sessions, Darious	1	1	3		
Parks, Isaac	1	2	5		
Lee, Joel	1	5	7		
Gay, Richard	2		3		
Learned, Danl	3	5	4		
Gimman, George	1	1	7		
Brown, Joseph	2	3	4		
Larned, Simon	2	3	4		
Gay, Ebene	2	2	5		
Willis, Joab	1	6	2		
Lee, Allen		1	4		
Lee, Joseph	1	3	2		
Woodward, John	1	2	3		
Record, Joseph	1				
Thayer, Reubin	1	1	3		
Lee, Jonath	3	1	3		
Thayer, Nathl	1	3	3		
Ruggles, Saml	1	1	1		
Demon, Joseph	1	2	2		
Converse, Payne	3	4	4		
Davis, Simon	3	2	8		
Paul, David	1	2	6		
Griggsby, Nathl	1	2	2		
Merriam, Benja	3	1	4		
Wilson, John	1	2	5		
Learned, Henry	1	2	5		
Whitmore, Jabez	1	3	4		
Wilson, Saml	2	3	6		
Paul, Jonathan	1	3	2		
Cleft, Obedh	5	2	8		
Learned, Benjn	2	3	5		
Russell, Jona, Jnr	3	2	4		
Briggs, Jona	1	1	4		
Russell, Danl	2	1	6		
Russell, Jona	3	1	2		
Hicks, Chase	1	1	5		
Hopkins, Jereh	1	4	2		
Cutlar, Solomon	1	2	4		
Blackmore, Ezekel	1	2	3		
Reynolds, Jacob	1	1	1		
Green, Seth	1	2	4		
Green, Pheneas	1		3		
Leonard, Giliver	1	2	3		
Plank, John	1		1		
Richmond, Michael	2		4		
Richmond, Oliver	1	2	5		
Westcoat, Amos	2	1	4		
Converse, Jacob	3	3	6		
Comstock, Israel	3	2	3		
Benson, Barack	1	2	3		
Coats, Benjn	1	1	6		
Robins, Seth	1	1	1		
Robins, John	2	1	2		
Knap, Lemuel	2	1	6	2	
Gleason, John	1	1	4		
Robins, David	1	2	2		
Mason, Abraham	2		6		
Jocelin, Edward	1	2	5		
Jocelin, Israel	1	2	7		
Porter, Jonan	2	1	6		
Cole, Isaac	2	1	3		
Porter, Flint	1	1	4		
Jinkham, Abel	1	3	3		
Coats, James	1		1		
Cutlar, Amos	3	2	4		
Polluck, Charles	2		4		
Coats, Hezh	1		1		
Jocelin, Joseph	3	2	2		
Wheeler, Jeremiah	1	3	2		
Jacobs, Asa	1				
Joslin, Jesse	1		3		
Emerson, Simeon	2	3	3		
Leggs, Thomas	1	1	1		
Hoyle, Richard	1	2	4		
Hoyle, Wm	1		3		
Covil, Ebenr	2	3	5		
Allen, Abraham	2	7	8		
Green, Benjn	2	1	4		
Fitz, Ebenr	2	1	2		
Green, Amos	4	2	2		
Barret, John	2	2	2		
Burrall, Jacob	1	1	1		

THOMPSON TOWN—con.

NAME OF HEAD OF FAMILY.	Free white males of 16 years and upward, including heads of families.	Free white males under 16 years.	Free white females, including heads of families.	All other free persons.	Slaves.
Green, Ebenr	1		1		
Moffat, Micajah	3	1	2		
Burrall, John	2	3	5		
Wakefield, John	2	1	4		
Green, Dexter	1	2	2		
Whitmon, John	1		1		
Cutlar, Saml	1		1		
Blackman, Jacob	1	2	5		
Moffat, Eli	1	1	2		
Wilson, James	2	2	4		
Marrion, Joseph, Jnr	4	3	6		
Marrion, Israel	1	2	4		
Marrion, Joseph	1		1		
Marrion, Benjn	1	1	1		
Harriss, Joseph	2	1	3		
Carrol, Amos	4		2		
Richard, Danl	1		2		
Russell, Joseph	2	3	4		
Richards, Israel	1	4	6		
Smith, Abraham	2	1	2		
Burral, Benjamin	1		4		
Wood, Ephraim A	1		3		
Morse, Joshua	3		3		
Dike, Thomas	1	3	5		
Dike, James	1	1	4		
Bigsby, Saml	1		2		
Bigsby, Jacob	1	3	1		
Bigsby, Moses	1	1	1		
Pratt, John	1	1	4		
Rodes, James	2		1		
Burlingham, Ezekiel	1	6	6		
Turtolot, Israel	1	3	3		
Kimball, Saml	1	2	4		
Jacob, John	4	1	1		
Atwell, John	2	2	2		
Bales, Elijah	3	5	3		
Martin, John	3	1	4		
Mason, Hale	1	2	1		
Cummins, Josiah	2		4		
Bigsby, Nathan	3	2	5		
Watson, Mathew	2		2		
Town, Archelous	2	2	3		
Duncan, William	1	1	6		
Wilson, Sharp					2
Watson, Abigal	6	4	5		
Luther, Isaac	1		1		
Bailey, John	2	1	3		
Keith, John	4	3	6		
Russell, Noadiah	3	1	2		1
Dresser, Asa	1		2		
Dresser, Jacob	3	2	7		6
Cooper, John	1	2	2		
Flint, Joseph	2		4		
Flint, Davis	1	2	7		
Wilson, Jonathan	2		6		
Keith, Stephen	3	3	4		
Bartholomew, Benjamin	1	2	4		
Nichols, Elijah	3	1	1		
Elliot, Thomas	2	2	2		
Elliot, John	1	2	2		
Elliot, Joel	2	1	3		
Green, John	2	2	3		
Bates, Isackas	2	2	3		
White, David	1	3	1		
White, Jonath	2		3		
Johnson, Jotham	1	2	2		
Starr, Ebenr	2	6	3		
Woodward, Comfort	1	2	3		
Stockwell, Peter	2	2	5		
Plummer, Israel	1		3		
Stockwell, Israel	2		5		
Beston, Jeremiah	2	3	5		
Walker, Andrew	1	4	3		
Robinson, Aaron	2	1	4		
Robinson, Moses	2	1	10		
Cole, Isaac	2	2	3		
Plumber, John	1	3	6		
Porter, Jonathan	3	1	9		
Carrol, Nathl	1	2	4		
Bigsby, Aaron	1	1	3		
Bigsby, Jesse	1	3	1		
Billows, Heza	1	2	1		
Bigsby, Amos	1	3	3		
May, Saml	2	4	2		
Rich, Israel	3		5		
Brown, Rufus	1	2	2		
Howard, Simon	1	2	4		
Howard, Ebenr	1		7		
Bates, John	2	2	3		
Cummins, Amos	1	1	2		
Brown, Stephen	1		4		
Ballard, Zachus	2	1	3		
Stone, Henry & Co	3	4	5		
Carrol, John	1	3	3		

THOMPSON TOWN—con.

NAME OF HEAD OF FAMILY.	Free white males of 16 years and upward, including heads of families.	Free white males under 16 years.	Free white females, including heads of families.	All other free persons.	Slaves.
Gleason, Nathl	1	2	4		
Turtolot, Erick	1		1		
Turtolot, Joshua	2	1	5		
Turtolot, Barnabas	2	2	5		
Turtolot, Michl	2	1	3		
Turtolot, Isaac	1	2	4		
Newall, Saml	2	2	4		
Jacobs, John, Jnr	1	4	3		
Russell, William	2	2	2		
Smith, Israel	1	2	5		
Cummins, Josiah, Jr	1	1	5		
Haskall, Jonh	1	4	8		
Soams, Consider	2	1	3		
Jammes, Solomon	1	6	4		
Fay, Saml	2	2	5		
Freeman, Joseph	3	2	2		
Haskall, David	1	2	1		
Alton, David	1	2	7		
Davis, Thomas	1	3	1		
Trumbull, John	1	2	3		
Town, Joseph	3	1	6		
Town, Joseph, Jnr	1	2	2		
Grant, Thos & co	2		5		
Prince, Saml	1	3	3		
Elliot, Saml	1	1	2		
Elliot, Thos, Jnr	1	3	2		
Stone, Jona	1	1	4		
Town, William	1	2	1		
Stone, Levi	1	2	5		
Beston, Asa	1		2		
Whittemore, Caleb	1	2	1		
Fay, Nehh, Senr	1		1		
Belcher, David	2	2	3		
Prince, Robert	1	4	3		
Prince, Joseph	2	1	3		
Prince, Ebenr	2		2		
Whitmore, William	1		2		
Whitmore, William, Jnr	2	4	4		
Ormsbe, Thos	2	2	2		
Crosby, Elijah	1	2	2		
Elliot, Roger	1	2	3		
Stone, Barsom	3	3	4		
Upham, Ivory	2		5		
Upham, Luther	3		7		
Curtiss, Japhet	1	3	6		
Upham, Jonathn	1		2		
Upham, Isaac	1	3	1		
Alby, Joseph	2	2	4		
Childs, Nathl	2	2	3		
Shiffields, Nathl	2		3		
Child, Elijah	1	3	2		
Converse, Elijah	1	2	3		
Curtiss, Charles	1	2	3		
Haughton, Edward	1	3	4		
Payne, Joseph	1		1		
Hendrick, Danl	1	1	1		
Copeland, William	1	1	2		
Stone, Simon	2	1	6		
Corban, Moses	2	1	1		
Atwood, Francis	1		2		
Bowen, Asa	1	2	4		
Ormsby, Jesse	1	1	1		
Jewit, Joseph	2	2	7		
Blackmar, Jonath	1		3		
Carpenter, Elijah	1	2	2		
Potter, Edmond	1		2		
Barret, John	1	1	2		
Elliot, Francis	2		2		
Elithorp, Nathl	3		3		
Elithorp, Henry	3	3	3		
Barrows, Printrise	3	1	3		
White, Jacob	2	1	1		
Elliot, John	1	3	2		
Nichols, Elijah	3	1	2		
Gay, Richard	3	1	5		
Luther	3	1	5		
Lee, Joel	2	1	3		
Parks, Isaac	2	1	6		
Cady, John	2	2	3		
Bundy, Ebenr	5		7		
Ellis, Jonath	4		3		
Keith, Peter	3	1	5		
Keith, Barack	1	1	3		
Dwight, William	2	5	3		
Nichalls, Jona, Jnr	3	1	4		
Prince, Abel	1	2	2		
Barret, Joseph	2		3		
Everden, Walter	1	1	2		
Perrin, Danl	2	5	4		
Elliot, Asael	2		3		
Thayer, Phillip	2	1	2		
Alger, Nathl	2	3	4		
Alger, Abraham	1	2	1		
Chaffee, Abiel	2	3	8		

NAME OF HEAD OF FAMILY.	Free white males of 16 years and upward, including heads of families.	Free white males under 16 years.	Free white females, including heads of families.	All other free persons.	Slaves.
THOMPSON TOWN—continued.					
Hosmer, David	1	1	3		
Bennet, James	2	2	4		
Barret, Moses	1	4	5		
Spalding, Sam¹	1	1	1		
Barret, Lemu¹	3	4	7		
Alton, William	3	2	5		
Carpenter, Sam¹	3	3	6		
Alton, John	3	3	4		
Barret, Oliver	3	3	4		
Hosmer, James	3	1	2		
Corban, Moses	4	2	7		
Corban, Clement	2	5	3		
Houghton, Ephraim	3		4		
Palmer, Sam¹	3	2	4		
Corban, Jonaᵗʰ	1	3	4		
Corban, Peleg	2	3	5		
Chaffee, Thomas	1	2	4		
Childs, Nath¹	2	1	3		
Childs, Elijah	1	3	2		
Converse, Elijah	1	1	3		
Hebard, Jonª	1		1		
Winter, Asa	1	1	4		
Humes, Sam¹	2	1	3		
Chaffee, Chester	2	2	3		
Chaffee, James	1	1	6		
Chaffee, Calvan	1	1	2		
Chaffee, Sam¹	1	2	3		
Winter, Amasa	1	2	1		
Webster, John	3		5		
Perry, Josiah	2	1	4		
Brown, Joseph	1		1		
Brown, Joseph, Jnr	1	1	2		
Brown, Henry	1	1	4		
Thayer, Oliver	3	1	3		
Rawson, Nath¹	1	1	1		
Fairbanks, Benjª	2		3		
Bowers, John, Jnr	1	3	4		
Palmer, Sam¹	1		1		
Phips, Jason	4	2	5		
Whitmore, John	2	2	2		
Brown, Nathan	2	1	2		
Brown, Rufus	1	4	2		
Brown, Charles	2	2	3		
Bowers, John	1	2	5		
Bowers, Alpheus	1		1		
Houghton, Ephraim	2		3		
Holbrook, Thoˢ	1		2		
Corban, Ezra	1	2	3	1	
Brown, Aaron	1		6		
Holbrook, John	5	1	6		
Green, Ira	1	2	2		
Blackmore, Levi	3		2		
Bugbee, Cathareˢ	1		2		
Sumner, Dan¹	1	2	4		
Gleason, William	2	1	5		
Chandler, Theophilus	2	2	3		
Sabin, Peter	1	1	3		
VOLUNTOWN TOWN.					
Dorrance, Archibald	3	1	3	1	
Hard, Josiah	3	1	3		
Spener, George	1	3	4		
Henry, John	3	1	4	1	
Kenyon, John	2	3	7		
Kenyon, Sam¹	1	3	3		
Smith, Ebenʳ	3	3	3		
Burlingham, Nathan	4	1	3		
Potter, Phillip	3	2	5		
Tuckerman, Benjamin	1	2	1		
Dixon, Robert	5	2	7		11
Amy, Elisha	2	1	8		
Smith, Francis	3	2	6		
Avery, Joseph	2	1	4		
Green, John	2	2	2		
Dorrance, Lemuel	2	3	5		2
Smith, Phebe	2		2		
Pearks, Robert	1	1	3		
Dixon, Thomas	2	1	2		
Gallop, David	2		1		
Dixon, John	3	4	7		
Gordon, Thomas	2		1		2
Edmonds, Andrew	3	4	4		
Gordon, Archibald	1	1	4		
Gallop, Isaac	3		3		
Gallop, Nath¹	2		2		
Gallop, William	2	1	1		
Cole, Thomas	2	1	3		
Douglass, John	3	4	5		
Gallop, Nath¹	2	1	3		
Gallop, Sam¹	1	1	2		
Dow, Benjª	2	1	3		
Frink, Matthias	2	2	3		
Dow, Ebenʳ	3	1	3		
Dow, Nathan	2		2		

NAME OF HEAD OF FAMILY.	Free white males of 16 years and upward, including heads of families.	Free white males under 16 years.	Free white females, including heads of families.	All other free persons.	Slaves.
VOLUNTOWN TOWN—continued.					
Stiles, Amos	1		3	1	
Gordon, John	1		3		
Cambell, Joseph	3		4		
Gordon, John, Jnr	2	2	3		
Douglass, John, Senr	2	3	3		
Kegwin, William	2		6		
Kegwin, Nicholas	2		6		
Frink, Usual	2	1	3		
Frink, Zachʰ	2		2		
Dixon, John, Senr	1		1		
Kennedy, David	3	3	4		
Stuart, Sam¹	2	3	8		1
Frink, Dan¹	1	1	4		
Campbell, Noble	1	2	6		
Wyley, Joseph	4		6		
Pulman, John	1	4	3		
Budlong, Joseph	2	2	4		
Budlong, David	1	1	1		
Rode, William	1		1		
Lewis, Caleb	1	1	1		
Adams, Stephen	3	2	2		
Adams, William	1	1	1		
Adams, Reubin	1		4		
Wilkinson, William, Jnr	2	1	4		
Campbell, John	1	3	3		
Kennedy, Daniel	2	2	6		
Partelow, Jonas	1	1	3		
Partelow, Thomas	2		6		
Wedge, Amos	2	1	6		
Kennedy, Joseph	1	2	3		
Gates, Phineas	1	3	2		
Alexander, Joseph	3		4		
Campbell, Amos	4	1	7		
Alexander, James, Jnr	2	1	1		
Campbell, James, Jnr	1		2		
Hunter, John	1		3		
Stanton, Joseph	1	4	4		
Sweet, Ezekiel	2	2	4		
Alexander, John	1	2	7		
Wyley, Moses	1	4	5		
Swift, James	1		1		
Lewis, Eleazr	1	3	5		
Bowdist, Joseph	1	1	1		
Colegrove, Benjª, Jnr	1	1	1		
Rhodes, John	4	4	3		
Rodes, John, Jnr	1		2		
Coats, Hezª	1	1	1		
Brown, John	3		3		
Robins, Sam¹	3	2	6		
Morgan, Peter	2	1	3		
Lewis, Nathan	2		2		
Robins, Sam¹, Jnr	1	2	3		
Cady, Martha	4	2	4		
Kenney, Sam¹	2	2	5		
Kenney, James	3	3	5		
Morgan, Eleanor	1		3		
Fish, Sam¹	2	1	4		
Robins, Lorin	4	2	4		
Kenney, Abel	1	3	6		
Kenney, Ira	3	3	5		
Robins, Moses	2	2	3		
Fisk, Elias, &c	3	4	7		
Peirce, William	1	1	2		
Fisk, Moses, Senr	1		2		
Fisk, Moses, Jnr	1	3	3		
Wilkinson, William	2		2		
Houston, John	1	1	3	1	1
Gallop, Benjª	3	1	11		
Davis, Bill	2	3	3		
Palmer, Benjª	3		3	1	
Palmer, Elihu	2	2	5		
Hillyard, Jonathan	1	1	5		
Ray, Gershom	1	2	3		
Palmer, Jonaᵗʰ	1	3	6		
Palmer, Joseph	2	2	3		
Gilman, Robert	2	1	4		
Randall, Amos	2	4	5		
Randall, Peleg	1	3	5		
Randall, Nicholas	2	4	3		
Gallop, William	2	2	3		
Gallop, Jabez	1	1	2		
Gallop, Lyda	1	2	4		
Newton, Mathew	3	2	2		
Corning, Benjª	1	2	2		
Newton, Jabez	1	1	3		
Brown, John, Jnr	1	2	2		
Palmer, Elyʰ	1	3	5		
Stanbury, John	1	2	3		
Safford, Mary			3		
Palmer, Ziba	1	4	1		
Randall, Joseph	2	1	3		
Palmer, Uriel	1	3	1		
Palmer, Pheneas	1	1	2		
Newton, Desire		2	2		
Coon, Joseph	1	1	2		

NAME OF HEAD OF FAMILY.	Free white males of 16 years and upward, including heads of families.	Free white males under 16 years.	Free white females, including heads of families.	All other free persons.	Slaves.
VOLUNTOWN TOWN—continued.					
Griffin, George	2	3	4		
Stephens, Simon	2	2	4		
Green, Jonathan	1	3	2		
Green, Benjn	1		1		
Peirce, Preserved	1	1	1		
Randall, Isaac	1		1		
Crandal, Ezra	1	1	2		
Bligh, Benjn	4	3	2		
Campbell, Allen	2	4	7		
Larkham, John	2	1	5		
Shepard, Nath¹	2	1	4		
Larkham, Lott	2	1	3		
Colegrove, Benjn	3		3		
Green, Sam¹	1	2	5		
Douglass, William	2	1	4		
Lewis, Sam¹	2	2	5		
Wintor, Weedon	1	2	1		
Poplestone, Gideon	1		1		
Weaver, Thoˢ	3	5	3		
Douglass, William, Jnr	1	1	2		
Peirce, Edward	1	2	2		
Martin, Stephen	2	2	5		
Campbell, James	3		6		
Palmer, Roswill	1		1		
Campbell, William	1	3	5		
Campbell, Partrick	1	1	1		
Blyth, Joseph	1	2	2		
Jackson, Elias	1	3	4		
Hoxey, Joseph	3	1	4		
Gallop, Sam¹	1	3	8		
Campbell, Archibald	2	2	5		
Wilkinson, James Y	1		2		
Lewis, Caleb	1	1	1		
Layton, Noyes	1	1	3		
Lewis, Asa	1	1	1		
Mathewson, Joshua	1	2	2		
Gorton, William	2	1	3		
Stewart, John	2	1	6		
Briggs, James	2	1	4	1	
Campbell, John	3		4		
Jackson, Robert	1		2		
Gallop, John	1	3	4		
Briggs, William	1	4	2		1
Montgomery, John	1	1	2		
Porter, Micaiah	2	4	2		
Gordon, Maryam	4		2		
Gallop, Wheeler	2	1	4	1	
Hutchinson, Elisha	1	4	3		
Gallop, Bennadam	1	2	2	1	
Prince (Negro)				3	
Button, Newberry	1	4	3		
McGollsgal, James	2	1	4		
Busey, Titus	2	3	1		3
Matthewson, George	1	1	7		
Mathewson, Dutifull	1	1	2		
Mathewson, Reuben	1	1	1		
Sweet, Ebenr	1	1	1		
Smith, John				3	
Bailey, Adonijah	2		1		
Congdoll, Benjª	2	2	2		
Wilson, Robert	3	1	3		
Vaughn, Dan¹	2	3	4		
Vaughn, Jesse	5	3	6		
Mathson, Thomas	1	2	3		
Mathewson, Caleb	1	1	3		
Whitford, Asa	1	2	4		
Wilbar, Oliver	2	3	3		
Marcy, Jereʰ	2				
Wyley, John	1	1	4		
Mathewson, Jesse	2	1	2		
Harris, Jonathª	2	3	3		
Green, Jonathan	1	1	1		
Stone, William	1	1	1		
Douglass, Sam¹	3	2	5		
Thompson, Thomas	2	1	4		
Pentnode, George	1	1	1		
Peavey, Ichabd	2	3	3		
Bennet, William	1	1	3		
Bennet, Benjn	1	2	2		
Knox, James	1	2	3		
Knox, Andrew	1	1	3		
Montgomery, Robert	2	1	4		
Montgomery, Asa	2	1	6		
Riser, Thoˢ	1	1	1		
Gibson, James	1	1	1		
Angell, Thoˢ	1	1	1		
Kinyon, Sylvester	3	2	2		
Burges, Thoˢ	2	1	4		
Burges, Beneyʰ	2	2	4		
Montgomery, Josiah	1	1	1		
Spence, Joshua	2	3	8		
Green, Thoˢ	1		4		
Frink, Joshua	3	4	5		
Montgomery, Sarah	2	1	4		
Phillips, John	1	1	3		

WINDHAM COUNTY—Continued.

VOLUNTOWN TOWN—continued.

NAME OF HEAD OF FAMILY.	Free white males of 16 years and upward, including heads of families.	Free white males under 16 years.	Free white females, including heads of families.	All other free persons.	Slaves.
Stedman, Harry	2	1	2		
Perkins, Amos	2	4	3		
Perkins, Newman	1	1	2		
Perkins, Elisha	1	1	2		
Perkins, Oliver	3	1	3		
Franklin, Abel	1		1		
Franklin, Uriah	2	2	3		
William, William	3	1	3		
Williams, Benja	1		5		
Williams, William, Ju	1		2		
Denison, Nathl	1		3		
Boyd, Joseph	1	2	2		
Wood, Elisha	1	1	1		
Dixon, John	1	1	1		
Geary, Ezekiel	2	3	5		
Dixon, Thos	5	1	5		
Bennet, Ezra	1	2	3		
Coloil, Saml	3	1	3		
Knight, John	1		2		
Mansfield, John	1	2	2		
Mansfield, Calvin	1	2	2		
Dorrance, James	2	1	4		
Gastin, John	2		2		
Cole, John	1		1		
Cole, Heza	2		3		
Hitt, John	1	1	2		
French, Isaac	1	3	4		
Young, Jonah	1	3	7		
Titus, Simon	1	2	2		
Titus, Ebenr	1		1		
Titus, Comfort	3	2	2		
Kenyon, Giles	1	2	4		
Kenyon, Freeman	1		2		
Kenyon, Azariah	1		2		
Kenyon, Gardiner	1	1	3		
Gore, Saml	2		2		
Adams, Silas	1		4		
Mason, Jinks	1	1	3		
King, Jonathn	1	1	2		
James, Anthony	1		1		
Seldon, Charles	1	4	4		
Bennet, John	1	1	3		
Rhodes, John	1	1	2		
Cole, Noah	4	5	2		
Hill, Robert	2	2	2		
Hill, Aves	1		2		
Hill, Danl	1		6		
Hill, Parker	1	1	4		
Hill, Jonathn	1	2	6		
James, Zephh	1	4	1		
Eaton, Joshua	1	1	1		
Henry, James	3		3		
Whiton, Amos	3	1	3		
Covill, Abraham	1		2		
Colvil, Ephriam	1	1	1		
Winston, Azariah	1	2	2		
Hammond, Saml	1	1	3		
Jocelin, Thos	1	3	4		
Howard, Jesse	1	2	3		
Brown, Anthony	1	2	4		
Bennet, Joseph	1	3	4		
Hill, Cromwell	1	1	2		
Newton, Isaac	1	1	1		
Hyde, Squire	1		3		
Millar, John	1		2		

WINDHAM TOWN.

NAME OF HEAD OF FAMILY.	Free white males of 16 years and upward, including heads of families.	Free white males under 16 years.	Free white females, including heads of families.	All other free persons.	Slaves.
Dyer, Hone Eliphalet	1		1	1	8
Staniford, John	3	2	4		
Backus, Bela	3	2	4		
Elderkin, Jedediah	1	2	3		
Carey, Marey	1		2		
Abbe, Pheneas	1	7	4		
Fitch, Eleazr, Jr	2	2	3		
Kennedy, Isaac	2	2	4		
Tileston, Thomas	2	1	3		
Brewster, Benjamin	4		2		1
Gray, Saml	1		4		
Clark, Jabez	1		3		
Backus, Nathl	3	1	5		
Fitch, John	1	3	4		
Webb, Peter	1	1	3		
Barker, John	1		2		
Hebard, Jonathan	1	1	1		
Stanley, Fredrick	1		1		
Clark, John	1	1	2		
Badger, Edmond	4	2	4		
Brown, Edward	1		4		
Abbe, Shubael	2		7		2
Miner, Stephen	2	1	3		
Webb, Nathl	1	2	4		
Ripley, Ralph	1	4	3		
Backus, Ebene	3	2	2		
Huntington, Roger	2	1	3		
Reed, Thomas	1	3	3		

WINDHAM TOWN—continued.

NAME OF HEAD OF FAMILY.	Free white males of 16 years and upward, including heads of families.	Free white males under 16 years.	Free white females, including heads of families.	All other free persons.	Slaves.
Jennings, Eunice	1		3		
Abbe, Elisha	3	2	6		
Hebard, Paul	2		1		1
Ripley, John	1	3	3		
Frink, Andrew	2	2	4		
Huntington, Solomon	2	1	4		
Webb, Samuel	3	2	7		
Ripley, Hezekiah	1	3	5		
Elderkin, Joshua	1		2		
Brewster, Asa	1	1	2		
Robinson, Deborah			2		
Lee, Samuel	4	2	6		
Skinner, Jonath	2	1	4		
Follet, Abner	1	2	8		
Crane, Eunice	1		5		
Buck, Daniel	3	2	3		
Robinson, Eleazer	1	1	1		
Flint, John	1	3	3		
Ormsby, Eliphalet	1	2	4		
Badger, Saml	1		1		
Young, William	1		4		
Perkins, Daniel	1	1	6		1
Elderkin, Joshua B	2	2	6		
Badger, Joseph	2	1	2		
Francis, David	1		2		
Lord, Solomon	2		2		
Hovey, Jacob	4	3	4		
Wales, Nathaniel	4	3	8		
Wales, Jonathan	2	2	6		
Wales, William	1	1	4		
Spafford, John	2	1	7		
Palmer, Enos	2	2	5		
Palmer, Seth	2	1	3		
Palmer, Joseph	3	1	5		
Palmer, Eliphalet	1	2	5		
Palmer, Eleazer	1	2	3		
Kingsley, Ezra	1	5	3		
Burnet, James	5	3	6		
Manning, Josiah	2		5		1
Church, Lemuel	1	2	2		
Manning, Joel	1	1	4		
Kingley, Eliphaz	2	2	5		
Palmer, Josiah	2	4	3		
Hebard, Jared	1	4	4		
Spencer, David	1		4		
Spencer, Jeduthan	1	4	2		
Carey, Nathl	2	1	1		
Hebard, Zebulon	3	2	4		
Hebard, Samuel	2	1	4		
Huntington, Nathan	4		7		
Cleft, Waterman	3	1	8		
Carey, Hezekiah	1	1	3		
Tracy, Percy	2		3		
Reed, David	2	3	4		
Reed, Beriah	2		4		
Spencer, Samuel	1		3		
Fitch, Christopher	1	2	3		
Fitch, Eleazr, 3d	1		3		
Bingham, Alfred	1	1	1		
Flint, James	1	1	2		
Backus, Calvin	1		3		
Ormsby, John	1		4		
Smith, Miner	1		4		
Backus, Abner	1	1	4		
Manning, Fredrick	1	2	3		
Miner, Rufus	2		5		
Taylor, Nathan	2		1		
Gray, Thomas	1		5		
Gilbert, Jabez	2		2		
Huntington, John	2	3	3		
Denison, Susanna			3		
Sawyer, Elijah	2	1	8		
Ripley, Eleazr	3		1		
Ripley, Ebenezer	2		2		
Barrows, Sylvanus	1		1		
Frink, Lathrop	1		3		
Elderkin, Lyda			4		
Larrabe, Timothy	4	2	5		5
Page, John	3	2	2		
Johnson, Joseph	1	1	3		
Duvit, Henry	2	2	6		
Warren, Nathl	2	1	4		
Flint, Jemima	2		4		
Jennings, Jonath	1	2	3		
White, Stephen	4		6		2
Clark, John	1		6		
Fitch, Olive		1	6		
Huntington, Heza	1		4		
Jones, John	1	4	4		
Dyer, Thomas	2	4	4		
Lathrop, Benjamin	2		3		
Ormsby, Stephen	1	1	5		
Elderkin, Alfred	1	1	5		
Hebard, Nathl	4	1	1		
Tozier, Charles	1	1	4		
Barrows Sylvanus Jnr.	1	1	3		

WINDHAM TOWN—continued.

NAME OF HEAD OF FAMILY.	Free white males of 16 years and upward, including heads of families.	Free white males under 16 years.	Free white females, including heads of families.	All other free persons.	Slaves.
Swift, Zeph	1	1	2		
Robinson, Daniel	2	2	7		
Bingham, Ebenzr	2	2	3		
White, Elisha	1	3	1		
Spafford, Asa	3		2		
Spafford, Pheneas	1	2	2		
Spafford, Eliphalet	2	1	4		
Sawyer, Joshua	4	2	4		
Downing, Benjan	1	2	4		
Fitch, Eleazr, Senior	1		2		
Cuningham, Robert	1	3	1		
Fitch, Shubael	1	2	4		
Backus, Demetrious	1		6		
Calkins, Nathl S	1	3	3		
Sawyer, Mathius	2		1		
Balcam, Azariah	1	4	2		
Millard, Benja	2	3	3		
Sawyer, Asael	1	1	4		
Skiffe, Joseph	2		2		
Molton, James	2		2		
Robinson, Isaac	2	1	8		
Abbe, Saml	1	1	3		
Carey, Zurveyh	2		3		
Elderkin, Bela	2	6	4		
Bingham, John	1	1	3		
Bingham, Elias	1	1	2		
Howes, Zenas	3	3	3		
Fitch, Roswell	1	1	3		
Hewit, Lewis	1	1	3		
Simons, Nathan	1		6		
Fitch, Jesse	2	4	3		
Fitch, Stephen	1	2	4		
Howes, Zachh	1		2		
Crowel, John	2	1	3		
Molton, William	3		5		
Shaw, Thomas	2	1	3		
Tracy, Prince	3		3		
Allen, Daniel	4	1	2		
Howes, Zachh	1	2	5		
Wills, Jacob	2		2		
Clark, Abel	1	1	5		
Hebard, Joseph	2	1	1		
Young, Saml	4	3	5		
Brown, Stephen	3	2	4		
Brown, John	5	1	6		
Murdock, Eliphalet	3		8		1
Tracy, Prince	3		3		
Murdock, Anne	1	1	3		
Young, William	3	3	3		
Woodward, Cathrine			3		
Dunham, George	1		3		
Spafford, Moses	3	1	8		
Warner, Nathl	2	2	7		
Howes, Zachh, Jnr	1	2	5		
Hovey, David	4	3	4		
Maxwell, Joshua	2	1	3		
Bingham, Joseph	2		1		
Bingham, Ralph	1	1	2		
Bingham, Gideon	2		6		
Button, Joshua	1	3	3		
Jennings, Zephh				5	
Spafford, Oliver	1		2		
Dewey, Alpheus	2	1	4		
Mingo, Primus				4	
Philps, Paul	2	6	2		
Gaser, Jason	2	4	4		
Smith, Oliver	2		4		
Robinson, William	2	1	3		
Huntington, Nathl	2	1	5		
Bass, Ebenr	5	4	8		
Manning, Hezekiah	2	2	4		
Carey, Oliver	2		2		
Perrit, John	3	2	3		2
Smith, Eleazer	1		1		
Tracy, Zebh	1	2	2		1
Lillie, Jared	1	2	2		
Parsons, Jesse	2		7		
Abbe, Sampson				2	
Smith, Ephraim	1	3	5		
Persons, Theodotious	1	1	4		
Cogshall, James	1	1	2		1
Devotion, Ebenezr	5	3	4		
Manning, Seabury	1		2		
Kingsley, Elisha	2	1	3		
Webb, Abner	2	3	2		
Cheney, Pemul	3		3		
Palmer, Marshal	2	4	2		
Dorrance, David	2	4	2		1
Kyes, John	1	1	5		1
Webb, John	2	1	2		
Lillie, Chester	1	4	2		
Ripley, Gamaliel	2	4	4		1
Hovey, Saml	1		2		
Giles, William	1		3		
Webb, Lebeus	1	2	2		
Webb Jared	2	1	4		

NAME OF HEAD OF FAMILY.	Free white males of 16 years and upward, including heads of families.	Free white males under 16 years.	Free white females, including heads of families.	All other free persons.	Slaves.	NAME OF HEAD OF FAMILY.	Free white males of 16 years and upward, including heads of families.	Free white males under 16 years.	Free white females, including heads of families.	All other free persons.	Slaves.	NAME OF HEAD OF FAMILY.	Free white males of 16 years and upward, including heads of families.	Free white males under 16 years.	Free white females, including heads of families.	All other free persons.	Slaves.
WINDHAM TOWN—con.						WINDHAM TOWN—con.						WINDHAM TOWN—con.					
Mudge, Charles	1	3	3			Kimball, Peltiah	3	1	4			Wheeler, David	1	2	1		
Hurlbert, Alfred	1	1	3			Huntington, Elipht	1		3			Bibbens, William	2	3	4		
Palmer, John	2	1	3			Robinson, Abner	4	1	7	1		Welch, Reuben	1	1	7		
Waldon, John	1	1	2			Burnam, John	2	3	2			Welch, Jeremiah	2	3	4		
Waldon, John, Jnr	1		6			Robinson, Experience	2	1	3			Dyer, Benjamin	1	2	5		
Bingham, Jereh	1	2	2			Robinson, Elias	1	1	3			Gray, Ebenezr	1	1	3		
Kimball, Deliverance			3			Webb, Stephen	5	3	8								
White, Asa	3	4	5			Luce, Mehitable	1	2	5			WOODSTOCK TOWN.					
Bingham, Uriah	1	3	2			Meachum, Joseph	3	1	8								
Bingham, Jereh	1	2	3			Kingsley, Jonath	2	3	5			Chandler, Anne	1	1	6		
Pettingall, Solomon	1		4			Ripley, William	2	2	3			Brock, David	2		3		
Allen, Joseph	1	2	4			Fox, Jabez	1	2	5			Morse, Abiel	2	5	7		
Allen, Asael	3	2	3			Walker, Asael	1	1		2		Tucker, Stephen	6	4	5		
Adams, Asa	1		1			Lathrop, Roswell	2	5	2			May, Caleb	3	1	4		
Smith, Nathl	1		1			Jennings, John	1	1	5			May, Thos	3	1	4		
Lasell, Josiah	2	3	4			Hutchins, Elizabeth			1			Russell, William	2	2	5	2	
Kingsley, John	1	2	4			Cross, John	1	1	2			Tucker, Zephh	2	1	4		
Kingsley, Asael	1		1			Bingham, Jonath	3	1	5			May, Stephen	3	1	4		
Lillie, Elisha	2	1	5			Cross, William	2	1	2			Childs, Elisha	3	3	8		
Carey, William	1	5	5			Johnson, David	2	1	3			May, Silas	1	2	4		
Rudd, Nathl	2		3			Cross, Joseph	1	2	1			Taylor, Micah	1	2	2		
Walton, Joseph	1	2	3			Linkon, Nathl	3		3			Johnson, Joshua	2	2	5		
Lillie, Nathan	1		5			Flint, John, Senr	1	4	4			Torrey, Elisha	3	3	2		
Webb, Ebenezr	1		2			Stowel, Jonath	2	2	6			Allard, Uriah	2		3		
Baker, Walter	1	1	7			Tilden, Littice			4			Comstock, John	3		6		
Rudd, William	2	2	5			Kingsbury, Thomas	1	1	6			Carpenter, Ephraim	1	2	3		
Rudd, Jonathan	3	2	5			Linkon, John	3	4	2			Rawney, William	1	3	3		
Waldo, Zachus	4	1	2			Dains, Ephm	2	3	4			Childs, Abiel	2	2	5		
Waldo, Zachus, Jnr	1	2	3			Abbe, Joshua	2	4	3			Blackmar, Adonijah	3		5		
Bingham, Jedediah	1	2	7			Abbe, Joshua, Jnr	2	3	8			Haven, Abraham	2	1	4		
Bingham, Saml	2	2	5			Sessions, Joseph	1		3			Chanler, Seth	3	3	6		
Baker, Saml	3	5	7			Geer, Aaron	2	2	2			Sumner, Moses	1	1	3		
Baker, John	2	4	6			Geer, Saml	2	3	6			Dayley, Jacob	3	1	5		
Hebard, Nathan	3	2	7			Perkins, Cudge				6		Sumner, Sarah			3		
Bingham, Nathl	2	1	3			Welch, Peter				2		Bullard, Asa	2	1	1		
Bingham, Isaac	1		4			Geer, Amos	1	1	2			Child, Obediah	2	2	2		
Smith, Benjn	1	3	5			Orcutt, John	2		1			Williams, David	2	1	4		
Wood, Isaih	2	1	2			Walcott, Nathl	1	1	3			Allard, Danl	1	2	4		
Wood, Mary			6			Kennedy, David	1	1	3			May, Joshua	3	3	4		
Smith, Jonah	2		7			Kennedy, John	1		1			May, Joseph	1	1	2		
Jackson, Andrew				2		Gennings, Zebulon	2	1	1			Allard, William	2	1	2		
White, Prince				5		Dains, Axenbridge	1		1			Dawson, Ebenr	3	3	5		
Geer, Saml	2	3	7			Dains, Thomas	1		5			Buckman, Stephen	2	3	5		
Linkon, Thomas	4	4	2			Neff, Benjn	2	2	1			Murry, James	1	1	4		
Rouse, Jabez	1		1			Neff, Oliver	1		3			Cheamberlin, Abiel	1	3	3		
Cuningham, Anne			3			Spalding, James	1	5	8			Child, Elias	2	3	2		
Hanson, Edward				8		Dain, Lemuel	1	3	3			Long, Josiah	2		2		
Phillips, Saml				2		Colburn, Robert	1		1			Fox, Joseph	1	1	3		
Lynes, John				6		Colburn, Sylvanus	1		4			Bacon, Benjn	2	2	5		2
Robinson, Asa, Jnr	2	4	3			Rogers, Oliver	2	1	6			Childs, Nathl	5	1	5		
Linkon, Nathan	2	2	4			Colburn, Ithamar	1	1	1			Childs, Alpha	2	3	3		
Linkon, Jonah	1		4			Robinson, Simeon, Jnr	1	2	5			Walker, Leonard	2		1		
Bebbons, Benjn	1		1			Jinnings, Menoah	1		1			Jones, Samuel	1	2	3		
Martin, Jonathan	2	2	6			Chester, Jonathan	1	1	2			Bacon, Parker	3	1	4		
Welch, John	2		3			Jennings, Ebenezr	1	2	2			White, Peregrine	5	2	4		
Spafford, Jehiel	1	3	3			Smith, Mathew	1	1	3			Lyon, Danl	3	2	8		
Rathborne, Ezra				6		Huntley, Elijah	1		6			Lyon, Stephen	1	1	1		1
Phillips, John				4		Robinson, Simeon	1		1			Child, Timothy	3		5		
Hebard, Gideon	2	2	5			Walcott, Jabez	1		3			Stone, Isaac	3		1		
Welch, John, Jnr	1	2	5			Aims, William	1	1	2			Morris, William	1	5	3		
Snow, Thomas	1	1	6			Aims, Asa	1	3	2			Bradford, Samuel	1	3	4		
Wheeler, David	1	2	1			Abbe, Nathl	1		6			May, Eleakin	2	3	4		
Carey, Roger	1	2	5	2		Neff, John	1	5	1			Rawson, William	2	2	2		
Littlefield, Ebenezr	1	1	4			Kinsbury, Saml	1	1	4			Brown, Andrew	2	2	5		
Francis, Manning	1	1	7			Parrish, John	2	1	1			Carpenter, Davis	2	3	7		
Gennings, McHanah	1		3			Jennings, John	2	1	1			Marcy, Uriah	1		2		
Robinson, Asa	2		5			Linkon, Danl	1	1	3			Marcy, Elisha	1	2	1		
Robinson, Levi	1		2			Fisk, John	1	2	3			Phillips, William	3	4	4		
Robinson, James	2	3	5			Larrabe, Sith	3	2	3			Perrin, John	3		1		
Robinson, Reubin	2	1	2			Preston, William	1		7			Tucker, Stephen, Senr	3		3		
Robinson, Rubin, Jnr	1	1	4			Badcock, Joseph, Jnr	2	2	5			Goodale, Lemuel	2		6		
Baker, Elijah	1	3	3			Badcock, Joseph	1		2			Foster, Jacob	1	1	2		
Robinson, Jacob	3	1	1			Badcock, Nathan	2	3	2			Child, Amasa	2	1	6		
Morgan, Saml	2	1	4			Badcock, Danl	3	2	2			Plummer, Ebenr	1	1	1		
Morgan, Nathan	1	1	4			Warner, William	3	3	4			Vinton, Timothy	1				
Bingham, Thomas	2	2	2			Cartright, Cyrus	1	3	2			Eddy, Benjn	2		4		
Luce, Ebenezer	2	1	7			Fox, Jesse	3	1	7			Eddy, Lew	1	2	4		
Smith, Josiah	1	2	6			Kidder, Luther	3		3			Child, Henry	6	2	8		
Bottom, Asa	2	5	3			Allen, William	1	2	6			Child, Peter	4	1	4		
Palmer, Veniah	1	1	3			Allen, Abner	1	2	4			Gould, Besaliel	1	2	4		
Palmer, Jonah	3	1	5			Fuller, Nathl	1	2	3			Lyon, Nehemiah	4	3	4		
Robinson, Saml	1		2			Robinson, Andrew	1	2	1			Richmond, Edward	2	5	5		
Ringe, Amy			2			Ashley, Jonathan	1	2	5			Walker, Pheneas	6	3	4		
Morgan, Asher	1	1	3			Ashley, David	3	3	2			Child, Asa	3		2	1	
Carey, Jonath	1	4	2			Parrish, John, Jnr	2	2	8			Allard, Peter	3	1	3		
Lathrop, Ebenezer	3	2	4	1		Blackman, Jonath	1	1	1			Jackson, Benjn	1		2		
Southward, William	1	4	2			Flint, Saml	1	1	2			Corban, Abijah	1	1	5		
Burnam, Andrew	3	1	4			Jennings, Stephen	1	4	2			Carpenter, Ezekiel	2	2	4		
Badcock, Beriah	1	1	2			Martin, George	1	3	1			Bacon, Saml	2	2	4		
Burnam, James	1	1	2			Bibbens, Elijah	3	1	8			Sibley, Asa	2	1	4		
Johnson, Levi	3		6			Bibbens, Benjn	1		1			White, Cornelious	1	3	4		
Lease, John	1	1	1			Spafford, Oliver	1		2	1		Barret, Ephraim	1	2	1		
Carey, James	1	3	4	1		Thatcher, Asa	2	1	3			Barret, John	2	4	2		
Holt, Benjamin	2		2			Snow, Thomas	1	1	6			Barret, Danl	2	4	5		

WINDHAM COUNTY—Continued.

WOODSTOCK TOWN—continued.

NAME OF HEAD OF FAMILY.	Free white males of 16 years and upward, including heads of families.	Free white males under 16 years.	Free white females, including heads of families.	All other free persons.	Slaves.
Holmes, Ebenr	1	1	1	1	
Holmes, Ebenr, Jnr	1	4	3		
Chapman, Wm	1	1	2		
Chapman, William, Jnr	2	3	4		
Bowen, William	2	1	3		
Nigas, Silas	1		3	1	
Sanger, Pearley	2	2	2		
Woodbury, David	2	1	3		
Torrey, Saml	2	1	6		
Kimball, Jedd	3		2		
Howlet, Saml	2		1		
Bugbee, James	3	3	8		
Chaffee, Stephen	2		1		
Chaffee, Josiah	2	2	5		
Tucker, Ephm	3	1	2		
Cummins, Perker	2	1	4		
Hosmer, Abel	1	2	7		
Perrin, Wm	2		4		
Perrin, Amos	3	3	4		
Child, Nathl	5		4		
Hosmer (Wido.)	1	2	2		
Allen, Jonathan	2		3		
Bartholomew, Leonard	1	1	2		
Peak, Joseph, &c	3	2	5		
Bartholomew, Benjn	1		4		
Frisell, Joseph	4	2	2		
Payne, Danl	3	2	8	1	
Johnson, Uriah	1		9		
Griggs, Abijah	2		1		
Sanger, John	2	1	7		
Holmes, David	3	2	5		
Riley, Saml	1		3		
Lindley, Danl	3	2	3		
McClallen, Saml	6	2	4	1	2
Newell, Thos	2	1	3		
Bowen, Mathew	2	2	3		
Carryl, Ephraim	4	4	4		
William, David	3	2	3		
Hammond, Josiah	2	1	2		
Lyman, Eliphalet	2	2	5		
Bartholomew, John	2	1	5		
Chandler, Meriam	3	1	7		2
Fox, Thos	2	1	6		
Kingsley, Rufus	1		2		
Merey, John	3	3	2		
Holmes, William	1	2	3		
Easterbrooks, Peleg	2	2	2		
Fairfield, David	2		3		
Bolls, Jesse	3	5	4		
Sprague, John	1	1	6		
Leonard, Mary	1	2	4		
Badcock, Nathanl	2	3	3		
Easterbrook, Moses	3	3	4		
Barret, Smith	1	1	2		
Holebrook, Jobe	2	4	6		
Lathrop, Benjn	1	3	3		
Lyon, Nathl	1	1	3		
Trisdal, Darias	1	3	2		
Holbrook, Calvan	1	2	3		
Judge (Negro)				4	
Simons, Asael	1	1	2		
Chaffee, Noah	1	2	6		
Bugbee, Jedh	1	3	5		
Bugbee, Thomas	2	1	3		
Bugbe, Thomas, Jnr	2	1	1		
Manning, Bela	2	1	4		
Howlet, Saml, Junr	1	4	3		
Gay, Calvin	1	3	4		
Spears, Mary	1	1	3		
Cheamberlin, John	2	1	3		
Skinner, William	2	2	5		
Chaffee, Saml	3	1	6		
Chaffee, Benjr	2		5		
Bradford, George	1		2		
Skinner, Priscilla			4		
Darke, Alpheus	2	1	3		
Martin, William	4	1	4		
Lyon, George	2		5		
Willowbe, Isaac	1		3		
Hurlburt, Elijah	1		5		
Payson, Asa	1	3	1		
Manning, William	1	1			

WOODSTOCK TOWN—continued.

NAME OF HEAD OF FAMILY.	Free white males of 16 years and upward, including heads of families.	Free white males under 16 years.	Free white females, including heads of families.	All other free persons.	Slaves.
Mercy, Ichabod	2	3	3		
Clark, Nathl	1		2		
Flyn, John	2	2	6		
Child, Rufus	2	1	1		
Williams, Elijah	3	2	1		
Horton, Jonas	2	1	6		
Richardson, John	2	2	2		
Lyon, Isaiah	2	2	2		
Lyon, Jonath	5	2	8		
Lyon, Wm	1	3	4		
Lyon, Elijah	2	3	1		
Lyon, Benjamin	5		3		
Mason, Elias	3	2	5		
Kingsley, Uriah	1		2		
Martin, David	1	3	1		
Mascroft, Jacob	4	3	11		
Morse, Jedediah	3	4	8		
Lyon, William, Jnr	1	4	5		
Lyon, Thos	1	1	1		
Johnson, Willard	1		3		
Skinner, William, Jnr	1	2	5		
Nicholls, Ezekiel	2	3	5		
Ainsworth, Darious	2	4	3		
Coburn, Ebenr	2	5	5		
Coburn, David	1		3		
Dewing, Heza	1	1	2		
Dewing, Michael	1		1		
Lyon, Wareham	2	1	6		1
Paul, Daniel	1	1	4		
Coats, Saml	2	1	4		
Doyt, Abiel	2	1	6		
Morris, Saml	3		2		
Peabody, Richard	2		5		
Abbot, Nathan	5	3	3		
William, Stephen	3		3	1	
Bugbee, Elijah	2	4	5		
Johnson, William	1	1	2		
Linkon, Zephh	3		4		
Blanchard, John	2	1	5		
Lyon, Ebenr	2	6	3		
Barton, Michael	1	2	3		
Bugbee, Jonathn	2	1	7		
Richmond, Abner	1	2	1		
Richmond, Joseph	2	1	4		
Bowen, Henry	2	4	2		
Morse, Lyda	2		3		
Bartholomew, Sarah			3		
Ferker, Eleazr	5	4	5		
Perrin, Moses	2		2		
Lillie, Ebenr	3	1	6		
Chandler, Moses	3		7		
Johnson, Peter	1		4		
Johnson, Stephen	1	3	2		
Skinner, Abraham	2		4		1
Payne, Stephen	1		1		
Mercy, Nathl	2	2	3		
Wilkinson, Rhodes	2	2	4		
Bradford, George	3	1	4		
Bradford, Essick	1		2		
Coltney, George	4		7		
Perrin, Elijah	2	1	4		
Howlet, John	2	4	3		
Fuller, Nathl	1	1	3		
Greggs, Ichabod	2	3	5		
Smith, Ebenr	3	2	9		1
Morris, Lemuel	5	4	5		
Bugbe, Rufus	2	3	7		
Mathewson, Israil	1	3	7		
Skinner, Stephen	2	3	3		
Payne, Luter	2	1	6		
Salisbury, Richard	1	1	6		
Martin, Henry	1	5	3		
Barber, William	3		4		
Howard, Peter	3	3	2		
Carpenter, Joseph	1	1	4		
Perrin, David	5	1	6		
Perrin, Stephen	2	1	3		
Childs, Elias	3		1		
Sheppard, William	2	3	3		
Perrin, Timothy	2	1	4		
Bugbee, William	2	3	4		
Childs, Jacob	2	3	4		

WOODSTOCK TOWN—continued.

NAME OF HEAD OF FAMILY.	Free white males of 16 years and upward, including heads of families.	Free white males under 16 years.	Free white females, including heads of families.	All other free persons.	Slaves.
Grosvener, Caleb	1	3	3		
Perry, Elijah	1		5		
Clark, Joseph	2	1	3		
Perrin, Danl	2	3	4		
Camp, Simeon	1		4		
Bugbe, Caleb	3	2	6		
Stoddard, Ebene	1	2	3		
Dean, Abiel	3		4		
Carpenter, Dan	1	1	1		
Austin, Jacob	4		3		
Dean, Zephh	3	2	3		
Howard, Benjn	6	2	5		
Howard, Amasa	1		7		
Howard, David	2	1	7		
Wally, John				4	
Green, Charles	2	1	3		
Mason, Noah	4	2	6		
Wheeler, James	2	2	3		
Hosmer, Menassah, Senr	2	4	6		
Hosmer, Menassah	2	1	2		
Macy, Asael	2	4	7		
Wilbar, William	2	1	4		1
Corbin, William	3	3	5		
Corban, Asael	3		3		
Corban, John	2	1	2		
Morse, David	1	1	4		
Cutlar, Jesse	1	2	2		
Bartholomew, Saml	1	1	3		
Lyon, Amos	3	1	4		
Underwood, Lemuel	1	2	3		
Bartholomew, Saml	1	2	6		
Leonard, Jacob	3	3	4		
Mercy, Israel	2	1	6		
Macy, Jonath	2	1	6		
Thayer, Mebisheth	1	1	3		
Morse, John	3		3		
Cheamberlin, Elisha	3	2	4		
Easterbrooks, Oliver	3	1	5		
Cheamberlin, Rubin	1	1	4		
Mercy, Abraham	1	2	2		
Smith, Danl	1	2	6		
Dodge, Eunice	1	2	3		
Broughton, Amos	1	2	5		
Gage, Joel	2	2	4		
Gage, Thaddeus	1	1	2		
Gage, Elisha	1	3	4		
Underwood, Josiah	1	3	2		
Goodale, Asa	3		5		
Clark, David	1	2	3		
Clark, Seth	2		3		
Gage, Aaron	1	2	1		
Mercy, Israel, Jnr	1	1	6		
Craft, David	1	1	2		
Clark, Asael	3		3		
Cady, Luther	1	1	2		
Ainsworth, Joseph	2	3	3		
Key, Joseph	1	2	2		
Cole, Nathan	2	2	5		
Thompson, Ichabod	1	1	2		
Lyon, Danl	2	2	2		
Jackson, Nehemiah	2	2	3		
Eddy, Levy	1	2	3		
Mashcraft, John	2	1	3		
Goodale, John	3	1	4		
Doyt, James	3	3	3		
Fox, John	2	5	3		
Child, Thos	1	1	4		
Child, Lem	2	2	5		
Underwood, Neheh	3	4	4		
Bugbee, Danl	5	1	4		
Lyon, Sabry	1	2	3		
Perrin, John	3		1		
Broadwav, Eleazr	2	1	3		
Ainsworth, William	1	1			1
Ferrin, Isaiah	1		2		
Corban, Silas	4	2	7		
Childs, Shubael	1				
Hull, Amos				3	
Fairfield, Eleanor	1	1	3		
Barret, Joseph	1	2	4		
Barret, Hannah		1	2		

INDEX.[1]

[1] No attempt has been made in this publication to correct mistakes in spelling made by the deputy marshals, but the names have been reproduced as they appear upon the census schedules.

Bibbons, Timothy, 30.
Bicket, David, 110.
Bicknal, Moses, 147.
Bicknall, John, 140.
Bicknall, Zachʰ, 140.
Bidwel, Eliezer, 68.
Bidwel, Joseph, 68.
Bidwell, Allyn, 42.
Bidwell, Amos, 47.
Bidwell, Asenath, 36.
Bidwell, Ashbel, 36.
Bidwell, Ashbell, 87.
Bidwell, Daniel, 79.
Bidwell, David, 37.
Bidwell, David, 42.
Bidwell, Elijah, 66.
Bidwell, Elisha, 36.
Bidwell, Eodias, 36.
Bidwell, Ephraim, 37.
Bidwell, Ephraim, 42.
Bidwell, Epiphras, 64.
Bidwell, Hezekiah, 42.
Bidwell, Isaac, 40.
Bidwell, Isaac, 42.
Bidwell, Jacob, 75.
Bidwell, James, 48.
Bidwell, Jeremiah, 75.
Bidwell, John, 36.
Bidwell, John, 79.
Bidwell, Jonathan, 36.
Bidwell, Jonathan, 42.
Bidwell, Jonathan, 55.
Bidwell, Joseph, 36.
Bidwell, Joseph, 42.
Bidwell, Mary, 36.
Bidwell, Rebecca, 42.
Bidwell, Riverious, 60.
Bidwell, Samuel, 36.
Bidwell, Samuel, 42.
Bidwell, Stephen, 37.
Bidwell, Stephen, 37.
Bidwell, Theodore, 40.
Bidwell, Thomas, 48.
Bidwell, Thomas, 60.
Bidwell, Zebulon, 37.
Bierce, Austin, 56.
Bierce, Hezekiah, 57.
Bierce, Isaih, 56.
Bierce, Jeames, 56.
Bierce, Joseph, 56.
Bierr, Hial, 60.
Bigalow, Asa, 122.
Bigalow, Azariah, 121.
Bigalow, Bond, 122.
Bigalow, Daniel, 121.
Bigalow, Ezra, 121.
Bigalow, Ira, 120.
Bigalow, James, 121.
Bigalow, John, 121.
Bigalow, Jonathan, 121.
Bigalow, Sarah, 121.
Bigelow, Alvin, 46.
Bigelow, Daniel, 45.
Bigelow, David, 43.
Bigelow, Elisha, 46.
Bigelow, Elisha, 83.
Bigelow, Elisha, Jr., 46.
Bigelow, Elizabeth, 85.
Bigelow, Frederick, 87.
Bigelow, Jame, 46.
Bigelow, Joel, 83.
Bigelow, John, 46.
Bigelow, Jonathan, 46.
Bigelow, Joseph, 46.
Bigelow, Josiah, 46.
Bigelow, Otis, 145.
Bigelow, Timothy H., 85.
Bigford, Thomas, 144.
Biggs, Adam, 143.
Biggs, Willᵐ, 89.
Bigsbee, Jnᵒ, 134.
Bigsbee, Solᵐ, 136.
Bigsbie, Ebenezer, 31.
Bigsby, Aaron, 150.
Bigsby, Amos, 150.
Bigsby, Gracy (Wᵈ), 22.
Bigsby, Green, 121.
Bigsby, Jacob, 150.
Bigsby, Jesse, 150.
Bigsby, Moses, 150.
Bigsby, Nathan, 150.
Bigsby, Samˡ, 150.
Bilbert, John, 33.
Bill, Aaron, 42.
Bill, Abial, 146.
Bill, Annis, 120.
Bill, Benaijah, 118.
Bill, Benjamin, 119.
Bill, Charles, 125.
Bill, Daniel, 69.
Bill, Elijah, 1ˢᵗ, 57.
Bill, Elijah, 2ᵈ, 57.
Bill, Elisha, 144.
Bill, Elizur, 42.
Bill, Ephraim, 131.
Bill, Erastus, 80.
Bill, Isaac, 42.
Bill, James, 80.
Bill, Jonathan, 62.
Bill, Jonaᵗʰ, 145.
Bill, Jonathan, 2ᵈ, 62.
Bill, Joseph, 116.
Bill, Joshua, 118.

Bill, Martha, 86.
Bill, Phineas, 118.
Bill, Roswell, 143.
Bill, Samuel, 86.
Bill, Solomon, 86.
Bill, Thomas, 146.
Bill, Timothy, 127.
Billing, Jnᵒ, 136.
Billinghast, John, 117.
Billings, Alpheus, 130.
Billings, Amos, 117.
Billings, Benaijah, 115.
Billings, Benaijah, Junʳ, 115.
Billings, Benjamin, 114.
Billings, Daniel, 115.
Billings, Eli, 40.
Billings, Elijah, 136.
Billings, Elisha, 115.
Billings, Henry, 131.
Billings, John, 118.
Billings, Joseph, 114.
Billings, Lament, 129.
Billings, Mary, 120.
Billings, Mary, 131.
Billings, Mathew, 125.
Billings, Nathan, 115.
Billings, Nathaniel, 40.
Billings, Otis, 115.
Billings, Randall, 114.
Billings, Samuel, 115.
Billings, Samˡ, 136.
Billings, Samuel, Junʳ, 115.
Billings, Sanford, 115.
Billings, Solⁿ, 136.
Billings, Stephen, 118.
Billings, Stephen, 125.
Billings, Thaddeus, 40.
Billings, William, 114.
Billows, Hezᵃ, 150.
Bills, Benajah, 61.
Bills, John, 37.
Bills, Joshua, 61.
Bills, Thomas, 104.
Bills, Thomas, 2ⁿᵈ, 104.
Bills, William, 103.
Bim, David, 101.
Bin, Isaac, 107.
Bindy, Nathan, 29.
Bingham, Abel, 81.
Bingham, Alfred, 152.
Bingham, Asa, 132.
Bingham, Banajah, 63.
Bingham, Daniel, 69.
Bingham, Daniel, 2ᵈ, 69.
Bingham, David, 126.
Bingham, Ebenzʳ, 152.
Bingham, Eleazʳ, 147.
Bingham, Elias, 152.
Bingham, Elijah, 122.
Bingham, Gideon, 152.
Bingham, Gidion, 142.
Bingham, Gurdon, 142.
Bingham, Isaac, 153.
Bingham, Ithᵐ, 134.
Bingham, Ithᵐ, 134.
Bingham, Jedediah, 153.
Bingham, Jereʰ, 153.
Bingham, Jereʰ, 153.
Bingham, John, 152.
Bingham, John, Junʳ, 112.
Bingham, Jonaᵗʰ, 153.
Bingham, Joseph, 152.
Bingham, Luther, 142.
Bingham, Nathan, 126.
Bingham, Nathˡ, 153.
Bingham, Oliver, 147.
Bingham, Ralph, 152.
Bingham, Samˡ, 153.
Bingham, Simeon, 131.
Bingham, Stephen, 135.
Bingham, Thomas, 153.
Bingham, Uriah, 153.
Bingley, Hannah, 105.
Bino, Ruth, 112.
Bino, Samuel, 112.
Bino, Watham, 101.
Birchard, Elijah, 73.
Birchard, Isaiah, 29.
Birchard, James, 23.
Birchard, Jemima (Wᵈ), 23.
Birchard, Jeremiah, 29.
Birchard, Jesse, 22.
Birchard, John, 130.
Birchard, Joseph, 147.
Birchard, Prince, 140.
Birchard, Uriah, 29.
Birchird, Ezra, 126.
Birchird, Jesse, 126.
Bird, Amy, 48.
Bird, Atwood, 56.
Bird, Ephraim, 35.
Bird, James, 66.
Bird, John, 35.
Bird, Joseph, 41.
Bird, Lucy, 66.
Bird, Sarah, 104.
Bird, Thomas, 66.
Birdsay, Hannah, 89.
Birdsey, Abel, 89.
Birdsey, Abigail, 89.
Birdsey, David, 89.
Birdsey, Ebenezer, 57.
Birdsey, John, 18.

Birdsey, John, 89.
Birdsey, John, Junʳ, 89.
Birdsie, Ezra, 31.
Birdsie, Thadeus, 31.
Birdsie, William, 30.
Birdslee, Joseph, 18.
Birdwell, John, 47.
Birdwell, Ozeas, 37.
Birdwell, Stephen, 70.
Birkingham, Hosmer, 90.
Birkshop, Abraham, 68.
Birrchard, Daniel, 21.
Bisco, Ruth, 101.
Biscow, John, 21.
Biscow, Sarah (Wid.), 20.
Bishnel, Alexander, 62.
Bishop, Abel, 106.
Bishop, Abijah, 24.
Bishop, Alexander, 24.
Bishop, Amos, 56.
Bishop, Benjamin, 41.
Bishop, Benjamin, 106.
Bishop, Betsy, 126.
Bishop, Billy, 56.
Bishop, Caleb, 112.
Bishop, Calvin, 66.
Bishop, Caty (Wᵈ), 26.
Bishop, Charles, 97.
Bishop, Clemment, 124.
Bishop, Dan., 56.
Bishop, Daniel, 56.
Bishop, Daniel, 103.
Bishop, Daniel, 124.
Bishop, David, 98.
Bishop, David, 98.
Bishop, Deborah, 56.
Bishop, Ebenezar, 34.
Bishop, Ebenezer, 99.
Bishop, Ebenezer, 99.
Bishop, Ebenezer, 113.
Bishop, Eleazer, 37.
Bishop, Eler, 71.
Bishop, Elias, 99.
Bishop, Elizabeth, 98.
Bishop, Elizabeth, 99.
Bishop, Eneas, 99.
Bishop, Ezra, 100.
Bishop, Ezra, 113.
Bishop, Hannah, 98.
Bishop, Hannah, 99.
Bishop, Icabod, 97.
Bishop, Isaac, 103.
Bishop, Israel, 102.
Bishop, Jacob, 22.
Bishop, James, 40.
Bishop, James, 96.
Bishop, James, 98.
Bishop, James, 99.
Bishop, Jarad, 92.
Bishop, Jerad, 98.
Bishop, Jereʰ, 140.
Bishop, Jesse, 68.
Bishop, Jesse, 99.
Bishop, John, 99.
Bishop, John, 113.
Bishop, John, 124.
Bishop, Jnᵒ, 132.
Bishop, John, 2ᵈ, 99.
Bishop, Johson, 97.
Bishop, Joiner, 98.
Bishop, Jonas, 96.
Bishop, Jonathan, 24.
Bishop, Jonathan, 98.
Bishop, Jonᵃ, 127.
Bishop, Jonathan A., 11.
Bishop, Joseph, 111.
Bishop, Joseph, 124.
Bishop, Joshua, 112.
Bishop, Joy, 106.
Bishop, Joy, 2ⁿᵈ, 106.
Bishop, Leveritt, 87.
Bishop, Lines, 98.
Bishop, Mary, 112.
Bishop, Miles, 59.
Bishop, Mimsa, 63.
Bishop, Nathan, 11.
Bishop, Nathaniel, 100.
Bishop, Nathˡ, 112.
Bishop, Nero, 99.
Bishop, Parker, 144.
Bishop, Parsons, 26.
Bishop, Peter, 26.
Bishop, Ruben, 100.
Bishop, Russell, 98.
Bishop, Samuel, 24.
Bishop, Samuel, 37.
Bishop, Samuel, 41.
Bishop, Samuel, 99.
Bishop, Samuel, 103.
Bishop, Samuel, 112.
Bishop, Samˡ, 132.
Bishop, Sarah, 124.
Bishop, Seth, 98.
Bishop, Seth, 2ᵈ, 60.
Bishop, Silas, 24.
Bishop, Silvanus, 66.
Bishop, Simion, 106.
Bishop, Stephen, 25.
Bishop, Stephen, Junʳ, 25.
Bishop, Susanna, 127.
Bishop, Sussannah, 99.
Bishop, Sylvanus, 103.

Bishop, Tabitha, 98.
Bishop, Thalmeno, 84.
Bishop, Thomas, 124.
Bishop, Thoˢ, 132.
Bishop, Thomas F., 41.
Bishop, Timothy, 100.
Bishop, William, 77.
Bishshop, Samuel, 52.
Bishshop, Seth, 60.
Bissel, Abagail, 64.
Bissel, Archulus, 64.
Bissel, Benjamin, 59.
Bissel, Benjamin, 60.
Bissel, Benjamin, 64.
Bissel, Benjamin, 69.
Bissel, Colvis, 64.
Bissel, Ebenezer, 69.
Bissel, Ebenr F., 54.
Bissel, Ebinr F., Ju., 54.
Bissel, Elijah, 69.
Bissel, Eliphet, 69.
Bissel, Ezekiel, 69.
Bissel, Hezekiah, 69.
Bissel, Hezekiah, 135.
Bissel, Heziʰ (Wid.), 54.
Bissel, John, 62.
Bissel, John, 71.
Bissel, Joseph, 64.
Bissel, Josiah, 54.
Bissel, Luthry, 133.
Bissel, Mathew, 133.
Bissel, Zebulon, 64.
Bissell, Aaron, 38.
Bissell, Benjamin, 146.
Bissell, Daniel, 38.
Bissell, Dan., 39.
Bissell, Daniel, 145.
Bissell, David, 38.
Bissell, Ebenezer, 38.
Bissell, Elisha, 38.
Bissell, Elisha, 146.
Bissell, Epaphras, 38.
Bissell, Hannah, 39.
Bissell, Hezekiah, 38.
Bissell, Col. Hezʰ, 55.
Bissell, Isaac, 52.
Bissell, Jerijah, 38.
Bissell, Jerijah, Jr., 38.
Bissell, John, 38.
Bissell, Jonathan, 38.
Bissell, Joseph F., 146.
Bissell, Joseph W., 145.
Bissell, Justus, 38.
Bissell, Moses, 38.
Bissell, Nathaniel, 38.
Bissell, Noah, 38.
Bissell, Ozias, 37.
Bissell, Partridge, 146.
Bissell, Roswold, 38.
Bissell, Russell, 37.
Bissell, Timothy, 39.
Bissell, William, 38.
Bissenton, Asael, 107.
Bissinton, Heil, 107.
Bissinton, Robert, 107.
Bivins, Ebenʳ, 88.
Black, Esther, 77.
Black, Step (negro), 22.
Blackesley, Mathew, 69.
Blackley, Admer, 22.
Blackley, Asa, 93.
Blackley, John, 129.
Blackley, Margaret, 129.
Blacklidge, George, 18.
Blacklidge, Pamey, 18.
Blackman, Aaron, 134.
Blackman, Ager, 18.
Blackman, Asahel, 17.
Blackman, Benjⁿ, 134.
Blackman, Benjⁿ, Jr., 134.
Blackman, Daniel, 32.
Blackman, David, 18.
Blackman, David, 18.
Blackman, Ebenezer, 10.
Blackman, Edward, 19.
Blackman, Eli, 17.
Blackman, Ephraim, 18.
Blackman, Jacob, 150.
Blackman, James, 21.
Blackman, James, 29.
Blackman, James, 29.
Blackman, Joel, 18.
Blackman, John, 13.
Blackman, John, 20.
Blackman, John, Junʳ, 21.
Blackman, Jonas, 18.
Blackman, Jonaᵗʰ, 153.
Blackman, Joseph, 20.
Blackman, Josiah, 20.
Blackman, Lemuel, 73.
Blackman, N. Cady, 74.
Blackman, Nehemiah, 32.
Blackman, Niram, 10.
Blackman, Peter, 63.
Blackman, Philo, 10.
Blackman, Phineas, 30.
Blackman, Reuben, 20.
Blackman, Ruth, 17.
Blackman, Samuel, 18.
Blackman, Samuel, 18.
Blackman, Timothy, 17.
Blackman, Treuman, 21.
Blackman, Truman, 63.

Blackman, William, 18.
Blackman, Wᵐ, 135.
Blackman, Zacheriah, 31.
Blackmar, Adonijah, 153.
Blackmar, Jonaʰ, 150.
Blackmon, Ezekel, 150.
Blackmore, Levi, 151.
Blackslee, Daniel, 84.
Blacksly, Benjamin, 23.
Blackston, John, 91.
Blague, Giles, 89.
Blague, Joseph, 79.
Blake, David, 94.
Blake, Elijah, 69.
Blake, Freelove, 87.
Blake, Isaac, 96.
Blake, John, 87.
Blake, Marana, 62.
Blake, Richard, 59.
Blake, Ruben, 96.
Blake, Samuel, 87.
Blakelee, David, 84.
Blakeley, Abner, 50.
Blakeley, Abram, 77.
Blakeley, Adna, 75.
Blakeley, Amos, 75.
Blakeley, Annis, 75.
Blakeley, Ashur, 75.
Blakeley, Bela, 75.
Blakeley, Dan, 77.
Blakeley, Eli, 75.
Blakeley, Enos, 57.
Blakeley, Jared, 76.
Blakeley, Jeames, 75.
Blakeley, Joel, 75.
Blakeley, Jonathan, 57.
Blakeley, Judah, 75.
Blakeley, Micajah, 75.
Blakeley, Moses, 75.
Blakeley, Samuel, 75.
Blakeley, Silas, 57.
Blakeley, Solomon, 75.
Blakeley, Thomas, 76.
Blakeley, Tilley, 77.
Blakeley, Zelus, 106.
Blakely, Abigal, 99.
Blakely, Baley, 51.
Blakely, Joseph, 107.
Blakely, Laban, 50.
Blakely, Moses, 93.
Blakely, Obidiah, 16.
Blakely, Oliver, 98.
Blakely, Ruben, 110.
Blakely, Sola, 75.
Blakeman, Elijah, 134.
Blakesley, Abraham, 106.
Blakesley, Amos, 106.
Blakesley, Caleb, 106.
Blakesley, Deborah, 100.
Blakesley, Enos, 106.
Blakesley, Isaac, 106.
Blakesley, Joel, 106.
Blakesley, John, 106.
Blakesley, Jonah, 106.
Blakesley, Philomen, 106.
Blakesley, Samuel, 61.
Blakesley, Samˡ, 64.
Blakesley, Samˡ, 68.
Blakesley, Seth, 106.
Blakesley, Thomas, 67.
Blakesley, Zopher, 106.
Blakley, Ebenezer, 109.
Blakley, Joseph, 99.
Blakley, Joseph, 2ᵈ, 107.
Blakley, Joshua, 99.
Blakley, Moses, 99.
Blakley, Tilley, 104.
Blakmore, Simeon, 62.
Blakston, Stephen, 91.
Blakston, Timothy, 91.
Blanchard, Elias, 143.
Blanchard, Jacob, 25.
Blanchard, Jere, 55.
Blanchard, John, 143.
Blanchard, John, 154.
Blanchard, William, 25.
Blancher, Nathaniel, 77.
Blancherd, Eunice, 36.
Bland, James, 125.
Blanott, James, 45.
Blaxton, Sarah, 91.
Bligh, Benjⁿ, 151.
Blin, David, 54.
Blin, Gershom, 52.
Blin, Hezekiah, 54.
Blin, Hosea, 52.
Blin, Hosea, 65.
Blin, James, 54.
Blin, Jonathan, 54.
Blin, Justus, 54.
Blin, Martha, 54.
Blin, Peter, 54.
Blin, Peter, Jr., 54.
Blin, Samuel, 52.
Blin, Solomon, 52.
Blin, Unni, 53.
Blin, William, 52.
Blish, David, 43.
Blish, John, 121.
Blish, Thomas, 43.
Bliss, Abel, 135.
Bliss, Abraham, 126.
Bliss, Amos, 145.

Bradley, Nathan, 13.
Bradley, Nathaniel, 49.
Bradley, Nathaniel, 75.
Bradley, Nehemiah, 49.
Bradley, Noah, 99.
Bradley, Obed, 106.
Bradley, Oliver, 93.
Bradley, Peleg, 92.
Bradley, Peter, 13.
Bradley, Phillip B., Esqr, 28.
Bradley, Philo, 75.
Bradley, Phineas, 104.
Bradley, Richard, 77.
Bradley, Roswell, 93.
Bradley, Ruben, 93.
Bradley, Ruben, 111.
Bradley, Ruben, 134.
Bradley, Samuel, 13.
Bradley, Samuel, 28.
Bradley, Samuel, 97.
Bradley, Sarah, 97.
Bradley, Searl, 77.
Bradley, Seth, 13.
Bradley, Silas, 111.
Bradley, Simeon, 97.
Bradley, Simry, 98.
Bradley, Soloman, 105.
Bradley, Stephen, 28.
Bradley, Stephen, 92.
Bradley, Stephen, 97.
Bradley, Stephen, 103.
Bradley, Stephen, Junr, 97.
Bradley, Thomas, 106.
Bradley Timothy, 50.
Bradley, Timothy, 71.
Bradley, Timothy, 98.
Bradley, Timothy, 111.
Bradley, Timothy, 2nd, 111.
Bradley, Tina, 66.
Bradley, Titus, 106.
Bradley, Walter, 13.
Bradley, William, 53.
Bradley, William, 96.
Bradley, Wilmot, 111.
Bradley, Zalmon, 13.
Bradley, Zewer, 106.
Bradly, Alling, 111.
Bradly, Charles, 111.
Bradly, David, 32.
Bradly, Gershom, 32.
Bradly, Isaac, 109.
Bradly, Joseph, 106.
Bradly, Timothy, 91.
Bradly, William, 31.
Bradshaw, William, 71.
Brag, Benjamin, 96.
Brag, Edwd, 134.
Bragg, Thomas, 140.
Bragnord, Othniah, 69.
Brainard, Aaron, 84.
Brainard, Adonejah, 46.
Brainard, Amos, 83.
Brainard, Bushnell, 84.
Brainard, Cornelius, 83.
Brainard, Daniel, 80.
Brainard, Daniel, 84.
Brainard, David, 84.
Brainard, David, 107.
Brainard, Dudley, 83.
Brainard, Eber, 83.
Brainard, Eliakim, 83.
Brainard, Eliakim, Junr, 83.
Brainard, Elijah, 84.
Brainard, Ezra, 36.
Brainard, Ezra, Esqr, 83.
Brainard, Gideon, 83.
Brainard, Gideon, Junr, 83.
Brainard, Heman, 84.
Brainard, Hen'y, 74.
Brainard, Hezh, Esqr, 83.
Brainard, Isaac, 83.
Brainard, James, 80.
Brainard, James, 83.
Brainard, Jedediah, 83.
Brainard, Jedediah, Junr, 84.
Brainard, Jepthia, 80.
Brainard, Jeremiah, 84.
Brainard, Jeremiah, 126.
Brainard, Jessey, 83.
Brainard, Jessey, 83.
Brainard, John, 81.
Brainard, John, 84.
Brainard, Jona, 83.
Brainard, Joshua, 104.
Brainard, Josiah, 83.
Brainard, Josiah, Junr, 83.
Brainard, Josiah, 3d, 84.
Brainard, Martha, 84.
Brainard, Nathan, 80.
Brainard, Nathaniel, 47.
Brainard, Nathaniel, 84.
Brainard, Nehemiah, Esqr, 83.
Brainard, Oliver, 83.
Brainard, Othniel, 80.
Brainard, Ozias, 80.
Brainard, Phinehas, 84.
Brainard, Phinehas, Junr, 83.
Brainard, Prosper, 84.
Brainard, Robert, 83.
Brainard, Samuel, 84.
Brainard, Seth, 80.
Brainard, Simeon, 80.
Brainard, Simeon, Junr, 80.
Brainard, Stephen, 75.
Brainard, Stephen, 81.
Brainard, William, 83.
Brainard, William, 84.
Brainard, William, 121.
Brainard, Zachariah, 84.
Brainard, Zadock, 83.
Brainerd, Amasa, 81.
Brainerd, Bezaleel, 81.
Brainerd, Eleazer, 81.
Brainerd, Enoch, 82.
Brainerd, Jared, 82.
Brainerd, John, 81.
Brainerd, Joshua, 81.
Brainerd, Joshua, 2d, 81.
Brainthwait, Robert, 45.
Braman, Daniel, 112.
Braman, Jos., 134.
Bramble, John, 124.
Bramin, John, 114.
Bramin, Paul, 127.
Bramin, Prudence, 113.
Branch, Moses, 148.
Branch, Stephen, 113.
Branch, Thomas, 113.
Brand, Benjamin, 119.
Brand, Lucy, 117.
Brand, Thomas, 116.
Brandier, Elishama, 33.
Branton, Michael, 70.
Brau, Abel, 68.
Brau, Ariel, 68.
Brau, Charles, 61.
Brau, Hanah (Wid.), 19.
Brau, Henry, 47.
Brau, John, 46.
Brau, Jonathan, Esqr, 42.
Brau, Lenas, 47.
Brau, Moses, 47.
Brau, Orange, 68.
Brau, Thomas, 47.
Braughton, Nathan, 63.
Bray, Asa, 50.
Bray, John, 50.
Bray, Thomas W., 99.
Brayman, Daniel, 38.
Brayne, Asahel, 62.
Brayton, David, 149.
Brayton, Thos, 149.
Breant, Alexander, 69.
Brecket, Zenus, 109.
Breed, Newell, 104.
Breford, Benjamin, 107.
Brendly, John, 53.
Breneson, Ozias, 67.
Bret, William, 130.
Breto, Isaac, 23.
Brewer, Benjamin, 44.
Brewer, Daniel, 36.
Brewer, Daniel, 37.
Brewer, Daniel, 37.
Brewer, David, 79.
Brewer, Dorothy, 43.
Brewer, Hezekiah, 79.
Brewer, John, 12.
Brewster, Asa, 152.
Brewster, Benjamin, 145.
Brewster, Benjamin, 152.
Brewster, Comfort, 145.
Brewster, David, 77.
Brewster, Elisha, 87.
Brewster, Experience, 146.
Brewster, Ichabod, 146.
Brewster, Israel, 133.
Brewster, Jacob, 133.
Brewster, Jane, 85.
Brewster, Jededih, 142.
Brewster, John, 143.
Brewster, Nathl, 143.
Brewster, Peleg, 142.
Brewster, Peter, 133.
Brewster, Saml, 146.
Brewster, Wadsworth, 146.
Brewster, Walter, 142.
Briant, Danl D., 134.
Brice, Robart, 120.
Brick, Moses, 60.
Brickwell, Zebulon, 99.
Bride, Ann, 132.
Bridge, Asa, 136.
Bridges, Edmund, 120.
Bridgham, George, 86.
Brigden, Jonathan, 104.
Brigden, Michael, 52.
Brigden, Thomas, 86.
Brigden, Timothy, 132.
Brigden, William, 103.
Briggs, Caleb, 25.
Briggs, Ezra, 25.
Briggs, Hannah (Wd), 25.
Briggs, Hannah, Jr (Wd), 25.
Briggs, James, 151.
Briggs, John, 140.
Briggs, Jona, 150.
Briggs, Stephen, 25.
Briggs, William, 129.
Briggs, William, 151.
Briggs, Zepheniah, 19.
Briggsby, Hopkins, 22.
Briggsby, John, 22.
Briggsby, John, 22.
Briggsby, Joseph, 22.
Briggsby, Moses, 22.
Brigh, Elijah, 76.
Brigham, Don, 133.
Brigham, Gersham, 133.
Brigham, Stephen, 147.
Brigham, Thos, 133.
Brigham, Tiphet, 133.
Brightman, Henry, 120.
Brightman, Henry, Junr, 120.
Brigs, Ithamer, 116.
Brindsmaid, Cyrus, 31.
Brindsmde, Josiah, 31.
Brinsley, Daniel, 30.
Brinsmade, Daniel, 74.
Brinsmade, Daniel N., 74.
Brinsmade, John, 66.
Brinsmade, Saml, 66.
Brintnal, William, 103.
Brises, Isaac, 73.
Brister, Bozaleel, 84.
Brister, David, 41.
Brister, Isarel, 10.
Brister, John, 63.
Brister, Joseph, 20.
Brister, Soloman, 26.
Bristo (Negro), 35.
Bristo (Negro), 132.
Bristol, Amos, 57.
Bristol, Arial, 71.
Bristol, Austin, 92.
Bristol, Benjamin, 92.
Bristol, Daniel, 71.
Bristol, David, 102.
Bristol, David, 105.
Bristol, David, 2nd, 105.
Bristol, Dick (Negroe), 93.
Bristol, Eliphlet, 73.
Bristol, Eunice, 111.
Bristol, Ezra, 93.
Bristol, Gad, 73.
Bristol, Gad, 2d, 73.
Bristol, George A., 100.
Bristol, Gideon, 93.
Bristol, John, 57.
Bristol, Jonathan, 92.
Bristol, Justus, 73.
Bristol, Nathan, 57.
Bristol (Negro), 145.
Bristol (Negroe), 95.
Bristol (Negroe), 100.
Bristol, P. Brigs, 73.
Bristol, Phico, 102.
Bristol, Reuben, 1st, 57.
Bristol, Reuben, 2d, 57.
Bristol, Richard, 71.
Bristol, Richard, 99.
Bristol, Ruben, 94.
Bristol, Samuel, 77.
Bristol, Samuel, 98.
Bristol, Sarah, 56.
Bristol, Simeon, 100.
Bristol, Thankfull, 93.
Bristol, Thomas, 73.
Bristol, Thomas, 93.
Bristol, Truman, 73.
Bristol, Zelus, 92.
Briston & Philup (Negro), 115.
Bristor, Elizabeth, 102.
Bristor, John, 60.
Bristow, John, 101.
Bristow, Nathan, 102.
Bristow, Richard, 102.
Bristow, Stephen, 109.
Britt, Em, 139.
Britterfield, Simeon, 71.
Britton, Newton, 101.
Broach, Mary, 32.
Broadway, Eleazr, 154.
Brock, David, 153.
Brock, Phillis, 35.
Brockway, Abner, 122.
Brockway, Benjamin, 123.
Brockway, Clark, 122.
Brockway, Ebenezer, 90.
Brockway, Ebenezer, 122.
Brockway, Edward, 61.
Brockway, Edward, 124.
Brockway, Elias, 123.
Brockway, Elijah, 90.
Brockway, Eliphelet, 122.
Brockway, Elisha, 123.
Brockway, Enoch, 82.
Brockway, Ezra, 122.
Brockway, Ezra, 122.
Brockway, Gamaliel, 122.
Brockway, John, 122.
Brockway, Joseph, 41.
Brockway, Joseph, Jr., 41.
Brockway, Lowis, 122.
Brockway, Moses, 61.
Brockway, Richard, 122.
Brockway, Richard, 2d, 122.
Brockway, Samuel, 35.
Brockway, Samuel, 35.
Brockway, Simeon, 35.
Brockway, Thomas, 146.
Brockway, William, 122.
Brockway, Woolston, 124.
Brockway, Zebulun, 122.
Brockwey, Watston, 69.
Brokes, Limeuel, 106.
Bromley, David, 116.
Bromley, Dewey, 114.
Bromley, Israel, 114.
Bromley, Jabez, 115.
Bromley, Jesse, 115.
Bromley, John, 115.
Bromley, Preserved, 113.
Bromwell, Ichabod, 67.
Bronson, Alford, 19.
Broock, Abraham, 34.
Brook, Abijah, 140.
Brooker, Abraham, 84.
Brooker, Abraham, 84.
Brooker, John, 62.
Brookes, Anna (Wd), 24.
Brookes, Timothy, 82.
Brooks, Abigail, 84.
Brooks, Abijah, 30.
Brooks, Abijah, 100.
Brooks, Abijail (Wid.), 30.
Brooks, Abraham, 84.
Brooks, Amassa, 93.
Brooks, Amos, 83.
Brooks, Asahel, 67.
Brooks, Asshael, 111.
Brooks, Benjamin, 30.
Brooks, Benjamin, 100.
Brooks, Benjamin, 131.
Brooks, Chancey, 35.
Brooks, Cloe, 93.
Brooks, Daniel, 87.
Brooks, Daniel, 126.
Brooks, David, 87.
Brooks, David, 93.
Brooks, David, 2d, 93.
Brooks, David S., 99.
Brooks, Ebenezer B., 93.
Brooks, Ezekiel, 128.
Brooks, Ezekiel, 2d, 128.
Brooks, Gideon, 93.
Brooks, Gurdon, 130.
Brooks, Guy, 131.
Brooks, Henry, 93.
Brooks, Henry, 2nd, 93.
Brooks, Isaac, 30.
Brooks, Isaac, 34.
Brooks, Isaac, 144.
Brooks, Jabez, 83.
Brooks, Jabez, 87.
Brooks, Jabez, 87.
Brooks, Jabez, Junr, 87.
Brooks, James, 83.
Brooks, James, 90.
Brooks, James, 128.
Brooks, Jerry, 93.
Brooks, Joel, 42.
Brooks, Joel, 93.
Brooks, John, 30.
Brooks, John, 62.
Brooks, John, 144.
Brooks, Jonathan, 52.
Brooks, Jonathan, 83.
Brooks, Jonathan, 128.
Brooks, Joseph, 65.
Brooks, Joseph, Esqr, 83.
Brooks, Joseph B., 87.
Brooks, Joshua, 84.
Brooks, Josiah, 43.
Brooks, Lemuel, 22.
Brooks, Lemuel, Junr, 22.
Brooks, Louis, 100.
Brooks, Martha, 87.
Brooks, Mary, 81.
Brooks, Nathan, 83.
Brooks, Nathl, 140.
Brooks, Noah, 87.
Brooks, Noah, 124.
Brooks, Polly (Wid.), 30.
Brooks, Porter, 84.
Brooks, Samuel, 34.
Brooks, Samuel, 43.
Brooks, Samuel, 80.
Brooks, Samuel, 84.
Brooks, Samuel, 87.
Brooks, Saml, 122.
Brooks, Samuel, Jr., 34.
Brooks, Samuel, Jr., 43.
Brooks, Samuel, Junr, 84.
Brooks, Silas, 123.
Brooks, Simeon, 90.
Brooks, Soloman, 92.
Brooks, Thadeus, 129.
Brooks, Thomas, 10.
Brooks, Thomas, 35.
Brooks, Thomas, 93.
Brooks, Thomas, 146.
Brooks, Thomas, Jur, 10.
Brooks, Timothy, 87.
Brooks, Wakeman, 83.
Brooks, William, 11.
Brooks, William, 30.
Brooks, William, 39.
Brooks, William, 43.
Brooks, William, 129.
Brooks, Zerah, 39.
Broome, Samuel, 102.
Brothington, Daniel, 12.
Brothington, Samuel, 32.
Brothwell, Benjamin, 15.
Brothwell, F. Joseph, 77.
Brothwell, Hezekiah, 29.
Brothwell, Joseph, 15.
Brothwell, Thomas, 14.
Broughton, Amos, 154.
Broughton, John, 140.
Broughton, William, 104.
Brougtron, Amos, 77.
Brown, Aaron, 151.
Brown, Abigail (Wd), 26.
Brown, Abm, 133.
Brown, Alpheus, 56.
Brown, Alpheus, 141.
Brown, Amasa, 121.
Brown, Amasa, 135.
Brown, Ambrose, 140.
Brown, Amos, 114.
Brown, Amos, 120.
Brown, Amos, Junr, 114.
Brown, Amos, Junr, 114.
Brown, Amy, 125.
Brown, Andrew, 144.
Brown, Andrew, 153.
Brown, Ann, 118.
Brown, Anthony, 152.
Brown, Asa, 109.
Brown, Asa, 115.
Brown, Asher, 116.
Brown, Asoph, 109.
Brown, Azariah, 146.
Brown, Bazaleel, 15.
Brown, Benjamin, 37.
Brown, Benjn, 56.
Brown, Benjamin, 58.
Brown, Benjamin, 103.
Brown, Benja, 128.
Brown, Benjn, 142.
Brown, Benjamin, Jr., 37.
Brown, Benjn, Ju., 56.
Brown, Bersheba, 105.
Brown, Charles, 19.
Brown, Charles, 127.
Brown, Charles, 151.
Brown, Christopher, 115.
Brown, Cumfort, 118.
Brown, Cumfort, 2d, 120.
Brown, Cumstock, 125.
Brown, Daniel, 57.
Brown, Daniel, 76.
Brown, Danl, 82.
Brown, Daniel, 109.
Brown, Daniel, 109.
Brown, Danl, 115.
Brown, Danl, 135.
Brown, Danl, 141.
Brown, Daniel, 2nd, 109.
Brown, Daniel, 2d, 125.
Brown, David, 16.
Brown, David, 56.
Brown, David, 57.
Brown, David, 114.
Brown, David, 116.
Brown, David, 124.
Brown, David, 140.
Brown, David, 144.
Brown, David, 149.
Brown, Ebenezer, 79.
Brown, Ebenezer, 109.
Brown, Ebenezer, 118.
Brown, Ebenr, 133.
Brown, Ebenr, 142.
Brown, Eber, 132.
Brown, Edmond, 68.
Brown, Edward, 53.
Brown, Edward, 152.
Brown, Eleazer, 48.
Brown, Eleazer, 116.
Brown, Eleazer, 127.
Brown, Elepht, 133.
Brown, Elias, 54.
Brown, Elias, 109.
Brown, Elias, 114.
Brown, Elias, 117.
Brown, Elijah, 75.
Brown, Elisha, 18.
Brown, Elisha, 32.
Brown, Elisha, 35.
Brown, Elizur, 102.
Brown, Elkanah, 118.
Brown, Enos, 24.
Brown, Ephm, 54.
Brown, Ephraim, 121.
Brown, Eunice, 114.
Brown, Ezekiel, 118.
Brown, Ezekiel, 135.
Brown, Ezra, 55.
Brown, Ezra, 121.
Brown, Francis, 26.
Brown, Francis, 103.
Brown, George, 103.
Brown, George, 114.
Brown, Gershom, Junr, 120.
Brown, Geshom, 118.
Brown, Hannah, 97.
Brown, Hannah, 118.
Brown, Hannah (Wid.), 48.
Brown, Henry, 102.
Brown, Henry, 123.
Brown, Henry, 143.
Brown, Henry, 151.
Brown, Hezekiah, 75.
Brown, Hugh, 88.
Brown, Humphrey, 115.
Brown, Isaac, 26.
Brown, Isaac, 29.
Brown, Isaac, 94.
Brown, Isaac, 103.
Brown, Isaiah, 144.
Brown, Jabez, 102.
Brown, Jabez, 115.

Gibson, Roger, 127.
Gibson, Samuel, 43.
Gibson, Timothy, 88.
Gibson, William, 75.
Giddeons, Jonathan, 19.
Giddeons, Joseph, 19.
Giddeons, William, 19.
Giddeons, Zebulon, 19.
Giddings, Benjamin, 61.
Giddings, Joshua, 61.
Gideons, David, 66.
Gideons, Joseph, 114.
Gideons, Nathl, 129.
Gideons, Solomon, 114.
Gifford, Caleb, 121.
Gifford, Siba, 134.
Gifford, Stephen, 126.
Gifford, Susanna, 126.
Giffords, Jeremiah, 130.
Giffords, John, 130.
Giffords, Samuel, 130.
Giffords, Saml, Junr, 132.
Gilbart, Abner, 28.
Gilbart, David, 28.
Gilbart, Ebenezer, 28.
Gilbert, Abner, 71.
Gilbert, Abraham, 18.
Gilbert, Abraham, 100.
Gilbert, Abraham, 2nd, 100.
Gilbert, Ager, 18.
Gilbert, Allen, 88.
Gilbert, Amos, 101.
Gilbert, Amos, 104.
Gilbert, Andrew, 32.
Gilbert, Asa, 86.
Gilbert, Asa, 101.
Gilbert, Benjamin, 24.
Gilbert, Benjamin, 47.
Gilbert, Benjamin, 88.
Gilbert, Burr, 32.
Gilbert, Caleb, 104.
Gilbert, Calvin, 71.
Gilbert, Charles, 47.
Gilbert, Daniel, 101.
Gilbert, David, 68.
Gilbert, David, 96.
Gilbert, David, 104.
Gilbert, Ebenezer, 32.
Gilbert, Ebenezer, 88.
Gilbert, Eleazr, 141.
Gilbert, Elihue, 17.
Gilbert, Elisha, 76.
Gilbert, Elisha, 104.
Gilbert, Elizabeth, 104.
Gilbert, Ely, 111.
Gilbert, Ezra, 74.
Gilbert, George, 130.
Gilbert, Grigson, 100.
Gilbert, Hezekiah, 71.
Gilbert, Hooker, 34.
Gilbert, Ichabod, 45.
Gilbert, Isaac, 104.
Gilbert, Jabez, 58.
Gilbert, Jabez, 74.
Gilbert, Jabez, 152.
Gilbert, James, 101.
Gilbert, James, 104.
Gilbert, Jessee, 63.
Gilbert, Joel, 18.
Gilbert, John, 17.
Gilbert, John, 20.
Gilbert, John, 31.
Gilbert, John, 70.
Gilbert, John, 87.
Gilbert, John, 100.
Gilbert, John, 123.
Gilbert, Jno, 135.
Gilbert, Jno, 135.
Gilbert, John, 147.
Gilbert, Jonathan, 34.
Gilbert, Jonathan, 47.
Gilbert, Jonathan, 87.
Gilbert, Jona, 125.
Gilbert, Jonathan, Jr., 34.
Gilbert, Jonathan, Junr, 87.
Gilbert, Joseph, 31.
Gilbert, Joseph, 67.
Gilbert, Joseph, 86.
Gilbert, Joseph, 100.
Gilbert, Joseph, 100.
Gilbert, Joseph, 141.
Gilbert, Katey, 101.
Gilbert, Lemwell, 18.
Gilbert, Lewis, 32.
Gilbert, Linus, 111.
Gilbert, Margaret, 104.
Gilbert, Mary, 34.
Gilbert, Mathew, 101.
Gilbert, Miriam, 103.
Gilbert, Moses, 34.
Gilbert, Moses, 100.
Gilbert, Nathan, 21.
Gilbert, Obediah, 17.
Gilbert, Rachel, 62.
Gilbert, Reubin, 31.
Gilbert, Rhoda, 88.
Gilbert, Roda, 67.
Gilbert, Saml, 82.
Gilbert, Samuel, 111.
Gilbert, Saml, 135.
Gilbert, Seth, 20.
Gilbert, Seth, 34.
Gilbert, Soloman, 111.

Gilbert, Stephen, 20.
Gilbert, Sylvester, 135.
Gilbert, Thadeus, 31.
Gilbert, Theodosia, 67.
Gilbert, Thodah, 67.
Gilbert, Thomas, 18.
Gilbert, Thomas, 31.
Gilbert, Thomas, 34.
Gilbert, Timothy, 104.
Gilbert, Truman, 74.
Gilbert, Wilks, 141.
Gilbert, Zalmon, 31.
Gilchrist, Damaras, 78.
Gilden, Issabell, 131.
Gildersleaves, Obadiah, 61.
Gildersleeves, Obediah, 79.
Gildersleeves, Phillip, 79.
Gildersleeves, Phillip, 80.
Gildersleve, Finch, 23.
Giles, John, 123.
Giles, Samuel, 52.
Giles, Thomas, 118.
Giles, Thomas, Junr, 119.
Giles, William, 86.
Giles, William, 152.
Gilkie, Peter, 93.
Gill, Abigail, 86.
Gill, Ebenezer M., 100.
Gill, John, 100.
Gill, John, 2nd, 100.
Gillam, Benjamin, 96.
Gillet, Aaron, 135.
Gillet, Abel, 71.
Gillet, Abraham, 41.
Gillet, Alme, 54.
Gillet, Amos, 65.
Gillet, Benjamin, 37.
Gillet, Danl, 55.
Gillet, Daniel, 124.
Gillet, David, 78.
Gillet, Ebenezer, 50.
Gillet, Ela, 120.
Gillet, Eliphalet, 102.
Gillet, Ellick, 35.
Gillet, Ezra, 124.
Gillet, Isaac, 41.
Gillet, Isaac, 51.
Gillet, Isaac, 146.
Gillet, Isaac, 146.
Gillet, Jabes, 69.
Gillet, John, 63.
Gillet, John, 69.
Gillet, Jno, 135.
Gillet, Jonah, 55.
Gillet, Jonah, 2d, 55.
Gillet, Jonathan, 58.
Gillet, Jonathan, 60.
Gillet, Jonathan, 62.
Gillet, Jonathan, 102.
Gillet, Joseph, 121.
Gillet, Joseph, 124.
Gillet, Joseph, Junr, 121.
Gillet, Lydia, 121.
Gillet, Mary (Wido.), 146.
Gillet, Matthew, 67.
Gillet, Michael, 67.
Gillet, Nehemiah, 121.
Gillet, Noah, 41.
Gillet, Oliver, 45.
Gillet, Reuben, 35.
Gillet, Reynold, 124.
Gillet, Stephen, 69.
Gillet, Wheelor, 56.
Gillet, William, 24.
Gillet, William, 66.
Gillet, Zacheus, 44.
Gillett, Adne, 44.
Gillett, Amos, 44.
Gillett, Azariah, 44.
Gillett, Benoni, 44.
Gillett, Buckler, 44.
Gillett, Calvin, 51.
Gillett, Daniel, 51.
Gillett, Elihu, 51.
Gillett, Elijah, 43.
Gillett, Ephraim, 44.
Gillett, Isaac, 44.
Gillett, Jabash, 44.
Gillett, Jacob, 44.
Gillett, Jeremiah, 35.
Gillett, Joab, 45.
Gillett, Joseph, 44.
Gillett, Levi, 44.
Gillett, Nathan, 44.
Gillett, Nathan, 50.
Gillett, Nathaniel, 45.
Gillett, Nathaniel, Jr, 45.
Gillett, Noadiah, 41.
Gillett, Othenial, 44.
Gillett, Othenial, Jr, 44.
Gillett, Timothy, 45.
Gillett, Zachariah, 50.
Gillit, Aaron, 55.
Gillit, Abel, 55.
Gillit, Abel, Ju., 55.
Gillit, Amasa, 135.
Gillit, Amos, 55.
Gillit, Charles, 135.
Gillit, Deborah, 55.
Gillit, Ezekl, 135.
Gillit, Levi, 55.
Gillitt, Joab, 48.
Gillman, Asher, 96.

Gillon, James, 96.
Gillott, Joel, 58.
Gilman, Benjamin, 38.
Gilman, David, 36.
Gilman, Elihu, 69.
Gilman, Elizabeth, 36.
Gilman, Evans, 24.
Gilman, George, 36.
Gilman, Jonah, 36.
Gilman, Nathaniel, 36.
Gilman, Oliver, 36.
Gilman, Robert, 151.
Gilman, Solomon, 37.
Gilman, Solomon, Jr, 37.
Gilman, Wm, 137.
Gilson, Jona, 132.
Gimman, George, 150.
Ginnason, Lucy, 86.
Ginnings, Jonathan, 114.
Ginnings, Zephaniah, 131.
Gion, Luke, 114.
Gipson, John, 88.
Gipson, Samuel, 57.
Gitchel, Joseph, 126.
Gitteau, Ephraim, 66.
Givins, Shelden, 76.
Gladden, Jedidiah, 34.
Gladden, Josiah, 52.
Gladden, Samuel, 33.
Glading, Ebenezer, 89.
Glading, Joseph, 90.
Glading, Rebekah, 89.
Glading, Silas, 89.
Glading, Wye, 89.
Glasier, Jacob, 73.
Glasier, John, 76.
Glason, Moses, 37.
Glass, James, 64.
Glass, John, 71.
Glass, Silas, 142.
Glayer, Silas, 139.
Glazier, John, 55.
Gleason, Arial, 67.
Gleason, Chancey, 49.
Gleason, David, 41.
Gleason, Elezer, 139.
Gleason, Elisha, 149.
Gleason, Ephraim, 69.
Gleason, Isaac, 40.
Gleason, Isaac, 41.
Gleason, John, 150.
Gleason, Jonah, 40.
Gleason, Joseph, 40.
Gleason, Joseph, 79.
Gleason, Joseph, Jr., 40.
Gleason, Margarett, 86.
Gleason, Nathl, 150.
Gleason, Ruful, 61.
Gleason, Samuel, 41.
Gleason, Solomon, 40.
Gleason, William, 151.
Glenny, William, 146.
Gloding, Daniel, 83.
Glosender, John, 42.
Glover, Benjamin, 20.
Glover, Budsery, 78.
Glover, Christopher, 12.
Glover, Daniel, 20.
Glover, Edward, 64.
Glover, Elias, 20.
Glover, Henery, 20.
Glover, James, 20.
Glover, Jeremiah, 123.
Glover, John, 20.
Glover, Lemuel, 27.
Glover, Nathan, 144.
Glover, Solimon, 20.
Glover, Zalmon, 20.
Gobine, Nicholas, 103.
Goddard, Ebenezer, 128.
Godfry, Cristopher, 32.
Godfry, Daniel, 32.
Godfry, David, 32.
Godfry, David, 32.
Godfry, Ebenezer, 13.
Godfry, Eleazer, 32.
Godfry, Elias, 32.
Godfry, Hannah, 14.
Godfry, Isaac, 32.
Godfry, John, 14.
Godfry, Jonathan, 13.
Godfry, Jonathan, 32.
Godfry, Mary, 12.
Godfry, Moses, 31.
Godfry, Nathan, 13.
Godfry, Samuel, 27.
Godfry, Silliman, 32.
Godfry, Stephen, 13.
Godman, Jno, 139.
Goff, Aaron, 43.
Goff, Benjamin, 81.
Goff, Charles, 121.
Goff, Cumfort, 121.
Goff, Cumfort, Junr, 121.
Goff, David, 87.
Goff, Elisha, 42.
Goff, Ezekiel, 80.
Goff, Gansey, 121.
Goff, Gideon, 53.
Goff, Gideon, 81.
Goff, Gideon, 83.
Goff, Jacob, 81.
Goff, James, 81.

Goff, John, 80.
Goff, Jonathan, 81.
Goff, Joshua, 121.
Goff, Josiah, 53.
Goff, Josiah, 81.
Goff, Peter, 15.
Goff, Phillip, 80.
Goff, Phillip, Junr, 80.
Goff, Samuel, 81.
Goff, Saml, 121.
Goff, Squire, 121.
Goff, William, 125.
Goit, Richard, 64.
Gold, Benjamin, 57.
Gold, Gurdon, 43.
Gold, Hezekiah, 57.
Gold, Joseph Wakefield, 57.
Gold, Nathan, 31.
Gold, Peter, 104.
Gold, Samuel, 27.
Gold, Thomas, 91.
Gold, Thomas, 103.
Gold, William, 91.
Goldsmith, Gilbert, 101.
Goldsmith, James, 101.
Goldsmith, James, 2nd, 101.
Goldsmith, John, 97.
Goldsmith, John, 2nd, 97.
Goldsmith, Joseph, 101.
Goldsmith, William, 101.
Gonyard, Spensor, 68.
Goodale, Aaron 143.
Goodale, Abijah, 141.
Goodale, Amasa, 149.
Goodale, Asa, 154.
Goodale, Avary, 43.
Goodale, Caleb, 149.
Goodale, Danl, 149.
Goodale, David, 149.
Goodale, Ebenezer, 39.
Goodale, Ebenezer, 43.
Goodale, Eler, 134.
Goodale, Henery, 43.
Goodale, Henry, 79.
Goodale, Isaac, 43.
Goodale, Jno, 139.
Goodale, John, 154.
Goodale, Joseph, 43.
Goodale, Joseph, Jr., 43.
Goodale, Lemuel, 153.
Goodale, Meachum, 149.
Goodale, Richard, 149.
Goodale, Thomas, 43.
Goodale, Walter, 39.
Goodale, Zachh, 149.
Goodard, Mary, 129.
Goodel, Ruben, 113.
Goodel, Silas, 131.
Goodell, Benjamin, 130.
Goodfaith, David, 129.
Goodhue, David, 65.
Goodin, William, 146.
Goodluck, London, 18.
Goodman, Asa, 47.
Goodman, Moses, 47.
Goodman, Richard, 45.
Goodman, Richard, 47.
Goodman, Thomas, 47.
Goodman, Thomas, 60.
Goodrich, Abigail, 42.
Goodrich, Abigail, 52.
Goodrich, Abner, 63.
Goodrich, Alpheus, 53.
Goodrich, Asahel, 34.
Goodrich, Ashbel, 60.
Goodrich, Barsheba, 87.
Goodrich, Benjamin, 62.
Goodrich, Bethrolma, 91.
Goodrich, Chancey, 45.
Goodrich, Charles, 79.
Goodrich, Charles, Junr, 79.
Goodrich, Crafts, 132.
Goodrich, David, 33.
Goodrich, David, 42.
Goodrich, David, 53.
Goodrich, David, 54.
Goodrich, David, Jr., 42.
Goodrich, Ebenezer, 53.
Goodrich, Eliakim, 42.
Goodrich, Elias, 34.
Goodrich, Elihu, 53.
Goodrich, Elijah, 41.
Goodrich, Elijah, 53.
Goodrich, Elijah H., 43.
Goodrich, Elijur, 104.
Goodrich, Elisha, 42.
Goodrich, Elisha, 63.
Goodrich, Elizabeth, 63.
Goodrich, Elizur, 53.
Goodrich, Elizur, 96.
Goodrich, Gidion, 91.
Goodrich, Giles, 68.
Goodrich, Gurden, 54.
Goodrich, Gurdin, Jr., 53.
Goodrich, Hezekiah, 79.
Goodrich, Hosea, 88.
Goodrich, Ichabod, 53.
Goodrich, Isaac, 33.
Goodrich, Isaac, 42.
Goodrich, Isaac, 53.
Goodrich, Isaac, 70.
Goodrich, Israel, 53.

Goodrich, Israel, 53.
Goodrich, James, 91.
Goodrich, Jediahah, 33.
Goodrich, Jehiel, 42.
Goodrich, Jeremiah, 79.
Goodrich, Jeremiah, Junr, 79.
Goodrich, Jerusha, 53.
Goodrich, Joel, 63.
Goodrich, John, 34.
Goodrich, John, 52.
Goodrich, John, 52.
Goodrich, John, 54.
Goodrich, John, 80.
Goodrich, John, 104.
Goodrich, Joseph, 53.
Goodrich, Joshua, 79.
Goodrich, Josiah, 53.
Goodrich, Moses, 132.
Goodrich, Nathaniel, 53.
Goodrich, Nathaniel, Jr., 53.
Goodrich, Noah, 42.
Goodrich, Oliver, 53.
Goodrich, Phineas, 91.
Goodrich, Reuben, 79.
Goodrich, Richard, 79.
Goodrich, Roger, 53.
Goodrich, Roswell, 42.
Goodrich, Salmon, 34.
Goodrich, Samuel, 85.
Goodrich, Revd Samuel, 28.
Goodrich, Seth, 33.
Goodrich, Seth, 54.
Goodrich, Seth, 69.
Goodrich, Solomon, 67.
Goodrich, Solomon, 79.
Goodrich, Stephen, 47.
Goodrich, Temperance, 53.
Goodrich, Thilcon, 53.
Goodrich, Thos, 134.
Goodrich, Wait, 42.
Goodrich, Wait, Jr., 42.
Goodrich, Waitstill, 56.
Goodrich, William, 53.
Goodrich, William, 63.
Goodrich, Zenas, 33.
Goodsall, Lidia, 92.
Goodsel, Isaac, 75.
Goodsel, Thomas, 75.
Goodsel, Timothy, 75.
Goodsell, Daniel, 97.
Goodsell, David, 13.
Goodsell, Epaphras, 13.
Goodsell, James, 13.
Goodsell, John, 12.
Goodsell, John, 62.
Goodsell, John, 97.
Goodsell, John Junr, 97.
Goodsell, Levi, 104.
Goodsell, Lewis, 13.
Goodsell, Samuel, 31.
Goodsell, Samuel, 50.
Goodsell, Samuel, 97.
Goodsell, Thomas, 13.
Goodshell, Daniel, 97.
Goodspead, Nathl, 138.
Goodspeed, Nathan, 81.
Goodwin, Abigal, 69.
Goodwin, Allyn, 45.
Goodwin, Anna (Wid.), 45.
Goodwin, Asher, 45.
Goodwin, David, 45.
Goodwin, Ebenr, 63.
Goodwin, Ebenr, 63.
Goodwin, Elizabeth, 64.
Goodwin, Elzer, 61.
Goodwin, George, 45.
Goodwin, Isaac, 70.
Goodwin, Jacob, 86.
Goodwin, James, 45.
Goodwin, Jessee, 63.
Goodwin, John, 36.
Goodwin, John, 45.
Goodwin, John, 63.
Goodwin, John P., 63.
Goodwin, Johnath, 146.
Goodwin, Jonathan, 45.
Goodwin, Jonothan, 61.
Goodwin, Joseph, 36.
Goodwin Joseph, 48.
Goodwin, Joseph, 64.
Goodwin, Levi, 36.
Goodwin, Mary, 45.
Goodwin, Mary, 45.
Goodwin, Michael, 61.
Goodwin, Morgan, 41.
Goodwin, Moses, 61.
Goodwin, Nathaniel, 64.
Goodwin, Russell, 45.
Goodwin, Samuel, 45.
Goodwin, Samuel, 86.
Goodwin, Saml, 146.
Goodwin, Seth, 62.
Goodwin, Sukey, 86.
Goodwin, Theodore, 45.
Goodwin, Thomas, 64.
Goodwin, Thomas, 86.
Goodwin, Thomas, Junr, 86.
Goodwin, Timothy, 45.
Goodwin, Tiras, 61.
Goodwin, Titus, 47.
Goodwin, William, 45.
Goodwin, William, 61.
Goodyear, Asa, 100.

Hitchcock, David, 72.
Hitchcock, David, 93.
Hitchcock, David, 94.
Hitchcock, Easter, 93.
Hitchcock, Ebenezer, 95.
Hitchcock, Ebenezer, 112.
Hitchcock, Ebenezur, 100.
Hitchcock, Ebenezur, 2nd, 100.
Hitchcock, Eliakim, 103.
Hitchcock, Eneas, 111.
Hitchcock, Eneas, 111.
Hitchcock, Hannah, 104.
Hitchcock, Hannah, 108.
Hitchcock, Harvey, 93.
Hitchcock, Harvie, 34.
Hitchcock, Icobed, 93.
Hitchcock, Ira, 72.
Hitchcock, Jabez, 100.
Hitchcock, Jared, 56.
Hitchcock, Joash, 108.
Hitchcock, Joel, 35.
Hitchcock, John L., 93.
Hitchcock, Jonathan, 74.
Hitchcock, Jonathan, 94.
Hitchcock, Jona, 137.
Hitchcock, Jonathan, 2nd, 94.
Hitchcock, Joseph, 15.
Hitchcock, Joseph, 112.
Hitchcock, Joseph, 112.
Hitchcock, Josiah, 49.
Hitchcock, Jotham, 103.
Hitchcock, Lemuel, 94.
Hitchcock, Levi, 93.
Hitchcock, Lidia, 100.
Hitchcock, Lidia, 100.
Hitchcock, Lydia, 56.
Hitchcock, Mary, 93.
Hitchcock, Medad, 112.
Hitchcock, Nathan, 72.
Hitchcock, Nathaniel, 108.
Hitchcock, Phineas, 111.
Hitchcock, Rufus, 93.
Hitchcock, Samuel, 49.
Hitchcock, Samuel, 76.
Hitchcock, Samuel, 95.
Hitchcock, Samuel, 100.
Hitchcock, Samuel, 102.
Hitchcock, Samuel, Jr., 49.
Hitchcock, Stephen, 50.
Hitchcock, Stephen, 100.
Hitchcock, Thomas, 15.
Hitchcock, Valantine, 93.
Hitchcock, William, 72.
Hitchcock, William, 112.
Hitchcock, Zachariah, 76.
Hitchcocks, Saml, 67.
Hitchcok, Amos, 49.
Hitchcox, Nathaniel, 34.
Hitchwick, Jason, 93.
Hitt, John, 152.
Hix, John, 120.
Hix, John, Junr, 120.
Hoadley, Amasia, 112.
Hoadley, Asa, 109.
Hoadley, Culpeper, 110.
Hoadley, Ebenezer, 110.
Hoadley, Ebenezur, 92.
Hoadley, Jehiel, 88.
Hoadley, Philo, 110.
Hoadley, Timothy, 92.
Hoadley, William, 110.
Hoadly, Abigal, 91.
Hoadly, Abigal, 91.
Hoadly, Benjamin, 91.
Hoadly, Daniel, 92.
Hoadly, Isaac, 91.
Hoadly, James, 91.
Hoadly, John, 91.
Hoadly, Jonathan, 91.
Hoadly, Jude, 110.
Hoadly, Lemuel, 109.
Hoadly, Nathl, 109.
Hoadly, Ralph, 91.
Hoadly, Rufus, 92.
Hoadly, Samuel, 91.
Hoadly, Samuel, 91.
Hoadly, Samuel, 97.
Hoady, Silas, 91.
Hoanmen, Wait, 65.
Hoase, Sarah, 105.
Hobart, Saml, 123.
Hobbs, Edmond, 145.
Hobby, Abraham, 15.
Hobby, Benjamin, 15.
Hobby, Charles, 15.
Hobby, David, 16.
Hobby, Ebenezer, 15.
Hobby, Henry, 24.
Hobby, Hezekiah, 15.
Hobby, Jabez Mead, 15.
Hobby, John, 15.
Hobby, Jonathan, 16.
Hobby, Joseph, 15.
Hobby, Joseph, Junr, 15.
Hobby, Mills, 15.
Hobby, Seymore, 16.
Hobby, Thomas, 15.
Hobby, Thomas, Junr, 15.
Hobby, Winsley, 85.
Hochkins, Joseph, 57.
Hoddy, Daniel, 67.
Hodg, Jno, 137.
Hodgden, David, 14.
Hodge, Abel, 19.
Hodge, Benjamin, 43.
Hodge, Benjamin, 115.
Hodge, Benjamin, Jr., 43.
Hodge, Eli, 42.
Hodge, Elijah, 42.
Hodge, Job, 23.
Hodge, John, 42.
Hodge, Jonathan, 42.
Hodge, Philo, 78.
Hodge, Roswell, 42.
Hodge, Samuel, 81.
Hodge, Thomas, 19.
Hodgekiss, James, 35.
Hodges, Ellane, 68.
Hodges, Ephram, 147.
Hodges, Ezra, 10.
Hodges, Thaddeus, 19.
Hodgkins, Thomas, 143.
Hodgkiss, Ambrose, 44.
Hodley, Andrew, 109.
Hoel, Edwd, 82.
Hoel, Ephraim, 149.
Hoffman, Samuel, 92.
Hogden (Widow), 29.
Hoit, Deodate, 25.
Hoit, Ebenezer, 59.
Hoit, Eli, 29.
Hoit, Mary, 24.
Hoit, Nezer, 25.
Hokim, David, 68.
Hokim, Eli, 66.
Holbrock, Joseph, 73.
Holbrook, Abel, 94.
Holbrook, Calvan, 154.
Holbrook, Daniel, 94.
Holbrook, Daniel, 95.
Holbrook, Elias, 138.
Holbrook, John, 94.
Holbrook, John, 151.
Holbrook, John, 2nd, 94.
Holbrook, Nathan, 94.
Holbrook, Philo, 95.
Holbrook, Thos, 151.
Holbrooks, Nathaniel, 61.
Holcomb, Abel, 44.
Holcomb, Abel, 2d, 44.
Holcomb, Abraham, 62.
Holcomb, Adonijah, 44.
Holcomb, Ahas, 44.
Holcomb, Amasa, 68.
Holcomb, Asa, 44.
Holcomb, Asahel, Jr., 45.
Holcomb, Asahel, Jr., 45.
Holcomb, Asahel, 3d, 44.
Holcomb, Asahel, 4th, 45.
Holcomb, Benajah, 44.
Holcomb, Benajah, 48.
Holcomb, Benajah, Jr., 48.
Holcomb, Caleb, 43.
Holcomb, Consider, 44.
Holcomb, Criss, 44.
Holcomb, Daniel, 43.
Holcomb, Dan., 44.
Holcomb, David, 44.
Holcomb, David, Jr., 44.
Holcomb, Ebenezer, 44.
Holcomb, Eli, 44.
Holcomb, Elihu, 43.
Holcomb, Elijah, 44.
Holcomb, Elijah, 54.
Holcomb, Elijah, 55.
Holcomb, Elijah, 62.
Holcomb, Elijah, Jr., 44.
Holcomb, Ezekiel, 44.
Holcomb, Ezekiel, Jr., 44.
Holcomb, Ezra, 45.
Holcomb, Hezekiah, 43.
Holcomb, Hezekiah, Jr, 43.
Holcomb, Jesse, 43.
Holcomb, John, 57.
Holcomb, John G., 44.
Holcomb, Joseph, 45.
Holcomb, Joseph, 55.
Holcomb, Joseph, Jr, 45.
Holcomb, Joshua, 43.
Holcomb, Judah, Esqr, 45.
Holcomb, Judah, Jr, 45.
Holcomb, Luther, 12.
Holcomb, Martha (Wid.), 45.
Holcomb, Martin, 55.
Holcomb, Martin, Jur, 55.
Holcomb, Masa (Wid.), 44.
Holcomb, Nahum, 44.
Holcomb, Nathan, Jr, 44.
Holcomb, Nathaniel, 44.
Holcomb, Noadiah, 44.
Holcomb, Noah, 43.
Holcomb, Noah, 62.
Holcomb, Obed, 44.
Holcomb, Oliver, 45.
Holcomb, Ozias, 44.
Holcomb, Ozias, Jr., 44.
Holcomb, Peter, 44.
Holcomb, Peter, Jr, 44.
Holcomb, Phineas, 44.
Holcomb, Reuben, 44.
Holcomb, Roderick, 55.
Holcomb, Roger, 44.
Holcomb, Roger, Jr, 44.
Holcomb, Saml, 55.
Holcomb, Silus, 44.
Holcomb, Simeon, 44.
Holden, John, 43.
Holden, Jonathan, 43.
Holden, Jonathan, Jr., 43.
Holden, Phineas, 130.
Holdridge, Hezekiah, 75.
Holdridge, Nathl, 116.
Holdrige, Benaijah, 118.
Holdrige, Phineas, 120.
Holdrige, Rufus, 118.
Holdrige, Saml, 120.
Holdrige, Saml, Junr, 120.
Holdrige, William, 114.
Holdrige, William, 118.
Holebrook, Abijah, 65.
Holebrook, Jobe, 154.
Holeburd, Timothy, 62.
Holeburd, William, 62.
Holeburton, Thomas, 14.
Holeburton, William, 14.
Holerige, Elisha, 114.
Holibard, David, 80.
Holibard, Elisha, 80.
Holibard, Jehiel, 80.
Holibard, Reuben, 80.
Holibard, William, Junr, 80.
Holibart, Martin, 63.
Holibert, Elisha, 63.
Holibert, Saml, 63.
Holiburd, John, 62.
Holiburt, Martin, 63.
Holiburt, Saml, 63.
Holiday, Naoma, 52.
Holiday, William, 52.
Holidy, Amos, 44.
Holidy, John, 44.
Holkins, Elijah, 39.
Holkins, Joel, 39.
Holkins, Joel, Jr., 39.
Holkins, Joseph, 39.
Holland, Benjamin, 46.
Hollebut, Daniel, 106.
Hollester, David B., 80.
Hollester, Lucretia, 123.
Hollester, Nathan, 60.
Hollett, John, 86.
Holley, Elnathan, 64.
Holley, Joseph, 120.
Holley, Stephen, 2nd, 112.
Hollibert, Daniel, 24.
Hollibert, James, 23.
Hollibert, John, 24.
Hollibert, Joseph, 21.
Hollibert, Stephen, 24.
Hollida, Daniel, 56.
Hollister, Aaron, 43.
Hollister, Abel, 72.
Hollister, Abraham, 42.
Hollister, Amos, 42.
Hollister, Appleton, 132.
Hollister, Asahel, 43.
Hollister, David, 42.
Hollister, David, 60.
Hollister, David, Jr., 43.
Hollister, David, 3d, 42.
Hollister, Elisha, 43.
Hollister, Elisha, 60.
Hollister, Elizur, 43.
Hollister, Ephraim, 34.
Hollister, George, 43.
Hollister, Gershom, 57.
Hollister, Gideon, 43.
Hollister, Gideon, 75.
Hollister, Gideon, 2d, 75.
Hollister, Ichabod, 43.
Hollister, Isaac, 63.
Hollister, Israel, 43.
Hollister, John, 37.
Hollister, John, 42.
Hollister, Jonathan, 42.
Hollister, Joseph, 42.
Hollister, Joseph, Jr., 42.
Hollister, Joshua, 60.
Hollister, Josiah, 37.
Hollister, Nathaniel, 43.
Hollister, Nehemiah, 43.
Hollister, Rebecca, 33.
Hollister, Roswell, 42.
Hollister, Solomon, 34.
Hollister, Stephen, 33.
Hollister, Stephen, 42.
Hollister, Theodore, 43.
Hollister, Thomas, 33.
Hollister, Thomas, 43.
Holloway, Danl, 137.
Holloway, John, 75.
Holly, Abel, 107.
Holly, Abraham, 25.
Holly, Abraham, Junr, 26.
Holly, David, 24.
Holly, Enoch, 26.
Holly, Francis, 25.
Holly, Increas, 26.
Holly, John, 23.
Holly, John, 26.
Holly, John, 94.
Holly, John, Junr, 26.
Holly, John W., 24.
Holly, Josiah, 103.
Holly, Lois (Wd), 15.
Holly, Manchester, 113.
Holly, Martha (Wd), 24.
Holly, Miller, 106.
Holly, Nathan, 24.
Holly, Numan, 24.
Holly, Stephen, 25.
Holly, Stephen, 112.
Holly, Stephen, Jr, 25.
Holman, Ebenezar, 37.
Holmbeck, Abraham, 68.
Holmes, Abel, 139.
Holmes, Anne, 89.
Holmes, Benjamin, 15.
Holmes, Benjn, 149.
Holmes, Charles, 43.
Holmes, Christopher, 82.
Holmes, Cornelius, 85.
Holmes, Daniel, 53.
Holmes, David, 149.
Holmes, David, 154.
Holmes, Ebenezer, 16.
Holmes, Ebenr, 149.
Holmes, Ebenr, 154.
Holmes, Ebenr, Jnr, 154.
Holmes, Elephalet, Esqr, 82.
Holmes, Gershom, 74.
Holmes, Isaac, 15.
Holmes, Isaac, 23.
Holmes, Israel, 74.
Holmes, Israel, 109.
Holmes, Jabez, 16.
Holmes, James, 129.
Holmes, Jazaniah, 137.
Holmes, Jeremiah, 71.
Holmes, Joel, 102.
Holmes, John, 26.
Holmes, John, 36.
Holmes, John, 54.
Holmes, Jonas, 53.
Holmes, Jona, 137.
Holmes, Jonathan, 149.
Holmes, Josi, 137.
Holmes, Lemuel, 54.
Holmes, Levi, 53.
Holmes, Nathan, 71.
Holmes, Nathl, 141.
Holmes, Nathel, 137.
Holmes, Peleg, 74.
Holmes, Reuben, 16.
Holmes, Seth, 68.
Holmes, Stephen, 15.
Holmes, Thatford, 19.
Holmes, Thomas, 53.
Holmes, Urial, 68.
Holmes, William, 43.
Holmes, William, 154.
Holms, George, 121.
Holms, James, 65.
Holms, Saml, 121.
Holscombe, James, 65.
Holt, Abiel, 143.
Holt, Andrew, 139.
Holt, Aron, 107.
Holt, Asa, 127.
Holt, Benjamin, 107.
Holt, Benjamin, 153.
Holt, Caleb, 139.
Holt, Daniel, 13.
Holt, Daniel, 76.
Holt, Daniel, 97.
Holt, Daniel, 107.
Holt, Daniel, 127.
Holt, Daniel, 2nd, 107.
Holt, Eben, 128.
Holt, Ebenezer, 38.
Holt, Ebenezer, 97.
Holt, Ebenezer, 128.
Holt, Elijah, 139.
Holt, Eliza, 67.
Holt, Elizabeth, 128.
Holt, Ezekiel, 141.
Holt, Isaac, 63.
Holt, Isaac, 67.
Holt, Isaac, 139.
Holt, James, 129.
Holt, James, 139.
Holt, Jesse, 114.
Holt, Jonathan, 128.
Holt, Jonath, 143.
Holt, Joseph, 97.
Holt, Joshua, 143.
Holt, Josiah, 34.
Holt, Nathaniel, 107.
Holt, Nathl, 113.
Holt, Nathl, 139.
Holt, Nathl, 2d, 139.
Holt, Nehemiah, 143.
Holt, Nehemh, Jnr, 143.
Holt, Nicholas, 67.
Holt, Paul, Jnr, 143.
Holt, Paul, Senr, 143.
Holt, Philn, 139.
Holt, Samuel, 97.
Holt, Seth, 139.
Holt, Stephen, 128.
Holt, Thomas, 128.
Holt, Timo, 139.
Holt, Wm, 127.
Holt, William, 128.
Holt, William, Jnr, 143.
Holt, Zebeh, 143.
Holton, Elisha, 39.
Holton, Timo, 134.
Hombbord, Isaac, 134.
Homer, David, 60.
Homer, James, 69.
Homerston, John, 68.
Homes, Appleton, 43.
Homes, Daniel, 31.
Homes, Edward, 116.
Homes, Elisha, 125.
Homes, Jabez, 118.
Homes, Jabez, 125.
Homes, James, 116.
Homes, Jared, 116.
Homes, Jeremi, 116.
Homes, John, 116.
Homes, John, 121.
Homes, Joshua, 116.
Homes, Samuel, 125.
Homes, Seth W., 125.
Homes, Silas, 117.
Homes, Thomas, 115.
Homestead, Joseph, 96.
Homestone, Abel, 76.
Homestone, Abram, 58.
Homestone, Abram, 2d, 58.
Homestone, David, 76.
Homestone, Eliphet, 76.
Homestone, Jose, 76.
Homestone, Joseph, 58.
Homestone, Thomas, 76.
Homestone, Timothy, 58.
Hond, John, 94.
Honferd, Rubin, 108.
Hood, George, 67.
Hood, Richard, 102.
Hood, Samuel, 102.
Hood, William, 102.
Hoods, Catherine, 101.
Hoogaboom, Jeremiah, 67.
Hooker, Bryon, 50.
Hooker, Daniel, 47.
Hooker, Elijah, 33.
Hooker, Elnathan, 41.
Hooker, Hezekiah, 112.
Hooker, Horrace, 54.
Hooker, James, 54.
Hooker, Jessee, 63.
Hooker, John, 102.
Hooker, Joseph, 41.
Hooker, Noadiah, 41.
Hooker, Roger, 41.
Hooker, Samuel, 33.
Hooker, William, 33.
Hooker, William, 46.
Hoolbrook, Abel, 146.
Hoolbrook, John, 146.
Hoolbrook, Timoy, 146.
Hooper, Asahel, 40.
Hooper, James, 91.
Hoopkins, Stephen, 61.
Hop, John, 81.
Hopkins, Asa, 45.
Hopkins, Benjamin, 33.
Hopkins, Benjamin, 58.
Hopkins, Benjamin, 74.
Hopkins, Benjamin, 125.
Hopkins, Caleb, 33.
Hopkins, Charles, 144.
Hopkins, Consider, 67.
Hopkins, David, 110.
Hopkins, Elijah, 74.
Hopkins, Elisha, 147.
Hopkins, George, 148.
Hopkins, Harriss, 68.
Hopkins, Harriss, 2d, 68.
Hopkins, Hezekiah, 58.
Hopkins, Isaac, 110.
Hopkins, Jenks, 144.
Hopkins, Jereh, 150.
Hopkins, Jesse, 109.
Hopkins, John, 110.
Hopkins, Jonathan, 51.
Hopkins, Joseph, 74.
Hopkins, Joseph, 109.
Hopkins, Joseph, 2nd, 110.
Hopkins, Josiah, 57.
Hopkins, Lemuel, 46.
Hopkins, Moses, 46.
Hopkins, Nathan, 74.
Hopkins, Noah, 59.
Hopkins, Prince, 74.
Hopkins, Richard, 144.
Hopkins, Roodrick, 67.
Hopkins, Samuel, 61.
Hopkins, Simeon, 110.
Hopkins, Stephen, 47.
Hopkins, Thomas, 45.
Hopkins, Thomas, 64.
Hopkins, Thomas, 74.
Hopkins, Thomas, 102.
Hopkins, Uriah, 58.
Hopkins, William, 47.
Hoppen, Benjamin, 93.
Hopson, Alvanus, 108.
Hopson, Amelia, 99.
Hopson, Ashbel, 108.
Hopson, Clement, 108.
Hopson, Ebenezer, 98.
Hopson, John, 59.
Hopson, John, 99.
Hopson, John, 121.
Hopson, Rue, 108.
Hopson, Samuel, 108.
Hopson, Simeon, 68.
Hopson, William, 75.
Horcheild, William, 103.
Horford, David, 65.

Sealee, Abel, 19.
Sealee, Bradley, 19.
Sealee, Deborah, 15.
Sealee, Ezra, 14.
Sealee Giddeon, 17.
Sealee, James, 12.
Sealee, Liman, 18.
Sealee, Seth, 15.
Sealy, Benjamin, 72.
Sealy, David, 31.
Sealy, Ephraim, 31.
Sealy, Jesse, 31.
Sealy, Joseph, 31.
Sealy, Nathaniel, Junr, 31.
Searls, John, 115.
Searls, Jno, 137.
Searls, Salter, 141.
Searls, William, 115.
Sears, Bartholomew, 17.
Sears, Charles, 84.
Sears, Comfort, 29.
Sears, Daniel, 29.
Sears, David, 81.
Sears, Ebenezer, 81.
Sears, Elijah, 17.
Sears, Elisha, 87.
Sears, Elkanah, 81.
Sears, Francis, 101.
Sears, Gershom, 17.
Sears, Hezekiah, 80.
Sears, Isaac, 81.
Sears, John, 72.
Sears, John, 87.
Sears, Knowles, 29.
Sears, Matthew, 81.
Sears, Nathan, 87.
Sears, Peter, 88.
Sears, Remington, 115.
Sears, Richard, 17.
Sears, Stephen. 87.
Sears, Willard, 81.
Sebens, Josiah, 27.
Sebor, Jacob, 85.
Sebor, Jacob, 129.
Sedgwick, Abram, 47.
Sedgwick, John, 57.
Sedgwick, Mary, 61.
Sedgwick, Samuel, 35.
Sedgwick, William, 47.
Sedgwik, John A., 57.
Sedgwith, Stephen, 41.
Sedgwith, Stephen, Jr., 41.
Seeley, Abner, 72.
Seeley, David, 66
Seeley, Ebenezer, 64.
Seeley, Elizabeth, 59.
Seeley, John, 69.
Seeley, John, 106.
Seeley, Joseph, 72.
Seeley, Nathaniel, 64.
Seelly, Isaac, 100.
Seely, Abijah, 26.
Seely, Abijah, Junr, 26.
Seely, Agar, 29.
Seely, Benjamin, 29.
Seely, Benjamin, 64.
Seely, David, 30.
Seely, Ebenezer, 26.
Seely, Elijah, 30.
Seely, Eliphalet, 26.
Seely, Elnathan, 29.
Seely, Esther (Wd), 26.
Seely, John, 25.
Seely, Jonas, 26.
Seely, Joseph, 26.
Seely, Justice, 64.
Seely, Nathan, 26.
Seely, Obadiah, 25.
Seely, Samuel, 26.
Seely, Silvanus, 26.
Seely, Silvanus, Junr, 26.
Seely, Wix, 26.
Seers, Stephen, 62.
Segar, Augustus, 44.
Segar, John, 44.
Segar, Joseph, 59.
Seger, Daniel, 10.
Seger, Eli, 11.
Seger, Joseph, 48.
Seger, Michael, 48.
Seir, James, 10.
Seirs, James, 29.
Selbe, Jereh, 81.
Selbe, Wm, 81.
Selby, Abraham, 106.
Selby, Abraham, 2nd, 106.
Selby, David M., 36.
Selden, Caleb, 144.
Selden, David, 80.
Selden, Dudley, 122.
Selden, Edward, 83.
Selden, Elias, 84.
Selden, Elisabeth, 122.
Selden, Ely, 122.
Selden, Ezra, 123.
Selden, Joseph, 41.
Selden, Joseph, 83.
Selden, Samuel, 122.
Seldon, Aaron, 80.
Seldon, Charles, 152.
Seldon, Elijah, 122.
Seldon, Joseph, 82.
Seldon, Seephas, 83.

Seldon, Thomas, 80.
Selleck, Daniel, 26.
Selleck, Edward, 26.
Selleck, Gershom, 26.
Selleck, Isaac, 23.
Selleck, Jacob, 23.
Selleck, James, 23.
Selleck, Jesse, 27.
Selleck, Joseph, 15.
Selleck, Mary (Wd), 26.
Selleck, Nathan, 26.
Selleck, Nathaniel, 22.
Selleck, Peter, 24.
Selleck, Samuel, 26.
Selleck, Seymore, 26.
Selleck, Silvanus, 15.
Selleck, Simeon, 26.
Selleck, Stephen, 24.
Selleck, Stephen, Jr, 26.
Selleck, Thaddeus, 23.
Selleck, Uriah, 22.
Selleck, Wray, 27.
Sellers, Phillip, 42.
Sellew, John, 42.
Sellick, Jesse, 28.
Sellick, Noah, 67.
Selm, Patience, 53.
Selvey, Ephraim, 62.
Selvey, William, 62.
Seman, Abraham, 19.
Semans, Abel, 139.
Semour, John, 79.
Semour, John, 2d, 79.
Semour, Joseph, 79.
Senior, Danl, 62.
Senot, Thomas, 126.
Senter, John, 130.
Sergeants, Isaac, 147.
Sergeants, Isaac, Jnr, 147.
Sergeants, Saml, 147.
Servant, James, 64.
Sessions, Amasa, 138.
Sessions, Amasa, 149.
Sessions, Darious, 150.
Sessions, Ebenr, 138.
Sessions, Jno, 139.
Sessions, John, 143.
Sessions, Joseph, 153.
Sessions, Leonard, 147.
Sessions, Nathl, 139.
Sessions, Nathl, 139.
Sessions, Saml, 134.
Sessions, Squire, 149.
Sessions, Waller, 139.
Sessons, Abijah, 138.
Sessons, Benj., 137.
Setle, Thomas, 19.
Sevans, David, 21.
Seward, Amos, 110.
Seward, Charles, 48.
Seward, Daniel, 62.
Seward, David, 98.
Seward, David, 2nd, 98.
Seward, John, 83.
Seward, Moses, 96.
Seward, Nathan, 57.
Seward, Samuel, 74.
Seward, Samuel, 96.
Seward, Solomon, 74.
Seward, Timothy, 98.
Sexton, Asabel, 40.
Sexton, Betsy, 121.
Sexton, George, 121.
Sexton, Jessey, 81.
Sexton, Joseph, 136.
Sexton, Joseph, 2d, 136.
Sexton, Samuel, 81.
Sexton, Simeon, 33.
Sexton, Stephen 136.
Sexton, Thomas, 40.
Seymore, Abijah, 22.
Seymore, Anne (Wd), 22.
Seymore, Daniel, 24.
Seymore, David, 22.
Seymore, David, 62.
Seymore, Elias, 63.
Seymore, Elijah, 59.
Seymore, Ezra, 22.
Seymore, Hezekiah, 63.
Seymore, James, 22.
Seymore, Jared, 26.
Seymore, John, 22.
Seymore, John, 22.
Seymore, Jonathan, 21.
Seymore, Moses, 65.
Seymore, Noah, 60.
Seymore, Phebe (Wd), 22.
Seymore, Rebecca (Wd), 22.
Seymore, Roger, 92.
Seymore, Samuel, 15.
Seymore, Samuel, 22.
Seymore, Samuel, 65.
Seymore, Seth, 22.
Seymore, Stephen, 64.
Seymore, Thomas, 22.
Seymore, Uriah, 63.
Seymore, William, 22.
Seymour, Aaron, 47.
Seymour, Aaron, 47.
Seymour, Allyn, 47.
Seymour, Asa, 46.
Seymour, Asa, 47.
Seymour, Ashbel, 54.

Seymour, Calvin, 47.
Seymour, Charles, 47.
Seymour, Charles, 47.
Seymour, Daniel, 47.
Seymour, Eli, 47.
Seymour, Elias, 54.
Seymour, Elisha, 52.
Seymour, Freeman, 47.
Seymour, George, 47.
Seymour, Hezekiah, 46.
Seymour, John, 47.
Seymour, Jonathan, 33.
Seymour, Joseph, 68.
Seymour, Joseph, 2d, 68.
Seymour, Joseph Whiting, 47.
Seymour, Lewis, 33.
Seymour, Matthew. 28.
Seymour, Michael, 47.
Seymour, Moses, 47.
Seymour, Nathaniel, 47.
Seymour, Norman, 47.
Seymour, Richard, 47.
Seymour, Robert, 46.
Seymour, Thankfull, 54.
Seymour, Thomas, 28.
Seymour, Thomas, Esqr, 46.
Seymour, Thomas, 2d, 28.
Seymour, Thomas Y., 47.
Seymour, Timothy, 47.
Seymour, Uriah, 28.
Seymour, Zebulon, 47.
Shaddock, Joseph, 63.
Shaddock, Moses, 52.
Shadrack (Negro) 120.
Shaler, Aaron, 83.
Shaler, Asa, 83.
Shaler, Bezeleel, 83.
Shaler, Ezra, 83.
Shaler, Hezekiah, 83.
Shaler, Hezekiah, Junr, 83.
Shaler, James, 83.
Shaler, Jeremiah, 83.
Shaler, Nathaniel, 86.
Shaler, Reuben, 83.
Shaler, Samuel, 83.
Shaler, Simon, 83.
Shaler, Thomas, 83.
Shally, Ebenezer, 97.
Shapley, John, 145.
Shapley, Mary, 129.
Sharkweather, Anne, 148.
Sharkweather, Richard, 148.
Sharman, James, 62.
Sharp, Abigail, 149.
Sharp, Asa, 149.
sharp, Caleb, 149.
Sharp, David, 149.
Sharp, Eliakim, 19.
Sharp, Eliakim, 75.
Sharp, Gershom, 19.
Sharp, Gershom, Secnd, 149.
Sharp, Jesse, 19.
Sharp, Joab, 74.
Sharp, John, 149.
Sharp, Joseph, 126.
Sharp (Negro), 115.
Sharp, Reubin & co., 144.
Sharp, Robert, 149.
Sharp, Ruth, 149.
Sharp, Solomon, 140.
Sharp, Thomas, 20.
Sharp, William, 75.
Sharp, William, 150.
Sharper (Negroe), 103.
Sharper (Negroe), 109.
Shatdock, William, 60.
Shatlief, Nathaniel, 110.
Shattuck, David, 121.
Shattuck, Randal, 81.
Shattuck, Robart, 121.
Shattuck, Robert, 87.
Shaw, Amos, 116.
Shaw, Benjn, 142.
Shaw, Daniel, 127.
Shaw, David, 38.
Shaw, Gid, 139.
Shaw, James, 26.
Shaw, John, 69.
Shaw, Peleg, 117.
Shaw, Thomas, 126.
Shaw, Thomas, 152.
Shaw, Thomas, 2d, 126.
Shaw, William, 142.
Shayler, Joseph, 107.
Sheers, Rebecca, 86.
Sheet, Hester, 108.
Sheffield, Achors, 117.
Sheffield, Amos, 118.
Sheffield, George, 117.
Sheffield, Isaac, 118.
Sheffield, Isaac, Junr, 118.
Sheffield, Paul, 14.
Sheffield, Paul, 119.
Sheffield, Robart, Junr, 117.
Sheffield, Saml, 125.
Sheffield, William, 117.
Sheffield, William, 2d, 117.
Shelbey, Ebenezer, 29.
Shelden, Ephephsas, 62.
Shelden, Moses, 62.
Shelden, Roger, 63.
Sheldon, Asher, 91.
Sheldon, Benjamin, 50.

Sheldon, Charles, 136.
Sheldon, Daniel, 50.
Sheldon, Daniel, 64.
Sheldon, Ebenezer, 50.
Sheldon, Elijah, 51.
Sheldon, Elisha, 69.
Sheldon, Elisha, 2d, 69.
Sheldon, Ely, 69.
Sheldon, Eunice, 148.
Sheldon, Ezra, 62.
Sheldon, George, 61.
Sheldon, Gersham, 50.
Sheldon, Hannah, 101.
Sheldon, Jacob, 50.
Sheldon, James, 46.
Sheldon, John, 46.
Sheldon, John, 51.
Sheldon, John, Jr., 46.
Sheldon, Jonathan, 50.
Sheldon, Jonathan, Jr., 50.
Sheldon, Joseph, 47.
Sheldon, Joseph, Jr., 47.
Sheldon, Josiah, 51.
Sheldon, Martin, 50.
Sheldon, Oliver, 51.
Sheldon, Phineas, 50.
Sheldon, Prince, 47.
Sheldon, Rachel, 50.
Sheldon, Remember, 54.
Sheldon, Roderic, 47.
Sheldon, Selah, 55.
Sheldon, Simeon, 50.
Sheldon, Thomas, 51.
Sheldon, William, 113.
Sheldorn, Saml, 65.
Shelley, Abram, 72.
Shelly, Edmond, 98.
Shelly, Joel, 97.
Shelly, John, 98.
Shelly, Lucy, 98.
Shelly, Medad, 98.
Shelly, Ruben, 98.
Shelly, Ruben, 2nd, 98.
Shelly, Shubal, 98.
Shelly, Timothy, 97.
Shelp, Joseph, 25.
Shelton, Abijah, 18.
Shelton, Abijah, 2d, 18.
Shelton, Ager, 18.
Shelton, Andrew, 17.
Shelton, Benjamin, 17.
Shelton, Daniel, 17.
Shelton, Daniel, 18.
Shelton, Daniel, 79.
Shelton, Elisha, 18.
Shelton, Eunice, 18.
Shelton, Gershom, 79.
Shelton, Isaac W., 34.
Shelton, James, 18.
Shelton, Jeremiah, 17.
Shelton, Joane, 18.
Shelton, Noah, 18.
Shelton, Philo, 14.
Shelton, Samuel, 17.
Shelton, Sealee, 18.
Shelton, Thaddeus, 18.
Shelton, William, 18.
Shelton, William, 78.
Shelton, Zacheriah, 17.
Shepard, Amos, 40.
Shepard, Ashbel, 46.
Shepard, Ashbel, 47.
Shepard, Benjn, 141.
Shepard, Charles, 46.
Shepard, Elisha, 46.
Shepard, Isaiah, 33.
Shepard, Jesse, 40.
Shepard, John, 47.
Shepard, Luther, 40.
Shepard, Mary, 47.
Shepard, Nathaniel, 50.
Shepard, Nathl, 151.
Shepard, Noah, 40.
Shepard, Noah, 40.
Shepard, Richard, 46.
Shepard, Samuel, 50.
Shepard, Samuel, Jr., 50.
Shepard, Sarah, 47.
Shepard, Stephen, 47.
Shepard, Stephen, 97.
Shepard, Thomas, 41.
Shepard, Timothy, 46.
Shepard, Uriah, 46.
Shepard, Whitmore, 141.
Shephard, Ebemener, 57.
Shephard, Eldad, 67.
Shephard, Isaac, 136.
Shepherd, Abel, 80.
Shepherd, Abraham, 20.
Shepherd, Amos, 20.
Shepherd, Amos, 80.
Shepherd, Benoni, 138.
Shepherd, Billy, 80.
Shepherd, Daniel, Junr, 80.
Shepherd, Daniel, Junr, 80.
Shepherd, David, 20.
Shepherd, Edward, 80.
Shepherd, Edward, Junr, 80.
Shepherd, Elisha, 80.
Shepherd, Elisha, Junr, 80.
Shepherd, Elisha, Junr, 80.
Shepherd, George, 20.
Shepherd, George, 80.

Shepherd, Gideon, 20.
Shepherd, Jacob, 136.
Shepherd, James, 20.
Shepherd, Jered, 88.
Shepherd, John, 20.
Shepherd, John, 80.
Shepherd, John, 128.
Shepherd, John, Junr, 80.
Shepherd, Revd John, 25.
Shepherd, Joseph, 88.
Shepherd, Merrit, 20.
Shepherd, Moses, 20.
Shepherd, Noah, 80.
Shepherd, Simeon, 21.
Shepherd, Stephen, 20.
Shepherd, Stephen, 68.
Shepherd, Thomas, 80.
Shepherd, Thomas, 81.
Sheppard, Abraham, 149.
Sheppard, Asa, 142.
Sheppard, Daniel, 63.
Sheppard, Isaac, 108.
Sheppard, James, 118.
Sheppard, James, 141.
Sheppard, John, 97.
Sheppard, John, 149.
Sheppard, John, 149.
Sheppard, Joseph, 64.
Sheppard, Joseph, 97.
Sheppard, Joseph, 148.
Sheppard, Josiah, 59.
Sheppard, Lyda, 149.
Sheppard, Moses, 64.
Sheppard, Olver, 62.
Sheppard, Phinehas, 59.
Sheppard, Reubin, 148.
Sheppard, Samuel, 97.
Sheppard, Simon, 148.
Sheppard, Stephen, 60.
Sheppard, Stephen, 149.
Sheppard, Thomas, 97.
Sheppard, William, 154.
Sheppard, Zebulon, 61.
Sheppardson, Jno, 83.
Sheppardson, Willm, 83.
Shepperd, Joseph, 66.
Sherborn, Benjamin, 20.
Sheridan, Mary, 122.
Sherman, Amos, 111.
Sherman, Benjamin, 83.
Sherman, Daniel, 72.
Sherman, Daniel, 74.
Sherman, Daniel, 79.
Sherman, Daniel, 2d, 79.
Sherman, David, 79.
Sherman, Eli, 72.
Sherman, Elijah, 79.
Sherman, Elisabeth, 113.
Sherman, Ephraim, 19.
Sherman, Ezra, 72.
Sherman, Jabez, 133.
Sherman, James, 128.
Sherman, Jese, 111.
Sherman, Jesse, 19.
Sherman, John, 28.
Sherman, John, 79.
Sherman, John, 104.
Sherman, John, 131.
Sherman, John, 2d, 79.
Sherman, Lemuel, 103.
Sherman, Mathew, 79.
Sherman, Molly, 102.
Sherman, Nathanel, 17.
Sherman, Nathanel, Jur, 17.
Sherman, Nathaniel, 38.
Sherman, Peter, 75.
Sherman, Philo, 17.
Sherman, Phineus, 17.
Sherman, Reuben, 79.
Sherman, Roger, 104.
Sherman, Rufus, 10.
Sherman, Samuel, 10.
Sherman, Samuel, 103.
Sherman, Sarah, 89.
Sherman, Solomon, 79.
Sherman, Taylor, 23.
Sherman, Tesna, 59.
Sherman, Vincen, 18.
Sherman, Walker, 17.
Sherman, William, 103.
Sherman, Zadock, 10.
Shermon, Andrew, 31.
Shermon, David, 20.
Shermon, David, 29.
Shermon, Ebenezer, 20.
Shermon, Elijah, 20.
Shermon, Ezra, 20.
Shermon, Filo, 19.
Shermon, Filo, 20.
Shermon, James, 30.
Shermon, John, 20.
Shermon, John, 30.
Shermon, Josiah, 31.
Shermon, Jotham, 20.
Shermon, Lemuel, 20.
Shermon, Lewis, 19.
Shermon, Lymon, 19.
Shermon, Lymon, 20.
Shermon, Matthew, 21.
Shermon, Nathan, 20.
Shermon, Nathan, 30.
Shermon, Sarah, 32.
Shermon, Seth, 20.